INTERNATIONAL HUMAN-RIGHTS LAW

INTERNATIONAL HUMAN RIGHTS LAW

Second Edition

EDITED BY

DANIEL MOECKLI

University of Zurich

SANGEETA SHAH

University of Nottingham

SANDESH SIVAKUMARAN

University of Nottingham

CONSULTANT EDITOR:

DAVID HARRIS

Professor Emeritus and Co-Director,
Human Rights Law Centre, University of Nottingham

OXFORD
UNIVERSITY PRESS

OXFORD
UNIVERSITY PRESS

Great Clarendon Street, Oxford, OX2 6DP,
United Kingdom

Oxford University Press is a department of the University of Oxford.
It furthers the University's objective of excellence in research, scholarship,
and education by publishing worldwide. Oxford is a registered trade mark of
Oxford University Press in the UK and in certain other countries

Published in the United States of America by Oxford University Press
198 Madison Avenue, New York, NY 10016, United States of America

British Library Cataloguing in Publication Data

Data available

Library of Congress Control Number: 2013943732

ISBN 978–0–19–965457–4

Printed in Great Britain by
Ashford Colour Press Ltd, Gosport, Hampshire

1006961887

OUTLINE CONTENTS

Preface   xxiii

Notes on contributors   xxiv

Abbreviations   xxix

Table of international instruments   xxxv

Table of cases   xlv

WHAT ARE HUMAN RIGHTS FOR?
THREE PERSONAL REFLECTIONS

NAVANETHEM PILLAY   3
   United Nations High Commissioner for Human Rights

KENNETH ROTH   7
   Executive Director of Human Rights Watch

HINA JILANI   10
   Director of AGHS Legal Aid Center and Advocate of the Supreme Court of Pakistan

PART I FOUNDATIONS

1 HISTORY   15
   Ed Bates

2 JUSTIFICATIONS   34
   Samantha Besson

3 CRITIQUES   53
   Marie-Bénédicte Dembour

PART II INTERNATIONAL LAW

4 SOURCES   75
   Christine Chinkin

5 NATURE OF OBLIGATIONS   96
   Frédéric Mégret

6 SCOPE OF APPLICATION   119
   Sarah Joseph and Adam Fletcher

PART III SUBSTANTIVE RIGHTS

7   CATEGORIES OF RIGHTS   143
    Theo van Boven

8   EQUALITY AND NON-DISCRIMINATION   157
    Daniel Moeckli

9   INTEGRITY OF THE PERSON   174
    Nigel S Rodley

10 ADEQUATE STANDARD OF LIVING   195
    Asbjørn Eide

11 THOUGHT, EXPRESSION, ASSOCIATION, AND ASSEMBLY   217
    Kevin Boyle and Sangeeta Shah

12 EDUCATION AND WORK   238
    Fons Coomans

13 DETENTION AND TRIAL   259
    Sangeeta Shah

14 CULTURAL RIGHTS   286
    Julie Ringelheim

15 SEXUAL ORIENTATION AND GENDER IDENTITY   303
    Michael O'Flaherty

16 WOMEN'S RIGHTS   316
    Dianne Otto

17 GROUP RIGHTS   333
    Robert McCorquodale

PART IV PROTECTION

18 UNITED NATIONS   359
    Jane Connors and Markus Schmidt

19 THE AMERICAS   398
    Jo Pasqualucci

20 EUROPE   416
    Steven Greer

21 AFRICA   441
    Christof Heyns and Magnus Killander

22 WITHIN THE STATE   458
    Andrew Byrnes and Catherine Renshaw

PART V LINKAGES

23 INTERNATIONAL HUMANITARIAN LAW   479
    Sandesh Sivakumaran

24 INTERNATIONAL CRIMINAL LAW   496
    Robert Cryer

25 INTERNATIONAL REFUGEE LAW   513
    Alice Edwards

PART VI CHALLENGES

26 NON-STATE ACTORS   531
    Andrew Clapham

27 TERRORISM   550
    Martin Scheinin

28 POVERTY   567
    Stephen P Marks

29 ENVIRONMENTAL DEGRADATION   590
    Malgosia Fitzmaurice

Index   611

DETAILED CONTENTS

Preface   xxiii

Notes on contributors   xxiv

Abbreviations   xxix

Table of international instruments   xxxv

Table of cases   xlv

WHAT ARE HUMAN RIGHTS FOR?
THREE PERSONAL REFLECTIONS

NAVANETHEM PILLAY   3
  United Nations High Commissioner for Human Rights

KENNETH ROTH   7
  Executive Director of Human Rights Watch

HINA JILANI   10
  Director of AGHS Legal Aid Center and Advocate of the Supreme Court of Pakistan

PART I FOUNDATIONS

1 **HISTORY**   15
   Ed Bates

   Summary   15

   1 Introduction   15

   2 Human rights on the domestic plane   16
      2.1 The enlightenment thinkers   17
      2.2 Human rights transformed into positive law   18
      2.3 Nineteenth-century challenges to natural rights   21
      2.4 Domestic protection of human rights today   21

   3 Human rights on the international plane before the Second World War   23
      3.1 International humanitarian law and the abolition of the slave trade   24
      3.2 The protection of minorities and the League of Nations   26

   4 Human rights on the international plane after the Second World War   28
      4.1 Crimes against humanity   29
      4.2 The UN Charter   29
      4.3 The Universal Declaration of Human Rights   30

   5 Conclusion   32

   Further reading   32
   Useful websites   33

2 JUSTIFICATIONS   34
Samantha Besson

Summary   34

1 Introduction   34

2 Why justify human rights   36
   2.1 Explaining justification   36
   2.2 Justifying justification   38

3 How to justify human rights   39
   3.1 Justifications of moral and legal rights   39
   3.2 Moral and legal justifications of moral and legal rights   41

4 Which justifications for human rights   41
   4.1 A plurality of justifications   41
   4.2 Two potential justifications   44

5 What follows from the justification of human rights   47
   5.1 Human rights justifications and the universality of human rights   47
   5.2 Human rights justifications and the strength of human rights   49

6 Conclusion   52

Further reading   52
Useful websites   52

3 CRITIQUES   53
Marie-Bénédicte Dembour

Summary   53

1 Introduction   53

2 Early critiques   55
   2.1 The realist critique   55
   2.2 The utilitarian critique   58
   2.3 The Marxist critique   60

3 More recent critiques   62
   3.1 The cultural relativist or particularist critique   62
   3.2 The feminist critique   65
   3.3 The post-colonial critique   67

4 Conclusion   70

Further reading   71

PART II INTERNATIONAL LAW

4 SOURCES   75
Christine Chinkin

Summary   75

1 Introduction   75

2 Formal sources   76

3 Treaties   77
   3.1 The principal treaties   77
   3.2 The importance of treaties   79
   3.3 Revitalizing the treaty system   79

    4   Customary international law   81
    5   *Jus cogens*   84
    6   General principles of law   85
    7   Judicial decisions   86
        7.1 Interaction at the international and regional levels   86
        7.2 Interaction between national courts   87
        7.3 Human rights litigation   88
    8   Writings of jurists   88
    9   Other sources   89
        9.1 Work of treaty bodies   89
        9.2 Resolutions of international institutions   90
        9.3 Other forms of soft law   91
    10 Conclusion   94
    Further reading   94
    Useful websites   95

5   NATURE OF OBLIGATIONS   96
    Frédéric Mégret

    Summary   96
    1   Introduction   96
    2   The 'special character' of human rights obligations   98
    3   Implementation of human rights obligations   101
        3.1 Respect   102
        3.2 Protect   102
        3.3 Fulfil   103
        3.4 Margin of appreciation   104
    4   Reservations   105
        4.1 Permissibility   106
        4.2 Responsibility for assessment   108
        4.3 Consequences   108
    5   Limitations and derogations   110
        5.1 Limitations   110
        5.2 Derogations   113
    6   Withdrawal   114
    7   Remedies for violations of human rights obligations   115
    8   Conclusion   118
    Further reading   118

6   SCOPE OF APPLICATION   119
    Sarah Joseph and Adam Fletcher

    Summary   119
    1   Introduction   119
    2   Who has human rights obligations?   120
    3   Who has human rights?   120
        3.1 Non-nationals   120

3.2	The unborn	121
3.3	Artificial entities	122
4	For which entities is a state responsible?	123
4.1	Private actors	123
4.2	International organizations	125
4.3	Other states	127
5	Where do human rights apply?	129
5.1	ECHR	129
5.2	ACHR	132
5.3	African Charter on Human and Peoples' Rights	132
5.4	ICCPR	133
5.5	ICESCR	134
5.6	Overall assessment	136
6	Conclusion	138
	Further reading	138

PART III SUBSTANTIVE RIGHTS

7 CATEGORIES OF RIGHTS   143
Theo van Boven

	Summary	143
1	Introduction	143
2	Categories of human rights	144
2.1	Economic, social, cultural rights/civil, political rights	144
2.2	Rights of individuals/rights of collectivities	145
2.3	One-dimensional/composite rights	147
3	Interdependence and indivisibility of all human rights	147
4	Core rights	150
5	New human rights?	152
6	Conclusion	155
	Further reading	155

8 EQUALITY AND NON-DISCRIMINATION   157
Daniel Moeckli

	Summary	157
1	Introduction	157
2	The meaning of equality and non-discrimination	158
2.1	Formal equality	158
2.2	Substantive equality	159
3	Equality and non-discrimination in international law	160
3.1	Sources	160
3.2	Scope: subordinate and autonomous norms	161
3.3	Prohibited grounds of distinction	163
4	Direct and indirect discrimination	164
4.1	Direct discrimination	164
4.2	Indirect discrimination	165
4.3	Discriminatory intention	166

5 Justified and unjustified distinctions   167
  5.1 The justification test   167
  5.2 Standard of review   168
  5.3 Evidence and proof   169

6 Positive action   170
7 Conclusion   172

Further reading   173
Useful websites   173

9 INTEGRITY OF THE PERSON   174
   Nigel S Rodley

Summary   174

1 Introduction   174
  1.1 Respect for human dignity   174
  1.2 The right to integrity of the person   175

2 The right to be free from torture and ill-treatment   175
  2.1 Sources   176
  2.2 Legal status   176
  2.3 Components   177
  2.4 Types of obligation   182
  2.5 Relationship with other human rights   183

3 The right to life   184
  3.1 Sources   184
  3.2 Legal status   185
  3.3 Scope: beginning and end of life   185
  3.4 Components   186
  3.5 Types of obligation   191
  3.6 Relationship with other human rights   192

4 Conclusion   192

Further reading   193
Useful websites   194

10 ADEQUATE STANDARD OF LIVING   195
    Asbjørn Eide

Summary   195

1 Introduction   195

2 Meaning and features   196
  2.1 Duties of the individual   197
  2.2 State obligations   198
  2.3 Equality and non-discrimination as an overarching principle   198

3 Normative content   199
  3.1 The right to food   199
  3.2 The right to housing   202
  3.3 The right to health   204

4 Categories and groups of people   206
  4.1 Women   207
  4.2 Children   207

4.3 Indigenous peoples 208

4.4 Dalits in South Asia and Roma in Europe 209

5 Relationship with other human rights 210

5.1 The right to social security and social assistance 211

5.2 Civil and political rights 212

6 Progressive implementation 212

7 The importance of international monitoring and recourse procedures 213

8 Conclusion 215

Further reading 215

Useful websites 216

11 THOUGHT, EXPRESSION, ASSOCIATION, AND ASSEMBLY 217
Kevin Boyle and Sangeeta Shah

Summary 217

1 Introduction 217

1.1 Four freedoms and their relationships 217

1.2 Limitations 218

2 Freedom of thought, conscience, and religion 219

2.1 Sources 219

2.2 Scope 220

2.3 Freedom of religion or belief 220

2.4 Limitations 223

3 Freedom of opinion and expression 225

3.1 Sources 225

3.2 Scope 225

3.3 Limitations 228

4 Freedom of association 231

4.1 Sources 231

4.2 Scope 231

4.3 Limitations 233

5 Freedom of assembly 234

5.1 Sources 234

5.2 Scope 234

5.3 Limitations 235

6 Conclusion 236

Further reading 237

Useful websites 237

12 EDUCATION AND WORK 238
Fons Coomans

Summary 238

1 Introduction 238

2 The Right to Education 239

2.1 Sources 239

2.2 Features 241

2.3 The aims of education   242
2.4 Components   242
2.5 Types of obligations   246
2.6 Relationship with other human rights   248

3 The right to work and work-related rights   249
   3.1 Sources   249
   3.2 Features   252
   3.3 Components   253
   3.4 Obligations   255
   3.5 Relationship with other human rights   256

4 Conclusion   257

Further reading   257
Useful websites   258

13 DETENTION AND TRIAL   259
    Sangeeta Shah

    Summary   259

    1 Introduction   259

    2 Freedom from arbitrary detention   260
       2.1 Sources   260
       2.2 Scope and types of obligations   261
       2.3 Permissible deprivations of liberty   262
       2.4 Guarantees to those deprived of their liberty   264
       2.5 Emergency detention powers   268

    3 Enforced disappearance   269

    4 Security of the person   270

    5 The right to a fair trial   270
       5.1 Sources   270
       5.2 Scope and types of obligations   271
       5.3 Generally applicable fair trial guarantees   272
       5.4 Fair trial guarantees in criminal proceedings   278

    6 Conclusion   284

    Further reading   284
    Useful websites   285

14 CULTURAL RIGHTS   286
    Julie Ringelheim

    Summary   286

    1 Introduction   286

    2 What is *cultural life*?   288
       2.1 From high culture to popular culture   289
       2.2 From culture as the life of the mind to culture as a way of life 289

    3 The right to take part in cultural life   290
       3.1 The normative content of the right to take part in cultural life 291
       3.2 Groups requiring special attention   294
       3.3 Limitations of the right   295

    4 The right to science   296

5　The rights of authors and inventors 297
　　5.1　Human rights and intellectual property 298
　　5.2　The content and limitations of the right under
　　　　　Article 15(1)(c) ICESCR 299

6　Conclusion 301

Further reading 301
Useful websites 302

15　SEXUAL ORIENTATION AND GENDER IDENTITY 303
　　Michael O'Flaherty

Summary 303

1　Introduction 303

2　Forms of vulnerability to human rights attack 304

3　Review of law and jurisprudence 305
　　3.1　Protection of privacy rights 306
　　3.2　Discrimination 307
　　3.3　General human rights protection 310

4　Legal initiatives to bridge the gap between law and practice 312

5　Conclusion 314

Further reading 315
Useful websites 315

16　WOMEN'S RIGHTS 316
　　Dianne Otto

Summary 316

1　Introduction 316

2　A new era of non-discrimination on the ground of sex and
　　equality with men 319
　　2.1　The position prior to 1945 319
　　2.2　The UDHR and the international covenants 319

3　The substantive equality approach of CEDAW 322
　　3.1　Towards a robust understanding of equality 322
　　3.2　Limitations of the CEDAW approach 324

4　Mainstreaming women's human rights 328
　　4.1　Re-imagining the universal subject: the approach of the
　　　　　Human Rights Committee 328
　　4.2　Analysing the relationship between gender and racial discrimination:
　　　　　the approach of the Committee on the Elimination of
　　　　　Racial Discrimination 329
　　4.3　Addressing the inequality of both women and men: the approach
　　　　　of the Committee on Economic, Social and Cultural Rights 330
　　4.4　Recognizing gender as a key factor: the approach of the
　　　　　Committee against Torture 330

5　Conclusion 331

Further reading 332
Useful websites 332

17 GROUP RIGHTS   333
    Robert McCorquodale

    Summary   333

    1 Introduction   333
       1.1 Group rights   333
       1.2 Group rights v rights of individuals   334
       1.3 Relevance of group rights   335

    2 The right of self-determination   335
       2.1 Concept   335
       2.2 Definitions   336

    3 The application of the right of self-determination   338
       3.1 Colonial context   338
       3.2 Outside the colonial context   340

    4 The exercise of the right of self-determination   341
       4.1 External and internal self-determination   341
       4.2 Procedures for exercising the right of self-determination   343

    5 Limitations on the exercise of the right of self-determination   345
       5.1 Rights of others   345
       5.2 Territorial integrity   346
       5.3 Other limitations   347

    6 Minorities   348
       6.1 Defining 'minorities'   348
       6.2 Rights of minorities   349
       6.3 Exercise of minority rights   350
       6.4 Individual v group rights   350

    7 Indigenous peoples   351
       7.1 Defining 'indigenous peoples'   351
       7.2 The rights of indigenous peoples   352
       7.3 Exercise of indigenous peoples' rights   353

    8 Conclusion   354

    Further reading   355

PART IV PROTECTION

18 UNITED NATIONS   359
    Jane Connors and Markus Schmidt

    Summary   359

    1 Introduction   359

    2 The Human Rights Council   360
       2.1 1946–2006: from the Commission on Human Rights to the
            Human Rights Council   360
       2.2 Composition, working methods, and mandate   361
       2.3 Universal periodic review   363
       2.4 Responses to urgent situations   365
       2.5 Special procedures   367
       2.6 Complaint procedure   370

	2.7 Human Rights Council Advisory Committee	372
	2.8 Review	373
	2.9 In conclusion	374
3	The treaty-based bodies	375
	3.1 State reporting	376
	3.2 General comments	379
	3.3 Inquiries	380
	3.4 Complaints procedures	381
	3.5 Treaty body coordination, harmonization, reform, and strengthening	384
	3.6 In conclusion	387
4	The Office of the UN High Commissioner for Human Rights	388
5	Human rights activities in other parts of the UN	391
	5.1 General Assembly	391
	5.2 Security Council	392
	5.3 Secretary-General	394
	5.4 International Court of Justice	395
6	Conclusion	395
	Further reading	396
	Useful websites	397

19 THE AMERICAS — 398
Jo Pasqualucci

	Summary	398
1	Introduction	398
2	Historical overview	399
3	American Convention on Human Rights	400
4	Inter-American Commission on Human Rights	402
	4.1 Structure and composition	402
	4.2 Individual complaints procedures	402
	4.3 Other roles of the Commission	404
5	Inter-American Court of Human Rights	404
	5.1 Structure and composition	406
	5.2 Contentious cases	406
	5.3 Court-ordered reparations and state compliance	408
	5.4 Interim measures	410
	5.5 Advisory jurisdiction	411
6	Challenges to the Inter-American system	412
7	Conclusion	413
	Further reading	414
	Useful websites	415

20 EUROPE — 416
Steven Greer

	Summary	416
1	Introduction	416
2	The Organization for Security and Cooperation in Europe	417

3 The Council of Europe   417
  3.1 Origins   418
  3.2 Key institutions   419
  3.3 Key instruments   420

4 The European Convention on Human Rights   422
  4.1 Substantive rights   422
  4.2 Institutional and procedural background   423
  4.3 Complaints procedure   426
  4.4 Resolution of complaints   430
  4.5 Supervision of the execution of judgments   433

5 The European Union   435
  5.1 Human rights and the Court of Justice of the European Union 436
  5.2 The Charter of Fundamental Rights   437
  5.3 The Fundamental Rights Agency and the Commissioner for
      Justice, Fundamental Rights and Citizenship   438

6 Conclusion   438

Further reading   439
Useful websites   440

21 AFRICA   441
   Christof Heyns and Magnus Killander

   Summary   441

   1 Introduction   441

   2 Historical overview   442

   3 The African Charter and other relevant treaties   444
     3.1 Norms recognized in the African Charter   444
     3.2 Duties and limitations   446
     3.3 Protection of women, children, and vulnerable groups   446

   4 The protective mechanisms   448
     4.1 The African Commission   448
     4.2 The African Court on Human and Peoples' Rights   452
     4.3 The AU main organs and human rights   454
     4.4 The African Peer Review Mechanism   455

   5 Conclusion   456

   Further reading   457
   Useful websites   457

22 WITHIN THE STATE   458
   Andrew Byrnes and Catherine Renshaw

   Summary   458

   1 Introduction   458

   2 Substantive protections   459
     2.1 Incorporation of international human rights norms into
         domestic law   460
     2.2 Constitutional guarantees of human rights   465
     2.3 Legislative protection of human rights   467
     2.4 Common law protection of human rights   468

3 Institutional protections 469
  3.1 The courts 469
  3.2 The executive 470
  3.3 The legislature 470
  3.4 Other bodies 471
4 Conclusion 474
Further reading 474
Useful websites 475

PART V LINKAGES

23 INTERNATIONAL HUMANITARIAN LAW 479
   Sandesh Sivakumaran

Summary 479
1 Introduction 479
2 What is international humanitarian law? 480
3 Different histories; shared values 481
4 Reasons for the application of human rights law in armed conflict 483
  4.1 Non-applicability of international humanitarian law 483
  4.2 Duty to investigate 485
  4.3 Enforcement 486
5 The relationship between the two bodies of law 487
  5.1 Rights exclusively matters of international humanitarian law 488
  5.2 Rights exclusively matters of international human rights law 489
  5.3 Rights matters of both international human rights law and
      international humanitarian law 489
  5.4 An alternative approach: regulation through application of
      international human rights law 492
6 Difficulties with the application of international human rights law
  to armed conflict 492
  6.1 Asymmetrical obligations between the parties 493
  6.2 Differential obligations within a coalition 493
  6.3 Sphere of applicability: the extraterritorial application of human
      rights treaties 494
7 Conclusion 494
Further reading 495
Useful websites 495

24 INTERNATIONAL CRIMINAL LAW 496
   Robert Cryer

Summary 496
1 Introduction 496
2 Human rights law and international crimes 497
  2.1 Genocide 498
  2.2 Crimes against humanity 501
  2.3 War crimes 505
  2.4 Aggression 506

3 Prosecutions: international and national   507

4 Non-prosecutorial options   510
   4.1 Amnesties   510
   4.2 Truth and reconciliation commissions   511

5 Conclusion   511

Further reading   512
Useful websites   512

25 INTERNATIONAL REFUGEE LAW   513
   Alice Edwards

Summary   513

1 Introduction   513

2 What is international refugee law?   514

3 Fundamental elements of international refugee law   515

4 Relationship between the two bodies of law   516

5 Human rights and refugee status   518

6 Refugee *non-refoulement* and human rights   520

7 The protections accorded to refugees   523

8 The end of refugee status and solutions for refugees   524

9 Conclusion   526

Further reading   526
Useful websites   527

PART VI CHALLENGES

26 NON-STATE ACTORS   531
   Andrew Clapham

Summary   531

1 Introduction   531

2 The challenge of non-state actors   533
   2.1 Globalization   533
   2.2 Privatization   534
   2.3 Fragmentation of states   535
   2.4 Feminization   535

3 The legal framework   535

4 The obligations of international organizations   538

5 International criminal responsibility of non-state actors   540

6 Corporate social responsibility and the move towards accountability   541

7 Armed opposition groups   543
   7.1 The UN Security Council on children and armed conflict 544
   7.2 UN special procedures   545
   7.3 NGOs and the example of Geneva Call   547

8 Conclusion   548

Further reading   549
Useful websites   549

27 TERRORISM 550
Martin Scheinin

Summary 550

1 Introduction 550

2 Is terrorism a violation of human rights? 551

3 Applicability of human rights law in the fight against terrorism 553
   3.1 Times of armed conflict or emergency 553
   3.2 Extraterritorial applicability of human rights law 554

4 The notion of terrorism and its misuse 554

5 Substantive challenges to human rights law in the fight against terrorism 556
   5.1 Freedom from torture and cruel, inhuman, or degrading treatment 557
   5.2 Right to liberty and right to a fair trial 558
   5.3 Right to non-discrimination 560
   5.4 Other human rights 561

6 An institutional challenge: terrorist listing by the security council 562

7 Conclusion: is the pendulum already swinging back? 564

Further reading 565
Useful websites 566

28 POVERTY 567
Stephen P Marks

Summary 567

1 Introduction 567

2 Human rights and poverty in the global economy 569
   2.1 Poverty and its significance for human rights 569
   2.2 Development, social justice, and human rights 571
   2.3 The context of poverty and human rights: globalization 572

3 Divergence of poverty reduction and human rights agendas 573
   3.1 Resistance to human rights discourse in economic thinking 573
   3.2 The perspective of central banks and ministries of finance 575

4 Convergence of poverty reduction and human rights agendas 578
   4.1 Trends in economic thinking congruent with human rights 578
   4.2 Human rights approaches in poverty reduction policies 579

5 Conclusion 587

Further reading 589
Useful websites 589

29 ENVIRONMENTAL DEGRADATION 590
Malgosia Fitzmaurice

Summary 590

1 Introduction 590

2 Substantive environmental rights 592
   2.1 African Charter 592
   2.2 San Salvador Protocol to the American Convention on Human Rights 593
   2.3 Progress at the UN 594
   2.4 Indirect substantive environmental rights 596

2.5 Substantive environmental rights at the national level   600
2.6 Is there a need for a substantive environmental right?   601

3 Procedural environmental rights   603
3.1 The Aarhus Convention   604
3.2 Indirect procedural environmental rights   607

4 Conclusion   608

Further reading   609
Useful websites   609

Index   611

PREFACE

Human rights mean different things to different people. From the woman on the street to the UN High Commissioner for Human Rights, from the local human rights activist to the government official, each of us has a different conception of the origin, purpose, and function of human rights. To reflect this diversity of views, we have invited a range of practitioners and academics with different regional, theoretical, and professional backgrounds to contribute chapters to this textbook on their respective fields of expertise.

The book follows the same format as the first edition. It opens with personal perspectives on what human rights are for from three leading human rights practitioners. It then covers the key elements of a typical international human rights law course. Part I seeks to show how human rights have developed over time, how they can be justified, and on what basis they may be criticized. Today, human rights are firmly located in international law and Part II explores the key international law aspects of human rights. Part III considers some of the rights guaranteed to individuals and groups by international human rights law. Part IV addresses the systems of human rights protection at the UN, regional, and national levels. Part V examines the linkages between international human rights law and three other areas of international law: international humanitarian law, international criminal law, and international refugee law. Finally, the book concludes, in Part VI, with a consideration of some of the major challenges to the protection of human rights. For want of space, it is impossible to cover all substantive rights, protected groups, systems of protection, linkages, and challenges. This is not meant to reflect in any way the importance, or lack thereof, of the omitted issues.

There are some changes to the book for this second edition. The most obvious is the addition of chapters on Justifications by Samantha Besson, Cultural Rights by Julie Ringelheim, and International Refugee Law by Alice Edwards. Furthermore, each of the original chapters has been thoroughly updated to take account of developments since the publication of the first edition in September 2010. Many chapters have also been expanded or elaborated in response to helpful comments received about the first edition. We are grateful to friends and colleagues for these comments. There have also been some changes in authors. Sadly, Kevin Boyle passed away in January 2011 and his chapter has been updated by one of the editors. We wish to extend our thanks to Joan Boyle for her agreement that we might update the chapter. Jane Connors of the UN Office of the High Commissioner for Human Rights has updated the chapter on the UN and Sarah Joseph has been joined by Adam Fletcher in the update of her chapter on Scope of Application.

Many people have supported us in various ways throughout the process of producing this textbook. We are particularly grateful to the contributors to the book for their enthusiasm and support, to our consulting editor, David Harris, for his guidance throughout the process, to Ioannis Athanasopoulos, Lea Raible, Raphael Keller, and Raffael Fasel for their editorial assistance, and to Emily Uecker, Hannah Marsden, and their team at Oxford University Press for steering us through the various editorial stages.

DM/SS/SS
Zurich/Nottingham, July 2013

NOTES ON CONTRIBUTORS

Ed Bates is a Senior Lecturer at the University of Southampton. He is a co-author of Harris, O'Boyle, Warbrick, Bates, and Buckley, *The Law of the European Convention on Human Rights* (Oxford University Press, 2009) and author of *The Evolution of the European Convention on Human Rights* (Oxford University Press, 2010).

Samantha Besson is Professor of Public International Law and European Law and Co-Director of the European Law Institute at the University of Fribourg, Switzerland.

The late **Kevin Boyle** was Professor of Law, University of Essex and director of the University's Human Rights Centre until 2007. He was senior adviser to Mary Robinson, then UN High Commissioner for Human Rights, 2001–2. He was Chair of the International Council of Minority Rights Group and founding director of Article 19, the Global Campaign for Freedom of Expression. He litigated before the European Court of Human Rights, including on freedom of expression cases.

Andrew Byrnes is Professor of International Law at the Faculty of Law, The University of New South Wales (UNSW), and Chair of the Management Committee of the Australian Human Rights Centre, UNSW. Since late 2012 he has served as external legal adviser to the Australian Parliamentary Joint Committee on Human Rights. His chapter with Catherine Renshaw draws on research conducted under two Australian Research Council-funded Linkage projects (LP0776639 and LP0989167) on national human rights institutions in the Asia Pacific, and economic, social and cultural rights, respectively.

Christine Chinkin, FBA, is Professor of International Law, London School of Economics and Political Science, and William W. Cook Global Law Professor, University of Michigan Law School.

Andrew Clapham is a Professor of International Law at the Graduate Institute of International and Development Studies and Director of the Geneva Academy of International Humanitarian Law and Human Rights. He is also a Commissioner of the International Commission of Jurists in 2013. His publications include *Brierly's Law of Nations: An Introduction to the Role of International Law in International Relations* (7th ed, 2012), *Human Rights Obligations of Non-State Actors* (2006), and *International Human Rights Lexicon* (2005), with Susan Marks.

Jane Connors is currently the Chief of the Special Procedures Branch of the United Nations Office of the High Commissioner for Human Rights (OHCHR). She has worked in the UN since 1996 when she took up the post of Chief of the Women's Rights Section in the Division for the Advancement of Women. She transferred to OHCHR in 2002 and until 2009 she was a senior human rights officer in the Human Rights Treaties Branch. Before joining the UN, she taught at the School of Oriental and African Studies in the University of London, Lancaster University, the University of Nottingham, the University of Canberra, and the Australian National University. She has written widely on the work of the human rights treaty bodies, violence against women, and the human rights of women.

Fons Coomans holds the UNESCO Chair in Human Rights and Peace at the Department of International and European Law of Maastricht University. He is also the coordinator of the Maastricht Centre for Human Rights, Senior Researcher at the Netherlands School of Human Rights Research, and Visiting Professor at the University of Cape Town. His research focuses on economic, social, and cultural rights and international human rights monitoring procedures.

Robert Cryer is Professor of International and Criminal Law at the University of Birmingham. He teaches international law, criminal law, and international criminal law.

Marie-Bénédicte Dembour is Professor of Law and Anthropology at the University of Brighton. She has published widely, including most prominently in the field of human rights a monograph entitled *Who Believes in Human Rights? Reflections on the European Convention* (Cambridge University Press, 2006). She is currently preparing a study which analyses the approach of the European Court of Human Rights to migrant cases since the inception of the Strasbourg system and contrasts it with the approach of the Inter-American Court (Oxford University Press, forthcoming).

Alice Edwards, PhD, is Senior Legal Coordinator and Chief of Law and Policy at the United Nations High Commissioner for Refugees (UNHCR) in Geneva, Switzerland, responsible for the organization's core legal and policy work, including doctrinal guidelines, legal and policy advice, advocacy, and litigation. She is the author of inter alia *Violence against Women under International Human Rights Law* (Cambridge University Press, 2011). She has previously held academic positions at the Universities of Oxford and Nottingham.

Asbjørn Eide is former Director and presently Professor Emeritus at the Norwegian Center for Human Rights at the University of Oslo. He has been Torgny Segerstedt Professor at the University of Gothenburg, Sweden, visiting professor at the University of Lund, and is adjunct professor at the College of Law, American University in Washington. He is author and editor of several books and numerous articles on human rights, and was for 20 years an expert member of the UN Sub-Commission on Promotion and Protection of Human Rights.

Malgosia Fitzmaurice is Professor of Public International Law at the Department of Law, Queen Mary, University of London. She has published widely in the areas of international environmental law, the law of treaties, water law, and indigenous peoples law. In July 2001, she delivered lectures on 'International Protection of the Environment' at the Hague Academy of International Law. In 2013 (with Professor Valsamis Mitsilegas) she was awarded a grant from the EU to research environmental crimes.

Adam Fletcher was formerly an intern at the United Nations High Commissioner for Refugees, an officer in the Australian Government's Office of International Law, and a legal adviser to the Association for the Prevention of Torture in Geneva. He is currently a PhD candidate in the Faculty of Law at Monash University, having previously held a Research Fellowship as Manager of the Accountability Project at the Castan Centre for Human Rights Law. His thesis is on the implementation of international human rights obligations through parliamentary scrutiny of legislation.

Steven Greer is Professor of Human Rights at the University of Bristol Law School and Academician at the UK's Academy of Social Sciences. He studied Law at the University of Oxford, Sociology at the London School of Economics and Political Science, and has a PhD in Law from the Queen's University of Belfast. He has taught at several universities in the UK—and in Germany, France and Australia—and acted as consultant/advisor to various organizations including the Council of Europe and others in Northern Ireland, Palestine, and Nepal. He was a Nuffield Foundation Visiting Research Fellow at the Oñati International Institute for the Sociology of Law (Spain) and a British Academy Research Fellow at the University of Bristol. He has published widely, particularly in the fields of criminal justice, human rights, and law and terrorism. Two of his books have been shortlisted for book prizes and some of his published and other work has been translated into half a dozen languages. Current research projects include a book, co-authored by Professor Andrew Williams (University of Warwick), about human rights in the Council of Europe and the European Union.

Christof Heyns is Professor of Human Rights Law and a director of the Institute for International and Comparative Law in Africa at the University of Pretoria. He is also United Nations Special Rapporteur on extrajudicial, summary or arbitrary executions.

Sarah Joseph is a Professor of International Human Rights Law and, since 2005, the Director of the Castan Centre for Human Rights Law at Monash University, Melbourne. She has written extensively in the area of human rights, including in relation to global trade and investment, multinational corporations, and terrorism. She is the main author of *The International Covenant on Civil and Political Rights: Cases Materials and Commentary* (Oxford University Press, 3rd ed, 2013). Her latest research is in the area of media, including social media, and human rights.

Magnus Killander is Senior Lecturer and Head of Research at the Centre for Human Rights at the University of Pretoria Faculty of Law.

Stephen P Marks is the François-Xavier Bagnoud Professor of Health and Human Rights at the Harvard School of Public Health, where he directs the Program on Human Rights in Development. He also teaches human rights in the Faculty of Arts and Sciences at Harvard University. He served in the United Nations system for 12 years, including in Unesco, in peace-keeping operations, and recently as member and chair of the UN High-level Task Force on the Implementation of the Right to Development (2004–2010). Among his recent publications as editor or co-editor are *Development as a Human Right: Legal, Political and Economic Dimensions* (2nd ed, 2010), *Health and Human Rights: Basic International Documents* (3rd ed, 2012), *Achieving the Human Right to Health* (2013), *Realizing the Right to Development: Essays in Commemoration of 25 Years of the United Nations Declaration on the Right to Development* (2013, as editorial consultant to the OHCHR), and *Research Handbook on Human Rights and Development* (in preparation for 2014).

Robert McCorquodale is the Director of the British Institute of International and Comparative Law in London. He is also Professor of International Law and Human Rights, and former Head of the School of Law, University of Nottingham. Previously he was a Fellow and Lecturer in Law at St. John's College, University of Cambridge and at the Australian National University in Canberra. Before embarking on an academic career, he worked as a qualified lawyer in commercial litigation in Sydney and London. Robert's research and teaching interests are in the areas of public international law and human rights law, including the role of non-state actors. He has published widely on these areas, including being co-author of *Cases and Materials on International Law* (Oxford University Press, 5th ed, 2011), and has provided advice to governments, corporations, international organizations, non-governmental organizations and peoples concerning international law and human rights issues, including advising on the drafting of new constitutions and conducting human rights training courses.

Frédéric Mégret is an Associate Professor at McGill University's Faculty of Law, and the holder of the Canada Research Chair in the Law of Human Rights and Legal Pluralism. He holds a PhD from the Université de Paris I and the Geneva Graduate Institute of International Studies.

Daniel Moeckli is an Assistant Professor of Public International Law and Constitutional Law at the University of Zurich and a Fellow of the University of Nottingham Human Rights Law Centre. He is the author of *Human Rights and Non-discrimination in the 'War on Terror'* (Oxford University Press, 2008).

Michael O'Flaherty is Established Professor of Human Rights Law and Director of the Irish Centre for Human Rights at the National University of Ireland, Galway. He also serves as Chief Commissioner of the Northern Ireland Human Rights Commission. From 2004–2012 he was a member, and latterly Vice Chair, of the United Nations Human Rights Committee. He was Rapporteur for the 2007 Yogyakarta Principles on the Application of International Human Rights Law Regarding Sexual Orientation and Gender Identity.

Dianne Otto is Director of the Institute for International Law and the Humanities (IILAH) at Melbourne Law School. She researches in the areas of public international law and human rights law, drawing upon and developing a range of critical legal theories particularly those influenced by feminism, postcolonialism, poststructuralism, and queer theory. Her current research focus is on gender and sexuality issues in the context of the UN Security Council, peacekeeping, counter-terror measures, people's tribunals and the work of the human rights treaty bodies. Dianne's scholarship explores how international legal discourse reproduces hierarchies of nation, race, gender, and sexuality, and aims to understand how the reproduction of such legal knowledge can be resisted. Her recent publications include 'Transnational Homo-Assemblages: Reading "gender" in counter-terrorism discourses' (Jindal Global Law Review, 2013) and 'International Human Rights Law: The Perils of Sex/Gender Dualism and Asymmetry' (Margaret Davies and Vanessa Munro (eds), *A Research Companion to Feminist Legal Theory*, Ashgate 2013). Dianne has recently edited three volumes on Gender Issues and Human Rights (Edward Elgar, Human Rights Law Series, 2013) and prepared a bibliographic chapter, 'Feminist Approaches', in *Oxford Bibliographies Online: International Law*, ed. Tony Carty (Oxford University Press, 2012). She also helped draft a General Comment on women's equality for the Committee on Economic, Social and Cultural Rights and a General Recommendation on treaty obligations for the Committee on the Elimination of Discrimination Against Women.

Jo M. Pasqualucci is a Professor of Law at the University of South Dakota. She earned her JD at the University of Wisconsin and her SJD in International and Comparative Law at George Washington University Law School. She clerked at the Inter-American Court of Human Rights and is the author of *The Practice and Procedure of the Inter-American Court of Human Rights* (Cambridge University Press, 2nd ed, 2013) and several articles on the Inter-American human rights system.

Catherine Renshaw is an Associate of the Sydney Centre for International Law at the University of Sydney. Between 2008 and 2010, she was Director of an Australian Research Council-funded Linkage Project (LP0776639) on national human rights institutions in the Asia Pacific region.

Julie Ringelheim is Senior Researcher with the Belgian National Fund for Scientific Research (FNRS) and with the Centre for Philosophy of Law of Louvain University. She is also Professor of International Human Rights Law at Louvain University.

Sir Nigel S Rodley is Professor of Law and Chair of the Human Rights Centre at the University of Essex. From 1992 to 2001 he served as UN Commission on Human Rights Special Rapporteur on the question of torture. He has been a member of the UN Human Rights Committee since 2001 and is currently its Chair. He is also President of the International Commission of Jurists.

Martin Scheinin is, since 2008, Professor of Public International Law at the European University Institute in Florence. He served as the UN Special Rapporteur on human rights and counter-terrorism (2005–2011). He has a doctorate in law from the University of Helsinki (1991) and was from 1997–2004 a member of the UN Human Rights Committee and from 1998–2008 Director of the Institute for Human Rights at Åbo Akademi University.

Markus Schmidt is senior legal officer for the UN Office at Geneva since 2010. Until December 2009, he was senior human rights officer in the Office of the UN High Commissioner for Human Rights (OHCHR). He served as secretary of the Human Rights Committee from 2001 to 2005 and was team leader of the Petitions Unit of OHCHR from 2002 to 2009.

Sangeeta Shah is a Lecturer in the School of Law, University of Nottingham and Member of the Human Rights Law Centre, University of Nottingham. She is the co-editor of the Recent Developments Section of the *Human Rights Law Review*.

Sandesh Sivakumaran is Associate Professor and Reader in Public International Law, and Member of the Human Rights Law Centre, University of Nottingham. He has worked at the

International Court of Justice, the International Criminal Tribunal for the former Yugoslavia, and the Special Court for Sierra Leone. His publications include *The Law of Non-International Armed Conflict* (Oxford University Press, 2012).

Theo van Boven is Professor Emeritus of International Law at Maastricht University, the Netherlands. Over the years he has been closely associated with the human rights programme of the UN, notably as Director of Human Rights, member of the Commission and the Sub-Commission for Human Rights, member of the Committee on the Elimination of Racial Discrimination, and Special Rapporteur on Torture.

ABBREVIATIONS

AAA	American Anthropological Association
ACHPR	African Charter on Human and Peoples' Rights
ACHR	American Convention on Human Rights
ACommHPR	African Commission on Human and Peoples' Rights
ADHR	American Declaration of the Rights and Duties of Man
AIDS	Acquired Immunodeficiency Syndrome
AJIL	American Journal of International Law
APRM	African Peer Review Mechanism
ASEAN	Association of Southeast Asian Nations
ASIL	American Society of International Law
AU	African Union
BBC	British Broadcasting Corporation
BC	Before Christ
BGE	Bundesgerichtsentscheid (Swiss Federal Supreme Court decision)
BYIL	British Year Book of International Law
CAT	Committee Against Torture
CDDH	Steering Committee for Human Rights
CEDAW	Convention on the Elimination of All Forms of Discrimination Against Women
CEDAW-OP	Optional Protocol to the CEDAW
CEJIL	Center for Justice and International Law
CERD	Committee on the Elimination of Racial Discrimination
CESCR	Committee on Economic, Social and Cultural Rights
CFI	Court of First Instance
CHR	UN Commission on Human Rights
CIDA	Canadian International Development Agency
CJEU	Court of Justice of the European Union
CLP	Current Legal Problems
CPED	International Convention for the Protection of all Persons from Enforced Disappearance
CPPEVAW	Inter-American Convention on the Prevention, Punishment and Eradication of Violence Against Women
CRC	Convention on the Rights of the Child
CRNZ	Criminal Reports of New Zealand

CRPD	Convention on the Rights of Persons with Disabilities
CRPD-OP	Optional Protocol to the CRPD
CSCE	Conference on Security and Cooperation in Europe
CTC	Counter-Terrorism Committee
CUP	Cambridge University Press
DANIDA	Danish International Development Agency
Dec	Decision
DFID	UK Department for International Development
DPKO	UN Department of Peacekeeping Operations
DRC	Democratic Republic of Congo
EACJ	East African Court of Justice
EC	European Community
ECHR	European Convention on Human Rights
ECJ	European Court of Justice
ECommHR	European Commission on Human Rights
ECOMOG	Economic Community of West African States Monitoring Group
ECOSOC	UN Economic and Social Council
ECOSOCC	Economic, Social and Cultural Council of the African Union
ECOWAS	Economic Community of West African States
ECPT	European Convention for the Prevention of Torture and Inhuman or Degrading Treatment or Punishment
ECSR	European Committee of Social Rights
EEC	European Economic Community
EHRLR	European Human Rights Law Review
EHRR	European Human Rights Reports
EIA	Environmental Impact Assessment
EJ	European Journal
EJIL	European Journal of International Law
ELJ	European Law Journal
ELR	European Law Review
EPO	European Patent Office
EU	European Union
EWCA	England and Wales Court of Appeal
EWHC	England and Wales High Court
FAO	Food and Agriculture Organization of the UN
FARC	Revolutionary Armed Forces of Colombia
FRA	Fundamental Rights Agency
FRY	Federal Republic of Yugoslavia
G-20	The Group of Twenty
GA	General Assembly of the UN

GDR	German Democratic Republic
HDCA	Human Development and Capability Association
HHRJ	Harvard Human Rights Journal
HIPC	Highly Indebted Poor Countries
HIV	Human Immunodeficiency Virus
HLR	Harvard Law Review
HMSO	Her Majesty's Stationery Office
HRBA	Human Rights-Based Approach
HRC	Human Rights Committee
HR Council	UN Human Rights Council
HRLJ	Human Rights Law Journal
HRLR	Human Rights Law Review
HRQ	Human Rights Quarterly
IACtHR	Inter-American Court of Human Rights
IACommHR	Inter-American Commission on Human Rights
ICC	International Criminal Court
ICCPR	International Covenant on Civil and Political Rights
ICCPR-OP1	First Optional Protocol to the ICCPR
ICCPR-OP2	Second Optional Protocol to the ICCPR
ICERD	International Convention on the Elimination of All Forms of Racial Discrimination
ICESCR	International Covenant on Economic, Social and Cultural Rights
ICESCR-OP	Optional Protocol to the ICESCR
ICLQ	International and Comparative Law Quarterly
ICJ	International Court of Justice
ICRC	International Committee of the Red Cross
ICRMW	International Convention on the Protection of the Rights of All Migrant Workers and Members of Their Families
ICTR	International Criminal Tribunal for Rwanda
ICTY	International Criminal Tribunal for the former Yugoslavia
IDC	International Disability Caucus
IDEA	International Development Ethics Association
IJHR	International Journal of Human Rights
IJRL	International Journal of Refugee Law
ILC	International Law Commission
ILM	International Legal Materials
ILO	International Labour Organization
IMF	International Monetary Fund
INSC	Supreme Court of India
IR	International Relations

IRA	Irish Republican Army
IRRC	International Review of the Red Cross
JCHR	Joint Committee on Human Rights (UK)
JCSL	Journal of Conflict and Security Law
JHR	Journal of Human Rights
JICJ	Journal of International Criminal Justice
KFOR	Kosovo Force
KLA	Kosovo Liberation Army
LGBT	Lesbian, Gay, Bisexual, and Transgender
LJIL	Leiden Journal of International Law
LNOJ	League of Nations Official Journal
LTTE	Liberation Tigers of Tamil Eelam
LQR	Law Quarterly Review
MCC	Millennium Challenge Corporation
MDGs	Millennium Development Goals
MJIL	Michigan Journal of International Law
MINURCAT	UN Mission in the Central African Republic and Chad
MINUSTAH	UN Mission in Haiti
MLR	Modern Law Review
MONUC	UN Mission in the Democratic Republic of Congo
NAACP	National Association for the Advancement of Colored People
NATO	North Atlantic Treaty Organization
NEPAD	New Partnership for Africa's Development
NGO	Non-Governmental Organization
NHRIs	National Human Rights Institutions
NJIL	Nordic Journal of International Law
NPMs	National Preventive Mechanisms
NQHR	Netherlands Quarterly of Human Rights
Nuremberg IMT	Nuremberg International Military Tribunal
NYU	New York University
NYUJILP	New York University Journal of International Law and Politics
OAS	Organization of American States
OAU	Organization of African Unity
ODIHR	Office for Democratic Institutions and Human Rights
OECD	Organization for Economic Co-operation and Development
OHCHR	Office of the UN High Commissioner for Human Rights
OJLS	Oxford Journal of Legal Studies
OPT	Occupied Palestinian Territory
OSCE	Organization of Security and Co-operation in Europe
OUP	Oxford University Press

PACE	Parliamentary Assembly of the Council of Europe
PAP	Pan-African Parliament
PCIJ	Permanent Court of International Justice
PKK	Kurdistan Workers' Party
PL	Public Law
PLD	Pakistan Legal Decisions
PRSPs	Poverty Reduction Strategy Papers
PRWA	Protocol of the Rights of Women in Africa
PSC	Peace and Security Council
Rec des Cours	Recueil des Cours de l'Académie de Droit International
RECs	Regional Economic Communities
Res	Resolution
SADC	Southern African Development Community
SC	Security Council
SCSL	Special Court for Sierra Leone
SGBV	Sexual and Gender-Based Violence
SSR	Soviet Socialist Republic
Tokyo IMT	Tokyo International Military Tribunal
UDHR	Universal Declaration of Human Rights
UK	United Kingdom
UKHL	United Kingdom House of Lords
UN	United Nations
UNAMA	UN Mission in Afghanistan
UNAMI	UN Nations Mission in Iraq
UNCAT	Convention against Torture and Other Cruel, Inhuman or Degrading Treatment or Punishment
UNCAT OP	Optional Protocol to the UNCAT
UNDAT	UN Declaration against Torture
UNDG	UN Development Group
UNDG-HRM	UN Development Group Human Rights Mainstreaming Mechanism
UNDP	UN Development Programme
UNECE	UN Economic Commission for Europe
UNESCO	UN Educational, Scientific and Cultural Organization
UNFPA	UN Population Fund
UNHCR	UN High Commissioner for Refugees
UNICEF	UN Children's Fund
UNIFEM	UN Development Fund for Women
UNMIK	UN Interim Administration Mission in Kosovo
UNMIS	UN Mission in Sudan
UNRWA	UN Relief and Works Agency for Palestine Refugees in the New East

UP	University Press
UPR	Universal Periodic Review
USA	United States of America
USC	United States Code
USSR	Union of Soviet Socialist Republics
VCLT	Vienna Convention on the Law of Treaties
WGC	Working Group on Communications
WGS	Working Group on Situations
WHO	World Health Organization
WLR	Weekly Law Reports
WTO	World Trade Organization
YB	Year Book
YJIL	Yale Journal of International Law

TABLE OF INTERNATIONAL
INSTRUMENTS

African Charter on Human and Peoples' Rights
    1981 (ACHPR) . . . 79, 113, 132, 152, 200, 203,
    442, 443, 444–6, 450, 452, 592–3, 602
    Art 1 . . . 449
    Art 2 . . . 161, 162, 163, 166, 447
    Art 3 . . . 161, 162, 166
    Art 4 . . . 184, 187, 188, 190
    Art 5 . . . 25, 174, 176
    Art 6 . . . 260, 262
    Art 7 . . . 190, 271, 283
        (1)(a) . . . 282
        (b) . . . 279
        (c) . . . 280
        (2) . . . 282
    Art 8 . . . 219, 446
    Art 9 . . . 225
        (2) . . . 446
    Art 10 . . . 231, 446
    Art 11 . . . 234, 240, 446
        (2)(c),(f) . . . 240
        (6) . . . 240
    Art 12 . . . 446
        (3) . . . 517
    Art 13 . . . 445
    Art 15 . . . 251, 254, 445
    Art 16 . . . 205, 445, 593
    Art 17 . . . 445
        (1) . . . 240
        (2) . . . 288
        (3) . . . 245
    Art 18(2) . . . 446
        (3)–(4) . . . 161
        (3) . . . 447
        (4) . . . 447
    Art 19 . . . 445
    Art 20 . . . 336, 445
    Art 21 . . . 445, 446
    Art 22 . . . 445, 586
    Art 23 . . . 445
    Art 24 . . . 445, 446, 592, 593, 608
    Art 27 . . . 446
        (2) . . . 446
    Art 28 . . . 161, 446
    Art 29 . . . 446
        (6) . . . 251
    Art 30 . . . 448
    Art 45 . . . 448
    Arts 47–49 . . . 450
    Art 50 . . . 450

Art 52 . . . 450
Art 53 . . . 450
Art 55 . . . 448, 450
Art 56 . . . 448, 449, 450
Art 57 . . . 448
Art 58 . . . 448
Art 59(1) . . . 450
Protocol on the African Court of Human and
    Peoples' Rights 1998 . . . 453
    Art 4(1) . . . 454
    Art 5 . . . 450
        (3) . . . 450
    Art 18 . . . 453
    Art 27(1) . . . 453
        (2) . . . 454
    Art 29(2) . . . 454
    Art 34(6) . . . 450
Protocol on the Rights of Women in Africa
    2003 (PRWA) . . . 93, 161, 325, 327, 447
    Art 1(j) . . . 326
    Art 2(1)(c) . . . 171
        (d) . . . 170
        (2) . . . 170
    Art 3(4) . . . 326
    Arts 3–24 . . . 170
    Art 4 . . . 326
    Art 5(d) . . . 326
    Art 6(c) . . . 447
    Art 11(3) . . . 326
    Art 20 . . . 327
    Art 22(b) . . . 326
    Art 23(b) . . . 326
    Art 24 . . . 327
African Charter on the Rights and Welfare of the
    Child 1990 . . . 447
    Art 15 . . . 251
African Union Convention for the Protection
    and Assistance of Internally Displaced Persons
    in Africa 2009
    Art 1 . . . 531
American Convention on Human Rights
    1969 (ACHR) . . . 79, 88, 91, 100, 109, 115,
    132, 133, 150, 152, 234, 263, 399, 400–1, 402,
    403, 404, 405, 406, 407, 409, 410, 411, 412,
    413, 462, 487
    Art 1 . . . 161, 162, 163
        (1) . . . 132, 401, 594
        (2) . . . 122, 594
    Art 2(1) . . . 122

Art 4 . . . 175, 184, 185, 189, 594
  (1) . . . 121, 191
  (2) . . . 188, 189
  (3) . . . 189
  (4) . . . 189
  (5) . . . 190
  (6) . . . 190
Art 5 . . . 174, 175, 176, 182, 594
  (2) . . . 265
Art 6 . . . 25
Art 7 . . . 260, 262, 267
  (4) . . . 265, 280
  (5) . . . 267
  (6) . . . 266
Art 8 . . . 241, 271, 278, 594
  (1) . . . 272, 273, 276, 277
    (a) . . . 261
  (2) . . . 279
    (c) . . . 280
    (d) . . . 280
    (e) . . . 281
    (f) . . . 281
    (g) . . . 279
    (h) . . . 282
  (3) . . . 279
  (4) . . . 282
  (5) . . . 278
Art 9 . . . 271, 283
Art 10 . . . 266, 282
Art 11 . . . 306, 594
Art 12 . . . 219
Art 13 . . . 225, 241, 594
  (5) . . . 170
Art 14 . . . 225
Art 15 . . . 234
Art 16 . . . 231
Art 17 . . . 489
Art 18 . . . 489
Art 22(7) . . . 517
Art 24 . . . 161, 162, 163
Art 25 . . . 594
Art 27 . . . 113, 185, 487
Arts 34–37 . . . 402
Art 44 . . . 117, 122
Art 45(1) . . . 403
Art 46(1) . . . 403Art 63(1)408
  (2) . . . 410
Art 78 . . . 114
San Salvador Protocol 1999 . . . 400,
  592, 593–4
  Art 6 . . . 251
    (1) . . . 251
  Art 7 . . . 251
    (a) . . . 254
    (h) . . . 251
  Art 9 . . . 211
  Art 10 . . . 205, 594
  Art 11 . . . 593, 594, 602
  Art 12 . . . 200
  Art 13 . . . 241

Art 19(6) . . . 241
Protocol No 2 to Abolish the Death Penalty
  1991 . . . 185, 400
Additional Protocol in the Area of
  Economic, Social and Cultural Rights
  Art 14 . . . 288
American Declaration on the
  Rights and Duties of
  Man 1948 . . . 91, 398–9, 521
  Art I . . . 260
  Art II . . . 161
  Art XIII . . . 288
  Art XVI . . . 211
  Art XXVII . . . 517
Arab Charter on Human Rights 2004
  Art 2 . . . 161
  Art 9 . . . 161
  Art 12 . . . 271
  Art 13 . . . 271
  Art 14 . . . 260
  Art 16 . . . 271
  Art 17 . . . 271
  Art 24 . . . 231
  Art 30 . . . 219
  Art 32 . . . 225
  Art 34 . . . 251
  Art 35 . . . 161
  Art 37 . . . 586
  Art 41 . . . 241
ASEAN Human Rights Declaration
  Arts 1, 2, 3, 9 . . . 161
  Art 22 . . . 219
  Art 23 . . . 225
  Art 24 . . . 234
  Art 31 . . . 241

Charter of Fundamental Rights of the
  European Union 2000 . . . 437–8
  Art 5 . . . 251
  Art 6 . . . 260
  Art 10 . . . 219, 225
  Art 11 . . . 225
  Art 12 . . . 231
  Art 13 . . . 291
  Art 14 . . . 240
    (2) . . . 240
  Art 18 . . . 517
  Art 20 . . . 161
  Art 21(1) . . . 161
  Art 23 . . . 161
  Art 27 . . . 251
  Art 30 . . . 251
  Art 51(1) . . . 438
  Art 52 . . . 437
    (3) . . . 437
Charter of the International Military Tribunal
  1945 (Nuremberg)
  Art 6 . . . 82
Charter of the Organization of African Unity
  1963 (OAU Charter) . . . 442

Charter of the Organization of American States
    1948 (OAS Charter) . . . 399–400, 402
Convention on Access to Information, Public
    Participation in Decision-making and Access
    to Justice in Environmental Matters 1998
    (Aarhus) . . . 603, 604–7, 608
    Art 3(4) . . . 606
        (9) . . . 606
    Art 4 . . . 604
    Art 5 . . . 604
        (3) . . . 604
    Art 6 . . . 605, 607
    Art 7 . . . 605
    Art 8 . . . 605
    Art 9 . . . 605
        (1) . . . 605
        (2) . . . 605
        (3) . . . 605
    Protocol . . . 604
Convention on the Elimination of All Forms
    of Discrimination Against Women 1979
    (CEDAW) . . . 78, 80–1, 92, 105, 148, 160, 168,
    170, 317, 318, 322–8, 331, 377, 447
    Art 1 . . . 81, 163, 166, 322
    Art 2(e) . . . 323
        (f) . . . 323
    Art 3 . . . 170, 172, 323
    Art 4(1) . . . 171, 323
        (2) . . . 323, 324
    Art 5 . . . 170, 323
        (a) . . . 327
        (b) . . . 324
    Art 6 . . . 170, 323
    Art 10 . . . 239, 243
        (c) . . . 242, 323, 324
        (f) . . . 323
        (h) . . . 324, 325
    Art 11 . . . 250
        (1)(e) . . . 211
        (f) . . . 324
        (2) . . . 323
        (c) . . . 324
    Art 12 . . . 205, 207
        (1) . . . 325
        (2) . . . 324
    Art 13(a) . . . 211
        (c) . . . 287
    Art 14 . . . 207, 327
        (1) . . . 325
        (2) . . . 203
        (c) . . . 211
    Art 15(2) . . . 274
        (3) . . . 324
    Art 16(1) . . . 326
        (d) . . . 326
        (e) . . . 325
    Optional Protocol 1999
        (CEDAW-OP) . . . 78, 377
        Art 8 . . . 92
        Art 16 . . . 325

Convention on Environmental Impact
    Assessment in a Transboundary Context
    1991 (Espoo) . . . 605, 608
Convention on Preventing and Combating
    Violence against Women and Domestic
    Violence 2011 . . . 93
    Art 4(3) . . . 93
    Art 5 . . . 93
    Art 6 . . . 326
    Art 9 . . . 327
    Art 12(6) . . . 326
    Art 18(3) . . . 326
Convention on the Prevention and
    Punishment of the Crime of Genocide
    1948 . . . 31, 78, 99, 100, 109, 116
Convention on the Prohibition of the
    Development, Production and Stockpiling
    of Bacteriological (Biological) and
    Toxin Weapons and on their Destruction
    1972 . . . 481
Convention on the Prohibition of the
    Development, Production and Stockpiling
    and Use of Chemical Weapons and on their
    Destruction 1993 . . . 481
Convention on the Protection of the Underwater
    Cultural Heritage 2001 . . . 292
Convention concerning the Protection of
    the World Cultural and Natural Heritage
    1972 . . . 291–2
Convention on the Rights of the Child 1989
    (CRC) . . . 78, 80, 91, 94, 148, 160, 201, 220,
    240, 377, 447
    Art 2 . . . 161, 243
        (1) . . . 162, 163
    Art 3 . . . 463
    Art 6 . . . 208
    Art 7(1) . . . 462
    Art 12 . . . 225, 462
    Art 13 . . . 225
    Art 23 . . . 462
    Art 24 . . . 199, 205, 208
        (2)(a) . . . 208
    Art 26 . . . 211, 462
    Art 27 . . . 196, 199, 203, 207
        (2) . . . 207
        (3) . . . 207
    Art 28 . . . 161, 240
    Art 29(1) . . . 240
        (a) . . . 242
        (2) . . . 240
    Art 31(2) . . . 288
    Art 32 . . . 250, 251
        (1) . . . 240
    Art 37 . . . 190
    Art 38(1) . . . 483
    Art 40 . . . 271, 283
    Optional Protocol on the Involvement of
        Children in Armed Conflict 2000 . . . 78,
        377, 383, 483, 547
        Art 4(1) . . . 483

Optional Protocol on the Sale of
Children, Child Prostitution and Child
Pornography ... 78, 377
Optional Protocol on a Communications
Procedure 2011 ... 78, 375, 377, 381
  Art 12 ... 381
Convention on the Rights of Persons
with Disabilities 2006 (CRPD) ... 78, 91, 94,
148, 153, 160, 169, 377
  Art 1 ... 163
  Art 2 ... 171
  Art 3 ... 250
  Art 5 ... 163
  Art 13 ... 271
  Art 14 ... 260
    (1)(b) ... 262
  Art 27 ... 250
  Art 30 ... 294, 288
    (1) ... 288
  Art 43 ... 77, 120
  Optional Protocol 2006 (CRPD-OP) ... 78, 377
Convention on the Safeguarding of
Intangible Cultural Heritage 2003 ... 292
Convention relating to the Status of Refugees
1951 ... 78, 513, 514, 515, 517, 518, 524, 526
preamble ... 513, 516, 517
  Art 1(A)(2) ... 515, 518
  Art 1C(1)–(4), (5)–(6) ... 524
  Arts 1D, 1F ... 515
  Art 2 ... 516
  Art 3 ... 523
  Arts 3–34 ... 516, 523
  Art 5 ... 513, 517, 523
  Art 6 ... 518
  Art 9 ... 516
  Arts 10, 11 ... 518
  Arts 13, 14, 15, 16 ... 523
  Arts 17–19 ... 523
  Art 19 ... 518
  Art 20–24 ... 518, 523
  Art 21 ... 203
  Art 22 ... 523
  Art 25 ... 518
  Arts 28, 29, 30 ... 518
  Art 31 ... 518, 523
  Art 31(1) ... 516
  Art 33 ... 520, 521, 523
  Art 33(1) ... 514, 520, 521, 522
  Art 33(2) ... 522
  Art 34 ... 518, 525
  Arts 35, 36 ... 515
  Protocol 1967 ... 514, 515
    Art 1 ... 515
Convention Against Torture and Other
Cruel, Inhuman or Degrading Treatment
1984 (UNCAT) ... 78, 87, 91, 94, 99, 113, 161,
175, 176, 179, 180, 182, 192, 330, 331, 377,
381, 395, 497, 558
  Art 1 ... 87, 178, 557, 491
    (1) ... 491

Art 2(2) ... 557
Art 3 ... 128, 183
Arts 5–8 ... 183
Art 6 ... 128, 129
Art 7 ... 129, 183
Art 15 ... 271, 279
Art 16 ... 179
Art 21 ... 381
Optional Protocol 2002 (UNCAT-OP) ... 78,
175–6, 377, 380
Cotonou Agreement between the Members of
the African, Caribbean and Pacific Group of
States and the European Community and its
Member States 2000
  Art 6 ... 531
Covenant of the League of Nations 1919 ... 27

Dayton Peace Agreement for Peace in Bosnia and
Herzegovina 1995 ... 78–9
Declaration by United Nations 1942 ... 29, 31

European Charter for Regional or Minority
Languages 1992 ... 349
  Art 8 ... 246
European Convention on Human Rights 1950
(ECHR) ... 65, 78–9, 83, 88, 90, 100, 101, 107,
119, 120, 126, 132, 150, 152, 162, 168, 234, 245,
288, 291, 384, 417, 418, 419, 420, 422–35, 437,
438, 462, 508, 522, 596, 597, 601
  Art 1 ... 125, 129, 131, 422, 485
  Art 2 ... 184, 185, 186, 187, 189, 192, 492,
  539, 596, 599
    (1) ... 191
  Arts 2–13 ... 422
  Art 3 ... 87, 128, 176, 177, 182, 186, 190,
  521, 596
  Art 4 ... 25
  Art 5 ... 126, 260, 261, 431
    (1) ... 125, 262, 263, 490
      (f) ... 263
    (2) ... 265, 279
    (3) ... 267, 599
    (4) ... 266
    (5) ... 266
  Art 6 ... 162, 189, 271, 272, 278, 431
    (1) ... 271, 273, 276, 277, 278, 279
    (3)(a) ... 280
      (b) ... 280
      (c) ... 280
      (d) ... 281
      (e) ... 281
  Art 7 ... 271, 283
    (2) ... 283
  Art 8 ... 127, 245, 306, 596, 597, 598, 599, 607
  Art 9 ... 219, 245
  Art 10 ... 225, 245, 423, 596, 607
  Art 11 ... 231, 232, 234, 310, 423
  Art 13 ... 127
  Art 14 ... 161, 162, 163, 164, 166, 167, 423, 599
  Art 15 ... 113, 185, 423, 487, 599

Art 16 . . . 423
Art 17 . . . 423
Art 18 . . . 423
Art 24 . . . 117
Art 27(1) . . . 429
  (2) . . . 429
Art 28 . . . 426
  (1)(a) . . . 426, 429
    (b) . . . 429
Art 29(1) . . . 429
  (2) . . . 427
Art 30 . . . 427, 429
Art 31(a) . . . 427, 429
Art 33 . . . 427
Art 34 . . . 429, 431
Art 35(3)(b) . . . 425, 428
  (4) . . . 427, 429
Art 39(1) . . . 427, 429
  (3) . . . 427, 429
  (4) . . . 429
Art 42 . . . 427, 429
Art 43 . . . 427, 429(2)433
  (5) . . . 427, 429
Art 44 . . . 427, 429
  (1) . . . 427, 429
  (2)(c) . . . 427, 429
Art 46(2) . . . 427, 429, 434
  (3) . . . 427, 429, 434
  (4) . . . 427, 429
Art 56 . . . 129
Art 57 . . . 106
Art 58 . . . 114
Art 59(2) . . . 77
Protocol No 1 . . . 423
  Art 1 . . . 431, 596
  Art 2 . . . 219, 240, 245
Protocol No 4 . . . 423
Protocol No 6 . . . 185, 188, 423
Protocol No 7 . . . 423
  Art 2 . . . 282
  Art 3 . . . 282
  Art 4 . . . 282
Protocol No 11 . . . 424, 425, 426
Protocol No 12 . . . 161, 162, 163, 423
Protocol No 13 . . . 185, 188, 423, 494
Protocol No 14 . . . 423, 425, 426, 428, 436,
  438, 540
Protocol No 14bis . . . 423, 425, 430
Protocol No 15 (draft) . . . 423, 438
  Art 1 . . . 432
  Art 3 . . . 430
  Art 4 . . . 428
  Art 5 . . . 428
European Convention for the Prevention of
  Torture and Inhuman or Degrading Treatment
  or Punishment 1987 (ECPT) . . . 418, 421
European Social Charter 1961 . . . 152, 251, 418,
  420, 437
  Art 10 . . . 240
  Art 11 . . . 205

Art 12 . . . 211
Art 13 . . . 211
Art 14 . . . 211
Art 31 . . . 203
Additional Protocol 1988 . . . 251
European Social Charter (Revised)
  1996 . . . 251, 257
  Art 1 . . . 251
  Art 4 . . . 254
  Art 15(3) . . . 288
  Art 23 . . . 288

Framework Convention for the Protection
  of National Minorities 1995 . . . 288, 329,
  418, 421
  Arts 12–14 . . . 240, 246
  Art 13 . . . 240
Framework Convention on the
  Value of Cultural Heritage for Society
  2005 . . . 292

Geneva Conventions 1949 . . . 24, 31, 480, 509
  Common Art 3 . . . 176, 480, 491
    (1)(c) . . . 483
  Additional Protocol I relating to the Protection
    of Victims of International Armed Conflicts
    1977 . . . 348, 480, 483
    Art 1(4) . . . 348, 480
    Art 10 . . . 481
    Art 15 . . . 481
    Art 35(2) . . . 481
    Art 39 . . . 481
    Art 40 . . . 481
    Art 41 . . . 481
    Art 51(2) . . . 481
      (4) . . . 481
      (5)(b) . . . 481, 482
      (6) . . . 486
    Art 52(1) . . . 481
    Art 57 . . . 481
    Art 72 . . . 488
    Art 75 . . . 481, 484
    Art 76 . . . 481
    Art 77 . . . 481
  Additional Protocol II relating to
    the Protection of Victims of
    Non-International Armed Conflicts
    1977 . . . 480, 483, 484
    preamble . . . 483, 488
    Art 1(1) . . . 484
    Art 4 . . . 481, 484
    Art 6(2)(a) . . . 491
    Arts 7–9 . . . 481
    Art 13(2) . . . 481
    Art 16 . . . 291
Geneva Convention for the Amelioration
  of the Wounded and Sick in the Field (First)
  1949 . . . 482
  Art 12 . . . 176
  Art 50 . . . 176

Geneva Convention for the Amelioration of the
  Wounded, Sick and Shipwrecked Members of
  Armed Forces at Sea (Second) 1949
    Art 12 . . . 176
    Art 51 . . . 176
Geneva Convention Relative to the Treatment of
  Prisoners of War (Third) 1949
    Art 17 . . . 176
    Art 21 . . . 490
    Art 87 . . . 176
    Art 121 . . . 485
    Art 130 . . . 176
Geneva Convention Relative to the Protection of
  Civilian Persons in Time of War (Fourth) 1949
    Art 32 . . . 176
    Arts 41–43 . . . 490
    Art 147 . . . 176
Geneva Protocol for the Prohibition of the Use
  in War of Asphyxiating, Poisonous or Other
  Gases, and of Bacteriological Methods of
  Warfare 1925 . . . 481

Hague Convention 1899 . . . 480, 492
    Art 46 . . . 319
    Art 56 . . . 291
Hague Convention (IV) Respecting the Laws and
  Customs of War on Land 1907 . . . 480
    Art 46 . . . 319
    Art 56 . . . 291
    Regulations
      Art 52 . . . 489
      Art 53 . . . 489
      Art 55 . . . 489

ICC Statute *see* Rome Statute of the International
  Criminal Court 1998
ILC Articles . . . 123
    Arts 5, 8, 11 . . . 123
ILO Constitution
    Art 19(3) . . . 252
    (8) . . . 252
ILO Convention No 1 Limiting the
  Hours of Work in Industrial Undertakings
  1919 . . . 252
ILO Convention No 2 concerning
  Unemployment 1919 . . . 252
ILO Convention No 3 concerning Maternity
  Protection 1919 . . . 319
ILO Convention No 4 concerning
  Employment of Women during the Night
  1919 . . . 254, 319
ILO Convention No 29 on Forced Labour 1930
    Art 2(1) . . . 253
    (2) . . . 253
ILO Convention No 45 on the Employment of
  Women on Underground Work in Mines of
  All Kinds 1935 . . . 319
ILO Convention No 87 concerning Freedom of
  Association and Protection of the Right to
  Organise 1948 . . . 232

ILO Convention No 90 on Equal
  Remuneration 1951
    Art 2 . . . 256
ILO Convention No 100 concerning Equal
  Remuneration for Men and Women Workers
  for Work of Equal Value 1951 . . . 78
ILO Convention No 105 concerning the
  Abolition of Forced Labour 1957
    Art 1 . . . 253
ILO Convention No 107 concerning Indigenous
  and Tribal Populations
  1957 . . . 351, 352
ILO Convention No 111 concerning
  Discrimination in Respect of Employment
  and Occupation 1958 . . . 254
ILO Convention No 122 concerning
  Employment Policy 1964 . . . 254
ILO Convention No 142 concerning
  Vocational Guidance and Vocational Training
  in the Development of Human Resources
  1975 . . . 256
ILO Convention No 158 concerning Termination
  of Employment at the Initiative of the
  Employer 1982 . . . 255
ILO Convention No 169 concerning Indigenous
  and Tribal Peoples in Independent Countries
  1989 . . . 208, 288, 351, 352, 599
ILO Convention No 171 concerning Night Work
  1990 . . . 254
ILO Convention No 176 concerning Safety and
  Health of Workers in Mines 1995 . . . 252
ILO Convention No 182 concerning the
  Prohibition and Immediate Action for the
  Elimination of the Worst Forms of Child
  Labour 1999 . . . 252
    Art 3(d) . . . 255
ILO Convention No 184 concerning
  Safety and Health in the Agricultural Sector
  2001 . . . 252
ILO Convention No 189 concerning decent work
  for domestic workers 2011 . . . 252
ILO Declaration concerning Aims and Purposes
  1944 (Declaration of Philadelphia) . . . 250
ILO Declaration on Fundamental Principles and
  Rights at Work 1998 . . . 255
ILO Declaration on Social Justice for a Fair
  Globalization 2008 . . . 249
Inter-American Convention on the Elimination
  of All Forms of Discrimination Against
  Persons with Disabilities 1999 . . . 161
Inter-American Convention Against All
  Forms of Discrimination and Intolerance
  2013 . . . 161
    Art 1(2) . . . 166
    Art 5 . . . 172
Inter-American Convention on Forced
  Disappearance of Persons 1994 . . . 400
Inter-American Convention to Prevent and
  Punish Torture 1985 . . . 400
    Art 2 . . . 179

Inter-American Convention on the Prevention,
Punishment and Eradication of Violence
against Women 1994 (CPPEVAW) . . . 93,
326, 400
Art 1 . . . 326
Art 7(b) . . . 326
Inter-American Convention against Racism,
Racial Discrimination and Related Forms of
Intolerance 2013 . . . 161
Inter-American Declaration of Principles on
Freedom of Expression 2000 . . . 400
International Agreement for the Suppression of
the White Slave Traffic 1904 . . . 319
International Convention on the Abolition of
Slavery and the Slave Trade 1926 . . . 25
Art 1(1) . . . 253
International Convention on the Elimination
of All Forms of Racial Discrimination
(ICERD) . . . 78, 116, 122, 148, 153, 160, 329,
375, 377, 381
Art 1(1) . . . 163, 166
(4) . . . 171
Art 2 . . . 162
(1)(d) . . . 170
(e) . . . 170
(2) . . . 170, 172
Art 4 . . . 170, 225, 230
Art 5 . . . 162
(a) . . . 271, 274
(e) . . . 170
(i) . . . 250
(ii) . . . 250
(iii) . . . 203
(iv) . . . 205, 287
Art 7 . . . 170
Arts 12–13 . . . 381
Art 21 . . . 114
International Convention for the Protection of
All Persons from Enforced Disappearance
2006 . . . 78, 113, 154, 161, 375, 377, 380, 381,
383, 497
Art 1 . . . 269
Art 2 . . . 559
Art 30 . . . 380
Art 32 . . . 381
Art 33 . . . 380
Art 34 . . . 381
International Convention on the Protection
of the Rights of All Migrant Workers
and Members of their Families 1990
(ICRMW) . . . 78, 79, 148, 160–1, 163,
377m381
Art 1(1) . . . 161, 163
Art 5 . . . 250
Art 7 . . . 161, 162, 163, 250
Art 16 . . . 260
(6) . . . 268
Art 18 . . . 161, 250
Art 25 . . . 161, 250
Art 27 . . . 161

Art 28 . . . 161
Art 30 . . . 161
Art 31 . . . 294
Art 43 . . . 161
(1)(g) . . . 288
Art 45 . . . 161
Art 52 . . . 250
Art 54 . . . 161
Art 55 . . . 161
Arts 57–63 . . . 250
Art 70 . . . 161
International Convention for the Suppression of
White Slave Traffic 1910 . . . 319
International Convention on the Suppression
and Punishment of the Crime of Apartheid
1973 . . . 78
International Convention for the Suppression
of the Traffic in Women and Children
1921 . . . 319
International Convention for the Suppression of
the Traffic in Women of Full Age 1933 . . . 319
International Covenant on Civil and Political
Rights 1966 (ICCPR) . . . 31, 78, 81, 83, 87, 91,
101, 105, 107, 108, 110, 112, 113, 115, 122, 123,
125, 129, 133–4, 144, 149, 150, 151, 163, 166,
167, 171, 174, 175, 232, 253, 311, 320, 321, 328,
329, 335, 360, 375, 377, 383, 384, 466, 467, 469,
482, 494, 517, 535, 546, 553–4, 558
preamble . . . 35, 483
Art 1 . . . 122, 336, 350
(1) . . . 336
(2) . . . 151
(3) . . . 339
Art 2 . . . 99, 144, 160, 219, 308, 492, 519
(1) . . . 120, 129, 133, 161, 320, 553
(2) . . . 316
Art 3 . . . 160, 219, 316, 320
Art 4 . . . 113, 150, 185, 487
(2) . . . 150, 557, 558
Art 5(1) . . . 345
Art 6 . . . 80, 114, 184, 187, 188, 189, 190, 191,
328, 490
(1) . . . 185, 188, 191
(2) . . . 188, 189
(4) . . . 190
(5) . . . 190
Art 7 . . . 105, 114, 174, 176, 182, 185, 187,
190, 265, 279, 329, 557
Art 8 . . . 25
(1) . . . 114, 253
(2) . . . 114
(3) . . . 250, 253
Art 9 . . . 192, 260, 261, 558, 559
(1) . . . 262, 264
(2) . . . 265
(3) . . . 267
(4) . . . 266, 273
(5) . . . 266
Art 10 . . . 176
(1) . . . 174, 265, 266

(2)(a) ... 267
   (b) ... 267
   (3) ... 268
Art 11 ... 114, 234, 262, 489
Art 12 ... 311, 563
   (3) ... 11
   (4) ... 120
Art 13 ... 121
Art 14 ... 189, 271, 276, 278, 558, 559
   (1) ... 271, 273, 276, 277, 278
   (2) ... 279
   (3)(a) ... 280, 463
   (b) ... 280
   (c) ... 277, 463
   (d) ... 273, 280, 281
   (e) ... 281
   (f) ... 281, 463
   (g) ... 279
   (4) ... 283
   (5) ... 190, 282
   (6) ... 282
   (7) ... 282
Arts 14–15 ... 491
Art 15 ... 114, 189, 283, 508, 556, 558
   (2) ... 283
Art 16 ... 114, 489
Art 17 ... 234, 306, 563
Art 18 ... 114, 219, 220, 221, 223, 234
   (1) ... 223
   (2) ... 222, 223
   (3) ... 223
   (4) ... 220, 223, 249
Art 19 ... 225, 226, 264, 307
   (1) ... 226
   (2) ... 154, 226
   (3) ... 228, 230
Art 20 ... 124, 170, 225, 230
Art 21 ... 234, 235, 236
   (2) ... 235
Art 22 ... 122, 231, 250
   (2) ... 312
Art 23(1) ... 312, 320
   (2) ... 312
   (4) ... 317, 320
Art 24(2) ... 311
Art 25 ... 120, 523
Art 26 ... 160, 162, 163, 164, 165, 169, 219,
   243, 273, 274, 308, 309, 312, 519
Art 27 ... 122, 146, 219, 246, 288, 292, 348,
   349, 350
Art 41 ... 381
Art 50 ... 123
1st Optional Protocol (ICCPR-OP1) ... 78,
   149, 334, 377, 381, 383
2nd Optional Protocol on the Abolition of the
   Death Penalty 1989 (ICCPR- OP2) ... 78,
   80, 115, 175, 185, 188, 377
   Art 2(1) ... 106
International Covenant on Economic, Social and
   Cultural Rights 1966 (ICESCR) ... 31, 35, 78,

80, 83, 91, 92, 101, 113, 122, 127, 134–6,
138, 144, 149, 151, 152, 174, 200, 201, 204,
213, 214, 232, 244, 250, 287, 289, 295, 320,
321, 330, 335, 360, 375, 377, 463, 466, 469,
482, 524, 562
preamble ... 483
Art 1 ... 336
   (1) ... 336
   (2) ... 151
   (3) ... 339
Art 2 ... 92, 144, 213, 297
   (1) ... 134, 239, 246, 255, 316
   (2) ... 145, 160, 162, 163, 199, 209, 243, 255,
   307, 320
   (3) ... 121, 145, 243, 523
Art 3 ... 160, 199, 243, 308, 316, 320
Art 4 ... 247, 295
Art 5(1) ... 345
Art 6 ... 321
   (1) ... 254
   (2) ... 255
Arts 6–8 ... 121, 250
Art 7 ... 321
   (a)(i) ... 145, 254
   (ii) ... 207
   (b) ... 252
Art 8 ... 145, 231, 321
Art 9 ... 211, 256
Art 10 ... 211
   (2) ... 321
   (3) ... 145, 250
Art 11 ... 196, 199, 200, 201, 202, 203, 256
   (1) ... 199, 204, 321
   (2) ... 199
Art 12 ... 196, 201, 205
   (1) ... 205
   (2) ... 205
   (a) ... 208
   (c) ... 463
   (d) ... 297
Art 13 ... 239, 240, 241, 245, 246, 247, 287
   (1) ... 239, 242, 248
   (2) ... 239, 241, 248
   (a) ... 145, 244, 247
   (b) ... 247
   (c) ... 463
   (d) ... 244
   (e) ... 121
   (3) ... 145, 239, 241, 248, 249
   (4) ... 145, 239, 241, 248
Art 14 ... 239, 241, 245, 246, 287
Art 15 ... 210, 287, 288, 289, 290, 297, 301
(1) ... 294
(1)–(4) ... 287
(1)(a) ... 290
   (b) ... 296, 297
   (c) ... 297, 298, 299, 300
(2) ... 291
(3) ... 291, 297
(4) ... 297

Optional Protocol 2008 (OP-ICESCR) . . . 78,
80, 149, 150, 375, 377, 381, 383
Art 2 . . . 134
Art 10 . . . 381

Maritime Labour Convention 2006 . . . 252
Millennium Declaration 2000 . . . 389

OAU Convention Governing the Specific
Aspects of Refugee Problems in Africa
1969 . . . 447, 514
Art I(2) . . . 448, 515
Art II . . . 517, 522

Rome Statute of the International Criminal
Court 1998 (ICC Statute) . . . 6, 82, 501, 503,
505, 509, 552
Art 5(1) . . . 506, 509
Art 6 . . . 499
Arts 6–8 . . . 509
Art 7 . . . 151, 176, 179, 180, 501
(1) . . . 502, 552
(h) . . . 502
(2)(a) . . . 503
Art 8 . . . 176
Art 12 . . . 509
Art 17 . . . 509
Art 66(1) . . . 279

Social Charter of the Americas . . . 400
St Petersburg Declaration Renouncing the Use,
in Time of War, of Explosive Projectiles Under
400 Grammes Weight 1868 . . . 482
Statute of the African Court of Justice and
Human Rights 2003
Art 53(1) . . . 454
Statute of the International Court of Justice 1945
Art 38
(1) . . . 75, 76, 77, 81, 85, 86, 89, 90
(d) . . . 88, 89
Art 59 . . . 76, 86
Statute of the International Criminal Tribunal
for the Prosecution of Persons Responsible
for Genocide and Other Serious Violations of
International Humanitarian Law Committed
in the Territory of Rwanda and Rwandan
citizens responsible for genocide and other
such violations committed in the territory of
neighbouring States, between 1 January 1994
and 31 December 1994 (ICTR) . . . 505
Art 2 . . . 499
Art 3 . . . 505
Art 20 . . . 271
(3) . . . 279
Statute of the International Tribunal for the
Prosecution of Persons Responsible for Serious
Violations of International Humanitarian Law
Committed in the Territory of the Former
Yugoslavia since 1991 (ICTY) . . . 505
Art 4 . . . 499

Art 21 . . . 271
(3) . . . 279

Treaty of Berlin (1878) . . . 26
Treaty on European Union 1992
Art 6(2) . . . 436
Art 7 . . . 438
Treaty on the Functioning of the European
Union 2008
Arts 263, 267 . . . 436
Treaty of Lisbon Amending the Treaty
on European Union and the Treaty
Establishing the European Community
2009 . . . 437
Treaty of Nice Amending the Treaty on European
Union, the Treaties Establishing the European
Communities and Certain Related Acts
2001 . . . 437
Treaty of Utrecht 1713 . . . 26
Treaty of Westphalia 1648 . . . 26

UN Charter 1945 . . . 29–30, 31, 76, 77, 316, 319,
335–6, 348, 363
preamble . . . 29, 360
Chap VII . . . 90, 508, 550, 562
Art 1 . . . 30, 359
(2) . . . 336
(3) . . . 77, 160
(4) . . . 316
Art 2(7) . . . 30
Art 13 . . . 30, 391
Art 41 . . . 393
Art 55 . . . 30, 77, 360
(c) . . . 30
Art 56 . . . 30, 77, 360
Art 62(2) . . . 30
Art 68 . . . 30
Art 76 . . . 30
Art 97 . . . 394
UN Declaration on the Elimination of All Forms
of Intolerance and Discrimination Based on
Religion or Belief 1981 . . . 168
UN Declaration on the Elimination of Violence
against Women 1993 . . . 93
UN Declaration on the Right to Development
1986 . . . 147, 389, 585
Art 4 . . . 587
Art 9 . . . 587
UN Declaration on the Right of Peoples to Peace
1984 . . . 146
UN Declaration on the Rights of Indigenous
Peoples 2007 . . . 148, 352–3
Art 1 . . . 146, 352
Art 3 . . . 146, 352
Art 4 . . . 352
Art 7 . . . 145, 260
UN Declaration on the Rights of Persons
Belonging to National or Ethnic, Religious or
Linguistic Minorities 1992 . . . 146
Art 4 . . . 246

UN Declaration against Torture
(UNDAT) . . . 179
Art 1(2) . . . 178
UN Declaration of the UN Conference
on the Human Environment 1972
(Stockholm) . . . 590
Principle 1 . . . 594
UN Declaration on the Use of Scientific or
Technological Progress in the Interests
of Peace and for the Benefit of Mankind 1975
Art 2 . . . 297
UNESCO Convention against Discrimination in
Education 1960 . . . 78, 239
Art 1 . . . 247
(1) . . . 243
Art 3 . . . 247
UNESCO Convention for the Protection of
Cultural Property in the Event of Armed
Conflict
1954 . . . 291
UNESCO Convention on the Protection and
Promotion of the Diversity of Cultural
Expressions 2005
Art 1 . . . 292
UNESCO Universal Declaration on Cultural
Diversity 2001 . . . 289, 290
Universal Declaration of Human Rights 1948
(UDHR) . . . 5, 15, 18, 30–2, 34, 55, 56, 78, 90,
91, 145, 155, 172, 174, 187, 218, 236, 244, 250,
319, 320, 359, 360, 363, 375, 388, 395, 466, 481,
482, 533, 546, 571, 588, 605
preamble . . . 35, 57, 195
Art 1 . . . 3, 46, 160, 196
Art 2 . . . 150, 184, 218, 316, 320
(1) . . . 160, 162, 163
Art 3 . . . 146, 184, 192
Arts 3–18 . . . 574
Art 4 . . . 25
Art 5 . . . 150, 175
Art 6 . . . 62
Art 7 . . . 160, 162

Art 9 . . . 260
Art 10 . . . 270
Art 12 . . . 320
Art 14 . . . 517
(1) . . . 515
Art 15 . . . 62
Art 16(1) . . . 317, 320
(3) . . . 320
Art 18 . . . 218, 219, 220, 221
Art 19 . . . 218, 225, 226
Art 20 . . . 218, 231, 234
(2) . . . 232
Art 21 . . . 218
Art 22 . . . 196, 211
Art 23 . . . 62, 250
(4) . . . 231
Art 24 . . . 150, 251
Art 25 . . . 196, 199, 202, 205, 211, 256, 568
(1) . . . 195
Art 26 . . . 239, 241, 242
Art 27 . . . 210, 287, 288, 289, 301
(2) . . . 297
Art 28 . . . 145, 588
Art 29(2) . . . 111

Vienna Convention on Consular Relations
1963 . . . 411
Art 36(1) . . . 268
Vienna Convention on the Law of Treaties 1969
(VCLT) . . . 97
Art 2 . . . 105
Art 19 . . . 106
Art 20(2) . . . 108
(4)(b) . . . 110
(c) . . . 108, 109
Arts 39–41 . . . 79
Art 53 . . . 84
Art 60 . . . 115
(5) . . . 116
Vienna Declaration and Programme of Action
1993 . . . 147, 157, 210, 359, 388, 579

TABLE OF CASES

NATIONAL

A v Secretary of State for Home Affairs [2005]
  UKHL 71 . . . 279
A and Others v Secretary of State for the Home
  Department (No 2) [2005] UKHL 71 . . . 84
Abtan et al. v Blackwater Worldwide, Case
  1:07-cv-01831 (RBW) (US) . . . 536
Acosta, A-24159781, US Board of Immigration
  Appeals, 1 March 1985 . . . 520
Al-Skeini v Secretary of State for Defence [2007]
  UKHL 26 . . . 131, 138
Applicant A v Minister for Immigration and
  Ethnic Affairs (1997) 190 CLR 225 . . . 520

Brown v Board of Education 347 US 483
  (1954) . . . 22
Bundesamt für Sozialversicherung v K,
  8C_295/2008 . . . 462

Cal (Aurelio) and the Maya Village of Santa Cruz
  v Attorney General of Belize and Manuel
  Coy and Maya Village of Conejo v Attorney
  General of Belize (Consolidated) Claim Nos
  171 and 17, 18 October 2007 . . . 353
Campbell v MGN Ltd [2004] UKHL 22 . . . 538
Campodónico de Beviacqua, Ana Carina v
  Ministerio de Salud y Acción Social Secretaria
  de Programas de Salud y Banco de Drogas
  Neoplásicas, 24 October 2000 (Sup Ct,
  Arg) . . . 463
Canada (Attorney General) v Ward [1993] 2
  S.C.R. 689 . . . 520
Case of Julio Hector Simon/ recurso de hecho,
  No.17.768, 14 June 2005 (Arg) . . . 409
Chen Shi Hai v The Minister for Immigration
  and Multicultural Affairs [2000]
  HCA 19 . . . 520

DaimlerChrysler AG v Bauman, US Supreme
  Court Docket No 11-965 . . . 537
Doe I v Unocal Corp, 18 September 2002
  (US) . . . 536
Dred Scott v Sandford 60 US 393 (1857) . . . 22
Drustva Ecology Slovenje, Case No
  U-I-30/95 . . . 606

Employees of the Pakistan Law Commission v
  Ministry of Works 1994 SCMR 1548
  (Pak) . . . 600

Farooque v Secretary, Ministry of
  Communication, Government of the People's
  Republic of Bangladesh WP No 300 of 1995
  (Bangladesh) . . . 600
Filartiga v Peña-Irala 630 F 2d 876 (2d Cir
  1980) . . . 82, 83

Government of the Republic of South
  Africa v Grootboom, 2000 (11) BCLR
  1169 . . . 88

Herewini v Ministry of Transport (1992) 9 CRNZ
  307 . . . 468

Ibrahim v Titan; Saleh v Titan, Case
  1:05-cv-01165-JR, Order 6 November 2007
  (DC, Dist of Columbia, US) . . . 536
Islam (A.P.) v Secretary of State for the Home
  Department; R v Immigration Appeal Tribunal
  and Another, Ex Parte Shah (A.P.) (conjoined
  appeals) [1992] 2 WLR 1015 . . . 519, 520

John Doe VIII et al. v Exxon Mobil et al.
  (pending before DC Circuit) . . . 537

Kadic v Karadzic 70 F 3d 232 (2d Cir 1995,
  US) . . . 536
Kiobel v Royal Dutch Petroleum (2013) 569 US,
  Slip Opinion 14 . . . 537
Krishnan (Unni) v State of Andhra Pradesh
  [1993] INSC 60, (1993) 1 SCC 645 (Sup Ct,
  India) . . . 243, 466
Kumar v State of Bihar AIR 1991 SC 420 (Sup Ct,
  India) . . . 600

Mabo v Queensland (No 2) (1992) 175 CLR 1
  (HC, Aus) . . . 465
Marbury v Madison 1 Cranch 137
  (1803) . . . 22, 470
Minister for Immigration & Ethnic Affairs v Teoh
  [1995] HCA 20, (1995) 183 CLR 273 (HC,
  Aus) . . . 465
Minister for Immigration and
  Multicultural Affairs v Khawar [2002]
  HCA 14 . . . 519, 520
Minister for Immigration and Multicultural and
  Indigenous Affairs v QAAH of 2004 (2006)
  231 CLR 1 . . . 524
Minister of Health v Treatment Action Campaign
  (TAC) (2002) 5 SA 721 (CC, SA) . . . 88

Mullin (Francis Coralie) v Administrator, Union
    of Territory Delhi [1981] INSC 12, (1981)
    2 SCR 516 (Sup Ct, India) . . . 466

Oposa v Factoran GR No 101083, 30 July 1993
    (Sup Ct, Philippines) . . . 600

Palmer v Thompson 403 US 217
    (1971) . . . 159
Pasikrisie belge 1984 I, 524, 17 January 1984
    (C de Cass, Belg) . . . 463
Pasikrisie belge 1985 I, 239, 16 October 1984
    (C de Cass, Belg) . . . 463
Pinochet Case see R v Bow Street Metropolitan
    Stipendiary Magistrate, ex parte Pinochet
    Ugarte (No 3)
Plessy v Ferguson 163 US 537 (1896) . . . 22
Public Committee Against Torture in Israel v
    Government of Israel, HCJ 769/02
    (2006) . . . 485
Public Prosecutor v X (1980) 11 Netherlands YB
    of IL 301 (CA, Arnhem) . . . 463

R v Bow Street Metropolitan Stipendiary
    Magistrate, ex parte Pinochet Ugarte
    (No 3) [1999] UKHL 17; [1999] 2 WLR
    827 . . . 88, 177, 183
R v Director of Immigration, ex parte Simon Yin
    Xiang-Jiang (1994) 4 HKPLR 264
    (CA, HK) . . . 465
R v Immigration Officer at Prague Airport, ex
    parte European Roma Rights Centre [2005]
    2 WLR 1 (HL) . . . 92, 521–2
R v Jones [2007] 1 AC 136 (HL) . . . 82, 83
R v Zardad, 7 April 2004 (CCC) . . . 540
R (Ullah) v Special Adjudicator [2004]
    UKHL 26 . . . 129
Rio Tinto PLC v Sarei, US Supreme Court
    Docket No 11-649 . . . 537
Roe et al. v Bridgestone Corp 492 F Supp 2d 988
    (26 June 2007) . . . 536
Roe v Wade 410 US 113 (1973) . . . 466

Secretary of Security v Sakthevel Prabakar [2005]
    1 HKLRD 289 . . . 380
Secretary of State for the Home Department
    (Respondent) v K (FC) (Appellant); Fornah
    (FC) (Appellant) v Secretary of State for the
    Home Department (Respondent) [2006]
    UKHL 46 . . . 520
Shehla Zia v WAPDA, PLD 1994 SC 693 (Sup
    Ct, Pak) . . . 466
Somersett's case, 20 State Trials 1 . . . 24
Sosa v Alvarez-Machain 542 US 692
    (2004) . . . 536

Vega (Victor Ramon Castrillon) v Federacio
    Nacional de Algodoneros y Corporacion
    Autonoma regional del Cesar (1997)
    Case No 4577 (Colombia) . . . 600

Verband Studierender an der Universität Zürich
    v Regierungsrat des Kantons Zürich, BGE 120
    Ia 1 (Sup Ct, Swiss) . . . 463
Viceconte (Mariela) v Estado Nacional
    (Ministerio de Salud y Ministerio de
    Economía de la Nación), No 31.777/96, 2 June
    1998 (CA, Arg) . . . 464
Vishaka v State of Rajasthan [1997] INSC 665,
    (1997) 6 SCC 241 (Sup Ct, India) . . . 380, 465

Wargraft (Ricardo Fliman) v Director y el Jefe
    de la Sección de Opciones a Naturalizaciones,
    Constitutional Chamber of the Supreme Court of
    Justice of Costa Rica, 11 November 1992 . . . 412
Washington v Davis 426 US 229 (1976) . . . 166
Wiwa v Royal Dutch Shell Petroleum, 28
    February 2002 (DC, NY) . . . 536

YL (by her litigation friend the Official
    Solicitor) (FC) (Appellant) v Birmingham
    City Council (Respondents) [2007]
    UKHL 27 . . . 537

INTERNATIONAL

A v Australia, CCPR/C/59/D/560/1993, 30 April
    1997 . . . 120, 263, 264
A v Australia, CCPR/C/76/D/900/1999, 28
    October 2002 . . . 264
A v UK (1999) 27 EHRR 611 (ECtHR) . . . 124
A and Others v UK (2009) 49 EHRR 29
    (ECtHR) . . . 113, 263, 266
A, B, C v Ireland (2011) 53 EHRR 13 . . . 121
A-G of Israel v Eichmann (1968)
    36 ILR 18 . . . 508
Abdulaziz, Cabales and Balkandali v UK
    (1985) 7 EHRR 471 (ECtHR) . . . 168
Abdussamatov et al. v Kazakhstan, CAT/
    C/48/D/400/2010, 1 June 2012 . . . 381
Abella v Argentina, IACommHR Rep No 55/97,
    18 November 1997 . . . 487
Aber v Algeria, CCPR/C/90/D/1439/2005, 16
    August 2007 . . . 181
Adam v Czech Republic, CCPR/
    C/57/D/586/1994, 25 July 1996 . . . 120, 166
Adonis v The Philippines, CCPR/
    C/103/D/1815/2008/Rev.1,
    26 April 2012 . . . 229
Agiza v Sweden, CAT/C/34/D/233/2003,
    24 May 2005 . . . 128
Airey v Ireland (1979–80) 2 EHRR 305
    (ECtHR) . . . 273
Aksoy v Turkey (1997) 23 EHRR 553
    (ECtHR) . . . 180
Aktas v France, Baryak v France, Gamaleddyn v
    France, Ghazal v France, J Singh v France, R
    Singh v France, App nos 43563/08, 18527/08,
    29134/08, 25463/08 and 27561/08, 17 July
    2009 (ECtHR) . . . 224

Al-Adsani v UK (2002) 34 EHRR 11
(ECtHR) . . . 177, 274

Al-Jedda v UK (2011) 53 EHRR 23 . . . 125,
127, 490

Al-Khawaja and Tahery v UK (2012) 54
EHRR 23 . . . 282

Al-Saadoon and Mufdhi v UK (2011) 53 EHRR
9 . . . 125, 188, 493

Al-Skeini and Others v UK (2011) 53
EHRR 18 . . . 494

Alejandre v Cuba, IACommHR Rep No 86/99, 29
September 1999 . . . 132

Alekseyev v Russia, AppNos 4916/07, 25924/08,
and 14599/09, Judgment of 21 October 2010
(ECtHR) . . . 310

Alexandridis v Greece, App no 19515/06, 21
February 2008 (ECtHR) . . . 223

Aliboeva v Tajikstan, CCPR/C/85/D/985/2001,
18 October 2005 . . . 189

Aliev v Ukraine, CCPR/C/78/D/781/1997, 7
August 2003 . . . 189

Allenet de Ribemont v France (1995) 20 EHRR
557 (ECtHR) . . . 279

Althammer v Austria, CCPR/C/78/D/998/2001, 8
August 2003 . . . 165, 166

Amekrane v UK (1973) 16 YB 356
(ECommHR) . . . 183

Amirov v Russian Federation, CCPR/
C/95/D/1447/2006, 2 April 2009 . . . 191

AP v Italy, CCPR/C/OP/2 at 67 (1990), 2
November 1987 . . . 282

Appleby v UK (2003) 37 EHRR 38
(ECtHR) . . . 534

Application of the Convention on the Prevention
and Punishment of the Crime of Genocide
see Bosnia and Herzegovina v Serbia and
Montenegro

Application of the International Convention
on the Elimination of All Forms of Racial
Discrimination see Georgia v Russian
Federation

Armed Activities on the Territory of the Congo
see Democratic Republic of the Congo v
Rwanda and Democratic Republic of Congo
v Uganda

Ashby v Trinidad and Tobago, CCPR/
C/74/D/580/1994, 19 April 2002 . . . 190

Asylum Case see Colombia v Peru

AT v Hungary, CEDAW/C/36/D/2/2003, 26
January 2005 . . . 92, 102, 124, 325

Ato del Avellanal v Peru, A/44/40 (1988)
196 . . . 273

Austin v UK (2012) 55 EHRR 14,
(ECtHR) . . . 261

Austria v Italy (1961) 4 YB 116
(ECommHR) . . . 100, 432

Autronic AG v Switzerland (1990) 12 EHRR 485
(ECtHR) . . . 334

Avena and other Mexican Nationals see Mexico v
United States

Axel Springer AG v Germany (2012) 55 EHRR 6
(ECtHR) . . . 229

Axen v Germany (1984) 6 EHRR 195
(ECtHR) . . . 278

Ayder v Turkey, App no 23656/94, 8 January 2004
(ECtHR) . . . 177

Aydin v Turkey (1998) 25 EHRR 251
(ECtHR) . . . 180

Baban v Australia, CCPR/C/78/D/1014/2001,
6 August 2003 . . . 264

Baby Boy Case, IACommHR Res 23/81,
6 March 1981 . . . 121, 185

Baczkowski v Poland, App no 1543/06,
3 May 2007 (ECtHR) . . . 235

Bahamonde v Equatorial Guinea, CCPR/
C/49/D/468/1991, 20 October 1993 . . . 275

Ballantyne, Davidson, McIntyre v Canada,
CCPR/C/47/D/359/1989, 5 May 1993 . . . 123

Bámaca-Velásquez v Guatemala, IACtHR Series
C No 70, 25 November 2000 . . . 487

Banković v Belgium (2002) 44 EHRR SE5
(ECtHR) . . . 130, 131, 132, 137, 138

Barcelona Traction, Light and Power Co Ltd
(Second Phase) see Belgium v Spain

Barrett and Sutcliffe v Jamaica, CCPR/
C/44/D/271/1998, 30 March 1992 . . . 384

Barrios Altos v Peru IACtHR Series C No 75
(2001) . . . 409, 510

Baumgarten v Germany, CCPR/
C/78/D/960/2000, 19 September 2003 . . . 283

Bayatyan v Armenia (2012) 54 EHRR 15
(ECtHR) . . . 225

BdB et al. v The Netherlands, CCPR/
C/35/D/273/1988, 2 May 1989 . . . 164

Behrami and Behrami v France; Saramati v
France, Germany and Norway (2007) 45
EHRR SE10 (ECtHR) . . . 125, 127, 539

Belgian Linguistics Case (1979–80) 1 EHRR 241
(ECtHR) . . . 104

Belgian Linguistics Case (No 2) (1968) 1 EHRR
252 (ECtHR) . . . 166, 167, 240, 245–6

Belgium v Senegal [2012] ICJ Rep para 159
(ICJ) . . . 84, 101, 177, 183, 395

Belgium v Spain [1970] ICJ Rep 3
(ICJ) . . . 100, 161

Belilos v Switzerland (1988) 10 EHRR 466
(ECtHR) . . . 107

Benham v UK (1996) 22 EHRR 293
(ECtHR) . . . 281

Biscet (Oscar Elías) v Cuba, IACommHR Rep No
57/04, 14 October 2004 . . . 236

Blagojević v The Netherlands, App no 49032/07,
Admissibility Decision of 9 June 2009
(ECtHR) . . . 125, 126, 127

Bodrozic v Serbia and Montenegro, CCPR/
C/85/D/1180/2003, 31 October 2005 . . . 229

Bosnia and Herzegovina v Serbia and
Montenegro [2007] ICJ Rep 108 (ICJ) . . . 81,
116, 499, 501

Bosphorus v Ireland (2006) 42 EHRR 1
  (ECtHR) . . . 126, 127
Bozano v France (1987) 9 EHRR 297
  (ECtHR) . . . 192
Brannigan and McBride v UK (1994) 17 EHRR
  539 (ECtHR) . . . 269
Broeks v The Netherlands, CCPR/
  C/29/D/172/1984 (9 April
  1987) . . . 162, 168
Brogan v UK (1989) 11 EHRR 117
  (ECtHR) . . . 267
Broniowski v Poland (2005) 40 EHRR 495
  (ECtHR) . . . 433
Budayeva v Russia, App nos 15339/02,
  20058/02 and 15343/02, 16 October 2003
  (ECtHR) . . . 598, 607
Bukta v Hungary, App no 25691/04, 17
  September 2007 (ECtHR) . . . 235
Burkina Faso v Mali [1986] ICJ Rep 554
  (ICJ) . . . 346, 347
Buscarini v San Marino (2000) 30 EHRR 208
  (ECtHR) . . . 223

Caesar v Trinidad and Tobago, IACtHR Series C
  No 123, 11 March 2005 . . . 177, 182
Cagas v The Philippines, CCPR/
  C/63/D/788/1997,
  23 October 2001 . . . 279
Campbell and Cosans v UK (1982) 4 EHRR 293
  (ECtHR) . . . 240
Campbell (Pvt) Ltd and Others v Zimbabwe
  [2007] SADCT 1 (28 November 2008); (2008)
  AHRLR 199 . . . 444
Casanovas v France, CCPR/C/51/D/441/1990, 26
  July 1994 . . . 511
Castells v Spain (1992) 14 EHRR 445
  (ECtHR) . . . 227
Catan and Others v Moldova and Russia, App
  nos 43370/04, 8252/06 and 18454/06, 19
  October 2012 (ECtHR) . . . 130
Celepli v Sweden, CCPR/C/51/D/456/91, 18 July
  1994 . . . 261
Celiberti de Casariego v Uruguay, CCPR/
  C/13/D/56/1979, 29 July 1981 . . . 133
Centre for Minority Rights Development (Kenya)
  and Minority Rights Group International on
  behalf of Endorois Welfare Council v Kenya,
  27th Activity Report of the ACommHPR
  (2009); (2009) AHRLR 75 . . . 446, 586
Chahal v UK (1997) 23 EHRR 413
  (ECtHR) . . . 177, 183, 522
Chang (Myrna Mack) v Guatemala,
  IACtHR Series C No 101, 25 November
  2003 . . . 409, 485
Chaparro-Alvarez and Lapo-Iniguez v Ecuador,
  IACtHR Series C No 170, 21 November
  2007 . . . 268
Chaparro (José Vicente and Amado Villafañe) v
  Colombia, CCPR/C/60/D/612/1995, 14 June
  1994 . . . 180

Chikunova v Uzbekistan, CCPR/
  C/89/D/1043/2002, 16 March
  2007 . . . 190
Children and Adolescents Deprived of Liberty
  in the 'Tautuapé Complex' of the CASA
  Foundation (Brazil) (Provisional Measures)
  IACtHR, 3 July 2007 . . . 411
Chocrón Chocrón v Venezuela, IACtHR Series C
  No 227, 1 July 2011. . . . 275
Coard v USA, IACommHR Rep No 109/99, 29
  September 1999 . . . 132
Colombia v Peru [1950] ICJ Rep 266
  (ICJ) . . . 81
Commission Nationale des Droits de l'Homme et
  des Libertés v Chad, ACommHR 9thActivity
  Rep (1995) . . . 485, 487
Community of La Oroya v Peru, IACommHR
  Report No 76/09, 5 August 2009 . . . 594
Constitutional Rights Project v Nigeria 60/91,
  8thActivity Report of the ACommHPR
  (1995) 13 . . . 282
Continental Shelf Case see Libyan Arab
  Jamahiriya v Malta
Coordinamento v Italy CCPR/C/21/D/163/1984,
  10 April 1984 . . . 122
Coronel v Columbia, CCPR/C/76/D/778/1997,
  24 October 2002 . . . 269
Costello Roberts v UK (1995) 19 EHRR 112
  (ECtHR) . . . 245
Cyprus v Turkey (1982) 4 EHRR 482
  (ECtHR) . . . 113
Cyprus v Turkey (2002) 35 EHRR 30
  (ECommHR) . . . 129, 168

Danev v Bulgaria, App no 9411/05, 2, September
  2010 (ECtHR) . . . 266
Dann (Mary and Carrie) v USA, IACommHR
  Rep No 75/02, 27 December 2002 . . . 208
Danning v The Netherlands, CCPR/C/OP/2, 9
  April 1987 . . . 164
Deisl v Austria, CCPR/C/81/D/1060/2002, 23
  August 2004 . . . 277
Delgado Páez v Colombia, CCPR/
  C/39/D/195/1985, 12 July 1990 . . . 192
Democratic Republic of the Congo v Burundi,
  Rwanda and Uganda, 227/99, 20th Activity
  Report of the ACommHPR (2006) . . . 448
Democratic Republic of the Congo v Rwanda
  [2006] ICJ Rep 3 (ICJ) . . . 84, 499
Democratic Republic of the Congo v Uganda
  [2005] ICJ Rep 168 (ICJ) . . . 132, 134, 487,
  490, 494
Detention Centre of Catia see
  Montero-Aranguren v Venezuela
DH and Others v Czech Republic(2008) 47
  EHRR 3 (ECtHR) . . . 165–6, 169–70, 243
Diallo (Ahmadou Sadio) see Republic of Guinea
  v Democratic Republic of Congo
Dickson v UK (2008) 46 EHRR 41
  (ECtHR) . . . 182

Dubetska and Others v Ukraine App no
30499.03, 9 September 2010 . . . 598
Dudgeon v UK (1981) 4 EHRR 149
(ECtHR) . . . 104, 112, 169, 306
Durand and Ugarte v Peru, IACtHR Series C No
68, 16 August 2000 . . . 276

East African Asians v UK (1973) 3 EHRR 76
(ECtHR) . . . 168, 177
East Timor Case *see* Portugal v Australia
EB v France (2008) 47 EHRR 21
(ECtHR) . . . 309
Ecuador v Colombia, IACommHR Report No
112/10 (21 October 2010) . . . 404
Effect of Reservations on the Entry into Force
of the American Convention (Arts 74 and
75), OC-2/82, IACtHR Series A No 2, 24
September 1982 . . . 100
Egmez v Cyprus (2002) 34 EHRR 29
(ECtHR) . . . 180
El-Masri v the Former Yugoslav Republic of
Macedonia, App no 39630/09, 13 December
2012 (ECtHR) . . . 262
El Salvador v Honduras [1992] ICJ Rep 355
(ICJ) . . . 347
Elmi v Australia, CAT/C/22/D/120/1998, 14 May
1999 . . . 493
Enhorn v Sweden (2005) 41 EHRR 633
(ECtHR) . . . 212
Estrella v Uruguay, CCPR/C/18/D/74/1980, 23
March 1983 . . . 180
Ethiopia v South Africa; Liberia v South Africa
[1966] ICJ Rep 6 (ICJ) . . . 86, 117, 161
Eweida and Others v UK, App nos 4820/10,
59842/10 and 36156/10, Judgment of 15
January 2013 (ECtHR) . . . 224
Exceptions to the Exhaustion of Domestic
Remedies, OC-11/90, IACtHR Series A No 11,
10 August 1990 . . . 273

Fadeyeva v Russia (2007) 45 EHRR 10
(ECtHR) . . . 598
Faurisson (Robert) v France, CCPR/
C/58/D/550/1993, 8 November
1996 . . . 230
Federal Republic of Germany v Denmark;
Federal Republic of Germany v The
Netherlands [1969] ICJ Rep 3 (ICJ) . . . 81, 82
Fedotova (Irina) v Russian Federation,
CCPR/C/106/D/1932/2010, 30 November
2012 . . . 310
Fei v Colombia, CCPR/C/53/D/514/1992, 4 April
1995 . . . 277
Fermín Ramírez, IACtHR Series C No 126, 20
June 2005 . . . 409
Fernando v Sri Lanka, CCPR/C83/D/1189/2003,
31 March 2005 . . . 263
Fillastre and Bizouarn v Bolivia, CCPR/
C/43/D/336/1988, 5 November 1991 . . . 268

Forensic Anthropology Foundation regarding
Guatemala (Provisional Measures) IACtHR,
21 April 2006 . . . 410
Fox, Campbell and Hartley v UK (1991) 13
EHRR 157 (ECtHR) . . . 265
Fredin v Sweden (1991) 13 EHRR 784
(ECtHR) . . . 164
Frette v France (2004) 38 EHRR 21
(ECtHR) . . . 104, 309
Frontier Dispute *see* Burkina Faso v Mali

Gangaram Panday v Suriname, IACtHR Series C
No 16, 21 January 1994 . . . 263
Garcia v Peru, IACommHR Rep No 1/95 . . . 263
Gas and Dubois v France, App No 25951/07,
Judgment of 15 March 2012 (ECtHR) . . . 312
Gaygusuz v Austria (1996) 23 EHRR 364
(ECtHR) . . . 169
Georgia v Russia (No 1) (2011) 52 EHRR SE 14
(ECtHR) . . . 426
Georgia v Russia (No 2) (2012) 54 EHRR SE10
(ECtHR) . . . 426
Georgia v Russian Federation [2011] ICJ Rep
(ICJ) . . . 116, 426, 494
Germany v Italy: Greece intervening [2012] ICJ
Rep, para 93 (ICJ) . . . 84, 85, 86
Germany v USA [1999] ICJ Rep 9
(ICJ) . . . 116, 268
Gillot v France, A/57/40, 15 July 2002 . . . 167
Giménez v Argentina, IACommHR Rep No
12/96, 1 March 1996 . . . 268
Goekce v Austria, CEDAW/C/39/D/5/2005, 6
August 2007 . . . 92, 124, 325, 327
Goiburu v Paraguay, IACtHR Series C No 202, 22
September 2009 . . . 270
Gomez Paquiyauri Brothers v Peru, IACtHR
Series C No 110, 8 July 2004, para 165 . . . 79
González et al. ('Cotton Field') v Mexico
(Preliminary Objection, Merits, Reparations,
and Costs) IACtHR Series C No 205, 16
November 2009 . . . 93, 384
Goodwin v UK (2002) 35 EHRR 18
(ECtHR) . . . 104, 306
Grant v Jamaica, CCPR/C/56/D/597/1994, 22
March 1996 . . . 265
Greek Case (1969) 12 YB 468
(ECommHR) . . . 178
Gridin v Russian Federation, CCPR/
C/69/D/770/1997, 20 July 2000 . . . 274, 279
Gryb v Belarus, CCPR/C/103/D/1316/2004, 26
October 2011 . . . 236
Guerra and Others v Italy (1998) 26 EHRR 357
(ECtHR) . . . 607
Guerrero v Colombia, CCPR/C/15/D/45/1979,
31 March 1982 . . . 186–7, 492
Gueye v France, CCPR/C/35/D/196/1985, 6 April
1989 . . . 120, 164, 168, 554
Gül v Turkey (2002) 34 EHRR 435
(ECtHR) . . . 187

Gunme v Cameroon, 266/03, 26th
    Activity Report of the ACommHPR
    (2008-2009) . . . 264, 445
Gustafsson v Sweden (1993) 16 EHRR 462
    (ECtHR) . . . 232

H v Norway (1992) 73 DR 155
    (ECommHR) . . . 121
Haitian Centre for Human Rights et al. v United
    States, IACommHR Report No 51/96, 13
    March 1997 . . . 521
Hajrizi Dzemajl v Yugoslavia, CAT/
    C/29/D/161/2000, 2 December
    2002 . . . 177
Handölsdalen Sami Village and Others v
    Sweden, CCPR/C/33/D/197/1985, 27 July
    1988 . . . 350
Handyside v UK (1979) 1 EHRR 737
    (ECtHR) . . . 112, 226, 296
Harward v Norway, CCPR/C/51/D/451/1991, 16
    August 1994 . . . 280
Hasan v Bulgaria (2000) 24 EHRR 55
    (ECtHR) . . . 112
Hasan and Chaush v Bulgaria (2002) 34 EHRR
    1339 (ECtHR) . . . 222
Hatton v UK (2002) 34 EHRR 1
    (ECtHR) . . . 597, 598
Helmers v Sweden (1993) 15 EHRR 285
    (ECtHR) . . . 278
Hénaf v France (2005) 40 EHRR 44
    (ECtHR) . . . 180
Hilaire, Constantine and Benjamin v Trinidad
    and Tobago, IACtHR Series C No 94, 21 June
    2002 . . . 188
Hill and Hill v Spain, CCPR/C/59/D/526/1993, 2
    April 1997 . . . 265
Hirsi Jamaa and Others v Italy, App no
    27765/09, Judgment of 23 February
    2012 . . . 521, 522
Hoffmann v Austria (1993) 17 EHRR 293
    (ECtHR) . . . 169
Huamán v Peru, CCPR/C/85/D/1153/2003, 22
    November 2005 . . . 121
Hudoyberganova v Uzbekistan, CCPR/
    C/82/D/931/2000, 5 November 2004 . . . 223
HvdP v The Netherlands, CCPR/
    C/29/D/217/1986, 8 April 1987 . . . 125

I v UK (2002) 35 EHRR 18 (ECtHR) . . . 306
IA v France, App no 28213/95, 23 September
    1998 (ECtHR) . . . 267
IA v Turkey (2007) 45 EHRR 30
    (ECtHR) . . . 231
IHRDA and Open Society Justice Initiative
    (OSJI) (on behalf of children of Nubian
    descent in Kenya) v Kenya (22 March
    2011) . . . 447
Ilascu v Moldova and Russia (2005) 40 EHRR 46
    (ECtHR) . . . 129, 137

Ilombe and Shandwe v Democratic Republic of
    Congo, CCPR/C/86/D/1177/2003, 17 March
    2006 . . . 265
Incal v Turkey (2000) 29 EHRR 449
    (ECtHR) . . . 276
International Pen v Nigeria, 137/94, 139/94,
    154/96 and 161/97, 12th Activity Report of the
    ACommHPR (1998–1999) . . . 190, 235
Interpretation of the American
    Declaration of the Rights and Duties of
    Man within the Framework of Article 64 of the
    American Convention on Human
    Rights, OC-10/89, IACtHR Series
    A No 10, 14 July 1989 . . . 91
Inze v Austria (1988) 10 EHRR 394
    (ECtHR) . . . 168, 169
Ireland v UK (1980) 2 EHRR 25
    (ECtHR) . . . 178, 179, 432
Isayeva v Russia (2005) 41 EHRR 38
    (ECtHR) . . . 485, 492
Işik (Sinan) v Turkey, App no 21924/05,
    Judgment of 2 February 2010
    (ECtHR) . . . 223
Ismayilov v Azerbaijan, App no 4439/04, 17
    January 2008 (ECtHR) . . . 233
Issa v Turkey (2005) 41 EHRR 27
    (ECtHR) . . . 130, 131
Ivantoc and Others v Moldova and Russia,
    App no 23687/05, Judgment of 15 November
    2011 (ECtHR) . . . 130
Ivcher-Bronstein v Peru, IACtHR Series C No 74,
    6 June 2001 . . . 226
Iwanczuk v Poland (2004) 38 EHRR 8
    (ECtHR) . . . 181

Jacobs v Belgium, CCPR/C/81/D/943/2000, 7
    July 2004 . . . 171
Jallow v Bulgaria, CEDAW/C/52/D/32/2011, 23
    July 2012 . . . 92, 325
James v UK (1986) 8 EHRR 123
    (ECtHR) . . . 169
James, Wells and Lee v UK (2013) 56 EHRR 12
    (ECtHR) . . . 264
Jawara v The Gambia, 147/95 and 149/96,
    13th Activity Report of the ACommHPR
    (2000) . . . 445, 449
Jayawardena v Sri Lanka, CCPR/
    C/75/D/916/2000, 22 July 2002 . . . 270
JB et al. v Canada, CCPR/C/OP/1, 18 July
    1986 . . . 232
Jeong et al. v Republic of Korea, CCPRC/C/101/
    D1642-1741/2007, 24 March 2011 . . . 225
Jewish Community of Oslo v Norway, CERD/
    C/67/D/30/2003, 15 August 2005 . . . 122
John Murray v UK (1996) 22 EHRR 29
    (ECtHR) . . . 280
Johnson, Clive v Jamaica, CCPR/
    C/64/D/592/1994, 25 November
    1998 . . . 190

Jordan v UK (2003) 37 EHRR 2
(ECtHR) . . . 191
Jorgić v Germany (2008) 47 EHRR 6
(ECtHR) . . . 498
Joslin v New Zealand, CCPR/C/75/D/902/1999,
30 July 2002 . . . 309, 311
JRT and the WG Party v Canada, CCPR/
C/18/D/104/1981, 6 April 1983 . . . 122
Judge v Canada, CCPR/C/78/D/829/1998, 20
October 2003 . . . 189
Juridical Condition and Rights of Undocumented
Migrants, OC-18/03, IACtHR Series A No 18,
17 September 2003 . . . 85, 161, 172
Jurisdictional Immunities of the State *see*
Germany v Italy
Juvenile Reeducation Institute v Paraguay,
IACtHR Series C No 112, 2 September
2004 . . . 410

Kadi v Council of the EU and Commission
of the EC (T-315/01) [2005] ECR II-3649
(CFI) . . . 85
Kadi and al Barakaat International Foundation v
Council of the European Union (C-402/05
P and C-415/05 P), 3 September 2008
(ECJ) . . . 564
Kanana v Zaire, CCPR/C/49/D/366/1989, 2
November 1993 . . . 264
Kang v Republic of Korea, CCPR/
C/78/D/878/1999, 15 July 2003 . . . 268
Karker v France, CCPR/C/70/D/833/98, 26
October 2000 . . . 261
Karner v Austria (2003) 38 EHRR 24
(ECtHR) . . . 309
Katabazi v Secretary General of the East African
Community [2007] EACJ 3 . . . 444
Katangese Peoples' Congress v Zaire, 75/92,
8th Activity Report of the ACommHPR
(1995) . . . 445
Kavanagh v Ireland, CCPR/C/71/D/819/1998, 4
April 2001 . . . 274
Kawas Fernández v Honduras, IACtHR Series C
No. 196, 3 April 2009 . . . 409
Kaya v Turkey (1999) 28 EHRR 1
(ECtHR) . . . 191, 485
Kell v Canada, CEDAW/C/51/D/19/2008, 17
April 2012 . . . 327
Kelly v UK, App no 30054/96, 4 May 2001
(ECtHR) . . . 191
Khashiyev and Akayeva v Russia (2006) 42
EHRR 20 (ECtHR) . . . 191
Kichwa Indigenous People of Sarayuku v
Ecuador, IACtHR Series C No 245, 27 June
2012 . . . 292, 293, 353, 354
Kitok v Sweden, CCPR/C/33/D/197/1985,
27 July 1988 . . . 350
Kivenmaa v Finland, CCPR/C/50/D/412/1990,
9 June 1994 . . . 235
Kiyutin v Russia (2011) 53 EHRR 364
(ECtHR) . . . 169

Kjeldsen, Busk Madsen and Pedersen v Denmark
(1979–80) 1 EHRR 711 (ECtHR) . . . 104,
240, 245
KL v Peru, CCPR/C/85/D/1153/2003, 22
November 2005 . . . 185
Klein v Slovakia (2010) 50 EHRR 15
(ECtHR) . . . 295
Kokkinakis v Greece (1994) 17 EHRR 397
(ECtHR) . . . 222
Koky and Others v Romania, App no 13642/03,
Judgment of 12 June 2012 (ECtHR) . . . 348
Kononov v Latvia (2011) 52 EHRR 21
(ECtHR) . . . 283
Koraou v Niger, ECW/CCJ/JUD/06/08, 27
October 2008 . . . 444
Korneenko v Belarus, CCPR/C/88/D/1274/2004,
10 November 2006 . . . 233
Krasnova v Kyrgyzstan, CCPR/
C/101/D/1402/2005, 27 April 2010 . . . 265
Krasovsky v Belarus, CCPR/C/104/D/1820/2008,
26 March 2012 . . . 125
Krone Verlag GmbH and Co KG v Austria (2003)
36 EHRR 57 (ECtHR) . . . 229
Kulomin v Hungary, CCPR/C/50/D/521/1992, 22
March 1996 . . . 267
Kuok Koi v Portugal, CCPR/C/73/D/925/2000, 8
February 2002 . . . 129
Kurt v Turkey (1999) 27 EHRR 373
(ECtHR) . . . 269
Kyrtatos v Greece (2005) 40 EHRR 16
(ECtHR) . . . 599

L v Lithuania (2008) 46 EHRR 22
(ECtHR) . . . 306
L and V v Austria (2003) 36 EHRR 55
(ECtHR) . . . 309
LaGrand, *see* Germany v USA
Lamagna v Australia, CCPR/C/65/D/737/1997,
30 April 1999 . . . 122
Lamby Longa v The Netherlands (2013) 56
EHRR SE1 (ECtHR) . . . 126, 127
Land, Island and Maritime Dispute *see* El
Salvador v Honduras
Las Palmeras v Colombia, IACtHR Series C No
67, 4 February 2000 . . . 487
'Last Temptation of Christ' v Chile (Olmeda
Bustos et al.), IACtHR Series C No 73, 5
February 2001 . . . 104
LaVende v Trinidad and Tobago, CCPR/
C/61/D/554/1993, 17 November 1997 . . . 189
Lawless v Ireland (1979–80) 1 EHRR 15
(ECtHR) . . . 113
Lawyers for Human Rights v Swaziland,
18th Activity Report of the ACommHPR
(2005) . . . 275
Legal Consequences for States of the Continued
Presence of South Africa in Namibia (South
West Africa) notwithstanding Security
Council Resolution 276 (1970) (Advisory
Opinion) [1971] ICJ Rep 16 (ICJ) . . . 339

Legal Consequences of the Construction of a
Wall in the Occupied Palestinian Territory
(Advisory Opinion) [2004] ICJ Rep 136
(ICJ) . . . 86, 134, 340, 395, 487, 488, 490,
494, 562
Legality of the Threat or Use of Nuclear Weapons
(Advisory Opinion) [1996] ICJ Rep 226
(ICJ) . . . 83, 84, 86, 480, 488, 490
Letellier v France (1992) 14 EHRR 83
(ECtHR) . . . 267
Leyaeva v Russia, App nos 53157/99, 53247/99,
53695/00 and 56850/00, 26 October 2006
(ECtHR) . . . 598
Libyan Arab Jamahiriya v Malta [1985] ICJ Rep
29 (ICJ) . . . 81
Lingens v Austria (1986) 8 EHRR 407
(ECtHR) . . . 229
Lithgow v UK (1986) 8 EHRR 329
(ECtHR) . . . 164
LMR v Argentina, CCPR/C/101/D/1608/2007, 28
April 2011 . . . 121
Loayza-Tamayo v Peru, IACtHR Series C No 33,
17 September 1997 . . . 181, 408
Loizidou v Turkey (Preliminary Objections)
(1995) 20 EHRR 99 (ECtHR) . . . 79, 101,
109, 110
Loizidou v Turkey (1997) 23 EHRR 513
(ECtHR) . . . 107, 129, 130, 343
Loor (Vélez) v Panama, IACtHR Series C No 218,
23 November 2010 . . . 265
Lopez Burgos v Uruguay, CCPR/
C/13/D/52/1979, 29 July 1981 . . . 133,
137, 554
Lopez Ostra v Spain (1995) 20 EHRR 277
(ECtHR) . . . 124, 597, 598
Lovelace v Canada, A/36/40 (1981) . . . 350
Lubuto v Zambia, CCPR/C/55/D/390/1990/
Rev.1, 30 June 1994 . . . 188, 277
Lustig-Prean and Beckett v UK (1999) 29 EHRR
548 (ECtHR) . . . 306
Lyashkevich v Belarus, CCPR/C/77/D/887/1999,
24 April 2003 . . . 190

MAB, WAT and JAYT v Canada, CCPR/
C/50/D/570/1993, 25 April
1994 . . . 221, 222
Madani v Algeria, CCPR/C/89/D/1172/2003, 21
June 2007 . . . 261, 276
Malawi African Association v Mauritania,
54/91, 98/93, 164/97–196/97, 210/98, 13th
Activity Report of the ACommHPR
(1999–2000) . . . 276
Maleki v Italy, CCPR/C/66/D/699/1996, 15 June
1999 . . . 276
Mamatkulov and Askarov v Turkey (2005)
41 EHRR 25 (ECtHR) . . . 431
Mangouras v Spain (2012) 54 EHRR 25
(ECtHR) . . . 599
Manneh v The Gambia, ECW/CCJ/JUD/03/08,
5 June 2008 . . . 444

Mansaraj v Sierra Leone, CCPR/
C/72/D/841/1998, 16 July 2001 . . . 190
Marckx v Belgium (1979–80) 2 EHRR 330
(ECtHR) . . . 434
Maritza Urrutia v Guatemala, IACtHR
Series C No 103, 27 November 2003 . . . 180
Markin (Konstantin) v Russia (2013) 56 EHRR 8
(ECtHR) . . . 168
Maya Indigenous Community of the Toledo
District v Belize, IACommHR Rep No 40/40,
12 October 2004 . . . 593
Mayagna (Sumo) Awas Tigni Community v
Nicaragua, IACtHR Series C No 79, 31 August
2001 . . . 208, 593
Mbenge v Zaire, CCPR/C/18/D/16/1977, 25
March 1983 . . . 189
MC v Bulgaria (2005) 40 EHRR 20
(ECtHR) . . . 87
McCann v UK (1996) 21 EHRR 97
(ECtHR) . . . 187, 507
McKerr v UK (2002) 34 EHRR 20
(ECtHR) . . . 191
Mejía v Peru, IACommHR Rep No 5/96, 1 March
1996 . . . 180
Metropolitan Church of Bessarabia v Moldova
(2002) 35 EHRR 306 (ECtHR) . . . 222
Mexico v United States [2004] ICJ Rep 12
(ICJ) . . . 268
Miguel Castro-Castro Prison v Peru,
IACtHR Series C No 160,
25 November 2006 . . . 180
Military and Paramilitary Activities in and
against Nicaragua see Nicaragua v USA
Minority Schools in Albania, Advisory Opinion,
PCIJ Series A/B No 64 (1935) (PCIJ) . . . 27,
86, 246
Modinos v Cyprus (1993) 16 EHRR 485
(ECtHR) . . . 306
Mojica v Dominican Republic, CCPR/
C/51/D/449/1991, 25 July 1994 . . . 269
Molnár (Eva) v Hungary, App no 10346/05, 7
October 2008 (ECtHR) . . . 236
Monagas Detention Center ('La Pica')
(Venezuela) (Provisional Measures) IACtHR, 3
July 2007 . . . 411
Montero v Uruguay, CCPR/C/18/D/106/1981, 31
March 1983 . . . 133, 137
Montero-Aranguren v Venezuela, IACtHR Series
C No 150, 5 July 2006 . . . 187
Morales de Sierra (María Eugenia) v Guatemala,
IACommHR Rep No 4/00, 19 January
2001 . . . 168
Moscow Branch of the Salvation Army v Russia
(2006) 44 EHRR 912 (ECtHR) . . . 222
Mouvement Burkinabé des Droits de l'Homme
et des Peuples v Burkina Faso, 14th
Activity Report of the ACommHPR
(2000–2001) . . . 269, 536
MSS v Belgium and Greece (2011) 53 EHRR 28
(ECtHR) . . . 517

Mukong v Cameroon, CCPR/C/51/D/458/1991, 10 August 1994 . . . 182, 264

Müller and Engelhard v Namibia, CCPR/C/74/D/919/2000, 26 March 2002 . . . 168, 169

Müller and Others v Switzerland (1991) 13 EHRR 212 (ECtHR) . . . 291

Munaf v Romania, CCPR/C/96/D/1539/2006, 21 August 2009 . . . 133

Musayeva and Others v Russia (2008) 47 EHRR 25 (ECtHR) . . . 191

Myrie v Jamaica, Case 12.417, IACommHR Report No 41/04, 12 October 2004 . . . 281

Nachova v Bulgaria (2006) 42 EHRR 43 (ECtHR) . . . 187

Nada v Switzerland (2013) 56 EHRR 18 (ECtHR). . . . 126–7, 563, 564

Naranjo (Mery) (Provisional Measures) IACtHR, 31 January 2008 . . . 410

Ng v Canada, CCPR/C/49/D/469/1991, 7 January 1994 . . . 183, 187, 190, 191

Nguyen v The Netherlands, A/61/38, Annex VIII, 14 August 2006 . . . 327

Nicaragua Case see Nicaragua v USA

Nicaragua v Costa Rica, IACommHR Rep No 11/07, 8 March 2007 . . . 403–4

Nicaragua v USA [1986] ICJ Rep 14 (ICJ) . . . 83

Niemietz v Germany (1993) 16 EHRR 97 (ECtHR) . . . 306

Norris v Ireland (1988) 13 EHRR 186 (ECtHR) . . . 306

North Sea Continental Shelf Cases see Federal Republic of Germany v Denmark; Federal Republic of Germany v The Netherlands

Norwood (Mark Anthony) v UK (2005) 40 EHRR SE11 (ECtHR) . . . 230

Novotka v Slovakia, App no 47244/99, 4 November 2003 (ECtHR) . . . 261

Nystrom v Australia, CCPR/C/102/D/1557/2007, 18 August 2011 . . . 120

Öcalan v Turkey (2005) 41 EHRR 45 (ECtHR) . . . 130, 190

Ogoniland see Social and Economic Rights Action Center (SERAC) and the Center for Economic and Social Rights (CESR) v Nigeria

Öllinger v Austria (2008) 46 EHRR 38 (ECtHR) . . . 235

Olsson v Sweden (1988) 11 EHRR 259 (ECtHR) . . . 596

Ominayak and the Lubicon Lake Band v Canada, A/45/40 (Vol II) Annex IX, 1 . . . 334, 350

Öneryıldız v Turkey (2005) 41 EHRR 20 (ECtHR) . . . 598, 607

Opuz v Turkey (2010) 50 EHRR 28 (ECtHR) . . . 93, 124, 384

Organisation Mondiale Contre La Torture v Rwanda, 27/89, 46/91, 49/91 and 99/93, 10th Activity Report of the ACommHPR (1996–1997) . . . 264

Osman v UK (2000) 29 EHRR 245 (ECtHR) . . . 102, 124, 192

Othman (Abu Qatada) v UK (2012) 55 EHRR 1 (ECtHR) . . . 128, 262, 272, 279

Otto-Preminger Institut v Austria (1995) 19 EHRR 34 (ECtHR) . . . 104, 295

Oulajin and Kaiss v The Netherlands, CCPR/C/46/D/406/1990 and 426/1990, 23 October 1992 . . . 169

Ould Dah v France, App no 13113/03, 30 March 2009 (ECtHR) . . . 84

Ouranio Toxo v Greece (2007) 45 EHRR 8 (ECtHR) . . . 218, 233

Páez (William Eduardo Delgado) v Colombia, CCPR/C/39/D/195/1985, 12 July 1990 . . . 102, 270

Paton v UK (1981) 3 EHRR 408 (ECtHR) . . . 121

PB and JS v Austria (2012) 55 EHRR 31 (ECtHR) . . . 312

Peace Community de San José de Apartadó (Colombia) (Provisional Measures) IACtHR, 24 November 2000 . . . 411

Peart v Jamaica, CCPR/C/54/D/464/1991, 24 July 1995 . . . 281

Pfunders Case see Austria v Italy

Piandiong v The Philippines, CCPR/C/70/D/869/1999, 19 October 2000 . . . 382

Piersack v Belgium (1983) 5 EHRR 169 (ECtHR) . . . 275

Pillai v Canada, CCPR/C/101/D/1763/2008, 25 March 2011 . . . 128

Pinkney v Canada, CCPR/C/OP/1 (1985) . . . 277

Plattform 'Ärzte für das Leben' v Austria (1991) 13 EHRR 204 (ECtHR) . . . 102, 234

Poma Poma (Angela_v Peru, CCPR/C/95/D/1457/2006, 27 March 2009 . . . 292, 293

Portugal v Australia [1995] ICJ Rep 90 (ICJ) . . . 340, 347

Powell and Raynor v UK (1990) 12 EHRR 355 (ECtHR) . . . 596

Pratt and Morgan v Jamaica, CCPR/C/35/D/210/1986, 6 April 1989 . . . 190

Pretty v UK (2002) 35 EHRR 1 (ECtHR) . . . 185, 186

Prieto (Glora Giralt de García) et al. (Provisional Measures) IACtHR, 26 September 2006 . . . 410

Proposed Amendments to the Naturalization Provisions of the Constitution of Costa Rica, Advisory Opinion OC-4/84, IACtHR Series A No 4, 19 January 1984 . . . 158, 166, 412

Prosecutor v Akayesu, IT-96-4-T, 2 September 1998 (ICTR) . . . 499, 500

Prosecutor v al Bashir, ICC-02/05-01/09, 4 March 2009 (ICC) . . . 501, 502

Prosecutor v Blaskić, IT-95-14-A, 29 July 2004 (ICTY) . . . 503, 505

Prosecutor v Brđanin, IT-99–36-A, 3 April 2007
    (ICTY) . . . 503
Prosecutor v Furundžija, IT-95–17/1-T, 10
    December 1998 (ICTY) . . . 84, 177
Prosecutor v Jelesić, IT-95–10-A, 5 July 2001
    (ICTY) . . . 500
Prosecutor v Kallon and Kamara, SCSL-2004-15-
    AR72(E) and SCSL-2004-16-AR72(E), 13
    March 2004 . . . 510
Prosecutor v Kondewa, SCSL-2004-14-AR72(E),
    25 May 2004 . . . 507
Prosecutor v Katanga and Ngudjolo,
    ICC-01/04–01/07–1497, 25 September 2009
    (ICC) . . . 509
Prosecutor v Krajišnik, IT-00–39-T, 27
    September 2006 (ICTY) . . . 503
Prosecutor v Krstić, IT-98–33-T-2, 2 August 2001
    (ICTY) . . . 501
Prosecutor v Krstić, IT-98–33-A, 19 April 2004
    (ICTY) . . . 499, 500
Prosecutor v Kunarac, Kovać and Vuković,
    IT-96–23-T, 22 February 2001
    (ICTY) . . . 87, 503
Prosecutor v Kunarac, Kovać and Vuković,
    IT-96–23/1-A, 12 June 2002 (ICTY) . . . 87,
    491, 502, 506
Prosecutor v Kupreškić, Kupreškić, Kupreškić,
    Papić and Šntić, IT-95–16-T, 14 January 2000
    (ICTY) . . . 503
Prosecutor v Martić, IT-95–11-A, 8 October 2008
    (ICTY) . . . 486
Prosecutor v Mucić, IT-96–21/T, 16 November
    1998 (ICTY) . . . 87
Prosecutor v Nahimana, Barayagwiza and
    Ngeze, ICTR-99–52-A, 28 November 2007
    (ICTR) . . . 504
Prosecutor v Sam Hinga Norman,
    SCSL-2004–14-AR72(E), 31 May 2004
    (SCSL) . . . 544
Prosecutor v Semanza, ICTR-97–20-T, 15 May
    2003 (ICTR) . . . 500
Prosecutor v Tadić, IT-94–1-A, 15 July 1999
    (ICTY) . . . 504
Prosecutor v Tadić, IT-94–1-AR72, 2 October
    1995 (ICTY) . . . 484, 508
Purohit v The Gambia, 241/01, 16th
    Activity Report of the ACommHPR
    (2002–2003) . . . 166, 449

Quaranta v Switzerland, A 205 (1991)
    (ECtHR) . . . 281
Queenan v Canada, CCPR/C/84/D/1379/2005,
    23 August 2005 . . . 121
Questions relating to the Obligation to Prosecute
    or Extradite see Belgium v Senegal

Rameka v New Zealand, CCPR/
    C/79/D/1090/2002, 6 November 2003 . . . 264
Rantsev v Cyprus and Russia (2010) 51 EHRR 1
    (ECtHR) . . . 89

Rasmussen v Denmark (1984) 7 EHRR 371
    (ECtHR) . . . 162, 164
Raxcacó-Reyes v Guatemala, IACtHR Series C
    No 133, 15 September 2005 . . . 182, 189, 409
Refah Partisi (The Welfare Party) v Turkey (2003)
    37 EHRR 1 (ECtHR) . . . 122, 233
Republic of Guinea v Democratic Republic of
    Congo [2010] ICJ Rep para 77 (ICJ) . . . 261,
    380, 395
Reservations to the Genocide Convention,
    Advisory Opinion [1951] ICJ Rep 15
    (ICJ) . . . 99
Restrepo (Vélez) v Colombia IACtHR Series C
    No 248, 3 September 2012 . . . 227
Reyes (Claude) v Chile, IACtHR Series C No 151,
    19 September 2006 . . . 228, 408
Richards v Jamaica, CCPR/C/59/D/535/1993/
    Rev.1, 29 April 1997 . . . 189
Riffo (Atala) and daughters v Chile (Merits),
    IACtHR Series C No 239, 24 February
    2012 . . . 305, 306, 309, 312
Right to Information on Consular Assistance
    in the Framework of Guarantees of the Due
    Process of Law, OC-16/99, IACtHR Series
    A No 16, 1 October 1999 . . . 189
Rights of Minorities in Upper Silesia, PCIJ Series
    A No 15 (1928) (PCIJ) . . . 27
Roach and Pinkerton v USA, IACommHR Res
    3/87, 22 September 1987 . . . 399
Ross v Canada, CCPR/C/70/D/736/1997, 18
    October 2000 . . . 230
RS v Trinidad and Tobago, CCPR/
    C/74/D/684/1996, 2 April 2002 . . . 190

Saadi v Italy, App no 37201/06, 28 February 2008
    (ECtHR) . . . 177, 183, 558
Sahin (Leyla) v Turkey (2007) 44 EHRR 5
    (ECtHR) . . . 223, 240
Saidova v Tajikstan, CCPR/C/81/D/964/2001, 8
    July 2004 . . . 189
Sakik v Turkey (1998) 26 EHRR 662
    (ECtHR) . . . 113
Saldano v Argentina, IACommHR Rep No 38/99,
    11 March 1999 . . . 132
Salduz v Turkey (2008) 49 EHRR 421
    (ECtHR) . . . 181
Sale (Chris), Acting Commissioner, Immigration
    and Naturalization Service, et al. v Haitian
    Centers Council, Inc et al. (1993) 509 US
    155 . . . 521
Salguiero da Silva Mouta v Portugal (1999) 31
    EHRR 1055 (ECtHR) . . . 309
Salinas v Peru, IACommHR Rep No 27/94
    (1994) . . . 276
Saramaka People v Suriname, IACtHR Series C
    No 172, 28 November 2007 . . . 292, 353
Sarma v Sri Lanka, CCPR/C/78/D/950/2000, 16
    July 2003 . . . 123, 269
Saunders v UK (1996) 23 EHRR 313
    (ECtHR) . . . 279

Sayadi and Vinck v Belgium, CCPR/
    C/94/D/1472/2006, 29 December
    2008 . . . 127, 563
Schalk and Kopf v Austria (2011) 53 EHRR 20
    (ECtHR) . . . 311–12
Schmitz-de-Jong v The Netherlands, CCPR/
    C/72/D/855/1999, 16 July 2001 . . . 164
Sechremelis v Greece, CCPR/
    C/100/D/1507/2006, 30 November
    2010 . . . 274
Selmouni v France (2000) 29 EHRR 403
    (ECtHR) . . . 179, 180
SERAC see Social and Economic Rights Action
    Center (SERAC) and the Center for Economic
    and Social Rights (CESR) v Nigeria
SERAP v Nigeria, ECW/CCj/JUD/07/10, 30
    November 2010 . . . 247
Serif v Greece (1999) 31 EHRR 561
    (ECtHR) . . . 222
Shanagan v UK, App no 37715/97, 4 May 2001
    (ECtHR) . . . 191
Sigurjonsson v Iceland (1981) 4 EHRR 38
    (ECtHR) . . . 232
Simunek v Czech Republic, CCPR/
    C/54/D/516/1992, 19 July 1995 . . . 166
Singer v Canada, CCPR/C/51/D/455/1991, 8
    April 1993 . . . 122, 334
Singh v France, CCPR/C/106/D/1852/2008, 4,
    February 2013 . . . 224
Singh Binder v Canada, CCPR/C/37/D/208/1986,
    9 November 1989 . . . 165
Singh (Ranjit) v France, CCPR/
    C/102/D/1876/2009, 27 September
    2011 . . . 224
SL v Austria (2003) 37 EHRR 39
    (ECtHR) . . . 309
SM v Barbados, CCPR/C/50/D/502/1992,
    4 April 1994 . . . 122
Smith and Grady v UK (1999) 29 EHRR 493
    (ECtHR) . . . 306
Social and Economic Rights Action Center
    (SERAC) and the Center for Economic and
    Social Rights (CESR) v Nigeria, 155/96, 16th
    Activity Report of the ACommHPR (2002–
    2003) . . . 125, 200, 203, 334, 445, 446, 449,
    592–3, 607
Soering v UK (1989) 11 EHRR 439
    (ECtHR) . . . 120, 128, 190, 191, 384, 522
Sorguç v Turkey, App no 17089/03, Judgment of
    23 June 2009 (ECtHR) . . . 291
South-West Africa Cases (Second Phase) see
    Ethiopia v South Africa; Liberia v South Africa
Stafford v UK (2002) 35 EHRR 32
    (ECtHR) . . . 264
Stalla Costa v Uruguay, CCPR/C/30/D/198/1985,
    9 July 1987 . . . 171
Stanev v Bulgaria (2012) 55 EHRR 22
    (ECtHR) . . . 264, 265
Stec v UK (2006) 43 EHRR 47 (ECtHR) . . . 172

Streletz, Kessler and Krenz v Germany (2001) 33
    EHRR 751 (ECtHR) . . . 283
Suárez-Rosero v Ecuador, IACtHR Series C No
    35, 12 November 1997 . . . 181
Sunday Times v UK (1979–80) 2 EHRR 245
    (ECtHR) . . . 104, 112, 122, 219
Szijjarto v Hungary, A/61/36, Annex VIII, 14
    August 2006 . . . 327

Tabacalera Boqueron SA v Paraguay,
    IACommHR Rep 47/97, 16 October
    1997 . . . 122
Társaság a Szabadságjogokért v Hungary, App no
    37374/05, 14 April 2009 (ECtHR) . . . 228
Taskin v Turkey (2006) 42 EHRR 50
    (ECtHR) . . . 607, 608
Tatar v Romania, App no 67021/01, 18 October
    2007 (ECtHR) . . . 607
Tatlav v Turkey, App no 50692/99, Judgment of 2
    May 1996 (ECtHR) . . . 295
Taxquet v Belgium (2012) 54 EHRR 26
    (ECtHR) . . . 278
Teixera v Brazil, CEDAW/C/49/D/17/2008, 27
    September 2011 . . . 327
Teruel (Pacheco) et al. v Honduras, IACtHR
    Series C No 241, 27 April 2012 . . . 266
Thlimmenos v Greece (2000) 31 EHRR 411
    (ECtHR) . . . 225
Thomas (Douglas Christopher) v USA,
    IACommHR Rep No 100/03, 29 December
    2003 . . . 85
Thompson v St Vincent and the Grenadines,
    CCPR/C/70/D/806/1998, 18 October
    2000 . . . 188
Thorgeirson (Thorgeir) v Iceland (1992) 14
    EHRR 843 (ECtHR) . . . 226
Timishev v Russia (2007) 44 EHRR 37
    (ECtHR) . . . 168, 169
Timurtas v Turkey (2001) 33 EHRR 6
    (ECtHR) . . . 269
Toonen v Australia, CCPR/C/50/D/488/1992, 4
    April 1994 . . . 123, 164, 306, 308, 310
Trijonis v Lithuania, App no 2333/02, 17 March
    2005 (ECtHR) . . . 261
Tyrer v UK (1978) 2 EHRR 1 (ECtHR) . . . 182

Ülke v Turkey (2009) 48 EHRR 48
    (ECtHR) . . . 225
Unión de Pequeños Agricultores v Council, Case
    C-50/00 P [2002] ECR I-6677 (ECJ) . . . 437
United Communist Party of Turkey v Turkey
    (1998) 26 EHRR 121 (ECtHR) . . . 233

Van Alphen v The Netherlands, CCPR/
    C/39/D/305/1988, 23 July 1990 . . . 263
Van Kuck v Germany (2003) 37 EHRR 51
    (ECtHR) . . . 306
Van Meurs v The Netherlands, CCPR/
    C/39/D/215/1986, 13 July 1990 . . . 278

Velásquez-Rodríguez v Honduras (Merits), IACtHR Series C No 4, 29 July 1988 . . . 93, 102, 103, 124, 183, 269, 399, 403, 507

Vera (Christián Daniel Sahli) v Chile, IACommHR Rep No 43/05, 10 March 2005 . . . 225

Vertido v Philippines, CEDAW/C/46/D/18/2008, 22 September 2010 . . . 92

VK v Bulgaria, CEDAW/C/49/D/20/2008, 27 September 2011 . . . 92, 325

Vo v France (2005) 10 EHRR 12 (ECtHR) . . . 121

Von Hannover v Germany (2005) 40 EHRR 1 (ECtHR) . . . 229

Vojnity v Hungary, App no 29617/07, Judgment of 12 February 2013 (ECtHR) . . . 169

VS v Belarus, CCPR/C/103/D/1749/2008, 21 November 2011 . . . 122

Waite and Kennedy v Germany (2000) 30 EHRR 261 (ECtHR) . . . 539

Waldman v Canada, CCPR/C/67/D/694/1996, 5 November 1999 . . . 123, 245

Wallman v Austria, CCPR/C/80/D/1002/2001, 29 April 2004 . . . 122

Wanza v Trinidad and Tobago, CCPR/C/74/D/683/1996, 26 March 2002 . . . 266

Warsame v Canada, CCPR/C/102/D/1959/2010, 21 July 2011 . . . 120

WBE v The Netherlands, CCPR/C/46/D/432/1990, 23 October 1993 . . . 267

Wemhoff v Germany (1979–80) 1 EHRR 55 (ECtHR) . . . 268

Western Sahara Case [1975] ICJ Rep 12 (ICJ) . . . 339, 344, 347

WJH v The Netherlands, CCPR/C/45/D/408/1990, 22 July 1992 . . . 282

Word 'Laws' in Article 30 of the American Convention on Human Rights,

OC-6/86, IACtHR Series A No 6, 9 May 1986 . . . 111

X v Austria, App No 19010/07, Judgment of 19 February 2013 (ECtHR) . . . 310

X v Colombia, CCPR/C/89/D/1361/2005, 14 May 2007 . . . 308, 312

X v Sweden (1959) 2 YB 354 (ECommHR) . . . 277

X and Y v Federal Republic of Germany 15 DR 161 (1976) (ECommHR) . . . 596

X and Y v The Netherlands (1986) 8 EHRR 235 (ECtHR) . . . 102, 536

Yakye Axa Indigenous Community v Paraguay, IACtHR Series C No 125, 17 June 2005 . . . 208–9

Yanomami v Brazil, IACommHR Res 12/85, 5 March 1985 . . . 593

Yeo-Bum Yoon (Mr) and Myung-Jin Choi (Mr) v Republic of Korea, CCPR/C/88/D/1321–1322/2004, 23 January 2007 . . . 225

Yildirim v Turkey, App no 3111/10, Judgment of 18 December 2012 (ECtHR) . . . 226

Yildirim (deceased) v Austria, CEDAW/C/39/D/6/2005, 1 October 2007 . . . 92, 124, 325, 327

Young v Australia, CCPR/C/78/D/941/2000, 6 August 2003 . . . 308, 312

Young, James and Webster v UK (1982) 4 EHRR 38 (ECtHR) . . . 102, 232

Zambrano Vélez v Ecuador, IACtHR Series C No 166, 4 July 2007 . . . 187

ZH v Hungary, App no 28973/11, 8 November 2012 (ECtHR) . . . 265

Zimmermann v Switzerland (1994) 6 EHRR 17 (ECtHR) . . . 277

WHAT ARE HUMAN RIGHTS FOR? THREE PERSONAL REFLECTIONS

NAVANETHEM PILLAY

UNITED NATIONS HIGH COMMISSIONER
FOR HUMAN RIGHTS

The editors of this textbook on international human rights law asked me to provide some thoughts on the question 'What are human rights for?' and to do so from the perspective of personal experience. I will begin by noting that I count myself among the lucky ones— those who against the odds of multiple discrimination, based on gender, race, and social class, came to enjoy the benefits of civil and political liberties, as well as economic, social, and cultural rights.

I was born a non-white in apartheid South Africa. My ancestors were sugarcane cutters. My father was a bus driver. We were poor.

At age 16 I wrote an essay which dealt with the role of South African women in educating children on human rights and which, as it turned out, was indeed fateful. After the essay was published, my community raised funds in order to send this promising, but impecunious, young woman to university. My people perhaps did not know that a right to education actually existed and that it was enshrined in international law; but they believed in education. They understood that it creates paths out of poverty and discrimination.

Despite their efforts and goodwill, I almost did not make it as a lawyer, because when I entered university during the apartheid regime everything and everyone was segregated. The registrar actually discouraged me from becoming a lawyer. He argued that I could not expect white secretaries to take instructions from a person of my background. However, I persevered. After my graduation I sought an internship, which was mandatory under the law; but then as a black woman I had to fight against multi-layered forms of discrimination and barriers. Finally, it was a black lawyer who agreed to take me on board, but he first made me promise that I would not become pregnant. And when I started a law practice on my own, it was not out of choice but because no one would employ a black woman lawyer.

Yet, in the course of my life, I had the privilege to see and experience a complete transformation in my country. South Africa now has one of the strongest constitutions in the world, and while it struggles, as many countries do, to turn legal rights into reality, watching such amazing change over a single decade and through a relatively peaceful evolution gives me great hope. Indeed, I offer a living testimony of rights realized.

Against this background it is no surprise that when I read or recite Article 1 of the Universal Declaration of Human Rights, I intimately and profoundly feel its truth. The article states that: 'All human beings are born free and equal in dignity and rights. They are endowed with reason and conscience and should act towards one another in a spirit of brotherhood.' These words resonate today as widely and as movingly as they did in 1948 when the Universal Declaration came into being. They affirmed the force of ideas and a vision of respectful and peaceful coexistence in the aftermath of utter brutality and destruction. The Universal Declaration's words speak with timeless and unalterable force of both the power of rights and of our kinship in rights.

THE POWER OF RIGHTS AND
OUR KINSHIP IN RIGHTS

The power of rights made it possible for an ever-expanding number of people, people like myself, to claim freedom, equality, justice, and well-being. All human rights—civil, political, economic, social, and cultural—were recognized as inherent and inalienable entitlements of all people, rather than privileges magnanimously bestowed upon them or denied to them at the caprice of the powerful.

The language of human rights makes manifest the relationship between fundamental freedoms and social justice, and the connection of these elements with peace and security. It is reflected in a wide and growing legal architecture, as well as advocacy vehicles for the promotion and protection of all rights.

Today, dedicated international, regional, and national mechanisms, including the UN Office of the High Commissioner for Human Rights and the UN Human Rights Council with its independent experts, have been put in place to be both the custodians and the monitors of human rights, to promote and protect all these rights. Civil society everywhere promotes vigilance of rights implementation with growing capacity and influence.

The protective canvas of human rights jurisprudence and implementing mechanisms recognizes the natural and social bonds of human destiny everywhere, that is, our kinship in rights. It empowers all of us to claim our entitlement to a life of dignity, our right to count and be counted irrespective of our ancestry, gender, colour, status, and creed.

Human rights underpin the aspiration to a world in which every man, woman, and child lives free from hunger and protected from oppression, violence, and discrimination, with the benefits of housing, healthcare, education, and opportunity. A human rights approach shines a light over the critical vulnerabilities of individuals and groups at risk of abuse. It engages them as active participants and generators of change. For the opposite of marginalization, discrimination, and neglect is not only equality in rights and opportunities, but also the ability to make one's voice heard and to be counted. Such participation requires the twin freedoms of expression and association. All over the world, the growth of organized civil society, as well as of a combative press that speaks truth to power, testifies to the vitality and enduring appeal of these principles. Indeed, information and the freedom to organize and express views openly are vital for good policy-making and the measurable implementation of human rights policies. This encapsulates the global culture of human rights towards which we strive.

Yet for too many people in the world, human rights remain an unfulfilled promise, as the political will to give effect to states' human rights obligations lags lamentably behind their pledges. We live in a world where crimes against humanity are ongoing, where mass rape and murder continue with impunity, and where the most basic economic rights critical to survival are not realized and often not even accorded the high priority they warrant.

The UN Secretary-General noted that the recent food emergencies, degradation of the natural environment, current economic crisis, and the unrest that they engender all underscore that those who are at the frontlines of hardship are also likely to be the victims of the ripple effects of human rights violations.

GIVING EFFECT TO RIGHTS:
MECHANISMS AND RESPONSIBILITIES

The challenge for all of us—states, international organizations, and civil society—remains in implementing human rights and ensuring that they are given effect without ranking them. The question is: how?

To begin to answer it, I will tap into the wisdom of Eleanor Roosevelt, leader of the Universal Declaration process, who once said, 'Where, after all, do universal human rights begin?... In small places, close to home.' Until these rights touch the lives of every man, woman, and child, everywhere, our work is not done.

The years to come are crucial for sowing the seeds of an improved international partnership that, by drawing on individual and collective resourcefulness and strengths, can meet the global challenges of poverty, discrimination, conflict, scarcity of natural resources, recession, and climate change.

In defeating fear and want and in dissuading potential perpetrators from committing human rights violations, we can be assisted not only by existing human rights and international humanitarian law, as well as existing institutions of justice, but also by innovative and evolving mechanisms.

In 2005, the world leaders at their summit created the UN Human Rights Council, an intergovernmental body which replaced the much-criticized UN Human Rights Commission, with the mandate of promoting 'universal respect for the protection of all human rights and fundamental freedoms for all'. The Council began its operations in June 2006. Since then, it has equipped itself with its own institutional architecture and has been engaged in an innovative process known as the Universal Periodic Review (UPR). The UPR is the Council's assessment at regular intervals of the human rights record of all UN member states. With time, I am confident that the review will help effectively to change for the better the human rights situation on the ground. We should recognize that this initiative carries a promising potential and is taken very seriously.

In addition, at each session of the Council several country-situations are brought to the fore in addresses and documents delivered by member states, independent experts, and the Office of the High Commissioner for Human Rights. Civil society eagerly contributes to the Council's work. Indeed, the Council is one of the pre-eminent international fora, attracting hundreds of representatives from NGOs, as well as individuals, whose clout and proposals are reflected in the decision-making processes. The Council also offers them a venue to channel comments and reflections, concerns and grievances.

Further, unlike the previous Commission, the Council is virtually a standing body. The frequency of its meetings—both in formal and informal gatherings—creates more opportunities for honing operations and responses to both chronic human rights conditions and crises. Among the latter, the Council tackled the recent food emergencies and the economic downturn with the sense of urgency they deserved. The assiduity of the Council's meetings may also help to build a firmer ground of understanding among the Council's members than sporadic interactions would permit.

If the Human Rights Council is the premier intergovernmental body for the promotion and protection of human rights, the Office of the High Commissioner for Human Rights, as part of the UN Secretariat, is their leading international advocate and independent champion.

As the UN Secretary-General noted, since its creation in 1993 the Office of the High Commissioner has grown to become a powerful driver of change. It has expanded dramatically, elevated the profile of human rights all over the world, provided expertise for capacity building both to states and within the UN system, and preserved the autonomy of judgement and scope of action that are indispensible to human rights work and advocacy.

Today, the Office of the High Commissioner is in a unique position to assist governments and civil society in their efforts to protect and promote human rights. The expansion of its field offices and its presence in more than 50 countries, as well as its increasing and deepening interaction with UN agencies and other crucial partners in government, international organizations, and civil society are important steps in this direction. With these steps we can more readily strive for practical cooperation leading to the creation of national systems which promote human rights and provide protection and recourse for victims of human rights violations.

Deterring the most flagrant human rights violations through the application of international criminal responsibility has also been a critical component of human rights advocacy. The International Criminal Court plays a central role in this regard. The Statute of the Court is a major step forward in that, for the first time, a major multilateral treaty unequivocally recognizes acts committed in non-international armed conflicts as war crimes. It is encouraging that an increasing number of states are signing and ratifying the Statute.

In the final instance, however, it is the duty of states, regardless of their political, economic, and cultural systems, to promote and protect all human rights and fundamental freedoms. Our collective responsibility is to assist states to fulfil their obligations and to hold them to account when they do not.

The roster of distinguished contributors to this textbook is very impressive. These experts will expand and clarify some of the thoughts that here I can only sketch. The readers of such an important contribution to human rights education are indeed in good hands.

KENNETH ROTH

EXECUTIVE DIRECTOR OF HUMAN RIGHTS WATCH

The modern state can be a source of both good and evil. It can do much good—protecting our security, ensuring our basic necessities, nurturing an environment in which people can flourish to the best of their abilities. But when it represses its people, shirks its duties, or misapplies its resources, it can be the source of much suffering.

International human rights law sets forth the core obligations of governments toward their people, prescribing the basic freedoms that governments must respect and the steps they must take to uphold public welfare. But the application of that law often differs from the enforcement of statutes typically found in a nation's law books.

In countries that enjoy the rule of law, the courts can usually be relied on to enforce legislation. The rule of law means that courts have the independence to apply the law free of interference, and powerful actors, including senior government officials, are expected to comply with court orders.

In practice, there is no such presumption in most of the countries where my organization, Human Rights Watch, works, and where international human rights law is most needed. The judges are often corrupt, intimidated, or compromised. They may not dare hold the government to account, or they may have been co-opted to the point that they do not even try, or the government may succeed in ignoring whatever efforts they make. It is worth noting that this problem is not limited to dictatorships or tyrannical governments. Even in functioning democracies, the courts do not always succeed in enforcing rights for the poor, the marginalized, and the unpopular. In those circumstances, the process of building political pressure through investigation, reporting and advocacy is often all we have. While it may not offer as simple a solution as a trip to the courthouse, it can still be quite powerful. Understanding how it works can be key to appreciating the significance of human rights law.

International human rights law should be seen as a backstop in such cases, a law of last resort when domestic rights legislation fails. Judicial enforcement is always welcome, but when it falls short, human rights law provides a basis that is distinct from domestic legislation for putting pressure on governments to uphold their obligations. It is easy for many who live in rule-of-law countries to assume that the enforcement of rights is a purely judicial function. In fact, the government as a whole is responsible for defending rights; after all, the political branches of government, not the courts, sign and ratify human rights treaties. The pressure techniques developed by the human rights movement could theoretically be applied on behalf of any body of law, but international human rights law, with obligations that many governments are particularly prone to shirk, has been the context in which these techniques have been most refined.

The key to this enforcement pressure is exposure and shame. Human rights groups investigate and report on situations in which governments fall short of their obligations. The resulting publicity, through the media and other outlets, can undermine a government's standing and credibility, embarrassing it before its people and peers and generating pressure for reform. This reporting can also convince other governments and institutions to use their influence with the target government to promote change.

There is a different dynamic to this shaming process than to the enforcement of law in regular courts. Any law weakens when its dictates deviate too far from the public's moral judgments. Even judges in rule-of-law countries tend to be attentive to public opinion with respect to certain controversial issues.

But when it comes to enforcing the law through shaming rather than litigation, public morality plays an even more important role. To put it simply, there can be no shame if the public approves of the conduct in question. The law may say that certain governmental conduct is wrong, but if the public disagrees, if it applauds the conduct, the government will feel no pressure to comply with the law.

The law is not irrelevant to the shaming process. It helps to shape public morality, and thus to promote a sense of shame, particularly in areas, such as warfare, where the norms governing conduct might be complex. But it is important not to equate law with public morality, or to delude ourselves into thinking that the mere existence of a law translates into the type of extra-judicial pressure that human rights groups can generate.

Beyond documenting and reporting violations of human rights law, human rights groups, thus, must shape public opinion to ensure that the exposure of government misconduct is met with opprobrium rather than approval. In part that is done by citing international law to convince the public of a global consensus about what is right or wrong in a given context. By presenting an issue in terms of rights, human rights groups help the public to develop a moral framework for assessing governmental conduct beyond public sentiment in any particular case or incident.

For example, many people might tend to believe that in an armed conflict, anything goes. International human rights law (as well as its sister body of law, international humanitarian law) makes clear that torture and other ill-treatment are prohibited, even in time of war. That is not necessarily an intuitive concept. But the unequivocal prohibition in international law helps to build a public morality that rejects all such mistreatment of detainees.

Or a public may feel that custom legitimizes the subordination of women. Human rights law provides an alternative moral framework to that custom and helps to build a public morality that finds such discrimination and inequality wrong.

For the law to play this role of moral instruction, it is not enough simply to recite it. When people's security or traditions are at stake, it takes more than a mere reference to the law to change the public's sense of moral propriety. Human rights groups must be creative in moving the public to embrace what the law demands.

One key to that effort is personifying the victim. When human rights abuses remain abstract—mere recitations of detention statistics or violated provisions of a penal code—it is far more difficult to mobilize public outrage than if the public can identify with the target of the abuse. The more compelling the story, the more likely there will be public outrage, whether about a political prisoner sentenced to a long prison term, a rape victim denied justice, or a child unable to obtain medical care despite adequate government resources. Here the media play an essential role in bringing the plight of these victims to the public's attention. Ideology, routine, or indifference can often be made to give way to human suffering made palpable.

Sometimes consequentialist arguments are required as well. After the September 11 attacks in the USA, many Americans were willing to contemplate torture because they thought it made them safer. It was not enough to ask Americans to identify with the primary victims—the foreign Muslim terrorist suspects, the supposed 'worst of the worst', because most Americans felt no such identity. But the public gradually rejected torture, in part out of a growing sense that it is not what the USA should stand for, but also, to a large degree, out of a growing belief that torture was making the public less safe by facilitating terrorist recruiters and discouraging the international cooperation needed to curb terrorism.

Sometimes the challenge is convincing the public to apply a broad concept to a particular situation. For example, international humanitarian law has long prohibited indiscriminate attacks, but few thought that this prohibition was violated by antipersonnel landmines or cluster munitions, even though these weapons are incapable of precise targeting of combatants. It took extensive factual reporting on the indiscriminate consequences of these weapons systems for the public to agree that their use was wrong. That public pressure, in turn, led governments to adopt treaties banning these weapons.

Sometimes it is difficult to convince a local public to disapprove of its government's conduct. In those cases, one option is to convince a more sympathetic external public to exert pressure indirectly, usually through its own government. Shaming is usually most powerful when the disapproving public is domestic. But even in the absence of domestic shame—for example, if a government succeeds in controlling its domestic media so that its public does not learn of its shameful conduct—surrogate publics can be a source of pressure. Any public whose views the target government cares about can play this surrogate role—because the target government fears that the surrogate public opinion might seep back home and influence domestic opinion, or because the surrogate public might influence its own government whose good graces matter to the target government.

Thus, the great challenge facing human rights groups is often less concerned with arguing the law's fine points or applying them to the facts of a case than with convincing the public that violations are wrong. That requires the hard work of helping the public to identify with the victim's plight, making the law come alive, and generating outrage at its violation with some public of relevance. When human rights law can be made to correspond with the public's sense of right and wrong, governments face intense pressure to respect that law. Shame can be a powerful motivator.

HINA JILANI

DIRECTOR OF AGHS LEGAL AID CENTER AND
ADVOCATE OF THE SUPREME COURT OF PAKISTAN

What are human rights for? The answer seems fairly obvious to those who have spent many years striving to promote values and principles they consider essential for progress, peace, and social justice. Yet when asked to articulate a response to this question in a manner that connects concepts with the reality of everyday life, it becomes complex, with so many challenges emanating from different experiences determined by the political, social, and economic conditions in which the struggle for the promotion and protection of human rights is being conducted.

From the perspective of human rights defenders, support for human rights is essential to create the environment in which they are able to exercise the freedoms necessary to carry out their activities for advocacy, monitoring, and reporting on respect for human rights. For instance, the freedoms of expression, assembly, association, and access to information are indispensable for the defence of human rights. From the perspective of victims of violations, the human rights framework provides the essential components for effective remedies in the form of redress, compensation, and reparation, through institutions that are independent and impartial and adhere to the basic principles of human dignity, equality, and non-discrimination. The human rights framework also provides the standards that must be reached in order that rights can be realized through the combined medium of state responsibility and the rule of law. It is in this aspect that international law becomes most relevant to domestic legal frameworks by allowing people to have the same expectations from the law, national institutions, state policy, and methods of governance.

The truth of these arguments and fulfilment of these expectations will, nevertheless, only be borne out if individuals' experiences show that what human rights represent has enabled them to obtain justice or has protected them from harm to their dignity, security, or liberty. The abstract promotion of human rights seldom garners the credibility gained when human rights are put to the test and applied to concrete situations involving a quest for their realization.

Human rights defenders have a significant role to play in raising public support for human rights. Their actions and choices regarding the means of promoting human rights often determine popular perceptions about those rights. When called upon to respond to a situation concerning the promotion or protection of rights—individual or collective— human rights defenders are faced with the initial task of choosing the forum in which to raise their concerns. Their choices are largely dependent on their assessment of the surrounding environment, the efficacy of the tools available, and their own capacity to sustain action. As a lawyer and a human rights defender, I have frequently had to choose between political action, by way of advocacy or protest, and legal action, by seeking to assert rights through legal process.

One of the primary considerations in making that choice has always been: what is the best way of linking the search for justice, and the result achieved, to respect for human rights? Another consideration is how to maximize public consciousness about the inter-connectedness of a public debate and the persons who suffer the consequences of human rights violations. In other words, 'giving the problem a human face' is more likely to result in the public relating directly to the issue at hand and having a stake in the outcome of the action taken. Sometimes, though, this may imply a complicated management of the role of a human rights defender as a lawyer *and* an activist, as it becomes necessary to take public action as well as to seek a judicial confirmation of rights on the same issue to maximize the impact of the campaign.

I recall our engagement in the 1980s with the pernicious and widespread practice of bonded labour in Pakistan. The human rights community began a public campaign to raise awareness of the issue and mobilize public opinion against the practice. While the process did take time to achieve a level of public sentiment that served as a pressure on the government and state institutions to take action, the objective was achieved and a public debate on the issue emerged from the campaign launched by human rights defend-ers. However, the public sentiment was focused on the moral wrongdoing in the practice but the essence of the rights to dignity, liberty, and security, and connected social and economic rights, was still not recognized as being at the core of the issue. Furthermore, although violations had been exposed, the practice of bonded labour persisted because of the failure of the government to respond with appropriate laws, policies, or enforcement mechanisms to eliminate the practice. It was through the courts that this was eventually achieved. A judgment of the Supreme Court of Pakistan spelled out the violations of fun-damental freedoms and human rights that the practice entailed with reference to interna-tional human rights standards and constitutional guarantees, and laid down guidelines for legislation to outlaw the practice and the requirements for its effective enforcement. More importantly, several hundred petitions on behalf of bonded labourers raised the awareness of their rights amongst victims. This was instrumental in the formation of victim associa-tions to protect their human rights as well as their rights under the law.

Where discrimination is inherent in social attitudes it becomes more difficult to strive for social justice for the more marginalized sections of the population on the basis of human rights. In many societies, women's rights are not considered an inalienable part of human rights. Constitutional guarantees, even though prescribed, are often not applied to women's fundamental rights. In the context of Pakistan, I have found it more difficult to promote women's rights in the abstract and achieved better results when the plight of actual victims and the gross injustice and cruelty suffered by some of them was made vis-ible through advocacy and litigation. The cumulative effect was more pronounced in terms of attitudinal changes and resulted in a slow, but very positive, change in public perception of the status and rights of women.

One particular case is that of a young woman at risk of 'honour killing', whose situation was given media exposure. More importantly, her case resulted in a landmark judicial decision, which set the tone for state responsibility in holding non-state actors accountable for violating the rights to life, physical security, and liberty of women on misconceived notions of culture and harmful social practices.

It is these experiences that give convincing illustrations of why human rights principles and values matter in the struggle for human rights. If these principles are covered com-prehensively in national laws, the potential for social justice increases. At the same time the international human rights system presents an option if national systems are flawed or unable to protect against violation of rights or to offer redress.

PART I

FOUNDATIONS

1

HISTORY

Ed Bates

SUMMARY

This chapter tells the story of the historical development of the concept of human rights and their status in international law. It is divided into three main sections. As the human rights story began on the domestic plane, the chapter starts by considering this. The focus is on the key developments since the seventeenth century, but in particular since the late eighteenth century. The chapter then turns to international law, examining it from the perspective of human rights over the period up to the Second World War. Finally, it focuses on the efforts to create international human rights law in the 1940s, culminating with the proclamation of the Universal Declaration of Human Rights in 1948.

1 INTRODUCTION

As an esteemed professor of international law and (later) international judge, Hersch Lauterpacht wrote in 1945: 'any attempt to translate the idea of an International Bill of the Rights of Man into a working rule of law is fraught with difficulties which disturb orthodox thought to the point of utter discouragement'.[1] The transformation of relations between a state and its nationals into international legal obligations by which the international community could derive a respectable and meaningful level of control and censure would, Lauterpacht argued, engender 'restrictions on sovereignty more far-reaching in their implications than any yet propounded in the annals of international utopias'.[2]

To be clear, Lauterpacht was firmly committed to the establishment of international human rights law, as his books of 1945 and 1950,[3] and his other work,[4] revealed. His 1945 study was published at a time when hopes were high that there would soon be established an International Bill of Rights. It was a pioneering work as not only did it address the substance of a proposed International Bill, but it also provided a detailed discussion of how it might be implemented and enforced at the international level. The dramatic quotations above were not intended to strike a pessimistic chord. Instead, the aim was to emphasize the extent of the task ahead for the international community. Lauterpacht was calling upon the international community, and leading states in particular, to face up to

---

[1] Lauterpacht, *An International Bill of Rights of Man* (Columbia University Press, 1945) 9–10.
[2] Lauterpacht (1945), 14.
[3] Lauterpacht, *International Law and Human Rights* (Stevens and Sons, 1950).
[4] See Simpson, 'Hersch Lauterpacht and the Genesis of the Age of Human Rights' (2004) 120 *LQR* 49.

that task as the Second World War came to an end and plans for a 'new world order' started to take shape.

We will return to the successes and failures of the immediate post-war effort as regards international human rights law in Section 4. However, in order to obtain a better perspective on this, and the other chapters in this book, we should trace the story of the protection of human rights, first, in domestic law and then in international law prior to 1945.

2 HUMAN RIGHTS ON THE DOMESTIC PLANE

Where should an analysis of the history of human rights begin?[5] One could go back several thousand years and find concepts related to human rights in ancient civilizations across the world, as with the Law Code of Hammurabi, created by the Babylonian king Hammurabi in the eighteenth century BC. The origins of human rights might also be traced back to various religious codes through the ages. By contrast, if the point of departure is the idea that human beings have natural rights, then the story commences at least as far back as the time of the Greek city states and the thinking of the Stoics.[6]

Finding a precise point of departure for 'a history of human rights' is an inherently controversial matter. It is probably quite unrealistic to credit any one culture, religion, or region of the world with the origins of human rights. Moreover, as a leading expert has put it, an attempt to do so would be 'politically charged'.[7] It inevitably risks privileging 'a particular world view' of human rights; it might be viewed as 'a way either to defend a specific status quo or value system against possible challenges'.[8] Two points must therefore be made at the outset. First, there are many different threads to the human rights idea as it exists today, and it is invidious to locate any one specific thread as *the* beginning. Second, the account that follows focuses especially on the origins of legal measures in the field of human rights. In that regard the first part of this chapter looks to the early developments in the Western world in particular, and to the extent that it might convey a Western bias, this is not the author's intention.[9]

From the perspective of legal measures championing the rights of the common person against the state, the starting point of the history of human rights is typically taken to be the Magna Carta of 1215. Yet this is somewhat erroneous. The Magna Carta resounds with statements that have since come to be celebrated: 'To none will we sell, to none deny or delay, right or justice'; and 'No freeman shall be taken, or imprisoned, or disseized, or outlawed, or exiled, or in any way harmed ... save by the lawful judgment of his peers or by the law of the land.' But the rights to trial by jury and of habeas corpus for all were hardly established by the Magna Carta. It had little to do with the rights of the common man, and much to do with securing rights for powerful barons against an overbearing king of England. The enduring significance of the Magna Carta, and other similar documents of this age,[10] for the history of human rights lies in the fact that it has come to be seen as a

---

[5] See Ishay, *The History of Human Rights: From Ancient Times to the Globalization Era* (University of California Press, 2004) ch 1; Ishay, *The Human Rights Reader* (Routledge, 2007) chs 1–4. For a useful 'timeline' on the history of human rights, see <http://www.facinghistory.org/udhr-timeline>.

[6] See n 3, ch 5.   [7] Ishay, n 5, xxii.   [8] Ishay, n 5, xxii.

[9] For much broader perspectives on the history of human rights, see n 5.

[10] Eg the King's agreement with the Cortes of Leon (1188, Spain) and the Magnus Lagaboters Landslov (1275, Norway).

starting point—the beginning of the limitation of absolute and arbitrary power of the sovereign. It therefore earns its place as the traditional point of departure in the story of how domestic law has addressed the enduring struggle of the individual against the tyranny and oppression of the state. This is a story that has lasted many centuries for some states and is still very much continuing in others.

We advance to the latter half of the seventeenth century for the next chapter in the overall story. The context was the English Civil War and the so-called 'Glorious Revolution', culminating in the Bill of Rights of 1689. Despite its name, that document was really a constitutional settlement that championed the sovereignty of Parliament. It set the seal on the absolute power of the Stuart kings after the myth of their 'divine power' had been debunked—in England at least, for it would last many more decades in France. So the bill of 1689 was no bill of rights in the sense that would be understood in modern democratic societies today.[11] Nonetheless it was the source of a limited number of defined rights, for example that 'cruel and unusual punishments [should not be] inflicted', which were applicable to all, at least in theory. Moreover, there were other important developments in this era such as the eradication of the practice of torture from the legal system of England in 1641 and the Habeas Corpus Act of 1679. The Bill of Rights of 1689 therefore saw the assertion of human liberty progress a stage further but, above all, its significance lay in its confirmation of a fundamental idea: that the absolute power of the state should be limited *for the sake of the individuals within it*. This idea had been prevalent in the contemporary writing of Thomas Hobbes and especially John Locke. And it deserves special emphasis since it is arguably the foundation stone upon which all progress in the field of human rights has been built.

2.1 THE ENLIGHTENMENT THINKERS

Hobbes' *Leviathan*,[12] published in 1651, soon after the beheading of Charles I, spoke of a world in which there was an imperative for absolute power; it was needed to keep society from the very type of disorder that had afflicted England in the 1640s. The *Leviathan* world did not accept the idea of formal restraints on power. It envisaged few if any natural rights for the individual, for all were subservient to the ruler. A level of abuse on the part of the ruler vis-à-vis his subjects might almost be expected; it was the price to be paid for the greater collective gain for a society that was protected from the much greater evil of mass disorder. Having said this, the ruler was expected to exercise his authority responsibly, and in accordance with the laws of God and of nature, and in turn this placed theoretical restraints on his authority. Hobbes' *Leviathan* is therefore credited with introducing the concept of the 'social contract', that is, the idea that power to govern is to some extent derived from the consent of the governed.

However, it was Locke who carried this concept very much further, above all in his *Two Treatises of Government*,[13] published in 1690, shortly after the overthrowing of another English king in 1688 (James II) and the approval of the Bill of Rights by Parliament in 1689. Locke advocated the natural liberty and equality of human beings: '[m]an' was *born* with 'a title to perfect freedom, and an uncontrolled enjoyment of all the rights and privileges of the law of nature, equally with any other man, or number of men in the world';

---

[11] For modern bills of rights, see Chapter 22. For a highly readable account of events and legal milestones related to this period, from the perspective of human rights and the rule of law, see Bingham, *The Rule of Law* (Penguin, 2010) ch 2.

[12] Many modern versions of the text are available, see eg Hobbes, *Leviathan* (OUP, 2009).

[13] Eg Laslett (ed), *Locke: Two Treatises of Government* (CUP, 1988).

he had '*by nature* a power...to preserve his property, that is, his life, liberty and estate, against the injuries and attempts of other men'.[14] Locke was therefore a strong advocate of natural rights, and in particular the right to property in the broad sense identified here, and, as he saw things, it was the state's duty to provide an environment in which such rights could flourish. His enduring contribution to the ideas that fuelled human rights thinking, however, lay in his theory of government, for it is in Locke that we see the origins of the idea of limited constitutional government and the fuller development of the idea of government by consent. Locke wrote that the 'end of government is the good of mankind', so rulers 'should be sometimes liable to be opposed, when they grow exorbitant in the use of their power, and employ it for the destruction, and not the preservation of the properties of their people'.[15] Within Locke's writing therefore were the seeds to the idea of modern democratic governance, although how much Locke expounded the democratic ideal through the idea of government by consent should not be exaggerated. He did not advocate universal suffrage and was, after all, writing in the seventeenth century when the right to vote remained a privilege of very few in England. But it is surely Locke we recall first when we read from the preamble to the Universal Declaration of Human Rights (UDHR) of almost three hundred years later: 'Whereas it is essential, if man is not to be compelled to have recourse, as a last resort, to rebellion against tyranny and oppression, that human rights should be protected by the rule of law'.

On the continent of Europe, the major historical contribution to ideas concerning the state and its relationship with the individual came in the eighteenth century. Authors such as Baron de Montesquieu (*The Spirit of Laws*, 1748), Jean-Jacques Rousseau (*The Social Contract*, 1762), Voltaire (*Philosophical Dictionary*, 1769), and Immanuel Kant (*On the Relationship of Theory to Practice in Political Right*, 1792) were leading figures in a movement which was later called 'the Enlightenment'. Montesquieu's contribution remains best known for his thoughts on the structures of government and his emphasis on the separation of powers. Rousseau advanced the theory of the 'social contract', but justice cannot be done in a few sentences here to the immense contribution made by him and others. It must suffice to say that the essence of all these philosophers' thinking was to place a new importance on the intrinsic value of man in society. There was thus further emphasis on the idea that everyone was born with certain natural rights which no authority could take away. This thinking was the intellectual force behind the French Declaration of the Rights of Man and Citizen (1789), but of course its impact was felt far beyond France. Indeed as one author has neatly put it:

> Natural rights were the cutting edge of the ax of rationalization that toppled many of the inherited medieval traditions of eighteenth-century Europe. They were part of that general aspiration toward bringing peace and order to the world that led Immanuel Kant to think that royal dynasties were the cause of war, and that a world of republics would bring a peaceful era to mankind.[16]

2.2 HUMAN RIGHTS TRANSFORMED INTO POSITIVE LAW

It was, however, in the 'new world' where the 'ax of rationalization' first achieved practical effect in a constitutional document. Locke's influence was unmistakable, and immortalized, in the US Declaration of Independence of 1776. That document listed grievances against

---

[14] Laslett (ed), ch VII, para 87 (emphasis added).   [15] Laslett (ed), ch XIX, para 229.
[16] Minogue, 'The History of the Idea of Human Rights' in Laqueur and Rubin (eds), *The Human Rights Reader* (Meridian, 1977) 11.

George III and inspired the successful prosecution of the American War of Independence. Its opening words are now infamous:

> We hold these truths to be self-evident, that all men are created equal, that they are endowed by their Creator with certain unalienable Rights; that among these are Life, Liberty and the Pursuit of Happiness. That to secure these rights, governments are instituted among men, deriving their just powers from the consent of the governed; that whenever any form of government becomes destructive of these ends, it is the right of the people to alter or to abolish it, and to institute new government, laying its foundation on such principles and organizing its powers in such form, as to them shall seem most likely to effect their safety and happiness.

Even before Thomas Jefferson and others penned these words on 4 July 1776, the process of drafting the constitutions of the newly independent individual states in what would become the United States of America was well underway. In 1776, five would be drafted so as to enshrine the protection of human rights, and by 1783 all states would have done so in one form or another. Probably the most celebrated example was the Virginia Declaration of Rights of 12 June 1776, regarded by many as the first 'proper' bill of rights. Its first article proclaimed that:

> all men are by nature equally free and independent, and have certain inherent rights, of which, when they enter into a state of society, they cannot, by any compact, deprive or divest their posterity; namely, the enjoyment of life and liberty, with the means of acquiring and possessing property, and pursuing and obtaining happiness and safety.

The Virginia Declaration then set out the idea of government by consent ('all power is vested in, and consequently derived from, the people') and separation of powers ('the legislative and executive powers of the state should be separate and distinct from the judicative'), before listing a number of human rights including, for example, basic due process rights and freedom of expression ('the freedom of the press is one of the greatest bulwarks of liberty and can never be restrained but by despotic governments').

Events in France would help to ensure that the end of the eighteenth century was a defining time in the history of human rights. The years 1789–91 stand out above all. The French Revolution swept away any notions of absolute monarchical power, replacing it with the philosophy of the French Declaration of the Rights of Man and Citizen. With this Declaration on 26 August 1789, the French National Assembly pronounced that 'ignorance, forgetfulness, or contempt of the rights of man' were 'the sole causes of public misfortunes and of the corruption of governments'. It therefore:

> resolved to set forth in a solemn declaration the natural, inalienable, and sacred rights of man, in order that such declaration, continually before all members of the social body, may be a perpetual reminder of their rights and duties; in order that the acts of the legislative power and those of the executive power may constantly be compared with the aim of every political institution and may accordingly be more respected; in order that the demands of the citizens, founded henceforth upon simple and incontestable principles, may always be directed towards the maintenance of the Constitution and welfare of all.

Article 16 French Declaration provided a classic formulation of the link between institutional limitations on state power and protecting human rights: 'Any society', it proclaimed, 'in which no provision is made for guaranteeing rights or for the separation of powers, has no Constitution.'[17]

---

[17] See also the French Declaration of the Right of Man and Citizen of 1793, a redraft of the 1789 text with an added emphasis on the principle of equality.

Today, a study of the French Declaration would form a good starting point for any course on human rights and, no doubt, stimulate much debate. The Declaration defined 'liberty' as 'the power to do whatever is not injurious to others'. It followed that 'the enjoyment of the natural rights of every man has for its limits only those that assure other members of society the enjoyment of those same rights'. According to the Declaration 'such limits may be determined only by law'. A flavour of what followed may be gleaned from paragraphs in the Declaration setting out due process rights such as the presumption of innocence and to the effect that free speech was 'one of the most precious of the rights of man', so 'every citizen may speak, write, and print freely', 'subject to responsibility for the abuse of such liberty in cases determined by law'. More generally the Declaration profoundly announced that: 'The law has the right to forbid only actions which are injurious to society. Whatever is not forbidden by law may not be prevented, and no one may be constrained to do what it does not prescribe.'

Against this background, the US Constitution of 1789 might, at first sight, have been regarded as a disappointment. There was no grand statement about the theory of government along the lines of the Declaration of Independence. Moreover, it provided for the protection of just a few rights; for example, the right to trial by jury (Article III, Section 2) and a right of habeas corpus, not to be suspended unless 'in cases of rebellion or invasion the public safety may require it' (Article I, Section 9). However, in 1791 the first ten amendments to the Constitution came into force having been ratified by three-quarters of the states. The (US) Bill of Rights, as it became known, began in now celebrated tones: 'Congress shall make no law respecting an establishment of religion, or prohibiting the free exercise thereof; or abridging the freedom of speech, or of the press; or the right of the people peaceably to assemble and to petition the government for a redress of grievances.' Among other things, the bill included the famous right to bear arms (Amendment II), protection from unreasonable search and seizure (Amendment IV), various protections relating to due process and fair trial (Amendments V and VI), and a prohibition on 'cruel and unusual punishments' (Amendment VIII). It should be added, however, that at this stage such rights were to be protected only at the federal level. It was in the individual constitutions of the states, with their own bills of rights, that the expression of the rights of man was really seen in the USA in the late eighteenth century.

These comments on the French and US experiences would not be complete without paying tribute to the work of Thomas Paine. Paine's 1776 work *Common Sense* set out the case for US democracy in the lead up to 4 July 1776. In 1791–2 he published *The Rights of Man*, which was in part a response to Edmund Burke's attack on the French Revolution. But he also subjected England's constitutional arrangements to severe criticism: 'government without constitution, is power without a right'. *The Rights of Man*, perhaps the first book ever to use the phrase 'human rights',[18] is said to have sold over 250,000 copies, making it a huge bestseller in today's terms. Paine did not invent the human rights thinking that was distilled into the landmark documents referred to here. But, as Louis Henkin has observed, his writing 'did much to spread and root' the idea of human rights: 'he provided us a theology and a terminology, guiding principles as well as blueprints'.[19] Paine remains revered in the USA, as was evidenced when he was quoted by President Obama in his inauguration speech in 2009. But he remains little known in his native England where, in his lifetime, he was considered as a dangerous revolutionary and convicted of seditious libel.[20]

---

[18] See Lauren, *The Evolution of International Human Rights: Visions Seen* (University of Pennsylvania Press, 1998) 20.

[19] Henkin, *The Rights of Man Today* (Stevens and Sons, 1978) 135.   [20] Lauren, n 18, 21.

2.3 NINETEENTH-CENTURY CHALLENGES TO NATURAL RIGHTS

The French Declaration and the US Bill of Rights were landmarks in the history of human rights for they transformed the philosophy espoused by the likes of Locke and Rousseau, and the thinking behind natural rights, into positive law. Nonetheless, during the nineteenth century the idea of natural rights came under attack from a new generation of philosophers.

The critics were led by Jeremy Bentham who famously criticized the idea of natural, God-given rights obtained by virtue of birth as 'nonsense upon stilts'.[21] His point was that natural rights counted for nothing on their own. To mean something, they required the protection of the law; so the real issue for Bentham, expounding a very British 'rights and remedy' approach to things, was what the law actually protected. As he famously put it: 'from real law come real rights; but from imaginary laws, from laws of nature, fancied and invented by poets, rhetoricians, and dealers in moral and intellectual poisons, come imaginary rights'.[22] For Bentham natural rights were dangerous since they fuelled revolutions such as those in France and so ultimately caused great social damage, hence the title of his famous work *The Anarchical Fallacies* (1843). Criticism of this type had already been made by another Englishman at the very time of the French Revolution. In his *Reflections on the Revolution of France*, Burke attacked the French Declaration as a 'monstrous fiction'. It inspired 'false ideas and vain expectations into men destined to travel in the obscure walk of laborious life' and had 'serve[d] to exaggerate and embitter that real inequality, which it can never remove'.[23]

The nineteenth century also saw an altogether different type of opposition to natural rights in the writing of Karl Marx. His 1844 work *On the Jewish Question* asked what use the French Declaration would be for Jews such as himself. As he saw it, it was found completely wanting for in reality the rights of man were the privileged rights of the bourgeoisie. According to Marx, rights were for egotistical men; they did not truly free the individual at all.[24]

As shown in Chapter 3, the longer term legacy of Bentham's and Marx's attacks on natural rights and the perspective they offer to contemporary thinking on human rights is still keenly debated today.

2.4 DOMESTIC PROTECTION OF HUMAN RIGHTS TODAY

We have seen, then, that for domestic law the human rights story really began in the seventeenth and eighteenth centuries. History will record the tribute to be paid to the visionaries of that age, such as Locke and Rousseau, many of whom were treated as dissidents at the time. The Bill of Rights of 1689, and in particular the American Declaration of Independence (1776), the French Declaration of the Rights of Man and Citizen (1789), and the US Bill of Rights (1791) were milestones in constitutional history, curtailing the sovereign power of the state in various ways, including by reference to the basic rights of the individual. This constitutional model certainly caught on as was evident by the constitutional arrangements secured in the Netherlands in 1798, Sweden in 1809, Spain in 1812, Norway in 1814, Belgium in 1831, Liberia in 1847, Sardinia in 1848, Denmark in 1849, and Prussia in 1850. In fact, it has been suggested that over 80 per cent of national

---

[21] See Chapter 3.
[22] Waldron (ed), *Nonsense upon Stilts: Bentham, Burke and Marx on the Rights of Man* (Routledge, 1987) 69.
[23] Burke, *Reflections on the Revolution in France* (Rivington, 1868) 46.   [24] See Chapter 3.

constitutions adopted between 1778 and 1948 provided a human rights guarantee in one form or another, and that between 1949 and 1975 the figure was 93 per cent.[25] That this upward trend continued was evident in the 1990s with the new constitutions of those states which were formerly part of the Soviet Union.

As we look back on the achievements secured in the eighteenth century via the French and US settlements, one should be careful to keep them in perspective. They were certainly landmarks, but it would be wrong to exaggerate the practical effects that they had at the time. Indeed one does not have to look far in French and US history to see that in practical terms the idea of human rights had made only relatively limited headway at this stage—at least, that is, compared to how we would view things today. The inferior position of women both in society generally and in law stirred women's rights campaigners such as Mary Wollstonecraft (*Vindication of the Rights of Women*, 1792). Moreover, at this stage the idea of judicial protection of human rights was virtually non-existent. The French Declaration had been incorporated as the first part of the formal French Constitution in 1791, but it was not enforceable by the courts at that time. As Lauren observed, the French Declaration, 'reflected far more vision than reality'. It 'emerged not out of long tradition or wide-spread experience or inclusive election, but rather out of … revolution and had to be nurtured in the face of overwhelming opposition'.[26]

The USA was quite exceptional in that judicial protection of constitutional safeguards came in 1803 with the US Supreme Court's watershed decision in *Marbury v Madison*, holding that it had an inherent power of judicial review by which it could even declare acts of Congress unconstitutional.[27] Nonetheless, this was of limited use for individuals in human rights terms, for at this stage the Bill of Rights was an instrument that applied overwhelmingly at the federal, not the individual state, level. Of course, the individual state constitutions guaranteed rights, as noted already, but slavery was flourishing in many such states in the late eighteenth century and would continue to do so for decades into the nineteenth century. In fact, when the controversy about slavery was reaching its peak the contribution made by the US Supreme Court served to perpetuate the practice. In *Dred Scott v Sandford* in 1857, it ruled that the Bill of Rights protected the right of slaveholders to their property, which included slaves, and that, in effect, Congress had acted illegally by outlawing slavery in Northern states.[28] Neither slaves 'nor their descendants, were embraced … [by] the Constitution',[29] the Court held. That is, they had no protection under the Bill of Rights. It would take a civil war and further amendments to the Constitution to secure the abolition of slavery in the 1860s. And it would take the better part of the next century for the Supreme Court to finally start to use the Bill of Rights to attack grossly unfair and discriminatory practices suffered by the black population of certain states. The breakthrough case was *Brown v Board of Education*[30] of 1954 bringing an end to the 'separate but equal' doctrine previously upheld by the Court in *Plessy v Ferguson*.[31]

The point of this digression is not to single out the practice of the USA in any way. If this chapter were to attempt to provide even the broadest of overviews of the failures of other states to protect human rights over the same timeframe, it would no doubt run into dozens of pages. What has been said here, however, provides a very useful perspective on Section 3, which looks at the international protection of human rights. It helps us to understand how very recent the protection of human rights is by domestic courts (see Table 1.1) and by reference to bills of rights in the overall story of the history of human rights. In the

---

[25] Van Maarseveen and van der Tang, *Written Constitutions: A Computerized Comparative Study* (Oceana, 1978) 191–5.

[26] n 18, 32.   [27] 1 Cranch 137 (1803).   [28] 60 US 353 (1857).

[29] 60 US 353 (1857), Taney, J.   [30] 347 US 483 (1954).   [31] 163 US 537 (1896).

Table 1.1 Human rights on the domestic plane: key dates

1215	Magna Carta
1689	English Bill of Rights
1776	US Declaration of Independence
	Virginia Declaration of Rights
1789	French Declaration of the Rights of Man and Citizen
	US Constitution
1791	US Bill of Rights

UK, for example, there existed a long tradition of Parliament and the courts protecting the rights of individuals by various statutes and under the common law. But only in 2000, with the entry into force of the Human Rights Act 1998, did the UK obtain something akin to a modern bill of rights encompassing judicial protection of a select number of human rights against the acts of public authorities, albeit not against parliamentary acts.[32] In France, the 1958 Constitution refers in its preamble to the French people's commitment to the Declaration of 1789, but only a limited challenge to the authority of the legislature is possible via the *Conseil Constitutionnel*.[33] Finally, the USA is without doubt the most celebrated exponent of the judicial protection of human rights. Yet only since around 1925 has the Supreme Court begun to use the Bill of Rights more widely to protect the rights of individuals against encroachments by the individual states themselves. Indeed, the story of human rights protection by the Supreme Court is overwhelmingly a post-Second World War phenomenon.[34]

The perspective we might take with us as we turn to the story of the *international* protection of human rights is therefore this: how incredibly grand the idea of an International Bill of Rights must have been in the 1940s when it was first proposed.

3 HUMAN RIGHTS ON THE INTERNATIONAL PLANE BEFORE THE SECOND WORLD WAR

Even if within domestic law there was a greater recognition of individual human rights by the start of the twentieth century, this was certainly not the case for international law. Prior to the 1940s there was no real conception in international law of the idea that one state had a right to interfere in the sovereign affairs of another state as regards how it treated its own citizens. International law was virtually a blank canvas as far as the protection of human rights was concerned. We say this from the perspective of a basic definition of human rights as the rights owing to human beings by nature of their humanity. Historically, international law could touch on or address the plight of human beings only in very limited ways.

---

[32] See Human Rights Act 1998, ss 3 and 4.

[33] For important recent developments see Hunter-Henin, 'Constitutional Developments and Human Rights in France: One Step Forward, Two Steps Back' (2011) 60 *ICLQ* 167.

[34] In 1935–6 only two of the 160 signed written opinions of the Supreme Court covered 'basic human freedoms', but by 1979–80 the ratio had increased to 80 out of 149. See Abraham and Perry, *Freedom and the Court* (OUP, 1998) 5.

For example, the inkling of the idea of certain minimal rights for certain human beings was present in customary international law in the guise of the doctrine of 'diplomatic protection', or the treatment of aliens. This doctrine has deep historical roots. It basically requires a state to treat foreigners in accordance with an 'international minimum standard' of protection,[35] at least as regards life, liberty, property, and protection from manifest denial of justice, regardless of how the state treats its own nationals. The point to note, then, is that the protection concerned is not afforded to the individuals as human beings, but because they are nationals of a foreign state. Moreover, it falls to that foreign state, not the individual, to pursue the enforcement of any claims. In the absence of such support, historically the foreigners concerned had no one to speak for them. As such they were placed in the same position as the nationals of the host state, for the traditional, pre-war position of customary international law was that it simply had nothing to say about the way that a state could treat its own nationals.

3.1 INTERNATIONAL HUMANITARIAN LAW AND THE ABOLITION OF THE SLAVE TRADE

Of course, states could enter into legal relations with each other motivated by a desire to relieve human suffering in certain ways. In this regard an apparently compassionate dimension to international law had been evident in the nineteenth century, first with the movement towards the abolition of the slave trade and, second, with the first steps that were taken in the field of international humanitarian law.

The second of these is addressed in Chapter 23 and all that need be said here is that the nineteenth century saw increasing international activity which expressed a concern with the plight of the individual subjected to the ravages of war—prisoners of war and soldiers above all. The founding father of this movement was Henry Dunant, who was so shocked by scenes of the wounded and vanquished he witnessed at the Battle of Solferino (1859) that he later helped to establish the International Committee of the Red Cross. The Geneva Conventions of the mid-nineteenth century soon followed, while the Hague Conventions were opened for signature at the start of the twentieth century. Perhaps the most significant achievements of this sector of international law from the perspective of human rights, however, were secured with the Geneva Conventions of 1949 and the Additional Protocols thereto.

The nineteenth century also saw remarkable progress in the abolition of the slave trade. Slavery became illegal in England in 1771 after *Somersett's case*.[36] The UK and the USA subsequently passed legislation at the start of the nineteenth century to outlaw the trade of slaves within their own jurisdictions, which included the British colonies. Yet international action was required to abolish the trade altogether, and here progress was slow. Despite the campaigning efforts of figures such as William Wilberforce, the best that could be achieved by the major European states at the Congress of Vienna (1815) was a mere declaration expressing a commitment to the abolition of the slave trade. There then followed more than half a century in which the British made great diplomatic efforts to secure dozens of bilateral treaties with trading nations principally in the European and Latin American regions, and other agreements with native chiefs from the African coast. In each instance there was an agreement to abolish the slave trade but also, where relevant, various measures of enforcement were provided for. Typically, the treaties provided for the inspection of ships if there was a suspicion that a merchant vessel was engaging in

---

[35] See Shaw, *International Law* (CUP, 2008) 824–5.   [36] 20 State Trials 1.

illicit activity. The abolition of the slave trade was therefore one of the earliest, if not the first, human rights related British foreign policy initiatives. This period also witnessed the establishment of Anti-Slavery International, the oldest human rights NGO in the world; its origins go back to 1839.[37]

The list of states committed to abolishing the trade slowly grew, but a sufficient global consensus on abolition of the slave trade did not emerge until the last decades of the nineteenth century. Only in 1885 did the Conference on Central Africa, held in Berlin, see in its General Act a commitment by states 'to help in suppressing slavery, and especially the slave trade' and their recognition that 'trading in slaves is forbidden in conformity with the principles of international law as recognized by the Signatory Powers'. Five years later, negotiations in Brussels saw the conclusion of the 1890 General Act, which included an Anti-Slavery Act ratified by 18 states stipulating specific measures for countering slavery and the slave trade. By this stage the great majority of states had made slavery illegal in their own jurisdictions. The experience of the USA, with President Lincoln's Emancipation Proclamation of 1863, is known best. Yet even after the US Civil War, Cuba and Brazil maintained domestic slavery into the 1880s.

In the twentieth century, the international abolition of the slave trade and slavery was taken up by the League of Nations, the key international organization established after the First World War with the principal objective of maintaining peace and stability in the world. There followed the International Convention on the Abolition of Slavery and the Slave Trade of 1926. The declared aim of this treaty was 'the complete suppression of slavery in all its forms and of the slave trade by land and sea'. There have been further international agreements since.

The international effort toward the abolition of the slave trade and slavery provides some interesting general lessons for students of international human rights law. The abolition of the trade evidenced why international law, in the form of bilateral treaties, was needed to improve the protection of individuals when the activities of more than one state were involved. But it also demonstrated that general international agreements may only follow a consensus being reached across a sufficient number of states, and that this may take a considerable time to achieve. The abolition of slavery itself inevitably required action on the part of the individual states—in some cases prompted, no doubt, by the growing body of international opinion encouraging them to do so. State practice in this field became so clearly defined that the prohibition of slavery became part of customary international law. Hence an absolute prohibition on 'slavery and servitude' passed without controversy into the main post-Second World War human rights documents, with images of Nazi concentration camps still fresh in the mind.[38] Finally, however, it would be wrong to assume that such documents have in themselves magically abolished slavery and servitude (and forced labour) in all its forms.[39] The creation of international standards for the protection of human rights may be one thing; their actual implementation and enforcement is another.

---

[37] For further details see <http://www.antislavery.org>.

[38] See UDHR, Art 4. See also International Covenant on Civil and Political Rights, Art 8; European Convention on Human Rights, Art 4; American Convention on Human Rights, Art 6; African Charter on Human and Peoples' Rights, Art 5.

[39] Slavery persists today, in modern forms, see <http://www.antislavery.org>, including in connection with human trafficking. On 'slavery' and 'forced and compulsory labour' see Chapter 12.

3.2 THE PROTECTION OF MINORITIES AND THE LEAGUE OF NATIONS

Resuming our analysis of the position of international law with respect to human rights before 1945, the protection of minorities should now be discussed. Here we need to recall the pre-Second World War stance of international law whereby, in effect, states had free rein to abuse their own citizens behind their own borders. Indeed, stories of oppression directed toward national and religious minorities in particular fill many pages of our history books.

The first, rather sporadic, efforts to provide a level of protection for religious minorities may be traced back to the end of the Thirty Years War with the Treaty of Westphalia (1648) and, subsequently, those of Utrecht (1713) and Berlin (1878).[40] But it was not until the early twentieth century that international law saw a much more organized, institutionalized approach to the minorities issue. It was prompted by the end of the First World War and in particular the significant redrawing of the political map of parts of Europe. This involved, for example, the restoration of Poland and for some states, Germany in particular, a rather radical redrawing of their boundaries. Given how mixed the population was in parts of Europe, no matter how those boundaries were (re)shaped, the result was that a significant number of minorities found themselves displaced. As Tomuschat has described it, 'ethnic Hungarians found themselves all of a sudden in Romania or Czechoslovakia, ethnic Germans became Polish citizens, and, on the other hand, ethnic Poles continued to live in Germany'.[41]

President Wilson is reported to have said at the Paris Peace Conference of 1919, '[n]othing…is more likely to disturb the peace of the world, than the treatment which might in certain circumstances be meted out to the minorities'.[42] It being recognized then that Europe's peaceful future could be jeopardized by the abuse of minorities by the dominant majority, arrangements were made to try to safeguard against this. As part of the various peace settlements ending the First World War, nine states[43] were required to enter into specific treaty obligations for the protection of minorities and, between 1921 and 1923, a further five[44] were required to settle upon similar arrangements as a condition of their membership of the League of Nations. The arrangements were complex and here we will identify only three main aspects.[45]

First, the individual peace treaties required that as part of their constitutional arrangements respective states should provide basic guarantees of protection as to life, liberty, and equality before the law for all inhabitants within their borders. There were also more specific guarantees which were particularly relevant for minorities including, for example, provisions guaranteeing the enjoyment of freedom of religion, use and recognition of minority languages, and various freedoms in the field of education. Second, when the League of Nations was set up, the Council of the League of Nations was mandated to make

---

[40] See Ezejiofor, *Protection of Human Rights under the Law* (Butterworths, 1964) 35–8.

[41] Tomuschat, *Human Rights: Between Idealism and Realism* (OUP, 2008) 18.

[42] Ezejiofor, n 40, 38.

[43] The treaties were concluded between 1919 and 1923. Czechoslovakia, Greece, Poland, Romania, and Yugoslavia entered into specific minority treaty arrangements with the Principal and Allied Powers. For Austria, Bulgaria, Hungary, and Turkey special chapters were inserted into the General Peace Treaties. Additionally special chapters were inserted into the German Polish Convention concerning Upper Silesia, and for the Memel Territory.

[44] Declarations undertaking to protect the rights of minorities were made by Albania, Estonia, Finland, Latvia, and Lithuania.

[45] The classic account is De Azcarate, *League of Nations and National Minorities* (trans Broke) (Carnegie, 1945). See also Simpson, *Human Rights and the End of Empire* (OUP, 2001) 121–45.

arrangements for the supervision of the aforementioned obligations at the international level. The states which were subjected to the treaty arrangements acknowledged that the guarantees constituted 'obligations of international concern' for the League of Nations, albeit only insofar as they affected persons belonging to racial, religious, or linguistic minorities, and therefore not for individuals forming part of the majority population. Third, oversight and possible measures of implementation with respect to the aforementioned obligations were envisaged. Arrangements were put in place to allow members of the minorities to directly petition the Council of the League about actual or potential infractions of the obligations.[46] If a petition was not settled, then the Permanent Court of International Justice was given competence to adjudicate upon the dispute. In fact, this occurred on only one occasion in a dispute concerning Germany and Poland regarding minority schools in Upper Silesia.[47] However, the Court could also deliver advisory opinions upon a request from the Council, and there were a small number of these, the most well-known of which concerned the treatment of Greek minorities in Albania.[48]

Details of the successes and failures of these minority treaties can be found elsewhere.[49] Our concern here is to reflect on their significance from an historical perspective. So what should we say about these treaties today?

An extreme view might be that the treaties were not really about human rights at all, given that they applied only to certain geographical areas and that the petitions system developed by the League of Nations depended on status (belonging to a national minority). A sceptic would also point out that the motive for the creation of the treaties was not so much the protection of the minorities for humane reasons, but for the broader aim of regional stability.

A less cynical perspective would point to the significant advances made by the treaties. For the first time, international law imposed on the sovereign states concerned certain obligations to treat their inhabitants in certain ways—a stark contrast to the 'blank canvas' position noted already. Equally radical for its time was the idea of institutionalized oversight of such obligations, especially the notion that individuals could petition international organs, potentially challenging the actions of their own national authorities. In this way the treaties started to challenge the orthodox view that individuals simply could not be the subjects of international law. Such notions had underpinned Oppenheim's confident dismissal, in 1905, of the contention that 'the law of nations' guaranteed individuals 'at home and abroad the so-called rights of mankind' (alleged to be 'the right of existence, the right to protection of honour, life, health, liberty and property, the right of practicing [sic] any religion one likes, the right of emigration, and the like'). Such rights, it had been argued, 'cannot enjoy such guarantee, *since the Law of Nations is a law between States, and since individuals cannot be subjects of this Law*'.[50]

Such a view had prevailed as far as most states were concerned when the Covenant of the League of Nations was concluded in 1919. As its preamble recited, the main aim of that organization was 'to promote international co-operation and to achieve international peace and security'. Talk that all states should protect minorities along the lines of the

---

[46] Such arrangements were the product of procedures settled upon by the League itself. Only the treaty concerning Upper Silesia actually conferred a right of petition, although Finland was also obliged to forward petitions in relation to the Aaland Islands.

[47] *Rights of Minorities in Upper Silesia*, PCIJ Rep Series A No 15 (1928).

[48] *Minority Schools in Albania case*, PCIJ Rep Series A/B No 64 (1935).

[49] See n 45 and MacCartney, 'League of Nations' Protection of Minority Rights' in Luard (ed), *The International Protection of Human Rights* (Thames and Hudson, 1967) 22, 34–7.

[50] Oppenheim, *Treatise on International Law, Vol I, Peace* (1905) 346 (emphasis added).

minority treaties was quickly dismissed; therefore no guarantees for the protection of individuals generally were imposed on states after the First World War. Quite simply, outside the discrete context of the minority treaties, the notion that international bodies could or should have an influence on how the state treated its own nationals was not developed at the general level at this stage. Hence, governments and the League of Nations made little attempt to intervene in what would today be seen as the human rights abuses that occurred in countries such as Germany, the Soviet Union, and Italy in the lead up to the Second World War. As Luard once put it, this was not because people did not care, rather:

> The assumptions of national sovereignty were almost everywhere still accepted. Regulations restricting freedom of the press, of speech and assembly, imprisonment for political offences, persecution on racial grounds, all these things were deplored and denounced. But it was widely accepted that they were ultimately the sole responsibility of the legal government of the territory in question: and not therefore matters over which foreign individuals or governments could legitimately take action.[51]

4 HUMAN RIGHTS ON THE INTERNATIONAL PLANE AFTER THE SECOND WORLD WAR

> And here, over an acre of ground, lay dead and dying people. You could not see which was which, except perhaps by a convulsive movement, or the last quiver of a sigh from a living skeleton, too weak to move. The living lay with their heads against the corpses, and around them moved the awful ghostly procession of emaciated, aimless people, with nothing to do, and no hope of life, unable to move out of your way, unable to look at the terrible sights around them...Babies had been born here, tiny wizened things that could not live. A mother, driven mad, screamed at a British sentry to give her milk for her child, and thrust the tiny mite into his arms and ran off, crying terribly. He opened the bundle, and found the baby had been dead for days. This day at Belsen was the most horrible of my life.[52]

These were the words of Richard Dimbleby reporting for the BBC at the time of the liberation of the Nazi concentration camp in Belsen. Such human rights atrocities, and countless others committed during the Second World War, were a galvanizing force that would help to ensure a new approach for international law after 1945 as regards the rights of the individual. They would prompt the first steps towards a modern international law of human rights.

The first proposals for an international code of human rights can be traced at least as far back as 1929, when in New York the Institute of International Law adopted 'An International Declaration of the Rights of Man'. Soon after the outbreak of war, the British author HG Wells campaigned for a Declaration of Rights; his book *HG Wells on the Rights of Man* sold well in the UK and 'in an act of utter optimism'[53] the war ministry had German translations dropped on the advancing German forces on the continent. Also dropped were leaflets from the White Rose Movement—a body made up of a small group of students and some academics at the University of Munich. In 1942–3 they courageously

---

[51] Luard, 'The Origins of International Concern over Human Rights' in Luard, n 49, 21. The League of Nations did take some notable steps in the fields of anti-slavery law, refugee law, and trafficking in drugs.

[52] Richard Dimbleby, BBC News (13 May 1945), available at: <http://news.bbc.co.uk/1/hi/in_depth/4445811.stm>.

[53] Robertson, *Crimes Against Humanity* (Penguin, 2006) 28.

produced and distributed a series of leaflets in defiance of the Nazi regime, calling for democracy in Germany and for the protection of certain fundamental rights in a new Europe. Six of the student authors and one academic were captured by the Gestapo in 1943; they were summarily tried and executed.[54]

Back in January 1941, in his message to Congress, US President Roosevelt spoke of a world founded on 'four essential human freedoms' ('freedom of speech and expression', 'freedom of every person to worship God in his own way', 'freedom from want', and 'freedom from fear'). Later that year, on 14 August, Roosevelt and the British Prime Minister Winston Churchill proclaimed the Atlantic Declaration; they hoped to see a world where 'the men *in all lands* may live out their lives in freedom of fear and want'.[55] This was followed in 1942 by the Declaration of the United Nations (UN). Not to be confused with the UN Charter of some three years later, the Declaration of 1942 was signed by 47 alliance states all prepared to subscribe to the principle that 'complete victory over their enemies [was] essential to defend life, liberty, independence and religious freedom, and to preserve human rights and justice in their own lands as well as in other lands'. 'Human rights' and democracy therefore became one of the moral bases upon which the Second World War was fought; Churchill even spoke of a time when the world's struggle ended with 'the enthronement of human rights'.[56] Passages such as these were quoted by Lauterpacht in his 1945 book, referred to in Section 1, as he looked forward to the post-war world.

So what happened when the conflict finally ended? To what extent were these lofty ambitions realized in the war-shattered world?

4.1 CRIMES AGAINST HUMANITY

A very important step was taken in 1945 when the victorious powers decided that the major war criminals of the German Third Reich should be brought to justice. The Four-Power Agreement of 8 August 1945 provided for the establishment of the International Military Tribunal for the Prosecution and Punishment of Major War Criminals of the European Axis (Nuremberg Tribunal). The crimes in question were primarily those of planning and waging a war of aggression and the committal of war crimes, but they also included 'crimes against humanity'. The Nuremberg Tribunal eventually interpreted these crimes in a rather restrictive way. Nonetheless, the concept of such crimes was very significant for international human rights law, for it realized the possibility of international accountability and punishment for appalling crimes committed against individuals. More detailed discussion of the Nuremberg Tribunal can be found in Chapter 24.

4.2 THE UN CHARTER

The main focus of the immediate post-war story for international human rights law concerned the attempts made to create legal instruments protecting human rights. Of course, this meant securing agreement on what that concept actually covered. The framing of the UN Charter in San Francisco in 1945 was the obvious starting point in this endeavour. Its preamble stated that the peoples of the UN were:

> determined to save succeeding generations from the scourge of war, which twice in our lifetime has brought untold sorrow to mankind, and to reaffirm faith in fundamental human

---

[54] See Dumbach and Newborn, *Sophie Scholl and the White Rose* (Oneworld, 2006).
[55] 35 AJIL (1941), Supplement, 191, principle six (emphasis added).
[56] *The Times* (30 October 1942), quoted by Lauterpacht, n 1, 6.

rights, in the dignity and worth of the human person, in the equal rights of men and women and of nations large and small.

Therefore, with the framing of the UN Charter human rights had finally become a subject of official concern for the international community. Nonetheless, Article 2(7) UN Charter, the 'domestic jurisdiction' clause,[57] cast something of a shadow over this, while the six references to 'human rights' in the main body of the Charter itself did not appear to commit member states to very much.[58] At most, members of the UN would be required to 'promote' human rights in accordance with Article 55(c) read with Article 56. There had been proposals to go further than this; Chile and Cuba, for example, had been prepared to accept provisions in the Charter to guarantee *specified* rights, and there had been a Panamanian proposal to include a bill of rights in the Charter. But this was all far too ambitious for the majority of states, which thwarted such proposals given the radical implications they had for state sovereignty. This was an inauspicious beginning. However, there remained hope that a more faithful consummation of the place of human rights in the new world order would follow. After all, President Truman's address to the San Francisco conference, which had concluded the Charter, had spoken of an International Bill of Rights 'acceptable to all the nations involved' to follow soon, one which would be 'as much part of international life as our own Bill of Rights is a part of our Constitution'.[59]

4.3 THE UNIVERSAL DECLARATION OF HUMAN RIGHTS

In 1946 the UN Commission on Human Rights was instituted and given the task of working on an International Bill of Rights. The task, to create a human rights instrument applicable to all states and peoples across the globe, threw up a series of difficult philosophical and political questions.[60]

Even before the Commission began its work, the politics of international human rights protection had become apparent, but by 1947 'human rights' was rapidly becoming an ideological weapon in the war of words between East and West.[61] So the idea of an International Bill of Rights was an attractive one in principle, but there were major difficulties when it came to putting in place concrete measures, especially international legal obligations.

The Commission quickly decided that the International Bill should have three parts: a declaration, a convention containing legal obligations, and 'measures of implementation', that is, a system of supervision and control. A drafting committee of eight members (from Australia, Chile, China, France, Lebanon, the UK, the USA, and the Soviet Union) was appointed to formulate the declaration. Its chair was Eleanor Roosevelt. The Universal Declaration of Human Rights (UDHR) was subsequently formulated from an initial outline produced by John Humphrey, as well as a British draft.[62] Following many sessions of the drafting committee and approval by the plenary Commission, on 10 December 1948, the UDHR was proclaimed by 48 states in the UN General Assembly. Indeed, the years 1948–9 proved to be remarkable ones for human rights standard-setting (see Table 1.2 for

---

[57] Art 2(7) reads (in part): 'Nothing contained in the present Charter shall authorize the United Nations to intervene in matters that are essentially within the domestic jurisdiction of any state'.

[58] See Arts 1, 13, 55, 56, 62(2), 68, and 76. See also the preamble to the Charter.

[59] UN Information Organisation, Documents of the UN Conference on International Organisation (1945), Vol I, 717, cited by Sohn, *The United Nations and Human Rights* (Oceana Publications, 1968) 55.

[60] Lauren, n 18, 219.   [61] Lauren, 228.

[62] See Humphrey, *Human Rights and the United Nations: A Great Adventure* (Transnational Publishers, 1984) 42–3.

Table 1.2 Human rights on the international plane: key dates

1941	Roosevelt's Four Freedoms speech
1942	Declaration of the UN
1945	UN Charter
1948	Universal Declaration of Human Rights
	Convention on the Prevention and Punishment of the Crime of Genocide
1949	Four Geneva Conventions
1966	ICCPR and ICESCR opened for signature
1976	ICCPR and ICESCR enter into force

key dates). The Convention on the Prevention and Punishment of the Crime of Genocide[63] was opened for signature on 11 December 1948 and the four Geneva Conventions in 1949.

The UDHR had been accepted by the General Assembly without any dissenting votes, although there had been eight abstentions from the six communist states which were then members of the UN (Byelorussian SSR, Czechoslovakia, Poland, Ukrainian SSR, USSR, and Yugoslavia), plus Saudi Arabia and South Africa. The 48 states had nevertheless backed the UDHR as a 'common standard of achievement for all peoples and all nations'. Eleanor Roosevelt famously told the General Assembly that the Declaration 'might well become the *Magna Carta* of all mankind'. Yet as she herself was quick to acknowledge, in her capacity as a US representative, the basic character of the UDHR had to be kept in mind. It was not, she stressed, a treaty; it did not 'purport to be a statement of law or of legal obligations'. Similarly, most of the delegates at the General Assembly were ready to applaud the UDHR, but quick to deny that it had legal force. In fact the emphatic and repeated denials that the UDHR had legal force were probably part of the efforts that were necessary for its acceptance by the 48 states in the first place.[64]

Writing less than two years after the UDHR had been proclaimed, Lauterpacht dismissed it as being of 'controversial moral authority'.[65] He was not alone in his criticism of the Declaration. Events, it seemed, had confirmed that states had failed to rise to the challenge foreseen by Lauterpacht in his 1945 book. From the perspective of 1950, Lauterpacht's disappointment can be appreciated. No International Bill of Rights was secured in the 1940s. Moreover, in 1950 the prospects for the remainder of the bill looked bleak. It took until 1954 for the UN Commission to complete the drafts of what would become the International Covenant on Civil and Political Rights (ICCPR) and the International Covenant on Economic, Social and Cultural Rights (ICESCR). However, they would not be opened for signature until 1966 and it would take until 1976 before they entered into force for the 35 states that were prepared to ratify them. The drafting history of the two Covenants reveals the many compromises and amendments that were necessary to secure their acceptability to the members of the UN, especially as the size of that organization grew significantly in the post-colonial era. A similar point may be made about the relatively weak enforcement regimes that were eventually agreed for both treaties. They revealed how unrealistic it had been in the mid-1940s to assume that classic features of state sovereignty could be pushed aside easily when it came to establishing an effective International Bill of Rights.

[63] See Chapter 24.   [64] Moskowitz, *Human Rights and World Order* (Stevens and Sons, 1959) 79.
[65] Lauterpacht, n 3, 279. He was highly critical of the leading nations for their limited achievements. See Lauterpacht, 397–408.

5 CONCLUSION

More than 60 years on from when Eleanor Roosevelt unveiled the UDHR, it seems that her description of it as a possible Magna Carta for mankind was most apt. After all, as already noted, the document of 1215 was but the start of the story of the domestic protection of human rights. Can the same comment not be made for the UDHR today with respect to the international protection of human rights?

As the subsequent chapters in this book will reveal, the rights protected by the UDHR, and the two Covenants more generally, which today have been ratified by a large majority of states, have become part of a body of international law the scope, breadth, and general significance of which would have been impossible to predict in the late 1940s. And if these are the achievements of only the last 60 years, then what further progress can we expect in this century and beyond?

Of course, none of this is to suggest that things are anywhere near perfect today. We know that serious human rights violations occur across the globe every day. We may nevertheless compare the situation now with that existing before 1945. Today, there are international legal obligations that restrain how a sovereign state may treat individuals within its jurisdiction. This is now a matter for legitimate international concern, and international human rights law represents the standard by which the conduct of states may be judged. Today, even the most authoritarian of regimes would not publicly oppose the principle that their citizens have certain fundamental rights, even though the actions of many such governments may not always faithfully uphold such ideals. Certainly much more needs to be done to see the proper enforcement of the international standards that have been created. But here we may recall the words of Lauterpacht; the history of human rights law, both at the domestic and the international level, confirms that '[t]he vindication of human liberties does not begin with their complete and triumphant assertion at the very outset'. Rather, 'it commences with their recognition in *some* matters, to *some* extent, for *some* people, against *some* organ of the State'.[66] The story of the history of human rights is, therefore, most certainly an ongoing one.

FURTHER READING

BINGHAM, *The Rule of Law* (Penguin, 2010) (esp ch 2).

HENKIN, *The Rights of Man Today* (Stevens and Sons, 1978).

HUMPHREY, *Human Rights and the United Nations: A Great Adventure* (Transnational Publishers, 1984).

ISHAY, *The History of Human Rights: From Ancient Times to the Globalization Era* (University of California Press, 2004).

ISHAY, *The Human Rights Reader* (Routledge, 2007).

LAUREN, *The Evolution of International Human Rights: Visions Seen* (University of Pennsylvania Press, 2003).

ROBERTSON, *Crimes Against Humanity* (Penguin, 2006).

ROBERTSON and MERRILLS, *Human Rights in the World* (Manchester University Press, 1996) ch 1.

SIMPSON, *Human Rights and the End of Empire* (Oxford University Press, 2001) especially chs 2–5.

TOMUSCHAT, *Human Rights: Between Idealism and Realism* (Oxford University Press, 2008) ch 2.

---

[66] Lauterpacht, n 1.

USEFUL WEBSITES

Avalon Project: Documents in Law, History and Diplomacy (many of the 'constitutional' documents referred to in this chapter are available on this site): <http://avalon.law.yale.edu>

Official UN website on the UDHR, with links to audiovisual materials on the UDHR: <http://www.ohchr.org/EN/UDHR/Pages/introduction.aspx>

2

JUSTIFICATIONS

Samantha Besson

SUMMARY

International human rights are often criticized. Proponents of human rights usually have a hard time responding to critiques that bear on their justifications. They may say that human rights are self-justificatory or justified by being themselves justifications (for example, of the authority of domestic or international law), and hence do not regard them as being in need of justification. Human rights theorists do not necessarily fare any better: some human rights theories do not include the justification of human rights among their aims, while others justify human rights albeit without clarifying why justifications are needed in the first place or what they are actually justifying, thereby often talking at cross purposes with each other. This chapter purports to explain: first, why we need to justify human rights; second, what it means to justify them; third, what the different justifications for human rights may be; and, finally, what some of the implications of the justifications of human rights could be.

1 INTRODUCTION

International human rights law[1] has come under critique for quite some time now.[2] Curiously, however, proponents of human rights have not, by and large, responded to those critiques. Nor, more importantly, have they tried to justify human rights in the first place. This may be because they think human rights are self-justificatory,[3] an irreducible value that is not in need of further justification, justified by being themselves justifications (for example, of the authority of domestic or international law), or justified by reference to another value that does not itself need justification (for example, dignity or equality). Others have hinted at the need to agree on human rights without even asking why.[4] These various positions come close to

---

[1] This chapter pertains to the justification of *international* human rights *law*. See on those two dimensions of human rights: Besson, 'Human Rights – Ethical, Political...or Legal? First Steps in a Legal Theory of Human Rights' in Childress (ed), *The Role of Ethics in International Law* (CUP, 2011) 211; Besson, 'Human Rights and Constitutional Law – Patterns of Mutual Validation and Legitimation' in Liao and Renzo (eds), *The Philosophical Foundations of Human Rights* (OUP, 2014).   [2] See Chapter 3.

[3] This could be, for instance, because they are rights human beings have by virtue of their human nature and they hence find their justification in human nature itself. On the dangers of the naturalistic fallacy (that is, deriving an 'ought' from an 'is') in the human rights context, see, however, Beitz, *The Idea of Human Rights* (OUP, 2009) 49 ff.

[4] In 1949, after the adoption of the Universal Declaration on Human Rights, Jacques Maritain wrote: 'We agree about the rights but on condition that no one asks us why.' Maritain, *Man and the State* (Hollis and Carter, 1954) 70.

making human rights a matter of faith rather than of reason.[5] And this in turn may explain why many human rights activists tend to see inquiries into the justification of human rights as quasi-blasphematory or, at the least, a waste of time and energy that would be better channelled towards working for and enforcing human rights in practice.

International human rights law is itself of no avail in this respect. It cannot provide justifications external to the law. Generally speaking, the law provides reasons for action that are independent of its content. Therefore, the justifications for its authority should not be identified with moral justifications for the content of legal norms. True, the justifications for the law's authority depend on those moral justifications and thus presume their existence. International human rights law is no exception. As a result, legal reasoning on human rights, like legal reasoning in general, is a special kind of moral reasoning. Human rights justifications and critiques are inherent to human rights legal reasoning just as justification and critique are inherent to the law in general. Interestingly, international human rights law does more than other international law in this respect as it refers expressly to the independent existence of various moral justifications for human rights. In particular, preambles to human rights instruments refer to concepts such as dignity, equality, or autonomy,[6] and use foundational or derivational language.[7] In short, international human rights law does not, itself, morally justify human rights and one should not expect it to do so. However, the way human rights law works and the manner in which its authority is justified do not only confirm the need to justify such rights, but also provide the institutional and deliberative space to do so.

The obvious place to turn to for justification then is human rights philosophy or theory. After all, justifying is what moral philosophers and philosophers of law do. Curiously, however, human rights theorists do not necessarily fare much better on this count.[8] Of course, they disagree about the justifications of human rights, but that is not the problem. On the contrary, human rights are essentially contestable concepts, and so should their justifications be. Rather, the concern is that, while the majority of human rights theorists do justify human rights, they do so without clarifying why justifications are needed in the first place or what exactly they are justifying (for example, human rights *law* or human rights as either legal or moral rights or both),[9] thereby often talking at cross purposes.[10] This is a shame as a lot in human rights theory depends on the justification(s) given to human rights. For instance, their justification(s) affect the kind of guidance human rights theory may give to human rights practice with respect to difficult questions such as the strength of specific human rights duties, the resolution of conflicts between human rights or between human rights and other moral considerations, the allocation of human rights duties, or the prioritization among human rights duties.

---

[5] See Ignatieff, 'Human Rights: The Midlife Crisis' (1999) 46 *NY Review of Books* 58.

[6] Eg UDHR, ICCPR, and ICESCR, preambles.

[7] Eg ICESCR and ICCPR, preambles: '... *recognition* of the inherent dignity and of the equal and inalienable rights of all members of the human family is the *foundation* of freedom, justice and peace in the world' (emphases added).

[8] There are important exceptions, of course. See eg Buchanan, 'Why International Legal Human Rights?' in Liao and Renzo (eds), *The Philosophical Foundations of Human Rights* (OUP, 2014); Waldron, 'Is Dignity the Foundation of Human Rights?' (2013) *NYU School of Law, Public Law Research Paper No 12–73*.

[9] Eg Griffin, *On Human Rights* (OUP, 2008); Tasioulas, 'Are Human Rights Essentially Triggers for Intervention?' (2009) 4 *Philosophical Compass* 938; Wellman, *The Moral Dimensions of Human Rights* (OUP, 2011).

[10] See also Buchanan, n 8; Buchanan and Sreenivasan, 'Taking International Legality Seriously: A Methodology for Human Rights' forthcoming (manuscript on file with author).

Despite the importance of justification in human rights theory, it is important not to be too disappointed by the indeterminate state of the debate. One should not lose sight of the reverse impact of one's respective theoretical approach to the nature, object, or scope of human rights on their justification. Justifications may engage with human rights at very different levels depending on what one understands their nature and content to be. And those features of human rights work as constraints on potential justifications in return. For instance, endorsing the universality or generality of human rights conditions the kind of justifications that may be given to those rights if their scope is to be sufficiently universal or general. Furthermore, human rights are usually understood as giving rise to strong, if not exclusionary, duties, and this in turn affects the kind of justifications that may warrant such correlative duties. As a result, if it is true that the justifications of human rights and their role are indeterminate and contested, it should be a consolation to realize that so is the rest of human rights theory. All aspects of human rights need to be worked on at the same time to identify the right justifications of human rights.

As a matter of fact, and more generally, the way in which one approaches the nature and role of human rights *theory* itself also affects one's understanding of the *justification* of human rights, and vice-versa.[11] For instance, since arguably the best human rights theory ought to attempt to account for our contemporary human rights practice, the justification of human rights should also be about the point of our human rights practice. This in turn means looking for human rights justifications in the normative practice of human rights themselves, and in particular in human rights legal reasoning.

In the light of these preliminary observations, this chapter explains why we need to justify human rights (Section 2), what it means to justify them (Section 3), what the different justifications for human rights may be (Section 4), and, finally, what some of the implications of the justifications of human rights may be for other key issues in human rights theory (Section 5).

2 WHY JUSTIFY HUMAN RIGHTS

2.1 EXPLAINING JUSTIFICATION

Justifying means more than explaining or accounting for something. It means giving reasons for action or belief. Moral justification, then, amounts to giving moral reasons for action or belief. In the legal context, moral justification is about understanding the point of the legal norms we have.[12]

Depending on one's moral theory, justifying may equate with 'founding', 'basing', 'deriving', or 'grounding'. As a matter of fact, those terms are used interchangeably by many authors.[13] It is important to be cautious, however, especially if one wants to distance oneself from foundationalist approaches to morality. In short, foundationalism is a characteristic of those moral theories that claim there are foundations in morality and hence that attempt to derive moral values or entities from other foundational ones that are non-derivative.[14] There is nothing, however, in the enquiry into the justifications of human rights that necessarily implies foundationalism.

---

[11] Contrast Beitz, n 3, or Raz, 'Human Rights in the Emerging World Order' (2010) 1 *Transnational Legal Theory* 31 with Griffin, n 9, or Tasioulas, 'Towards a Philosophy of Human Rights' (2012) 65 *CLP* 1.

[12] Eg Waldron, n 8, on human rights; and Waldron, *Dignity, Rank and Rights* (OUP, 2012) on dignity.

[13] Eg Tasioulas, 'The Moral Reality of Human Rights' in Pogge (ed), *Freedom from Poverty as a Human Right: Who Owes What to the Very Poor?* (OUP, 2007) 75; Griffin, n 9.

[14] See Nickel, *Making Sense of Human Rights* (Blackwell, 2007) ch 4; Waldron, n 8.

In the case of human rights, justifying implies giving reasons for human rights. Because human rights are grounds for duties in concrete circumstances, and hence reasons for action, justifying human rights comes close to providing an abstract justification for a further concrete justification. Abstract justifications of human rights may themselves be general or specific, depending on whether they pertain to all human rights or to some in particular. Considerations about the abstract justification of human rights as justifications for concrete duties that correspond to concrete human rights enable us to draw two key distinctions.

First, the justification of human rights should not be conflated with the *object* of human rights. It often is, however. This may be because the object of human rights is generally perceived as a normatively loaded question. Not everything can be protected by a human right, precisely because human rights justify duties. However, the object of a human right, that is, the concrete content of the duties corresponding to a specific human right, is identified by reference to the threats against which the right protects the interests of its holder in concrete circumstances and not abstractly. All the same, the equation of the justification and object is often made in pluralistic accounts of the justifications of human rights.[15] Those authors argue for a plurality of justifications in order to match the plurality of objects of human rights. However, the reading proposed here is equally reconcilable with a monist approach to the justification of human rights. This would be the case in particular with an account that justifies human rights by reference to one single value such as dignity, but also understands that every particular right protects, and hence has as an object, something specifically required by dignity in a particular area. The loose relationship between the object and the justification of human rights also means that the correlation often made between the justification of human rights and their fundamental or intangible core is not a direct one. They are related, of course, and it will be explained how in this chapter, but not directly, and certainly not by reference to the object of the human right in question.

Second, and more generally, the justification of human rights should be carefully distinguished from other elements in the *moral structure* of human rights. Those elements are constitutive of any given human right in general and necessary for the recognition of a specific human right. They are, in a nutshell: the existence of an interest equally fundamental to all people, the existence of standard threats to that interest, the fair burden of the protection of the interest against those threats, and the abstract feasibility of that protection. Often, human rights theorists conflate some elements in the structure of human rights with their justification.[16] This is particularly the case with interest-based accounts of human rights. In the interest-based approach to human rights, as opposed to the choice-based or will-based approach,[17] human rights protect fundamental human interests that all human beings have. More precisely, a human right exists when a fundamental and general human interest is a sufficient reason to hold someone else (the duty-bearer) under a duty to respect that interest vis-à-vis the right-holder. Just as the choice-based approach does not necessarily mean that human rights are justified by autonomy, the interest-based approach does not imply that they are justified by reference to well-being. Of course, identifying interests as fundamental and general, threats as standard, and burdens as fair are matters of specific justification as well, but they are distinct from the general justification of human rights and can be established by analysis at a general level.

---

[15] See eg Tasioulas', n 9, critique of Griffin's autonomy-based account of human rights.
[16] See eg Tasioulas, n 11, on the dual root of human rights (interests and dignity).
[17] See Waldron, 'Introduction' in Waldron (ed), *Theories of Rights* (OUP, 1984) 1, 9–12.

Furthermore, it is important not to conflate the justification of human rights with other connected endeavours.

First, the justification of human rights does not equate with their *history*. The former is normative, whereas the latter is descriptive. Of course, human rights theory and human rights history ought to inform each other to be successful in their respective projects.[18] Not only because human rights history is also a kind of intellectual history, and hence the history of justifications, but also because human rights theory contributes to determining the object of human rights history. However, their aims and methods are clearly different.

Second, justifying human rights does not amount to explaining the *sources* of human rights. Their sources as legal norms are the sources of international human rights law, that is, treaties, customary international law, and general principles, as identified, specified, and interpreted by international judicial decisions.[19] Of course, those law-making processes and their normative outcome may themselves be morally justified, and often will be, as their content may correspond to that of universal moral rights. However, this is not a condition for the validity of the corresponding legal norms. True, this is a resolutely legal positivist take on international human rights. Some, albeit presumably very few, natural law accounts of international human rights law may condition the legal validity of human rights on their moral justification.

Finally, justifying human rights does not amount to accounting for their *legitimacy*, and hence to justifying their authority. Admittedly, their legitimacy is not entirely distinct from their moral justification, to the extent that the reasons given by a legal norm should match pre-existing reasons of those subject to the law and depend on these pre-existing reasons. The search for the moral justification of human rights remains distinct from that of the legitimacy of international human rights law, however, even if the former will eventually inform the latter.

2.2 JUSTIFYING JUSTIFICATION

The next question is why we should care about justifying human rights.

The first argument lies in the nature of human rights as rights. Rights protect interests that are recognized as sufficiently important to give rise to duties. As normative relationships, they are grounds for reasons for action and are in themselves justifications as a result. Every time a right gives rise to specific duties in concrete circumstances, a justification is provided. This turns the law into a forum of justification for human rights duties. And this in turn requires a justification: the justification of abstract human rights themselves.

Second, the legality of human rights also explains why we should justify them. International human rights law does not provide external justifications of human rights, but makes it clear that we need to justify them. This is because of the relationship between law and morality generally, and in particular between the justifications for the law's authority and moral justifications. The justifications for the law's authority are content-independent and do not amount to moral justifications of the content of any given legal norm, but the reasons for action it gives have to match pre-existing moral reasons of those bound by it. This so-called dependence condition of legitimacy in turn implies that the law's content be also justified morally, not so much to be valid law but for the authority it claims ever to be justifiable.

---

[18] Besson and Zysset, 'Human Rights History and Human Rights Theory: A Tale of Two Odd Bedfellows' (2012) *Ancilla Juris*, available at: <http://www.anci.ch/_media/beitrag/ancilla2012_204_besson.pdf>.

[19] See Chapter 4.

Finally, international human rights law refers expressly to the independent existence of various moral justifications for human rights. It does so mostly in preambles to human rights instruments.[20] International human rights law invites us, therefore, to explore those justifications further.

Of course, justifications may themselves call for further justifications. Thus, one value may be given as a justification for something and itself be regarded as having to be justified. Usually, at this stage, alternatives for further 'justifications of justifications' are suggested. The choice lies between either a metaphysical[21] or religious[22] route.[23] They are indeed the only ones able to provide these kinds of bedrock foundations. If neither approach is taken, however, there is no reason why the search for justification should be one for ultimate foundations and why a failure to identify those ultimate foundations should be a problem. The regress in the search for justifications has to halt at some stage. One may be satisfied with pausing at, for instance, equality or dignity without further justification and without searching for a master-justification or master-value. This may be because those moral values and principles are so widely accepted as part of people's moralities that one does not have to argue for them before using them to argue for human rights.[24]

3 HOW TO JUSTIFY HUMAN RIGHTS

3.1 JUSTIFICATIONS OF MORAL AND LEGAL RIGHTS

Human rights mean different things to different people. Some regard human rights as rights in the strict sense, while others do not see them as rights beyond their name. And those who understand them as rights may conceive them as legal rights, as moral rights, or as both.

The moral justifications of human rights will differ significantly depending on how one understands them. For instance, there may be moral justifications of legal human rights that are distinct from the moral justifications of corresponding moral rights. One may consider that international human rights law is justified by reference to peace, independently of whether it entails rights in the strict sense, whether those are also moral rights, and whether they have separate justifications as such. Or one may justify international human rights law by reference to their specifying role of universal moral rights or to their entrenching a canonical version of them.[25]

It is submitted here that we should understand the justification of human rights as a justification of rights, and of legal and moral rights at the same time. Further, as rights, human rights should also be regarded as grounds for duties, and hence their justification as a justification of a justification.

First, human rights understood as *rights*. The practice of international human rights law treats human rights as rights. Of course, sometimes they go by other names such as principles or, at least, are applied as principles and not as subjective and claimable rights. In most cases, however, human rights legal reasoning, and especially judicial reasoning about

---

[20] See n 6–7.

[21] Eg Habermas, 'The Concept of Human Dignity and the Realistic Utopia of Human Rights' (2010) 41 *Metaphilosophy* 464.

[22] Eg Waldron, *God, Locke, and Equality: Christian Foundations in Locke's Political Thought* (CUP, 2002) ch 3.

[23] See Tasioulas, 'Justice, Equality and Rights' in Crisp (ed), *The Oxford Handbook of the History of Ethics* (OUP, 2013) 768.

[24] See Nickel, n 14, 61.   [25] Eg Buchanan and Sreenivasan, n 10.

human rights, is rights-based reasoning. In a practice-sensitive human rights theory like the proposed one, human rights ought, therefore, to be understood as rights.

Second, human rights understood as *legal and moral rights*. As rights guaranteed by legal norms, international human rights are clearly legal rights. The question is whether they also correspond to moral rights. Just as moral rights are moral propositions and sources of moral duties, legal rights are legal propositions and sources of legal duties. They are moral interests recognized by the law as sufficiently important to generate moral duties.[26] The same may be said of legal *human* rights: legal human rights are fundamental and general moral interests recognized by the law as sufficiently important to generate moral duties. Generally speaking, moral rights can exist independently from legal rights, but legal rights recognize, modify, or even create moral rights by recognizing certain moral interests as sufficiently important to generate moral duties. As such, legal rights are always also moral rights, whether by recognition of pre-existing moral rights or by creation of moral rights. Of course, there may be ways of protecting moral interests or even independent moral rights legally without recognizing them as legal rights. Conversely, some legal rights may not actually protect pre-existing moral rights or create moral rights, thus only bearing the name of rights and generating legal duties at the most. However, the same cannot be said of human rights. The universal moral rights that will become human rights create moral duties for institutions, and hence for the law as well, to recognize and protect human rights.[27] This is the only way to give them their central egalitarian dimension, and to assess, for instance, whether the interests and threats at stake are general and to specify and allocate the corresponding duties in an egalitarian fashion. In other words, human rights as a subset of universal moral rights are also of an inherently legal nature. The law makes universal moral rights human rights, either by recognizing them as legal rights or by creating them in recognition of certain fundamental universal moral interests. This understanding of the relationship between moral and legal human rights is one of mutuality. It goes beyond the traditional understanding of a one-way relationship of translation or enforcement of moral rights through legal rights.

Finally, human rights understood as *grounds for duties*. As normative relationships, human rights imply duties. There are three remarks one should make about the correlativity between human rights and duties. First, while human rights can be abstract, there can be no abstract human rights duties; since they may only be specified by reference to a concrete threat to the protected interest, they are always context-specific and concrete. As a result, a human right may be justified, recognized, and protected before specifying which duties correspond to it. This is what we refer to as the justificatory priority of rights over duties.[28] Once a duty is specified, however, it will be correlative to the (specific) right. Second, a human right is a sufficient ground for holding duty-bearers under all the duties necessary to protect the interest against standard threats. It follows that a right might provide for the imposition of many duties and not only one. As a result, those duties will evolve with time and place.[29] This is what one refers to as the pluralism of human rights duties. Third, human rights have a dynamic nature. As such, successive specific duties can be grounded on the same right depending on the circumstances. This application indeterminacy of rights also implies that rights need to be localized to be fully effective; it is only in local circumstances that the allocation and specification of duties can take place.

---

[26] Raz, 'Legal Rights' (1984) 4 *OJLS* 1, 12; Raz, n 11.

[27] See Raz, 'Human Rights without Foundations' in Besson and Tasioulas (eds), *The Philosophy of International Law* (OUP, 2010) 321.

[28] See MacCormick, 'Rights in Legislation' in Hacker and Raz (eds), *Law, Morality and Society: Essays in Honour of HLA Hart* (OUP, 1977) 189, 199–202; Raz, 'On the Nature of Rights' (1984) 93 *Mind* 194, 196, and 200.

[29] See Beitz and Goodin (eds), *Global Basic Rights* (OUP, 2009) 10.

3.2 MORAL AND LEGAL JUSTIFICATIONS
OF MORAL AND LEGAL RIGHTS

Moral justifications of human rights ought to be distinguished from legal justifications of human rights as legal rights, that is, justifications entirely internal to the law.

Moral justifications of human rights are moral justifications of those rights as moral and/or legal rights. Depending on whether it is the moral or the legal dimension of human rights that is justified, different moral justifications may be proposed. The justifications of human rights that matter are those that pertain to human rights in general, that is, human rights as moral *and* legal rights.

Moral justifications of human rights as moral and legal rights may be articulated, in an ideal fashion, as external moral justifications. This is what most human rights theorists have done so far.[30] They treat justifications as a basis for the 'top-down' derivation of human rights. However, in a theory of human rights that takes their legal dimension seriously it is important to assess the moral justifications that one finds embedded in the legal practice of human rights. As explained in the introduction to this chapter, moral justifications and critiques of human rights are inherent to human rights law and legal reasoning. It is this kind of law-immanent moral justification that is relevant to accounting for human rights practice and explaining its point from within.

The best way to capture the moral justifications of human rights present in legal practice in a 'bottom-up' fashion is to focus on human rights legal reasoning and in particular on the interpretation, especially judicial interpretation, of human rights. This kind of justification of human rights is normative in kind and cannot be reduced to some kind of descriptive account of human rights practice. The legal practice of moral justification of human rights is now reverted to with respect to the two justifications that are discussed here, namely equality and dignity.

Last but not least, one should emphasize that human rights do not exhaust morality. As a result, their justifications do not either. They may, therefore, conflict with those of other moral and legal norms. One may think of considerations of justice or democracy that often conflict with human rights whatever their justifications. For instance, the protection of specific human rights, such as the right to property, may conflict with concerns of distributive equality in practice. This explains how human rights are wrongly accused of epitomizing moral individualism at any price. It is quite the contrary actually, as they have to be interpreted in the broad context of morality, including by reference to the collective dimensions of morality.

4 WHICH JUSTIFICATIONS FOR
HUMAN RIGHTS

4.1 A PLURALITY OF JUSTIFICATIONS

Moral justifications of human rights may be of various types, and a few clarifying distinctions are in order.

The first distinction is between *religious* and *non-religious* justifications of human rights. It follows from the structure of human rights presented in Section 2 that human rights protect fundamental human interests. Of course, this does not exclude providing

---

[30] Eg Nickel, n 14; Griffin, n 9; Tasioulas, n 11; Wellman, n 9. Note that some have done so taking as their object human rights as moral rights, as legal rights, or as both.

religious justifications of human rights.[31] As a matter of fact, religious approaches often converge on the same list of rights as secular ones. It suffices to think here of the right to life or freedom of religion. It is key, however, that the interests protected be humanistic interests, that is, interests that individuals have as human beings, and not extra-human concerns including the will of God.[32] In this section, and for reasons that pertain to the antecedence of morality over religion,[33] the focus will be on non-religious justifications of human rights.

A second distinction opposes *prudential* justifications of human rights to *objective* ones. Prudential reasons are reasons relating to a person's own prospects for a good life and what is in his or her subjective interest as a result. Prudential reasons for human rights may be, for instance, that human rights contribute to making society safer both for individuals and for the group. Focusing on prudential reasons for human rights is attractive because their existence confirms that the feasibility of human rights ought to matter for their justification, and that their cost is not too high for our societies. In addition, they confirm that there are psychological patterns in place to support those rights in practice. Those reasons also demonstrate the importance of the collective dimension of human rights, and that it is necessary to factor it into any justification of human rights whether prudential or not. However, there are various difficulties with prudential justifications of human rights. One is their relativity, and the problem this creates when accounting for the universality of human rights. Another one is the instability of these justifications when majorities and power shift. In the remainder of this chapter, I will focus on objective justifications of human rights, that is, those arguments that appeal directly to what is reasonable from the interpersonal moral point of view. Again, of course, many prudential reasons for human rights may correspond to those objective justifications.

Third, among objective justifications of human rights, it is useful to distinguish *consequentialist* justifications from *non-consequentialist* ones. Consequentialist justifications refer to results and support human rights because they make the societies that respect them more peaceful or prosperous. A common example may be utilitarian justifications, according to which human rights are justified by reference to their consequences for the general welfare.[34] The main difficulty with utilitarian justifications of human rights lies in their quantitative approach: human rights, and their corresponding duties, are regarded as commensurable and as having to be balanced against considerations of utility or other human rights, with the potential consequence of justifying grave restrictions to certain human rights or even emptying them of their whole purpose by reference to the general welfare. This contradicts an important dimension of human rights in practice: their demanding normative nature and their alleged resistance to trade-offs. In this section, therefore, the focus will be on non-consequentialist, that is deontological, justifications of human rights. Of course, this does not exclude convergence with consequentialist considerations, and in particular the importance of paying due attention to the egalitarian, and hence collective, dimension of human rights.

Finally, among non-consequentialist justifications, one may distinguish between *instrumental* and *inherent* justifications. Instrumental justifications account for one

---

[31] Eg Villey, *Le droit et les droits de l'homme* (PUF, 2008); Perry, *Toward a Theory of Human Rights: Religion, Law, Courts* (CUP, 2006).

[32] See Buchanan, *Justice, Legitimacy, and Self-determination: Moral Foundations for International Law* (OUP, 2004) 130–1, 141–2.

[33] See Dworkin, 'Religion without God' (2013) 60 *NY Review of Books*.

[34] Eg Talbott, *Human Rights and Human Well-being* (OUP, 2010).

human right by reference to its relationship to others, thus making the former a more fundamental right. Certain human rights are regarded as being instrumental to others when they are necessary to their effective implementation or enjoyment. One may think here of the human rights to security and subsistence and their necessity to the enjoyment of other human rights.[35] This is sometimes referred to as a linkage argument or a derivative justification for human rights. The supportive relationship between human rights may be unilateral or mutual.[36] Either way, it may be more or less strong depending on how important it is to the effective implementation of other rights in practice. Importantly, the instrumental justification needs to be assessed in the abstract when first justifying another human right. However, there are difficulties with the idea of instrumental justification of some human rights. One may mention, for instance, its all or nothing consequences for every given human right, and the indeterminacy of instrumental justifications at the abstract level of rights. In any case, no further conclusions may be drawn as to the abstract priority of non-instrumentally justified rights over instrumental ones.[37] Indeed, all human rights are equal and relationships among their justifications should not affect their relationships. This argument will be returned to in the context of the discussion of the strength of human rights, but for now the focus is on inherent justifications of human rights.

The next question is whether one should try to identify a single justification and defend a monist account of the justification of human rights or whether a pluralistic account is more plausible. Among the arguments put forward in favour of a single justification, one may mention the holistic approach to humanity or, better, moral personhood, and in particular the indivisibility of that basic moral status. In reply, one may stress not only the pluralism that characterizes morality, but also the plurality of the corresponding dimensions of moral personhood and hence presumably of moral justifications of the rights that correspond to those dimensions of personhood. Furthermore, the more justifications for human rights are identified, the more one enhances their potential subjective or psychological legitimacy. It is important to emphasize that one should differentiate between justifications articulated as such and those reached through overlapping consensus.[38] Not endorsing the latter and focusing on the former kind of justifications does not mean, however, that we should not be concerned with the widespread subjective recognition of the proposed objective justifications of human rights.

Of course, defending a pluralist account of the justification of human rights means that there could be conflicts between those justifications themselves, and not only between human rights duties. The connection between the two issues is discussed in Section 4.2. It suffices here to recognize that pluralism and the possibility of conflict in justifications of human rights are a quality of one's human rights theory, and in particular of its ability to account for the pluralist practice of human rights.

---

[35] See Nickel, n 14, 87–90; Shue, *Basic Rights: Subsistence, Affluence and US Foreign Policy* (Princeton UP, 1996) 11.

[36] When the linkage between human rights is strong and mutual, one may speak of indivisibility of human rights. Eg Nickel, 'Rethinking Indivisibility: Towards a Theory of Supporting Relations between Human Rights' (2008) 30 *HRQ* 984.

[37] See Waldron, 'Security as a Basic Right (After 9/11)' in Beitz and Goodin (eds), *Global Basic Rights* (OUP, 2009) 207.

[38] Eg Cohen, 'Minimalism about Human Rights: The most we can hope for?' (2004) 12 *J of Political Philosophy* 190. For a critique, eg Beitz, n 3; Forst, 'The Justification of Human Rights and the Basic Right to Justification: A Reflexive Approach' (2010) 120 *Ethics* 711.

4.2 TWO POTENTIAL JUSTIFICATIONS

The two moral grounds most commonly advanced for human rights are equality and dignity. Many other potential justifications could be mentioned, in particular autonomy and fairness. As pluralistic approaches to the justification of human rights are more promising, I will not address equality and dignity's virtues as monistic or sole justifications of human rights.

Equality and dignity constitute status-related justifications of human rights. This focus on status-related justifications should not be mistaken for a rejection of an interest-based approach to human rights. A basis in interests or status does not imply a justification only in interests or status. The moral structure of human rights endorsed in Section 2 regards human rights as based on objective interests. However, interests are part of the moral structure of human rights and do not justify them. Even if human rights are not status-based, they may be justified by reference to status. Human rights are constitutive of a status and that status amounts to those human rights in return. Human rights cannot, therefore, be based on that status, even though they are justified by reference to that status. It is the underlying idea informing that status and explaining how different rights constitute that status, and not the status itself, that justifies the rights constitutive of the status, whether it is equality or dignity.[39]

4.2.1 Equality

Human rights are sometimes justified by reference to equality, and in particular thin or basic moral equality. Basic moral equality is usually referred to as equal moral status.

The concept of equal moral status is best explained by separating the notion of moral status from that of *equal* moral status. In a nutshell, *moral status* pertains to the way in which a being is subject to moral evaluation, how it ought to be treated, whether it has rights, and what kind of rights it has.[40] Moral status goes further, therefore, than mere moral considerability: the latter is a standing that may be shared with many other sentient animals and even with things, whereas moral status only belongs to human beings. *Equal moral status* refers to the idea that 'all people are of equal worth and that there are some claims people are entitled to make on one another simply by virtue of their status as persons'.[41]

There are two, inseparable core ideas in this understanding of equal moral status: the idea that all persons should be regarded as having the same moral worth, and the idea that this equal moral worth is relational and the basis for mutual moral claims. The first core idea in equal moral status pertains to the inherent and non-instrumental value of personhood. According to that idea, no person may be deemed as morally inferior to another: all those who have the characteristics that are sufficient for being a person, and hence the capacity for rational and moral agency, have the same moral status.[42] Equal moral status is of course compatible with important inequalities on other counts such as health, beauty, luck, etc. It is important to stress that what matters here is personhood and not human nature. The former captures what ought to be protected morally in human beings as moral agents, and it escapes the naturalistic fallacy and many other misconceptions that come with the notion of human nature. The second core idea in equal moral status pertains to its relational dimension. One is at once a person valuable in him- or herself and a person

---

[39] See also Waldron, n 8.
[40] See Buchanan, 'Moral Status and Human Enhancement' (2009) 37 *Philosophy and Public Affairs* 346.
[41] Scheffler, 'What is Egalitarianism' (2003) 31 *Philosophy and Public Affairs* 5, 22.
[42] See Buchanan, n 40, 347.

equal to others, that is, a person whose status and moral worth is defined by one's moral relations to others. The relational or social nature of equal moral status explains why the latter amounts to more than mere autonomy or rational capacity that is covered by the first core idea.[43] The denial of equal moral status amounts to a judgment of exclusion and inferiority *to others* where this kind of judgment is 'thought to disqualify one from participation as an equal in important social practices or roles'.[44]

As a result, equal moral status does more than simply entitle persons to mutual claims. It is *defined* by reference to those mutual claims. The mutual entitlements inherent in equal moral status are usually described as mutual basic moral rights.[45] Human rights are among the basic moral rights that constitute one's equal moral status, although they may not exhaust them. What these basic moral rights or entitlements amount to are rights or entitlements to equal treatment or respect in a broad sense. It is one of the interesting features of equal moral status that it amounts both to a normative status, on the one hand, and to the entitlements stemming from that status and actually constituting that status in return, on the other. This relationship between equal status and rights explains how human rights protect only those interests that can give rise to mutual entitlements that are themselves constitutive of equal moral status, with that status itself amounting to those mutual entitlements in return. This is why human rights cannot be said to be 'grounded' in (political) equality, even though the latter can be a 'ground' or justification for the recognition of human rights[46] and human rights a 'ground' for the recognition of equal (political) status.

Political equality is indeed the kind of equality that matters in a legal order and, accordingly, in the context of human rights law. The passage from equality to political equality corresponds to that from basic moral rights to human rights. The relational or social nature of equal moral status alluded to before implies that 'the proper acknowledgement of a person's moral status requires some sort of fundamental public recognition of equality'.[47] Political, or public, equality implies that people can see that they are being treated as equals and takes the form of its recognition by the law and institutions. The political dimension of equal moral status leads to a further process: the struggle for equal participation rights. And this in turn implies struggling for the establishment of a democratic regime that includes all those subjected to a decision into the decision-making process. Democracy is indeed the way 'of publicly realizing equality when persons who have diverse interests need to establish rules and institutions for the common world in which they live',[48] in spite of persistent and widespread reasonable disagreement.

It is precisely in the equal political status of each individual as an equal member of the moral-political community that the threshold of importance and point of passage from a general and fundamental interest to a human right may be found. Only those interests that are recognized as sufficiently important by members of the community can be recognized as giving rise to duties and hence human rights. Each person's interests deserve equal respect by virtue of her status as member of the community and of his or her mutual relations to other members of the community. As a result, the recognition of human rights occurs not in a top-down fashion; they are not externally promulgated but mutually granted by members of a given political community.[49] This is particularly important as it allows for the mutual assessment of the general and standard nature of the threats to

---

[43] See Anderson, 'What is the Point of Equality?' (1999) 109 *Ethics* 287, 288–9 and 313.

[44] Buchanan, 'The Egalitarianism of Human Rights' (2010) 120 *Ethics* 679, 708–10.

[45] See Buchanan, *Beyond Humanity?* (OUP, 2011) 233.   [46] See Waldron, n 8.

[47] Buchanan, n 40, 379.

[48] Christiano, 'Democratic Legitimacy and International Institutions' in Besson and Tasioulas (eds), *The Philosophy of International Law* (OUP, 2010) 119, 121–2.   [49] See Forst, n 38.

certain interests that, therefore, deserve protection, on the one hand, and of the burdens and costs of the recognition of the corresponding rights and duties, on the other. As a matter of fact, human rights are not merely a consequence of individuals' equal political status, but also a way of earning that equal status and consolidating it. Without human rights, political equality would remain an abstract guarantee; through mutual human rights, individuals become actors of their own equality and members of their political community. Borrowing Hannah Arendt's words: 'we are not born equal; we become equal as members of a group on the strength of our decision to guarantee ourselves mutually equal rights.'[50]

Evidence of the egalitarian dimension of human rights may be found in practice. One may think, for instance, of the non-inherently individualistic nature of human rights that protect basic individual interests deemed comparatively important within the political community. Some human rights, like freedom of expression, protect individual interests in collective goods or individual interests whose social importance is also part of the reason to protect them as individual rights. The egalitarian dimension of human rights is also echoed in the idea of an inviolable core of human rights as a limit on restrictions to the enjoyment of human rights. Contrary to the standard inviolability approach to that core,[51] on the proposed account, each human right is based on an interest (rather than a status) that is deemed, when protected as a right, as fundamental and constitutive of one's political equality, and, as a result, status. What is inviolable is not the interest, but the fact that everyone ought to benefit from its protection and hence from the right to have rights that protect it.

4.2.2 Dignity

Dignity is sometimes invoked as another way of justifying human rights.[52] The problem is that dignity is an extremely indeterminate and historically complex concept, often used as placeholder in morality.[53]

It remains unclear, for instance, whether dignity does some work in the human rights context that equal moral status cannot do. To start with, authors use dignity to refer to what is unique in human beings and shared by all of them: their personhood and capacity for rational and moral agency. This is, however, the very idea captured by the concept of equal moral status.[54] Another important element about dignity as it is used in the human rights context is its comparative or relational dimension. However, the fact that authors usually use the term 'equal dignity'[55] to describe this dimension shows how the question of equality cannot be escaped by gesturing to dignity. Confirmation that 'equal dignity' is redundant if one adopts the proposed approach to equal moral status as equal universal moral rights may be found in Article 1 of the Universal Declaration of Human Rights that refers to human beings being born 'equal in dignity *and* rights'.[56]

If this argument against dignity as a foundation of human rights holds, one still needs to explain why dignity has been a key feature within major international and domestic human rights law instruments since 1945.[57]

---

[50] Arendt, *The Origins of Totalitarianism* (Penguin, 1951) 147.

[51] Eg Kamm, 'Rights', in Coleman and Shapiro (eds), *The Oxford Handbook of Jurisprudence and Philosophy of Law* (OUP, 2002) 476; Nagel, 'La valeur de l'inviolabilité', (1994) 99 *Revue de métaphysique et de morale* 149.

[52] Eg Waldron, n 12; Habermas, n 21; Forst, n 38; Habermas, *Zur Verfassung Europas: Ein Essay* (Suhrkamp, 2011); Tasioulas, n 11.   [53] Eg Pinker, 'The Stupidity of Dignity', *The New Republic* (28 May 2008).

[54] This becomes clear when one looks at Habermas, n 21, 468–9 and 472.

[55] Eg Gosepath, 'The Place of Equality in Habermas' and Dworkin's Theories of Justice' (1995) 3 *EJ of Philosophy* 2, 27.   [56] Emphasis added.

[57] Eg McCrudden, 'Dignity and Judicial Interpretation of Human Rights' (2008) 19 *EJIL* 655. Of course, there are also counter-arguments in international and domestic human rights practice, as not all constitutional traditions know dignity, and some have now abandoned it.

An historical explanation is the post-Second World War political convergence of two extremely powerful traditions: Christian theology and Kantian philosophy.[58] Yet historical compromises do not necessarily make for good moral interpretations of law, and historical understandings do not necessarily stick in judicial interpretations of legal norms. As to the resurgence of interest in dignity these days, explanations are easy to find. Legal reasons may lie in the development of comparative constitutional law, and the influence of German constitutional law (where dignity is a central concept) in that context, but also within EU fundamental rights law and international human rights law. Morally, one may find explanations in the return of the religious or at least of the sacred, but also in the coming under threat of Kantian moral philosophy within moral philosophy in general. Those debates within morality ensure that the fascination for dignity can endure. And this may not necessarily be a regrettable state of affairs given the role such essentially contestable concepts play in a democratic legal order. Besides, if dignity works as a moral placeholder and 'status-indicator',[59] then its resilience may be good news for the protection of equal moral status and human rights.

All of this is not to say, of course, that dignity does not have a moral existence of its own besides equal moral status, but merely that it is redundant to equal moral status in its relationship to human rights. For instance, dignity is a way to be treated. That meaning of dignity corresponds to the idea of being treated with dignity or dignified respect. It usually takes the shape of a duty to dignified treatment, as opposed to a right.

5 WHAT FOLLOWS FROM THE JUSTIFICATION OF HUMAN RIGHTS

5.1 HUMAN RIGHTS JUSTIFICATIONS AND THE UNIVERSALITY OF HUMAN RIGHTS

The justifications of human rights have to be such that they can account for the claim to universality of human rights, or, at least, provide an explanation of why that claim is made in practice and cannot be justified.

A well-known challenge to the legitimacy, but also to the moral justification, of the universality of international human rights law is based on a brand of moral relativism. In short, the objection is that international human rights law embodies a 'parochial' (that is, limited or narrow) set of values (or ordering of such values) that it unjustifiably imposes, through its claim to a universal personal scope, on people and societies who do not share it. If one refers to the conditions of justified authority or legitimacy in Joseph Raz's conception of authority (that is, the dependence condition and the normal justification condition),[60] the claim made by parochialism is that international law does not have legitimate authority over certain subjects of international law. The parochialist complaint can be read as denying that international law facilitates conformity with pre-existing objective reasons, as opposed to the reasons asserted by certain dominant groups. In other words, parochialism denounces the legitimacy of international law for disregarding the dependence condition.

---

[58] See Rosen, *Dignity: Its History and Meaning* (Harvard UP, 2012) 53, 80 ff and 90 ff. See also Moyn, 'Personalism, Community and the Origins of Human Rights' in Hoffmann (ed), *Human Rights in the Twentieth Century* (CUP, 2011) 85.

[59] Ladwig, 'Menschenwürde als Grund der Menschenrechte' (2010) 1 *Zeitschrift für Politische Theorie* 51, 65. See also Habermas, n 52, 26.

[60] Raz, *The Morality of Freedom* (Clarendon, 1986); Raz, *Ethics in the Public Domain* (Clarendon, 1995).

There are three ways of understanding the moral relativist challenge: moral relativism in the strict sense, epistemological relativism, and social relativism. One may assume here that the parochialism objection is not based on a sceptical view of morality.[61] In respect of the first challenge, *moral relativism in the strict sense*, it may be pointed out that adopting an objective view of morality does not equate with adhering to a single conception of morality. The background to the present analysis is an objective, albeit pluralist, account of morality that can accommodate conflicts of values and different orderings between them. As to the second challenge, *epistemological relativism*, one may legitimately contend that the institutionalized intercultural dialogue and mutual adjustment promoted by democratic coordination in international human rights law-making, and international human rights decision-making generally, could pay sufficient attention to the issue of the diversity of perspectives and understandings when adopting or applying international human rights law.[62] Finally, with regard to the third challenge, that of *social relativism*, it should be emphasized that holding to moral objectivity does not mean denying the importance of the contextualization of moral values recognized by international human rights law at the domestic level, nor the possibility of the historical national localization of objective values and of historical changes in that localization over the course of time.[63] This is particularly appropriate in the context of human rights where duties can only be specified in a concrete political and, in particular, democratic context. In short, parochialism is a necessary component of human rights enforcement that requires contextualization and hence some form of vernacularization or adaptation to the local circumstances.[64]

It seems, therefore, that the difficulties raised by moral, epistemological, and social relativism can be adequately met. However, the critique based on moral relativism retains some of its original bite when it is understood as based on moral pluralism. This version of the challenge relies on the absence of correspondence between the basic values or reasons or, more often, their orderings or rankings imposed by international human rights norms, and those applying within any given political community. One may think, for instance, of collectivist moralities that give the group priority over the individual. This objection affects the plausibility of universal moral justification of international human rights law and cannot simply be put at rest by reference to the piecemeal or fragmented nature of the legitimate authority of international law. If successful, the challenge would preclude a whole set of international human rights, albeit abstract rights, from applying to a whole range of cultures (regions and countries).

Despite appearances, the moral pluralism objection can also be met. The situation differs, however, depending on the state and its existing level of human rights protection.

Those states that do not have domestic human rights norms do not yet have the duties that correspond to those rights. What they have, however, is a moral duty to protect fundamental universal interests and this ought to be done by recognizing those interests as

---

[61] Defeating a moral relativist objection would take us beyond the scope of this chapter. It is clear, however, that reasonable moral disagreement does not validate a moral relativist argument (see Griffin, n 9, 128–32). Nor actually does reasonable moral agreement validate a moral realist one. Acceptability and acceptance are deeply parochial. This is why, for instance, the legal universality of human rights may not be proposed as a solution to the problem of human rights parochialism, but is at its source.

[62] See Buchanan, n 32; Buchanan, 'Human Rights and the Legitimacy of the International Legal Order' (2008) 14 *Legal Theory* 39.

[63] See Williams, *In the Beginning was the Deed: Realism and Moralism in Political Argument* (Princeton UP, 2005) 62, 66.

[64] See also Buchanan, n 32; Merry, *Human Rights and Gender Violence: Translating International Law into Local Justice* (University of Chicago Press, 2006); Benhabib, 'The Legitimacy of Human Rights' (2008) 137 *Daedalus* 94.

human rights. In such cases, the dependence condition is met because the reason corresponding at least to the right to have rights is pre-existing. However, the other reasons corresponding to international human rights duties cannot match pre-existing state reasons. Thus, the inescapable parochialism of political equality that only exists within the bound of a given political community and that is hence ingrained in human rights defeats the universal justification and legitimacy of international human rights law, just as it conditions their very legalization as human rights in the first place. With respect to the right to have rights, in any case, it is important to work on substantive and institutional mechanisms of deliberation and inclusive transcultural dialogue that increase the epistemic virtues of international human rights law-making and can, therefore, minimize the discrepancies in the ordering of interests and of reasons between international human rights norms and domestic ones.

If, by contrast, a state already has a set of corresponding domestic human rights norms, the reasons stemming from those human rights duties can be matched by the reasons given by international human rights norms. It is the specific ordering of interests and reasons that may differ, however, in circumstances of moral pluralism. Given what was said before about the interdependence between human rights and political equality and given the role of the political community and hence of domestic law in identifying the egalitarian threshold of importance of those interests that need to be protected as human rights, international human rights norms are drafted as minimal and abstract legal norms. Their threshold may then be set higher by domestic law. Their ordering with other interests that is necessary to further specify the rights and identify the corresponding duties may depend on the contextualization made by domestic authorities. Since most of the legalization of human rights takes place at domestic level, this also makes domestic law the locus of justification and hence legitimization of international human rights norms.

International human rights law accommodates moral pluralism, in other words, by not forcing complete orderings of the same values. This minimizes the chances of disconnect between the ordering of interests in international human rights norms and states' pre-existing reasons for action. It should be added that the egalitarian justification of human rights proposed before grants human rights a relational and collective dimension that goes part of the way in accommodating collectivist and non-individualistic moralities and hence moral pluralism within human rights.

5.2 HUMAN RIGHTS JUSTIFICATIONS AND THE STRENGTH OF HUMAN RIGHTS

The justifications of human rights have to be such that they can account for the special strength and demanding normative nature of human rights in practice, but also provide an explanation of why and how they are being restricted in case of conflict with other moral considerations or other human rights.

It is commonly expected that human rights weigh as much as their justification and thus that conflicts between rights should be resolved by reference to that weight. This is, for instance, what many status-based approaches to the justification of human rights claim.[65] Those who defend the idea of a minimal core in every human right that is resistant to trade-offs also usually relate its special stringency to that of the justification of the human right (for example dignity). Other accounts that endorse linkage approaches to the

---

[65] Eg Kamm, n 51; Nagel, n 51.

justification of certain human rights see their priority in case of conflict as conditioned by whether they are instrumental rights or not.[66]

Things are not that straightforward, however. Human rights do not have a certain weight that may be quantitatively balanced and traded off like utility, but are described and relate by reference to their moral stringency. Actually, it is the concrete duties that have that stringency and not the abstract rights. And the different duties corresponding to any given human right may have very different stringencies depending on the threats against which they are shielding the protected interest. As a result, human rights should not be weighed and balanced quantitatively when they conflict with other rights or moral considerations, but their duties' respective and variable stringency should be assessed to reach a qualitative trade-off.

No wonder then that the stringency of human rights is only indirectly related to their moral justification. This dispels the apparent paradox that besets human rights theory according to which it is hard to understand why human rights justified by reference to extremely stringent values can be restricted on the basis of conflicting public interests and less stringent moral considerations, on the one hand, or how human rights that are equal in justification may have to be weighed against each other, on the other.[67] It is true that all equally justified human rights are equal in the abstract and have very stringent justifications, but this does not mean that their corresponding duties are of equal stringency and may not be restricted in a differentiated fashion. Nor does it mean that they may be restricted to any degree, however. They may be restricted, but in a manner that is justified by reference to the underlying justification of human rights.

The specific stringency of human rights pertains to the ranking or priority of human rights when they conflict with other moral considerations. It is part of the meaning of human rights that they should have a relationship of priority over certain other moral considerations. Human rights are often portrayed as resistant to 'changes on the scale of social costs'.[68] This was famously captured by Ronald Dworkin's idea of rights as trumps,[69] Robert Nozick's conception of rights as side-constraints,[70] or John Rawls' idea of lexical priority.[71]

The first question, however, is whether human rights should take priority over any other moral considerations or just some of them. Other moral considerations may include, depending on the accounts, moral interests, values, interests, goods, welfare, justice, utility, security, and so on. It may be useful to refer to Dworkin's idea of rights as trumps, as he is very careful when identifying the considerations he has in mind. His idea is to exclude merely external preferences, that is, others' preferences about how one should lead one's own life.[72] His argument for that exclusion is egalitarian. Rights should be invoked in cases where invocations of the common good or the general interest of the community are likely to have been contaminated by those external preferences and the latter granted more importance than they should as a result.

The next question pertains to the degree of stringency of human rights duties when they enter in relation with other moral considerations and to whether their stringency is

---

[66] Eg Shue, n 35; and a critique by Waldron, n 37.

[67] Eg Griffin, n 9, 76: 'Human rights are resistant to trade-offs, but not completely so'.

[68] See Waldron, 'Security and Liberty: The Image of Balance' (2003) 11 *J of Political Philosophy* 191, 196.

[69] Dworkin, *Taking Rights Seriously* (Harvard UP, 1977) 190 ff.

[70] Nozick, *Anarchy, State and Utopia* (Basic Books, 1974) 28 ff.

[71] Rawls, *The Law of Peoples* (Harvard UP, 1999) 36 ff.

[72] See Dworkin, 'Rights as Trumps' in Waldron (ed), *Theories of Rights* (OUP, 1984) 153, 165. See also Waldron, 'Rights in Conflict' in *Liberal Rights: Collected Papers* (CUP, 1993) 203, 220–1.

absolute or not. Here again, Dworkin's account is helpful as he does not preclude that, in some cases, some of the considerations *a priori* excluded from restricting human rights may be allowed to restrict them.[73] This is why some authors have referred to Dworkin's account as one that treats rights as 'shields' rather than trumps.[74] There are two ways in which this conclusion seems plausible. The first one pertains to the plurality of human rights duties at any given time and over time. Depending on the circumstances and the kinds of threats to the interest protected by the human right, different duties corresponding to the same right may be of different stringency, at least relatively to one another. The second one is that not all moral considerations that may be conflicting with human rights duties are of the same stringency. Some may be more important and weightier than others, depending on the circumstances.

The question, however, is how to structure the relationship between those moral considerations that are not trumped by human rights and the idea of human rights that work as trumps over moral considerations. As Jeremy Waldron demonstrates, the answer cannot lie in any quantitative assessment of the interest protected as this would bring back the dangers of the utilitarian weighing and balancing of interests.[75] The same may be said of any quantitative measurement of the degree of threat to the interest protected. The logic of the idea of weight would indeed suggest that ultimately any human rights duty associated with that interest may be dealt with in that way.

The answer to this dilemma lies arguably in the collective dimension of the interests protected by human rights and, more specifically, their egalitarian dimension. These two features are internal to human rights as rights and enable them to relate to other interests and moral considerations in their own way and within their specific moral category without threatening the special stringency of that moral category in general.

First, the collective dimension of some of the individual interests protected by human rights provides guidance as to how qualitative trade-offs may be operated and this within the rights themselves. Human rights are normative relations and have a socio-comparative dimension that incorporates a given relationship between the individual and the group. Thus, one may imagine that the collective dimension of the interest protected by freedom of expression in a democracy, that is, its contribution to political life, may allow for justified restrictions of some of its corresponding duties in circumstances where that collective dimension requires them. The role of the collective dimension of any given human right is precisely to help draw the line between what is collectively necessary in the protection of a right and what is not.

Second, the egalitarian idea underlying all human rights calls for egalitarian justifications of restrictions to human rights duties. All restrictions of human rights should be egalitarian, implying, for instance, that attention is paid to the distributive consequences of restrictions: the losers should not always be on the same side. The egalitarian justification of human rights also explains why the restriction of human rights duties by reference to other moral considerations may never lead to the complete erosion of any one of them or to the restriction of their fundamental core.[76] This would amount to denying equal rights-holders their equal rights and their equal moral status as members of the political community. Finally, in institutional terms, this egalitarian requirement of human rights restrictions also implies that democratic procedures are the adequate procedures in which to justify human rights restrictions. This is why most international and regional human

---

[73] See Dworkin, n 72, 191.
[74] See Schauer, 'A Comment on the Structure of Rights', (1993) 27 *Georgia LR* 415, 429.
[75] Waldron, n 72, 216 ff.   [76] See Waldron, n 37, 224–6. See also Shue, n 35, 114, 166.

rights instruments include a reference to democracy in the justification test they apply to human rights restrictions.

6 CONCLUSION

Human rights need to be justified, not the least because they have been under fierce critique lately. The purpose of this chapter was to explain what the justification of human rights amounts to, why it is necessary, how we should go about it, and what its implications are.

Of course, as it should have become clear in the course of the argument, the justification of human rights is so central to human rights theory that it is conditioned by, and conditions in return, other key issues in human rights theory. Those are not only the nature, object, scope, rights-holders, and duty-bearers of human rights, but also what we understand the project of human rights theorizing itself to be.

FURTHER READING

BEITZ, *The Idea of Human Rights* (Oxford University Press, 2009).

BUCHANAN, 'The Egalitarianism of Human Rights' (2010) 120 *Ethics* 679–710.

BUCHANAN, 'Why International Legal Human Rights?' in Liao and Renzo (eds), *The Philosophical Foundations of Human Rights* (Oxford University Press, 2014).

FORST, 'The Justification of Human Rights and the Basic Right to Justification. A Reflexive Approach', (2010) 120 *Ethics* 711–40.

GRIFFIN, *On Human Rights* (Oxford University Press, 2008).

HABERMAS, 'The Concept of Human Dignity and the Realistic Utopia of Human Rights' (2010) 41 *Metaphilosophy* 464–80.

IGNATIEFF, *Human Rights as Politics and Idolatry* (Princeton University Press, 2003).

NICKEL, *Making Sense of Human Rights* (Blackwell, 2007).

RAZ, 'Human Rights without Foundations' in Besson and Tasioulas (eds), *The Philosophy of International Law* (Oxford University Press, 2010) 321–37.

ROSEN, *Dignity: Its History and Meaning* (Harvard University Press, 2012).

TALBOTT, *Human Rights and Human Well-being* (Oxford University Press, 2010).

TASIOULAS, 'Towards a Philosophy of Human Rights', (2012) 65 *CLP* 1–30.

WALDRON, 'Is Dignity the Foundation of Human Rights?' (2013) *NYU School of Law, Public Law Research Paper No 12–73*.

WELLMAN, *The Moral Dimensions of Human Rights* (Oxford University Press, 2011).

USEFUL WEBSITES

Stanford Encyclopedia of Philosophy: <http://plato.stanford.edu>

Routledge Encyclopedia of Philosophy: <http://www.rep.routledge.com/>

3

CRITIQUES

Marie-Bénédicte Dembour

SUMMARY

Whether they are conceived as the rights that every human being has, thus 'naturally' setting limits to the legitimate action of states and others, or as principles of good political action which society agrees to adopt and follow, human rights have always been subjected to intense and perceptive critiques. This chapter reviews six such critiques, deriving from realist, utilitarian, Marxist, particularist (cultural relativist), feminist, and post-colonial theoretical perspectives. The first three critiques emerged in reaction to the (successive) French Declarations of the Rights of Man of the late eighteenth century; the last three were fully developed in reaction to the International Bill of Rights enacted after the Second World War. Each of these critiques reveals a gap between what human rights claim to be or achieve, on the one hand, and what human rights are or do in practice, on the other. The question arises as to whether this gap is bridgeable. The critiques answer this question in various ways.[1]

1 INTRODUCTION

Human rights, for those who believe in them, embody the promise of a better world. However, there always have been and continue to be persuasive critiques of the concept of human rights. This chapter reviews six such critiques, emanating respectively from realist, utilitarian, Marxist, particularist (cultural relativist), feminist, and, finally, post-colonial theoretical perspectives.

Before understanding a critique, the concept it is critiquing first needs to be understood. This is not the context, however, to discuss in detail what human rights are.[2] Suffice it to say here that this chapter is written with the understanding that human rights orthodoxy has been moving from conceiving human rights as a given ('natural school') to conceiving them as values and principles which are agreed upon ('deliberative school'). For ease of terms, the natural school will be referred to as the 'old orthodoxy' and the deliberative school as the 'new orthodoxy', even though this terminology may suggest that the understanding of human rights at any one time is clearly set. It is not. Human rights are a highly contested concept.[3]

---

[1] Parts of this chapter draw upon *Who Believes in Human Rights?: Reflections on the European Convention* © Marie-Bénédicte Dembour (CUP, 2006) extracts reproduced with permission. [2] But see Chapter 2.
[3] See further Dembour, 'What are Human Rights? Four Schools of Thought' (2010) 32 *HRQ* 1.

In one way or another, each of the six critiques reviewed in this chapter points to a gap between the promise that every human being enjoys a number of fundamental rights and a world where human rights violations abound and many people are excluded from the enjoyment of human rights; that is, a gap between the human rights ideal and practice. Why is there such a gap? Two rather different answers are possible. The gap can be thought to exist *either* because the practice has, so far, failed to live up to the theory, but without this affecting the validity of the concept of human rights, *or* because human rights cannot be what they are said to be, making the concept invalid. In other words, critiques of human rights can either require human rights to be true to their word or reject them as constructed on unsound premises. These two positions correspond to what will be called in this chapter the practical and the conceptual critiques of human rights.

Practical critiques conceive of problems with human rights as demanding that a better practice be elaborated. The problems that such critiques identify are various and include, in a non-exhaustive list, the existence of double standards in the application of human rights, the fact that powerful non-state actors largely remain outside the human rights compass, the relative neglect of economic and social rights, the status of collective rights, the implications of environmental degradation, overzealous responses to the terrorist threat, and so on.[4] Practical critiques accept the idea of human rights, but demand that human rights be made to work better in the face of challenges. Crucially, they do not suggest that the concept is irretrievably defective. They 'simply' ask for the gap between what the concept promises and what it delivers to be closed, believing that human rights must and *can* be improved.

In contrast, conceptual critiques conceive of the concept of human rights as fundamentally flawed. They regard problems of bad governance as requiring a solution that lies outside the human rights logic. For them, human rights are not the best way to try to implement the ideas of justice, equality, and humanity which human rights supposedly stand for; better ways have to be found. Obviously those who embrace these views are not *against* human rights in the sense that their aim is not to call for the supposed binary opposite of human rights, namely, violations of human rights. Rather, their view is that the route towards emancipation need not, or even, *should not*, take the form of human rights.

The critiques reviewed in this chapter have both conceptual and practical variants. To complicate matters further, they often overlap. At the risk of caricature, but in order to introduce them, an attempt can be made to encapsulate each of them in one sentence. Realists reject the idea that human rights are natural, simply existing out there to be recognized and implemented; they argue that human rights cannot be 'above' or 'beyond' the state but necessarily originate from and are enmeshed within the state. Utilitarians, seeking the common good, oppose the granting of individual rights regardless of the consequences for the common good; they think it is impossible for human rights to be absolute and/or inalienable. Marxists view rights as sustaining the bourgeois order and thus feeding oppression by privileging a particular class to the detriment of the oppressed majority. Particularists object to the idea that moral judgments can be made that hold true across cultures; they call for tolerance of practices that are not comprehensible within the dominant perspective and denounce what they see as the inherent imperialism of human rights, which are not universal but the product of the society which has created them. Feminists dispute the idea that human rights are gender-neutral; they attack human rights' pretence of equality and neutrality by observing that rights, which have generally been defined by

---

[4] Some of these problems are discussed in Chapters 26–9.

men, tend to regulate the so-perceived public sphere, thereby bypassing the interests and concerns of women, typically associated with the private sphere. Post-colonial theorists link human rights to imperialism; they observe that the International Bill of Rights was developed outside any concern for the inequities arising from the colonial situation and that the rise of human rights in political discourse has not signalled an end to inequality.

These critiques encompass variants which dismiss the concept of human rights altogether. When they are conceptual, the critiques tend to hold the human rights logic to be defective in at least four respects. First, the human rights logic is said to present the concept as universal, while the claim that human rights are relevant to all human beings across time and space is not credible in the face of human history. Second, the logic is criticized for celebrating the individual to the neglect of solidarity and other social values. Third, the human rights logic is found to be derived from an abstract reasoning about 'man' which is ill-equipped to assess both the reality of political life and the requirements of social justice. Fourth, the human rights logic is denounced for being oblivious to the way it directly participates in sustaining power relationships and thus fails to produce equality.

For some thinkers, there is a very close connection—almost a conflation—between human rights and liberalism, understood as the political philosophy that either holds that government should interfere as little as possible in the lives of its citizens or signifies, more broadly, 'an order in which the state exists to secure the freedom of individuals on a formally egalitarian basis'.[5] For example, Jack Donnelly refuses to say of the USA that they are a liberal society because they do not realize the very high human rights benchmarks he associates with a liberal society.[6] At the opposite end of such a conflation, it is increasingly common for scholars to bemoan the 'hijacking' of human rights by liberalism.[7] This position might suggest that conceptual critiques of human rights necessarily stand opposed to or outside liberalism. However, it is possible to oppose the concept of human rights (as understood under the old orthodoxy) on liberal grounds. A resounding illustration is provided by Jeremy Bentham, a utilitarian firmly belonging to the liberal tradition, who, as we shall see in Section 2, famously qualified human rights as 'nonsense upon stilts'.[8]

2 EARLY CRITIQUES

2.1 THE REALIST CRITIQUE

Considering the old orthodoxy, which viewed human rights as a given, it is not surprising that human rights have typically first been *declared* before being turned into conventional law. This practice can be traced back to the two French Declarations of the Rights of Man and the Citizen of the eighteenth century (French Declarations) and, in the contemporary era, the 1948 Universal Declaration of Human Rights (UDHR) (which was directly inspired by the French Declarations). Why is there this tradition of 'declaring' rights? In contemporary international law it is, of course, important to distinguish between a declaration,

---

[5] In a definition borrowed from Brown, 'Neo-Liberalism and the End of Liberal Democracy' (2003) 7 *Theory & Event* 6.

[6] Donnelly, *Universal Human Rights in Theory and Practice* (Cornell University Press, 1989) 68 and 73.

[7] Eg Douzinas, *Human Rights and Empire: The Political Philosophy of Cosmopolitanism* (Routledge-Cavendish, 2007) 24; Stammers, *Human Rights and Social Movements* (Pluto, 2009).

[8] Bentham, 'Anarchical Fallacies. An Examination of the Declaration of the Rights of the Man and the Citizen Decreed by the Constituent Assembly in France' in Bentham, *Selected Writings on Utilitarianism* (Wordsworth, 2000) 381, 405.

which has no binding force, and a convention, which has binding force for those states that have ratified it. This crucial distinction, however, cannot have been the reason why the French National Assembly entitled the document it adopted in 1789 'Declaration'. The preamble of the Declaration spoke of the need to 'set forth in a solemn declaration, the natural, inalienable, and sacred rights of man'. It purported to have done this 'in the presence and under the auspices of the Supreme Being'. Clearly, the intention was to spell out the belief that human rights were being *declared* rather than created. This idea is also found in the UDHR, albeit more implicitly, in line with the fact that an exact convergence on the foundations of human rights was lacking, in the more plural context of the United Nations (UN). The UDHR laconically refers to a 'faith in fundamental human rights'.[9]

The implications of believing that human rights pre-exist any legislative or social recognition have been helpfully spelled out by Louis Henkin: 'Implied in one's humanity, human rights are inalienable and imprescriptible: they cannot be transferred, forfeited, or waived; they cannot be lost by having been usurped, or by one's failure to exercise or assert them.'[10] This is another way of saying that human rights are 'natural', existing irrespective of social recognition and so discoverable through reason. These assumptions were at the core of the old human rights orthodoxy. But they have not been without their detractors. Among these is what is referred to here as the realist critique of human rights, which stresses the man-made origin of human rights and argues that they are not obvious at all.

For present purposes, Jeremy Bentham, popularly known as the father of utilitarianism, can be qualified as a realist. His virulent critique of the 1789 French Declaration argued:

> [F]rom *real* laws come real rights; but from *imaginary* laws, from laws of nature, fancied by poets, rhetoricians, and dealers in moral and intellectual poisons, come *imaginary* rights, a bastard brood of monsters, 'gorgons and chimeras dire'[11]

For Bentham, it was clear that the French Declaration was 'nonsense upon stilts' and the rights it declared imaginary. Not only did these rights not exist, but making people believe they existed was dangerous, for their inevitable disrespect would lead to discontent, and possibly in turn, insurrection. Bentham's critique was published under the title 'Anarchical Fallacies', which said it all. The Declaration was *conceptually* fallacious—a nonsensical flow of words amounting to nothing more than a bundle of contradictions. It also presented a *practical* problem as the promise of rights that could not be respected in practice invited a perpetual overthrowing of political institutions. As far as Bentham was concerned, the rights proclaimed in the Declaration were a 'mere effusion of imbecility'.[12] For him, the way to deal with abusive government was to induce the legislator to change the law, not to call for its abandonment in the name of non-existent natural rights.

Bentham argued that the rights of the French Declaration, if taken literally, meant nothing. For example, he noted that, contrary to what the Declaration stated, human beings are obviously not born equal. In Bentham's opinion, the drafters of the Declaration were constantly oscillating between a utopian world, where all men would be equal, and the real world, where they clearly were not. This led them to use ambiguous wording, for example, 'can' instead of 'ought' (as in 'every man can do this' instead of 'every man ought to be able to do this').[13] If the rights of the Declaration were not to be taken literally, then they still meant nothing as they would need to be given limits. For example, Article 10 guaranteed freedom of expression and religion. However, it accepted exceptions governed by public order considerations. Bentham derided: 'Disturb the public order?—what does that mean?

---

[9] Preambular para 5.   [10] Henkin, *The Age of Rights* (Columbia University Press, 1990) 2.
[11] Henkin, n 10, 458 (original emphases).   [12] Henkin, n 10, 441.   [13] Henkin, n 10, 402 and 393.

Louis XIV need not have hesitated about receiving an article thus worded into his code.'[14] Of liberty, he said:

> Suppose a declaration to this effect—no man's liberty shall be abridged in any point. This, it is evident, would be an useless extravagance, which must be contradicted by every law that came to be made. Suppose it to say—no man's liberty shall be abridged, but in such points as it shall be abridged in, by the law. This, we see, is saying nothing: it leaves the law just as free and unfettered as it found it.[15]

Giving or recognizing supposedly 'natural', 'superior', 'inalienable', 'fundamental' rights which can then be defeated through legislation amounts to *nothing*. Bentham concluded: 'Look to the letter, you find nonsense—look beyond the letter, you find nothing.'[16]

Bentham's critique was very much directed at the old human rights orthodoxy, which regarded human rights as natural—a given. For a realist critique of human rights in their new, increasingly dominant conception—as agreed upon through a deliberative process—one can turn to International Relations (IR). IR realism holds the state as the key actor on the international scene, and one which always follows its own interests.[17] According to one of its long dominant variants, the state does whatever is required to ensure its own survival and, what is more, acts morally when it does as, in this pursuit, it should not be guided by private morality. The idea that political ethics should be brought into line with private ethics is thought 'not only ill-advised but also irresponsible... not only mistaken intellectually but also fundamentally wrong morally'.[18] In this perspective, given the ill-advisability of cooperation with other states that by definition also follow their own interests and cannot be trusted, *raison d'état* (literally, reason of state, an idea linked to realpolitik) is a fundamental concept and state sovereignty a chief concern. Human rights have no real place.

Not all IR realist scholars are of the persuasion described here. For some, that states are unwilling to act in ways which restrict their power is an empirical fact, but not a moral precept. Starting from the observation that states cling to power as much and as long as they can, these scholars argue that if states act in apparently immoral ways, it is because it is in their interests to do so, not because they (should) follow a public morality different from the one governing relations between individuals. Realism, in this variant, is not a moral vision but an inescapable fact. These realists are wary of the idea that states might ever truly approach a document such as the UDHR as 'a common standard of achievement for all peoples and all nations'—whatever its preamble asserts. They would be quick to point out how human rights law is yet another sphere where states play their power games, as evidenced by reservation clauses and derogations which let them off the hook or the double standards they apply.[19] At best, then, human rights provide protection akin to a sandbag, holding back the bulk of the water/government's arbitrariness and oppression—for as long as the tide/repressive impulse is not too strong.

Like all 'isms', realism can mean many things. What the realisms of Bentham and IR have in common is that, taking a realistic look at the world, they reject the idea that human rights could somehow exist 'above' or 'aside from' the state. For them, human rights belong to the imagination of utopian dreamers. In Bentham's case, this is because the French Declaration did not provide a positive legal framework which made the declared rights real. In the case of today's realists, it is because they do not believe that states wish to

---

[14] Henkin, n 10, 435.   [15] Henkin, n 10, 387.   [16] Henkin, n 10, 397.
[17] Jackson and Sørensen, *Introduction to International Relations* (OUP, 1999) 96.
[18] Jackson and Sørensen, n 17, 77.
[19] Eg Mertus, *Bait and Switch: Human Rights and US Foreign Policy* (Routledge, 2004).

submit to either the spirit or the letter of the human rights declarations and conventions that are supposedly now guiding the international community.

2.2 THE UTILITARIAN CRITIQUE

Bentham, a towering figure of the utilitarian movement, dismissed the predecessor of human rights (the rights of man) as 'nonsense upon stilts'. Does this mean that utilitarianism is irretrievably opposed to human rights? Yes and no. On the one hand, the logic of utilitarianism is such that it cannot accept the idea of absolute and inalienable rights, which at first sight seems central to human rights orthodoxy—at least in its old version. On the other hand, individual rights being obviously conducive to the happiness of a great number of individuals, utilitarianism can act as a strident defender of human rights. Appreciating why these two apparently contradictory positions coexist requires understanding the nature of both utilitarianism and human rights orthodoxy.

Utilitarianism is the ethical philosophy that posits that an action must be judged morally by reference to the welfare (utility) it produces. It holds that the good act is the one that maximizes happiness. Such a philosophy is consequentialist: it judges actions by reference to their consequences. Before deciding on a course of action, utilitarianism demands that the action's likely effects on various interests be considered and weighed. In other words, it does not believe in *a priori* judgments as to the value of some good (in the sense of an interest worthy of protection) over other goods.

The trade-offs that utilitarianism never rules out have led its detractors to intimate that it allows the individual to be sacrificed to the collective interest. One healthy person, so the argument goes, could be killed under utilitarianism for the benefit of a number of people who depend for their survival on the transplant of various organs. In a similar vein, an innocent could be found guilty in order to defuse a riotous situation when his condemnation would appear to facilitate a return to peace and order. These kinds of scenarios, however, are more often than not put forward by thinkers who oppose utilitarianism. Self-declared utilitarians observe that they are unlikely to present themselves in the clear-cut form imagined by their detractors.[20] Utilitarians are quick to note that repeated sacrifices of individuals would immediately generate a substantial decrease in general happiness because of the sense of insecurity it would foster across the population.

Many utilitarians are thus wary of the concept of individual sacrifice for the collective good which utilitarianism supposedly supports. Nonetheless, it remains that utilitarianism does not accept the idea that some rights are absolute and inalienable. By contrast, this idea is at the core of (the old) human rights orthodoxy. To understand the crucial difference between these two positions, one must understand what makes a right absolute.

For a right to be absolute, the corresponding duty to which it gives rise must be expressed in a negative form. Let us take the example of the right to be free from torture, one of the few rights to be considered absolute in human rights orthodoxy. To respect this right, it might be thought that governments must do one thing and one thing only: *refrain from* inflicting torture. Clearly, this is a negative duty: that of *not acting* in a certain way. If this reasoning is followed, there is only one way to respect the right not to be tortured; hence its infringement is easy to establish (at least in principle). Now, rights which are not absolute are relative. Their respect is relative to many things; it is never easy, in the sense of clear-cut, to establish when they are, in fact, respected. A standard example of relative

---

[20] Häyri, *Liberal Utilitarianism and Applied Ethics* (Routledge, 1994) 80.

rights is economic and social rights. Their respect requires the state to provide education, healthcare, and so on, that is, *to act* in a certain way. Endless discussions can be had as to whether a state has done enough to fulfil its positive obligations in that respect. A positive obligation is by nature unclear, in the sense of never strictly defined.

Logically, only a negative obligation can give rise to an absolute right. In turn, thinking in these terms entails categorical reasoning. To return to the example of the prohibition of torture, human rights orthodoxy considers torture to be intrinsically wrong: it considers that torture is and always will be wrong, whatever the circumstances. This is based on deontological philosophy, which holds that some things have an intrinsic, categorical, non-consequential value.[21]

By contrast, utilitarianism is a consequentialist theory which evaluates the morality of an action by reference to its consequences. Utilitarianism does not ask, 'Is this wrong?' but, 'Is this *causing* wrong?' It does not hold anything to have intrinsic value as such. A utilitarian cannot rule out, once and for all, the possibility that one day utility will require a right to be set aside in order to further the collective good. This is true in particular of the right to be free from torture, even though it is difficult to imagine *sound* utilitarian reasoning justifying it easily. It is worth stressing in this respect that the would-be convincing scenario of the ticking bomb is not very convincing at all: the police would know everything, including who has the vital information, except for the single element of where the bomb is—how likely is this? Even if this unlikely scenario were to happen in practice, there would still be strong utilitarian arguments against the use of torture, including the corrupting effect of having to train officials to inflict it.[22] Having said this, it remains that the consequential logic of utilitarianism makes it ill-fitted to defend human rights in all cases. Does this mean that there is an unbridgeable divide between utilitarianism and human rights orthodoxy?

In many ways, utilitarianism and human rights have in practice always been largely compatible. A long tradition within utilitarianism, going back to John Stuart Mill, has never stopped to defend human rights for being conducive to the common good. Allan Gibbard argues, from a self-avowed utilitarian perspective, that rights contribute to good institutional design.[23] Conversely, starting from the other end of the relationship, the human rights orthodoxy has always been replete with utilitarian considerations, as the numerous possible limitations of human rights in the name of public considerations (such as public order, health, or morality) and the concept of proportionality (requiring different interests to be balanced), central to human rights law, readily demonstrate.[24] More generally, the old human rights orthodoxy has had to give way: while its emphasis on clear-cut negative rights should have generated a relatively well-delimited list of 'core' rights,[25] what has happened instead is a continual identification of 'new' rights as well as a recognition that positive obligations attach to *all* rights—including the right to be free from torture, which also entails action by the state, such as appropriate training of the police force, for its full implementation.[26]

The compatibility between human rights and utilitarianism is arguably deepening today as human rights orthodoxy increasingly slides from 'natural' logic into 'deliberative' mode. The latter tends to regard human rights as guiding principles of good

---

[21] See Chapter 2.   [22] Brecher, *Torture and the Ticking Bomb* (Blackwell, 2007) ch 2.

[23] Gibbard, 'Utilitarianism and Human Rights' in Paul, Miller Jr, and Paul (eds), *Human Rights* (Blackwell, 1984) 92.   [24] See Chapter 5.

[25] Dembour, *Who Believes in Human Rights? Reflections on the European Convention* (CUP, 2006) 87. See also Chapter 7.   [26] See Chapter 9.

governance (rather than firm entitlements). It conceives of human rights as being agreed upon, the result of a consensus most evident in the development of international human rights law, rather than constituted as a universal given that exists outside social recognition. The 'deliberative' orientation of the new orthodoxy makes it possible for some thinkers to refer explicitly to utilitarian considerations (admittedly alongside other ones) in order to justify human rights.[27] This would have been unthinkable under the old orthodoxy. The divide between utilitarianism and human rights is ceasing to be the great chasm once intimated both by 'the father of utilitarianism' (as Bentham came to be known) and by human rights defenders. Having said this, it remains relatively rare for human rights to be defended today from a perspective which is conspicuously utilitarian in its inspiration.

2.3 THE MARXIST CRITIQUE

For Karl Marx, far from being nonsense, the French Declaration was problematic because it made too much sense in the political order of the so-called 'free state' which had followed the French Revolution but had not succeeded in emancipating man. (Marx did not think much about women.)

Marx's essay 'On the Jewish Question', written at the tender age of 23, was implacable in its critique of the French Declaration of the Rights of Man and the Citizen of 1791. The essay denounced the rights of man as being 'nothing but the rights of the member of civil society, i.e. egoistic man, man separated from other men and the community'.[28] The right to liberty, the young Marx argued, was the right to do anything which does not harm others, that is, the liberty of man 'as an isolated monad...withdrawn into himself'; the right to private property was the right to enjoy and dispose of one's possessions 'arbitrarily, without regard for other men, independently from society, the right of selfishness'. The right to equality represented nothing else but access to liberty as described already; the right to security provided the guarantee of egoism.[29] Marx concluded:

> Thus none of the so-called rights of man goes beyond egoistic man, man as he is in civil society, namely an individual withdrawn behind his private interests and whims and separated from the community. Far from the rights of man conceiving of man as a species-being, species-life itself, society, appears as a framework exterior to individuals.[30]

A question mark has been raised on the value to be assigned to Marx's initial writings in Marxist theory. Marx's early work grappled with philosophy and was explicitly interested in discussing the nature of man; his mature work was devoted to the 'scientific' study of material conditions, leading him to identify the 'laws of motion' of capitalism and to elaborate a theory of history as progress through stages conditioned by society's attained level of productivity and the requirements of increase. While Louis Althusser forcefully rejected the relevance of Marx's 'pre-scientific' writings, Erich Fromm relied on these early works to develop a humanist interpretation of Marxism and denounce the claims of 'scientific Marxism', especially as propounded in the Soviet Union.

If the absence of a break in Marx's works is accepted, 'On the Jewish Question' appears recognizably Marxian in its denunciation of human alienation. The essay cautions that man is not yet free in the free state.[31] While it recognizes that political emancipation

---

[27] Nickel, *Making Sense of Human Rights* (Blackwell, 2007) 58–61.
[28] 'On the Jewish Question', reproduced in McLellan, *Karl Marx: Selected Writings* (OUP, 2000) 46, 60.
[29] 'On the Jewish Question', n 28, 46, 60.   [30] 'On the Jewish Question', n 28, 61.
[31] 'On the Jewish Question', n 28, 51.

may have been achieved, it argues that this falls short of human emancipation. The rights granted in the political state newly created in France supposedly endow man with freedom; but, in fact, they alienate him. Why? Because they split the 'citizen' from the 'bourgeois' in the individual. The 'citizen' part of man corresponds to the public self and belongs to the political state; the 'bourgeois' part corresponds to the private self and belongs to civil society.[32] In the political state, Marx argues, man is condemned to lead a double life. This is the more serious since the citizen (the part where man regards himself as a communal being) is put at the service of the bourgeois (the part where man acts as a private individual and leads an egoistic life). Man is thus alienated from his true self which is to be a species-being where the individual interest corresponds to everyone else's interest.

'On the Jewish Question' can also be read in the light of the concept of ideology which Marx developed fully in his later work. As an ideology, the rights declared in France announce and guarantee man's liberty. However, what they really do is to mask and sustain the inequality and oppression characteristic of capitalist society. Applying this reading to the contemporary era, the anthropologist Talal Asad urges us to 'examine critically the assumption that…human rights always lead in an emancipatory direction, that they enable subjects to move beyond controlling power into the realm of freedom.'[33] In Asad's view, the language of human rights 'articulates inequalities in social life.'[34] It is therefore doubtful that the human rights project could bring about 'practical equality and an end to all suffering.'[35]

That real emancipation cannot be expected through human rights is an idea that was explicitly stated in 'On the Jewish Question'. Marx believed that true emancipation would come through the establishment of a society where man would be able to 'take the abstract citizen back into himself and…become a species-being', recognizing his own forces as social forces.[36] Under communism, he believed, the institutions of state, law, and property would have withered away. The political state—and its declaration of the rights of man and citizen—represented a necessary stage in the progression towards communism. But it was only a step. In Marx's words: 'Political emancipation is of course a great progress. Although it is not the final form of human emancipation in general, it is nevertheless the final form of human emancipation inside the present world order.'[37]

History has shown that Marx's belief in the establishment of a communist society true to his words was ridiculously naive. Not surprisingly perhaps given the utopian character of his project, Marx failed to indicate anywhere in his work how the transformation from bourgeois man to species-being would be achieved. He did mention 'a political transition period in which the state [could] be nothing but the revolutionary dictatorship of the proletariat',[38] but without working out its details. Taken as a political programme, Marx's writings were at best hollow, at worst dangerous. Had they had little impact, this would not have mattered much. But Marx, who died in 1883, inspired revolutions and dictatorships throughout the world, starting in 1917 in what became the Soviet Union. The most appalling acts were committed in the twentieth century in the name of Marxism and communism. It is probably disingenuous to criticize a thinker for ideas that have been used in a way that he could not have imagined and to hold him partly, if unwillingly, responsible

---

[32] 'On the Jewish Question', n 28, 53; see also 57.

[33] Asad, 'What Do Human Rights Do? An Anthropological Enquiry' (2000) 27 *Theory and Event* 40.

[34] Asad, n 33, 43.   [35] Asad, n 33, 57.   [36] n 28, 64.   [37] n 28, 54.

[38] Marx, 'Critique of the Gotha Programme' reproduced in McLellan, n 28, 610, 611.

for the Stalinist gulag. But many did exactly that. At the same time, during the Cold War, others continued to profess their faith in Marxism, refusing to acknowledge the terror which Marxist ideas, taken to a logical extreme, could inspire.

There were exceptions. For example, the British Marxist historian EP Thompson did not end *Whigs and Hunters*, his study of the eighteenth-century 'Black Act',[39] with a conventional Marxian conclusion. This would have been that 'law is an instrument of brute force by which the ruling class consolidates and reinforces its hegemony'.[40] In an afterword which made him controversial in Marxist circles, Thompson stated instead that the rule of law is an 'unqualified human good'.[41] This qualification was spurred by his disturbing experience of the Soviet regime which had led him to resign his membership of the Communist Party in 1956. Thompson wanted to stress the 'very large difference... between arbitrary extra-legal power and the rule of law [which] may disguise the true realities of power, but, at the same time,... may curb that power and check its intrusions'.[42] He declared the rule of law—to which he would likely have readily associated human rights law—'a cultural achievement of universal significance'.[43] This attracted the ire of many fellow Marxist thinkers.

It could be asked, 'Who were/are the true Marxists?' This question is controversial, with one person often accusing another of abusing Marxism. What is not disputed, however, is that the way Marx analysed power relationships and examined how things are not as they seem left a mark on all the social sciences. This is clear, in particular, in respect of the human rights critiques reviewed in Section 3.

3 MORE RECENT CRITIQUES

3.1 THE CULTURAL RELATIVIST OR PARTICULARIST CRITIQUE

The universal versus cultural relativist debate can be said to have been spurred by discussions generated by the UDHR. In 1947, the year before the UDHR was adopted, the American Anthropological Association (AAA) addressed a 'Statement on Human Rights' to the UN Commission on Human Rights, which was drafting the Universal Declaration.[44] The Statement asked: 'How can the proposed Declaration be applicable to all human beings, and not be a statement of rights conceived only in terms of the values prevalent in the countries of Western Europe and America?'[45] It argued for the need to seek respect for the individual both as individual and as member of 'his' society (at a time when feminist concerns were still very much out of public consciousness). Bearing in mind the cultural destruction heralded by colonialism, imperialism, and the very establishment of the USA (not least in respect of native Americans), it called for 'respect for the cultures of differing human groups'.

The AAA Statement was right in arguing that the formulation of human rights cannot but derive from a particular culture. The UDHR is replete with concepts, such as legal personality (Article 6), nationality (Article 15), and protection against unemployment (Article 23), which are simply not known to most human societies. The concept of human

---

[39] Thompson, *Whigs and Hunters: The Origins of the Black Act* (Allen Lane, 1975).
[40] Cole, '"An Unqualified Human Good": EP Thompson and the Rule of Law' (2001) 28 *J Law & Soc* 177, 181.
[41] Thompson, n 39, 266.   [42] Thompson, n 39, 265.   [43] Thompson, n 39, 265.
[44] See 'Statement on Human Rights' (1947) 49 *American Anthropologist* 539.
[45] 'Statement on Human Rights', n 44.

rights itself is not incontrovertible in humankind's repertoire. If the Statement rightly cautioned that no declaration could ever manage to identify universal human rights valid for all humankind across time and space, it was nonetheless problematic in other respects. It treated culture as a static and homogeneous 'thing' rather than the dynamic and contested process that anthropologists have now demonstrated culture always is.[46] Moreover, it lent itself to be taken to call for the respect of any cultural trait, simply because of its cultural nature; which is ethically unacceptable. In other words, the Statement bore the mark of cultural relativism, the core tenet of US anthropology in the 1920s and 1930s which, with time, increasingly came to appear untenable.

But what do we mean by 'cultural relativism'? The theory is founded on the double observation that moral systems are embedded in culture and that different cultures produce different moralities. However, to become an 'ism', ethical inferences must be derived from these (assuredly sound) empirical observations. What are these inferences? According to its detractors, cultural relativism would dictate tolerance of any culturally embedded moral system on earth, perhaps even any morality. However, whether self-declared cultural relativists hold this position is doubtful.[47]

Recognizing that different societies hold different values need not logically lead to the conclusion that all these different values and practices must be tolerated. The observation that cultures produce different moral norms does not say anything about the respective value of these norms.[48] Despite this, and no doubt also due to excessive formulations by its proponents, cultural relativism came to be denigrated for demanding that the intolerable be tolerated. The doctrine is even said to have been an embarrassment to anthropologists, because of the indifference and/or inaction which it advocated.[49] It has also been criticized for lending itself to abuse, allowing those in power to make spurious or disingenuous cultural arguments in pursuit of their own political ends.[50] Undoubtedly, cultural relativism, like other theories, has been abused, and the last point must indeed be conceded. This, however, should not detract from appreciating what the doctrine offers.

In the words of anthropologist Elvin Hatch, the 'good side' of relativism is that it highlights the difficulty of 'establishing reasonable and general grounds for making moral judgments about the actions of others' and the 'strong tendency among the more powerful peoples of the world to use their own standards, or standards favourable to them, in their relations with others'.[51] Put more simply, the doctrine acts as a counterpart to the arrogance and abusive effect of universalism. This is vital, given the imperialism which has accompanied and still accompanies human rights enunciation and practice.

The universality of human rights is *not* a fact. At best, human rights universal*ism* is a theory. It is a worthwhile project, directed at discussing, agreeing upon, and practising principles of governance which should benefit all individuals equally, but which also has a dark side which it would be either disingenuous or naive not to recognize. This dark side includes the inherent danger not to respect the ways of others, if not an active collusion

---

[46] Cowan, Dembour, and Wilson (eds), *Culture and Rights: Anthropological Perspectives* (CUP, 2001).

[47] Eg Herskovits, *Cultural Relativism: Perspectives in Cultural Pluralism* (Random House, 1972) 64.

[48] Renteln, 'Relativism and the Search for Human Rights' (1988) 90 *American Anthropologist* 56, 64.

[49] Engle, 'From Skepticism to Embrace: Human Rights and the American Anthropological Association from 1947–1999' (2001) 23 *HRQ* 536. For a more nuanced view, see Goodale, *Surrendering to Utopia: An Anthropology of Human Rights* (Stanford University Press, 2009) ch 2.

[50] Pollis, 'Cultural Relativism Revisited: Through a State Prism' (1996) 18 *HRQ* 316.

[51] Hatch, 'The Good Side of Relativism' (1997) 53 *J Anthropological Research* 371, 372.

in their destruction. Universalists too often assume that they are on firm ground in making judgments about others. They can easily end up imposing their ways on others for no other reason than sheer dominant position, without even realizing it, so full are they of their good intentions. By contrast, instead of saying 'we know best' or 'we know', relativism poses the question, 'What do we know?'

Universalism has a good side—the elaboration of minimal common standards—but it also has a bad side—arrogance. Similarly, relativism has a good side—respect for different ways—but it also has a bad side—inaction or indifference. Let us think about the implications of this conceptual matrix with a concrete example. In 1994, an 18-year-old US citizen was sentenced in Singapore to six lashes for spray-painting parked cars.[52] Let us first judge the caning abhorrent, assaulting the dignity of the young man. If so, universalism should be applauded for making it possible to condemn the punishment, while relativism would show only its bad side by calling for inaction when resistance is needed. Another assessment, however, is to say that the caning is a legitimate element in the disciplinary framework put in place in a society largely different from ours. If so, universalism would be showing its bad side by condemning the practice while it is relativism which should be welcome for letting the punishment be. What some regard as an expression of the good side of relativism is *always* regarded by others as an expression of its bad side, and the same is true of universalism (see Table 3.1). Applying the conceptual matrix to concrete situations and deciding which position is which is rarely easy; nor is it uncontroversial.

Wishing the controversy away will not do. It arises *every time* common standards are predicated, whatever the limits of the constituency—the whole world, a regional system, a nation, a village. Establishing common standards is never completely unproblematic because minimal common standards are never entirely common. However small the relevant constituency, it always stands in the way of more peculiar, or particular, norms.

Universalism cannot exist independently of its opposite, most aptly named 'particularism'. (Etymologically, what is not universal is special, specific, or particular; what is not relative is absolute. Using the word 'particularism' presents the further advantage of avoiding both the possibly reifying tone of the reference to 'culture' and the embarrassment of the faint moral position commonly associated with 'cultural relativism'.) It is in opposition to practices that appear abhorrent that universal norms are being set, and it is by reference to local particularities that these universal norms are implemented. The reverse is true. Particularism does not exist independently of universalism. As moral beings concerned with ethics, we are not just beings of culture but respond to what could be termed the call of universalism. This is to say that we are always somewhere between the ideal represented by universalism (which should be recognized as an ideal) and the reality of our being embedded in culture (which is inescapable). We are bound to oscillate between the two positions in a pendulum-like motion.[53]

Table 3.1 The universalism vs relativism matrix

	Universalism	Relativism
Good side	Respect for common standards (*caning is abhorrent*)	Respect for difference (*caning is OK*)
Bad side	Arrogance (*caning is abhorrent*)	Indifference (*caning is OK*)

[52] Hubbard, 'Singapore shrugs off uproar over "barbaric" flogging', *The Independent* 2 April 1994.
[53] Dembour, 'Following the Movement of the Pendulum: Between Universalism and Relativism' in Cowan *et al.*, n 46, 56.

Contrary to a commonly held assumption, the debate between universalism and particularism is not primarily concerned with the reaction by the rest of the world to something which originated in the West. Its essence is to capture the difficult and always controversial accommodation of unity and diversity in mankind. While the debate was obviously pertinent under the old orthodoxy where human rights were conceived as a given, it remains relevant under the new orthodoxy. The reason why the debate cannot be put to rest once and for all is that we do not have a choice between being either universalists or particularists: we must be both at the same time. Similarly, human rights law must accommodate both positions—whether it does so explicitly or not. (This contributes to an explanation of, for example, the development of the doctrine of the margin of appreciation in the European Convention system whereby the European Court of Human Rights often asserts that local authorities are in principle in a better position than an international court to assess local requirements.) Properly understood, the particularist critique is less a critique than a corrective to the ever-possible excesses of universalism. These excesses remain a danger under the new human rights orthodoxy, for the human rights values supposedly agreed upon at any given level (international, regional, or national) rarely derive from a consensus as broad as believed by those who unreservedly declare their commitment to them.

3.2 THE FEMINIST CRITIQUE

In 1789, the first article of the French Declaration proudly stated: 'Men are born and remain free and equal in rights.' One year later, Olympe de Gouges asserted in a 'Declaration of the Rights of Woman', of her own making: 'Women are born free and remain equal to men in rights.'[54] This stance did not go down well. On 3 November 1793, de Gouges was guillotined—like a man—for having forgotten the virtues of her sex and inappropriately sought to become a statesman. A feminist critique of human rights was then largely silenced, but it has now become vigorous. Can the argument that human rights remain predominantly male in their conception and implementation be dismissed in an age when women, especially in the West, have successfully fought for the rights to vote, be educated, manage their property, open a bank account, exercise a profession, keep their nationality upon marriage with a foreign man, claim equal pay for equal work, and so on? The answer is a resounding no. The affirmation in law of women's entitlement to equal rights is assuredly a momentous achievement. While it must be celebrated, it should not lead to complacency. Feminist analyses demonstrate human rights law to have been and continue to be male-oriented.

Before turning to these analyses, it is worth pondering what feminism is. As noted in Section 2.1, virtually all 'isms' have more than one variant. This is certainly the case with feminism, of which the variants are so pronounced that for someone to declare herself— and possibly, though more rarely, himself—a feminist does not say much about her position. One can nonetheless tentatively speak of feminism in the singular. Janet Halley has identified its components as follows:

> First, to be feminism, a position must make a distinction between *m* and *f*. Different feminisms do this differently: some see men and women; some see male and female; some see masculine and feminine... And secondly, to be a feminism..., a position must posit some

[54] De Gouges's Declaration is reproduced in Ishay (ed), *The Human Rights Reader: Major Political Writings, Essays, Speeches and Documents. From the Bible to the Present* (Routledge, 1997) 140–7. My translation of Art 1 is slightly different from that of Ishay, who offers: 'Woman is born free and lives equal to man in her rights.'

kind of subordination as between m and f, in which f is the disadvantaged or subordinated element. At this point feminism is both descriptive and normative... Feminism is feminism because, as between m and f, it carries a brief for f.[55]

Feminism is a way of looking at the world, seeing it as organized along gendered lines which benefit men, and trying to change it so that women are empowered. In the human rights field, feminist critique has taken a long time to be expressed—or, perhaps more accurately, to be heard. For two centuries, the vibrant and clear message sent by Olympe de Gouges in her Declaration of 1790 remained dormant in human rights scholarship. In the last 30 years, however, feminist critiques of human rights have become inescapable. In 1989, a working bibliography on women's international human rights contained a mere 142 publications and a list of 15 international governmental and NGOs and other sources of information; by 2003, it included approximately 700 articles and 246 links to websites.[56] No doubt the increase has continued to be exponential.

The feminist critique to which human rights have increasingly been subjected does not mean that an agreement has emerged as to what constitutes, and what should be done in respect of, a human rights situation analysed as problematic for women. This is because there are many different ways of being a feminist. Following an admittedly limited, but nonetheless useful, classification followed in various synthesizing works, this section first discusses the liberal, cultural, and radical strands of feminism before highlighting more recent (post-modern) trends.

At the core of the *liberal* feminist strand is the assumption that women are equal to men, with the consequence that women must not in principle be excluded from the rights enjoyed by men—and vice versa. In other words, liberal feminism asks for liberalism to be true to its fundamental intuition that everyone must have their rights guaranteed. Laws that explicitly guarantee, or implicitly endorse, the principle of sex and gender equality constitute its great achievement. Today, this principle is for the most part accepted. However, assessing what it requires in the practice of actual rights is riddled with difficulties. The implementation of a feminist liberal agenda is far from a straightforward matter, the more so since liberal feminism is concerned not simply with the formal allocation of rights but also with the under-representation of women in politically and socially significant positions, as well as their over-representation among the poor.

'But why should a woman want to be treated like a man?', asks a second strand of feminism. In 1982, the book *In a Different Voice* contrasted the logical, abstract, deductive reasoning favoured by boys to the emotional, concrete, and contextual reasoning favoured by girls.[57] Its author, the social psychologist Carol Gilligan, concluded that the masculine model of an 'ethic of rights' is not universal and called for the feminine model of an 'ethic of care' to be valued. Her book established the feminist strand generally known as *cultural* feminism, in recognition of the fact that men and women develop different patterns of thinking and acting due to being educated into different social roles which are culturally evolved. This strand of feminism has clear implications for human rights. As with other areas of law, human rights law tends to look at individuals as individuals, to decontextualize situations, and to be confrontational; it accordingly has—so the cultural feminist argument goes—nothing or little to offer to women who are 'naturally'/'culturally' inclined to think their problems through contextually, for example by assessing the implications of

---

[55] Halley, 'Take a Break from Feminism?' in Knop (ed), *Gender and Human Rights* (OUP, 2004) 57, 61.

[56] Knop, 'Introduction' in Knop (ed), *Gender and Human Rights* (OUP, 2004), 1.

[57] Gilligan, *In a Different Voice: Psychologist Theory and Women's Development* (Harvard University Press, 1982).

any possible solution for the people for whom they care (including, but not only, their children). Human rights law should either be rejected, or at the very least transformed, in order to accommodate the female way of thinking and acting.[58]

For the leading *radical* feminist Catharine MacKinnon, however, getting women to think of themselves as carers is, in itself, a male trick. The problem is not whether women are equal or different to men; the problem is that men subordinate women. The key issue is women's oppression, whereby men reduce women to their sexuality and use them as sexual objects. In MacKinnon's phrase, 'Man fucks woman: subject, verb, object.'[59] The aim of the radical feminist movement, led in law by MacKinnon, is therefore the empowerment of women—even those who are not aware of the continual sexual oppression to which men subject them because of 'false consciousness'. MacKinnon asks that women become women on their own terms: feminism 'unmodified'. One can again immediately see the implications of this strand of feminism for our subject. Far from being neutral, human rights theory and law are on the whole made by men for men. They do not adequately address women's concerns, such as sexual violence in the home, and rely on concepts, such as the public–private dichotomy, which tend to perpetuate men's sexual subordination of women.

With the *post-modern* turn of the late 1980s and early 1990s in the social sciences, the failure by the feminist strands discussed above to acknowledge that the situation of one woman was not that of another became glaringly obvious: clearly, no woman could speak for all women.[60] Post-modern feminists deconstructed the categories of 'woman' and 'gender'. Listening to the 'Other', they explored rather than explained. As meta-narratives were distrusted, myths debunked, basic concepts questioned, post-modern feminism did not produce a definite political agenda. Its resistance to claims of universal truths was critiqued for being relativist. On the positive side, however, its insights generated new awareness, including the obvious fact that various factors of marginality intersect. Put in simple terms, the situation and experiences of a white middle-class woman are hardly comparable to those of a black poor woman; other factors, such as sexual orientation, nationality, disability, and so on, come to play a role, too. In the wake of intersectionality, current directions in feminist critiques of human rights—sometimes called 'black' or 'Third World'—are at the forefront of arguing for 'the transformative potential of a feminist human rights praxis' that embraces collective justice.[61]

The theoretical framework presented here is simplistic. Feminist scholars are not necessarily encompassed by it nor do they all fit neatly within the reviewed categories. Nonetheless, this section should have indicated that there are many ways in which feminists will wish to challenge the human rights orthodoxy, both in its old and new guises.

3.3 THE POST-COLONIAL CRITIQUE

It is often remarked that it was the atrocities of the Second World War that brought into being the International Human Rights Bill. Some would be ready to thank, admittedly not

[58] Eg Hardwig, 'Should Women Think in Terms of Rights?' (1984) 94 *Ethics* 441.

[59] MacKinnon, *Feminism Unmodified: Discourses on Life and Law* (Harvard University Press, 1987) 71. See also her *Toward a Feminist Theory of the State* (Harvard University Press, 1989).

[60] Eg Mohanty, 'Under Western Eyes: Feminist Scholarship and Colonial Discourses' (1988) 30 *Feminist Review* 61.

[61] Collins, Falcón, Lodhia, and Talcott, 'New Directions in Feminism and Human Rights: An Introduction' (2010) 12 *International Feminist Journal of Politics* 298. Thanks are due to Helen Dancer for a most enlightening discussion on feminist critiques of human rights that directed me to this article.

without irony, Hitler and Stalin for this gift.[62] Others bitterly note that it took the suffering of whites to force the powers that be into action; by comparison, slavery and colonialism left the world indifferent.[63] The post-colonial critique teases out the implications of this observation. At its core is the argument that there were, and continue to be, direct connections between the Enlightenment universalizing project and the history of European and Western conquest. A mild post-colonial critique of human rights shows human rights, as a child of the Enlightenment, not to have been completely immune to the colonial logic which long governed the world. Deeper critiques go further than this and argue that human rights are, to this day, irretrievably entrenched in a colonial logic.

The term 'post-colonial' has been used in many different ways. It emerged first to denote the condition that succeeded the formal passing of colonial rule, but soon came to denote a variety of theoretical perspectives. The three towering figures of post-colonialism in its theoretical form are commonly recognized to be the late Edward Said, Gayatri Spivak, and Homi Bhabha, three scholars of southern origin who have pursued an academic career in the West and grappled with the question of how the post-colonial subject can understand and overcome the condition of having been born into the abjection of colonialism. Said forever changed the way we look at representation with the publication in 1978 of *Orientalism*: after this book, the way we (academics, journalists, novelists, film makers, and common people) represent (study, report, discuss, portray, and talk about) the 'Other' could never again appear as a neutral exercise.[64] Spivak asked: 'Can the Subaltern Speak?', directly pointing at the mutedness suffered by those who are not in a position to speak or be heard.[65] More optimistically, Bhabha's development of the concept of 'hybridity' (meaning mixture) seems to promise the possibility of finding a space where we shall be able to speak of Ourselves and Others.[66]

Post-colonialism is many different things. What these things have in common is a commitment 'to critique, expose, deconstruct, counter and (in some claims) to transcend, the cultural and broader ideological legacies and presences of imperialism'.[67] In this phrasing, imperialism is understood as the source of power at the receiving end of which are the colonized, in their physical but also cultural and mental self; colonialism is not understood as pertaining exclusively to the formal colonial era—it existed in the past and continues to exist today under many guises. Post-colonialism is committed to a double task: revealing how the colonial logic imbibes ideas and behaviours, even ones which seemingly have nothing to do with colonialism, and trying to make it possible to hear the experiences of the colonized.

How does this relate to human rights? Listen to Makau Mutua, born 'in a part of colonial Africa that the British had named Kenya'.[68] Mutua recalls how colonialism stripped him of his identity, forcing him to take a Christian name to enter the Church, and then argues:

> There was a basic assumption that Christianity was *superior* to, and better than, any African spirituality. It was presented as a cultural package. What is interesting are the parallels

[62] Sieghart, *The Lawful Rights of Mankind: An Introduction to the International Legal Code of Human Rights* (OUP, 1985) 38.

[63] Mutua, *Human Rights: A Political and Cultural Critique* (University of Pennsylvania Press, 2002) 16.

[64] Said, *Orientalism* (Routledge and Kegan Paul, 1978).

[65] Spivak, 'Can the Subaltern Speak?' in Nelson and Grossberg (eds), *Marxism and the Interpretation of Culture* (University of Illinois Press, 1998).

[66] Bhabha, *The Location of Culture* (Routledge, 1994).

[67] In a formulation borrowed from Sidaway, 'Postcolonial Geographies: An Exploratory Essay' (2000) 24 *Progress in Human Geography* 591, 594.   [68] Mutua, n 63, x.

between Christianity's violent conquest of Africa and the modern human rights crusade. The same methods are at work and similar cultural dispossessions are taking place, without dialogue or conversation. The official human corpus, which issues from European predicates, seeks to supplant all other traditions, while rejecting them. It claims to be the only genius of the good society.[69]

Contrary to its claims of being inclusive, the idea of human rights was always an exclusionary concept—as Marx and feminists such as de Gouges had perceived from the start. Post-colonial perspectives broaden these early critiques by showing how the supposedly universal and all-encompassing liberal tradition in which human rights were developed nurtured stark differences between 'us' and 'them' on the basis of arguments about civilization, cultural backwardness, and racial superiority. The Enlightenment figure of 'the individual', bearer of human rights, suddenly appears to be full of the arrogance of the West, rather than neutral and innocent. Moreover, even if the presumed existence of an essential difference between us and them is no longer referred to in the explicit language used in the formal colonial era, this arrogance is not something of the past but something which carries on, albeit in new forms. The conduct of international relations in the post-Cold War era has been characterized as follows:

'We' of the West are not inefficient, corrupt or dependent on a benevolent international society for our existence. 'We' are the unquestioned upholders of human rights. 'We' attained positions of privilege and authority as a result of our capacities. 'We' of the West are different from 'them'. 'Their' fate could not befall 'us'. 'They' can succeed only if 'they' become more like 'us'.... The North is constituted vis-à-vis the South as modern, efficient, competent. The South is constituted as its lack, its other.... The incapacity to exercise agency in the same manner as the Western 'self' is repeatedly inscribed in the identity of non-Western 'other'.[70]

The 'civilizing mission' was at the very heart of colonialism's justification and remains so in the deployment of new imperial forms. The bringing of law, and rights, and gender equality are some of its key elements. But the overall achievements of human rights are dubious in the face of continual oppression, hurry for wars, rampant poverty, persistent inequalities in trade, lack of attention to the consequences of global warming, and, more generally, rejection of the 'Other'. In this light, trumpeting the rise of human rights as 'one of the great civilising achievements of the modern era'[71] appears problematic. Post-colonialism asks, 'Is there a sense in which human rights have been "civilizing"?'

A post-colonial critique intimates that the human rights logic has all too often led to the annihilation of the 'Other'. This has occurred not only in respect of their identity—for example, through 'assimilation' and the imposition of a Christian name as in Mutua's experience—but also in their physicality—still holding true when, among other current atrocities taking place in the world, wars conducted in the name of human rights entail 'collateral damage' which refer to the death of the 'Other'. There is also a whole spectrum of exclusionary discourse and practices, which the treatment of the deemed illegal or suspected terrorist migrant—barred from entry, detained, deported, subjected to extraordinary rendition, tortured, or simply left to die—exemplifies today.

The crucial question for post-colonial critiques therefore is, 'Can human rights be redeemed?' Most seem unwilling to reject human rights outright. In the words of Ratna

---

[69] Mutua, n 63, xi (original emphasis).

[70] Doty, *Imperial Encounters: The Politics of Representation in North-South Relations* (University of Minnesota Press, 1996) 162.　　　[71] Gearty, *Can Human Rights Survive?* (CUP, 2006) 1.

Kapur: 'We "cannot not want" human rights. Rights are radical tools for those who have never had them. Human rights seems a preferable, though a flawed ideal, to no rights at all'.[72] According to her, 'the centering of excluded subjects, excluded zones and excluded histories can bring the project back to a space of greater optimism and lesser despair'.[73] This, however, is easier said than done. This is to say that the post-colonial critique hits at the new—not to mention the old—human rights orthodoxy very hard. Those ready to see that a colonial logic remains pertinent in understanding today's world would all agree that managing 'to give the human rights body a soul'[74] is a challenge which, if at all successful, will need to be taken up over and over again, rather than being met once and for all.

4 CONCLUSION

Human rights accounts are generally celebratory and triumphalist. This is so much the case that a student can take a course entirely devoted to human rights without ever being introduced to some of the critiques reviewed in this chapter. Admittedly, it has become politically incorrect for human rights tutors not to refer, at least in passing, to the feminist critique. A lack of formal reference to the IR realist critique is not very damaging, given that most students are attuned to its suggestions. This may also largely be true of the utilitarian perspective: students perceive immediately, especially in the context of the war on terror, its relevance (and difficulties). Grasping the implications of the Marxist critique is already more difficult. And is it not irresponsible to relegate the particularist (cultural relativist) critique to something worthy of discussion only if time allows, which it apparently does not (in a manifestation of what I have called elsewhere 'the footnote 10 phenomenon')?[75] As for the post-colonial critique, its neglect is even more staggering: this critique is hardly mentioned in human rights courses, leaving not only the 'Other' but also those in the privileged world moved by the idea of a social justice project more disempowered than if they had been made aware of the critique.

Such silences are unfortunate because all the critiques reviewed in this chapter (as well as others) are worth pondering. They each make important points. Some critiques are more profound than others that can be, and indeed have already been, absorbed in human rights theory. Bentham's objection to the rights of man as 'imaginary' falls in the face of the new orthodoxy and the constant definition, re-definition, and implementation of 'real' rights. The utilitarian perspective is capable of being accommodated in the new orthodoxy—as has already started to happen.[76] In a different mode, this is also the case of the particularist (cultural relativist) critique, which this chapter has argued is in need of being constantly considered by human rights theory and practice, thus hopefully making it possible to keep in check the possible excesses of universalism.

The other human rights critiques that have been reviewed are less easily absorbed. The Marxist critique remains as pertinent as ever, pointing as it does to the exclusion that the human rights discourse continues to encompass. This insight penetrates the critiques that have been developed in the last decades. Radical feminists, some IR realists, and some post-colonial theorists posit that human rights will *never* be able to live up to the promises it makes, so that it is hardly a project worth pursuing.[77] Others, again found across

---

[72] Kapur, 'Human Rights in the 21st Century: Take a Walk on the Dark Side' (2006) 28 *Sydney LR* 665, 682.
[73] Kapur, n 72, 687.   [74] In a paraphrase of Kapur's concluding sentence, in Kapur, n 72, 687.
[75] Dembour, n 53, 72.   [76] Eg Nickel, n 27.
[77] See Brown, '"The Most We Can Hope For...": Human Rights and the Politics of Fatalism' (2004) 103 *South Atlantic Quarterly* 451.

a broad theoretical spectrum that includes realism, feminism, and post-colonialism, are less extreme in their critique and argue that human rights has contradictory effects, which make it an inherently ambiguous project or discourse, sometimes worth pursuing and sometimes not.[78] Still others believe in the intrinsic value of human rights but call for them to be, or to become, true to themselves, which in their view means doing the protest work that brought them into being in the first place.[79] What is nonetheless clear is that recent important grassroots protests such as the Occupy movement against neo-liberalism have not relied much on human rights.

FURTHER READING

BAXI, *The Future of Human Rights* (Oxford University Press, 2006).

BHAMBRA and SHILLIAM (eds), *Silencing Human Rights: Critical Engagements with a Contested Project* (Palgrave, 2009).

BREMS, 'Human Rights: Minimum and Maximum Perspectives', (2009) HRLR 349.

BROWN, '"The Most We Can Hope For..." Human Rights and the Politics of Fatalism' (2004) 103 *South Atlantic Quarterly* 451.

CAMPBELL, *Rights: A Critical Introduction* (Routledge, 2006).

COLLINS, FALCÓN, LODHIA and TALCOTT, 'New Directions in Feminism and Human Rights: An Introduction' (2010) 12 *International Feminist Journal of Politics* 298.

DEMBOUR, *Who Believes in Human Rights? Reflections on the European Convention* (Cambridge University Press, 2006).

DOUZINAS, *Human Rights and Empire: The Political Philosophy of Cosmopolitanism* (Routledge, 2007).

KAPUR, 'Human Rights in the 21st Century: Take a Walk on the Dark Side' (2006) 28 *Sydney LR* 665.

LANGLOIS, 'Human Rights in Crisis? A Critical Polemic Against Polemical Critics' (2012) 11 *J of HR* 558.

MERTUS, *Bait and Switch: Human Rights and US Foreign Policy* (Routledge, 2004).

MOYN, 'The First Historian of Human Rights', (2011) 116 *American Historical Review* 58.

MUTUA, *Human Rights: A Political and Cultural Critique* (University of Pennsylvania Press, 2002).

NASH, *The Cultural Politics of Human Rights: Comparing the US and UK* (Cambridge University Press, 2009).

STAMMERS, *Human rights and Social Movements* (Pluto Press, 2009).

WALDRON (ed), *'Nonsense upon Stilts': Bentham, Burke and Marx on the Rights of Man* (Methuen, 1987).

[78] Eg Cowan, 'Ambiguities of an Emancipatory Discourse: The Making of a Macedonian Minority in Greece' in Cowan *et al.*, n 46, 152; Bhambra and Shilliam, 'Introduction: "Silence" and Human Rights' in Bhambra and Shilliam (eds), *Silencing Human Rights: Critical Engagements with a Contested Project* (Palgrave, 2009) 1, 9; Nash, *The Cultural Politics of Human Rights: Comparing the US and UK* (CUP, 2009) vii.

[79] See eg Douzinas, n 7; Stammers, n 7; Bowring, *The Degradation of the International Legal Order? The Rehabilitation of Law and the Possibility of Politics* (Routledge-Cavendish, 2009).

PART II

INTERNATIONAL LAW

4

SOURCES

Christine Chinkin

SUMMARY

This chapter outlines the sources of international human rights law that are listed in Article 38(1) Statute of the International Court of Justice: treaties, custom, general principles of law, and, as subsidiary means for determining the law, judicial decisions and the writings of jurists. The chapter also considers how so-called 'soft law' instruments, such as resolutions of the UN General Assembly and the work of human rights expert bodies, may also be regarded as sources of human rights law.

1 INTRODUCTION

A source of law identifies what constitutes law, that is, how decision-makers can determine what instruments, practices, or policies constitute legally binding obligations as opposed to moral, political, or other social commitments. Sources of law provide us with the basis of legal obligation: they are 'really all about the provenance of norms'.[1] In practical terms, the sources of law tell us how new rules are made and existing rules are repealed or abrogated.

International human rights law is a specialist regime within general public international law. Its prescribed or *formal sources* are, therefore, the same as those for other subject areas of international law, such as international environmental law, trade law, or the law of the seas. Unlike national legal systems, international law lacks a central legislative body (comparable to a national parliament), an executive (a government), and a general court of compulsory jurisdiction. International law—and hence international human rights law—must, therefore, derive from other sources.

These are set out in Article 38(1) Statute of the International Court of Justice (ICJ Statute). This provision directs the judges of the International Court on where they should turn when deciding a dispute brought before them. However, Article 38 has long been accepted as providing the authoritative statement of the sources of international law. It states that the Court shall apply:

a. international conventions, whether general or particular, establishing rules expressly recognized by the contesting states;
b. international custom, as evidence of a general practice accepted as law;
c. the general principles of law recognized by civilized nations;

---

[1] Higgins, *Problems and Process: International Law and How We Use it* (OUP, 1994) 17.

d. subject to the provisions of Article 59, judicial decisions and the teachings of the most
   highly qualified publicists of the various nations, as subsidiary means for the determination of rules of law.

As well as stipulating the formal sources of international law, this statement contains elements of both law-making and what are often termed material sources of law. *Law-making*
is the 'how' of international law, the methods adopted by the relevant participants in
the international arena through which international law is made.[2] The *material sources*
of international law are the 'where' of international law: where to look for evidence of
the content of a rule—the words of a treaty, the resolution of an international organization, a statement by the Prime Minister or Foreign Secretary to Parliament or UN General
Assembly. Material sources are numerous and diverse.

These initial definitions do not indicate the complexity or diversity of contemporary
international human rights law, which are reflected in contestations about its content
and sources. Like other areas of international law, in the decades since 1945 international
human rights law has grown exponentially and on an essentially ad hoc basis. There has
been no overarching plan or design; rather it has developed through a range of processes
and in response to demands from numerous participants. Human rights offer a vision of
the 'good life' and engender an almost messianic zeal among their proponents. People seek
to ground claims in the language of human rights so as to gain the 'high moral ground'
against governments, against corporations, against faceless bureaucrats, against anyone
that they deem to have violated their rights. To this end, multiple actors operating within
an array of institutions—civil society activists, legal advocates, the media, individual
lobbyists—draw on material far beyond the formal sources listed in Article 38(1) ICJ
Statute and engage a variety of instruments and statements to bolster their arguments that
a particular matter can be cast as a binding rule of international human rights law.

Human rights generate claims and counterclaims. Those against whom claims are
made—primarily governments—seek to contain their human rights obligations within
the formal sources of law to which they have agreed, while claimants may receive support
from the growing body of specialist human rights experts mandated to monitor human
rights compliance. There is no 'litmus test'[3] for determining claims of new rights or arbiter
with comprehensive authority to make such decisions. The sources of international human
rights law, and thus its substantive content, are often hotly contested and, in the absence of
any final authoritative global decision-maker, are likely to remain so.

This chapter first discusses the formal sources of international human rights law as set
out in Article 38(1) ICJ Statute. It then examines other more contested sources so as to give
a fuller picture of contemporary international human rights law.

2 FORMAL SOURCES

What we now regard as the international human rights story largely dates from the adoption of the UN Charter in 1945,[4] although the underlying ideas are much older.[5] What
has occurred since 1945 has been the legalization of human rights within global and regional

---

[2] Boyle and Chinkin, *The Making of International Law* (OUP, 2007).

[3] Koskenniemi, 'Human Rights Mainstreaming as a Strategy for Institutional Power', (2010) 1 *Humanity: An International Journal of Human Rights, Humanitarianism, and Development* 477.

[4] Moyn argues that it was not until the late 1970s that human rights became a significant force in international relations: Moyn, *The Last Utopia* (Harvard University Press, 2010).   [5] See Chapter 1.

institutional frameworks. Today, it is widely accepted that international human rights law is based on state consent as expressed through the forms outlined in Article 38(1) ICJ Statute.

This was not always the case. The idea of human rights derives its inspiration from multiple sources, including religious creed, natural law, and the nature of society. Natural law sources of rights have long been influential. They rest in the concept of a higher law than that made through human agency, although the content of such law must be mediated through the exercise of human reason.[6] A natural law basis for rights is incapable of empirical proof and its legitimacy rests upon societal agreement on what constitutes the common good, or on the exercise of power in its assertion. In the eighteenth century natural law theories evolved away from reliance on the state of nature through to concepts of the social contract, while in the nineteenth century positivist views based on state consent prevailed. Natural law was to some extent reinvigorated after the horrors of the Second World War and the judgments of the International Military Tribunals at Nuremburg and Tokyo revealed the potential moral abyss of excessive adherence to positivist law.

Nevertheless, although the UN Charter was adopted in a climate of revulsion at the extremism of some state law, the foundations of contemporary human rights law lie in positivist law, based on state consent. The primary way in which states express that consent is through the first instrumentality listed in Article 38(1), the negotiation and adoption of treaties.

3 TREATIES

International human rights law today primarily derives from international and regional treaties. An agreement between states may be termed a treaty, convention, charter, covenant, or pact. The chosen term does not denote any legal difference. Generally only states can become parties to treaties, but exceptionally other actors may be authorized to become parties.[7] States are bound by the treaties to which they have given formal consent, generally through ratification or accession. This is done by the constitutionally appropriate state organ depositing an instrument of ratification with the body so designated within the treaty, in the case of UN human rights treaties generally the UN Secretary-General.[8] International human rights treaties are unlike many other treaties in that they do not provide for a reciprocal exchange of rights and duties between states parties.[9] Instead, by accepting the terms of such treaties, states accept legal constraints upon their treatment of individuals within their territory and subject to their jurisdiction.

3.1 THE PRINCIPAL TREATIES

The UN Charter provides the first guarantees of human rights and fundamental freedoms within a global treaty, albeit in general and indeterminate language.[10] The immediate

---

[6] See Chapter 2.

[7] Convention on the Rights of Persons with Disabilities, Art 43 provides for regional integration organizations to do so; European Convention for the Protection of Human Rights and Fundamental Freedoms (ECHR), Art 59(2) allows for the European Union to do so.

[8] Ratification is the name of the process where a state has previously signed the treaty text while the same process is called accession in the case of a non-signatory state. [9] See Chapter 5.

[10] UN Charter, Art 1(3) provides that one of the purposes of the UN is '[t]o achieve international co-operation in . . . promoting and encouraging respect for human rights and for fundamental freedoms for all without distinction as to race, sex, language, or religion'. See also Arts 55 and 56.

follow up to the Charter was the adoption by the General Assembly of the non-binding Universal Declaration of Human Rights (UDHR), in 1948, eventually followed in 1966 by the adoption of two UN Covenants, the International Covenant on Civil and Political Rights (ICCPR) and its First Optional Protocol and the International Covenant on Economic, Social and Cultural Rights (ICESCR). These three instruments—the UDHR, ICCPR, and ICESCR—are often referred to as the International Bill of Rights.

There has since followed a large number of multilateral treaties that complement the International Bill of Rights by adding new rights, by identifying categories of people who are especially vulnerable to violations of their rights, and by refining the obligations of those first treaties. The multilateral treaties that share some common features are widely regarded as constituting the UN human rights treaty system. In addition to the ICCPR and ICESCR, in chronological order these treaties are: the International Convention on the Elimination of All Forms of Racial Discrimination (1965) (ICERD); the Convention on the Elimination of All Forms of Discrimination Against Women (1979) (CEDAW) and its Optional Protocol (1999); the Convention against Torture and Other Cruel, Inhuman or Degrading Treatment (1984) (UNCAT) and its Optional Protocol (2002); the International Convention on the Rights of the Child (1989) (CRC) and three Optional Protocols (on the Involvement of Children in Armed Conflict (2000); on the Sale of Children, Child Prostitution and Child Pornography (2000); and on a Communications Procedure (2011)); the International Convention on the Protection of the Rights of All Migrant Workers and Members of their Families (1990); the Convention on the Rights of Persons with Disabilities (2006) (CRPD) and its Optional Protocol (2006); and the International Convention for the Protection of All Persons from Enforced Disappearance (2006). A Second Optional Protocol (ICCPR-OP2) to the ICCPR was adopted by the General Assembly in 1989 and an Optional Protocol to the ICESCR (ICESCR-OP) was adopted by the General Assembly in 2008.

The most important of the common features shared by the treaties comprising the UN human rights system is the establishment of specialist committees ('treaty bodies') in accordance with their terms.[11] Each committee, whose members serve in their personal capacity, monitors implementation of the relevant treaty and their work has been central to the development of international human rights law. No account of the sources of human rights law at the global level is complete without taking the work of the treaty bodies into account.

There are many other multilateral treaties that include human rights obligations but which do not have such monitoring mechanisms. Other treaties adopted by the General Assembly include the Convention on the Prevention and Punishment of the Crime of Genocide (1948), the International Convention on the Suppression and Punishment of the Crime of Apartheid (1973), and the Convention relating to the Status of Refugees (1951). Specialist bodies within the UN system have adopted important human rights treaties, notably the International Labour Organisation with respect to workers' rights and the UN Educational, Scientific and Cultural Organisation (UNESCO) on rights to education and information.[12] Human rights obligations for particular states may also derive from peace agreements, which now almost routinely incorporate existing human rights treaties or set out specific rights. For example, the Dayton Peace Accords, which terminated the armed conflict in Bosnia-Herzegovina, gives the European Convention on Human Rights

---

[11] See Chapter 18.
[12] Eg ILO Convention No 100, Equal Remuneration Convention, 1951; UNESCO Convention Against Discrimination in Education, 1960.

(ECHR) priority over all other domestic law, incorporates certain specific rights enumerated in the Convention, and requires the state to become (or to remain) a party to listed UN and regional human rights instruments.[13]

Regional institutions have developed their own human rights systems through the adoption of treaties that are limited to states within the region. Today the ECHR, the American Convention on Human Rights (ACHR), and the African Charter on Human and Peoples' Rights are principal sources of human rights obligations for states parties.

3.2 THE IMPORTANCE OF TREATIES

Treaty law is indisputably the most significant source of international human rights law today. It has a number of advantages. Potentially a large number of states may become parties to a treaty, thereby accepting its provisions as binding legal obligations. After a somewhat slow start (the two UN Covenants each took ten years to receive the required number of parties to come into force), the objective of widespread—ideally universal—adherence to the human rights treaties has been largely successful: only South Sudan is not a party to at least one UN human rights treaty. Widespread treaty adherence provides for a degree of uniformity between states in their understanding of the requirements of international human rights law, which undermines arguments of cultural or other specificity. Treaty ratification and accession also allow for certainty in identifying states parties and written texts set out the obligations accepted.

But there are also some downsides. The authority of a treaty as a source of law lies in states' consent to be bound. Some treaties may not be widely accepted; for example, the Migrant Workers Convention has fewer than 50 states parties. Treaty language is open to differing interpretations, so states may agree to be bound by the same obligations but may differ on their precise meaning. Further, as an expression of their consent states may make reservations to their acceptance of a treaty. Allowing states to make reservations recognizes the many interests of over 190 states and that concessions may have been made during the negotiation process. But reservations also eat away at the integrity of the text and may undermine any serious obligation.[14]

3.3 REVITALIZING THE TREATY SYSTEM

It is evident that many human rights treaties are now relatively old. The International Bill of Rights was negotiated between 1945 and 1966 when the global, political, and economic environments were very different from those of today. There is a dilemma for the development of human rights law. On the one hand, the early conventions have acquired a significant authority and status but, on the other hand, they risk becoming outdated. While international law provides recognized procedures for treaty amendment,[15] the process risks dilution (or even rejection) of existing obligations. Other techniques have been sought for ensuring that the legal guarantees of human rights retain their relevance within a dynamic system. This entails the articulation of new rights as societal conditions demand them, the refinement and extension of existing rights through treaty interpretation,[16] and

---

[13] Framework Agreement for Peace in Bosnia and Herzegovina, 1995.   [14] See Chapter 5.

[15] Vienna Convention on the Law of Treaties, 1969, Arts 39–41.

[16] The regional human rights courts have often referred to human rights treaties as 'living' instruments, eg *Gomez Paquiyauri Brothers v Peru*, IACtHR Series C No 110 (8 July 2004) para 165; *Loizidou v Turkey* (Preliminary Objections) (1995) 20 EHRR 99, para 71.

the enhancement of implementation mechanisms. A number of such techniques have been developed, which add to the richness of the sources of human rights law.

3.3.1 Additional protocols

One such technique comes directly within the ambit of treaty law and that is the adoption of additional protocols to an existing treaty. This has been done at both the UN and regional levels. An additional protocol is essentially a new treaty. States may select whether (and when) to become a party to a protocol in exactly the same way as they do for the main treaty. Protocols to the human rights treaties serve one of two functions: they either provide for rights not included within the original treaty or provide for new methods of enforcement.

An example of the former is ICCPR-OP2 aiming at the abolition of the death penalty. Abolition of the death penalty is controversial, with its proponents claiming that capital punishment is contrary to the right to life while those committed to its use deny that this is the case. Article 6 ICCPR recognizes the continued existence of the death penalty. The adoption of OP2 allows each state to choose its legal stance on the subject. For those states that become a party, the protocol is the formal source of a legal obligation not to execute any person within their jurisdiction. Other states can remain parties to the ICCPR without accepting this additional obligation. Similarly, states parties to the CRC have the choice whether to accept additional legal obligations relating to the recruitment and use of children in armed forces and hostilities and to the economic and sexual exploitation of children. An unusual situation is that of the USA which has chosen to become a party to these two Optional Protocols to the CRC, but not to the 'parent' Convention.

An example of the latter is the ICESCR-OP, which entered into force in May 2013. It makes three new procedures available with respect to states parties to it: communications from an individual, or group of individuals, alleging violation of the ICESCR; inquiry into situations that appear to constitute a consistent pattern of gross or systematic violations of economic, social, and cultural rights within a state party; and inter-state complaints.

3.3.2 General comments

Another technique through which states' treaty obligations have arguably evolved is the adoption of general comments or recommendations on the part of treaty bodies, which set out their understanding of the treaty language. The status of such general comments, of which there are now many,[17] as a source of human rights law is uncertain. While general comments are readily cited by advocates as sources of human rights law, and may be relied upon by decision-makers, any assertion of legally binding effect must depend upon states' consent to their terms. Where a general comment clarifies treaty provisions it might be seen as a form of secondary treaty law, deriving its authority from the binding nature of the treaty and the implied consent of states to it. However, the treaty bodies have not been bestowed with law-making competence and in some instances states may consider a particular treaty body to have exceeded its competence. It must then be doubtful whether any such consent can be assumed.

Two examples illustrate the different possibilities. The CEDAW has no provision directly addressing gender-based violence against women as a violation of women's human rights. In its General Recommendation 19, the CEDAW Committee asserted that the Convention did indeed prohibit such violence as a form of discrimination against women within the terms of

---

[17] The human rights treaty bodies' general comments are collected annually in UN Doc HRI/GEN/1/Rev.9 (Vol I).

Article 1. The Committee required states to include the measures they had taken to combat violence against women in their reports. States have responded positively to this recommendation and have engaged in dialogue with the Committee on the issue. It seems that they have consented to an interpretation of the CEDAW that includes violence against women.

In contrast is the response of at least some states to the Human Rights Committee's General Comment on treaty reservations. The Committee asserted that the special nature of human rights treaties and its need to be able to perform adequately its monitoring tasks mean that it 'necessarily falls to the Committee to determine whether a specific reservation is compatible with the object and purpose of the [ICCPR]'.[18] This assertion has been challenged, in particular by the USA, the UK, and France.[19] State consent to the Human Rights Committee's interpretation of its role is thus lacking, at least in the case of these states. Nevertheless the General Comment formed part of the 'dialogue' on the effect of reservations, which was taken up by the International Law Commission (ILC) and culminated in the Guide to Practice on Reservations to Treaties.[20] In this sense it has contributed to the evolving law on reservations.

Other general comments (or statements) relate to the status of human rights treaties, such as their continuing validity following state succession or the effect of withdrawal from a treaty. Judge Weeramantry of the ICJ noted that such statements are 'not authoritative in themselves' but nevertheless contribute to the understanding of the relevant principle. He was mindful of the fact that the treaty bodies 'are all committees with special experience of handling problems in the human rights area'.[21]

General comments may be considered as sources of human rights law where they are treated by states as coming within the terms of the treaty, but this is less likely where the particular committee is considered to have overstepped its competence. A general comment may also become the basis of state practice, which leads on to the next source of international human rights law—customary international law.

4 CUSTOMARY INTERNATIONAL LAW

The second source of international law, and, therefore, also international human rights law, listed in Article 38(1) ICJ Statute is customary international law. While treaties are binding only on states that have chosen to become parties, custom is binding upon all states with limited exceptions.[22] A treaty may codify customary international law or come to be accepted as customary international law. It is then binding on all states as custom. Customary international law is unwritten. Just as there are regional human rights treaties there may also be regional customary law.[23]

The ICJ has affirmed that customary international law—whether global or regional—comprises two components: an extensive and virtually uniform and consistent state practice and the belief that the practice is required by law (*opinio juris*),[24] rather than for some

---

[18] HRC, General Comment 24, HRI/GEN/1/Rev.9 (Vol I) 210.

[19] See A/50/40, 126 (USA), 130 (UK); A/51/40, 104 (France).

[20] Report of the ILC on the work of its 63rd session, 2011, A/66/10, para 75.

[21] *Application of the Convention on the Prevention and Punishment of the Crime of Genocide (Bosnia and Herzegovina v Serbia and Montenegro)* [1996] ICJ Rep 43, 654 (Sep Op Judge Weeramantry).

[22] One exception is the so-called persistent objector rule. See Cassese, *International Law* (OUP, 2005) 162–3. The rule appears to have little application to human rights. Eg, South Africa persistently objected to the designation of apartheid as contrary to customary international law but was nevertheless held to be in violation.

[23] *Asylum Case (Columbia v Peru)* [1950] ICJ Rep 266.

[24] Eg *North Sea Continental Shelf Cases (FRG v Denmark) (FRG v The Netherlands)* [1969] ICJ Rep 3, para 77; *Continental Shelf (Libyan Arab Jamahiriya v Malta)* [1985] ICJ Rep 29, para 27.

other reason such as diplomatic nicety or etiquette. But these two requirements are not easily applied, and determining the content of customary international law is strewn with practical and theoretical difficulties. The first problem is selecting from among the daily activities and statements made by states, those that constitute evidence of state practice. Places where one might look to discover evidence of custom include diplomatic correspondence, government policy statements, press releases, the opinions of government legal advisers, official manuals, and government comments on international drafting processes. In the context of human rights, other materials may be included such as the behaviours described in states' reports to the UN treaty bodies, material gathered for the Human Rights Council Universal Periodic Review (UPR) process, and the work and documentation of national human rights institutions. Unlike the state treaty reporting process, the UPR does not rest on any specific treaty but on states' general human rights obligations including, therefore, customary international law. As a peer (state) review process, both the reports and recommendations can provide evidence of practice and *opinio juris*.

Two examples illustrate how some decision-makers have approached the task of deciding whether a customary rule of international law exists and some of the theoretical quandaries in so deciding. In *Filartiga v Peña-Irala*, a US judge had to decide whether torture is contrary to customary international law. The case was in 1980, four years before the adoption of the UNCAT. Judge Kaufman sought to find international consensus on the prohibition of torture. He looked to General Assembly resolutions (including the UDHR), 'numerous international treaties and accords', and their reiteration in municipal law, including the constitutions of over 55 states. In sum, he found evidence of state practice in 'the usage of nations, judicial opinions and the work of jurists'.[25]

In *R v Jones*, the House of Lords determined the crime of aggression to be established under customary international law. Lord Bingham referred to what he called the 'major milestones along the road leading to this conclusion'.[26] These included a mix of treaties and statements: a draft Treaty of Mutual Assistance in 1923 (which never came into force); descriptions by the League of Nations Assembly; a resolution of the Pan-American Conference (1928); the Charter of the International Military Tribunal, Article 6; decisions of the International Military Tribunal; General Assembly Resolutions dating from 1946; the work of the International Law Commission; and the Rome Statute of the International Criminal Court (1998). In neither of these cases did the judge have to decide when the rule of custom had emerged; it was sufficient that it had done so by the time of the litigation.

Two further issues emerge from these examples. The first issue is that treaties, including treaties that never came into force, were drawn upon as evidence of state practice. It might be argued that a treaty that has not come into force is evidence of what states have not accepted, rather than of what they have. Further, the practice of states parties to treaties is not evidence of state practice for the purpose of establishing a rule of custom, because it must be assumed that such states are acting in accordance with their treaty obligations, not because they consider themselves bound by custom to do so.[27] They, therefore, lack the requisite *opinio juris*. States' reports to the treaty bodies are relevant as they provide a wealth of information about that state's policies, practices, and legislation, including changes that can be traced through the multiple rounds of reporting that many states have now undergone. If states have changed their practices in response to the concluding comments addressed to them by the relevant treaty bodies, this too must be viewed

---

[25]   (1980) 630 F2d 876.   [26]   [2007] 1 AC 136.
[27]   *North Sea Continental Shelf Cases*, n 24, para 76.

as action taken for treaty compliance, not as evidence of state practice for the purpose of establishing a rule of customary international law. Nevertheless, in terms of human rights policy, changed behaviour towards implementation is precisely the desired objective and if consistency in state practice can be identified it seems artificial to discount it as evidence of customary international law.

The second issue is the problem caused by the divergence between what states do and what states say. In *Filartiga*, Judge Kaufman noted that he had not been 'directed to any assertion by any contemporary state of a right to torture its own or another nation's citizens'.[28] But this optimistic statement is contradicted by reports of torture evidenced by human rights organizations. In 2011, Amnesty International documented cases of torture and other ill-treatment in at least 98 countries.[29] For evident policy reasons—the desire not to deny the existence of a rule of customary international law prohibiting torture—custom may be asserted by reference to states' words rather than the reality of their actions. As will be seen in this chapter, General Assembly resolutions are formally non-binding, but these statements are often used as evidence of *opinio juris*, overriding inconsistent practice.[30] Both Judge Kaufman and Lord Bingham in *R v Jones* referred to General Assembly resolutions in determining customary international law. The desire to hold states to their words, particularly when pronounced in the formal setting of the General Assembly, is especially strong where the conduct is 'violative of the basic concept of human dignity', which is at the core of human rights.[31]

Treaties and custom coexist and despite the wide adherence by states to human rights treaties, customary international law retains some considerable importance as a source of human rights law.[32] A claim of obligation under custom may be made against a state that has not become a party to a particular treaty, or which has made a reservation to a treaty provision as a state cannot reserve out of customary international law. A binding treaty may not yet have been concluded on the topic in question. Rules of customary international law may be held to bind non-state actors that cannot be parties to treaties. In a number of states, including the UK, treaty law creates rights and obligations that can be relied on in national courts only if the treaty has been made part of national law through incorporating legislation. A state may thus become a party to a treaty but have failed to take the requisite action to allow it to be relied on within its own courts, as was the case in the UK before the passing of the Human Rights Act in 1998 to give domestic effect to the ECHR, which it had ratified in 1951. It has still not taken such action with respect to the ICCPR or ICESCR. In contrast, customary international law may be accepted as the law of the land without any such act of incorporation.

---

[28] Filartiga, n 25, 884.   [29] Amnesty International, *State of the World's Human Rights* (2011).

[30] In the *Nicaragua* case, the ICJ found that, despite numerous examples of armed conflict, there was sufficient evidence of contrary *opinio juris* in General Assembly resolutions to support principles of customary law prohibiting the use of force and wrongful intervention: *Military and Paramilitary Activities in and against Nicaragua (Nicaragua v US)* [1986] ICJ Rep 14, paras 186–90. However, in *Legality of the Threat or Use of Nuclear Weapons* the ICJ considered that 'although those [General Assembly] resolutions are a clear sign of deep concern regarding the problem of nuclear weapons, they still fall short of establishing the existence of an *opinio juris* on the illegality of the use of such weapons': [1996] ICJ Rep 226, para 71.

[31] Schachter, 'International Law in Theory and Practice: General Course in Public International Law' (1982) 178 *Rec des Cours* 21, 334–8. In such instances Schachter considered that 'statements of condemnation are sufficient evidence of its illegitimacy under customary international law'.

[32] See Clapham, *Human Rights Obligations of Non-State Actors* (OUP, 2006) 85–6.

5 JUS COGENS

A *jus cogens* norm is a 'peremptory norm of general international law…accepted and recognized by the international community of states as a whole as a norm from which no derogation is permitted and which can be modified only by a subsequent norm of general international law having the same character'.[33] *Jus cogens* norms or 'intransgressible principles of customary international law'[34] constitute the pinnacle of the hierarchy of sources of international law. They both limit states' freedom to enter into treaties by reference to fundamental values of the international community and bind all states regardless of whether they have ratified the treaties that contain them. They import notions of universally applicable norms into the international legal process.

Until relatively recently candidates for *jus cogens* norms were designated by commentators or scholars but had had relatively little application. Many of the norms most commonly asserted to have this status were those of human rights, including the prohibitions of genocide, slavery and the slave trade, murder/disappearances and torture, prolonged arbitrary detention, and systematic racial discrimination.[35] Indeed, it has been remarked that there is 'an almost intrinsic relationship between peremptory norms and human rights'.[36] Since the 1990s, international, regional, and national courts have recognized—albeit belatedly in the case of the ICJ[37]—certain norms as *jus cogens*, including the prohibitions against torture,[38] genocide,[39] and fundamental rules of humanitarian law.[40] Such judicial recognition has an important symbolic effect, signifying the seriousness with which the international community regards certain behaviours. It also has practical consequences, including making illegitimate any national legislative, administrative, or judicial act authorizing such acts, subjecting alleged perpetrators to universal criminal jurisdiction, and forbidding their exclusion from extradition under any political offence exemption.

States are bound by *jus cogens* norms whether or not they have expressly consented to them. For example, the 40 or so states that are not parties to the UNCAT remain subject to the prohibition of torture: they cannot derogate from it through international treaties, through local or special customs, or even 'through general customary rules not endowed with the same normative force'.[41] Although the grounding of *jus cogens* norms in fundamental interests of the wider international community overrides the requirement for individual state consent,

---

[33] Vienna Convention on the Law of Treaties, Art 53.

[34] *Legality of the Threat or Use of Nuclear Weapons*, n 30, para 79.

[35] American Law Institute, *Restatement (Third) of the Foreign Relations Law of the United States* (1987) para 702.   [36] Bianchi, 'Human Rights and the Magic of Jus Cogens' (2008) 19 *EJIL* 491.

[37] Judge Cançado Trindade noted that 'it has taken more than six decades for [the ICJ] to acknowledge its existence…, in spite of its being one of the central features of contemporary international law.' *Questions relating to the Obligation to Prosecute or Extradite (Belgium v Senegal)* [2012] ICJ Rep (Sep Op Judge Cançado Trindade) para 159.

[38] Eg *A and others v Secretary of State for the Home Department (No 2)* [2005] UKHL 71; *Prosecutor v Furundžija*, Judgment, IT-95-17/1-T, 10 December 1998 (ICTY); *Ould Dah v France*, app no 13113/03, Decision of 30 March 2009 (European Court of Human Rights); *Questions relating to the Obligation to Prosecute or Extradite*, para 99 ('[T]he prohibition of torture is part of customary international law and it has become a peremptory norm *(jus cogens)*').

[39] Eg *Armed Activities on the Territory of the Congo* (New Application 2002) *(Democratic Republic of the Congo v Rwanda)* [2006] ICJ Rep 3, para 64.

[40] *Legality of the Threat or Use of Nuclear Weapons*, n 30, para 79; *Jurisdictional Immunities of the State (Germany v Italy: Greece intervening)* [2012] ICJ Rep, para 93 (with respect to 'rules of the law of armed conflict which prohibit the murder of civilians in occupied territory, the deportation of civilian inhabitants to slave labour and the deportation of prisoners of war to slave labour').   [41] *Furundžija*, n 38, para 153.

the threshold is high. These norms must be accepted as such by the 'international community of states as a whole' indicating widespread general consent.

However, there remains controversy over which human rights norms have this status and over some of its implications. There is widespread agreement on the *jus cogens* quality of certain rights such as the prohibition of torture and genocide, but others that have been accepted by some bodies are more controversial; for example, all forms of discrimination,[42] the death penalty for those under 18,[43] and the right to property.[44] With respect to the legal consequences of a determination of *jus cogens*, it seems that it does not override jurisdictional requirements. On its detailed analysis of state practice as evidenced by national legislation and decisions of national courts, as well as the jurisprudence of the regional human rights courts, the ICJ has concluded that there is no rule of customary international law displacing state immunity for torts allegedly committed on the territory of another state by state organs during armed conflict, nor that this is changed by the status of the relevant norms as *jus cogens*.[45]

6 GENERAL PRINCIPLES OF LAW

The meaning of 'general principles of law' as listed in Article 38(1)(c) ICJ Statute remains controversial and has had little practical application. One view is that this expression refers to principles found in most, if not all, national legal systems, such as notions of procedural fairness or equity, while another view is that they include 'general principles applicable directly to international legal relations',[46] for example, the principle that treaties are binding upon states parties. In both cases, human rights are more likely to be applied as general principles rather than general principles constituting a source of human rights.[47]

Simma and Alston have argued for greater use of general principles as a contemporary source of human rights law and that general principles derived from the international plane should be expanded:

> Principles brought to the fore in this 'direct' way... would (and should) then percolate down into domestic fora, instead of being elevated from the domestic level to that of international law by way of analogy.[48]

General principles drawn from international arenas may be found in statements of consensus, such as those expressed at global summits, and in the resolutions of UN organs. Simma and Alston reason that this would retain the consensual basis of international law while overcoming many of the conceptual and practical problems of customary international law, in particular the need to prove state practice and *opinio juris*. However, it does not seem that their position has influenced decision-makers.

---

[42] *Juridical Conditions and Rights of Undocumented Migrants*, IACtHR Series A No 18 (2003) paras 82–110.

[43] Case 12.240, *Douglas Christopher Thomas v United States*, IACommHR Report No 100/03, OEA/Ser./L/V/II.114 Doc.70 rev.1 (2003) 790, para 52.

[44] The European Court of First Instance suggested this in *Kadi v Council of the EU and Commission of the EC* (T-315/01) [2005] ECR II-3649, 293, at least where there is arbitrary deprivation.

[45] *Jurisdictional Immunities of the State*, n 40.

[46] Thirlway, 'The Sources of International Law' in Evans (ed), *International Law* (OUP, 2006) 128.

[47] But see Capaldo, *The Pillars of Global Law* (Ashgate, 2008) ch 1.

[48] Simma and Alston, 'The Sources of Human Rights Law: Custom, *Jus Cogens* and General Principles' (1992) 12 *Australian YIL* 82, 102.

7 JUDICIAL DECISIONS

There is no dedicated international human rights court. However, a feature of the international legal system over the past few decades has been the proliferation of judicial bodies, many of which determine questions of human rights that arise before them. There is no hierarchy between these courts but their interaction has contributed to the dynamic quality of human rights law.

Article 38(1)(d) ICJ Statute provides that judicial decisions are 'subsidiary means' for determining rules of international law. The article does not clarify which courts it is referring to or the weight that should be given to judicial decisions. It does, however, refer to Article 59, which rejects any doctrine of precedent before the ICJ.[49] The formal position is that international courts do not make law and that their decisions are binding only on the parties to the particular case and can be discounted in subsequent cases. However, this ignores the reality that, through the interpretation and application of treaties and custom, judicial decisions elucidate and develop international law. In a decentralized legal system that lacks a legislature and where unwritten law is developed through the amorphous processes of state practice and *opinio juris*, judicial decision-making carries great weight through exposition of the law and accelerates the formation of customary international law.[50] At the national, regional, and international levels courts play an especially important role in developing and moulding human rights law in accordance with changing social circumstances and understandings of rights. The ICJ has noted their relevance as evidence of customary international law.[51]

7.1 INTERACTION AT THE INTERNATIONAL AND REGIONAL LEVELS

The ICJ is the only international court with jurisdiction over all questions of international law, which includes issues relating to human rights.[52] It has, for example, asserted the applicability of human rights law in armed conflict and in occupied territories.[53] The Human Rights Committee has adopted a similar approach as seen in its General Comment 31,[54] in its practice, and in its express comments to Israel in its 2003 concluding observations to Israel's report submitted under Article 40 ICCPR. The Committee had concluded that the ICCPR applies 'to the benefit of the population of the Occupied Territories'.[55] The Court likewise considered that the ICCPR 'is applicable in respect of acts done by a State in the exercise of its jurisdiction outside its own territory'.[56] The Human Rights Committee did not refer to the Court's advisory opinion on the *Threat or Use of Nuclear Weapons* in its General Comment 31, which was adopted shortly before the advisory opinion on Israel's security wall, while the Court did draw upon the Committee's practice and observations in

---

[49] Art 59 states that '[t]he decision of the Court has no binding force except between the parties and in respect of that particular case'.

[50] Clapham, *Brierly's Law of Nations* (7th edn, 2012) 65.

[51] *Jurisdictional Immunities of the State*, n 40.

[52] Eg the former Permanent Court of International Justice made an important contribution to the understanding of equality and difference: *Minority Schools in Albania, Advisory Opinion*, PCIJ Series A/B No 64 (1935). Dissenting Judge Tanaka in the *South West Africa Cases* (second phase) [1966] ICJ Rep 6, 305–6 did likewise.

[53] *Legality of the Threat or Use of Nuclear Weapons*, n 30; *Legal Consequences of the Construction of a Wall in the Occupied Palestinian Territory* [2004] ICJ Rep 136.

[54] HRC, General Comment 31, HRI/GEN/1/Rev.9 (Vol I) 243, para 11.

[55] *Wall*, n 53, para 109.   [56] *Wall*, n 53, para 111.

that case. The consistency between the two bodies strengthens and adds legitimacy to the emergent law. Decisions of the ICJ may also contribute to state practice where its decisions are followed by national courts, although there is no guarantee that this will be the case.

International human rights law and international criminal law are companion legal regimes and developments in one area may impact on the other, adding to the richness of the sources of each. Thus, international criminal courts may consider human rights law as a potential source of international criminal law. For example, the sources of the prohibition of torture, as a human rights violation, are customary international law, the ICCPR, and the UNCAT. The human rights definition of torture can be found in Article 1 UNCAT. Torture is also an international crime and the International Criminal Tribunal for the former Yugoslavia (ICTY) has had to determine whether the international crime of torture has the same definition as the human rights violation. The ICTY first looked to human rights law and accepted the UNCAT definition as customary international law.[57] It subsequently changed its stance and adapted the definition to suit its own context—armed conflict—and the requirement that it apply international humanitarian law.[58] The ICTY Appeals Chamber affirmed that the UNCAT definition remains important as customary international law when considering state responsibility—the domain of human rights— but not for individual criminal responsibility—the domain of international criminal law.[59]

Similarly, decisions of international criminal tribunals may be turned to by human rights courts as a subsidiary source of human rights law. For example, in *MC v Bulgaria* the European Court of Human Rights noted the jurisprudence of the ICTY in determining that rape constituted treatment incurring positive obligations under Article 3 ECHR. While accepting that the ICTY was dealing with the particular context of rape in armed conflict, the European Court considered that its jurisprudence 'reflected a universal trend' that was relevant to its own determination of rape as a human rights violation.[60] The decisions of international criminal courts may be a subsidiary source of human rights law, but their different legal focus means that there cannot be an automatic transposition between the two legal regimes.

7.2 INTERACTION BETWEEN NATIONAL COURTS

The same processes can be observed across national courts. Many states have adopted international human rights standards into their constitutions and legislation, requiring national courts to interpret and apply the relevant provisions. In some cases international human rights treaties are incorporated into national law, while in others language is simply taken from them. In either event, judges in different jurisdictions must interpret and apply similarly worded provisions and may look to each other's decisions in doing so. The jurisprudence of regional and national courts is authoritative only within their own legal system, but careful judicial analysis can be influential in the decision-making by courts in other regions and states that are faced with comparable problems and must apply similar language. Judicial decisions can carry persuasive weight across national and regional boundaries and it is becoming commonplace for judges in one jurisdiction 'to refer extensively to the decision of the courts of foreign jurisdictions when interpreting human rights guarantees'.[61] Especially when deciding a novel point, judges may feel that drawing on

---

[57] *Prosecutor v Mucić et al.*, Judgment, IT-96-21-T, 16 November 1998, para 459.

[58] *Prosecutor v Kunarac*, Judgment, IT-96-23-T and IT-96-23/1-T, 22 February 2001, paras 465 ff.

[59] *Prosecutor v Kunarac*, Judgment, IT-96-23 and IT-96-23/1-A, 12 June 2002, para 146.

[60] (2005) 40 EHRR 20.

[61] McCrudden, 'A Common Law of Human Rights? Transnational Judicial Conversations on Constitutional Rights' (2000) 20 *OJLS* 499, 506.

a decision, or reasoning, of another court bestows legitimacy on their own judgment. Nevertheless, this process must not be taken for granted and research is required on specific issues to determine whether there is judicial consistency on a particular point and its extent. Where there is such consistency, it can be used as evidence of uniform state practice.

The reputation of certain courts, or the novelty of the point of human rights law under consideration, may give some decisions additional persuasive weight. They may also be used in advocacy and in writings and reports by human rights groups. For example, the decision of the House of Lords in the *Pinochet* case[62] has been widely cited and referred to by courts elsewhere, although subsequent decisions have narrowed its potential scope and limited its impact on the evolution of customary international law.[63] Similarly, the decisions of the South African Constitutional Court with respect to the understanding of economic and social rights have been influential.[64] The importance of this jurisprudence may have been enhanced because of the lack of judicial decision-making on these rights at the international and regional levels: the Committee on Economic, Social and Cultural Rights historically has not had the competence to hear individual complaints, and the ECHR and ACHR are primarily focused on civil and political rights.

7.3 HUMAN RIGHTS LITIGATION

Human rights litigation is a comparatively new phenomenon but one that has rapidly evolved, thereby increasing the availability of argument, interpretation, and application of norms and enhancing the value of judicial decisions as a source of human rights law. Electronic information means that pleadings and decisions from numerous fora are readily available and accessible. Global networks of human rights activists devise litigation strategies, seek out test cases, and publicize successful claims so that similar arguments may be made elsewhere. There is now a body of judges and experts in global and regional institutions who regularly hear cases involving claims of violations of human rights. These are complemented by judges in national courts responsible for the judicial enforcement of human rights. They too form networks through bodies such as the International Bar Association, and can thus support and reinforce each other. They may attend training sessions on international human rights law. While they must all work within the constraints of their particular institution and legal framework, they face similar issues and may turn to the decisions of other bodies in determining their own approach. In all these ways judicial decision-making fleshes out and develops international human rights treaties and custom and, thus, has a greater influence than might be expected of a 'subsidiary means for the determination of rules' of human rights law.

8 WRITINGS OF JURISTS

Article 38(1)(d) ICJ Statute includes the 'teachings of the most highly qualified publicists' as another subsidiary means for determining the law. Within the international and regional human rights systems there are now a plethora of expert bodies and

---

[62] *R v Bow Street Metropolitan Stipendiary Magistrate, ex parte Pinochet Ugarte (No 3)* [1999] 2 WLR 827.

[63] Wuerth, '*Pinochet's* Legacy Reassessed', (2012) 106 *AJIL* 731.

[64] *Government of the Republic of South Africa & Ors v Grootboom & Ors* 2000 (11) BCLR 1169; *Minister of Health v Treatment Action Campaign (TAC)* (2002) 5 SA 721 (CC).

individuals who produce important reports and commentaries on a wide range of human rights issues. These include the UN Human Rights Council special procedures (Special Rapporteurs, fact-finding missions, working groups, expert meetings), the reports of the former Sub-Commission on Human Rights (now advisory council), human rights work of UN specialized agencies, and NGO reports such as those of Human Rights Watch and Amnesty International. Such works are often scholarly, well researched, and analytical. They are compiled for many purposes: to expose a particular violative practice, to provide an academic analysis of an issue, or to gain media attention. They may also consciously seek to develop human rights law, by bringing together examples of state practice and *opinio juris* and arguing that these are sufficiently consistent to found a new rule of custom, or to demonstrate the need for a treaty on the subject. Writings of this type are not binding and do not constitute a formal source of human rights law, but may be relied upon by decision-makers as sources of information and for analysis.[65] The result is that there is a wealth of literature that may be understood as a subsidiary means for determining the law. The persuasiveness of any one piece of writing depends upon the quality of research and analysis and the authority of the relevant institution or author. There may be deliberate strategies to enhance the authority of a particular piece of work; for example, the growing practice of reports by multiple Special Rapporteurs.[66] As with judicial decisions, much depends on the use made of such works by states and other actors. Today, such works are more influential in developing human rights law than the writings of more traditional publicists referred to in Article 38(1)(d).

9 OTHER SOURCES

In addition to the formal sources of international law as spelled out in Article 38(1) ICJ Statute, other methods of developing human rights law must be identified.

9.1 WORK OF TREATY BODIES

The role of the UN treaty bodies in developing human rights law has been mentioned. The different activities of these bodies cut across the different sources. The treaty bodies elucidate states' obligations under the various treaties through the adoption of general comments and concluding observations in response to states' reports. These might be described as secondary treaty law, in that state consent can be implied from their acceptance of the treaties and the authority of the expert committees. This is reinforced where states comply with the reporting requirements.

Some of the treaty bodies also have a form of quasi-judicial competence. This is the individual complaint or communication procedure, which is primarily a written procedure and concludes with views and recommendations by the relevant committee.[67] Can such opinions be regarded as judicial decisions under Article 38(1)(d)? On the one hand, they are non-binding and in many instances include only limited reasoning. On the other hand, the monitoring role accorded by treaty to the expert committees means that their opinions

---

[65] Eg the European Court of Human Rights referred to reports of the European Commissioner for Human Rights and the Cypriot Ombudsman to highlight the nature of human trafficking in Cyprus: *Rantsev v Cyprus and Russia* (2010) 51 EHRR 1.

[66] Eg Situation of detainees at Guantánamo Bay, joint report of five holders of mandates of special procedures of the Commission on Human Rights, E/CN.4/2006/120 (27 February 2006).   [67] See Chapter 18.

cannot be easily disregarded. The individual complaint procedure allows the treaty bodies to develop jurisprudence on the interpretation and application of the relevant convention and their opinions may be cited before decision-makers, or used as supporting evidence of current human rights law. The Human Rights Committee has described its views as having some of the characteristics of judicial decisions in that they 'are arrived at in a judicial spirit, including the impartiality and independence of Committee members, the considered interpretation of the language of the Covenant, and the determinative character of the decisions' and as such provide 'an authoritative determination by the organ established under the Covenant itself charged with the interpretation of that instrument.'[68] This view appears to be accepted by the ICJ, which has stated that the opinion of the Human Rights Committee—'an independent body established specifically to supervise the application of that treaty'—should be given 'great weight.'[69] The weight given to their output varies according to the strength of the argument, the esteem accorded to the particular committee, and the extent to which their work is in tune with other developments in human rights law.

Another individual complaints mechanism is the Human Rights Advisory Panel in Kosovo. Its authority ultimately derives from Security Council Resolution 1244 (1999), which mandated the international civil presence in Kosovo (the UN Interim Administration Mission in Kosovo (UNMIK)) with, inter alia, 'protecting and promoting human rights'. The first Regulation promulgated by UNMIK affirmed that the Mission 'shall observe internationally recognized human rights standards.'[70] In 2006 UNMIK established the Panel 'to examine alleged violations of human rights by UNMIK' and to issue opinions in accordance with a list of applicable instruments, including UN human rights treaties, the ECHR, and the formally non-binding UDHR.[71] As an international organization the UN cannot become party to a human rights treaty (unless explicitly provided for), but in this way the treaties listed are made an applicable source of law for the performance of the mandate of a UN mission. The Panel's opinions largely follow the jurisprudence of the European Court of Human Rights, but go beyond it in considering the human rights standards required of a UN mission in the field. The reasoned opinions may be influential in developing the law in this area.

9.2 RESOLUTIONS OF INTERNATIONAL INSTITUTIONS

An important omission from Article 38(1) ICJ Statute is resolutions of international institutions. Security Council resolutions adopted under UN Charter Chapter VII are binding on states parties; by specifying the human rights obligations of non-state actors (for instance armed militia groups) the Council has contributed to the expanding applicability of human rights law.[72] Of much greater significance are the numerous resolutions of the General Assembly and Human Rights Council, which have widened the scope of human rights, set standards for states and non-state actors, and provided aspirations and goals. The status of the Human Rights Council as a subsidiary body of the General Assembly may add greater authoritative weight to its resolutions than those of its predecessor, the Commission on Human Rights. Indeed, the foundational document of international human rights law—the UDHR—is in the form of a General Assembly resolution. Such

---

[68] HRC, General Comment 33, CCPR/C/GC/33, 5 November 2008, paras 11–13.
[69] *Ahmadou Sadio Diallo (Republic of Guinea v Democratic Republic of the Congo)* [2010] ICJ Rep para 66.
[70] UNMIK/REG/1999/1, 25 July 1999.   [71] UNMIK/REG/2006/12, 23 March 2006.
[72] Clapham, 'Human Rights Obligations of Non-state Actors in Conflict Situations' (2006) 88 *IRRC* 491.

non-binding instruments (often termed 'soft law') may be the basis for binding norms where they are declaratory of custom, or are subsequently transformed into a treaty or custom. The UDHR was followed, albeit 18 years later, by the ICCPR and ICESCR, treaties binding on states parties. It is also regarded by many commentators as having become customary international law. This transformation into formal sources, however, fails to indicate its own abiding authority and status.

The same pattern—resolution followed by treaty—has occurred in many other instances: the Declaration on Torture was followed by the UNCAT; many resolutions on the rights of the child were followed eventually by the CRC; resolutions on the rights of persons with disabilities were followed by the CRPD. In other cases no treaty has been adopted on the subject matter addressed in a General Assembly resolution. There has been no global treaty on the rights of minorities following the General Assembly Declaration on the Rights of Persons belonging to National, Ethnic, Religious and Linguistic Minorities, or on those of indigenous peoples following the General Assembly Declaration on the subject. Even where a treaty has followed a resolution, it is unlikely that all states will become parties. Individuals may, therefore, wish to argue that the resolution has crystallized into customary international law. Criteria for determining that a resolution has become customary international law have been put forward. They include adoption of the resolution by consensus, the inclusion of normative language, and follow-up procedures—all factors that indicate states' consent to be bound.

Another way in which a non-binding resolution may be understood as a source of human rights law is where it provides an authoritative interpretation of a treaty. This was the approach taken by the Inter-American Court of Human Rights in considering the status of the American Declaration of the Rights and Duties of Man. The Court considered that for

> member states of the Organization, the Declaration is the text that defines the human rights referred to in the [OAS] Charter…with the result that…the American Declaration is for these States a source of international obligations related to the Charter of the Organization…. That the Declaration is not a treaty does not, then, lead to the conclusion that it does not have legal effect.[73]

The Inter-American Commission has accordingly determined that the USA has human rights obligations under the Declaration despite it not having become a party to the ACHR.

9.3 OTHER FORMS OF SOFT LAW

There are multiple other forms of soft law. They include resolutions of the Human Rights Council, guidelines,[74] codes of conduct[75] and standards of behaviour,[76] and the final

---

[73] OC-10/89, *Interpretation of the American Declaration of the Rights and Duties of Man within the Framework of Article 64 of the American Convention on Human Rights*, Series A No 10 (1989), paras 45–7.

[74] Eg Basic Principles and Guidelines on the Right to a Remedy and Reparation for Victims of Gross Violations of International Human Rights Law and Serious Violations of International Humanitarian Law, GA Res 60/147, 16 December 2005; Guiding Principles on Business and Human Rights: Implementing the United Nations 'Protect, Respect and Remedy' Framework, A/HRC/17/31, 21 March 2011.

[75] Eg Code of Conduct for Law Enforcement Officials, GA Res 34/169, 17 December 1979; Basic Principles on the Use of Force and Firearms by Law Enforcement Officials, 1990.

[76] Eg Standard Minimum Rules for the Treatment of Prisoners, 1955.

instruments of global summit meetings held under UN auspices. The last have become noteworthy features of the international landscape since the 1990s. They have typically generated great energy through the establishment of a conference secretariat, wide participation, intensive preparations, lobbying, and intense (often heated) negotiations. They have culminated in declarations and programmes of action directed to states, intergovernmental organizations, and NGOs.[77] There have been follow-up procedures, normally at five-year intervals.

It is noticeable that many of these instruments are negotiated with as much care and attention to detail as binding texts and states also make reservations to them, undermining the formal position that they lack legal authority. The practical difference in impact between treaties and non-binding instruments may not be great, especially where treaty language is imprecise and seems to deny legal obligation. For example, under Article 2 ICESCR, each state party undertakes to 'take steps...to the maximum of its available resources, with a view to achieving progressively the...rights recognized...by all appropriate means'. Phrases such as 'take steps', 'progressively', and 'appropriate means' lack clear legal content. As there was originally no right of individual complaint under the ICESCR, the treaty might be considered as imposing only a 'soft' obligation despite its legal form.[78] There are advantages to the 'soft' form: it may facilitate reaching a political consensus, bring an issue onto the international agenda, define the area of international concern, and provide guidelines for behaviour that may generate the requisite practice for a rule of customary international law. Judges and other decision-makers may turn to formally non-binding instruments in much the same way as treaties,[79] and there is often little distinction in terms of compliance.[80]

What might be termed a 'fusion' of soft law sources can lead to the emergence of new norms without input from 'formal' sources, for instance where negotiation of a convention remains politically contested. The example of violence against women illustrates how the different procedures of a specialist UN human rights treaty body, the CEDAW Committee, in conjunction with other non-binding processes, may work together to produce binding norms. The Committee has used its General Recommendation 19 on violence against women, its concluding observations on states parties' reports, an inquiry procedure,[81] and its decisions in individual complaints of brutal domestic violence sustained over many years,[82] to develop the understanding that gender-based violence is discrimination within the terms of the CEDAW and that states have an obligation to exercise due diligence to protect women from such violence, prosecute it, and punish

---

[77] Eg World Conference on Human Rights, Vienna, 1993; Fourth World Conference on Women, Beijing, 1995; and review conferences. [78] See Chapter 7.

[79] Eg in *R v Immigration Officer at Prague Airport, ex parte European Roma Rights Centre and Others* [2005] 2 WLR 1, the UK House of Lords referred to a range of formally non-binding documents, including a UN High Commissioner for Refugees *Handbook on Procedures and Criteria for Determining Refugee Status*; the Declaration on Territorial Asylum, 1967; American Law Institute, *Restatement of the Foreign Relations Law of the United States (Third)*; resolutions of the Committee of Ministers of the Council of Europe; reports of the International Law Association; HRC, General Comment 31; reports by the Inter-American Commission for Human Rights and UN Committee on the Elimination of Racial Discrimination; academic articles.

[80] Shelton (ed), *Commitment and Compliance: The Role of Non-Binding Norms in the International Legal System* (OUP, 2000).

[81] Report on Mexico produced by the CEDAW Committee under Art 8 of the Optional Protocol to the Convention, and reply from the Government of Mexico, CEDAW/C/2005/OP8/Mexico (27 January 2005).

[82] *Ms AT v Hungary*, CEDAW/C/36/D/2/2003 (26 January 2005); *Şahide Goecke v Austria*, CEDAW/C/39/D/5/2005 (6 August 2007); *Fatma Yildirim (deceased) v Austria*, CEDAW/C/39/D/6/2005 (6 August 2007); *Vertido v Philippines*, CEDAW /C/46/D/18/2008 (22 September 2010); *VK v Bulgaria*, CEDAW/C/49/D/20/2008 (27 September 2011); *Isatou Jallow v Bulgaria*, CEDAW/C/52/D/32/2011 (23 July 2012).

it. The concept of due diligence was embedded in the international law principle of state responsibility for wrongful treatment of aliens, formulated in an expert report on disappearances,[83] developed by the Inter-American Court of Human Rights (also in the context of disappearances),[84] conceptualized in the context of violence against women in a report of the Special Rapporteur on violence against women,[85] and incorporated into jurisprudence of regional human rights courts[86] and treaty law within the Council of Europe framework,[87] a trajectory that illustrates how diverse bodies draw upon and explicate concepts developed elsewhere. The Committee's work has been reinforced by General Assembly resolutions,[88] resolutions of the Commission on Human Rights (and now Council), including the adoption of a mandate for a Special Rapporteur on the causes and consequences of violence against women, the final instruments of global conferences, and ongoing work by the General Assembly, including commissioning the Secretary-General to prepare an 'In-Depth Study on Violence against Women' and an annual report on implementation of its recommendations. These non-binding processes taken together have strong accumulative effect in determining that violence against women violates human rights law.[89] At the very least, these expressions by states of the wrongfulness of failing to prevent and punish such behaviour constitute considerable evidence of *opinio juris* of an international norm prohibiting violence against women, despite its continuing prevalence.

Another example is non-discrimination on the grounds of sexual and gender identity. The treaty bodies, and in particular the European Court of Human Rights, have found such discrimination to be in violation of the various conventions. Following a controversial resolution of the UN Human Rights Council,[90] the Office of the High Commissioner for Human Rights produced a detailed report entitled Discriminatory Laws and Practices and Acts of Violence against Individuals based on their Sexual Orientation and Gender Identity. This demonstrated the extent of harmful discriminatory practices and violence, analysed the practice of the treaty bodies in developing a coherent and consistent approach to condemnation of such discrimination, and generated a panel discussion at the Council.[91] Although the issue continues to divide states, there is hope that this is a step towards further legal development.[92]

---

[83] Report of the Special Rapporteur on extrajudicial, summary or arbitrary executions, E/CN.4/2005/7 (22 December 2004) para 73. Alston attributes the formulation in the human rights context to Abdoulaye Dieye of Senegal, in his capacity as an expert in relation to the situation in Chile (A/34/583/Add.1, para 124).

[84] *Velásquez Rodriguez v Honduras (Merits)*, IACtHR Series C No 4, 29 July 1988.

[85] Report of the Special Rapporteur on violence against women, E/CN.4/2006/6 (20 January 2006).

[86] *Opuz v Turkey*, App no 33401/02, Judgment of 9 June 2009; see also *Case of González et al. ('Cotton Field') v Mexico (Preliminary Objection, Merits, Reparations, and Costs)*, IACtHR Series C No 205, 16 November, 2009.

[87] Council of Europe Convention on Preventing and Combating Violence against Women and Domestic Violence, CETS No 210, 11 May 2011, Art 5.

[88] Most importantly the Declaration on the Elimination of Violence against Women, GA Res 48/104, 20 December 1993.

[89] Regional treaties on violence against women are the Inter-American Convention on the Prevention, Punishment and Eradication of Violence against Women, Belém do Pará, 1994 and the Protocol to the African Charter on Human and Peoples' Rights on the Rights of Women in Africa, 2003; Council of Europe Convention on Preventing and Combating Violence against Women and Domestic Violence, 2011. See Chapter 16.

[90] Res A/HRC/17/L.9/Rev.1.   [91] A/HRC/19/41, 17 November 2011.

[92] Council of Europe Convention on Preventing and Combating Violence against Women and Domestic Violence, 2011, Art 4(3) is the first treaty provision prohibiting discrimination on the grounds of sexual orientation and gender identity with respect to the provisions of the Convention.

10 CONCLUSION

The formal sources of international human rights law derive from state consent: states negotiate and enter into treaties; custom is drawn from state behaviour and intent. However, this conclusion should be treated with some caution for two reasons. First, the requirement for state consent may be weakening through the turn to international community interests and values as in the concept of *jus cogens*. Long a theoretical concept that held little attraction for judges and decision-makers, *jus cogens* has been more widely appealed to since the 1990s. Second, human rights law speaks to people who appeal to its standards against what they regard as unwarranted state intrusion into their lives. It provides a language, a methodology, and techniques for challenging state action. Working as individuals and through human rights NGOs, they seek to influence the development of human rights law through a range of activities. The practice and statements of these non-state actors do not constitute formal sources of human rights law but they should not be ignored. NGOs have been the driving force in the negotiation of a number of treaties (for example, the UNCAT, the CRC, and the CRPD) and their recommendations and monitoring activities may influence state practice.[93]

Contemporary human rights law is dynamic and evolving through claims for new rights, additional instruments, and practices. Decision-makers have a choice: they can be rigid and rely strictly on formal sources which they interpret narrowly; or they may interpret open-ended and indeterminate treaty language, or move beyond treaties to the range of other instruments that are out there to capture a wide range of behaviours and assert them to be contrary to international law.

FURTHER READING

ALVAREZ, *International Organizations as Law-Makers* (Oxford University Press, 2005).

BRILMAYER, 'From "Contract" to Pledge": The Structure of International Human Rights Agreements' (2006) 77 *BYBIL* 163.

BOYLE and CHINKIN, *The Making of International Law* (Oxford University Press, 2007).

CASSESE, *International Law* (Oxford University Press, 2005) chs 8–11, 19.

CLAPHAM, 'Human Rights Obligations of Non-state Actors in Conflict Situations' (2006) 88 *IRRC* 491.

CRAWFORD, *Brownlie's Principles of Public International Law* (Oxford University Press, 8th edn 2012) ch 2.

GOWLLAND-DEBBAS (ed), *Multilateral Treaty-Making* (Martinus Nijhoff, 2000).

INTERNATIONAL LAW ASSOCIATION, *Final Report of the Committee on Formation of Customary (General) International Law* (2000) available at <http://www.ila-hq.org/en/committees/index.cfm/cid/30>.

MECHLEM, 'Treaty Bodies and the Interpretation of Human Rights' (2009) 42 *Vanderbilt J Trans'l L* 905.

MOYN, *The Last Utopia* (Harvard University Press, 2010).

ORAKHELASHVILI, *Peremptory Norms in International Law* (Oxford University Press, 2008).

---

[93] NGOs and expert groups produce carefully researched and drafted statements that they hope may lead to formal acceptance, or at the least influence state behaviour. A recent example is the Maastricht Principles on Extraterritorial Obligations of States in the Area of Economic, Social and Cultural Rights. See De Schutter et al., 'Commentary to the Maastricht Principles on Extraterritorial Obligations of States in the Area of Economic, Social and Cultural Rights' (2012) 34 *HRQ* 1084.

Roberts and Sivakumaran, 'Lawmaking by Nonstate Actors: Engaging Armed Groups in the Creation of International Humanitarian Law' (2012) 37 *Yale JIL* 107.

Simma and Alston, 'The Sources of Human Rights Law: Custom, *Jus Cogens* and

General Principles' (1992) 12 *Australian YIL* 82.

Teitel, *Humanity's Law* (Oxford University Press, 2011).

Wuerth, '*Pinochet's* Legacy Reassessed' (2012) 106 *AJIL* 731.

USEFUL WEBSITES

For the work of the UN treaty bodies, see the website of the Office of the High Commissioner for Human Rights, Human Rights bodies: **<http://www.ohchr.org/EN/HRBodies/Pages/ HumanRightsBodies.aspx>**

For the UN Human Rights Council, see: **<http://www.ohchr.org/EN/HRBodies/HRC/ Pages/HRCIndex.aspx>**

For human rights treaties, see the University of Minnesota human rights library: **<http:// www1.umn.edu/humanrts/>**

5

NATURE OF OBLIGATIONS

Frédéric Mégret

SUMMARY

Human rights obligations have a special status in international law because they are, in some ways, fundamentally different from other international law obligations. States that ratify international human rights treaties are not primarily committing to respect human rights vis-à-vis other states, but vis-à-vis persons within their jurisdiction. This is what is sometimes known as the 'special character' of international human rights obligations and it has concrete implications. States must implement human rights domestically in particular ways, even though they may have a 'margin of appreciation' in doing so. When ratifying human rights treaties, states must be particularly careful of what reservations they make, as many reservations have been found to be incompatible with the 'object and purpose' of such treaties. Human rights obligations can be limited on the basis of certain needs justifiable in a democratic society, and can even be derogated from in very exceptional circumstances, but it is likely that a state cannot withdraw entirely from a human rights treaty if the treaty does not contain a clause on denunciation.

1 INTRODUCTION

What is the fundamental nature of human rights obligations? What does it mean to be bound by international human rights law? Obligations can be defined in terms of their duty-holders and their beneficiaries. In trying to assess the 'nature' of human rights obligations, this chapter will go beyond assessing duty-holders and beneficiaries to understand what *sort* of obligations are involved. For example, are human rights obligations fundamentally unilateral or multilateral, reciprocal or non-reciprocal, temporal or eternal, conditional or unconditional, relative or absolute? The main idea in this chapter is that human rights obligations are in some ways very distinct from other types of obligations existing under general international law.

Why does this matter and why should general international law be the standard of comparison? First, international human rights law is a branch of public international law. When human rights lawyers sought to internationalize the human rights project in the middle of the twentieth century, they had no choice but to draw on the body of law existing at the global level.[1] Only public international law could bind states 'from above' and change domestic practices. However, international law as a legal system is far from

---

[1] See Chapter 1.

neutral. It comes with its own legal assumptions, preferences, and logic, some of which, as will be seen, might be at odds with the very idea and purpose of human rights. It must be remembered that, classically, international law was a law created by, between, and for states. Its cardinal concept was state sovereignty, and the typical source of obligation was state voluntarism (that is, states are only bound by those obligations to which they have consented). International law was, in a sense, dedicated to ensuring that state sovereignty and state voluntarism would not be undermined. It would be surprising, therefore, if these origins did not lead to some tensions with the human rights project, the goal of which is very much geared towards redefining sovereignty.

Although the stark divide between public international law and international human rights law has lessened over time as the development of the former has been influenced by the growth of the latter, some tensions between these bodies of law remain. The problem can be analysed as one of tension between substance and form, where ideally in any given legal system the two should be aligned. Substantively, the projects of public international law and international human rights law could not be more at odds. Human rights law is concerned with proclaiming and enforcing certain fundamental guarantees for individuals against the state. As such, it is both radical and revolutionary. The strict international protection of sovereignty is, in principle, largely incompatible with a strong stance in favour of human rights, in that human rights deal with issues that are essentially domestic and traditionally considered to be part of states' exclusive purview.

Formally, human rights law and general international law differ very significantly. International law is the slow maturing of ancient customary practice. It emphasizes states' obligations, and it is marked by a high degree of flexibility. Human rights law emerges from the proclamation of rights, usually in declarations. It outlines minimum rights with a strong principled component, and its focus is on the beneficiaries of obligations (individuals). However, the two have converged formally, at least to the extent that human rights obligations are typically given their binding character internationally by being recognized in international sources, such as custom and treaty.

Inevitably, this creates a tension between the *substance* of human rights, and the *form* they take, between the idea of rights as inherent to the human person and the fact that they only have traction internationally to the extent they are recognized in, especially, treaties. Historically, international law has been seen as neutral about political ends, essentially only offering states the means for a very basic interaction that safeguarded their sovereignty by allowing them to coexist. International norms emerged from consent between equals. The model for them was the *contract*, that is, an obligation based on reciprocity. In other words, the obligations of each party are entered into in exchange for the other party undertaking similar obligations, and each party is bound to the extent that the other respects its own obligations.

Some of the implications of this included the fact that states could subscribe to whatever obligations they freely agreed to, modify the content of their obligations through consensus, and even under certain conditions cease to respect certain obligations. A further consequence was that international legal instruments only created obligations between states, at the expense of individuals who were considered mere 'objects' of international law, at best unintended and collateral beneficiaries of obligations undertaken by sovereigns. Although international law diversified substantively over time—regulating ever more areas of international life—it did and largely still does claim to lay the ground rules for all thematic branches of international law. For example, the Vienna Convention on the Law of Treaties (VCLT) is not interested in the particular content of treaties, whether they deal with trade, the environment, or diplomatic immunities; it lays down the same basic rules which apply to all treaties.

The problem is that the international law form—the particular expression international commitments take legally—is not substantively neutral and the substance of human rights does not always fit this form. The point has been made eloquently by Craven in the context of human rights treaties:

> [In human rights] treaties the two elements of 'form' and 'function' appear to be fundamentally at odds with one another. On the one hand, the form in which the rights are expressed—the treaty—supposes that human rights are merely the incidental subject of a contractual bargain between states. Individual 'right-holders' are therefore simply the fortuitous beneficiaries of a regime that is otherwise concerned with promoting the rights and interests of states. The teleology of the regime on the other hand—focused as it is on individual or group 'human rights'—supposes that the treaties are quasi-constitutional in character.[2]

Historically, this has created a very significant conceptual and practical challenge for human rights lawyers: how can we avoid the human rights project being stultified, or even absorbed, by the language of traditional international law? The answer generally has been to redefine human rights obligations, particularly treaty obligations, as having a 'special character'. Thus, human rights obligations are dependent on, and yet also crucially distinct from, the way in which international legal obligations typically operate. But this idea that human rights obligations are somehow 'special' needs to be grounded and explained, to understand exactly what its basis and implications are.

This chapter will introduce the basic idea of what it means for a legal obligation to be described as 'special' in nature in international law (Section 2). It will then identify several key consequences that can be said to flow from this character in terms of implementing human rights obligations (Section 3), reservations (Section 4), limitations and derogations (Section 5), withdrawal (Section 6), and enforcement (Section 7).

2 THE 'SPECIAL CHARACTER' OF HUMAN RIGHTS OBLIGATIONS

Defining in general terms the 'special character' of human rights obligations is a difficult exercise. The fundamental idea is that international human rights obligations differ from normal international law obligations in that they deal with the obligations of states towards individuals rather than between states.

At a certain level, international human rights law is hardly a rejection of all the rules of public international law. As has been seen in Chapter 4, for example, there is no reason to think that the list of existing sources of the 'branch' that is international human rights law is entirely different from the 'trunk' of public international law. International human rights treaties borrow much from the traditional law of treaties, including the way treaties come into existence, the simple idea that states are bound by treaties they ratify (the *pacta sunt servanda* rule), and that states should discharge their obligations in good faith. Many of the key aspects of state responsibility (that is, what happens when a state violates its obligation), moreover, are applicable in the field of human rights. There is no reason to think that any of these rules apply in markedly different ways simply because the subject matter of a treaty is human rights.

---

[2] Craven, 'Legal Differentiation and the Concept of the Human Rights Treaty in International Law' (2000) 11 *EJIL* 489, 493.

However, there are also clearly some ways in which human rights obligations are different. A traditional treaty is one that creates rights and obligations between states, to the broad exclusion of any other actor, even if that other actor may objectively benefit from such arrangements. States typically *exchange* such rights and obligations, with a view to securing an advantage commensurate with their costs. Moreover, treaties are often quite strictly relational: states enter into treaties only with those states with which they want to enter into such treaties. Finally, as states are not normally interested in the substantive content of contracts concluded between private parties, international law traditionally does not have a significant stake in the subject matter to which states commit (as opposed to the fact that they should honour whatever commitments they make).

Human rights treaties, of which there are many, superficially borrow the idea of an agreement between states as the basis of international human rights obligations. But they are also strikingly different. They are agreements, typically between states, the beneficiaries of which are in fact third parties, namely 'all individuals within [the state's] territory'.[3] Indeed, human rights treaties create rights specifically for individuals who are not normally subjects of international law generally or treaties specifically. To describe human rights treaties as contractual, moreover, would be profoundly misleading. It is wrong to say that states commit to respecting certain human rights obligations in exchange for other states doing the same. Rather states are formally binding themselves to other states, even though they in fact mostly create rights for individuals within their jurisdiction. From a practical point of view, international human rights obligations are not as dependent on the idea of reciprocity as most ordinary treaties, where the interest of incurring an obligation will very quickly lapse if the other party or parties do not comply with their obligations. For example, one would hope that a state would not simply feel it is no longer bound by the obligation not to torture simply because other states party to the UN Convention against Torture engage in torture. Finally, human rights lawyers think that human rights treaties have a substance that is inherently of a high normative worth, above and beyond states' consent to be bound by them.

All these differences are very important, because they have an impact on the way international human rights obligations are understood, administered, and interpreted. To capture what makes human rights different, human rights lawyers have forged the unique notion of the 'special character' of human rights obligations. At first, the meaning of 'special character' was unclear. It seemed to be one of those 'catch-all' phrases that merely seemed to imply that ordinary rules of international law did not apply when it came to human rights. However, human rights bodies have refined the idea over the years to reflect what is distinctive about human rights, and the idea now has a quite distinct doctrinal content.

The first reference to the special character of a human rights treaty occurred when the General Assembly sought an advisory opinion from the International Court of Justice (ICJ) on reservations to the Genocide Convention. The Court distinguished between ordinary treaties and those of a humanitarian or human rights character. In the case of the latter:

> [T]he contracting States do not have any interests of their own; they merely have, one and all, a common interest, namely, the accomplishment of those high purposes which are the *raison d'être* of the convention. Consequently, in a convention of this type one cannot speak of individual advantages or disadvantages to States, or of the maintenance of a perfect contractual balance between rights and duties.[4]

---

[3] ICCPR, Art 2.
[4] *Reservations to the Genocide Convention* (Advisory Opinion) [1951] ICJ Rep 15, para 23.

The idea was that the Genocide Convention created something greater than the sum of each party's will. Moreover, there was a certain vertical element involved: states were not so much bargaining between each other horizontally, as solemnly committing themselves to a certain supranational standard of behaviour.

A similar approach was taken by the European Commission of Human Rights in 1961, when it affirmed that:

> The obligations undertaken by the High Contracting Parties in the [European] Convention [on Human Rights] are essentially of an objective character, being designed rather to protect the fundamental rights of individual human beings from infringements by any of the High Contracting Parties than to create subjective and reciprocal rights for the High Contracting Parties themselves.[5]

In this context, 'objective' does not mean that the obligations in question are absolute or that they are scientifically proven. Rather, it should be understood in the legal meaning of not strictly dependent on the commitments of other states ('subjective'). Again, the idea is that, despite appearances of a treaty being concluded with other states, there is something relatively unilateral about states' adherence to a treaty like the European Convention on Human Rights (ECHR). States are better understood as making a solemn promise to the international community, and indeed to individuals within their jurisdiction.

The Inter-American Court of Human Rights has added its own views on the idea of special character. As the Court put it in one of its advisory opinions:

> [M]odern human rights treaties in general, and the American Convention in particular, *are not multilateral treaties of the traditional type concluded to accomplish the reciprocal exchange of rights for the mutual benefit of the contracting States.* Their object and purpose is the protection of the basic rights of individual human beings irrespective of their national-ity, both against the State of their nationality and all other contracting States. In concluding these human rights treaties, the States *can be deemed to submit themselves to a legal order within which they, for the common good, assume various obligations, not in relation to other States, but towards all individuals within their jurisdiction.*[6]

The special character of human rights suggests that states' human rights obligations are in some ways independent of their consent to be bound by them. Human rights obligations have a life of their own that takes over as soon as states have manifested their initial com-mitment to be bound. This is also linked to old claims about human rights pre-existing their legal recognition (the idea, for example, that rights exist 'in nature'). States are sol-emnly committing to something which they were already, at least morally or philosophi-cally, obliged to recognize. Another way of putting it would be to say that becoming a party to a human rights treaty is *declaratory* of states' obligations rather than *constitutive* of them.[7]

Moreover, the objective character of human rights obligations points to their *erga omnes* status. The ICJ famously suggested that certain obligations may have an *erga omnes* char-acter in that they are owed 'towards the international community as a whole' so that 'by their very nature, (they) are the concern of all States'.[8] What was a slightly puzzling obiter

---

[5] *Austria v Italy (Pfunders Case)* (1961) 4 YB 116, para 138.

[6] OC-2/82, *The Effect of Reservations on the Entry into Force of the American Convention (Arts 74 and 75)*, IACtHR Series A No 2 (24 September 1982) paras 29–30 (emphases added).   [7] See Chapter 2.

[8] *Barcelona Traction, Light and Power Company, Limited (Belgium v Spain)* (New Application: 1962) [1970] ICJ Rep 3, para 33.

dictum in the general international law context, has become relatively mainstream in the human rights environment, where it is understood that, precisely as a result of the special character of human rights obligations, each and every state (that is a party to the human rights system) has an interest in their enforcement. Indeed, it could be said that international human rights obligations have become a typical example of *erga omnes* obligations. This, in turn, justifies routine scrutiny by states of the human rights record of others even though they have not directly suffered a prejudice, something that would be unthinkable in general international law.[9]

Another dimension of the 'special character' is the idea that human rights instruments are more like legislative, or even constitutional, norms than the treaties they are embedded in would suggest. The ECHR has been described by the European Court of Human Rights as a 'constitutional instrument of European public order'.[10] The reference to this constitutional character also underlines the extent to which international human rights treaties, perhaps especially regional ones, are part of governance structures and, beyond that, one of the normative foundations of particular political communities (for example, that of the Council of Europe in the case of the ECHR, or the entire international community in the case of the International Covenant on Economic, Social and Cultural Rights (ICESCR) and the International Covenant on Civil and Political Rights (ICCPR)). International human rights thus appear as the cement that binds groups of states together in a collective project that is both domestic and supranational, rather than international in the strict sense of the term.

Although the special nature of human rights obligations might at first appear to be a mere doctrinal construct, what is remarkable is the extent to which concrete consequences have flowed from this idea. In Sections 3, 4, 5, 6, and 7 we will see some of the manifestations of the special character of human rights obligations, and the considerable impact it has had on the implementation of human rights.

3 IMPLEMENTATION OF HUMAN RIGHTS OBLIGATIONS

Typically, under traditional international law the manner in which an obligation is supposed to be discharged is not specified. States simply have to do what they commit themselves to do, and considerable discretion is left as to the means by which they do so. When it comes to human rights, this traditional laissez-faire approach will not do because of the broad and comprehensive character of the obligations involved. International human rights law has thus come up with a complex concept of how obligations are to be discharged and a new vocabulary of obligations has emerged. Typically, states are supposed to 'respect and ensure rights to all individuals'.[11] However, this is a very broad obligation and in practice the UN human rights treaty bodies have adopted a tripartite typology of how human rights obligations should be secured. According to that typology, states must respect, protect, and fulfil human rights.

---

[9] See *Questions Relating to the Obligation to Prosecute or Extradite (Belgium v Senegal)* [2012] ICJ Rep, paras 68–69.

[10] *Loizidou v Turkey* (Preliminary Objections) (1995) 20 EHRR 99, para 75.   [11] Eg ICCPR, Art 2.

3.1 RESPECT

The duty to secure human rights is, perhaps first and foremost, a duty to 'respect' human rights. Thus, states have a negative obligation not to take any measures that result in a violation of a given right. They should not consciously violate rights, either through their organs (for example, parliament or the executive) or through their agents (such as, civil servants, the police, or the army). This obligation not to interfere is perhaps the most classical one.

3.2 PROTECT

In addition, and this notion is becoming ever more important, states must 'protect' individuals from human rights violations.[12] This means that the state needs to proactively ensure that persons within its jurisdiction do not suffer from human rights violations at the hands of third parties. This is much more akin to creating an environment in which rights are enjoyed. Of course, the state does not become liable for every adverse interference with individuals' rights by private actors. However, the state *is* liable for those failures that can be traced to its shortcomings in protecting individuals from other individuals, for example because it has adopted a law that made the violation possible, or because it has failed to do something that would have prevented the violation from happening.[13] This is known as the indirect horizontal effect of human rights. States have been found liable for failing to protect demonstrators from third parties,[14] for failing to protect an individual from murder despite the fact that the police knew the victim's life had been threatened,[15] and, in cases of domestic violence, for failing to provide adequate structures or legal protection to abused women.[16] As the Inter-American Court of Human Rights put it in the landmark case of *Velásquez Rodríguez v Honduras*, which involved the forced disappearance by unidentified abductors of a student activist:

> An illegal act which violates human rights and which is initially not directly imputable to a State (for example, because it is the act of a private person or because the person responsible has not been identified) can lead to international responsibility of the State, not because of the act itself, but because of the lack of due diligence to prevent the violation or to respond to it as required by the [American] Convention..... [The state is liable when it] allows private persons or groups to act freely and with impunity to the detriment of the rights recognized by the Convention.[17]

The obligation to protect has been particularly instrumental in connecting states to violations of the rights of women, in cases where states were found not to have made adequate provision to protect women from violence, typically in the home. Violations that occur *a priori* in the private sphere (and were as a result traditionally neglected by human rights law), have thus been linked to the public sphere. The obligation to protect is also very

---

[12] This specific doctrinal meaning of the obligation to protect is very different and quite unrelated to the idea of the 'Responsibility to Protect', which has recently become quite popular in international circles, and which deals with state and international community responsibility to avert atrocities.

[13] Eg *X and Y v The Netherlands* (1986) 8 EHRR 235; *Young, James and Webster v UK* (1982) 4 EHRR 38. See also Chapter 6.

[14] *Plattform 'Ärzte für das Leben' v Austria* (1991) 13 EHRR 204.

[15] *Osman v UK* (2000) 29 EHRR 245; *William Eduardo Delgado Páez v Colombia*, CCPR/C/39/D/195/1985 (12 July 1990).

[16] *AT v Hungary* A/60/38 (Part I) Annex III (26 January 2005).

[17] *Velásquez Rodríguez v Honduras* (*Merits*), IACtHR Series C No 4 (29 July 1988), paras 172 and 176.

important in the disability context where it is understood to impose obligations on the state to create an environment that is conducive to the enjoyment of their rights by persons with disability.

3.3 FULFIL

The obligation to 'respect' human rights is a primarily negative one (to not actively violate rights). Treaty bodies, however, have also long emphasized the existence of an obligation to 'fulfil' human rights, by which it is understood that states should take positive steps that have as a consequence the greater enjoyment of rights. Some civil and political rights, such as the right to vote, are meaningless if the state does nothing to implement them. Similarly, the right to be free from torture entails not only an obligation not to torture but also an obligation to adopt all types of concrete measures to prevent and sanction torture (for example, training of police or prison officers, rules on the non-admissibility of evidence obtained under torture, and so on).[18]

In formal terms, the obligation to fulfil involves an obligation on states to adopt appropriate laws that implement their international undertakings. This may involve incorporating the very rights protected by the international instrument into domestic law. However, treaty bodies, confronted with claims by states that rights were effectively protected simply because they were formally incorporated in the constitution, have insisted that the duty to secure human rights includes an obligation to adopt, not just legislative measures, but also 'judicial, administrative and educative and other appropriate measures',[19] and an obligation to organize the structure of the state apparatus in a way that ensures the full exercise of human rights.

In particular, the obligation to fulfil entails provision of a remedy, whether judicial or administrative, to all victims of human rights violations. In the *Velásquez Rodríguez* case, the Inter-American Court of Human Rights insisted that:

> The State is obligated to investigate every situation involving a violation of the rights protected by the Convention. If the State apparatus acts in such a way that the violation goes unpunished and the victim's full enjoyment of such rights is not restored as soon as possible, the State has failed to comply with its duty to ensure the free and full exercise of those rights to the persons within its jurisdiction.[20]

Economic and social rights are the prime example of rights which entail a positive obligation to adopt specific measures and where 'not doing anything' is not an option. The obligation to fulfil has been understood in the context of the right to food as entailing both an obligation to *facilitate* individuals' ability to access resources and means to ensure their livelihood and an obligation to *provide* them with adequate food whenever they are unable to enjoy the right to food 'for reasons beyond their control'.[21] At its most general, the obligation to fulfil is considered also to involve an obligation to *promote* human rights, which means that states should adopt policies that promote rights both domestically (for example, human rights education) and internationally (such as a foreign policy conducive to human rights).

In practice, the obligations to 'respect', 'protect', and 'fulfil' are closely interrelated and it may not always be easy to make a clear-cut distinction between these different aspects.

---

[18] See Chapter 9.   [19] HRC, General Comment 31, HRI/GEN/1/Rev.9 (Vol I) 243, para 7.
[20] *Velásquez Rodríguez*, n 17, para 176.
[21] CESCR, General Comment 12, HRI/GEN/1/Rev.9 (Vol I) 55, para 15.

Nevertheless, the typology is a helpful conceptual device to identify the various ways in which states can and must discharge their obligations that are specific to international human rights law.

3.4 MARGIN OF APPRECIATION

Whereas general international law obligations are typically not susceptible to fine-tuning by states, international human rights law has been at the forefront of efforts to develop a geographically and culturally plural notion of implementation. Particularly in the European context, there is no expectation of absolute uniform implementation. Instead, a certain minimum standard should be achieved, while respecting the cultural, legal, and political specificity of each state. This is what the European Court of Human Rights describes as states having a 'margin of appreciation' in how they implement their obligations, taking into account their historical, social, political, and legal specificities. As the European Court put it:

> the main purpose of the Convention is 'to lay down certain international standards to be observed by the Contracting States in their relations with persons under their jurisdiction'. This does not mean that absolute uniformity is required and, indeed, since the Contracting States remain free to choose the measures which they consider appropriate, the Court cannot be oblivious of the substantive or procedural features of their respective domestic laws.[22]

This is often related to the jurisdictional notion that 'the machinery of protection established by the Convention is subsidiary to the national systems safeguarding human rights'.[23] The European Court views the margin as 'go(ing)...hand in hand with a European supervision'.[24]

One rationale for the margin of appreciation is that states and domestic courts are better suited to assess local peculiarities and that there is simply too much uncertainty about how human rights are to be implemented in practice for international supervision to exercise more than relatively minimal control. Issues of legitimacy also arise, as international bodies might provoke political backlash if they delve too deeply in matters that are seen as culturally specific.

Margin of appreciation reasoning has featured prominently in cases involving sexual minorities,[25] and the place of religion in society,[26] to mention only some examples. The margin of appreciation involves an assessment of the degree of consensus (a minimum common denominator) about a certain practice across member states. In the absence of such consensus and, more importantly, in the presence of significant divisions, the European Court will hesitate to impose on a minority (let alone a majority) of states a particular understanding of rights. It is important to note that whether there is a margin of appreciation for a particular issue is something that can evolve over time. For example, states parties to the ECHR may have had a certain margin of appreciation 50 years ago when it came to criminalizing homosexuality, but the very same treaty is interpreted radically differently today given changes in the European consensus on the issue, so that criminalizing same-sex relations between consenting adults is now a violation of several rights.

---

[22] *Sunday Times v UK* (1979–80) 2 EHRR 245, para 61.
[23] *'Belgian Linguistics' Case* (1979–80) 1 EHRR 241.
[24] *Kjeldsen, Busk Madsen and Pedersen v Denmark* (1979–80) 1 EHRR 711, para 49.
[25] *Dudgeon v UK* (1981) 4 EHRR 149; *Frette v France* (2004) 38 EHRR 21; *Goodwin v UK* (2002) 35 EHRR 18.
[26] *Otto-Preminger-Institut v Austria* (1995) 19 EHRR 34; *Wingrove v UK* (1997) 24 EHRR 1, para 57; *'The Last Temptation of Christ' v Chile* (*Olmedo Bustos et al.*), IACtHR Series C No 73 (5 February 2001), para 64.

One of the consequences of this is that the margin of appreciation militates in favour of a conservative international assessment of rights. The European Court of Human Rights has often been less of a pioneer than a safe endorser of existing trends and developments. But on a more positive note, the margin of appreciation also reinforces the sense of human rights being rooted in a community of reference (which is also a community of interpretation), dynamic in time, and a product of a constant interaction between rights and ideas about society and justice.

The idea of the margin of appreciation is not universally accepted beyond the European context. It has been criticized as leading to an excessively relativistic application of human rights that may even contain the seeds of the project's dissolution. The Human Rights Committee, in particular, has expressed scepticism about the notion.[27]

4 RESERVATIONS

States may modify their obligations under international human rights treaties by entering reservations. Reservations are a particularly technical area of international law, but the study of this rather dry subject in the context of international human rights law is enlightening. A reservation is defined in Article 2 VCLT as a 'unilateral statement, however phrased or named, made by a State, when signing, ratifying, accepting, approving or acceding to a Treaty, whereby it purports to exclude or to modify the legal effect of certain provisions of the Treaty in their application to that State.' The aim of a reservation is to limit a state's obligations under a particular treaty. International law is not formalistic about what constitutes a reservation: it does not matter whether a state presents it as a 'general political statement' or a 'declaration of interpretation'. If the result is exclusion or modification of the legal effect of certain provisions, it will be considered a reservation.

In the international human rights context, states have availed themselves broadly of the possibility of reservations, both quantitatively and qualitatively. For example, as of October 2009, 38 of the 165 state parties to the ICCPR had, between them, entered more than 200 reservations. A typical reservation is one whereby a state purports to interpret an internationally protected right only in accordance with its domestic, often constitutional or religious, law. For example, the USA has entered a reservation to the ICCPR that its obligations under Article 7, regarding the prohibition of torture and other cruel, inhuman, and degrading treatment, are to be interpreted in the light of its constitutional protections of rights.[28] A problematic reservation from some states has been to the effect that accession to a human rights treaty, such as the Convention on the Elimination of Discrimination against Women (CEDAW), is 'subject to the general reservation that such accession cannot conflict with the laws on personal status derived from Islamic Sharia'.[29]

There are, of course, valid reasons why a state may wish to enter reservations to human rights treaties. A state may generally be committed to human rights but have problems with one particular provision, and therefore want to exclude or limit the application of that provision in order to be able to become a party to the treaty. The state may wish to inject a certain cultural understanding of a particular obligation, or guard against an expansive interpretation by international human rights bodies by pre-empting the meaning of a

---

[27] See HRC, General Comment 34, CCPR/C/GC/34 (12 September 2011), para 36.

[28] See US reservations, declarations, and understandings, International Covenant on Civil and Political Rights, 138 Cong Rec S4781-01 (2 April 1992).

[29] Such is the wording of the Libyan reservation to the CEDAW.

particular provision. States may know in advance that part of their domestic law is incompatible with a provision of a treaty and seek some temporary accommodation. This sort of international legal flexibility is something that human rights lawyers may want to allow, if only to encourage states to ratify treaties.

However, there is no doubt that reservations are problematic for international human rights law, perhaps even more so than they are for general international law.[30] Human rights are clearly more of a 'package' than most international normative instruments. There is a very real tension between the idea of human rights and the notion that a state may, through reservations, pick and choose the obligations to which it wishes to be bound or interpret them as it so wishes, at the risk of emptying some of their content. It is the very universality of human rights and the whole point of international human rights treaties which is threatened if states do not agree to honour the same rights. Moreover, there is a sense that some states may 'free ride' human rights treaties, by obtaining the benefits broadly associated with being a party to them, whilst subscribing only to an eviscerated set of obligations. Finally and crucially, reservations also create problems of legal certainty, making it difficult for individuals to ascertain the exact scope of the rights they have been guaranteed.

Accordingly, human rights supervisory bodies have frequently deplored the abundance and scope of reservations, and urged states to repeal them. This is in itself a departure from ordinary international treaties, where few bodies are authorized or would see fit to criticize a practice that is largely seen as within a state's prerogative. In fact, international human rights law has also evolved specific notions of what reservations are permissible, who may decide on their permissibility, and what consequences flow from reservations.

4.1 PERMISSIBILITY

The general regime under Article 19 VCLT is that states may formulate reservations to a treaty, unless a reservation is prohibited by the treaty or, more ambiguously, is incompatible with its object and purpose. Although Article 19 provides 'relevant guidance',[31] and some states have insisted that the general regime of international law is sufficient,[32] human rights bodies have nonetheless developed quite a specific approach to permissible reservations. Most human rights treaties neither allow nor specifically exclude reservations.[33] Therefore, most of the discussion has focused on whether certain reservations are compatible with the 'object and purpose' of the respective treaties.

One of the most important sources on the issue is the Human Rights Committee's general comment on reservations, General Comment 24, the very existence of which is an indication of how seriously the issue is taken by the UN treaty monitoring bodies. According to the Committee:

> In an instrument which articulates very many civil and political rights, each of the many articles, and indeed their interplay, secures the objectives of the Covenant. *The object and purpose of the Covenant is to create legally binding standards for human rights* by defining certain civil and political rights and placing them in a framework of obligations which

---

[30] The ILC Guide to Practice on Reservations to Treaties suggests a certain wariness of reservations and reflects the evolution of international law towards a relatively narrow concept of permissible reservations. See ILC, Guide to Practice on Reservations to Treaties, 2011.

[31] HRC, General Comment 24, HRI/GEN/1/Rev.9 (Vol I) 210, para 6.

[32] Eg Observations on General Comment 24 (1996) 3 IHHR 261, para 4.

[33] There are a few exceptions. See Second Optional Protocol to the ICCPR, aiming at the abolition of the death penalty, Art 2(1); ECHR, Art 57.

are legally binding for those States which ratify; and to provide an efficacious supervisory machinery for the obligations undertaken.[34]

The Human Rights Committee defines the object and purpose of the ICCPR very broadly. Moreover, the sheer interdependence of rights suggests that it will be difficult to make reservations to one right without altering the entire content of the obligations contained in a treaty. The Committee has also specifically excluded a number of reservations which it considers would be incompatible per se with the object and purpose of human rights treaties, such as those violating peremptory norms, customary international law, or non-derogable norms.

States may not make reservations relating to certain basic guarantees associated with the rights protected, such as the right to an effective remedy. Defined as 'supportive guarantees', these provisions are seen to provide 'the necessary framework for securing the rights in the Covenant and are thus essential to its object and purpose'.[35] In fact, they 'are an integral part of the structure of the Covenant and underpin its efficacy' so that to limit them would defeat the purpose of the ICCPR.[36] Finally, states cannot make reservations to institutional arrangements designed to supervise the implementation of treaties. For example, a state cannot become a party to one of the universal human rights treaties and make a reservation to the effect that it does not consider itself bound by the obligation to submit periodic reports to its corresponding supervisory body.

This leaves very few areas where reservations might be valid. The Human Rights Committee does give a few examples of reservations that would be considered acceptable, such as a reservation saying that communications can be heard by the Committee only after the entry into force of the ICCPR for the state party, or that communications cannot be examined if they are already being examined by a comparable international procedure. These reservations are procedural rather than substantive in nature. Even assuming a reservation is permitted, the Human Rights Committee has added a number of formal and substantive requirements to the type of reservations that can be made, for example: that they must be 'specific and transparent', cannot be 'general', and must 'refer to a particular provision'. Moreover, states should 'take into consideration the overall effect of a group of reservations', and avoid committing to treaties only to the extent that these conform with their domestic law.[37]

The European Court of Human Rights has also considered invalid a number of reservations that were 'too vague or broad for it to be possible to determine their exact meaning and scope'.[38] In *Loizidou v Turkey*, for example, it found that the 'special character of the Convention as an instrument of European public order' meant that Turkey's attempt to exclude the application of the ECHR to Northern Cyprus by a reservation was invalid.[39]

The grounds for such limitations to the ability to make reservations are easily understandable. International human rights bodies have sought to protect international treaties from crippling reservations that lead to 'a perpetual non-attainment of international human rights standards'[40] and protect beneficiaries from uncertainty about the exact scope of their rights. Thus, the use of reservations is tightly constrained by numerous rules

---

[34] General Comment 24, n 31, para 7 (emphasis added).
[35] General Comment 24, n 31, para 11.
[36] General Comment 24, n 31, para 11.   [37] General Comment 24, n 31, para 19.
[38] *Belilos v Switzerland* (1988) 10 EHRR 466, para 55.
[39] *Loizidou v Turkey* (1997) 23 EHRR 513, para 43.   [40] General Comment 24, n 31, para 19.

that suggest that the object and purpose of the human rights treaty would be defeated by selective assumption of human rights obligations.

4.2 RESPONSIBILITY FOR ASSESSMENT

In a typical international law scenario, the invalidity of reservations will be raised by other states parties. However, one can see how the dependence on state objections to reservations is problematic for the protection of human rights. In the human rights context, states might be less likely to object to other states' reservations, for the simple reason that generally they are not impacted by these reservations. States have occasionally manifested their rejection of other states' reservations, but this is a haphazard process. In fact, as the Human Rights Committee has pointed out, the pattern is so unclear that it is not safe to assume that a non-objecting state thinks that a particular reservation is acceptable.[41]

These key differences have led the Human Rights Committee to opine that 'the operation of the classic rules on reservations is inadequate for the [ICCPR]'.[42] Consequently, a new rule has emerged in the human rights context, whereby a purely consensual approach to reservations (reservations are accepted or not) has been replaced by an increasingly axiological one (reservations are valid or not). States are asked to act as the guardians of the integrity of human rights treaties and judge whether reservations are valid, rather than simply be the keepers of their own national interest. Moreover, human rights bodies, whether judicial or supervisory organs, have seen themselves as the defenders of the *ordre public* of international human rights law and raised issues of invalid reservations before actual disputes arise. The particular interest that the international community has in the integrity of human rights treaties necessitates that reservations fall under a strong system of international supervision.

4.3 CONSEQUENCES

The consequences that flow from reservations are complex, particularly if reservations turn out to be invalid. This matter raises different problems for the treaty, the reserving state, and third states. There is a fundamental tension between, on the one hand, the desire to have as many states as possible ratify a treaty, thereby allowing it to enter into force as quickly as possible and in relation to as many parties as possible, and, on the other hand, the risk of a treaty's integrity being compromised by too many reservations.

As regards the effects of reservations on the entire treaty, Article 20(2) VCLT provides that only where 'it appears from the limited number of the negotiating States and the object and purpose of a treaty that the application of the treaty in its entirety between all the parties is an essential condition of the consent of each one to be bound by the treaty' do all state parties to a treaty need to accept a reservation. This would be typical of treaties between very few parties. However, international human rights treaties are the exact opposite, since they are intended to become universal. Therefore, reservations do not have to be accepted by all states for a human rights treaty to enter into force. This explains why so many human rights treaties have entered into force despite considerable numbers of reservations.

The second question is what happens to reserving states. Under general international law, the position is that the reserving state becomes bound by the treaty if at least one other state accepts the reservation.[43] However, in the context of treaties of a humanitarian

---

[41] General Comment 24, n 31, para 17.   [42] General Comment 24, n 31, para 17.
[43] VCLT, Art 20(4)(c).

or human rights character, the ICJ has held that states can in fact become party to a treaty even if other state parties object to its reservation:

> The object and purpose of the Genocide Convention imply that it was the intention of the General Assembly and of the States which adopted it that as many States as possible should participate. The complete exclusion from the Convention of one or more States would not only restrict the scope of its application but would detract from the authority of the moral and humanitarian principles which are its basis. It is inconceivable that the contracting parties readily contemplated that an objection to a minor reservation should produce such a result.[44]

Not only is there an interest in states being bound as soon as possible, notwithstanding the reservations of a few, but the specific nature of human rights treaties suggests that approval by other parties should really be seen as a secondary matter. This was further clarified by the Inter-American Court of Human Rights. The Inter-American Commission asked the Court for an advisory opinion on whether the American Convention on Human Rights (ACHR) would enter into force as soon as the requisite number of states had ratified it, or whether ratifications accompanied by reservations should be considered complete only when at least one state had accepted them (or, as the VCLT stipulates, all states parties had failed to object to them within a year of the ratification).[45] The Inter-American Court found that because of the special character of the ACHR as 'a multilateral legal instrument or framework enabling States to make binding unilateral commitments not to violate the human rights of individuals within their jurisdiction', it would enter into force regardless of whether any other state accepted reservations appended to an instrument of ratification as 'no useful purpose would be served by such a delay'.[46] In other words, states became bound the moment they deposited their instrument of ratification, notwithstanding the fact that their reservations were not accepted and might even be invalid. This again underlines the strictly non-relational character of human rights treaties.

One of the problems created by this approach is that the actual validity of reservations will only be examined at a later date. This can create complex issues of retroactive application when a reservation turns out to have been invalid all along. A state that has ratified a treaty with a reservation may insist that it ratified the treaty only on the basis of such a reservation and that if the latter is then found to be invalid, it is either not bound by the provision to which the reservation relates or not bound by the treaty at all. The opposite stance is that invalid reservations are 'severable' from the commitment to be bound by a treaty so that the reservation can be 'quarantined' and the overall commitment to the treaty preserved.

This last proposition was illustrated in the *Loizidou* case. The European Court of Human Rights held that Turkey's reservation excluding its activities in Northern Cyprus from the supervision of the European Court was invalid. The Court was then required to ascertain whether Turkey's broader recognition of jurisdiction was nonetheless valid. Under normal international law rules, the tendency would be to consider that the whole consent to the treaty had been contaminated by the invalidity of the reservation. Against Turkey's arguments, however, the Court considered that the reservation could be severed from the recognition of jurisdiction, so that Turkey would still be considered to have accepted the compulsory jurisdiction of the European Court. This was all the more so since, the Court

---

[44] *Reservations to the Genocide Convention*, n 4, para 24.
[45] VCLT, Art 20(4)(c).   [46] *Effect of Reservations*, n 6, para 33.

argued, Turkey must have known at the time that its reservation was invalid, especially in view of protests by several state parties.[47]

Finally, the situation of a state accepting another's reservation is perhaps the simplest. Under normal international law, a state that agrees to another state's reservation is bound in its relations with the other state by that reservation.[48] However, that is not a very helpful way of thinking about human rights treaties, for which it should not make a difference to states' commitment to individuals within their jurisdiction whether other states have sought to limit their ratification. In particular, the fact that a state accepts another state's invalid reservation certainly does not make that reservation applicable between them. Similarly, a state that objects to another state's reservation, even on grounds of invalidity, cannot draw on this to then claim that it is not bound in its relations with the other state by the relevant provision, or that it is not bound at all by the relevant provision, or that it is not bound by the treaty at all. It should again make no difference for the entry into force of a human rights treaty that a state is objecting to a reservation, precisely because such a reservation cannot in any significant way be said to affect the interests of that state as they are normally understood in treaty law. For example, the UK could not say that it is not bound by the ECHR or its recognition of the European Court's jurisdiction simply because it objects to Turkey having limited its jurisdiction to its continental territory.

One can see from such examples how the application of normal principles of international law to human rights treaties is almost nonsensical. As the Human Rights Committee put it:

> Human rights treaties, and the [ICCPR] specifically, are not a web of inter-State exchanges of mutual obligations. They concern the endowment of individuals with rights. The principle of inter-State reciprocity has no place.[49]

Therefore, a state is not released from its general obligation to abide by the ICCPR, merely because it disapproves of a reservation made by another state.

5 LIMITATIONS AND DEROGATIONS

Despite what is sometimes suggested, the vast majority of human rights are not absolute in the sense that they can never be limited. One of the only absolute rights is the right to be free from torture, which is absolute in the sense that no social goal or emergency can ever limit the categorical prohibition of torture. For the rest, there are two ways in which human rights can be limited. First, some treaty provisions explicitly provide circumstances in which the enjoyment of a right may be limited. These are known as limitations. Second, states have the possibility of derogating from their obligations in a time of emergency justifying exceptional measures.

5.1 LIMITATIONS

Although human rights stipulate certain forms of minimum treatment, the nature of this minimum treatment will vary somewhat. This is especially the case when human rights do not operate in an 'either/or' fashion (to be tortured or not to be tortured), but where the question is the scope of a right (for example, the degree of privacy to which one is

---

[47] *Loizidou v Turkey*, n 10, para 96.   [48] VCLT, Art 20(4)(b).   [49] General Comment 24, n 31, para 17.

entitled). Human rights obligations inevitably raise tensions between individual and social imperatives. To take an easy example, an individual who is imprisoned for having committed a crime following a fair trial cannot invoke a violation of his or her right not to be detained. It is understood that the right to liberty is limited by the exigencies of public order, as manifested through the operation of the criminal law. Moreover, it is primarily for the state to define the framework of collective life that constrains certain rights, in ways that other states will have little cause to complain about (unlike a normal international treaty situation based on exact reciprocity).

Limitations do not grant states the ability to abuse rights; they simply define the actual scope of rights. Rights are limited in a number of ways. Sometimes, because a right is crucial—and all rights relating to integrity and security of the person are—permitted limitations will be spelled out in detail. This is the case for the right to life (which is limited by the possibility of imposing the death penalty in some cases, killings in armed conflict situations, and the use of reasonable force by law enforcement agents)[50] or the right to be free from detention (which is limited by, for example, the possibility of being sentenced to imprisonment for a criminal offence, pursuant to a fair trial).[51]

Some instruments contain a general limitation clause. The Universal Declaration of Human Rights (UDHR), for example, proclaims that:

> In the exercise of his rights and freedoms, everyone shall be subject only to such limitations as are determined by law solely for the purpose of securing due recognition and respect for the rights and freedoms of others and of meeting the just requirements of morality, public order and the general welfare in a democratic society.[52]

A similar formulation is used for specific provisions of the ICCPR. For example, Article 12(3) ICCPR provides limitations to the right to liberty of movement, providing that the right 'shall not be subject to any restrictions except those which are provided by law, are necessary to protect national security, public order (*ordre public*), public health or morals or the rights and freedoms of others, and are consistent with the other rights recognized in the Covenant.'[53] The possibility of such limitations has been confirmed by international and domestic case law, but is typically subject to a tripartite test that ensures that the limitations are in conformity with human rights. Thus, limitations to rights have to be justified by the fact that they (1) are prescribed by law, (2) pursue a legitimate aim, and (3) are necessary in a democratic society.

5.1.1 Prescribed by law

The requirement that limitations be prescribed by law has been understood by the Inter-American Court to mean that they must be based on laws as instruments adopted by parliament, not merely that they are 'part of the Law'.[54] Given that limitations are those 'necessary in a democratic society', it is logical that they should be adopted by a legislative body rather than, for example, the executive. Nonetheless, it is accepted in the European context that the common law, for example, can constitute a sufficient basis for a rights limitation. What seems to matter is that limitations should either be democratically adopted or have a certain historical pedigree. The requirement that limitations be stipulated in

---

[50] See Chapter 9.   [51] See Chapter 13.   [52] UDHR, Art 29(2).

[53] See also ICCPR, Art 19 (freedom of expression), Art 21 (peaceful assembly), and Art 22 (freedom of association).

[54] OC-6/86, *The Word 'Laws' in Article 30 of the American Convention on Human Rights*, IACtHR Series A No 6 (9 May 1986).

law also guarantees a certain foreseeability of the law and the rights guaranteed. The law should be:

> adequately accessible: the citizen must be able to have an indication that is adequate in the circumstances of the legal rules applicable to a given case. Secondly, a norm cannot be regarded as a 'law' unless it is it is formulated with sufficient precision to enable the citizen to regulate his conduct: he must be able—if need be with appropriate advice—to foresee, to a degree that is reasonable in the circumstances, the consequences which a given action may entail.[55]

Unfettered executive discretion, even if granted by the law, would not satisfy this requirement.[56]

5.1.2 Legitimate aim

According to the European Court of Human Rights, a legitimate aim must be a 'pressing social need'.[57] A state cannot overturn human rights simply for idiosyncratic policy preferences that are not themselves for the benefit of rights. Typically, pressing social needs are identified by human rights treaties themselves as grounds for limitations of rights that are prima facie valid. For example, the ICCPR mentions 'national security, public order (ordre public), public health or morals or the rights and freedoms of others'. These are then expanded through interpretation by human rights bodies. The protection of democracy, pluralism, or secularism have all been presented at various times as being legitimate goals. It is interesting that human rights law, which is often recognized as being against the state, is also very much about legitimizing a certain state role.

5.1.3 Necessary in a democratic society

The limitation has to be 'necessary'. It does not suffice simply to allege a desirable social policy and then adopt a measure that is in fact not truly connected to that goal. Many laws that criminalized homosexuality, for example, which were presented as in pursuance of the legitimate aim of maintaining public morals, were struck down because they were not related to that goal at all, especially since they stigmatized homosexuality in the private sphere.[58]

The necessity test also implies that the relevant measure must be proportionate to the goal sought. Proportionality involves a delicate equation evaluating the importance of the social aim, the importance of the right guaranteed, and the degree of encroachment. Certain rights are very inelastic to even the most important social goals. Others will be more responsive to limitations. For example, the right to demonstrate will be quite sensitive to states' invocation of public order or the need to protect the rights of others.

The onus to prove any limb of the test is typically on states, which cannot simply claim that they 'know better'. But by what standard are such limitations to be judged? After all, what is necessary for some might be seen as perfectly abusive by others. Several human rights instruments suggest that the key threshold is that of a 'democratic society'. In other words, limitations are justified on all the grounds that have just been introduced, if they conform to what would be considered necessary in a 'democratic society'. This is certainly a standard that can be criticized as vague (not to mention one that raises the problem of tensions between democracy and human rights), but at least such limitation clauses acknowledge that human rights are not simply about upholding absolutes but very often about the complex exercise of balancing individual rights against legitimate social

---

[55] *Sunday Times v UK*, n 22, para 49.   [56] *Hasan v Bulgaria* (2000) 24 EHRR 55.
[57] *Handyside v UK*, (1979–80) 1 EHRR 737, para 48.   [58] *Dudgeon v UK*, n 25.

priorities. Obviously, human rights should be taken seriously, but the emphasis is on state justification, transparency, and accountability, in circumstances in which states may otherwise gladly invoke the priority of politics over rights.

5.2 DEROGATIONS

The law of state responsibility in general international law traditionally contemplates that a defence of necessity is available to states in limited circumstances. However, international human rights treaties often have their own regime to deal with states of exception, known as the 'derogation' regime, which better takes into account the special character of human rights obligations.[59] Essentially, states are permitted to suspend some of their obligations under human rights treaties if a state of emergency requires them to do so. The consequence of recognizing states' power to derogate from human rights treaties in times of emergency is an increased regulation and supervision of such derogations by international organs. The regime applicable in situations of emergency is typically more constraining than for ordinary international law obligations.

First, a situation of public emergency under international human rights law needs to exist. It must be declared in advance, and its existence (and abrogation) notified to relevant international authorities (for example, the Secretary-General of the UN as the depository of the ICCPR and ICESCR).[60] A situation of public emergency can only be invoked where there exists a threat to 'the life of the nation' itself. This is clearly a high threshold, and such a threat cannot be inferred from 'every disturbance or catastrophe'. Not even an armed conflict will automatically justify the recognition of a public emergency.[61] The European Court of Human Rights, for example, has described a public emergency under Article 15 ECHR as 'an exceptional situation of crisis or emergency which affects the whole population and constitutes a threat to the organized life of the community of which the State is composed.'[62] Adjudicators will look, as they did when the UK invoked a situation of public emergency following the attacks of 11 September 2001, at whether other similarly situated states deemed it necessary to invoke a situation of emergency. However, they often place much weight on the determinations of national governments who are the 'guardian of their own people's safety.'[63]

Second, the public emergency should be invoked only insofar and for as long as is strictly necessary to return to a situation of normalcy. Indeed, 'the restoration of a state of normalcy where full respect for the [ICCPR] can again be secured must be the predominant objective of a State party derogating from the Covenant.'[64] In other words, human rights can be suspended only in order for the state to be able to guarantee them as soon as the danger has passed, not to achieve something that is in itself alien to human rights. Derogations should specify their territorial[65] and temporal[66] reach, and can only be of an

---

[59] Eg ICCPR, Art 4; ECHR, Art 15; ACHR, Art 27. The ACHPR does not have a derogation regime. Other human rights treaties, such as UNCAT or CPED, do not have a derogation regime, but this is because they protect non-derogable rights.

[60] *Cyprus v Turkey* (1982) 4 EHRR 482, para 526.

[61] HRC, General Comment 29, HRI/GEN/1/Rev.9 (Vol I) 234, para 3.

[62] *Lawless v Ireland* (1979–80) 1 EHRR 15, para 28.

[63] *A and others v UK* (2009) 49 EHRR 29, para 180.   [64] General Comment 29, n 61, para 1.

[65] Eg as the European Court recognized in *Sakik and others v Turkey* (1998) 26 EHRR 662, the fact that Turkey had declared a state of emergency in Kurdistan did not mean that it was therefore in a similar state of exception in Northern Cyprus.

[66] This is particularly important in light of the tendency of states of emergency to prolong themselves far beyond what is strictly necessary. 'Sunset clauses', eg, should indicate the exact date or the occurrence of the event which will bring an end to the public emergency.

exceptional and temporary nature. A standard provision in several international human rights treaties, for example, is that emergencies should only be proclaimed 'to the extent strictly required by the exigencies of the situation'.

Third, situations of national emergency can only be invoked to suspend (at best) a limited set of so-called derogable rights. For example, it may be legitimate for a state confronting an armed conflict or a major natural catastrophe to suspend the right to demonstrate or the right to vote. Conversely, there are a number of 'non-derogable' rights that can never be suspended. The list varies slightly from treaty to treaty, but the ICCPR mentions the following provisions: Articles 6 (life), 7 (torture), 8(1) and (2) (slavery), 11 (imprisonment for failure to fulfil a contractual obligation), 15 (*nullum crimen sine lege*), 16 (recognition as a person under the law), and 18 (freedom of thought, conscience, and religion). Derogation measures, furthermore, should not be inconsistent with states' other obligations under international law and should not involve discrimination solely on the ground of race, colour, sex, language, religion, or social origin. The former means that states cannot use derogations, for example, to violate international humanitarian law or commit crimes against humanity. Even in situations of emergency, moreover, states are to provide remedies, particularly judicial guarantees, to individuals whose rights may have been violated.

This intense regulation of situations of emergency is designed to ensure that exceptional situations are not maintained indefinitely, which can have a catastrophic impact on rights. The Human Rights Committee, for example, has frequently deplored that some states have been operating under states of emergency for decades, leading to situations in which rights can be easily trampled.

6 WITHDRAWAL

In international law, withdrawal from a treaty under certain conditions is always an option and is generally known as the possibility of 'denouncing' a treaty. This is consonant with the fact that general international law is not particularly concerned with the substantive content of obligations and, therefore, sees withdrawing from a particular set of obligations as not raising fundamental issues of principle. The situation is more complicated when it comes to international human rights treaties. Withdrawals can have the effect of leaving populations legally vulnerable to violations, especially since supervisory machinery is often attached to substantive human rights commitments. The position of international human rights law on this matter is not entirely settled, but there appear to be two possibilities, depending on whether denunciation is explicitly anticipated by the relevant treaty.

Some international human rights instruments contain denunciation clauses. For example, Article 21 of the Convention on the Elimination of Racial Discrimination provides that '[a] State Party may denounce this Convention by written notification to the Secretary-General of the United Nations'. Similarly, the ECHR[67] and ACHR[68] also include denunciation clauses. It should be noted, nonetheless, that despite the existence of such provisions, straightforward withdrawal is quite unlikely.

Even though a state may do so for other alleged reasons, withdrawal from a human rights treaty is likely to be seen as an admission that a state is up to no good. At the time of writing, only two states have availed themselves successfully of the possibility of denouncing a human rights treaty, namely Greece, which denounced the ECHR from 1969 to 1974

---

[67] Art 58.   [68] Art 78.

following a military coup, and Trinidad and Tobago, which denounced both the Optional Protocol to the ICCPR and the ACHR from 1998 to 1999 as a result of wanting to proceed in the execution of the death penalty without the oversight of the Inter-American Commission. In both cases, the denunciations would not have had retroactive effect and, therefore, these states could not escape liability for violations committed prior to withdrawal.

As regards human rights treaties that do not explicitly allow for denunciation, there is a view that denunciation is simply not an option. There is only one case to date of the issue being decided internationally, but it is an interesting and unusual one. In 1998, North Korea sought to withdraw entirely from the ICCPR, after becoming upset about the Human Rights Committee's criticism of its record. The question of whether this was possible was referred to the UN Secretary-General, as depository of the treaty, who promptly returned an opinion to the effect that states could not withdraw from the ICCPR. According to the Human Rights Committee's general comment on the issue, 'it is clear that the Covenant is not the type of treaty which, by its nature, implies a right of denunciation'.[69] Moreover, in what was quite a bold move, the Human Rights Committee went on to note that:

> the rights enshrined in the Covenant belong to the people living in the territory of the State party. The Human Rights Committee has consistently taken the view, as evidenced by its long-standing practice, that once the people are accorded the protection of the rights under the Covenant, such protection devolves with territory and continues to belong to them, notwithstanding change in government of the State party.[70]

In other words, and in striking contrast to normal international law treaties, rights once recognized (rather than granted) cannot subsequently be withdrawn. This suggests a unique 'stickiness' to international human rights commitments, which cannot be undone even when states desire to do so formally. The Secretary-General did point out, however, that North Korea could withdraw from the ICCPR if all states parties agreed, obviously an unlikely prospect.

This has not prevented discussion about withdrawal from international human rights instruments in countries as different as the UK and Venezuela. The latter country denounced the ACHR on 10 September 2012, to come into effect a year later. Ironically, this withdrawal may be an indirect consequence of an earlier failed attempt by Peru to withdraw from the contentious jurisdiction of the Inter-American Court, which the court dismissed as not anticipated by the ACHR. Although both Trinidad and Tobago and Venezuela have withdrawn from the ACHR, neither have withdrawn from the Organization of American States, which means that they still come under the Inter-American Commission's scrutiny in relation to the American Declaration of Human Rights.[71]

7 REMEDIES FOR VIOLATIONS OF HUMAN RIGHTS OBLIGATIONS

A typical way in which international law obligations are enforced, traditionally, is through termination, suspension,[72] or even, under customary international law, counter-measures (ie measures that would be otherwise unlawful) by the party that considers that it has suffered from an internationally wrongful act. This is appropriate in an inter-state world

---

[69] HRC, General Comment 26, HRI/GEN/1/Rev.9 (Vol 1) 222, para 3.
[70] General Comment 26, n 69, para 4.   [71] See Chapter 19.
[72] The possibility is anticipated by VCLT, Art 60.

in which the dominant model is contractual and where states are really only bound to the extent that other parties respect their 'side of the bargain'. It is also a consequence of the fact that quite often enforcement bodies will not be available, so that each state has to decide for itself whether obligations owed to it have been violated and whether one of these remedies is justified. This is what is sometimes known as the 'decentralized' enforcement of international law.

This is, of course, always problematic under classical international law, but it is arguably even more so when it comes to international human rights obligations. In fact, quite strikingly, Article 60 VCLT, which provides for the possibility of termination or suspension of a treaty, is said not to be applicable 'to provisions relating to the protection of the human person contained in treaties of a humanitarian character, in particular to provisions prohibiting any form of reprisals against persons protected by such treaties'.[73]

The idea is simple enough: whereas under general international law it is reasonable that a violating state suffer the consequences of its unwillingness or inability to respect its obligations, the same cannot be said if it violates a human rights obligation, which is not primarily secured for the benefit of other states. Several scenarios are conceivable. For example, in a context where state A violates the human rights of citizens of state B on its territory, one can imagine that state B could cease to honour its human rights obligations vis-à-vis the citizens of state A. However, this would clearly run against the object and purpose of human rights treaties, the obligations of which are not primarily owed to other states parties.

Even more nonsensical is the possibility that state A would cease to respect its international human rights obligations vis-à-vis its own nationals as a counter-measure to state B not respecting its own obligations vis-à-vis persons within its jurisdiction. This would result in the state essentially punishing persons within its jurisdiction, and would have no effect on the offender state. It would be absurd from a human rights point of view.

Non-execution is thus clearly not an adequate remedy in the case of human rights violations. Because human rights obligations are primarily incurred by states vis-à-vis persons within their jurisdiction, the inter-state element in human rights enforcement has tended to recede.[74] Nevertheless, inter-state procedures do exist in the international human rights context. In theory, nothing prevents states from bringing cases before the ICJ for violations of various international human rights instruments. They have certainly done so in relation to the Genocide Convention in the *Bosnia Genocide* case;[75] or the Convention on the Elimination of Racial Discrimination in the case of *Georgia v Russia*;[76] or sometimes indirectly as in the cases brought by Germany and Mexico against the USA concerning foreign nationals who had been sentenced to capital punishment following violations of the Vienna Convention on Consular Relations on the part of the USA.[77] Several human rights instruments specifically envisage inter-state procedures, whether before regional courts or treaty bodies.[78]

---

[73] VCLT, Art 60(5).   [74] See Chapters 18–21 for a detailed discussion.

[75] *Application of the Convention on the Prevention and Punishment of the Crime of Genocide* (*Bosnia and Herzegovina v Serbia and Montenegro*) [2007] ICJ Rep 108.

[76] *Application of the International Convention on the Elimination of All Forms of Racial Discrimination* (*Georgia v Russian Federation*) [2011] ICJ Rep.

[77] *Case Concerning the Vienna Convention on Consular Relations* (*Germany v USA*) (*Request for the Indication of Provisional Measures: Order*) [1999] ICJ Rep 9.

[78] Eg ACHR, Art 44; ECHR, Art 24.

Inter-state procedures provide evidence of the communal interest in the enforcement of a human rights guarantee. For example, the notion of *locus standi* (that is, standing to appear before a court or tribunal) has been adapted to fit the concerns of international human rights law. Under traditional international law, the only subjects able to invoke a breach of an obligation are those that are directly its beneficiaries and, therefore, directly affected by its breach. Third parties do not normally have a general interest in the law's enforcement such that they could bring a sort of *actio popularis*. The ICJ famously considered that Liberia and Ethiopia did not have standing in the *South-West Africa* case because they could not adduce a violation of a specific interest.[79] However, because of the largely *erga omnes* character of human rights obligations, a third state *can* bring a case against a violating state even if none of its nationals were affected. It is assumed that states parties to human rights treaties are affected by a human rights violation committed by any state, even if it is against its own citizens.

This *erga omnes* nature of human rights obligations, incidentally, has implications not only for formal inter-state mechanisms but more generally for human rights foreign policy. By making human rights (regardless of where they may be violated) a matter of concern for all, the law profoundly redefines the notion of sovereignty and what constitutes the internal affairs of states. Normatively this should make it more difficult for states to claim that other states that criticize their human rights record are meddling in their internal affairs (although in practice and politically, of course, it may not be that difficult to make such claims).However, it should be said that resort to inter-state human rights procedures has in practice been very much the exception. There have been fewer than two dozen inter-state procedures before the European Commission and Court of Human Rights, while no inter-state dispute regarding a violation of a human rights treaty obligation has been referred to a UN treaty body.

Instead, a number of important, innovative, *sui generis* mechanisms for enforcement have been pioneered in the international human rights field that emphasize the role of supranational institutions and jurisdictions. First are various mechanisms through which states are required to provide periodic reports to international committees, outlining how they have complied with their treaty obligations. These mechanisms are described in more detail in Chapters 18–21, but it is interesting to note here that they create a situation where states, in contrast to the tradition in international law, have to report on their behaviour even if there has been no dispute or litigation. This undeniably reflects the higher interest in preventing violations of human rights, rather than simply adjudicating upon them. Second, and this must surely count as international human rights' greatest innovation in terms of enforcement, many instruments create a right of petition for individuals before international bodies (or at least the possibility of such a right if it is recognized by state parties). This is inconceivable in the inter-state context where the possibility of individuals, or even significant non-state actors, intervening before the ICJ, for example, is never seriously entertained. There are relatively stringent conditions to appearing directly before international human rights bodies, but it is a remarkable characteristic of international human rights law that under certain conditions it allows individuals to directly sue their state at the international level.

---

[79] *South-West Africa Cases (Ethiopia v South Africa; Liberia v South Africa)* (Second Phase) [1966] ICJ Rep 6.

8 CONCLUSION

This chapter has presented some key ways in which international human rights obligations differ from mainstream international law obligations. Human rights obligations may allow for a degree of flexibility in their application, but they are also highly binding, regardless of how other state parties conform to their duties. The root of the tension lies in the fact that human rights are intrinsically different in nature and belong to a very different history than general international law. Although typically expressed through treaties, human rights obligations norms have a logic of their own.

It is testimony to the flexibility of international law that it has adapted itself to this new subject matter, in the process changing many rules and practices. In return, human rights law has also significantly shaped the evolution of public international law, and contributed to redefine it less as a project of coexistence between equal states, and more as a common effort to achieve certain universal minimal standards of treatment of the individual.

FURTHER READING

CRAVEN, 'Legal Differentiation and the Concept of the Human Rights Treaty in International Law' (2000) 11 *EJIL* 489.

GARDBAUM, 'Human Rights as International Constitutional Rights' (2008) 19 *EJIL* 749.

GOODMAN, 'Human Rights Treaties, Invalid Reservations, and State Consent' (2002) 96 *AJIL* 531.

HUMAN RIGHTS COMMITTEE, General Comment 24, HRI/GEN/1/Rev.9 (Vol I) 210.

HUMAN RIGHTS COMMITTEE, General Comment 31, HRI/GEN/1/Rev.9 (Vol I) 243.

KAMMINGA and SCHEININ (eds), *The Impact of Human Rights Law on General International Law* (Oxford University Press, 2009).

KOJI, 'Emerging Hierarchy in International Human Rights and Beyond: From the Perspective of Non-Derogable Rights' (2001) 12 *EJIL* 917.

LIJNZAAD, *Reservations to UN-Human Rights Treaties: Ratify and Ruin?* (Martinus Nijhoff, 1995).

MAHONEY, 'Marvellous Richness of Diversity or Invidious Cultural Relativism' (1998) 19 *HRLJ* 1.

MOWBRAY, 'The Creativity of the European Court of Human Rights' (2005) 5 *HRLR* 57.

MULLER, 'Limitations to and Derogations from Economic, Social and Cultural Rights' (2009) *HRLR* 557.

SHELTON, *Remedies in International Human Rights Law* (Oxford University Press, 1999).

6

SCOPE OF APPLICATION

Sarah Joseph and Adam Fletcher

SUMMARY

A state is clearly not responsible for every act or omission which harms human rights, regardless of location. Therefore, it is necessary to examine the scope of application of a state's obligations under international human rights law. That is, when do human rights duties apply? This chapter first defines key concepts and identifies the duty-bearers and beneficiaries of human rights law. Then it explains the instances in which a state will be held responsible for the actions or omissions of particular persons or entities. Finally, it addresses the scope of the territorial application of a state's human rights duties.

1 INTRODUCTION

It is necessary to clarify some key concepts for the purposes of the discussion in this chapter: those of 'state responsibility' and 'jurisdiction'.

'State responsibility' refers to the circumstances in which a state will be held liable for a violation of its international obligations. For example, a state will be held to have breached international human rights law if an act or omission, which is wrongful under human rights law, is attributable to that state. The state will not be held in breach if the act or omission cannot be attributed to it.

The concept of 'jurisdiction' is very complex. It can refer, for example, to the circumstances in which a state is recognized under its own domestic law, or under international law, as having a right to prescribe and enforce its laws. In this chapter, it is used in a limited context to refer to a state's authority over a particular act or omission. As discussed here, the most common view of a state's jurisdiction extends it to acts and omissions over which a state exercises effective control, regardless of the control exercised by the state in the territory in which the act or omission takes place. The European Court of Human Rights may adopt a more conservative approach, extending jurisdiction only where a state exercises 'effective control' over a particular territory. However, the current state of European Convention on Human Rights (ECHR) law regarding extraterritoriality is somewhat uncertain.

A state is not responsible under human rights law for every act or omission by any person that arises within its jurisdiction. However, a state's responsibility under human rights law is limited by its jurisdiction. That is, a state is not responsible for acts or omissions under human rights law that fall outside its jurisdiction.

2 WHO HAS HUMAN RIGHTS OBLIGATIONS?

States have duties under human rights treaties if they are party to them. Human rights treaties generally do not bind entities other than states. However, Article 43 Convention on the Rights of Persons with Disabilities provides for formal confirmation and accession by regional integration organizations and the European Union has so formally confirmed.[1] The ECHR also provides for accession by the European Union—a process which is underway at the time of writing.[2]

Under customary international law, the principal duty-bearers of human rights obligations are again states. There are rare exceptions under customary international law where entities other than states have direct human rights obligations. Examples include the duties not to perpetrate genocide, certain war crimes, or crimes against humanity.[3] In this chapter, the focus is on the scope of application of a state's duties under human rights treaties.[4]

3 WHO HAS HUMAN RIGHTS?

As noted in Section 2, states generally have duties under international human rights law. To whom are these duties owed? That is, who is recognized as a person with human rights under international human rights law?

Individuals within a state's jurisdiction are generally recognized as having human rights. For example, Article 2(1) International Covenant on Civil and Political Rights (ICCPR) requires states parties to respect and ensure the human rights of 'all individuals' within their territory and jurisdiction.

3.1 NON-NATIONALS

One does not have to be a national of a state in order to be able to claim human rights against that state. Numerous international human rights decisions and judgments have confirmed that non-nationals have human rights.[5] In most instances, they enjoy civil and political rights to the same extent as nationals.[6] However, rights of political participation, such as those found in Article 25 ICCPR, including the right to vote and stand for election, may legitimately be restricted to citizens. Similarly, non-citizens do not have the same rights to enter or remain in a state as nationals,[7] though that is not

---

[1] Formal Confirmation (23 December 2010). See <http://treaties.un.org/Pages/ViewDetails.aspx?src=TREATY&mtdsg_no=IV-15&chapter=4&lang=en>

[2] Council of Europe, *ECHR: Accession of the European Union* <http://hub.coe.int/what-we-do/human-rights/eu-accession-to-the-convention>.

[3] See Joseph, *Corporations and Transnational Human Rights Litigation* (Hart, 2004) 48–9.

[4] See Chapter 26 for a discussion of the human rights duties of non-state actors.

[5] Eg *Gueye v France*, CCPR/C/35/D/196/1985 (6 April 1989); *A v Australia*, CCPR/C/59/D/560/1993 (30 April 1997); *Adam v Czech Republic*, CCPR/C/57/D/586/1994 (25 July 1996); *Soering v UK* (1989) 11 EHRR 439.

[6] HRC, General Comment 15, HRI/GEN/1/Rev.9 (Vol 1) 189.

[7] See the interpretation of Art 12(4) ICCPR in *Nystrom v Australia* CCPR/C/102/D/1557/2007 (18 August 2011) and *Warsame v Canada* CCPR/C/102/D/1959/2010 (21 July 2011).

to say that states have an absolute right under international human rights law to expel them. Due to their special vulnerability to deportation, non-nationals have unique procedural rights with regard to deportation under Article 13 ICCPR and similar provisions.

Under Article 2(3) International Covenant on Economic, Social and Cultural Rights (ICESCR), 'developing countries' are permitted to determine the extent to which they guarantee 'economic rights' to non-nationals, taking into account 'human rights and their national economy'. Economic rights have been defined by one commentator as those ICESCR rights 'that enable a person to earn a living or that relate to that process', that is, the employment rights in Articles 6 to 8 and perhaps Article 13(2)(e).[8] Article 2(3) has not been authoritatively interpreted by the Committee on Economic, Social and Cultural Rights. The Committee did not even mention Article 2(3) in its General Comment 18 on the right to work,[9] and it receives only the briefest of mentions and no explication in its General Comment 20 on non-discrimination.[10] Hence, the extent of developing states' discretion under Article 2(3) is unclear. Dankwa describes the provision as transitional, designed to permit post-colonial states to favour local people in employment to redress the balance in economies dominated by ex-patriot populations.[11] A report by the UN Special Rapporteur on the rights of non-citizens suggests that this 'exception to the general rule on equality' should be interpreted narrowly.[12]

3.2 THE UNBORN

Do human rights extend to the unborn? The American Convention on Human Rights (ACHR), in Article 4(1), explicitly contemplates life beginning from conception rather than birth, and thus seems to confer human rights on unborn children.[13] The European Court of Human Rights and the European Commission of Human Rights have found that a foetus is not a person protected by the right to life, and, in any case, its right would not automatically override the rights and interests of its mother. Accordingly, the European human rights bodies have found complaints brought on behalf of a foetus to be inadmissible.[14] They have also declined to decide whether the right to respect for private and family life extends to unborn children.[15] In *Queenan v Canada*, the Human Rights Committee found that a claim could not be brought on behalf of unborn children against the practice of abortion.[16]

---

[8] Dankwa, 'Working Paper on Article 2(3) of the International Covenant on Economic, Social and Cultural Rights' (1987) 9 *HRQ* 230, 240.

[9] CESCR, General Comment 18, HRI/GEN/1/Rev.9 (Vol 1) 139.

[10] CESCR, General Comment 20, E/C.12/GC/20.   [11] Dankwa, n 8, 246–9.

[12] Final report of the Special Rapporteur on the rights of non-citizens, E/CN.4/Sub.2/2003/23 (26 May 2003) para 19.

[13] The right to life in Art 4(1) applies 'in general, from the moment of conception': Case 2141, *The Baby Boy Case*, IACommHR Res 23/81 (6 March 1981) Annual Report 1980–1.

[14] *Vo v France* (2005) 10 EHRR 12; *Paton v United Kingdom* (1981)3 EHRR 408; *H v Norway* (1992) 73 DR 155.   [15] *A, B, C v Ireland* (2011) 53 EHRR 13.

[16] *Queenan v Canada*, CCPR/C/84/D/1379/2005 (23 August 2005). The HRC found the application of a prohibition on abortion to breach various rights in the ICCPR in *Huamán v Peru*, CCPR/C/85/D/1153/2003 (22 November 2005) and made similar findings concerning denial of a legal abortion in *L.M.R. v Argentina*, CCPR/C/101/D/1608/2007 (28 April 2011).

3.3 ARTIFICIAL ENTITIES

Do artificial entities such as corporations and associations, including NGOs, have human rights? Corporations and associations have standing to make claims on their own behalf before the European Court of Human Rights. Examples include *Sunday Times v UK*,[17] a case concerning a media corporation's freedom of expression, and *Refah Partisi (The Welfare Party) v Turkey*,[18] a case concerning the rights of a political party. In contrast, the UN human rights treaties generally protect only individual rights. Though some rights can clearly be enjoyed in conjunction with other people, such as freedom of association in Article 22 ICCPR or minority rights in Article 27 ICCPR,[19] the only collective right recognized in the global treaty system is that of self-determination in Article 1 ICCPR and Article 1 ICESCR.[20] Corporations and other artificial entities do not have rights under the UN treaties,[21] though an organization can submit a complaint under the Convention on the Elimination of All Forms of Racial Discrimination as the representative of a group of individuals.[22] Similarly, the Inter-American system is concerned with the rights of individuals,[23] though complaints may be submitted in respect of those rights by others, such as corporations or other artificial entities.[24]

However, restrictions on the rights of a corporation may, in some instances, inevitably impact severely on the rights of a person, such as a director or shareholder, such that that person may bring a claim of abuse of his or her own rights. *Singer v Canada* concerned a complaint under the ICCPR by one Alan Singer about Quebec laws that banned businesses from advertising outdoors in a language other than French.[25] Canada responded that the real 'victim' of this limit to freedom of expression was Singer's company, Alan Singer Ltd, which owned the relevant business. The Human Rights Committee disagreed, noting that freedom of expression was 'inalienably linked to the person' and that person's 'freedom to impart information concerning his business in the language of his choice'.[26] It is likely that the Committee's decision was influenced by the fact that Singer's company was a small family business, such that breaches of its rights necessarily impacted on his enjoyment of those same rights. The same might not apply, for example, in regard to large listed companies.[27]

In contrast, other cases before the Human Rights Committee, such as *S.M. v Barbados*[28] and *Lamagna v Australia*,[29] which have concerned allegations of the unfair treatment of small one-person companies, have been dismissed for want of personal jurisdiction. Emberland has criticized these decisions, particularly *Lamagna*, on the basis that the Committee adopted an overly formal approach to the issue at hand, leaving Ms Lamagna

---

[17] (1980) 2 EHRR 317.   [18] (2003) 37 EHRR 1.

[19] HRC, General Comment 31, HRI/GEN/1/Rev.9 (Vol 1) 243, para 9.   [20] See Chapter 17.

[21] *SM v Barbados*, CCPR/C/50/D/502/1992 (4 April 1994) (regarding a corporation); *JRT and the WG Party v Canada*, CCPR/C/18/D/104/1981 (6 April 1983) (regarding a political party); *Coordinamento v Italy*, CCPR/C/21/D/163/1984 (10 April 1984) (regarding a NGO), *Wallman v Austria*, CCPR/C/80/D/1002/2001 (29 April 2004) (regarding a partnership); *V.S. v Belarus* CCPR/C/103/D/1749/2008 (21 November 2011) (regarding a religious organization).

[22] *Jewish Community of Oslo v Norway* CERD/C/67/D/30/2003 (15 August 2005).

[23] ACHR, Art 2(1) clarifies that a person for the purposes of that Convention is a 'human being'.

[24] ACHR, Arts 1(2) and 44. See eg *Tabacalera Boqueron SA v Paraguay*, IACommHR Report 47/97 (16 October 1997) Annual Report 1997, paras 29 and 35.   [25] CCPR/C/51/D/455/1991 (15 August 1994).

[26] CCPR/C/51/D/455/1991 (15 August 1994), para 11.2.

[27] Joseph and Castan, *The International Covenant on Civil and Political Rights: Cases Commentary and Materials* (OUP, 2013) 78.

[28] n 21.   [29] CCPR/C/65/D/737/1997 (30 April 1999).

without any relevant human rights protection simply because she chose to use the corporate form to arrange her business affairs.[30] While Emberland does not recommend the conferral of rights on companies under the ICCPR, he recommends a less legalistic approach in the case of small businesses.

4 FOR WHICH ENTITIES IS A STATE RESPONSIBLE?

This section considers the responsibility of states under international human rights law for the acts of a person or entity. The key question is: when is an act or omission attributable to the state?

A state is clearly responsible under international human rights law for the actions of its organs, such as its executive, legislature, judiciary, and its bureaucracy.[31] Thus, breaches of human rights law may arise from actions taken by leaders, police officers, the army, judges, administrative officers, and so on. States remain responsible for the actions of their agents even when they act beyond their authority, as long as they are purportedly acting in an official capacity.[32]

Provincial government entities in a federal state are treated as emanations of the national government for the purposes of international human rights obligations. A federal division of powers is not deemed to alter a state's human rights obligations at all.[33] For example, Tasmanian anti-gay legislation gave rise to a breach of the ICCPR by Australia in *Toonen v Australia*,[34] even though the national government neither enacted nor approved of the impugned laws. Indeed, the national government of Canada has been found in breach of the ICCPR on numerous occasions due to provincial laws, even though it lacks, in some instances, the domestic constitutional power to alter those laws.[35]

Thus, states are clearly responsible for actions of their organs. But to what extent, if at all, are they responsible for the actions of other persons or entities such as private actors, international organizations, or other states?

4.1 PRIVATE ACTORS

Governments are not the only threat to human rights. The right of non discrimination, for example, is a very limited right if it has no impact in the private sector. According to the Articles on State Responsibility, a state is responsible for the acts of a private actor if that actor is acting in a governmental capacity, or under its direction and control, or where it adopts a person's actions as its own.[36] Such situations might arise, for example, when private contractors carry out governmental functions.

---

[30] Emberland, 'Corporate Veil in the Jurisprudence of the Human Rights Committee and the Inter-American Court and Commission of Human Rights' (2004) 4 *HRLR* 257, 272.

[31] HRC, n 19, para 4. See also International Law Commission (ILC), Articles on Responsibility of States for Internationally Wrongful Acts, A/56/10, ch IV.E.1, Art 4.

[32] Eg *Sarma v Sri Lanka*, CCPR/C/78/D/950/2000 (31 July 2003); see also ILC Articles, on Responsibility of States for Internationally Wrongful Acts, A/56/10, ch IV.E.1, Art 7.

[33] Eg ICCPR, Art 50.   [34] CCPR/C/50/D/488/1992 (4 April 1994).

[35] Eg *Ballantyne et al. v Canada*, CCPR/C/47/D/385/1989 (5 May 1993); *Waldman v Canada*, CCPR/C/67/D/694/1996 (5 November 1999).

[36] ILC Articles, n 31, Arts 5, 8, and 11. The Articles were drafted by the ILC, an expert group with a mandate under the UN Charter to develop and codify international law, over a number of decades, and were adopted in 2001. Most aspects of the Articles are recognized as customary international law.

Furthermore, the application of human rights within the private sphere is now well recognized in international human rights law.[37] Some human rights provisions, such as Article 20 ICCPR, explicitly require the regulation of private actors by the state.[38] The classical tripartite description of a state's human rights duties, that is, to respect, protect, and fulfil human rights, reveals a more general duty with regard to private actors. As part of a state's duty to protect a person's enjoyment of a human right, it must exercise due diligence by taking reasonable measures to prevent and punish actions by a private actor that prejudice the human rights of another. The Inter-American Court of Human Rights enunciated the duty in the following way in *Velasquez-Rodriguez v Honduras*:

> An illegal act which violates human rights and which is initially not directly imputable to a State (for example, because it is the act of a private person or because the person responsible has not been identified) can lead to international responsibility of the State, not because of the act itself, but because of the lack of due diligence to prevent the violation or to respond to it as required by the [American] Convention.[39]

The Human Rights Committee explained in General Comment 31:

> [T]he positive obligations on States Parties to ensure Covenant rights will only be fully discharged if individuals are protected by the State, not just against violations of Covenant rights by its agents, but also against acts committed by private persons or entities that would impair the enjoyment of Covenant rights in so far as they are amenable to application between private persons or entities. There may be circumstances in which a failure to ensure Covenant rights as required by article 2 would give rise to violations by States Parties of those rights, as a result of States Parties' permitting or failing to take appropriate measures or to exercise due diligence to prevent, punish, investigate or redress the harm caused by such acts by private persons or entities.[40]

In *Osman v UK*, the European Court of Human Rights confirmed that states have duties to do all that can reasonably be expected to prevent human rights abuses by private actors. The expectations upon a state increase if the state knows, or should know, that a person or entity poses a risk to another's enjoyment of human rights.[41]

The following are examples of this application of human rights within the private sphere. *A v UK* concerned a young boy who had been hit with a garden cane by his stepfather. The stepfather was acquitted of assault in the UK, where the court found he had merely engaged in 'reasonable chastisement'. The European Court found that the UK, in acquitting the stepfather in its courts, had failed properly to protect the boy's right to be free from inhuman and degrading treatment.[42] Various human rights bodies have held that states must take reasonable and effective measures to protect a person from domestic violence: failure to do so will result in violations of the rights of the person subjected to such violence, such as the right to life if the person is killed, or the right to be free from torture or other ill-treatment.[43] In *Lopez Ostra v Spain*, the European Court found that Spain had failed to take reasonable measures to prevent the spread of severe air pollution

---

[37] See Chapter 5.

[38] See also Convention on the Elimination of All Forms of Discrimination Against Women (CEDAW) Arts 6 and 11; and Convention on the Elimination of All Forms of Racial Discrimination (ICERD) Art 5.

[39] IACtHR Series C No 4 (29 July 1988) para 172.   [40] n 19, para 8.

[41] (2000) 29 EHRR 245, para 116.   [42] (1999) 27 EHRR 611, 624.

[43] eg *Opuz v Turkey (2010)* 50 EHRR 28; *AT v Hungary*, CEDAW/A/61/38/2006 (26 January 2005); *Goekce v Austria*, CEDAW/C/39/D/5/2005 (6 August 2007); *Yildirim v Austria*, CEDAW/C/39/D/6/2005 (6 August 2007). See also CEDAW, General Recommendation 19, HRI/GEN/1/Rev.9 (Vol II) 331.

from a privately owned waste treatment plant, which breached the rights to privacy and family life of those who lived in the plant's vicinity.[44] Similarly, in *SERAC v Nigeria*, the African Commission on Human and Peoples' Rights found that Nigeria had failed to protect indigenous peoples in Ogoniland from harmful actions by an oil consortium, which breached the peoples' rights to health, property, housing, food, and freedom from forced deprivation of wealth and resources.[45] Finally, in *Krasovsky v Belarus*, the Human Rights Committee found the State in breach of the ICCPR due to its failure to properly investigate the disappearance of the victim, even though it had earlier failed to find that the disappearance was the work of State agents.[46]

4.2 INTERNATIONAL ORGANIZATIONS

To what extent, if at all, are states responsible for the actions of international organizations of which they are a member? *H v d P v Netherlands* concerned a complaint to the Human Rights Committee about the recruitment practices of the European Patent Office (EPO), an international organization of which the Netherlands was one of five member states.[47] The complaint was dismissed as it was aimed at the EPO and thus concerned issues beyond the jurisdiction of the Netherlands. However, the Committee has since stated that states are responsible for the actions of 'forces constituting a national contingent of a State party assigned to an international peace-keeping or peace-enforcement operation'.[48] One must, therefore, inquire as to when a state's personnel are its own and when they are the responsibility of an international organization.

The European Court, in the joined cases of *Behrami and Behrami v France* and *Saramati v France, Germany and Norway*, found that complaints against various European states that had contributed personnel to peacekeeping forces in Kosovo (KFOR) and to the UN interim administration in Kosovo (UNMIK), in respect of certain acts and omissions of KFOR and UNMIK, were inadmissible *ratione personae*.[49] The Court found that the activities of KFOR and UNMIK were attributable to the UN Security Council. It went on to find that it was not competent to review the actions of states parties in respect of actions taken by their personnel on behalf of the UN as part of KFOR and UNMIK.

The European Court distinguished *Behrami and Saramati* in its 2011 judgment in *Al-Jedda v UK*, which concerned the imprisonment of the applicant (a UK citizen) in Basrah between 2004 and 2007. The Court held that the situation in Iraq in 2004 was different from that in Kosovo in 1999 because the Security Council had 'effective control' and 'ultimate authority' in the latter situation but not the former.[50] It also held that, in the case of any ambiguity, Security Council resolutions ought to be interpreted compatibly with human rights, and it criticized the UK's interpretation of Resolution 1546 as authorizing the indefinite detention of terrorist suspects in Iraq.[51] The Court concluded that the UK was responsible under the ECHR for Mr Al-Jedda's detention, which violated his right to liberty under Article 5(1).

In *Blagojević v The Netherlands*, the European Court found that a suspect in the custody of the International Criminal Tribunal for the former Yugoslavia was not within the Netherlands' jurisdiction for the purposes of Article 1 of the Convention, despite his physical presence in The Hague. The Court reasoned that the Tribunal was set up by the

---

[44] (1995) 20 EHRR 277.   [45] Communication No 155/96 (2002).
[46] CCPR/C/104/D/1820/2008 (26 March 2012), paras 8.2 and 8.3.
[47] CCPR/C/29/D/217/1986 (8 April 1987).   [48] n 19, para 10.
[49] (2007) 45 EHRR SE10.   [50] (2011) 53 EHRR 23, para 84 of majority judgment.
[51] (2011) 53 EHRR 23, paras 102–6. See also *Al-Saadoon and Mufdhi v UK* (2011) 53 EHRR 9.

Security Council under Chapter VII of the UN Charter, and that its actions were attributable to the UN.[52] The Court also adverted to the fact that the legal provisions governing the Tribunal's operation provided appropriate human rights guarantees.[53]

Lambi Longa v The Netherlands concerned a witness for the defence of Thomas Lubanga Dyilo, the Congolese militia leader who was the first person to be convicted by the International Criminal Court (ICC). The applicant had been arrested in the Democratic Republic of the Congo (DRC) on charges related to the murders of UN personnel (which he denied). He claimed that the last valid detention order expired in 2007, yet he remained in detention in the DRC in 2011, when he was transferred to detention in The Hague to give evidence in the Lubanga trial. The applicant then claimed asylum from the Netherlands during the trial, but the Dutch Government refused to process his claim on the basis that he was outside its jurisdiction. In response, the applicant applied to the European Court alleging a breach of Article 5 ECHR due to unlawful detention. The Court held that the power to keep witnesses in custody was a 'necessary corollary' of the ICC's operations, and that (as in *Blagojević*) his physical presence in The Hague did not suffice to establish jurisdiction.[54] The applicant also claimed that the law governing the ICC failed to protect his human rights, but the Court rejected this argument.[55] *Blagojević* and *Lambi Longa* indicate that states parties to the ECHR will not be held responsible for those under the control of international organizations operating within their territory, so long as the organizations provide appropriate human rights guarantees to ensure against a 'legal vacuum'.

It appears that a state can be held responsible under human rights treaties for its own actions taken in order to implement a Security Council resolution and, by implication, other international obligations. In *Bosphorus v Ireland*, the European Court of Human Rights found a complaint regarding the seizure in Ireland of the applicant's leased aircraft to be admissible. The seizure took place pursuant to a ministerial decision that implemented an EC Council regulation which itself applied a Security Council resolution that had imposed sanctions on the Federal Republic of Yugoslavia. Ireland was bound under EC law to implement the regulation. Nevertheless, the impugned actions were deemed to be those of Ireland and the complaint was admissible. However, no violation (of the right to property) was ultimately found. The Court found that there was a presumption that actions taken to implement international obligations as a member of an international organization were compatible with the ECHR if the relevant organization provided equivalent or comparable protection of the rights recognized in the ECHR.[56] The presumption can be rebutted where protection of ECHR rights is 'manifestly deficient'. The presumption was not rebutted in *Bosphorus*.

In contrast, the European Court found that Swiss implementation of a Security Council resolution relating to al-Qaida and the Taliban violated a number of ECHR provisions in *Nada v Switzerland*.[57] The complainant, Nada, lived in a tiny Italian enclave surrounded by the Swiss canton of Ticino. From 2002 he was prevented from entering Switzerland (and thus leaving that enclave) for any purpose—including visiting his family or his Italian doctor—by a Federal Ordinance enacted in order to implement the Security Council resolution. In May 2005 the Swiss authorities determined that allegations against Nada of links with terrorism were unfounded, but refused to lift the travel ban, arguing that they could not do so until the Security Council removed Nada from the relevant sanctions list. The Security Council's Sanctions Committee did not remove Nada's name until September

---

[52] App no 49032/07, Admissibility Decision of 9 June 2009, paras 31–46.
[53] App no 49032/07, Admissibility Decision of 9 June 2009, para 46.
[54] (2013) 56 EHRR SE1, paras 69–75.   [55] (2013) 56 EHRR SE1, paras 77–80.
[56] (2006) 42 EHRR 1, paras 155–6.   [57] (2013) 56 EHRR 18.

2009. Switzerland claimed that it was not responsible for any violations of Nada's rights, as it was compelled to act as it did by the Security Council. The Court did not make a finding on the hierarchy of Switzerland's conflicting international obligations relating to compliance with the Security Council resolution and with the ECHR. Instead, it found that Switzerland had not done all it could, within the scope of discretion permitted to it by the Security Council, to protect Nada's rights. For example, it could have informed Italian authorities more quickly of its 2005 findings: after all Nada's name was removed from the UN Sanctions List quickly after Italy's request in 2009. It ultimately found that Switzerland had breached Articles 8 and 13 of the ECHR.[58] A similar decision was reached by the Human Rights Committee in *Sayadi and Vinck v Belgium*.[59]

In *Nada* and *Sayadi and Vinck*, the European Court and the Human Rights Committee found that the relevant Security Council resolution did not compel the rights abusive actions at issue. Hence, neither case addressed how a conflict between a Security Council resolution and human rights obligations would be resolved. *Bosphorus* goes further. It indicates that a state can be held responsible for human rights violations even if those violations are necessitated by its implementation of obligations to another international organization (though it benefits in this regard from a presumption of compatibility). However, *Behrami and Saramati* indicates that a state will not be held responsible for human rights violations by its personnel, such as its troops, if command of those people is given to an international body: those personnel are held to be beyond the jurisdiction of that particular state. Similarly, the Netherlands is not responsible for the actions of the many international courts located within its territory, according to *Blagojević* and *Lambi Longa*. On the other hand, *Al-Jedda* shows that the context is important, and that a state cannot assume its responsibility has passed entirely to the international organization in every instance.

A state, which is a member of an international organization, is not per se responsible for the actions of that organization under international human rights law. Can a state be held responsible for its own actions within the organization, such as its votes, or even its decision to join a particular organization? The Committee on Economic, Social and Cultural Rights has stated, regarding the right to food, that states violate that right if they fail to take it into account 'when entering into agreements with other States or with international organisations'.[60] Therefore, for example, a state must take its ICESCR obligations into account when joining the World Trade Organization (WTO) or signing a free trade deal with another state.[61] The Committee has also strongly implied that members of the Security Council must take ICESCR rights into account when imposing economic sanctions on a state.[62]

4.3 OTHER STATES

To what extent is a state responsible for the actions of another state? A state is responsible for those of its acts which expose a person to a real risk of a violation of his or her rights

---

[58] (2013) 56 EHRR 18, paras 187–199.

[59] CCPR/C/94/D/1472/2006 (29 December 2008). See also Chapter 27.

[60] CESCR, General Comment 12, HRI/GEN/1/Rev.9 (Vol 1) 55, para 19. See also CESCR, General Comment 14, HRI/GEN/1/Rev.9 (Vol 1) 78, para 39.

[61] See generally Howse and Teitel, 'Beyond the Divide: The Covenant on Economic, Social and Cultural Rights and the World Trade Organization' (Occasional Paper No 30, Friedrich Ebert Stiftung, 2007), available at <http://library.fes.de/pdf-files/iez/global/04572.pdf/>.

[62] CESCR, General Comment 8, HRI/GEN/1/Rev.9 (Vol 1) 43, esp para 8. This statement also raises issues regarding the extraterritorial obligations of states, an issue which is discussed further in this chapter.

by another state, where that breach was reasonably foreseeable at the time of the relevant act. The classic situation where such issues arise is in the context of refoulement: where a state deports a person to another state in circumstances where 'the necessary and foreseeable consequence of the deportation would be a real risk of the killing or torture'.[63] States are thus under a duty not to put individuals into such situations. This duty is explicit in Article 3 Convention against Torture and Other Cruel, Inhuman or Degrading Treatment or Punishment (UNCAT).

In *Soering v UK*, the European Court of Human Rights found that the extradition of Soering, a young man accused of murder, to the USA would amount to inhuman and degrading treatment contrary to Article 3 ECHR.[64] This was because the UK would have knowingly exposed Soering to a real possibility of experiencing the death row phenomenon, that is, a prolonged period of time on death row characterized by mounting anguish at the inevitable prospect of death.

Agiza v Sweden concerned the expulsion of a terrorist suspect, one Ahmed Hussein Agiza, from Sweden to Egypt.[65] He was transported to Egypt by US agents. Sweden was found to have violated Article 3 UNCAT by allowing Agiza to be transported from Sweden to Egypt where it could reasonably foresee that he was at risk of being tortured. Sweden also breached the prohibition on cruel, inhuman, and degrading treatment in Article 16 by handing Agiza over to US agents in Sweden, and apparently acquiescing in his inhuman and degrading treatment by US agents while he remained on Swedish soil prior to his removal to Egypt.[66] The Article 16 finding thus manifested a different type of responsibility of a state for the human rights violations of another state.

In *Othman (Abu Qatada) v UK*,[67] the European Court held that the UK could not legally deport the terrorist suspect applicant to his country of nationality, Jordan, due to the risk that he would face an unfair trial there (contrary to the requirements of Article 6 of the Convention). In particular, Abu Qatada alleged that some of the evidence likely to be used against him in Jordan had been obtained by torture. The UK conceded that he might not receive a fair trial, but denied that it would amount to a 'flagrant denial of justice'.[68] The European Court disagreed, finding that the real risk of evidence obtained by torture being adduced at trial went to the 'very essence' of Article 6, and that the UK would itself breach the Article by deporting Abu Qatada to face a trial which would be 'not only immoral and illegal, but also entirely unreliable in its outcome'.[69]

Until *Othman*, the case law from all international human rights tribunals had only established that a sending state's non-refoulement obligations protected prospective deportees from foreseeable violations of the right to life and the right to be free from torture and other cruel, inhuman, and degrading treatment in the receiving state. *Othman* extended the non-refoulement obligation under the ECHR to cases in which a 'flagrant denial of justice' was likely to occur in breach of fair trial guarantees. In General Comment 31, the Human Rights Committee described the obligation not to deport as arising when

---

[63] *Pillai v Canada* CCPR/C/101/D/1763/2008 (25 March 2011), concurring opinion of Ms Keller, Ms Antoanella Motoc, Messrs Neuman and O'Flaherty, and Sir Nigel Rodley.

[64] (1989) 11 EHRR 439.   [65] CAT/C/34/D/233/2003 (24 May 2005).

[66] Agiza was stripped, blindfolded, and hooded for his flight to Egypt by US agents.

[67] (2012) 55 EHRR 1.

[68] The European Court had suggested in *Soering*, n 64 at para 113 that extradition would be precluded if a person foreseeably faced a 'flagrant denial of justice' in the receiving country.

[69] n 67, paras 265–7. The Court also stated that evidence obtained through other forms of ill-treatment (cruel, inhuman or degrading treatment or punishment) may also give rise to 'flagrant denials of justice,' but found it unnecessary to decide the issue (para 267).

deportation would give rise to a real risk of irreparable harm, such as that contemplated by Articles 6 and 7 of the Covenant.[70] It seems doubtful that many other human rights violations can be characterized as 'irreparable'.[71] It is, however, assumed that the obligations are more extensive if the sending state somehow colludes with the receiving state in bringing about violations of those other rights.

5   WHERE DO HUMAN RIGHTS APPLY?

What is the territorial scope of a state's jurisdiction for the purposes of human rights law? Clearly, a state has jurisdiction over its own territory. For example, Article 2(1) ICCPR specifies the duties owed to individuals within a state's territory. What is the scope, if any, of a state's extraterritorial jurisdiction under human rights treaties?

Before moving on, it is important to set the limits of what is meant by 'extraterritorial jurisdiction'. Cases such as those concerning refoulement mentioned in Section 4.3 involve intra-territorial acts which generate extraterritorial consequences. They do not involve instances of extraterritorial jurisdiction. The actual breach by the sending state in such cases arises at the time of its intra-territorial act of expelling the person, rather than when (or even if) the receiving state perpetrates the anticipated human rights abuse (for example, an act of torture upon the deported person).

So, what about a state's jurisdiction outside its own territory? A state's obligations under the ICCPR are generally presumed to extend to its colonies unless it has made a contrary declaration at the time of ratification.[72] On the other hand, under Article 56 ECHR, a state must specifically extend the application of the Convention to its dependent territories.

The approaches to the extraterritorial application of rights adopted by the European Court of Human Rights, the Inter-American human rights bodies, and the UN Committees established under the two Covenants are discussed in Sections 5.1 and 5.2.

5.1 ECHR

Article 1 ECHR states that '[t]he High Contracting Parties shall secure to everyone within their jurisdiction the rights and freedoms' in the Convention. No territorial limit is expressed therein. The extraterritorial application of the ECHR in certain circumstances was confirmed in *Loizidou v Turkey*[73] and *Cyprus v Turkey*[74] where the acts of the authorities in Northern Cyprus were held to be within Turkey's jurisdiction due to the 'effective control' exercised over those authorities by Turkey. Similarly, the actions of the authorities in the Transdniestrian separatist region in Moldova were held in *Ilascu v Moldova and Russia* to be within Russia's jurisdiction, due to Russia's 'effective authority', or at the very least decisive influence' over those authorities, due to its 'military, economic, financial and

---

[70] n 19, para 12. Due process guarantees also apply to extradition hearings; see for example Article 13 of the ICCPR. However, these guarantees relate to the receiving state's own behaviour rather than the foreseeable behaviour of another state, the subject matter of this section.

[71] See, however, *R (Ullah) v Special Adjudicator* [2004] UKHL 26, where the UK House of Lords indicated that non-refoulement may apply to prevent exposure to very serious breaches of other rights, such as one's right to freedom of religion.

[72] The HRC's decision in *Kuok Koi v Portugal*, CCPR/C/73/D/925/2000 (8 February 2002) seems somewhat confused on the matter, but on balance favours this conclusion. See Joseph, 'Human Rights Committee: Recent Cases' (2002) 2 *HRLR* 287, 287–95. See also ICCPR, Art 1(3).

[73] (1997) 23 EHRR 513.   [74] (2002) 35 EHRR 30.

political support'.[75] It seems that this threshold of 'effective authority' over Transdniestrian authorities is similar, or even slightly lower, than the requirement of 'effective control' over a territory in *Loizidou*.[76]

Banković et al. v Belgium et al. concerned a complaint about the actions of North Atlantic Treaty Organization (NATO) troops in bombing Radio Television Serbia in Belgrade during the airstrikes against the Federal Republic of Yugoslavia (FRY) in 1999. The complaint was issued against 17 European states that were members of NATO.[77] The Grand Chamber of the European Court of Human Rights concluded that the complaint was inadmissible for want of territorial jurisdiction. Extraterritorial jurisdiction was limited to instances where a respondent state is in 'effective control' of a particular territory through, for example, military occupation. The firing of missiles was not enough to establish such a level of control. Furthermore, the Court went on to state that the ECHR was a regional treaty confined to a particular 'legal space (*espace juridique*)',[78] of which the FRY was not part. It stated: 'The Convention was not designed to be applied throughout the world, even in respect of the conduct of Contracting States'.[79] *Banković* thus seemed to close the door on claims under the ECHR with regard to the behaviour of contracting states outside the area of the Council of Europe.

However, the European Court has since retreated from this position. *Öcalan v Turkey*, decided soon after *Banković*, concerned the arrest of the leader of the Kurdistan Workers' Party (PKK), Abdullah Öcalan, by Turkish agents at Nairobi airport in Kenya and his blindfolded flight back to Turkey. The European Court found that Turkey had jurisdiction over the actions that took place at Nairobi airport and duly considered the complaint of unlawful detention in this regard.[80]

Issa v Turkey concerned an allegation of killings by Turkish soldiers in northern Iraq. The applicants argued that that area was under the effective control of Turkish troops. On the issue of the Convention's 'legal space', the European Court stated that if the deceased had been under the effective control of Turkey at the relevant time, 'it would follow logically that they were within the jurisdiction of Turkey (and not that of Iraq, which is not a Contracting State and clearly does not fall within the legal space (*espace juridique*) of the Contracting States'.[81] This argument renders the issue of 'legal space' irrelevant when a contracting state is in fact exercising 'effective control' over any area anywhere in the world. The Court also adopted a very broad concept of 'effective control' to include 'overall control' so that a contracting party did not need to exercise 'detailed control over the policies and actions of the authorities' in the relevant area.[82] The Court also stated:

> [A] State may also be held accountable for violation of the Convention rights and freedoms of persons who are in the territory of another State but who are found to be under the former State's authority and control through its agents operating—whether lawfully or unlawfully—in the latter State ... Accountability in such situations stems from the fact that Article 1 of the Convention cannot be interpreted so as to allow a State party to perpetrate

---

[75] (2005) 40 EHRR 46, para 392. The court confirmed this line of reasoning in *Ivanţoc and Others v Moldova and Russia*, App no 23687/05, Judgment of 15 November 2011 and *Catan and Others v Moldova and Russia*, App nos 43370/04, 8252/06 and 18454/06, Judgment of 19 October 2012.

[76] Cerone, 'Human Dignity in the Line of Fire: The Application of International Human Rights Law during Armed Conflict, Occupation, and Peace Operations' (2006) 39 *Vanderbilt JTL* 1446, 1491.

[77] A separate issue regarding the responsibility of these states for NATO actions was not considered by the Court.   [78] *Bankovic et al. v Belgium et al.* (2007) 44 EHRR SE5, para 80.

[79] *Bankovic et al. v Belgium et al.* (2007) 44 EHRR SE5, para 80.

[80] (2005) 41 EHRR 45. Ultimately, that particular complaint was not upheld.

[81] (2005) 41 EHRR 27, para 74.   [82] (2005) 41 EHRR 27, para 70.

violations of the Convention on the territory of another State, which it could not perpetrate on its own territory.[83]

Thus, according to *Issa*, effective control can arise when a state's agents have effective control over a person (or persons) rather than over a particular area. According to that reasoning, in the *Banković* case, the people who were in Radio Television Serbia were arguably under the control of NATO forces when the latter decided to target that building with airstrikes.[84]

The conflicting European jurisprudence was reviewed by the UK House of Lords in *Al-Skeini v Secretary of State for Defence*. That case concerned a claim under the Human Rights Act 1998, which incorporates the ECHR into domestic law, concerning the deaths of six Iraqi civilians at the hands of British troops in Iraq. Five of the deceased had allegedly been killed by British forces in the streets of Basra, while the sixth was allegedly detained and mistreated before dying in British custody at a military base in Basra. The House of Lords, applying the principles in *Banković* and sidelining those in *Issa*, held that the UK did not have jurisdiction over the five street deaths, but it accepted that the death in detention was within UK jurisdiction. The applicants in *Al-Skeini* subsequently took their case to the European Court, which held that all six victims had been within the UK's jurisdiction for the purposes of Article 1 of the ECHR.[85] The Court's reasoning was somewhat confusing, such that it is difficult to now know the ECHR rules regarding extraterritorial jurisdiction.

It seems that *Al-Skeini* moved away from the *espace juridique* concept, though, frustratingly, it did not do so expressly. The European Court seemed to reinterpret the concept as meaning that the Convention does not 'govern the actions of States not Parties to it, nor does it purport to be a means of requiring the Contracting States to impose Convention standards on other States'.[86] Such a principle is uncontroversial, and was irrelevant on the facts in *Banković*—that complaint was not against or about the behaviour of a non-party. In a remarkably unacknowledged obliteration of *Banković*, the Court went on to say that the principle 'does not imply...that jurisdiction under Article 1 of the Convention can never exist outside the territory covered by the Council of Europe Member States. The Court has not in its case-law applied any such restriction'.[87] The European Court seemed to allude to two separate bases for extraterritorial jurisdiction, that is where a 'State through its agents exercises control and authority over an individual', and where a State 'exercises effective control of an area outside that national territory'. The difference between these two bases is made clear by the fact that the second is described as being '[a]nother exception' to the principle that jurisdiction is generally intra-territorial.[88] If the two bases are distinct, extraterritorial jurisdiction under the ECHR is in fact as broad as indicated in *Issa*, and significantly broader than signalled in *Banković*. However, the matter is confused by the fact that the Court, in its analysis of the facts, conflated the two tests and focused heavily on the actual territorial control exercised by the UK in southern Iraq in order to establish UK jurisdiction in the case. Hence, it is arguably uncertain whether jurisdiction can lie under the ECHR in the absence of effective control of a territory.

---

[83] (2005) 41 EHRR 27, para 71.

[84] Ultimately, the Court in *Issa* could not find any evidence that the Turkish forces were in the area at the relevant time, so the case was dismissed for lack of evidence that the relevant events occurred within Turkish jurisdiction.   [85] (2011) 53 EHRR 18.

[86] (2011) 53 EHRR 18, para 141.   [87] (2011) 53 EHRR 18, para 142.

[88] (2011) 53 EHRR 18, paras 137–8.

As stated by the ECHR, the matter is 'determined with reference to the particular facts' of a case:[89] the fact-specific nature of such inquiries renders it difficult to predict the outcome of future cases.

5.2 ACHR

Article 1(1) ACHR requires states to respect and ensure the rights to 'all persons subject to their jurisdiction', so, as with the ECHR, no territorial limit is expressed. In *Coard et al. v United States*, the Inter-American Commission on Human Rights found that the USA exercised jurisdiction over persons in Grenada during its 1983 invasion for the purposes of the American Declaration of Human Rights.[90] The USA is not a party to the ACHR and no jurisdictional clause is contained within the American Declaration. On the facts in *Coard*, it does not seem debatable that the USA had jurisdiction over the relevant persons. They were detained on a US military ship, and the USA arguably had effective control over Grenada at the time.[91] Nevertheless, neither fact was explicitly referenced in the Commission's decision. It found that people could come within US jurisdiction through the actions of US agents, namely the US military in Grenada.

Alejandre v Cuba concerned the shooting down of unarmed civilian aircraft by Cuban aircraft.[92] The case again concerned findings under the American Declaration, as Cuba was not a party to the ACHR. The Inter-American Commission found that Cuba had jurisdiction over the four deceased occupants of the airplanes. The shootings took place in international airspace, and two of the deceased were not Cubans. The only potential basis for jurisdiction lay 'in the relationship between the agents of Cuba and the victims in the circumstances at the time of the incident'.[93] Indeed, the degree of control exercised over the victims seems analogous to that exercised by the NATO troops over the victims in *Bankovic*.

The Commission indicated that the ACHR had similar extraterritorial application to the American Declaration in *Saldano v Argentina*, stating that extraterritorial jurisdiction arose 'under certain circumstances for the acts and omissions of [state agents] which produce effects or are undertaken outside that State's own territory'.[94] Hence, the test adopted seems to be one of effective control over a person rather than effective control over the territory in which a violation takes place. The Inter-American bodies have not yet confronted the issue of whether Inter-American human rights law might be confined to the Inter-American 'legal space'.

5.3 AFRICAN CHARTER ON HUMAN AND PEOPLES' RIGHTS

In *Democratic Republic of the Congo v Burundi, Rwanda, and Uganda*, the respondent states were found responsible by the African Commission on Human Rights for the actions of their occupying troops in the Democratic Republic of the Congo.[95] Indeed, the respondent states did not dispute the admissibility of the complaint on the grounds of extraterritoriality. The case seems a fairly clear instance of 'effective control' being exercised in an extraterritorial context.

---

[89] (2011) 53 EHRR 18, para 132.   [90] Case 10.951, IACommHR Report No 109/99 (29 September 1999).
[91] Cerone, 'The Application of Regional Human Rights Law Beyond Regional Frontiers: The Inter-American Commission on Human Rights and US Activities in Iraq', *ASIL Insights* (25 October 2005) 3.
[92] Case 11.589, IACommHR Report No 86/99 (29 September 1999).   [93] Cerone, n 91, 4.
[94] IACommHR Report No 38/99 (11 March 1999) para 17.
[95] Communication No 227/99 (May 2003).

5.4 ICCPR

The UN treaties are logically unaffected by any 'legal space' argument, given their global reach. Article 2(1) ICCPR requires states to respect and ensure ICCPR rights 'to all individuals within its territory *and* subject to its jurisdiction'.[96] Thus, the language of the ICCPR arguably limits a state's responsibility under the ICCPR to its territory. Nevertheless, the Human Rights Committee has confirmed the extraterritorial impact of the ICCPR in a number of cases. The Committee (and other UN human rights treaty bodies) have confirmed Israel's responsibility for human rights abuses in the Occupied Territories,[97] and the same for the USA regarding its detention camp in Guantánamo Bay in Cuba.[98] In numerous cases, such as *Montero v Uruguay*, states have been held responsible for the actions of their overseas consulates in unreasonably refusing to renew a passport.[99] In *Lopez Burgos v Uruguay*, Uruguay was held responsible for the kidnap in Argentina of a man by its agents.[100]

In General Comment 31, the Human Rights Committee described the extraterritorial impact of the ICCPR as follows:

[A] State party must respect and ensure the rights laid down in the Covenant to *anyone within the power or effective control* of that State Party, even if not situated within the territory of the State Party...... This principle also applies to those within the power or effective control of the forces of a State Party acting outside its territory, regardless of the circumstances in which such power or effective control was obtained.[101]

Thus, the ICCPR and the ACHR apply extraterritorially where an affected person is under the effective control of a state's agents, rather than only where an affected person is within territory that is effectively controlled by a state. The focus of the Committee in defining the extent of jurisdiction seems to be on the state's relationship with the relevant impugned act and the person affected, rather than its relationship with the territory where a relevant act takes place.

The extent of a state's possible extraterritorial responsibilities was tested in *Munaf v Romania*.[102] The allegation in that case was that the Romanian embassy in Iraq wrongly released the complainant Munaf into the hands of the US embassy, where he was ultimately handed over to Iraqi authorities and charged with capital crimes. Ultimately, the claim of a breach of the right to life (and other rights) was not upheld, as Romania was found not to be in a position to have foreseen the events following its release of Munaf. However, the admissibility decision indicated that a state could, in principle, be held responsible for extraterritorial acts which facilitate the predictable abusive actions of another state (at least with regard to torture or killing).

In Concluding Observations on Germany in 2012, the Human Rights Committee expressed concern at 'German companies acting abroad allegedly in contravention of relevant human rights standards' (referring to complaints of forcible evictions in Uganda to

---

[96] Emphasis added.

[97] Eg HRC, Concluding observations of the Human Rights Committee: Israel, CCPR/C/ISR/CO/3 (3 September 2010). See also *Legal Consequences of the Construction of a Wall in the Occupied Palestinian Territory* (Advisory Opinion) [2004] ICJ Rep 36.

[98] Eg HRC, Concluding observations: US, CCPR/C/USA/CO/3 (15 September 2006) paras 14–15.

[99] CCPR/C/18/D/106/1981 (31 March 1983).

[100] CCPR/C/13/D/52/1979 (29 July 1981). A similar decision arose in *Celiberti de Casariego v Uruguay*, CCPR/C/13/D/56/1979 (29 July 1981), concerning the kidnapping of a person from Brazil.

[101] n 19, para 10 (emphasis added).　　[102] CCPR/C/96/D/1539/2006 (21 August 2009).

make way for a coffee plantation owned by a German conglomerate) and made the following recommendation:

> While welcoming measures taken by the State party to provide remedies against German companies acting abroad allegedly in contravention of relevant human rights standards, the Committee is concerned that such remedies may not be sufficient in all cases (art. 2, para. 2).
>
> The State party is encouraged to set out clearly the expectation that all business enterprises domiciled in its territory and/or its jurisdiction respect human rights standards in accordance with the Covenant throughout their operations. It is also encouraged to take appropriate measures to strengthen the remedies provided to protect people who have been victims of activities of such business enterprises operating abroad.[103]

This Concluding Observation may signal an extension of a state's extraterritorial obligations. Thus far, extraterritorial obligations have concerned the actions or omissions of a state's own agents. In these 2012 comments, the HRC *encouraged* Germany to exert extraterritorial control over its private corporate citizens so as to constrain them from harming the human rights of people in other states. It remains to be seen whether such 'encouragement' will evolve into a legal expectation.[104]

5.5 ICESCR

The extraterritorial scope of the ICESCR is more open to debate due to the current lack of case law under that treaty. Furthermore, the ICESCR does not contain a provision relating to jurisdictional or territorial scope.[105] Article 2(1) does, however, say that states must progressively realize ICESCR rights through steps taken individually 'and through international assistance and cooperation'. Those words seem to imply that states should at least refrain from actions which harm those rights abroad, as such measures are decidedly non-cooperative.

The International Court of Justice confirmed in its advisory opinion on the *Legal Consequences of the Construction of a Wall in the Occupied Palestinian Territory* that states have duties under the ICESCR to 'territories over which a State party has sovereignty and to those over which that State exercises territorial jurisdiction'.[106] Ultimately, the Court found that Israel had violated a number of rights in the ICESCR by building part of its wall in the Occupied Territory and, for example, hindering access to educational facilities, places of employment, health services, agricultural land, and sources of water. In *Democratic Republic of Congo v Uganda* the International Court stated that states are responsible under international human rights treaties for acts done in the exercise of jurisdiction outside their territory, especially in occupied territories.[107] The *Wall* standard focused on territorial control (which Israel exercised over the West Bank), at least in respect of the ICESCR, while the *Congo* standard seemed to focus on extraterritorial acts with regard to all human rights treaties.

Given that extraterritorial jurisdiction under the ICESCR exists, one may readily assume that states are required to *respect* ICESCR rights outside their borders, that is, to refrain from harming such rights. In fact, the most important aspects of a duty to respect

---

[103] Concluding Observations on Germany, CCPR/C/DEU/CO/6, para 16.

[104] Compare text at n 109.

[105] ICESCR-OP Art 2 provides that communications may be received on behalf of people 'under the jurisdiction of a State party'.   [106] n 98, paras 111–13.

[107] *Armed Activities on the Territory of the Congo* (*Democratic Republic of the Congo v Uganda*) (Judgment, Merits) [2005] ICJ Rep 168, para 216.

may arise with regard to intra-territorial acts which have an extraterritorial effect, rather than with extraterritorial acts as such. For example, the adoption by a state of protectionist measures within its territory will often cause harm to the right to work of those in export industries outside its territory. Indeed, a state's intra-territorial acts are more likely to impact detrimentally (or beneficially) on economic, social, and cultural rights abroad than civil and political rights. The comparable analysis is arguably that of the refoulement cases, meaning that harm amounts to a breach of ICESCR obligations if a real risk of breach is reasonably foreseeable. On the other hand, the connection between the state and the expelled person is clearer than in the case of an external person who suffers economic harm, as the impugned act of refoulement initially occurs while the person is within the state's territory, and the act is clearly aimed at that person such as to cause harm to his or her rights. Therefore, the crucial jurisdictional issue in this context concerns the identification of circumstances when a state owes obligations to persons outside its territory such that it must avoid acts, whether occurring inside or outside its territory, that cause harm to their ICESCR rights. That is, the question may be more one of 'who has rights' rather than 'where has the impugned act occurred'.

The Committee on Economic, Social and Cultural Rights has indicated that states parties also have duties to *protect* ICESCR rights in other states. For example, it stated in General Comment 15 on the right to water that states should take steps 'to prevent their own citizens and companies from violating the right to water of individuals and communities in other countries'.[108] On the other hand, the UN Special Representative on the issue of human rights and transnational corporations concluded that 'States are not [presently] generally required under international human rights law to regulate the extraterritorial activities of businesses domiciled in their territory and/or jurisdiction'.[109] Such a duty is easier to maintain if a state is actively facilitating its corporations' overseas activities, such as through the provision of export credits.

The most controversial aspect of potential extraterritorial duties under the ICESCR relates to *fulfilling* ICESCR rights in other states. Such a duty would imply that rich states are obliged to provide aid to assist poorer countries. Rich states predictably resist such a characterization of their ICESCR duties. Such a duty is more evident in the words of the Declaration on the Right to Development,[110] as well as the Millennium Development Goals.[111] For its part, the Committee has indicated that states have a duty to assist other states to provide international assistance when they are in a position to do so.[112] On the other hand, the parameters of such a duty are difficult to determine. When, precisely, would state X have a duty to a person in state Y to take positive actions to fulfil his or her rights? And when could that person's socio-economic deprivation be held to come within the responsibility of a particular external state?[113]

---

[108] CESCR, General Comment 15, HRI/GEN/1/Rev.9 (Vol 1) 97, para 33. See also CESCR, General Comment 19, HRI/GEN/1/Rev.9 (Vol 1) 152, para 54.

[109] See Report of the Special Representative of the Secretary-General on the issue of human rights and transnational corporations and other business enterprises: 'Guiding Principles on Business and Human Rights: Implementing the United Nations "Protect, Respect and Remedy" Framework', A/HRC/17/31 (21 March 2011), Principle 2. Compare with the text at n 104.

[110] Declaration on the Right to Development, esp Art 4.

[111] See Alston, 'Ships Passing in the Night: The Current State of the Human Rights and Development Debate seen through the Lens of the Millenium Development Goals' (2005) 27 *HRQ* 778. See also Charter of Economic Rights and Duties of States, Art 24.

[112] Eg CESCR, General Comment 3, HRI/GEN/1/Rev.9 (Vol 1) 7, para 14; CESCR General Comment 12, n 60, para 35; CESCR General Comment 15, n 108, para 38.

[113] See Salomon, *Global Responsibility for Human Rights* (OUP, 2007) 184–93.

In September 2011, the *Maastricht Principles on the Extraterritorial Obligations of States in the Area of Economic, Social and Cultural Rights* (Principles) were adopted by a group of legal experts under the auspices of Maastricht University and the International Commission of Jurists. The preamble sets out the drafters' intention to address the actions of states in a globalized world which increasingly affect the economic, social, and cultural rights of individuals outside their borders. Principle 3 provides that '[a]ll States have obligations to respect, protect and fulfil human rights, including civil, cultural, economic, political and social rights, both within their territories and extraterritorially.' Principle 9 clarifies:

> A State has obligations to respect, protect and fulfil economic, social and cultural rights in any of the following:
>
> a) situations over which it exercises authority or effective control, whether or not such control is exercised in accordance with international law;
>
> b) situations over which State acts or omissions bring about foreseeable effects on the enjoyment of economic, social and cultural rights, whether within or outside its territory;
>
> c) situations in which the State, acting separately or jointly, whether through its executive, legislative or judicial branches, is in a position to exercise decisive influence or to take measures to realize economic, social and cultural rights extraterritorially, in accordance with international law.

The Principles also provide that states remain responsible for their own conduct even when they are acting as members of international organizations (Principle 15); that states must interpret and apply other international instruments (such as trade agreements) consistently with their human rights obligations (Principle 17); that states must refrain (and require non-state actors under their power to refrain) from actions which nullify or impair others' enjoyment of economic, social, and cultural rights (Principles 20 and 24); and that states must take steps to create an 'international enabling environment conducive to the universal fulfilment of economic, social and cultural rights' (Principle 29).[114] The Principles are not binding at international law, nor are they open for signature by states. The OHCHR describes such instruments as having 'an undeniable moral force' and providing 'practical guidance to States in their conduct.'[115] The Principles may also play a role in developing and crystallizing customary international law in the area, given they represent a statement by eminent experts of their opinion as to what that law is.

5.6 OVERALL ASSESSMENT

Wilde has put forward a convincing argument that the focus on jurisdiction over a person, rather than territory, is the preferred determinant of establishing when a state has extraterritorial jurisdiction. He claims, correctly, that a territorial focus inevitably discriminates against non-nationals, as states are far more likely to be in control of territory populated by nationals. Furthermore, a solely territorial focus would permit states to dictate that their agents behave on foreign-controlled soil in a manner that is not permitted under human

---

[114]   De Schutter *et al.*, 'Commentary to the Maastricht Principles on Extraterritorial Obligations of States in the Area of Economic, Social and Cultural Rights' (2012) 34 *HRQ* 1084.

[115]   See OHCHR, *International Law*: <http://www2.ohchr.org/english/law>.

rights law at home. Finally, the territorial approach might regrettably generate legal vacuums where no human rights law applies.[116]

An issue arises as to the comprehensiveness of a state's extraterritorial human rights obligations. Within its territory, a state must respect, protect, and fulfil human rights. One might imagine that, extraterritorially, a sliding scale of duties applies according to the degree of control a state has over a particular situation.[117] For example, the detainees in Guantánamo Bay are under the total control of the USA and, therefore, should be entitled to claim the full range of treaty rights against the USA, regardless of their Cuban location. On the other hand, one might assume that Israel's human rights responsibilities in Gaza are not as comprehensive since its withdrawal from that territory. While Israel is obliged to refrain from measures which harm rights in Gaza, it seems unlikely that Israel retains the same obligation to fulfil the right to education in Gaza, where educational facilities are essentially controlled by Hamas, an entity that is hostile to Israel. Similarly, while the victim in *Montero v Uruguay* could claim the right to freedom of movement against the Uruguayan consulate in Germany with regard to a refusal to renew his passport, Montero could not claim that the consulate was required to take measures to protect the full range of his rights while he was in Germany. When jurisdiction is tied to an act with respect to a person, rather than effective control over territory, 'it would seem that the individual is within the jurisdiction of that state only for the purposes of that act',[118] with the relevant act in *Montero*, for example, being the refusal to renew the passport.

In *Banković*, the European Court of Human Rights denied that a state's obligations could 'be divided and tailored in accordance with the particular circumstances of the extra-territorial act in question'.[119] However, this 'all or nothing' approach seems unduly strict. There seems little difficulty, for example, in imposing a duty on states to respect human rights, and therefore refrain from actions which harm human rights outside their territory. On the other hand, the extent of extraterritorial positive obligations (to protect and fulfil) seem logically more dependent upon a greater degree of control over a situation.

Indeed, the European Court seemed to depart from its strict *Banković* position in *Ilascu*, with regard to the scope of Moldova's human rights responsibilities on the facts of that case. The complaint against Moldova in *Ilascu* concerned its jurisdiction over an area within its own territory, but where it plainly lacked control. Analogous situations include Cuba's responsibility for Guantánamo Bay and Cyprus's responsibility for Northern Cyprus. Does a state retain jurisdiction over such areas for human rights purposes? In *Ilascu*, the European Court conceded that Moldova did not have effective control over Transdniestria so the scope of its jurisdiction was reduced,[120] but it retained 'a positive obligation...to take diplomatic, economic, judicial or other measures that [were] within its power to take...to secure the rights guaranteed in the Convention'.[121] The concession that jurisdiction can be retained in a reduced form cut against the Court's 'all or nothing' approach in *Banković* that jurisdiction is not divisible.

In *Al-Skeini*, the European Court explicitly confirmed that its view had changed, stating:

> It is clear that, whenever the State through its agents exercises control and authority over an individual, and thus jurisdiction, the State is under an obligation under Article 1 to secure to that individual the rights and freedoms under Section 1 of the Convention that are relevant

---

[116] Wilde, 'Legal "Black hole"? Extraterritorial State action and international treaty law on civil and political rights' (2005) 26 *Michigan JIL* 1, 25–8. See also *Lopez Burgos*, n 100, including the concurring opinion of Mr Tomuschat.

[117] Wilde, 'Triggering State Obligations Extraterritorially: the Spatial Test in Certain Human Rights Treaties' (2007) 40 *Israel LR* 503, 524.

[118] Cerone, n 76, 1497.   [119] n 78, para 75.   [120] n 75, para 333.   [121] n 75, para 331.

to the situation of that individual. In this sense, therefore, the Convention rights can be 'divided and tailored' (compare *Banković*, cited above, § 75).[122]

6 CONCLUSION

Generally, states owe human rights duties to individuals and groups within their jurisdiction. However, the extent of a state's jurisdiction for the purposes of its human rights treaty obligations is a complex and evolving concept. There would be gaping lacunae in human rights protection if a state's jurisdiction, and consequent responsibility, only arose in connection with its own acts and omissions within its own territory.

Therefore, human rights law has evolved to generate the concept of due diligence to ensure some accountability for human rights abuses in the private sphere. In contrast, the extent of state responsibility for the acts of international organizations is less clear.

The broader view of extraterritorial jurisdiction, which clearly prevails within the UN treaty bodies, the Inter-American bodies, and probably the International Court of Justice, holds that such jurisdiction arises when a state has effective control over the enjoyment of a particular right by an individual. This view has significant ramifications for the extraterritorial scope of the ICESCR, given the ubiquity of external economic impacts, and consequent effects on economic, social, and cultural rights, caused by state actions in today's interconnected global economy. The European Court seems to adopt a narrower approach, though the precise meaning of *Al-Skeini* is unclear. It has now abandoned the conservative *espace juridique* approach, originally adopted in *Banković*. However, it is not certain that it has completely abandoned its test of 'effective control of territory' in favour of the broader 'effective control of the person' test adopted in other international tribunals.

FURTHER READING

CERONE, 'Human Dignity in the Line of Fire: The Application of International Human Rights Law during Armed Conflict, Occupation, and Peace Operations' (2006) 39 *Vanderbilt JTL* 1446.

COOMANS and KAMMINGA (eds), *Extraterritorial Application of Human Rights* (Intersentia, 2004).

CRAVEN, 'The Violence of Dispossession: Extra-Territoriality and Economic, Social and Cultural Rights' in Baderin and McCorquodale (eds), *Economic Social and Cultural Rights in Action* (Oxford University Press, 2007).

HATHAWAY et al., 'Human Rights Abroad: When Do Human Rights Treaty Obligations Apply Extraterritorially?' (2011) 43 *Arizona State LJJ* 389.

INTERNATIONAL LAW COMMISSION, *Articles on Responsibility of States for Internationally Wrongful Acts*, A/56/10, ch IV.E.1.

KAMCHIBEKOVA, 'State Responsibility for Extraterritorial Human Rights Violations' (2007) 13 *Buffalo HRLR* 87.

KNOX, 'Horizontal Human Rights Law' (2008) 103 *AJIL* 1.

MCCORQUODALE and SIMON, 'Responsibility beyond Borders: State Responsibility for Extraterritorial Violations by Corporations under International Human Rights Law' (2007) 70 *MLR* 599.

---

[122] See *Al-Skeini and Others v UK*, n 85, para 137.

SALOMON, *Global Responsibility for Human Rights* (Oxford University Press, 2007).

SARI, 'Jurisdiction and International Responsibility in Peace Support Operations: the *Behrami* and *Saramati* cases' (2008) 8 *HRLR* 151.

SKOGLY, 'Extraterritoriality: Universal Human Rights without Universal Obligations?' in Joseph and McBeth (eds), *Research Handbook on International Human Rights* (Edward Elgar, 2010).

WILDE, 'Legal "Black Hole"?: Extraterritorial state action and international treaty law on civil and political rights' (2005) 26 *Michigan JIL* 739.

PART III
SUBSTANTIVE RIGHTS

7

CATEGORIES OF RIGHTS

Theo van Boven

SUMMARY

This chapter seeks to identify different categories of human rights, but in doing so recognizes the indivisibility, interdependence, and interrelatedness of all human rights. A first categorization distinguishes civil and political rights from economic, social, and cultural rights. This distinction is, however, increasingly contested and should not disguise the mutual relationship between these rights as essential conditions for the life and well-being of the human person. A second distinction is that between the rights of individuals and the rights of collectivities, in particular indigenous peoples. Collective rights offer parameters for the effective enjoyment of individual rights. A third distinction is that between core rights and other rights, raising the issue of whether there is a ranking among human rights as to their fundamental nature. It is argued that basic substantive rights determining the life, survival, dignity, and worth of individuals and peoples may be considered as core rights. The chapter finally discusses the question of whether 'new human rights' are emerging. It advises that this question be approached with caution and that human rights should be understood in an inclusive and newly focused manner, encompassing hitherto marginalized and excluded groups and human beings.

1 INTRODUCTION

There is a certain uneasiness about classifying human rights in different categories. Leading UN documents state that all human rights are *indivisible*, *interdependent*, and *interrelated*. Whatever categories of human rights one may have in mind—civil, political, economic, social, or cultural rights; individual or collective rights; core or non-core rights—intersections bear out that all rights are interlinked and that categories or classifications correspond more to conceptual premises than to realities. The relative inadequacy of human rights categories and classifications becomes evident when the focus is on the human being whose enjoyment of rights and freedoms depends on prevailing conditions of freedom from fear and freedom from want. Domestic and international policies, insofar as they take into account the holistic nature of human rights, transcend human rights categorizations and classifications.

The comprehensive and holistic nature of human rights was recognized by US President Franklin D Roosevelt when, in his famous speech of 1941, he mentioned 'four essential freedoms' that must be guaranteed to all persons everywhere in the world: freedom of speech and expression, freedom of worship, freedom from want, and freedom from fear.[1] This

---

[1] Commager, *Documents of American History* (Crofts, 1946) 634.

forward-looking four freedoms message served as one of the sources of inspiration for the UN International Bill of Rights and continues to inspire policy-makers. For example, former UN Secretary-General Kofi Annan, in his landmark report *In Larger Freedom: Towards Development, Security and Human Rights for All*, drew extensively on the freedom from want and freedom from fear paradigm.[2] A major thrust thereof is that development, security, and human rights are not only interlinked, they also reinforce each other.[3] In order to attain larger freedom, human rights must be an integral part of development and security policies. Even though this chapter reviews various categories of human rights, this should neither distract from the indivisibility of all human rights, nor from their comprehensive and holistic nature.

2 CATEGORIES OF HUMAN RIGHTS

2.1 ECONOMIC, SOCIAL, CULTURAL RIGHTS/CIVIL, POLITICAL RIGHTS

Much attention has been given over the years to the distinction between, on the one hand, *economic, social, and cultural rights* (such as the rights to an adequate standard of living, education and work, dealt with in Chapters 10 and 12) and, on the other, *civil and political rights* (such as the rights to life and integrity of the person, the freedoms of thought, expression, association, and assembly, and the rights to liberty and a fair trial, dealt with in Chapters 9, 11, and 13).[4] There is indeed a significant difference between the two as far as the nature of states parties' obligations under the International Covenant on Economic, Social and Cultural Rights (ICESCR) and the International Covenant on Civil and Political Rights (ICCPR) are concerned. While Article 2 ICESCR provides for the *progressive realization* of economic, social, and cultural rights and acknowledges the constraints due to limits of available resources, the parallel Article 2 ICCPR prescribes the obligation to respect and ensure all civil and political rights as an *immediate* obligation. Accordingly, the Committee on Economic, Social and Cultural Rights has viewed the concept of progressive realization as a recognition that full realization of all economic, social, and cultural rights will generally not be achieved in a short period of time. Since progressive realization is an essential objective, not in the abstract but to the maximum of available resources, a question arises regarding how such an obligation of the state is to be interpreted in times of economic depression and shrinking resources as experienced at the end of the first decade of the twenty-first century. An essential bottom-line to be respected under all circumstances, even in times of shrinking resources, is that of non-discrimination, which the Committee termed 'an immediate and cross-cutting obligation in the [ICESCR]'.[5]

Nevertheless, the Committee on Economic, Social and Cultural Rights has pointed out that, despite this difference, there are also significant similarities between the ICESCR and the ICCPR. In particular, the ICESCR imposes various obligations of *immediate effect*.[6] Thus, there are a number of provisions in the ICESCR that, as the Committee has pointed out in its General Comment 3, would seem to be capable of immediate application by

---

[2] A/59/2005 (21 March 2005).

[3] See World Summit outcome document, GA Res 60/1 (24 October 2005) para 9.

[4] van Boven, 'Distinguishing Criteria of Human Rights' in Vasak and Alston (eds), *The International Dimensions of Human Rights: Vol 1* (UNESCO/Greenwood Press 1982) 87.

[5] CESCR, General Comment 20, E/C.12/GC/20 (2009) para 7.

[6] CESCR, General Comment 3, HRI/GEN/1/ (Vol 1) 7, para 1.

judicial and other organs in many domestic legal systems. Among these are the elimination of discrimination (Articles 2(2) and (3)), the right to form and join trade unions and to strike (Article 8), protection of children and young persons from economic and social exploitation (Article 10(3)), equal remuneration for work of equal value without distinction of any kind (Article 7(a)(i)), the provision of free and compulsory primary education for all (Article 13(2)(a)), the liberty of parents to choose schools for their children, other than those established by public authorities (Article 13(3)), and the liberty of individuals and bodies to establish and direct educational institutions which conform to certain minimum standards (Article 13(4)).[7]

In addition to the difference between obligations of immediate effect and progressive realization, it is quite common to advance further criteria to distinguish civil and political rights from economic and social rights by contrasting the concept of freedom rights with that of welfare rights or by referring to duties of the state not to intervene as opposed to duties to take positive measures. Such distinctions are helpful but do not apply across the board insofar as there is no strict dividing line between civil and political rights on the one hand and economic and social rights on the other.

While the status of civil and political rights as human rights is largely uncontested, this is less true for economic, social, and cultural rights.[8] The latter are sometimes referred to as 'aspirations' phrased in terms of rights but without legal enforceability. The media, many NGOs, public officials, as well as public opinion generally understand human rights in terms of the right to life, the abolition of the death penalty, the prohibition of torture, the right to privacy, freedom of information and expression, freedom of religion or belief, and the right to vote and to be elected. The rights to food, healthcare, housing, and employment are considered much less part of the human rights package. However, this perception of human rights overlooks the comprehensive nature of the Universal Declaration of Human Rights (UDHR) and notably its Article 28, which provides that everyone is entitled to a social and international order in which the rights and freedoms set forth in the Declaration can be fully realized. Over the years, as the human rights discourse became part of processes towards widening categories of entitlements and beneficiaries and linking human rights to the promotion of peace, security, and sustainable development, as well as preserving a healthy environment, a comprehensive human rights approach has evolved, encompassing the broad and interlinked scale of civil, political, economic, social, and cultural rights.

2.2 RIGHTS OF INDIVIDUALS/RIGHTS OF COLLECTIVITIES

The same process has also had an impact on another traditional categorization of human rights, namely the distinction between *rights of individuals* and *rights of collectivities*. In the frame of reference of the UDHR and the international covenants, with their emphasis on human dignity and the worth and uniqueness of every human being, the focus is on the rights of every individual person. Of course, in many ways individual human beings live and work in community and partnership with other human beings, in family and similar relations, in the exercise of religion or belief, in educational settings, and in forming and

---

[7] CESCR, General Comment 3, HRI/GEN/1/ (Vol 1), paras 1 and 5.
[8] See Robinson, 'Advancing Economic, Social and Cultural Rights: The Way Forward' (2004) 26 *HRQ* 866; Roth, 'Defending Economic, Social and Cultural Rights: Practical Issues Faced by an International Human Rights Organization' (2004) 26 *HRQ* 63.

joining trade unions. Yet it is the individual person, while part of social or cultural relations of a community nature, who is the beneficiary of rights.

The same construction has been used, at least in the UN terminology, where rights of peoples and minority groups, addressed in Chapter 17, are involved. Minorities, as collectivities, are not referred to as beneficiaries of rights. This is so that any separatist ambitions that they may pursue in the states where they live are not legitimized. Accordingly, the relevant provision of the ICCPR, Article 27 reads: 'In those States in which ethnic, religious or linguistic minorities exist, *persons belonging to such minorities* shall not be denied the right, in community with other members of their group, to enjoy their own culture, to profess and practise their own religion, or to use their own language.'[9] This provision is phrased in very restrained terms and avoids, at least in theory, the recognition of collective rights. Similarly, the UN Declaration on the Rights of Persons Belonging to National or Ethnic, Religious and Linguistic Minorities (1992) cautiously and consistently refers to 'persons belonging to minorities', thereby focusing on individuals rather than collectivities.

A different approach, one that is more collectivist or peoples-oriented, is to be found in the UN Declaration on the Rights of Indigenous Peoples (2007). The text of this declaration was negotiated over a period of more than 20 years with considerable input from indigenous peoples themselves. In the preamble of the Declaration, the rights of individuals and the rights of collectivities are brought together in a dialectical fashion by 'recognizing and reaffirming that indigenous individuals are entitled without discrimination to all human rights recognized in international law and that indigenous peoples possess collective rights which are indispensable for their existence, well-being and integral development as peoples'.[10] Throughout the text of the Declaration, rights are attributed to indigenous peoples as well as to indigenous individuals, with the indigenous peoples as principal rights-holders and the express recognition of the right to self-determination as the cornerstone of their rights. Article 3 of the Declaration restates the wording of common Article 1 of the international covenants, applying it to the particular case of indigenous peoples: 'Indigenous peoples have the right to self-determination. By virtue of that right they freely determine their political status and freely pursue their economic, social and cultural development.' In many ways, the Declaration on the Rights of Indigenous Peoples brings together peoples' rights and individual rights in a spectrum of mutual relationship and reach. A good illustration of this is Article 7, which, echoing Article 3 UDHR, provides that 'indigenous individuals have the rights to life, physical and mental integrity, liberty and security of person', while at the same time making it clear, in language similar to the UN Declaration on the Right of Peoples to Peace (1984),[11] that 'indigenous peoples have the collective right to live in freedom, peace and security as distinct peoples'.

This collective dimension of the rights of peoples and populations, for present and future generations, recognizes that the realization and enjoyment of individual rights are conditioned by the attainment of peace, security, and development. The same notion is embodied in the right to self-determination, defined in terms of free determination of political status and free pursuance of economic, social, and cultural development. Peoples' right to self-determination is recognized as a leading and underlying principle for the enjoyment of civil, political, economic, social, and cultural rights and was therefore included in both international covenants as the first substantive provision. Against this background, the 1993 Vienna World Conference on Human Rights considered the denial

---

[9] Emphasis added.   [10] GA Res 61/295 (13 September 2007) preamble.
[11] GA Res 39/11 (12 November 1984).

of the right of self-determination as a violation of human rights.[12] Similarly, it is significant that the UN Declaration on the Right to Development (1986) places the individual and collective aspects of this right in a mutual relationship and seeks to link the conditions of life of the human person with the welfare and well-being of peoples.[13] Thus, the right to development is defined as an inalienable human right with the proviso that equality of opportunity for development is a prerogative both of nations and of individuals who make up nations. Further, the Declaration states that 'the human person is the central subject of development and should be the active participant and beneficiary of the right to development'.[14]

2.3 ONE-DIMENSIONAL/COMPOSITE RIGHTS

As compared to rights such as freedom of expression or the right to a fair trial, the rights to self-determination and development, as well as the right to peace, are of a more complex nature. Therefore, they are often described as composite rights. The question may be asked what the legal significance of such rights is. While they condition the life and welfare of individual human beings, they are not rights inherent in the human person. Their realization depends on political, economic, social, and cultural policies deployed by national and international organs and institutions. These rights do not lend themselves to enforcement by legal authorities. Nevertheless, gross violations of the right to peace, the right to self-determination, or the right to development may, under given circumstances, incur state responsibility as well as civil responsibility of other major actors, or, if they amount to aggression, genocide, or crimes against humanity, even criminal responsibility of natural persons. While these rights primarily represent major policy objectives of a national and international order, their legal implications are not without significance and may be tested in political or judicial settings in case of their breach or gross denial.

3 INTERDEPENDENCE AND INDIVISIBILITY OF ALL HUMAN RIGHTS

The previous section identified different categories of human rights: civil and political rights as compared to economic, social, and cultural rights; rights of individuals as compared to rights of collectives; one-dimensional rights as compared to rights of a composite nature. But it has also already been made clear that all these rights are intersected and interrelated. They condition each other, with the human person, as the UN Declaration on the Right to Development puts it, as 'the central subject' and 'beneficiary' of rights,[15] and, in the words of the preambles of the international covenants, with a focus on 'the ideal of free human beings enjoying freedom from fear and want'.

Against this background, the interdependence and indivisibility of all human rights, whether or not classified in various categories, has become a leading axiom in the international human rights discourse. A number of examples taken from UN instruments, statements, and practices can be advanced to underline this interdependence and indivisibility. The Proclamation of Teheran, adopted at the first world conference on human

---

[12] Vienna Declaration and Programme of Action, A/CONF.157/23 (25 June 1993) para 2.
[13] GA Res 41/128 (4 December 1986).   [14] GA Res 41/128 (4 December 1986), Art 2(1).
[15] GA Res 41/128 (4 December 1986), Art 2(1).

rights in 1968, stated that human rights and fundamental freedoms are indivisible.[16] The second world conference held in Vienna in 1993 stated with greater emphasis that '[a]ll human rights are universal, indivisible, and interdependent and interrelated'.[17] The outcome document of the 2005 World Summit reaffirmed this statement.[18] The General Assembly resolution of 2006 establishing the Human Rights Council again reaffirmed that 'all human rights are universal, indivisible, interrelated, interdependent and mutually rein-forcing, and that all human rights must be treated in a fair and equal manner, on the same footing and with the same emphasis'.[19]

It may be argued that reiterating and reaffirming the same phrase does not—necessarily make it a reality. Perhaps more convincing are the language and contents of specific legal instruments on non-discrimination and the rights of vulnerable persons and persons in need of special recognition and protection. Thus, the International Convention on the Elimination of All Forms of Racial Discrimination, the Convention on the Elimination of All Forms of Discrimination Against Women, the Convention on the Rights of the Child, the International Convention on the Protection of the Rights of All Migrant Workers and Members of Their Families, and the Convention on the Rights of Persons with Disabilities all recognize the full scope of human rights in a comprehensive interrelationship. Finally, as already noted, it can be argued that the UN Declaration on the Rights of Indigenous Peoples is in its scope and wording the most far-reaching illustration of the interdepend-ence and interrelatedness of all human rights, be they economic, social, cultural, civil, or political rights; rights of individuals or collectivities; or composite rights such as the right to self-determination and the right to development. More concretely, the interrelationship between economic, social, and cultural rights, on the one hand, and civil and political rights, on the other, may be demonstrated through Table 7.1, which illustrates how the for-mer set of rights can be protected by invoking the latter—in other words, how economic, social, and cultural rights can be framed in terms of civil and political rights.[20]

Table 7.1 Indirect protection of economic, social, and cultural rights through civil and political rights

Invoked civil and political rights	Protected economic, social, cultural rights
Right to life	Rights to health, food, water, education
Freedom from torture/degrading treatment	Rights to health, housing
Right to private/family life and home	Rights to health, housing
Right to property	Right to social security, housing; collective right to ancestral land of indigenous people
Protection of the child	Rights to health, food, education
Freedom of movement, residence	Right to housing; collective right to ancestral land of indigenous people
Freedom of association	Right to form and join trade unions; rights to collective bargaining
Freedom from forced/compulsory labour	Right to work/to fair conditions of work

[16] UN, *Compilation of International Instruments, Vol 1 (First Part)* (1993) 51–4, Art 13.
[17] n 12, para 5.   [18] n 3, para 13.   [19] GA Res 60/251 (3 April 2006) preambular para 3.
[20] This illustration is reproduced from International Commission of Jurists, *Courts and the Legal Enforcement of Economic, Social and Cultural Rights; Comparative Experiences of Justiciability* (2008) 72 (© Copyright International Commission of Jurists, 2008).

In line with the interdependence and indivisibility of all human rights, a significant evolution has occurred over the years towards the *enhanced status of economic, social, and cultural rights.* Thus, UN supervisory mechanisms and procedures, including those relating to violations of human rights, have progressively brought economic, social, and cultural rights on a par with civil and political rights. Further, while initially, after the entry into force of the ICESCR, the UN Economic and Social Council was entrusted with general monitoring tasks, it soon became clear that it lacked the capacity and expertise to carry out these tasks effectively. Therefore, the Council established a supervisory committee of independent experts, the Committee on Economic, Social and Cultural Rights, with similar tasks and responsibilities as the Human Rights Committee under the ICCPR. More recently, the UN General Assembly adopted an Optional Protocol to the ICESCR, which provides for the right to petition by individuals or groups of individuals claiming to be victims of a violation of any of the rights set forth in the Covenant by a state party that has accepted the Optional Protocol. This new legal instrument, which entered into force in 2013, can be considered as a counterpart to the previously established First Optional Protocol to the ICCPR. It will help to strengthen the legal protection of economic, social, and cultural rights by the development of case law which will enhance, domestically and internationally, the justiciability of economic, social, and cultural rights. Although the Optional Protocol to the ICESCR was finally, after lengthy and protracted negotiations, adopted without a vote, it did not attract unreserved support of the entire UN membership. A number of states would have preferred an *à la carte* instrument which would expressly allow states to select the rights they would accept as falling under the operation of the Protocol. This view, however, did not prevail and the Protocol, therefore, covers all the rights included in the ICESCR.

The same tendency of rendering a more prominent status to economic, social, and cultural rights is also apparent in the system of special procedures developed under the former UN Commission on Human Rights and now operating under the authority of the Human Rights Council. These special procedures with geographic or thematic mandates were established to respond to gross and consistent patterns of human rights violations. They initially concentrated on violations of civil and political rights, notably enforced disappearances, extrajudicial, summary, and arbitrary executions, torture and ill-treatment, arbitrary arrests and detention, freedom of religion or belief, and freedom of opinion and expression.[21] Gradually, however, during the last decade of the twentieth century and in later years, civil and political rights mandates were complemented by mandates in the area of economic, social, and cultural rights, notably dealing with the right to adequate housing, the right to food, human rights and extreme poverty, the right to physical and mental health, the right to education, and the right to water. Other thematic mandates dealing with contemporary forms of racism, indigenous people, minority issues, and the rights of migrants cover a whole range of human rights, not limited to civil and political rights or economic, social, and cultural rights.

A significant role in identifying and supporting the normative content of economic, social, and cultural rights was played by the Limburg Principles on the Implementation of the ICESCR, drawn up in 1986 by a group of experts.[22] The Limburg Principles were instrumental in helping to frame the conceptual work of the Committee on Economic, Social and Cultural Rights so as to clarify the obligations of states under the ICESCR, including their legal duties arising from violations of economic, social, and cultural rights.

---

[21] See Gutter, *Thematic Procedures of the United Nations Commission on Human Rights and International Law: In Search of a Sense of Community* (Intersentia, 2006). [22] (1987) 9 *HRQ* 121.

Ten years later, the Maastricht Guidelines on Violations of Economic, Social and Cultural Rights underscored the violations component by spelling out that violations can occur through both acts of commission and omissions by the state, and by providing guidance on states' responsibility for violations, the notion of victims, and remedies and other responses to violations.[23] More recently, the Maastricht Principles on Extraterritorial Obligations of States in the area of Economic, Social and Cultural Rights were drawn up to clarify the content of extraterritorial state obligations to realize economic, social, and cultural rights.[24]

The focus on violations is linked with the issue of the 'justiciability' of economic, social, and cultural rights. Justiciability refers to the ability of an independent and impartial body to provide a remedy for individuals in case of a violation of a right.[25] The general comments by treaty bodies, notably the Committee on Economic, Social and Cultural Rights and the Committee on the Rights of the Child, have helped to define the content of economic, social, and cultural rights in view of their justiciability.[26] The Optional Protocol to the ICESCR will most likely contribute to a broader acceptance of the notion of justiciability of economic, social, and cultural rights.

4 CORE RIGHTS

While the principle of interdependence and indivisibility of all human rights has become axiomatic and largely uncontested, the issue remains whether certain human rights rank higher than other rights because they are more essential for the preservation of human life and the upholding of human dignity and human welfare. For instance, there is little doubt that the right to life and the prohibition of torture, enshrined in Articles 2 and 5 of the UDHR, are more fundamental or basic than the right to rest and leisure, set out in Article 24. Widely-ratified human rights instruments and their interpretation by judicial and quasi-judicial human rights bodies clearly indicate that certain human rights represent or embody core attributes of human life and human dignity, so that violations of these rights entail a special and imperative responsibility to prevent, to protect, and to remedy. The following examples illustrate that in international human rights law certain rights and their protection rank particularly high on the scale of basic values of human life and existence and can thus be classified as core rights.[27]

Major human rights treaties, notably the ICCPR, the European Convention on Human Rights (ECHR), and the American Convention on Human Rights (ACHR), recognize a set of core rights from which no derogation is permitted, not even during times of public emergency. Thus, Article 4(2) ICCPR lists as non-derogable the right to life, the prohibition of torture or cruel, inhuman, or degrading treatment or punishment, the prohibition of slavery, the prohibition of imprisonment because of inability to fulfil a contractual obligation, the principle of legality in criminal law, the recognition of everyone as a person before the law, and the freedom of thought, conscience, and religion. In its General Comment 29, the Human Rights Committee has analysed the implications of Article 4 in

---

[23] (1998) 20 *HRQ* 691.   [24] (2011) 34 *HRQ* 1084.

[25] See Coomans (ed), *Justiciability of Economic and Social Rights; Experiences from Domestic Systems* (Intersentia, 2006).

[26] n 5. See further Committee on the Rights of the Child, General Comment 5, HRI/GEN/1/ (Vol II) 421.

[27] See also Seiderman, *Hierarchy in International Law: The Human Rights Dimension* (Intersentia, 2001).

detail.[28] It notes that the enumeration of non-derogable provisions is related to, but not identical with, the question of whether certain human rights obligations have the nature of peremptory norms of international law (*jus cogens*) and recognizes that some of the non-derogable ICCPR rights also fall into that category, notably the right to life and the prohibition of torture or cruel, inhuman, or degrading treatment or punishment.

Core rights entail essential obligations on the part of states that have undertaken to respect, protect, and fulfil them. Such obligations are not limited to the field of civil and political rights but extend to economic, social, and cultural rights. Thus, the Committee on Economic, Social and Cultural Rights has stated in its General Comment 3 that 'a minimum core obligation to ensure the satisfaction of, at the very least, minimum essential levels of each of the [ICESCR] rights is incumbent upon every State party'.[29] For example, a state party in which a significant number of individuals are deprived of essential food-stuffs, essential primary healthcare, basic shelter and housing, or the most basic forms of education would, according to the Committee, prima facie be failing to discharge its obligations under the Covenant. The formulation of these core obligations relating to basic conditions of human life corresponds to the phrase in common Article 1(2) of both international covenants concerning the right of all peoples to self-determination that 'in no case may a people be deprived of its own means of subsistence'. Consequently, basic subsistence rights which determine the life, the dignity, and the well-being of individuals and peoples should be considered as core rights.

Furthermore, with the development of international criminal law through standard-setting and national and international adjudication, violations of internationally protected basic human rights may amount to crimes under international law, with the corresponding duty of states to carry out an effective and prompt investigation and to prosecute and punish the perpetrators.[30] Another corresponding duty involves the provision of effective remedies to victims, including reparation for harm suffered. As the Human Rights Committee has stated in its General Comment 31, these obligations arise notably in relation to those violations of ICCPR provisions that are recognized as criminal under domestic or international law, such as torture, summary and arbitrary killing, and enforced disappearance.[31] When such violations of the Covenant are committed as part of a widespread or systematic attack on a civilian population, they are crimes against humanity under Article 7 Statute of the International Criminal Court.[32] While the violation of all human rights entails legal consequences in terms of effective remedies, the violation of core rights requires legal action so as to combat impunity and to make reparations. Moreover, the evolving practice of international human rights bodies, notably the European Court of Human Rights, the Inter-American Court of Human Rights, and the Human Rights Committee, makes it abundantly clear that in cases where core rights such as the right to life and the right to be free from torture or ill-treatment are at stake, urgent preventive action by way of provisional or interim measures are called for in order to avoid irreparable harm to persons.[33]

Finally, the newly evolving doctrine of the Responsibility to Protect, set out in the outcome document of the 2005 UN World Summit, attributes special responsibility to protect populations from genocide, war crimes, ethnic cleansing, and crimes against humanity. This responsibility rests primarily with individual states but may also require collective action, through the UN, should national authorities manifestly fail to protect their

---

[28] HRC, General Comment 29, HRI/GEN/1/ (Vol I) 234. See also Chapter 5.   [29] n 6, para 10.

[30] See Chapter 24.   [31] HRC, General Comment 31, HRI/GEN/1/ (Vol I) 243.

[32] HRC, General Comment 31, HRI/GEN/1/ (Vol I) 243.

[33] Rieter, *Preventing Irreparable Harm: Provisional Measures in International Human Rights Adjudication* (Intersentia, 2010).

populations from such crimes.[34] The doctrine of the Responsibility to Protect represents a common *opinio juris* in theory but still needs affirmation and implementation in practice. However, what is important for present purposes is that it implies that core rights and core values pertaining to the very existence and survival of populations may, in situations where national authorities are failing to respect these rights and values, prevail over invocations of national sovereignty.

5 NEW HUMAN RIGHTS?

It may be argued that the standard-setting or codification process of human rights was completed with the adoption and entry into force of the general and comprehensive human rights instruments, notably the international covenants and regional instruments such as the ECHR, the European Social Charter, the ACHR, and the ACHPR. However, while a broad corpus of internationally recognized standards has taken shape in these instruments, the standard-setting process did not stop but continued progressively in order to respond to widely felt needs to further define the normative scope of basic rights and principles and to provide more explicit protection for vulnerable and marginalized people.

Examples of the further elaboration of the normative scope of human rights include instruments relating to the abolition of the death penalty, the prohibition of torture or cruel, inhuman, or degrading treatment or punishment, and the elimination of discrimination on the grounds of race, religion, and gender. More explicit protection of specific groups of people is envisaged in instruments relating to the rights of women, children, migrant workers, persons with disabilities, persons subjected to enforced disappearance, and indigenous peoples. These instruments do not define new rights but re-define and re-conceptualize existing human rights in order to make them more explicit and more inclusive and to extend their reach to persons in need of special care, attention, and protection. This is a dynamic process that involves the shaping of the normative content of rights and basic principles such as the best interests of the child, the absolute prohibition of gender-based violence, and the relevance of the right to self-determination.

Human rights treaty bodies, as authoritative interpreters and custodians of treaty norms, have drawn up general comments and recommendations so as to further define or refine the scope and reach of the human rights norms already embodied in legal instruments. Do treaty bodies thereby create new human rights norms? This would not seem to be the purpose and task of treaty bodies. Rather, the purpose of general comments and recommendations is to clarify the normative scope of human rights. For instance, in its General Comment 15, the Committee on Economic, Social and Cultural Rights made it clear that there is a right to water, although such a right is not explicitly referred to in the ICESCR.[35] The Committee did not proclaim this right as a new human right, but defined it as emanating from, and indispensable for, the realization of the right to an adequate standard of living and as inextricably related to the rights to the highest attainable standard of health, adequate housing, and adequate food.[36] Similarly, the Committee on

---

[34] n 3, paras 138–40. See further Evans, *The Responsibility to Protect: Ending Mass Atrocity Crimes Once and For All* (Brookings Institution Press, 2008).

[35] See Chapter 10.   [36] CESCR, General Comment 15, HRI/GEN/1/ (Vol I) 97, para 3.

the Elimination of Racial Discrimination, in its General Recommendations on the rights of indigenous peoples, on discrimination against Roma, on descent-based discrimination, and on discrimination against non-citizens,[37] clearly set out the relevance and the applicability of the International Convention on the Elimination of All Forms of Racial Discrimination with respect to groups of marginalized and vulnerable people. It did this, not by the creation of new rights, but by explaining the normative content and the implications of the Convention in support of these groups.

In the human rights discourse and campaigns entertained by proponents of a rights-based strategy on behalf of marginalized and excluded groups, claims are often framed as being part of a 'struggle for new rights'.[38] The rights of children born of wartime rape, Dalits, lesbian, gay, bisexual, and transgender (LGBT) people, mentally and physically disabled people, people living with HIV and AIDS, and other stigmatized minorities are advocated under this label. These campaigns have greatly contributed to awareness-building and the broadening and deepening of a rights-based approach in support of people who for a long time had been neglected and treated as outsiders or even outcasts. They constitute another step in the lengthy process from exclusion to inclusion, with due regard for the specific situation and the specific interests of the people concerned.

This newly developed reach of human rights has found expression in a series of new instruments and documents such as the Convention on the Rights of Persons with Disabilities, the General Recommendations of the Committee on the Elimination of Racial Discrimination on discrimination against Roma and descent-based discrimination, the General Recommendation of the Committee on the Elimination of Discrimination against Women on the avoidance of discrimination against women in national strategies for the prevention and control of AIDS, as well as the General Comment of the Committee on the Rights of the Child on HIV/AIDS and the rights of the child.[39] The Yogyakarta Principles on the Application of International Human Rights Law in Relation to Sexual Orientation and Gender Identity are a further example illustrating this new human rights focus.[40] While in all these instances the focus and scope of human rights is newly-defined and developed to underline their relevance and applicability to people hitherto neglected, ignored, or degraded, their basic thrust lies in the recognition that all people, without discrimination or exclusion, are entitled to the full benefit of all human rights, notably the right to be equal before the law and non-discrimination. It appears, therefore, that in these instances the term 'new human rights' is conceptually not called for. Instead, the better term might be 'newly focused human rights'. The concept of 'new human rights' should be approached with caution.

Attention may also be drawn to victims' rights in this context. Victims of gross human rights violations have been largely overlooked, both at the national and the international level. Only in recent decades, in particular in the context of transitional justice processes in societies scarred by serious crimes under international law, has there been some tentative movement towards the express recognition of victims' rights

[37] Committee on the Elimination of Racial Discrimination, General Recommendation XXIII, HRI/GEN/1/ (Vol II) 285, General Recommendation XXVII, HRI/GEN/1/ (Vol II) 289, General Recommendation XXIX, HRI/GEN/1/ (Vol II) 296, General Recommendation XXX, HRI/GEN/1/ (Vol II) 301.

[38] See in particular Bob (ed), *The International Struggle for New Human Rights* (University of Pennsylvania Press, 2009).

[39] Committee on the Elimination of Racial Discrimination, General Recommendation XXVII, n 36; Committee on the Elimination of Discrimination against Women, General Recommendation 15, HRI/GEN/1/ (Vol II) 327; Committee on the Rights of the Child, General Comment 3, HRI/GEN/1/ (Vol II) 398.

[40] Available at: <http://www.yogyakartaprinciples.org/>. See Chapter 15.

as a main condition for the attainment of reconciliation and justice.[41] This new emphasis on victims' rights is duly reflected in the UN Basic Principles and Guidelines on the Right to a Remedy and Reparation to Victims of Gross Violations of International Human Rights Law and Serious Violations of International Humanitarian Law (2005) (Reparation Principles).[42] This instrument is not intended to define new victims' rights but to identify mechanisms, modalities, procedures, and methods for the implementation of victims' rights.[43] Another normative document of particular relevance to transitional justice situations is the Updated Set of Principles for the Protection and Promotion of Human Rights Through Actions to Combat Impunity (2005) (Impunity Principles).[44] This document provides for the right to know, the right to justice, and the right to reparation, and guarantees of non-recurrence. Under the right to know, the inalienable right to know the truth figures prominently. This right has a collective dimension. Every people has the right 'to know the truth about past events concerning the perpetration of heinous crimes and about the circumstances and reasons that led . . . to the perpetration of those crimes'.[45] But the right to truth also includes the right of victims and their families 'to know the truth about the circumstances in which violations took place and, in the event of death or disappearance, about the victims' fate'.[46] In line with the Reparation Principles and Impunity Principles, the new International Convention for the Protection of All Persons from Enforced Disappearance affirms the right of each victim to know the truth regarding the circumstances of the enforced disappearance, the progress and results of the investigation, and the fate of the disappeared person. Finally, it also spells out the right of victims to obtain reparation and prompt, fair, and adequate compensation.[47]

These normative developments raise the question of whether the right to know the truth, as a collective and individual right, qualifies as a 'new human right'. It may be argued in this connection that this right is a corollary of the freedom to seek, receive, and impart information and ideas of all kinds set out in Article 19(2) ICCPR. Technically speaking, this argument is correct, although it insufficiently appreciates the existential life and death dimensions that lie at the basis of the right to know the truth. Nevertheless, it can be argued that the right to know the truth is a basic principle that already forms part of existing human rights law. In fact, the International Convention for the Protection of All Persons from Enforced Disappearance gives support to this reasoning insofar as its preamble 'affirms' the right of any victim to know the truth.[48] Therefore, the right to know the truth should not be qualified as a 'new human right' as if it had only emerged recently. Such a classification would fail to do justice to efforts to seek and uncover the truth about many historical wrongs that still beleaguer past and present generations. Rather, there are good reasons to state, in consonance with the Impunity Principles, that there is an inalienable right to know the truth. This right is in need of recognition and renewed emphasis and is thus correctly affirmed in a legal document such as the International Convention for the Protection of All Persons from Enforced Disappearance.

---

[41] van Boven, 'Reparative Justice: Focus on Victims' (2007) 25 *NQHR* 723.
[42] GA Res 60/147 (16 December 2005).   [43] GA Res 60/147 (16 December 2005), preambular para 7.
[44] E/CN.4/2005/102/Add.1, endorsed by UN Commission on Human Rights Res 2005/81 (21 April 2005).
[45] E/CN.4/2005/102/Add.1, Principle 2.   [46] E/CN.4/2005/102/Add.1, Principle 4.   [47] Art 24.
[48] International Convention for the Protection of All Persons from Enforced Disappearance, preambular para 8.

6 CONCLUSION

All human rights are indivisible, interdependent, and interrelated. This chapter fully sub-scribes to this postulate, not as a method to put all rights in a melting-pot where they lose their own distinct character, but as a means to reinforce the validity and impact of all rights. Classifying human rights in various categories—civil, political, economic, social, and cul-tural; individual and collective; one-dimensional and composite—is not as such a reduction of the indivisibility, interdependence, and interrelatedness of human rights. Such classifica-tions or categorizations are not meant to store human rights in watertight compartments. Their merit lies in their capacity to operationalize human rights, to make rights and respon-sibilities more specific and transparent, with corresponding claims and obligations.

Neither does the maxim of indivisibility, interdependence, and interrelatedness of all human rights stand in the way of the notion of core rights as distinct from other human rights. It is true that the notion of core rights presumes a ranking or hierarchy of human rights. Such ranking is inherent in essential rights and entails corresponding core obliga-tions on the part of states and non-state actors. It runs across all human rights categories and classifications, with the right to life, the inviolability of the human person, and the very existence of people as cornerstones.

It is self-evident that human rights, in whatever manner they are classified or subdi-vided, are the rights of individuals and collectivities. But it has been less obvious, under past and present policies and practices of exclusion and discrimination, that human rights are the inalienable rights of all members of the human family. The UDHR proclaimed human rights as the rights of all human beings and set into motion a major trend towards the inclusion of all people in human rights documents. It is in keeping with this trend to grant explicit recognition to people who had been, over the years and in many places if not eve-rywhere, the subject of exclusion, discrimination, neglect, or treatment as inferiors. It was also in line with the same trend that the call was widely heard: women's rights are human rights, children's rights are human rights, indigenous rights are human rights, Roma rights are human rights, Dalits rights are human rights, and so on. International instruments with a specific focus on the human rights of particular categories of people were drawn up, most recently of persons with disabilities. Rather than labelling the rights of these persons as 'new human rights', they should be denominated as the rights of newly identified categories of people, as inclusive rights. In sum, categories of human rights are not abstract concepts. Human rights relate to all people, including categories of people who belong to the down-trodden, the disadvantaged, and the discarded in national and international society.

FURTHER READING

ALSTON, 'Conjuring up New Human Rights: A Proposal for Quality Control' (1984) 78(3) *AJIL* 607.

BOB (ed), *The International Struggle for New Human Rights* (University of Pennsylvania Press, 2009).

COOMANS (ed), *Justiciability of Economic and Social Rights: Experiences from Domestic Systems* (Intersentia, 2006).

INTERNATIONAL COMMMISSION OF JURISTS, *Courts and the Legal Enforcement of Economic, Social and Cultural Rights* (Geneva, 2008).

MAHON, 'Progress at the Front: The Draft Optional Protocol to the International Covenant on Economic, Social and Cultural Rights' (2008) 8(4) *HRLR* 617.

MERON, 'On a Hierarchy of International Human Rights' (1986) 80(1) *AJIL* 1.

OHCHR, *Report on the Right to the Truth*, A/ HRC/12/19 (21 August 2009).

QUANE, 'A Further Dimension to the Interdependence and Indivisibility of Human Rights? Recent Developments Concerning the Rights of Indigenous Peoples' 25 (2012) *Harvard HRJ* 49.

SEIDERMAN, *Hierarchy in International Law: The Human Rights Dimension* (Intersentia, 2001).

VANDENBOGAERDE and VANDENHOLE, 'The Optional Protocol to the International Covenant on Economic, Social and Cultural Rights: An *Ex Ante* Assessment of its Effectiveness in Light of the Drafting Process' (2010) 10(2) *HRLR* 207.

8

EQUALITY AND NON-DISCRIMINATION

Daniel Moeckli

SUMMARY

The international human rights system is founded on the idea that all human beings have the same set of fundamental rights. Accordingly, almost all general human rights instruments guarantee the right to equality and non-discrimination, and several specialized treaties provide protection against particular forms of discrimination. International human rights law prohibits discrimination in treatment (direct discrimination) as well as in outcome (indirect discrimination), regardless of whether it is intended or unintended. Yet it also acknowledges that it may sometimes be justified to classify people: differences in treatment or outcome are permissible as long as they pursue a legitimate aim in a proportionate manner. Indeed, the right to equality may *require* states to treat people differently in order to overcome historical patterns of disadvantage and achieve real equality.

1 INTRODUCTION

The notion that all human beings are equal and therefore deserve to be treated equally has a powerful intuitive appeal. It is one of the central ideals of the Enlightenment and at the heart of liberal theories of the state.[1] The US Declaration of Independence of 1776 famously proclaimed that 'all men are created equal', and today virtually every liberal democratic state guarantees equality in its constitution. The principle of equality and non-discrimination has gained a similarly important status in international law. It is included in the key human rights instruments and the Vienna Declaration and Programme of Action, adopted by the World Conference on Human Rights in 1993, describes it as 'a fundamental rule of international human rights law'.[2]

What this fundamental rule entails in practice, however, is difficult to establish. For, of course, no two human beings are equal in the sense that they are identical. We might be able to say that two people are equal in respect of some measurable characteristic ('they both weigh 82 kilograms'), but they will always be different in some other respects (income, political opinion, and so on). In order to apply the principle of equality we first need to define the relevant criterion in respect of which people should be judged to be alike or different. And even when two persons can be said to be alike, it might still be questionable

---

[1] See Chapter 1.   [2] A/CONF.157/23 (25 June 1993) para 15.

whether they should always be treated equally. Furthermore, we need to decide what kind of equality we seek to achieve. Do we mean by equality that people should be treated identically? Or that they should be given the same opportunities? Or that they should be placed in the same position? Equality can be formulated in different ways, and deciding which concept of equality to use is not a question of logic but a political choice. In this sense, equality is an 'empty idea'[3]—it does not answer the questions of who are equals and what constitutes equal treatment. External values, not derivable from the concept of equality, are necessary to answer these questions.

The challenge, therefore, is to give substance to the abstract notion of equality by translating it into concrete legal formulations that make clear which forms of unequal treatment are legitimate because they are based on morally acceptable criteria and which ones are wrongful. This chapter explains how this challenge has been addressed in international human rights law.

Section 2 discusses what, in general terms, equality and non-discrimination can be interpreted to mean. Section 3 gives an overview of the different norms guaranteeing equality and non-discrimination in international human rights law. Section 4 explains the concepts of direct and indirect discrimination. Section 5 considers the requirements for a difference in treatment to be justified under international human rights law. Section 6 sets out the different sorts of obligations that the right to equality imposes on states, in particular their duty to take positive action to ensure everyone can enjoy this right.

2 THE MEANING OF EQUALITY AND NON-DISCRIMINATION

The terms 'equality' and 'non-discrimination' have often been used interchangeably and described as the positive and negative statement of the same principle: whereas the maxim of equality requires that equals be treated equally, the prohibition of discrimination precludes differential treatment on unreasonable grounds.[4] In recent years, however, there has been an increased emphasis on the positive formulation. This shift in terminology highlights that equality implies not only a negative obligation not to discriminate, but also a duty to recognize differences between people and to take positive action to achieve real equality. Thus, whereas 'non-discrimination' corresponds to the more limited concept of *formal equality*, usage of the term 'equality' stresses the need for a more positive approach aimed at *substantive equality*.

2.1 FORMAL EQUALITY

Formal equality refers to Aristotle's classical maxim according to which equals must be treated equally or, more precisely, likes must be treated alike.[5] This notion of equality as consistency focuses on the process rather than the outcome: equality is achieved if individuals in a comparable situation are treated equally, regardless of the result. The values underpinning

---

[3] Westen, 'The Empty Idea of Equality' (1982) 95 *Harvard LR* 537.

[4] Eg OC-4/84, *Proposed Amendments to the Naturalization Provisions of the Constitution of Costa Rica*, IACtHR Series A No 4 (1984), Separate Opinion of Rodolfo E Piza, J, para 10 ('it appears clear that the concepts of equality and non-discrimination are reciprocal, like the two faces of one same institution. Equality is the positive face of non-discrimination. Discrimination is the negative face of equality').

[5] Aristotle, *The Nicomachean Ethics of Aristotle* (JM Dent, 1911) Book V3, paras 1131a–b.

formal equality are the liberal ideals of state neutrality and individualism, that is, the notion that the state should not give preference to any one group and that people should be treated exclusively on their individual merits and regardless of group membership.

However, as noted already, this idea of equality raises the question of when two cases can be said to be alike. It is inevitable that laws and government action classify persons into groups that are treated differently. Under a progressive taxation system, for example, people are treated differently according to their income. In states with a juvenile justice system, people are treated differently according to their age. These distinctions are generally seen as perfectly legitimate because they are based on morally acceptable grounds. Accordingly, at least in common language, the word 'discrimination' also has a positive connotation ('to discriminate between right and wrong'). But which differences in treatment are legitimate and which ones are not? The principle that likes should be treated alike does not, by itself, answer this question.

There are a number of other problems with the concept of equality as consistency.[6] First, since it is not concerned with the outcome, it does not matter whether two parties are treated equally well or equally badly. Thus, it is compatible with this understanding of equality that a city closes all its swimming pools rather than open its 'whites only' pools to black people ('levelling down').[7] Second, inconsistent treatment can only be demonstrated if the complainant can find a comparably situated person who has been treated more favourably. Yet for a woman in a low-paid position, for instance, it may be difficult to find a man doing the same job. Third, treating people apparently consistently regardless of their differing backgrounds may have a disparate impact on particular groups. A law which, in the famous words of Anatole France, 'forbids the rich as well as the poor to sleep under bridges, to beg in the streets, and to steal bread' will in fact entrench inequality.[8]

2.2 SUBSTANTIVE EQUALITY

Proponents of a substantive conception of equality recognize that a merely formal notion of equality as procedural fairness can in fact perpetuate existing patterns of disadvantage. Drawing on values such as human dignity, distributive justice, and equal participation, they argue that equality must go beyond consistent treatment of likes. There are two main variants of substantive equality: equality of opportunity and equality of results.

According to the notion of equality of opportunity, true equality can only be achieved if people are not only treated equally but are also given the same opportunities. Like competitors in a race, everyone should be able to begin from the same starting point. Equality of opportunity requires the removal of barriers to the advancement of disadvantaged groups, such as upper age limits for employment that may disadvantage women with childcare responsibilities. According to a broader, substantive understanding of the concept, it may also require positive measures such as training. But equality of opportunity does not aim to achieve equality of outcome. Once the race has started, everyone is treated the same. Thus, while equality of opportunity is to some extent about redressing past discrimination, it also stresses individual merit.

Equality of results goes further than this and aims to achieve an equal distribution of social goods such as education, employment, healthcare, and political representation. It recognizes that removing barriers does not guarantee that disadvantaged groups will in fact be able to take advantage of available opportunities. Abolishing upper age limits, for

---

[6] See Fredman, *Discrimination Law* (OUP, 2011) 8–15.
[7] See *Palmer v Thompson* 403 US 217 (1971).   [8] France, *Le Lys Rouge* (Calmann-Lévy, 1894) ch 7.

example, does not, by itself, ensure that more women with childcare responsibilities will be able to apply for the respective jobs. Equality of results can be understood and achieved in different ways. In its strongest form, it explicitly aims to increase the representation of disadvantaged groups in educational institutions, employment, or public office through preferential treatment and quota systems.

These differing conceptions of equality find their reflection in different forms of legal regulation. Formal equality forms the conceptual basis of the requirement of equality before the law and prohibitions of direct discrimination, whereas prohibitions of indirect discrimination are supported by a substantive notion of equality (see Section 4 for the distinction between direct and indirect discrimination). 'Affirmative action' programmes (see Section 6) can be justified on the basis of a substantive notion of equality, but they are incompatible with a formal conception of equality as consistency. In any jurisdiction, a range of regulations that reflect different conceptions of equality will be found; no legal system relies exclusively on simply one approach to equality.

3 EQUALITY AND NON-DISCRIMINATION IN INTERNATIONAL LAW

The right to equality and non-discrimination gives concrete expression to the basic idea on which the whole international human rights system is founded: that all human beings, regardless of their status or membership of a particular group, are entitled to a set of rights. Since it underlies all other human rights, equality is often described not only as a 'right' but also as a 'principle'. The foundational significance of equality is reflected in the fact that it is proclaimed in the very first article of the Universal Declaration of Human Rights (UDHR): 'All human beings are born free and equal in dignity and rights'.

This section first gives an overview of the different sources of the right to equality and non-discrimination in international law. Next, it considers the scope of these norms: do they guarantee equality and non-discrimination only in the context of other human rights or across the board? Finally, the prohibited grounds of distinction are explored: which groups are protected against discrimination?

3.1 SOURCES

Article 1(3) of the UN Charter makes it clear that one of the basic purposes of the UN is the promotion of the equal guarantee of human rights for all without any distinction. Numerous instruments aimed at the realization of this notion have been adopted under the auspices of the UN. The general human rights instruments guarantee the right to equality and non-discrimination in several of their provisions: the UDHR in Articles 1, 2(1), and 7; the International Covenant on Civil and Political Rights (ICCPR) in Articles 2, 3, and 26; and the International Covenant on Economic, Social and Cultural Rights (ICESCR) in Articles 2(2) and 3. As far as the specialized human rights treaties are concerned, at least three of them are specifically devoted to addressing certain forms of discrimination: the International Convention on the Elimination of All Forms of Racial Discrimination (ICERD), the Convention on the Elimination of All Forms of Discrimination Against Women (CEDAW), and the Convention on the Rights of Persons with Disabilities (CRPD). The Convention on the Rights of the Child (CRC) and the International Convention on the Protection of the Rights of All Migrant Workers and

Members of Their Families (ICRMW) at least partly pursue the same objective and contain explicit provisions on equality and non-discrimination.[9] The only international human rights treaties without explicit non-discrimination clauses are the Convention against Torture and Other Cruel, Inhuman or Degrading Treatment or Punishment (UNCAT) and the International Convention for the Protection of All Persons from Enforced Disappearance (CPED).

The right to equality and non-discrimination is also guaranteed by all major regional human rights instruments: the African Charter on Human and Peoples' Rights (ACHPR) (Articles 2, 3, 18(3)–(4), and 28), the American Convention on Human Rights (ACHR) (Articles 1 and 24), the American Declaration of the Rights and Duties of Man (Article II), the Arab Charter on Human Rights (Articles 2, 9, and 35), the ASEAN Human Rights Declaration (Articles 1, 2, 3, and 9), the European Convention on Human Rights (ECHR) (Article 14 and Protocol No 12), and the Charter of Fundamental Rights of the European Union (Articles 20, 21(1), and 23). In addition, the Inter-American Convention against All Forms of Discrimination and Intolerance provides protection against discrimination based on a long list of criteria, while several specialized regional treaties, such as the Protocol to the ACHPR on the Rights of Women in Africa, the Inter-American Convention against Racism, Racial Discrimination, and Related Forms of Intolerance and the Inter-American Convention on the Elimination of All Forms of Discrimination against Persons with Disabilities, protect against particular forms of discrimination.

Finally, it is now widely acknowledged that, at the very least, the right to non-discrimination on the grounds of race, sex, and religion binds all states, irrespective of their ratification of human rights treaties, because it has become part of customary international law.[10] The Inter-American Court of Human Rights has gone further than this and held that also the guarantee against discrimination on other grounds, including language, political or other opinion, national, ethnic or social origin, nationality, age, economic situation, property, civil status, birth, or any other status, forms part of general international law and, indeed, is a norm of *jus cogens* that cannot be set aside by treaty or acquiescence.[11]

3.2 SCOPE: SUBORDINATE AND AUTONOMOUS NORMS

Non-discrimination provisions can be subdivided into subordinate and autonomous (or free-standing) norms. *Subordinate norms* prohibit discrimination only in the enjoyment of the rights and freedoms otherwise set forth in the respective instrument. An example of a subordinate norm is Article 2(1) ICCPR, which states:

> Each State Party to the present Covenant undertakes to respect and to ensure to all individuals within its territory and subject to its jurisdiction the rights recognized in the present Covenant, without distinction of any kind, such as race, colour, sex, language, religion, political or other opinion, national or social origin, property, birth or other status.

---

[9] CRC, Arts 2 and 28; ICRMW, Arts 1(1), 7, 18, 25, 27, 28, 30, 43, 45, 54, 55, and 70.

[10] For race, see eg *South-West Africa Cases (Second Phase)* [1966] ICJ Rep 6, 293 and 299–300 (Tanaka, J dissenting); *Barcelona Traction (Second Phase)* [1970] ICJ Rep 3, 32. For the other grounds, see Shaw, *International Law* (CUP, 2008) 287 and references cited there.

[11] OC/18, *Juridical Condition and Rights of the Undocumented Migrants*, IACtHR Series A No 18 (2003) paras 100–1 and 173.4.

Other subordinate norms include Article 2(1) UDHR, Article 2(2) ICESCR, Article 2(1) CRC, Article 7 ICRMW, Article 1 ACHR, Article 2 ACHPR, and Article 14 ECHR.[12] As the ECHR does not contain an autonomous norm in addition to its subordinate provision in Article 14, the jurisprudence of the European Court of Human Rights interpreting it is of particular importance. According to the European Court, in order to invoke Article 14, an applicant must show that the facts of the case fall 'within the ambit' of another substantive Convention right.[13] However, there is no need to show that there has been *a violation* of that Convention right. A measure that in itself is in conformity with the requirements of a given ECHR right, but is of a discriminatory nature, will violate that right *when read in conjunction with Article 14*. For example, it does not as such amount to a violation of Article 6 ECHR (the right to a fair trial) if a state fails to establish a system of appeals. However, when a state does establish such a system, then this is a matter falling within the ambit of Article 6, and there is a violation of that article read in conjunction with Article 14 if, without a legitimate reason, certain persons are given the right to appeal while others are denied it.

Article 7 UDHR, Article 26 ICCPR, Articles 2 and 5 ICERD, Article 24 ACHR, and Article 3 ACHPR, on the other hand, are *autonomous norms*: they guarantee non-discrimination not only in the context of other rights but in general. For example, Article 26 ICCPR provides:

> All persons are equal before the law and are entitled without any discrimination to the equal protection of the law. In this respect, the law shall prohibit any discrimination and guarantee to all persons equal and effective protection against discrimination on any ground such as race, colour, sex, language, religion, political or other opinion, national or social origin, property, birth or other status.

The UN Human Rights Committee elaborated on the scope of this provision in *Broeks v The Netherlands*.[14] Mrs Broeks had been denied unemployment benefits on the basis of legislation that provided that married women could only claim benefits if they could prove that they were 'breadwinners'—a requirement that did not apply to married men. The Netherlands argued that Mrs Broeks could not rely on Article 26 ICCPR as it could only be invoked in the sphere of civil and political rights; Mrs Broeks' complaint, however, related to the right to social security, which was specifically provided for under the ICESCR. The Human Rights Committee rejected the government's argument, holding that it did not matter whether a particular subject matter is covered by the ICCPR or some other international instrument. It stressed that 'Article 26 does not merely duplicate the guarantees already provided for in Article 2' but instead 'prohibits discrimination in law or in practice in any field regulated and protected by public authorities'.[15] The Committee confirmed this finding in its General Comment 18.[16] Thus, states parties to the ICCPR have a general obligation neither to enact legislation with a discriminatory content nor to apply laws in a discriminatory way.

As noted already, the ECHR only contains a subordinate non-discrimination guarantee. This gap is partially addressed by Protocol No 12 to the ECHR. The Protocol, which entered into force in 2005 but has not been widely ratified so far, contains a non-discrimination

---

[12] ECHR, Art 14 reads: 'The enjoyment of the rights and freedoms set forth in this Convention shall be secured without discrimination on any ground such as sex, race, colour, language, religion, political or other opinion, national or social origin, association with a national minority, property, birth or other status.'

[13] *Rasmussen v Denmark* (1984) 7 EHRR 371, para 29.

[14] CCPR/C/29/D/172/1984 (9 April 1987).   [15] CCPR/C/29/D/172/1984 (9 April 1987), para 12.3.

[16] HRC, General Comment 18, HRI/GEN/1/Rev. 9 (Vol I) 195, para 12.

guarantee that is not limited to the enjoyment of Convention rights.[17] However, this guarantee is still narrower than the general right to equality before the law and equal protection of the law under Article 26 ICCPR in that it only applies to the enjoyment of rights set forth by (national) law.

3.3 PROHIBITED GROUNDS OF DISTINCTION

Which grounds of distinction are unacceptable and should, therefore, be prohibited? There is no straightforward answer to this question as, depending on one's moral and political views, any criterion may be regarded as either relevant or irrelevant. There is certainly broad consensus today that normally a person's inherent characteristics such as race, colour, or sex are not acceptable criteria for differential treatment. In addition, grounds such as membership of a particular group, holding certain beliefs, and national or social origin are outlawed by most human rights treaties. But as is evident from a comparison between the ICCPR, adopted in 1966, and the ICRMW, adopted in 1990, what is seen as unacceptable can change over time: the ICRMW has considerably expanded the list of prohibited grounds by adding the criteria of conviction, ethnic origin, nationality, age, economic position, and marital status. Today, further criteria, including disability[18] and sexual orientation and gender identity,[19] would have to be added. In addition, discrimination may be intersectional, that is, based on a combination of characteristics that form an individual's identity rather than a single ground.[20] Intersectional discrimination often occurs based on sex in combination with one or more other grounds.[21]

Equality and non-discrimination norms vary widely in their approaches to defining the prohibited grounds of distinction. A first type of norm provides for a *general guarantee of equality*, without specifying any particular prohibited grounds. Article 24 ACHR, for instance, simply states: 'All persons are equal before the law. Consequently, they are entitled, without discrimination, to equal protection of the law.' Such norms leave it to the relevant body to decide which distinctions are acceptable and which ones are not.

A second category of norms uses a diametrically opposed approach: these norms contain an *exhaustive list* of prohibited grounds. The CEDAW, for instance, prohibits only distinctions based on 'sex' (Article 1), the ICERD those based on 'race, colour, descent, or national or ethnic origin' (Article 1(1)), and the CRPD those based on 'disability' (Articles 1 and 5). Article 2(2) ICESCR, Article 2(1) CRC, and Article 1 ACHR contain lists that are much longer but still fixed (in the case of the ICESCR, 'race, colour, sex, language, religion, political or other opinion, national or social origin, property, birth or other status').

Steering a middle course between these two extremes, there is a third category of norms which contain a list of prohibited grounds but one that is *open-ended*. For instance, Article 14 ECHR (as well as its Protocol No 12) prohibits 'discrimination on *any* ground *such as* sex, race, colour, language, religion, political or other opinion, national or social origin, association with a national minority, property, birth or other status'. Similarly, Article 2(1) UDHR, Articles 1(1) and 7 ICRMW, and Article 2 ACHPR provide for non-discrimination

---

[17] Protocol No 12 to the Convention for the Protection of Human Rights and Fundamental Freedoms, Art 1 ('(1) The enjoyment of any right set forth by law shall be secured without discrimination on any ground such as sex, race, colour, language, religion, political or other opinion, national or social origin, association with a national minority, property, birth or other status. (2) No one shall be discriminated against by any public authority on any ground such as those mentioned in paragraph 1').

[18] See CRPD.   [19] See Chapter 15.

[20] See Crenshaw, 'Mapping the Margins: Intersectionality, Identity Politics, and Violence Against Women of Color' (1991) 43 *Stanford LR* 1241.   [21] See Chapter 16.

'without distinction of *any* kind, *such as…*'. As a consequence, even distinctions made on grounds that are not explicitly listed may engage these provisions. The European Court of Human Rights sometimes does not even find it necessary to state the particular ground of distinction involved when considering a case under Article 14 ECHR.[22]

The text of Article 26 ICCPR ('discrimination on *any* ground *such as* race, colour, sex, language, religion, political or other opinion, national or social origin, property, birth or other status') suggests that this provision is also open-ended. Nevertheless, the Human Rights Committee has often been at pains to fit a particular distinction within one of the listed grounds, be it the specific ones or the broad rubric of 'other status'. Thus, it has found that the reference to 'sex' also includes 'sexual orientation'[23] and that 'other status' covers grounds such as nationality,[24] age,[25] and marital status.[26] But it has never clarified how it decides whether a difference in treatment comes within the reference to 'other status'. Its efforts to apply one of the listed grounds suggest that the Committee regards the list of Article 26 as exhaustive and it has accordingly stated that an applicant is required to show that the difference in treatment was based on one of the enumerated grounds.[27]

4 DIRECT AND INDIRECT DISCRIMINATION

At the heart of all non-discrimination norms is the formal equality requirement that likes should be treated alike. It is, therefore, clear that international human rights law prohibits direct discrimination (Section 4.1). But human right bodies and courts have acknowledged that the requirement of consistent treatment is not sufficient to achieve true equality: not only discriminatory treatment but also a discriminatory outcome (indirect discrimination) is prohibited (Section 4.2). Finally, it is important to note that international human rights law prohibits both intended and unintended discrimination (Section 4.3).

Whether there has been a difference in treatment or result is the first question that a court needs to assess when considering a discrimination claim under international human rights law. Once a prima facie case of direct or indirect discrimination has been made out, the court must decide whether there is a justification for the difference in treatment or outcome. This second element of the test is discussed in Section 5.

4.1 DIRECT DISCRIMINATION

Direct discrimination occurs when a person, *on account of one or more of the prohibited grounds*, is treated less favourably than someone else in comparable circumstances. Thus, the complainant must show, first, that others have been treated better because they do not share the relevant characteristic or status and, second, that these others are in a comparable, or, in the terminology of the European Court of Human Rights, 'analogous'[28] or 'relevantly similar',[29] situation. In practice, international human rights bodies often tend to merge the comparability test with the test for whether there is an objective justification for the difference in treatment, explained in Section 5.

---

[22] Eg *Rasmussen v Denmark*, n 13, para 34.
[23] *Toonen v Australia*, CCPR/C/50/D/488/1992 (31 March 1994) para 8.7.
[24] *Gueye v France*, CCPR/C/35/D/196/1985 (3 April 1989) para 9.4.
[25] *Schmitz-de-Jong v The Netherlands*, CCPR/C/72/D/855/1999 (16 July 2001).
[26] *Danning v The Netherlands*, CCPR/C/OP/2 (9 April 1987).
[27] *BdB et al. v The Netherlands*, CCPR/C/35/D/273/1988 (2 May 1989) para 6.7.
[28] *Lithgow v UK* (1986) 8 EHRR 329, para 177.
[29] *Fredin v Sweden* (1991) 13 EHRR 784, para 60.

A classic example of direct discrimination is when members of a certain ethnic group are denied access to a public facility, such as a swimming pool, which is open to everyone else. But most cases of direct discrimination are not as straightforward as this. More often, direct discrimination occurs covertly: the 'discriminator' will not admit that the difference in treatment was based on a prohibited ground, making it difficult for the complainant to provide sufficient evidence. Furthermore, as explained already, it may not always be easy to identify a person who is in a comparable situation. How can a woman establish pay discrimination when there are hardly any men doing the same job?

4.2 INDIRECT DISCRIMINATION

Indirect discrimination occurs when a practice, rule, or requirement that is outwardly *'neutral'*, that is, not based on one of the prohibited grounds of distinction, has a disproportionate impact on particular groups defined by reference to one of these grounds. Thus, although there is no difference in treatment, due to structural biases, treating unequals equally leads to unequal results.

The concept of indirect discrimination has its origins in US and European Community (EC) law but has now also found its way into the jurisprudence of international and regional human rights bodies. The Human Rights Committee recognized the possibility of indirect discrimination, albeit without explicitly referring to the concept, for the first time in *Singh Bhinder v Canada*.[30] The case concerned a Sikh who was dismissed from his employment with the Canadian Railway because he refused to comply with a legal requirement that safety headgear be worn at work, as his religion required him to wear only a turban. The Committee found that the legislation may amount to de facto discrimination: although it was neutral in that it applied to all persons without distinction, it disproportionately affected persons of the Sikh religion. (There was nevertheless no violation of Article 26 ICCPR as the safety headgear requirement was based on reasonable and objective grounds.) But only much later, in *Althammer v Austria*, a case concerning the abolition of household benefits that affected retired persons to a greater extent than active employees, did the Committee expressly refer to the concept of 'indirect discrimination':

> The Committee recalls that a violation of article 26 can also result from the discriminatory effect of a rule or measure that is neutral at face value or without intent to discriminate. However, such indirect discrimination can only be said to be based on the grounds enumerated in Article 26 of the Covenant if the detrimental effects of a rule or decision exclusively or disproportionally affect persons having a particular race, colour, sex, language, religion, political or other opinion, national or social origin, property, birth or other status.[31]

Similarly, it was only in 2007 that the European Court of Human Rights, in its groundbreaking ruling in *DH and others v Czech Republic*, came up with an explicit definition of 'indirect discrimination'. Several Roma children had complained that the manner in which statutory rules governing assignment to schools were applied in practice resulted in the placement of a disproportionate number of Roma pupils in 'special schools' for children with 'mental deficiencies'. Referring to the definition of 'indirect discrimination' in EC law, the Grand Chamber of the European Court of Human Rights stated:

> The Court has already accepted in previous cases that a difference in treatment may take the form of disproportionately prejudicial effects of a general policy or measure which,

---

[30] CCPR/C/37/D/208/1986 (9 November 1989).
[31] CCPR/C/78/D/998/2001 (8 August 2003) para 10.2.

though couched in neutral terms, discriminates against a group... In accordance with, for instance, Council Directives 97/80/EC and 2000/43/EC and the definition provided by ECRI [the European Commission against Racism and Intolerance], such a situation may amount to 'indirect discrimination', which does not necessarily require a discriminatory intent.[32]

The African Commission on Human and Peoples' Rights seems also to have recognized the concept of indirect discrimination when it found a violation of Articles 2 and 3 ACHPR in a case where legal remedies, even though guaranteed to everyone by law, were in practice 'only...available to the wealthy and those that can afford the services of private counsel'.[33] The Inter-American Convention against All Forms of Discrimination and Intolerance of 2013 contains, in Article 1(2), an explicit definition of 'indirect discrimination'.

4.3 DISCRIMINATORY INTENTION

In some legal systems, such as the USA, complainants need to show a discriminatory intention or purpose to establish discrimination.[34] There is no such requirement under international human rights law, the reason why someone has been treated less favourably is irrelevant.

That both intended and unintended discrimination are prohibited under international law is apparent from the explicit definitions of discrimination contained in some of the human rights treaties. The ICERD defines discrimination as any distinction based on one of the listed grounds 'which has the purpose *or effect* of nullifying or impairing the recognition, enjoyment or exercise, on an equal footing, of human rights and fundamental freedoms'.[35] The CEDAW definition is almost identical.[36] The Human Rights Committee, in its General Comment on non-discrimination, has adopted the same definition for the purposes of the ICCPR[37] and has made it clear in its jurisprudence that discriminatory intention is not a necessary element of discrimination.[38] Equally, the European Court of Human Rights has indicated that discrimination under Article 14 ECHR may also relate to the *effects* of state measures.[39]

As is illustrated by the rulings in *Althammer* and *DH* described in Section 4.2, indirect discrimination is often equated with unintended discrimination. Conversely, it is normally assumed that where there is direct discrimination, there is a discriminatory intention. Although it is true that these concepts will often correlate, this is not always the case. There may be cases of direct discrimination—for example, the exclusion of pregnant women and mothers from certain types of work—where the intention is to protect the respective groups rather than to discriminate against them. On the other hand, a 'neutral' criterion such as a literacy test for job applicants may well be used as a pretext for excluding certain ethnic groups, amounting to intended indirect discrimination.

---

[32] (2008) 47 EHRR 3, para 184.

[33] *Purohit and Moore v The Gambia*, Communication No 241/2001, 16th Activity Report (2002) paras 53–4.

[34] The leading case is *Washington v Davis* 426 US 229 (1976).

[35] Art 1(1) (emphasis added).   [36] Art 1.   [37] n 16, para 7.

[38] Eg *Simunek et al. v The Czech Republic*, CCPR/C/54/D/516/1992 (19 July 1995) para 11.7; *Adam v The Czech Republic*, CCPR/C/57/D/586/1994 (23 July 1996) para 12.7.

[39] *Case Relating to Certain Aspects of the Laws on the Use of Languages in Education in Belgium (Belgian Linguistics Case) (No 2)* (1968) 1 EHRR 252, 284 para 10.

5 JUSTIFIED AND UNJUSTIFIED DISTINCTIONS

Once it is established that there has been a difference in treatment or outcome, the next question that needs to be answered is whether there is a justification for it. As explained already, it is to some extent inevitable that states classify people into different groups. The crucial question is whether there are objective and reasonable criteria for these distinctions. This section first explains the relevant test under international human rights law. Next, it explores what standard of review human rights bodies or courts apply to carry out this test. Finally, it considers matters concerning evidence and proof.

5.1 THE JUSTIFICATION TEST

The Human Rights Committee, in its General Comment on non-discrimination, has stressed that, for the purposes of the ICCPR, 'not every differentiation of treatment will constitute discrimination, if the criteria for such differentiation are reasonable and objective and if the aim is to achieve a purpose which is legitimate under the Covenant.'[40] But it is in the jurisprudence of the European Court of Human Rights that the criteria for distinguishing between justified and unjustified distinction have been most clearly articulated. The Court interpreted Article 14 ECHR for the first time in the *Belgian Linguistics Case* and has since repeatedly confirmed those conclusions:

> [T]he Court, following the principles which may be extracted from the legal practice of a large number of democratic states, holds that the principle of equality of treatment is violated if the distinction has no objective and reasonable justification. The existence of such a justification must be assessed in relation to the aim and effects of the measure under consideration, regard being had to the principles which normally prevail in democratic societies. A difference of treatment in the exercise of a right laid down in the Convention must not only pursue a legitimate aim: Article 14 is likewise violated when it is clearly established that there is no reasonable relationship of proportionality between the means employed and the aim sought to be realised.[41]

This two-limb test, requiring that any difference in treatment must (1) pursue a legitimate aim and (2) be proportionate, is very similar to the test used in the context of other rights to assess the permissibility of limitations, described in Chapter 5. The test formulated by the European Court has been adopted, explicitly or implicitly, by most other human rights bodies. While the Human Rights Committee had originally failed to provide a clear and consistent explanation of what it means by 'reasonable and objective criteria', it has later increasingly started to interpret these terms as requiring a legitimate aim and proportionality.[42] The Committee on the Elimination of Racial Discrimination and the Committee on Economic, Social and Cultural Rights have embraced the same approach,[43] as has the Inter-American Court of Human Rights.[44]

In terms of what exactly this test involves, its first limb will not usually be very difficult for states to meet: most distinctions can be argued to pursue some aim that qualifies as legitimate, for example the protection of public order or tailoring the education system to

---

[40] n 16, para 13.   [41] n 39, para 10.   [42] Eg *Gillot v France*, A/57/40 (15 July 2002) para 13.2.

[43] CERD, Concluding observations: Australia, CERD/C/AUS/CO/14 (14 April 2005) para 24; CESCR, General Comment 20, E/C.12/GC/20, para 13.

[44] *Proposed Amendments to the Naturalization Provisions of the Political Constitution of Costa Rica*, n 4, paras 56–7.

children's differing learning capabilities. More difficult to satisfy is the second element of the test, the proportionality requirement. This requirement reflects the basic notion that a fair balance ought to be struck between the interests of the community and respect for individual rights. A wide range of factors may need to be considered to assess proportionality, including the suitability of a distinction to achieve the aim pursued, the availability of alternative means, and the question of whether the disadvantage suffered by the affected individuals or groups is excessive in relation to the aim. Whilst this assessment inevitably turns on the specific facts of a given case, international human rights bodies have been consistent in their characterization of certain reasons as not sufficient to justify differential treatment; these include, among others, mere administrative inconvenience,[45] existence of a longstanding tradition,[46] prevailing views in society,[47] stereotypes,[48] or convictions of the local population.[49]

5.2 STANDARD OF REVIEW

The stringency with which human rights courts or bodies review the existence of a justification will vary according to a number of factors.

Most importantly, certain grounds of distinction are generally regarded as inherently suspect and therefore require particularly strict scrutiny. The grounds attracting the greatest degree of attention and most likely to be declared unjustified are race, ethnicity, sex, and religion. That *race* is among these 'suspect classifications' is indicated by the general acceptance of the prohibition of racial discrimination as forming part of customary international law, the widespread ratification of the ICERD, and the finding of the European Commission of Human Rights, later endorsed by the Court, that 'a special importance should be attached to discrimination based on race' and that it may amount to degrading treatment.[50] The Inter-American Commission on Human Rights also applies a strict standard of scrutiny to distinctions based on race.[51]

With regard to the related notion of *ethnicity*, the European Court has stressed that 'no difference in treatment which is based exclusively or to a decisive extent on a person's ethnic origin is capable of being objectively justified in a contemporary democratic society built on the principles of pluralism and respect for different cultures'.[52] That distinctions based on *sex* are particularly suspect is underlined by the wealth of international treaties addressing the problem of sexual discrimination, including the CEDAW.[53] The Inter-American Commission has stated that distinctions based on sex 'necessarily give rise to heightened scrutiny'[54] and the European Court has observed that 'very weighty reasons would have to be advanced before a difference in treatment on the ground of sex could be regarded as compatible with the [ECHR]'.[55] Finally, the suspect nature of distinctions based on *religion* can be concluded from the unanimous adoption by the General Assembly of the Declaration on the Elimination of All Forms of Intolerance and Discrimination Based on Religion or Belief[56] and the European Court's finding that '[n]otwithstanding

---

[45] *Gueye v France*, n 24, para 9.5.

[46] *Müller and Engelhard v Namibia*, CCPR/C/74/D/919/2000 (26 March 2002) para 6.8.

[47] *Broeks v The Netherlands*, n 14.   [48] *Konstantin Markin v Russia* (2013) 56 EHRR 8, paras 141–3.

[49] *Inze v Austria* (1988) 10 EHRR 394, para 44.

[50] *East African Asians v UK* (1973) 3 EHRR 76, paras 207–8; *Cyprus v Turkey* (2002) 35 EHRR 30, para 306.

[51] Case 11.625, *María Eugenia Morales de Sierra v Guatemala*, IACommHR Report No 4/01 (19 January 2001) para 36.   [52] *Timishev v Russia* (2007) 44 EHRR 37, para 58.

[53] See Chapter 16.   [54] *María Eugenia Morales de Sierra v Guatemala*, n 51, para 36.

[55] *Abdulaziz, Cabales and Balkandali v UK* (1985) 7 EHRR 471, para 78.

[56] GA Res 36/55 (25 November 1981).

any possible arguments to the contrary, a distinction based essentially on a difference in religion alone is not acceptable'.[57]

As far as other grounds of distinction are concerned, it is difficult to discern a consistent approach in international case law. The Human Rights Committee, for instance, has indicated that any distinction based on one of the grounds explicitly listed in Article 26 ICCPR 'places a heavy burden on the State party to explain the reason for the differentiation',[58] but that does not seem to mean that differential treatment on grounds other than race, sex, and religion are subject to the same intense scrutiny. The European Court, on the other hand, has suggested that also distinctions based on nationality,[59] illegitimacy,[60] and, more generally, membership of any 'particularly vulnerable group in society that has suffered considerable discrimination in the past' (such as people with HIV or a disability and members of sexual minorities) should be treated as inherently suspect.[61] Lists of suspect classifications are, in any event, not fixed but can change as international law on these matters develops. Given the recent emergence of new international norms against discrimination on grounds such as disability,[62] sexual orientation,[63] and age,[64] it seems likely that these classifications will soon more widely be regarded as suspect.

Apart from the ground of distinction, the intensity of review may also depend on a number of other factors. For example, most courts and human rights bodies tend to apply a lenient standard as far as matters of social or economic policy are concerned,[65] whereas classifications affecting fundamental individual interests entail particularly strict scrutiny.[66] Furthermore, it will generally be more difficult for states to justify direct rather than indirect discrimination. The Declaration of Principles on Equality, an important but non-binding document signed by numerous human rights and equality experts, states that 'direct discrimination may be permitted only very exceptionally'.[67]

5.3 EVIDENCE AND PROOF

According to established human rights jurisprudence, it is up to the individual complaining of discrimination to establish a difference in treatment or outcome, the ground of distinction, and the existence of comparably situated groups. Having done so, the burden of proof shifts to the state to show that there is a justification for the distinction.[68]

In cases of alleged indirect discrimination, however, complainants may find it very difficult to prove that a neutral measure has a disproportionate impact on particular groups. Therefore, the European Court of Human Rights has held that less strict evidential rules should apply in these cases: 'statistics which appear on critical examination to be reliable and significant' may be sufficient prima facie evidence of indirect discrimination.[69] Thus,

---

[57] *Hoffmann v Austria* (1993) 17 EHRR 293, para 36. See also *Vojnity v Hungary*, App no 29617/07, Judgment of 12 February 2013, para 36.   [58] *Müller and Engelhard v Namibia*, n 46, para 6.7.

[59] *Gaygusuz v Austria* (1996) 23 EHRR 364, para 42.   [60] *Inze v Austria*, n 49, para 41.

[61] *Kiyutin v Russia* (2011) 53 EHRR 26, paras 63–4 and references cited there.   [62] See the CRPD.

[63] See Chapter 15.   [64] See UN Principles for Older Persons, GA Res 46/91 (16 December 1991).

[65] Eg *Oulajin and Kaiss v The Netherlands*, CCPR/C/46/D/406/1990 and 426/1990 (23 October 1992), individual opinion submitted by Committee members Herndl, Müllerson, N'Diaye, and Sadi, and *James v UK* (1986) 8 EHRR 123, para 46 (stating that 'the margin of appreciation available to the legislature in implementing social and economic policies should be a wide one').

[66] Eg *Dudgeon v UK* (1981) 4 EHRR 149, para 52.

[67] Equal Rights Trust, Declaration of Principles on Equality, available at <http://www.equalrightstrust.org/endorse/index.htm>, Principle 5.

[68] Declaration of Principles on Equality, n 67, Principle 21. For the ECHR, see *Timishev v Russia*, n 52, para 57.

[69] *DH v Czech Republic*, n 32, para 188.

in *DH*, even though the statistical figures submitted by the applicants were contentious, the Court still thought that they revealed a dominant trend and thus accepted them as sufficient to establish a presumption of disproportionate numbers of Roma children being placed in 'special schools'. As a consequence, the burden of proof shifted to the government to show that there was a justification for the disparate impact of the legislation.[70]

DH demonstrates that statistical evidence may be of decisive importance to the outcome of cases of alleged indirect discrimination. Yet often the data required to establish a presumption that a measure has a discriminatory effect can, unlike in *DH*, only be collected by state authorities. The UN treaty bodies, therefore, regularly stress in their concluding observations that states have a duty to collect and analyse relevant statistical data, disaggregated by grounds of distinction.[71] Such a duty to gather information has also been included in the Declaration of Principles on Equality.[72]

6 POSITIVE ACTION

As with any other human right, the right to equality and non-discrimination entails state obligations of different types.[73] The *obligation to respect* requires states to refrain from any discriminatory action and to ensure that all their laws and practices comply with the right to non-discrimination. The *obligation to protect* imposes a duty on states to prevent discrimination by non-state actors. According to the consistent jurisprudence of the UN treaty bodies, this means that states must introduce comprehensive legislation prohibiting discrimination in fields such as employment, education, healthcare, housing, and the provision of goods and services. This conclusion is supported by various provisions in the respective human rights treaties themselves. Article 2(d) ICERD, for example, explicitly states that '[e]ach State Party shall prohibit and bring to an end, by all appropriate means, including legislation as required by circumstances, racial discrimination by any persons, group or organization'; the CEDAW contains a parallel provision in Article 2(e); and most treaties are scattered with norms requiring states to prohibit particular actions of private parties that are discriminatory or may contribute to discrimination, such as racial hate speech (Article 20 ICCPR, Article 4 ICERD, Article 13(5) ACHR), trafficking in women and exploitation of prostitution of women (Article 6 CEDAW), or racial discrimination with regard to employment, housing, or education (Article 5(e) ICERD).

However, an exclusively prohibitory approach is severely limited in that it focuses on discrimination understood as individual, isolated events that can be remedied through penalizing the perpetrators and compensating the victims. In fact discrimination is often the consequence of deeply embedded patterns of disadvantage and exclusion that can only be addressed through changes to social and institutional structures. Accordingly, it is now well established in international human rights law that it is not sufficient for states to have anti-discrimination legislation in place. Instead, they also have an *obligation to promote, guarantee, and secure* equality by taking proactive steps to eliminate structural patterns of disadvantage and to further social inclusion.[74] This obligation, often referred to as the

---

[70] *DH v Czech Republic*, n 32, paras 191–5.
[71] Eg CEDAW Committee, Report on twenty-ninth session, A/58/38 (part II), para 134 (Brazil).
[72] Declaration of Principles on Equality, n 67, Principle 24.   [73] See Chapter 5.
[74] Eg ICERD, Arts 2(1)(e), 2(2), and 7; HRC, General Comment 4, HRI/GEN/1/Rev. 9 (Vol I) 175, para 2; HRC, General Comment 18, n 16, paras 5 and 10; CEDAW, Arts 3 and 5; CERD, General Recommendation XXIX, HRI/GEN/1/Rev. 9 (Vol II) 296, paras 5, 6, 8, 9, 17, 33–5; Protocol to the African Charter on Human and Peoples' Rights on the Rights of Women in Africa, Arts 2(1)(d), 2(2), 3–24.

duty to take 'positive action', may cover a huge variety of legislative, administrative, and policy measures, ranging from the restructuring of institutions to the provision of 'reasonable accommodation'[75] for individuals in particular circumstances, from educational campaigns to the use of public procurement to promote equality, and from the 'mainstreaming'[76] of equality issues in public policy to encouraging participation of affected groups in relevant decision-making processes.

One important aspect of 'positive action' are 'affirmative action programmes' or, as they are generally called in international law, *special measures of protection*. These are 'measures...aimed specifically at correcting the position of members of a target group in one or more aspects of their social life, in order to obtain effective equality'.[77] In their strongest form, such special measures involve the preferential treatment of members of a previously disadvantaged group over others in the allocation of jobs, university places, and other benefits (often referred to as 'positive' or 'reverse discrimination'). For example, when two equally qualified persons apply for a job, priority is given to the female applicant, or a certain number of university places are reserved for racial minorities.

Although such preferential treatment is clearly incompatible with a formal notion of equality, international human rights law permits it, thus recognizing that it may be legitimate to prioritize the achievement of substantive equality over the requirement of consistent treatment. Article 1(4) ICERD, for example, provides:

> Special measures taken for the sole purpose of securing adequate advancement of certain racial or ethnic groups or individuals requiring such protection as may be necessary in order to ensure such groups or individuals equal enjoyment or exercise of human rights and fundamental freedoms shall not be deemed racial discrimination, provided, however, that such measures do not, as a consequence, lead to the maintenance of separate rights for different racial groups and that they shall not be continued after the objectives for which they were taken have been achieved.

The CEDAW contains a similar provision in Article 4(1). For purposes of the ICCPR, the Human Rights Committee has made it clear that special measures are permissible as long as they meet the general justification test described in Section 5.1, that is, as long as they pursue a legitimate aim in a proportionate manner.[78] Proportionality in this context means, among other things, that the preferential treatment must be introduced for the benefit of genuinely disadvantaged groups, be temporary and cease once the objectives have been achieved, and not result in the maintenance of separate rights for different groups.

Not only does international human rights law permit but to some extent it even *requires* states to adopt special measures of protection. As the Human Rights Committee's General Comment on non-discrimination states:

> [T]he principle of equality sometimes requires States parties to take affirmative action in order to diminish or eliminate conditions which cause or help to perpetuate discrimination

---

[75] For a definition of 'reasonable accommodation', see CRPD, Art 2.

[76] For 'gender mainstreaming', that is, the integration of a gender perspective in all legislation and public policies, see Report of the Fourth World Conference on Women, A/Conf.177/20 (1995), strategic objective H.2. The Protocol to the African Charter on Human and Peoples' Rights on the Rights of Women in Africa contains, in Art 2(1)(c), an explicit obligation of gender mainstreaming. See further Chapter 16.

[77] Progress report on the concept and practice of affirmative action by the Special Rapporteur of the Sub-Commission on the Promotion and Protection of Human Rights, E/CN.4/Sub.2/2001/15 (26 June 2001) para 7.

[78] Eg *Stalla Costa v Uruguay*, CCPR/C/30/D/198/1985 (9 July 1987) para 10; *Jacobs v Belgium*, CCPR/C/81/D/943/2000 (7 July 2004) para 9.5.

prohibited by the Covenant. For example, in a State where the general conditions of a certain part of the population prevent or impair their enjoyment of human rights, the State should take specific action to correct those conditions. Such action may involve granting for a time to the part of the population concerned certain preferential treatment in specific matters as compared with the rest of the population.[79]

That states may need to adopt special measures has also been highlighted by the Committee on Economic, Social and Cultural Rights.[80] As far as racial groups and women are concerned, the duty follows from Article 2(2) ICERD and Article 3 CEDAW, respectively. At the regional level, the Inter-American Court of Human Rights has observed that 'States are obliged to take affirmative action to reverse or change discriminatory situations that exist in their societies to the detriment of a specific group of persons',[81] and this obligation is now codified in the Inter-American Convention against All Forms of Discrimination and Intolerance.[82] The European Court, finally, has stressed that 'a failure to attempt to correct inequality through different treatment' may amount to a violation of the right to non-discrimination.[83]

7 CONCLUSION

The concept of equality and non-discrimination in international human rights law has evolved significantly since the adoption of the UDHR. Detailed legal standards have been drawn up and human rights bodies and courts have developed a rich jurisprudence, giving concrete substance to the notion of equality. Nevertheless, considerable gaps, inconsistencies, and uncertainties remain: the concept of indirect discrimination was developed in other jurisdictions and has only very recently been acknowledged by international human rights bodies; details of the justification test, such as the applicable standard of review and evidentiary rules, need further elaboration; and, as far as implementation at the national level is concerned, numerous states do not yet have comprehensive legislation to combat discrimination.

The most important challenge, however, is to ensure that every human being is in fact able to enjoy her or his right to equality. In a world in which the poorest 30 per cent collectively own only 1 per cent of the global household wealth and thus 32 times less than the richest 1 per cent,[84] equal rights remain an unfulfilled promise for large sections of the population. Recent developments in international human rights law are evidence of a growing recognition that, while prohibitions of discrimination play a crucial role in achieving equality, states also have an obligation to proactively tackle structural patterns of disadvantage—in other words, formal and substantive approaches to equality need to be combined. One key component of such a proactive strategy must be to ensure that all people can participate on an equal basis in all areas of economic, social, and political life, including in the very decisions on how equality should be realized.

---

[79] n 16, para 10.   [80] Eg CESCR, General Comment 16, HRI/GEN/1/Rev. 9 (Vol I) 113, paras 15 and 35.
[81] *Juridical Condition and Rights of the Undocumented Migrants*, n 11, para 104.   [82] Art 5.
[83] *Stec and Others v UK* (2006) 43 EHRR 47, para 51.
[84] Davies *et al.*, 'The Level and Distribution of Global Household Wealth' (2010) 121 *Economic J* 223, 244.

FURTHER READING

ARNARDÓTTIR, *Equality and Non-discrimination under the European Convention on Human Rights* (Martinus Nijhoff, 2003).

BAYEFSKY, 'The Principle of Equality or Non-Discrimination in International Law' (1990) 11 *HRLJ* 1.

CHOUDHURY, 'Interpreting the Right to Equality under Article 26 of the International Covenant on Civil and Political Rights' [2003] *EHRLR* 24.

FREDMAN (ed), *Discrimination and Human Rights: The Case of Racism* (Oxford University Press, 2001).

FREDMAN (ed), *Discrimination Law* (Oxford University Press, 2011).

GERARDS, 'The Discrimination Grounds of Article 14 of the European Convention on Human Rights' (2013) 13 *HRLR* 99.

LERNER, *Group Rights and Discrimination in International Law* (Martinus Nijhoff, 2003).

MCCRUDDEN (ed), *Anti-Discrimination Law* (Ashgate, 2004).

MCKEAN, *Equality and Discrimination under International Law* (Clarendon Press, 1983).

O'CONNELL, 'Cinderella Comes to the Ball: Art 14 and the Right to Non-discrimination in the ECHR' (2009) 29 *LS* 211.

USEFUL WEBSITES

UN Committee on the Elimination of Racial Discrimination (CERD): **<http://www2.ohchr.org/english/bodies/cerd/>**

European Commission Against Racism and Intolerance (ECRI): **<http://www.coe.int/ecri>**

Equal Rights Trust: **<http://www.equalrightstrust.org>**

9

INTEGRITY OF THE PERSON

Nigel S Rodley

SUMMARY

This chapter examines the right to be free from torture and cruel, inhuman, or degrading treatment or punishment and the right to life, arguably the core rights understood within the concept of integrity of the person. These rights also have a direct pedigree to the principle of respect for human dignity that is at the heart of the International Bill of Human Rights. The complex definitional issues of what constitutes torture and other ill-treatment are addressed, mainly in light of treaty definitions and case law of courts and other bodies charged with applying relevant treaties. The same approach is taken with respect to the right to life, where the central issues of the limits international law places on the death penalty and on the use of force by security forces and law enforcement officials are considered. Both rights are considered to be rules of customary international law and probably peremptory norms of international law (*jus cogens*).

1 INTRODUCTION

1.1 RESPECT FOR HUMAN DIGNITY

Respect for human dignity is the one explicit underlying principle of the International Bill of Human Rights. It is invoked in the first preambular paragraph of the Universal Declaration of Human Rights (UDHR) and the second preambular paragraphs of both the International Covenant on Economic, Social and Cultural Rights (ICESCR) and the International Covenant on Civil and Political Rights (ICCPR).

The prohibition of torture and cruel, inhuman, or degrading treatment or punishment ('torture and ill-treatment') and the right to life both have an immediate link to the principle of human dignity. Thus, the African Charter on Human and Peoples' Rights (ACHPR) places the prohibition of torture and ill-treatment in its Article 5 that guarantees 'respect of the dignity inherent in a human being'. In a more limited way, the analogous Article 5 of the American Convention on Human Rights (ACHR), after stating the basic prohibition on torture and ill-treatment, provides that all persons deprived of liberty are to be 'treated with respect for the inherent dignity of the human person'. A similar requirement is found in Article 10(1) ICCPR. While this is separate from Article 7 containing the prohibition of torture and ill-treatment, it has long been treated by the Human Rights Committee as intimately linked to Article 7.[1] With regard to the

---

[1] HRC, General Comment 20, HRI/GEN/1/Rev.9 (Vol I) 200, para 2; General Comment 21, HRI/GEN/1/Rev.9 (Vol I) 202, para 3.

right to life, the first preambular paragraph of the Second Optional Protocol to the ICCPR (ICCPR-OP2), aimed at the abolition of the death penalty, affirms that abolition 'contributes to enhancement of human dignity'.

1.2 THE RIGHT TO INTEGRITY OF THE PERSON

The prohibition of torture and ill-treatment and the right to life are at the core of the notion of integrity of the person. Article 5 ACHR, for example, which guarantees the right to humane treatment, provides in its first paragraph: 'Every person has the right to have his physical, mental, and moral integrity respected.' The link between the right to humane treatment and personal integrity is established. The same is true for the link between the right to life and integrity of the person. Thus, Article 4 ACHPR stipulates the right of every human being 'to respect for his life and the integrity of his person'. Here the link is essential.

This chapter deals, first, with the right to be free from torture and ill-treatment (Section 2) and, then, with the right to life (Section 3).

2 THE RIGHT TO BE FREE FROM TORTURE AND ILL-TREATMENT

Article 5 UDHR provides: 'No-one shall be subjected to torture or to cruel, inhuman or degrading treatment or punishment.' Verbally inspired by the prohibition of 'cruel and unusual punishments' in the English and American Bills of Rights, the direct stimulus for this provision was the Nazis' use of torture. Related vivid concerns included the use of harmful and painful medical experiments, such as those conducted by the notorious Dr Josef Mengele. This breadth of concern explains the expansive, non-technical language of the prohibition.

While torture had been legal under certain circumstances in Europe from at least Roman times, it had been abolished virtually everywhere by the end of the eighteenth century.[2] Its re-emergence in the heart of Europe in a post-Enlightenment world was a matter for shock and felt to be an aberration. Accordingly, after the prohibition's inclusion in the UDHR, it found its way uncontroversially, in almost identical language, into the ICCPR and the principal regional treaties.

That the use of torture may not have been such an aberration became clear in the 1970s when Amnesty International published a report documenting the practice of torture in many countries from all regions of the world and led a campaign on the issue. Demonstrably in response to this campaign, and a successor one in 1984–5,[3] the UN began sustained activities, first in the field of standard-setting, then in the area of developing an institutional response. There were also activities at the regional level to the same effect.

The product of the standard-setting is referred to in Section 2.1. The institutional output has included the creation of the mandate of the UN Special Rapporteur on the question of torture, the establishment of the Committee against Torture under the UN Convention against Torture and Other Cruel, Inhuman or Degrading Treatment or Punishment (UNCAT), and a Sub-Committee on the Prevention of Torture created by the Optional

---

[2] Torture seems to have been alien to Islamic tradition from its beginnings, albeit not, in practice, to various governments claiming to apply Islamic law in their legal systems.

[3] See Amnesty International, *Report on Torture* (1973) and *Torture in the Eighties* (1984).

Protocol to UNCAT (UNCAT-OP). The latter was inspired by the work of the European Committee for the Prevention of Torture and Inhuman or Degrading Treatment or Punishment that was put in place by the European Convention of the same name adopted by the Council of Europe in 1987.

2.1 SOURCES

The right to be free from torture and ill-treatment is guaranteed by the general universal and regional human rights treaties: Articles 7 and 10 ICCPR, Article 3 European Convention on Human Rights (ECHR), Article 5 ACHR, and Article 5 ACHPR. In addition, a human rights treaty specifically designed to ensure protection of the right to be free from torture and ill-treatment has been adopted: UNCAT. Key UN 'soft law' sources include the Standard Minimum Rules for the Treatment of Prisoners (1955), the Declaration on the Protection of All Persons from Being Subjected to Torture and Other Cruel, Inhuman or Degrading Treatment or Punishment (1975), the Code of Conduct for Law Enforcement Officials (1979), the Principles of Medical Ethics relevant to the Role of Health Personnel, particularly Physicians, in the Protection of Prisoners and Detainees against Torture and Other Cruel, Inhuman or Degrading Treatment or Punishment (1982), the Body of Principles for the Protection of All Persons under Any Form of Detention or Imprisonment (1988), and the Principles on the Effective Investigation and Documentation of Torture and Other Cruel, Inhuman or Degrading Treatment or Punishment (Istanbul Principles) (2000). There are also treaty provisions in the field of international humanitarian law that prohibit torture, cruel treatment, inhuman treatment, and humiliating and degrading treatment.[4] As with the human rights treaties, the terms are undefined. Finally, there is international criminal law, which covers, among other aspects, crimes against humanity and war crimes. Torture and other forms of ill-treatment may amount to war crimes and, when committed as part of a widespread or systematic attack against a civilian population, crimes against humanity. The case law of the International Criminal Tribunal for the former Yugoslavia and the International Criminal Tribunal for Rwanda, therefore, also provide helpful guidance in determining the normative content of the right to be free from torture and ill-treatment. Furthermore, the Rome Statute of the International Criminal Court (ICC Statute) has both codified crimes against humanity and war crimes and provided definitions for some components, including torture.[5]

2.2 LEGAL STATUS

There is no doubt that the prohibition of torture and other ill-treatment is a norm of customary international law. Relevant indications are: the fact that the rule is couched in absolute terms, brooking no exception (such as for public order or national security purposes, as allowed for in some rights, notably the freedoms covered in Chapter 11), not even the spurious 'ticking bomb' situation;[6] the non-derogability of the rule even in time

---

[4] Geneva Convention I, Arts 12 and 50; Geneva Convention II, Arts 12 and 51; Geneva Convention III, Arts 17, 87, and 130; Geneva Convention IV, Arts 32 and 147; and Common Art 3 to all four Geneva Conventions, which is understood as reflecting the 'fundamental principles of international humanitarian law'. See Chapter 23.   [5] Arts 7 and 8. See Chapter 24.

[6] This posits the extremely hypothetical situation that a person in custody knows where a bomb that would cause great loss of life has been placed and the aim is to locate it and prevent it from going off. In reality, the person's knowledge will be doubtful and the person will be able to prevaricate until the bomb goes off, even in the unlikely event that a 'specialist' interrogation team is available.

of war or other public emergency;[7] and the fact that states do not claim a right to torture. One might also look to the prohibition in international humanitarian law and its criminal nature under international criminal law.

It is also beyond peradventure that the prohibition of torture is a rule of *jus cogens*, a peremptory rule of international law which cannot even be modified by treaty.[8] It has been described as such by the International Court of Justice, as well as by the European Court of Human Rights, the Inter-American Court of Human Rights, the Human Rights Committee, the Committee Against Torture, the International Criminal Tribunal for the former Yugoslavia, the International Law Commission, and the UK House of Lords.[9] It is worth noting that, not only has the influential American Law Institute long ago espoused this position, in its third Restatement of US Foreign Relations Law,[10] so has one of the controversial legal memoranda from the US Department of Justice that provided the basis for the temporary use of 'enhanced interrogation techniques' by US personnel of certain 'high value' detainees held in the context of the 'global war on terror'.[11] All that remains unsettled is whether the prohibition of other ill-treatment has the same status. The American Restatement makes no distinction. Most of the other sources cited focus on torture, without necessarily excluding other ill-treatment.

2.3 COMPONENTS

We have seen that the treaty prohibitions of torture and cruel, inhuman, or degrading treatment or punishment were drafted broadly with a view to avoiding an overly technical or narrow approach. Indeed, international bodies have found an extensive range of practices to fall foul of it. For instance, in the late 1960s and early 1970s the UK refused to admit British nationals being deported from Uganda, resulting in their 'shuttlecocking' between the two countries. In 1973, the (former) European Commission of Human Rights found the practice to violate Article 3 ECHR.[12] Another type of concern was highlighted when a team of UN Special Rapporteurs found that the widespread property destruction carried out by East Timorese paramilitaries in Dili engaged the prohibition of torture and ill-treatment.[13] Nevertheless, the earliest case law, especially by the European Commission of Human Rights and the European Court of Human Rights, started to break down the prohibition into its component limbs, mostly in connection with cases dealing with prisoners.

---

[7] See case law listed in n 9. See also *Chahal v UK* (1997) 23 EHRR 413; *Saadi v Italy* (2009) 49 EHRR 30.

[8] See Chapter 4.

[9] Eg ICJ, *Questions relating to the Obligation to Prosecute or Extradite (Belgium v Senegal)* [2012] ICJ Rep, para 99; *Al-Adsani v United Kingdom* (2002) 34 EHRR 273, para 61; *Caesar v Trinidad and Tobago*, IACtHR Series C No 123 (11 March 2005); HRC, General Comment 29, HRI/GEN/1/Rev.9 (Vol I) 234, para 3; CAT, General Comment 2, HRI/GEN/1/Rev.9 (Vol I) 376 para 1; *Prosecutor v Furundzija* (1998), No 17-95-17/1, Trial Judgment, paras 153–7; International Law Commission, Draft Articles on State Responsibility, A/56/10, ch IV.E.2; *Regina v Bow Street Metropolitan Stipendiary Magistrate, ex parte Pinochet Ugarte (No 3)* [1999] UKHL 17.

[10] American Law Institute, Restatement of the Law: Restatement (Third) of the Foreign Relations Law of the United States, Vol II (1987) s 702.

[11] See Memorandum from Daniel P Levin to James B Comey (30 December 2004) 1 and n 2, available at <http://www.usdoj.gov/olc/18usc23402340a2.htm>.

[12] *East African Asians v UK* (1973) 3 EHRR 76.

[13] Joint report of the Special Rapporteurs on extrajudicial, summary or arbitrary executions, torture, and violence against women, A/54/660 (10 December 1999) paras 70–1. See also, for the Committee Against Torture, *Hajrizi Dzemajl v Yugoslavia*, CAT/C/29/D/161/2000 (2 December 2002) and, for the European Court, *Ayder and others v Turkey*, App no 23656/94, Judgment of 8 January 2004, paras 104–11.

2.3.1 Definition of 'torture' and 'cruel, inhuman, and degrading treatment or punishment'

In the *Greek Case*, arising out of treatment inflicted on political opponents by the military regime that seized power in Greece in 1967, the European Commission distinguished between various kinds of ill-treatment. In particular, it characterized *falanga* (beatings on the soles of the feet) as 'torture *and* inhuman treatment' while it considered some extremely severe beatings as 'torture *or* inhuman treatment'.[14]

The landmark case of *Ireland v UK* concerned the treatment by UK security forces of suspected Irish Republican Army (IRA) prisoners in Northern Ireland. Again the European Commission distinguished between treatment amounting to torture and other ill-treatment. While it assigned serious physical beatings to the category of inhuman treatment, it concluded that five special interrogation techniques amounted to torture. The five techniques were:

1) wall-standing: forcing the detainees to remain for periods of some hours in a 'stress position', spread-eagled against the wall, with their fingers put high above the head against the wall, the legs spread apart and the feet back, causing them to stand on their toes with the weight of the body mainly on the fingers;

2) hooding: putting a bag over the detainees' heads and, at least initially, keeping it there all the time except during interrogation;

3) subjection to noise: pending their interrogations, holding the detainees in a room where there was a continuous loud and hissing noise;

4) deprivation of sleep: pending their interrogations, depriving the detainees of sleep;

5) deprivation of food and drink: subjecting the detainees to a reduced diet.[15]

The European Court of Human Rights, however, decided in 1978 that these techniques should be considered as inhuman treatment rather than torture. It invoked the definition of torture found in the recently adopted UN Declaration against Torture (UNDAT). Article 1(2) UNDAT had defined torture as an aggravated and deliberate form of cruel, inhuman, or degrading treatment or punishment. For the European Court, the five techniques did not meet this criterion 'as so understood', the techniques being undeserving of the 'special stigma' of torture.[16] This was a controversial decision. After all, the definition of torture in the UNDAT had made clear that the pain or suffering inflicted did not have to be physical. It could also be *mental* pain or suffering. Many found it hard to understand what kind of mental pain or suffering might be required if the mixed mental *and* physical pain and suffering caused by interrogation techniques did not constitute torture.

The year 1984, also the title of George Orwell's futuristic novel which has his hero, Winston Smith, tortured by being in a room full of rats to which he was known to be phobic, brought us the UNCAT and its authoritative definition of torture. According to Article 1:

> For the purposes of this Convention, the term 'torture' means any act by which severe pain or suffering, whether physical or mental, is intentionally inflicted on a person for such purposes as obtaining from him or a third person information or a confession, punishing him for an act he or a third person has committed or is suspected of having committed, or intimidating or coercing him or a third person, or for any reason based on discrimination of any

---

[14] *The Greek Case* (1969) 12 YB 468, 504 (emphases added).
[15] See *Ireland v UK* (1978) 2 EHRR 25, para 96.   [16] *Ireland v UK* (1978) 2 EHRR 25, para 167.

kind, when such pain or suffering is inflicted by or at the instigation of or with the consent or acquiescence of a public official or other person acting in an official capacity. It does not include pain or suffering arising only from, inherent in or incidental to lawful sanctions.

While the definition is formally only applicable to the states parties to the UNCAT and the Committee against Torture that monitors its implementation, it has proven to be the first port of call for most bodies seeking to identify practices of torture. The definition largely follows that of UNDAT, with one notable exception: it does not describe torture as an aggravated and deliberate form of inhuman treatment. The definition has three core elements:

1. pain or suffering that must be severe; it may be physical or mental;
2. it must be inflicted for a certain kind of purpose, that is, the sort of public purpose traditionally associated with torture; and
3. it must be inflicted by or under the aegis of public officialdom.

Each of these elements will be considered briefly. The first element, *severity of pain or suffering*, is common to most understandings of the term torture[17] and is found in the Article 7 ICC Statute definition of torture as a crime against humanity and in the definition of torture as a war crime in the Elements of Crimes adopted under the ICC Statute.[18] As indicated, there is no requirement for aggravation of pain or suffering. However, it should be noted that Article 16 UNCAT does make provision for cruel, inhuman, or degrading treatment or punishment that 'does not amount to torture'. This can lend itself to an interpretation that would reintroduce the idea of aggravation, but the better view is that it does not.

It is unclear to what extent the practice of the European Court of Human Rights may have been influenced by this evolution. Certainly, it has seen fit at least to attenuate the application of its distinction between torture and inhuman treatment. In the 1999 *Selmouni* case, it decided that the kind of serious beatings that had occurred in a number of cases, including *Ireland v UK*, and would earlier have been classified as inhuman treatment, would now be considered as torture. It invoked its doctrine of the ECHR as 'a living instrument' and argued that the definition of torture had to evolve with democratic society's understanding of the term.[19] It is probable that the European Court was also signalling that it would have been prepared to treat practices such as the five interrogation techniques similarly. The Court continues to distinguish torture from inhuman treatment that 'does not reach the level of severity' to constitute torture. However, it gives little away as to what is the criterion for inhuman treatment. Earlier, inhuman treatment had to be severe, thus requiring torture to be more than severe. It is possible that it may now require a certain level of seriousness of pain or suffering, but without rising to the level of 'severe', for treatment to be considered 'inhuman'. What is clear is that, after *Selmouni*, the Court has brought down the threshold of pain or suffering required for a finding of torture.

The second element, *purpose*, was always part of European Commission and Court case law and it is found in all but one of the existing definitions of torture. Indeed, in the definition of torture as a war crime in the Elements of Crimes adopted under the ICC Statute, the only distinction between torture and inhuman (or cruel) treatment is the purposive element. However, there is one definition that omits the purposive element, namely that in

---

[17] Inter-American Convention to Prevent and Punish Torture, Art 2 refers to 'physical or mental pain' without qualification.

[18] Elements of Crimes, Arts 8(2)(a)(ii)-1 and 8(2)(c)(i)-4.   [19] (2000) 29 EHRR 403, para 101.

Article 7 ICC Statute defining torture as a crime against humanity. This may be explained by the fact that crimes against humanity can be committed by unofficial groups, thus making the attribution of motivation more difficult than in respect of states or other officially constituted bodies. Also, unlike the other definitions, that of Article 7 is limited to persons in custody or under the control of the accused, thus implicitly assigning some public purposive context. The definition remains an unsatisfactory outlier. The approach taken by UNCAT and the ICC Elements of Crime, making purpose the key distinguishing factor between torture and cruel or inhuman treatment, may be the more satisfactory one.

Finally, as a third element, the UNCAT definition requires public *official responsibility* for the pain or suffering. This is not found in the ICC-related definitions. This is perhaps inevitable as crimes against humanity and war crimes are not necessarily committed by public officials in the sense of state officials. A party to an armed conflict may well not be a state. However, it must have sufficient elements of organization such as to endow it with the status of party to an armed conflict within the meaning of international humanitarian law. Similarly, a crime against humanity must also be committed in the context of an attack against a civilian population. This institutional dimension should be seen as substituting for the public official requirement, as is the case in respect of war crimes.

2.3.2 Specific practices

While most findings of torture have involved an accumulation of cruel acts, some specific practices have been found to be torture. We have already seen this in respect of the *falanga* and sustained beatings with instruments. Others include water suffocation,[20] 'Palestinian hanging' (tying a person's hands behind their back and suspending them in the air),[21] and rape.[22]

Since the suffering involved in torture can be physical or mental, it is clear that psychological torment, such as that to which Orwell subjected his fictional hero Winston Smith, may fall within the legal definition of torture. The classic example is the Human Rights Committee finding that the threat of amputation of a concert pianist's hands constituted torture.[23] Explicit and implicit threats of torture and death in circumstances where the threats were credible were found by the Inter-American Court of Human Rights to be torture.[24]

As far as other ill-treatment is concerned, it includes, first, any treatment that would amount to torture, but was not inflicted for a public purpose. Even since *Selmouni*, the European Court of Human Rights has found some beatings to be inhuman or degrading rather than torture. The reluctance to find torture may be attributable to the fact that in these cases there seem to be circumstances in which the facts, including the behaviour of the affected individual, are in doubt.[25] The unnecessary use of handcuffs or other physical restraints may, under certain circumstances, amount to prohibited ill-treatment,[26] as can

---

[20] *José Vicente and Amado Villafañe Chaparro and others v Colombia*, CCPR/C/60/D/612/1995 (14 June 1994). The case is evidently consistent with the proposition that 'waterboarding'—briefly authorized for use by US personnel in the reaction to the atrocities of 11 September 2001—is torture.

[21] *Aksoy v Turkey* (1997) 23 EHRR 553, para 64.

[22] Case 10.970, *Mejía v Peru*, IACommHR Report No 5/96 (1 March 1996) Annual Report 1995, 157, 186–7; *Case of the Miguel Castro-Castro Prison v Peru*, IACtHR Series C No 160 (25 November 2006) para 311; *Aydin v Turkey* (1998) 25 EHRR 251, para 86.

[23] *Estrella v Uruguay*, CCPR/C/18/D/74/1980 (23 March 1983), para 8.3.

[24] *Maritza Urrutia v Guatemala*, IACtHR Series C No 103 (27 November 2003) paras 91–5.

[25] Eg *Egmez v Cyprus* (2002) 34 EHRR 29, paras 78–9.

[26] *Hénaf v France* (2005) 40 EHRR 44, paras 55–60.

unnecessary or oppressive strip-searching,[27] and displaying an alleged terrorist in prison garb.[28]

As far as persons in detention are concerned, they are at particular risk of ill-treatment during the *investigative phase* of detention, when the police or other detaining authority is seeking information of concern or a confession. This is because during this phase normal safeguards are not always respected. Thus, instead of detainees having prompt access to a lawyer and others from outside the place of detention, such as family members, or a medical practitioner, the detaining authority holds them at its sole mercy. This is generally called 'incommunicado detention'. Rules concerning the right to liberty aim at restricting this period of detention.[29] However, there is strong treaty body authority for the proposition that prolonged incommunicado detention in itself can violate the right of detainees to be treated with humanity and respect for their human dignity and the prohibition of torture and other ill-treatment.[30] Moreover, the UN Human Rights Council has clearly stated that prolonged incommunicado detention can amount to torture or other ill-treatment.[31] The Human Rights Committee has found that the US practice of capturing and detaining terrorist suspects in various parts of the world, as well as transferring them from place to place, violated the prohibition on torture and ill-treatment.[32] The European Court of Human Rights has gone as far as generally requiring assistance of a lawyer from the first police interview of a suspect.[33]

The second phase of detention is the *remand phase*, the phase in which, typically, a judicial authority will order continued detention on criminal charges. As in this phase the detaining authority will usually be different from the investigating authority (the prison authorities rather than the police or security services), detainees are generally better protected from ill-treatment. However, even after being formally remanded in custody, people may remain in the hands of the police or other investigating authority. Therefore, human rights bodies tend to recommend that the period of pre-remand detention not exceed a very few days (typically not more than two or three)[34] and that places of remand be under an authority administratively separate from that responsible for the police or similar security agency.

The *post-conviction phase* raises two kinds of issue. The first is the conditions of detention, the second is the nature of the punishment.

As to the first, the fact that someone has been sentenced to a term of imprisonment does not mean that there are no limits to how the prisoner may then be treated. On the contrary, the basic principle is that conditions should be no more oppressive than those necessary to maintain the deprivation of liberty which is the object of the punishment.[35] Accordingly, standards have been developed to assist in this, notably the UN Standard Minimum Rules for the Treatment of Prisoners.[36] These cover such matters as avoidance

---

[27] *Iwanczuk v Poland* (2004) 38 EHRR 8.

[28] *Loayza-Tamayo v Peru*, IACtHR Series C No 33 (17 September 1997), paras 46(d) and 58.

[29] See Chapter 13.

[30] *Aber v Algeria*, CCPR/C/90/D/1439/2005 (16 August 2007), para 7.3; *Suárez-Rosero v Ecuador*, IACtHR Series C No 35 (12 November 1997), paras 90–1.

[31] Human Rights Council Res 8/8 (18 June 2008), para 7(c).

[32] Concluding observations: US, CCPR/C/USA/CO/3/Rev.1 (18 December 2006) paras 12 and 16.

[33] *Salduz v Turkey* (2008) 49 EHRR 421.

[34] Eg Report of the Special Rapporteur on torture, E/CN.4/2003/68 (17 December 2002) para 26(g); ECPT Standards, CPT/Inf/E (2002) I-Rev 2006, paras 40–6.

[35] Eg the UN Basic Principles for the Treatment of Prisoners, GA Res 45/111 (14 December 1990) para 5.

[36] At the European level, the Council of Europe has adopted the European Prison Rules (2006).

of overcrowding, recreation, education and work, limits to time spent confined in cells, fair administration of discipline, and the limits to disciplinary punishment (including solitary confinement or segregation). Not every breach of every rule will necessarily involve a violation of the prohibition of torture or ill-treatment or the right to treatment with respect for humanity and human dignity. However, the more serious or widespread the breach of the Rules, the more likely will be a finding of a violation of one of these human rights. Treaty bodies now routinely invoke the Standard Minimum Rules in finding prison conditions to violate these rights.[37]

With regard to the second issue, the nature of the punishment, it will be recalled that the UNCAT definition of torture excludes 'lawful sanctions'. Does that mean that the prohibition of cruel, inhuman, and degrading *punishment* can only apply either to oppressive prison conditions or punishment inflicted extrajudicially, for example by the police? The answer has to be negative. There is extensive treaty body authority finding various forms of corporal punishment to violate the prohibition. The first was the 1978 *Tyrer* case in which the European Court of Human Rights found the infliction of a judicially ordered three strokes of the birch on a young person to be a degrading punishment violating Article 3 ECHR.[38] More recently, the Inter-American Court of Human Rights found the lashing of a naked adult strapped to a metal contraption, until he fainted, to be torture in violation of Article 5 ACHR.[39] The Human Rights Committee has long been clear in its rejection of corporal punishment as a violation of Article 7 ICCPR.[40] Similarly, the Human Rights Council has reminded governments that 'corporal punishment can amount to cruel, inhuman or degrading punishment or even to torture'.[41] This begs the question of the exclusion of lawful sanctions from the definition of torture. The proper understanding is that the exclusion refers to those sanctions that are lawful under both national *and* international law. Since it is widely accepted that corporal punishment at least amounts to cruel, inhuman, or degrading punishment, it does not qualify as a 'lawful sanction' and, accordingly, is not immunized against being categorized as torture.

2.4 TYPES OF OBLIGATION

The prohibition of torture is in formal terms primarily a negative obligation. The state is required to refrain from engaging in the practices concerned, either directly through its agents' acts or indirectly by its agents' omissions when there is a duty to act. However, the latter dimension already can be understood as an embryonic positive obligation. It arises to avoid the circumvention of the rule by simply blaming the acts on others (paramilitary groups, 'death squads', vigilantes, and so on), in circumstances in which the acts may well have been committed with 'a nod and a wink' from state authorities. Because such collusion is hard to prove, other positive obligations have been developed.

Thus, it is generally accepted that where there are grounds for believing that torture has taken place, there is an obligation on the state to initiate an effective investigation into the situation, typical elements of which are reflected in the Istanbul Principles. Moreover, not only should such an investigation be capable of sustaining a prosecution of those found to be responsible, there seems to be an obligation to initiate such prosecutions when the

---

[37] Eg *Mukong v Cameroon*, CCPR/C/51/D/458/1991 (10 August 1994); *Greek Case*, n 14; *Dickson v UK* (2008) 46 EHRR 41, para 30 (note the Court relied more heavily, as it generally does, on the European Prison Rules; see paras 31–6); *Raxcacó-Reyes v Guatemala*, IACtHR Series C No 133 (15 September 2005) paras 99–102.
[38] *Tyrer v UK* (1978) 2 EHRR 1.   [39] *Caesar*, n 9, paras 49(27) and (28).
[40] General Comment 20, n 1.   [41] Human Rights Council Res 8/8 (18 June 2008) para 7(a).

facts permit. Indeed, it is this very obligation that is increasingly seen as the basis for the impermissibility of granting amnesties to persons responsible for torture (and probably other ill-treatment).[42] The obligation to prosecute is reinforced by Article 7 UNCAT, which requires states parties to submit for prosecution the case of anyone in their jurisdiction against whom there is sufficient evidence of having committed torture, regardless of the jurisdiction in which the torture was committed and the nationality of the perpetrator (a form of universal jurisdiction). This applies unless the person is extradited to another state wishing to exercise jurisdiction. It was on this basis that in 1999 the UK House of Lords upheld the detention order made by a magistrate against former Chilean President Augusto Pinochet Ugarte, pending processing of an extradition request from Spain.[43] Similarly, the International Court of Justice found Senegal in breach of Article 7 UNCAT for failure either to prosecute or extradite former Chadian President Hissène Habré.[44] A further arguably positive obligation is to refrain from exposing a person to torture or ill-treatment by sending that person to a country where he or she faces a real risk of treatment in violation of the prohibition (*non-refoulement*). Interestingly, the case law began in cases involving the death penalty.[45] It was consolidated in the 1996 *Chahal v UK* case in which a Sikh former torture victim from India could not, according to the European Court of Human Rights, be returned to India even on national security grounds.[46] Requested by the UK to revisit the issue, especially in relation to terrorism cases, the Court in the 2008 case of *Saadi v Italy* resoundingly and unanimously reaffirmed its position.[47] This dimension of the prohibition is codified for states parties to UNCAT in its Article 3. It is to be noted that this provision applies to torture, but not expressly to other cruel, inhuman, or degrading treatment or punishment.

What the limits of positive obligations are is unclear. In principle, the question to be asked is: how far are the acts in question attributable to the state? But, once acts of omission rather than commission are in question and once we envisage an obligation to prevent torture and ill-treatment, the harder it becomes to identify the borderlines of responsibility. As is reflected in the practice of the Human Rights Committee, the obligations may extend to action to prevent such phenomena as human trafficking and domestic violence.[48] It is not controversial that such obligations are ones of means, not of result, often known as 'due diligence'.[49] What means may be appropriate in any given situation, or what diligence is due, may well be far from evident. One factor that may be relevant in making any assessment is the extent to which the state may be said to have an interest in the perpetration or continuation of the harm suffered by the victims. The less the interest, the higher may be the threshold to attribute responsibility to the state.

2.5 RELATIONSHIP WITH OTHER HUMAN RIGHTS

There are various connections between the prohibition of torture and ill-treatment and other human rights. For example, one of the rules for a fair trial is that one may not be compelled to testify against oneself. Clearly, testimony coerced by prohibited ill-treatment would fall foul of that prohibition.[50] As already seen, rules relating to the right to liberty

---

[42] Eg HRC, General Comment 31, HRI/GEN/1/Rev.9 (Vol I) 243, para 18.

[43] *Pinochet (No 3)*, n 9. See UNCAT, Arts 5–8.

[44] ICJ, *Questions relating to the Obligation to Prosecute or Extradite*, n 9.

[45] *Amekrane v UK* (1973) 16 YB 356; *Soering v UK* (1989) 11 EHRR 439; *Ng v Canada*, CCPR/C/49/D/469/1991 (7 January 1994). See also HRC, General Comment 31, n 42, para 12.   [46] n 7.

[47] n 7.   [48] Eg HRC, General Comment 28, HRI/GEN/1/Rev.9 (Vol I) 228, paras 11–12.

[49] Eg *Velásquez-Rodríguez v Honduras*, IACtHR Series C No 4 (29 July 1988) para 172. See also Chapter 5.

[50] See Chapter 13.

provide an essential guarantee against prohibited ill-treatment. Moreover, some forms of arbitrary detention such as prolonged detention may amount to a violation of the prohibition of ill-treatment. This will be especially true in respect of the most extreme form of detention, namely enforced disappearance. In that case, among other rights, the right to life may also be engaged, as it evidently is when death occurs under torture.

3   THE RIGHT TO LIFE

The right to life is dealt with very early and summarily in the UDHR. According to Article 3, '[e]veryone has the right to life, liberty and security of person'. There is no further reference to the right to life in the UDHR. This nevertheless leaves it as the first substantive right, after the Article 2 affirmation of the principle of non-discrimination. It was not further developed partly because of a lack of consensus as to what issues it covers, notably the death penalty.

The right to life has been considered the 'supreme human right'[51] and 'the fountain from which all human rights spring'.[52] On the other hand, treaty provisions giving effect to it are not couched in the same absolute language as those prohibiting torture. Typically, they will insist that 'no-one shall be arbitrarily deprived' of life. Indeed, it is not hard to think of circumstances in which states may be expected to sanction the taking of life. Warfare is the most obvious example and killings committed lawfully under international humanitarian law will not in principle be considered as violating the right to life. The forces of law may also sometimes be required to take life, notably to protect the lives of others. And, of course, for centuries the death penalty, though now on the retreat, figured in most national legislation.

These considerations make the right to life a more complex concept than the prohibition of torture and ill-treatment. This in turn may help to explain why the right as a whole has not been the object of the same sustained campaigning and attention as that prohibition. Rather, work has focused on particular aspects, with the major emphasis being on the death penalty, as reflected in abolitionist protocols to general human rights treaties. Some 'soft law' instruments have been adopted, notably in relation to deprivation of life in law enforcement situations. Moreover, the second earliest thematic mechanism created by the UN Commission on Human Rights in 1982 was the mandate of Special Rapporteur on extrajudicial, summary, and arbitrary executions.

In practice, most of the case law concerns the central issues of deprivation of life by state authorities, either by the maintenance of law and public order or by recourse to the death penalty. This will, accordingly, be the principal focus of this section.

3.1   SOURCES

Article 6 ICCPR, Article 4 ACHR, and Article 4 ACHPR all guarantee the right not to be 'arbitrarily deprived of life'.[53] In contrast, Article 2 ECHR prohibits any intentional deprivation of life except for certain, listed purposes. In the practice of other treaty bodies, those

---

[51]   HRC, General Comment 6, HRI/GEN/1/Rev.9 (Vol I) 176, para 1.

[52]   Report of the UN Special Rapporteur on summary and arbitrary executions, E/CN.4/1983/16 (31 January 1983) para 22.

[53]   ACHPR, Art 4 reads: 'Human beings are inviolable. Every human being is entitled to respect for his life and the integrity of his person. No one may be arbitrarily deprived of this right.'

purposes would take the killing out of the designation of 'arbitrary'. All these articles make, in various ways, provision for the death penalty. The ICCPR-OP2, the Sixth and Thirteenth Protocols to the ECHR, and the Second Protocol to the ACHR all contemplate abolition of the death penalty. The main 'soft law' sources protecting the right to life are the UN Basic Principles on the Use of Force and Firearms by Law Enforcement Officials (1990), the UN Principles on the Effective Prevention and Investigation of Extra-legal, Arbitrary and Summary Executions (1989), and the UN Economic and Social Council's Safeguards guaranteeing protection of the rights of those facing the death penalty (ECOSOC Safeguards) (1984).

3.2 LEGAL STATUS

There can be little doubt that the right to life is a rule of customary international law, even if it has not received the same legislative attention, for example by way of treaty-making, as the prohibition of torture. This is even suggested in the specific wording of the language of Article 6(1) ICCPR, which speaks of the 'inherent right to life'. Less certain is whether it is a rule of *jus cogens*. It has not had the same degree of case law so asserting as the prohibition of torture, but then the occasion has not arisen. It is true that the core content of the rule has not been defined with the same precision. Nevertheless, because of its importance, it is non-derogable in those treaties that contemplate derogations.[54] Murder, in the context of a widespread or systematic attack against a civilian population, is a crime against humanity and, together with wilful killing, a war crime. The prohibition of murder is treated as a *jus cogens* rule in the American Law Institute's Restatement of US Foreign Relations Law.[55] It cannot seriously be contested that this core content of the right is *jus cogens*, and the same must apply to the prohibition of the death penalty without basic fair trial standards; so, the prohibition of unnecessary and disproportionate killings deserves to fall into the same category.

3.3 SCOPE: BEGINNING AND END OF LIFE

When does life begin? If, as according to Article 4 ACHR, life is protected 'in general, from the moment of conception' then state-tolerated abortion could be held to violate the right. In practice, only one case is believed to have dealt with the merits of the issue so far, and no violation was found. This was despite the fact that the Inter-American Commission on Human Rights had recourse to, though was not applying, the ACHR.[56]

Euthanasia and assisted suicide, both illegal in many states, but permitted in some, also raise questions. On the one hand, a genuine right (to life) cannot comfortably be considered to be not only an entitlement but also an obligation imposed on the right-holder. However, this did not deter the European Court of Human Rights from insisting that Article 2 ECHR does not comprehend a right to die.[57] Yet there is an issue of human dignity and possibly degrading treatment if one is denied the option of a longed-for death just because one is no longer physically capable of killing oneself. It is troubling that the European Court has refused to accept that denial of the right to needed assistance to

---

[54] ICCPR, Art 4; ECHR, Art 15; ACHR, Art 27.   [55] n 10.

[56] Case 2141, *Baby Boy Case* (USA), IACommHR Res 23/81 (6 March 1981). See also *KL v Peru*, CCPR/ C/85/D/1153/2003 (22 November 2005) para 6.3 (distress caused by refusal of medical authorities to carry out an apparently legal therapeutic abortion violates Art 7 ICCPR).

[57] *Pretty v UK* (2002) 35 EHRR 1, paras 39–41.

commit suicide infringes Article 3.[58] On the other hand, the vulnerability of many people to improper influence means that the law should be very careful to contemplate any intentional third-party involvement in a deprivation of life.

3.4 COMPONENTS

3.4.1 Protection against killings by security forces

Different bodies use different terms to describe unlawful killings by agents of public authority: 'extra-legal' or 'extrajudicial' 'killings' or 'executions'. Regardless of terminology, wherever there is intentional resort to outright killings of those considered undesirable, be they street children, political opponents, or suspected organized criminals, this is clearly murder by any definition and is at the core of the prohibition of arbitrary deprivation of life.

The central question is: what other killings fall into this category? Here, guidance may be sought from the deprivations of life not regarded as contravening Article 2 ECHR, which include those resulting 'from the use of force which is no more than absolutely necessary: (a) in defence of any person from unlawful violence; (b) in order to effect a lawful arrest or to prevent the escape of a person lawfully detained; (c) in action lawfully taken for the purpose of quelling a riot or insurrection.'

It is generally accepted that law enforcement measures must conform to the principles of necessity and proportionality. The Article 2 ECHR limitation of force to the minimum necessary clearly meets the *necessity* principle, requiring that the means used is no more than necessary to achieve the objective. Less reassuringly, the text of Article 2 does not guarantee the test of *proportionality*; it does not explicitly require the level of force to be no more than the harm to be avoided. Clearly, the use of lethal force could be the only way to stop a pub brawl, or to prevent the escape of someone imprisoned for contempt of court, but it would evidently be disproportionate.

The UN Basic Principles on the Use of Force and Firearms come to our assistance here. Principle 9 reads:

> Law enforcement officials shall not use firearms against persons except in self-defence or defence of others against the imminent threat of death or serious injury, to prevent the perpetration of a particularly serious crime involving grave threat to life, to arrest a person presenting such a danger and resisting their authority, or to prevent his or her escape, and only when less extreme means are insufficient to achieve these objectives. In any event the intentional lethal use of firearms may only be made when strictly unavoidable in order to protect life.

It is clear from this text that the principle of proportionality is strictly drawn. Not only may *potentially* lethal force be used solely to protect life and limb from *imminent* threat, but *intentional* lethal force may only be used to protect life. Principles 14 and 16 reaffirm this standard in respect of dispersal of unlawful, violent assemblies, and avoidance of escape from custody, respectively.

The practice of treaty bodies is consistent with the Principles. An early example of the principle of necessity is found in the Human Rights Committee case of *Guerrero v*

---

[58] *Pretty v UK* (2002) 35 EHRR 1, paras 54–6. Compare the more nuanced approach in the HRC, Concluding Observations: the Netherlands, CCPR/CO/72/NET (27 August 2001) para 5; CCPR/C/NLD/CO/4 (11 August 2009) para 7.

Colombia, where the state was found to have violated Article 6 ICCPR as the police had waited in a location inhabited by suspected terrorists and, on their arrival, shot them without making any attempt to arrest them.[59] An even more stringent application of the principle is found in the case of *McCann and others v UK* before the European Court of Human Rights. British security personnel summarily killed IRA members avowedly on 'mission' to detonate a bomb in a crowded place in Gibraltar. The security personnel had been briefed to believe that the victims were armed, that there was a bomb in their car, and that they could detonate it from a remote control device on their person. In fact it turned out that they were not armed, there was no bomb in the car, nor did they have a detonator. The Court found that the UK had violated Article 2 ECHR by failing to take various planning measures that could have avoided the fatal outcome.[60]

The clearest example of the proportionality principle is found in the case of *Nachova and others v Bulgaria*. Invoking the UN Basic Principles, the European Court found that 'recourse to potentially deadly force cannot be considered as "absolutely necessary" where it is known that the person to be arrested poses no threat to life or limb and is not suspected of having committed a violent offence'.[61] Here the Court is evidently using the language of necessity in Article 2 to embrace proportionality. In the case of *Detention Centre of Catia*, in which Venezuelan prison guards fired indiscriminately into prisoners they suspected of being involved in an escape, the Inter-American Court of Human Rights applied the principles of necessity and proportionality, finding that 'the actions of the security forces...were neither proportionate to the existing threat or danger, nor strictly necessary to keep the peace and order in the Detention Centre of Catia'.[62]

3.4.2 Protection against the death penalty

Inconsistent as it may seem, while international law apparently rules out corporal punishment as a cruel, inhuman, or degrading punishment—or even torture—it has not yet done so in respect of the death penalty. While the framers of the UDHR may have contemplated that at some time international law would reach that point, it had not then and still has not. This is because international law is not a system that operates by majority rule. State practice is a key element and as long as a substantial minority of states maintain the death penalty—especially states as influential as China, India, and the USA—international law will have to reflect that reality.

All the human rights treaty norms guaranteeing the right to life, except Article 4 ACHPR, contemplate the possibility of the death penalty. Since any treaty provision has to be interpreted in the context of the treaty as a whole, this means that it is not possible to interpret the provisions on treatment of prisoners without reference to those on the right to life. The Human Rights Committee has indeed made the point that, but for the death penalty provisions of Article 6 ICCPR, it would find the death penalty to violate Article 7.[63]

Nevertheless, the last quarter of the twentieth century witnessed a trend towards abolition that is steady and sustained. The fact that the community of states was willing to adopt abolitionist protocols to human rights treaties makes it increasingly difficult for abolitionist states to deny that the death penalty is a human rights issue. Promoting ratification of the protocols has also become a focus of abolitionist campaigning activities.

---

[59] CCPR/C/15/D/45/1979 (31 March 1982). For reckless lethal attacks on premises violating the right to life, see *Gül v Turkey* (2002) 34 EHRR 435, paras 79–83; *Zambrano Vélez and others v Ecuador*, IACtHR Series C No 166 (4 July 2007) para 108.

[60] (1996) 21 EHRR 97.   [61] (2006) 42 EHRR 43, paras 71–4, 96, 107.

[62] *Montero-Aranguren and others (Detention Centre of Catia) v Venezuela*, IACtHR Series C No 150 (5 July 2006) paras 69–74.   [63] *Ng v Canada*, n 45, para 16.2.

Even before the adoption of the ICCPR-OP2, the Human Rights Committee had felt that the actual language of Article 6 preserving the death penalty permitted it to conclude that 'all measures of abolition should be considered as progress in the enjoyment of the right to life'.[64] Meanwhile, at the political level, the UN General Assembly long ago accepted that the objective should be 'progressive restriction' of the number of offences to which the punishment applies 'with a view to the desirability of abolishing this punishment in all countries'.[65] It has, more recently, called on states that retain the death penalty to adopt moratoria on its use.[66]

As to the abolitionist protocols themselves, all but one envisage commitments that permit states to carve out an exception for wartime situations (few have done so in fact). The exception is Protocol 13 to the ECHR, adopted precisely to fill this gap left by Protocol 6. It is worth noting that, insofar as a commitment to adherence at least to Protocol 6 is a condition of membership of the Council of Europe, the 47-country area of Europe, from the Atlantic to the Urals, is now effectively a death-penalty-free zone.[67]

If the death penalty as such remains a permissible exception to the right to life, it is clear that states do not have a free hand to resort to it at will. There is a range of far-reaching substantive, procedural, and personal limitations that have to be respected.

Substantive limitations

The most important substantive limitation is that of Article 6(2) ICCPR and Article 4(2) ACHR, requiring that imposition of the death penalty be limited to 'the most serious crimes'. The prohibition of arbitrary deprivation of the right to life of Article 4 ACHPR may be expected to be understood at least as strictly as the ICCPR and ACHR provisions. The first paragraph of the ECOSOC Safeguards endorses the notion of 'the most serious crimes'. Underlying these words is an implicit invocation of the principle of proportionality. The death penalty should not be disproportionate to the offence for which it is applicable.

The treaty provisions offer no definition of what elements would place a crime among the most serious. The ECOSOC Safeguards are helpful here. For them, the scope of the term 'should not go beyond intentional crimes with lethal or other extremely grave consequences'.[68] The Human Rights Committee has found a mandatory death penalty for armed robbery where death did *not* result to contravene Article 6(2) ICCPR.[69] It has subsequently also found the mandatory death penalty, even in murder cases, to violate Article 6(1).[70] It is not clear whether it does so by virtue of its not being covered by Article 6(2) because of its non-serious nature. The latter is the position taken by the Inter-American Court of Human Rights.[71] This would mean that not even all murders would be sufficiently serious to fall within the category. It is worth noting that the same court also found the 'simple

---

[64] HRC, General Comment 6, n 51, para 6.   [65] GA Res 2857 (XXVI) (20 December 1971).

[66] GA Res 62/149 (18 December 2007) and 63/168 (18 December 2008).

[67] The Russian Federation, despite its commitment, has not yet ratified Protocol 6 but has implemented a formal moratorium. On 2 March 2010, the European Court of Human Rights concluded that the death penalty is no longer permitted, even under Article 2 ECHR. *Al-Saadoon and Mufdhi v UK* (2010) 51 EHRR 9.

[68] Para 1.   [69] *Lubuto v Zambia*, CCPR/C/55/D/390/1990/Rev.1 (30 June 1994) para 7.2.

[70] *Thompson v St Vincent and the Grenadines*, CCPR/C/70/D/806/1998 (18 October 2000) para 8.2.

[71] *Hilaire, Constantine and Benjamin et al. v Trinidad and Tobago*, IACtHR Series C No 94 (21 June 2002) paras 106–7. According to Christof Heyns, the UN Special Rapporteur on extrajudicial, summary and arbitrary executions, 'intentional killing' is a condition for the applicability of the death penalty. Report of the Special Rapporteur on extrajudicial, summary or arbitrary executions, A/67/275 (9 August 2012), para 67.

crime of kidnapping' to fall outside the notion of 'most serious' and so a death penalty imposed for it violated Article 4 ACHR.[72]

Further substantive limitations following from Articles 6(2) and 15 ICCPR are that both the crime and the prescribed punishment must be non-retroactive, that is, provided by law at the time of the commission of the acts in question. In addition, under Article 4(2) ACHR, the death penalty may not be extended to crimes to which it does not 'presently' apply, while Article 4(3) ACHR prohibits reintroduction in states that have abolished it. It is also possible to interpret Article 6(2) ICCPR in the same way. Since it refers to 'countries which have not abolished the death penalty', it may be logical to infer that the possibility is not available to countries that *have* abolished the penalty.[73] Article 4(4) ACHR also prohibits the use of the death penalty for 'political offenses or related common crimes'.

Procedural limitations

The main procedural limitation is that the death penalty may only be imposed after a fair trial, as provided for under Article 14 ICCPR, including a right of appeal. While this is not stated in Article 6 ICCPR directly, Article 6(2) provides that the death penalty must not be contrary to the provisions of the Covenant. The General Assembly has called on all states to respect 'as a minimum' Articles 6, 14, and 15.[74] The Human Rights Committee has made clear its view that this means that, not only is Article 6 non-derogable, but so is Article 14 when it comes to the application of the death penalty.[75]

A few of the many examples of findings of a violation of Article 6 because of a violation of Article 14 in death penalty cases are: a trial in absentia ending in a death sentence in the absence of any effective attempt to notify the person accused;[76] a murder trial after the accused had pleaded guilty to manslaughter in a case involving the same incident;[77] and deficient or non-existent legal representation.[78] The right of a foreign national to consular assistance may also fall within Article 14. This was the opinion of the Inter-American Court of Human Rights applying the comparable Article 4 ACHR and also referring to Article 14 ICCPR.[79]

Remarkably, despite the absence of a verbal linkage in the ECHR and the ACHPR, the European Court of Human Rights and the African Commission on Human and Peoples' Rights have read the respective fair trial provisions together with the right to life provisions. So, in the case of Abdullah Öcalan, the leader of the Turkish PKK movement, the European Court held that implementation of the death penalty would be impermissible under Article 2 ECHR as he had not received a fair trial according to Article 6: Öcalan had been held in incommunicado detention for ten days, then allowed only two one-hour supervised meetings per week with his lawyers before his trial, which took place in a special

---

[72] *Raxcacó-Reyes*, n 37, paras 67–72.

[73] See also *Judge v Canada*, CCPR/C/78/D/829/1998 (20 October 2003) para 6.1 (holding that an abolitionist state that sends someone to another country to face the death penalty cannot benefit from the exception of Art 6(2) ICCPR for states that have not abolished the death penalty and so violates Art 6(1)).

[74] GA Res 35/172 (15 December 1980); this was the first of several resolutions to the same effect.

[75] HRC, General Comment 29, n 9, para 15.

[76] *Mbenge et al. v Zaire*, CCPR/C/18/D/16/1977 (25 March 1983) paras 14(1)–(2) and 17.

[77] *Richards v Jamaica*, CCPR/C/59/D/535/1993/Rev.1 (29 April 1997) paras 7.2 and 7.5.

[78] Eg *LaVende v Trinidad and Tobago*, CCPR/C/61/D/554/1993 (17 November 1997) para 5.8; *Aliev v Ukraine*, CCPR/C/78/D/781/1997 (7 August 2003) para 7.3; *Saidova v Tajikistan*, CCPR/C/81/D/964/2001 (8 July 2004) para 68; *Aliboeva v Tajikistan*, CCPR/C/85/D/985/2001 (18 October 2005) para 6.4.

[79] Advisory Opinion OC-16/99, *The Right to Information on Consular Assistance in the Framework of Guarantees of the Due Process of Law*, IACtHR Series A No 16 (1 October 1999) paras 68–87.

security court that initially included a military judge.[80] Similarly, the African Commission found a violation of Article 4 ACHPR in respect of the execution of celebrated playwright Ken Saro-Wiwa after a summary trial for murder by a special court whose members were chosen by the executive and without right of appeal that involved multiple violations of the fair trial guarantee of Article 7.[81]

The right of appeal is explicitly guaranteed by Article 14(5) ICCPR, so its denial in death penalty cases is a violation not only of that provision but also of Article 6.[82] The ECOSOC Safeguards contain the same guarantee.[83] The right has to be effective, so both the trial court and an appeal court must provide a written judgment where that is a condition for further appeal.[84] In addition, Article 6(4) ICCPR and Article 4(6) ACHR require the possibility of submitting a clemency petition. The Human Rights Committee has found violations in cases where executions took place while appellate or clemency procedures were underway.[85]

A further procedural dimension is that the process in which the death penalty is carried out must cause the minimum possible suffering if it is not to violate the prohibition of ill-treatment. Thus, the Human Rights Committee held that execution by gas asphyxiation was incompatible with Article 7 ICCPR.[86] The method of execution is not the only relevant factor. The leading European Court of Human Rights case, *Soering v UK*, found that sending a young German man to face death row conditions in Virginia for six to eight years, when he could be tried in (abolitionist) Germany, would violate Article 3 ECHR.[87] Finally, where the death penalty is shrouded in secrecy, close family members of the executed person can be victims of inhuman treatment. This has been the case with the practice that was common in the former Soviet Union of treating the date of execution and place of burial as a state secret, thus causing an unacceptable 'state of uncertainty and mental distress' to family members.[88]

Personal limitations

The main personal limitation on the application of the death penalty is that, under Article 6(5) ICCPR, Article 4(5) ACHR, and Article 37 Convention on the Rights of the Child, it may not be imposed on persons under 18. The Human Rights Committee has found the very imposition of a death sentence on a person under 18 at the time of the offence to violate the ICCPR, despite later commutation of the sentence.[89]

According to Article 6(5) ICCPR, Article 4(5) ACHR, and paragraph 3 ECOSOC Safeguards, the death penalty may also not be carried out on pregnant women and, according to the ECOSOC Safeguards, recent mothers. The ECOSOC Safeguards also immunize 'persons who have become insane', and the Human Rights Committee has decided that the reading of a death warrant for the execution of a mentally incompetent person was a violation of Article 7 ICCPR.[90] Under Article 4(5) ACHR, states parties may not execute persons over 70 at the time of the offence.

---

[80] *Öcalan v Turkey* (2005) 41 EHRR 985, para 166.
[81] *International Pen et al. v Nigeria*, Communication nos 137/94, 154/96, and 161/97.
[82] *Mansaraj et al. v Sierra Leone*, CCPR/C/72/D/841/1998 (16 July 2001) paras 5.6 and 6.2.   [83] Para 6.
[84] *Pratt and Morgan v Jamaica*, CCPR/C/35/D/210/1986 (6 April 1989) paras 13.5, 14(b).
[85] *Ashby v Trinidad and Tobago*, CCPR/C/74/D/580/1994 (19 April 2002) para 10.8; *Chikunova v Uzbekistan*, CCPR/C/89/D/1043/2002 (16 March 2007) para 7.6.   [86] *Ng v Canada*, n 45, para 16.4.
[87] n 45, paras 106–11.   [88] *Lyashkevich v Belarus*, CCPR/C/77/D/887/1999 (24 April 2003) para 9.2.
[89] *Johnson, Clive v Jamaica*, CCPR/C/64/D/592/1994 (25 November 1998) para 10.3.
[90] *RS v Trinidad and Tobago*, CCPR/C/74/D/684/1996 (2 April 2002) para 7.2.

3.5 TYPES OF OBLIGATION

As with the prohibition of torture and ill-treatment, the right not to be arbitrarily deprived of life is primarily a negative obligation. To the extent that there is no treaty obligation prohibiting the use of the death penalty, states are simply obliged to refrain from having recourse to it when not respecting the legal limitations that apply to it. Other deprivations of life involving the intentional killing of people by public authorities are to be avoided, if they do not meet the criteria of necessity or proportionality already considered here.

It is notable that three of the provisions guaranteeing the right to life (Article 6(1) ICCPR, Article 2(1) ECHR, and Article 4(1) ACHR) stipulate that the right 'shall be protected by law'. Such language has the connotation of positive obligation. It clearly lends itself to an interpretation, confirmed by practice, that states must investigate apparent unlawful killings. This is the thrust of the UN Principles on the Effective Prevention and Investigation of Extra-legal, Arbitrary and Summary Executions.

Thus, there have been numerous findings of state violations of the right to life because of the absence of an effective investigation, even when the killing could not be found on the evidence to be firmly attributable to the state. The European Court of Human Rights has found violations where the state was unable to show serious activity by investigating prosecutors,[91] or where the prosecutors confined themselves to interviewing the relevant security units involved without interviewing relevant non-official witnesses,[92] or where they made no effort to identify the unit responsible.[93] The UK coroners' inquest system was also found wanting in a series of Northern Ireland cases in which there was an alleged 'shoot-to-kill' policy by the security forces. This was because the inquiry could not compel the presence of police and other security force witnesses, could not make a finding of 'unlawful killing', and was neither prompt nor expeditious.[94]

In the case of *Amirov v Russian Federation*, the Human Rights Committee found a failure of effective investigation and so a violation of Article 6 ICCPR, where prosecutors opened and closed the investigation into the rape and murder of a woman in the Chechen Republic, numerous times, but without securing the testimony of federal agents who had seen the body at the time it was found.[95] The UN Principles and findings by treaty bodies are clear in understanding that there is an obligation on states to prosecute when an investigation determines that individuals are responsible for an unlawful killing. For example, the failure to do this was part of the violation in *Amirov*.[96]

As with the prohibition of ill-treatment, exposing someone to the threat of a violation of the right to life is itself a violation of the prohibition or ill-treatment, as well as presumably of the right to life. The cases of *Soering* and *Ng* already discussed are the leading cases on the matter.[97]

There is also an evident obligation to protect people from death from third parties. But, as with the prohibition of torture, it is an obligation of means, not of result. The question will always be: did the state exercise 'due diligence' when apprised of circumstances that may have suggested that a person's life required protection? While finally not finding a violation, the European Court of Human Rights essentially followed this approach in respect of a schoolmaster who stalked a former student and then killed her. The Court

---

[91] *Kaya v Turkey* (1999) 28 EHRR 1, paras 86–92.

[92] *Musayeva and others v Russia* (2008) 47 EHRR 25, para 162.

[93] *Khashiyev and Akayeva v Russia* (2006) 42 EHRR 20, para 158.

[94] *Jordan v UK* (2003) 37 EHRR 2, para 142; *Kelly and others v UK*, App no 30054/96, Judgment of 4 May 2001, para 136; *McKerr v UK* (2002) 34 EHRR 20, para 157; *Shanagan v UK*, App no 37715/97, Judgment of 4 May 2001, para 122.   [95] CCPR/C/95/D/1447/2006 (2 April 2009) para 11.4.

[96] CCPR/C/95/D/1447/2006 (2 April 2009) para 11.4.   [97] n 45.

held that the stalking itself did not suggest likely lethal consequences, but it was clear that if there had been evidence of impending harm, the state would have violated Article 2 ECHR.[98] Also, if it is difficult to justify rules permitting euthanasia and assisted suicide, it is because of the positive obligation on states to protect life and the need to avoid people being improperly influenced to seek or accept aid in terminating their lives.

3.6 RELATIONSHIP WITH OTHER HUMAN RIGHTS

The links with the prohibition of torture and ill-treatment have already been discussed. An additional dimension here is the need even for the death penalty to avoid unnecessary suffering. The connection with the right to a fair trial is of central importance as regards the lawfulness (or otherwise) of the death penalty.

There is also a connection with the notion of security of person, as suggested by Article 3 UDHR. Although the European Court of Human Rights has not been willing to give content to the idea outside the context of deprivation of liberty, the Human Rights Committee has done so. For example, failure to give adequate protection to a person receiving death threats has been found to violate the Article 9 ICCPR guarantee of security of person.[99] To the uncertain extent that the right to life may be engaged in situations of economic and social deprivation, there is a connection with the corresponding economic and social rights.

4 CONCLUSION

The prohibition of torture and ill-treatment and the right to life are both situated by the language of the International Bill of Human Rights and other international instruments as directly based on the concept of human dignity, which inspires the whole corpus of human rights law, and as at the core of the right to personal integrity.

The understanding of the scope of the prohibition of torture and ill-treatment is capable of much elasticity and was indeed drafted in language intended to avoid rigid definitions of what might technically be called torture. Nevertheless, in the light of sustained attention to the problem of torture, notably of people deprived of liberty, there has been a focus on definitions of that concept, the UNCAT definition being the most influential. On the key issue of what the borderline may be between torture and other ill-treatment, this definition seems to avoid the approach of the European Court of Human Rights, according to which torture is seen as requiring even greater pain or suffering than that already required for the treatment to be considered inhuman. Rather, it is the purpose of the treatment (for example, obtaining information or confessions) that marks the treatment out as being torture or not. Also, the mental form of torture as exemplified by the Orwellian rats should not be downplayed. While a few states retain corporal punishment in their legislation and apply it in practice, the consistent view of human rights bodies has been to find such punishment to be cruel, inhuman, or degrading. Indeed, the Inter-American Court of Human Rights has found a manifestation of it to be torture.

As to the right to life, the aspects that have received most attention have been those relating to the limits on lethal force that can be used in the maintenance of law and public

---

[98] *Osman v UK* (1998) 29 EHRR 245, paras 121–2.
[99] Compare *Delgado Páez v Colombia*, CCPR/C/39/D/195/1985 (12 July 1990) paras 5.5, 5.6, 6 with *Bozano v France* (1987) 9 EHRR 297, para 53.

order and to the applicability of the death penalty. In the absence of authoritative defini-tions in treaties, international 'soft law' standards and the practice of human rights bodies have provided the principal guidance, especially in the area of recourse to lethal force. The crucial tests of whether a particular use of such force is lawful are those of necessity and proportionality. That is, the force must not only be the least harmful necessary to achieve a legitimate law enforcement objective, it must furthermore not exceed the harm to be avoided by its use. The right to life does not as yet rule out recourse to the death penalty. However, many states are parties to protocols to human rights treaties that prohibit the death penalty. The other states are bound to respect a number of substantive limitations (notably, the death penalty must be used only for the most serious crimes), procedural limitations (notably, the rules concerning the rights to a fair trial, to appeal, and to seek clemency), and personal limitations (notably, the lower age limit of 18).

There is no serious doubting that the prohibition of torture is a rule of *jus cogens*. There is persuasive authority suggesting this also applies to other prohibited ill-treatment. While there is not as much explicit evidence in respect of the right to life (apart from with regard to outright official murder), the better view is that its status as 'the supreme human right' that, like the prohibition of torture and ill-treatment, is non-derogable must put it on a par with that prohibition.

FURTHER READING

EVANS, 'Getting to Grips with Torture' (2002) 51 *ICLQ* 365.

EVANS and MORGAN, *Preventing Torture: A Study of the European Convention for the Prevention of Torture and Inhuman or Degrading Treatment or Punishment* (Oxford University Press, 1998).

GINBAR, *Why Not Torture Terrorists? Moral, Practical, and Legal Aspects of the 'Ticking Bomb' Justification for Torture* (Oxford University Press, 2008).

HOOD and HOYLE, *The Death Penalty: A Worldwide Perspective* (Oxford University Press, 2008).

INGELSE, *The UN Committee against Torture: An Assessment* (Kluwer Academic Publishers, 2001).

KRETZMER, 'Targeted Killing of Suspected Terrorists: Extra-Judicial Executions or Legitimate Means of Defence?' (2005) 16 *EJIL* 171.

MELZER, *Targeted Killing in International Law* (Oxford University Press, 2008).

NOWAK, 'What Practices Constitute Torture?: US and UN Standards' (2006) 28 *HRQ* 809.

NOWAK and MCARTHUR, *The United Nations Convention against Torture: A Commentary* (Oxford University Press, 2008).

RODLEY, 'The Prohibition of Torture: Absolute Means Absolute' (2006) 34 *Denv J Int'l L & Pol'y* 145.

RODLEY and POLLARD, *The Treatment of Prisoners under International Law* (Oxford University Press, 2009).

SCHABAS, *The Abolition of the Death Penalty in International Law* (Cambridge University Press, 2002).

SCHACHTER, 'Human Dignity as a Normative Concept' (1983) 77 *AJIL* 848.

WALDRON, 'Is Dignity the Foundation of Human Rights?', NYU School of Law, Public Law Research Paper No 12-73 (3 January 2013), available at SSRN: <http://papers.ssrn.com/sol3/papers.cfm?abstract_id=2196074> or <http://dx.doi.org/10.2139/ssrn.2196074>.

WICKS, 'The Meaning of "Life": Dignity and the Right to Life in International Human Rights Treaties' (2012) 12 *HRLR* 199.

USEFUL WEBSITES

Association for the Prevention of Torture: <http://www.apt.ch>

Amnesty International: <http://www.amnesty.org>

European Committee for the Prevention of Torture and Inhuman or Degrading Treatment or Punishment: <http://www.cpt.coe.int/en/>

Hands Off Cain: <http://www.handsoffcain.info>

Human Rights Watch: <http://www.hrw.org>

UN Special Rapporteur on Torture: <http://www2.ohchr.org/english/issues/torture/rapporteur/index.htm>

UN Committee against Torture: <http://www2.ohchr.org/english/bodies/cat/index.htm>

UN Sub-Committee on Prevention of Torture: <http://www2.ohchr.org/english/bodies/cat/opcat/index.htm>

10

ADEQUATE STANDARD OF LIVING

Asbjørn Eide

SUMMARY

This chapter considers the right to an adequate standard of living and its components, namely, the rights to food, housing, and health. These rights are, in whole or in part, contained in principal international and regional human rights instruments, which impose an obligation on states to take a range of measures to ensure everyone can enjoy them. A particular challenge is to ensure the right to an adequate standard of living to those groups of people who have special needs or are particularly vulnerable. The chapter explores the relationship between the right to an adequate standard of living and other human rights and highlights the need for international action in the progressive implementation of the right.

1 INTRODUCTION

The right to an adequate standard of living was first introduced into international human rights law through the Universal Declaration of Human Rights (UDHR), Article 25(1) of which provides:

> Everyone has the right to a standard of living adequate for the health and well-being of himself and his family, including food, clothing, housing and medical care and necessary social services, and the right to security in the event of unemployment, sickness, disability, widowhood, old age or other lack of livelihood in circumstances beyond his control.

Among the main inspirations for this provision was US President Franklin D Roosevelt's 'Four Freedoms' address to Congress in 1941.[1] In that speech, Roosevelt referred to four fundamental human freedoms: freedom of speech, freedom of religion, *freedom from want*, and freedom from fear. The inspirational legacy of that speech is expressly recognized in the preamble to the UDHR:

> Whereas disregard and contempt for human rights have resulted in barbarous acts which have outraged the conscience of mankind, *and the advent of a world in which human beings*

---

[1] On the origin of Roosevelt's concern with freedom from want, see McGovern, *The Third Freedom: Ending Hunger in Our Time* (Simon & Schuster, 2001).

*shall enjoy freedom of speech and belief and freedom from fear and want has been proclaimed
as the highest aspiration of the common people.*[2]

Article 25 UDHR can also be seen as an elaboration of Article 1 UDHR, which states that
'All human beings are born free and equal in dignity and rights. They are endowed with
reason and conscience and should act towards one another in a spirit of brotherhood.'
A life in dignity requires an adequate standard of living. Human rights are based on the
assumption that individuals are not only rational but also have a social conscience, and
are, therefore, concerned with the dignity of their fellow human beings. Such concern has
to be put into practice through appropriate state implementation of human rights as public goods of society as a whole. The right to an adequate standard of living is also closely
linked to Article 22 UDHR, which states that everyone is entitled to the realization of economic, social, and cultural rights indispensable for their dignity and the free development
of their personality, and guarantees a right to social security.

This chapter starts, in Section 2, with an analysis of the meaning and key features of
the right to an adequate standard of living. Section 3 examines the normative content of
this right and its components, namely, the rights to food, housing, and health. The right to
water is a necessary component of each of these rights, and is briefly addressed under the
right to food. Section 4 explores the difficulties and special obligations in ensuring the right
to an adequate standard of living for particular groups of people. Section 5 addresses the
relationship between the right to an adequate standard of living and other human rights.
Section 6 examines the question of progressive implementation of this right. Section 7
addresses the justiciability of the right to an adequate standard of living and the need for
international action in its implementation.

2 MEANING AND FEATURES

Article 25 UDHR has been legally strengthened through subsequent guarantees of an adequate standard of living, including Article 11 of the International Covenant on Economic,
Social and Cultural Rights (ICESCR) and Article 27 of the Convention on the Rights of
the Child (CRC). None of these instruments precisely define the term 'adequate standard
of living', but it can to some extent be understood from the context. Article 25 UDHR
refers to 'a standard of living adequate for the health and well-being of himself and of his
family, including food, clothing, housing and medical care and necessary social services'.
According to Article 11 ICESCR, an adequate standard of living includes 'adequate food,
clothing and housing'. In addition, under Article 12 of the same covenant, states parties
have recognized the right of everyone to the highest attainable standard of health. The
standard of living guaranteed to every child by Article 27 CRC is one that is 'adequate for
the child's physical, mental, spiritual, moral and social development'.

While the basic necessities referred to in these instruments include food, clothing,
housing, and healthcare, an adequate standard of living requires more than simply these.
Precisely how much more is required cannot be stated in general terms, but will depend
on the conditions in the society concerned. The essential point is that everyone should
be able, without shame and without unreasonable obstacles, to be a full participant in
ordinary, everyday interaction with other people. In other words, everyone should be
able to enjoy their basic needs under conditions of dignity. No one should have to live

---

[2] UDHR, second preambular para (emphasis added).

under conditions whereby the only way to satisfy their needs is by degrading or depriving themselves of their basic freedoms, such as through begging, prostitution, or bonded labour. In purely economic terms, an adequate standard of living implies a living above the poverty line of the society concerned, which according to the World Bank comprises two elements:

> The expenditure necessary to buy a minimum standard of nutrition and other basic necessities and a further amount that varies from country to country, reflecting the cost of participating in the everyday life of society.[3]

2.1 DUTIES OF THE INDIVIDUAL

The enjoyment of the right to an adequate standard of living depends on a combination of efforts by every adult individual to take care of her or his own needs and the needs of their children, together with measures taken by the state or public authorities to ensure everyone's enjoyment of that right. The obligations of the state are, therefore, to some extent, subsidiary to the efforts of the individual: *state* obligations come fully into play only when individuals cannot or do not manage by themselves to secure their own or their dependants' standard of living. The obligations of the *international community* are of an even more subsidiary nature, namely to encourage and assist states in implementing their obligations, to criticize them if they fail to do so, to abstain from harmful action that prevents other states from fulfilling their obligations, and to assist those states whose resources are too limited to fulfil their obligations under international human rights law.

Thus, individuals are expected, wherever possible through their own efforts and through the use of their own resources, to find ways to ensure the satisfaction of their needs. Use of one's resources presupposes that the person has resources that can be used—such as land, other capital or assets, and labour. Access to food and housing, for example, depends, first, on the assets held by the individual (ownership of land or capital) or her or his rights to common resources (for example, fishing grounds). Second, it depends on income from work (in the formal or informal sector, whether employed by others or self-employed). Third, it may depend on income in the form of social assistance or social security.

For most children, their standard of living depends primarily on that of their parents. If a child does not have parents or the parents fail to support the child, the state has an obligation to assist or provide. In many societies, women have been dependent on their family, or husband, for their standard of living. This was certainly not always the case—in the past, in many agricultural societies women were the main breadwinner. In modern post-industrial societies, women are now increasingly regaining their economic autonomy and becoming less dependent on the efforts of their husband, although in most societies the standard of living of families still depends on the joint effort of husband and wife. In pre-industrial society, the elderly were to a large extent taken care of by their offspring, just as they had taken care of their children. In many modern societies this is no longer practical, due in part to increased mobility. The standard of living of the elderly has, therefore, increasingly been secured through various forms of social security, such as old-age pensions.

---

[3] World Bank, *World Development Report 1990* (OUP, 1990) 26.

2.2 STATE OBLIGATIONS

The nature of state obligations varies greatly, depending on the nature and level of its social development, the differences in the needs of individuals, the resources at the disposal of the state, and the different components of the right. In most societies there is a considerable difference between the role played by the state regarding the realization of the right to food or to housing, on the one hand, and the realization of the right to health, on the other hand. In economic terms, food and housing are mainly considered to be private goods which people are generally expected to obtain through their own efforts, whereas the right to health is widely associated with publicly organized healthcare as a public good and, therefore, a duty of the state. In spite of these differences, states do have obligations under international human rights law in regard to all these rights, although the content of the obligations varies from one to the other.[4]

Under the right to an adequate standard of living, states must, first, *respect* the individual's freedom to take the necessary action and use the necessary resources, alone or in association with others. It is in regard to the latter that collective or group rights become important: resources belonging to, or controlled by, a collective of persons, such as an indigenous population, must be respected if such a population is to satisfy its needs through their use. Similarly, the rights of peoples to exercise permanent sovereignty over their natural resources may be essential for them to be able, through their own collective efforts, to satisfy their needs.

Second, states have an obligation to *protect* individuals' freedom of choice and use of resources necessary to secure their basic needs. For example, states may be required to provide protection against fraud, unethical behaviour in trade and contractual relations, the marketing of dangerous products, and the dumping of hazardous waste. States are also obliged to protect against discrimination that directly or indirectly prevents particular groups of people from having access to food or housing. Generally, this is the most important aspect of the rights to food, housing, and water, requiring the state to act not as provider but as protector. This function is similar to the obligation of states to protect civil and political rights, such as the right to life or freedom from slavery, from violation by third parties.

Third, states have, when this is necessary, the obligation to *fulfil* everyone's right to an adequate standard of living—that is, to function as the provider. This may take two forms. First, states may have to *facilitate* people's access to resources and means to ensure their livelihood if they lack the opportunity to do so themselves. Second, states may have to directly *provide* the means and resources for the satisfaction of basic needs (in the form of direct aid or social security) to supplement the efforts of individuals. Extensive direct provision of resources may become necessary during periods of widespread unemployment (such as during a recession), sudden crises or disasters, or with regard to the disadvantaged, the elderly, or others who have been marginalized.

2.3 EQUALITY AND NON-DISCRIMINATION AS AN OVERARCHING PRINCIPLE

The duty of states to ensure equality and non-discrimination runs through all human rights instruments as a core principle and is essential to the enjoyment of economic,

---

[4] On the origins of the analysis that follows, see Eide, 'State Obligations Revisited' in Barth Eide and Kracht (eds), *Food and Human Rights in Development*, Vol I (Intersentia, 2007) 137. See also Chapter 5.

social, and cultural rights, including the right to an adequate standard of living. Article 2(2) ICESCR obliges states parties 'to guarantee that the rights enunciated in the present Covenant will be exercised without discrimination of any kind as to race, colour, sex, language, religion, political or other opinion, national or social origin, property, birth or other status'. More specifically, Article 3 requires states to ensure the equal right of men and women to enjoy all Covenant rights. The obligations arising from the principle of equality and non-discrimination have been elaborated by the Committee on Economic, Social and Cultural Rights in its General Comment 20, adopted in May 2009.[5] The Committee has made it clear that states must eliminate formal and substantive, as well as direct and indirect, discrimination.[6] The Committee has also elaborated the meaning of equality and non-discrimination in the context of specific Covenant rights, including the rights to housing,[7] food,[8] health,[9] and water.[10]

3 NORMATIVE CONTENT

This section explains the different elements of the right to an adequate standard of living, namely the rights to food, housing, and health. The main legal sources and different components of each of these rights are considered and challenges to their realization set out. However, these rights should not be seen in isolation, but need to be seen in conjunction with other rights such as the rights to work, to social security, and to education and other rights that will be briefly touched upon in this chapter.

3.1 THE RIGHT TO FOOD

At the core of the right to an adequate standard of living is the right to food. While human beings do not live by bread alone, without food there is no life, and with the wrong food, life is shorter and more prone to ill-health. Access to adequate food and to food security has been a dominant concern in the evolution of civilizations and in the formation of states. Neglect or violation of the right to food is probably the most serious global human rights issue in terms of the number of people whose rights are not ensured. Nearly a billion people suffer from hunger and under-nutrition. For them, the right to food is the most important of all rights. Access to water is of crucial importance for the enjoyment of all the elements of the right to an adequate standard of living, including the right to food, and is therefore also briefly dealt with in this section.

3.1.1 Sources

The guarantee of the right to food of Article 25 UDHR is further elaborated in Article 11 ICESCR. While Article 11(1) recognizes everyone's right to adequate food, Article 11(2) obliges states parties to adopt more immediate and urgent steps to ensure 'the fundamental right of everyone to be free from hunger'. The right to food is also contained in other international human rights instruments, such as the CRC (Articles 24 and 27), and regional

---

[5] CESCR, General Comment 20, E/C.12/GC/20 (2 July 2009).
[6] See Chapter 8 for an explanation of these concepts.
[7] CESCR, General Comment 4, HRI/GEN/1/Rev.9 (Vol I) 11; General Comment 7, HRI/GEN/1/Rev.9 (Vol I) 38.   [8] CESCR, General Comment 12, HRI/GEN/1/Rev.9 (Vol I) 55.
[9] CESCR, General Comment 14, HRI/GEN/1/Rev.9 (Vol I) 78.
[10] CESCR, General Comment 15, HRI/GEN/1/Rev.9 (Vol I) 97.

instruments such as in Article 12 of the Additional Protocol to the American Convention on Human Rights in the Area of Economic, Social and Cultural Rights ('Protocol of San Salvador'). While the African Charter on Human and Peoples' Rights (ACHPR) does not contain an express reference to the right to food, the African Commission on Human and Peoples' Rights, in its decision in *SERAC v Nigeria*, has suggested that the right is implicit in the ACHPR because it is inextricably linked to human dignity and is essential for the enjoyment of other rights.[11]

3.1.2 Components and obligations

In its General Comment 12, the Committee on Economic, Social and Cultural Rights defined the right to food as follows: 'The right to adequate food is realized when every man, woman and child, alone or in community with others, has physical and economic access at all times to adequate food or means for its procurement'.[12] According to the Committee, 'adequate food' implies, first, 'the *availability* of food in a quantity and quality sufficient to satisfy the dietary needs of individuals, free from adverse substances, and acceptable within a given culture'.[13] *Availability* means that either people must be able to feed themselves directly from natural resources or well-functioning distribution and processing systems must exist; *dietary needs* implies that the diet as a whole contains all the necessary nutrients for physical and mental growth, development, and maintenance; *free from adverse substances* sets requirements for food safety; and *cultural or consumer acceptability* implies the need also to take into account perceived non nutrient-based values attached to food.[14] Second, the right to food requires 'the *accessibility* of such food in ways that are sustainable and that do not interfere with the enjoyment of other human rights',[15] encompassing both physical and economic accessibility.[16]

The legal obligations of states parties to the ICESCR under the right to food have been interpreted by the Committee in paragraph 15 of the same General Comment:

> The obligation to *respect* existing access to adequate food requires States parties not to take any measures that result in preventing such access. The obligation to *protect* requires measures by the State to ensure that enterprises or individuals do not deprive individuals of their access to adequate food. The obligation to *fulfil (facilitate)* means the State must pro-actively engage in activities intended to strengthen people's access to and utilization of resources and means to ensure their livelihood, including food security. Finally, whenever an individual or group is unable, for reasons beyond their control, to enjoy the right to adequate food by the means at their disposal, States have the obligation to *fulfil (provide)* that right directly. This obligation also applies for persons who are victims of natural or other disasters.[17]

The Committee has pointed out that some of the measures required from states are of a more immediate nature, while others are more long term in character.[18] The right to food is violated when a state fails to ensure the satisfaction of, at the very least, the minimum essential level required to be free from hunger. Resource constraints do not absolve the state from responsibility; it still has to show that every effort has been made to use all the resources at its disposal in an effort to satisfy, as a matter of priority, those minimum obligations.[19] Furthermore, any discrimination in access to food or to means and entitlements for its procurement constitutes a violation of Article 11 ICESCR.[20] The Committee has

---

[11] Communication No 155/96 (27 May 2002).   [12] General Comment 12, n 8, para 6.
[13] General Comment 12, n 8, para 8 (emphasis added).   [14] General Comment 12, n 8, paras 9–12.
[15] General Comment 12, n 8, para 8 (emphasis added).   [16] General Comment 12, n 8, para 13.
[17] Original emphases.   [18] General Comment 12, n 8, para 16.
[19] General Comment 12, n 8, para 17.   [20] General Comment 12, n 8, para 18.

emphasized that violations can occur through the direct action of states or other entities insufficiently regulated by states. Non-state actors also have responsibilities in the realization of the right to food, and states should provide an environment that facilitates implementation of these responsibilities.[21]

3.1.3 The right to water

An adequate standard of living requires access to adequate water for personal and domestic use. While the right to water is not expressly mentioned in either Article 11 or 12 ICESCR, it is clearly implied. The availability and accessibility of safe and potable water throughout the day is essential for health. Water is required in producing, preparing, and consuming food. Water is necessary for personal hygiene and sanitation and is also, therefore, an integral part of the right to health.

As with the right to food, the Committee on Economic, Social and Cultural Rights has spelled out the different components of the right to adequate water in a General Comment, namely General Comment 15. According to the Committee, adequacy implies that the water supply for each person must be sufficient and continuous (*availability*), that water must be safe (*quality*), and that water and water facilities have to be within physical reach and affordable for all, without discrimination (*accessibility*).[22] The Committee has emphasized that the right to water includes freedoms, for example the right to be free from interferences such as disconnections or contamination of water supplies, as well as entitlements, such as the right to a system of water supply and management that provides equality of opportunity for people to enjoy the right to water.[23]

3.1.4 Realization

Extensive international attention has been paid to the right to food since the World Food Summit, held at the invitation of the Food and Agriculture Organization of the UN (FAO) in Rome in November 1996. At that summit, governments from all parts of the world declared it unacceptable that more than 800 million people throughout the world, particularly in developing countries, did not have enough food to meet their basic nutritional needs. They recognized that this was not the result of a lack of food supplies, which in fact had increased substantially, but due to a lack of physical or economic *access* to food. Governments at the summit committed themselves to achieving food security for all and to an on-going effort to eradicate hunger in all countries, with an immediate view to reducing the number of undernourished people to half the 1996 level no later than the year 2015. Regrettably, this target will not be met. The real number of seriously undernourished persons has not been reduced—on the contrary, the figure at the end of 2012 was 870 million. It should be noted, however, that the world population as a whole has steeply increased since 1996. It now stands at more than 7 billion, which means that the proportion of undernourished people has decreased, but much less than what was hoped for in 1996.

Conditions differ widely between states, and, therefore, the most appropriate ways in which to implement the right to adequate food also vary considerably. Nevertheless, all states parties to the ICESCR and the CRC are obliged to take the measures required to ensure that everyone is free from hunger, and thereupon move as quickly as possible to a situation where everyone can enjoy their right to adequate food. In so doing, the different

---

[21] General Comment 12, n 8, paras 19–20. [22] General Comment 15, n 10, para 12.
[23] General Comment 15, n 10, para 10.

levels of state obligations discussed here should be applied, using the particular combination of measures warranted by the national situation.

Therefore, every state should have, or should develop, a national strategy to implement the right to food. The first step in any such strategy should be to map the situation for different groups and regions within the country, taking into account the differences that might exist on the basis of gender, ethnicity, or race, and between rural and urban areas. Such mapping is necessary to identify those who are food-insecure and to develop appropriate responses to food insecurity. Having identified the groups that are food-insecure, the national strategy should create or recreate food security for those groups and for the population as a whole. When resource constraints emerge, measures should be undertaken to ensure, as a minimum, that vulnerable population groups and individuals do not face hunger. This should be achieved through social programmes, safety nets, and international assistance.

In the elaboration and implementation of national strategies for the right to food, people's informed participation is essential. Thus, states must ensure that particular conditions in different regions of the country are taken into account. Furthermore, attention must be given to all aspects of the food chain, from production to consumption. This includes paying attention to the processing of food in order to ensure food safety and the physical distribution of food in order to enable access for all. Finally, any national strategy should give particular attention to the need to prevent discrimination in access to food or resources for food.

In November 2004 the FAO Council adopted the 'Voluntary guidelines to support the progressive realization of the right to adequate food in the context of national food security'.[24] The objective of these guidelines, elaborated by an intergovernmental working group, is to provide practical guidance to states in the realization of the right to food. They are based on the legal standards mentioned already. The guidelines deal with general enabling conditions, but more importantly, they include a set of practical measures to be carried out. These include measures relating to access to resources and assets (labour, land, water, genetic resources for food and agriculture, and so on), food safety and consumer protection, nutrition policies, education and awareness-raising, national monitoring, and the setting of benchmarks for progressive realization.[25] The guidelines also underline the importance of ensuring that national human rights institutions address the realization of the right to food as part of their work.[26] Finally, they contain a section on international measures, which deals with international cooperation and unilateral measures, the role of the international community, international trade, external debt, international food aid, partnerships with NGOs, civil society organizations, and the private sector (corporations, enterprises).

3.2 THE RIGHT TO HOUSING

Second only to the enjoyment of the right to food, an adequate standard of living requires that everyone has a place to live—a physical space which provides personal and family security, basic infrastructure, satisfactory privacy, necessary warmth on cold days, and protection against heat on warm days.

3.2.1 Sources

The right to housing forms part of the guarantees set out in Article 25 UDHR and Article 11 ICESCR. Furthermore, it is either expressly referred to or implied in other

---

[24] Available at <http://www.fao.org/docrep/meeting/009/y9825e/y9825e00.htm>.
[25] FAO Council, n 24, Guidelines 8–17.   [26] FAO Council, n 24, Guideline 18.

international instruments such as the Convention on the Elimination of All Forms of Racial Discrimination (ICERD) (Article 5(e)(iii)), the CRC (Article 27), the Convention on the Elimination of All Forms of Discrimination Against Women (CEDAW) (Article 14(2)), and the Convention Relating to the Status of Refugees (Article 21). At the regional level, the right to housing is contained in the European Social Charter (Article 31). As with the right to food, the African Commission on Human and Peoples' Rights held in its decision in *SERAC v Nigeria* that, although there is no express reference to the right to housing in the ACHPR, the Charter must be interpreted to include such a right.[27]

3.2.2 Components and obligations

The Committee on Economic, Social and Cultural Rights has elaborated on the content of the right to housing in its General Comment 4.[28] In terms of the holders of the right, it has pointed out that the right applies to everyone. According to the Committee, the reference to 'himself and his family' in Article 11 ICESCR reflects traditional assumptions regarding gender roles and economic activity patterns, but cannot be read today as implying any limitations upon the applicability of the right to individuals or to female-headed households or collective groups. The concept of 'family' must, therefore, be understood in a wide sense and enjoyment of this right must not be subject to any form of discrimination.[29]

Adequate housing requires more than mere shelter in the sense of having a roof over one's head—it must be seen as the right to live somewhere in security, peace, and dignity. According to the Committee, the requirements for adequate housing are the following:

- *Legal security of tenure*: whatever the type of tenure, all persons should possess a degree of security of tenure which guarantees legal protection against forced eviction, harassment, and other threats.

- *Availability of services, materials, facilities, and infrastructure*: this includes safe drinking water, energy for cooking, heating and lighting, sanitation and washing facilities, means of food storage, refuse disposal, site drainage, and emergency services.

- *Affordability*: personal or household financial costs associated with housing should not be such that the attainment and satisfaction of other basic needs is threatened or compromised.

- *Habitability*: the housing must provide the inhabitants with adequate space and protection from cold, damp, heat, rain, wind, or other threats to health, structural hazards, and disease vectors.

- *Accessibility*: housing laws and policies must take into account the special needs of disadvantaged groups to ensure that such groups have full access to adequate housing resources.

- *Location:* adequate housing must be in a location which allows access to employment options, healthcare services, schools, childcare centres, and other social facilities.

- *Cultural adequacy*: the way housing is constructed, the building materials used, and the relevant policies must appropriately enable the expression of cultural identity and diversity of housing.[30]

In market economies, housing is generally considered to be a private good. However, the right to housing implies that the state has a duty to protect against discrimination in access to

---

[27] n 11.   [28] n 7.   [29] General Comment 4, n 7, para 6.   [30] General Comment 4, n 7, para 8.

housing and to facilitate access to housing for all. To that extent, human rights makes housing a public good. That does not necessarily mean that states have an obligation to provide housing. Most people find their own way to obtain and secure their preferred place to live. As with other human rights, state obligations under the right to housing are a combination of passive and active duties. States have, first, a duty to *respect* the housing found by people themselves by abstaining from forcible evictions and displacements. Second, they must *protect* the tenure of existing housing against interference or unjustified evictions by third parties and adopt and enforce the necessary regulations to ensure the necessary quality of housing. Third, they have an obligation through regulatory functions to *facilitate* the opportunity of everyone to find affordable housing. Fourth, in exceptional circumstances and in regard to particularly vulnerable groups, they have to *provide* necessary housing when individuals or groups cannot manage to do so themselves. State measures to implement the right to housing will, therefore, normally reflect a mixture of provisions regulating the private sector ('enabling strategies') and public or state-driven measures (public housing). In essence, the obligation on states is to demonstrate that they have done enough to realize the right for every individual in the shortest possible time, prioritizing for that purpose the use of available resources.[31]

3.2.3 Realization

The Committee on Economic, Social and Cultural Rights has pointed out that there remains a disturbingly large gap between the standards set out in Article 11(1) ICESCR and the situation prevailing in many parts of the world. This refers principally to developing countries, which confront major resource and other constraints, but there is also a significant and growing problem of homelessness and inadequate housing in some of the most economically developed societies. According to some UN estimates, there are over 100 million homeless persons worldwide and over 1 billion who are inadequately housed, with millions of homeless or inadequately housed persons located in Europe and North America.

Besides homelessness, forced evictions are the most severe violation of the right to housing. Forced evictions have been carried out against squatters, low-income renters, indigenous peoples, and other vulnerable groups with no or inadequate legal security of tenure. In its General Comment 7, the Committee on Economic, Social and Cultural Rights called for strict legislation to prevent unjustified evictions. Similarly, the Commission on Human Rights adopted a resolution in 2004 calling for a wide range of measures, including legislation, to prohibit forced evictions unless justified under strict limitations. It requested governments to eliminate the practice of forced evictions by 1) repealing existing plans involving, as well as any legislation allowing for, forced evictions and 2) adopting and implementing legislation ensuring the right to security of tenure for all residents.[32]

No state party to the ICESCR is free of significant problems of one kind or another in relation to the right to housing. The Committee on Economic, Social and Cultural Rights has, therefore, expressed regret that many states do not acknowledge their difficulties in ensuring the right to adequate housing in their reports to the Committee.[33]

3.3 THE RIGHT TO HEALTH

The term 'right to health' can be misleading. There is no human right to be healthy. Due to genetics, risky behaviour, accidents, and other factors, it is not within the capacity of states

---

[31] General Comment 4, n 7, para 14.   [32] CHR Res 2004/28, E/CN.4/RES/2004/28 (16 April 2004), para 2.
[33] General Comment 4, n 7, para 4.

to ensure that everyone lives a full and lengthy life. What is envisaged in international human rights law is that everyone shall have a right to the highest attainable standard of health—attainable both in terms of the individual's potential, the social and environmental conditions affecting the health of the individual, and in terms of health services. For reasons of convenience, this chapter refers to the 'right to health', but this term should be understood in its proper sense of the right to the highest attainable standard of health.

3.3.1 Sources

The right to health is guaranteed as part of Article 25 UDHR. In the case of the ICESCR, it is contained in a separate, comprehensive provision (Article 12). Further human rights standards on the right to health include Article 12 CEDAW, Article 5(e)(iv) ICERD, Article 24 CRC, Article 11 of the European Social Charter, Article 10 of the Protocol of San Salvador, and Article 16 ACHPR.

3.3.2 Components and obligations

Under Article 12(1) ICESCR, states parties recognize the right of everyone to the enjoyment of the highest attainable standard of physical and mental health. The right to health extends to adequate healthcare, the underlying preconditions for health, and adequate fulfilment of the social determinants of health. Article 12(2) ICESCR sets out the main directions for state action in fulfilling this right. According to this provision, states must take steps for:

(a) the provision for the reduction of the stillbirth-rate and of infant mortality and for the healthy development of the child; (b) the improvement of all aspects of environmental and industrial hygiene; (c) the prevention, treatment and control of epidemic, endemic, occupational and other diseases; (d) the creation of conditions which would assure to all medical service and medical attention in the event of sickness.

In its General Comment 14, the Committee on Economic, Social and Cultural Rights has specified that the right to health involves the following elements and state obligations:

- *Availability*: states must ensure that functioning public health and healthcare facilities, goods, and services are available in sufficient quantity. The precise nature of these facilities, goods, and services will vary depending on numerous factors, including the state party's level of development.

- *Accessibility*: health facilities, goods, and services have to be accessible to everyone. Accessibility has four overlapping dimensions: (1) non-discrimination; (2) physical accessibility; (3) economic accessibility (affordability); and (4) information accessibility (the right to seek, receive, and impart information and ideas concerning health issues).

- *Acceptability*: all health facilities, goods, and services must be respectful of medical ethics and culturally appropriate, sensitive to gender and lifecycle requirements, as well as being designed to respect confidentiality and improve the health status of those concerned.

- *Quality*: health facilities, goods, and services must be scientifically and medically appropriate and of good quality. This requires, inter alia, skilled medical personnel, scientifically approved and unexpired drugs, appropriate hospital equipment, safe and potable water, and adequate sanitation.[34]

---

[34] General Comment 14, n 9, para 12.

The right to health requires states to adopt and implement measures ensuring the right of access to health facilities, goods, and services to all on a non-discriminatory basis, including to vulnerable or marginalized groups that otherwise might not have such access. This also requires the equitable distribution of all health facilities, which are often concentrated in the main urban areas, leaving rural and less important urban areas unattended.

As the Committee has pointed out, a state is in violation of its obligation to protect individuals' health if it fails to take all necessary measures to safeguard persons within its jurisdiction from infringements of the right to health by third parties. This may include omissions such as the failure to discourage production, marketing, and consumption of tobacco, narcotics, and other harmful substances; the failure to discourage the continued observance of harmful traditional medical or cultural practices; or the failure to enact or enforce laws to prevent the pollution of water, air, and soil by extractive and manufacturing industries.[35]

3.3.3 Realization

Realization of the right to health is closely linked to the realization of other economic and social rights. It is crucial that states ensure freedom from hunger and access for all to essential and sufficient food, which is nutritionally adequate and safe. The high level of child mortality, particularly in developing countries, is caused primarily by insufficient or inadequate food and unsafe and polluted water. Furthermore, realization of the right to health depends on access to basic shelter, housing, and sanitation, as well as an adequate supply of safe and potable water.

The Committee on Economic, Social and Cultural Rights has urged all states parties to adopt and implement a national public health strategy and plan of action, on the basis of epidemiological evidence, addressing the health concerns of the entire population. It has pointed out that the strategy and plan of action should be devised, and periodically reviewed, on the basis of a participatory and transparent process. They should include methods, such as right-to-health indicators and benchmarks, by which progress can be monitored, and should give particular attention to all vulnerable or marginalized groups. In addition, everyone should be ensured access to essential drugs as defined under the World Health Organization Action Programme on Essential Drugs.[36]

Of key importance is, finally, the task of ensuring reproductive, maternal (pre-natal as well as post-natal), and child healthcare. Maternal mortality is the leading cause of death among women and girls of reproductive age. It is estimated that half a million women and girls die annually from complications related to pregnancy and childbirth. If pregnancy-related injuries and disabilities are included, such as haemorrhage, infection, brain seizures, hypertension, anaemia, and obstetric fistulae, it is probable that tens of millions of women and girls are affected.

4 CATEGORIES AND GROUPS OF PEOPLE

Human rights, including the right to an adequate standard of living, are equally applicable to everyone. In practice, however, it has proved necessary to pay special attention to the situation of some categories or groups of people, because they are vulnerable, have been neglected, or have particular needs. It has been recognized that separate attention has to be given to the standard of living of different members of the family, including women and

---

[35] General Comment 14, n 9, para 51.   [36] General Comment 14, n 9, para 43.

children. In addition, three particularly vulnerable groups of people will be discussed in this section: indigenous peoples, Dalits in South Asia, and the Roma in Europe.

4.1 WOMEN

International human rights bodies have recognized that women may face greater difficulties than men in securing an adequate standard of living. The Committee on Economic, Social and Cultural Rights has, therefore, urged states to include in their national strategies to implement the right to food guarantees of women's full and equal access to economic resources, including the right to inheritance and ownership of land and other property, credit, natural resources, and appropriate technology. Such strategies should also contain measures to respect and protect self-employment and work which provides adequate remuneration to ensure a decent living for wage-earners and their families (as stipulated in Article 7(a)(ii) ICESCR).[37]

Healthcare is of particular importance for motherhood and childhood. Article 12 CEDAW requires states to 'take all appropriate measures to eliminate discrimination against women in the field of health care in order to ensure, on a basis of equality between men and women, access to health care services, including those related to family planning' and to ensure women have access to appropriate services in connection with pregnancy, confinement, and the post-natal period. The Committee on Economic, Social and Cultural Rights has underlined the need to develop and implement a comprehensive national strategy for promoting women's right to health to meet these requirements. It has pointed out that the realization of women's right to health requires the removal of all barriers interfering with access to health services, education, and information, including in the area of sexual and reproductive health. It has also emphasized the importance of preventive, promotional, and remedial action to shield women from the impact of harmful traditional cultural practices and norms that deny them their full reproductive rights.[38]

Article 14 CEDAW requires states to pay special attention to the particular problems faced by rural women. In particular, states must ensure such women have the right to adequate living conditions, particularly in relation to housing, sanitation, electricity and water supply, transport, and communications. Furthermore, they must be given the right to participate in the elaboration and implementation of development planning at all levels and to have access to adequate healthcare facilities, including information, counselling, and services in family planning.

4.2 CHILDREN

Article 27 CRC guarantees 'the right of every child to a standard of living adequate for the child's physical, mental, spiritual, moral and social development'. This involves adequate food, housing, nursing, and care. Article 27(2) provides that the parent(s) or others responsible for the child have the primary responsibility to secure the conditions of living necessary for the child's development.

While ensuring the child's right to an adequate standard of living is the primary duty of parents, it is not exclusive. According to Article 27(3) CRC, states must take appropriate measures to assist parents to implement this right. If necessary, they have to provide material assistance and support programmes, particularly with regard to nutrition, clothing, and housing. In addition, many children grow up in single-parent households, or are orphaned

---

[37] General Comment 12, n 8, para 26.   [38] General Comment 14, n 9, para 21.

or have parents that have absconded or neglect their duty, and, in such situations, where other relatives do not take it over, the state has a primary duty to ensure for the child an adequate standard of living through appropriate institutions or placement with foster parents.

Under the right to health, states have a duty to diminish infant and child mortality. Article 12(2)(a) ICESCR expressly requires states to make 'provisions for the reduction of the still-birth rate and of infant mortality and for the healthy development of the child'. Similar obligations are contained in Article 24(2)(a) CRC and flow from Article 6 CRC, which provides that every child has the inherent right to life and that states 'shall ensure to the maximum extent possible the survival and development of the child'. This obligation may be understood as requiring measures to improve child and maternal health, sexual and reproductive health services, pre- and post-natal care, access to information, as well as to resources necessary to act on that information.

More generally, Article 24 CRC guarantees the right of the child to the enjoyment of the highest attainable standard of health and to facilities for the treatment of illness and rehabilitation of health. Thus, states must ensure that no child is deprived of his or her right of access to healthcare services. Furthermore, they have an obligation to ensure the provision of necessary medical assistance and healthcare to all children, combat disease and malnutrition, and develop preventive healthcare. The obligation of state parties to combat disease and malnutrition reflects the dominant problems facing children in many developing countries. A large number of children, particularly in the poorer sector of the population, die before the age of five, due to a combination of malnutrition, unsafe water and sanitation, and communicable diseases. The risks can be substantially reduced through readily available technology such as oral rehydration therapy and immunization against the common childhood diseases, but this alone is not enough. It is also essential to ensure provision of adequate nutritious food and clean drinking water.

4.3 INDIGENOUS PEOPLES

The indigenous peoples of the world are generally among the most impoverished.[39] Many of them are struggling to maintain and preserve their own culture. Since much of their land and resources has been taken away from them, the little that is left cannot provide them with enough to satisfy an adequate standard of living. While efforts to strengthen their rights have had some positive results in recent years, such as the adoption in 1989 of the ILO Convention on the Rights of Tribal and Indigenous Peoples (No 169) and in 2007 the adoption by the UN General Assembly of the Universal Declaration on the Rights of Indigenous Peoples, they still suffer from severe deprivation. When they are displaced and live on 'welfare', their culture is undermined and the alien lifestyle leads to high degrees of alcoholism, suicide, and sometimes criminal behaviour. In line with the UN Declaration on the Rights of Indigenous Peoples, conditions must be established, including through recognition of their rights to land and natural resources which enable them to preserve their culture while sustaining a livelihood that ensures for them an adequate standard of living. This close link between rights to land and natural resources on the one hand and economic survival on the other hand has been highlighted by the Inter-American human rights bodies in a number of cases.[40] In the *Yakye Axa Indigenous Community* case, the

---

[39] For the definition of 'indigenous peoples', see Chapter 17.

[40] See Case 11.140, *Mary and Carrie Dann v United States*, IACommHR Report No 75/02 (27 December 2002); *Mayagna (Sumo) Awas Tingni Community v Nicaragua*, IACtHR Series C No 79 (31 August 2001); *Yakye Axa Indigenous Community v Paraguay*, IACtHR Series C No 125 (17 June 2005).

Inter-American Court of Human Rights held that Paraguay had violated the rights of the members of that community to live a dignified existence, which follows from the right to life, by delaying the restitution of their ancestral lands and thus making it difficult for them to obtain food, clean water, adequate housing, and healthcare.[41]

The Committee on Economic, Social and Cultural Rights has repeatedly addressed the problems faced by indigenous peoples in its General Comments. It has drawn attention to the particular vulnerability of indigenous peoples whose ancestral land may be threatened. In several places corporations involved in oil or other mineral extraction have aggravated the situation of indigenous peoples, degraded their land, and caused their displacement.[42] The Committee has also emphasized that as part of their obligations to protect people's resource base for food, states parties should take appropriate steps to ensure that activities of the private business sector are in conformity with the right to food.[43] With regard to the right to housing, it has pointed out that indigenous peoples are among those vulnerable groups who suffer most from evictions.[44] Finally, the Committee has called on states to take particular care to ensure that indigenous peoples and ethnic and linguistic minorities are not excluded from social security systems through direct or indirect discrimination, particularly through the imposition of unreasonable eligibility conditions or lack of adequate access to information.[45]

Indigenous peoples often live in remote areas with the lowest level of access to modern healthcare, and when they can reach healthcare stations there is often a poor understanding of, and respect for, their cultural requirements. The Committee has argued that indigenous peoples have the right to specific measures to improve their access to health services and care. Health services should be culturally appropriate and thus take into account traditional preventive care, healing practices, and medicines. States should provide resources for indigenous peoples to design, deliver, and control such services. The Committee has noted that, in indigenous communities, the health of the individual is often linked to the health of the society as a whole and has a collective dimension. Therefore, development-related activities that lead to the displacement of indigenous peoples, denying them their sources of nutrition and breaking their symbiotic relationship with their lands, have a deleterious effect on their health.[46]

4.4 DALITS IN SOUTH ASIA AND ROMA IN EUROPE

Many other minorities are subject to persistent discrimination, undermining their standard of living. These include the low-castes or Dalits in South Asia—particularly in India—who, as a result of social practices, are often marginalized, deprived of access to the means of adequate food and housing, and given access only to the lowest, most menial work. While such practices are generally prohibited under the respective national laws, enforcement of the law is often weak and segments of the police and other law enforcement agencies are themselves socialized in the same discriminatory attitudes that keep such practices alive. In its General Comment 20 of 2009, the Committee on Economic, Social and Cultural Rights pointed out that the prohibited ground of discrimination of 'birth' listed in Article 2(2) ICESCR also includes *descent*, especially on the basis of caste and analogous systems of inherited status. Therefore, states parties should take steps to prevent, prohibit,

---

[41] *Yakye Axa Indigenous Community v Paraguay*, paras 164–8 and 176.
[42] General Comment 12, n 8, para 13.   [43] General Comment 12, n 8, para 27.
[44] General Comment 7, n 7, para 10.
[45] General Comment 19, HRI/GEN/1/Rev.9 (Vol I) 152, para 35.
[46] General Comment 14, n 9, para 27.

and eliminate discriminatory practices directed against members of descent-based communities and act against dissemination of ideas of superiority and inferiority on the basis of descent.[47]

A somewhat comparable situation exists in many parts of Europe, where the Roma and the Sinti are subject to widespread social discrimination, and where governments are unable fully to eradicate these practices. In 2012 the Commissioner for Human Rights of the Council of Europe presented a comprehensive report detailing extensive racially motivated violence against Roma and Travellers, police abuse of these groups, discrimination in access to adequate housing and to employment, denial of and discrimination by emergency medical health services and by health providers, exclusion from healthcare as a result of physical distance from healthcare facilities, and serious impediments to their access to social security.[48] Multiple initiatives have been taken by the Council of Europe, the European Union, and by the Organisation for Security and Cooperation in Europe (OSCE), but the persistent prejudices against, and exclusion of, the Roma and Sinti have made progress difficult.

5 RELATIONSHIP WITH OTHER HUMAN RIGHTS

As pointed out in the conclusions of the 1993 Vienna World Conference on Human Rights, '[a]ll human rights are universal, indivisible, interdependent and interrelated.'[49] It is easy to show that the right to an adequate standard of living is closely linked to other human rights. Most obviously, it is heavily dependent on the realization of other economic and social rights, such as the rights to work, education, and property. Of particular importance is the right to social security, dealt with in Section 5.1. Economic rights have a dual function, most clearly demonstrated in regard to the right to property. On the one hand, this right serves as a basis for entitlements which can ensure an adequate standard of living, while on the other hand it is a basis of independence and, therefore, freedom. Similarly, the right to work is also a basis of both independence (provided the work is freely chosen by the person concerned) and an adequate standard of living (provided that sufficient income is obtained from work).

The right to an adequate standard of living is also linked to cultural rights, which, according to Article 27 UDHR and Article 15 ICESCR, contain the following elements: the right to take part in cultural life, the right to enjoy the benefits of scientific progress and its applications, the right to benefit from the protection of the moral and material interests resulting from any scientific, literary, or artistic production of which the beneficiary is the author, and the freedom indispensable for scientific research and creative activity.[50] These rights intersect in several ways with the right to an adequate standard of living. To mention one example: the right to benefit from advances in scientific progress can be a basis for claiming a right of access to affordable new medicine, which may be crucial in treating diseases such as HIV and AIDS.

---

[47] E/C.12/GC/20, para 26.

[48] Commissioner for Human Rights of the Council of Europe, *Human Rights of Roma and Travellers in Europe* (Council of Europe Publications, 2012).

[49] Vienna Declaration and Programme of Action, A/CONF.157/23 (25 June 1993) para 5. See Chapter 7 and Eide, 'Interdependence and Indivisibility of Human Rights' in Donders and Volodin (eds), *Human Rights in Education, Science and Culture* (UNESCO Publishing/Ashgate, 2007).   [50] See Chapter 14.

Finally, as explained in Section 5.2, the right to an adequate standard of living may also coincide or, on the other hand, clash with civil and political rights.

5.1 THE RIGHT TO SOCIAL SECURITY AND SOCIAL ASSISTANCE

The right to social security is essential when people are not able to secure an adequate standard of living themselves, particularly when they do not have the necessary property or are not able to work due to unemployment, old age, or disability. The drafters of the UDHR considered social security to be one of the core guarantees for the right of everyone to an adequate standard of living.

The general guarantee of an adequate standard of living set out in Article 25 UDHR includes 'the right to security in the event of unemployment, sickness, disability, widowhood, old age or other lack of livelihood in circumstances beyond his control'. But the UDHR also contains a separate guarantee of the right to social security that uses stronger terms. Article 22 states that '[e]veryone, as a member of society, has the right to social security'. Article 9 ICESCR guarantees 'the right of everyone to social security, including social insurance', while Article 10 of the same covenant refers to social security within the context of the protection of the family, mothers, and children. CEDAW contains a range of social security guarantees relevant to women, including the right of women to social security, particularly in cases of retirement, unemployment, sickness, invalidity and old age, and other incapacity to work, as well as the right to paid leave (Article 11(1)(e)), the right to family benefits (Article 13(a)), and the right of rural women to benefit directly from social security programmes (Article 14(2)(c)). The CRC provides for the right of the child to benefit from social security, including social insurance (Article 26). The right to social security is also explicitly mentioned in regional human rights instruments, including the American Declaration of the Rights and Duties of Man (Article XVI), the Protocol of San Salvador (Article 9), and the European Social Charter (Articles 12, 13, and 14).

Social security must be distinguished from social assistance and charity. Charity is irrelevant in the present context, because it involves neither a right of the individual nor a duty imposed on the state. It is, therefore, not a human rights issue. Social assistance is often discretionary and, therefore, neither a right nor a duty, but in some states it is sufficiently well regulated in law and practice to make it conform to requirements of human rights law.

Measures to implement the right to social security as set out in Article 9 ICESCR can include contributory or non-contributory schemes, or a combination of the two. The Committee on Economic, Social and Cultural Rights, in its General Comment 19, has defined these two types of provision of social security benefits as follows. *Contributory* (or insurance-based) schemes, such as social insurance, which is expressly mentioned in Article 9, generally involve compulsory contributions from beneficiaries, employers, and, sometimes, the state, in conjunction with the payment of benefits and administrative expenses from a common fund. *Non-contributory* schemes include universal schemes, which provide the relevant benefit to everyone who experiences a particular risk or contingency, and targeted social assistance schemes, where benefits are received by those in a situation of need.

In recent years, an embryonic form of social security under the name of 'cash transfer programmes' has emerged, particularly in the least developed countries where the social security system has limited reach. These programmes, which provide payments in cash to individuals or households, are normally targeted at the poorest and most vulnerable sections of the population. The transfers may be in the form of non-contributory old-age pensions, disability grants, child support grants, widow's allowances, or household trans-fers to persons in extreme poverty. Some of these programmes are conditional, for example requiring that the supported children attend school. The UN Independent Expert on the question of extreme poverty has recognized that these cash transfer programmes can assist states in fulfilling their human rights obligations. However, she has also pointed out that this requires that the programmes are fully integrated within broader social protection systems. Their legal and institutional frameworks must take into account the international and national standards regarding the right to social security.[51]

The Committee on Economic, Social and Cultural Rights has expressed its concern over the very low levels of access to social security. About 80 per cent of the global population currently lack access to formal social security, with 20 per cent living in extreme poverty. The Committee has emphasized that this denial of, or lack of access to, adequate social security has undermined the realization of many Covenant rights.[52]

5.2 CIVIL AND POLITICAL RIGHTS

Civil and political rights are essential in order to achieve the realization of an adequate standard of living. The availability of independent courts and other institutions such as human rights commissions are essential in order to have remedies available when rights to housing or to food are unjustifiably denied or neglected. Civil and political rights have been extensively used to advance the realization of economic and social rights, including the right to an adequate standard of living.[53]

More specifically, torture and ill-treatment is not only a violation of core civil rights but also a violation of the right to health. Severe violations of the right to health or the right to be free from hunger may lead, in turn, to violations of the right to life, which is a civil right. On the other hand, there can also be conflicts between these different categories of rights. To give just one example, while the state has an obligation under international human rights law to take measures to protect the right to health, such measures must comply with the rights of people who carry infectious diseases such as their rights to physical integrity, privacy, and liberty. In each specific case, the need to protect the health of the public at large has to be balanced against individual interests. Thus, the European Court of Human Rights has held that an individual can only be compulsorily isolated to prevent him or her from spreading the HIV virus *as a last resort*, that is, where less severe measures are insuf-ficient to safeguard the public interest.[54]

6 PROGRESSIVE IMPLEMENTATION

It is obvious that the right of everyone to an adequate standard of living is still far from realized. Nearly 1 billion people suffer from hunger and malnutrition and the number is probably growing. Possibly 2 billion, out of the total of 7 billion now living on earth, have substandard housing or no housing at all. There are enormous gaps between the standards set by international human rights law and the reality that many people face. This is also the case for many civil and political rights. Some may consider that human rights that are not applied in practice do not deserve the name 'rights'.

---

[51] Report of the Independent Expert on the question of human rights and extreme poverty, A/HRC/11/9 (27 March 2009).   [52] General Comment 19, n 45, paras 7 and 8.

[53] See Chapter 7.   [54] *Enhorn v Sweden* (2005) 41 EHRR 633.

It has to be borne in mind that economic and social rights were adopted as 'standards of achievement' to be achieved through progressive measures both at the national and international level. Article 2 ICESCR envisages a progressive realization of the Covenant rights and acknowledges the constraints due to the limited available resources. However, it also imposes obligations which are of immediate effect. In particular, states parties must guarantee that the rights will be exercised without discrimination of any kind and must take immediate and progressive steps towards full realization of the relevant rights by all appropriate means, including particularly the adoption of legislative measures. The Committee on Economic, Social and Cultural Rights has pointed out that such steps should be deliberate, concrete, and targeted as clearly as possible towards meeting the obligations recognized in the Covenant.[55]

Full realization would require that human rights are given priority in development processes. Regrettably, this has often not been the case. Both at the national and international level, there are serious maldevelopments. The most pressing problem is the unregulated and misdirected process of globalization culminating in the recent financial crisis, which has led to a tremendous increase in inequality worldwide, particularly within states. Development can produce not only wealth but also poverty, unless development projects themselves are human rights based.[56]

As explained already, violations imputable to the state can occur either by direct action by the state and its agencies or by its failure to ensure economic and social rights. The Committee on Economic, Social and Cultural Rights has pointed out that in determining which actions or omissions amount to a violation, it is important to distinguish the inability of a state party to comply from its unwillingness to do so. Should, for instance, a state party argue that resource constraints make it impossible to provide access to food for those who are unable by themselves to secure such access, then it has to demonstrate that every effort has been made to use all the resources at its disposal in an effort to satisfy, as a matter of priority, its minimum obligations. A state claiming that it is unable to carry out its obligation for reasons beyond its control has the burden of proving that this is the case and that it has unsuccessfully sought to obtain international support to ensure the availability and accessibility of the necessary food. Furthermore, any discrimination in access to food, as well as to means and entitlements for its procurement, constitutes a violation of the ICESCR.[57]

7 THE IMPORTANCE OF INTERNATIONAL MONITORING AND RECOURSE PROCEDURES

Most states have some legislation relating to the rights to food, housing, and health. However, such legislation is often fragmented, does not guarantee them as proper entitlements, and is often weakly enforced or not enforced at all. International economic, social, and cultural rights constitute a comprehensive normative framework that guides the content of national legislation in this area. In the absence of sufficient national legislation

---

[55] General Comment 3, HRI/GEN/1/Rev.9 (Vol I) 7, para 2.

[56] See further Eide, 'Human Rights-Based Development in the Age of Economic Globalization: Background and Prospects' in Andreassen and Marks (eds), *Development as a Human Right: Legal, Political, and Economic Dimensions* (Harvard UP, 2007) 220, and Salomon, *Global Responsibility for Human Rights: World Poverty and the Development of International Law* (OUP, 2007). See also Chapter 28.

[57] CESCR, General Comment 12, n 8, paras 17 and 18.

or its enforcement, the economic, social, and cultural rights contained in international instruments can play an important role for the individual. But are these rights justiciable? Behind this widely discussed question is a more fundamental one: what is the nature of international economic, social, and cultural rights?

The answer is not as difficult as is often thought. International human rights law serves two functions. First, it provides directive principles. Second, under some conditions, it provides subjective rights or genuine entitlements, provided national courts treat them as such. National courts have, to an increasing extent, enforced international guarantees of economic, social, and cultural rights.[58] This issue is further discussed in Chapter 22, so the discussion here will focus on the first issue.

The notion of directive principles is well-known from constitutional law. In India, for example, directive principles of state policy are contained in the constitution as guidelines to the central and state governments, to be considered when framing laws and policies. These provisions are not directly enforceable by any court, but they are considered to be fundamental principles of governance that must be applied by state authorities.[59] Similar principles are also found in other constitutions, such as that of Ireland, which focus on social justice and economic welfare. Such directive principles play an important role in the political process, but there are normally no national monitoring authorities supervising their implementation. In addition, they are often general and vague in their wording and, therefore, leave a wide margin for political disagreement concerning their implementation.

This is where international human rights law, and in particular guarantees of economic, social, and cultural rights, have an important additional value. International monitoring bodies can pursue a dialogue with each state on the optimal implementation of the directive principles and can elaborate and clarify the content of state obligations under international human rights standards. This is what the Committee on Economic, Social and Cultural Rights has done by issuing its General Comments, several of which concern the right to an adequate standard of living, and by adopting concluding observations and recommendations upon examination of state reports.

This monitoring through examination of state reports has been supplemented by a new procedure created by the Optional Protocol to the ICESCR, which was adopted in December 2008 and came into force in May 2013. Under the Optional Protocol, individuals who claim that their economic, social, and cultural rights have been violated can bring a complaint to the Committee after having exhausted available domestic remedies. This new procedure will undoubtedly add to the impact of economic, social, and cultural rights. Regrettably, the number of ratifications is still rather small, but will hopefully grow as the procedure becomes better known. In any case, it will not reduce the importance of the monitoring process, which in some respects can produce more comprehensive effects than complaint procedures.[60]

In addition, the UN Human Rights Council and its predecessor, the Commission on Human Rights, have developed important thematic mechanisms to report on and promote the implementation of the right to an adequate standard of living. The reports by these Special Rapporteurs or Independent Experts play a very important role in advancing the enjoyment of the right to an adequate standard of living. There are Special Rapporteurs on the right to food, the right to housing, and the right to health; and Independent Experts

---

[58] See Langford (ed), *Social Rights Jurisprudence: Emerging Trends in International and Comparative Law* (CUP, 2008).   [59] See further Chapter 22.

[60] See Langford, 'Closing the Gap? – An Introduction to the Optional Protocol to the International Covenant on Economic, Social and Cultural Rights' (2009) 27 *Nordic JHR* 1.

on the right to water and on extreme poverty. All of these mechanisms perform important work in highlighting in their reports shortcomings in the implementation of the right to an adequate standard of living in different parts of the world. Thereby, they make a significant contribution to the worldwide realization of this right.

8 CONCLUSION

Intended to promote and ensure freedom from want, the right to an adequate standard of living was given a central place in the proclamation of universal human rights from the very beginning in 1948. It has since been elaborated in international standards and clarified in detailed General Comments and practice. Several guidelines have been adopted for the implementation of the different components of an adequate standard of living, namely, the rights to food, water, housing, and health. The relevant international human rights standards serve both as directive principles and as subjective rights. While their main function has been as directive principles pursued through international monitoring and reporting, there is an emerging trend also to use them as subjective rights in adjudicative bodies.

Enormous gaps remain, however, in the implementation of the right to an adequate standard of living. Regrettably, this right is not given the priority it should have in development processes. The creation of wealth for some is often associated with the creation of poverty for others, at least in the relative sense and sometimes even in the absolute sense.

FURTHER READING

ALBUQUERQUE with ROAF, *On the Right Track: Good Practices in the Realization of the Right to Water and Sanitation*, available at <**http://www.ohchr.org/Documents/Issues/Water/BookonGoodPractices_en.pdf**>.

CRAVEN, *The International Covenant on Economic, Social and Cultural Rights* (Oxford University Press, 2002).

BARTH-EIDE and KRACHT (eds), *Food and Human Rights in Development: Volume I: Legal and Institutional Dimensions* (Intersentia, 2005).

BARTH-EIDE and KRACHT (eds), *Food and Human Rights in Development: Volume II: Evolving Issues and Emerging Applications* (Intersentia, 2007).

DE SCHUTTER, 'The Right of Everyone to Enjoy the Benefits of Scientific Progress and the Right to Food: From Conflict to Complementarity' (2011) 33 *HRQ* 304.

EIDE, KRAUSE, and ROSAS (eds), *Economic, Social and Cultural Rights* (Martinus Nijhoff, 2001).

HEALTH AND HUMAN RIGHTS: AN INTERNATIONAL JOURNAL (Francois-Xavier Bagnaud Centre for Health and Human Rights).

KENT (ed), *Global Obligations for the Right to Food* (Rowman & Littlefield, 2008).

LANGFORD (ed), *Social Rights Jurisprudence* (Cambridge University Press, 2008).

LANGFORD et al. (eds), *Global Justice, State Duties: The Extraterritorial Scope of Economic, Social and Cultural Rights* (Cambridge University Press, 2013).

LECKIE (ed), *Housing, Land, and Property Restitution Rights of Refugees and Displaced Persons: Laws, Cases, and Materials* (Cambridge University Press, 2007).

SKOGLY, 'The Requirement of Using the "Maximum of Available Resources" for Human Rights Realisation: A Question of Quality as Well as Quantity?' (2012) 12 *HRLR* 393.

TOBIN, *The Right to Health in International Law* (Oxford University Press, 2012).

TOEBES, *The Right to Health as a Human Right in International Law* (Intersentia, 1999).

UNESCO ETXEA, *The Human Right to Water: Current Situation and Future Challenges* (Icaria Editorial, 2008).

USEFUL WEBSITES

UN Committee on Economic, Social and Cultural Rights: <http://www2.ohchr.org/english/bodies/cescr/index.htm>

UN Special Rapporteur on the right to food: <http://www.ohchr.org/EN/issues/food/Pages/FoodIndex.aspx>

UN Special Rapporteur on adequate housing as a component of the right to an adequate standard of living: <http://www.ohchr.org/en/issues/housing/pages/housingindex.aspx>

UN Special Rapporteur on the right of everyone to the enjoyment of the highest attainable standard of physical and mental health: <http://www.ohchr.org/EN/Issues/Health/Pages/SRRightHealthIndex.aspx>

UN Independent Expert on the issue of human rights obligations related to access to safe drinking water and sanitation: <http://www.ohchr.org/EN/Issues/WaterAndSanitation/SRWater/Pages/SRWaterIndex.aspx>

UN Independent Expert on human rights and extreme poverty: <http://www.ohchr.org/EN/Issues/Poverty/Pages/SRExtremePovertyIndex.aspx>

European Committee of Social Rights: <http://www.coe.int/t/dghl/monitoring/socialcharter/ecsr/ecsrdefault_EN.asp>

11
THOUGHT, EXPRESSION, ASSOCIATION, AND ASSEMBLY

Kevin Boyle and Sangeeta Shah

SUMMARY

The four freedoms introduced in this chapter—thought, expression, association, and assembly—are interrelated and fundamental freedoms of the individual. They are essential for the exercise of all other rights. None are absolute in the sense that their exercise may never be restricted. International law provides the grounds on which each freedom may be required to be balanced against the rights of others or broader community interests. It also offers principles to safeguard against abuse of restrictions by the state. Freedom of thought includes freedom of conscience, religion, or belief. Freedom of expression includes freedom of opinion and freedom of information. Media freedom is also protected in international human rights law as essential for the enjoyment of freedom of expression. Freedom of association concerns the right to establish autonomous organizations through which individuals pursue common interests together. The right of assembly protects non-violent, organized, temporary gatherings in public and private, both indoors and outdoors.

1 INTRODUCTION

1.1 FOUR FREEDOMS AND THEIR RELATIONSHIPS

The freedoms of thought, expression, association, and assembly, often described as fundamental freedoms, are closely related civil and political rights. The guarantee of each is necessary for the enjoyment of the other and indeed for the exercise of all human rights. Thus, freedom of expression is necessary if freedom of thought is to be exercised. In turn, freedom of expression has little meaning without the individual having freedom to think and have an opinion. The right to practise or to teach a religion includes the freedom to publish religious literature or broadcast religious programmes. If religious communities or denominations are to exist, their freedom of association is essential, as is their right to assemble for religious purposes. Freedom of expression is essential when people come together to pursue their interests through other associations, such as trade unions, political parties, or community groups. The European Court of Human Rights has defined one of the objectives of the freedom of association as the protection of opinions and the freedom to express them.[1] Freedom of expression is essential also to the freedom to assemble and the right to demonstrate over grievances. Thus, while each freedom is distinct in theory, in practice they are interrelated and interdependent.

The consecutive location of the freedoms in all international human rights texts, beginning with the Universal Declaration of Human Rights (UDHR), reflects their complementary nature. Article 18 UDHR proclaims freedom of thought, conscience, religion, or belief, Article 19 freedom of opinion and expression, and Article 20 the freedoms of association and assembly. Each of the freedoms is pivotal for the individual's right to democratic participation, a right proclaimed in Article 21 UDHR. Each freedom needs also to be understood as integrating the right to equality and non-discrimination in Article 2 UDHR. Denials of the freedoms often occur in the context of discriminatory policies directed at particular groups or minorities, for example religious or ethnic minorities.

Each freedom, as defined in international law, is expressed as a freedom of the individual but also has a collective dimension. Thus, Article 18 UDHR provides that freedom of thought, religion, or belief is to be enjoyed 'alone or in communion with others'. Freedom of expression includes not only the right of a speaker to communicate with others but the right of others to hear what the speaker has to say. By definition the freedom of association or assembly concerns the collective activities of individuals.

1.2 LIMITATIONS

A common feature of these freedoms is that none is unconditional in the sense that its exercise by the individual or group cannot be limited by the state. International human rights standards set out the grounds of permitted limitation or restriction. Two categories of restriction are envisaged. First, the freedoms may legitimately be regulated by law to protect the rights and freedoms of others. Second, restriction may be justified for different public interest reasons, namely, public order, health, morality, or national security. The constant challenge arising in practice is how to strike a balance, which is acceptable in a democratic society, between the right to exercise the freedom, on the one hand, and the need to protect the rights of others and the public interest, on the other hand.

Most violations of these freedoms arise over patently unjustified restrictions by governments. The killing of journalists, censorship of the Internet, or the arbitrary banning of political movements or religious denominations occur with depressing frequency. But, even where these freedoms are broadly respected, difficult questions can arise over how to respond to direct conflict between the freedoms themselves or with other rights. In the case of the news media, for example, conflict arises on a daily basis between freedom of the press and the right to privacy. The tensions and misunderstandings which can arise between freedom of religion and freedom of expression were vividly demonstrated in the worldwide controversy over the publication of cartoons of the Prophet Mohammad in a Danish newspaper in 2005.[2] Another contemporary example, which is discussed further in Section 2.4, concerns the display of religious symbols or wearing of religious dress in the classroom. In several countries the wearing of the Islamic headscarf (*Hijab*) has been prohibited in schools or universities. This interference with freedom of religion, as it is, has been held to be justified on various grounds including the maintenance of a state's secular principles. In other countries, such as the UK, the balance has been drawn differently.

---

[1] *Ouranio Toxo and Others v Greece* (2007) 45 EHRR 8, para 35.
[2] Cram, 'The Danish Cartoons, Offensive Expression, and Democratic Legitimacy' in Hare and Weinstein (eds), *Extreme Speech and Democracy* (OUP, 2009) 311.

Religious symbols and dress are accommodated, to some extent, within school policy on uniforms.[3] In summary, a society which enjoys the freedoms under discussion is not one in which there are no restrictions on their exercise. It is rather one in which the boundaries of freedom are openly debated and democratically resolved under the rule of law.

Limitations will be discussed further as regards each freedom but some general principles applicable to all can be set out here:[4]

- *Legality*: any limitation on a freedom must be set down or prescribed in law. A restriction cannot be legitimate where it is the arbitrary whim of an official. National law must set out the ground of restriction in clear and precise terms.

- *Legitimate aim*: the interference or restriction must follow a legitimate purpose, that is, be based on one of the exhaustive grounds of limitation listed in the international standards which define the freedom.

- *Proportionality*: the restriction must be 'necessary' in the sense that there is 'a pressing social need' for it and that any measure taken is the minimum required to achieve the purpose of the limitation in a democratic society.

- *Presumption of freedom*: freedom is the rule, its limitation the exception. In the *Sunday Times Case*, which involved a claim of justified judicial restriction on the publication of information by a newspaper, the European Court of Human Rights noted that freedom of expression is not a right that is to be balanced equally with the permissible restrictions. It is rather a right that is subject to a limited number of restrictions that must be narrowly construed and convincingly justified, ultimately to a court.[5] Thus one should start with a strong presumption in favour of the freedom in question. The onus is on the authorities in the particular case to show that it is legitimate to restrict it.

The following sections consider, in turn, the right to freedom of thought (Section 2), freedom of expression (Section 3), freedom of association (Section 4), and freedom of assembly (Section 5). Each section explains the sources of the respective right, its scope, and the limitations that can be imposed on it.

2 FREEDOM OF THOUGHT, CONSCIENCE, AND RELIGION

2.1 SOURCES

This freedom is enshrined in Article 18 UDHR and in Article 18 of the International Covenant on Civil and Political Rights (ICCPR) as well as its Article 27 concerning the rights of minorities. It is also to be found in all regional human rights instruments.[6] The equality and non-discrimination provisions of the ICCPR (Articles 2, 3, and 26) and

---

[3] Bacquet, 'Manifestation of Belief and Religious Symbols at Schools: Setting Boundaries in English Courts' (2009) 4 *Religion and HR* 121; Howard, 'School Bans on the Wearing of Religious Symbols: Examining the Implications of the Recent Case Law from the UK' (2009) 4 *Religion and HR* 7. See also the Report of the Special Rapporteur on Freedom of Religion or Belief, A/HRC/16/53 (15 December 2010) 13–15.

[4] See also Chapter 5.   [5] *Sunday Times v UK* (1979) 2 EHRR 245, para 65.

[6] ECHR, Art 9; Protocol 1 to the ECHR, Art 2; Charter of Fundamental Rights of the European Union, Art 10; ACHR, Art 12; ACHPR, Art 8; Arab Charter on Human Rights, Art 30; ASEAN Human Rights Declaration, Art 22.

their equivalents in the regional instruments are vital for the enjoyment of the freedom as they prohibit unjustified differential treatment on the basis of religion. The Human Rights Committee has adopted a General Comment on the scope and meaning of Article 18 of the Covenant.[7] No international human rights treaty specifically devoted to freedom of thought, conscience, and religion has ever been adopted. However, an important Declaration was agreed by the UN General Assembly in 1981,[8] which provides the mandate of the Special Rapporteur on freedom of religion or belief, appointed by the UN Human Rights Council.[9]

2.2 SCOPE

Article 18 UDHR proclaims:

> Everyone has the right to freedom of thought, conscience and religion; this right includes freedom to change his religion or belief, and freedom, either alone or in community with others and in public or private, to manifest his religion or belief in teaching, practice, worship and observance.

The UDHR by its nature could not specify fully the substance of this freedom in international law. That came with the drafting of Article 18 ICCPR. The predominant focus of both texts is on freedom of religion. However, the scope of the right is wider. It protects freedom of thought, that is, the right of the individual to have independent thoughts, ideas, and beliefs. This includes, for instance, an individual's right not to have to accept a political ideology or a religion with which he or she disagrees. Freedom of conscience, the individual's moral sense of right and wrong, is also explicitly recognized and protected. One common instance, considered in Section 2.4, in which this freedom is invoked arises where a citizen refuses on grounds of conscience to undertake compulsory military service. Finally, Article 18(4) ICCPR offers specific safeguards against the indoctrination of children. It establishes a duty on the state to respect the liberty of parents or guardians to determine the religious and moral education of their children in conformity with their own convictions. The child's right to freedom of thought, conscience, and religion is provided for in the Convention on the Rights of the Child (CRC).[10]

2.3 FREEDOM OF RELIGION OR BELIEF

While freedom of religion is the central concern of Article 18 ICCPR, that provision speaks of 'religion or belief', thus underlining the intention of the drafters that all beliefs, including beliefs other than religious, are protected. The Human Rights Committee has confirmed this understanding in its General Comment: 'Article 18 protects theistic, non-theistic and atheistic beliefs, as well as the right not to profess any religion or belief.'[11]

There is no definition of religion offered in any international human rights instrument. It is probably impossible to agree a definition given the sheer diversity of religious ideas in the world. However, the significance of religion as one of the 'fundamental elements in [the] conception of life' for believers is recognized in international human rights law.[12]

---

[7] HRC, General Comment 22, HRI/GEN/1/Rev.9 (Vol I) 204.

[8] Declaration on the Elimination of All Forms of Intolerance and Discrimination Based on Religion or Belief, GA Res 36/55 (25 November 1981).

[9] HR Council Res 22/20 (12 April 2013). See Wiener, 'The Mandate of the Special Rapporteur on Freedom of Religion or Belief—Institutional, Procedural and Substantive Legal Issues' (2007) 2 Religion and HR 3.

[10] Art 14.   [11] General Comment 22, n 7, para 2.   [12] 1981 Declaration, n 8, preamble.

Freedom of religion is an individual right but has a collective aspect also. It means the right to hold spiritual beliefs and *to live by them*, whether in private or in public, alone or in community with others. The Human Rights Committee has stated that the term religion or belief is to be broadly construed. It is not limited to traditional religions.[13] New religions are as entitled to protection as old ones. But there are limits. A Canadian group, the 'Assembly of the Church of the Universe', whose beliefs required the cultivation and worship of marijuana which they termed 'God's tree of life' had a complaint of a violation of their freedom of religion dismissed. The Committee thought it inconceivable that the cultivation and worship of a narcotic drug could be a protected religion or belief under Article 18 of the Covenant.[14]

2.3.1 Manifestation of religion

Article 18 ICCPR speaks of the right to manifest religion through 'worship, observance, practice and teaching'. The Human Rights Committee has offered guidance as to the wide range of activities encompassed by these words:

> The concept of *worship* extends to ritual and ceremonial acts giving direct expression to belief, as well as various practices integral to such acts, including the building of places of worship, the use of ritual formulae and objects, the display of symbols, and the observance of holidays and days of rest. The *observance and practice* of religion or belief may include not only ceremonial acts but also such customs as the observance of dietary regulations, the wearing of distinctive clothing or head coverings, participation in rituals associated with certain stages of life, and the use of a particular language customarily spoken by a group. In addition, the *practice and teaching* of religion or belief includes acts integral to the conduct by religious groups of their basic affairs, such as the freedom to choose their religious leaders, priests and teachers, the freedom to establish seminaries or religious schools and the freedom to prepare and distribute religious texts or publications.[15]

Practices that are merely *motivated* by religious belief are not protected. There must be an intimate connection between the act and the belief.

2.3.2 Freedom to change religion or belief

It follows from the freedom of thought and conscience that one may decide to change one's beliefs. The individual's right to change or choose religious belief is contested particularly by the Islamic faith. In some Muslim majority countries conversion to another religion constitutes the offence of apostasy, punishable by death. Freedom to change a religion or belief is stated explicitly in Article 18 UDHR. However, reflecting Muslim sensitivities over the issue,[16] Article 18 ICCPR speaks of 'freedom to have or to adopt a religion or belief of his choice'. But despite this difference of language, the Human Rights Committee has confirmed that Article 18 guarantees that anyone may replace a current religion with another religion or become an atheist.[17] States must respect this right by abolishing state-sanctioned punishments for conversion and ensuring that there are no administrative obstacles to changing religion. There is also a positive obligation to protect individuals from harassment or violence from third parties that arises as a consequence of conversion.

---

[13] General Comment 22, n 7, para 2.

[14] *MAB, WAT and JAYT v Canada*, CCPR/C/50/D570/1993 (25 April 1994).

[15] General Comment 22, n 7, para 4 (emphases added).

[16] Boyle, 'Freedom of Religion in International Law' in Rehman and Breau (eds), *Religion, Human Rights and International Law* (Brill, 2007) 37–40.   [17] General Comment 22, n 7, para 5.

2.3.3 Proselytism

Article 18(2) ICCPR stipulates that there must be no coercion of the individual in the decision to either retain or to change beliefs. Subject to this prohibition on forced conversion, the right to spread one's faith and to seek to persuade others to convert to it is protected as the manifestation of religion.[18] Proselytism or missionary activity by religious groups is, however, a controversial matter according to some religions. Conversion from Islam is prohibited for Muslims and in India several states have passed anti-conversion laws aimed primarily at inhibiting conversion from Hinduism to Christianity. Some religious communities, inter-faith organizations and NGOs have proposed various voluntary codes of conduct for religious conversion.[19]

2.3.4 Religion and the state

International human rights law does not require a separation between religion and the state. Such separation is to be found in the constitutional arrangements of many states, following the long-established examples of France and the USA. But in other states the relationships range from fusion of state and religion to formal recognition in law of the majority faith. The sole principles on religion and the state that international human rights law insists upon are those of pluralism and non-discrimination. Thus, the existence of a state church should not entail the suppression of, or discrimination against, minority faiths or new religions.[20] It is the duty of the state to defend religious diversity in a democratic society, and to insist on the values of pluralism and tolerance should tensions arise from the coexistence of different faiths or beliefs.[21] The European Court of Human Rights has ruled that for democracy to function properly, the state has to remain neutral and impartial in its relations with various religions, denominations, and beliefs.[22] In states that require the registration of religions to give legal status to a denomination, neither the law nor its application should discriminate between religions by refusing, for example, to register some faiths while recognizing others. All religions must have the freedom to establish communities or organizations and these should be autonomous in their activities, including in determining their own leadership without interference from the state.[23]

While there may be exceptional cases,[24] the state has no general authority to decide whether or not a religion is legitimate. In *Moscow Branch of the Salvation Army v Russia*, the branch was refused registration by the city authorities. The authorities claimed that it was a paramilitary organization because of the word 'army' in its name and because its members wore uniforms and had ranks similar to those used in the military.[25] The branch complained to the European Court of Human Rights, which found a violation of its freedom of association in the context of the guarantee of freedom of religion. The Court emphasized that the guarantee of freedom of religion meant the state had no discretion to decide whether religious beliefs or the means used to manifest them were legitimate. It could not be credibly argued that the Salvation Army advocated the violent overthrow of the constitution or threatened the security of the state.

---

[18] *Kokkinakis v Greece* (1994) 17 EHRR 397.

[19] See Richards, Svendsen, and Bless, 'Voluntary Codes of Conduct for Religious Persuasion: Effective Tools for Balancing Human Rights and Resolving Conflicts?' (2011) 6 *Religion and HR* 151; Report of the Special Rapporteur on Freedom of Religion or Belief, A/67/303 (13 August 2012).

[20] General Comment 22, n 7, para 9.

[21] *Serif v Greece* (1999) 31 EHRR 561; *Metropolitan Church of Bessarabia and others v Moldova* (2002) 35 EHRR 306.

[22] *Hasan and Chaush v Bulgaria* (2002) 34 EHRR 1339.   [23] *Hasan and Chaush v Bulgaria*, n 22.

[24] *MAB, WAT and JAYT v Canada*, n 14.   [25] (2006) 44 EHRR 912.

2.4 LIMITATIONS

2.4.1 *Forum internum* and *forum externum*

An important distinction is to be drawn between those dimensions of the freedom of religion or belief which may be subject to limitation and those which may never be limited. Under Article 18(3) ICCPR it is the manifestation of the freedom of religion or belief in 'worship, observance, practice and teaching' (the forum externum) which may be limited. The individual's freedom of thought, conscience, religion, or belief (forum internum), guaranteed in Article 18(1), must be respected by the state unconditionally, and that includes the freedom to have or adopt a religion or belief of one's choice. Thus, no one may be compelled to reveal his or her thoughts or beliefs, for example by a requirement to swear a religious oath or to carry a religious affiliation in an identity card.[26] Equally, as Article 18(4) makes clear, there may be no restriction on the liberty of parents in regard to the moral and religious education of their children.

2.4.2 Grounds of limitation

Manifestation of religious belief may be limited on the grounds set out in Article 18(3) ICCPR: 'public safety, order, health, or morals or the fundamental rights and freedoms of others'. National security, however, is not included as a permissible ground in the case of freedom of religion, whereas it is a permissible ground with the other freedoms. As explained already, any restriction applied on one of the permitted grounds must be prescribed by law and be necessary in a democratic society.

Religious clothing and symbols

A contemporary and complex issue regarding religious manifestation concerns regulation of the wearing of religious dress or symbols in public spaces, which amounts to an interference with the believer's freedom to express their religious beliefs or identity. For example, the injunction to women in the Koran of *Hijab* or modesty is the religious source of the headscarf or the *burka* worn by some Muslim women.[27] International human rights bodies have taken different positions as to whether the wearing of the veil in public may be restricted by the state. They all agree that such restrictions are an interference with the right to manifest religious belief but differ on whether such interferences can be justified.

The Human Rights Committee found that the exclusion from a university in Uzbekistan of a practising Muslim student for wearing a headscarf interfered with her rights under Article 18 ICCPR.[28] The Committee held in line with its General Comment[29] that the freedom to manifest her religion encompasses the right to wear clothes or attire in public that was in conformity with her religion. The Committee was also of the view that her exclusion from studies amounted to a violation of her right to be free from coercion in matters of religion under Article 18(2). In contrast, in *Leyla Sahin v Turkey*, the European Court of Human Rights upheld a similar Turkish regulation which prevented the applicant from continuing her medical studies at Istanbul University because she refused to remove her headscarf on religious grounds.[30] The majority of the judges considered that

---

[26] General Comment 22, n 7, para 3; *Buscarini and Others v San Marino* (2000) 30 EHRR 208; *Alexandridis v Greece*, App no 19516/06, Judgment of 21 February 2008; *Sinan Işik v Turkey*, App no 21924/05, Judgment of 2 February 2010.

[27] McGoldrick, 'Extreme Religious Dress: Perspectives on Veiling Controversies' in Hare and Weinstein (eds) n 2, 400.

[28] *Hudoyberganova v Uzbekistan*, CCPR/C/82/D/931/2000 (5 November 2004).   [29] See n 7.

[30] (2007) 44 EHRR 5.

the interference with her religious freedom was justified in the interests of the rights and freedoms of others, which it linked to the Turkish constitutional principles of equality and secularism.

Issues regarding regulation of religious dress are not limited to Islamic dress. In 2004 a French law banned the wearing of conspicuous religious symbols in state schools invoking the constitutional principle of secularism. The law prohibited not only the Islamic veil but also Jewish skullcaps, Sikh turbans, and Christian crosses. The European Court of Human Rights rejected complaints over this law brought by several Muslim girl pupils and Sikh boys over their expulsion from school. The children had worn substitute headwear, kerchiefs in the case of the girls and under-turbans in the case of the boys, which they refused to remove.[31] Noting that the pupils could still continue their schooling by correspondence courses, the Court found that the interference with their freedom to manifest their religion was justified and proportionate to the aims pursued, namely the rights and freedoms of others and public order. However, the Human Rights Committee took a different view in a communication based on similar facts, holding that expulsion could neither be considered necessary nor proportionate.[32] Where restrictions upon religious dress in the workplace were imposed by a private company, the European Court has confirmed that the state still has a duty to ensure that a 'fair balance' is struck between the interests of the individual and those of the company.[33]

The Human Rights Committee has also held that a requirement for a Sikh man to appear bareheaded in an identity card photograph constitutes a continuing interference with his right to freedom of religion. The Committee noted that:

> even if the obligation to remove the turban for the identity photograph might be described as a one-time requirement, it would potentially interfere with the author's freedom of religion on a continuing basis because he would always appear without his religious head covering in the identity photograph and could therefore be compelled to remove his turban during identity checks.[34]

In some Muslim majority countries it is compulsory for women to wear a veil, a requirement which may also violate the freedom of religion. A human rights approach would argue that it should be for the individual to decide whether to wear religious dress or not. States should respect and seek to accommodate that choice.

Conscientious objection to military service

In a number of states, conscription laws require that male adult citizens (in the case of Israel females also) have a legal duty to undertake a period of military training or service. For some individuals such a duty conflicts with their conscience due to their religious or philosophical beliefs, and they assert the right to refuse to undertake military service. International human rights standards are evolving in the direction of accepting that such refusal is a manifestation of the individual's conscience and should be protected under the guarantee of freedom of thought, conscience, and religion. The right to conscientious

---

[31] *Aktas v France, Bayrak v France, Gamaleddyn v France, Ghazal v France, J Singh v France, R Singh v France*, App nos 43563/08, 14308/08, 18527/08, 29134/08, 25463/08, and 27561/08, Admissibility Decision of 17 July 2009.   [32] *Singh v France*, CCPR/C/106/D/1852/2008 (4 February 2013).

[33] *Eweida and Others v UK*, App nos 48420/10, 59842/10, 51671/10, and 36156/10, Judgment of 15 January 2013.

[34] *Ranjit Singh v France*, CCPR/C/102/D/1876/2009 (27 September 2011) para 8.4.

objection to military service has been recognized by the Human Rights Committee and other UN bodies.[35] The Committee has recognized that states may, instead, require individuals to undertake alternative service. However, this service must not be punitive in nature. Rather, it must be a real service to the community and compatible with respect for human rights.[36] Similarly, the European Union (EU) Charter of Fundamental Rights and Freedoms recognizes a right to conscientious objection to military service. All member states of the Council of Europe, except Turkey, have recognized such a right.[37] In *Bayatyan v Armenia*, the European Court of Human Rights relied upon this fact when holding that compulsory military service can only be justified where convincing and compelling reasons suggest that there is a pressing social need for conscription.[38] On the other hand, the Inter-American Commission on Human Rights has declined to accept that obligatory military service may conflict with freedom of conscience.[39]

3 FREEDOM OF OPINION AND EXPRESSION

3.1 SOURCES

This freedom is contained in Article 19 UDHR and in Articles 19 and 20 ICCPR. Detailed and authoritative guidance on states' obligations under these provisions can be found in the Human Rights Committee's General Comment 34.[40] Similar but not identical formulations of the freedom can be found in the regional human rights instruments.[41] There are also important provisions in the UN Convention on the Elimination of Racial Discrimination (ICERD), in particular Article 4, which concerns the prohibition of racist speech and organizations. The CRC recognizes the child's right to freedom of expression.[42] Since 1993 there exists the position of Special Rapporteur on the promotion and protection of the right to freedom of opinion and expression, who is now appointed by the Human Rights Council.[43]

3.2 SCOPE

Freedom of expression has been described as the touchstone of all rights. Not only is freedom of expression inseparable from freedom of thought, association, and assembly, it is essential for the enjoyment of all rights, including economic, social, and cultural rights. It is a vital freedom for development, the functioning of democracy, and modern economies.

---

[35] General Comment 22, n 7, para 11; *Mr Yeo-Bum Yoon and Mr Myung-Jin Choi v Republic of Korea*, CCPR/C/88/D/1321–1322/2004 (23 January 2007). See also CHR Res 1998/77 (22 April 1998); UN Working Group on Arbitrary Detention, Recommendation 2, E/CN.4/2001/14, paras 91–4; OHCHR, *Conscientious Objection to Military Service* (2012).

[36] *Jeong et al. v Republic of Korea*, CCPRC/C/101/D/1642-1741/2007 (24 March 2011).

[37] EU Charter of Fundamental Rights, Art 10.

[38] (2012) 54 EHRR 15. See also, *Thlimmenos v Greece* (2000) 31 EHRR 411; *Ülke v Turkey* (2009) 48 EHRR 48.

[39] Case 12.219, *Cristián Daniel Sahli Vera et al. v Chile*, IACommHR Report No 43/05 (10 March 2005).

[40] HRC, General Comment 34, CCPR/C/GC/34 (12 September 2011). This replaced General Comment 10, HRI/GEN/1/Rev.9 (Vol 1) 181.

[41] ECHR, Art 10; EU Charter of Fundamental Rights, Art 11; ACHR, Arts 13 and 14; ACHPR, Art 9; Arab Charter on Human Rights, Art 32; ASEAN Human Rights Declaration, Art 23.

[42] Arts 12 and 13.   [43] HR Council Res 16/4 (8 April 2011).

Article 19 UDHR provides the foundation for the fuller definition of the freedom in the ICCPR:

> Everyone has the right to freedom of opinion and expression; this right includes freedom to hold opinions without interference and to seek, receive and impart information and ideas through any media and regardless of frontiers.

Although this text was drafted over 60 years ago, it powerfully expresses the ideal of freedom of speech in today's era of the Internet and other digital communication technologies. Freedom of expression is an individual right. It means the freedom, without interference or penalty, to speak one's mind. Freedom of expression also has its collective components. Human beings communicate with others, not with themselves. The freedom includes the right to hear other views and to exchange ideas and information with others. It also includes the right to inform oneself and to be informed. Hence, the crucial importance of all media as means of communication.

3.2.1 Freedom of opinion

Article 19 ICCPR guarantees freedom of opinion as well as expression. Human beings have diverse and differing opinions on all kinds of subjects, including political and social affairs. Article 19(1) provides that everyone is entitled to hold such views without interference. No one can be forced to think in a particular way. Nor should anyone suffer prejudice, discrimination, or repression because of their views or opinions. The freedom to hold opinions may not be restricted. In the words of the Human Rights Committee: 'it is a right to which the Covenant admits no exception or restriction'.[44] In other words people may think what they like.

3.2.2 Freedom of expression

Article 19(2) ICCPR sets out the positive meaning of freedom of expression under international law. Its scope is extensive. The right is defined as including freedom to seek, receive, and impart information and ideas of all kinds. Freedom *to seek* includes active and investigative journalism in the public interest. Freedom *to receive* has been interpreted by the European Court of Human Rights as including the right of the public to be informed and the duty of the mass media to impart information to the public.[45] The freedom to *impart* extends to every kind of information and idea expressed through any media of choice, 'either orally, in writing or in print, [or] in the form of art'.[46] As the European Court has noted, the freedom 'is applicable not only to "information" or "ideas" that are favourably received or regarded as inoffensive or as a matter of indifference, but also to those that offend, shock or disturb the State or any sector of the population'.[47]

All forms of expression are protected. These include spoken and written language, as well as art and images. The manner in which these are transmitted, that is through books, newspapers, the Internet, leaflets, film, paintings, sculpture, song, and so on, is also protected. The Internet has become 'one of the principal means by which individuals exercise their right to freedom of expression and information; it provides essential tools for taking part in activities and discussions concerning political issues or matters of public interest'.[48] In 2011 a Joint Declaration on Freedom of Expression and the Internet was adopted by the UN Special Rapporteur on freedom of expression and Special Rapporteurs on freedom of expression from the Organization of American States, the Organization for Security and

---

[44] General Comment 34, n 40, para 9.

[45] *Thorgeir Thorgeirson v Iceland* (1992) 14 EHRR 843, para 63.   [46] ICCPR, Art 19(2).

[47] *Handyside v UK* (1976) 1 EHRR 737, para 49. See also *Ivcher-Bronstein v Peru*, IACtHR Series C No 74 (6 June 2001).   [48] *Yildirim v Turkey*, App no 3111/10, Judgment of 18 December 2012, para 54.

Cooperation in Europe, and the African Commission on Human and Peoples' Rights. The Declaration sets out that freedom of expression must apply to the Internet in the same way that it applies to any other media.[49]

There is no human right to access the Internet. However, given the increasing importance of the Internet in daily lives, particularly in terms of participation and facilitating governmental transparency and access to diverse sources of information, some have argued that the positive obligations of states to promote and facilitate the right to freedom of expression must include facilitating access to the Internet.[50]

Freedom of expression is to be enjoyed 'without regards to frontiers', in other words it does not stop at the borders of the state. This clause was intended to outlaw forms of censorship such as the Cold War practice of radio jamming of foreign broadcast signals and extends in today's digital age, for example, to the blocking of access to the Internet or mobile phones. So, completely blocking access to the Internet during times of social unrest, as took place during the anti-government protests arising in various countries in the Arab world in 2011, known as the Arab Spring, or the blocking of content of particular web sites, such as YouTube, Facebook, or Twitter, constitute interferences with the right.

3.2.3 Media freedom

There is no explicit recognition or protection offered to the press and other media in international human rights standards, although such is often to be found in national laws and constitutions. At the international level, the freedoms and responsibilities of the press have been developed from the guarantee of freedom of expression of the individual. The protection afforded under human rights standards to all media—modern mass electronic and print media and the new information communication technologies—is justified because of their role in making people's freedom of expression meaningful and their contribution to democratic life. All such means of communication provide access to news and to opportunities to exchange information and ideas. International and national standards on freedom of expression have largely been shaped by the struggle for journalistic and artistic independence against government licensing and censorship of media. That struggle continues in different parts of the world. Media freedom is thus inseparable in practice from the enjoyment of freedom of expression in society. The media has a watchdog role on the exercise of power in society, and free media facilitates political debate. As the European Court of Human Rights has put it:

> Freedom of the press affords the public one of the best means of discovering and forming an opinion of the ideas and attitudes of political leaders. In particular it gives politicians the opportunity to reflect and comment on the preoccupations of public opinion; it thus enables everyone to participate in the free political debate which is at the core of the concept of a democratic society.[51]

States must, therefore, protect journalists from threats, violence, or other acts of harassment that stop them from fulfilling this essential role.[52] Human rights bodies have

---

[49] Available at: <http://www.oas.org/en/iachr/expression/showarticle.asp?artID=848&lID=1>. See also, Report of the Special Rapporteur on the promotion and protection of the right to freedom of expression and opinion, A/HRC/17/27 (16 May 2011).

[50] See Report of the Special Rapporteur on the promotion and protection of the right to freedom of opinion and expression, A/66/290 (10 August 2011), paras 61–63.

[51] *Castells v Spain* (1992) 14 EHRR 445, para 43.

[52] General Comment 34, n 40, para 23; *Vélez Restrepo v Colombia* IACtHR Series C No 248 (3 September 2012) para 209.

adopted an expansive definition of the term 'journalists', which includes: 'professional full-time reporters and analysts, as well as bloggers and others who engage in forms of self-publication in print, on the Internet or elsewhere'.[53]

But media in all its forms is also a source of considerable power, including economic power. The international standards speak, therefore, of the media's duties and responsibilities. Media regulation is necessary to ensure democratic accountability and to guard against excessive concentration of ownership. Regulatory regimes, whether self-regulation or established by legislation, will differ according to different media. Thus, public, private, or community broadcasting systems and the print media will often be subject to different regulatory codes. But all such regulatory systems should protect editorial freedom, promote plurality of the media, and operate independent of government.

3.2.4 Freedom of information laws

The most striking advance in the norms on freedom of expression over recent years has been the growth of laws implementing the right to access official information held by governments. Democracies, both new and old, have come to understand that transparency affords governments and public administration legitimacy in the eyes of the public. In all regions of the world, governments have established 'the right to know' through legislation. An 'access to information law' works on the principle of maximum disclosure: all official information should be made public as a matter of principle, unless there are legitimate reasons justifying non-disclosure.

In *Claude Reyes and others v Chile* the Inter-American Court of Human Rights became the first international tribunal to hold that there is a right to access information held by the government, derived from the guarantee of freedom of expression.[54] The case originated in a request for information made by three environmental activists about a controversial deforestation project, which was ignored by the government. The Human Rights Committee has also confirmed that states must 'proactively put in the public domain Government information of public interest . . . [and] enact the necessary procedures, whereby one may gain access to information, such as by means for freedom of information legislation'.[55] In 2009, the Council of Europe adopted the first international treaty on access to official documents.[56]

3.3 LIMITATIONS

If people may think what they like, they may not always say or write what they like. As opposed to freedom of opinion, freedom of expression is not an absolute right. Under Article 19(3) ICCPR its exercise carries with it 'special duties and responsibilities'. Such language acknowledges the power of the media, but also the justification of restriction where it is necessary to respect the rights or reputations of others, and where it is necessary on grounds of national security, public order, public health, or morals. It is possible to examine only some of these grounds here. But as discussed already, it is crucial how restrictions are applied because if wrongly or excessively invoked, they can 'chill' the freedom or even

---

[53] General Comment 34, n 40, para 44; Report of the Special Rapporteur on the promotion and protection of the right to freedom of opinion and expression, A/HRC/20/17 (4 June 2012).
[54] IACtHR Series C No 151 (19 September 2006). See also *Társaság a Szabadságjogokért v Hungary* (2011) 53 EHRR 3.   [55] General Comment 34, n 40, para 19.
[56] Council of Europe Convention on Access to Official Documents.

eliminate it. Thus, a ground such as national security in the context of counter-terrorism is often misapplied or abused to the detriment of freedom of expression.[57]

3.3.1 Privacy

One right which may clash with freedom of expression is privacy.[58] In *Von Hannover v Germany*, Princess Caroline of Monaco, who had campaigned for many years over paparazzi taking pictures for publication in European magazines of her and her children, complained to the European Court of Human Rights.[59] The Court found that her right to privacy was violated. There was no justification for the constant media intrusion into her private life. The public interest was not advanced since the photographs were published to satisfy public curiosity, not to contribute to public debate. The Court considered that the Princess, although a member of a royal family, exercised no official functions and was thus a private person. While public figures such as politicians and popular celebrities do have a right to private life, it is less extensive given that they are willingly in the public arena.[60] Therefore, when considering whether the correct balance has been struck between freedom of expression and privacy, regard should be had to the following issues: whether the expression contributes to a debate of general interest; how well-known the person concerned is; the nature of the activities that are the subject of the report and how they link to the role of the person concerned; the prior conduct of the person concerned; how the information was obtained and its veracity; the content, form, and consequences of publication; and finally the severity of the sanction imposed.[61]

3.3.2 Defamation

To publish a false statement about another which damages his or her reputation is a civil and often a criminal wrong. But the implementation of laws which impose liability for defamation can, and often do, undermine the freedom of the media to fulfil their function of informing the public and to comment critically on public affairs. Given the vital importance of free media in a democracy, international human rights standards have been directed at ensuring that national laws on defamation are applied as narrowly as possible as regards 'political speech'. Robust criticism of the government or a politician should be tolerated in the interests of open debate on political issues. In *Lingens v Austria*, a journalist was convicted of criminal libel because he had accused a former Prime Minister of Austria of political opportunism and of using his influence to prevent an investigation of a political ally for Nazi crimes. The European Court of Human Rights found that Austrian law, which required Lingens to prove the truth of what were his opinions, operated as an excessive interference with press freedom.[62] There is an increasing trend towards the abolition of criminal penalties for defamatory statements based on the argument that civil remedies such as the payment of damages is a sufficient sanction and the threat of criminal prosecution has a chilling effect on freedom of expression. This approach has garnered the support of the Human Rights Committee.[63]

---

[57] General Comment 34, n 40, para 46. See also Barendt, 'Incitement to, and Glorification of, Terrorism' in Hare and Weinstein (eds), n 2, 446.

[58] ICCPR, Art 17.　　[59] (2005) 40 EHRR 1.

[60] General Comment 34, n 40, para 38; *Krone Verlag GmbH and Co KG v Austria* (2003) 36 EHRR 57.

[61] *Axel Springer AG v Germany* (2012) 55 EHRR 6, paras 89–95.

[62] (1986) 8 EHRR 407. See also *Bodrozic v Serbia and Montenegro*, CCPR/C/85/D/1180/2003 (31 October 2005).

[63] General Comment 34, n 40, para 47; *Adonis v Philippines*, CCPR/C/103/D/1815/2008/Rev.1 (26 April 2012).

3.3.3 Hate speech

Control of the advocacy of violence, hatred, and discrimination against individuals or groups on the basis of their race, colour, ethnicity, religious beliefs, sexual orientation, or other status presents a challenge to all states. The Internet has added a global dimension to the availability of propaganda advocating violence or hatred of others. Article 20 ICCPR and Article 4 ICERD *oblige* states to criminalize speech that amounts to war propaganda or that advocates racial hatred. However, these limitations on expression must be compliant with Article 19(3) and thus be provided by law and be the least restrictive means of achieving the relevant aim. The use of speech to incite violence is a criminal offence in virtually all states. But to strike an acceptable balance between the right to freedom of expression and restraint on other forms of objectionable speech is in practice often difficult.[64]

Islamophobia and anti-Semitism

Incitement to ethnic, racial, or religious hostility, hatred, and discrimination is not protected speech. A current concern is the widespread expression, particularly in Europe, of prejudice and hostility towards Muslims, sometimes termed Islamophobia. In 2001–2, a member of the British National Party displayed a large poster in his flat window with a photograph of the Twin Towers in flames with the caption 'Islam out of Britain—Protect the British People' and a symbol of a crescent and star in a prohibition sign. He was convicted of displaying hostility to a racial or religious group. His complaint to the European Court of Human Rights that his freedom of expression was infringed was dismissed.[65] The poster, the Court held, represented a vehement attack against Muslims linking the group as a whole with a grave act of terrorism.

Like Islamophobia, anti-Semitism is a widespread phenomenon, which frequently finds expression in Holocaust denial. Holocaust denial or negationism denies the Nazi genocide against Jews during the Second World War or seeks to minimize its true scale. Such speech is a criminal offence in several European states. A French historian, Robert Faurisson, in an interview with a magazine said it was his personal conviction that there were no homicidal gas chambers for the extermination of Jews in Nazi concentration camps. When convicted over these comments, he claimed before the Human Rights Committee that his freedom of expression had been violated. The Committee upheld the conviction as a justifiable interference with his freedom of expression under Article 19 ICCPR.[66] It was persuaded by the French government's argument that holocaust denial is the main vehicle of anti-Semitism in France.[67]

Blasphemy

Criticism of religion, as distinct from incitement to hatred of people because of their religious beliefs, is currently a highly contested freedom of expression issue at the international level. For example, the 1988 publication of *The Satanic Verses* by Salman Rushdie and the 2005 Danish cartoons that depicted the Prophet Mohammed were both considered to be 'insulting' to the Islamic faith.[68] Such incidences, amongst others, led to calls for a restriction on

---

[64] See Report of the Special Rapporteur on the promotion and protection of the right to freedom of opinion and expression, A/67/357 (7 September 2012).
[65] *Mark Anthony Norwood v UK*, App no 23131/03, Admissibility Decision of 16 November 2004.
[66] *Robert Faurisson v France*, CCPR/C/58/D/550/1993 (8 November 1996).
[67] See also *Ross v Canada*, CCPR/C/70/D/736/1997 (18 October 2000).
[68] Cram, n 2; Keane, 'Cartoon Violence and Freedom of Expression' (2008) 30 *HRQ* 845.

freedom of expression in order to suppress 'defamation of religions' and the Human Rights Council and General Assembly, led by Muslim majority states, has passed resolutions supporting such an approach.[69] But others, mostly Western states, have rejected the need to protect religious institutions or doctrines from robust criticism, satire, or even ridicule. In 2011, the Human Rights Council moved away from the terminology of 'defamation of religion', returning to the idea of protecting believers from intolerance and violence.[70] This is a more convincing approach. Human rights law protects those individuals who have a religious belief rather than the religion itself. Therefore, blasphemy laws are, according to the Human Rights Committee, incompatible with the right to freedom of expression.[71] Nevertheless, a number of states still retain offences of blasphemy in their criminal codes and the European Court of Human Rights has accepted the legitimacy of a prosecution for blasphemy where 'believers may legitimately [have felt] themselves to be the object of unwarranted and offensive attacks' and the punishment imposed was an 'insignificant fine'.[72]

4 FREEDOM OF ASSOCIATION

4.1 SOURCES

Freedom of association is proclaimed as an individual right in Article 20 UDHR and is included in both international covenants and regional instruments.[73] Article 22 ICCPR provides a general guarantee of freedom of association. It also includes the right to form and join trade unions, a right independently recognized in Article 23(4) UDHR. Article 8 of the International Covenant on Economic, Social and Cultural Rights (ICESCR) provides for the association rights of trade unions. Trade union rights are more fully protected in the international agreements of the International Labour Organization (ILO).[74] The ILO Committee on Freedom of Association, comprising an equal number of representatives of governments, employers, and unions, oversees the protection of trade union freedoms.[75]

4.2 SCOPE

Freedom of association is the freedom to pursue collective action. It protects the right of individuals to form associations for common purposes, free from government interference. It includes the right of the association independently to determine its membership, appoint officers, employ staff, and generally conduct its own affairs subject only to the law. While linked historically with trade unions, the freedom includes the freedom to establish and belong to political parties, which are vital for the functioning of democracy. But the right of the individual to establish and participate in all manner of civil society associations or voluntary organizations is equally part of this freedom. Article 16 of the American Convention on Human Rights (ACHR) speaks of the right to establish associations for 'ideological, religious,

---

[69] Eg GA Res 62/154 (6 March 2008); HR Council Res 7/36 (28 March 2008). See Parmar, 'The Challenge of "Defamation of Religions" to Freedom of Expression and the International Human Rights System' [2009] EHRLR 353.

[70] HR Council Res 16/18 (12 April 2011).   [71] General Comment 34, n 40, para 48.

[72] I.A. v Turkey (2007) 45 EHRR 30, paras 29 and 32.

[73] ECHR, Art 11; EU Charter of Fundamental Rights, Art 12; ACHR, Art 16; ACHPR, Art 10; Arab Charter on Human Rights, Art 24.

[74] Freedom of Association and Protection of the Right to Organize Convention 1948 (No 87); Right to Organize and Collective Bargaining Convention 1949 (No 98).   [75] See also Chapter 12.

political, economic, labor, social, and cultural, sports, or other purposes'. This freedom is also of central importance to the activities of human rights defenders. The Declaration on Human Rights Defenders, passed by the UN General Assembly in 1999, affirms the right of human rights activists to form, join, and participate in NGOs for the purpose of, inter alia, seeking and imparting information about human rights, discussing and developing new ideas on human rights, and advocating on issues of human rights.[76]

4.2.1 The right not to associate

The right to associate includes the negative freedom to choose not to belong to an association and not to be compelled to join one. The negative formulation of the right is included in the UDHR (Article 20(2)) but not in the ICCPR. The explanation for its absence concerns the status of collective bargaining agreements between trade unions and employers over the employment of union members only (closed shop agreements). For the same reason the right to freedom of association under Article 11 ECHR is also silent on the right not to associate. The European Court of Human Rights has approached compulsory union membership on a case-by-case basis. In *Young, James and Webster v UK*, the Court found that the dismissal of individuals employed prior to a closed shop agreement violated the right to freedom of association of the dismissed employees.[77] In *Sigurjonsson v Iceland*, the same Court examined an Icelandic law that made taxi drivers' licences contingent upon membership of a union.[78] The applicant had been licensed before the regulation came into force, had principled reasons for objecting to union membership, and lost his licence as a result of his refusal to join. The Court found that the government interest in this rule— facilitating the regulation of public transport—was relevant but not sufficient to justify the extreme consequence of non-membership of the union.

In *Gustafsson v Sweden* the applicant owned a restaurant. He was not a member of the restaurant employers association and was not bound by any collective agreement which the union representing restaurant workers had agreed with the association. Because he refused to enter into a substitute agreement recognizing the rights of his workers to collective bargaining, his business was placed under a boycott by the union. The applicant complained that the union's actions violated his negative freedom of association, which the state should have protected. The European Court noted the special role in Sweden of collective agreements in labour relations and held that there had not been a violation of the negative right of association.[79] These cases illustrate the tension which can arise between the individual and collective dimensions of the freedom of association.

4.2.2 The right to strike

The Human Rights Committee has held that the right to association in the ICCPR does not include a right to strike. In *JB et al. v Canada*, the Committee noted that ILO Convention No 87 had been interpreted to provide such a right and that the ICESCR includes the right to strike along with its recognition of trade union rights.[80] The Committee pointed out that 'each international treaty, including the [ICCPR] has a life of its own and must be interpreted in a fair and just manner'.[81] Having been drafted in parallel discussions, the inclusion of the right to strike in the ICESCR without similar language in the ICCPR suggested that the right of association in that covenant was not intended to protect the right to strike.

---

[76] GA Res 53/144 (8 March 1999).   [77] (1981) 4 EHRR 38.   [78] (1993) 16 EHRR 462.
[79] (1996) 22 EHRR 409.   [80] CCPR/C/OP/1 (18 July 1986).
[81] *J.B. et al. v Canada*, n 80, para 6.2.

4.3 LIMITATIONS

The Human Rights Committee addressed the type of activities that constitute an interference with the right of association in *Korneenko et al. v Belarus*. In that case, the authorities stripped a human rights organization, 'Civil Initiatives', of its recognition because it had violated domestic regulations governing associations. Its official documentation was said to suffer from 'deficiencies' and it was accused of using equipment purchased with foreign grants for propaganda purposes. A domestic court ordered the dissolution of the group. The key determination for the Committee was whether the dissolution of the organization amounted to an interference with the right of association. The Committee held that the ICCPR protected all activities of an association. Dissolution of a group amounts to a severe interference with the freedom and must be strictly justified by reference to the grounds of limitation in Article 22(2). The government had failed to do this. Even if the NGO's documentation had been defective the extreme step taken of dissolving it was a disproportionate response. The Committee found a violation.[82]

Where domestic law requires registration of civic associations in order to obtain legal personality, a refusal or delay by the authorities in registration may constitute an interference with the freedom of association.[83]

4.3.1 Banning political parties

Political parties are an essential form of association if democracy is to exist. Without an effective democracy, human rights cannot be guaranteed. Political parties thus must be guaranteed the fullest freedom of association and compelling reasons must be given for any interference with the freedom. That principle applies most particularly where political parties are banned or dissolved.

In *Refah Partisi (the Welfare Party) and Others v Turkey*, the European Court of Human Rights upheld the decision of the Turkish Constitutional Court to disband the largest political party in the state.[84] The judgment sparked considerable controversy as at the time the Refah party was serving in a coalition government. Certain of its leaders were accused of advocating the introduction of Islamic law (*Sharia*) in Turkey, and violating the secular principles of the Turkish Constitution. The Court recognized that closure constituted an extreme interference in the right of association, but concluded unanimously that it was justifiable. It noted that 'protection of public safety and the rights and freedoms of others and the prevention of crime might depend on safeguarding the principle of secularism'.[85] The Refah party was likely poised to be able to implement policies that could undermine the democratic and secular nature of Turkey and threaten the rights of others.

The decision in *Refah* can be contrasted with an earlier Turkish case, *United Communist Party of Turkey and Others v Turkey*.[86] The Turkish Constitutional Court dissolved this political party on the basis that the party advocated class domination and threatened the territorial integrity of the state. The European Court found that the dissolution of the party was disproportionate. The party had not undertaken activities or adopted stances that would threaten the territorial integrity or national security of the state and the use of terminology that the state found offensive or threatening was not enough to justify the extreme step of dissolution of a political party.

Thus, unless a party threatens the democratic nature of a state, it cannot be suppressed, even if the party espouses offensive ideas. In *Ouranio Toxo and Others v Greece*, a political

---

[82] CCPR/C/88/D/1274/2004 (10 November 2006).
[83] *Ismayilov v Azerbaijan*, App no 4439/04, Judgment of 17 January 2008.   [84] (2003) 37 EHRR 1.
[85] (2003) 37 EHRR 1, para 66.   [86] (1998) 26 EHRR 121.

party representing the Macedonian minority adopted a name that was deemed offensive to the majority Greek population. The government removed a sign with the party's name on it, claiming that the name—written in Macedonian—was specifically intended to elicit memories of a violent battle between the Greek and Macedonian people and exacerbated tensions in the region. The party replaced the sign. In response, citizens, including political leaders, attacked the headquarters of the party and destroyed its equipment. The Court determined that the removal of the sign constituted an arbitrary interference. Concerns over regional tensions did not justify removing the sign. The use of a minority language, regardless of its ability to inflame the sentiments of others, could not be said to constitute a threat to democratic society. The Court again noted the essential role played by political parties in democratic systems and emphasized the importance of political pluralism for democracy. It found that Article 11 had been violated by both the government's acts and its failure to protect the party's premises.[87]

4.3.2 Additional limitations applicable to military and police

Article 22(2) ICCPR provides that members of the armed forces and of the police may be restricted by law in their exercise of the right of association. The provision, however, does not deny the right of military and police to freedom of association. It recognizes only that the state may regulate the exercise of that freedom. There are similar restrictions in the ECHR and the ACHR.

5 FREEDOM OF ASSEMBLY

5.1 SOURCES

The freedoms of assembly and association are contained in one provision in the UDHR and the ECHR,[88] and the Human Rights Council has created a single special procedure mandate for both rights.[89] The ICCPR (Article 21) and other regional instruments separate the rights.[90] While the rights of assembly and association are closely connected, they are distinct. They are both vital democratic freedoms that enable individuals to act collectively to promote their interests. Freedom of assembly is qualified as a right of 'peaceful assembly' or in the ACHR a right to 'peaceful assembly, without arms'. Specific types of assemblies, such as religious assemblies, are additionally protected by Article 18 ICCPR, as are private assemblies in one's home by Article 17 ICCPR.

5.2 SCOPE

The right of peaceful assembly protects non-violent, organized gatherings in public and private, both indoors and outdoors. A broad range of assemblies is encompassed, including political, economic, artistic, and social gatherings. The right also extends to counter-protests, though states have an obligation to ensure counter-demonstrators do not interfere with the initial demonstration.[91] Thus, states must not only abstain from interfering with the right, but are also required to take positive measures to protect

---

[87] n 1.   [88] UDHR, Art 20; ECHR, Art 11.
[89] Special Rapporteur on the rights to freedom of peaceful assembly and of association. See HR Council Res 15/21 (6 October 2010).
[90] ACHR, Art 15; ACHPR, Art 11; ASEAN Human Rights Declaration, Art 24.
[91] *Plattform 'Ärzte Für Das Leben' v Austria* (1988) 13 EHRR 204.

peaceful assemblies. Although the right envisages temporary gatherings, it also protects mass political protests that may last for weeks or months.

The African Commission on Human and Peoples' Rights found that the convictions and executions of four indigenous Ogoni activists violated their right to life and also their right of assembly. The Nigerian government alleged that the activists were responsible for the deaths of four men following a rally for indigenous rights. The activists were not accused of perpetrating the deaths, but held responsible because their peaceful assembly 'incited' the killings. The Commission held that the executions were part of a widespread attempt to intimidate protestors and limit demonstrations.[92]

5.3 LIMITATIONS

Restrictions on peaceful assembly may be imposed under Article 21(2) ICCPR, provided these are prescribed by law and necessary in a democratic society in the interests of national security or public safety, public order, the protection of public health or morals, or the protection of the rights and freedoms of others. Outright banning of a demonstration may prove necessary, but clearly requires the strongest justification. In *Öllinger v Austria*, the European Court of Human Rights held that the state's duty to protect the right of assembly as far as possible should have included considering alternatives to a total ban on a small counter-protest at a cemetery on All Saints Day where a commemoration was to take place for former SS soldiers.[93]

5.3.1 Prior notifications and permits

Regulation of demonstrations or gatherings through prior notification or issuing of a permit by the authorities before a march or public meeting can take place is compatible with the freedom to assemble. In *Kivenmaa v Finland*, the Human Rights Committee accepted that a requirement to notify the police of an intended demonstration in a public place in Helsinki six hours before its commencement would be compatible with the permitted limitations laid down in Article 21 ICCPR.[94] Such administrative procedures enable other rights and interests to be balanced with the right to assemble, for example the freedom of movement of others, national security, public order, and the normal circulation of traffic. Undue delays or arbitrariness in the issuance of permits, however, can constitute a violation of the right. In *Baczkowski v Poland*, the European Court of Human Rights heard a complaint over the mayor of Warsaw's refusal to authorize a march and different other public gatherings to protest over discrimination, including against homosexual people. The mayor had said publicly before considering the applications for permits that he would ban any public propaganda for homosexuality. The Court found, inter alia, that the mayor's refusal to permit the demonstrations constituted a discriminatory interference with the right to freedom of assembly.[95]

The dispersal of a spontaneous peaceful demonstration, one that occurs, for example, in response to an unexpected political event, solely because of the absence of prior notice may amount to a disproportionate restriction on freedom of peaceful assembly.[96] However, the police can disperse a demonstration where there was ample time to file notice of a public

---

[92] 137/94, 149/94, 154/96, and 161/97, *International Pen, Constitutional Rights Project, Interights on behalf of Ken Saro-Wiwa Jr and Civil Liberties Organisation v Nigeria*, 12th Activity Report of the ACommHPR (1998–1999) paras 1–2, 106.   [93] (2008) 46 EHRR 38.
[94] CCPR/C/50/D/412/1990 (9 June 1994).   [95] (2009) 48 EHRR 19.
[96] *Bukta and Others v Hungary* (2010) 51 EHRR 25.

demonstration in advance but this was not done.[97] Should dispersal of a peaceful assembly take place through violent means, including the use of tear gas, this will not be proportionate.[98] Therefore, some of the military responses to the protests that took place during the Arab Spring were criticized because the protests were largely peaceful and the security forces had responded with excessive force.[99]

5.3.2 Repressive restrictions

Any restriction on assembly must be shown to be necessary in a democratic society. In *Oscar Elías Biscet et al. v Cuba*, the Inter-American Commission on Human Rights held that restrictions on the right of assembly are illegal if used solely to suppress the opposition.[100] The petitioners claimed they were arrested, detained, and intimidated because they discussed dissident publications at their weekly meetings. The Commission concluded that the convictions were an arbitrary restraint on freedom of assembly since their primary purpose was to constrain political opposition.

Even where an assembly is unauthorized, the penalties for participation must be justified and necessary. The Human Rights Committee has found a violation of Article 21 ICCPR where an individual had been refused a 'lawyers licence' following the imposition of a fine for his participation in an unauthorized rally. Although the imposition of the fine was appropriate, it was not clear to the Committee how the non-issuance of the licence was necessary for the purposes of Article 21.[101]

6 CONCLUSION

In this chapter four freedoms—freedom of thought, expression, association, and assembly—were introduced. The freedoms were discussed along with the body of international human rights norms and jurisprudence, which have helped to define their scope since each was proclaimed in the UDHR in 1948. Each freedom was examined as a discrete freedom of the individual. But it was also noted that each has a collective component. All are interrelated and mutually reinforcing. The freedoms share the common feature that they are not unconditional entitlements. In practice their exercise needs balancing against the rights and freedoms of others and against certain public interest considerations, which are carefully and exhaustively set out in the international standards governing each freedom. A challenge common to all the freedoms is how to ensure that, where such restrictions are in principle necessary, they are implemented by the state in a proportionate manner. That requires a democratic society and one built on the rule of law. The freedoms are, in turn, part of the foundations of a democratic society. The right to dissent and to speak out, the freedom to come together with others in independent associations to promote common interests, and the freedom to demonstrate are all essential if a democratic society based on the participation of its members is to function successfully.

---

[97] *Éva Molnár v Hungary*, App no 10346/05, Judgment of 7 October 2008.

[98] Report of the Special Rapporteur on the rights to freedom of peaceful assembly and of association, A/HRC/20/27 (21 May 2012) paras 33–8.

[99] Eg OHCHR Press Release, 'UN human rights chief calls for investigation into deaths in Tunisia' (12 January 2011); OHCHR Press Release, 'Tunisia: "Words must become reality, excessive use of force must end" – UN human rights experts' (14 January 2011).

[100] Cases 771/03 and 841/03, IACommHR Report No 57/04 (14 October 2004).

[101] *Gryb v Belarus*, CCPR/C/103/D/1316/2004 (26 October 2011).

FURTHER READING

BARENDT, *Freedom of Speech* (Oxford University Press, 2007).

BIELEFELDT, 'Misperceptions of Freedom of Religion or Belief' (2013) 1 *HRQ* 33.

EVANS, *Freedom of Religion under the European Convention on Human Rights* (Oxford University Press, 2001).

EVANS, *Religious Liberty and International Law in Europe* (Cambridge University Press, 1997).

EVANS, *Manual on the Wearing of Religious Symbols in Public Areas* (Council of Europe, 2009).

GROSSMAN, 'Challenges to Freedom of Expression Within the Inter-American System: A Jurisprudential Analysis' (2012) 34 *HRQ* 361.

HARE and WEINSTEIN (eds), *Extreme Speech and Democracy* (Oxford University Press, 2009).

INTERNATIONAL LABOUR ORGANIZATION, *Law on Freedom of Association: Standards and Procedures* (Geneva, 1995).

LEADER, *Freedom of Association: A Study in Labor Law and Political Theory* (Yale University Press, 1992).

McDONAGH, 'The Right to Information in International Human Rights Law' (2013) 13 *HRLR* 25.

O'FLAHERTY, 'Freedom of Expression: Article 19 of the International Covenant on Civil and Political Rights and the Human Rights Committee's General Comment No 34' (2012) 12 *HRLR* 627.

OSCE, *Guidelines on Freedom of Peaceful Assembly*, available at: <http://www.osce.org/item/23835.html>.

OSCE, *Venice Commission Guidelines for Review of Legislation Pertaining to Religion or Belief*, available at: <http://www.osce.org/publications.odihr/2004/>.

REHMAN and BREAU (eds), *Religion, Human Rights and International Law: A Critical Examination of Islamic State Practices* (Brill, 2007).

USEFUL WEBSITES

International Labour Organization: <http://www.ilo.org>

On Freedom of Religion or Belief

Human Rights Without Frontiers: <http://www.hrwf.net/>

Forum 18: <http://www.forum18.org/>

On Freedom of Expression

Article 19: Global Campaign for Freedom of Expression: <http://www.article19.org/>

Amnesty International, Learn about Human Rights: Freedom of Expression: <http://www.amnesty.org/en/freedom-of-expression>

On Freedom of Information

Access Info Europe: <http://www.access-info.org/>

Freedom Info.org: <http://www.freedominfo.org/countries/index.htm>

12

EDUCATION AND WORK

Fons Coomans

SUMMARY

This chapter focuses on the normative content of the right to education and the right to work. It discusses the sources of these rights under international human rights law and their main features and components. Both rights should be understood in terms of different entitlements and freedoms. Next, the obligations resulting from each right are set out, demonstrating that states have both negative and positive obligations. Finally, the relationship of each right with other human rights is highlighted, thus illustrating that all human rights are interrelated and interdependent.

1 INTRODUCTION

This chapter discusses two human rights that belong to the category of economic, social, and cultural rights, namely the right to education and the right to work. It was long argued that this category of human rights is different from civil and political rights. The latter were said to be capable of immediate implementation, cost-free, and only entailing negative obligations (obligations not to interfere) for states. Economic, social, and cultural rights, on the other hand, were seen as subject to progressive realization, requiring financial resources, and entailing positive obligations (obligations to actively take measures). These differences were also said to imply that civil and political rights could be enforced by courts, whereas economic, social, and cultural rights were seen as non-justiciable, that is, not suitable for review by courts. This traditional view, which emphasized the inherent differences between the two categories of rights, dominated until the late 1980s. Gradually, however, this approach has given way to a view that stresses the unity, equality, and interdependence of all human rights.[1]

Section 2 deals with the right to education and Section 3 with the right to work and work-related rights. The chapter explains how the modern view of the nature of economic, social, and cultural rights can be applied to these rights. Each section first discusses the sources of the right under international human rights law, its main features, and components. Next, the obligations resulting from each right are discussed. Finally, the relationship of each right with other human rights is highlighted. Both rights are crucial for one's ability to live a life in dignity and develop one's personality.[2]

---

[1] See Chapter 7.   [2] See UDHR, Art 22.

2 THE RIGHT TO EDUCATION

The right to education has been included in many constitutions and international treaties. States have agreed that illiteracy must be eliminated and that all children must attend
school. However, there is a big gap between theory and reality. Worldwide there are still
100 million children of primary school age who do not have access to education. The right
to education is crucial for a person's self-fulfilment and the development of society as a
whole. This section explains what the right to education is and what states should do to
make this key right a reality for those who lack access to education.

2.1 SOURCES

2.1.1 Universal instruments

Article 26 of the Universal Declaration of Human Rights (UDHR) has been the basis for
further guarantees of the right to education in later human rights instruments. It provides
for the three basic characteristics of the right to education, namely, recognition of the right
to receive an education, a guarantee for the exercise of parental rights in matters of education, and a reference to the aims of education.

Article 26 UDHR was transformed into legally binding form through two provisions of
the International Covenant on Economic, Social and Cultural Rights (ICESCR), which in
comparison to other Covenant rights are rather detailed: Articles 13 and 14. The right to
education laid down in Article 13 ICESCR is a universal right, granted to every person,
regardless of age, language, social or ethnic origin, or other status. Article 13(1) lists the
aims that education should achieve in society. Article 13(2) enumerates the different steps
that states must take to achieve the full realization of the right to education, in particular
the specific obligation to make education available and accessible in a non-discriminatory
way. In performing this duty, states have a degree of discretion within the limits of the
standards of Article 13 and the key provision of Article 2(1), which states:

> Each State Party to the present Covenant undertakes to take steps, individually and through
> international assistance and co-operation, especially economic and technical, to the maxi-
> mum of its available resources, with a view to achieving progressively the full realization of
> the rights recognised in the present Covenant by all appropriate means, including particu-
> larly the adoption of legislative measures.

Article 14 deals with the implementation of primary education in states that have not yet
realized this goal. It requires states to adopt a plan of action for the introduction of free
and compulsory primary education. Article 13(3) and (4) guarantees the rights of parents
in matters of education and the freedom to establish schools outside the public school
system.

Other relevant universal instruments include the UN Educational, Scientific and
Cultural Organization (UNESCO) Convention against Discrimination in Education,
adopted in 1960, which aims to eliminate discrimination in education and promote equality of opportunity and treatment. The historical background of this Convention is the
discrimination and segregation in education under the *apartheid* regime in South Africa.
It remains relevant today as an important interpretation of the phenomenon of discrimination and exclusion in education. Article 10 of the Convention on the Elimination of
All Forms of Discrimination Against Women (CEDAW) requires states to ensure that
women have equal rights with men in the field of education. It lists a number of particular

measures and goals, such as access to the same curricula and reduction in female student drop-out rates. The Convention on the Rights of the Child (CRC) also contains a number of provisions relating to the right to education. Article 28 lists the measures that states must take progressively to realize this right. It includes one new element that is lacking in previous instruments, namely the obligation to ensure that school discipline is administered in a manner consistent with the child's dignity. This may be understood as a ban on applying corporal punishment in schools. Article 29(1) deals with the aims of education, while Article 29(2) guarantees the freedom of individuals and bodies to establish schools. Finally, Article 32(1) calls for protective measures against economic exploitation of children (child labour) which may interfere with the child's education.

2.1.2 Regional instruments

The right to education is also guaranteed by regional human rights instruments. In Europe, the relevant provision is Article 2 of the First Protocol to the European Convention on Human Rights (ECHR). This norm guarantees access to public educational institutions without discrimination and requires states to abstain from interference in the free exercise and free choice of education by pupils and parents. The European Commission and the European Court of Human Rights have interpreted this provision as requiring states only to maintain the level of educational services existing at a given time, without imposing an obligation to expand educational facilities or to increase funding for education.[3] Access to education within the context of labour and other professional activities is covered by the right to vocational training laid down in Article 10 of the European Social Charter (1961). Educational rights of national minorities are guaranteed by Articles 12 to 14 of the Council of Europe Framework Convention for the Protection of National Minorities (1995). For example, Article 13 recognizes the right of persons belonging to a national minority to set up and manage their own (private) educational institutions, without entailing any financial obligations for state parties. Finally, the EU Charter of Fundamental Rights guarantees the right to education in Article 14. This provision contains the key elements of the ECHR and the European Social Charter relating to education, but it adds that the right to education includes the possibility of receiving free compulsory education (Article 14(2)). The latter element is also a key part of Article 13 ICESCR.

Article 17(1) of the African Charter on Human and Peoples' Rights (ACHPR) provides that '[e]very individual shall have the right to education'. The Charter does not elaborate on this brief and generally worded provision. However, the African Charter on the Rights and Welfare of the Child contains a detailed provision on the right to education in Article 11. It is modelled on other human rights instruments, in particular the ICESCR and the CRC. It also contains some elements that are relevant from an African perspective. These include a clause that education shall be directed to the preservation and strengthening of positive African morals, traditional values, and cultures, and to the promotion and achievements of African unity and solidarity (Article 11(2)(c) and (f)). Furthermore, Article 11(6) stipulates that states parties shall take all appropriate measures to ensure that children who become pregnant before completing their education shall have an opportunity to continue their education on the basis of their individual ability. This means that they should not be banned from attending school.

---

[3] The European Court of Human Rights has interpreted the meaning and scope of Art 2 in a number of leading judgments: *Case relating to certain aspects of the laws on the use of languages in education in Belgium* (*Belgian Linguistics Case No 2*) (1968) 1 EHRR 252; *Kjeldsen, Busk Madsen and Pedersen v Denmark* (1976) 1 EHRR 711; *Campbell and Cosans v UK* (1982) 4 EHRR 293; and *Leyla Sahin v Turkey* (2007) 44 EHRR 5.

The Additional Protocol to the American Convention on Human Rights in the Area of Economic, Social and Cultural Rights (Protocol of San Salvador) deals with the right to education in Article 13. This provision is very similar to Article 13 ICESCR. It includes the rights to receive an education and to choose an education. What is special about this Protocol is that the complaints procedure of the American Convention on Human Rights (ACHR) applies to two of its provisions, namely certain trade union rights (Article 8a) and the right to education (Article 13). That means that there is a mechanism open to individuals to enforce these rights in case they 'are violated by action directly attributable to a State Party to this Protocol'.[4]

Article 41 of the Arab Charter on Human Rights, adopted in 2004, provides for the right to education and requires states to eradicate illiteracy. It contains references to free primary and fundamental education and the aims of education. However, it lacks a provision guaranteeing parental rights and the freedom to establish schools.

Finally, the non-binding Association of Southeast Asian Nations (ASEAN) Human Rights Declaration, adopted in November 2012, provides for the right to education in Article 31. Its structure and content are similar to other international provisions on the right to education.

From this overview, it becomes clear that Article 26 UDHR has been, and still is, a major source of inspiration for the drafting of universal and regional provisions on the right to education. However, subsequent developments, changing views, and regional particularities have been taken into account in more recent instruments.

2.2 FEATURES

Two aspects of the right to education as laid down in international documents can be identified. On the one hand, realization of the right to education demands an effort on the part of the state to make education available and accessible. It implies a positive state obligation. This may be defined as the *right to receive an education* or the *social dimension* of the right to education. On the other hand, there is the personal freedom of individuals to choose between state-organized and non-public education, which can be translated, for example, in parents' freedom to ensure their children's moral and religious education according to their own beliefs. From this stems the freedom of natural persons or legal entities to establish their own educational institutions. This is the *right to choose an education* or the *freedom dimension* of the right to education. It requires the state to follow a policy of non-interference in private matters. It implies a negative state obligation. Both aspects can be found in Articles 13 and 14 ICESCR. Article 13(2) and Article 14 cover the social dimension, while Article 13(3) and (4) embodies the freedom dimension.

In addition, the right to education has been explained by the Committee on Economic, Social and Cultural Rights and the UN Special Rapporteur on the right to education to include four interrelated features:

- *Availability*: functioning educational institutions and programmes have to be available in sufficient numbers, through a public educational system and allowing private parties to establish non-public schools.

- *Accessibility*: educational institutions and programmes have to be accessible to everyone, without discrimination on any ground, also implying physical and economic accessibility.

---

[4] Protocol of San Salvador, Art 19(6).

- *Acceptability*: the form and substance of education, including curricula and teaching methods, have to be relevant, culturally appropriate, of good quality, and in accordance with the best interests of the child; this includes a safe and healthy school environment.

- *Adaptability*: education has to be flexible, so that it can adapt to the needs of changing societies and communities and respond to the needs of students within their specific social and cultural context, including the evolving capacities of the child.[5]

This '4-A' scheme is a useful device to analyse the content of the right to receive an education and the obligations of states parties resulting from it as well as to measure the level of its realization.

2.3 THE AIMS OF EDUCATION

Education can be used or abused to prepare children well or badly for life.[6] Education in Germany during the Nazi regime was an example of brainwashing children. Indeed, the formulation of the aims of education as contained in international human rights instruments reflects the aftermath of the Second World War. This is clear from Article 26 UDHR, which provides that education should contribute to avoiding conflicts between nations, groups, and people by promoting understanding, tolerance, and friendship and the maintenance of peace. In addition, education must be directed to the full development of the human personality and to strengthening respect for human rights. By emphasizing the individual's sense of dignity and ability to participate in a free society, Article 13(1) ICESCR makes it clear that the interests of the individual should be central to education.

It is noteworthy that some instruments emphasize specific aims, such as the elimination of stereotyped concepts of the role of men and women at all levels and in all forms of education (Article 10(c) CEDAW) or the development of a child's personality, talents, and mental and physical abilities through education (Article 29(1)(a) CRC). The CRC also adds further goals for education, such as the development of respect for the natural environment and for people of indigenous origin. These common aims, laid down in a number of international instruments, reflect a 'broad universal consensus on the major aims and objectives of the right to education'.[7] They also constitute the foundation for education about human rights in schools worldwide.[8]

2.4 COMPONENTS

On the basis of treaty law, general comments of the Committee on Economic, Social and Cultural Rights, and case law, the following four key components of the right to education can be identified.

---

[5] CESCR, General Comment 13, HRI/GEN/1/Rev.9 (Vol I) 63. Preliminary Report of the Special Rapporteur on the Right to Education, E/CN.4/1999/49 (13 January 1999) part II.

[6] Tomasevski, *Education Denied* (Zed Books, 2003) 60.

[7] Nowak, 'The Right to Education' in Eide, Krause, and Rosas (eds), *Economic, Social and Cultural Rights* (Martinus Nijhoff, 2001) 251.

[8] Eg UNESCO/OHCHR, Plan of Action: World Programme for Human Rights Education (2006).

2.4.1 Access to education on a non-discriminatory basis

The essence of the right to education is the right to access available educational facili-ties. In more concrete terms, this means the right of access to existing public educational institutions on a non-discriminatory basis.[9] This right is violated, for example, if people belonging to a specific ethnic, linguistic, or religious group have restricted access to exist-ing public educational institutions, as is the case for Roma children in some European countries.[10] In addition, education provided by the state should be of the same quality for all groups. Girls, for example, should not be given education of an inferior quality com-pared to boys.[11] Another, extreme, example was the situation in Afghanistan where the Taliban regime banned girls and women from all types of educational institutions.[12] The case of the young Pakistani girl, Malala, who advocated for the right to education for girls and was shot in the head by the Taliban in 2012, shows that this right is still far from being accepted by everyone as a human right.[13] In some African countries, female students are forced to disclose a pregnancy and leave school once the pregnancy has been discovered. This practice was found to be discriminatory by the Botswana Court of Appeal.[14] Finally, at the time of writing, in Iran, members of the Bahá'i religious minority are barred from access to institutions for higher education, because of their religious convictions and polit-ical views.[15]

2.4.2 The right to enjoy free and compulsory primary education

A second key component of the right to education is the right to enjoy primary educa-tion in one form or another, not necessarily in the form of traditional classroom teaching. Primary education is so fundamental for the development of a person's abilities that it can be rightfully defined as a minimum claim. Accordingly, the Supreme Court of India has held the right to (primary) education to be implicit in the right to life.[16] International human rights law does not define the term 'primary education', but guidelines have been developed by international organizations such as UNESCO.[17] Primary education relates to the first layer of a formal school system and usually begins between the ages of five and seven and lasts approximately six years, but in any case no fewer than four years.[18] Primary education includes the teaching of basic education or covering basic learning needs.

The term 'basic education' is frequently used, for example in outcome documents of international conferences such as the World Declaration on Education for All, but it is not

---

[9] ICESCR, Arts 2(2) and 3; ICCPR, Art 26; CRC, Art 2.

[10] See *DH and Others v Czech Republic* (2009) 47 EHRR 3; Coomans, 'Discrimination and Stigmatisation Regarding Education: The Case of the Romani Children in the Czech Republic' in Willems (ed), *Developmental and Autonomy Rights of Children: Empowering Children, Caregivers and Communities* (Intersentia, 2002).

[11] UNESCO Convention Against Discrimination in Education, Art 1(1) and CEDAW, Art 10.

[12] Human Rights Watch, *1999 World Report*. See also Report of the UN Secretary-General on the situation of women and girls in Afghanistan, E/CN.4/Sub.2/2000/18 (21 July 2000).

[13] 'Pakistani girl shot over activism in Swat valley, claims Taliban', *The Guardian*, 9 October 2012, available at: <http://www.guardian.co.uk/world/2012/oct/09/pakistan-girl-shot-activism-swat-taliban>.

[14] Quansah, 'Is the Right to Get Pregnant a Fundamental Right in Botswana?' (1995) 39 *J Afr L* 97.

[15] See the report, *Punishing Stars*, available at: <http://www.iranhumanrights.org/2010/12/punishing-stars-dec2010/>.

[16] *Unni Krishnan and Others v State of AP and Others*, 1 SCC 645 (4 February 1993).

[17] UNESCO, Statistical Yearbook and Revised Recommendation concerning the Standardization of Educational Statistics (1978).

[18] Preliminary Report of the Special Rapporteur on the Right to Education, n 5, paras 75–9; Melchiorre, 'At what age?...' (2004) available at: <http://www.right-to-education.org>.

part of international human rights law.[19] Basic education relates to the content of education rather than the form it takes (formal or non-formal schooling). Apart from a school and classroom system, basic education may be given in less traditional forms, such as village- or community-based, or in the open air. Usually, basic education is aimed at children within the framework of primary schooling. However, basic education is also relevant for other persons who lack basic knowledge and skills. This dimension is referred to as 'fundamental education' in Article 13(2)(d) ICESCR. The enjoyment of this right is not limited by age or gender; it extends to children, youth, and adults, including older persons; it is an integral component of adult education and life-long learning.[20]

The right to free and compulsory primary education also implies that no one, for example parents or employers, can withhold a child from attending primary education.[21] It is the only provision in the UDHR and the ICESCR in which the exercise of a right is linked to meeting an obligation, namely to attend primary education. States have an obligation to protect this right from encroachments by third persons. According to Article 13(2)(a) ICESCR, primary education shall be compulsory. There is a worldwide trend to extend compulsory schooling beyond primary schooling. The rationale for a minimum length of compulsory schooling beyond 11 years of age is that it should last at least to the minimum age of employment.[22] Obviously it is not sufficient that primary education is compulsory by law. What is also necessary is an official state inspection service to supervise and enforce this duty with respect to parents, schools, employers, and pupils themselves.

There are a number of factors that may influence actual attendance of children at school. These include inadequacy of school services, such as the distance between a student's home and the school, lack of transportation facilities, lack of running water and sanitation facilities at school, teaching in a language other than the child's mother tongue, and teaching materials and methods that do not fit in with the cultural background of children and their parents (adaptability of education). Other factors relate to the socio-economic and cultural status of parents, including their inability to pay for school attendance of their children, traditional attitudes regarding the education of girls, and loss of family income that a child attending classes would otherwise earn.

Article 13(2)(a) ICESCR also stipulates that primary education shall be free. The rationale behind this entitlement is that:

> children would not have to pay for their schooling or remain deprived of it when they cannot afford the cost. Children cannot wait to grow, hence their prioritized right to education in international human rights law. The damage of denied education while they are growing up cannot be retroactively remedied.[23]

The degree to which primary education is really free is determined by a number of direct and indirect costs, such as school fees, expenses for textbooks, extra lessons, meals at school canteens, school transport, school uniforms, medical expenses, and boarding fees. In some countries it is the practice that the village community or parents provide labour for constructing, running, or maintaining the school, which may be seen as a form of indirect cost. Another form of indirect cost for parents is taxation. Its effects upon the

---

[19] Millennium Development Goal No 2 aims at achieving 'universal primary education'. See <http://www.un.org/millenniumgoals>.

[20] CESCR, General Comment 13, n 5.

[21] See CESCR, General Comment 11, HRI/GEN/1/Rev.9 (Vol I) 52.

[22] See Progress report of the Special Rapporteur on the Right to Education, E/CN.4/2000/6 (1 February 2000) para 46 and Table 3. See also Melchiorre, n 18.

[23] Report of the Special Rapporteur on the Right to Education, E/CN.4/2004/45 (15 January 2004) para 8.

accessibility of education will depend upon the progressiveness of the tax system: do low income groups pay less, in absolute and relative terms, compared to high income groups?[24]

Primary education must be a priority when allocating resources, because it deals with the fundamental basis for a person's development and the development of society as a whole.[25] It is the responsibility of states to provide for primary education and maintain educational services. They cannot waive that responsibility by giving more room to the private sector or by stimulating public–private partnerships for the financing of the educational infrastructure. With respect to the right to education in the ECHR, the European Court of Human Rights has held that a state cannot absolve itself of responsibility by delegating its obligations to private school bodies.[26] UNICEF has emphasized that 'only the State…can pull together all the components into a coherent but flexible education system'.[27] The Committee on Economic, Social and Cultural Rights has stressed that 'Article 13 [ICESCR] regards States as having principal responsibility for the direct provision of education in most circumstances'[28] and that states have an immediate duty to provide primary education for all.[29] For those states that have not yet realized compulsory and free primary education, there is an 'unequivocal obligation' to adopt and implement a detailed plan of action as provided for in Article 14 ICESCR.[30] After a long delay, in 2009, India finally adopted an Act to implement the right to free and compulsory education for children of the age of six to fourteen years.[31]

2.4.3 Free choice of education

Yet another key component of the right to education is free choice of education without interference by the state or a third person, in particular, but not exclusively, with regard to religious or philosophical convictions. This component is violated when a state fails to respect the free choice of parents with regard to religious instruction of their children. Public education entails the danger of political goals, that is, the danger that the state will promote the most influential 'philosophy of life'.[32] Thus, a state must ensure an objective and pluralist curriculum and avoid indoctrination in this dominant philosophy.[33] However, in many states there is only limited, or no, opportunity to attend education of one's own choice: there may only be state-controlled education or, where available, private education is too expensive for parents. There is no obligation under international human rights law for states to provide financial support to private educational institutions. If they do, however, they must do so in a non-discriminatory way.[34]

2.4.4 The right to be educated in the language of one's own choice

A more controversial question is whether the right to be educated in the language of one's own choice is a key component of the right to education. In the *Belgian Linguistics* case,

---

[24] See background paper prepared by the Special Rapporteur on the Right to Education, E/C.12/1998/18 (30 November 1998) para 12.

[25] See CESCR, General Comment 13, n 5, para 51: 'States parties are obliged to prioritise the introduction of compulsory, free education'.   [26] *Costello-Roberts v UK* (1993) 19 EHRR 112.

[27] UNICEF, *The State of the World's Children 1999*, 63.   [28] CESCR, General Comment 13, n 5, para 48.

[29] CESCR, General Comment 13, n 5, para 51.   [30] CESCR, General Comment 11, n 21, para 9.

[31] Act No 35 of 2009, *The Gazette of India* No 39, 27 August 2009.

[32] See ACHPR, Art 17(3): 'The promotion and protection of morals and traditional values recognized by the community shall be the duty of the State'.

[33] *Kjeldsen, Busk Madsen and Pedersen*, n 3. The Court emphasized that Art 2 of the First Protocol should be interpreted in light of Art 8 (right to privacy), Art 9 (freedom of conscience and religion), and Art 10 (freedom to receive information) ECHR.   [34] *Waldman v Canada*, CCPR/C/67/D/1996 (5 November 1999).

the European Court of Human Rights stated that 'the right to education would be meaningless if it did not imply, in favour of its beneficiaries, the right to be educated in the
national language or in one of the national languages, as the case may be'.[35] This means that
it is the state that determines whether a specific language is to be a national or official language as a medium of instruction in education. In addition, the European Court stressed
that individuals cannot claim a right to state-funded education in the language of their
own choice, thus rejecting claims of a positive state obligation in that regard.

On the other hand, a state must respect the freedom of individuals to teach, for instance,
a minority language in schools established and directed by members of that minority.
This does not imply, however, that a state must allow the use of this language as the only
medium of instruction; this would be dependent on the educational policy of the state. As
a minimum, states must not frustrate the right of members of national, ethnic, or linguistic
minorities to be taught in their mother tongue at institutions outside the official system
of public education, albeit they are not obliged to fund these institutions. This right of
minorities is solidly established in international law.[36] It was a cornerstone of the minority
protection system established under the auspices of the League of Nations after the First
World War. Moreover, the right of minorities to establish educational institutions in which
they are entitled to use their own language was characterized by the Permanent Court of
International Justice in 1935 as 'indispensable to enable the minority to enjoy the same
treatment as the majority, not only in law but also in fact'. The Court considered these
institutions as 'suitable means for the preservation of their racial peculiarities, their traditions and their national characteristics'.[37] It is in this sense that the right to be educated in
the language of one's own choice belongs to the key components of the right to education.

2.5 TYPES OF OBLIGATIONS

Obligations of states resulting from Articles 13 and 14 ICESCR may be derived from these
treaty provisions themselves, Article 2(1) ICESCR, and General Comments 3, 11, and 13
of the Committee on Economic, Social and Cultural Rights. They may be divided into
general obligations and specific obligations. *General obligations* include immediate obligations to prohibit discrimination in law and in fact, in the area of education, and to take
steps to make primary education compulsory and free. Moreover, states are obliged not
to take retrogressive measures, such as the introduction of school fees where previously
education was free, and to protect the most vulnerable groups in society through special
programmes, such as schooling for street children. *Specific obligations* include obligations
to draft, adopt, and implement a comprehensive national education strategy, to establish
minimum standards for private educational institutions, to develop curricula that conform to the purposes of education, and to set up a school inspection system.

The typology of obligations introduced by the Committee on Economic, Social and
Cultural Rights (obligations to respect, to protect, and to fulfil)[38] can be used to further
define and refine the nature of states' obligations.

---

[35] n 3, para 3.
[36] Eg ICCPR, Art 27; Document of the Copenhagen Meeting of the Conference on the Human Dimension
of the CSCE (1990) sections 32–4; Declaration on the Rights of Persons Belonging to National or Ethnic,
Religious and Linguistic Minorities, Art 4; European Charter for Regional or Minority Languages, Art 8;
Framework Convention for the Protection of National Minorities, Arts 12–14.
[37] *Minority Schools in Albania*, PCIJ, Advisory Opinion, Series A/B No 64 (1935) 17.
[38] See Chapter 5.

The obligation to *respect* the right to education requires states to abstain from interference. They must not prevent children from attending education, for example by closing educational institutions in times of political tension without complying with the limitations clause of Article 4 ICESCR.[39] In addition, states must not discriminate on the basis of sex or ethnic origin with respect to admission to public schools. Detailed standards of non-discrimination and equal treatment of individuals in education are laid down in the UNESCO Convention against Discrimination in Education, particularly in its Articles 1 and 3. The obligation to respect can be characterized as an obligation of conduct: it requires the state to follow the specific course of action specified in the treaty provision.

The obligation to *protect* requires states to guarantee the exercise of the right to education in horizontal relations (between private groups or individuals). For example, they must protect against discrimination of students in obtaining access to non-public schools. Other examples of the obligation to protect are the adoption and enforcement of legislation to combat child or bonded labour in private labour relations, or arrangements for monitoring and enforcing compulsory primary education.

The nature of the right to education is such that positive state action is needed to achieve the full realization of this right. In the view of the Committee on Economic, Social and Cultural Rights, 'it is clear that article 13 regards States as having principal responsibility for the direct provision of education in most circumstances.'[40] This statement can be seen as a confirmation of the obligation to *fulfil*. The obligation to fulfil requires states to make the various types of education available and accessible for all and to maintain that level of realization, which may involve a variety of measures. While it may be necessary to adopt legislation to provide a legal framework, the primary means of realizing the right to education are policy measures as well as financial and material support. It is clear that the embezzlement of public education funds will have a negative impact on the enjoyment of the right to education, because fewer resources will be available for the provision of education.[41] The obligation to fulfil implies that states have a substantial degree of latitude, depending also on the specific level of education and the wording of the respective treaty obligation. Compare, for example, the following clauses: 'primary education shall be compulsory and available free to all' (Article 13(2)(a) ICESCR); 'secondary education...shall be made generally available and accessible to all by every appropriate means, and in particular by the progressive introduction of free education' (Article 13(2)(b) ICESCR). Implementation of the latter clause gives more latitude to states than the former. Therefore, the obligation to fulfil should be characterized as an obligation of result, leaving the choice of means to the state, providing the result achieved conforms to international standards.

Particular elements of the right to education give rise to *minimum core obligations* as defined by the Committee on Economic, Social and Cultural Rights in its General Comment on the nature of states parties' obligations.[42] Such obligations are not limited to cost-free (negative) obligations to respect but also include positive obligations to protect and to fulfil. Minimum core obligations emanating from the right to education apply irrespective of the availability of resources.[43] According to the Committee, the minimum core obligations with respect to the right to education include obligations:

> to ensure the right of access to public educational institutions and programmes on a non-discriminatory basis; to ensure that education conforms to the objectives set out in

---

[39] CESCR, General Comment 13, n 5, para 59.   [40] CESCR, General Comment 13, n 5, para 48.
[41] ECOWAS Community Court of Justice, *SERAP v Nigeria*, ECW/CCj/JUD/07/10 (30 November 2010), para 19.   [42] CESCR, General Comment 3, HRI/GEN/1/Rev.9 (Vol I) 7.
[43] 'Maastricht Guidelines on Violations of Economic, Social and Cultural Rights' (1998) 20 *HRQ* 691.

article 13(1) [ICESCR]; to provide primary education for all in accordance with article 13(2)(a); to adopt and implement a national educational strategy which includes provision for secondary higher and fundamental education; and to ensure free choice of education without interference from the State or third parties, subject to conformity with 'minimum educational standards' (article 13(3) and (4)).[44]

It is obvious that for many states meeting these core obligations is a challenge from legal, policy, and financial points of view.

2.6 RELATIONSHIP WITH OTHER HUMAN RIGHTS

Education is a social good in that it creates opportunities and provides choices to people. In this sense, education is an end in itself. However, it is also a means to an end, because it helps to achieve economic growth, health, poverty reduction, personal development, and democracy. Therefore, the right to education should be characterized as an 'empowerment right'. Such a right 'provides the individual with control over the course of his or her life, and in particular, control over . . . the state'.[45] In other words, exercising an empowerment right enables a person to experience the benefit of other rights: 'the key to social action in defense of rights . . . is an educated citizenry, able to spread its ideas and to organize in defense of rights'.[46] Education enables people to make a contribution to society as independent and emancipated citizens. Civil and political rights, such as freedom of expression, freedom of association, or the right to political participation only obtain substance and meaning when a person is educated. Galbraith has emphasized that 'education not only makes democracy possible; it also makes it essential. Education not only brings into existence a population with an understanding of the public tasks; it also creates their demand to be heard.'[47] In this sense, education is a threat to autocratic rule. Governments have used the education system for building nations, for instance through the introduction of a national language. Often this happened to the detriment of the languages and cultures of ethnic minorities and indigenous groups. For such groups, the right to education is an essential means to preserve and strengthen their cultural identity.

Education enhances social mobility: it helps people to escape from discrimination based on social status and to move up the social ladder. Moreover, education promotes the realization of other social, economic, and cultural rights, such as the right to work, the right to food, or the right to health: an educated person will have a greater chance of finding a job, will be better equipped to secure his or her own food supply, and is more aware of public health dangers. In general, education promotes the fulfilment of the right to an adequate standard of living; it provides people with access to the skills and knowledge for full membership of society. From the perspective of the rights of the child, education contributes to socializing children into understanding and accepting views different from their own. In other words, education unlocks the enjoyment of other human rights and contributes in an important way to the promotion of the essence of human rights, namely living in human dignity.

---

[44] CESCR, General Comment 13, n 5, para 57.
[45] Donnelly and Howard, 'Assessing National Human Rights Performance: A Theoretical Framework' (1988) 10 *HRQ* 214, 215.   [46] Donnelly and Howard, 234–5.
[47] Galbraith, *The Good Society: The Humane Agenda* (Houghton Mifflin, 1996).

Finally, the right to education has a clear overlap with civil rights, such as freedom of religion and the right to privacy: the freedom of parents to determine the (religious) education of their children is not only part of the right to education but also of the freedom of religion[48] and is an issue belonging to people's private lives. Similarly, the right to education is linked to the freedom of association through the freedom to establish private educational institutions.

The right to education, through its links with other rights, accentuates the unity, indivisibility, and interdependence of all human rights. It is related to civil and political rights by its freedom dimension and the obligation of states to abstain from interference with that freedom. It is also linked to other economic, social, and cultural rights through its social dimension which calls for state action to make the right to receive an education effective.

3 THE RIGHT TO WORK AND WORK-RELATED RIGHTS

In the age of economic globalization, millions of workers in many parts of the world experience the flexibility of the world labour market on a daily basis. They may benefit from new jobs created as a result of foreign direct investment, or they may lose their job, because their employer fires them and moves the company to a country where labour is cheaper. Some countries rely on cheap labour and weak trade unions as a comparative advantage to attract foreign investments. As jobs move from one part of the world to another, so too do workers. Many migrant workers from developing countries try to find a living in rich countries by taking on work that is badly paid and often of an inferior status and quality. It is particularly in this type of situation that workers' rights come to the fore. These rights are meant to counter the negative consequences of economic globalization for labour, such as extreme forms of income inequality, exploitation of workers (including women, children, and migrant workers), and high levels of unemployment. The reaction of the international community to these consequences has been the call for social justice and decent work.[49] Workers' rights are crucial in this respect. They aim at protecting and promoting working conditions by laying down international minimum standards. The International Labour Organization (ILO) has played, and continues to play, a key role in setting, implementing, and monitoring these standards. This section of the chapter discusses the right to work and so-called work-related rights, including, among others, the right to the enjoyment of just and favourable working conditions, the right to strike, and trade union rights.

3.1 SOURCES

3.1.1 Universal instruments

A discussion of the right to work and work-related rights should start with the origins of the ILO, which was established in 1919 after the First World War. From the preamble to its constitution it is clear that the achievement of social justice was considered to be crucial for the establishment of lasting peace between states. In addition, it was deemed important to improve labour conditions of workers in order to prevent social unrest, which could possibly result in social and political revolutions such as the one that took place in

---

[48] See ICESCR, Art 13(3) and ICCPR, Art 18(4).
[49] See ILO Declaration on Social Justice for a Fair Globalization (2008).

Russia in 1917.[50] Thus, governments at that time had a self-interest in improving labour conditions, although sentiments of justice and humanity were also mentioned as guiding concerns in the preamble. In this respect, it is interesting to note that in 1944 the ILO stated explicitly that 'labour is not a commodity'.[51] Hundreds of binding conventions and non-binding recommendations have been adopted within the framework of the ILO over the years. The tripartite structure of the organization provides a framework for representatives of governments, workers, and employers to agree on new rules. These are usually called international labour standards.

The early establishment of the ILO meant that it was far ahead in laying down work-related rights when the UN started its normative human rights activities after the Second World War. The ILO contributed actively to the drafting of both the UDHR and the ICESCR. Article 23 UDHR and Articles 6 to 8 ICESCR contain a number of elements that relate to the protection of the right to work, such as the free choice of work, equal pay for equal work, and trade union rights. Trade union rights are also part of the International Covenant on Civil and Political Rights (ICCPR), Article 22 of which recognizes the right to form and join trade unions. The ICCPR also provides for the prohibition of forced labour in Article 8(3). There are a number of further universal human rights instruments that deal with work-related rights. Pursuant to Article 5(e)(i) and (ii) ICERD, states have an obligation to prohibit and eliminate racial discrimination in the enjoyment of the right to work and the right to form and join trade unions. Article 11 CEDAW lays down detailed obligations for states aimed at eliminating discrimination in the field of employment. Article 32 CRC recognizes the right of children to be protected from economic exploitation and hazardous work. There is a clear link here with the elimination of child labour. Article 10(3) ICESCR serves a similar purpose, adding that states 'should set age limits below which the paid employment of child labour should be prohibited and punishable by law'. Note the use of the permissive 'should' instead of the more mandatory 'shall'.

The work-related rights of migrant workers are of particular importance. The International Convention on the Protection of the Rights of All Migrant Workers and Members of their Families lays down a number of relevant rights. Its main feature is the principle of non-discrimination with respect to rights granted to migrant workers and members of their families (Article 7). This principle has been elaborated for matters of employment and labour conditions in Article 25. However, Article 52 allows for restrictions that states of employment may impose on migrant workers' free choice of remunerated activities. Furthermore, the Convention contains a number of provisions that are applicable to particular categories of migrant workers, such as frontier workers and seasonal workers.[52] Some aspects of the Convention do not apply to migrant workers and members of their families who are non-documented or in an irregular situation.[53]

The Convention on the Rights of Persons with Disabilities is based on the principles of, among others, non-discrimination, full and effective participation and inclusion of disabled people in society, and equality of opportunity (Article 3). As is made clear by Article 27, these principles also apply to matters of work and employment. This means, for example, that states have to prohibit discrimination on the basis of disability with respect to conditions of recruitment for jobs and to promote employment opportunities and career advancement for persons with disabilities in the labour market. Among numerous

---

[50] The text of the Constitution is available at: <http://www.ilo.org>.

[51] Declaration Concerning the Aims and Purposes of the International Labour Organization (Declaration of Philadelphia) (1944).

[52] CRPD, Arts 57–63.   [53] CRPD, Art 5.

other positive obligations, states must also ensure that reasonable accommodation is provided to persons with disabilities in the workplace.

3.1.2 Regional instruments

The European Social Charter (1961), the Additional Protocol to the European Social Charter (1988), and the Revised European Social Charter (1996) all aim at protecting the rights of workers. They extensively regulate various aspects of the right to work, employment conditions, vocational training, participation of workers in the determination of labour issues, and access to social security, social assistance, and welfare services. The Charter also identifies specific groups that need special protection, such as women, children, elderly persons, and migrant workers. The Charter does not recognize individual rights that are directly enforceable against the state. Although rights language is used, its provisions are framed as state obligations rather than individual rights. For example, Article 1 Revised European Social Charter, dealing with the right to work, reads: 'With a view to ensuring the effective exercise of the right to work, the Contracting Parties undertake...to accept as one of their primary aims and responsibilities the achievement and maintenance of as high and stable a level of employment as possible, with a view to the attainment of full employment.' The Charter of Fundamental Rights of the European Union stipulates in Article 5 that no one shall be required to perform forced or compulsory labour. In addition, it contains a number of workers' rights, including protection in the event of unjustified dismissal (Article 30) and the right of workers to information and consultation (Article 27).

Article 15 ACHPR provides that every individual shall have the right to work under equitable and satisfactory conditions and receive equal pay for equal work. Interestingly, the Charter also contains duties that are imposed on the individual, one of them being 'to work to the best of his abilities and competence' (Article 29(6)). Article 15 African Charter on the Rights and Welfare of the Child provides protection against child labour in similar terms to those of Article 32 CRC. Measures to protect children cover both the formal and informal sectors of employment.

In the Americas, the Protocol of San Salvador provides for the right to work in Article 6. Its wording is quite modern in that it refers to the notions of dignity and decency that have been essential features of recent debates about the right to work.[54] Article 7 lists a range of labour conditions that should be just, equitable, and satisfactory. Like Article 24 UDHR, it recognizes that workers have a right to rest, leisure, and paid holidays, and remuneration for national holidays (Article 7(h)).

In the Arab Charter on Human Rights, one comprehensive article deals with a number of aspects of the right to work. Article 34 provides that the right to work is a natural right of every citizen. It also requires states to provide, to the extent possible, a job for the largest number of those willing to work. The reference to 'those willing to work' is unique in the texts of human rights instruments. Article 34 also prescribes non-discriminatory treatment of men and women in matters of training, employment, job protection, and remuneration.

3.1.3 ILO conventions

Conventions adopted within the framework of the ILO are special conventions, because they deal with one or more particular labour issue(s). As the ILO has always stated, labour

---

[54] Art 6(1) reads: 'Everyone has the right to work, which includes the opportunity to secure the means for living a dignified and decent existence by performing a freely elected or accepted lawful activity.'

standards included in its conventions and recommendations are universal in nature. They are deliberately set low in order to achieve a worldwide reach, although more favourable national working conditions remain applicable.[55] The ILO conventions recognize that there are economic disparities between states and that these differences may have an impact on the way states implement their obligations.[56] What is decisive in the end is whether a state has complied with its treaty obligations. The conventions address diverse issues relating to the right to work and work-related rights, and many of them have a long history. The first ILO convention, adopted in 1919, dealt with the regulation of hours of work in industrial plants,[57] while another early convention was designed to counter unemployment.[58] More recent conventions deal with the elimination of the worst forms of child labour, the safety and health of workers in mines, and the rights of domestic workers.[59]

3.2 FEATURES

The right to work has a number of special features. First of all, it is an aggregate right, that is, it includes a number of components, such as claims to employment, free choice of work, improvement of working conditions, and trade union rights. Furthermore, the nature of the right to work, understood as a claim to employment, is such that it is not possible to enforce it directly against the state. It is not a subjective right enforceable by courts. Most people are employed by private employers rather than the state. This means that the state must regulate, monitor, and enforce labour rules by laying down mechanisms that workers can use to enforce their rights against employers. Many labour standards thus apply in horizontal relationships between employers and employees. To implement the ILO conventions, states have to bring their domestic law and practice into conformity with the international standards and employers have to comply with the domestic law. The advantage of ILO standards is that they are specific and detailed, thus giving clear guidance to states as to how to implement them. Consequently, compared to other economic, social, and cultural rights, the right to work and work-related rights are well developed in terms of their normative content.

The detailed nature of ILO standards has helped to clarify the meaning of relevant provisions in human rights instruments. For example, Article 7(b) ICESCR mentions safe and healthy working conditions as a component of just and favourable conditions of work, without further explanation. ILO conventions and recommendations have been helpful in defining what this means for specific types of activity or categories of workers. For example, there is a convention on safety and health in the agricultural sector,[60] and a convention on the labour conditions of seafarers.[61] These detailed rules may be used by human rights supervisory bodies to explain the nature and scope of human rights obligations.

Traditionally, there was little cooperation and coordination between international labour circles, on the one hand, and the human rights movement, on the other hand. The ILO and trade unions paid little attention to the use of human rights language to promote their cause and human rights activists largely ignored labour rights issues in their campaigns.[62] This situation has changed gradually over time. The ILO has been devoting special attention to the role of human rights in achieving social justice. For example, in 2010 it

---

[55] ILO Constitution, Art 19(8).   [56] See also ILO Constitution, Art 19(3).
[57] Hours of Work (Industry) Convention 1919 (No 1).   [58] Unemployment Convention 1919 (No 2).
[59] Convention No 182 (1999), Convention No 176 (1995), and Convention No 189 (2011) respectively.
[60] Convention No 184 (2001).   [61] Maritime Labour Convention (2006).
[62] Leary, 'The Paradox of Workers' Rights as Human Rights' in Compa and Diamond (eds), *Human Rights, Labor Rights, and International Trade* (University of Pennsylvania Press, 1996) 22.

adopted an international Recommendation on HIV/AIDS and the World of Work, which is meant to give impetus to anti-discrimination policies at the workplace level.[63] On the other hand, the human rights community is focused increasingly on violations of workers' rights, which often result as a negative consequence of the globalization of production and trade. For example, Amnesty International has broadened its mandate to include economic, social, and cultural rights and has drawn attention to the discrimination and abuse of internal migrant workers in China as a side-effect of uncontrolled business practices and economic growth.[64]

3.3 COMPONENTS

The right to work is composed of several key components. One of the most fundamental rights is the *freedom from slavery*, guaranteed by Article 8(1) ICCPR. Slavery is 'the status or condition of a person over whom any or all of the powers attaching to the right of ownership are exercised'.[65] Thus, a slave is unable to exercise the right of individual self-determination. Although slavery has been eradicated in many countries, it still exists in parts of Asia and Africa. For example, caste and ethnic status underpin the use of slavery in Niger, Mauritania, and Mali, where tens of thousands of people are ascribed slave status at birth and are then considered to be the property of their 'masters' who force them to work without pay.[66] In India many children work long hours in the cotton industry to pay off the debts of their parents. This is not freely chosen work, but bonded labour.

Forced or compulsory labour has also been banned under international human rights law. 'Forced or compulsory labour' is 'all work or service which is exacted from any person under the menace of any penalty and for which the said person has not offered himself voluntarily'.[67] In 1957, ILO member states agreed on new standards concerning the abolition of forced labour, committing themselves not to use forced labour as a means of political coercion or education or as a punishment for holding or expressing certain views; as a method of mobilizing and using labour for purposes of economic development; as a means of labour discipline; as a punishment for having participated in strikes; or as a means of racial, social, national, or religious discrimination.[68] The convention was directed against communist states that imposed forced labour in so-called labour camps for political opponents and states such as Rhodesia and South Africa that applied forced labour of black workers as part of their discriminatory laws and practice. Not all forms of 'compulsory' labour qualify as prohibited labour under international labour law and human rights law. Today China still applies the 'Re-Education Through Labor' system which imposes forced labour on persons in detention under a severe regime. It has been used to silence and suppress political dissidents.[69] Both the 1930 Forced Labour Convention and the ICCPR provide for exceptions, including compulsory military service and work required of persons in detention.[70]

The counterpart of the prohibition of slavery and forced labour is the *freedom to work*, which means the right to free choice of work or occupation. Workers have a right,

---

[63] ILO Recommendation 200 (2010).
[64] Amnesty International, *China: Internal Migrants: Discrimination and Abuse* (1 March 2007).
[65] Slavery Convention (1926), Art 1(1).
[66] See <http://www.antislavery.org> for more information on current forms of slavery.
[67] See ILO Forced Labour Convention (No 29) (1930), Art 2(1).
[68] ILO Convention Concerning the Abolition of Forced Labour (No 105) (1957), Art 1.
[69] Lu, *The Right to Work in China* (Intersentia, 2011).
[70] Forced Labour Convention (No 29), Art 2(2) and ICCPR, Art 8(3).

not a duty, to work. This right is codified in several human rights instruments, such as Article 6(1) ICESCR and Article 1(2) Revised European Social Charter. An example of a restriction of the free choice of work is the prohibition of night work for women, as originally required by ILO standards.[71] This was meant to protect women from the adverse consequences night work would have on their health. Today, the prohibition of night work for women has been increasingly relaxed with a reference to the equality of treatment and opportunity between men and women. Recent standards provide for the regulation and protection of night work of both women and men.[72]

Another key component of the right to work and work-related rights is the principle of *non-discrimination and equal treatment*, which is part of every human rights treaty. For example, Article 7(a)(i) ICESCR provides for 'equal remuneration for work of equal value without distinction of any kind, in particular women being guaranteed conditions of work not inferior to those enjoyed by men, with equal pay for equal work'. ILO standards lay down more specific rules and other grounds of discrimination that are prohibited.[73] Examples include trade union membership and action, marital status, pregnancy, and family responsibilities.

The right to work also includes the *right to seek work*, which implies that states must design, adopt, and implement active employment policies aimed at creating jobs and reducing unemployment. States are under a duty to act, not to succeed in providing everyone with a job. In some communist states, the right to work was constitutionally guaranteed and the authorities claimed that there was full employment, when in reality there was hidden unemployment. Today, the internationalization of economic processes has limited the role of governments to influence employment through national measures, but raising employment figures remain one of the major concerns.[74] The ILO has said that job creation for young people must be a top priority.[75]

The right to work implies a right to, not just any kind of work but, *decent work*. Although there is no conclusive definition of 'decent work', this concept, which is at the heart of current ILO policies and programmes, implies that work has to be of an acceptable quality in terms of conditions of work, feelings of value and satisfaction, relations between employer and employee, and remuneration.[76] The right to a fair remuneration is part of several human rights instruments.[77] It includes, inter alia, the right to equal pay for work of equal value. Fair remuneration is meant to guarantee to workers and their families a decent standard of living. The wage level is subject to a number of factors, such as the standard of living in a country, the type of work, and the situation on the labour market. For the European region, the European Committee on Social Rights has determined that the net minimum wage should amount to at least 60 per cent on the net national average wage.[78] Decency also implies that a certain minimum level of protection has to be met. For example, there is agreement that certain forms of child labour do not meet that standard, as is

---

[71] ILO Night Work (Women) Convention (No 4) (1919).

[72] ILO Night Work Convention (No 171) (1990). For a discussion, see Servais, *International Labour Law* (Kluwer Law International, 2011) 196–8.

[73] See ILO Discrimination (Employment and Occupation) Convention (No 111) (1958).

[74] See ILO Employment Policy Convention (No 122) (1964) and Revised European Social Charter, Art 1(1).

[75] ILO Global Employment Trends 2013, available at: <http://www.ilo.org/global/research/global-reports/global-employment-trends/2013/WCMS_202326/lang--en/index.htm>.

[76] See Servais, n 72, 345–6.

[77] Eg ICESCR, Art 7(a)(i); Revised European Social Charter, Art 4; Protocol of San Salvador, Art 7(a); ACHPR, Art 15.

[78] Digest of the Case Law of the European Committee on Social Rights (2008) 43.

evidenced by the ILO Convention on the Worst Forms of Child Labour.[79] According to this convention, the worst forms of child labour include work which, by its nature or the circumstances in which it is carried out, is likely to harm the health, safety, or morals of children (Article 3(d)).

Other components of the right to work include the right to have access to free employment services in order to find a job as guaranteed by Article 1(3) Revised European Social Charter, and protection of employment security, that is, protection against unjustified dismissal. ILO Convention No 158 (1982) sets out reasons that cannot be invoked to justify a dismissal, such as union membership or the exercise of a right by a worker, such as maternity leave.

Finally, there are some instrumental rights, such as the freedom of association, the right to bargain collectively, and the right to strike that serve the purpose of promoting and protecting the right to work and work-related rights.

The critical importance of some fundamental work-related rights has been proclaimed and confirmed in a key Declaration adopted by all member states of the ILO in 1998. The Declaration on Fundamental Principles and Rights at Work establishes an obligation of member states, arising from the very fact of membership of the ILO, to respect, promote, and realize a number of *core principles and rights* laid down in ILO conventions. These include:

- freedom of association and effective recognition of the right to collective bargaining;
- elimination of all forms of forced or compulsory labour;
- effective abolition of child labour; and
- elimination of discrimination in respect of employment and occupation.

The significance of this Declaration lies in the fact that states agreed that they have these obligations even if they have not ratified the relevant conventions.[80] Furthermore, the principles referred to here have universal reach and application, applying to all member states of the ILO with respect to both their domestic and international policies and practice. As a consequence, for example, importing and exporting states may not benefit from commodities produced through the use of forced labour or the worst forms of child labour.

3.4 OBLIGATIONS

Obligations resulting from the right to work and work-related rights can be derived from the treaty provisions themselves as well as the explanations given by the Committee on Economic, Social and Cultural Rights, for example in its General Comment 18. However, these obligations have been formulated in general terms, often making it difficult to monitor implementation.

As explained already, pursuant to Article 2(1) ICESCR, states must progressively realize the rights included in the ICESCR by taking appropriate measures, such as the adoption of legislation. Article 6(2) ICESCR lists a number of steps that states parties must take to achieve the full realization of the right to work, such as setting up vocational guidance and training programmes. Some obligations are not subject to progressive realization, but have an immediate effect. One example is the obligation to guarantee that the right to work can be exercised 'without discrimination of any kind', as provided for in Article 2(2) ICESCR.

[79] ILO Convention No 182 (1999).
[80] ILO Declaration on Fundamental Principles and Rights at Work and Its Follow-Up (1998).

The Committee on Economic, Social and Cultural Rights has identified further obligations resulting from the right to work by using the typology of obligations 'to respect,
to protect and to fulfil'.[81] These entail both negative obligations to abstain from interference and positive obligations to act. Under the obligation to *respect* the state must not, for
example, apply forced or compulsory labour and must allow the establishment and functioning of trade unions. The obligation to *protect* requires states to lay down in domestic
law standards for labour relations between private employers and employees (for example minimum wages, working hours, and safety rules), to monitor compliance with the
law, and to enforce it in case of infringement. The obligation to *fulfil* requires states, for
instance, to develop an active employment policy to counter unemployment.

The Committee on Economic, Social and Cultural Rights has characterized some obligations as *minimum core obligations*, which must be realized under all circumstances. These
include, for example, the obligation to ensure non-discrimination and equal opportunity
in matters of employment, for instance with respect to the right of access to employment
for women, migrants, and disabled people.[82] Another core obligation is the obligation to
abolish the worst forms of child labour pursuant to applicable ILO standards.

As far as the obligations arising from ILO conventions are concerned, two broad categories can be distinguished. First, some of the conventions entail immediate obligations
for states. An example is the Equal Remuneration Convention (No 90) (1951), which
stipulates in Article 2 that states shall ensure the application to all workers of the principle
of equal remuneration for men and women workers for work of equal value. States may
use different methods to implement this principle, including national laws or regulations,
legally established or recognized machinery for wage determination, or collective agreements between employers and workers. Other conventions, in contrast, contain obligations that are programmatic in nature, that is, they provide for programmes of action that
set general objectives for domestic policy. These conventions allow for policy freedom and
discretion for authorities regarding how best to implement the standards. An example is
the Human Resources Development Convention (No 142) (1975), which requires states
to adopt and develop policies and programmes of vocational guidance and vocational
training.

3.5 RELATIONSHIP WITH OTHER HUMAN RIGHTS

The right to work and work-related rights are linked to the enjoyment of other human
rights. They play a key role in facilitating the right to an adequate standard of living laid
down in Article 25 UDHR and Article 11 ICESCR. When people earn money through
work, they are in a much better position to get access to food, medical care, housing, and
education. Income generated through work is instrumental in acquiring property, such as
a house or land. In addition, decent work, not any kind of work, and just and favourable
working conditions contribute to living in dignity. There are also links with the right to
social security, that is, the right to access and maintain benefits in order to secure protection from a lack of work-related income, caused by illness, disability, maternity, employment injury, unemployment, old age, or death of a family member.[83] This right is thus
complementary to the right to work and work-related rights. The right of children not to

---

[81] CESCR, General Comment 18, HRI/GEN/1/Rev.9 (Vol I) 139, paras 22–8.
[82] CESCR, General Comment 18, HRI/GEN/1/Rev.9 (Vol I) 139, para 31.
[83] CESCR, General Comment 19, HRI/GEN/1/Rev.9 (Vol I) 152, para 2. (This General Comment deals with
the right to social security laid down in Article 9 ICESCR.) See Chapter 11.

be subject to child labour is closely linked to the need to make the right to education a reality.[84]

There are also relationships with civil and political rights, such as the right to information concerning work-related issues, freedom of expression to speak out about abuses at the workplace, and freedom of association with regard to trade unions. Finally, the enjoyment of other rights has an impact on the enjoyment of the right to work. Workers who are well trained and in good health will probably find it easier to find a suitable job and will perform better. This relationship has been acknowledged in international human rights law, including in the ILO Conventions[85] and the Revised European Social Charter.[86]

Due to its different dimensions and its links to other work-related rights, the right to work is a composite and complex right. In practice, it is particularly relevant to the horizontal relationships between employers and employees. Similar to the right to education, it becomes clear with the right to work that all human rights are interrelated and interdependent. International human rights law is less developed with regard to the right to work than the international standards established within the framework of the ILO. The implementation of the right to work at the domestic level can benefit from the detailed rights and obligations laid down in ILO conventions. Similarly, it can be argued that ILO standards should be seen and applied as human rights norms, because they touch upon the protection of human dignity.

4 CONCLUSION

This chapter has demonstrated that both the right to education and the right to work are important for living a life in dignity. Both rights are critical for the development of society as a whole, but also for achieving self-fulfilment and 'moving up the social ladder'. Their content, but also their realization, reflects the idea that all human rights are indivisible, interdependent, and interrelated. The modern approach to economic, social, and cultural rights emphasizes the importance of clarifying the normative content of each right by identifying its different dimensions, framed as entitlements and freedoms. These give rise to positive and negative obligations for states. It is a challenge for states to phrase, implement, and monitor their domestic policies in accordance with international standards. This is particularly so when implementation requires allocation of scarce (financial) resources in a period of economic recession. Human rights monitoring bodies, international organizations, and NGOs should be aware of these different dimensions when monitoring implementation of these rights by states.

FURTHER READING

ALSTON, 'Core Labour Standards and the Transformation of the International Labour Regime' (2004) 15 *EJIL* 457.

CHAPMAN and RUSSELL (eds), *Core Obligations: Building a Framework for*

Economic, Social and Cultural Rights (Intersentia, 2002).

COOMANS (ed), *Justiciability of Economic and Social Rights—Experiences from Domestic Systems* (Intersentia, 2006).

---

[84] See Worst Forms of Child Labour Convention (No 182) (1999), Art 7(2).
[85] See Servais, n 72, 210–12.   [86] Revised European Social Charter, Arts 10–13.

COOMANS, 'Justiciability of the Right to Education' (2009) 2 *Erasmus LR* 427.

DONDERS and VOLODIN (eds), *Human Rights in Education, Science and Culture* (UNESCO/Ashgate, 2007).

EIDE, KRAUSE, and ROSAS (eds), *Economic, Social and Cultural Rights* (Martinus Nijhoff, 2001).

HOWARD-HASSMANN and WELCH, JR (eds), *Economic Rights in Canada and the United States* (University of Pennsylvania Press, 2006).

INTERIGHTS, 'Litigating the Right to Education in Africa' (2013) 17 *Interights Bulletin*, available at: <http://www.interights.org/document/259/index.html>.

KALANTRY, GETGEN, and KOH, 'Enhancing Enforcement of Economic, Social and Cultural Rights Using Indicators: A Focus on the Right to Education in the ICESCR' (2010) 32 *HRQ* 253.

MACNAUGHTON and FREY, 'Decent Work, Human Rights, and the Millennium Development Goals' (2010) 7 *Hastings Race & Poverty LJ* 303.

MUNDLAK, 'The Right to Work: Linking Human Rights and Employment Policy' (2007) 146 *Intl Lab Rev* 189.

RODGERS, LEE, SWEPSTON, and VAN DALE, *The ILO and the Quest for Social Justice, 1919–2009* (International Labour Office, 2009).

SERVAIS, *International Labour Law* (Kluwer Law International, 2011).

TOMASEVSKI, *Education Denied* (Zed Books, 2003).

USEFUL WEBSITES

ILO: <http://www.ilo.org>

UNESCO: <http://www.unesco.org>

International Network for Economic, Social & Cultural Rights: <http://www.escr-net.org>

Anti-Slavery Society: <http://www.antislavery.org>

Right to Education Project: <http://www.right-to-education.org>

13

DETENTION AND TRIAL

Sangeeta Shah

SUMMARY

This chapter investigates two rights: the right to liberty and the right to a fair trial. The right to liberty regulates state powers of detention and provides safeguards against ill-treatment of detainees. The right to a fair trial sets out how court proceedings should be conducted and court systems organized. Both these rights set out extensive guarantees for individuals who are subjected to state-sanctioned detention regimes or national justice systems, as well as specific guarantees for those suspected of having committed a criminal offence. These rights seek to prevent the arbitrary use of executive power and create a climate conducive to the realization of human rights.

1 INTRODUCTION

When in detention, the liberty of individuals has been curtailed and they are at their most vulnerable. They are at the complete mercy of their captors. Therefore detention powers should only be exercised when actually necessary. Similarly, the determination of disputes by judicial bodies also subjects individuals to the authority of the state. Such proceedings must be conducted so that this authority is not exercised in an arbitrary manner. The rule of law can only be secured if trials are conducted fairly. Therefore, there is a need to regulate how individuals should be treated under national justice systems.

These concerns were recognized as early as 1215 in the Magna Carta, which gave certain individuals what can now be considered to be the origins of the rights to liberty and fair trial.[1] The rights to liberty and fair trial set out safeguards to ensure that notions of 'due process' are adhered to in the operation of regimes of detention, the investigation and prosecution of criminal charges, and the conduct of court proceedings. This chapter considers the content of the right to liberty, including freedom from arbitrary detention (Section 2), freedom from enforced disappearance (Section 3), and security of the person (Section 4), as well as the right to a fair trial (Section 5).

---

[1] The rights were only accorded to noblemen. See Chapter 1.

2 FREEDOM FROM ARBITRARY DETENTION

The ideal is that no one should be deprived of their liberty. However, there may be valid reasons for a state to assume custody of an individual. For example, it may be necessary to detain convicted criminals who pose a threat to the community. As such, traditionally, the main concern of human rights activists has been the capricious use of detention powers by oppressive governments in order to subdue their opponents. Beyond this, it is recognized that restrictions on liberty are permitted and may even be required. However, even where the grounds for detention may be justified, individuals in detention are susceptible to violations of their human rights. They are regularly 'forgotten', left to languish in prisons or mental health facilities, or may be subjected to torture or ill-treatment, either at the hands of their captors or by virtue of the conditions in which they are held.[2] The right to liberty recognizes these concerns. It is an umbrella of protections, which seeks to prevent the arbitrary use of detention powers and provide safeguards to eradicate ill-treatment or 'disappearance' from instances of permitted detention. This section first surveys the sources of the right and then considers how these two aims are realized.

2.1 SOURCES

Article 9 of the Universal Declaration of Human Rights (UDHR) provides that: 'No one shall be subjected to arbitrary arrest, detention or exile'. This pithy yet powerful provision was extended and its protections elaborated in Article 9 of the International Covenant on Civil and Political Rights (ICCPR). The Human Rights Committee has since articulated a general comment on the right to liberty[3] and the right has been guaranteed in other UN human rights treaties and declarations, including the Convention on the Protection of the Rights of Migrant Workers (Article 16), the Convention on the Rights of Persons with Disabilities (Article 14), and the Declaration on the Rights of Indigenous Peoples (Article 7). All regional human rights instruments also guarantee the right to liberty.[4] Freedom from arbitrary detention is a rule of customary international law[5] and the Human Rights Committee has claimed that this rule is peremptory in nature, that is, it is a *jus cogens* norm.[6]

There are a number of non-binding instruments that serve to elaborate upon the implications of the right, including the UN Standard Minimum Rules for the Treatment of Prisoners,[7] UN Body of Principles for the Protection of All Persons under Any Form of Detention or Imprisonment,[8] UN Basic Rules for the Treatment of Prisoners,[9] UN Rules for the Protection of Juveniles Deprived of their Liberty,[10] the Council of Europe Minimum Rules for the Treatment of Prisoners,[11] and the Inter-American Commission

---

[2] See Chapter 9.

[3] HRC, General Comment 8, HRI/GEN/1/Rev.9 (Vol I) 179. At the time of writing, the General Comment is being updated, see HRC, Draft General Comment 35, CCPR/C/107/R.3 (28 January 2013).

[4] ECHR, Art 5; Charter of Fundamental Rights of the European Union, Art 6; ADHR, Art I; ACHR, Art 7; ACHPR, Art 6; Arab Charter on Human Rights, Art 14.

[5] HRC, General Comment 24, HRI/GEN/1/Rev.9 (Vol I) 210, para 8. See also WGAD, Deliberation No 9, A/HRC/22/44 (24 December 2012).   [6] HRC, General Comment 29, HRI/GEN/1/Rev.9 (Vol I) 234, para 11.

[7] ECOSOC Res 663C(XXIV) (31 July 1957).   [8] GA Res 43/173 (9 December 1988).

[9] GA Res 45/111 (14 December 1990).   [10] GA Res 45/113 (14 December 1990).

[11] Committee of Ministers Res (73)5 (19 January 1973).

of Human Rights' Principles and Best Practices on the Protection of Persons Deprived of Liberty in the Americas.[12]

Given the importance of the concerns regarding arbitrary detention, in 1991 the UN Commission on Human Rights created a Working Group on Arbitrary Detention,[13] whose mandate has been renewed by the UN Human Rights Council.[14] The Working Group receives and investigates communications regarding possible cases of arbitrary detention, and also issues its own form of general comment: 'deliberations', on issues concerning arbitrary detention, which are an invaluable source of information.

2.2 SCOPE AND TYPES OF OBLIGATIONS

Although most issues concerning the right to liberty involve the arrest and detention of an individual in the context of criminal proceedings, the protections afforded by the right to liberty are not restricted to such situations. Rather, the Human Rights Committee has stressed that Article 9 ICCPR is applicable to 'all deprivations of liberty, whether in criminal cases or in other cases such as, for example, mental illness, vagrancy, drug addiction, educational purposes, immigration control etc'.[15] This is not an exhaustive list and there may be other situations where a deprivation of liberty may occur. A deprivation of liberty becomes a human rights issue when it takes place without the consent of the individual detained.

It is important to note the objective limits of the scope of right to liberty provisions. House arrest has been considered to be a deprivation of liberty,[16] while restrictions upon movement which confined an individual to his home during non-working hours was not a deprivation of liberty but a restriction upon the right to freedom of movement.[17] Similarly, restrictions upon movement within a state, a city, or even parts of a city have been held to be restrictions on freedom of movement and not deprivations of liberty.[18] Crowd-control techniques may give rise to a deprivation of liberty, but it will depend on the context in which they are used. The European Court of Human Rights has held that the 'kettling'—or confinement—of persons inside a police cordon for up to seven hours did not constitute a deprivation of liberty when it took place in dangerous conditions that may have led to serious injury or damage.[19] Thus, right to liberty provisions are concerned with narrow notions of detention involving the imposition of severe restrictions upon a person's physical being, where the intensity of the restriction depends on its duration, effects, and manner of implementation. However, this does not mean that short periods of detention are excluded. Detention for a period of 55 minutes has been held to engage Article 5, the arbitrary detention provision, of the European Convention on Human Rights (ECHR).[20]

The nature of the obligations corresponding to the right to liberty is primarily negative; that is, states should *respect* the right and not arbitrarily deprive an individual of their liberty. States must also *protect* the right. Where private actors undertake detention functions on behalf of the state, there is an obligation to ensure that all such instances of detention

---

[12] OEA/Ser/L/V/II.131 doc.26 (March 2008).   [13] CHR Res 1991/42 (5 March 1991).

[14] HR Council Res 15/18 (30 September 2010).

[15] General Comment 8, n 3, para 1. See also *Case Concerning Ahmadou Sadio Diallo (Republic of Guinea v Democratic Republic of the Congo)* [2010] ICJ Rep 639, para 77.

[16] *Madani v Algeria*, CCPR/C/89/D/1172/2003 (21 June 2007).

[17] *Trijonis v Lithuania*, Application no 2333/02 (17 March 2005).

[18] *Celepli v Sweden*, CCPR/C/51/D/456/91 (18 July 1994); *Karker v France*, CCPR/C/70/D/833/98 (26 October 2000).   [19] *Austin v UK* (2012) 55 EHRR 14.

[20] *Novotka v Slovakia*, App no 47244/99, Judgment of 4 November 2003.

are compliant with the right to liberty. All other forms of detention by private actors, such as abduction and kidnapping, must be criminalized. The European Court of Human Rights has held that states have an obligation not to return an individual to a country where there is a 'real risk' that there may be a 'flagrant breach' of the right to liberty, such as indefinite or incommunicado detention for many years without the prospect of being brought to trial.[21] The Human Rights Committee, though, has not yet found a violation of the right to liberty in such circumstances, preferring instead to label such treatment as inhuman treatment. A clear violation of the positive obligations inherent in the right to liberty is state participation in extraordinary rendition processes, whereby the state detains an individual who is handed over to foreign officials outside of ordinary legal processes.[22] *Fulfilling* the right is essentially achieved through the establishment of procedural safeguards that are explicitly spelt out within the various international law provisions on liberty. These will be examined in Section 2.4.

2.3 PERMISSIBLE DEPRIVATIONS OF LIBERTY

Article 9(1) ICCPR provides that: 'No one shall be subjected to arbitrary arrest or detention. No one shall be deprived of his liberty except on such grounds and in accordance with such procedures as are established by law.' Therefore, not all deprivations of liberty at the hands of the state will constitute a violation of a state's obligations. Only where a deprivation of liberty is unlawful and/or arbitrary, will it constitute a violation of Article 9(1). Other international treaties have similar provisions on arbitrary detention.[23] However, some grounds for detention are prohibited by international human rights law. If detention is solely on the basis of a disability or failure to fulfil a contractual obligation it will be unlawful.[24]

The ECHR sets out a more restrictive approach to detention. Rather than simply protecting individuals against illegal and/or arbitrary detention, Article 5(1) ECHR provides an exhaustive list of grounds upon which detention is justified. These are:

1. execution of a sentence after conviction by a competent court;
2. non-compliance with a lawful court order or legal obligation;
3. reasonable suspicion of having committed an offence, to prevent flight having done so, or to prevent the commission of an offence where the ultimate aim is to bring the person before a competent court;
4. educational supervision in the case of minors;
5. prevention of the spread of infectious diseases;
6. where persons are of unsound mind, alcoholics, drug addicts, or vagrants; and
7. prevention of unauthorized entry into the state or where action is being taken with a view to deportation or extradition.

Detention on grounds other than those listed is not permissible under the ECHR.

If the detention does not meet the specific Article 5(1) ground upon which it was justified it will not be permitted. For example, in the wake of the attacks of 11 September 2001, a law was passed in the UK which authorized the detention of non-UK nationals

---

[21] *Othman v UK* (2012) 55 EHRR 1; see also the opinion of the WGAD, A/HRC/4/40 (9 January 2000), para 47.
[22] *El-Masri v the Former Yugoslav Republic of Macedonia*, App no 39630/09, Judgment of 13 December 2012.
[23] eg ACHR, Art 7; ACHPR, Art 6.   [24] ICCPR, Art 11; CRPD, Art 14(1)(b).

who were suspected terrorists and could not be deported for fear that they may suffer torture abroad. The UK government justified these measures on the basis that they were immigration measures and as such were permitted under Article 5(1)(f) ECHR. However, in *A and others v UK* the European Court of Human Rights disagreed, holding that the detention measures were not measures taken with a view to deportation as there was no prospect that the detained individuals could be removed from the UK. Therefore, the powers of detention were considered to be a violation of Article 5(1) ECHR.[25]

None of the grounds set out in Article 5(1) ECHR by itself is enough to justify detention. As with the other treaties, the detention must also be lawful and not arbitrary.

2.3.1 Legality

Any deprivation of liberty must be pursuant to domestic law. It must be both sanctioned by and in conformity with any procedural requirements set out in national legislation or an equivalent norm of common law. Such a law must be formulated with sufficient precision to prevent arbitrary or overbroad application. So, the involuntary detention of psychiatric patients in secure hospitals should only take place where there is a legal basis to do so, which clearly sets out the situations under which such detention will take place. Similarly, where arrest warrants are mandatory and arrest takes place without one, a violation of the right to liberty will be found.[26] For example, in an attempt to arrest former President Garcia, the Peruvian army arrested his wife and children. As the army lacked constitutional authority to arrest individuals and the arrests were not based upon a court order, the Inter-American Commission of Human Rights held that the arrests were unlawful and thus in violation of the arbitrary detention provisions of the American Convention on Human Rights (ACHR).[27]

2.3.2 Arbitrariness

Whether detention is arbitrary will depend upon considerations of 'inappropriateness, injustice and lack of predictability' as well as 'unreasonableness'.[28] Thus, detention is arbitrary not only when it takes place without a legal basis but also where 'it is not necessary in all the circumstances of the case'.[29] In order to assess the necessity of detention measures, some form of proportionality assessment must take place. This assessment involves consideration of whether, *in the specific circumstances*, the detention regime is fit for the purported aim and whether there is a less invasive method of achieving that aim. So, the Human Rights Committee held that detention was a disproportionate punishment in *Fernando v Sri Lanka* where the author had been sentenced to one year of 'rigorous imprisonment' for contempt of court on the grounds of repeated applications to court, raising his voice, and refusing to apologize to the court. A fine would have sufficed.[30] The Australian policy of compulsory detention of asylum-seekers until their status has been determined has also been held to be disproportionate and thus arbitrary. The Human Rights Committee held that although it is permissible to detain individuals requesting asylum for an initial period

[25] *A and others v UK* (2009) 49 EHRR 29.
[26] *Gangaram Panday v Suriname*, IACtHR Series C No 16 (21 January 1994).
[27] *Garcia v Peru*, Case 11.006, IACommHR Report No 1/95.
[28] *Van Alphen v Netherlands*, CCPR/C/39/D/305/1988 (23 July 1990).
[29] *A v Australia*, CCPR/C/59/D/560/93 (3 April 1997) para 9.2. See also *Garcia v Peru*, n 27, para 47.
[30] *Fernando v Sri Lanka*, CCPR/C/83/D/1189/2003 (31 March 2005).

to record claims, confirm identity, and so on, detention beyond this period without good reasons that are specific to the individual, such as a risk of criminal behaviour, would be considered arbitrary.[31]

Where the detention of an individual would lead to a violation of another human right or is the result of a violation of another human right, such as the right to a fair trial, it will be considered arbitrary. As such violations of Article 9(1) ICCPR have been found when individuals were arrested for their political views in contravention of Article 19 ICCPR.[32] Similarly, detention on the basis of ethnic origin alone will be arbitrary.[33] Therefore, arrests on the basis of racial profiling, without further evidence, are prohibited.[34]

A detention that is legitimate at the outset may become arbitrary over time. The rationale for detention may cease to be relevant. As a safeguard against this there is a right to *periodic* review of detention in certain circumstances. If the circumstances surrounding the detention have not changed, or the detention has only been for a short period of time, then there is no requirement of periodic review. For example, where a person is serving a sentence of detention as a punishment which has been imposed by a court of law, it is assumed that the court that imposed the sentence has reviewed the necessity of the detention. However, in cases of life imprisonment, or where there is a discretionary 'preventive' sentence of detention to be served after a mandatory 'tariff' or 'punitive' period, human rights bodies have clearly stated that there should be periodic reviews of the necessity of the 'preventive' period of detention.[35] The key question is: does the detainee remain such a danger to society as to warrant continued detention? Furthermore, the European Court of Human Rights has held that the 'preventive' period of detention may become arbitrary if no reasonable effort is made to rehabilitate offenders and address the risks that they pose to society.[36] Similar principles apply to detention on grounds other than criminal conviction.

2.4 GUARANTEES TO THOSE DEPRIVED OF THEIR LIBERTY

Even if a state is justified in depriving someone of their liberty, the state's obligations regarding that individual do not end. Although states may legitimately restrict the enjoyment of some rights, such as freedom of expression, when necessary, the general position is that individuals do not lose their human rights as a consequence of detention. In addition to these general protections, there are a number of specific guarantees of treatment that must be accorded to detainees. Most of these are entitlements for those individuals who have been arrested or detained pursuant to a criminal charge, although some are safeguards of general application to all detainees. States should take into account specific vulnerabilities of individuals when fulfilling these guarantees to ensure their effective protection. So, the European Court of Human Rights has held that where individuals have been declared 'partially incapacitated' and placed in a psychiatric institution 'special

---

[31] *A v Australia*, n 29; *C v Australia*, CCPR/C/76/D/900/1999 (28 October 2002); *Baban v Australia*, CCPR/C/78/D/1014/2001 (6 August 2003).

[32] *Mukong v Cameroon*, CCPR/C/51/D/458/1991 (21 July 1994); *Kanana v Zaire*, CCPR/C/49/D/366/1989 (2 November 1993). See also 266/03, *Gunme v Cameroon*, 26th Activity Report of the ACommHPR (2009).

[33] 27/89, 46/91, 49/91, and 99/93, *Organisation Mondiale Contre La Torture v Rwanda*, 10th Activity Report of the ACommHPR (1997).

[34] CERD Committee, General Recommendation XXXI, HRI/GEN/1/Rev.9 (Vol II) 306, para 20.

[35] *Rameka v New Zealand*, CCPR/C/79/D/1090/2002 (6 November 2003); *Stafford v UK* (2002) 35 EHRR 32. In the mental health context see *Stanev v Bulgaria* (2012) 55 EHRR 22.

[36] *James, Wells and Lee v UK* (2013) 56 EHRR 12.

procedural safeguards may be called for in order to protect the interests of persons who, on account of their mental disabilities, are not fully capable of acting for themselves.'[37]

2.4.1 Rights of all detainees

Right to be informed of reasons for detention

Article 9(2) ICCPR provides that '[a]nyone who is arrested shall be informed, at the time of arrest, of the reasons for his arrest'. Similar guarantees can be found in Article 5(2) ECHR and Article 7(4) ACHR. This elementary safeguard exists to ensure that individuals know why they are being detained, which serves both to reduce the distress of being incarcerated, as well as to allow detainees to challenge the reasons for their detention. Thus, it applies to anyone who is in detention, not just those who are arrested pursuant to a criminal charge. However, in the context of detention on the basis of a criminal charge, individuals should be informed not just of the reasons for arrest, but also of the charges that they face. The reasons for arrest must be communicated in a language that the detainee understands and must contain sufficiently detailed information to indicate why the individual is being incarcerated. So when individuals were told that they had breached state security, but no further details were given, the Human Rights Committee held that a violation of Article 9(2) ICCPR had occurred.[38] For this right to be effective for certain categories of detainees, such as those with certain mental disabilities or children, reasons for detention ought to be provided to an appropriate representative who can represent their interests.[39] The reasons for arrest must be communicated to the detainee promptly, though not necessarily at the moment of arrest. So, while a delay of seven days has been considered too long,[40] a period of seven hours has been considered satisfactory.[41] Where overnight delays have occurred because of the need for an interpreter, this has been considered acceptable.[42]

Right to humane treatment

Article 10(1) ICCPR provides that all detainees must be 'treated with humanity and with respect for [their] inherent dignity'.[43] This fundamental protection has implications for the treatment of the individual as well as the conditions of detention. While most cases of severe ill-treatment will be considered inhuman treatment or torture contrary to Article 7 ICCPR, Article 10(1) is triggered by attacks on dignity that do not reach the severity of suffering threshold required by Article 7 ICCPR.[44] States are obliged to protect all individuals from 'any hardship or constraint other than that resulting from the deprivation of liberty'.[45]

Fulfilment of a detainee's right to humane treatment is inextricably linked to the conditions of detention in which they are held. States must ensure that these conditions are adequate, and so detention facilities must not be over-crowded and must provide satisfactory light, ventilation, bedding, sanitary facilities, food, and clothing, as well as access to

---

[37] *Stanev v Bulgaria*, n 35, para 170.

[38] *Ilombe and Shandwe v Democratic Republic of Congo*, CCPR/C/86/D/1177/2003 (17 March 2006).

[39] *Krasnova v Kyrgyzstan*, CCPR/C/101/D/1402/2005 (27 April 2010); *Z.H.v Hungary*, App no 28973/11, Judgment of 8 November 2012.

[40] *Grant v Jamaica*, CCPR/C/56/D/597/1994 (22 March 1996) para 8.1.

[41] *Fox, Campbell and Hartley v UK* (1991) 13 EHRR 157, para 42.

[42] *Hill and Hill v Spain*, CCPR/C/59/D/526/1993 (2 April 1997) para 12.2.

[43] See also ACHR, Art 5(2).   [44] See Chapter 9.

[45] HRC, General Comment 21, HRI/GEN/1/Rev.9 (Vol I) 202, para 3; *Vélez Loor v Panama*, IACtHR Series C No 218 (23 November 2010) para 198.

appropriate medical care where necessary.[46] Although ensuring such minimum conditions may be financially expensive, the Human Rights Committee has emphasized that the 'fundamental nature of the right means that the application of this rule...cannot be dependent on the material resources available in the State Party'.[47] The Committee found a violation of Article 10(1) ICCPR in *Wanza v Trinidad and Tobago* where the author was detained in a windowless cell, ventilated by an 18 x 18 inch opening, for between 22 and 23 hours a day, whilst on weekends or holidays, when the number of prison staff was too low, he was not permitted to leave the cell at all.[48] A number of the recommendations and declarations adopted by the UN and regional bodies listed in Section 2.1 set out minimum standards of detention below which a violation would be found. There must be strict state regulation of *all* detention facilities, even where they are run by private organizations, to ensure that conditions of detention are appropriate. Furthermore, the Inter-American Commission has stressed that states must exercise overall effective control over prisons and prevent systems of self-government whereby prison life is governed by 'gangs' of prisoners. In such situations, the state is simply unable to protect the dignity of prisoners.[49]

Right to challenge legality of detention

A further element of the guarantees against arbitrary detention is the right to bring *habeas corpus* proceedings; that is, detainees should have the opportunity to challenge the *legality* of their detention, and be released should it be considered unlawful.[50] This right of challenge aims to provide redress where incarceration is not necessary. Review of the legality of detention must be conducted by an independent court of law,[51] not by an administrative or executive body, and must take place without delay. In order for the right to be effective, detainees must have access to a lawyer, and individuals cannot be kept incommunicado. The right to bring such proceedings is considered to be part of customary international law and cannot be derogated from in times of emergency.[52]

Remedies for unlawful detention

Articles 9(4) and 9(5) ICCPR provide for two specific remedies where detention is found to be unlawful: release and compensation for pecuniary and non-pecuniary harm suffered. Similar rights are provided for in Article 10 ACHR and Article 5(5) ECHR. Thus, national courts must have the power to order release and award compensation. In the case of *A and others v UK*, discussed in Section 2.3, the European Court of Human Rights found a violation of Article 5(5) ECHR. The individuals concerned had been released from detention as a result of a national court decision, but they had not been paid any compensation for the time they spent in unlawful detention.[53]

2.4.2 Rights of those detained on a criminal charge

In addition to those rights discussed already, human rights law provides specific protections to individuals who are detained pursuant to a criminal charge, or who have been arrested on the basis of a suspicion that they have committed a criminal offence. Prevention and punishment of crimes is one of the broadest bases upon which states may ground

---

[46] See *Pacheco Teruel et al. v Honduras*, IACtHR Series C No 241 (27 April 2012).

[47] HRC General Comment 21, n 45, para 4.   [48] CCPR/C/74/D/683/1996 (26 March 2002).

[49] IACommHR, *Report on the Human Rights of Persons Deprived of Liberty in the Americas* (OAS, 2011), para 14.   [50] ICCPR, Art 9(4); ECHR, Art 5(4); ACHR, Art 7(6).

[51] On the meaning of 'independent court', see Section 5.3.2.

[52] WGAD Deliberation No 9, n 21, para 47.

[53] n 26. See also *Danev v Bulgaria*, App no 9411/05, Judgment of 2 September 2010.

detention. The considerable powers of the state in these circumstances must be kept in check with mechanisms for accountability of law enforcement officers and safeguards for arrested persons. All individuals who are arrested pursuant to a criminal charge must be brought 'promptly before a judge or other officer authorized to exercise judicial power'.[54] This should be an automatic process and not one which is dependent upon a request by the arrested individual. The initial days of detention are often those when a detainee is at his most vulnerable; the probability that torture or ill-treatment will occur is at its highest at this time. Thus, the aim of bringing a detainee before a judge is to ensure independent judicial supervision of the actions of law enforcement officers and to confirm the legal basis for detention. The judge or judicial officer should be empowered to order the release of detainees where detention is not appropriate. If they cannot do so, the protections provided by this right will be illusory. Furthermore, the judge or other officer should be 'independent, objective and impartial in relation to the issues dealt with'.[55] A public prosecutor who is involved in the proceedings or receives instruction from the public prosecutor's office is not sufficiently independent to exercise this role of review. With regard to the requirement of 'promptness', the Human Rights Committee has stated that 'forty-eight hours is ordinarily sufficient to transport the individual and to prepare for the judicial hearing; any delay longer than forty-eight hours should be justified by exceptional circumstances'.[56] The European Court of Human Rights has taken a strict approach also, finding that even in the exceptional circumstances of detention for terrorism-related offences, four days and six hours was too long.[57]

Protections afforded to those detained on a criminal charge continue beyond this first appearance before a judge. Article 9(3) ICCPR provides that such persons 'shall be entitled to trial within a reasonable time or to release' pending trial. Article 5(3) ECHR and Article 7 ACHR provide similar guarantees. The general rule is that individuals should not be kept in pre-trial detention unless it is really necessary to do so. Essentially these provisions provide a qualified right to release pending trial where exceptions are permitted 'to ensure the presence of the accused at the trial, to avert interference with witnesses and other evidence, or the commission of other offences'.[58] 'Public order', where the release of a suspected offender may give rise to a social disturbance,[59] and the 'personal safety of the suspect', where release of suspects may leave them vulnerable to attack, will also be relevant considerations.[60] International human rights bodies have advocated the use of financial guarantees or the removal of travel papers and passports, rather than pre-trial detention, to secure the attendance of a suspect at trial.

Where individuals are held in pre-trial detention, as part of the right to humane treatment and in order to maintain the presumption of innocence, they should be kept segregated from convicted criminals (Article 10(2)(a) ICCPR). They are to be treated as innocent individuals until proven guilty of an offence. Article 10(2)(b) ICCPR also provides that '[a]ccused juveniles shall be separated from adults and brought as speedily as possible for adjudication'. Furthermore, where release is not possible, the trial of the accused must take place within a reasonable period of time. What is considered *reasonable* is a matter to be determined on a case-by-case basis, but factors that will be taken into account include: the complexity of the case, the conduct of the accused (have they delayed

---

[54] ICCPR, Art 9(3); ACHR, Art 7(5); ECHR, Art 5(3).
[55] *Kulomin v Hungary*, CCPR/C/50/D/521/1992 (22 March 1996) para 11.3.
[56] HRC Draft General Comment 35, n 3, para 34 [footnotes omitted].
[57] *Brogan and others v UK* (1989) 11 EHRR 117.
[58] *WBE v Netherlands*, CCPR/C/46/D/432/1990 (23 October 1992), para 6.3.
[59] *Letellier v France* (1992) 14 EHRR 83.
[60] *IA v France*, App No 28213/95, Judgment of 23 September 1998.

the proceedings with challenges or by subverting investigations), and the efficiency of national authorities (a 'lack of budgetary appropriations for the administration of criminal justice...[will] not justify unreasonable delays').[61] Of primary concern is 'whether the time that has elapsed, for whatever reason, before judgment is passed on the accused has at some stage exceeded a reasonable limit whereby imprisonment without conviction imposes a greater sacrifice than could, in the circumstances of the case, reasonably be expected of a person presumed innocent'.[62]

Finally, Article 10(3) ICCPR obliges states to ensure that detention following a conviction for a criminal offence is aimed at the reformation and social rehabilitation of offenders, not simply punishment. So, in *Kang v Republic of Korea*, the Human Rights Committee found a violation of this provision where the author had been held in solitary confinement for 13 years for failing to abandon his political views.[63]

2.4.3. Rights for foreign nationals

Foreign detainees are particularly vulnerable. They may have problems of participation in different and often disorientating legal systems, including a lack of knowledge of the official language of the host state. Therefore, all foreign nationals who are 'arrested or committed to prison or to custody pending trial or...detained in any other manner' are entitled to access to a consular official from their home state.[64] Foreign detainees have the right to request that consular officials of their home state are notified of their arrest without delay and that all communications between the detainee and consular officials are forwarded without delay. All foreign detainees must be informed of these entitlements. This 'right' has been confirmed by the International Court of Justice to apply in all cases of detention of foreign nationals.[65]

2.5 EMERGENCY DETENTION POWERS

The right to liberty has been the subject of many derogations by states from their human rights obligations.[66] Detention, particularly indefinite detention without charge, is often seen as an important tool by states to deal with emergencies, particularly in the fight against terrorism. On a purely textual basis derogation from the right to liberty is permitted. However, any emergency deprivation of liberty measures must fulfil the requirements for a valid derogation, that is, the measures must be a necessary and proportionate response to the emergency faced. It would appear then that any such deprivations of liberty must not be arbitrary, and thus that the right to freedom from arbitrary detention is not derogable. Rather, it is the determination of what is arbitrary that changes when a state faces an emergency that threatens the life of the nation. So, in a time of armed conflict what constitutes an arbitrary detention will need to be determined by reference to the relevant rules of international humanitarian law.[67] Furthermore, the essential protections that

---

[61] *Fillastre and Bizouarn v Bolivia*, CCPR/C/43/D/336/1988 (5 November 1991) para 6.5.

[62] *Wemhoff v Germany* (1979–80) 1 EHRR 55; Case 11.245, *Giménez v Argentina*, IACommHR Report No 12.96 (1 March 1996) para 83.   [63] CCPR/C/78/D/878/1999 (15 July 2003).

[64] Vienna Convention on Consular Relations, Art 36(1); ICRMW, Art 16(7).

[65] *LaGrand (Germany v United States)* [2001] ICJ Rep 466; *Avena and other Mexican Nationals (Mexico v United States)* [2004] ICJ Rep 12; *Ahmadou Sadio Diallo*, n 15, para 91. In these cases the ICJ failed to confirm that the rights were human rights, however, the Inter-American Court has done so: see *Chaparro-Alvarez and Lapo-Iniguez v Ecuador*, IACtHR Series C No 170 (21 November 2007).   [66] See Chapter 6.

[67] Eg *Precautionary Measures in Guantanamo Bay, Cuba*, IACommHR (13 March 2002). See also Chapter 23.

the right to liberty affords serve to prevent violations of rights which are not derogable, such as freedom from torture and ill-treatment. Recognizing these further positive effects of the right to liberty, human rights bodies have stated that the procedural safeguards discussed already, including judicial oversight of arrests and the right to bring *habeas corpus* proceedings, must remain in place during times of emergency. For example, the Human Rights Committee has confirmed that '[i]t is inherent in the protection of rights explicitly recognized as non-derogable... that they must be secured by procedural guarantees, including, often, judicial guarantees' and so 'the right to take proceedings before a court to decide without delay on the lawfulness of detention must not be diminished by a State party's decision to derogate from the [ICCPR]'.[68] The Inter-American Court[69] and the European Court of Human Rights have made similar statements.[70]

3 ENFORCED DISAPPEARANCE

The most egregious violation of the right to liberty is an 'enforced disappearance', which comprises the secret deprivation of a person's liberty by state agents who refuse to inform anyone of the arrest.[71] As such, at least insofar as the friends and family of the individual is concerned, the individual has effectively disappeared. In such a situation, the victim is removed from the protection of the law and cannot make use of the judicial safeguards described in Section 2. Such abductions often result in the death of the victim. This practice of enforced disappearance was used systematically in Latin America in the 1960s and 1970s, and its usage has spread across the globe. Given its experience of the practice, the OAS was the first international organization to adopt a treaty specifically directed at the eradication of the practice: the Inter-American Convention on Forced Disappearance of Persons.

Each of the international human rights bodies has confirmed that enforced disappearance will constitute a violation of multiple human rights, including: the right to liberty, the right to humane conditions of detention, the right to recognition before the law, the right not to be tortured, and possibly the right to life.[72] Enforced disappearance may also result in violations of the prohibition of torture and ill-treatment both in respect of the victim and family members who are left worrying about the fate of abducted individuals.[73] The UN Convention for the Protection of All Persons against Enforced Disappearance has now confirmed that individuals have a 'free-standing' right not to be subjected to enforced disappearance.[74] Parties to the UN Convention or the Inter-American Convention are obliged to criminalize the practice of enforced disappearance and adopt further administrative

---

[68] General Comment 29, n 6, paras 15–16.
[69] OC-8/87, *Habeas Corpus in Emergency Situations*, IACtHR Series A No 8 (30 January 1987); OC-9/87, *Judicial Guarantees in States of Emergency*, IACtHR Series A No 9 (6 October 1987).
[70] *Brannigan and McBride v UK* (1994) 17 EHRR 539, para 62.
[71] See CPED, Art 2; Inter-American Convention on Forced Disappearance of Persons, Art II; Rome Statute of the International Criminal Court, Art 7(2)(i); Working Group on Enforced or Involuntary Disappearances, General Comment on the definition of enforced disappearance, A/HRC/7/2 (10 January 2008).
[72] *Sarma v Sri Lanka*, CCPR/C/78/D/950/2000 (16 July 2003); *Coronel v Columbia*, CCPR/C/76/D/778/1997 (24 October 2002); *Velásquez-Rodriguez v Honduras*, IACtHR Series C No 4 (29 July 1988); 24/97, *Mouvement Burkinabé des Droits de l'Homme et des Peuples v Burkina Faso*, 14th Activity Report of the ACommHPR (2001); *Kurt v Turkey* (1999) 27 EHRR 373; *Timurtas v Turkey* (2001) 33 EHRR 6.
[73] Eg *Mojica v Dominican Republic*, CCPR/C/51/D/449/1991 (25 July 1994).   [74] CPED, Art 1.

and legal measures, in addition to those which exist to prevent arbitrary detention, to bring to an end the practice of 'secret detention'. The obligations to criminalize, investigate, and punish enforced disappearance have, according to the Inter-American Court of Human Rights, attained the status of *jus cogens*.[75]

4 SECURITY OF THE PERSON

Treaty provisions on the right to liberty invariably contain a reference to protection of the 'security of the person', which is concerned with freedom from injury. States are obliged to refrain from inflicting bodily injury on individuals, to investigate threats to the person from both state and non-state actors, and to provide protection for individuals where such threats are credible. Some human rights bodies have restricted the right to security of the person to those individuals who are threatened with arbitrary detention. In the *Garcia* case discussed in Section 2.3, the Inter-American Commission decided that there had been a violation of the right to personal security because Garcia was 'threatened with arbitrary and unlawful arrest'.[76] The Human Rights Committee, extending the protections beyond the detention context, has stated that '[i]t cannot be the case that, as a matter of law, States can ignore known threats to the life of persons under their jurisdiction, just because he or she is not arrested or otherwise detained'.[77] Therefore, it has found violations of the right to security where there was a failure to investigate credible death threats.[78]

5 THE RIGHT TO A FAIR TRIAL

The right to a fair trial is 'aimed at the proper administration of justice' and securing the rule of law.[79] Human rights treaty provisions on fair trial establish a complex set of rules that cover two aspects of how the right is to be secured. First, there are rules which specify how court proceedings should be conducted. In general, fair trial guarantees are not primarily concerned with the *outcome* of judicial proceedings, but rather the *process* by which the outcome is achieved. Fairness of outcome is not guaranteed. Second, there are structural rules regarding the organization of domestic court systems. Securing the right to a fair trial can require a high level of investment in the court system and many states fail to fulfil their obligations because of serious structural problems. It should be noted that human rights law does not seek to impose a particular type of court system on states, but rather implements the principle that there should be a separation of powers between the executive and the judiciary.

5.1 SOURCES

Article 10 UDHR provides that '[e]veryone is entitled in full equality to a fair and public hearing by an independent and impartial tribunal, in the determination of his rights and obligations and of any criminal charge against him'. The UDHR also provides further, more specific protections applicable when determining a criminal charge, in Article 11. The

---

[75] *Goiburu v Paraguay*, IACtHR Series C No 202 (22 September 2009).   [76] n 27, 100.

[77] *Delgado Páez v Columbia*, CCPR/C/39/D/195/1985 (12 July 1990) para 5.5.

[78] *Jayawardena v Sri Lanka*, CCPR/C/75/D/916/2000 (22 July 2002).

[79] HRC, General Comment 13, HRI/GEN/Rev.9 (Vol I) 184, para 1.

general and specific criminal protections are merged into one, extremely detailed, provision of the ICCPR: Article 14. Due to their importance, aspects of fair trial guarantees can be found in most of the UN human rights treaties, including: Article 40 of the Convention on the Rights of the Child (CRC), Article 18 of the Migrant Workers Convention, Article 5(a) of the Convention on the Elimination of Racial Discrimination (ICERD), Article 15 of the Convention against Torture (UNCAT), and Article 13 of the Convention on the Rights of Persons with Disabilities. All regional treaties guarantee the right to a fair trial.[80]

Despite the sophisticated treaty provisions on the right to a fair trial, this is an area that has evolved by means of considerable elaboration by international human rights bodies. The 'fundamental principles of fair trial' form part of customary international law and the Human Rights Committee considers them to be peremptory norms of international law.[81] Although not listed within derogation clauses, the Committee has held that such principles are non-derogable in times of emergency because they ensure that 'the principles of legality and the rule of law' are respected. As such, these fundamental principles create safeguards for those norms that are explicitly listed as non-derogable, such as the right to life and the prohibition against torture.[82]

Particular aspects of the right to a fair trial are also elaborated upon in numerous declarations and guiding principles, including the Basic Principles on the Independence of the Judiciary,[83] the Basic Principles on the Role of Lawyers,[84] and the UN Standard Minimum Rules for the Administration of Juvenile Justice.[85]

Not all prosecutions will take place nationally. International law imposes liability on individuals for international crimes,[86] and these crimes are sometimes tried at the international level. International criminal tribunals must also ensure a fair trial of the accused and fair trial guarantees are provided in the relevant statutes and rules of procedure.[87] These rules are based upon the protections found in Article 14 ICCPR and customary international law.

5.2 SCOPE AND TYPES OF OBLIGATIONS

Though concerns regarding the conduct of judicial proceedings have traditionally focused on how *criminal* trials should be conducted, the right to a fair trial extends beyond such trials to civil and certain administrative proceedings. Article 14(1) ICCPR provides that guarantees should apply to the determination of both rights and obligations in a 'suit at law' as well as criminal charges, while Article 6(1) ECHR refers to the determination of both criminal charges and 'civil rights and obligations'. What is meant by the terms 'suit at law' and 'civil rights and obligations' has been a difficult question to answer.

The Human Rights Committee has interpreted the term 'suit at law' widely:

[T]he concept...is based on the nature of the right in question rather than on the status of one of the parties or the particular forum provided by domestic legal systems for the determination of particular rights. The concept encompasses (a) judicial procedures aimed

---

[80] ECHR, Arts 6 and 7; ACHR, Arts 8 and 9; ACHPR, Art 7; Arab Charter, Arts 12, 13, 16, and 17. The protections in the ACHPR are augmented by the African Commission Principles and Guidelines on the Right to a Fair Trial and Legal Assistance in Africa, DOC/OS (XXX) 247 (2003).

[81] General Comment 29, n 6, para 11.

[82] General Comment 29, n 6, para 15; see also HRC, General Comment 32, HRI/GEN/1/Rev.9 (Vol I) 248, para 6.   [83] GA Res 40/32 (29 November 1985) Annex.

[84] A/CONF.144/28/Rev.1, 118 (1990).   [85] GA Res 45/100 (14 December 1990) Annex.

[86] See Chapter 24.

[87] Eg ICTY Statute, Art 21 and ICTR Statute, Art 20. See Cassese and Gaeta, *International Criminal Law* (OUP, 2013) ch 19; Zappalà, *Human Rights in International Criminal Proceedings* (OUP, 2005).

at determining rights and obligations pertaining to the areas of contract, property and torts in the area of private law, as well as (b) equivalent notions in the area of administrative law such as the termination of employment of civil servants for other than disciplinary reasons, the determination of social security benefits or the pension rights of soldiers, or procedures regarding the use of public land or the taking of private property. In addition it may (c) cover other procedures which, however, must be assessed on a case by case basis in the light of the nature of the right in question.[88]

Similarly, Article 8(1) ACHR specifies that fair trial guarantees are to be accorded in all proceedings which involve 'the determination of . . . rights and obligations of a civil, labour, fiscal, or any other nature'. The case law of the European Court of Human Rights suggests that the reference to 'civil rights and obligations' means that 'most substantive rights that an individual may arguably claim under national law fall within Article 6 [ECHR] unless they quintessentially concern the exercise of the public power of the state'.[89] Most importantly, for all the international bodies, the application of fair trial rights to a 'suit at law' or the determination of 'civil rights and obligations' does not depend on whether national law has provided that the issue should be determined by a court or another body.

Similarly, what constitutes a criminal charge is not restricted to what national law considers 'criminal' and thus punishable under the law. If this were the case, then states could avoid some of their human rights obligations by simply designating certain charges as something other than criminal. Rather, the idea of 'criminal charge' extends to those offences which are criminal in nature, because they apply to the population at large, and are accompanied by sanctions that 'must be regarded as penal because of their purpose, character or severity'.[90] The expulsion of aliens or disciplinary measures against soldiers, however, will not be considered 'criminal'. In the criminal context, the right to a fair trial is triggered at the moment official notification of a charge is given. Therefore, there may be some overlap with the protections granted by the right to liberty.

Fair trial norms oblige states to secure the right through a number of different guarantees. As stated already, these norms are very detailed in the treatment that individuals must experience in order to enjoy a fair trial. There are both negative obligations to *respect* these guarantees by not interfering in their enjoyment and positive obligations to *fulfil* them through investment, monetary and otherwise, in the court system. States must also *protect* the rights. Although one might assume that justice is only administered by the state, there are instances where the state must protect fair trial rights from interference by other actors. For example, where states recognize religious courts or those based on customary law, it must ensure that these tribunals adhere to fair trial guarantees.[91] In addition, states must not transfer an individual to a jurisdiction where an individual may face a 'flagrant denial of justice', whereby there is a 'destruction of the very essence' of the right to a fair trial.[92]

5.3 GENERALLY APPLICABLE FAIR TRIAL GUARANTEES

What does the right to a fair trial entail? Article 14 ICCPR provides fair trial guarantees of general application that apply to all types of judicial proceedings (considered in this section) as well as detailed guarantees specific to criminal trials (considered in Section 5.4).

---

[88] General Comment 32, n 82, para 16 (footnotes omitted).

[89] Harris *et al.*, *Harris, O'Boyle and Warbrick: The Law of the European Convention on Human Rights* (OUP, 2009) 212.

[90] General Comment 32, n 82, para 15.   [91] General Comment 32, n 82, para 24.

[92] *Othman v UK*, n 21, para 260. See also *Soering v UK* (1989) 11 EHRR 439, para 113.

The generally applicable guarantees are set out in Article 14(1) ICCPR, which provides, inter alia, that '[a]ll persons shall be equal before the courts and tribunals. . . . everyone shall be entitled to a fair and public hearing by a competent, independent and impartial tribunal established by law'.[93] It should be noted that procedural aspects of a number of human rights obligations include recourse to judicial procedures and the general rights of due process will apply in these contexts. To take an example referred to already, Article 9(4) ICCPR provides that detainees have the right to have the legality of their detention determined by a court. Such review proceedings must be conducted according to the fundamental principles relating to a fair trial. Failure to do so will constitute violations of both Articles 9(4) and 14(1) ICCPR.

5.3.1 Equality before the courts

The right to equality before courts and tribunals is a specific application of the right to non-discrimination, contained in Article 26 ICCPR, to judicial proceedings.[94] It incorporates (1) the right of equal access to courts, and (2) the rights of all parties to proceedings to equality of arms and to be treated without discrimination.

Equal access

Although not explicitly provided for in fair trial provisions, all human rights bodies have confirmed that there is a right to access courts of first instance to determine a criminal charge or rights and obligations in a suit at law. All individuals must have an equal chance to pursue their legal rights. As the Human Rights Committee has stated, 'access to administration of justice must be effectively guaranteed in all such cases to ensure that no individual is deprived, in procedural terms, of his/her right to claim justice'.[95]

Ensuring equal access to courts and tribunals involves substantial activity on the part of states. They must ensure that judicial systems are organized so that 'all individuals. . . who may find themselves in the territory or subject to [their] jurisdiction' can access the courts.[96] This involves ensuring that there are no legal impediments to accessing justice. For example, statutory provisions that only allow for husbands (and not wives) to bring proceedings regarding matrimonial property in the courts have been found to violate Article 14(1) ICCPR.[97] But it is not just legal impediments that the state must remove. Access to courts and tribunals can be severely hampered if no legal assistance is available or only available at a prohibitively high cost. Article 14(3)(d) ICCPR obliges states to provide free legal aid in criminal cases where the interests of justice so demand and the individual concerned cannot afford to pay. Although there is no corresponding provision for civil proceedings, the Human Rights Committee has encouraged states 'to provide free legal aid. . . for individuals who do not have sufficient means to pay for it'.[98] Furthermore, where there are cultural practices or norms that exclude certain vulnerable groups from accessing justice, the state must make efforts to overcome these. For example, in Luxembourg free information is provided once a week for women on issues that might affect them, such as divorce and domestic violence, and how to access judicial help.[99]

---

[93] See also ECHR, Art 6(1); ACHR, Art 8(1).   [94] See Chapter 8.
[95] General Comment 32, n 82, para 9.   [96] General Comment 32, n 82, para 9.
[97] *Ato del Avellanal v Peru*, A/44/40 (1988) 196.
[98] General Comment 32, n 82, para 10. See also *Airey v Ireland* (1979–80) 2 EHRR 305; OC-11/90, *Exceptions to the Exhaustion of Domestic Remedies*, IACtHR Series A No 11 (10 August 1990) para 28.
[99] Report of the Special Rapporteur on the independence of judges and lawyers, A/HRC/17/30 (29 April 2011) para 75.

However, states may restrict access to courts where such restrictions are based on law, can be justified on objective and reasonable grounds, and are not discriminatory.[100] One area where the issue of restricting access to justice has been extremely contentious is where claims of state immunity have barred judicial proceedings. *Al Adsani v UK* concerned a claim in tort that had been initiated before the courts in the UK regarding torture alleged to have been committed by the government of Kuwait. The Kuwaiti government relied upon the customary international law rule of state immunity, which provides that a state is immune from proceedings in foreign courts regarding certain official acts. This claim of immunity was upheld by the UK courts. The European Court of Human Rights held, by nine votes to eight, that restricting access to the courts by virtue of the rule of state immunity was permissible because it pursued the legitimate aim of 'complying with international law to promote comity and good relations between states through the respect of another's state sovereignty'.[101] Thus, applying the customary rule of state immunity to civil proceedings for torture did not violate the right to a fair trial.[102]

Equality of arms and treatment without discrimination

The right to equality before the courts also includes protections of equality of arms and treatment without discrimination. Equality of arms means that all parties should be provided with the same procedural rights unless there is an objective and reasonable justification not to do so and there is no significant disadvantage to either party. The essence of the guarantee is that each side should be given the opportunity to challenge all the arguments put forward by the other side.[103] Where courtroom conditions are not conducive to securing equality of arms there will be a violation. For example, in *Gridin v Russian Federation* the author of the communication was the defendant of multiple rape allegations and his trial had attracted much media publicity. The courtroom was filled with people who shouted that the author should be sentenced to death. The Human Rights Committee held that 'the failure of the trial court to control the hostile atmosphere and pressure created by the public in the courtroom, which made it impossible for defence counsel to properly cross-examine the witnesses and present his defence...violated the author's right to a fair trial'.[104]

There should be no differential treatment of persons during court proceedings. Like cases should be treated alike unless there are objective and justifiable reasons not to do so. On this basis, the Human Rights Committee held in *Kavanagh v Ireland* that a situation where the Director of Public Prosecutions decided, with unfettered discretion, whether or not individuals accused of certain crimes would face a jury trial raised issues of equality before the law.[105] The treaties aimed at eradicating specific forms of discrimination, such as the ICERD and the Convention on the Elimination of All Forms of Discrimination Against Women (CEDAW), explicitly emphasize that there should not be distinction as to race, colour, national origin, heritage, or sex during court proceedings.[106] Distinction on these grounds will never be justifiable.

---

[100] General Comment 32, n 82, para 9.   [101] (2002) 34 EHRR 11, para 54.
[102] See also *Sechremelis v Greece*, CCPR/C/100/D/1507/2006 (30 November 2010).
[103] General Comment 32, n 82, para 13.   [104] CCPR/C/69/D/770/1997 (20 July 2000) para 8.2.
[105] CCPR/C/71/D/819/1998 (4 April 2001). Although note that the majority found a violation of ICCPR, Art 26 and decided not to go on and examine whether there had been a breach of Art 14(1).
[106] See ICERD Art 5(a); CEDAW Art 15(2). See also General Recommendation XXXI, n 34.

5.3.2 Hearing by a competent, independent, and impartial tribunal

The courts and tribunals before which claims are heard and criminal charges are determined must be 'competent, independent and impartial' and established pursuant to national law. Courts and tribunals are those institutions which are empowered to make legally binding decisions on the basis of the rules of law applicable within a state. Therefore, a panel which can make recommendations as to a particular course of action but not binding decisions, such as a parole board, will not be considered a *competent* court or tribunal for the purposes of fair trial provisions. The requirement that tribunals be *established by law* means that the basic rules on jurisdiction, organization, and membership of the court should be contained in legislation. This acts as a safeguard against executive abuse of court procedures.

The requirement of independence refers to the institutional setup of the courts. States are obliged to establish courts so that any form of interference with the activities of judges is thwarted. There are essentially two aspects to this. First, the courts should be fully independent of the executive and the parties to a dispute. Thus, courts should not take direction from government ministers or departments on how to decide a case.[107] Second, states must ensure that there are safeguards in place to preserve the independence of the judiciary, including 'clear procedures and objective criteria for the appointment, remuneration, tenure, promotion, suspension and dismissal of the judiciary and disciplinary sanctions taken against them'.[108] Providing such procedures and guarantees aims to remove the threat that justice may be subverted by appointing 'sympathetic' judges, corruption, or the removal of judges from their post. A clear violation of this principle, and thus breach of fair trial guarantees, was seen in *Lawyers for Human Rights v Swaziland* where the King assumed all judicial power, including the ability to remove judges as well as exercise judicial authority.[109]

Related to the consideration of independence is the idea of *impartiality* of the courts. There are two aspects to this. First, judges of the court must be *subjectively* impartial. That is, they must act without any personal bias towards either party in a case. Similarly, they must not harbour preconceptions about the action before them and must remain uninfluenced by the media and public perception. In general, there will be a presumption that judges are impartial unless there is evidence to the contrary. The court should also be *objectively* impartial, so that the court and its judges must *appear* to the impartial observer to be free from bias. Justice must be seen to be done. For example, in *Piersack v Belgium* the presiding judge in the applicant's case had been the head of the public prosecutor's department during the investigation of the case. Although there was no evidence that the judge had knowledge of the investigation, the European Court of Human Rights held that he was not objectively impartial.[110] Where there is a perceived lack of independence and impartiality, people are wary of having recourse to justice systems and thus access to justice is affected.

Concerns have been expressed by international human rights bodies regarding the use of military courts to try civilians. There are two grounds for such concerns. First, it is argued that military courts violate the principle of equality before the law because military trials deviate from the normal criminal trial procedures in a state, creating a distinction in the manner in which individuals are tried. As such there need to be justifications for their

---

[107] Eg *Bahamonde v Equatorial Guinea*, CCPR/C/49/D/468/1991 (20 October 1993).
[108] General Comment 32, n 82, para 19. See also the UN Basic Principles on the Independence of the Judiciary; *Chocrón Chocrón v Venezuela*, IACtHR Series C No 227 (1 July 2011).
[109] 251/02, 18th Activity Report of the ACommHPR (2005).   [110] (1983) 5 EHRR 169.

use which are based on objective and reasonable grounds. The Human Rights Committee has stated that '[t]rials of civilians by military or special courts should be exceptional, i.e. limited to cases where the State party can show that resorting to such trials is necessary and justified by objective and serious reasons, and where with regard to the specific class of individuals and offences at issue the regular civilian courts are unable to undertake the trials'.[111]

The second concern is that military courts are not sufficiently impartial to fulfil the requirements of fair trial provisions. In the words of the African Commission of Human Rights:

> Withdrawing criminal procedure from the competence of the courts established within the judicial order and conferring [it] onto an extension of the executive necessarily compromises the impartiality of the courts. Independent of the qualities of the persons sitting in such jurisdictions, their very existence constitutes a violation of the principles of impartiality and independence of the judiciary.[112]

Thus, some have argued that military trials of civilians are, of themselves, a violation of the right to be tried by an independent and impartial court. There may even be concerns regarding impartiality where only one member of the court is a serving military officer while the others are civilians.[113]

The Human Rights Committee has held that a state must demonstrate that there is both a need for the military trial, and, if this is demonstrated, that the military courts have afforded the full protection of the rights of the accused according to Article 14 ICCPR.[114] Thus, according to the Committee, if it can be shown that the military trial is necessary, has maintained impartiality, and afforded the civilian a fair trial in procedural terms, then the military trial will not result in a violation of Article 14(1) ICCPR. The procedural requirements of a fair trial are considered in Section 5.3.3.

5.3.3 Fair and public hearing

'Fair'

Fair trial guarantees explicitly provide for a right to a fair hearing in both civil and criminal proceedings.[115] The content of this right is ever-evolving as new situations are considered by international human rights bodies, though there is a core minimum for criminal trials. The principle of fairness includes 'the absence of any direct or indirect influence, pressure or intimidation or intrusion from whatever side and for whatever motive'.[116] All judicial proceedings must adhere to this principle. Other aspects of a fair hearing include, inter alia, the right to equality of arms discussed already, the right to attend hearings, and the expeditious disposal of proceedings.[117]

The right to attend hearings is based on the idea that individuals will wish to monitor proceedings concerning their interests. However, it is not an absolute guarantee. In criminal trials, a hearing in the absence of the defendant (*in absentia*) is generally not compatible with the idea of a fair hearing.[118] However, there are three exceptions to this general

---

[111] General Comment 32, n 82, para 22 (footnotes omitted).

[112] 54/91, *Malawi African Association v Mauritania*, 13th Activity Report of the ACommHPR (2000) para 98. See also Case 11.084, *Salinas v Peru*, IACommHR Report No 27/94 (30 November 1994); *Durand and Ugarte v Peru*, IACtHR Series C No 68 (3 December 2001), para 125.

[113] *Incal v Turkey* (2000) 29 EHRR 449, paras 71–2.

[114] See *Madani v Algeria*, n 16, para 8.7.   [115] ICCPR, Art 14(1); ECHR, Art 6(1); ACHR, Art 8(1).

[116] General Comment 32, n 82, para 25.   [117] See further Harris *et al.*, n 89, 246–71.

[118] *Maleki v Italy*, CCPR/C/66/D/699/1996 (15 June 1999).

position. First, an individual may waive his or her right to be at the trial. Second, where the authorities have tried diligently but failed to inform the individual of the trial date because, for example, he or she has moved away from their stated address, then there will be no violation of fair trial guarantees. Finally, if an individual aims to evade justice by not attending the trial, there will be no violation. As regards civil proceedings, the right to be present at proceedings has been interpreted flexibly in accordance with different national legal systems. The presence of legal representatives may suffice. However, the European Commission of Human Rights has stated that where 'the personal character and manner of life of the party concerned is directly relevant to the formation of the court's opinion', for example in child custody hearings, then there is a right to be present.[119]

A further aspect of the right to a fair trial is that there should be no excessive procedural delays in the resolution of a dispute. Delays call the effectiveness of the judicial system into question. Furthermore, it is clear that a delay in determining a criminal charge will leave the defendant unsure of his or her fate and, although the guilt or innocence of the defendant is yet to be determined, public perceptions of guilt are often encouraged by long delays. Thus, there is a specific provision in the ICCPR (Article 14(3)(c)) that provides that everyone charged with a criminal offence should 'be tried without delay'. Although there is no comparable explicit protection in Article 14(1), the Human Rights Committee has interpreted the notion of 'fair hearing' to include the expeditious disposal of proceedings and so it is applicable to civil proceedings also.[120] The entire duration of proceedings, from the moment an individual is informed of a criminal charge or civil proceedings are initiated until a final appeal decision is made, is taken into account when deciding whether there has been undue delay. In addition, there may be a determination that the reasonable time guarantee has been violated for a particular stage of the judicial process. For example, a violation was found in *Pinkney v Canada* because appeals proceedings were delayed by nearly three years owing to the transcripts of the trial proceedings taking 29 months to prepare.[121] There is no absolute time limit within which judicial proceedings should take place. Instead, there are a number of considerations that need to be taken into account when assessing the reasonableness of a delay. These include: the length of each stage of the proceedings, the complexity of the legal issues at stake, the detrimental effects on the individual concerned caused by the delay, the availability of remedies to accelerate proceedings, and the outcome of any appeal proceedings.[122]

The organization of a state's judicial system is implicated in the enjoyment of this right. Where delays to the administration of justice are caused by budgetary constraints, states must ensure that more resources are allocated to the judicial system. The Human Rights Committee has not accepted the argument of lack of financial resources as a valid excuse for a delay in the determination of criminal charges.[123] States are obliged to take appropriate measures to deal with temporary backlogs of cases.[124]

'Public'

Article 14(1) ICCPR also provides all individuals with a right to a public trial. Trials that are shrouded in secrecy are more likely to involve, or be perceived to involve, manipulation of the justice system; such trials have been used to suppress 'dissident' groups in some

---

[119] *X v Sweden* (1959) 2 YB 354, 370.
[120] *Fei v Columbia*, CCPR/C/53/D/514/1992 (4 April 1995). ACHR, Art 8(1) and ECHR, Art 6(1) explicitly provide this protection for both the determination of civil claims and criminal charges.
[121] CCPR/C/OP/1 at 95 (1985).   [122] *Deisl v Austria*, CCPR/C/81/D/1060/2002 (23 August 2004).
[123] *Lubuto v Zambia*, CCPR/C/55/D/390/1990/Rev.1 (31 October 1995) para 7.3.
[124] *Zimmermann v Switzerland* (1994) 6 EHRR 17.

states. There are two elements to this right. First, the trial itself should be conducted publicly and orally. Therefore, information regarding upcoming court proceedings should be made readily available in good time and sufficient facilities should be provided in courtrooms to allow the press and other members of the public to observe the proceedings.[125] However, this aspect of the right is qualified and Article 14(1) contains an exhaustive list of situations where hearings can be conducted without public scrutiny: 'for reasons of public morals, public order (ordre public) or national security in a democratic society, or when the interest of the private lives of the parties so requires, or to the extent strictly necessary in the opinion of the court in special circumstances where publicity would prejudice the interests of justice'. The language of these restrictions implies that a condition of holding a trial without public scrutiny is that the principles of a democratic society must be upheld, so that questions of proportionality will come into play. Furthermore, for pre-trial proceedings or appellate proceedings based on purely written submissions, there is no need for public access.[126]

The second element to the right to a public trial provides that judgments should be made available to the public. Article 14(1) ICCPR provides that there may be exceptions to this rule where 'the interest of juvenile persons otherwise requires or the proceedings concern matrimonial disputes or the guardianship of children'.[127] In all other circumstances no restrictions to access to judgments are permitted. Therefore, even where the trial has been conducted without public scrutiny, the Human Rights Committee has stated that 'the judgment, including the essential findings, evidence and legal reasoning must be made public'.[128] A question recently arose before the European Court of Human Rights regarding the finding of guilt or innocence in criminal cases by lay juries. In such cases no reasons for the final verdict were given. In order to avoid arbitrariness in the final decision, the Court held that it was necessary to ensure that a framework was established within which the verdict could stand. The use of procedural safeguards such as directions or guidance provided by the presiding judge to the jurors on the legal issues or evidence presented, and precise, unequivocal questions put to the jury by the judge, would provide such a framework.[129]

5.4 FAIR TRIAL GUARANTEES IN CRIMINAL PROCEEDINGS

A detailed account of what constitutes a fair criminal trial is to be found in most human rights treaty provisions on the right to a fair trial. In addition to the generally applicable principles discussed already, Article 14 ICCPR, for example, contains a further six paragraphs regarding the rights of defendants in criminal trials. Similar detailed guidance can be found in Article 6 ECHR, Article 8 ACHR, and the African Commission's Principles and Guidelines on the Right to a Fair Trial and Legal Assistance in Africa. The conduct of investigations often impacts upon criminal trials, and so to ensure that these rights are effective, they have been interpreted, where appropriate, to apply to the pre-trial phase as well.

---

[125] *Van Meurs v The Netherlands*, CCPR/C/39/D/215/1986 (13 July 1990).
[126] *Axen v Germany* (1984) 6 EHRR 195; *Helmers v Sweden* (1993) 15 EHRR 285.
[127] ECHR, Art 6(1) does not allow for any exceptions to this right, while the ACHR only provides this guarantee in the criminal context: see Art 8(5). No equivalent protections are set out in the ACHPR.
[128] General Comment 32, n 82, para 29.   [129] *Taxquet v Belgium* (2012) 54 EHRR 26.

5.4.1 Presumption of innocence

All treaty provisions on the right to a fair trial contain a guarantee of the right to be presumed innocent until proven guilty.[130] The Human Rights Committee has stated that this guarantee is one of the 'fundamental principles of fair trial' and constitutes a rule of *jus cogens*.[131] This right applies from the moment that an individual is accused, even before a formal criminal charge is issued, until a determination of the charge by the final appeal court. State authorities, including judges, must refrain from any conduct that would influence the outcome of a trial to the defendant's disadvantage. Therefore, declarations of the guilt of an individual before trial[132] and excessively long periods of pre-trial detention that affect perceptions of innocence will constitute violations of this right.[133] Similarly, judges should not begin a trial with a preconceived idea of guilt. Investigatory actions, such as fingerprinting, taking DNA samples, and searches of property, however, do not violate the presumption. As the presumption of innocence must be maintained at all times during the trial, the burden of proof rests upon the prosecution to prove guilt. If there is insufficient evidence, the court must decide in favour of the accused.

5.4.2 Freedom from self-incrimination

Closely related to the presumption of innocence is the right not to be compelled to incriminate oneself. This right is provided for in Article 14(3)(g) ICCPR as well as Articles 8(2)(g) and 8(3) ACHR, and has been read into what constitutes a fair trial for the purposes of Article 6(1) ECHR.[134] This right is 'to be understood in terms of the absence of any direct or indirect physical or undue psychological pressure from the investigating authorities on the accused, with a view to obtaining a confession of guilt'.[135]

Article 15 UNCAT prohibits the use of evidence obtained by torture 'in any proceedings, except against a person accused of torture as evidence that the statement was made', while the Human Rights Committee has gone further to state that any evidence arising from treatment contrary to Article 7 ICCPR, that is torture *or* inhuman or degrading treatment or punishment, should be excluded from evidence.[136] In fact, the UK House of Lords has held that even evidence obtained by a third party, who is not involved in the proceedings, by means of torture should not be admissible in court.[137] The African Commission has taken a strong position on this, assuming that any confession obtained during incommunicado detention shall be considered to have been obtained by coercion. It has held that 'where a confession is obtained in the absence of certain procedural guarantees against [torture or ill-treatment], it should not be admitted as evidence.'[138] However, disappointingly perhaps, the European Court of Human Rights has held that where evidence is secured as an *indirect* result of torture or ill-treatment—so-called 'fruit of the poisonous tree'—it may be admissible. In *Gäfgen v Germany*, the applicant was suspected of having kidnapped a young boy. He was threatened with torture in order to provide information regarding the boy's whereabouts. Although the confessions provided by the applicant following this threat were considered inadmissible, real evidence which had been found as a result of the confessions was admissible during the applicant's trial.

---

[130] ICCPR, Art 14(2); ACHR, Art 8(2); ACHPR, Art 7(1)(b); ECHR, Art 6(2). See also ICTY Statute, Art 21(3); ICTR Statute, Art 20(3); ICC Statute, Art 66(1).   [131] General Comment 29, n 6, para 11.

[132] See *Gridin v Russian Federation*, n 104; *Allenet de Ribemont v France* (1995) 20 EHRR 557.

[133] Eg *Cagas v Philippines* CCPR/C/63/D/788/1997 (23 October 2001), para 7.3.

[134] Eg *Saunders v UK* (1996) 23 EHRR 313.   [135] General Comment 32, n 82, para 41.

[136] See also *Othman v UK*, n 21, paras 263–7.

[137] *A v Secretary of State for Home Affairs* [2005] UKHL 71.

[138] 334/06, *Egyptian Initiative for Personal Rights and Interights v Egypt*, 29th Activity Report of the ACommHPR (2011) para 218.

The European Court held that as this evidence was not the only evidence pointing to guilt, its admissibility was not a violation of the right to a fair trial.[139]

Other instances of improper pressure will be decided on a case-by-case basis, examining whether the 'very essence of the right' not to incriminate oneself has been destroyed. So where adverse inferences are drawn in court from a suspect's silence during questioning, whether a violation has occurred will depend on whether there was other evidence pointing to guilt.[140]

5.4.3 Right to be informed of the charge

Individuals accused of a criminal offence have the right to be informed of the charge that they are facing. This is in addition to the right of those detained to know the charge against them (see Section 2.4.1), and applies to an individual whether in detention or not from the moment he or she is formally charged or publicly named as an accused person.[141] This right, provided for in Article 14(3)(a) ICCPR, Article 7(4) ACHR, and Article 6(3)(a) ECHR, must be fulfilled promptly, without inexcusable delay. At the stage of being formally charged, suspects are entitled to be informed of the full details of the charge against them, including the type of offence and the elements upon which the accusation has been founded, in a language that they understand, so that they may begin to formulate a defence.

5.4.4 Right to an adequate defence

Beyond these protections are those that elaborate on the principle of equality of arms. So, for example, Article 14(3)(b) ICCPR provides that everyone is entitled 'to have adequate time and facilities for the preparation of his defence and to communicate with counsel of his own choosing'. Article 8(2)(c) ACHR, Article 7(1)(c) ACHPR, and Article 6(3)(b) ECHR contain similar provisions. What is considered adequate time will depend upon the nature and complexity of the case. There are certain minimum levels of facilities, however, that must be accorded to all defendants for their defence to be effective. Explicitly provided for is the guarantee that defendants must be able to communicate with their counsel. They must also be provided with all the materials that the prosecution is to use in court as well as any other material that may be exculpatory. Exculpatory evidence does not only include evidence that suggests innocence, but also material regarding the gathering of evidence which may show some impropriety. For example, where there is information that the evidence against the defendant has been obtained by torture, this should be transmitted to the defence. The materials must be presented so that the defendant *or* his counsel is able to understand them. Therefore, where the defendant requires translation of documents but his counsel does not, there is no obligation on the state to provide such translations.[142]

There are other rights associated with aspects of an adequate defence guaranteed by international human rights law. Defendants have the right to be present at their trial and to defend themselves personally or to have counsel represent them.[143] Although the key principle is that individuals must be allowed to defend themselves, this right is not unlimited. If the interests of justice require a lawyer to represent the accused, then a lawyer may be assigned against the wishes of the accused. Such interests apply when an individual is charged with a serious offence but unable to act in his or her own interests, when the

[139] (2011) 52 EHRR 39.   [140] *John Murray v UK* (1996) 22 EHRR 29.

[141] General Comment 32, n 82, para 31.

[142] *Harward v Norway*, CCPR/C/51/D/451/1991 (16 August 1994).

[143] ICCPR, Art 14(3)(d); ACHR, Art 8(2)(d); ACHPR, Art 7(1)(c); ECHR, Art 6(3)(c).

defendant is obstructing justice, or in order to prevent intimidation of witnesses if they are examined by the accused during the trial.[144] Any restriction on the choice of representation must be strictly proportionate to the serious purpose articulated.

Should the defendant require legal representation in order to exercise his or her defence but does not have the means to pay, states are obliged to provide legal aid where the interests of justice so require.[145] The seriousness of the offence and the possible punishment will be relevant to this consideration. So, where 'deprivation of liberty is at stake, the interests of justice...call for legal representation'.[146] Similarly, free legal assistance should be given if the proceedings may result in the death penalty.[147] The interests of justice may also require legal aid where the personal circumstances of the defendant require it. For example, the case of *Quaranta v Switzerland* concerned a young adult with a drug addiction from an underprivileged background who was convicted for drugs offences. The European Court of Human Rights held that he was not capable of presenting his case in an adequate manner and that the Swiss authorities should have provided him with legal assistance.[148] The legal assistance provided must be effective. If the counsel provided is negligent in their duties, then the state will have breached its obligation. In *Myrie v Jamaica* the state-appointed counsel was absent from the courtroom for significant periods of the trial. The Inter-American Commission on Human Rights held that although the state cannot be held responsible for *all* deficiencies in state-provided legal assistance, it was required to 'intervene if a failure by legal aid counsel to provide effective representation is manifest or sufficiently brought to their attention'.[149] Furthermore, where court proceedings are conducted in a language which the defendant cannot understand, interpreter assistance must be offered free of charge.[150]

The right to an effective defence also includes the right of the defendant 'to examine, or have examined, the witnesses against him and to obtain the attendance and examination of witnesses on his behalf under the same conditions as witnesses against him'.[151] Essentially this secures the same powers for the defendant to compel witnesses to appear and cross-examine them as are granted to the prosecution. What is key is that the principle of fairness is upheld at all times. For example, in *Peart v Jamaica* the principal witness for the prosecution had made a written statement that indicated a person other than the defendant had committed the relevant crime.[152] However, the statement was not made available to the defence until after an appeal to the conviction had been rejected. The Human Rights Committee held that this was a serious obstruction of the defence in its cross-examination of the lead witness and thus precluded a fair trial of the defendant. Where cross-examination may lead to serious concerns for the safety of the witness, then restrictions upon the right to examine may be implemented. The interests of the defence must be balanced against those of a witness called to testify and so, in extreme cases, witnesses may remain anonymous. However, even where the witness remains anonymous to the public and the defendant, an effective examination of their testimony must still be facilitated. Where witnesses are completely absent from the trial, for example where they have died during the course of the investigation, and a conviction is based 'solely or decisively' on their evidence, a violation of this right will be found unless 'there are sufficient

---

[144] General Comment 32, n 82, para 37.
[145] ICCPR, Art 14(3)(d); ECHR, Art 6(3)(d). ACHR, Art 8(2)(e) leaves it to states to decide whether to provide legal aid.   [146] *Benham v UK* (1996) 22 EHRR 293, para 61.
[147] General Comment 32, n 82, para 38.   [148] A 205 (1991).
[149] Case 12.417, IACommHR Report No 41/04 (12 October 2004), para 63.
[150] ICCPR, Art 14(3)(f); ACHR, Art 8(1)(a); ECHR, Art 6(3)(e).
[151] ICCPR, Art 14(3)(e). See also ACHR, Art 8(2)(f); ECHR, Art 6(3)(d).
[152] CCPR/C/54/D/464/1991 (24 July 1995).

counterbalancing factors in place, including measures that permit a fair and proper assessment of the reliability of that evidence to take place.'[153]

5.4.5 Right to review

Everyone convicted of a crime is entitled to have the conviction reviewed by a higher
court in accordance with procedures set out in national law. This right is aimed at correcting miscarriages of justice, so higher courts are required to conduct an evaluation of the
evidence presented at the trial and the conduct of the trial. This right is set out in Article
14(5) ICCPR and Article 8(2)(h) ACHR, while a more restrictive version of the right is
to be found in Article 2 Protocol 7 ECHR. The African Commission on Human Rights
confirmed in *Constitutional Rights Project v Nigeria* that this right is also protected by the
ACHPR. The Commission criticized certain provisions of Nigerian law that precluded
any judicial appeal of convictions for which the death penalty was imposed. It held that
'to foreclose any avenue of appeal to "competent national organs" in criminal cases bearing such penalties clearly violates Article 7(1)(a) of the African Charter, and increases the
risk that severe violations may go unaddressed'.[154] Obviously all review proceedings must
adhere to the principles of a fair trial discussed already.

Where a newly discovered fact shows conclusively that there has been a miscarriage of
justice and hence a conviction is overturned or a pardon given, all affected individuals are
entitled to compensation for the punishment already endured.[155] In *WJH v Netherlands*
the author had been convicted of a number of offences but served no time in detention.
Following a challenge to the conviction, the Dutch Supreme Court set aside the verdict
and remitted the case back for consideration by a lower court, which acquitted him on
procedural grounds. The Human Rights Committee rejected a claim that the Netherlands
had violated its obligation to grant compensation for the initial conviction as 'the final
decision in this case…acquitted the author, and since he did not suffer any punishment
as a result of his earlier conviction'.[156] Therefore, miscarriages of justice must be distinguished from acquittals on appeal. It is only for miscarriages of justice that compensation
is due.

5.4.6 *Ne bis in idem*

All major human rights treaties provide that the principle of *ne bis in idem* is applicable
to all individuals who are charged with a criminal offence.[157] The principle essentially
maintains that no person shall be tried twice for the same offence in the same jurisdiction.
There are certain exceptions to this general rule. If there is evidence of newly discovered
facts or there were serious defects in the earlier proceedings that affected the outcome of
the case, the interests of justice may demand that cases should be reopened. Furthermore,
individuals may be tried for the same offence in different jurisdictions. In the case of *AP v
Italy* the author of the communication was convicted by a Swiss court of being involved in
a kidnapping conspiracy which had taken place in Italy. Four years later, after the author
had served his sentence, an Italian court convicted him of the same offence. The Human
Rights Committee held that Article 14(7) ICCPR was not engaged in this case because it

---

[153] *Al-Khawaja and Tahery v UK* (2012) 54 EHRR 23, para 147.
[154] 60/91, 8th Activity Report of the ACommHPR (1994–1995) 13.
[155] ICCPR, Art 14(6); ACHR, Art 10; ECHR Protocol No 7, Art 3.
[156] CCPR/C/45/D/408/1990 (22 July 1992).
[157] ICCPR, Art 14(7); ECHR Protocol No 7, Art 4; ACHR, Art 8(4); ACHPR, Art 7(2).

'does not guarantee *ne bis in idem* with regard to the national jurisdiction of two or more States'.[158]

5.4.7 'No Punishment without law'

The fundamental right of 'no punishment without law' is protected by all human rights treaties and serves to protect individuals from being held guilty of criminal behaviour without adequate legal basis.[159] States may not derogate from this obligation in times of emergency. To mete out punishment without legal basis to do so is an obvious abuse of state power. Therefore, laws that are so vague that individuals cannot know how to regulate their actions in order to act in accordance with the law will constitute a violation of the right.

The right also includes the prohibition of retroactive legislation. This encompasses, first, a guarantee not to be punished for acts or omissions that 'did not constitute a criminal offence under national or international law' at the time of the offence (*nullum crimen sine lege*). Second, where harsher penalties are introduced after the commission of an offence, they may not be applied (*nulla poena sine lege*). There are two restrictions upon this aspect of the right. First, retroactive legislation will be permitted where the new law is more lenient than the old one. Second, legislation that is enacted to introduce criminal sanctions for international crimes, such as war crimes, can be applied retrospectively as long as the conduct was a crime under international law at the time of commission.[160]

The question of the application of retrospective legislation has arisen before both the European Court of Human Rights and the Human Rights Committee in cases concerning convictions for the killings of individuals who had attempted to flee the former German Democratic Republic (GDR) in the period from the early 1960s to 1989. In *Streletz, Kessler and Krenz v Germany* the applicants, senior party officials and members of the GDR National Council, argued that their conduct was not one that had attracted criminal prosecution at the time.[161] However, the convictions were based on the GDR criminal code of 1968, which explicitly stated that anyone who committed crimes against human rights would be punished. The European Court noted that the reason prosecutions had not been forthcoming at the time of the killings was because the individuals concerned, by virtue of their high status within the state apparatus, had maintained a situation of impunity. It was quite clear to the Court that the killings had been disproportionate and a violation of the right to life and, therefore, attracted criminal punishment under the GDR criminal code. The Human Rights Committee arrived at a similar conclusion in *Baumgarten v Germany*.[162] However, this is not to say that violations of human rights always give rise to retrospective criminal responsibility—these findings are restricted to the application of the GDR criminal code.

5.4.8 Protection of juveniles

Juveniles, that is, those individuals who have not yet reached the age of majority, require special protection in criminal procedures. Recognition of this fact is set out in Article 40 CRC and Article 14(4) ICCPR. Underpinning both these provisions is the idea that children should be spared the stigma of being labelled criminals as far as possible and where offences are made out they should be met with educational rehabilitation rather than punitive measures. Thus, states should establish 'an appropriate criminal justice system, in

---

[158] CCPR/C/OP/2 at 67 (1990).   [159] ICCPR, Art 15; ACHR, Art 9; ACHPR, Art 7; ECHR, Art 7.
[160] ICCPR, Art 15(2); ECHR, Art 7(2). See *Kononov v Latvia* (2011) 52 EHRR 21.
[161] (2001) 33 EHRR 751.   [162] CCPR/C/78/D/960/2000 (19 September 2003).

order to ensure that juveniles are treated in a manner commensurate with their age' where measures such as mediation between the perpetrator and the victim are contemplated as an alternative to criminal trials.[163] Where criminal trials are held, juveniles should:

> be informed directly of the charges against them and, if appropriate, through their parents or legal guardians, be provided with appropriate assistance in the preparation and presentation of their defence; be tried as soon as possible in a fair hearing in the presence of legal counsel, other appropriate assistance and their parents or legal guardians, unless it is considered not to be in the best interest of the child, in particular taking into account their age or situation.[164]

6 CONCLUSION

Rights regarding the administration of justice are some of the oldest protections granted by law to individuals. Today, it is recognized that securing the rights to liberty and a fair trial is a necessary pre-requisite for the enjoyment of all other human rights. Since the drafting of the Magna Carta, a substantial body of norms, guidelines, and jurisprudence regarding these rights has been developed to give more specific protections to all individuals. As criminal justice systems are often manipulated to the detriment of the enjoyment of human rights, a significant proportion of the human rights framework for the administration of justice is devoted to this area. However, rights regarding the administration of justice are also concerned with issues such as the judicial resolution of civil disputes and the use of detention powers beyond the criminal justice context. Any failure to regulate these concerns is bound to raise questions about the credibility of a justice system.

FURTHER READING

CASSEL, 'International Human Rights Law and Security Detention' (2009) 40 *Case Western JIL* 383.

COOK, 'Preventive Detention – International Standards and the Protection of the Individual' in Frankowski and Shelton (eds), *Preventive Detention: A Comparative and International Law Perspective* (Martinus Nijhoff, 1992).

DÖRR, 'Detention, Arbitrary' in Wolfrum (ed), *Max Planck Encyclopaedia of International Law* (Oxford University Press, 2012).

DOSWALD-BECK and KOLB (eds), *Judicial Process and Human Rights: UN, European, American and African Systems: Texts and Summaries of International Case-Law* (Engel, 2004).

INTER-AMERICAN COMMISSION ON HUMAN RIGHTS, *Report on the Human Rights of Persons Deprived of Liberty in the Americas* (Organization of American States, 2011).

RODLEY and POLLARD, *The Treatment of Prisoners under International Law* (Oxford University Press, 2009) chs 8, 9, 11.

SCOVAZZI and CITRONI, *The Struggle Against Enforced Disappearance and the 2007 United Nations Convention* (Martinus Nijhoff, 2007).

TRECHSEL, 'Why Must Trials be Fair?' (1997) 31 *Israel LR* 94.

——, *Human Rights in Criminal Proceedings* (Oxford University Press, 2005).

---

[163] General Comment 32, n 82, paras 43 and 44.   [164] General Comment 32, n 82, para 42.

UDOMBANA, 'The African Commission on Human and Peoples' Rights and the Development of Fair Trial Norms in Africa' (2006) 6 *African HRLJ* 299.

WEISSBRODT, *The Right to a Fair Trial: Articles 8, 10 and 11 of the Universal Declaration of Human Rights* (Martinus Nijhoff, 2001).

WEISSBRODT and WOLFRUM (eds), *The Right to a Fair Trial* (Springer, 1997).

USEFUL WEBSITES

UN Working Group on arbitrary detention: <http://www2.ohchr.org/english/issues/detention/index.htm>

UN Special Representative on independence of the judiciary: <http://www2.ohchr.org/english/issues/judiciary/index.htm>

14

CULTURAL RIGHTS

Julie Ringelheim

SUMMARY

While cultural rights have long been neglected in human rights theory and practice, they are attracting growing attention today. This chapter examines the sources of this category of rights in international human rights law, describes their evolution, and highlights the major debates their interpretation has given rise to. It discusses more specifically the content and meaning of the three following rights: the right to take part in cultural life, the right to enjoy the benefits of scientific progress and its applications, and the rights of authors and inventors to the protection of their moral and material interests.

1 INTRODUCTION

A certain degree of fuzziness surrounds the notion of cultural rights. The source of the problem lies with the concept of culture itself. In the course of its history, the term 'culture' has been endowed with different meanings, each of which continues to coexist today.[1] First, at the time of the Enlightenment, that is, in the seventeenth and eighteenth centuries, the term culture began to be used in France in a metaphorical sense to mean the *cultivation of the mind* as well as the result of intellectual development, namely the knowledge of a person who is well versed in arts, letters, and science. During the nineteenth century, in an era of rising nationalism, the German term *Kultur* came to mean the intellectual and moral achievements of a whole nation. This new definition progressively permeated other languages. While in the earlier understanding culture was seen as an individual characteristic of universal relevance—the culture one could acquire was supposed to be common to the whole mankind—this newer conception of culture was a collective phenomenon associated with a particular group. Yet, in both cases, the notion referred to a distinct set of social activities: it only included intellectual, artistic, or moral expressions, in other words 'the life of the mind', to the exclusion of material or technical aspects of social life. A third usage of the term emerged in the late nineteenth century in the nascent field of anthropology. Culture, in this context, was redefined as encompassing *all* manifestations of the social life of a given population.[2] This last understanding of the term spread during the twentieth century in common language. Thus conceived, culture became synonymous with the specific *way of life* of a community.

---

[1] See Beneton, *Histoire de mots. Culture et civilisation* (Presses de la fondation nationale des sciences politiques, 1975).

[2] The British anthropologist Edward B. Tylor is widely considered as the first author to propose this new definition of culture in *Primitive Culture* (John Murray, 1871).

This plurality of meanings of the concept of culture presents a persistent challenge for the conceptualization of cultural rights.[3] The difficulty involved in defining the subject matter of this category of rights partly explains the often-noted fact that cultural rights have long been neglected.[4] But other factors have also contributed to this neglect. Culture is often seen as a luxury compared to more 'classic' human rights issues, such as the right to life or freedom from torture. Besides, the idea of recognizing a *right to culture* in the anthropological sense has been viewed by many as entailing the risk of legitimizing cultural practices that conflict with particular human rights, such as female genital mutilation.[5] Attitudes, however, seem to be changing. Since 2000, cultural rights have attracted increasing attention from human rights experts and international bodies. The decision of the UN Human Rights Council in 2009 to appoint an independent expert in the field of cultural rights is a sign of this rising interest.[6]

Among international treaties dealing with human rights, the International Covenant on Economic, Social, and Cultural Rights (ICESCR) is the only one to refer to *cultural rights* in its title. It is generally considered that cultural rights under this convention include the right to education (Articles 13 and 14) and the rights spelled out in Article 15. The latter provision is inspired by Article 27 of the Universal Declaration of Human Rights (UDHR) which lays down that everyone has 'the right freely to participate in the cultural life of the community, to enjoy the arts and to share in scientific advancement and its benefits' as well as 'the right to the protection of the moral and material interests resulting from any scientific, literary or artistic production of which he is the author.' Building upon this provision, Article 15(1) ICESCR recognizes three different rights: the right (a) to take part in cultural life; (b) to enjoy the benefits of scientific progress and its applications; and (c) to benefit from the protection of the moral and material interests resulting from any scientific, literary, or artistic production of which he or she is the author. Articles 15(2) to 15(4) provide additional clarifications as to what these rights require from states parties:

2. The steps to be taken by the States Parties to the present Covenant to achieve the full realization of this right shall include those necessary for the conservation, the development and the diffusion of science and culture.

3. The States Parties to the present Covenant undertake to respect the freedom indispensable for scientific research and creative activity.

4. The States Parties to the present Covenant recognize the benefits to be derived from the encouragement and development of international contacts and co-operation in the scientific and cultural fields.

Echoing this provision, the specialized United Nations (UN) human rights conventions— the International Convention on the Elimination of All Forms of Racial Discrimination (ICERD) (Article 5(e)(iv)); the Convention on the Elimination of All Forms of Discrimination Against Women (CEDAW) (Article 13(c)); the Convention on the Rights

---

[3] McGoldrick, 'Culture, Cultures, and Cultural Rights', in Baderin and McCorquodale (eds), *Economic, Social and Cultural Rights in Action* (OUP, 2007) 447.

[4] Symonides, 'Cultural Rights: A Neglected Category of Human Rights' (1998) 158 *International Social Science J* 559; McGoldrick, n 3, 447.

[5] Stamatopoulou, *Cultural Rights in International Law. Article 27 of the Universal Declaration of Human Rights and Beyond* (Martinus Nijhoff, 2007) 4–6.

[6] HR Council Res 10/23, (26 March 2009). The mandate of the Independent Expert was extended for three years in 2012: HR Council Res 19/6 (16 March 2012).

of the Child (CRC) (Article 31(2)); the International Convention on the Protection of the Rights of All Migrant Workers and Members of their Families (ICRMW) (Article 43(1)(g)); and the Convention on the Rights of Persons with Disabilities (CPRD) (Article 30(1))— guarantee the right to participate in cultural life without discrimination of the specific categories of people they protect. At the regional level, the right to take part in the cultural or artistic life of the community is recognized in the American Declaration of the Rights and Duties of Man (Article 13), which preceded the UDHR, as well as in the Additional Protocol to the American Convention on Human Rights in the Area of Economic, Social and Cultural Rights, Article 14 of which is very similar to Article 15 ICESCR. It is also proclaimed in the African Charter on Human and Peoples' Rights (Article 17(2)). By contrast, the European Convention on Human Rights (ECHR) contains no similar provision, while the Revised European Social Charter only mentions an obligation for states to take measures to enable persons with disabilities to access cultural activities (Article 15(3)) and elderly persons to play an active part in cultural life (Article 23).

In addition, in the human rights literature, it has become increasingly common to speak of *cultural rights* when referring to the special rights recognized to minorities and indigenous peoples in order to enable them to preserve their distinct identity.[7] International instruments relating to these groups, like Article 27 of the International Covenant on Civil and Political Rights (ICCPR), the ILO Convention No. 169 concerning Indigenous and Tribal Peoples in Independent Countries, or the Council of Europe Framework Convention on the Protection of National Minorities, do not explicitly label the rights they lay down as *cultural rights*. Yet, they contain numerous references to the notions of *culture*, *cultural identity*, or *cultural practices*. Thus, Article 27 ICCPR recognizes the rights of people belonging to minorities to enjoy *their own culture*. As we shall see, the evolution of the understanding of the right to take part in cultural life under Article 15 ICESCR has provided further support for this usage of the phrase *cultural rights*.

Since the right to education and the rights of minorities and indigenous peoples are dealt with in other chapters of this book,[8] this chapter focuses on the rights recognized in Article 27 UDHR and Article 15 ICESCR. One notion is central to these provisions, that of 'cultural life'. Accordingly, Section 2 retraces the evolution of the interpretation of this concept. The three sections that follow analyse the content and scope of the three rights protected in these two articles: the right to take part in cultural life (Section 3), the right to science (Section 4), and the right of authors and inventors to the protection of their moral and material interests (Section 5).

2 WHAT IS *CULTURAL LIFE*?

The *travaux préparatoires* of the UDHR indicate that for its framers, the notion of 'cultural life' appearing in Article 27 meant intellectual and artistic activities.[9] More precisely, it was 'high culture' that they had in mind, that is, the traditional canons of literature, music, art, and so on.[10] The provision was primarily aimed at recognizing the right of the masses to access lofty cultural resources, that had so far been the privilege of an elite.[11]

---

[7] Eg Stamatopoulou, n 5; Francioni and Scheinin (eds), *Cultural Human Rights* (Martinus Nijhoff, 2008); and Eide, 'Cultural Rights as Individual Human Rights', in Eide, Krause, and Rosas (eds), *Economic, Social and Cultural Rights. A Textbook* (Martinus Nijhoff, 2001) 289.

[8] See Chapter 12 and Chapter 17.

[9] Morsink, *The Universal Declaration of Human Rights. Origins, Drafting and Intent* (University of Pennsylvania Press, 1999) 217–19.

[10] O'Keefe, 'The Right to Take Part in Cultural Life under Article 15 of the ICESCR' (1998) 47 *ICLQ* 904, 905.

[11] O'Keefe, n 10, 906; Donders, *Towards a Right to Cultural Identity?* (Intersentia, 2002) 141.

With time, however, the interpretation of the term 'cultural life' used in Article 27 UDHR and Article 15 ICESCR has undergone a double evolution. First, the notion has been extended beyond *high culture* to include *popular* or *mass culture*. Second, it has been progressively acknowledged that the concept does not only refer to the idea of culture as intellectual and artistic expressions (culture as the *life of the mind*) but also covers culture in an anthropological sense (culture as a *way of life*).

2.1 FROM HIGH CULTURE TO POPULAR CULTURE

The work of the United Nations Educational, Scientific and Cultural Organisation (UNESCO) had an important influence on the evolution of the interpretation of 'culture' and 'cultural life' in the context of UN human rights instruments. Departing from the vision of the UDHR drafters, the UNESCO Recommendation on Participation by the People at Large in Cultural Life and their Contribution to It (1976) states that 'culture is not merely an accumulation of works and knowledge which an élite produces, collects and conserves in order to place it within the reach of all'.[12] Rather, it includes 'all forms of creativity and expression of groups or individuals'.[13] Thus:

> by participation in cultural life is meant the concrete opportunities guaranteed for all groups or individuals to express themselves freely, to communicate, act, and engage in creative activities with a view to the full development of their personalities, a harmonious life and the cultural progress of society.[14]

This text clearly asserts that cultural life is not restricted to high culture but also extends to non-elitist cultural expressions. This broader approach to cultural life was taken up by the Committee on Economic, Social and Cultural Rights. In the Revised Guidelines regarding the reports to be submitted by states under the ICESCR, adopted in 1991, the right to take part in cultural life is described as 'the right of everyone to take part in the cultural life *which he or she considers pertinent*', including popular forms of culture such as cinema and traditional arts and crafts.[15] Under the current Guidelines, drafted in 2008, states are requested to provide information on the measures taken to promote popular participation in, and access to, concerts, theatre, cinema, and sport events, as well as information technologies such as the Internet.[16]

2.2 FROM CULTURE AS THE LIFE OF THE MIND TO CULTURE AS A WAY OF LIFE

The second transformation affecting the concept of cultural life was more profound. The inclusion of popular cultural expressions within the notion of cultural life did not modify its basic nature: cultural life was still conceived as a specific sphere of activities within society, relating to creativity, imagination, and artistic or intellectual endeavours. By contrast, the endorsement of an anthropological conception of culture entailed a considerable expansion of its scope: this latter notion of culture basically embraces the whole way of

---

[12] Preamble, 5th recital, subpara (c).   [13] Para 3(a).

[14] Art 2(b). See also the UNESCO Universal Declaration on Cultural Diversity (2001).

[15] Revised Guidelines regarding the form and contents of reports to be submitted by states parties under Arts 16 and 17 of the International Covenant on Economic, Social and Cultural Rights, E/1991/23, 88, at 108. See also O'Keefe, n 10, 913–14.

[16] Revised Guidelines on treaty-specific documents to be submitted by States Parties under Articles 16 and 17 of the International Covenant on Economic, Social and Cultural Rights. E/C.12/2008/2, at 15.

life of a social group. It can encompass *any* social activity or expression that is specific
to a given population: from art, language, or religion to techniques, economic activities,
customs, laws, conception of the family, and so on. At the same time, the anthropological
approach to culture focuses on traits which are *specific* to a given community. The right to
culture in this latter sense becomes the right to one's *own* culture. It overlaps with minority
protection and indigenous peoples' rights.

Here too, UNESCO had a leading role in this evolution. As early as 1982, the Mexico City
Declaration on Cultural Policies defined culture as 'the whole complex of distinctive spiritual, material, intellectual and emotional features that characterize a society or social group',
including 'not only the arts and letters, but also modes of life, the fundamental rights of the
human beings, value systems, traditions and beliefs'.[17] The UNESCO Universal Declaration
on Cultural Diversity (2001) embraces the same conception of culture.[18] A similar approach
was progressively endorsed by the Committee on Economic, Social and Cultural Rights.
During the day of general discussion on the right to take part in cultural life, organized by
the Committee in 1992, various members declared that 'culture meant a way of life' and that
taking part in cultural life 'embraced all the activities of the individual'.[19] The Committee's
General Comment 21 on the right of everyone to take part in cultural life, adopted in 2009,
confirms this evolution. Culture is described in it as 'encompassing all manifestations of
human existence'.[20] For the purpose of Article 15 ICESCR, it includes:

> inter alia, ways of life, language, oral and written literature, music and song, non-verbal com-
> munication, religion or belief systems, rites and ceremonies, sport and games, methods of
> production or technology, natural and man-made environments, food, clothing and shelter
> and the arts, customs and traditions through which individuals, groups of individuals and
> communities express their humanity and the meaning they give to their existence, and build
> their world view representing their encounter with the external forces affecting their lives.[21]

This expansion of the concept of cultural life, while encouraged by many authors,[22] has been
criticized by some.[23] Critics argue that the definition proposed in the General Comment is
so broad that it is very difficult to identify specific individual entitlements and state obligations. Moreover, some fear that the emphasis now put in the context of Article 15 ICESCR
on the protection of minorities and indigenous peoples, two subjects already covered by
more specialized international instruments, risks reinforcing the traditional neglect affecting
what initially was the main objective of this provision: promoting access to and participation
of everyone, including the most disadvantaged, to culture in its artistic and intellectual sense.[24]

3 THE RIGHT TO TAKE PART IN CULTURAL LIFE

The Committee on Economic, Social and Cultural Rights has endeavoured to clarify
the content, scope, and implications of the right to take part in cultural life protected by
Article 15(1)(a) ICESCR in General Comment 21. In line with the evolution described

---

[17] Para 6. See also *Our Creative Diversity. Report of the World Commission on Culture and Development*
(UNESCO, 1995).   [18] Preamble, para 5.

[19] E/1993/22, para 213.   [20] E/C.12/GC/21 (21 December 2009), para 11.

[21] General Comments 21, n 20, para 13.

[22] Eg Stamatopoulou, n 5; Eide, n 7; Stavenhagen, 'Cultural Rights: A Social Science Perspective', in Eide,
Krause and Rosas (eds), n 7, 85.

[23] McGoldrick, n 3, 450–1; Romainville, *Le droit à la culture. Une réalité juridique* (Bruylant, forthcoming).

[24] Romainville, n 23.

in Section 2, it attempts to do this on the basis of what can be termed a 'bi-dimensional' conception of culture, as meaning *both* the life of the mind and ways of life.

3.1 THE NORMATIVE CONTENT OF THE RIGHT TO TAKE PART IN CULTURAL LIFE

General Comment 21 distinguishes between three main components of the right to take part in cultural life.[25] First, *participation* in cultural life means the right to freely choose one's identity and engage in one's own cultural practices as well as to express oneself in the language of one's choice. Second, *access* to cultural life covers the right to know one's own culture and that of others through education and information, the right to follow a way of life associated with the use of cultural goods and resources such as land, water, biodiversity, language, or specific institutions, and the right to benefit from the cultural heritage and creations of others. Finally, *contribution* to cultural life refers to the right to be involved in creating the spiritual, material, intellectual, and emotional expressions of the community. This is supported by the right to take part in the elaboration and implementation of policies that have an impact on cultural rights.

The Committee on Economic, Social and Cultural Rights has applied the tripartite distinction—*respect*, *protect*, and *fulfil*—to specify the corresponding obligations of state parties to the right to take part in cultural life.[26] The *obligation to respect* requires states to refrain from interfering with the enjoyment of the right.[27] This entails a duty to guarantee various rights and freedoms inherent in the right to participate in culture: the right to freely choose one's own cultural identity; the freedom to create, which implies the abolition of censorship of cultural and artistic activities; freedom of expression in the language of one's choice; the right to access one's own cultural heritage and that of others; and the right to take part freely in decision-making processes that may have an impact on cultural rights. Freedom to create and to research is explicitly protected in Article 15(3) ICESCR, under which states must undertake 'to respect the freedom indispensable for scientific research and creative activity.' It can, moreover, be seen as a particular application of the right to freedom of expression.[28] The European Court of Human Rights has indeed acknowledged that free speech under the ECHR covers freedom of artistic expression[29] as well as academic freedom.[30]

To meet their *obligation to protect*, states must take measures to prevent third parties, such as private enterprises, from interfering in the exercise of the rights listed here. In addition, they need to protect cultural heritage in all its forms at all times, whether in time of war or peace and in case of natural disasters.[31] This can be related to the duty incumbent upon states under Article 15(2) ICESCR to take the necessary steps to ensure, inter alia, the conservation of culture. Moreover, UNESCO's initiatives on the concept of cultural heritage and its protection are especially relevant in this regard. This includes the UNESCO Convention for the Protection of Cultural Property in the Event of Armed Conflict (1954);[32] the Convention concerning the Protection of the World Cultural and

---

[25] General Comment 21, n 20, para 15. [26] See Chapter 5.
[27] General Comment 21, n 20, para 49. [28] See Chapter 11.
[29] *Müller and others v Switzerland* (1991) 13 EHRR 212, para 27.
[30] *Sorguç v Turkey*, App no 17089/03, Judgment of 23 June 2009, para 35. See more generally European Court of Human Rights, Research Division, *Cultural Rights in the Case-law of the European Court of Human Rights* (Council of Europe, 2011). See also Charter of Fundamental Rights of the European Union, Art 13, which recognizes artistic and academic freedom. [31] General Comment 21, n 20, para 50(a).
[32] On the protection of cultural heritage during armed conflicts, see also the The Hague Conventions of 1899, Art 56, and 1907, Art 56; Protocol I Additional to the Geneva Conventions of 12 August 1949, and relating to the Protection of Victims of International Armed Conflicts, 53; and Protocol II Additional to the Geneva Conventions of 12 August 1949, and relating to the Protection of Victims of Non-International Armed Conflicts, Art 16.

Natural Heritage (1972); the Convention on the Protection of the Underwater Cultural Heritage (2001); and the Convention for the Safeguarding of Intangible Cultural Heritage (2003). At the European level, the Council of Europe has also adopted relevant instruments, notably the Framework Convention on the Value of Cultural Heritage for Society (2005).

Another aspect of the obligation to protect concerns the protection of cultural resources in the context of economic development. The General Comment insists that 'particular attention should be paid to the adverse consequences of globalization, undue privatization of goods and services and deregulation on the right to participate in cultural life.'[33] The Committee here alludes to several highly complex phenomena. There is first of all the problem of homogenization and standardization of culture resulting from an unbalanced globalization, which favours cultural products and models of rich countries to the detriment of those of poor countries. This concern is echoed in Article 1 UNESCO Convention on the Protection and Promotion of the Diversity of Cultural Expressions (2005), which aims to ensure 'wider and balanced cultural exchanges in the world in favour of intercultural respect and a culture of peace'; 'to give recognition to the distinctive nature of cultural activities, goods and services as vehicles of identity, values and meaning'; and 'to reaffirm the sovereign rights of States to maintain, adopt and implement policies and measures that they deem appropriate for the protection and promotion of the diversity of cultural expressions on their territory'. Furthermore, the defence of the right to culture in the face of the power of private economic actors poses the more general question of the role of the state towards cultural production in a market economy. Artistic creation being heavily dependent upon financial factors—shooting a movie, producing a disk, staging a play, and so on all require financial means—some private cultural industries can acquire a disproportionate power to promote certain cultural expressions and marginalize others. Besides, cultural enterprises can compromise access of the most disadvantaged to culture if the price they set for cultural goods and services is too high. The protection of the right to take part in cultural life thus seems to require intervention by the state to support various forms of cultural creation and to regulate culture-related economic activities.[34] But such state intervention in the cultural field must remain compatible with respect for artistic freedom.

An additional dimension of the obligation to protect the right to take part in cultural life lies with the duty to defend the cultural productions of indigenous peoples, notably their traditional knowledge, natural medicines, folklore, and rituals. This includes protecting their lands and resources from illegal or unjust exploitation by state entities and private companies.[35] The Inter-American Court of Human Rights has established that when dealing with major development or investment plans that may have a profound impact on the traditional territory of an indigenous people, states must not only carry out prior consultation with this people, but also obtain their free, prior, and informed consent, in accordance with their traditions and customs.[36] This principle has also been endorsed by the Human Rights Committee in the context of Article 27 ICCPR.[37]

---

[33] General Comment 21, n 20, para 50(b).   [34] See Romainville, n 23.

[35] General Comment 21, n 20, para 50(c).

[36] *Case of the Saramaka People v Suriname*, IACtHR Series C No 172 (28 November 2007) para 137. In *Kichwa Indigenous People of Sarayuku v Ecuador*, IACtHR Series C No 245 (27 June 2012), the Court asserted that states' obligation to carry out prior consultation with indigenous communities on the exploitation of natural resources in their territory is a general principle of international law (para 164).

[37] *Angela Poma Poma v Peru*, CCPR/C/95/D/1457/2006 (27 March 2009) para 7.6.

Finally, the Committee on Economic, Social and Cultural Rights also mentions, as part of the obligation to protect, the duty to prohibit discrimination based on cultural identity and incitement to discrimination, hostility, or violence on the basis of national, racial, or religious features.[38]

The *obligation to fulfil* entails a duty for states to take appropriate legislative, administrative, budgetary, judicial, and other measures necessary for the full realization of the right. This level of obligations includes an obligation to *facilitate* and *promote* the right as well as, in some circumstances, to *provide* conditions under which the right can be enjoyed:

- To *facilitate* the exercise of the right to participate in cultural life, states should establish and support public cultural institutions; develop adequate policies for the protection of cultural diversity and grant assistance to individuals or organisations engaged in creative and scientific activities (artists, cultural associations, science academies, etc). They should also support minorities and other communities in their efforts to preserve their culture.[39]

- The obligation to *promote* requires states to ensure appropriate education and public awareness concerning the right to take part in cultural life, particularly in rural and deprived urban areas, as well as in relation to minorities and indigenous peoples.[40]

- Finally, states must *provide* individuals with the means necessary for the enjoyment of the right when, for reasons outside their control, they are unable to realize this right by themselves. The Committee ranks in this category the duty to preserve and restore cultural heritage; the duty to include cultural education, including history, literature, music, and teaching of other culture, in school curricula; and the obligation to guarantee access for all, including disadvantaged groups, to cultural institutions (museums, libraries, cinemas, theatres, etc) and activities. Effective mechanisms should moreover be established to allow persons, individually, in association with others, or within a group, to participate effectively in decision-making processes.[41] The Inter-American Court of Human Rights has especially insisted on the duty of states to carry out prior consultation with indigenous communities on the exploitation of natural resources in their territory. It considers this obligation to be a general principle of international law.[42]

Among these elements, the Committee on Economic, Social and Cultural Rights identifies 'core obligations', that is, minimum essential levels of the right which all states must immediately implement, by contrast with other obligations that may be achieved progressively, depending on available resources. States must at least create and promote an environment within which people can participate in the culture of their choice. This entails the immediately applicable obligations to guarantee non-discrimination and gender equality in the enjoyment of the right to take part in cultural life; to respect the right of everyone to identify or not identify with one or more communities; to respect and protect the right of everyone to engage in their own cultural practices, while respecting human rights; to eliminate barriers or obstacles to people's access to their own culture or other cultures; and to allow and encourage the participation of members of minorities,

---

[38] General Comment 21, n 20, para 50(d).   [39] General Comment 21, n 20, para 52.
[40] General Comment 21, n 20, para 53.   [41] General Comment 21, n 20, para 54.
[42] *Kichwa Indigenous People of Sarayaku v Ecuador*, n 36, para 164. The Human Rights Committee has also inferred from ICCPR, Art 27 a duty for states to take measures to ensure effective participation of indigenous peoples in decisions affecting their right to maintain a particular way of life associated with the use of land resources. See General Comment 23, HRI/GEN/1/Rev.9 (Vol I) 207, para 7; *Angela Poma Poma v Peru*, n 37.

indigenous peoples, or other communities in the design and implementation of laws and policies affecting them.[43]

3.2 GROUPS REQUIRING SPECIAL ATTENTION

For different reasons, certain groups require particular attention in the implementation of the right to take part in cultural life.

First of all, for some categories of people, special measures are needed to enable them to effectively access the cultural resources, activities, and infrastructures necessary for the enjoyment of the right. In the case of *persons with disabilities*, Article 30 CRPD requires steps to be taken to ensure the availability of cultural materials, television programmes, films, theatre, and other activities in accessible forms as well as the accessibility of cultural infrastructures, such as theatres, museums, cinemas, libraries, tourist services, and, as far as possible, monuments, and places of national cultural importance. Moreover, their specific cultural and linguistic identity, including sign language, should be recognized.[44] The Committee on Economic, Social and Cultural Rights has also emphasized the need to pay particular attention to the promotion of cultural rights of *older persons*. It refers to the Vienna International Plan of Action on Aging (1982), which encourages governments to support programmes aimed at providing these persons with easier physical access to cultural institutions, such as museums, theatres, concert halls, and cinemas and calls for the development of programmes featuring older persons as teachers and transmitters of knowledge, culture, and spiritual values.[45] Additionally, the Committee expresses concern at the situation of *persons living in poverty* and urges states parties to take concrete measures to bring culture within the reach of all and ensure the full exercise of the right to enjoy and take part in cultural life by persons living in poverty.[46]

Minorities, indigenous peoples, and *migrants* are in a specific situation from the viewpoint of the right to take part in cultural life because they are likely to be wanting to maintain a cultural tradition or heritage that differs from that of the majority. Accordingly, they are at risk of being subject to assimilation policies by the authorities. The Committee on Economic, Social and Cultural Rights insists that minorities should have the right to take part in the cultural life of the society at large as well as to conserve, promote, and develop their own culture.[47] In line with Article 31 ICRMW, it notes that the protection of cultural identities, language, religion, and folklore of migrants should receive particular attention.[48] In relation to indigenous peoples, the Committee considers that Article 15(1) ICESCR requires measures to be taken to protect their right to own, develop, control, and use their communal lands and resources as well as to act collectively to maintain and develop their cultural heritage, traditional knowledge, and cultural expressions.[49]

Finally, *women* and *children* must also be given special consideration. The Committee has highlighted the duty of states to eliminate institutional and legal obstacles as well as those based on customs and traditions that prevent women from participating fully in cultural life, science, education, and research.[50] As for children, they 'play a fundamental role as the bearers and transmitters of cultural values from generation to generation.'[51] The right to take part in cultural life in their case is closely linked to the right to education.

---

[43] General Comment 21, n 20, para 55.   [44] General Comment 21, n 20, paras 30–1.
[45] General Comment 21, n 20, para 28.   [46] General Comment 21, n 20, paras 38–9.
[47] General Comment 21, n 20, para 32.   [48] General Comment 21, n 20, para 34.
[49] General Comment 21, n 20, paras 36–7.
[50] General Comment 21, n 20, para 25. See CEDAW, Art 2(f).   [51] General Comment 21, n 20, para 26.

States should ensure that education is culturally appropriate, which means that it should enable children to develop their cultural identity and to learn about the culture of their own communities as well as of others.[52] Accordingly, school curricula for all children should respect the cultural specificities of minorities and indigenous peoples and incorporate their history, knowledge, cultural values, and aspirations.[53]

3.3 LIMITATIONS OF THE RIGHT

As with the other rights set out in the ICESCR, the right to take part in cultural life is not absolute. It may be subject to limitations. Such restrictions must, however, respect certain conditions: they must be determined by law, compatible with the nature of the right, and strictly necessary for the promotion of the general welfare in a democratic society.[54]

Of special concern here are cultural practices that conflict with certain human rights. The extension of the notion of 'cultural life' to culture in the anthropological sense has made this problem especially salient. Various practices anchored in cultural traditions are in tension with some human rights, in particular women's rights. The Committee has emphasized in this regard that limitations to the right to take part in cultural life may be necessary to counter 'negative practices, including those attributed to customs and traditions, that infringe upon other human rights.'[55] In another part of the General Comment, it goes even further and asserts that taking steps to combat customary or traditional practices harmful to the well-being of persons, such as female genital mutilation, would in fact be *required* by the right to take part in cultural life. Failing to do so would, according to the Committee, constitute a violation of this right insofar as such practices constitute barriers to the full exercise of the right by the affected persons.[56]

Interestingly, in some contexts, conflicts may arise between different aspects of the right to take part in cultural life. For instance, artistic freedom may in principle be limited by the prohibition of incitement to discrimination, hostility, and violence against an ethnic or religious group. Yet, evaluating whether a novel, song, or work of art constitutes such form of incitement may raise arduous questions. As recognized by the European Court of Human Rights, it is important to take into account the particular nature of artistic expression, which can take metaphorical or satiric forms.[57] One must also be mindful of the risk that state authorities instrumentalize the accusation of incitement to hostility or violence to justify censorship of artistic creations that touch upon sensitive issues. In some states, in the name of combating incitement to religious hatred or of protecting religious feelings of believers, penal sanctions are imposed on artists who mock or criticize religious doctrines.[58] But it is in the nature of art to challenge conventions, moral codes, and traditions. Artistic freedom must include the right to create works that 'offend, shock or disturb the State or any sector of the population', to use a famous quotation from the European Court of

---

[52] General Comment 21, n 20, para 26.   [53] General Comment 21, n 20, para 27.

[54] ICESCR, Art 4. See General Comment 21, n 20, para 19. See also Chapter 5.

[55] General Comment 21, n 20, para 19.   [56] General Comment 21, n 20, para 64.

[57] *Cultural Rights in the Case-law of the European Court of Human Rights*, n 30, 5–7.

[58] The European Court of Human Rights has admitted that the protection of 'the right of citizens not to be insulted in their religious feelings' can constitute a legitimate aim for the purposes of Article 10(2) ECHR (limitations to free speech): *Otto-Preminger-Institut v Austria* (1995) 19 EHRR 34, para 48. In its later case law it has, however, qualified this principle: see *Tatlav v Turkey*, App no 50692/99, Judgment of 2 May 1996; and *Klein v Slovakia* (2010) 50 EHRR 15.

Human Rights.[59] This discussion reveals a potential tension between the two approaches to culture now brought together in the interpretation of the right to take part in cultural life. Artistic freedom, which pertains to culture understood as artistic and intellectual activities, has a distinctly individualist character: it includes the freedom of individual artists to question, subvert, or contest dominant social norms and identities. By contrast, the right to enjoy one's own culture in the anthropological sense has a communitarian and somewhat conservative connotation: it is primarily the right to preserve a community's traditions and way of life inherited from the past. Finding the right balance between these two dimensions of the right to take part in cultural life may not always be easy.

4 THE RIGHT TO SCIENCE

The right of everyone 'to enjoy the benefits of scientific progress and its applications', protected in Article 15(1)(b) ICESCR, has long been overlooked by human rights advocates and institutions.[60] It was largely perceived as vague and obscure. Yet it was rediscovered in the 1990s in the context of the controversies generated by the expansion of the international intellectual property regime.[61] Many argued that this latter development restricted the ability of the general public, and especially the most disadvantaged, to benefit from scientific advancements, with a detrimental impact on the enjoyment of various rights (see Section 5). Against this background, the right provided for in Article 15(1)(b) started to attract more attention. Between 2007 and 2009, three expert meetings were convened by UNESCO, with the collaboration of academic institutions, resulting in the Venice Statement on the Right to Enjoy the Benefits of Scientific Progress and its Applications (2009), which attempts to clarify the normative content of this right.

One important question is how to construe the notion of 'scientific progress' for the purpose of this provision.[62] The Venice Statement observes that a human rights-based approach 'requires that science and its applications are consistent with fundamental human rights principles such as non-discrimination, gender equality, accountability and participation, and that particular attention should be paid to the needs of disadvantaged and marginalized groups'.[63] Some authors further argue that 'scientific progress' in this context should mean discoveries and technologies that contribute to the enjoyment of human rights, including by the most disadvantaged.[64] Some technologies, however, can have both positive and negative effects on human development. The rise of environmental concerns epitomizes this problem: technologies which do improve immediate well-being of individuals by making their life more comfortable can have a negative impact on the environment and, therefore, jeopardize their living conditions in the long term.[65] The implementation of the right under Article 15(1)(b) ICESCR is thus bound to raise dilemmas and controversies.

The obligations stemming from the right to benefit from scientific progress and its applications are potentially very wide. The obligation to *respect* entails that states should not

---

[59] *Handyside v UK* (1979–90) 1 EHRR 737, para 49.

[60] Chapman, 'Towards an Understanding of the Right to Enjoy the Benefits of Scientific Progress and Its Applications', (2009) 8 *Journal of HR* 1, 1.

[61] Plomer, 'The Human Rights Paradox: Intellectual Property Rights and Rights of Access to Science', (2013) 35 *HRQ* 143, 144.

[62] Eide, n 7, 296.   [63] Para 12(b).

[64] De Schutter, 'The Right of Everyone to Enjoy the Benefits of Scientific Progress and the Right to Food: From Conflict to Complementarity', (2011) 33 *HRQ* 304, 309; Chapman, n 60, 11.

[65] See Chapter 29.

interfere with the freedom of scientists to research, disseminate their results, and collaborate with other researchers across boundaries.[66] The obligation *to protect* requires states to safeguard people against harmful applications of scientific and technical progress.[67] Since 2008, the Committee on Economic, Social and Cultural Rights has asked states to indicate in their periodic reports the measures they have taken to prevent the use of scientific and technical progress for purposes that are contrary to the enjoyment of human dignity and human rights.[68] But the most distinctive contribution of Article 15(1)(b) certainly lies with the third level of obligation, namely the obligation to *fulfil* the right. This is interpreted as entailing a duty for states to take positive steps 'to ensure affordable access to the benefits of scientific progress and its applications for everyone, including disadvantaged and marginalized individuals and groups'.[69] The importance of science and technology for the realization of certain rights is already highlighted in two other provisions of the ICESCR. Under Article 11(2)(a), states must, in order to achieve the right to food:

> improve methods of production, conservation and distribution of food by making full use of technical and scientific knowledge, by disseminating knowledge of the principles of nutrition and by developing or reforming agrarian systems in such a way as to achieve the most efficient development and utilization of natural resources

The right to health commands 'the creation of conditions which would assure to all medical service and medical attention in the event of sickness' (Article 12(2)(d)). But promoting access to scientific innovations may be important for the realization of various other rights, such as the right to an adequate standard of living, to education, or to water.[70]

There is, however, an important limit to this obligation: Article 2 ICESCR requires states to act only *to the maximum of their available resources* to realize the rights recognized in the Covenant. Hence, states cannot be obliged to provide access to technologies that are disproportionately costly compared to their financial means.[71]

Beside the issue of cost, the will to ensure affordable access to the benefits of scientific progress and its applications may clash with intellectual property rules. This points towards a wider debate, which is at the core of current discussions on Article 15(1)(c) ICESCR, that of the relationship between intellectual property and human rights law.

5 THE RIGHTS OF AUTHORS AND INVENTORS

While the right to take part in cultural life and the right to science concern the whole population, the third right recognized in Article 15 ICESCR concerns a specific category of persons, namely scientists, writers, and artists. Similarly to Article 27(2) UDHR, Article 15(1)(c) ICESCR provides that everyone has the right to 'the protection of the moral and material interests resulting from any scientific, literary or artistic production of which he is the author.' This is an implicit reference to the notion of intellectual property. The insertion of this clause in the UDHR generated vociferous debates during the drafting process. Introduced at the insistence of the French delegation, Article 27(2) was strongly opposed

[66] Chapman, n 60, 18. See also ICESCR, Art 15(3) and (4).   [67] Venice Statement, para 15.

[68] Guidelines on treaty-specific documents to be submitted by States Parties under Articles 16 and 17 of the ICESCR, E/C.12/2008/2 (14 March 2009), para 70(b). See also the UN Declaration on the Use of Scientific or Technological Progress in the Interests of Peace and for the Benefit of Mankind (1975), Art 2.

[69] Guidelines on treaty-specific documents to be submitted by States Parties under Articles 16 and 17 of the ICESCR, n 68, para 70(a); Venice Statement, para 16(2).

[70] Venice Statement, para 12(d).   [71] Eide, n 7, 296.

by several delegations, including those of the UK and the US, who contested that intellectual property was a basic human right. Chile pointed out the potential conflict between the protection of intellectual work and freedom of access to literary, artistic, or scientific output. Nevertheless, a majority of states voted in favour of this right.[72]

5.1 HUMAN RIGHTS AND INTELLECTUAL PROPERTY

A crucial question raised by the right under Article 15(1)(c) ICESCR is that of its relationship with intellectual property law, which has been developed largely outside the human rights framework, through domestic legislation, bilateral agreements, and multilateral treaties.[73] Broadly stated, this body of law aims to safeguard the producers of intellectual goods or services by granting them certain time-limited rights that allow them to prohibit or authorize the use of those productions by others and to draw financial reward from such use.[74] Whereas *copyright* relates to literary and artistic creations (such as books and other writings, music, paintings, or films) and technology-based works like computer programs and electronic databases, *industrial property* covers the protection of inventions through patents as well as trademark and industrial design protection. Importantly, a patent holder may benefit from a right of exclusion: once a patent has been granted in a certain country, the patentee can exclude others from making, using, or selling the protected invention in that country.[75] To be sure, in all national systems, there are some exceptions and limitations to intellectual property rights.

While human rights and intellectual property rights have long developed in relative isolation from each other, this changed radically with the adoption of the Trade Related Aspects of Intellectual Property Rights (TRIPS) agreement by the World Trade Organization (WTO) in 1994. TRIPS had the effect of imposing high minimum standards of intellectual property on all WTO member states, including on developing countries where copyright and patent laws were, at that time, absent or very limited. This generated intense criticism. It was observed that strict intellectual property models were likely to significantly disadvantage less developed countries by increasing the costs of development, in a context where industrialized countries hold the overwhelming majority of the patents registered worldwide. Furthermore, it was realized that intellectual property norms could hamper the achievement of various human rights, in particular the rights to health and to food.[76] A number of UN human rights institutions expressed serious concerns about this development. In 2000, the Sub-Commission on the Promotion and Protection of Human Rights adopted Resolution 2000/7 on 'Intellectual Property Rights and Human Rights', stating that 'actual or potential conflicts exist between the implementation of the TRIPS Agreement and the realisation of economic, social and cultural rights'.[77] The following year, the UN High Commissioner for Human Rights drafted a report on the

---

[72] Morsink, n 9, 219–22 and Plomer, n 61, 171–5.

[73] Eg the Paris Convention for the Protection of Industrial Property (1883, last revised 1967); the Berne Convention for the Protection of Literary and Artistic Words (1886, last revised 1971); and the International Convention for the Protection of Performers, Producers of Phonograms and Broadcasting Organizations (1961).

[74] World Intellectual Property Organization (WIPO), *Introduction to Intellectual Property: Theory and Practice* (Kluwer, 1997) 3.

[75] WIPO, *Understanding Industrial Property*, WIPO Publication No. 895(E), 7–8.

[76] Chapman, 'The Human Rights Implications of Intellectual Property Protection', (2002) 5 *Journal of International Economic Law* 861; Helfer, 'Toward a Human Rights Framework for Intellectual Property', (2007) 40 *UC Davis LR* 971; Cullet, 'Human Rights and Intellectual Property Protection in the TRIPS Era', (2007) 29 *HRQ* 404; Plomer, n 61.   [77] E/CN.4/Sub.2/2000/7 (17 August 2000).

impact of TRIPS on human rights, focusing on the right to health.[78] Also in 2001, the UN Committee on Economic, Social and Cultural Rights adopted a statement on 'Human rights and intellectual property'.[79] All these documents insisted on the primacy of human rights obligations over TRIPS and called upon states to ensure that intellectual property regulations correspond with international human rights law.

The tensions between intellectual property rules and human rights are especially acute in the case of the right to health. The standard justification for the intellectual property system is that it creates an incentive for innovation, including in the pharmaceutical field. Yet, whereas affordability of medicines is a central component of the right to health, medical patents result in higher prices for drugs, which restrict access for the poor. The problem became particularly salient in relation to the HIV and AIDS pandemic that predominantly affects the populations of developing countries. Additionally, because it links innovation to commercial motivation, the system of intellectual property entails that research is directed first and foremost towards 'profitable' diseases, namely diseases that are prevalent in rich countries, where the return is likely to be the greater.[80]

The impact of intellectual property on the right to food has also become a source of major concern. In order to encourage innovation in agriculture, intellectual property has been extended to new plant varieties in the form of patents and plant breeders' rights. As a result, a few agricultural corporations have acquired virtual monopolies on the genome of important crops, enabling them to set prices at levels far exceeding actual costs. In consequence, poor farmers experience difficulties in accessing seeds and production resources. This situation, moreover, can lead to higher prices for food, making it less affordable for the poorest.[81]

Another crucial debate concerns the protection of traditional knowledge (relating to medicine, agriculture, etc.) and artistic creations of indigenous communities. These intellectual goods rarely qualify for intellectual property protection, because they are usually considered by the community to belong to the whole group whereas intellectual property rules presuppose a single owner. Accordingly, such knowledge and creations are considered to be part of the public domain, which makes them available for exploitation and appropriation by third parties. This leads to a situation called 'biopiracy', 'whereby traditional knowledge is expropriated and patented by outsiders without the indigenous sources receiving any benefit'.[82]

5.2 THE CONTENT AND LIMITATIONS OF THE RIGHT UNDER ARTICLE 15(1)(C) ICESCR

Against the backdrop of these controversies, the Committee on Economic, Social and Cultural Rights issued, in 2005, a General Comment on the right protected in Article 15(1)(c). At the outset, the Committee asserts that this right 'does not necessarily coincide with what is referred to as intellectual property rights under national legislation or international agreements.'[83] The right to benefit from the protection of the moral and material interests resulting from any scientific, literary, or artistic production of which she is the author is

---

[78] The Impact of the Agreement on Trade-Related Aspects of Intellectual Property Rights on Human Rights, Report of the High Commissioner, E/CN.4/Sub.2/2001/13 (27 June 2001).

[79] 'Human Rights and Intellectual Property: Statement by the Committee on Economic, Social and Cultural Rights', Follow-up to the day of general discussion on Article 15(1)(c), 26 November 2001, E/C.12/2001/15 (14 December 2001).

[80] Report of the High Commissioner, n 78, para 38.   [81] De Schutter, n 64.

[82] Chapman, n 76, 872–3. See also Helfer, n 76, 982–3.

[83] General Comment 17, HRI/GEN/1/Rev.9 (Vol I) 123, para 2.

a human right, which derives from the inherent dignity and worth of all persons, while intellectual property rights are first and foremost means by which states seek to advance societal interests, namely to 'provide incentive for inventiveness and creativity, encourage the dissemination of creative and innovative productions, as well as the development of cultural identities, and preserve the integrity of scientific, literary and artistic productions for the benefit of society as a whole.'[84] The right under Article 15(1)(c) is essentially aimed at safeguarding the personal link between authors and their creations and allowing them to enjoy an adequate standard of living, whereas intellectual property regimes 'primarily protect business and corporate interests and investments.'[85]

The Committee thus distinguishes the right under Article 15(1)(c) from intellectual property rights. Yet the approach developed in the General Comment denotes a conceptual framework that 'is still largely influenced by existing intellectual property rights frameworks.'[86] According to the Committee, the 'moral interests' referred to in the provision include the right of authors to be recognized as the creators of their intellectual productions and to object to any distortion, mutilation, or modification which would be prejudicial to their honour and reputation.[87] The protection of 'material interests' is meant to allow authors to enjoy an adequate standard of living.[88] Among the obligations imposed on states lies the duty to 'prevent the unauthorized use of scientific, literary and artistic productions that are easily accessible or reproducible through modern communication and reproduction technologies.' This may be achieved 'by establishing systems of collective administration of authors' rights or by adopting legislation requiring users to inform authors of any use made of their productions and to remunerate them adequately.'[89]

Furthermore, the Committee asserts that states should take action to effectively protect the interests of indigenous peoples in relation to their intellectual productions, which are often expressions of their cultural heritage and traditional knowledge.[90] As seen already, a similar obligation has also been derived by the Committee from the right to take part in cultural life, which in its view entails a duty to defend the cultural productions of indigenous peoples, including their traditional knowledge and natural medicines, against unjust exploitation by state entities or private companies.[91]

The rights of authors, scientists, and inventors can be subject to limitations provided they are compatible with the essential aims of the right, namely protecting their personal link with their creation and allowing them to enjoy an adequate standard of living.[92] Significantly, the Committee calls for an adequate balance to be struck between state obligations under Article 15(1)(c) and under the other provisions of the Covenant:

> In striking this balance, the private interests of authors should not be unduly favoured and the public interest in enjoying broad access to their productions should be given due consideration. States parties should therefore ensure that their legal or other regimes for the protection of the moral and material interests resulting from one's scientific, literary or artistic productions constitute no impediment to their ability to comply with their core obligations in relation to the rights to food, health and education, as well as to take part in cultural life and to enjoy the benefits of scientific progress and its applications, or any other right enshrined in the Covenant.[93]

---

[84] General Comment 17, n 83, para 1.   [85] General Comment 17, n 83, para 2.
[86] Cullet, n 76, 422.   [87] General Comment 17, n 83, para 13.
[88] General Comment 17, n 83, para 15.   [89] General Comment 17, n 83, para 31.
[90] General Comment 17, n 83, para 32.   [91] General Comment 21, n 20, para 50 (c).
[92] General Comment 17, n 83, para 23.   [93] General Comment 17, n 83, para 35.

In particular, states parties 'have a duty to prevent unreasonably high costs for access to essential medicines, plant seeds or other means of food production, or for schoolbooks and learning materials, from undermining the rights of large segments of the population to health, food and education.'[94]

Importantly, the Committee insists that the right to the protection of the moral and material interests resulting from the production of which one is the author is intrinsically linked to the other rights recognized in Article 15, the right of everyone to take part in cultural life, the right to enjoy the benefits of scientific progress and its applications as well as the right to artistic and academic freedom. The relationship between these rights 'is at the same time mutually reinforcing and reciprocally limitative.'[95] The Committee thereby calls for a holistic interpretation of Article 15 ICESCR, implying the search for a fair equilibrium between the rights of authors and inventors to the protection of their private interests and the right of the public to access culture and science.

6 CONCLUSION

The cultural rights recognized in Article 27 UDHR and Article 15 ICESCR have traditionally been neglected in human rights theory and practice. Today, however, these rights are attracting growing attention. They prove to be particularly relevant to some crucial debates of our time, such as how to protect local cultures in the face of economic globalization, how to safeguard indigenous peoples, minorities, and migrants' rights to preserve their cultural heritage, how to ensure access for all to essential scientific advancements, or how to prevent intellectual property rules from hindering the enjoyment of human rights. Nonetheless, many interpretive questions remain. Two issues in particular are likely to continue to generate discussions in the years to come. One is how to develop an effective protection of cultural life given the very broad conception that has been endorsed by the Committee on Economic, Social and Cultural Rights, as including both culture as intellectual and artistic expressions and culture in the anthropological sense. A second critical question is how to find the right balance between the different components of Article 15 ICESCR, in particular the right of authors and inventors to the protection of their interests, on the one hand, and, on the other hand, the right of everyone to access culture and science.

FURTHER READING

CHAPMAN, 'The Human Rights Implications of Intellectual Property Protection' (2002) 5 *Journal of International Economic Law* 861.

CHAPMAN, 'Towards an Understanding of the Right to Enjoy the Benefits of Scientific Progress and Its Applications' (2009) 8 *Journal of HR* 1.

CULLET, 'Human Rights and Intellectual Property Protection in the TRIPS Era' (2007) 29 *HRQ* 404.

HELFER, 'Toward a Human Rights Framework for Intellectual Property' (2007) 40 *UC Davis LR* 971.

EIDE, 'Cultural Rights as Individual Human Rights', in Eide, Krause, and Rosas (eds), *Economic, Social and Cultural Rights. A Textbook* (Martinus Nijhoff, 2001) 289.

FRANCIONI and SCHEININ (eds), *Cultural Human Rights* (Martinus Nijhoff, 2008).

---

[94] General Comment 17, n 83, para 35.   [95] General Comment 17, n 83, para 4.

McGoldrick, 'Culture, Cultures, and Cultural Rights', in Baderin and McCorquodale (eds), *Economic, Social and Cultural Rights in Action* (Oxford University Press, 2007) 447.

Plomer, 'The Human Rights Paradox: Intellectual Property Rights and Rights of Access to Science' (2013) 35 *HRQ* 143.

Stamatopoulou, *Cultural Rights in International Law. Article 27 of the Universal Declaration of Human Rights and Beyond* (Martinus Nijhoff, 2007).

Thornberry, 'Cultural Rights and Universality of Human Rights', Contribution to the Day of General Discussion on 'The right to take part in cultural life' organized by the UN Committee on Economic, Social and Cultural Rights (9 May 2008).

USEFUL WEBSITES

UN Committee on Economic, Social and Cultural Rights: <http://www2.ohchr.org/english/bodies/cescr/>

Day of General Discussion on 'The right to take part in cultural life', UN Committee on Economic, Social and Cultural Rights, 9 May 2008 (including background papers from experts): <http://www2.ohchr.org/english/bodies/cescr/discussion090508.htm>

UN Independent Expert in the field of cultural rights: <http://www.ohchr.org/EN/Issues/CulturalRights/Pages/FaridaShaheed.aspx>

Venice Statement on the Right to Enjoy the Benefits of Scientific Progress and its Applications: <http://shr.aaas.org/article15/Reference_Materials/VeniceStatement_July2009.pdf>

15

SEXUAL ORIENTATION AND GENDER IDENTITY

Michael O'Flaherty

SUMMARY

Worldwide, people are subject to persistent human rights violations because of their actual or perceived sexual orientation and gender identity. The range of violations demonstrates that the members of sexual minorities are highly vulnerable to human rights abuse. This chapter assesses the forms of their vulnerability and identifies the applicable international human rights law. It will be seen that the jurisprudence focuses on issues of non-discrimination and privacy and that important human rights protections can also be derived from the range of other civil, political, economic, social, and cultural human rights of general application. The chapter concludes with an examination of a recent exercise in the clarification of the application of human rights law concerning issues of sexual orientation and gender identity, the Yogyakarta Principles.

1 INTRODUCTION

Typically, to be different to the majority in any society is to be vulnerable to prejudice, discrimination, and even attack. The greater the difference, the greater the risk. The story of the human rights movement is replete with moments defined by the identification of such vulnerable minorities and efforts to protect them. Thus, today, treaties address the situation of ethnic, racial, indigenous, religious, and other communities. However, the protection afforded by international law is by no means confined to groups that have been explicitly recognized in the treaties. International human rights treaty law has proved itself to be flexible in addressing the plight of groups whose vulnerability may not have been in the minds of the treaty drafters. One of the most vibrant contemporary human rights debates concerns the extent to which international law offers protection to members of what are sometimes termed 'sexual minorities'—about whom there is no explicit reference whatsoever in the treaty law.

A wide range of terms are used to describe the diverse members of sexual minorities, such as homosexuals, bisexuals, gays, lesbians, transsexuals, transgender, and inter-sex. Other terms, such as 'queer', can be considered pejorative in some contexts and acceptable in others. The variety of designations and usages, as well as the manner in which some of them have changed over time, can give rise to confusion on the part of the lawyer seeking to identify applicable provisions of human rights law. With this in mind, recent discourse on the application of human rights law has tended to cluster issues around two categorizations: 'sexual orientation' and 'gender identity'. An authoritative document that we will consider in this chapter, the Yogyakarta Principles,[1] describes 'sexual orientation' as 'each person's capacity for profound emotional, affectional and sexual attraction to, and intimate sexual relations with, individuals of a different gender or the same gender or more than one gender'.[2] 'Gender identity' is described as:

> each person's deeply felt internal and individual experience of gender, which may or may not correspond with the sex assigned at birth, including the personal sense of the body (which may involve, if freely chosen, modification of bodily appearance or function by medical, surgical or other means) and other expressions of gender, including dress, speech and mannerisms[3]

Of course, these definitions are no more than intellectual constructs and, as such, can be subject to criticism. However, they have some force in that they tend to reflect the contexts in which affected people experience discrimination, exclusion, and attack in many societies. They also—and this is especially the case with regard to 'sexual orientation'—are grounded in the jurisprudence of human rights courts and treaty-monitoring bodies. To the extent possible, this chapter will employ these terms.[4]

2 FORMS OF VULNERABILITY TO HUMAN RIGHTS ATTACK

Before we examine the extent of applicable human rights law, it is important to take account of the situation in which people of diverse sexual orientations and gender identities find themselves. Even the briefest of global surveys demonstrates a remarkable degree of vulnerability and abuse.[5] Seven states maintain the death penalty for consensual same-sex practices and reports are commonplace of persons who are killed because of their sexual orientation or gender identity. Perpetrators often go unpunished. Persons with diverse gender identities are particularly likely to be targeted for violence. They are 'often subjected to violence in order to "punish" them for transgressing gender barriers or for challenging predominant conceptions of gender roles',[6] and transgender youth have been described as 'among the most vulnerable and marginalized young people in society'.[7] Violations directed against lesbians because of their sex are often inseparable from violations directed against them because of their sexual orientation. For example, there are accounts of multiple rape of a lesbian arranged by her family in an attempt to 'cure' her of her homosexuality.[8] Same-sex

---

[1] The Yogyakarta Principles on the Application of International Human Rights Law in Relation to Sexual Orientation and Gender Identity (2007), available at: <http://www.yogyakartaprinciples.org>.

[2] The Yogyakarta Principles, n 1, preamble.   [3] The Yogyakarta Principles, n 1, preamble.

[4] For a general discussion of this usage and its implications, see Hamzic, 'The Case of "Queer Muslims": Sexual Orientation and Gender Identity in International Human Rights Law and Muslim Legal and Social Ethos' (2011) 11 *HRLR* 237.

[5] For an extensive review of the forms of vulnerability, see O'Flaherty and Fisher, 'Sexual Orientation, Gender Identity and International Human Rights Law: Contextualising the Yogyakarta Principles' (2008) 8 *HRLR* 207.

[6] Report of the Special Rapporteur on the question of torture and other cruel, inhuman or degrading treatment or punishment, A/56/156 (3 July 2001) para 17.

[7] Report of the Special Rapporteur on the sale of children, child prostitution and child pornography, E/CN.4/2004/9 (5 January 2004) para 123.

[8] Report of the Special Rapporteur on violence against women, its causes and consequences, E/CN.4/2002/83 (31 January 2002) para 102.

sexual relations between consenting adults constitute a criminal offence in some 80 states. Some states apply laws against 'public scandals', 'immorality', or 'indecent behaviour' to punish people for looking, dressing, or behaving differently from what are considered to be the social norms.

Serious problems have also been identified regarding the enjoyment of economic, social, and cultural rights. For example, people have been denied employment or employment-related benefits or have faced dismissal because of their sexual orientation or gender identity. In the context of the right to adequate housing, lesbian and transgender women are reported to be at a high risk of homelessness; discrimination based on sexual orientation or gender identity when renting accommodation has been experienced both by individuals and same-sex couples; and children have been thrown out of the family home by their families upon learning of their sexual orientation or gender identity. Transgender persons often face obstacles in seeking access to gender-appropriate services at homeless shelters. Materials referencing issues of sexual orientation and gender identity have been banned from school curricula; student groups addressing sexual orientation and gender identity issues have been prohibited; students have faced high levels of bullying and harassment because of their actual or perceived sexual orientation or gender identity; and, in some cases, young persons who express same-sex affection have been expelled from school. In some countries, laws have prohibited the 'promotion of homosexuality' in schools. Numerous health-related human rights violations based on sexual orientation and gender identity have been documented. People have been forcibly confined in medical institutions, subjected to 'aversion therapy', including electroshock treatment, and inter-sex people have been subjected to involuntary surgeries in an attempt to 'correct' their genitals.

The plight in which people of diverse sexual orientations and gender identities find themselves is well summarized in a comment by an Indonesian human rights expert, Siti Musdah Mulia:

> I realise that compared to other minority groups, LGBT [Lesbian, Gay, Bisexual and Transgender] people suffer more stigmas, stereotypes and discriminatory treatment, and even ruthless exploitation. The majority community (in Indonesia) still considers homosexuality as illicit, often as unmentionable.[9]

3 REVIEW OF LAW AND JURISPRUDENCE

As we have already observed, there are no specific references to issues related to sexual orientation or gender identity in the regional and global human rights treaties. However, the UN human rights treaty-monitoring bodies and the European Court of Human Rights have developed a significant body of jurisprudence on the topics while the Inter-American Court of Human Rights issued its first, and wide-ranging, judgment on issues of sexual orientation in 2012.[10] The findings tend to be clustered in three groups: protection of privacy rights, combat of discrimination, and ensuring other general human rights protection to all, regardless of sexual orientation or gender identity. We will look at each of these in turn.

---

[9] Musdah Mulia, 'Promoting LGBT Rights through Islamic Humanism' (1–6 June 2008).
[10] *Atala Riffo and daughters v Chile (Merits)*, IACtHR, Series C No 239, 24 February 2012.

3.1 PROTECTION OF PRIVACY RIGHTS

The European Convention on Human Rights (ECHR), in Article 8, the American Convention on Human Rights (ACHR), in Article 11, and the International Covenant on Civil and Political Rights (ICCPR), in Article 17, contain provisions for the protection of an individual's privacy. These reflect a perception of the drafters that there is an autonomous zone within which a person may live a personal life and make choices without interference. While the scope and the limits of that private space are impossible to chart outside the context of specific cases, it is acknowledged that 'respect for private life must also comprise to a certain degree the right to establish and develop relationships with other human beings'.[11]

The first successful international human rights cases on issues of sexual orientation were brought under the ECHR and invoked the privacy argument with regard to same-sex sexual activity. In *Dudgeon v UK*[12] and *Norris v Ireland*,[13] the criminalization of such practices was deemed a violation of Article 8 ECHR. In *Modinos v Cyprus*, the European Court, taking account that many of the prohibitions were not actually enforced in practice, held that even a 'consistent policy' of not bringing prosecutions under the law was no substitute for full repeal.[14] Privacy arguments were also successful regarding a ban on recruitment to the military of homosexuals: *Smith and Grady v UK*[15] and *Lustig-Prean and Beckett v UK*.[16] The Inter-American Court of Human Rights, in its first ever finding of sexual orientation-related violations of the ACHR, identified a violation of the right to privacy in the case of the loss of parenting rights on the part of a woman, divorced from the father of her children, who was living with a same-sex partner.[17]

The European Court of Human Rights has been willing to recognize privacy protection with regard to issues of gender identity. The approach of the Court reflects a perception that privacy protection may extend to the choices one makes regarding one's own choice of gender identity or expression. Interestingly, the cases are not about any effort of states to prohibit forms of gender identity choices. Instead, they address the positive obligation on the state to take the administrative actions, such as amending identity documents, which are necessary for the affected individuals to live in their changed gender identity. In *Goodwin v UK*[18] and *I v UK*,[19] the European Court reversed a long line of previous case law and held that the UK's refusal to change the legal identities of two transsexual women constituted a violation of Article 8 ECHR. In *Van Kuck v Germany*, the Court considered the case of a transsexual woman whose health-insurance company had denied her reimbursement for costs associated with sex-reassignment surgery. It found a violation of Article 8, holding that the German courts had failed to respect 'the applicant's freedom to define herself as a female person, one of the most basic essentials of self-determination'.[20] In *L v Lithuania*, the Court considered that the state was required to legislate for the provision of full gender-reassignment surgery whereby a person in the 'limbo' of partial reassignment could complete the process and be registered with the new gender identity.[21]

The Human Rights Committee, in the communication *Toonen v Australia*, adopted the approach of the European Court of Human Rights and considered that a criminal prohibition on same-sex sexual activity, even if unenforced, constituted an unreasonable interference with Mr Toonen's privacy under Article 17 ICCPR.[22] It is sometimes suggested that *Toonen* turns on its facts in the particular context of a state that cherishes diversity and that the

---

[11] *Niemietz v Germany* (1993) 16 EHRR 97, para 29.   [12] (1982) 4 EHRR 149.
[13] (1988) 13 EHRR 186.   [14] (1993) 16 EHRR 485.   [15] (1999) 29 EHRR 493.
[16] (1999) 29 EHRR 548.   [17] *Atala Riffo and daughters*, n 10.   [18] (2002) 35 EHRR 447.
[19] (2002) 35 EHRR 18.   [20] (2003) 37 EHRR 51, para 73.
[21] (2008) 46 EHRR 22.   [22] CCPR/C/50/D/488/1992 (4 April 1994).

findings might have been very different in the case of, for example, an Islamic state with a dominant moral code that rejected homosexual acts.[23] However, this view is mistaken since it ascribes to the Human Rights Committee a doctrine of margin of appreciation such as that to be found in the practice of the European Court of Human Rights.[24] In 2011, in its General Comment 34 on Article 19 ICCPR, the Committee definitively repudiated such a doctrine in its practice. It also stated that morals may only be invoked to restrict rights where such morals are, inter alia, non-discriminatory in effect and compatible with the universality of human rights.[25]

The Human Rights Committee has not considered applications of the right to privacy other than with regard to criminalization. This, in itself, does not tell us anything on the position of the Committee, since it can only develop case-specific jurisprudence on the basis of the complaints that are submitted to it. More tellingly, the Human Rights Committee has never taken the opportunity to explore the range of applications of a privacy approach in the context of its review of periodic reports submitted by states parties to the ICCPR. Here it has addressed privacy rights exclusively in the context of the criminalization of same-sex sexual activity. Taking account of the relatively vigorous and wide-ranging engagement with privacy issues in the European context, including with regard to the duties that fall to states regarding issues of gender identity, this dearth of practice is notable and may reflect unease with the issues on the part of some members of the Committee.

3.2 DISCRIMINATION

As we have seen, people of diverse sexual orientations and gender identities are subject to multiple forms of discrimination. It is not surprising, then, that a considerable body of practice has developed in the work of the international human rights treaty-monitoring bodies. Again, though, as in the case of privacy, and probably for the same reasons as noted in Section 3.1, the focus has been on sexual orientation rather than gender identity. The Committee on Economic, Social and Cultural Rights has addressed sexual orientation-related discrimination in its general comments. In General Comments 18, on the right to work,[26] 15, on the right to water,[27] and 14, on the right to the highest attainable standard of health,[28] it has indicated that the International Covenant on Economic, Social and Cultural Rights (ICESCR) proscribes any discrimination on the basis of, inter alia, sex and sexual orientation, 'that has the intention or effect of nullifying or impairing the equal enjoyment or exercise of [the right at issue]'. The Committee has consistently based this prohibition on the terms of the anti-discrimination provision—Article 2(2) ICESCR—which prohibits discrimination on a variety of specified grounds as well as one termed 'other status'. In 2009, the Committee adopted a General Comment on non-discrimination specifying that, '"other status" as recognised in article 2(2) includes sexual orientation. States parties should ensure that a person's sexual orientation is not a barrier to realising Covenant rights.'[29] The Committee, in its General Comments, also invokes the provision

---

[23] Cowell and Millon, 'Decriminalization of Sexual Orientation Through the Universal Periodic Review' (2012) 12 *HRLR* 341.

[24] See Chapter 5.   [25] HRC, General Comment 34, CCPR/C/GC/34 (12 September 2011).

[26] CESCR, General Comment 18, HRI/GEN/1/Rev.9 (Vol I) 139.

[27] CESCR, General Comment 15, HRI/GEN/1/Rev.9 (Vol I) 97.

[28] CESCR, General Comment 14, HRI/GEN/1/Rev.9 (Vol I) 78.

[29] CESCR, General Comment 20, E/C.12/GC/20 (10 June 2009) para 32.

addressing the equal rights of men and women, Article 3 ICESCR, as a basis for its prohibition of sexual orientation-related discrimination.[30]

Two other treaty bodies have adopted similar positions in their General Comments. The Committee on the Rights of the Child, in its General Comment 4, stated that:

> [s]tate parties have the obligation to ensure that all human beings below 18 enjoy all the rights set forth in the Convention [on the Rights of the Child] without discrimination (art. 2), including with regard to 'race, colour, sex, language, religion, political or other opinion, national, ethnic or social origin, property, disability, birth or other status.' These grounds also cover [*inter alia*] sexual orientation.[31]

In 2010, the Committee on the Elimination of Discrimination Against Women (CEDAW Committee) issued two General Recommendations—one on the rights of older women and the other on the core obligations of states—in which it recognized that sexual orientation and gender identity are prohibited grounds of discrimination against women.[32]

All but one of the treaty bodies (the Committee on the Elimination of Racial Discrimination) have occasionally raised issues of sexual orientation-related discrimination when considering periodic reports of states parties. The Committee on Economic, Social and Cultural Rights did so regarding eight of the 70 states considered between 2000 and 2006, and the Committee on the Rights of the Child regarding five of the 186 states considered in the same period. In each case, the Committees expressed concern in their 'concluding observations'. Given the non-binding and flexible nature of these treaty body outputs, they are not always a useful indicator of formal obligations under the treaty. However, where the treaty body expresses concern about a specific practice, we can surmise that serious issues arise under the treaty. Examples include the Committee on Economic, Social and Cultural Rights' regret, in 2005, that Hong Kong's anti-discrimination legislation failed to cover sexual orientation-related discrimination,[33] and its concern, in 2000, that Kyrgyzstan classified lesbianism as a sexual offence in its penal code.[34] The CEDAW Committee, on a number of occasions, has criticized states for discrimination on the basis of sexual orientation. For example, it too addressed the situation in Kyrgyzstan and recommended that 'lesbianism be reconceptualised as a sexual orientation and that penalties for its practice be abolished'.[35]

Issues of sexual orientation-related discrimination have received extensive attention in the work of the Human Rights Committee. In *Toonen*, the Committee said that 'the reference to "sex" in articles 2, paragraph 1, and 26 is to be taken as including sexual orientation'. The Committee accordingly considered that sexual orientation-related discrimination is a suspect category in terms of the enjoyment of ICCPR rights (Article 2) and, more generally, for equality before and equal protection of the law (Article 26). A small number of individual cases have illustrated the Human Rights Committee's approach. In *Young v Australia*[36] and *X v Colombia*,[37] the Committee was of the view that distinctions made in law between same-sex partners who were excluded from pension benefits, and

---

[30] Eg General Comment 18, n 26, para 12(b)(i).

[31] CRC, General Comment 4, HRI/GEN/1/Rev.9 (Vol II) 410, para 6.

[32] CEDAW, General Recommendation 27, CEDAW/C/2010/47/GC (16 December 2010); CEDAW General Recommendation 28, CEDAW/C/2010/47/GC.2 (16 December 2010).

[33] CESCR, Concluding Observations: People's Republic of China (including Hong Kong and Macau), E/C.12/1/Add.107 (13 May 2005) para 78.

[34] CESCR, Concluding Observations: Kyrgyzstan, E/C.12/1/Add.49 (1 September 2000) para 17.

[35] CEDAW, Concluding Observations: Kyrgyzstan, A/54/38 (5 February 1999) para 128.

[36] CCPR/C/78/D/941/2000 (6 August 2003).   [37] CCPR/C/89/D/1361/2005 (14 May 2007).

unmarried heterosexual partners who were granted such benefits, constituted violations of the ICCPR. However, not every case has been successful. In *Joslin v New Zealand*, the differential treatment under taxation regulations of same-sex unmarried couples (for whom marriage was not available in law) and heterosexual married couples was considered not to constitute a violation of Article 26 ICCPR. And yet, an individual concurring opinion of two members observed that 'the Committee's jurisprudence supports the position that such differentiation may very well, depending on the circumstances of a concrete case, amount to prohibited discrimination.'[38]

The Human Rights Committee frequently raises the issue of discrimination on the basis of sexual orientation in its consideration of periodic reports. During the period 2000–6, it did so regarding 13 of the 84 states under review and, for example, criticized many states for the criminalization of homosexual sexual relations and the failure to incorporate sexual orientation into anti-discrimination legal frameworks. It also expressed concern regarding unequal ages of consent for sexual activity, failure to prohibit employment-related discrimination, and lack of education programmes to combat discriminatory attitudes.

The European Court of Human Rights has generated a substantial body of jurisprudence concerning discrimination both on the grounds of sexual orientation and gender identity. In *Salgueiro da Silva Mouta v Portugal*, it held that a judge's denial of child custody to a homosexual father on the ground of his sexual orientation was discriminatory.[39] The Inter-American Court adopted a similar line of reasoning in *Atala Riffo and daughters v Chile*.[40] In *Karner v Austria*, the European Court considered that the failure of Austria to permit a homosexual man to continue occupying his deceased partner's flat was discriminatory, since this entitlement, available to family members under Austrian law, did not apply to same-sex partners. Austria claimed that excluding homosexuals aimed to protect 'the family in the traditional sense', but the Court considered that it had not demonstrated how the exclusion was necessary to that aim.[41] In *L and V v Austria*[42] and *SL v Austria*,[43] the Court considered that Austria's differing age of consent for heterosexual and homosexual relations was discriminatory. As the Court put it, the differing age 'embodied a predisposed bias on the part of a heterosexual majority against a homosexual minority', which could not 'amount to sufficient justification for the differential treatment any more than similar negative attitudes towards those of a different race, origin or colour'.

One area of discrimination in which the European Court was slow to find a violation of the Convention concerned the adoption of children. In the case of *Frette v France*, a homosexual man complained regarding a refusal to allow him to adopt a child for reasons of his sexual orientation.[44] The Court found against him, referring to the fast-evolving and very diverse practice across Europe, as well as the conflicting views of experts as to what would be in the best interests of the child. The decision in *Frette* is unsatisfactory. It posits false dilemmas such as a supposed tension between the rights of the man and the child. There is no such tension. The tension is between the rights of homosexual and heterosexual prospective adoptive parents, with the best interests of the child as the overarching consideration. Issues such as these were handled in a better manner in *EB v France*. In that case, the Court, while maintaining the paramount principle of the best interests of the child, held that, 'in rejecting the applicant's application for authorisation to adopt, the domestic authorities made a distinction based on considerations regarding her sexual orientation, a distinction which is not acceptable under the Convention'.[45] In the later case

---

[38] CCPR/C/75/D/902/1999 (30 July 2002).   [39] (1999) 31 EHRR 1055.   [40] n 10.
[41] (2003) 38 EHRR 24.   [42] (2003) 36 EHRR 55.   [43] (2003) 37 EHRR 39.
[44] (2003) 38 EHRR 21.   [45] (2008) 47 EHRR 21, para 96.

of *X v Austria*, the Court held that a prohibition of the adoption of the child of a same-sex partner was in violation of the Convention since Austria extended such an entitlement to partners in different-sex relationships.[46]

Overall, we can consider that the regional courts and the treaty bodies have mapped out an extensive range of areas and contexts in which sexual orientation-related discrimination is prohibited. The European Court has extended this consideration also to discrimination on the grounds of gender identity. Furthermore, as we will see in Section 3.3, it can also be assumed that the protections extend very much further than is specifically indicated in the jurisprudence and the review of periodic reports: they apply for the non-discriminatory enjoyment of *all* human rights.

3.3 GENERAL HUMAN RIGHTS PROTECTION

The international monitoring bodies are increasingly addressing issues of the entitlement of people of diverse sexual orientations and gender identities to benefit from the protection of other human rights of general application. The European Court of Human Rights, in *Alekseyev v Russia*, ruled that a municipal ban on LGBT Pride marches violated various provisions of the ECHR, including Article 11 on freedom of assembly.[47] The Human Rights Committee, in *Fedotova v Russian Federation*, held that the prevention of a display of posters that declared, 'Homosexuality is normal' and 'I am proud of my homosexuality' near a secondary school building constituted a violation of the protester's right to freedom of expression. The Committee observed that the protester had 'not made any public actions aimed at involving minors in any particular sexual activity or at advocating any particular sexual orientation. Instead, she was giving expression to her sexual identity and seeking understanding for it'.[48]

The Human Rights Committee and the other treaty bodies have also generated significant practice in the context of the review of periodic reports. The Human Rights Committee has expressed concern to specific states regarding violent crimes perpetrated against persons of minority sexual orientation, including by law enforcement officials; the failure to address such crime in legislation on hate crime; the frequent failure of states to investigate such acts; and the need for training of law enforcement and judicial officials in order to sensitize them to the rights of sexual minorities. The Committee on the Rights of the Child has expressed concern that homosexual and transsexual young people often do not have access to the appropriate information, support, and necessary protection to enable them to live their sexual orientation. On a number of occasions, the Committee against Torture has expressed concern about the torture of homosexuals and regarding complaints of threats and attacks against sexual minorities and transgender activists.

The reports of the 'special procedures' of the Human Rights Council constitute a particularly valuable repository of examples of the application for people of diverse sexual orientations and gender identities of general human rights protections, as well as of the principle of non-discrimination. The Council's Working Group on Arbitrary Detention has frequently invoked *Toonen* as a basis for its finding of arbitrary detention of homosexuals. A former Independent Expert on the situation of human rights defenders was assiduous in condemning attacks on members of sexual minorities.[49] She drew attention to such

---

[46] Application No 19010/07, Judgment of 19 February 2013.

[47] *Alekseyev v Russia*, Application Nos 4916/07, 25924/08, and 14599/09, Judgment of 21 October 2010.

[48] *Irina Fedotova v Russian Federation*, CCPR/C/106/D/1932/2010 (30 November 2012).

[49] Report of the Special Representative of the Secretary-General on human rights defenders, E/CN.4/2006/95/Add.1 (22 March 2006).

human rights violations as summary execution; torture; arbitrary detention; unreasonable impediments to freedom of expression, movement, and association; and participation in public life.

A number of the 'special procedures' have drawn attention to the intersectional nature of many human rights violations, where already vulnerable people face heightened risk when promoting the rights of people of diverse sexual orientations and gender identities. For example, the Independent Expert on minority issues has referred to the multiple forms of exclusion of members of minority communities, based on aspects of their identities and personal realities such as sexual orientation or gender expression that challenge social or cultural norms.[50]

Some of the 'special procedures' that address economic, social, and cultural rights have indicated the extent to which violations of these rights are at issue for people of diverse sexual orientations and gender identities. The work of a former Special Rapporteur on the right to health is particularly notable. In 2004, he observed that:

> fundamental human rights principles, as well as existing human rights norms, lead ineluctably to the recognition of sexual rights as human rights. Sexual rights include the right of all persons to express their sexual orientation, with due regard for the well-being and rights of others, without fear of persecution, denial of liberty or social interference.[51]

A former Special Rapporteur on education has identified a right to comprehensive sexual education.[52]

A broad range of human rights are also increasingly engaged at the regional level. The Council of Europe Commissioner for Human Rights often refers to violations.[53] Country reports and follow-up reports of the Inter-American Commission on Human Rights comment on such violations as 'social-cleansing' (killing) of homosexuals and the treatment of lesbian prisoners.[54] The UN and regional level examples clearly reinforce the assertion that human rights of general application may not be constrained on the basis of sexual orientation or gender identity.

But how does one distinguish rights of general application from those that are intended only to benefit a certain category of people? The answer to this question will usually be straightforward. For instance, the ICCPR limits the right to participate in political life to citizens. The question arises though of when a generally stated human right is limited in terms of who may benefit. For our purposes, the issue concerns when a right exclusively addresses the situation and choices of what we might term sexual majorities. This is the context for one of the most charged of contemporary debates concerning the rights of sexual minorities: whether international human rights law recognizes a right of same-sex marriage or of same-sex family life.

The Human Rights Committee, in *Joslin*, has been unequivocal on the matter of same-sex marriage. It contends that the right to marriage (Article 24(2) ICCPR) refers to a right of a man and a woman and that same-sex marriage is thereby excluded from the protection of the Covenant. The position of the European Court of Human Rights is unclear. In its 2010 judgment in *Schalk and Kopf v Austria*, it observed that, '[it] would no longer consider that the right to marry enshrined in Article 12 must in all circumstances be limited to marriage between two persons of the opposite sex'. However, in the case before it, it concluded that

---

[50] Report of the Independent Expert on minority issues, E/CN.4/2006/74 (6 January 2006).

[51] Report of the Special Rapporteur on the right of everyone to the enjoyment of the highest attainable standard of physical and mental health, E/CN.4/2004/49 (16 February 2004) para 54.

[52] Report of the Special Rapporteur on the Right to Education, A/65/162 (23 July 2010).

[53] Memorandum to the Polish Government, CommDH(2007)13 (20 June 2007).

[54] Annual Report of the Inter-American Commission on Human Rights 2006, ch IIIC(1).

the diversity of practice across states parties to the European Convention was such that the matter of same-sex marriage 'is left to regulation by the national law'.[55] In a judgment delivered in 2012, the Court also felt it necessary to issue *obiter dicta* to the effect that the Convention does not require states to grant access to marriage to same-sex couples.[56]

When we turn to the related but distinct issue of the identification of the family in international human rights law, we may observe that the UN and regional human rights monitoring bodies are moving, albeit haltingly, towards recognition of the existence of and rights pertaining to same-sex unmarried families. Article 23(1) ICCPR states the fundamental importance of the family and its entitlement to protection by the state, without reference to the form of family under consideration. Only in Article 23(2) do we find reference to the right of men and women to marry and found families. It is not necessarily the case that Article 23(2) restricts the meaning of the word 'family' in Article 23(1). And the Human Rights Committee, in *Young* and in *X*,[57] has criticized state practices that impede same-sex couples from benefiting from family-related benefits, such as transfer of pension entitlements. These cases, however, only addressed issues of inequality before the law (Article 26 ICCPR) and, in *X*, in a dissenting opinion of two members, it was observed that 'a couple of the same sex does not constitute a family within the meaning of the Covenant and cannot claim benefits that are based on a conception of the family as comprising individuals of different sexes'.[58]

It is the regional judicial courts that are providing the clearest current guidance. The European Court of Human Rights in *Schalk and Kopf v Austria* reversed previous findings,[59] observing that, 'a cohabiting same-sex couple living in a stable de facto partnership, falls within the notion of "family life", just as the relationship of a different-sex couple in the same situation would'.[60] The Inter-American Court of Human Rights adopted similar reasoning in the *Atala Riffo and daughters* case.[61]

One final uncertainty may be observed concerning the reach of human rights law to address abuses related to sexual orientation or gender identity. It remains unclear how far a human rights approach can go in terms of the regulation of practices of non-state actors.[62] This issue is of obvious importance since so many of the forms of abusive behaviour are to be found outside the state sector, such as in the workplace, privately owned housing, religious communities, and so forth.

4 LEGAL INITIATIVES TO BRIDGE THE GAP BETWEEN LAW AND PRACTICE

This chapter's review of the law has shown the long reach of international human rights standards as regards the particular situation of people of diverse sexual orientations and gender identities. Fundamental principles, such as those of non-discrimination and of the universal application of general human rights standards, have been strongly affirmed. However, as has also been demonstrated, the courts, the treaty bodies, and the independent

---

[55] *Schalk and Kopf v Austria* (2011) 53 EHRR 20 para 61.
[56] *Gas and Dubois v France*, Application No 25951/07, Judgment of 15 March 2012.
[57] n 37 and n 38.   [58] n 38, separate opinion of Mr Abdelfattah Amor and Mr Ahmed Tawfik Khalil.
[59] See Walker, 'Moving Gaily Forward? Lesbian, Gay and Transgender Human Rights in Europe' (2001) 2 *Melbourne JIL* 122.
[60] *Schalk and Kopf v Austria* n 57, para 94. See also, *P.B. and J.S. v Austria* (2012) 55 EHRR 31.
[61] n 10.   [62] See Chapter 26.

experts, limited as they are by the facts before them or their various mandates, have only indicated the actual application of these principles to a limited number of circumstances.

As a result, a certain degree of legal uncertainty persists. That uncertainty is compounded by the terminological confusion, referred to already, which is to be found throughout the case law, comments of treaty bodies, and reports of special procedures. In particular, issues of gender identity have been little understood, with, for instance, some special procedures and states referencing transsexuality as a 'sexual orientation', and others frankly acknowledging that they do not understand the term.

There has been a significant initiative to address the uncertainty regarding the reach of the law (and the terminological confusion). In 2007, a group of 29 international human rights experts produced a text known as the Yogyakarta Principles on the application of international human rights law in relation to sexual orientation and gender identity.[63] This document has a tripartite function.[64] In the first place, it constitutes a 'mapping' of the experiences of human rights violations experienced by people of diverse sexual orientations and gender identities. Second, the application of international human rights law to such experiences is articulated. Finally, the Principles spell out the nature of the obligation on states for implementation of each of the human rights.

The Principles have no binding force. They are neither a treaty nor the finding of a judicial or quasi-judicial body. Nevertheless, they carry the authority of their expert authors and have been considered by many states and experts to constitute a careful articulation of the state of existing law. Accordingly, they bear examination in some detail. Each principle comprises a statement of the law, its application to a given situation, and an indication of the nature of the state's duty to implement the legal obligation. Principles 1 to 3 address the principles of the universality of human rights and their application to all persons without discrimination, as well as the right of all people to recognition before the law. The experts placed these elements at the beginning of the text in order to recall the fundamental significance of the universality of human rights and the scale and extent of discrimination against people because of their actual or perceived sexual orientation or gender identity, as well as the manner in which they are often rendered invisible within society and its legal structures. Principles 4 to 11 deal with the fundamental rights to life, freedom from violence and torture, privacy, access to justice, and freedom from arbitrary detention. Principles 12 to 18 address non-discriminatory enjoyment of economic, social, and cultural rights, including accommodation, employment, social security, health, and education. Principles 19 to 21 concern the importance of the freedom to express oneself, one's identity, and one's sexuality, without state interference, based on sexual orientation or gender identity, including the rights to participate peaceably in public assemblies and events and otherwise associate in community with others. Principles 22 and 23 address the right to seek asylum from persecution based on sexual orientation or gender identity. Principles 24 to 26 deal with the rights to participate in family life, public affairs, and the cultural life of the community, without discrimination based on sexual orientation or gender identity. Principle 27 recognizes the right to defend and promote human rights without discrimination based on sexual orientation and gender identity, and the obligation of states to ensure the protection of human rights defenders. Principles 28 and 29 affirm the importance of holding rights violators accountable, and of ensuring redress for those whose rights are violated.

A notable feature of the principles is the manner in which they spell out in some detail the legal obligations of the state with regard to each of the rights that are affirmed.

---

[63] n 1.　　[64] Address of the Rapporteur, launch event of the Principles (March 2007).

A general typology for the obligations can be observed. States must: (1) take all necessary legislative, administrative, and other measures to eradicate impugned practices; (2) take protection measures for those at risk; (3) ensure accountability of perpetrators and redress for victims; and (4) promote a human rights culture by means of education, training, and public awareness raising. Also, in the document's preamble, as we have already observed, the experts proposed the definition of the terms 'sexual orientation' and 'gender identity'. These formulations, drawing on their wide usage within academic writing and advocacy communities, establish a personal scope of application for the Principles. The preface also includes references that acknowledge the imperfections of the text and the need to keep its contents under review with a view to future reformulations that would take account of legal changes as well as developing understandings of the situation of people of diverse sexual orientations and gender identities.

5 CONCLUSION

This chapter has assessed the actual human rights situation of people of diverse sexual orientations and gender identities worldwide as well as the extent of the application to them of international human rights law. The gap between law and practice has been highlighted and a major initiative to address that gap, the Yogyakarta Principles, has been discussed. These Principles are presented as a form of *aide-mémoire* that indicates the contemporary state of the law and presents it in an integrated and coherent manner.

Also pertinent for this area of the law are the relevant national and international politics. It is of particular utility to study the practice in such international diplomatic fora as the United Nations Human Rights Council and the General Assembly. For instance, it will be of interest to examine and assess the debate at the Human Rights Council when, in 2012, the UN High Commissioner for Human Rights tabled an unprecedented report on violence and discrimination based on sexual orientation and gender identity.[65] On that occasion, Pakistan's representative to the Council addressed the session on behalf of the Organization of Islamic Cooperation, denouncing the discussion and questioning the concept of sexual orientation.[66] Four years earlier, a statement in support of full protection of human rights for persons of diverse sexual orientations and gender identities was proclaimed at the General Assembly on behalf of 66 states (the authors of which acknowledged the extent to which its contents were informed by the Yogyakarta Principles).[67] In a form of response, what is sometimes described as the 'counter-statement' was delivered on behalf of 57 other states.[68] These patterns of diplomatic practice recall the extent to which the subject area is highly controversial and in a state of political flux. We are thus precluded from drawing any firm conclusions as to prospects for better enforcement of the law or its further development. We can no more than observe that with regard to the plight of many members of sexual minorities, the universal enjoyment of human rights remains an elusive and distant goal.

---

[65] A/HRC/19/41 (17 November 2011). The debate at the Human Rights Council is summarized at: <http://www.ohchr.org/Documents/Issues/Discrimination/LGBT/SummaryHRC19Panel.pdf>.

[66] See <http://www.ohchr.org/en/NewsEvents/Pages/DisplayNews.aspx?NewsID=11920&LangID=E>.

[67] Statement of Argentina (18 December 2008) video-archived (at 2 hours, 25 mins), available at: <http://www.un.org/webcast/ga.html>.

[68] Statement of Syria (18 December 2008), video-archived (at 2 hours, 32 mins), available at: <http://www.un.org/webcast/ga.html>.

FURTHER READING

CORREA, PETCHESKY, and PARKER, *Sexuality, Health and Human Rights* (Routledge, 2008).

HAMZIC, 'The Case of "Queer Muslims": Sexual Orientation and Gender Identity in International Human Rights law and Muslim Legal and Social Ethos' (2011) 11 *HRLR* 237.

O'FLAHERTY and FISHER, 'Sexual Orientation, Gender Identity and International Human Rights Law: Contextualising the Yogyakarta Principles' (2008) 8 *HRLR* 207.

Report of the United Nations High Commissioner on Human Rights on violence and discrimination based on sexual orientation and gender identity, A/HRC/19/41 (17 November 2011).

WALKER, 'Moving Gaily Forward? Lesbian, Gay and Transgender Human Rights in Europe' (2001) 2 *Melbourne JIL* 122.

USEFUL WEBSITES

International Commission of Jurists: <http://www.icj.org>

Human Rights Watch: <http://www.hrw.org/en/category/topic/lgbt-rights>

International Lesbian, Gay, Bisexual, Trans and Intersex Association: <http://www.ilga.org>

ARC International: <http://www.arc-international.net>

16

WOMEN'S RIGHTS

Dianne Otto

SUMMARY

International human rights law prohibits discrimination against women in their enjoyment of all human rights and fundamental freedoms. While non-discrimination is an essential component to the realization of women's rights, its comparative approach measures women's equality against men's enjoyment of rights, reinforcing the masculinity of the universal subject of human rights law, whose rights are fully promoted and explicitly protected. To the extent that violations experienced exclusively or primarily by women are expressly recognized in the founding human rights instruments, they are treated as a sub-category of the universal and often formulated as 'protective' measures rather than as human rights. There have been many efforts to address the resulting marginalization of women's rights, including the adoption of the Convention on the Elimination of All Forms of Discrimination Against Women and the strategy of gender mainstreaming in the application of general human rights instruments. While these efforts have been successful in many respects, there are continuing conceptual and practical problems, including, not only the limitations of anti-discrimination law and dualistic conceptions of gender, but the danger that specific recognition of women's rights violations may simply reproduce women's secondary status.

1 INTRODUCTION

In 1945, the United Nations (UN) Charter recognized the principle that human rights and fundamental freedoms should be enjoyed by everyone 'without distinction as to...sex'.[1] Since then, international human rights instruments have repeatedly affirmed that women and men must equally enjoy the human rights they enumerate, without discrimination on the ground of sex.[2] The new era of universal human rights promised women, for the first time in international law, the full recognition of their humanity, marking a decisive break with the longstanding legal representation of women as lacking full legal and civil capacity. Significantly, the promise of equality also extended to the private realm of the

---

[1] UN Charter, Art 1(4).
[2] Eg Universal Declaration of Human Rights (UDHR), Art 2; International Covenant on Civil and Political Rights (ICCPR), Arts 2(2) and 3; International Covenant on Economic, Social and Cultural Rights (ICESCR), Arts 2(1) and 3.

family.[3] Women were no longer to be treated as the dependants of men, or as the property of their fathers or husbands.

Yet there has been widespread resistance to taking these obligations seriously, as evidenced by the many sweeping reservations to the Convention on the Elimination of All Forms of Discrimination Against Women (CEDAW). The CEDAW was adopted in 1979 to draw specific attention to the entrenched nature of women's inequality and the need for significant affirmative measures to address it. Unashamedly, some of the reservations to the CEDAW challenge the very idea of women's equality with men.[4] As UN High Commissioner for Human Rights, Navi Pillay, observed in a statement to the Human Rights Council (HRC) in 2012, which welcomed the creation of a mechanism to address discrimination against women in law and practice, the 'stubborn persistence and frequent resurgence [of women's inequality] requires our full and sustained attention'.[5] In some countries, historic hard-won advances towards the recognition of women's rights are now under threat, or have been wound back, in the face of cultural or religious 'fundamentalisms',[6] or in the name of thwarting international terrorism.[7]

The grim reality is that women fare considerably worse than men on almost every indicator of social well-being, despite the assumption by all states of at least some international legal obligations to promote their equal enjoyment of human rights and many good intentions. Everywhere, despite women's increasing participation in the workforce, their average wage is considerably less than that of men and they are concentrated in precarious work in the formal and informal sectors. Furthermore, many women do not receive any remuneration for work in family enterprises and have unequal access to social security assistance.[8] Violence against women continues to be pervasive, endangering women's lives in both public and private spheres.[9] The World Health Organization estimates that every day 1,500 women and girls die of preventable complications related to pregnancy and childbirth.[10] As an international group of eminent global leaders, brought together by Nelson Mandela, recently observed, religious teachings and customary practices 'have been [mis]used throughout the centuries to justify and entrench inequality and discrimination against women and girls', denying them 'fair access to education, health, employment, property and influence within their own communities'.[11] Women's inequality is still widely regarded as 'natural' and as prescribed by religious teachings and cultural traditions.

---

[3] UDHR, Art 16(1). See further ICCPR, Art 23(4).

[4] Clark, 'The Vienna Convention Reservations Regime and the Convention on Discrimination Against Women' (1991) 85 *AJIL* 281; Cook, 'Reservations to the Convention on the Elimination of All Forms of Discrimination Against Women' (1990) 30 *Virginia JIL* 643. On reservations to human rights treaties generally, see Chapter 5.

[5] Opening Statement by Ms Navi Pillay, UN High Commissioner for Human Rights, for the 19th Session of the Human Rights Council', 27 February 2012.

[6] Report of the Secretary-General, In-depth study on all forms of violence against women, A/61/122/Add.1 (6 July 2006) para 58.

[7] Report of the Special Rapporteur on the promotion and protection of human rights and fundamental freedoms while countering terrorism, Part III, 'A gender perspective on countering terrorism', A/64/211 (3 August 2009) paras 18-53.

[8] Razari *et al.*, *Gendered Impacts of Globalization – Employment and Social Protection*, UNSRID Research Paper 2012-3 (March 2012).   [9] Report of the Secretary-General, n 8, paras 363–4.

[10] Human Rights Council Res 11/8 (17 June 2008) paras 1 and 2.

[11] The Elders, 'Equality for Women and Girls', available at: <http://www.theelders.org/womens-initiatives>.

Yet, although the lack of political will presents an extremely significant barrier to the realization of women's rights and equality, it is not the only problem. International human rights law itself presents some obstacles. As Douzinas has observed, human rights 'construct humans', rather than the reverse, and it follows that '[a] human being is someone who can successfully claim rights'.[12] This recognition presents a conundrum for women's human rights advocates because, in crafting laws that respond to the gendered realities of women's lives, there is the risk of reconstituting gender stereotypes through reproducing those realities, rather than challenging them. At the same time, 'special' measures designed to address women's specific injuries and disadvantage continue to affirm the maleness of the universal subject of human rights law, as men need no special enumeration of their gender-specific injuries.[13] Charlesworth has called this the 'paradox of feminism'; whether women's rights are best protected through general norms that treat women as the same as men, or through specific norms applicable only to women.[14] Ultimately, the paradox forces us to ask hard questions about how women's inclusion as full subjects of the universal regime of human rights law might be achieved. One such question is whether the recognition of gendered harms suffered by everyone because of their gender identity, including men, women, trans, and other genders, would help to shift the harmful gender stereotypes that continue to reside in the idea of the universal human being.

This chapter critically examines the many efforts to achieve women's full inclusion in international human rights law. Section 2 describes the treatment of women in international law prior to the adoption of the UN Charter, in order to highlight the significance of the subsequent shift to the promotion of women's equality. It examines the non-discrimination approach favoured by the drafters of the founding human rights instruments, highlighting the importance of the approach as well as some of its limitations. Section 3 examines the innovative approach taken in the CEDAW, the drafters of which aimed to address the problems attending the concept of non-discrimination by promoting a strong version of women's substantive equality. Yet while the CEDAW fostered a better understanding of the measures that may be necessary to achieve women's equal enjoyment of human rights, it also reinforced the marginalization of women's rights practically and conceptually, and institutionalized the idea that gender was a duality that always worked to women's disadvantage. The other human rights treaty bodies tacitly used the existence of the CEDAW Committee as an excuse to continue their neglect of women's rights, and different administrative arrangements helped to 'ghettoize' both the CEDAW Committee and its work. To tackle this marginalization, a new strategy of 'gender mainstreaming' was adopted during the 1990s, which sought to reinterpret mainstream human rights to be inclusive of women's experiences. This strategy is examined in Section 4. The chapter concludes, in Section 5, by drawing attention to some continuing obstacles presented by the law itself, which prevent women from successfully claiming and enjoying human rights.

---

[12] Douzinas, 'The End(s) of Human Rights' (2002) 26 *Melbourne ULR* 445, 457.

[13] Otto, 'Lost in translation: re-scripting the sexed subject of international human rights law', in Orford (ed), *International Law and its Others* (CUP, 2006) 318–56.

[14] Charlesworth, 'Not Waving but Drowning: Gender Mainstreaming and Human Rights in the United Nations' (2005) 18 *HHRJ* 1.

2 A NEW ERA OF NON-DISCRIMINATION ON THE GROUND OF SEX AND EQUALITY WITH MEN

While the UN Charter was the first international treaty to promote women's equality with men, it was not the first time that women were constituted as a category in international law. This section will briefly describe how women appeared in earlier international legal texts before examining how women's rights were recognized by the foundational human rights instruments. While the idea of women's equality with men was a radical and visionary development, of great importance to women (and men), this approach failed to acknowledge the specificity of many human rights violations suffered exclusively or predominantly by women and, therefore, failed to construct them as fully human.

2.1 THE POSITION PRIOR TO 1945

Before 1945, international law had taken a paternalistic or 'protective' approach to women, treating them as the property, extension, or dependants of men, as primarily mothers and wives, and as incapable of full autonomy and agency.[15] Women were valued for their pre-marital chastity, their prioritization of motherhood and domesticity, and their acceptance of the heterosexual family hierarchy and the paternal protection of the state and its laws. The laws of war, for example, required an occupying power to respect 'family honour and rights', treating women as part of (male) family property and reputation, to be protected by the law.[16] Early international labour conventions prohibited women from certain types of work, such as night work and mining, on the basis that this interfered with their domestic and reproductive responsibilities.[17] Anti-trafficking conventions made women's consent to working in the sex industry irrelevant, thereby treating all sex workers as victims, needing rescue and rehabilitation.[18] None of these conventions constructed women as rights-bearers. Instead, women were granted 'protections', sometimes in the form of 'privileged' treatment, because of their socially ascribed secondary status.

2.2 THE UDHR AND THE INTERNATIONAL COVENANTS

Following the Second World War, the shift from protectionism to universal human rights promised to recognize women as fully human, for the first time, by granting them the same human rights as men. The primary means for achieving women's equality, adopted by the drafters of the UDHR, was to prohibit discrimination based on sex in the enjoyment of universal rights and freedoms which, notably, does not single women out as the

---

[15] Hevener, 'International Law and the Status of Women: An Analysis of International Legal Instruments Related to the Treatment of Women' (1978) 1 *Harvard Women's LJ* 131, 133–40.

[16] See Convention Respecting the Laws and Customs of War on Land (1899) (Hague Convention II) Art 46; and Convention Respecting the Laws and Customs of War on Land (1907) (Hague Convention IV), Art 46.

[17] Eg International Labour Organization, Maternity Protection Convention (1919) (Convention 3); International Labour Organization, Convention Concerning Night Work of Women Employed in Industry (1919) (Convention 4); International Labour Organization, Convention Concerning the Employment of Women on Underground Work in Mines of All Kinds (1935) (Convention 45).

[18] International Agreement for the Suppression of the White Slave Traffic (1904); International Convention for the Suppression of White Slave Traffic (1910); International Convention for the Suppression of the Traffic in Women and Children (1921); Convention for the Suppression of the Traffic in Women of Full Age (1933). See further, Doezema, 'Loose Women or Lost Women? The Re-Emergence of the Myth of White Slavery in the Contemporary Discourses of Trafficking in Women' (2000) 18 *Gender Issues* 23, 24.

disadvantaged gender group.[19] The decision not to recognize rights that were specific to women's experiences was deliberately made, informed by the concern that the latter would compromise the idea of 'universality' of rights and wrongly emphasize women's difference from men rather than their common humanity.[20]

In transforming the UDHR into legally binding instruments, the International Covenant on Economic, Social and Cultural Rights (ICESCR) and the International Covenant on Civil and Political Rights (ICCPR) followed suit, relying largely on the prohibition of sex discrimination in the enjoyment of the rights they enumerated to achieve women's equality.[21] As the Covenants did not define 'discrimination' or 'equality', many states parties interpreted their obligations narrowly, to require formal, rather than substantive, equality.[22] However, an additional provision was included as Article 3 common to the two Covenants, which required states parties to ensure 'the equal right of men and women to the enjoyment of all ... [rights] set forth in the present Covenant', indicating that special attention must be paid to achieving women's equality and, by the use of the term 'enjoyment', suggesting that equality in outcome (substantive equality) was the goal, although states parties were slow to embrace this interpretation.

The obligation to ensure that women enjoy the same rights as men was a very significant step forward for women. States parties are required to treat women and men alike when they are in a comparable situation. Think, for example, of the importance to women of the universal franchise, the freedom to move and to express their opinions to the same extent as men, of equal pay, and education on the same basis as men. In addition, the unprecedented acknowledgement that women and men 'are entitled to equal rights as to marriage, during marriage and at its dissolution',[23] broke through the tradition in liberal legal thinking that exempted the private sphere from legal scrutiny.[24] This provision opened the way for dispensing with the public–private dichotomy that has served to shield many of the human rights violations experienced by women in the 'private' realm of the family from public scrutiny and deliver impunity to perpetrators. However, as would soon become apparent, this development was in tension with states' responsibilities to protect the institution of the family and the right to privacy within families as also set out in the UDHR and ICCPR.[25] For many Third World women, the issue of private actors violating their rights is not only a concern within their communitarian and extended-family networks, but also an issue of the unregulated activities of global private actors, such as transnational corporations and banks.[26] The policies and practices of many global economic actors exploit local resources and labour, with highly gendered effects, compounding the difficulties that poor states have in complying with their human rights obligations. Yet the 'private' conduct of the marketplace is not directly regulated by human rights law.

---

[19] UDHR, Art 2. This type of non-discrimination provision is described as a 'subordinate norm' because it prohibits discrimination only with respect to the rights and freedoms set out in the instrument.

[20] Morsink, 'Women's Rights in the Universal Declaration' (1991) 13 *HRQ* 229. For a critical analysis see Bequaert Holmes, 'A Feminist Analysis of the Universal Declaration of Human Rights' in Gould (ed), *Beyond Dominance: New Perspectives on Women and Philosophy* (Rowman & Allanheld, 1983) 250.

[21] ICESCR, Art 2(2); ICCPR, Art 2(1).   [22] See Chapter 8.

[23] UDHR, Art 16(1); ICCPR, Art 23(4).

[24] Romany, 'State Responsibility Goes Private: A Feminist Critique of the Public/Private Distinction in International Human Rights Law' in Cook (ed), *Human Rights of Women: National and International Perspectives* (University of Pennsylvania Press, 1994) 85.

[25] UDHR, Arts 12 and 16(3); ICCPR, Arts 17(1) and 23(1).

[26] Oloka-Onyango and Tamale, '"The Personal is Political" or Why Women's Rights Are Indeed Human Rights: An African Perspective on International Feminism' (1995) 17 *HRQ* 691, 702.

Despite these shortcomings, the prohibition of sex discrimination left little doubt that the differences between women and men, which had previously been treated as immutable and used to justify women's inequality, were to be understood as socially constructed and, therefore, changeable. International human rights law had the potential to challenge the 'naturalness' of many discriminatory beliefs and practices, and assist in the task of changing oppressive stereotypes about 'women', simultaneously challenging dominating stereotypes about 'men'. While ground-breaking in many respects, the preferred method of realizing women's full legal subjectivity by promoting their equal and non-discriminatory enjoyment of human rights soon proved to be problematic, both conceptually and in practice.

Conceptually, non-discrimination was interpreted as a formal (*de jure*) rather than substantive (*de facto*) obligation, requiring only that women be granted the same rights as men, regardless of whether this achieved equality of outcome. Treating women in the same way as men works well when women's and men's experiences of human rights violations are directly comparable, as in the first communication concerning sex discrimination considered by the Human Rights Committee. The communication was brought by a group of Mauritian women, complaining that legislation discriminated against women because it granted automatic residency to the foreign wives of Mauritian men but denied automatic residency to the foreign husbands of Mauritian women.[27] On these facts, the Human Rights Committee easily found that the legislation made an 'adverse distinction based on sex' because it negatively affected married women's enjoyment of ICCPR rights related to privacy and family life, as compared to married men.[28]

However, a comparison with the rights that men enjoy does not help in situations where women's experiences are substantially different from men's, as in the case of work. Rights recognized by the ICESCR that protect the right to work assume a male model of employment, which makes women's unremunerated work in the family and their poorly remunerated work in the informal sector invisible.[29] This approach also fails to take account of women's often interrupted patterns of paid work, the problem of gender segregation in the workforce, and the need for maternity leave, childcare provision, and a radical change in the distribution of domestic and caring responsibilities. A further problem with the comparative approach of equality and non-discrimination is that, when the Covenants depart from it by explicitly referring to women's different experience, international law's discursive heritage of treating women protectively tends to re-emerge, as in the requirement that states parties ensure 'special protection' (rather than rights) for mothers for a period before and after childbirth.[30] The result is that women are included in the Covenants by reference to the gendered specificities of their lives, which need 'special' treatment to be addressed. This approach constructs women's experience as non-universal and has the effect of buttressing the masculinity of the universal subject. The ICESCR also describes the right of everyone to an adequate standard of living 'for himself [sic] and his family',[31] breathing life into the erroneous stereotype that all women are dependent on male household breadwinners, although the Committee on Economic, Social and Cultural Rights has since strongly repudiated this interpretation.[32]

In practice, drawing formal comparisons between women and men proved to be a blunt means of promoting women's substantive equality. The narrow focus of a comparison does

---

[27] *Aumeeruddy-Cziffra et al. v Mauritius*, CCPR/C/12/D/35/1978 (9 April 1981).

[28] *Aumeeruddy-Cziffra et al. v Mauritius*, n 27, paras 9.2(b)2(i)8 and 9.2(b)2(ii)4.

[29] ICESCR, Arts 6, 7, and 8. See further, Promoting Women's Enjoyment of their Economic and Social Rights: Expert Group Meeting, EGM/WESR/1997/Report (1–4 December 1997) paras 46–8.

[30] ICESCR, Art 10(2).   [31] ICESCR, Art 11(1).

[32] CESCR, General Comment 4, HRI/GEN/1/Rev.9 (Vol I) 11, para 6.

not take account of the need to redress the institutionalized history of discrimination and disadvantage that often affects women's ability to exercise their rights in the same way as men, for example by ensuring they have the information, autonomy, and mobility to exercise their right to vote. A formal comparison also ignores the need to create enabling circumstances that will make women's equal enjoyment of rights possible, which may involve changing deeply embedded social and cultural attitudes that stigmatize or punish women for exercising their rights.

The limitations of relying on the prohibition of sex discrimination to do all the work of ensuring that women fully enjoy universal human rights and fundamental freedoms was soon apparent.[33] In addition to interpreting equality as a formal rather than substantive obligation, women's human rights violations were rarely addressed by human rights treaty bodies in the early years of their operation because the comparative standard of non-discrimination did not force them to rethink their own gendered frameworks, and human rights NGOs were preoccupied with addressing Cold War violations experienced by men in the public sphere, such as the freedom of political expression and the release of political prisoners, which blinded them to what was happening to women, even where they too were political prisoners.

3 THE SUBSTANTIVE EQUALITY APPROACH OF CEDAW

Growing dissatisfaction with women's marginalization within the general framework and implementation of international human rights law led to the adoption of the CEDAW by the UN General Assembly in 1979. Although the CEDAW takes the same general approach as the Covenants by promoting non-discrimination, it is concerned specifically with discrimination against women and the promotion of women's equality with men, advancing a strong form of women's substantive equality as the international norm. This section discusses the positive features of the approach to women's equality taken by the CEDAW and then examines some of its limitations. It begins with a discussion of three strategies adopted by the CEDAW to promote a robust understanding of women's equality: the adoption of a comprehensive definition of discrimination against women; the promotion of the use of temporary and permanent 'special measures'; and the requirement that states parties tackle the causes of women's inequality by promoting social change relating to both women and men in all spheres of life, including in families.

3.1 TOWARDS A ROBUST UNDERSTANDING OF EQUALITY

The first step towards advancing women's substantive equality is the provision of a comprehensive definition of 'discrimination against women' in Article 1:

> [it] shall mean any distinction, exclusion or restriction made on the basis of sex which has the effect or purpose of impairing or nullifying the recognition, enjoyment or exercise by women, irrespective of their marital status, on a basis of equality of men and women, of human rights and fundamental freedoms in the political, economic, social, cultural, civil or any other field.

This definition covers a wide range of conduct and, importantly, prohibits discriminatory treatment (direct discrimination) as well as discriminatory outcome (indirect

---

[33] Petersen, 'Whose Rights? A Critique of the "Givens" in Human Rights Discourse' (1990) 15 *Alternatives* 303.

discrimination), and intended (purposive) discrimination as well as unintended discrimination (discrimination in effect). Both 'sex' and 'marital status' are specified as prohibited grounds of discrimination against women, and it should further be noted that other provisions in the CEDAW (for example, Article 11(2) in the field of employment) also prohibit discrimination on the grounds of 'pregnancy' and 'maternity'.

The definition specifically promotes substantive equality by requiring that women must be able to 'enjoy' or 'exercise' their human rights and fundamental freedoms, and makes it clear that the prohibition of discrimination against women applies to all fields of life, not only the public sphere. Indeed, the application of the CEDAW to private actors, including individuals and organizations, is made explicit in many instances in the text.[34] The CEDAW Committee, which monitors its implementation, has made it clear that states parties have the obligation to act with 'due diligence' to ensure that private actors do not violate the Convention.[35] The Committee has also clarified many of the other obligations required by its substantive approach to women's equality in its interpretations of the CEDAW, helping to constitute a more gender-inclusive subject of human rights law. For example, the Committee has urged states parties to adopt criteria in the determination of equal pay that facilitate the comparison of the *value* of the work usually done by women with the *value* of those more highly paid jobs usually done by men,[36] and to implement health measures that address 'the distinctive features and factors that differ for women in comparison with men'.[37]

The second way that the CEDAW promotes the norm of women's substantive equality is by making it clear that non-identical treatment aimed at addressing women's specific experiences of disadvantage may be necessary to achieve women's equality. The CEDAW distinguishes between temporary and permanent measures. Article 4(1) promotes the use of 'special temporary measures' (also known as 'affirmative action', 'positive action', or 'reverse discrimination'), which are directed towards 'accelerating de facto equality between women and men' by remedying the effects of past or present discrimination against women and promoting the structural, social, and cultural changes necessary to support the realization of women's substantive equality.[38] Such discriminatory measures are not prohibited, as long as they do not entail 'the maintenance of unequal or separate standards' for women and men and are discontinued when their objectives have been achieved. Thus, 'temporary' measures may result in the application of the measures for a sustained period of time, until their objectives have been realized.[39] Some specific references to temporary special measures can be found in the text of the CEDAW, such as measures in the field of education that increase women's functional literacy (Article 10(c)) and reduce the drop-out rates of female students (Article 10(f)). On many occasions the CEDAW Committee has advocated special temporary measures, such as the adoption of quotas to promote gender balance in political bodies.[40]

The CEDAW supports permanent 'special measures' to ensure that non-identical treatment of women, due to their biological differences from men, is not considered discriminatory and does not work to their disadvantage. Article 4(2) makes it clear that measures 'aimed at protecting maternity' are not discriminatory, and this point is reinforced by other

---

[34] Eg CEDAW, Arts 2(e), 2(f), 3, 5, and 6.

[35] CEDAW Committee, General Recommendation 19, HRI/GEN/1/Rev.9 (Vol II) 331, para 9.

[36] CEDAW Committee, General Recommendation 13, HRI/GEN/1/Rev.9 (Vol II) 325, para 2.

[37] CEDAW Committee, General Recommendation 24, HRI/GEN/1/Rev.9 (Vol II) 358, para 12.

[38] See further CEDAW Committee, General Recommendation 25, HRI/GEN/1/Rev.9 (Vol II) 365.

[39] General Recommendation 25, n 38, para 20.

[40] CEDAW Committee, General Recommendation 23, HRI/GEN/1/Rev.9 (Vol II) 347, para 29.

more specific provisions including measures safeguarding women's reproductive capacities in the field of employment (Article 11(1)(f)) and measures that provide women with appropriate reproductive health services (Article 12(2)). Recognizing that these provisions have a 'protective' orientation, the CEDAW Committee has emphasized that the term 'special', when used in the context of the CEDAW, breaks with the past paternalistic usage of the term to indicate that a group suffering discrimination is weak or vulnerable, and refers instead to measures designed to serve a specific human rights goal.[41] However, in practice, avoiding protective responses to women's specificities is a continuing challenge.

The third way that the CEDAW promotes women's substantive equality is by requiring that states parties address the underlying causes of women's inequality. As mentioned, religious teachings and cultural practices have often been (mis)used to reinforce dominant beliefs about women's secondary status, generating systemic discrimination against women, which may be perceived as 'natural'. To tackle systemic discrimination, Article 5(a) requires states parties to work towards 'the elimination of prejudices and customary and all other practices which are based on the idea of the inferiority or the superiority of either of the sexes or on stereotyped roles for men and women'. This obligation is echoed in other provisions, such as the requirement that gender stereotypes be removed from school programmes and textbooks (Article 10(c)) and the deeming of legal instruments to be null and void if they restrict the legal capacity of women (Article 15(3)). Article 5(b) builds further on states parties' social change obligations by requiring that they promote change in sex-stereotyped attitudes and practices in families, including by 'recognition of the common responsibility [of women and men] in the upbringing and development of their children'. Some specific aspects of this obligation are also spelled out in other provisions, such as the requirement to establish a network of childcare services 'to enable parents to combine family obligations with work responsibilities and participation in public life' (Article 11(2)(c)), and access to 'information and advice on family planning' that will help to ensure the health and well-being of families (Article 10(h)). Unfortunately, the CEDAW takes a consistently negative view of social, religious, and cultural traditions, yet it must be remembered that they can also lend valuable support to women's equality.[42]

3.2 LIMITATIONS OF THE CEDAW APPROACH

The approach taken by the CEDAW also has some limitations, four of which will be highlighted here: its continuing reliance on a comparison with men; the lack of reference to violence against women; the assumption of normative married heterosexuality; and the very limited acknowledgement of multiple and intersectional forms of discrimination. The CEDAW Committee has ameliorated many of these problems by treating the CEDAW as a dynamic instrument that must be read in light of changing circumstances, and progressively interpreting its provisions in Concluding Observations to states parties' periodic reports and in General Recommendations. However, it is difficult for these efforts to completely overcome the limitations in the CEDAW text without supporting interpretations from other human rights bodies and good faith implementation by states parties.

The first limitation is that the CEDAW still relies fundamentally on a comparison between women and men, like the Covenants. This is problematic for two reasons. First,

---

[41] General Recommendation 25, n 40, para 21.

[42] Nyamu-Musembi, 'Are Local Norms and Practices Fences or Pathways? The Example of Women's Property Rights' in An-Na'im (ed), *Cultural Transformation and Human Rights in Africa* (Zed Books, 2002) 126; Obiora, 'Feminism, Globalization, and Culture: After Beijing' (1997) 4 *Glob Legal Stud J* 355.

it does not allow women to claim rights that men do not enjoy, except as 'special measures'. Consider the example of women's reproductive rights, such as access to information, advice, and services related to family planning (Articles 10(h) and 12(1)) and the right to 'decide freely and responsibly [sic] on the number and spacing of their children' (Article 16(1)(e)), which are all to be enjoyed 'on a basis of equality of men and women'. This leaves little room, if any, for the recognition of women's specific, standalone reproductive rights, including abortion rights, unless they qualify as 'measures protecting maternity' (Article 4(2)). By contrast, the 2003 Protocol on the Rights of Women in Africa (PRWA) recognizes women's autonomous right to sexual and reproductive health, including the right to control their own fertility, to decide on the number and spacing of children, to choose any method of contraception, and to have family planning education.[43]

The CEDAW's primary reliance on comparing women with similarly situated men is also problematic because it does not address discrimination between different groups of women. For example, denying unmarried women access to reproductive technologies is prohibited by the CEDAW only if unmarried men (the relevant comparator) are able to access the technology. The comparison does not do justice to women's interests because men have very different needs for reproductive assistance than women. Another example is the cultural practice of evicting a widow from her deceased husband's family home, which is clearly adverse treatment due to sex and marital status, but is not discrimination prohibited by the CEDAW because there is no relevant male comparator.

A second limitation of the CEDAW is its lack of reference to violence against women. This is a silence that may be explained by the reliance on a comparative model, because gendered violence does not affect men in the same way as women—which is not to deny that men may also experience gendered violence. The failure in CEDAW to make specific reference to rights associated with security of the person suggests that, at the time of drafting, the prevalence of violence against women was unknown or simply accepted as the norm. Much has changed since then. The General Assembly adopted the Declaration on the Elimination of Violence Against Women in 1993, recognizing that gendered violence is 'one of the crucial social mechanisms by which women are forced into a subordinate position compared with men'.[44] In 1994, the Commission on Human Rights (now the Human Rights Council) established the mandate of the Special Rapporteur on violence against women, its causes and consequences, which continues today.[45] A couple of years earlier, in 1992, the CEDAW Committee pre-empted these developments by adopting General Recommendation 19, which interpreted gender-based violence as a form of 'discrimination against women' that is prohibited by the CEDAW. Thus, violence 'directed against a woman because she is a woman or that affects women disproportionately' breaches specific CEDAW provisions, even though the provisions do not expressly make reference to violence.[46] This approach has been applied in the jurisprudence of the CEDAW Committee under its Optional Protocol procedure, which has found violations of states obligations to eliminate discrimination against women in family relations (Article 16) where states parties have not acted positively, with due diligence, to protect complainants from domestic violence.[47]

[43] CEDAW, Art 14(1).

[44] Declaration on the Elimination of Violence Against Women, GA Res 48/104, 20 December 1993.

[45] Commission on Human Rights Res 1994/45, 4 March 1994, Chap XI, E/CN.4/1994/132. See further: <http://www.ohchr.org/EN/Issues/Women/SRWomen/Pages/SRWomenIndex.aspx>.

[46] General Recommendation 19, n 37, paras 1 and 6.

[47] *AT v Hungary*, A/60/38, Annex III (26 January 2005); *Goekce v Austria*, CEDAW/C/39/D/5/2005 (6 August 2007); *Yildrim v Austria*, CEDAW/C/39/D/6/2005 (1 October 2007); *VK v Bulgaria*, CEDAW/C/49/D/20/2008 (27 September 2011); *Jallow v Bulgaria*, CEDAW/C/52/D/32/2011 (28 August 2012).

Addressing violence against women as a human rights violation has been further expounded in three regional human rights instruments. The first, the 1994 Inter-American Convention on the Prevention, Punishment and Eradication of Violence Against Women (CPPEVAW) defines violence against women broadly as 'any act or conduct, based on gender, which causes death or physical, sexual or psychological harm or suffering to women, whether in the public or the private sphere'.[48] Importantly, this definition does not confine violence against women to a form of sex discrimination, but recognizes that it may constitute a human rights violation in itself, without the need for a male comparator. States parties must adopt a wide range of positive measures to eliminate such violence, including by applying 'due diligence' to 'prevent, investigate and impose penalties'.[49] The second regional human rights instrument to explicitly prohibit violence against women is the PRWA, which extends the definition even further by including acts which 'cause *or could cause* [women] physical, sexual, psychological, and *economic harm*', threats, and all such acts during armed conflict.[50] Violence against women is specifically recognized as a violation of the right to dignity,[51] the rights to life, integrity, and security of the person,[52] and the right to be protected from harmful practices.[53] The particular vulnerability of asylum-seeking and internally displaced women, and elderly and disabled women, is also acknowledged.[54] The Council of Europe's Convention on Preventing and Combating Violence Against Women and Domestic Violence 2011 (CPCVAW), the third regional instrument, identifies achieving women's empowerment and economic independence as one of its aims, in a new effort to counter protective responses.[55] These regional developments build on and complement the CEDAW and other international efforts.

A third limitation of the CEDAW is that, like the Covenants, women's experience of 'family life' is assumed to be married and heterosexual (Article 16(1)), except in their rights as a parent which are to be enjoyed regardless of marital status (Article 16(1)(d)). One result of the emphasis on 'marriage' and the equal rights of 'spouses' is that the diversity of family forms within which women live, including customary and de facto heterosexual and lesbian partnerships, is rendered invisible. Consequently, the text ignores human rights violations that take place within different family formations, like the unequal sharing of income and assets in a customary marriage or violence in a lesbian relationship, and fails to protect women's equal rights when a non-marital relationship breaks down. The CEDAW Committee has gone some way towards rectifying this problem by acknowledging that various forms of the family exist, by using the terminology of 'spouse or partner',[56] and by insisting that women and men be treated equally in families, whatever form they take.[57] However, it has not yet dealt explicitly with the issue of same-sex partnerships or families. Another repercussion of the CEDAW's normative focus on heterosexual marriage in the context of the family is that women's sexuality is reduced to issues of procreation, such as family planning and the spacing of children. This means that the CEDAW also fails to address the discrimination that many women face for expressing their sexuality outside marriage, whether in committed relationships, in pursuit of sexual pleasure, as lovers of other women, or as sex workers.

The fourth limitation is that the CEDAW largely treats 'women' as a homogeneous group who share the same experience of discrimination. Yet sex discrimination can

---

[48] CPPEVAW, Art 1.   [49] CPPEVAW, Art 7(b).   [50] PRWA, Art 1(j) (emphases added).

[51] PRWA, Art 3(4).   [52] PRWA, Art 4.   [53] PRWA, Art 5(d).

[54] PRWA, Arts 11(3), 22(b), and 23(b).   [55] CPCVAW, Arts 6, 12(6), and 18(3).

[56] Eg CEDAW Committee, General Recommendation 21, HRI/GEN/1/Rev.9 (Vol II) 337, para 22.

[57] CPCVAW, paras 13, 18, 29, 33, and 39.

intersect with other forms of discrimination and create experiences of discrimination that are not fully comprehended by the concept of sex discrimination. This has been called 'compound' or 'intersectional' discrimination,[58] and its most extreme forms are experienced by the most disadvantaged groups of women. While the CEDAW acknowledges some limited differences between women, on the basis of maternity for example, and age in respect of child marriage, there is only one significant exception to the general pattern of assuming homogeneity. Article 14 requires that states parties 'take into account the specific problems faced by rural women and the significant roles which rural women play in the economic survival of their families',[59] and many of the rights it goes on to enumerate do not rely on a comparison with men. This usefully enables the CEDAW Committee to draw comparisons between rural and urban women, and the Committee has interpreted 'rural' very broadly in many of its Concluding Observations in order to discuss intersectional forms of discrimination faced by women, on the basis of age, ethnicity, caste, and indigeneity.[60] The CEDAW Committee has also drawn attention to 'multiple' or 'double' discrimination faced by specific groups of women in the context of Article 5(a), which requires modification of social and cultural attitudes and practices that are inconsistent with women's equality.[61] Further, a number of General Recommendations emphasize the CEDAW's application to specific groups of women,[62] and others have stressed that special attention must be paid to the needs of women belonging to 'vulnerable' and 'disadvantaged' groups.[63] Recently, in a very positive move, the CEDAW Committee has drawn attention to intersectional discrimination under the Optional Protocol,[64] after failing to acknowledge intersectionality in four of its first five decisions on the merits which concerned immigrant or minority women.[65]

As with violence against women, the more recent regional women's rights instruments fill some of the gaps in the CEDAW. The CPPEVAW requires states parties to adopt measures that take 'special account' of women whose vulnerability to violence is compounded by such factors as their 'race or ethnic background', their 'status as migrants, refugees or displaced persons...while pregnant or...disabled, of minor age, elderly, socio-economically disadvantaged, affected by armed conflict or deprived of their freedom'.[66] The PRWA has provisions that address the rights of asylum-seeking and internally displaced women, elderly women, and women with disabilities and also recognizes specific rights that must be enjoyed by widows[67] and 'women in distress', which includes poor women, women heads of families, pregnant or nursing women, and women in detention.[68] Both instruments recognize women's diversity more fully than the CEDAW, and draw attention to the need to address the compound effects of other forms of discrimination.

---

[58] Crenshaw, 'Demarginalizing the Intersection of Race and Sex: A Black Feminist Critique of Anti-Discrimination Doctrine, Feminist Theory and Antiracist Politics' [1989] *U Chi LF* 139.

[59] There is also a reference to 'rural women' in CEDAW, Art 10(a) about vocational guidance and access to studies.

[60] Eg India, A/54/38, 1 February 2000 paras 51–3; China, A/54/38, 3 February 1999 para 294.

[61] Eg Sweden, A/56/38, 31 July 2001 para 356.

[62] CEDAW Committee, General Recommendation 18, HRI/GEN/1/Rev.9 (Vol II) 330 (disabled women); General Recommendation 26, CEDAW/C/2009/WP.1/R (women migrant workers). A General Recommendation on older women is forthcoming (at the time of writing).

[63] CEDAW Committee, General Recommendation 24, HRI/GEN/1/Rev.9 (Vol II) 358, para 6.

[64] See *Teixeira v Brazil*, CEDAW/C/49/D/17/2008 (27 September 2011) para 7.7; *Kell v Canada*, CEDAW/C/51/D/19/2008 (27 April 2012) para 10.2.

[65] See *Nguyen v The Netherlands*, A/61/38, 14 August 2006 Annex VIII; *Szijjarto v Hungary*, A/61/36, 14 August 2006 Annex VIII; *Goekce v Austria*, n 49; *Yildrim v Austria*, n 49. [66] CPPEVAW, Art 9.

[67] PRWA, Art 20. [68] PRWA, Art 24.

There is little doubt that the almost universal ratification of the CEDAW, the work of the CEDAW Committee, and the efforts of many women's rights and human rights NGOs[69] have advanced the project of making international human rights law more gender inclusive. However, the adoption of a specialist women's rights treaty has also, in many respects, reinforced women's marginalization. The high number of reservations to the CEDAW, particularly those that defeat its object and purpose, tends to undermine the idea that women's rights are as universal as 'men's'. Rather than prompting the other human rights treaty committees to take women's rights more seriously, the CEDAW has tended to have the opposite effect of reinforcing the marginalization of women's rights.[70] While a specific convention focusing on women's equality was necessary to address women's marginalization in international human rights law, it was not sufficient.

4 MAINSTREAMING WOMEN'S HUMAN RIGHTS

As a result of the CEDAW's limited impact, another major effort to advance the prospects of women successfully claiming their human rights emerged, which refocused attention on the general human rights instruments by promoting 'gender mainstreaming'.[71] The strategy was adopted by the 1993 Vienna World Conference on Human Rights and reaffirmed by the 1995 Beijing World Conference on Women. These developments prompted the chairpersons of the human rights treaty committees to commit to fully integrating gender perspectives into their working methods.[72] This led eventually to the adoption of General Comments by four treaty committees, which aim to comprehensively incorporate women's experience of human rights violations into the coverage of their respective treaty texts. This section examines each of these General Comments, noting the diversity of thinking about how to achieve gender mainstreaming that emerges. It also highlights the tenacity of protective representations of women, especially in the context of addressing gendered violence, and concludes that women are not yet constructed as fully human by international human rights law.

4.1 RE-IMAGINING THE UNIVERSAL SUBJECT: THE APPROACH OF THE HUMAN RIGHTS COMMITTEE

The Human Rights Committee led the way in 2000 with the adoption of General Comment 28 on equality between men and women.[73] The General Comment works through each of the ICCPR rights, bringing women-specific violations into the mainstream by re-imagining the subject of the ICCPR as a woman. For example, it is recognized that the right to life (Article 6) may be violated if women have no option but to resort to backyard abortions or if they are living in extreme poverty,[74] and the right to be free from torture and other cruel,

---

[69] Dairiam, 'From Global to Local: The Involvement of NGOs' in Schopp-Schilling (ed), *The Circle of Empowerment: Twenty-Five Years of the UN Committee on the Elimination of Discrimination Against Women* (Feminist Press, 2007) 313.

[70] Byrnes, 'The "Other" Human Rights Treaty Body: The Work of the Committee on the Elimination of Discrimination Against Women' (1989) 14 *YJIL* 1; Reanda, 'Human Rights and Women's Wrongs: the United Nations Approach' (1981) 3 *HRQ* 11.

[71] Bunch, 'Women's Rights as Human Rights: Towards a Re-Vision of Human Rights' (1990) 12 *HRQ* 486; Kouvo, *Making Just Rights? Mainstreaming Women's Human Rights and a Gender Perspective* (Iustus Forlag, 2004).

[72] Report of the Sixth Meeting of Persons Chairing the Human Rights Treaty Bodies, A/50/505, 4 October 1995 para 34(a)–(f).

[73] HRC, General Comment 28, HRI/GEN/1/Rev.9 (Vol I) 228.

[74] General Comment 28, n 73, para 10.

inhuman, and degrading treatment (Article 7) may be violated if a state party fails to protect women from domestic violence.[75] The General Comment clearly promotes women's
equality as a substantive concept and accepts that different treatment of women and men
may be necessary to achieve equality. The result is an ambitious and creative 'feminization'
of ICCPR rights.[76]

However, some of the problems associated with seeking to include women by reference
to their 'difference' are also evident. The extensive cataloguing of women's specific injuries
and disadvantages, particularly the emphasis on violence, threatens to reproduce women's
marginalization by inviting protective responses. Indeed, the frequent use of the language
of 'protection' is disquieting.[77] It revives the historically conditioned tendency to slide into
protective responses when thinking about women as 'victims' of gendered and sexual violence, working against legal responses that empower women as full legal subjects. This
tendency is compounded by the failure of the General Comment to identify any gendered
human rights abuses that may be specific to men, such as military conscription.

4.2 ANALYSING THE RELATIONSHIP BETWEEN GENDER AND RACIAL DISCRIMINATION: THE APPROACH OF THE COMMITTEE ON THE ELIMINATION OF RACIAL DISCRIMINATION

The Committee on the Elimination of Racial Discrimination, which monitors implementation of the International Convention on the Elimination of All Forms of Racial
Discrimination (ICERD), was initially resistant to the idea of gender mainstreaming.[78]
Despite this, General Recommendation XXV on the 'gender-related dimensions of racial
discrimination' was adopted in 2000.[79] In contrast to the Human Rights Committee's
General Comment 28, which identified the gender issues associated with each of the substantive rights recognized by the ICCPR, the ICERD Committee elaborates a methodology for analysing the relationship between gender and racial discrimination, with the
aim of developing 'a more systematic and consistent approach', in conjunction with states
parties.[80] The method requires particular consideration of gender in: (1) the form and
manifestation of racial discrimination; (2) the circumstances in which it occurs; (3) its
consequences; and (4) the availability and accessibility of remedies.[81]

This approach opens the way to a deeper understanding of the structural dimensions of
the intersection of race and gender discrimination and how they work together to inten-
sify women's inequality. The methodology is very flexible, allowing for diverse and shifting conceptions of race, which, like gender, is socially constructed. However, like General
Comment 28, the few examples of the intersectional discrimination provided are dominated by a concern with addressing violence against women,[82] also running the risk of
eliciting protective responses. While General Recommendation XXV is notable for its use

---

[75] General Comment 28, n 73, para 11.
[76] See further, Otto, ' "Gender Comment": Why Does the UN Committee on Economic, Social and Cultural Rights Need a General Comment on Women?' (2002) 14 *Can J Women & L* 1.
[77] General Comment 28, n 77, paras 8, 10, 11, 12, 16, and 22.
[78] Crooms, 'Indivisible Rights and Intersectional Identities or, "What Do Women's Human Rights Have to Do with the Race Convention?" ' (1997) 40 *Howard LJ* 619; Gallagher, 'Ending Marginalisation: Strategies for Incorporating Women into the UN Human Rights System' (1997) 19 *HRQ* 283.
[79] CERD, General Recommendation XXV, HRI/GEN/1/Rev.9 (Vol II) 287.
[80] General Recommendation XXV, n 97, para 3.   [81] General Recommendation XXV, n 79, para 5.
[82] General Recommendation XXV, n 79, para 2.

of the language of 'gender' rather than 'women', it is not at all clear that it is intended to recognize that men, as well as women, may suffer from discrimination in which race and gender intersect. The language of gender potentially enables the relational quality of the gender stereotypes, which usually privileges men and disadvantages women, to be acknowledged, pointing to the necessity of changing harmful stereotypes of both men and women. Unfortunately this potential remains inchoate in the General Recommendation.

4.3 ADDRESSING THE INEQUALITY OF BOTH WOMEN AND MEN: THE APPROACH OF THE COMMITTEE ON ECONOMIC, SOCIAL AND CULTURAL RIGHTS

A much fuller conception of 'gender' mainstreaming is evident in General Comment 16, adopted in 2005 by the Committee on Economic, Social and Cultural Rights.[83] In some respects, the approach taken is similar to General Comment 28 of the Human Rights Committee in the attention given to identifying the gender dimensions of each of the rights enumerated in the ICESCR and the emphasis on addressing gendered violence. However, its radical distinctiveness lies in its identification of men, as well as women, as potentially suffering sex discrimination and inequality in the enjoyment of ICESCR rights. For example, with respect to the right to social security, states parties are expected to guarantee 'adequate maternity leave for women, paternity leave for men, and parental leave for both men and women'.[84] General Comment 16 also recognizes that victims of domestic violence are 'primarily women', thereby acknowledging that men too may be victims.[85] This position would be highly controversial if it was a means to deny the general reality of women's inequality vis-à-vis men. However, it also has the potential to support a radical move towards recognizing men's gendered human rights abuses, as well as women's, which would help to eliminate protective approaches to women and point to the importance of changing the way 'men' are imagined in the process of re-imagining 'women' as equal.

4.4 RECOGNIZING GENDER AS A KEY FACTOR: THE APPROACH OF THE COMMITTEE AGAINST TORTURE

In 2008, the Committee against Torture adopted a General Comment on implementation obligations, which makes some important observations about the gender dimensions of the Convention Against Torture (UNCAT), conceiving the idea of gender mainstreaming even more inclusively.[86] General Comment 2 emphasizes that special attention must be given to protecting marginalized groups or individuals who are 'especially at risk of torture', including those who may be at risk because of '[race,] gender, sexual orientation, transgender identity…or any other status or adverse distinction'.[87] States parties are requested to provide additional information in their periodic reports about the implementation of UNCAT with respect to women, keeping in mind that 'gender is a key factor' that can intersect with other characteristics of a person to make them more vulnerable to torture or ill-treatment.[88] The Committee notes that women are particularly at risk in contexts that include 'deprivation of liberty, medical treatment, particularly involving reproductive decisions, and violence by private actors in communities and homes'.[89]

[83] HRI/GEN/1/Rev.9 (Vol I) 113.
[84] HRI/GEN/1/Rev.9 (Vol I) 113, para 26.   [85] HRI/GEN/1/Rev.9 (Vol I) 113, para 27.
[86] CAT, General Comment 2, HRI/GEN/1/Rev.9 (Vol II) 376.   [87] General Comment 2, n 86, para 21.
[88] General Comment 2, n 86, para 22.   [89] General Comment 2, n 86, para 22.

Notably, the Committee uses the terminology of 'gender' and takes a similar approach to the Committee on Economic, Social and Cultural Rights by observing that men too may be subject to gendered violations of UNCAT, 'such as rape or sexual violence and abuse', and, further, that men and boys, as well as women and girls, may be subject to violations 'on the basis of their actual or perceived non-conformity with socially determined gender roles'.[90] This approach is marked by the effort made to identify the specificity of human rights violations that are experienced solely or primarily by men and transgendered people, as well as by women.

While all the General Comments aimed at gender mainstreaming promote women's equal enjoyment of human rights in a substantive sense, taking their lead from the CEDAW, they also reinterpret mainstream human rights to be more inclusive of women's experience. These reinterpretations alleviate the need to compare women's experience with that of men's by reconstructing the universal standard itself, so that it is more gender-inclusive. Positive as these developments are, the real test is whether the Committees are able to integrate their new interpretations into all aspects of their work, and hold states parties accountable for their implementation. Although it is early days, the record so far has been patchy,[91] and the old urge to protect women rather than to recognize their rights continues to be seductive,[92] especially when it comes to women from the Third World.[93] The cost of women's inclusion may yet prove to be their continuing marginalization.

5 CONCLUSION

The history of women's rights in international human rights law reveals a conundrum: how to insist on the recognition of women's specific human rights abuses without reproducing women's secondary status and encouraging protective responses. While every effort to more fully recognize women's rights in the development, interpretation, and implementation of international human rights law has met with some success, these efforts have also highlighted new challenges. While anti-discrimination law can be a very powerful means of promoting women's enjoyment of human rights, the comparative standard that it relies upon presents quandaries about how best to frame, measure, and realize women's substantive equality, which have yet to be resolved. While recognizing gendered violence as a violation of women's human rights has been a massive achievement, the historical pull towards embracing protective responses highlights the challenge of promoting, instead, a rights-based response that takes women's sexual injuries seriously while also respecting women's sexual agency. While the need to take account of other forms of discrimination that intersect with or compound discrimination against women is increasingly acknowledged, there remain many conceptual and practical problems about how to make such discrimination legally cognizable and hold states parties accountable for addressing it. Finally, while gender mainstreaming has led to radical reinterpretations of mainstream human rights instruments, emphasizing the interdependence of ideas about 'men' and 'women' and the realization that women's equality depends on challenging accepted wisdom about dominant masculinities, it has also highlighted the dilemma of how fully to

---

[90] General Comment 2, n 86, para 22.   [91] Charlesworth, n 16; Kouvo, n 75.

[92] Otto, 'The Exile of Inclusion: Reflections on Gender Issues in International Law over the Last Decade' (2009) 10 *MJIL* 11.

[93] Kapur, 'The Tragedy of Victimisation Rhetoric: Resurrecting the "Native" Subject in International/ Postcolonial Feminist Legal Politics' (2001) 10 *Colum J Gender & L* 333.

embrace 'gender' as a socially constructed category and include the whole range of gender identities in its coverage. We need new thinking about legal representations of gender that challenges the dualistic and naturalized gender stereotypes that underpin gendered human rights abuses, before it will be possible for international human rights law to recognize women as fully human.

FURTHER READING

ANDERSON, 'Violence Against Women: State Responsibilities in International Human Rights Law to Address Harmful "Masculinities"' (2008) 26 *NQHR* 173.

BANDA, *Women, Law and Human Rights: An African Perspective* (Hart Publishing, 2005).

BUSS and MANJI (eds), *International Law: Modern Feminist Approaches* (Hart Publishing, 2005).

CHARLESWORTH, 'Not Waving But Drowning: Gender Mainstreaming and Human Rights in the United Nations' (2005) 18 *HHRJ* 1.

COOK and CUSACK, *Gender Stereotyping: Transnational Legal Perspectives* (University of Pennsylvania Press, 2009).

EDWARDS, 'The "Feminizing" of Torture under International Human Rights Law' (2006) 19 *LJIL* 349.

KAPUR, 'The Tragedy of Victimization Rhetoric: Resurrecting the "Native" Subject in International/Post-Colonial Feminist Legal Politics' (2002) 15 *HHRJ* 1.

MILLER, 'Sexuality, Violence against Women, and Human Rights: Women Make Demands and Ladies Get Protection' (2004) 7 *Health and HR* 16.

OTTO (ed), *Gender Issues and Human Rights*, vols I-III (Elgar, 2013).

VAN LEEUWEN, 'A Woman's Right To Decide? The United Nations Human Rights Committee, Human Rights of Women, and Matters of Human Reproduction' (2007) 25 *NQHR* 97.

USEFUL WEBSITES

Women's Human Rights Resources: <http://www.law-lib.utoronto.ca/diana/mainpage.htm>

CEDAW materials (OHCHR): <http://www2.ohchr.org/english/bodies/cedaw/index.htm>

United Nations Human Rights Treaties: <http://www.bayefsky.com/>

United Nations Entity for Gender Equality and the Empowerment of Women (UN Women): <http://www.un.org/womenwatch/daw/daw/index.html>

Women Watch (UN Inter-Agency Network on Women and Gender Equality): <http://www.un.org/womenwatch/>

International Women's Rights Action Watch (IWRAW): <http://www1.umn.edu/humanrts/iwraw/>

IWRAW Asia-Pacific (IWRAW-AP): <http://www.iwraw-ap.org/index.htm>

17

GROUP RIGHTS

Robert McCorquodale

SUMMARY

This chapter concerns the human rights of three particular groups: peoples with the right of self-determination, minorities, and indigenous peoples. The right of self-determination is a right that protects a group as a group entity in regard to their political participation, as well as their control over their economic, social, and cultural activity as a group. It is a right that applies to 'peoples' in all states and can be exercised in many ways, with most exercises of the right today being within the boundaries of a state. The right cannot be limited by the rights of others and by the general interests of the international community except in restricted circumstances. Rights of minorities can be seen as both individual and group rights, and have been the subject of increasing international human rights protection in recent years, as have the rights of indigenous peoples.

1 INTRODUCTION

1.1 GROUP RIGHTS

Most of the discussion in this book, and the focus of many of its chapters, is about the human rights of individual human beings. This is not surprising, as the historical and conceptual bases of human rights generally developed from considerations concerning the dignity and oppression of individuals, and almost all national constitutional and legislative protections of human rights have been drafted to protect the rights of individuals. Similarly, the vast majority of human rights protected in international and regional treaties, such as the right to life, the right to an adequate standard of living, the right to education, and the right to freedom of thought, protect the rights of individual human beings.

However, human rights are not limited to those of individual human beings. As long as each individual is a part of one or many groups, an individual's identities, histories, and engagements are affected by belonging to groups and by the communities within which they live. Human rights can be understood in terms of the need to protect the dignity of a group (or a 'people'), and a group's physical integrity, as well as its civil, cultural, economic, political, and social engagement. As human rights should reflect lived realities, it is necessary to see them as more than about individuals. After all, most societies accord an importance to communities, collectives, and families, and humans possess a general communal quality. International human rights law is conceived and exercised within the context of communities, with rights being limited (in all except a few instances) by the rights of others and the general interests of the relevant community. [1]

Yet in a number of situations it is a group of individuals who are discriminated against or oppressed because of the fact that they belong to a group or they have a group identity and sense of human dignity that is dependent on them belonging to a group. For example, the prohibition on genocide is a human right premised on the need to protect a group as a group from actions against the group's physical integrity and not only to protect the individual's right to life. Similarly, many indigenous communities have an identity that is dependent on them being a group rather than being a selection of individuals. Therefore, group rights (sometimes called 'collective rights') are intended to protect a group (for example, a people) from discrimination and oppression *as a group*.

1.2 GROUP RIGHTS V RIGHTS OF INDIVIDUALS

Many individual human rights do have the effect of protecting a group. For example, the right of freedom of assembly, the right to join a trade union, and the right of freedom of religion all enable groups to gather, have protection, and express their thoughts. Yet each of these rights is an individual right under international human rights law. It is an individual right exercised in concert with other individual human rights but it can only be held and claimed by an individual human being. While there is now some case law that enables legal entities, such as religious institutions and corporations, to bring claims on behalf of individuals (and perhaps even in their own right),[2] these remain individual rights that may lead indirectly to the protection of a group. They are not rights that directly protect a group as a group.

The UN Human Rights Committee considered the difference between group rights and individual rights when considering the right of self-determination (which is a group right), stating that:

> The right of self-determination is of particular importance because its realization is *an essential condition* for the effective guarantee and observance of individual human rights and for the promotion and strengthening of those rights. It is for that reason that States set forth the right of self-determination in a provision of positive law in both Covenants [the International Covenant on Civil and Political Rights and the International Covenant on Economic, Social and Cultural Rights] and placed this provision as article 1 apart from and before all of the other rights in the two Covenants.[3]

In making this statement, the Human Rights Committee both recognized the difference between group rights and individual rights, and acknowledged that when groups are subject to oppression as a group and their rights are not able to be exercised, then the individuals within those groups are also not able to exercise their individual rights. The Committee made the difference even clearer when it took the view that a group who brought a complaint under the Optional Protocol to the International Covenant on Civil and Political Rights (ICCPR-OP1) alleging a breach of the right of self-determination could not do so because the specific terms of the ICCPR-OP1 only enabled complaints by 'individuals'.[4]

---

[1] Limitations on human rights are discussed in Chapter 6.

[2] Eg *Autronic AG v Switzerland* (1990) 12 EHRR 485; *Singer v Canada*, CCPR/C/51/D/455/1991 (8 April 1993); and 155/96, *Social and Economic Rights Action Center and the Center for Economic and Social Rights (SERAC) v Nigeria*, 15th Activity Report of the ACommHPR (2001).

[3] HRC, General Comment 12, HRI/GEN/1/Rev.9 (Vol I) 183, para 1 (emphasis added).

[4] *Ominayak and the Lubicon Lake Band v Canada*, A/45/40 (Vol II) Annex IX, 1, para 32.1.

While there is some criticism of the Committee taking this stance, other international human rights treaties do not tend to contain the restriction that only individuals are able to bring a complaint.

1.3 RELEVANCE OF GROUP RIGHTS

While there are a range of group rights, such as the prohibition on genocide, the right to development, and the right to a clean environment, a specific focus of this chapter is on the right of self-determination (sometimes called the right *to* self-determination). This is because the right of self-determination is protected under the International Covenant on Civil and Political Rights (ICCPR) and the International Covenant on Economic, Social and Cultural Rights (ICESCR), it has been considered in case law and other jurisprudence, and it has wide and significant impacts across the international community, as will be shown.

The rights of minorities have similar wide and significant impacts, as there are minorities in every state. While these rights have often been seen as within the compass of individual rights, it will be shown that they are also now considered as group rights. One type of collective that has been especially affected by the development of peoples and minorities rights is indigenous peoples, and so they are also considered in this chapter.

The acknowledgment that peoples, minorities, and indigenous groups have human rights, and that their rights should be protected in international law, has taken a long time. They are still not fully understood and respected. However, they are important human rights that affect the whole of the international community. With the reality that almost every state in the world has some current or potential issue connected with group rights, it is important that these rights are understood, respected, and applied appropriately.

2 THE RIGHT OF SELF-DETERMINATION

2.1 CONCEPT

Claims have been made for centuries about matters that could now be seen in terms of self-determination, with some writers tracing it as far back as the early stages of the institution of government. However, the use of self-determination in an international legal context primarily developed during the immediate post-First World War period, with US President Wilson stating that, '[P]eoples may now be dominated and governed only by their own consent. "Self-determination" is not a mere phrase. It is an imperative principle of action, which statesmen will henceforth ignore at their peril.'[5]

At about the same time Marxist thought on national liberation took root in the USSR. The combined effect of these ideas (and others) was that self-determination, despite its vague content and the sense to which it could be applied to a range of situations, became an accepted term of use in international relations. Then in 1945 the UN Charter

---

[5] Wilson, *War Aims of Germany and Austria* (1918), reproduced in Baker, Dodd, and Leach (eds), *The Public Papers of Woodrow Wilson: War and Peace* (Harper and Brothers, 1927) 177 at 182. Wilson was supported by the British Prime Minister, Lloyd George, who declared that one reason for the UK entering the First World War had been the 'principle of self-determination' and that future territorial questions should be resolved by respecting 'the consent of the governed': address to the Trade Union Conference, 5 January 1918, reported in *The New York Times Current History* (New York) 270.

proclaimed that one of the purposes of the UN was 'respect for the principle of equal rights and self-determination of peoples'.[6]

Since that time, through resolutions of the Security Council and the General Assembly, in decisions and opinions of the International Court of Justice (ICJ), in treaties, and in state practice—some of which will be referred to below—the idea of self-determination of peoples has been restated, reinforced, and reinvigorated. It has also been used in diverse contexts, not least because 'couching political goals in the language of legal entitlement has an undisputed rhetorical appeal',[7] and has become part of international law.

2.2 DEFINITIONS

Despite the general acceptance that self-determination is part of international law, it was not until the conclusion of the two international human rights Covenants that it was accepted that self-determination was a human right and that some form of legal definition was provided. Article 1 ICCPR and ICESCR provides:

1. All peoples have the right of self-determination. By virtue of that right they freely determine their political status and freely pursue their economic, social and cultural development.

2. All peoples may, for their own ends, freely dispose of their natural wealth and resources without prejudice to any obligations arising out of international economic co-operation, based upon the principle of mutual benefit, and international law. In no case may a people be deprived of its means of subsistence.

3. The States Parties to the present Covenant, including those having responsibility for the administration of Non-Self-Governing and Trust Territories, shall promote the realization of the right of self-determination, and shall respect that right, in conformity with the provisions of the Charter of the United Nations.

The definition in Article 1(1) is largely repeated in all the subsequent international and regional human rights treaties and documents that contain a right of self-determination, although the African Charter on Human and Peoples' Rights (ACHPR) elaborates on it slightly.[8]

Yet this definition does not clarify all aspects of the right. While it is evident that it is a right that is relevant in political contexts, it is also applicable in economic, social, and cultural contexts, with, for example, Article 1(2) of the Covenants dealing with a particular economic manifestation of the right and Article 55 UN Charter referring to economic and social aspects of the right. It is also a right of peoples as distinct from individuals, although

---

[6] UN Charter, Art 1(2).

[7] Drew, 'Self-Determination, Population Transfer and the Middle-East Peace Accords' in Bowen (ed), *Human Rights, Self-Determination and Political Change in the Occupied Palestinian Territories* (Martinus Nijhoff, 1997) 127.

[8] ACHPR, Art 20 provides:
1. All peoples shall have the right to existence. They shall have the unquestionable and inalienable right to self-determination. They shall freely determine their political status and shall pursue their economic and social development according to the policy they have freely chosen.
2. Colonized or oppressed peoples shall have the right to free themselves from the bonds of domination by resorting to any means recognized by the international community.
3. All peoples shall have the right to the assistance of the States parties to the present Charter in their liberation struggle against foreign domination, be it political, economic or cultural.

the lack of further clarification as to who are the 'peoples' who have the right, has been a major ⟵
stumbling block for many diplomats and writers.

There have been many attempts to establish a definition of 'peoples'.[9] The definition often
referred to is that of an influential group of UNESCO experts:

A people for the [purposes of the] rights of people in international law, including the right
to self-determination, has the following characteristics:

(a) A group of individual human beings who enjoy some or all of the following common
features:

    (i)   A common historical tradition;

    (ii) Racial or ethnic identity;

    (iii) Cultural homogeneity;

    (iv) Linguistic unity;

    (v) Religious or ideological affinity;

    (vi) Territorial connection;

    (vii) Common economic life.

(b) The group must be of a certain number who need not be large (e.g. the people of micro
States) but must be more than a mere association of individuals within a State.

(c) The group as a whole must have the will to be identified as a people or the consciousness
of being a people—allowing that groups or some members of such groups, though sharing the foregoing characteristics, may not have the will or consciousness.

(d) Possibly the group must have institutions or other means of expressing its common
characteristics and will for identity.[10]

This definition appears to be an 'objective' one that can be applied to all relevant groups around
the world, by providing some criteria that should be met for a 'people' to be established.
However, an objective definition is impossible—and is likely to reinforce a developed-world,
colonial, male construct of a 'people'[11]—and there would be few groups who have been universally accepted as peoples having the right of self-determination (including some of those
who are in former colonies) who would meet all these criteria. This impossibility is acknowledged in paragraph (c) of the definition given here, where a 'subjective' criterion is included.
This is because a key aspect of 'self' is self-identification, where the group identifies themselves consciously as a 'people'. This is an essential part of the definition of a 'people', not least
because 'nations and peoples, like genetic populations, are recent, contingent and have been
formed and reformed constantly throughout history',[12] often due to the oppression that they
have received or to attain certain ends.[13]

---

[9] Eg Kiwanuka, 'The Meaning of "People" in the African Charter of Human and Peoples' Rights' (1988) 82
AJIL 80.

[10] Final Report and Recommendations of an International Meeting of Experts on the Further Study of the
Concept of the Right of People for UNESCO, SNS–89/CONF.602/7 (22 February 1990). For a similar definition,
see International Commission of Jurists, *Events in East Pakistan* (International Commission of Jurists, 1972) 49.

[11] See Charlesworth, Chinkin, and Wright, 'Feminist Approaches to International Law' (1991) 85 *AJIL* 613;
Gaete, 'Postmodernism and Human Rights: Some Insidious Questions' [1991] *Law and Critique* 149.

[12] Kamenka, 'Human Rights, Peoples' Rights' in Crawford (ed), *The Rights of Peoples* (Clarendon Press,
1988) 127 at 133. See also Allott, 'The Nation as Mind Politic' (1992) 24 *NYUJILP* 1361.

[13] Chinkin and Wright, 'Hunger Trap: Women, Food and Self-Determination' (1993) 14 *Michigan JIL* 262, 306,
propose that 'food, shelter, clean water, a healthy environment, peace and a stable existence must be the first priorities in how we define or "determine" the "self" of both individuals and groups, instead of the present definitions,
which are based on masculinist goals of political and economic aggrandizement and aggressive territoriality'.

In fact, in many situations, it is evident who are the 'peoples' with the right of self-determination. This can be because the relevant national constitution, legislation, or practice indicates this. For example, the Scots in the UK, the Basques in Spain, and the Aceh people in Indonesia, are all accepted as peoples with the right of self-determination. There is also, as will be shown in Section 3, universal acceptance that the right of self-determination applies to all peoples in colonial territories, as well as significant state practice that applies it beyond the colonial context. Consistent oppressive action by those in power over another group may also indicate an acceptance of the group as a 'people', not least because it may be a catalyst for the self-identification of the group as a people with the right of self-determination. External recognition by a state or group of states can be very useful for the group (such as the recognition by many states of the Palestinian people) but it is not conclusive of the group being a people for the purposes of the right of self-determination.

Indeed, if such external state recognition was conclusive it would allow the possibility of the existence of a human right (as distinct from the ability of a human right to be exercised) being dependent on the whims of governments. Above all, dependence on the government for the existence of a right would undermine the concept of a human right as being, for example, inherent in human dignity.[14]

Therefore, it is necessary to adopt a very flexible definition as to who are a 'people'. A definition is required that is broad and inclusive, not decided by states alone or imposed on a group, and is adaptable to the many circumstances that exist worldwide. The definition must respect the self-identification of a group as a people. There would need to be some territorial nexus for a 'people' with a right of self-determination. Yet a 'people' can include just a part of a population in a state and it can include groups that live across state territorial boundaries (which reflect the fact that in reality there is no 'nation-state'). It would include all those who are subject to 'alien subjugation, domination and exploitation'.[15]

If a broad and adaptable definition is adopted, then the focus on the right of self-determination under international human rights law is in relation to how and when the right can be exercised. As with all human rights, the concept of the right itself (being to protect the human dignity of the group as a group) cannot be dependent on governments or political considerrations alone. Further, a broad definition of the possessors of this human right is consistent with the need to protect as many people as possible from violations of human rights by a state, considering both the inequality of power between a state and its inhabitants and the non-reciprocal nature of human rights treaties. Such a broad definition would then be consistent with the approach to other human rights in this book.

3   THE APPLICATION OF THE RIGHT OF SELF-DETERMINATION

3.1   COLONIAL CONTEXT

From the earliest time that the UN focused on self-determination as part of international law, it applied it to colonial territories. In 1960 self-determination was considered in the context of 'the necessity of bringing to a speedy and unconditional end colonialism in all

---

[14]   See Chapter 2.

[15]   Declaration on Independence for Colonial Countries and Peoples, GA Res 1514 (XV) (14 December 1960).

its forms and manifestations'.[16] Article 1(3) ICCPR and ICESCR makes express reference to the special responsibility of colonial powers in regard to the right of self-determination:

> The States Parties to the present Covenant, including those having responsibility for the administration of Non-Self-Governing and Trust Territories, shall promote the realization of the right of self-determination, and shall respect that right, in conformity with the provisions of the Charter of the United Nations.[17]

The term 'Non-Self-Governing Territories' refers to the list of territories held by the UN that was meant to designate which were colonial territories. While this list was never comprehensive (especially as it was possible for states unilaterally to remove territories from the list), the term was a recognized UN abbreviation for colonial territories or colonies.

The ICJ has consistently held that the right of self-determination applies to all peoples in all colonial territories. In its *Namibia Opinion*, concerning the illegal presence of South Africa in Namibia, the Court's view was:

> [T]he subsequent development of international law in regard to non-self-governing territories, as enshrined in the Charter of the United Nations, made the principle of self-determination applicable to all of them.... The ultimate objective of the sacred trust was the self-determination and independence of the peoples concerned.[18]

This position was confirmed by the ICJ in the *Western Sahara Case*, with Judge Dillard stating that '[t]he pronouncements of the Court thus indicate, in my view, that a norm of international law has emerged applicable to the decolonisation of those non-self-governing territories which are under the aegis of the United Nations'.[19]

State practice confirms that the right of self-determination applies to all peoples in colonial territories. This is evident not only from the vast number of colonial territories that have exercised their right of self-determination to become new states, but also because of the acceptance by the colonial powers that they have a legal obligation to allow this exercise. For example, the British government stated in 1982:

> It is true that [the UK] took the position in the 1960s that self-determination was a principle and not a right.... Not only has my country [now] endorsed the right to self-determination in the sense of the [UN] Charter, the [International Human Rights] Covenants and the Friendly Relations Declaration [1970], but we have gone a great deal further to disprove the allegation that we are the colonial Power *par excellence*. Since General Assembly Resolution 1514 (XV) was adopted at the end of 1960, we have brought to sovereign independence and membership of [the UN] no less than 28 States. We are proud of our record, and I think we have every right to be.[20]

Some writers have concluded from this consistent state practice, *opinio juris*, and lack of any denial by states that the right of self-determination of colonial peoples is now a matter of *jus cogens*.[21]

---

[16] Declaration on Independence for Colonial Countries and Peoples, n 15, preamble.

[17] The special responsibility of colonial powers in regard to self-government of Non-Self-Governing Territories is also stated in UN Charter, Art 73.

[18] *Legal Consequences for States of the Continued Presence of South Africa in* Namibia *(South West Africa) notwithstanding Security Council Resolution 276 (1970)* [1971] ICJ Rep 16, para 52.

[19] *Western Sahara Case* [1975] ICJ Rep 12, per Judge Dillard at 121, and see Majority Opinion at paras 54–5.

[20] Statement by the UK's representative in the Security Council on 25 May 1982 (1983) 54 *BYBIL* 371–2.

[21] Eg Cassese, *Self-Determination of Peoples: A Legal Appraisal* (CUP, 1995) 140; Crawford, *The International Law Commission's Articles on State Responsibility: Introduction, Text and Commentaries* (CUP, 2002) in relation to Art 41; Saul, 'The Normative Status of Self-Determination in International Law: A Formula for Uncertainty in the Scope and Content of the Right?' (2011) 11 *HRLR* 609. See Chapter 4 for an explanation of *jus cogens*.

3.2 OUTSIDE THE COLONIAL CONTEXT

While it is clear that the right of self-determination applies to all colonial peoples as a part
of customary international law (and perhaps as a matter of *jus cogens*), there remains the
question as to whether it also applies outside the colonial context. State practice shows
that it has definitely been applied outside the colonial context. For example, when East and
West Germany were united into one state in 1990, it was expressly stated in a treaty signed
by four of the five permanent members of the UN that this was done as part of the exercise
of the right of self-determination by the German people.[22] The right of self-determination
was also referred to in the context of the dissolution of the USSR and Yugoslavia,[23] internally within states, and the ICJ confirmed that the right of self-determination applies to
the Palestinian people in its *Advisory Opinion on the Wall*.[24]

The ICJ has gone further and has declared that the right of self-determination is 'one of
the essential principles of contemporary international law' and has 'an *erga omnes* character'.[25] By having an *erga omnes* character it means that there is an obligation on *all states*
to protect and respect the right of self-determination. This makes clear that it is not only
an obligation on colonial powers and so the right applies to peoples beyond the colonial
context.

Indeed, since 1960 the right of self-determination has not been expressed in any international or regional instruments solely in the context of colonial territories but as a right of
'all peoples'. This is seen in the Declaration on Principles of International Law 1970 (which
is often considered as being internationally agreed clarifications of the principles of the
UN Charter) which provides:

> [All States should bear] in mind that subjection of peoples to alien subjugation, domi-
> nation and exploitation constitutes a violation of the principle [of equal rights and
> self-determination of peoples], as well as a denial of fundamental human rights, and is con-
> trary to the Charter of the United Nations.[26]

In fact, even the 1960 Declaration on Independence of Colonial Countries and Peoples
dealt with colonialism 'in all its forms and manifestations'. The forms and manifestations
of colonialism relevant to the application of the right of self-determination are about the
oppressive *nature* of the administrative power over a people and not simply about the
physical distance of the administering colonial power from the colonial territory. Hence,
where a group or groups in a state administer power in such a way that there is 'subjugation, domination and exploitation' of another group that oppresses, demeans, and undermines the dignity of that group, then the right of self-determination may apply to the latter
group. Therefore, the right of self-determination applies to any peoples in any territory
(including non-colonial territories) who are subjected to 'alien subjugation, domination
and exploitation'. Indeed, it would be contrary to the concept of a human right if the right

---

[22] Treaty on the Final Settlement With Respect to Germany (1990) 29 *ILM* 1186.

[23] Eg the terms of the European Community's Declaration on Yugoslavia and its Declaration on the
Guidelines on Recognition of New States in Eastern Europe and the Soviet Union (16 December 1991), (1992)
31 *ILM* 1486.

[24] *Legal Consequences of the Construction of a Wall in the Occupied Palestinian Territory* (Advisory Opinion)
[2004] ICJ Rep 136, paras 118 and 122.

[25] *East Timor Case (Portugal v Australia)* [1995] ICJ Rep 90, para 29. The HRC also requires all states
parties to the ICCPR to report on their protection of the right of self-determination: General Comment 12, n 3,
para 3.   [26] GA Res 2625(XXV) (1970) Annex.

of self-determination could only be exercised once (such as by a colonial territory) and then not again. So, all peoples in all states have the right of self-determination.

4 THE EXERCISE OF THE RIGHT OF SELF-DETERMINATION

4.1 EXTERNAL AND INTERNAL SELF-DETERMINATION

Under international human rights law, there is a concentrated focus on the *exercise* of a human right. This is usually because a particular issue has arisen due to an alleged restriction on the exercise of a right by a state. Similarly, the exercise of the right of self-determination is a crucial aspect in understanding the right.

The Declaration on Principles of International Law sets out the principal methods as to how the right of self-determination can be exercised. It provides that:

> The establishment of a sovereign and independent State, the free association or integration with an independent State or the emergence into any other political status freely determined by a people constitute modes of implementing the right of self-determination by that people.

While the vast majority of peoples in colonial territories exercised their right of self-determination by independence, this was not the only method of exercise that was either available or used. For example, the British and the Italian Somaliland colonies joined into one state of Somalia, part of the British colony of Cameroon merged with the French colony of Cameroun to form the new state of Cameroon and the remaining part joined with the existing state of Nigeria, and Palau and a number of other Pacific Ocean islands formed a free association with the USA (that is, they had general self-government but their foreign affairs and defence were controlled by the USA).

In non-colonial situations, a range of exercises of the right of self-determination have occurred. While many have been by independence, such as Bangladesh from Pakistan and Montenegro from its union with Serbia, others have been by merger (for example, the two Yemens), or by free association (for example, Bougainville with Papua New Guinea). Some have occurred after prolonged armed conflict, such as Eritrea from Ethiopia in 1993, or a period of international territorial administration, such as in Kosovo. In the latter instance, the Kosovo Assembly issued, on 17 February 2008, a unilateral declaration of independence from Serbia. A large number of states, including the UK and USA, recognized Kosovo as an independent state, while other states, including Serbia and Russia, rejected this independence on the grounds that it was contrary to international law. The ICJ was asked by the UN General Assembly to give its opinion. In the *Advisory Opinion on Kosovo*, the majority of the ICJ held:

> Whether, outside the context of non-self-governing territories and peoples subject to alien subjugation, domination and exploitation, the international law of self-determination confers upon part of the population of an existing State a right to separate from that State is, however, a subject on which radically different views were expressed...Similar differences existed regarding whether international law provides for a right of "remedial secession" and, if so, in what circumstances...The Court considers that it is not necessary to resolve these questions in the present case. The General Assembly has requested the Court's opinion only on whether or not the declaration of independence is in accordance with international law...[T]he Court considers that general international law contains no applicable

prohibition of declarations of independence. Accordingly, it concludes that the declaration of independence of 17 February 2008 did not violate general international law.[27]

This avoidance by the Court in deciding these issues has been, rightly, strongly criticized. Judge Simma took the view that:

> the Court could have delivered a more intellectually satisfying Opinion, and one with greater relevance as regards the international legal order as it has evolved into its present form, had it not interpreted the scope of the question so restrictively. To treat these questions more extensively would have demonstrated the Court's awareness of the present architecture of international law.[28]

Nevertheless, in these types of situation, there has been a change in the international relationships between the peoples exercising their right of self-determination and the original state/colonial power, as well as with other states and international actors. So these are considered exercises of *external* self-determination.

Yet, self-determination can also be exercised by *internal* means, where there is a change in the internal relationships and administrations within a state but no change in the external relationships. The Organization of Security and Co-operation in Europe (OSCE), which comprises all West and East European states, the then USSR, USA, and Canada, accepted that self-determination could be exercised by external and internal methods, when it declared:

> By virtue of the principle of equal rights and self-determination of peoples, all peoples have the right, in full freedom, to determine, when and as they wish, their internal and external political status, without external interference, and to pursue as they wish their political, economic, social and cultural development.[29]

The Declaration on Principles of International Law expresses internal self-determination as being where 'a government [is] representing the whole people belonging to the territory without distinction as to race, creed or colour'. The Canadian Supreme Court considered that internal self-determination in relation to the peoples of the province of Québec enabled the 'residents of the province freely [to] make political choices and pursue economic, social and cultural development within Québec, across Canada, and throughout the world. The population of Québec is [and should be] equitably represented in legislative, executive and judicial institutions.'[30]

Accordingly, there are a range of internal exercises of the right of self-determination. For example, outside the colonial context there has been devolution of some legislative powers to Scotland and Wales in the UK, control over cultural, linguistic and other matters within the Swiss cantons, and a form of federalism in Bosnia-Herzegovina and Iraq. These methods are often called forms of autonomy or governance. In many instances, the method of exercise has been by agreement with the government for significant autonomy within a state, such as the Crimea in Ukraine, Mindanao in the Philippines, and the northern regions of Mali.[31]

---

[27] *Accordance with International Law of the Unilateral Declaration of Independence in Respect of Kosovo, Advisory Opinion*, [2010] ICJ Reports, paras 82–4.

[28] Kosovo Advisory Opinion, n 27, Declaration of Judge Simma, para 7. See also, for example, Hannum, 'The Advisory Opinion on Kosovo: An Opportunity Lost, or a Poisoned Chalice Refused?' (2011) 24 *Leiden JIL* 155.

[29] Helsinki Final Act 1975, Principle VIII.

[30] *Reference Re Secession of Québec* [1998] 2 SCR 217, (1998) 37 ILM 1342, para 136.

[31] For details of these and other exercises, see Weller, 'Settling Self-Determination Conflicts: Recent Developments' (2009) 20 *EJIL* 111.

What is shown by all these examples is that there are many possible exercises by peoples of their right of self-determination. While independence—called 'secession' when it is from an existing independent state—is often seen as the only option in non-colonial contexts, it is but *one option* of very many forms of exercise, and not normally the first option lawfully able to be exercised under international law. The Supreme Court of Canada made this clear when it stated that:

> The recognized sources of international law establish that the right to self-determination of a people is normally fulfilled through internal self-determination—a people's pursuit of its political, economic, social and cultural development within a framework of an existing state. A right to external self-determination (which in this case potentially takes the form of the assertion of a right to unilateral secession) arises in only the most extreme of cases and, even then, under carefully defined circumstances.[32]

What the court is indicating is that, in most instances outside the colonial context, independence will not be considered to be the legitimate first step in the exercise of the right of self-determination. However, should other methods of exercise, such as internal self-determination, be made impossible due to the actions of the state, and if there is increased oppression of the group as a group, then it may be argued that, in those limited circumstances, the people could exercise their right of self-determination by seeking independence as a last resort.[33]

In any event, there must be flexibility in the forms of exercise of the right of self-determination. In many instances, the exercise will be dependent on the particular context and the resolution of a dispute. For example, the Badinter Committee, which was established by the European Community (now European Union) to clarify the legal position during the dissolution of Yugoslavia, held that:

> In the Committee's view one possible consequence of [the right of self-determination] might be for the members of the Serbian population in Bosnia-Herzegovina and Croatia to be recognized under agreements between the Republics as having the nationality of their choice, with all the rights and obligations which that entails with respect to the states concerned.[34]

This suggestion of different nationalities and sovereign powers within one state is a possibility that should be explored. It could also operate across states, as has happened to some extent with the peace agreements concerning Northern Ireland, where both the British and Irish governments were involved in the key negotiations and both signed the various peace agreements, even though Northern Ireland is entirely within the UK. While such solutions challenge traditional notions of sovereignty, they acknowledge the breadth of impact of the right of self-determination and seek to provide effective means to exercise the right as fully as possible.

4.2 PROCEDURES FOR EXERCISING THE RIGHT OF SELF-DETERMINATION

The exercise of the right of self-determination must be by the people themselves. The ICJ confirmed this when it emphasized 'that the application of the right of self-determination

---

[32] *Reference Re Secession of Québec*, n 30, paras 112, 126.

[33] See *Aaland Islands Opinion*, International Committee of Jurists (1920) LNOJ Spec Supp 3; *Loizidou v Turkey* (1997) 23 EHRR 513, per Judges Wildhaber and Ryssdal.

[34] Badinter Committee, Opinion 2, (1992) 31 ILM 1495, para 3.

requires a free and genuine expression of the will of the peoples concerned'.[35] In most instances the will of the people can be determined by a popular consultation, such as by referendum or elections. For example, the Badinter Committee decided that the will of the peoples in Bosnia-Herzegovina had to be ascertained, possibly by a referendum carried out under international supervision.[36]

However, there may be exceptional circumstances where there is no consultation, such as where the position is clear in all the circumstances. For example, during the dissolution of the USSR few referenda were held. Yet consultations can be manipulated. When Indonesia sought to integrate West Papua, which had been under a separate Dutch colonial administration from the rest of Indonesia, just a few indigenous leaders were asked their views as to whether they would accept Indonesian control and, probably under military threats, agreed to accept this control. Similarly, the people of Hong Kong were not fully consulted about the transfer of sovereignty of that separate, distinctive region to China. Even if the geopolitical situation is one where the choices of the people may be limited, they must be able to make a free and genuine decision on a clear question, which is their own decision and is not imposed by governments or others. In ensuring that the genuine will of the people is clear, it is important that the views of all within the group, including those of women and minorities, are heard and listened to equally.

In regard to the majority needed at a popular consultation, it must be at least 50 per cent plus one. It is not clear if this should be the majority of all people eligible to vote, the majority of people who do vote, or if it should be both or some other majority. The decision on the necessary majority and form of public consultation is important, especially as the numbers voting can be affected by a boycott (for example, by smaller groups who may seek a different exercise of their right of self-determination) or other circumstances. The practice during the dissolution of Yugoslavia varied considerably. In Bosnia-Herzegovina, it was assumed that 50 per cent plus one was sufficient and a boycott by the Serbian population (who comprised over 30 per cent of the population) did not affect the result, with over 60 per cent of all those eligible to vote voting in favour of independence. In Montenegro the EU stated that there had to be a majority of 55 per cent of votes cast and there had to be a participation of at least 50 per cent plus one of those eligible to vote. This required majority was probably based on the opinion polls suggesting that approximately half of the population supported independence while a relatively large share of the population strongly opposed it.[37]

The actual voters in the referendum may not always be easy to decide. This is seen in the debate over which people to include in a referendum on Western Sahara, being primarily whether those who could vote was limited to those who were living in Western Sahara at the time of the ICJ opinion or if it could include those (mainly Moroccans) who have moved there since.[38] Further, even if a majority of the people choose to exercise their right of self-determination by seeking secession from a state, this will not automatically lead to that result (though it may give a strong mandate to a people in their consultations with the relevant government), as there can be limitations on the exercise of the right of self-determination.

---

[35] *Western Sahara*, n 19, para 55.   [36] Badinter Committee, Opinion 4, (1992) 31 ILM 1495, para 4.
[37] See, Vidmar, *Democratic Statehood in International Law* (Hart, 2013).   [38] *Western Sahara*, n 19.

5 LIMITATIONS ON THE EXERCISE OF THE RIGHT OF SELF-DETERMINATION

5.1 RIGHTS OF OTHERS

Almost all human rights (with the exception of absolute rights such as the prohibition on torture) have limitations on their exercise. These limitations are to protect the rights of others or the general interests of the society (such as public order and public health). The right of self-determination is a human right and, because it is not an absolute right, it has limitations on its exercise. These are limitations on the ability of the peoples with the right to exercise that right fully and legitimately under international law.

In relation to the limitation in regard to the rights of others, each of the two international human rights Covenants provides:

> Nothing in the present Covenant may be interpreted as implying for any State, group or person any right to engage in any activity or perform any act aimed at the destruction of any of the rights and freedoms recognized herein or at their limitation to a greater extent than is provided for in the present Covenant.[39]

This limitation applies to the right of self-determination. Therefore, where there is another people with the right of self-determination within the state or region or a people who are few in number with the right of self-determination within a larger population (as with most colonial territories), then the right is limited in its exercise in order to take into account the right of the other people. As shown in other chapters, this right is limited only to the extent to which it enables all rights to be exercised as fully as possible in the circumstances.

An example of the operation of this limitation is found in the decision of the Canadian Supreme Court concerning the potential secession (through the exercise of the right of self-determination) of the people of the province of Québec. The Court noted that the rights of the indigenous ('aboriginal') peoples in the province were also affected:

> We...acknowledg[e] the importance of the submissions made to us respecting the rights and concerns of aboriginal peoples in the event of a unilateral secession, as well as the appropriate means of defining the boundaries of a seceding Québec with particular regard to the northern lands occupied largely by aboriginal peoples. However, the concern of aboriginal peoples is precipitated by the asserted right of Québec to unilateral secession. In light of our finding that there is no such right applicable to the population of Québec, either under the Constitution of Canada or at international law, but that on the contrary a clear democratic expression of support for secession would lead under the Constitution to negotiations in which aboriginal interests would be taken into account, it becomes unnecessary to explore further the concerns of the aboriginal peoples in this Reference.[40]

The Court not only acknowledged the rights of the indigenous peoples in this passage but also the human rights and constitutional rights of other parts of Canada. It determined that, even if there had been a clear majority of the people of Québec who wished to secede, they could not do so without negotiations with the other parts of Canada. However, this does not necessarily give a permanent veto power to the other parts of Canada, as the internal right of self-determination of the people of Québec must not be so restricted.

---

[39] ICESCR and ICCPR, Art 5(1).   [40] *Reference Re Secession of Québec*, n 30, para 139.

5.2 TERRITORIAL INTEGRITY

The limitation on the exercise of the external right of self-determination that is most often asserted by governments is 'territorial integrity'. This is a claim that asserts that the state itself should not be divided up and is broadly based on the general interests of international peace and security. This limitation on the right of self-determination was expressed in the Declaration on Principles of International Law:

> Nothing in the foregoing paragraph [recognizing the right of self-determination] shall be construed as authorizing or encouraging any action which would dismember or impair, totally or in part, the territorial integrity or political unity of sovereign and independent States conducting themselves in compliance with the principle of equal rights and self-determination of peoples as described above and thus possessed of a government representing the whole people belonging to the territory without distinction as to race, creed or colour.

This is an important potential limitation on the exercise of the right. However, it is only a justifiable limitation in certain situations, namely when an exercise of external self-determination (such as independence) is being sought and when a state is 'possessed of a government representing the whole people belonging to the territory without distinction as to race, creed or colour'. In other words, it can only be a legally justifiable limitation on the exercise of the right of external self-determination when a state is *already* enabling full internal self-determination for those people.

A particular aspect of this limitation on the exercise of the right of self-determination is the international legal principle of *uti possidetis juris*. This principle provides that states emerging from colonial administrative control must accept the pre-existing colonial boundaries. Its purpose is to achieve stability of territorial boundaries and to maintain international peace and security. This was made clear by a Chamber of the ICJ:

> The maintenance of the territorial *status quo* in Africa is often seen as the wisest course, to preserve what has been achieved by peoples who have struggled for their independence, and to avoid a disruption which would deprive the continent of the gains achieved by much sacrifice. The essential requirement of stability in order to survive, to develop and gradually to consolidate their independence in all fields, induced African states judiciously to consent to the respecting of colonial frontiers.[41]

While this has been uniformly accepted as a principle applicable solely to colonial territories, it was surprisingly applied by the Badinter Committee to the former Yugoslavia.[42] This latter application was probably incorrect, as it confused historically established boundaries with colonial boundaries (as the former will not have resulted from colonial determinations). There is some scope for considering that historically established boundaries (as was the case in much of the former Yugoslavia and the USSR) may be accepted as *prima facie* the appropriate territorial boundaries on independence even in non-colonial contexts, unless there are agreements to the contrary.

The principle of *uti possidetis juris* may appear to be a sound one in terms of preserving international peace and security at the time of independence. However, it has not prevented many boundary disputes.[43] This is mainly because many of these boundaries were created to preserve the interests of the colonial states and were not related to natural or

---

[41] *Frontier Dispute Case* (*Burkina Faso v Mali*) [1986] ICJ Rep 554 (Chamber of the ICJ), para 25.

[42] Badinter Committee, Opinion 2, n 34, para 1.

[43] See Craven, *The Decolonization of International Law* (OUP, 2007).

cultural boundaries understood by the peoples on the ground. As one of the architects of these boundary determinations said at the time:

> We have been engaged...in drawing lines upon maps where no white man's feet have ever trod; we have been giving away mountains and rivers and lakes to each other, but we have only been hindered by the small impediment that we never knew exactly where those mountains and rivers and lakes were.[44]

The ICJ recognized these problems when they stated that '*uti possidetis juris* is essentially a retrospective principle, investing as international boundaries administrative limits intended originally for quite other purposes'.[45] It could be argued that adoption of the principle today gives legitimacy to political or diplomatic actions purely on the basis that those actions occurred during the colonial era and were made without taking the views of the people on the territory into account.[46]

Therefore, the principle of *uti possidetis juris* is of questionable legitimacy as a limitation on the right of self-determination. It should only apply, if at all, in (the now very few) situations of decolonization or, perhaps, where the states involved in a dispute expressly choose to use a colonial boundary as relevant evidence for a boundary delimitation.[47]

5.3 OTHER LIMITATIONS

There are two other potential limitations on the exercise of the right of self-determination that are often raised: competing claims over the relevant territory by states; and the use of of force. It is not uncommon for there to be a situation where more than one state asserts sovereignty over a territory where there are people with a right of self-determination. The ICJ recognized this situation in the *East Timor Case*, where it accepted that Portugal, as the colonial power, and Indonesia, as the occupying power, had forms of sovereignty over the same territory, as did the people of East Timor, who had the right of self-determination.[48] In many instances, a state will assert that an early treaty enables it to gain sovereignty (as did China in relation to Hong Kong and as Spain does in relation to Gibraltar), notwithstanding the wishes of the people of that territory. This situation was considered in the *Western Sahara Case*:

> [T]he consultation of the people of a territory awaiting decolonization is an inescapable imperative.... Thus even if integration of territory was demanded by an interested State, as in this case, it could not be had without ascertaining the freely expressed will of the people— the very *sine qua non* of all decolonization.[49]

Therefore, even where there may be a lawful competing claim by another state over a particular territory, the peoples on that territory still have a right of self-determination that they must be able to exercise.

In relation to the use of force, it is not uncommon that the peoples seeking to exercise their right of self-determination use force and have force used against them.

---

[44] Lord Salisbury, speaking in 1890, as quoted in the Separate Opinion of Judge Ajibola, in *Territorial Dispute (Libya v Chad)* [1994] ICJ Rep 6, 53.

[45] *Land, Island and Maritime Dispute (El Salvador v Honduras)* [1992] ICJ Rep 355, 388.

[46] See *Frontier Dispute (Burkina Faso v Niger)* [2013] ICJ Rep, Declaration of Judge Bennouna.

[47] *Frontier Dispute (Burkina Faso v Niger)*, n 46, Judgment, para 63.

[48] *East Timor (Portugal v Australia)* [1995] ICJ Rep 90, para 32.

[49] *Western Sahara Case*, n 19, per Judge Nagendra Singh, 81.

The general position appears to be that set out in the Declaration on Principles of International Law:

> Every State has the duty to refrain from any forcible action which deprives peoples referred to above in the elaboration of the present principle of their right to self-determination and freedom and independence. In their actions against and resistance to such forcible action in pursuit of the exercise of their right to self-determination, such peoples are entitled to seek and to receive support in accordance with the purposes and principles of the Charter of the United Nations.

This makes clear that a state cannot use disproportionate force to prevent the exercise of the right of self-determination (which was one basis of criticism about Serbia's actions during the dissolution of Yugoslavia). The people themselves are entitled to support from other states when forcible action occurs against them as a people. That support must be in accordance with the purpose and principles of the UN Charter, so occupation by one state to 'support' a people's right of self-determination in another state would not be lawful. Significantly, when the Protocols to the Geneva Conventions 1949 were agreed in 1977, its protection extended to wars of national liberation, being 'armed conflicts which peoples are fighting against colonial domination and alien occupation and against racist regimes in the exercise of their right of self-determination.'[50] The restrictions on the use of force against peoples seeking to exercise the right of self-determination do not seem to restrict the peoples themselves using force to assert their right of self-determination, such as the people of Eritrea, though other human rights issues may then arise as their force cannot infringe the human rights of others, such as minorities.

6 MINORITIES

6.1 DEFINING 'MINORITIES'

Article 27 ICCPR and the Declaration on the Rights of Persons Belonging to National or Ethnic, Religious and Linguistic Minorities (Declaration on Minority Rights) provide protections for those who are 'ethnic, religious or linguistic' minorities. The Special Rapporteur of the UN Sub-Commission on Prevention of Discrimination and Protection of Minorities determined that:

> [Minorities are groups who are] numerically inferior to the rest of the population of a State, in a nondominant position, whose members—being nationals of the State—possess ethnic, religious, or linguistic characteristics differing from those of the rest of the population and show, if only implicitly, a sense of solidarity, directed towards preserving their culture, traditions, religion or language.[51]

However, there are other minorities who may be excluded from this definition, and it is not clear how minorities are determined. Are they the minority within the territorial boundaries of a state or are they minorities in a region within a state if that region has some of its own governance (or autonomy)? What if there is no majority as such because it is a multi-ethnic state or if the minority has been created by immigration? What about issues of integration and assimilation?[52] Indeed,

---

[50] Protocol Additional to the Geneva Conventions of 12 August 1949, and Relating to the Protection of Victims of International Armed Conflicts (Protocol I), Art 1(4).

[51] Capotorti, UN Special Rapporteur, Study on the Rights of Persons Belonging to Ethnic, Religious and Linguistic Minorities, E/CN.4/Sub.2/384/Rev.1 (1979), para 242.

[52] For example, the European Court of Human Rights has noted that, as a result of their turbulent history and constant uprooting, the Roma people have become a specific type of disadvantaged and vulnerable minority, and require special protection: see *Koky and Others v Romania*, App no 13642/03, Judgment of 12 June 2012.

[t]he difficulty in arriving at a widely acceptable definition lies in the variety of situations in which minorities live. Some live together in well-defined areas, separated from the dominant part of the population. Others are scattered throughout the country. Some minorities have a strong sense of collective identity and recorded history; others retain only a fragmented notion of their common heritage.[53]

Therefore, any determination as to the existence of a minority must take into account objective elements, such as shared ethnicity, language, or religion, and subjective considerations, such as the self-identification by individuals as members of a minority. While the Declaration on Minority Rights (see Section 6.2) is devoted to national, ethnic, religious, and linguistic minorities, it is also important to combat multiple discrimination and to address situations where a person belonging to a national, ethnic, religious, or linguistic minority is also discriminated against on other grounds such as gender, disability, or sexual orientation. Similarly, it is important to keep in mind that, in many states, minorities are often found to be among the most marginalized groups in society and severely affected by, for example, pandemic diseases, such as HIV and AIDS, and in general have limited access to health services. Undoubtedly, the state-focused nature of the international human rights legal system means that it is largely minorities within a state as a whole who are protected by this right.

6.2 RIGHTS OF MINORITIES

At the same time that self-determination was being developed as part of international law, rights relating to minorities were being set out in treaties. At the Paris Peace Conference in 1919 after the First World War a number of treaties were drafted to protect minorities in the new states being created, as a condition for settlement of territorial boundaries.[54] The obligations to protect minorities under these treaties largely related to giving minorities some autonomy.

However, significant development of minority rights did not occur until the adoption of the Article 27 ICCPR, which provides:

> In those States in which ethnic, religious or linguistic minorities exist, persons belonging to such minorities shall not be denied the right, in community with the other members of their group, to enjoy their own culture, to profess and practice their own religion, or to use their own language.

Subsequently, the Declaration on Minority Rights was adopted by the General Assembly in 1992.[55] The Declaration provides guidance about the development of law in this area—as do some regional treaties in this field.[56] There is now probably a customary international law obligation on all states to protect the rights of minorities.[57]

---

[53] OHCHR, *Minority Rights: International Standards and Guidance for Implementation* (2010) 2.

[54] See Macklem, 'Minority Rights in International Law' (2008) 6 *IJConL* 531; Berman, 'But the Alternative is Despair: European Nationalism and the Modernist Renewal of International Law' (1992–3) 106 *Harvard LR* 1792. [55] A/RES/47/135/Annex (18 December 1993).

[56] European Charter for Regional and Minority Languages; Framework Convention for the Protection of National Minorities; Document of the Copenhagen Meeting of the Conference on the Human Dimension of the Conference (now Organization) for Security and Co-operation in Europe, para 35; and Establishment of the OSCE High Commissioner on National Minorities, Helsinki Summit of Heads of State, 9–10 July 1992. In addition, protections of the rights of minorities were contained in the EC documents regarding the dissolution of the former Yugoslavia and the former USSR, and were applied by the Badinter Committee: EC's Declaration on Yugoslavia and its Declaration on the Guidelines on Recognition of New States in Eastern Europe and the Soviet Union (16 December 1991). [57] Badinter Committee Opinion 2, n 34, para 2.

6.3 EXERCISE OF MINORITY RIGHTS

The types of rights for which minorities have protection are, as Article 27 ICCPR provides, 'to enjoy their own culture, to profess and practice their own religion, or to use their own language'. The Declaration on Minority Rights adds to these: the rights to participate in cultural, religious, social, economic, and public life; to participate in decisions on the national and, where appropriate, regional level; and to associate with other members of their group and with persons belonging to other minorities.

In some instances the exercise of minority rights does raise issues of conflict between the individual and the group. In the case of *Lovelace*,[58] the claim by a divorced indigenous Canadian to return to the indigenous land was upheld by the Human Rights Committee despite Canadian law (intending to protect the indigenous minority) precluding her from so doing. However, a Swedish law that protected the identity of the Sami minority as a whole by revoking the reindeer husbandry rights of those who pursued more lucrative work was held to be valid despite the consequent restriction imposed on the individual Sami.[59] The Human Rights Committee's view was that 'a restriction upon the right of an individual member of a minority must be shown to have a reasonable and objective justification and to be necessary for the continued viability and welfare of the minority as a whole'.[60] Therefore, there are times when the minority rights protection of an individual will be limited by the broader interest of the group as a whole. These examples also show that indigenous peoples may be able to assert their human rights through the use of minority rights protections.[61]

6.4 INDIVIDUAL V GROUP RIGHTS

The concept of human rights of minorities embodies both the protection of the rights of individuals who are part of a minority group and of the minority group as a group, according minorities a collective right to enjoy the common traits of their group. There are two views as to how these rights should be approached. The individual rights approach to minority rights argues that such rights must be vested in, and be exercised by, the individual members claiming affiliation with the minority group rather than the minority group itself. In contrast, the group rights approach recognizes that the collective qualities that the minority possess, such as their group culture and their group language (being an inherent part of their human dignity), distinguishes them from the majority and so requires them to be protected as a group. However, it should be noted that, under both approaches, who is a minority may change over time and location, and this makes the right somewhat contingent on historical circumstances, which is unusual for a human right.[62]

It is clear that Article 27 ICCPR is solely an individual right for those who are part of a minority. For example, the Human Rights Committee has rejected group claims based on Article 1 (right of self-determination), as discussed already, but accepted the same claim under Article 27 as long as it was argued as an individual right.[63] However, there is a good argument that where 'national' minorities are concerned then treating the right as a group right is the appropriate approach. Indeed, it is strongly argued that minorities can form a 'people' for

---

[58] *Sandra Lovelace v Canada*, A/36/40 at 166 (1981).

[59] *Ivan Kitok v Sweden*, CCPR/C/33/D/197/1985 (27 July 1988); *Handölsdalen Sami Village and others v Sweden* App no 39013/04, Judgment of 30 March 2010; Report of the UN Special Rapporteur James Anaya, The situation of the Sami peoples in the Sápmi region of Norway, Sweden and Finland, A/HRC/18/XX/Add.Y (2011).   [60] *Ivan Kitok*, n 59, para 15.

[61] It has been argued that the UN approach has been to accommodate the rights of indigenous peoples but to seek assimilation of minorities more generally: Kymlicka, 'The Internationalization of Minority Rights' (2008) 6 *IJConL* 5.

[62] See Macklem, n 54.   [63] *Ominayak and the Lubicon Lake Band*, n 4, 27.

the purposes of the right of self-determination, especially as the definitions for each group are very similar, the right of self-determination is now more commonly exercised by internal means, and many minorities use the language of self-determination.[64] For example, the Badinter Committee considered that the shared ethnic, religious, and linguistic background of Serbians from Bosnia-Herzegovina and Croatia with Serbians in Serbia did not prevent them from being a 'people' for the purposes of the right of self-determination even though they had specific minority rights protection as well.[65] While the exercise by a minority of their right of self-determination may be limited to internal self-determination, in that minority groups would usually seek to exercise their right by enabling some degree of autonomy over matters of relevance to their culture, language, religion, or ethnic identity, it does not mean that they do not possess a right of self-determination.

7 INDIGENOUS PEOPLES

7.1 DEFINING 'INDIGENOUS PEOPLES'

There are significant similarities between minorities and indigenous peoples. Indigenous peoples have also been in a non-dominant position, and their cultures, languages, and religious traditions are normally different from the majority in the societies in which they live. International law has tended to recognize and protect indigenous rights separately. For example, the ILO adopted in 1957 and 1989 two treaties, ILO Convention No. 107 concerning Indigenous and Tribal Populations and ILO Convention No. 169 concerning Indigenous and Tribal Peoples, which apply to members of 'semi-tribal or tribal populations', 'tribal peoples', and 'groups regarded as indigenous', with specific characteristics.

However, no definition of 'indigenous peoples' has unanimously been adopted by the international community. Since the importance of maintaining their distinct identities and characteristics under the self-identification principle was accepted, the idea of a formal definition has deliberately been rejected.[66] Nevertheless, the recognition and protection of the rights of indigenous peoples under international law has not depended on a formal definition, and their main characteristics have been outlined widely in different instruments. The UN Working Group on Indigenous Populations listed the relevant factors to the understanding of the concept of 'indigenous', which have also been taken into account by international organizations and legal experts:

(a) Priority in time, with respect to the occupation and use of a specific territory;

(b) The voluntary perpetuation of cultural distinctiveness, which may include the aspects of language, social organization, religion and spiritual values, modes of production, laws and institutions;

(c) Self-identification, as well as recognition by other groups, or by State authorities, as a distinct collectivity; and

(d) An experience of subjugation, marginalization, dispossession, exclusion or discrimination, whether or not these conditions persist.[67]

---

[64] Thornberry, *International Law and the Rights of Minorities* (OUP, 1991).

[65] Badinter Committee, Opinion 2, n 34.

[66] See Workshop on data collection and disaggregation for Indigenous Peoples, 'The Concept of Indigenous Peoples, Background prepared by the Secretariat of the Permanent Forum on Indigenous Issues', PFII/2004/WS.1/3 (2004). My thanks to Gaia Hernández Palacios for her research on this section.

[67] Working Group on Indigenous Populations, Working paper by the Chairperson-Rapporteur, Mrs. Erica-Irene A. Daes, on the concept of 'indigenous people', E/CN.4/Sub.2/AC.4/1996/2 (1996).

7.2 THE RIGHTS OF INDIGENOUS PEOPLES

The main concern in relation to indigenous peoples has been the preservation of their views and traditions as a group:

Under the basic principles of universality, equality and non-discrimination, indigenous peoples are entitled to the full range of rights established under international law. However, indigenous peoples, as collectivities, have distinct and unique cultures and world views, and their current needs may differ from those of the mainstream population. Their equal worth and dignity can only be assured through the recognition and protection of not only their individual rights, but also their collective rights as distinct groups. It is when these rights are asserted collectively that they can be realized in a meaningful way. This has led to the development of a separate body of international instruments for the recognition and protection of the rights of indigenous peoples.[68]

Thus, indigenous peoples are entitled to the full range of individual human rights, including protection from discrimination, rights in relation to children, and cultural rights, as well as the rights of the indigenous peoples as a group.

The ILO Conventions remain the only international binding instruments that specifically provide a detailed list of rights and obligations of states in respect of indigenous peoples. The ILO Convention No. 107 covered a wide range of issues, such as traditionally occupied lands; social, economic, and cultural development; recruitment and conditions of employment; and social security and health. However, it had an integrationist approach that was gradually seen as outdated and so was modified by the ILO Convention No. 169, on the basis of the recognition of, and respect for, ethnic and cultural diversity of indigenous peoples as permanent societies. ILO Convention No. 169 acknowledges the rights of indigenous peoples to identity (in relation to the recognition of their legal capacity or juridical status), territory, autonomy, participation in the political and social national life, physical welfare, and cultural integrity.

The UN Declaration on the Rights of Indigenous Peoples 2007 represents the most comprehensive response to the issue of indigenous peoples at the universal level. The Declaration proclaims:

Article 1

Indigenous peoples have the right to the full enjoyment, as a collective or as individuals, of all human rights and fundamental freedoms as recognized in the Charter of the United Nations, the Universal Declaration of Human Rights and international human rights law.

Article 3

Indigenous peoples have the right to self-determination. By virtue of that right they freely determine their political status and freely pursue their economic, social and cultural development.

Article 4

Indigenous peoples, in exercising their right to self-determination, have the right to autonomy or self-government in matters relating to their internal and local affairs, as well as ways and means for financing their autonomous functions.

Its provisions are compatible with ILO Convention No. 169, although it does not provide a mechanism to monitor its implementation and it does not have a legally binding character. Nonetheless, the Declaration has been influential and its provisions have been

---

[68] UN Development Group, Guidelines on Indigenous Peoples Issues (2008) at 6.

reflected in some national laws,[69] and in the decisions of the Inter-American Court of Human Rights.[70] It is, therefore, clear that there is a general consensus, based on accept-ance of the UN Declaration and other state practice, that indigenous peoples have the right of self-determination.

In relation to other group rights of indigenous peoples, the Inter-American Court of Human Rights has accepted a right to collective property, noting the existence of a special relationship between the indigenous peoples and their traditional lands and resources:

> Among indigenous peoples there exists a communitarian tradition related to a form of col-lective land tenure, inasmuch as land is not owned by individuals but by the group and the community... [T]he protection of the territories of indigenous and tribal peoples also stems from the need to guarantee the security and continuity of their control and use of natural resources, which in turn allows them to maintain their lifestyle... This connection between territory and natural resources that indigenous and tribal peoples have traditionally main-tained, one that is necessary for their physical and cultural survival and the development and continuation of their worldview, must be protected under Article 21 of the Convention so that they can continue living their traditional lifestyle, and so that their cultural identity, social structure, economic system, customs, beliefs and traditions are respected, guaranteed and protected by States.[71]

The Court has also developed a system of reparations that are applicable in the cases of violations of indigenous peoples' rights.[72]

7.3 EXERCISE OF INDIGENOUS PEOPLES' RIGHTS

The exercise of indigenous peoples' rights follows similar patterns to those seen with regard to the right of self-determination and minority rights, with the same diversity of means of exercise. In addition, there is a specific right that is considered to be essential for protecting indigenous peoples, which finds its origins in the right to self-determination and has been recognized as a general international law obligation: consultation.

Because of their particular economic and social characteristics, including their vulner-able situation, indigenous peoples have the right to be consulted about decisions affecting their land. The Inter-American Court of Human Rights has stated:

> The Court has established that in order to ensure the effective participation of the members of an indigenous community or people in development or investment plans within their ter-ritory, the State has the obligation to consult the said community in an active and informed manner, in accordance with its customs and traditions, within the framework of continuing communication between the parties. Furthermore, the consultations must be undertaken in good faith, using culturally-appropriate procedures and must be aimed at reaching an agreement. In addition, the people or community must be consulted in accordance with

---

[69] Impacts on national law include Bolivia incorporating the Declaration into its Constitution on 7 November 2007 (adopted as Bolivian National Law 3760 on the Rights of Indigenous Peoples) and the Belize Supreme Court deciding that the property provisions of the Declaration embodied 'general principles of inter-national law' that had the same force as a treaty: *Aurelio Cal and the Maya Village of Santa Cruz v Attorney General of Belize; and Manuel Coy and Maya Village of Conejo v Attorney General of Belize*, (Consolidated) Claim Nos 171 and 17 (18 October 2007).

[70] *Kichwa Indigenous People of Sarayaku v Ecuador*, IACtHR Series C No 245 (27 June 2012) para 217.

[71] *Kichwa Indigenous People of Sarayaku*, n 70, paras 145–6.

[72] Eg *Saramaka People v Suriname*, IACtHR Series C No 172 (28 November 2007).

their own traditions, during the early stages of the development or investment plan, and not only when it is necessary to obtain the community's approval, if appropriate. The State must also ensure that the members of the people or the community are aware of the potential benefits and risks so they can decide whether to accept the proposed development or investment plan. Finally, the consultation must take into account the traditional decision-making practices of the people or community. Failure to comply with this obligation, or engaging in consultations without observing their essential characteristics, entails the State's international responsibility.[73]

This is a broad obligation on states and is reflective of the breadth of impact on indigenous peoples of the activities of states and of other actors, such as corporations.[74]

8 CONCLUSION

Human rights are not only in relation to rights of individual human beings; they can also protect a group as a group. One of these group rights is the right of self-determination. This right applies to a wide range of people, not just those in colonial territories and not just those recognized by some states as having the right. It is a right of all peoples in all territories. This right can be limited in its exercise due to others' rights (such as others' right of self-determination) and where the general interests of the relevant society is legitimately applied. In the exercise of this right, there are many alternatives, such as internal control over the people's own cultural affairs, with independence now being difficult to justify legally in the first instance in most contexts. Both indigenous groups and minorities can assert a right of self-determination. There are also individual minority rights protected under international human rights law, which encompass cultural, ethnic, linguistic, religious, and national minorities, and indigenous peoples have both individual and group rights. In exercising these individual rights, the collective rights of the group as a group will need to be taken into account.

With the right of self-determination, minority rights, and the rights of indigenous peoples, the intention is to enable the rights-holders to determine their political, economic, social, and cultural destiny as they wish, while not overriding the legitimate interests of others affected. These rights developed once it was generally accepted that the traditional approach to international law and to the determination of boundaries had a severe consequence on some groups.

These group rights are, therefore, a reflection of the changing of values in the international community away from a state-based and solely state-interested system towards a more flexible system. Indeed, the reason behind many of the claims relating to the right of self-determination, and those in relation to minority and indigenous rights, is that the unjust, state-based international legal order has failed to respond appropriately to the legitimate aspirations of peoples.

---

[73] *Kichwa Indigenous People of Sarayaku*, n 70, para 177. This is also recognised in the ILO Convention No. 169, Art 6.   [74] See Chapter 26.

FURTHER READING

ALSTON (ed), *Peoples' Rights* (Oxford University Press, 2001).

ANAYA, *Indigenous Peoples in International Law* (Oxford University Press, 2005).

CASSESE, *Self-Determination of Peoples: A Legal Reappraisal* (Cambridge University Press, 1995).

CHINKIN and WRIGHT, 'Hunger Trap: Women, Food and Self-Determination' (1993) 14 *Michigan JIL* 262.

CRAWFORD (ed), *The Rights of Peoples* (Oxford University Press, 1988).

ENGLE, 'On Fragile Architecture: The UN Declaration on the Rights of Indigenous Peoples in the Context of Human Rights' (2011) 22 *EJIL* 141.

GHANEA and XANTHAKI (eds), *Minorities, Peoples and Self-Determination: Essays in Honour of Patrick Thornberry* (Martinus Nijhoff, 2005).

KLABBERS, 'The Right to Be Taken Seriously: Self-Determination in International Law' (2006) 28 *HRQ* 186.

KYMLICKA, 'The Internationalization of Minority Rights' (2008) 6 *IJConL* 1.

MCCORQUODALE (ed), *Self-Determination in International Law* (Ashgate, 2000).

PAVKOVIĆ and RADAN (eds), *The Ashgate Research Companion to Secession* (Ashgate, 2011).

SAUL, 'The Normative Status of Self-Determination in International Law: A Formula for Uncertainty in the Scope and Content of the Right?' (2011) 11 *HRLR* 609.

SHELTON, 'Self-Determination in Regional Human Rights Law: From Kosovo to Cameroon' (2011) 105 *AJIL* 60.

WILDE, 'Self-Determination, Secession, and Dispute Settlement after the Kosovo Advisory Opinion' (2011) *Leiden JIL* 149.

XANTHAKI, 'Indigenous Rights in International Law over the Last 10 Years and Future Developments' (2009) 10 *Melbourne JIL* 27.

PART IV

PROTECTION

18

UNITED NATIONS

Jane Connors and Markus Schmidt

SUMMARY[1]

According to its Charter, the promotion and protection of human rights is one of the principal purposes of the United Nations (UN). This chapter considers the work of the UN in the field of human rights. Particular attention is given to the Human Rights Council and the treaty bodies that consider progress in the implementation of UN human rights treaties. The role of the Office of the High Commissioner for Human Rights is briefly described, as is that of the General Assembly, Security Council, Secretary-General, and International Court of Justice.

1 INTRODUCTION

Human rights have pervaded political discourse since 1945. The massive affront to human dignity of the Second World War and the need to prevent the recurrence of these horrors prompted the codification, at the international level, of human rights and fundamental freedoms. Thus, Article 1 UN Charter identifies 'promoting and encouraging respect for human rights and for fundamental freedoms for all without distinction as to race, sex, language or religion' as one of the principal purposes of the UN.

The Universal Declaration of Human Rights (UDHR), adopted on 10 December 1948, was the first step taken by the UN towards that objective. In 1948 most governments recognized the UDHR, but insisted that its provisions were not legally binding. Since then, human rights and fundamental freedoms have been codified in hundreds of universal, regional, and sub-regional, binding and non-binding, instruments. At the level of the UN, this process is still in progress, but the main challenge is implementation of existing standards at the national level. Another challenge is to enhance the effectiveness and the visibility of the UN mechanisms in the field of human rights, be they Charter or treaty based.

This chapter introduces the work of the UN in the field of human rights. It shows the progress that has been made, particularly since the adoption of the Vienna Declaration and Programme of Action (VDPA) by the World Conference on Human Rights 20 years ago.[2] This document reaffirms the commitment of all states to fulfil their obligations to promote universal respect for, observance, and protection of human rights and fundamental freedoms for all in accordance with the UN Charter, human rights instruments, and international law. It makes clear that all human rights are universal, indivisible, interdependent,

---

[1] The views expressed in this chapter are those of the authors and do not necessarily reflect the views of the United Nations.   [2] A/CONF.157/23 (25 June 1993).

and interrelated, and although the significance of national and regional particularities and various historical, cultural, and religious backgrounds must be borne in mind, it is the duty of states, regardless of their political, economic, and cultural systems, to promote and protect all human rights and fundamental freedoms.

2 THE HUMAN RIGHTS COUNCIL

The preamble to the UN Charter reaffirms 'faith in fundamental human rights, in the dignity and worth of the human person, [and] in the equal rights of men and women'. Article 1 UN Charter identifies respect for human rights as one of the purposes of the organization. To realize this purpose, Article 55 provides that the UN shall promote universal respect for, and observance of, human rights and fundamental freedoms for all without distinction as to race, sex, language, or religion, whilst Article 56 commits member states to take both joint and separate action in cooperation with the UN to achieve these goals. The UN has established bodies, known as 'Charter-based' bodies, to fulfil these functions, including the Commission on Human Rights, which was replaced in 2006 by the Human Rights Council.

2.1 1946–2006: FROM THE COMMISSION ON HUMAN RIGHTS TO THE HUMAN RIGHTS COUNCIL

In 1946 the UN Economic and Social Council (ECOSOC), one of the principal organs of the UN, created the Commission on Human Rights. For 60 years, the Commission, com- posed of 53 representatives of UN member states, performed countless activities aimed at the protection and promotion of human rights. It made important contributions to human rights standard-setting, including drafting the UDHR, the International Covenant on Civil and Political Rights (ICCPR), and the International Covenant on Economic, Social and Cultural Rights (ICESCR). The Commission also developed UN institutional capacity to promote and protect the full range of human rights: civil, cultural, economic, political, and social, including the right to development. It developed working methods and pro- cedures, creating a Sub-Commission on the Promotion and Protection of Human Rights to prepare thematic studies, and provided a forum for human rights discourse in which it allowed civil society to participate to an extent not known in other parts of the UN system. Through the establishment and operation of its special procedures system, consisting of experts mandated to investigate particular human rights issues or human rights violations in specific countries, and a confidential mechanism for individuals to report consistent patterns of gross and systematic violations of human rights in a country, the Commission helped to improve the human rights situation of many individuals in many countries.

However, the Commission became increasingly subject to criticism, with particular attention focused on the politicization of its work. In 2005, in a report on UN reform, former Secretary-General Kofi Annan considered the Commission to be:

> undermined by its declining credibility and professionalism...States have sought member- ship of the Commission not to strengthen human rights but to protect themselves against criticism or to criticize others. As a result, a credibility deficit has developed, which casts a shadow on the reputation of the United Nations system as a whole.[3]

---

[3] In Larger Freedom: Towards Development, Security and Human Rights for All, Report of the Secretary-General, A/59/2005 (21 March 2005) para 182.

The Secretary-General's report set the stage for the replacement of the Commission by a new body—the Human Rights Council—and had important implications for the direction of the UN human rights programme. His call for reform was underpinned by the assumption that the system should move from 'standard-setting', that is, the negotiation of new instruments, to implementation. This approach echoed that of a High-Level Panel of Experts mandated to formulate recommendations on systemic UN reform. In December 2004, the Panel made a number of recommendations for change to the UN human rights programme, including: overhaul of the Commission to allow for universal membership; the submission of an Annual Report by the UN High Commissioner for Human Rights to the General Assembly; and increased interaction between the High Commissioner and the Security Council.[4] The Secretary-General chose not to endorse the recommendation for a Commission on Human Rights based on universal membership, but proposed the creation of a smaller Human Rights Council, which would be a standing body and a subsidiary body of the General Assembly. Importantly, he suggested that the Human Rights Council should function as a 'chamber of peer review' and that its principal task would be the evaluation of the fulfilment by *all* states of *all* their human rights obligations.[5]

Substantive negotiations on the establishment of the Human Rights Council began in May 2005. Various issues proved contentious: the composition of the Council, including the number of members and their eligibility to serve; whether election of members by the General Assembly would be by simple or two-thirds majority; the functions and mandates of the Council; whether a peer review mechanism for monitoring state compliance with human rights obligations should be created; whether the Council would operate as a standing body, with several regular annual sessions and special sessions for urgent situations, or a body that would meet as required; and transitional measures and arrangements. With most of these concerns resolved, on 15 March 2006, the General Assembly adopted Resolution 60/251 establishing the Human Rights Council. The Resolution was adopted by 170 states voting in favour, four against, and three abstentions. The Commission was abolished on 16 June 2006, the same day as the first meeting of the Council.

2.2 COMPOSITION, WORKING METHODS, AND MANDATE

The Human Rights Council is composed of 47 members. All UN member states are eligible for membership, not only those with a good human rights track record or that have ratified the majority of international human rights instruments and cooperate with their respective mechanisms. Members are elected by a simple majority vote of the members of the General Assembly. However, when electing members, the 'contribution of candidates to the promotion and protection of human rights and their voluntary pledges and commitments made thereto' should be taken into account. Pledges and commitments are submitted by the vast majority of candidates and include promises of better cooperation with the UN human rights treaty bodies, standing invitations to special procedures mandate holders, ratification of international instruments, and promises of action at the national level.[6]

All Council members must uphold the highest standards in the promotion and protection of human rights, fully cooperate with the Council, and be reviewed under the Council's review mechanism during their membership. There is no formal mechanism to

---

[4] A More Secure World: Our Shared Responsibility, Report of the High-Level Panel on Threats, Challenges and Change, A/59/565 (2 December 2004).   [5] In Larger Freedom, n 3, Addendum 1.

[6] The pledges made by each candidate are available at: <http://www.un.org/en7ga/67/meetings/elections/hrc.shtml>.

hold members to account, but a member that has committed gross and systematic violations of human rights may be suspended by the General Assembly by a two-thirds majority of its members present and voting. This procedure was invoked in March 2011, when
the General Assembly, acting on a recommendation of the Human Rights Council, agreed
by consensus to suspend the membership of the Libyan Arab Jamahiriya.[7] The suspension,
described by some during the debate as unprecedented and not to be used lightly, was
reversed by the General Assembly in November 2011, again on a recommendation of the
Human Rights Council.[8]

Council membership is broken down into regional groupings. The African and Asian
groups are allocated 13 seats each. Eight seats are reserved for the Latin American and
Caribbean group, six for the Eastern European group, and seven for the West European
and others group. Members serve for a period of three years and are not eligible for
immediate re-election after two consecutive terms. Non-governmental organizations
(NGOs) may participate in the Human Rights Council as observers if they have been
granted consultative status with the ECOSOC.[9] Similarly, national human rights institutions (NHRIs) that are fully compliant with the Paris Principles may also participate in
Council meetings.[10]

The Human Rights Council meets regularly throughout the year, convening at least
three annual sessions. There must be at least ten weeks of scheduled sessions to allow the
Council to adopt a comprehensive approach to human rights and respond effectively to
human rights situations as they develop. Special sessions, lasting one or two days at a time,
may also be scheduled at the request of a Council member that has garnered the support
of at least one-third of the Council's membership.

The principal duties of the Human Rights Council are spelled out in General Assembly
Resolution 60/251. These include: promote universal respect for the protection of all
human rights and fundamental freedoms for all, without distinction of any kind and in
a fair and equal manner; address and make recommendations on situations of violations
of human rights, including gross and systematic violations; promote effective coordination and mainstreaming of human rights in the UN system; promote human rights
education and learning; help prevent human rights violations through advisory services,
technical assistance and capacity building in consultation with, and the consent of, the
states concerned; serve as a forum for dialogue on thematic issues; make recommendations to the General Assembly on developing new human rights standards; help prevent
human rights violations through dialogue and cooperation; and respond promptly to
human rights emergencies. In addition, paragraph 5(e) of the Resolution stipulates that
the Council shall undertake a 'universal periodic review' (UPR), based on objective and
reliable information, of the fulfilment by each state of its human rights obligations and
commitments in a way that ensures universality of coverage and equal treatment. In
fulfilling its mandate, the Council's work should be based on the principles of *universality, impartiality, objectivity, non-selectivity, constructive international dialogue*, and
cooperation.

---

[7] GA Res 65/265 (1 March 2011).   [8] GA Res 66/11 (18 November 2011).

[9] ECOSOC Res 1996/31 (25 July 1996). This resolution sets out the principles that are to be applied when
considering whether NGOs should be accorded consultative status.

[10] See Chapter 22 for a discussion of the Paris Principles and NHRIs.

2.3 UNIVERSAL PERIODIC REVIEW

The UPR mechanism was conceived as a form of 'peer review' of UN member states' action to fulfil their human rights obligations, as well as a means of identifying areas in which help and advice are required. The performance of states is measured against the relevant standards in the UN Charter, the UDHR, the UN human rights treaties to which the state is a party, and voluntary commitments and pledges made by the state in the field of human rights.

Resolution 60/251 left the modalities of the UPR procedure for the Council to work out. Between June 2006 and June 2007, the Council's 'institution-building period', during which it negotiated and agreed its rules, working methods, and tools, Council members discussed the way UPR was to be conducted and on 18 June 2007, the Human Rights Council adopted Resolution 5/1.[11] The framework of the UPR process is set out in the annex to this resolution, and subsequent Council resolutions and decisions regarding the Council and the UPR.[12] The first cycle of UPR began in April 2008 and was completed in October 2011. The second cycle of UPR began in June 2012 and is currently ongoing. During these, and subsequent cycles, each of the 193 UN member states will be reviewed once every four-and-a-half years.

Forty-two states are reviewed per year during three annual two-week sessions, with 14 states reviewed in each session. The review is conducted by a UPR Working Group, consisting of all members of the Council, chaired by its President. Three Council members, each from a different regional group and drawn by lot, known as the 'troika', facilitate each review. Reviews are based on three documents, which address implementation of recommendations accepted in previous cycles of the UPR and the development of the human rights situation in the state under review.[13] These are:

(1) The *National report* which is prepared by the state under review. This report should not exceed 20 pages. It should include developments since the previous review, details of human rights achievements, best practices, challenges and constraints in relation to implementation of accepted recommendations from earlier reviews, key priorities for the state, expectations in terms of capacity-building, and requests, if any, for technical assistance. In preparing their reports, states are encouraged to adopt a broad consultative process with relevant stakeholders, such as local NGOs and NHRIs.

(2) The *Compilation of UN information* gathers together relevant recommendations, observations, and comments on the state made since the last review by the UN treaty bodies, special procedures mandate holders, as well as summaries of other relevant UN documents. The report is produced by the Office of the High Commissioner for Human Rights (OHCHR) and should not exceed ten pages.

(3) The *Summary of stakeholders' information* is also prepared by the OHCHR and should not be longer than ten pages. It compiles additional 'credible and reliable' country information from relevant stakeholders such as NGOs, NHRIs, academic sources, and regional organizations. The contribution of NHRIs that are fully compliant with the Paris Principles are summarized in a separate section of this report. Stakeholders are encouraged to include information on follow-up to the preceding review in their submissions.

---

[11] HR Council Res 5/1 (18 June 2007). See Loulichki, 'The Universal Periodic Review or the Promise of a New Mechanism for the Protection of Human Rights' in Müller (ed), *The First 365 Days of the United Nations Human Rights Council* (Swiss Government, 2007) 80.

[12] See HR Council Dec 6/102 (27 September 2007); HR Council Res 16/2 (25 March 2011); HR Council Dec 17/119 (19 July 2011); A/HRC/PRST/20/1 (6 July 2012). [13] HR Council Dec 17/119 (17 June 2011).

The review itself consists of a three-and-a half hour interactive dialogue between the state under review and the UPR Working Group. All Council members and observers can participate in the dialogue, but interventions are subject to strict time-limits. After the review, the 'troika' submits an 'outcome report' (which summarizes the dialogue, recommendations made by the Working Group on how to improve human rights protection within the state, the state's responses to these recommendations, including those that at this initial stage it accepts or rejects and its voluntary commitments) for adoption by the UPR Working Group. A final outcome report is submitted to the next ordinary session of the Human Rights Council, where one hour is allowed for discussion of the report. The state under review has an opportunity to indicate whether it accepts, rejects, or reserves any recommendations and the reasons for its position. This is recorded in an amendment to the Working Group report. If the NHRI of the state under review is fully compliant with the Paris Principles, it is entitled to intervene immediately after the state's statement. Thereafter, all member states, observers, NGOs, and other stakeholders may comment at this stage. At the end of this discussion a final outcome report, containing the accepted and rejected recommendations, is adopted. This report serves as the basis for the next review the state undergoes.

In 2007, the Secretary-General characterized the UPR as a mechanism with 'great potential to promote and protect human rights in the darkest corners of the world'.[14] The first cycle was judged by most to be extremely positive. All UN member states participated, with the majority fielding representatives of a very high level and engaging in a constructive and open fashion. Many states created processes to allow for internal review across governmental bodies and between government and civil society. NHRIs, civil society organizations, UN entities, and development actors engaged with the mechanism, as did individuals on the ground, with many watching the proceedings via webcast. Over 20,000 recommendations were made, covering a broad range of human rights issues, with follow-up to these providing a means to initiate or strengthen human rights dialogue and cooperation at national, regional, and global levels. Some states made specific commitments in relation to human rights issues at various stages of the review,[15] while many adopted the practice, now encouraged by the Council, of submitting mid-term reports on implementation of recommendations.[16]

Experience of the UPR mechanism shows that it is complementary to, and not in competition with, the procedures of the UN treaty bodies (see Section 3). During UPR sessions, Council members frequently quiz states about their follow-up to treaty body recommendations, and the final outcome documents often contain concrete recommendations to this effect. The treaty bodies often raise the commitments made by states parties under the UPR process in their proceedings. Cooperation with treaty bodies, including submission of reports, as well as ratifications of human rights treaties and withdrawal of reservations to treaties often increases before a review or as a result of recommendations.

Nevertheless, critics have expressed concern that some states avoid negative UPR assessments by ensuring that friendly governments praise their human rights record and ignore their shortcomings. Thus, the outcome of the review may not address human rights violations that are occurring within the state. In addition, the response of the state under review to recommendations may not be clear. The proliferation of recommendations has

---

[14] Secretary-General's video message to the opening of the fourth Council session (12 March 2007), available at: <http://www.un.org/webcast/unhrc/archive.asp?go=004>.

[15] UPR Info has created a database of these commitments, available at: <http://www.upr-info.org/database/>.

[16] McMahon, 'The Universal Periodic Review: A Work in Progress, An Evaluation of the First Cycle of the New UPR Mechanism of the Human Rights Council' (Friedrich Ebert Stiftung, 2012).

also raised concern, as has the fact that some may be repetitive. Others raise the issue that some recommendations are so vague as to be unimplementable.

Follow-up to UPR recommendations will be the test of its success. One study reports positively that slightly over two-thirds of the recommendations made have been accepted, with acceptance rates increasing over the first cycle, and that implementation of these has been encouraging.[17] Implementation of recommendations is primarily for the state itself, but states are encouraged to conduct broad consultations with all stakeholders in this process. A voluntary fund exists to assist the least-developed and small-island developing states implement UPR recommendations.[18] The OHCHR, other UN entities, regional organizations, and civil society actors have invested significant energy into UPR follow-up, with the High Commissioner reporting to the General Assembly in 2012 that over 150 activities related to UPR in more than 60 countries had been undertaken.[19]

As a testimony to UPR's success, all states scheduled for review in the first two sessions of the second cycle participated, thereby maintaining the UPR's universality. However, sustaining this record may be a challenge. In early 2013, one state, Israel, decided not to participate in its second review. The Council adopted a decision on the non-cooperation of a state under review with the UPR, regretting the state's decision, calling on it to resume its cooperation, requesting its President to take steps to urge the state to resume cooperation and report on the results of these efforts, and rescheduling the review to later in 2013.[20] During the Council's 23rd session, the President presented a written report outlining steps he had taken to urge Israel to resume cooperation with the UPR and encouraging it to participate in its review in October 2013.[21] It remains to be seen how the Council will react if the state maintains its non-cooperative stance.

2.4 RESPONSES TO URGENT SITUATIONS

When responding to serious human rights situations, the Human Rights Council can convene for special sessions or hold urgent debates during regular sessions. Since June 2006, the Council has held 19 special sessions. This should be contrasted with the Commission on Human Rights, which between May 1990, when ECOSOC authorized it to hold such sessions,[22] and its replacement by the Council in June 2006, convened only five. Two of the Council's special sessions have had a thematic focus (the effects of the global economic crisis and the world food crisis), while the balance has addressed urgent human rights situations in countries. Five related to the human rights situation in the Israeli Occupied Territory, and one on Israeli military operations, and four have addressed the situation in the Syrian Arab Republic. The other sessions have concerned the human rights situation in Côte d'Ivoire, Darfur (Sudan), the Democratic Republic of Congo, the Libyan Arab Jamahiriya, Myanmar, Sri Lanka, and Haiti. The Council has also convened three urgent debates during its regular sessions: one in relation to Israel and two on Syria.

The outcomes of special sessions or urgent debates have included the creation of fact-finding missions by experts appointed by the Council President (Israeli military attacks against the Occupied Gaza Strip, 2009; Israeli attacks against the humanitarian

[17] UPR Info, 'Universal Periodic Review: On the road to implementation' (2012), available at: <http://www.upr-info.org>.

[18] HR Council Res 6/17 (28 September 2007). This resolution also creates a trust fund to assist states with their participation in the UPR.

[19] Report of the UN High Commissioner for Human Rights, A/67/36 (27 July 2012), para 20.

[20] A/HRC/OM/7/1 (28 January 2013).   [21] A/HRC/23/CRP.1

[22] ECOSOC Res 1990/48 (25 May 1990).

boat convoy, 2010),[23] which sometimes include the relevant Special Rapporteur (situation in the Occupied Palestinian Territory, 2006);[24] the creation of high-level independent international commissions of inquiry (situation in Lebanon caused by Israeli military operations, 2006; Israeli military incursions in the Occupied Palestinian Territory, including northern Gaza and Beit Hanoun, 2006; Darfur, 2006; Syria, 2011);[25] requests for the OHCHR to dispatch an urgent mission to the country to provide the Council with a preliminary report and oral update (Syria, 2011);[26] requests for the High Commissioner to report on the situation (Israeli military attacks in the Occupied Palestinian Territory, including Gaza strip, 2008; Democratic Republic of Congo, 2008; Côte d'Ivoire following the 2010 presidential election, 2010);[27] or that the situation be subject to urgent examination by special procedures mandate holders (Democratic Republic of Congo, 2008).[28]

In response to less urgent situations within countries, the Council can also create a commission of inquiry (Democratic Peoples' Republic of Korea, 2013) or mandate the High Commissioner to report on human rights concerns in individual countries,[29] including in relation to technical assistance and capacity building provided by OHCHR.[30] The Council is also able to create a special procedure to address country situations (see Section 2.5), and has done so increasingly since 2011. Resolutions establishing such procedures are unlikely to be adopted by consensus unless the country concerned is willing to agree to the mandate's creation and expresses its willingness to cooperate with the mandate holder. Where the country expresses such willingness, the scope of the mandate will be primarily technical assistance and capacity building. Whether the Council will address a country situation depends on the willingness of its membership. The operation of regional groups and alliances assumes particular importance here and it should be noted that, given the composition of the Council, the African and Asian groups have an automatic majority in Council decision-making. There have been charges that the Human Rights Council is selective and politically biased. Some point to the existence of its agenda item 7 on the human rights situation in Palestine and other occupied Arab territories and the fact that developing states with difficult human rights situations have largely escaped such scrutiny as evidence to support their claims. It is worth noting that no special session, nor special procedure, has been put forward regarding Western states. Proposals to examine a particular country situation are often opposed on the basis that 'cooperative' approaches to human rights should be used—that is, approaches with which the state concerned consents. Clearly, this is the preferred way forward, but workable only where the state has a true desire to improve human rights enjoyment. Some delegations also argue that UPR is the ideal mechanism to address country situations, as it is based on state cooperation, but the fact that it addresses individual states only periodically makes it unsuitable for urgent human rights concerns.

[23] HR Council Res S-9/1 (12 January 2009); HR Council Res 14/1 (2 June 2010).

[24] HR Council Res S-1/1 (6 July 2006).

[25] HR Council Res S-2/1 (11 August 2006); HR Council Res S-3/1 (15 November 2006); HR Council Dec S-4/101 (13 December 2006); HR Council Res S-17/1 (23 August 2011).

[26] HR Council Res S-16/1 (29 April 2011).

[27] HR Council Res S-6/1 (24 January 2008); HR Council Res S-8/1 (1 December 2008); HR Council Res S-14/1, (23 December 2010).   [28] HR Council Res S-8/1 (1 December 2008).

[29] Eg A/HRC/22/38 on promoting reconciliation and accountability in Sri Lanka (11 February 2013); A/HRC/22/33 on situation of human rights in the north of Mali (7 January 2013).

[30] Eg A/HRC/22/37 on situation of human rights in Afghanistan (28 January 2013); A/HRC/22/39 on situation of human rights in Guinea (21 January 2013).

2.5 SPECIAL PROCEDURES

The creation of the special procedures mechanisms was one of the major achievements of the Commission on Human Rights. From the establishment of the first special procedures mandate in 1980—the Working Group on Enforced and Involuntary Disappearances—to the end of the Commission's final session, the special procedures system evolved remarkably. These mechanisms, consisting of independent experts who work *pro bono*—either individually or as part of a five-member working group—address country-specific situations or thematic issues that concern all states. General Assembly Resolution 60/251 mandated the Human Rights Council to review and, where necessary, rationalize and improve all mandates and mechanisms of the former Commission 'in order to maintain a system of special procedures' within one year of its first session. Any decision to discontinue, merge, or streamline mandates must be guided by the need to enhance human rights protection and promotion.

Five country-specific mandates have been discontinued since 2006, although one was re-established in 2012,[31] and a further five have been created.[32] Eight thematic mandates have been added, and a single mandate holder on slavery has now replaced the Working Group on Contemporary Forms of Slavery of the Subcommission on the Promotion and Protection of Human Rights. At the end of June 2013, there were a total of 49 special procedures mandates: 13 on country situations;[33] 11 focussing on civil and political rights;[34] ten in the area of economic, social, and cultural rights;[35] and ten mandates that focus on specific groups.[36] The Working Group on the issue of human rights and transnational corporations and other business enterprises replaced the single mandate holder on that theme in 2010, while the remaining four mandates are: promotion of a democratic and equitable international order; promotion of truth, justice, reparation and guarantees of non-recurrence; human rights and international solidarity; and the Working Group on African Descent.

Mandate holders are experts in their respective fields. They are selected on the basis of technical criteria developed by the Human Rights Council.[37] Candidates for vacant posts may self-nominate or be nominated by governments, regional groups, international organizations, NGOs, NHRIs that are fully compliant with the Paris Principles, and other human rights bodies. Candidates must submit an application for each specific mandate, with their personal data and a motivation letter of no more than 600 words. A five-member Consultative Group, comprising representatives of each regional group who serve in their personal capacity, will conduct a selection process including an interview, and then propose a shortlist of experts for vacant mandates to the Council President. After broad

---

[31] The mandates on Belarus, Burundi, Cuba, the Democratic Republic of the Congo, and Liberia were discontinued; the Belarus mandate was re-established in 2012.

[32] Mandates relating to Côte d'Ivoire, Eritrea, Iran, Mali, and Syria, although the latter mandate holder will only take up his functions after the relevant Commission of Inquiry on that country has finished its work.

[33] Belarus, Cambodia, Côte d'Ivoire, Democratic Peoples' Republic of Korea, Eritrea, Haiti, Iran, Mali, Myanmar, Occupied Palestinian Territories, Somalia, Sudan, and Syria.

[34] Counter-terrorism, freedom of expression and opinion, freedom of religion, human rights defenders, independence of judges and lawyers, peaceful assembly and association, racism, summary executions, torture, Working Group on Arbitrary Detention, and the Working Group on Enforced and Involuntary Disappearances.

[35] Cultural rights, education, environment, extreme poverty, food, foreign debt, health, housing, safe drinking water and sanitation, and toxic waste.

[36] The Working Group on discrimination against women in law and in practice, indigenous peoples, internally displaced persons, migrants, minorities, sale of children, slavery, trafficking, violence against women, and the Working Group on Mercenaries.

[37] See HR Council Res 5/1, n 11, Annex; HR Council Dec 6/102, n 12.

consultation among Council members, the President will then put forward a candidate for each vacancy for the Council's approval, along with an explanation if the proposal differs from that of the Consultative Group. Throughout, consideration is given to gender balance, equitable geographic distribution, and representation of different legal systems.

Each mandate holder serves in his or her personal capacity and independently. They should not hold a decision-making position in government or any other body that may result in a conflict of interest. He or she must also respect the principle of non-accumulation of human rights functions. Thematic mandate holders may serve up to two three-year terms, and country mandate holders usually serve six one-year terms; the maximum term for both types of mandate holders is six years.[38] While the denomination of experts varies ('Special Rapporteur', 'Independent Expert', or 'member of working group'), their status is equal. They benefit from such diplomatic privileges and immunities as are required for the discharge of their duties.[39]

Since 1993, mandate holders have met annually for one week to discuss themes of common interest and harmonization of working methods. During these meetings they also interact with the High Commissioner for Human Rights, the Bureau of the Human Rights Council, and others. Their manual of operations was adopted and revised in the context of such a meeting.[40] A Coordination Committee of mandate holders was established in 2005 to represent the system, including by making statements on its behalf. The Committee meets regularly to discuss issues pertinent to the special procedures system. All mandate holders conduct *country visits*. Currently, 94 states have extended 'standing invitations', and so, in principle, any thematic special procedure may visit these states. However, in all circumstances a visit must be agreed. Where other states are concerned, a specific invitation must be extended. Before the start of a visit, its terms of reference are negotiated and agreed by the mandate holder and the government. During visits, mandate holders meet with relevant stakeholders and visit facilities relevant to their mandate. Before they leave, they debrief the authorities and the media on their (preliminary) findings and conclusions. A report on the visit, including conclusions and recommendations, is subsequently transmitted to the Human Rights Council, annexing any comments from the state. The report is presented during the Council's annual interactive debate on the mandate. During 2012 mandate holders carried out 80 visits to 55 countries.

Most mandate holders examine *complaints* from individuals, human rights defenders, or other interested persons regarding alleged human rights violations that fall within the area(s) of their mandate. The OHCHR channels these to the relevant mandate holders for action. 'Letters of allegation' are addressed to governments requesting clarification of the allegation. Where alleged violations are time-sensitive (imminent loss of life, life-threatening situations, ongoing or imminent damage of a severe nature) 'urgent appeals' are dispatched. Mandate holders also transmit 'other letters' that address non-state actors and thematic issues. In 2012, mandate holders sent 603 communications to 127 states, with over 74 per cent being transmitted jointly by two or more mandates. A report containing communications transmitted, and any replies received, is submitted to each session of the Human Rights Council. Two special procedures have developed sophisticated working practices and adopt reasoned opinions in response to complaints. The Working Group on

---

[38] Presidential Statement of the Human Rights Council on terms of office of special procedures mandate holders, A/HRC/8/PRST/2 (18 June 2008).

[39] Regulations Governing the Status, Basic Rights and Duties of Officials other than Secretariat Officials, and Experts on Mission, ST/SGB/2002/9 (18 June 2002).

[40] Manual of Operations of the Special Procedures of the Human Rights Council (August 2008), available at: <http://www.ohchr.org/Documents/HRBodies/SP/Manual_Operations2008.pdf>.

Enforced and Involuntary Disappearances receives reports of alleged disappearance, which it seeks to clarify. Since its establishment in 1980, it has transmitted almost 54,000 cases to states, of which approximately 43,000 are outstanding.[41] The Working Group on Arbitrary Detention adopts opinions on complaints regarding arbitrary arrest and detention. This Working Group was established in 1991, and, to date, has adopted over 600 opinions.[42]

Some mandate holders *develop authoritative opinions and standards*, thus contributing to the progressive development of international law. For example, the special procedure on internally displaced persons formulated Guiding Principles on Internal Displacement;[43] the former Special Representative of the Secretary-General on human rights and trans-national corporations and other business enterprises developed Guiding Principles on Business and Human Rights;[44] and the Independent Expert on the effects of foreign debt prepared Guiding Principles on Foreign Debt and Human Rights, which were endorsed by the Council in June 2012.[45] Others adopt 'deliberations' or general comments on specific themes.[46] Mandate holders often research a specific theme, either at the request of the Human Rights Council or on their own initiative, and present annual thematic reports to the Council and the General Assembly. Questionnaires are often transmitted to governments, NGOs, and other stakeholders and meetings convened to elicit comprehensive, up-to-date information. At the end of their tenure, mandate holders often present a report which analyses the global human rights situation as regards their mandate. They frequently organize, in conjunction with the OHCHR, governments, and NGOs, seminars or consultations which contribute to the analysis of human rights issues.

Mandate holders also *raise awareness of human rights concerns* by releasing joint or individual press statements and engaging in regular contact with the media, especially during country visits and Human Rights Council or General Assembly sessions. Attendance at activities and meetings organized by governments, NGOs, or academic institutions is used to raise awareness about their mandates, create and develop partnerships, and learn about new developments.

The Human Rights Council adopted a Code of Conduct for Special Procedures mandate holders in June 2007, which was designed to 'enhance the effectiveness of the system by defining the standards of ethical behaviour and professional conduct that special procedures mandate-holders... shall observe whilst discharging their mandates'.[47] The Code sets out general principles on the conduct, status, and prerogatives of mandate holders, and regulations on sources of information, communications, relations with states, and field visits. On occasion, states have used the Code in statements during Council sessions or correspondence with mandate holders, the Secretary-General, High Commissioner, or the Council President to found allegations that individual mandate holders have acted in contravention of the Code, often with a view to restricting their activities, and even to dismiss individual experts.[48] In June 2008 the Council adopted Presidential Statement 8/2, which

---

[41] Report of the Working Group on Enforced or Involuntary Disappearances, A/HRC/22/45 (28 January 2013) para 6.

[42] Report of the Working Group on Arbitrary Detention, A/HRC/22/44 (24 December 2012) para 6.

[43] E/CN.4/1998/53/Add.2 (11 February 1998).

[44] A/HRC/17/31 (21 March 2011).   [45] A/HRC/20/23 (10 April 2011).

[46] Eg, Report of the Working Group on Arbitrary Detention, Deliberation No.9 concerning the definition and scope of arbitrary detention under international law, A/HRC/22/44 (24 December 2012) 16–25.

[47] HR Council Res 5/2 (18 June 2007).

[48] See Baldwin-Pask and Scannella, 'The Unfinished Business of a Special Procedures System' in Bassiouni and Shabas (eds), *New Challenges for the UN Human Rights Machinery: What Future for the UN Treaty Body System and the Human Rights Council Procedures* 439, 463–70.

provides that the President will convey any information of persistent non-compliance by a mandate holder with the Code, especially prior to the mandate holder's renewal, to the Council for consideration and action as appropriate. A year later, the Council adopted Resolution 11/11, which notes that it is incumbent on mandate holders to exercise their functions with full respect for, and strict observance of, their mandates set out in the relevant Council resolutions and full compliance with the Code. It also requests the OHCHR to assist special procedures mandate holders in this regard.[49]

While the Code of Conduct was being negotiated, proposals were made for a body to oversee its implementation, but these were unsuccessful. Instead, in 2008, the special procedures' Coordination Committee adopted an 'Internal Advisory Procedure' (IAP) to review practices and working methods. The IAP includes a mechanism, facilitated by the Coordination Committee, to deal confidentially with issues that arise in the practices and working methods of the mandate holders. In early 2010, Philip Alston, then the Special Rapporteur on extrajudicial, summary, or arbitrary executions, suggested the creation of a committee to deal with complaints by governments and others of non-compliance with the Code by mandate holders and governments in a way that would protect mandate holders' independence and integrity, yet hold them accountable.[50] This proposal was rejected by other mandate holders, many states, and most civil society actors. Several states introduced this idea in a somewhat different form during the review of the Council that took place in 2011 (see Section 2.8) but it was not adopted.

Reference to the Code of Conduct by states in their interactions with special procedures is now less frequent. However, cooperation by some states with special procedures remains weak. There have also been instances where states' conduct towards mandate holders has been inappropriate, leading one state, France, to propose the introduction of a code of conduct for states themselves. This proposal was not taken up.

Successive UN Secretaries-General have described the special procedures as the 'eyes and ears' of the Human Rights Council. One commentator has labelled them 'catalysts for human rights', and argues that they play a critical role in shaping international human rights norms, shedding light on how states comply with these, as well as influencing government behaviour for the benefit of millions of people.[51] Mandate holders have generated positive changes in many countries, and these changes have been facilitated by their expertise, the quality of their recommendations, and the openness of states to co-operate. However, the full potential of the special procedures remains untapped, and the impact of their activities is negatively affected by lack of state cooperation, inadequate resources, and, as in the case of all human rights mechanisms, weak follow-up.

2.6 COMPLAINT PROCEDURE

The Council complaint procedure is based on the '1503 procedure' created by ECOSOC in May 1970, which was implemented by the Commission on Human Rights.[52] This confidential procedure, the oldest human rights complaint mechanism in the UN system, was concerned with patterns of gross violations of human rights rather than individual cases. Similarly, the Council complaint procedure is concerned with identifying 'consistent

---

[49] HR Council Res 11/11 (18 June 2009).

[50] His proposals are outlined in Alston, 'Hobbling the Monitors: Should UN Human Rights Monitors be Accountable?' (2011) 52 *Harvard ILJ* 563.

[51] Piccone, *Catalysts for Change: How the UN's Independent Experts Promote Human Rights* (Brookings Institution Press, 2012), viii.   [52] ECOSOC Res 1503 (XLVII) (27 May 1970).

patterns of gross and reliably attested violations of all human rights and all fundamental freedoms occurring in any part of the world and under any circumstances'.[53]

A complaint alleging a pattern of violation can be transmitted by a person, or group, claiming to be the victims of violations of human rights, or by any person or group of persons, including NGOs, who have direct and reliable knowledge of the alleged violations. Complaints will be considered inadmissible if they have manifestly political motivations or are inconsistent with the purposes of the UN. All complaints must give a factual description of the alleged violation and an indication of the rights violated. The language used must not be abusive, although such a complaint may be considered if it meets the other admissibility criteria after deletion of the abusive elements. Complaints should not be based solely on media reports. Domestic remedies should be exhausted before a complaint is submitted, unless it appears that such remedies would be ineffective or unreasonably prolonged, and situations being dealt with by a special procedure or other UN or regional human rights complaints mechanism will not be considered.

Complaints do not go directly to the Human Rights Council. Rather, they are pre-screened by the OHCHR, and two Council working groups: the Working Group on Communications (WGC) and the Working Group on Situations (WGS). Both working groups are composed of five members, each representing one of the five regional groups. WGC members are designated by the Human Rights Advisory Committee (see Section 2.7) from amongst its members, while the WGS is appointed by the regional groups of the member states of the Council. Complaints are pre-screened by the Chairperson of the WGC with the OHCHR. At this point those communications that are manifestly ill-founded or anonymous are dismissed. Those considered admissible are transmitted to the state concerned for observations. Complaints and state replies are examined by the WGC, which transmits cases it considers admissible, including its recommendations on the case, to the WGS. The WGS may dismiss a case, or keep it under review until its subsequent session, requesting further information from the state. The WGS also prepares a report for a closed session of the Human Rights Council plenary, including recommendations for action, usually in the form of a draft decision or resolution. Proceedings in both working groups are confidential. They are conducted on the basis of written materials alone, with neither governments nor complainants appearing before them. Unlike the '1503 procedure', both the author of the communication and the state are informed of the status of the proceedings at key stages, including when the communication is registered, deemed inadmissible by the WGC, taken up by the WGS, kept pending by either Working Group or the Council, as well as the final outcome.

The value of the complaint procedure has been questioned by some. However, it is often resorted to with the OHCHR receiving between 11,000 and 15,000 communications annually. During 2010–11, 1,451 of 18,043 complaints were submitted for further action by the WGC.

Increasing numbers of situations have been referred to the Council by the WGS since 2011, with four—the largest number so far—being considered during its 19th session in February–March 2012. Although most situations have been discontinued, the impact of the complaint procedure should not be underrated. Ninety-four per cent of states respond to the communications submitted to them. The confidential nature of the procedure may also encourage states to take remedial action in order to avoid public scrutiny. In some cases the Council has recommended the provision of technical assistance to states subject to communications.[54] Notably, during its 21st session in September 2012, the Council

---

[53] HR Council Res 5/1, n 11, annex para 85.
[54] Eg Democratic Republic of the Congo, A/HRC/18/2 (18 November 2011) para 210; and Iraq, A/HRC/19/2 (16 August 2012) para 324; and A/HRC/20/2 (3 August 2012) para 212.

decided to discontinue the review of complaints alleging widespread violations of human rights in Eritrea under the complaints procedure in order to consider the matter publicly in the context of the appointment of a Special Rapporteur on human rights in Eritrea.[55] The Council also decided to transmit the documentation received under the complaint procedure to the Special Rapporteur and invite her to investigate those allegations and report back.

2.7 HUMAN RIGHTS COUNCIL ADVISORY COMMITTEE

The Human Rights Council Advisory Committee was set up to operate as a 'think-tank' for the Council.[56] Consisting of 18 independent and impartial experts, the Advisory Committee replaced the 26-member Sub-Commission on the Promotion and Protection of Human Rights of the Commission on Human Rights. Committee members are elected by the Human Rights Council by secret ballot from a list of candidates who fulfil the requirements for nomination, which include high moral standing and recognized competence and expertise in the field of human rights.[57] All members must be independent and impartial, so those who hold decision-making positions in governments or any other entity that might give rise to a conflict are excluded. The geographic distribution of experts is: African states: five; Asian states: five; Eastern European states: two; Latin American and Caribbean states: three; and Western European and other states: three. All UN member states may propose and endorse candidates from their own region. They should consult their NHRIs and civil society organizations in the process, and include the names of those supporting their candidates. Members serve for a period of three years, are eligible for re-election once and may not accumulate other human rights functions during their tenure.

The Advisory Committee convenes two annual sessions, for a maximum of ten days per year. Additional sessions may be scheduled with the approval of the Council. The first annual session of the Committee takes place immediately prior to the March session of the Council, with the second session being held in August. The annual report of the Committee is submitted to the Council's September session and an interactive dialogue with the Committee's Chairperson is conducted during this session.

The role of the Advisory Committee is to provide expertise to the Council in the manner and form it requests, mainly through studies and research-based advice. Unlike its predecessor, the Sub-Commission, the Advisory Committee may not adopt resolutions or decisions, nor may it examine and decide on specific country situations. The Committee's expertise may only be provided to the Council on its request and under its guidance. However, the Committee may make proposals to the Council for the incremental enhancement of procedural efficiency, and research proposals within the scope of the work set out by the Human Rights Council. The Advisory Committee is actively to engage with states, NHRIs, NGOs, and other civil society stakeholders. Council members and observers, UN specialized agencies, other intergovernmental institutions, and NGOs may participate in the work of the Advisory Committee.

Since its first session in August 2008, the Advisory Committee has prepared a draft declaration on human rights education and training,[58] and a draft set of principles and

---

[55] HR Council Res 21/1 (27 September 2012).   [56] HR Council Res 5/1, n 11, paras 65–84.
[57] HR Council Dec 6/102, n 12.
[58] A/HRC/AC/4/4 (10 February 2010). The Declaration has been adopted by the GA: GA Res 66/137 (19 December 2011).

guidelines for the elimination of discrimination against persons affected by leprosy and their family members.[59] It has addressed subjects including missing persons; the protection of civilians in armed conflicts; the promotion of a democratic and equitable international order; human rights and international solidarity; aspects of the right to food; ways to further advance the rights of people working in rural areas; and promoting human rights and fundamental freedoms through a better understanding of traditional values of humankind. The Committee has worked at the Council's request on a declaration on the right to peace, the human rights of elderly people, international cooperation on human rights, human rights and terrorist hostage-taking, and promotion of the human rights of the urban poor. The Advisory Committee also works to mainstream a gender perspective and the human rights of persons with disabilities into its work.

Despite these important contributions, the fact that the Advisory Council is unable to initiate its own work or adopt resolutions or decisions has circumscribed its capacity to provide the Council with expertise. The Council's 'guidelines' on the way its requests to the Advisory Committee should be addressed are also prescriptive, thus affecting the way this expertise can be provided. To date, the Committee has not fully exploited its capacity to submit research proposals to the Council. However, this may be changing as the Advisory Committee has started to put forward priority proposals for the consideration of the Council, with the most recent being accompanied by detailed concept papers. It is important for the Committee to devise ways to strengthen its influence. These could include working with other mechanisms and in different frameworks, and perhaps convening panels or expert group meetings during its sessions. Committee members have valuable expertise, and while some states consider that the Committee's work replicates that of other bodies or goes beyond its mandate, the Council should explore ways to maximize its potential.

2.8 REVIEW

Resolution 60/251 provided that the Human Rights Council would review its work and functioning five years after its establishment and report to the General Assembly. In turn, the General Assembly was also to review the status of the Council. The outcome of the five-year review of the Council's work and functioning was adopted on 25 March 2011.[60] The review focused on five issues: the UPR; the special procedures; the Human Rights Council Advisory Committee, and the Council's complaints procedure; the agenda and framework for the programme of work; and methods of work and rules of procedure.

A myriad of proposals was put forward during review discussions, but few changes were actually agreed. Many states expressed dissatisfaction with the outcome, and the US disassociated itself from it. A group of influential NGOs described the result as a 'vital opportunity' to strengthen the Council's work and functioning...squandered.'[61] These reactions related predominantly to the fact that proposals for a mechanism to improve the Council's responsiveness to emergency and chronic human rights situations could not gain consensus.

---

[59] A/HRC/AC/5/2 (3 June 2010). The Guidelines were welcomed by the GA: GA Res 65/251 (21 December 2010).

[60] HR Council Res 16/21 (25 March 2011).

[61] Joint NGO Statement on the review of the Council's status by the General Assembly, IOR 41/006/2011, available at: <http://www.amnesty.org/en/library/asset/IOR41/006/2011/en/db1d6284-3340-43ae-b6fd-9361bba976cc/ior410062011en.html>.

Nonetheless, the outcome includes some important elements. For example, the role of NHRIs that are fully compliant with the Paris Principles in the UPR, and with regard to special procedures, was strengthened. Procedures for the selection and appointment of special procedures mandate holders were enhanced. States were urged to cooperate with and assist them by responding in a timely manner to requests for information and visits. Technical measures to streamline the work of the Council, including a voluntary yearly calendar of resolutions, were encouraged. A task force on accessibility of persons with disabilities to the Council and its mechanisms and the use of information technology, including video-conferencing or video-messaging to enhance participation of all stakeholders, was established.

Importantly, the outcome highlighted the issue of reprisals against individuals and groups who cooperate, or have cooperated, with the UN or its representatives and mechanisms in the field of human rights. States were urged to prevent and ensure adequate protection against such acts. Since the adoption of the review document, cross-regional statements on reprisals are now made by states during Council sessions and discussions have been held on ways to prevent reprisals.[62] During 2012, the President of the Council raised allegations of reprisals in Council sessions and with relevant delegations. Her successor has been similarly vigilant.

Disappointment was also expressed at the result of the General Assembly's review of the status of the Council.[63] Some states and many NGOs had hoped that the General Assembly review would lead to an enhanced election process for membership to the Council, perhaps by including a means by which the pledges put forward by states presenting their candidatures would be reviewed publicly. They had also hoped that 'open slates' for elections might be required. However, none of these proposals was adopted.

The outcome maintains the Council's status as a subsidiary body of the General Assembly, although this is to be reconsidered before 2026. Despite being labelled as 'technical and bureaucratic' by several NGOs, a number of changes have been introduced that make a practical difference to the work of the Council. The Council's annual report now covers the period from 1 October to 30 September, allowing the outcome of all of its sessions in any one year to be considered by the General Assembly that year. Its sessions are aligned to the calendar year, rather than starting in June as before; and the President of the Council presents its annual report to the Assembly's plenary and Third Committee, with the latter engaging in an interactive dialogue on the report. Importantly, the need to provide adequate financing to fund unforeseen and extraordinary expenses resulting from resolutions and decisions of the Council was recognized. These had been met previously by the OHCHR diverting funds from other activities.

2.9 IN CONCLUSION

Early in its life, several observers and NGOs criticized, or even dismissed outright, the activities of the Human Rights Council. They pointed to the fact that numerous states with questionable human rights records were members of the Council and that most of its special sessions unfairly 'targeted' Israel, whilst other serious country situations, such as that in Zimbabwe, had not been scrutinized, let alone criticized. These critiques should be reassessed in light of the Council's current performance, including its willingness to call for the suspension of a member that did not meet threshold membership criteria.

---

[62] Eg A/HRC/22/34 (17 December 2012).
[63] GA Res 65/281 (17 June 2011), adopted with 154 votes in favour and four against.

The Council has proved itself to be willing to address critical country situations. Indeed, in April 2011, it was the first UN intergovernmental body to address the profound human rights concerns in Syria. Its attention to this situation has been sustained: it has adopted strong resolutions, created a Country Rapporteur, and a Commission of Inquiry, the mandate of which has been extended. It has been equally strong in relation to the Democratic People's Republic of Korea, in respect of which it has also created a Commission of Inquiry. Other country situations have also been addressed, including Iran and Sri Lanka, and it has continued to establish country-specific special procedures mandates. It has supported countries in transition, encouraging accountability measures through technical assistance and capacity-building resolutions, which have led to domestic inquiry mechanisms.

The Council has also made progress on thematic issues through resolutions, annual discussions, and panels. The UN's first resolution on human rights, sexual orientation, and gender identity was adopted by the Council in July 2011,[64] and a panel discussion was convened on this subject a year later. Progress has been made on women's rights, including maternal mortality, the safety of journalists, and the rights of persons with disabilities, and the Council has worked hard to provide full access to its deliberations. In March 2011, it adopted, by consensus, a ground-breaking resolution on freedom of religion or belief, which dropped references to 'defamation of religions' and provides a comprehensive road map for coordinated national and international efforts to ensure that freedom of religion or belief is not undermined.[65] The Council has been swift to adopt new human rights instruments, such as the International Convention for the Protection of all Persons from Enforced Disappearance, the Optional Protocol to the ICESCR, and the third Optional Protocol to the Convention on the Rights of the Child.

The experience with the UPR mechanism has been extremely positive. The future of the special procedures system appears secure, and the interactive dialogue of Council members with mandate holders is substantive and, on the whole, respectful, although at times robust. Established practices for the participation of NGOs in the work of the Council have been maintained and the role of NHRIs strengthened. It is to be hoped that the Council builds on this progress, in particular by continuing to respond swiftly to human rights crises in countries and rejecting attacks on the universality of rights, to consolidate its role as the primary global human rights advocate and monitor.

3 THE TREATY-BASED BODIES

When the UDHR was adopted in December 1948, there was broad agreement that the rights it enshrined should be spelled out in treaties that would be binding on those states which ratified, acceded, or succeeded to them. The year 1965 saw the adoption of the International Convention on the Elimination of Racial Discrimination (ICERD) by the General Assembly, while the ICCPR and the ICESCR were adopted in 1966. Since then, a further seven 'core' UN human rights treaties have been adopted, as have substantive and procedural protocols, most under the auspices of the Commission on Human Rights and the Human Rights Council. All UN member states have ratified at least one of the core human rights treaties. While it is often argued that no further human rights standard-setting activities are required and that new instruments would duplicate rather than complement those which exist, new instruments have been proposed on topics such

---

[64] HR Council Res 17/19 (14 July 2011).   [65] HR Council Res 17/13 (24 March 2011).

as the human rights of older persons[66] and the regulation of private military and security companies.[67]

Where the core human rights treaties are concerned, an expert body composed of between 10 and 23 independent experts—a 'human rights treaty body'—examines the progress made by states parties in the implementation of the treaty guarantees (see Table 18.1 for an overview of UN treaty bodies). A 25-member treaty body also implements the mandates created by the Optional Protocol to the Convention against Torture. Treaty body experts are elected at biannual meetings of states parties to the instruments on the basis of their expertise in human rights.[68] Although they are nominated by states parties, experts are independent and not subject to instruction from any government. Each expert works *pro-bono* and is not an employee of the UN. The treaty bodies hold two or three regular sessions of two to four weeks' duration per year, in Geneva.

Each treaty body is invested with various tools to assist states parties' implementation of their treaty obligations, including consideration of state reports, the issuance of general comments, the conduct of inquiries, and individual communication procedures.

3.1 STATE REPORTING

States parties to the core UN human rights treaties undertake to report regularly on their implementation of the treaty.[69] Initial reports must generally be submitted to the relevant treaty body within one year of the treaty entering into force for the state concerned. Thereafter, periodic reports are due in accordance with the provisions of the treaty or the established practice of the treaty body concerned; periodicity varies from two to five years.

All treaty bodies have issued detailed reporting guidelines on the form and content of initial and periodic reports.[70] In general, states are to submit a 'Treaty Specific Document' setting out the legal, administrative, and judicial measures taken to give effect to the treaty provisions and any difficulties encountered in implementing the rights. States are also to submit a 'Common Core Document' to all the treaty bodies to which they report, which sets out the general domestic legal and constitutional framework for the protection of human rights and information on implementation of substantive treaty provisions which are common to all, or several, treaties.

State reports are prepared at the national level, usually under the direction of a lead ministry or an inter-ministerial committee. The UN High Commissioner for Human Rights encourages systematization of the preparation of reports through the establishment of a national reporting and coordination mechanism to facilitate national consultations and follow-up. The preparation of the report offers states parties the opportunity to undertake a comprehensive review of measures they have taken to harmonize national laws and policies with provisions of the relevant international human rights instrument; monitor the progress made in the enjoyment of the rights in the treaties; identify shortcomings and problems with the domestic implementation; and evaluate future needs. The reporting

---

[66] See GA Res 65/182 (21 December 2010).   [67] See HR Council Res 15/26 (7 October 2010).

[68] The only exception is the Committee on Economic, Social and Cultural Rights, established by ECOSOC Res 1985/17 (28 May 1985), whose members are elected by member states of ECOSOC. Unlike other treaty bodies, membership is subject to strict regional distribution.

[69] See also OHCHR Report on the working methods of the human rights treaty bodies relating to the state party reporting process, HRI/ICM/2011/4 (23 May 2011).

[70] Most are based on the Harmonized guidelines on reporting under the international human rights treaties, HRI/ICM/2006/3 and Corr 1 (10 May 2006).

Table 18.1 Overview of the UN treaty bodies

Instrument	Treaty body	Number of states parties
International Convention on the Elimination of Racial Discrimination (ICERD)	Committee on the Elimination of Racial Discrimination (18 members)	176
International Covenant on Civil and Political Rights (ICCPR)	Human Rights Committee (18 members)	167
First Optional Protocol to the ICCPR (ICCPR-OP1)	Human Rights Committee	114
Second Optional Protocol to the ICCPR on the Abolition of the Death Penalty (ICCPR-OP2)	Human Rights Committee	77
International Covenant on Economic, Social and Cultural Rights (ICESCR)	Committee on Economic, Social and Cultural Rights (18 members)	160
Optional Protocol to the ICESCR (ICESCR-OP)	Committee on Economic, Social and Cultural Rights	10
Convention against Torture and Other Forms of Cruel, Inhuman and Degrading Treatment (UNCAT)	Committee against Torture (10 members)	153
Optional Protocol to UNCAT (UNCAT-OP)	Subcommittee on Prevention of Torture (25 members)	69
Convention on the Elimination of All Forms of Discrimination against Women (CEDAW)	Committee on the Elimination of Discrimination against Women (23 members)	187
Optional Protocol to CEDAW (CEDAW-OP)	Committee on the Elimination of Discrimination against Women	104
Convention on the Rights of the Child (CRC)	Committee on the Rights of the Child (18 members)	193
Optional Protocol on Sale of Children, Child Prostitution and Child Pornography	Committee on the Rights of the Child	164
Optional Protocol on Children in Armed Conflict	Committee on the Rights of the Child	151
Optional Protocol to the Convention on the Rights of the Child on a communications procedure	Committee on the Rights of the Child	6 (not yet in force)
International Convention on the Rights of Migrant Workers and their Families (ICRMW)	Committee on the Rights of Migrant Workers (14 members)	47
Convention on the Rights of Persons with Disabilities (CRPD)	Committee on the Rights of Persons with Disabilities (18 members)	133
Optional Protocol to the CRPD (CRPD-OP)	Committee on the Rights of Persons with Disabilities	78
International Convention for the Protection of all Persons from Enforced Disappearance (CPED)	Committee on Enforced Disappearances (10 members)	40

guidelines urge states to provide concrete examples of treaty implementation, and not focus exclusively on the constitutional and legal framework.

Once submitted, the report is translated into the working languages of the committee concerned and scheduled for examination. There is usually a delay in the consideration of the report as most treaty bodies have many reports awaiting examination. Some treaty bodies, such as the Committee on the Rights of the Child, have adopted the strategy of periodically meeting in two chambers to ensure reports are considered promptly. Normally one or two sessions prior to the session at which it will consider the state report, the treaty body will adopt a 'list of issues' based on all available information, including that provided by entities other than the state such as NGOs and NHRIs, which is sent to the state party. In replying to this list, the state party may update the information contained in its report, or provide additional information omitted earlier or deemed necessary by the treaty body. In 2007, the Committee against Torture adopted an optional reporting procedure. The Committee prepares lists of issues *prior* to the submission of the state report that are based on all available information. A state's response to this list of issues constitutes its periodic report. The Human Rights Committee and the Committee on Migrant Workers have now also adopted this procedure.

Consideration of reports takes place in public session, in the presence of a delegation of the state party. To date, one state party has appeared before a Committee using video-conferencing facilities. Treaty body members aim to engage the delegation in a constructive dialogue on how the guarantees in the relevant instrument can be respected better. After the public consideration, treaty bodies adopt 'concluding observations'. These identify progress in implementation since the last report, and remaining problems and concerns. Each concern is matched by a specific recommendation or practical advice designed to give the state suggestions on further steps to improve implementation. There is a clear correlation between the substance of the treaty body–state dialogue and the substance and specificity of the recommendations in concluding observations, which should be as targeted, specific, pragmatic, and implementable as possible, so that the state party may follow-up. The treaty bodies have been encouraged to adopt concluding observations which focus on priority concerns, are more user-friendly, and are shorter.

All the treaty bodies with the competence to review state reports require information on implementation of recommendations in previous concluding observations in the next state periodic report. The Human Rights Committee, the Committee against Torture, the Committee on the Elimination of Racial Discrimination, and the Committee on the Elimination of Discrimination against Women have developed procedures for follow-up to their concluding observations, and the Committee on Economic, Social and Cultural Rights is considering such a procedure. These committees generally invite states to report back within one or two years on all follow-up action. Most have appointed a Special Rapporteur or Coordinator for follow-up who is in regular contact with states parties. Where follow-up information is deficient or not forthcoming despite reminders, this individual can organize meetings with government representatives to survey possible follow-up action and urge the state party to implement the committee's recommendations. Most of the treaty bodies that have developed follow-up procedures report on the status of follow-up to their concluding observations in a chapter of their annual reports to the General Assembly.

An important feature of the reporting process is the contribution that various stakeholders make. All treaty bodies have emphasized the importance of cooperation with NGOs, whether national or international, and the positive role NGOs can play at the domestic level in follow-up activities. In addition, most treaty bodies have instituted formal mechanisms for consultations with NGOs.[71] NGOs often submit 'alternative', 'parallel', or 'shadow' reports to treaty bodies, which analyse and often challenge the content of the state party's report. Many treaty body members rely on NGO information when preparing their dialogue with the state party, or during the questioning of state delegations. Treaty bodies also receive information from NHRIs, and some have adopted guidelines for these institutions.[72] Input is also provided by specialized agencies and other entities of the UN system, including UN Country Teams (UNCTs).

Reporting to the treaty bodies may be a challenge for states parties, particularly those that have ratified most or all of the core instruments. Many states face a serious reporting backlog. The reports of some states are more than a decade overdue, and some may have never submitted a report. This has prompted the treaty bodies to coordinate and streamline their procedures, and discuss options for reform. States that experience difficulties with the reporting procedures may solicit technical assistance from the OHCHR, which has conducted many reporting workshops for governments, often in partnership with other organizations and/or NGOs.

Where states fail to submit reports despite repeated reminders, the relevant treaty body may initiate a process, sometimes referred to as the 'review procedure', for consideration of the state's implementation in the absence of a report. The state party is notified of the intention of the treaty body to proceed with a review in the absence of a report. Should the state party submit a report at this time, or indicate that one will be submitted, the review procedure is suspended. Where no such response is received, the treaty body may formulate a list of issues and questions for the state party and invite a state delegation to attend a nominated session. Concluding observations are formulated on the basis of the dialogue with the state party and other information. However, where no response is received the review will proceed in the absence of the state party. The state's performance in the fulfilment of its treaty obligations is examined by the treaty body in public session on the basis of existing information from relevant stakeholders and the concluding observations adopted are communicated to the state concerned. The review procedure is used in exceptional cases only; although since October 2010 the Human Rights Committee has examined at least one state party per session in this way. In most cases, notification by a committee that it intends to consider a state in the absence of a report results in the state agreeing to present the overdue report within a short deadline.

3.2 GENERAL COMMENTS

All treaty bodies, with the exception of the Sub-Committee for the Prevention of Torture, issue 'general comments'. In the case of the Committee on the Elimination of Racial Discrimination and the Committee on the Elimination of Discrimination against Women these are termed 'general recommendations'. These comments are developed through consultative processes, often after general discussions or informal meetings with states and other stakeholders, with some committees calling for written comments on drafts. The comments or recommendations are adopted by consensus and provide authoritative guidance on the general treaty obligations of states parties or set out how the treaty body interprets the scope of the substantive provisions of their treaty. Thus, they offer helpful

---

[71] See *Working with the United Nations Human Rights Programme: A Handbook for Civil Society* (2008), available at: <http://www.ohchr.org/EN/AboutUs/Pages/CivilSociety.aspx>.

[72] Eg, HRC, Paper on the relationship of the Human Rights Committee with national human rights institutions, CCPR/C/106/3 (13 November 2012).

interpretative guidance to states and other stakeholders. General comments and recommendations frequently deal with wider thematic or cross-cutting issues, such as the role of NHRIs, the obligations of states during states of emergency, violence against women, or gender-related dimensions of racial discrimination. While not legally binding, these comments are often invoked by states and complainants in reporting and complaints procedures, and, increasingly, by international, regional, and national courts in their judgments.[73]

3.3 INQUIRIES

The Committee against Torture, the Committee on the Elimination of Discrimination against Women, the Committee on Economic, Social and Cultural Rights, the Committee on the Rights of Persons with Disabilities, and the Committee on the Rights of the Child[74] may initiate inquiries upon receipt of reliable, well-founded indications of serious, grave, or systematic violations of the respective conventions by a state party. Inquiries may only be conducted in relation to states that have recognized the competence of the relevant committee to conduct them. The inquiry procedures are confidential and the cooperation of the state party is required throughout. Once a state has consented to an inquiry, the relevant committee may urgently designate one or several members to undertake a confidential inquiry and report back. Where this is warranted and the state consents, this may include a visit to the state. The findings of the members are examined by the whole committee and transmitted to the state party with appropriate recommendations. A report on the inquiry can only be published, or summarized in the committee's annual report, with the state party's consent. The Committee against Torture has conducted inquiries in Brazil, Mexico, Nepal, Peru, Sri Lanka, Turkey, and the former Yugoslavia; the Committee on the Elimination of Discrimination against Women has conducted one inquiry, which took place in Mexico.

A similar inquiry procedure is created by Article 33 CPED, although states parties do not have to have recognized the competence of the Committee on Enforced Disappearance for it to conduct inquiries. In addition to the inquiry procedure, the Committee on Enforced Disappearance has two other innovative methods of dealing with urgent or severe violations of the CPED. First, the Committee may request for urgent action that a disappeared person be sought and found. Second, having sought information from the state concerned, the Committee may bring well-founded indications that enforced disappearance is being practised on a widespread or systematic basis by a state party to the attention of the General Assembly through the Secretary-General.[75]

The UNCAT-OP creates a novel preventative inquiry mechanism. It establishes a system of complementary regular visits to places of detention conducted by both independent international and national bodies. UNCAT-OP's two-pillar approach relies on an international body, the Subcommittee on Prevention of Torture, and 'national preventive mechanisms' (NPMs)—national bodies which must be established by each state party within one year of entry into force of the UNCAT-OP for the relevant state. NPMs should have unrestricted access to all places of detention and all relevant information about the treatment and conditions of detention of individuals deprived of liberty. In order to discharge its mandate to advise states on national mechanisms and supervise their work, the

---

[73] Eg *Case Concerning Ahmadou Sadio Diallo (Republic of Guinea v Democratic Republic of Congo)* [2010] ICJ Rep 639; *Secretary of Security v Sakthevel Prabakar* [2005] 1 HKLRD 289 (Hong Kong Court of Final Appeal); *Vishaka v State of Rajasthan* (1997) 6 SCC 241 (Supreme Court of India).

[74] Although this competence is not yet in force for the Committee on the Rights of the Child.

[75] CPED, Arts 30 and 34.

Subcommittee should have the same level of unrestricted access as the NPMs. Since the beginning of its activities in 2007, the Subcommittee has conducted 16 visits to states parties, one follow-up visit, and three visits to advise NPMs.

3.4 COMPLAINTS PROCEDURES

The ability to claim that human rights have been violated is an important part of the protection mechanisms of the UN human rights treaties. The ICCPR-OP1, ICESCR-OP, UNCAT, ICERD, CPED, and CRC-OP3 provide for a state party to complain to the relevant treaty body that another state party is not fulfilling its treaty obligations where both states concerned have accepted this competence.[76] These are known as inter-state complaints mechanisms. To date there have been no inter-state complaints to treaty bodies. Instead, attention has been focused on mechanisms for individuals to complain that their rights under a particular treaty have been violated by a state party.

Seven treaty bodies, the Human Rights Committee, the Committee against Torture, the Committee for the Elimination of Racial Discrimination, the Committee for the Elimination of Discrimination against Women, the Committee on the Rights of Persons with Disabilities, the Committee on Enforced Disappearances, and the Committee on Economic, Social and Cultural Rights, currently implement optional individual complaints procedures. These procedures allow individuals to complain that a state party has violated their convention rights. As these are optional mechanisms, states must accept the competence of the relevant committee to receive individual complaints. To date, there have been no individual complaints considered under the CESCR-OP or the CPED. The ICRMW and the CRC-OP3 also provide for optional individual complaints procedures, but these are not yet functioning as they have not been accepted by the required number of states.

The procedure for the examination of individual complaints is generally characterized as 'quasi-judicial'. It is written and confidential; and oral hearings are rare.[77] Complaints are pre-screened as to their compatibility with the provisions of the relevant treaty and fulfilment of basic admissibility requirements by the OHCHR. Complainants do not need to be legally represented, but this is advisable. However, there is no UN system of legal aid to help with this. Complaints may be brought by third parties on behalf of individuals provided they have given their written consent or are unable to do so.[78]

A treaty body member designated as Special Rapporteur for New Communications (Human Rights Committee, Committee against Torture), or a Working Group (Committee on the Elimination of Discrimination against Women) decides on the registration of complaints and issues instructions on how to proceed with new cases. Once formally registered, the complaint is normally transmitted to the respondent state party for observations. Deadlines for observations vary, but states generally have six months to submit observations on both the admissibility and merits of a communication. As the treaty bodies are careful to apply the principle of equality of arms, each party must be able to

---

[76] ICCPR, Art 41; ICESCR-OP, Art 10; UNCAT, Art 21; ICERD, Arts 12–13, CPED, Art 32; CRC-OP3, Art 12.

[77] On 8 May 2012, the Committee against Torture held its first oral hearing in *Abdussamatov et al. v Kazakhstan* (444/2010).

[78] Where the CRC-OP is concerned, the Committee's rules of procedure provide that if there is a concern that representation, despite the victim's consent, may be a result of improper pressure, the Committee may request additional information or documents to show that the submission of a complaint on the alleged victim's behalf is not a result of improper pressure or inducement and is in the best interests of the child. Complaints may also be submitted on behalf of the alleged victim without express consent, provided that the complainant can justify his or her action and the Committee deems it to be in the best interests of the child.

comment on the other's submissions and allegations. Therefore, the state party's observations are sent to the complainant for comments. If a state party fails to respond to a complaint, the relevant treaty body usually bases its assessment of the situation on the facts as submitted by the complainant, provided they are properly substantiated. A state party may request that the treaty body examine the admissibility of the communication separately from the merits should it believe that the communication is inadmissible. The state must set out the reasons for its view. In such circumstances the complainant is given the opportunity to respond to the claims of inadmissibility and it is then for the treaty body to decide whether to consider the admissibility and merits of the communication separately.

Treaty bodies may issue interim measures of protection in situations of particular urgency which require immediate action to prevent irreparable harm to the complainant. These are often issued in death penalty, life-threatening, and deportation or extradition cases.[79] The vast majority of states parties comply with such requests. Despite this, requests for interim measures should remain confined to the most urgent and exceptional situations—too liberal a practice may jeopardize the state party's compliance with the request. In the past, the Human Rights Committee and the Committee against Torture have been criticized for being over-generous with their requests for interim measures and they now issue requests for 'provisional measures of protection'. Such requests differ from interim measures as they indicate explicitly that they may be reviewed, at the request of the state, in light of information and comments received from it and further comments, if any, from the complainant. Treaty bodies regard compliance with interim measures requests as inherent in a state party's treaty obligations and any failure to comply with them a serious breach thereof.[80]

Decisions on admissibility are adopted either at the level of the Committee plenary (Committee on the Elimination of Racial Discrimination, Committee against Torture, Committee on the Elimination of Discrimination against Women, Committee on the Rights of Persons with Disabilities) or at the level of a working group (Human Rights Committee). The Committees examine a number of admissibility criteria.[81] First, the complainant must show that he or she is a 'victim' of a violation of provisions of the instrument he or she invokes. The complainant must be personally affected by the impugned state action. General claims by groups or an individual not affected by the alleged violation ('actio popularis') are not permissible.

Second, the complaint must relate to events which occurred *after* the entry into force of the complaint mechanism for the state party concerned (admissibility *ratione temporis*) unless these produce effects after the entry into force which constitute a violation of the relevant treaty.

Third, the complaint must relate to rights that are actually protected by the instrument invoked by the complainant (admissibility *ratione materiae*).

Fourth, the same matter must not have been examined by the treaty body concerned or by another international investigation or settlement procedure, such as the European Court of Human Rights, the Inter-American Court of Human Rights, or the African Commission on Human and Peoples' Rights, or be undergoing examination by such a

---

[79] Rules of Procedure of the Human Rights Committee, Rule 92; Rules of Procedure of the Committee against Torture, Rule 108(1); Rules of Procedure of the Committee on the Elimination of Racial Discrimination, Rule 94(3). Explicit powers to request interim measures are included in the CEDAW-OP, CRPD-OP, CPED, CESCR-OP, and CRC-OP.

[80] Eg *Piandiong v The Philippines*, CCPR/C/70/D/869/1999 (19 October 2000) para 5.2.

[81] These admissibility criteria are set out in the ICCPR-OP1; CERD, Art 14; UNCAT, Art 22; CEDAW-OP; CPRD-OP; CPED, Art 31.

procedure. In regard to ICCPR-OP1 and CPED, only those cases that are being examined by such a procedure at the same time as the communication to the UN treaty body will be excluded. Most European states parties have entered a reservation to the ICCPR-OP1 to the effect that once the European Court of Human Rights has disposed of a complaint, it cannot subsequently be considered by the Human Rights Committee.[82]

Fifth, the complainant must have exhausted all available domestic remedies. This means that, in principle, the highest court of the state party concerned must have considered and dismissed the case before a treaty body may consider it. The rule does not apply if the pursuit of domestic remedies has been 'unreasonably prolonged'. This is an assessment that must be made on a case-by-case basis. Such remedies must not only be available but also *effective*, thereby offering a reasonable prospect of actual redress.

Complaints that do not fulfil these criteria will be declared inadmissible and such decisions are final.[83] Those complaints declared admissible are referred to the state party for observations on the merits, if such observations have not already been given. Once provided and the complainant has been given a reasonable opportunity to comment on these observations, or the deadline for submission has expired, the treaty body will examine the merits of the case.

The CESCR-OP and CRC-OP provide that their respective committees shall make available their good offices to the parties with a view to reaching a friendly settlement of the matter of the communication. An agreement on a friendly settlement terminates consideration of the communication. Treaty bodies generally adopt decisions on complaints—called 'views' or 'opinions'—by consensus. Often those experts who do not share the opinion of the majority append individual (dissenting or concurring) opinions to the final decisions. This does not in any way undermine the authority of the decision. The participant judges of three judicial colloquia on the domestic application of international human rights norms and jurisprudence held in Nairobi (2006), Panama (2008), and Bangkok (2009) all underlined that treaty body decisions must be thoroughly and cogently argued for them to be useful as a potential judicial precedent for the national judge.[84]

One, if not the principal, weakness of the treaty body complaints procedures is that the final merits decisions are not strictly speaking legally binding and thus cannot be enforced. However, in its General Comment 33, the Human Rights Committee stated that although its views are non-binding they 'exhibit some important characteristics of a judicial decision'.[85] Furthermore, the Committee stated that its views are an authoritative interpretation of the ICCPR by a body entrusted by states parties to give such interpretations, and, as such, the principle of good faith to treaty obligations requires that states cooperate with the Committee and inform it of action taken to implement its views. In order to strengthen the legal value of their decisions, the treaty bodies have Special Rapporteurs mandated to consider state follow-up on views. These Rapporteurs monitor how states parties respond to the recommendations for a remedy and other measures to be taken following the finding of a violation. It is normally expected that states will submit follow-up information

---

[82] See Phuong, 'The Relationship Between the European Court of Human Rights and the Human Rights Committee: Has the "Same Matter" Already Been "Examined"?' (2007) 7 *HRLR* 385.

[83] CESCR-OP provides that the Committee on Economic, Social and Cultural Rights may decline to consider a communication of it does not reveal that the alleged victim has suffered a 'clear disadvantage', unless the Committee considers that the communication raises a serious issue of general importance.

[84] Judicial Colloquium on the Domestic Application of International Human Rights Norms, Outcome Document (23–5 March 2009) para 4(a).

[85] HRC, General Comment 33, CCPR/C/GC/33 (5 November 2008) para 11.

within a few months of a decision. The Special Rapporteurs are in regular contact with states parties and the annual reports of the treaty bodies to the General Assembly include a chapter in which state party follow-up to views is detailed. All follow-up information provided by the parties to a case is, in principle, public.[86]

It is difficult to categorize state party follow-up. Many states parties pay compensation to victims, even though some observe they do so not as a matter of legal obligation but *ex gratia*. Others have released individuals detained or imprisoned arbitrarily, or commuted death sentences. Others either do not provide follow-up information or challenge the findings of the treaty body concerned. 'Enabling legislation'—that is, legislation that makes decisions of treaty bodies enforceable at the national level—is rare. However, the fact that all treaty bodies which decide complaints have instituted and largely synchronized follow-up mechanisms has improved the level of compliance with recommendations.

For many years, the treaty bodies developed their jurisprudence under the complaints procedures in what could be called 'splendid isolation' from that of regional human rights mechanisms or national tribunals. This raised the spectre of conflicting interpretations of substantively very similar, if not identical, provisions of international or regional human rights instruments. One such example is the different treatment of the 'death row phenomenon' and the prohibition of torture and cruel, inhuman, and degrading treatment under the ICCPR and the European Convention on Human Rights by the Human Rights Committee and the European Court of Human Rights.[87] More recently, comparative analyses of jurisprudence prepared by the OHCHR have helped treaty bodies to keep abreast of relevant developments in regional and national tribunals. This has led to a welcome 'cross-fertilization' of human rights jurisprudence. The treaty bodies now take into account the relevant jurisprudence of regional courts and national tribunals when seized of complex or novel legal issues. Conversely, the regional mechanisms (for example, the European Court of Human Rights and the Inter-American Court of Human Rights)[88] and some national tribunals now regularly rely on, or cite, treaty body jurisprudence. This contributes to the emergence of substantively consistent and truly universal human rights jurisprudence.

3.5 TREATY BODY COORDINATION, HARMONIZATION, REFORM, AND STRENGTHENING

The treaty bodies have continuously sought to improve their effectiveness by streamlining and harmonizing their working methods and practices. Even so, differences remain in areas such as the treatment of NGO information, the preparation of lists of issues, or the procedure for the examination of reports. Many states parties complain of such procedural differences and urge further harmonization.

Since 1984, the treaty body chairpersons have assembled, first on an *ad hoc* basis, and then annually since 1994, to discuss issues of common concern, working methods, common approaches to thematic issues, and so on, with a view to enhancing the effectiveness of the treaty body system as a whole. In 2010 and 2012, the Annual Meeting of Chairpersons of Human Rights Treaty Bodies was held in Brussels and Addis Ababa, respectively, in

---

[86] Follow-up to Decisions, HRI/ICM/2009/7 (11 November 2009) para 5.

[87] Compare *Soering v UK* (1989) 11 EHRR 439 and *Barrett and Sutcliffe v Jamaica*, CCPR/C/44/D/270 and 271/1998 (30 March 1992).

[88] Eg IACtHR, *González (Claudia) et al. ('Cotton Field') v Mexico*, IACtHR Series C No 205 (16 November 2009); *Opuz v Turkey* (2010) 50 EHRR 28.

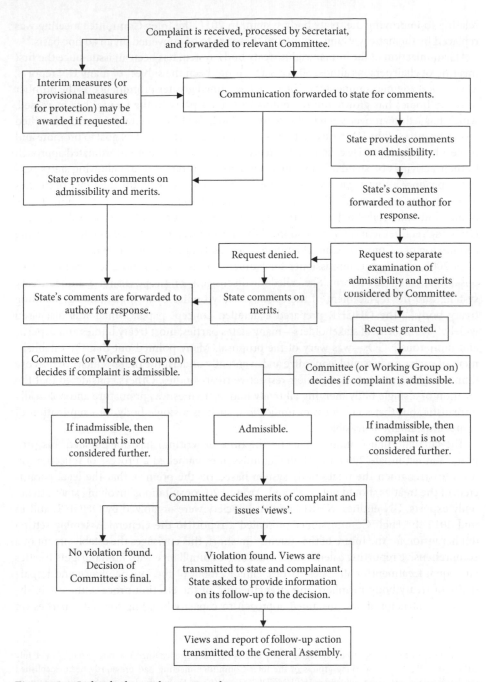

Figure 18.1 Individual complaints procedures

order to bring the treaty bodies closer to the site of implementation and strengthen links among international and regional mechanisms and institutions and stakeholders. In 2013, it met in New York to consider treaty body strengthening. In addition to the Annual Meeting, an 'Inter-Committee Meeting', in which the chairperson and two other members of each treaty body participated, was convened. These meetings took place prior to the Annual Meeting of Chairpersons and allowed for more detailed discussion of proposals relating to improving the treaty body system. In 2011, the Inter-Committee meeting was replaced by thematic working groups and these are to be convened on an ad hoc basis.[89]

Harmonization of the human rights treaty body system has been an issue since the first meeting of chairpersons almost 30 years ago. It has been the subject of many UN reports, as well as academic commentary. The issue has gained greater prominence as the number of treaty bodies has grown and the number of states party to the treaties has increased, which has led to an over-stretched system. In 2002, the UN Secretary-General identified modernization of the UN treaty system as a crucial element in the UN goal to promote and protect human rights. He called on the treaty bodies to craft a more coordinated approach to their activities by standardizing their reporting requirements and allowing states parties to produce a *single report* summarizing their compliance with the full range of treaties to which they are a party.[90] The idea of a single report did not gain favour with the treaty bodies and other stakeholders, but the treaty bodies were amenable to standardizing their reporting requirements and most adopted the harmonized reporting guidelines requiring submission of a Common Core Document and Treaty Specific Document.

In 2005, the High Commissioner for Human Rights made a more far-reaching, proposal for treaty body reform. She called for discussions on proposals for a unified treaty system, and the replacement of the existing treaty bodies by a single, unified, standing treaty body.[91] The OHCHR prepared a detailed concept paper, which was discussed widely.[92] A majority of stakeholders—many states parties, most treaty bodies and experts, and numerous NGOs—was wary of the proposal. Many pointed out that the establishment of such a body would jeopardize and eventually undermine the specificity of the core human rights instruments and their respective treaty bodies. Others considered that the creation of a single body merging all treaty body activities was premature and politically unrealistic, but that some form of unification, such as a single body for examination of complaints, might be feasible.

The current High Commissioner (at the time of writing) has not pursued this proposal. Rather, in late 2009, the High Commissioner launched a process of reflection on ways to strengthen the treaty body system based on the premise that the legal parameters of the treaties should not be altered. Around 20 consultations involving states, treaty body experts, UN entities, NHRIs, and civil society were organized by OHCHR, and in mid-2012 the High Commissioner presented a report to the General Assembly setting out her vision for the future of the system.[93] In short, this envisages the establishment of a comprehensive reporting calendar to ensure strict compliance with human rights treaties and equal treatment of all states parties; enhancement of the independence and impartiality of treaty body members and strengthening of the election process; the establishment of a structured and sustained approach to capacity-building for states parties on

---

[89] Report of the chairs of human rights treaty bodies on their twenty-third meeting, A/66/175 (21 July 2011), para 25. Ad hoc working groups of the Inter-Committee meeting had previously been established on: harmonized reporting guidelines (HRI/MC/2006/3 and Corr 1); harmonization of working methods (HRI/MC/2007/2); reservations (HRI/MC/2007/5); and follow-up to concluding observations, decisions on individual complaints and inquiries (HRI/ICM/2011/3-HRI/MC/2011/2).

[90] Strengthening of the United Nations: An Agenda for Further Change, A/57/387 (9 September 2002) paras 52–4.

[91] Plan of Action submitted by the High Commissioner for Human Rights. Annex to 'In Larger Freedom: Towards Development, Security and Human Rights for All', Report of the Secretary-General, A/59/2005/Add.3 (26 May 2006).

[92] Concept Paper on the High Commissioner's Proposal for a Unified Standing Treaty Body, HRI/MC/2006/CRP.1 (14 March 2006).

[93] High Commissioner for Human Rights, UN Reform: Measures and Proposals, A/66/960 (26 June 2012).

reporting; ensuring consistency of treaty body jurisprudence in individual communications; increasing coordination among the treaty bodies in respect of individual communications, including through adoption of common guidelines on procedural questions; increasing the accessibility and visibility of the system, including through webcasting and other technology; the introduction of a focused reporting procedure; alignment of working methods in compliance with the normative specificities of the treaties; and limitation of the length of documentation. The High Commissioner's proposals have been well received by treaty body members and others. In 2012, an inter-governmental process on strengthening and enhancing the effective functioning of the human rights treaty body system was established by the General Assembly.[94] This intergovernmental process is due to conclude during 2013 and, although the High Commissioner's proposals have been welcomed, it remains to be seen whether they will be adopted.

3.6 IN CONCLUSION

The activities of the human rights treaty bodies have developed greatly in terms of scope and sophistication. The reporting procedures are being increasingly harmonized to assist states parties with multiple reporting obligations, whilst the quality, specificity, and usability of concluding observations has gradually improved, making it possible for states parties to follow-up on recommendations meaningfully. Follow-up procedures have helped to keep those states parties that display little or no political will to implement treaty body recommendations engaged. In terms of individual complaints, the jurisprudence emanating from such procedures has improved substantively and qualitatively over the years. A very positive development has been the increasing 'cross fertilization' of human rights jurisprudence. Follow-up to decisions of the treaty bodies has also improved, with increasing numbers of states granting appropriate remedies following a finding of a violation.

Despite these achievements, the treaty bodies continue to face challenges. First, the state reporting procedures must be further harmonized and simplified to prompt *all* states parties to meet their reporting obligations and reduce the large number of overdue reports. Further efforts are necessary to encourage all states parties to report using the Guidelines for the Common Core Document and Treaty Specific reports. Second, some of the treaty-based complaints procedures face a backlog of pending communications that must be reduced as a matter of priority. While the quality of decisions has improved, consensual decision-making is slow and cumbersome. The non-binding nature of treaty body decisions remains a concern. Although it is currently politically unrealistic to call for treaty amendments that would make all final decisions under the treaty-based complaints procedures legally binding and executable, follow-up procedures that strengthen the domestic implementation of decisions should be developed further. Finally, endeavours with the ultimate objective of creating an holistic and harmonious functioning of the treaty body system should continue. This is all the more necessary with the entry into force of new instruments and the likely establishment of new mechanisms. In the long term, however, harmonization of working methods will not address the challenge posed by the existence of ten human rights treaty bodies enjoying similar competence and attracting wide acceptance.[95] This challenge can be met only by the provision of appropriate financial and human resources to the system or profound structural change.

---

[94] GA Res 66/254 (15 May 2012).

[95] Report of the Secretary-General, Measures to improve further the effectiveness and harmonization and reform of the treaty body system, A/66/344 (7 September 2011).

4 THE OFFICE OF THE UN HIGH COMMISSIONER FOR HUMAN RIGHTS

Since the adoption of the UDHR the international community sought to establish a body within the UN that could support implementation of human rights obligations by countries at the national level and effectively deal with human rights violations. Suggestions for the creation of a UN High Commissioner for Human Rights were advanced as early as 1947 and in the mid-1960s Costa Rica made a concrete proposal, but for political reasons it was dropped.[96]

The 1993 World Conference on Human Rights reactivated discussions about the institution and mandate of a High Commissioner for Human Rights. Paragraph 18 of the Vienna Declaration, adopted by the Conference, called on the General Assembly to 'begin, as a matter of priority, consideration of the question of the establishment of a High Commissioner for Human Rights'. The General Assembly reacted swiftly, establishing a working group on the issue, and, on 20 December 1993, General Assembly Resolution 48/141, which created the post of High Commissioner for Human Rights and set out its mandate, was adopted without a vote. The first UN High Commissioner for Human Rights, José Ayala Lasso from Ecuador, took office in April 1994. Since then there have been four High Commissioners.[97]

The High Commissioner has the responsibility of promoting and protecting the effective enjoyment by all of all human rights. In order to carry out this mandate, she is to liaise with competent UN bodies and issue recommendations on how to improve promotion and protection of human rights, as well as rationalize and strengthen the UN human rights machinery. The High Commissioner should also coordinate UN education and public human rights information programmes. States should be helped to realize their human rights obligations by providing advisory, technical, and financial services, and engaging governments in dialogue aimed at improving human rights protection. As well as enhancing international cooperation for the promotion of human rights, the High Commissioner should play an active role in removing current obstacles to the full realization of all human rights, and in preventing the continuation of human rights violations throughout the world. Finally, the High Commissioner is to promote the realization of the right to development. The High Commissioner reports annually to the Human Rights Council and the General Assembly on her activities and those of her office—the OHCHR.

The High Commissioner fulfils this extensive mandate through the OHCHR, which is part of the UN Secretariat. The OHCHR has developed greatly in terms of the scope of its activities, the mandates it supports and services, and the human and financial resources made available to it.[98] The headquarters of the OHCHR are located in Geneva, with an office in New York. In addition, the OHCHR has staff based in around 60 countries as part of regional offices, country offices, as human rights components of UN peace operations, and as part of UN country teams.

---

[96] Clapham, 'Creating the High Commissioner for Human Rights: The Outside Story' (1994) 5 *EJIL* 556.

[97] To date at the time of writing: Mary Robinson (Ireland); Sergio Vieira de Mello (Brazil); Louise Arbour (Canada); Navanethem Pillay (South Africa). Bertrand G. Ramcharan (Guyana) was Acting High Commissioner from August 2003 to June 2004.

[98] See OHCHR, *Report 2012* (2013), available at: <http://www2.ohchr.org/english/ohchrreport2011/web_version/ohchr_report2012_web>.

The work of the OHCHR focuses on three broad areas: human rights standard-setting, human rights monitoring, and supporting human rights implementation at the country level. Within these three areas, it provides expertise and substantive (research and analysis) and technical support to the UN human rights bodies described above and contributes to the monitoring of human rights situations and implementation of human rights standards at the national level. More specifically at the national level, the OHCHR provides technical expertise and capacity development on the ground, including in relation to laws, policies, and institutions. It also provides support to NHRIs, civil society, and individuals and groups in their advocacy and efforts to claim their rights, including through human rights education and information. The OHCHR responds to human rights emergencies with rapid deployments, and provides guidance regarding follow-up to UPR, treaty body, and special procedures mandate holders' recommendations. The OHCHR also supports the High Commissioner in her role as the global human rights conscience and advocate. Since 2010, the OHCHR has pursued six thematic priorities in its work, which reflect leading human rights challenges. These are: countering discrimination; combating impunity and strengthening accountability, the rule of law, and democratic society; pursuing economic, social, and cultural rights and combating inequalities and poverty; protecting human rights in the context of migration; protecting human rights in situations of conflict, violence, and insecurity; and strengthening international human rights mechanisms and the progressive development of international human rights law.

The UN Declaration on the Right to Development, adopted in 1986,[99] the Millennium Development Goals (MDGs), set out in the Millennium Declaration of September 2000,[100] and the discussions relating to the post-2015 agenda also have manifold implications for the work of the OHCHR. Development issues cut across much of the work of the OHCHR, and it works actively on the links between human rights and development activities, in particular the MDGs. The OHCHR provides methodological expertise and field support in the areas of the right to development, poverty and aid policy issues, human rights indicators, human trafficking, anti-corruption policies, globalization, and trade. The work programme of the OHCHR in this area is largely defined by reference to decisions of the General Assembly and the Human Rights Council, and the work and recommendations of the latter's Open-Ended Working Group on the Right to Development. The OHCHR provides methodological support to UN country teams and human rights field presences in respect of the MDGs and works on development policy and programming issues under the auspices of the UN Development Group, in particular with regard to the post-2015 agenda.

Much of the work of the OHCHR now takes place in the field and there has been an identifiable shift of emphasis away from headquarters. The importance of work in the field cannot be underestimated. For example, the genocide in Rwanda in 1994, which had been predicted by NGOs and development agencies on the ground, highlighted the need for the establishment of preventive mechanisms, of which human rights field presences were seen as part and parcel. The first High Commissioner made the creation of field presences a priority, and a field office in Rwanda was set up in 1994. Since then the OHCHR has taken numerous policy decisions designed to 'operationalize' its activities and create and strengthen field presences—whether country-specific, regional, or part of peacekeeping missions—throughout the world. By the end of 2012, the OHCHR ran or supported 59 field presences.

---

[99] GA Res 41/128 (4 December 1986).   [100] GA Res 55/2 (8 September 2000).

The decision to create a field presence is taken in consultation with the relevant government, taking into consideration the domestic human rights situation, security and political considerations, human and financial resources, administrative arrangements, and the scope of activities to be undertaken (whether monitoring and/or technical cooperation activities). The OHCHR country and stand-alone offices are established on the basis of a standard agreement between OHCHR and the host government that delineates the activities of the field presence: generally, human rights observation, technical cooperation activities, and public reporting. However, some field presences are restricted to technical cooperation only. Regional offices and centres are also established on the basis of an agreement with the host governments and in consultation with other countries in the region, and these focus on cross-cutting regional human rights concerns and assisting governments in their interaction with human rights mechanisms. Several regional human rights centres, such as those in Cambodia, Cameroon, and Doha, have been created by the General Assembly, and their mandates are set out in their constituent resolutions. Similarly, where there is a human rights component to a Security Council peacekeeping, special political, or peace-building mission, such as in Mali, Libya, and South Sudan, the mandate is governed by the Security Council resolution creating the mission. Finally, human rights advisers in UN country teams assist and support the integration of human rights into programming activities, and seek to build the human rights capacity of national stakeholders. Reports on the work of field presences are regularly presented to the Human Rights Council for consideration and possible action.

The variety and complexity of field presences have grown beyond expectation since 1994. While some standalone field presences are tiny and closely associated with the local UN country team, other field offices, for example in Cambodia and Colombia, are staffed by numerous human rights officers recruited both internationally and locally. Where larger country offices are actively engaged in monitoring human rights violations and regular reporting thereon, relations with the host state's authorities can become strained. Sometimes the re-negotiation with the relevant government of the agreement for the field presence may become a politically difficult exercise that requires the personal involvement of the High Commissioner. The 2005 World Summit recognized that human rights, peace and security, and development were the pillars of the UN system, and resolved to strengthen the OHCHR through the doubling of its regular budget resources over five years.[101] Yet less than 3 per cent of the total UN regular budget is allocated to OHCHR and much of its activities are funded by voluntary contributions. For example, in 2012, just over 40 per cent of OHCHR's funding needs were covered by the UN regular budget, with the remainder being made up of voluntary funding from states and other donors. Predominantly, extra-budgetary resources support work not covered by the regular budget, the majority of which is activities in the field. Voluntary contributions also assist the financing of implementation of mandates established by intergovernmental bodies, as frequently the regular budget allocation for these is insufficient. The dependence on voluntary contributions may be problematic because the OHCHR consistently relies on the contributions of major donors to implement essential activities and, thus, these will be affected in times of economic downturn when there is a funding shortfall. Indeed, in 2012, such a shortfall forced the OHCHR to cut posts and activities, with an appeal for funds being launched in 2013.[102] Furthermore, although the High Commissioner strongly

---

[101] GA Res 60/1 (24 October 2005) para 124.
[102] United Nations Human Rights Appeal 2013, available at: <http://www.ohchr.org/EN/PublicationsResources/Pages/AnnualReportAppeal/aspx>.

encourages unearmarked financing, major donor countries may be tempted to peg size-able voluntary contributions to achieve some political leverage over the content of pro-grammes, or influence staffing policy. This is a preoccupation voiced frequently by states, in particular non-donors.

5 HUMAN RIGHTS ACTIVITIES IN OTHER PARTS OF THE UN

In his first report on the renewal of the UN system published in 1997, former Secretary-General Kofi Annan advocated for the integration of human rights into the activities of other UN Departments and specialized agencies.[103] This process is known as 'mainstreaming' human rights and much progress has been made. General Assembly Resolution 60/251 tasks the Human Rights Council with an important role in promoting the effective coordination and mainstreaming of human rights within the UN system, and it convenes an annual discussion with heads of UN entities on this theme. Increased inte-gration of human rights standards and principles, including the right to development, into UN system policies relating to development, humanitarian action, peace and security, and economic and social issues, is one of the OHCHR's 11 global expected accomplishments, and much of the work of the OHCHR entails provision of guidance, policy advice, and technical support to implement the mainstreaming imperative. In addition, the OHCHR and other relevant UN entities have agreed a policy on human rights in UN peace opera-tions and political missions that provides guidance on how human rights are to be inte-grated into these activities.

In May 2008, the Secretary-General issued a policy decision reaffirming the central-ity of human rights in the development work of the UN and tasking OHCHR and the UN Development Group (UNDG) to initiate an inter-agency process to explore further system-wide coherence, collaboration, and support for Resident Co-ordinators and UN country teams in mainstreaming human rights. As a result, the UNDG Human Rights Mainstreaming Mechanism (UNDG-HRM), funded through a multi-donor trust fund, was established in 2009 to institutionalize human rights mainstreaming.[104] The Mechanism is made of up 19 UN agencies, funds, and programmes and is chaired by the OHCHR.

The OHCHR provides guidance, policy advice, and technical support in respect of the mainstreaming of human rights. This has influenced the approach of the main UN organs in the area of human rights, including the General Assembly, Security Council, Secretary-General, and International Court of Justice. These will be discussed in Sections 5.1, 5.2, 5.3, and 5.4.

5.1 GENERAL ASSEMBLY

The General Assembly, the UN's principal deliberative organ composed of all member states, is regularly seized of human rights issues. Article 13 UN Charter provides that the Assembly 'shall initiate studies and make recommendations for the purpose of... assisting in the realization of human rights and fundamental freedoms for all without distinction as to race, sex, language, or religion'. It is generally the Third Committee of the General

---

[103] Renewing the United Nations: A Programme for Reform, A/51/950 (14 July 1997) paras 78 and 79.
[104] See <http://hrbaportal.org/human-rights-mainstreaming-mechanism>.

Assembly, responsible for social, humanitarian, and cultural issues, which reviews human rights issues. The Third Committee receives and discusses the Human Rights Council's annual report (which is also considered by the General Assembly plenary); reports from the Council's special procedures; the annual report of the High Commissioner for Human Rights; annual reports of the treaty bodies; and reports on human rights issues considered by the Secretary-General. This Committee also negotiates and adopts resolutions on human rights issues.

The plenary General Assembly adopts human rights-related declarations or resolutions, such as on the right to development,[105] or on the outcome of the Council's review of its work and functioning.[106] It formally adopts new instruments in the field of human rights that have been adopted by the Council or other UN bodies. The General Assembly also discusses and endorses the results and outcome documents of international or world conferences dealing with human rights, such as the World Conference against Racism, Racial Discrimination, Xenophobia and Related Intolerance, held in Durban in 2001, and the Durban Review Conference, held in Geneva in 2009. Human rights instruments are also elaborated in ad hoc working groups of the General Assembly, while human rights considerations are also taken up during its High-level Meetings, for example the 2005 World Summit and the 2012 High-level Meeting on the Rule of Law. Finally, the General Assembly's Fifth Committee, on the advice of the Advisory Committee on Administrative and Budgetary Questions, approves the regular budget allocation to OHCHR on a biennial basis and each year considers the financial implications of the decisions and resolutions of the Human Rights Council.

5.2 SECURITY COUNCIL

The Security Council, the 15-member UN body with primary responsibility for the maintenance of international peace and security, has increasingly recognized the importance of the enjoyment of human rights for the fulfilment of its mandate. The Council has often characterized massive human rights violations as threats to international peace and its discussions and resolutions regarding situations in countries or regions, such as Afghanistan, the Democratic Republic of Congo, Haiti, Mali, Myanmar, the Middle East, including the Occupied Palestinian Territories, and Syria, frequently address human rights concerns. The Security Council also addresses several thematic issues with human rights dimensions. These include women, peace and security,[107] protection of civilians,[108] and sexual violence in armed conflict.[109] It has established a working group on children and armed conflict, made up of its 15 members, which examines reports of monitoring and reporting mechanisms in countries of concern and makes recommendations and monitors grave abuses of children that may occur in an armed conflict.[110] The Security Council has created mechanisms which touch on human rights issues. Thus, Council Resolution 1888 established a Special Representative of the Secretary-General on sexual violence in conflict who is empowered to report countries suspected to be responsible for such violence to the Security Council.[111] In addition, Security Council peacekeeping, or special political and peace-building support missions, increasingly have human rights promotion and

---

[105] n 99.   [106] n 63.   [107] SC Res 1325 (31 October 2000).
[108] SC Res 1674 (28 April 2006); SC Res 1894 (11 November 2009).
[109] SC Res 1820 (19 June 2008), SC Res 1888 (30 September 2009); SC Res 1889 (5 October 2009); SC Res 1960, (16 December 2010); SC Res 2106 (24 June 2013).
[110] SC Res 1612 (26 July 2005); SC Res 1882 (4 August 2009).   [111] SC Res 1888, n 109.

protection as part of their mandates. In early January 2013 there were 13 human rights components of such missions. The Security Council also conducts missions to the field during which human rights issues may be raised. Finally, the Council also has responded to impunity for massive human rights violations by establishing ad hoc international tribunals for the Former Yugoslavia and Rwanda and exercising its capacity to refer situations to the Prosecutor of the International Criminal Court in respect of Darfur[112] and Libya.[113] Its lack of action on Syria has led some critics to suggest that it fails to use this latter power consistently or well.

The High Commissioner for Human Rights and her senior staff regularly engage in open debates with the Security Council on protection of civilians and in formal meetings or informal consultations on country situations. Under the 'Arria formula',[114] which allows the Security Council to meet informally with non-members of the Council outside the Security Council Consultation Room, members of Human Rights Council commissions of inquiry, special procedures, and human rights components of peace missions have also provided human rights briefings that inform the work of the Security Council.[115]

Under Article 41 UN Charter, the Security Council may impose economic or other sanctions to quell a threat to peace. Examples of sanctions include those against Iraq during the regime of Saddam Hussein,[116] Angola during the civil war,[117] and Sudan for its policy in the Darfur region.[118] Although these sanctions were not adopted solely to stop human rights violations, the violations were taken into account. Sanctions have the potential to be a very important tool, but they may also harm innocent civilians rather than the political regime against which they are directed, as the devastating humanitarian results of 13 years of sanctions against Iraq demonstrate.[119] Accordingly, 'targeted' or 'smart' sanctions have been adopted by the Council, such as measures, including freezing of assets or travel bans, directed at those responsible for the violation of international law. These sanctions include humanitarian exemptions. A focal point to receive requests from most individuals and entities subject to sanctions to be 'de-listed' and grant humanitarian exemptions has been established by the Secretary-General at the request of the Security Council.[120]

In 2001 the Security Council adopted Resolution 1373, which requests that states take certain measures, such as financial, penal, and others, against those individuals listed as suspected terrorists, to enhance the international campaign against terrorism. States report to the Counter-Terrorism Committee (CTC) of the Security Council on their implementation of Resolution 1373, as well as other resolutions in the field of countering terrorism. However, as in the case of sanctions, such measures can adversely affect human rights enjoyment by individuals and Security Council Resolutions adopted since 2003 have reminded states that any measures they take to combat terrorism must comply

---

[112] SC Res 1593 (31 March 2005).   [113] SC Res 1970 (26 February 2011). See Chapter 24.

[114] Named after former Permanent Representative to the United Nations of Venezuela and Security Council President, Diego Arria.

[115] Breen, 'Revitalizing the United Nations Human Rights Special Procedures Mechanisms as a Means of Achieving and Maintaining International Peace and Security' (2008) 12 *Max Planck YB of UN Law* 177.

[116] SC Res 661 (6 August 1990).   [117] SC Res 864 (15 September 1993).

[118] SC Res 1591 (29 March 2005).

[119] See The adverse consequences of economic sanctions, E/CN.4/Sub.22000/33 (21 June 2000); CESCR, General Comment 8, HRI/GEN/1/Rev.9 (Vol I) 43, para 3.

[120] SC Res 1730 (2006). A dedicated ombudsperson deals with delisting requests from those on the Al-Qaida Sanctions List.

with their international obligations, in particular international human rights, refugee, and humanitarian law.[121]

5.3 SECRETARY-GENERAL

The Secretary-General of the UN is the 'chief administrative officer' of the organization and is appointed by the General Assembly upon the recommendation of the Security Council.[122] The role of the Secretary-General is rather loosely defined in the UN Charter, and each holder of the post has defined their role in different ways. Most importantly the Secretary-General is to uphold the values and authority of the UN in all his or her work.

The Secretary-General at the time of writing, Ban Ki Moon, frequently recalls the 2005 Summit's acknowledgment that peace and security, development, and human rights are the pillars of the UN system and are interlinked and mutually reinforcing. He reaffirmed the central role of human rights in the work of the UN in his Five-year Action Agenda in 2012 and often underlines the relevance of the 'Responsibility to Protect' as a tool for prevention and response. Indeed, he designated 2012 as the 'year of prevention'.

The Secretary-General regularly addresses the Human Rights Council and has taken up a range of human rights concerns, including discrimination and violence against women, reprisals against human rights advocates, and discrimination and violence based on sexual orientation and gender identity in this and other fora.[123] In addition, in 2011, the Secretary-General instituted a human rights due diligence policy, which provides guidance to those UN entities that support non-UN security forces. The policy sets out the measures UN entities must take to exercise 'due diligence' to ensure that UN support is not provided to non-UN security forces where there are substantial grounds for believing there is a real risk that they may commit grave violations of international humanitarian, human rights, or refugee law. The policy also sets out steps to be taken where grave violations are committed by such forces.[124] The Secretary-General also routinely focuses on human rights violations in country situations. For example, in 2010, with the agreement of the President of Sri Lanka, the Secretary-General established a Panel of Experts to advise him on the issue of accountability with regard to alleged violations of international human rights and humanitarian law during the final stages of the conflict on Sri Lanka. A second Panel was established to consider the response of the UN in this context, which reported to the Secretary-General on 14 November 2012.[125]

The Secretary-General chairs the UN system Chief Executives Board for Coordination, composed of the Executive Heads of all UN specialized agencies, funds, and programmes as well as of the World Bank, International Monetary Fund, International Atomic Energy Agency, and the World Trade Organization (WTO). The Chief Executives Board regularly discusses human rights issues, as do two of its subsidiary bodies: the High-level Committee on Programmes and the UNDG.

Finally, the 'good offices' of the Secretary-General may, in particular cases, help address and resolve human rights violations affecting particular individuals or groups. Such

---

[121] SC Res 1456 (20 January 2003); SC Res 1535 (26 March 2004); SC Res 1566 (8 October 2004); SC Res 1822 (30 June 2008); SC Res 1963 (20 December 2010). See Chapter 27.

[122] UN Charter, Art 97.

[123] Secretary-General Ban Ki-Moon, 'Remarks to the Human Rights Council,' 10 September 2012, available at: <http://www.un.org/apps/news/infocus/sgspeeches/statments_full.asp?statID=1643>.

[124] A/67/775-S/2013/110, Annex.

[125] Secretary-General, Ban Ki-Moon, Statement on the internal Review Panel Report on Sri Lanka, 14 November 2012, available at: <http://www.un.org//apps/news/infocus/sgspeeches/statments_full.asp?s>.

'good offices' tend to be reserved for politically sensitive and high visibility cases. The Secretary-General may also appoint special envoys or representatives for such cases, and direct them to broker a solution or compromise. For example, in March 2013, former President of Ireland and High Commissioner for Human Rights Mary Robinson was appointed as the Secretary-General's special envoy to the Great Lakes Region.

5.4 INTERNATIONAL COURT OF JUSTICE

The role of the International Court of Justice (ICJ), the principal judicial organ of the UN, is to settle legal disputes submitted to it by states and hand down advisory opinions on legal questions referred to it by authorized UN organs and specialized agencies. Individuals cannot bring cases to the Court. Recent judgments and advisory opinions have drawn on the provisions of the principal UN human rights instruments and pronouncements of the UN human rights treaty bodies. Judgments or advisory opinions may clarify the interpretation of provisions of international human rights instruments, or spell out the legal obligations of states under these instruments.[126] Some human rights treaties provide that inter-state disputes relating to the interpretation or application of the treaty concerned may be referred to the ICJ, usually after certain preconditions are fulfilled.[127] One such dispute led the Court to spell out the obligations of states parties to UNCAT to prosecute alleged perpetrators of torture or extradite them to another country with jurisdiction to prosecute.[128] Furthermore, the ICJ has developed an increasingly human rights sensitive jurisprudence. This may be attributable, in part, to the fact that several of the ICJ's judges, past or present, were members of the human rights treaty bodies, special procedures of the Commission on Human Rights, or judges in regional human rights courts prior to their election to the ICJ.[129]

6 CONCLUSION

The UN human rights protection system has grown in ways that could hardly have been predicted at the time of the adoption of the UDHR. It is now a multi-tiered and sophisticated system with numerous international human rights instruments and monitoring mechanisms, supported by a sizeable and increasingly operational OHCHR.

The growth of the UN human rights protection system has contributed to an improvement in the human rights situation in many countries and many thematic areas. So has the mainstreaming of human rights into other UN programmes, notably UN development, peace, and security activities. The UN's human rights work is now highly visible, particularly as a result of social media. This ensures dissemination of knowledge of international human rights standards and mechanisms. National-level implementation of recommendations and decisions of treaty bodies, special procedures, the UPR, and the Human

---

[126] Eg *Legal Consequences of the Construction of a Wall in the Occupied Palestinian Territory* [2004] ICJ Rep 136; *Ahmadou Sadio Diallo*, n 73. See Ghandhi, 'Human Rights and the International Court of Justice: The *Ahmadou Sadio Diallo* Case' (2011) 11 *HRLR* 527.

[127] Eg ICERD, Art 22; CEDAW, Art 29; CAT, Art 30.

[128] *Questions relating to the Obligation to Prosecute or Extradite (Belgium v Senegal)* [2012] ICJ Rep.

[129] Eg Judge Rosalyn Higgins, Judge Thomas Buergenthal, Judge Bruno Simma, Judge Peter Kooijmans, and Judge Antônio Cançade Trindade.

Rights Council improves steadily, even though there remains considerable room for the improvement of existing follow-up mechanisms, coordination amongst them, as well as identification of good practices.

Regardless of the budgetary constraints facing the UN and its human rights programme, demands for its support are unlikely to decrease, particularly as the Human Rights Council steps up efforts to address critical human rights issues, and other UN bodies, including the Security Council, and development mechanisms mainstream human rights into their work. Major challenges will be: avoiding politicization of the work of the Human Rights Council, as well as overlaps amongst the special procedures mandates that it creates; further harmonization of the procedures of the treaty bodies and treaty body strengthening; coordinated follow-up to, and encouraging implementation of, human rights mechanisms' recommendations; and the consolidation of the field presences of the OHCHR, especially through the establishment of regional and sub-regional offices in those parts of the world with currently limited or no OHCHR presence. If all these challenges are addressed and resolved, the UN human rights programme will fulfil its role of assisting to secure the protection of human rights where it matters most: at the national and grassroots levels.

FURTHER READING

ALSTON, 'Hobbling the Monitors: Should UN Human Rights Monitors be Accountable?' (2011) 52 *Harvard ILJ* 563.

BASSIOUNI and SCHABAS, *New Challenges for the UN Human Rights Machinery (What Future for the UN Treaty Body System and Human Rights Council Procedures?)* (Intersentia, 2011).

EGAN, *The UN Human Rights Treaty System: Law and Procedure* (Bloomsbury Professional, 2011).

FOOT, 'The United Nations, Counter Terrorism, and Human Rights: Institutional Adaptation and Embedded Ideas' (2007) 29 *HRQ* 489.

FREEDMAN, *The United Nations Human Rights Council: A Critique and Early Assessment* (Routledge, 2013).

HUMAN RIGHTS LAW REVIEW, Special Issue, 'Reform of the UN Human Rights Machinery' (2007) 7 *HRLR*.

INTERNATIONAL JOURNAL OF HUMAN RIGHTS, Special Issue, 'The Role of the Special Rapporteurs of the United Nations Human Rights Council in the Development and Promotion of International Human Rights Norms' (2011) 15 *IJHR*.

LAUREN, ' "To preserve and build on its achievements and to redress its shortcomings": The Journey from the Commission on Human Rights to the Human Rights Council' (2007) 29 *HRQ* 307.

MAHONY and NASH, *Influence on the Ground: Understanding and Strengthening the protection impact of United Nations Human Rights Field Presences* (Fieldview Solutions, 2012).

MORJIN, 'Reforming United Nations Human Rights Treaty Monitoring Reform' (2011) 58 *Netherlands ILR* 295.

ORGANIZATION INTERNATIONALE DE LA FRANCOPHONIE, *Practical Guide, Universal Periodic Review* (Organization Internationale de la Francophonie, 2013).

PICCONE, *Catalysts for Change, How the UN's Independent Experts Promote Human Rights* (Brookings Institution Press, 2012).

SIMMA, 'Mainstreaming Human Rights: The Contribution of the International Court of Justice' (2012) 3 *Journal of International Dispute Settlement* 7.

USEFUL WEBSITES

UPR-Info: <**http://www.upr-info.org**>

United Nations: <**http://www.un.org**>

Office of the High Commissioner for Human Rights: <**http://www.ohchr.org**>

Universal Human Rights Index: <**http://www.universalhumanrightsindex.org**>

International Court of Justice: <**http://www.icj-cij.org**>

19

THE AMERICAS

Jo Pasqualucci

SUMMARY

The Inter-American human rights system was created by the Organization of American States (OAS), an international organization comprised of all independent states in the Western hemisphere. The OAS has drafted and promulgated several human rights documents and treaties, primary of which are the American Declaration of the Rights and Duties of Man and the American Convention on Human Rights. The enforcement organs in the Inter-American system are the Inter-American Commission on Human Rights (the Commission) and the Inter-American Court of Human Rights (the Court). The Commission and the Court may consider individual complaints of human rights abuse. In addition, the Commission may conduct country studies or thematic studies, and the Court has advisory jurisdiction to assist the American states in complying with their global human rights obligations. Together, the Commission and the Court have made a major contribution to the recognition and protection of human rights in the Americas.

1 INTRODUCTION

The governance of many American states has evolved from the brutal dictatorships of the 1970s and 1980s to the democracies of today. Even in democracies, however, domestic judicial systems can be incapable of rectifying and putting an end to human rights abuses. Individuals can be powerless in the face of entrenched state errors or injustices. In some states there may not be laws that protect certain human rights. In most states, however, laws protect most human rights, but there may be insufficient political will to enforce them. Therefore, it is essential that the victims of human rights abuse have the opportunity to resort to regional systems, such as the Inter-American human rights system, to ensure and protect their rights when their domestic legal systems fail them.

Human rights protection in the Americas is governed by the Organization of American States (OAS), an international organization comprised of the independent states of the Western hemisphere. Cuba had been excluded from participating in the OAS because it adopted a Marxist-Leninist form of government. On 3 June 2009, however, the OAS General Assembly voted by acclamation to revoke the 1962 resolution that suspended Cuba, thereby allowing Cuba to again participate in the OAS, after negotiations, if it so chooses. As of August 2013, Cuba had not yet chosen to participate.

The OAS has promulgated several human rights treaties and documents. The most influential of these are the American Declaration of the Rights and Duties of Man (American

Declaration) and the American Convention on Human Rights (ACHR). The two enforcement bodies, the Inter-American Commission and the Inter-American Court, have different but complementary functions and powers in promoting state observance and ensuring human rights in the Americas. A primary role for both organs is the processing of individual complaints that allege that an American state is liable for the violation of protected human rights. All individual petitions must first be filed with the Commission. Once proceedings have been completed by the Commission, under certain circumstances, the case may be submitted to the Court.

The cases initially submitted to the Inter-American Court involved gross and systematic human rights violations including disappearances, torture, and extra-judicial executions. The Court has issued precedent-setting jurisprudence, especially in the area of state responsibility for forced disappearances.[1] In more recent years the Court's jurisprudence has expanded to encompass many of the rights protected by the American Convention. In particular, the Court has rendered landmark decisions on amnesty laws, the rights of children and women, communal property rights of indigenous peoples, and freedom of expression, especially in the area of criminal defamation against public officials. The Inter-American human rights system has made substantial progress in protecting civil and political rights and promoting their observance in the Americas.

The effectiveness of the Inter-American human rights system has been under study for many years. Under the auspices of the OAS Committee on Juridical and Political Affairs, OAS member states, members of the Commission, judges on the Inter-American Court, NGOs, and other groups from civil society participated in a broad-based transparent reappraisal of the system. As a result, the Commission and the Court have repeatedly modified their rules of procedure to enhance the role of victims, expedite the processing of cases, and provide for transparency.

2 HISTORICAL OVERVIEW

The OAS was formally created in 1948, when the sovereign states of the Americas adopted the Charter of the Organization of American States (OAS Charter). The OAS Charter is the constituent treaty that sets out the legal framework of the OAS. It is binding on all OAS member states. The purposes of the OAS include strengthening peace and security, promoting and consolidating representative democracy, and eradicating extreme poverty. One of the basic principles of the OAS Charter affirms the ideal that fundamental rights are due to every human being without distinction as to race, nationality, creed, or sex.[2]

The 1948 conference that approved the OAS Charter also adopted the American Declaration. The American Declaration, which was adopted six months before the adoption of the Universal Declaration of Human Rights, was the first international statement of human rights. The Inter-American Court and Commission have both held that, although the Declaration was not initially adopted as a legally binding treaty, the Declaration is now a source of legal obligations for OAS member states.[3] Not all American states, including the USA, agree with that conclusion. The Declaration sets forth civil and political rights as

---

[1] *Velásquez Rodríguez v Honduras* (Merits), IACtHR Series C No 4 (29 July 1988).

[2] OAS Charter, Art 3(l).

[3] OC-10/89, *Interpretation of the American Declaration of the Rights and Duties of Man within the Framework of Article 64 of the American Convention on Human Rights*, IACtHR Series A No 4 (14 July 1989) paras 35–45; and Case 9647, *Roach and Pinkerton v US*, IACommHR Res 3/87 (22 September 1987) paras 46–9.

well as economic, social, and cultural rights. In addition, it specifies corresponding duties owed by individuals to society and the state, such as the duties to vote, pay taxes, work, obey the law, and care for minor children and parents.

The Protocol of Buenos Aires, adopted in 1967, amended the OAS Charter to include the Inter-American Commission as a principal organ of the OAS. Under the Charter, the primary function of the Commission is to 'promote the observance and protection of human rights and to serve as a consultative organ of the Organization in these matters'.[4] At that time, no binding OAS human rights treaty was in effect in the Americas. In 1969 the ACHR was adopted. This Convention sets forth 23 civil and political rights that ratifying states (referred to as 'states parties') pledge to respect and ensure. Only one provision provides for the progressive development of economic, social, and cultural rights.

The OAS has adopted two Protocols to the American Convention: the Additional Protocol in the area of Economic, Social and Cultural Rights, also referred to as the 'Protocol of San Salvador', which entered into force in 1999; and the Protocol to Abolish the Death Penalty, which entered into force in 1991. Additional treaties adopted by the OAS are the Inter-American Convention on Forced Disappearance of Persons, which entered into force in 1996; the Inter-American Convention to Prevent and Punish Torture, which entered into force in 1987; the Inter-American Convention on the Prevention, Punishment and Eradication of Violence against Women, also known as the Convention of Belém Do Pará for the city in Brazil where it was adopted, which entered into force in 1995; and the Inter-American Convention on the Elimination of All Forms of Discrimination against Persons with Disabilities which entered into force in 2001. The OAS has also promulgated other human rights instruments. The most significant of these are the Inter-American Declaration of Principles on Freedom of Expression; the Principles and Best Practices on the Protection of Persons Deprived of Liberty in the Americas; the Social Charter of the Americas; the proposed American Declaration on the Rights of Indigenous Peoples; and the draft Inter-American Convention against Racism and All Forms of Discrimination.

The OAS, like the Council of Europe, has affirmed its commitment to democracy as the only acceptable type of political governance for a member state.[5] The OAS adopted the Inter-American Democratic Charter in 2001 to guarantee democracy in the region. The OAS Charter recognizes that representative democracy is essential for stability, peace, development, and the protection of human rights. The OAS General Assembly relied on the Inter-American Democratic Charter in 2009 when it temporarily suspended Honduras from OAS participation as a result of a coup d'état that deposed the constitutionally elected president.[6] The Inter-American Court has affirmed in an advisory opinion the fundamental principle that a democratic form of government is essential to the protection of human rights.[7]

3 AMERICAN CONVENTION ON HUMAN RIGHTS

Twenty-three of the 35 OAS member states are states parties to the American Convention. The treaty has not been ratified by Belize, Canada, the USA, and some Caribbean nations. Trinidad and Tobago, which had been a state party to the American Convention,

---

[4] OAS Charter, Art 106. The Commission was created by a resolution of the Fifth Meeting of Consultation of Ministers of Foreign Affairs in Santiago, Chile in 1959. [5] See Chapter 20.

[6] OAS Press Release, 'OAS Suspends Membership of Honduras', 5 July 2009.

[7] OC-6/86, *The Word 'Laws' in Article 30 of the American Convention on Human Rights*, IACtHR Series A No 6 (9 May 1986) para 35.

denounced the treaty in 1998. Venezuela denounced the Convention on 10 September 2012. Denunciations become effective one year from the date of communication.

Under the ACHR, states parties undertake to respect and ensure the human rights specified in the Convention to all persons who are subject to their jurisdiction.[8] Jurisdiction, within the context of a human rights treaty, is not limited to the physical territory of the state; rather, it is generally regarded that a state's jurisdiction includes all areas over which it has effective control.[9] As explained by the Inter-American Commission, the prisoners held by the USA in Guantanamo Bay, Cuba, although outside the physical territory of the USA, are 'wholly within the authority and control of the United States government'.[10] Therefore, the USA could be held responsible for human rights abuses taking place there. States parties also agree to give legal effect to the rights and freedoms set forth in the ACHR at the domestic level. In accordance with that provision, some American states have incorporated international human rights standards in their laws and constitutions and have provided for the execution of the judgments of the Inter-American Court at the domestic level.

The rights and freedoms protected by the ACHR include the right to life, humane treatment, personal liberty, a fair trial, privacy, conscience and religion, property, equal protection, assembly, and to participate in government. The Convention also ensures the freedoms of thought and expression, conscience and religion, association, movement and residence, and freedom from slavery and *ex post facto* laws. Rights of the family and of the child are likewise recognized.

The ACHR establishes two organs to protect and enforce the rights set forth in the Convention: the Inter-American Commission and the Inter-American Court. Although the Commission and the Court are empowered to enforce international human rights law in the Americas, the first and foremost authorities to deal with claims of human rights abuse are national authorities. Only when there are defects in the domestic system and its efforts are not effective can the case be referred to the Inter-American Commission and the Inter-American Court.

States parties to the ACHR automatically agree to the right of an individual to file a petition with the Inter-American Commission alleging state violations of individual human rights.[11] Even the right of individual petition, however, may not be sufficient to allow all persons to avail themselves of the protection of the ACHR. Many victims of human rights abuse in the Americas have a limited education and live in poverty. Although they are authorized to file a complaint, they do not have the knowledge or means to do so. Also, in some states, victims and their families are intimidated and justifiably fear retaliation if they file a complaint with the Inter-American Commission. Therefore, the ACHR permits parties that are unrelated to the victim to file human rights petitions. Any person or non-governmental entity legally recognized in an OAS member state may file a petition with the Commission denouncing human rights violations. Thus, NGOs such as Human Rights Watch (formerly Americas Watch), the Center for Justice and International Law (CEJIL), or the World Council of Journalists—organizations with experience litigating before the organs of the Inter-American system—are often the formal petitioners in cases. These organizations have more resources than most individuals, are less susceptible to intimidation, and can generate local and international publicity.

---

[8] ACHR, Art 1(1).   [9] See Chapter 6.
[10] Guantanamo Bay Precautionary Measures Communication of March 12, 2002 from IACHR President Juan E Méndez to US Secretary of State Colin Powell (2002) 96 *AJIL* 730. See Tittemore, 'Guantanamo Bay and The Precautionary Measures Of The Inter-American Commission On Human Rights: A Case For International Oversight In The Struggle Against Terrorism' (2006) 6 *HRLR* 378.   [11] ACHR, Art 4.

4 INTER-AMERICAN COMMISSION
ON HUMAN RIGHTS

The Inter-American Commission plays a dual role in the Inter-American human rights system. The Commission was created as a principal organ of the OAS under the OAS Charter, and it was also established as an organ for the protection of human rights under the ACHR. Under the Charter, the Commission has authority to oversee the human rights obligations of all member states of the OAS. Thus, every American state has accepted the competence of the Commission to consider individual complaints concerning alleged human rights violations that occur in its jurisdiction, simply by virtue of the ratification of the OAS Charter.

If a complaint is filed against a state that has not ratified the ACHR, the Commission will determine whether the state violated the protections set forth in the ADHR. For those 23 states that have ratified or acceded to the ACHR, however, the Commission determines whether there has been a violation of the Convention. The most complex aspect of the Inter-American system of individual petitions is that states have somewhat different human rights obligations depending on whether they have ratified the ACHR.

4.1 STRUCTURE AND COMPOSITION

The Inter-American Commission is composed of seven commissioners who are elected by secret ballot of all OAS member states at the OAS General Assembly. They are elected to four-year terms and may be re-elected once. Commissioners do not serve as representatives of states. They must be nationals of OAS member states, and no two commissioners may be nationals of the same state. Members of the Commission must be 'persons of high moral character and recognized competence in human rights'.[12]

The Commission is located at the OAS headquarters in Washington, DC. It is in session only on a part-time basis, but the Commission's Secretariat, composed of lawyers and human rights specialists, functions on a full-time basis. The Secretariat immediately consults the Commission in serious or urgent cases.

4.2 INDIVIDUAL COMPLAINTS PROCEDURES

The primary function of the Commission is the examination of individual petitions denouncing human rights violations. Complaints to the Inter-American system alleging that an American state has violated individual human rights must first be filed and processed by the Inter-American Commission. Except for requests for provisional measures, the Commission must complete its proceedings before a case may be referred to the Inter-American Court. In 2012, the Commission received 1,936 individual petitions alleging human rights abuse against 26 OAS member states.[13] The average time for the processing of a complaint from submission to the Commission to referral to the Inter-American Court has been over eight years.[14]

[12] ACHR, Arts 34–7.
[13] Annual Report of the Inter-American Commission on Human Rights 2012, chapter 3B, 52.
[14] CEJIL, Contributions to the Process of Reflection on Possible Reforms to the Procedures of the Inter-American Commission on Human Rights and the Inter-American Court of Human Rights (October 2008), available at: <http://www.civil-society.oas.org>.

Human rights petitions to the Commission must meet criteria of admissibility. A petition must state facts that tend to establish a violation of a guaranteed right. Also, to be admissible a petition must show that the petitioner has pursued and exhausted all remedies under domestic law when that is possible; that the petition was lodged within six months of the notification of a final judgment in the domestic court; that the subject of the petition is not pending in another international proceeding; and that the petition contains basic information such as the name, nationality, domicile, profession, and signature of the person who lodged the petition.[15] If the petition lacks the required content, the Commission may ask the petitioner to complete it. It is important that the Commission be flexible in this regard, as those who complain that their rights have been violated often do so without the assistance of attorneys. When the complaint is determined to be prima facie admissible, in that it satisfies the formal requirements of admissibility, the Commission will forward the pertinent portions of it to the state. The Commission then forwards the relevant parts of the government's response to the petitioner, along with a request for observations. If there is no governmental response, the Commission may treat the petitioner's allegations as presumptively true. States today generally respond to Commission requests for information.

After the Commission has made a formal decision that a case is admissible, it will consider the merits of the case. It may hold hearings for the purpose of receiving evidence. Occasionally, with the prior permission of the respondent state, and if the commissioners consider it to be necessary, the Commission may carry out an on-site investigation in the state where the violations allegedly occurred.

At the request of either party or on its own initiative, the Commission will attempt to bring about a friendly settlement between the petitioner and the state. Friendly settlements may be beneficial to both states and victims. Victims are more likely to receive the determined reparations when the state's express agreement is garnered through friendly settlement procedures. Friendly settlements also shorten the usually time-consuming nature of proceedings before the Commission. In the event that the parties reach a friendly settlement, the Commission will adopt a report, transmit it to the parties, and publish it.

In most cases, the petitioner and state do not reach a friendly settlement. In such instances, after consideration of the merits, if the Commission finds that the state has violated a right protected by the ACHR, it will recommend measures that the state should take to remedy the violation. If the state does not follow these recommendations, and it has accepted the jurisdiction of the Inter-American Court, the Commission's Rules of Procedure provide for the automatic referral of a case to the Court 'unless there is a reasoned decision by an absolute majority of the members of the Commission to the contrary'.[16] One of the Commission's primary concerns is whether the petitioner wishes the case to be referred to the Court. As a result, the Commission submits almost all such cases to the Court. Consequently, the Court's caseload has increased substantially.

In addition to authorizing individuals to file complaints of human rights abuses, the ACHR also authorizes inter-state complaints. State parties to the Convention may accept the competence of the Inter-American Commission to receive and examine communications in which one state alleges that another state party has violated individual human rights.[17] Inter-state complaints require reciprocity; both states must have made declarations accepting the competence of the Commission to examine state-to-state complaints. To date, only two inter-state complaints have been filed. The *Nicaragua v Costa Rica*

---

[15] ACHR, Art 46(1). *Velásquez Rodríguez*, n 1, para 61.
[16] Inter-American Commission Rules of Procedure, Art 44(1).   [17] ACHR, Art 45(1).

complaint was declared inadmissible,[18] while the complaint by Ecuador against Colombia was declared admissible.[19] States are often hesitant to file a complaint against another state for fear of jeopardizing trade or other relations. Consequently, the inter-state complaint process, which historically had been the only avenue available in international law to deal with disputes, has not proven to be an effective curb to human rights violations in the Americas.

4.3 OTHER ROLES OF THE COMMISSION

Although the primary function of the Commission is the examination of individual complaints of human rights abuse, the Commission also studies and reports on human rights in a broader context. The Commission may prepare a country study when there are alarming reports about the human rights situation in a member state. Country reports and the adverse publicity they generate have contributed significantly to the downfall of military dictatorships and the eventual democratization of several states in the Americas. For instance, during the 'dirty war' in Argentina, when thousands of people were forcibly disappeared by the government, the Inter-American Commission made an official visit to Argentina. The Commission met with government officials and also heard testimony from victims and their families. Thousands of people waited in the streets to give testimony before the Commission or to support those who did. Some commentators credit the Commission's visit as one factor in the downfall of the ruling junta.[20]

The Commission also conducts thematic studies concerning violations of certain types of rights throughout the hemisphere, and it monitors the situation of particularly vulnerable groups. Commissioners may serve as thematic rapporteurs who analyse and report on the rights of migrant workers, persons of African descent, prisoners, indigenous peoples, women, and children. The Commission also has a rapporteur on freedom of expression, and a special unit on human rights defenders.

5 INTER-AMERICAN COURT OF HUMAN RIGHTS

The Inter-American Court of Human Rights is the sole judicial organ of the OAS. The Court was created in 1979 following the entry into force of the ACHR. The Convention authorizes the Court to adjudicate contentious cases, issue advisory opinions, and order states to take provisional measures to protect persons who are in grave and imminent danger. A state is subject to the jurisdiction of the Court if it has ratified the ACHR and explicitly accepted the Court's contentious jurisdiction. This jurisdiction empowers the Court to adjudicate cases of alleged violations of individual human rights protected by the ACHR for which a state government is responsible. As of 1 May 2013, 20 of the 23 states parties to the ACHR had filed declarations accepting the Court's contentious jurisdiction. Other states parties to the ACHR may accept the Court's jurisdiction by special agreement for a specific case.

---

[18] Inter-State Case 01/06, *Nicaragua v Costa Rica*, IACommHR Report No 11/07 (8 March 2007).

[19] Inter-State Case IP-02, *Ecuador v Colombia*, IACommHR Report No 112/10 (21 October 2010).

[20] Weissbrodt and Bartolomei, 'The Effectiveness of International Human Rights Pressures: The Case of Argentina, 1976–1983' (1991) 75 *Minn LR* 1009.

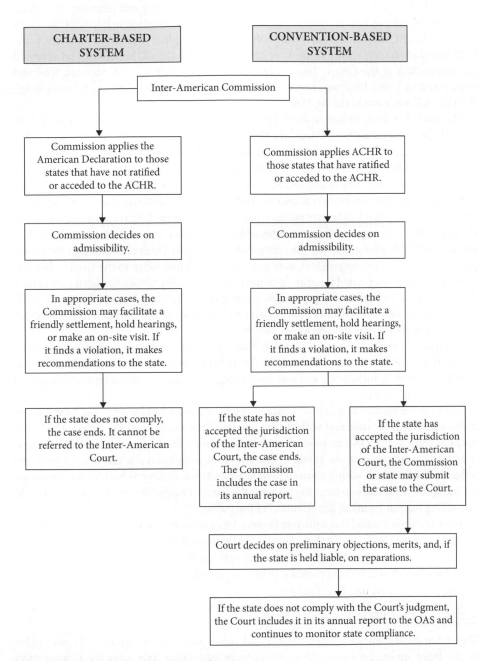

Figure 19.1 Individual petitions procedure

5.1 STRUCTURE AND COMPOSITION

The Court is composed of seven judges who are elected to a six-year term by a vote of the states parties to the ACHR. Judges may be re-elected for one additional term, and they continue to hear cases that they have begun to hear and that are still pending when their terms expire. The judges are elected by secret ballot by an absolute majority of the states parties to the ACHR. A state party may nominate an individual who is a national from any OAS member state, not only from those states that have ratified the ACHR and accepted the jurisdiction of the Court. Thus, Judge Thomas Buergenthal, a US national, who was nominated by Costa Rica, was one of the initial judges elected to the Court, even though the USA has not ratified the ACHR.

No two judges may be nationals of the same state. Judges are to be chosen from 'jurists of the highest moral authority' who are recognized for their competence in human rights law and who possess the qualifications to be a judge in the nominating state or the state of the nominee's nationality. There is no vetting procedure similar to that of the Council of Europe to ensure that judges and commissioners are well qualified for their positions. The judges serve in their individual capacities and do not represent the states that nominate them. Judges may not hold other positions incompatible with their responsibilities on the Court, such as serving as officers of international organizations or as high-ranking government officials who are under the control of the executive branch. Although the Court previously allowed the respondent state to appoint an ad hoc judge to the Court when the contentious case originated from an individual petition, this practice has been eliminated. The Court issued an advisory opinion interpreting the ACHR to permit ad hoc judges only in inter-state cases.[21] Even sitting judges who are nationals of the respondent state are not permitted to participate in individual cases.[22]

The Inter-American Court sits on a part-time basis and decides cases in plenary session. In addition to its four regular sessions, the Court held two special sessions in 2012. In that year, it rendered 21 judgments and was monitoring compliance with its reparations orders in 138 contentious cases.

The Court is located in San José, Costa Rica where it often holds its regular sessions, but at the invitation of a state and with the agreement of the majority of the judges, the Court may convene in any OAS member state. In recent years, for example, it has held sessions in at least 15 other countries. When holding sessions away from the seat of the Court, the judges will often meet with government officials and civil society as well as hold seminars on the Inter-American system. In this way, the Court brings the system and its work in protecting human rights to the attention of the public.

The Court has a small but full-time Secretariat of attorneys and other staff. The official languages of the Court are English, French, Portuguese, and Spanish. Each year the judges decide on the working languages. Persons appearing before the Court may use their own languages, which will be interpreted into one of the working languages.

5.2 CONTENTIOUS CASES

Under the ACHR only the Commission and states parties have authority to refer cases to the Inter-American Court. This referral may take place only after the Commission has completed its proceedings. The individual victim or petitioner does not have standing to bring a case before the Court. The Commission now refers almost all cases to the

---

[21] OC-20/09, *Article 55 of the American Convention on Human Rights*, Series A No 20 (29 September 2009).
[22] IACtHR, Rules of Procedure approved by the Court (24 November 2009), Art 19.

Court when the state involved has accepted the Court's jurisdiction and the state has not complied with the Commission's recommendations. The state may make preliminary objections to the admissibility of an application or to the Court's jurisdiction to hear a case. If a state does not submit preliminary objections, or the case is not dismissed at the preliminary objections stage, the Court will address the merits of the case.

At the merits stage of the proceedings, the Court considers written briefs, affidavits from witnesses, other documentary evidence, and often holds public hearings to take oral testimony from witnesses and experts. Oral proceedings are not mandated in the Inter-American system. As a result of the increase in its caseload and for purposes of procedural economy, the Inter-American Court has attempted to limit the number of days scheduled for public hearings and the number of witnesses testifying at the hearings. Thus, the Court often accepts sworn declarations or affidavits in place of live testimony. Public hearings may not be necessary at the preliminary objections stage when the issues presented are questions of law, which can be adequately briefed by the parties. Conversely, public hearings on the merits of the case, especially when the facts are disputed, are essential to provide a full factual record, allow the victims the opportunity to tell their stories, and attract media attention that will increase public understanding of the plight of victims and the overall situation in the state concerned.[23]

The alleged victim's role before the Court has been steadily enhanced, and the Commission's role has been minimized. Although the ACHR specifies that the Commission must appear before the Court in all cases, the Commission no longer represents the alleged victim, who has standing before the Court once the case has been submitted. At all stages of the Court's proceedings, the victims are represented by their own attorneys. If the alleged victims do not have legal representation, the Inter-American Court may, on its own motion, appoint Inter-American public defenders to represent them during the processing of the case.[24] Generally only representatives of the alleged victim and the state conduct interrogations of witnesses. At the opening of the public hearing, the Commission presents the grounds for the case and any other matter that it considers relevant for its resolution. The Commission may present its written observations in response to any preliminary objections made by the state or question any expert witnesses proposed by the Commission. After the oral arguments, the Commission presents its final observations. Judges may question any witness or party.

At the conclusion of the proceedings the judges hold private deliberations, which remain confidential. The Court's judgments are binding on the parties to the case and cannot be appealed. The Court can interpret a judgment at the request of one of the parties to the case if there is disagreement as to the meaning or scope of the judgment. Even when the state has accepted partial or full responsibility for the violations, the Court's judgment should fully recount the proven facts to set forth an authoritative record of the events. This record provides support to human rights advocates when generating public opinion. The average duration of proceedings before the Inter-American Court, from the presentation of the application to the final judgment, has been reduced to just over 16 months.[25]

---

[23] See generally Cavallaro and Brewer, 'Reevaluating Regional Human Rights Litigation in the Twenty-First Century: The Case of the Inter-American Court' (2008) 102 *AJIL* 768.

[24] IACtHR, Rules of Procedure approved by the Court (24 November 2009), Art 37. The Inter-American Court and the Inter-American Association of Public Defenders signed an Agreement of Understanding on 25 September 2009 to provide free legal assistance to alleged victims who lack economic resources or legal representation before the Court. See IACtHR Press Release 15–09 (29 September 2009).

[25] However, in 2012, the average duration of proceedings before the Court, from the presentation of the application to final judgment was 19.2 months, owing to one exceptionally long case. Annual Report of the Inter-American Court 2012, 8.

5.3 COURT-ORDERED REPARATIONS AND STATE COMPLIANCE

When the Inter-American Court determines that the state is liable for a violation of the victim's human rights, or the state voluntarily accepts responsibility for a violation, the Court orders the state to make reparations to the victim. One of the greatest contributions made by the Inter-American Court to international human rights law is the enhancement of the concept of reparations. The Court has ordered victim-centred reparations as well as reparations that will benefit specific communities or society as a whole.

Financial compensation was the traditional type of reparation when the state was held liable for a human rights violation, and it remains one aspect of reparations in the Inter-American system. The ACHR specifies that 'fair compensation be paid to the injured party'.[26] Financial compensation may cover loss of earnings, restitution of material property taken or destroyed, and payment for moral damages for emotional harm to the victim. Overall, states have complied with approximately 80 per cent of Court-ordered financial compensation awards, although payments are sometimes delayed beyond the period specified by the Court.[27] The state also must reimburse successful applicants for their costs and expenses. Financial compensation alone is not sufficient, however, for those who have suffered human rights abuses. As stated by the mother of a victim who had been executed by the Venezuelan military in El Amparo, '[m]y son was not a cow. I don't want money. What I want is justice'.[28]

The ACHR provision on reparations authorizes the Court 'to rule that the injured party be ensured the enjoyment of his right or freedom that was violated'. The Court drew on this aspect of its authority to order reparations when it ordered Peru to release Maria Elena Loayza Tamayo, a university professor who had been wrongfully imprisoned in Peru for several years.[29] Peru complied with the Court's order and released the prisoner.[30] Needless to say, not all states comply with all Court reparations orders. For instance, Paraguayan lawmakers voted against the return of ancestral lands to the Yakye Axa indigenous community, despite a judgment by the Inter-American Court ordering the state to return the land to the people.[31]

Another, and very important, aspect of reparations under the ACHR is that the 'consequences of the measure or situation that constituted the breach of such right or freedom be remedied'.[32] Pursuant to this authority, the Inter-American Court has held that a state law is without legal effect, that the state amend or repeal domestic legislation, and even that the state undertake constitutional reform of provisions that do not comply with the state's freely assumed human rights obligations under the ACHR. For instance, the Court ordered Chile to implement domestic legal measures to guarantee the right to access information and to adapt its laws to comply with the ACHR. Chile fully complied with the Court-ordered reparations when the Chilean President signed the Law on Transparency of Public Functions and Access to Information of the State Administration.[33] The legislation was enacted in response to the Inter-American Court's judgment in *Claude Reyes v Chile*, in which an environmental organization successfully challenged the Chilean government to release information regarding a deforestation project.[34] Chile's transparency law will limit governmental corruption by allowing the public access to information. Likewise, the Argentine

---

[26] ACHR, Art 63(1).   [27] Inter-American Court Annual Report 2010, 12.

[28] See Krsticevic, 'Conference on Reparations in the Inter-American System: A Comparative Approach' (2007) 56 *AmUniv LR* 1418, 1420–1.

[29] *Loayza Tamayo v Peru*, IACtHR Series C No 33 (17 September 1997).

[30] *Chicago Tribune* (17 October 1997) 28.

[31] See Amnesty International, 'Paraguayan Congress Risks Lives of 90 Indigenous Families' (28 June 2009).

[32] ACHR, Art 63(1).   [33] Inter-American Court Annual Report 2008, 26.

[34] IACtHR Series C No 151 (19 September 2006).

Supreme Court struck down Argentina's amnesty laws, citing the Inter-American Court's earlier decision in the *Barrios Altos* case.[35] In *Barrios Altos*, the Court declared that two amnesty laws promulgated by the government of then Peruvian President Alberto Fujimori in 1995 were incompatible with the ACHR and hence without legal effect.[36] Reparations that require modification to domestic laws that violate the state's international obligations have a broader impact than individual financial reparations. All of society benefits from the changes, and human rights are advanced because new violations are prevented.

The Inter-American Court may also find that a domestic court ruling was not made in accordance with the due process guarantees of the ACHR. Following the *Raxcacó Reyes* case, Guatemala complied with the Court order to annul the death sentence imposed on the victim.[37] Guatemala also complied with the Court-ordered reparations and held a new trial in the *Fermín Ramírez* case.[38]

When appropriate, the Court may order the state to undertake various remedies such as providing human rights training to the state's armed forces and police, giving free medical and psychological treatment to victims of violence or imprisonment, awarding grants for higher education, and creating funds for the collective interest of a community. The Inter-American Court has been creative in its reparations orders. In the *Kawas Fernández v Honduras* case, in which an environmental activist was murdered in Honduras, the Court ordered, as one form of reparations, that the state implement a national campaign to educate the public about the work of environmental activists and their contributions to the defence of human rights.[39]

In the interest of general deterrence, and in an attempt to clear the names of victims who have often been maligned by the state, the Court generally orders the state to publish pertinent parts of its judgment. The Court also may order the state to undertake a symbolic public act, such as participating in a public ceremony, so that society will learn the truth about the facts underlying the case. After the Court's judgment in the *Myrna Mack* case, Guatemala implemented one aspect of the Court's reparations order by holding a public function to acknowledge responsibility for the murder of the anthropologist and social activist. The President of Guatemala spoke at the meeting and hundreds of military personnel including high-ranking officers of the armed forces, the police, and members of the community attended.[40] Symbolic actions taken by states in compliance with Court-ordered reparations include naming streets or schools after victims or creating memorials. In addition, high-level state officials have apologized to victims in response to the Court's reparations decisions, and many are pre-empting such orders by apologizing to the victims during the Court's public hearings.

In an attempt to combat impunity, the Court regularly mandates that the state investigate human rights violations and identify, prosecute, and punish those responsible. The state's obligation persists until it has fully complied with this duty. However, states in many cases have not appeared to make good-faith efforts to fulfil such orders. The most likely reasons for this chronic failure are that either government or military personnel who are implicated in the human rights offences still wield power within the state, or that current officials do not want to set a precedent that could affect them in the future.

The Inter-American system lacks an effective formal institutional mechanism to enforce state compliance with its orders and judgments. It does not have an equivalent of the Committee of Ministers of the Council of Europe.[41] The ACHR provides that if a state

---

[35] Corte Suprema de Justicia [CSJN], 14/6/2005, 'Case of Julio Hector Simon/recurso de hecho', No 17.768 (Arg).

[36] IACtHR Series C No 75 (14 March 2001).   [37] Inter-American Court Annual Report 2008, n 33, 18.

[38] Inter-American Court Annual Report 2008, n 33, 17.

[39] (Merits, Reparations and Costs), IACtHR Series C No 196 (3 April 2009), operative para 14.

[40] See Krsticevic, n 28, 1420–1.   [41] See Chapter 20.

has not complied with judgments of the Inter-American Court, the Court should inform the OAS General Assembly of the failure in its Annual Report and make pertinent recommendations regarding the state. Unfortunately, the OAS political bodies, in general, and its General Assembly, in particular, do not have the political will to impose any sanctions on states that fail to comply with their human rights obligations. The Court has attempted to address this shortcoming by maintaining cases on its docket and overseeing state compliance with its judgments, a function which is overburdening the Court.[42] At the end of 2012, the Court was monitoring state compliance in 138 cases. The Court holds private hearings to monitor compliance with its judgments and raises public awareness of state compliance by including a 'compliance with judgments' section on its website.

5.4 INTERIM MEASURES

International proceedings may be too slow to prevent the victim's injury or death in urgent situations. The ACHR affords the Commission and the Court the authority to act more expeditiously when warranted. 'In cases of extreme gravity and urgency, and when necessary to avoid irreparable damage to persons', the Convention authorizes the Court to 'adopt such provisional measures as it deems pertinent.'[43] The Commission may request that the Court take such measures even when the case is not yet on the Court's docket, such as when the person or persons to be protected are petitioners or witnesses before the Commission. The Commission is also authorized under its Rules of Procedure to request that the state take precautionary measures.

Pursuant to the ACHR, the Court can order a state to take immediate action or to refrain from some action if an individual's life or physical integrity is threatened. Provisional measures ordered by the Inter-American Court are binding on states parties to the ACHR. The most common circumstance warranting provisional measures for those cases already on the Court's docket involves threats to past and future witnesses. The Inter-American Commission and Court are often called upon to issue precautionary or provisional measures to protect human rights activists, journalists, and news organizations. These persons and organizations who report on human rights abuses or official corruption may be considered by state agents to be traitors who have sullied the international reputation of the state. They may be subject to reprisals and, therefore, need special protection.[44]

Initially, the Inter-American Court restricted provisional measures to individually-named persons. This requirement proved problematic as naming individuals could have the opposite effect from that desired; rather than protecting them, it could subject them to reprisals. The Court subsequently changed its criteria, stating that potential victims must be identifiable but not necessarily named individually.[45] In this way, entire communities threatened by authorities and paramilitary groups have been granted protection. For example, the 1,200 members of a peace community in Colombia, which was attempting to maintain its neutrality in the midst of civil conflict, were identifiable as those living in the community.

---

[42] Remarks by Antônio Augusto Cançado Trindade, 'The Future of International Law' (2007) 101 *ASIL Proc* 238, 240.

[43] ACHR, Art 63(2). Interim measures are referred to as 'precautionary measures' when ordered by the Commission and as 'provisional measures' when ordered by the Court.

[44] See *Case of Gloria Giralt de García Prieto et al.* (Provisional Measures), IACtHR (26 September 2006); *Matter of Mery Naranjo et al.* (Provisional Measures), IACtHR (31 January 2008); *Matter of the Forensic Anthropology Foundation regarding Guatemala* (Provisional Measures), IACtHR (21 April 2006).

[45] *'Juvenile Reeducation Institute' v Paraguay*, IACtHR Series C No 112 (2 September 2004) para 108.

Forty-seven members of the community had been murdered in the nine-month period before provisional measures were ordered.[46]

The Court has also ordered provisional measures to protect the populations of prisons and children's detention centres where overcrowding, inadequate living conditions, and untrained or abusive personnel resulted in violent outbreaks and the murder and injury of inmates. Provisional measures in such cases commonly consist of orders to the state to reduce overcrowding, confiscate weapons from prisoners, adapt the detention facilities to international standards, provide adequate medical care, and separate those convicted from those awaiting trial.[47]

In 2012, in monitoring compliance with its judgments, the Court issued 32 orders, holding six hearings in 14 cases. In most cases, the Court orders the state to consult with the future beneficiaries of the measures to determine what protective measures would be most effective in the circumstances. Provisional measures have been unexpectedly effective in the Inter-American human rights system, although they can never serve as a solution for most human rights problems in the Western hemisphere.

5.5 ADVISORY JURISDICTION

A member state or organ of the OAS may request that the Inter-American Court issue an advisory opinion. An advisory opinion is an authoritative but non-binding explanation of a human rights provision or issue, which can assist American states in understanding and complying with their international human rights obligations. Requests to the Court may concern interpretations of certain rights or procedures set forth in the ACHR or in human rights provisions in other treaties. For example, in its request in the *Right to Information on Consular Assistance within the Framework of the Guarantees of Legal Due Process*, Mexico asked the Court's advice on whether the Vienna Convention on Consular Relations requires that an arresting state inform detained foreigners that they have the right to contact their national consulates.[48] The question arose because Mexican nationals, who had not had the opportunity to confer with the Mexican consulate, had been sentenced to death in the USA. The Inter-American Court interpreted the Vienna Convention to confer the right to receive consular assistance on detained foreign nationals.[49] Subsequent to the Court's advisory opinion, the US State Department issued and distributed a handbook to US law enforcement authorities informing them that foreign nationals have the mandatory right to assistance from their consulates.

At the request of a member state, the Court may also issue an advisory opinion regarding the compatibility of the state's domestic laws with international human rights instruments. For instance, the Costa Rican government requested an advisory opinion pursuant to this clause when it asked the Court whether a proposed naturalization amendment to its constitution was in accordance with the ACHR and with Costa Rica's other international human rights obligations. The amendment in question would have allowed foreign

---

[46] *Peace Community de San José de Apartadó (Colombia)* (Provisional Measures), IACtHR (24 November 2000).

[47] See *The Matter of the Monagas Detention Center ('La Pica')* (Venezuela) (Provisional Measures), IACtHR (3 July 2007); *The Matter of the Children and Adolescents Deprived of Liberty in the 'Tatuapé Complex' of the CASA Foundation (Brazil)* (Provisional Measures), IACtHR (3 July 2007).

[48] OC-16/99, *The Right to Information on Consular Assistance in the Framework of the Guarantees of Due Process of Law*, IACtHR Series A No 16 (1 October 1999).

[49] *The Right to Information*, n 48, para 82.

women who married Costa Rican nationals to become naturalized Costa Rican citizens, but would not have provided the same opportunity for foreign males. The Inter-American Court relied on both the ACHR and natural law to determine that although states have the right to confer and regulate nationality, they may not do so by violating superior norms such as the right to non-discrimination.[50] After the Inter-American Court's advisory opinion in *Proposed Amendments to the Naturalization Provisions of the Costa Rican Constitution*, the Constitutional Chamber of the Supreme Court of Justice of Costa Rica declared, in accordance with the Court's opinion, that a state law on the naturalization of spouses could not discriminate on the basis of gender.[51]

The Inter-American Court draws on the medium of an advisory opinion to make important contributions to the development and evolution of principles of international law. In the *Proposed Amendments* opinion, the Court went beyond the question asked and specified that not all differences in treatment per se violate non-discrimination provisions but only those that have 'no objective and reasonable justification'.[52] According to the Inter-American Court, some preferential and, thus, unequal treatment may be essential to obtain justice for those persons in a 'weak legal position'.[53] Although an advisory opinion does not create legal obligations for states, it often exerts moral authority over them. It encourages, rather than compels, a course of action.

6 CHALLENGES TO THE INTER-AMERICAN SYSTEM

One of the biggest challenges to the Inter-American human rights system is chronic underfunding, which imposes constraints on the functioning of the Inter-American Commission and the Inter-American Court. The increase in the number of contentious cases and requests for provisional measures, as well as the mounting number of judgments the Court is monitoring, stretch the Commission's and the Court's limited resources. Underfunding translates into fewer staff attorneys and an inadequate number of Commission or Court sessions. The workload warrants permanent sitting bodies to handle complaints expeditiously. The OAS General Assembly has resolved to examine the possibility that the Inter-American Commission and Court operate on a permanent basis, but funding is one of the major drawbacks to this consideration.[54]

For some years, the Commission and the Court have had to rely on voluntary contributions to supplement their allocation under the OAS budget. A percentage of these voluntary contributions come from OAS member states, some of which are subject to the jurisdiction of the Court. Voluntary contributions, particularly those from states that are accused of human rights violations, can compromise the integrity of the Inter-American protection organs. Even the appearance of impropriety should be avoided. Also, commitments to make voluntary contributions can be withdrawn leaving the organs without the necessary funding to carry out scheduled work.

[50] OC-4/84, *Proposed Amendments to the Naturalization Provisions of the Constitution of Costa Rica*, IACtHR Series A No 4 (19 January 1984).
[51] Exp 2965-S-91, Voto 3435–92, *Ricardo Fliman Wargraft v Director y el Jefe de la Sección de Opciones a Naturalizaciones*, Constitutional Chamber of the Supreme Court of Justice of Costa Rica (11 November 1992).
[52] *Proposed Amendments*, n 50, para 56.   [53] *Proposed Amendments*, n 50, para 56.
[54] OAS General Assembly, Strengthening of human rights systems pursuant to the mandates arising from the Summit of the Americas, thirty-ninth Regular Session, OEA/Ser.P, AG/doc 5006/09 (4 June 2009).

In the past, inadequate financial resources also negatively affected victim access to the Inter-American system. This problem may have been resolved in 2009 when the Permanent Council of the OAS created the Legal Assistance Fund of the Inter-American System of Human Rights to assist alleged victims of human rights abuse finance the cost of legal proceedings before the Inter-American Commission and Court.[55]

Another basic challenge to the optimal functioning of the Inter-American human rights system is the lack of universality. All states should undertake to uphold the same criteria and principles of human rights protection. Belize, Canada, the USA, and some Caribbean Island nations have not ratified the ACHR or accepted the contentious jurisdiction of the Inter-American Court. Another three states have ratified the ACHR but have not accepted the Court's jurisdiction. The lack of universality complicates the functioning of the Inter-American human rights system. The Inter-American Commission must apply different criteria when determining whether a state has violated individual rights depending on whether the state is a party to the ACHR. Moreover, the Commission cannot refer cases to the Inter-American Court if the respondent state has not accepted the jurisdiction of the Court. The lack of universal ratification provides an excuse to those states that have ratified human rights treaties that their treatment of human rights should not be judged to a greater extent than states that do not ratify. The Inter-American system for the protection of human rights will be more effective when all states in the Western hemisphere have ratified all Inter-American and universal human rights treaties and have accepted the jurisdiction of the Court.

States must do more, however, than merely ratify the ACHR and accept the jurisdiction of the Inter-American Court. States must also incorporate the substantive rights of the ACHR and the judgments of the Inter-American Court into their legal systems, and take the necessary legal measures to ensure that the judgments of the Inter-American Court are self-executing in domestic courts. States must also follow Commission recommendations. When states fulfil their duty to ensure and protect rights on the domestic plane there will be fewer cases wherein one state repeatedly engages in conduct that violates the same right of multiple victims. There will be fewer human rights abuses, and the burden on international enforcement organs, such as the Inter-American Court and Commission, will be eased.

7 CONCLUSION

The Inter-American human rights system has made significant progress in improving the human rights situation in the Americas, although there are many improvements still to be made. Initially it was feared that states would withdraw from the ACHR and the jurisdiction of the Inter-American Court if they were held liable for human rights violations and ordered to make reparations to victims. Trinidad and Tobago denounced the ACHR and the jurisdiction of the Inter-American Court in 1998 in a dispute over limitations on its death penalty and the length of proceedings before the Inter-American Commission. Venezuela denounced the ACHR in September 2012. Although Peru once attempted to withdraw from the jurisdiction of the Court without denouncing the Convention after the fall of President Fujimori, the subsequent government announced that it considered

[55] It is essential that States repay the Fund if it is to remain solvent. In 2012, of the thirteen cases that benefitted from access to the Fund, only one State, El Salvador, paid the amount ordered. Inter-American Court Annual Report 2012, n 25, 81.

itself subject to the jurisdiction of the Court. So, to date, the threat has not materialized to a substantial extent.

Even before a Court judgment, states now acquiesce or acknowledge partial or total international responsibility in almost half of the contentious cases referred to the Inter-American Court. In response to Court-ordered reparations, states have paid financial compensation to the victims in 81 per cent of the cases, amended or repealed national laws, and held that self-amnesty laws are without legal effect. In these aspects, at least, the Inter-American human rights system is proving effective. The problem of impunity for human rights violations is still to be conquered. States, in general, have not complied with Court orders to investigate the violations and prosecute and punish the offenders.

The jurisprudence and reforms to the Inter-American human rights system are proving to be relevant to other human rights systems. The Inter-American system was the first human rights system to function in an underdeveloped region of the world where human rights abuses such as extra-judicial killings, torture, and disappearances were prevalent. The European human rights system initially dealt with states that had a history of democracy, and its cases primarily involved violations of the individual's due process rights. Since the Council of Europe admitted member states from the former Soviet Union, however, the European system is confronting the type of endemic abuses that have been common in the Inter-American system. Also, the African human rights system is likely to confront similar gross and systematic abuses. Consequently, the jurisprudence established by the Inter-American system should serve as a model for other regional human rights systems around the world.

FURTHER READING

ANTKOWIAK, 'Remedial Approaches to Human Rights Violations: the Inter-American Court of Human Rights and Beyond' (2008) 46 *Colum J Transnatl L* 351.

BINDER, 'The Prohibition of Amnesties By The Inter-American Court Of Human Rights' (2011) 12 *German LJ* 1203.

BUERGENTHAL, 'Remembering the Early Years of the Inter-American Court of Human Rights' (2005) 2 *NYU J Intl Law and Politics* 37.

BUERGENTHAL and SHELTON, *Protecting Human Rights in the Americas: Cases and Materials* (NP Engel, 1995).

CAVALLARO and BREWER, 'Reevaluating Regional Human Rights Litigation in the Twenty-First Century: The Case of the Inter-American Court' (2008) 102 *AJIL* 768.

CERNA, 'Are We Headed in the Right Direction? Reflections on the New (2001) Rules of Procedure of the Inter-American Commission on Human Rights in Light of the Experience of the European System' in Bayefsky (ed), *Human Rights and Refugees, Internally Displaced Persons, and Migrant Workers: Essays in Memory of Joan Fitzpatrick and Arthur Helton* (Martinus Nijhoff, 2006) 387.

GARCÍA-SAYÁN, 'The Inter-American Court and Constitutionalism in Latin America' (2011) 89 *Texas LR* 1836.

GOLDMAN, 'History and Action: The Inter-American Human Rights System and the Role of the Inter-American Commission on Human Rights' (2009) 31 *HRQ* 856.

HARRIS and LIVINGSTONE (eds), *The Inter-American System of Human Rights* (Oxford University Press, 1998).

HUNEEUS, 'Courts Resisting Courts: Lessons from the Inter-American Court's Struggle to Enforce Human Rights' (2011) 44 *Cornell ILJ* 493.

KRSTICEVIC, 'Conference on Reparations in the Inter-American System: A Comparative Approach' (2007) 56 *AmUniv LR* 1418.

NEUMAN, 'Import, Export, and Regional Consent in the Inter-American Court of Human Rights' (2008) 19 *EJIL* 101.

PASQUALUCCI, *The Practice and Procedure of the Inter-American Court of Human Rights* (Cambridge University Press, 2013).

PASQUALUCCI, 'The Advisory Practice of the Inter-American Court of Human Rights: Contributing to the Evolution of International Human Rights Law' (2002) 38 *Stanford JIL* 241.

PASQUALUCCI, 'Criminal Defamation and the Evolution of the Doctrine of Freedom of Expression in International Law: Comparative Jurisprudence of the Inter-American Court of Human Rights' (2006) 39 *Vand J Trans L* 379.

PASQUALUCCI, 'The Evolution of International Indigenous Rights in the Inter-American Human Rights System' (2006) 6 *HRLR* 281.

USEFUL WEBSITES

Inter-American Commission on Human Rights: <**http://www.cidh.org**>

Inter-American Court of Human Rights: <**http://www.corteidh.or.cr**>

20

EUROPE

Steven Greer

SUMMARY

This chapter considers the origins, historical development, and key characteristics of Europe's two pre-eminent transnational organizations for the legal protection of human rights—the Council of Europe and the European Union—and the challenges they face. The European Court of Human Rights, the Council of Europe's most significant achievement, is universally celebrated by human rights scholars and activists as the world's most successful international human rights tribunal. The relatively recent, but rapidly developing, interest in human rights shown by the European Union has also been widely welcomed. However, in spite of some encouraging recent developments, the European Court of Human Rights continues to grapple with a case overload crisis, and the European Union's approach to human rights lacks coherence and principled consistency. There can be little doubt that both organizations face an increasingly interdependent future. But the form this should, and is likely to, take is only beginning to be debated.

1 INTRODUCTION

For two conflicting reasons Europe occupies a central and unique place in the history of international human rights law. First, it is, together with the USA, the birthplace of the now global processes of political, social, legal, and economic modernization which embody, amongst other things, liberalization, democratization, marketization, and internationalization. Second, and paradoxically, it was also the site of the Holocaust and a crucial theatre for the twentieth century's two world wars, events that together constituted or precipitated the most systematic and serious violations of human rights the world has ever seen.

In the second half of the twentieth century, this positive and negative heritage not only inspired and laid the foundations for international human rights law itself, it also led to increasing convergence in European political, constitutional, legal, and economic systems around a common institutional model formally defined by democracy, human rights, the rule of law, and the democratically regulated market. These processes now operate on three principal and overlapping dimensions: European states, the Council of Europe, and the European Union (EU). While this chapter is devoted to the last two of these, it should be recognized that other international institutions with a human rights brief, including the United Nations (UN) and the Organization for Security and Cooperation in Europe (OSCE), are also active across the continent. However, only the Council of Europe and the

EU have legislative and/or judicial functions, essential for the development of a distinctive European human rights law.

2 THE ORGANIZATION FOR SECURITY AND COOPERATION IN EUROPE

Apart from the Council of Europe and the EU, the most prominent pan-European inter-governmental organization with a human rights brief is the 57-member OSCE, the largest regional security organization in the world.[1] Participating states from Europe, Central Asia, and North America have equal status and take politically, but not legally, binding decisions on a consensual basis. The OSCE was established in December 1994 as a more permanent post-Cold War version of the Conference on Security and Cooperation in Europe (CSCE). The CSCE was created in the early 1970s as an ad hoc multilateral forum for dialogue and negotiation between East and West in the phase of the Cold War known as 'détente'. Its main achievements were the Helsinki Final Act, signed on 1 August 1975—which included key commitments on political, military, economic, environmental, and human rights issues central to the so-called 'Helsinki process'—and the Decalogue, ten fundamental principles governing the behaviour of states towards each other and towards their own citizens.

At its inception the OSCE was intended to assist in the management of the post-Cold War transition in Europe. Today, its main functions cover the three 'dimensions' of security: the politico-military; the economic and environmental; and the human. Within these fields the OSCE's activities range from traditional security issues such as conflict prevention, to fostering economic development, ensuring the sustainable use of natural resources, and promoting full respect for human rights and fundamental freedoms. Its four specialist human rights-related agencies are: the Office for Democratic Institutions and Human Rights (ODIHR), active in election observation, democratic development, and the promotion of human rights, tolerance, non-discrimination, and the rule of law; the Office of the Special Representative and Coordinator for Combating Trafficking in Human Beings, which supports the development and implementation of anti-trafficking policies; the OSCE Representative on Freedom of the Media who provides early warning on violations of freedom of expression and promotes full compliance with OSCE press freedom commitments; and the High Commissioner on National Minorities who seeks to identify and to resolve ethnic tensions which might endanger peace, stability, or friendly relations between participating states.

3 THE COUNCIL OF EUROPE

The Council of Europe was founded in Strasbourg in 1949 by ten West European liberal democracies as one of a number of Cold War initiatives to promote their interdependence, common identity, and collective security.[2] Its main achievements, and the principal focus of this chapter, were and remain the European Convention on Human Rights (ECHR), which, amongst other things, established the European Court of Human Rights.[3] The

---

[1] Galbreath, *The Organization for Security and Co-operation in Europe* (Routledge, 2007).
[2] Royer, *The Council of Europe* (Council of Europe, 2010).
[3] Greer, *The European Convention on Human Rights: Achievements, Problems and Prospects* (CUP, 2006).

Council of Europe has also been responsible for over 200 other treaties on a wide range of issues. Three of the most important of these—the European Social Charter, the European Convention for the Prevention of Torture and Inhuman or Degrading Treatment or Punishment, and the European Framework Convention for the Protection of National Minorities—are considered in Section 3.3. But first, the origins of the Council of Europe and its key institutions will be reviewed.

3.1 ORIGINS

At the core of the political history of Europe in the nineteenth and twentieth centuries is the story of the formation of nation-states and their struggles between competing conceptions of themselves—liberal or authoritarian—and their battles with each other. By the end of the twentieth century three main lessons, both for human rights and for international peace, had been learned. First, competitive European nationalism, unrestrained by effective international institutions, is likely to result in massively destructive international armed conflict. Second, the attempt after the First World War to protect national minorities and to secure European peace by establishing a collective complaints procedure to the League of Nations had failed.[4] Third, liberal democracies with regulated capitalist economies committed to the rule of law and constitutional rights are essential not only for national prosperity and justice but also for international peace.

Therefore, as the Second World War drew to a close, proposals for increased European collaboration were debated by the Western allies including the USA. Towards the end of 1948 the governments of Belgium, France, and the UK agreed to establish a Council of Europe and invited Denmark, Ireland, Italy, Norway, and Sweden to participate in the negotiations. Luxembourg and the Netherlands joined later. At its foundation, the Council had four main objectives: to contribute to the prevention of another war between West European states; to provide a statement of common values contrasting sharply with Soviet-style communism, hence the almost exclusive emphasis on civil and political rights in the ECHR; to re-enforce a sense of common identity and purpose should the Cold War become an active armed conflict; and to establish an early-warning device by which a drift towards authoritarianism in any member state could be detected and dealt with by complaints from other states to an independent transnational judicial tribunal. This early-warning function was also itself inextricably linked to the prevention of war, since the slide towards the Second World War indicated that the rise of authoritarian regimes in Europe made the peace and security of the continent more precarious. The Council of Europe's founding statute contains several core principles. Certain unspecified 'spiritual and moral values'—'the cumulative influence of Greek philosophy, Roman law, the Western Christian Church, the humanism of the Renaissance and the French Revolution'[5]—are said to constitute the 'common heritage' of the signatory states, to be the 'true source of individual freedom, political liberty and the rule of law', and to form the 'basis of all genuine democracy'. 'Closer unity' between like-minded European states is also deemed to be required in order to implement these principles and to promote 'economic and social progress'.[6]

---

[4] See Chapter 1.

[5] Robertson, *The Council of Europe: Its Structure, Functions and Achievements* (Stevens & Sons, 1961) 2.

[6] Statute of the Council of Europe, preamble.

3.2 KEY INSTITUTIONS

In addition to the European Court of Human Rights, considered in Section 4, the Council of Europe's key institutions are the Committee of Ministers, the Parliamentary Assembly, the Secretariat, the European Commissioner for Human Rights, the Congress of Regional and Local Authorities, and the Conference of International Non-Governmental Organizations.

The Committee of Ministers, the executive and formal policy and treaty-making body, consists of the foreign ministers of member states who usually meet in Strasbourg once a year at a ministerial level for a day or two half-days, and, at the level of Deputy Permanent Representatives, once a week in plenary session and several times a week in subsidiary groups. The Committee of Ministers also supervises execution of judgments of the European Court of Human Rights.

The Parliamentary Assembly of the Council of Europe (PACE) has 318 members (plus a further 318 substitutes) elected on a proportional basis by, and from, national parliaments. It meets four times a year in Strasbourg's Palais de l'Europe, which it shares with the European Parliament, the parliamentary body of the EU. PACE's chief functions are to make recommendations, to pass resolutions, and to express opinions about, and to monitor state compliance with, Council of Europe policy. It also elects the European Commissioner for Human Rights, the Secretary-General and Deputy Secretary-General of the Council of Europe, and judges to the European Court of Human Rights from the lists of three candidates presented by member states. It has no legislative powers.

The Secretary-General presides over the Secretariat, the Council of Europe's bureaucracy, and also has some formal monitoring responsibilities with respect to the ECHR. The post of European Commissioner for Human Rights—not to be confused with the now defunct European Commission of Human Rights (see Section 4.2)—was created in the Secretariat by resolution of the Committee of Ministers in 2000 to promote education and awareness of human rights in member states including collaborating with national and international human rights institutions and ombudsmen, identifying human rights shortcomings in the law and practice of member states, and promoting effective observance of all Council of Europe human rights instruments. As part of his or her general monitoring responsibility the Commissioner can also receive individual complaints but can neither adjudicate nor present them before any national or international court. Although Protocol No 14 now enables the Commissioner to submit written comments to the European Court of Human Rights, and to take part in Chamber and Grand Chamber hearings but not to initiate litigation, by the end of 2012 only one such intervention had been made.[7] The principal function of the 318-member Congress of Local and Regional Authorities (plus a further 318 substitutes), drawn from local and regional representatives, is to advise the Committee of Ministers, PACE, and member states on a wide range of local and regional issues. The 400 or so NGOs with participatory status at the Council of Europe meet four times a year at the Conference of International Non-Governmental Organizations, now an official Council of Europe institution, constituting civil society's contribution to the Council of Europe's 'quadrilogue' with the Committee of Ministers, the Parliamentary Assembly, and the Congress of Local and Regional Authorities.

---

[7] *The Centre for Legal Resources on Behalf of Valentin Câmpeanu v Romania*, App no 47848/08; Council of Europe Steering Committee for Human Rights (CDDH), CDDH report containing elements to contribute to the evaluation of the effects of Protocol No. 14 to the Convention and the implementation of the Interlaken and Izmir Declarations on the Court's situation, CDDH(2012)R76 Addendum II (30 November 2012) para 32.

It is unclear whether the Council of Europe could be said to have an overall human rights policy beyond the general one of drafting treaties and other documents and promoting state compliance with them. Nor is it clear which institution is most influential in policy formation. Some insiders claim specific policies are advocated by specific states, others that they originate in the various committees of the Secretariat, while still others believe the goals and agendas of particular individuals are central. However, it is widely acknowledged that integration and coordination between the activities of the Council's many different agencies and institutions could be improved. While some insiders consider that PACE has the greatest legitimacy regarding human rights policy formation—particularly as it consists of members of national legislatures—others believe the European Commissioner for Human Rights has the most credibility when it comes to identifying priorities.[8]

3.3 KEY INSTRUMENTS

As already indicated, while the ECHR, considered in Section 4, is the Council of Europe's principal achievement, three of its many other treaties—the European Social Charter, the European Convention for the Prevention of Torture and Inhuman or Degrading Treatment or Punishment, and the European Framework Convention for the Protection of National Minorities—also warrant brief discussion.

Among other differences between the ECHR and the European Social Charter 1961 (revised in 1996),[9] seven are particularly worthy of note. First, the ECHR contains mostly civil and political rights whereas the Charter contains a catalogue of social and economic rights, including those relating to housing, health, education, and work. Second, accession to the Charter, unlike the Convention, is not a condition of Council of Europe membership. To date, 43 of the Council's 47 states are bound by the original Charter, the revised version or both. Third, states can choose provisions they do not wish to accede to. Fourth, while the ECHR applies to all those within the jurisdiction of member states, the Charter only applies to citizens of signatory states and to foreign nationals of such states lawfully resident or working regularly within the territory of the state concerned. Fifth, the Charter has no judicial complaints process, nor, sixth, a right of individual complaint. Seventh, compliance is instead monitored in two ways by the 15 independent and impartial expert members of the European Committee of Social Rights (ECSR). Under the 'reporting procedure' the ECSR publishes its 'conclusions' every year based on annual state self-assessment reports. If the Committee of Ministers is dissatisfied with a state's response, it can make appropriate resolutions and recommendations guided by a Governmental Committee comprising representatives of Charter states and observers from European employers' organizations and trade unions. Second, under a complaints procedure provided by an optional protocol, ratified or acceded to by 14 states parties so far, the ECSR can also make decisions on applications—100 by May 2013[10]—received from employers' organizations, trade unions, and NGOs, which in turn may provide the basis for recommendations by the Committee of Ministers. Levels of compliance with both reporting and complaints processes are difficult to determine. Benelhocine claims that states generally respond

---

[8] Information for this paragraph was collected in July 2007 from interviews with some key Council of Europe officials in Strasbourg, generously funded by a Nuffield Foundation Social Sciences Small Grant.
    [9] See Benelhocine, *The European Social Charter* (Council of Europe, 2012); Harris and Darcy, *The European Social Charter* (Transnational, 2000).
    [10] See: <http://www.coe.int/t/dghl/monitoring/socialcharter/Complaints/Complaints_en.asp>.

positively to findings of violation including amending legislation if necessary.[11] However, as De Schutter and Sant'Ana point out: it is 'patently clear that findings of non-compliance can be ignored by the State with little cost'.[12]

The European Convention for the Prevention of Torture and Inhuman or Degrading Treatment or Punishment 1987 (ECPT), amended in 2002, aims to 'strengthen by non-judicial means of a preventive nature',[13] the right of everyone detained by a public authority in a member state not to be subjected to torture or to inhuman or degrading treatment or punishment. It seeks to do so by providing an enforcement regime based on unannounced visits to places of detention, particularly those holding vulnerable groups, by delegations from the 47 independent and impartial expert member European Committee for the Prevention of Torture and Inhuman or Degrading Treatment or Punishment, one per state party to the ECPT. The Committee is obliged to inform states of its intention to conduct a visit but not of the precise locations chosen for inspection. While all states are subject to periodic missions every four to six years, the Committee can, at its own discretion, make ad hoc visits and 'rapid reaction interventions', typically prompted by concerns expressed by individuals, groups, or other state parties that ill-treatment is a problem in the state concerned. The purpose of visits is to open up dialogue with states. Missions end with members of the delegation conveying initial impressions to officials in the expectation of a response to the subsequent report. Although formally confidential, publication of reports has become the rule rather than the exception. Following 'high level talks' the Committee is empowered to 'make a public statement' if a state fails to cooperate or to improve defects in compliance with the ECPT to which its attention has been drawn. Up to 2012 this had happened only six times—with respect to Russia (three times), Turkey (twice), and Greece (once).[14] Confidential reports are also submitted to the Committee of Ministers and follow-up visits can be made to assess progress. Now a condition of Council of Europe membership, the ECPT has been signed and ratified by every member state. Collectively the Committee's recommendations form 'part of a dynamic corpus of standards'.[15] However, although these and the Committee's other activities have influenced states and other European institutions, such as the European Prison Rules and the European Court of Human Rights, it is not clear if the ECPT has made any significant direct difference to preventing the torture or ill-treatment of detainees.[16]

The Framework Convention for the Protection of National Minorities 1995 marks a departure from the Council of Europe's commitment to individual rather than collective rights, prompted in the 1990s by the 'shock of interethnic violence that afflicted Eastern Europe with the unfreezing of the Cold War'.[17] The word 'Framework' indicates that the principles this instrument contains are not directly applicable in national legal systems but require implementation through legislation and national public policy. The Framework Convention aims to ensure that states respect the rights of national minorities and facilitate the protection and development of their culture and identity, including by combating discrimination, promoting equality, guaranteeing certain freedoms in relation to access to

[11] Benelhocine, n 9, 26 and 52.

[12] De Schutter and Sant'ana, 'The European Committee of Social Rights (the ECSR)' in de Beco (ed), *Human Rights Monitoring Mechanisms of the Council of Europe* (Routledge, 2012) 90.   [13] ECPT, preamble.

[14] Kicker, 'The European Committee for the Prevention of Torture and Inhuman or Degrading Treatment or Punishment (the CPT)' in de Beco, n 12, 63 (footnote 56).   [15] Kicker, n 14, 52.

[16] Kicker, n 14, 52–3, 62–3, 65; Evans and Morgan, *Preventing Torture: A Study of the European Convention for the Prevention of Torture and Inhuman or Degrading Treatment or Punishment* (Clarendon Press, 1998) 159.

[17] Verstichel et al. (eds), *The Framework Convention for the Protection of National Minorities* (Intersentia, 2008); Weller (ed), *The Rights of Minorities: A Commentary on the European Framework Convention for the Protection of National Minorities* (OUP, 2005) vii.

the media, minority languages, and education, and encouraging participation by national minorities in public life. The Committee of Ministers monitors national compliance with the assistance of an appointed Advisory Committee of between 12 and 18 independent and impartial experts.[18] The Advisory Committee examines the reports that states are required to submit at five-yearly intervals, or when the Committee of Ministers so requests. Meetings may also be held with officials and country visits conducted. Although the Advisory Committee does not deal with individual complaints, it may, nevertheless, receive information from individuals and other sources such as NGOs. In the light of the opinion of the Advisory Committee, the Committee of Ministers makes its final decision ('conclusion') concerning the adequacy of measures to implement the Framework Convention taken by any state party. Where appropriate, it may also make recommendations. Conclusions, recommendations, the Advisory Committee's opinions, and any comments by the state concerned are made public. By 2013 the Framework Convention had been signed and ratified by 39 of the Council of Europe's 47 member states. Assessing the effectiveness of the Framework Convention is next to impossible, not least because of its programmatic nature and because the term 'national minority' is not formally defined.

4 THE EUROPEAN CONVENTION ON HUMAN RIGHTS

The Convention for the Protection of Human Rights and Fundamental Freedoms (more commonly known as the 'European Convention on Human Rights' or 'ECHR') was drafted by the Council of Europe in 1950 and entered into force in 1953. Its ratification has been a condition of membership of the Council of Europe since the beginning. The central objective of the ECHR is to provide an independent judicial process at Strasbourg, which can authoritatively determine whether a Convention right has been violated by a given member state. This section considers the substantive rights the Convention contains, reviews the establishment and development of its key institutions and processes, describes the current inter-state and individual applications processes, discusses the resolution of complaints by friendly settlement and adjudication of the merits, and finally outlines how the Committee of Ministers supervises the execution of the Court's judgments.

4.1 SUBSTANTIVE RIGHTS

The ECHR is similar in content to other international and national instruments that deal with civil and political rights, particularly the International Covenant on Civil and Political Rights. Article 1 requires member states 'to secure to everyone within their jurisdiction' the rights and freedoms the Convention contains. Articles 2 to 13 provide the rights: to life; not to be subjected to torture or to inhuman or degrading treatment or punishment; not to be held in slavery or servitude or to be required to perform forced or compulsory labour; to freedom from arbitrary arrest and detention; to a fair trial; not to be punished without law; to respect for private and family life, home, and correspondence; to freedom of thought, conscience, and religion; to freedom of expression; to freedom

---

[18] de Beco and Lantschner, 'The Advisory Committee on the Framework Convention for the Protection of National Minorities (the ACFC)' in de Beco (ed), n 12.

of assembly and association; to marry; and to an effective national remedy for the violation of a Convention right. Article 14 states that the enjoyment of any Convention right
shall be secured without discrimination on any ground such as sex, race, colour, language,
religion, political or other opinion, national or social origin, association with a national
minority, property, birth, or other status. Article 15 provides for the suspension of all but
a handful of rights 'in time of war or other public emergency threatening the life of the
nation', provided such 'derogations' are 'strictly required by the exigencies of the situation'
and are not incompatible with the state's other international legal obligations. Article 16
provides that nothing in Articles 10, 11, and 14 shall be regarded as preventing restrictions
on the political activities of aliens. Article 17 prohibits the ECHR from being interpreted
to imply a right to engage in any activity, or to perform any act, aimed at the destruction of
any Convention right or freedom, or its limitation to a greater extent than the Convention
itself permits. Article 18 limits restrictions upon rights to those purposes the ECHR itself
expressly provides.

Sixteen subsequent protocols have either added further rights or instigated procedural
reforms. The former are optional and usually come into effect when a specified number of
states has completed the formalities. Protocol No 1, for example, contains rights to education, the peaceful enjoyment of possessions, and free elections; while Protocol No 4 provides the right not to be imprisoned for debt, the right to freedom of movement, the right
of nationals not to be expelled from the state to which they belong, and the right of aliens
not to be collectively expelled. Protocol No 6 abolishes the death penalty except in time of
war. Protocol No 7 contains procedural safeguards regarding the expulsion of aliens, the
right of appeal in criminal proceedings, the right to compensation for wrongful conviction, the right not to be tried or punished twice in the same state for the same offence, as
well as the equal right of spouses under the law. Protocol No 12 outlaws discrimination in
relation to any right 'set forth by law', in contrast with Article 14 ECHR which prohibits
discrimination only with respect to Convention rights. Protocol No 13 outlaws the death
penalty even in time of war. Protocol No 14bis applied for a year before Protocol No 14
came into effect in June 2010. Once a universal procedural protocol comes into effect, it
loses its separate identity and its provisions are seamlessly incorporated into the revised
text of the Convention.

4.2 INSTITUTIONAL AND PROCEDURAL BACKGROUND

At its inception it was agreed that the Convention's main *modus operandi* should be complaints brought by states against each other (the 'inter-state process'). Some also chose to
permit individual applications before this became compulsory in 1998. The ECHR was at
first, therefore, much more obviously about protecting the democratic identity of member
states through the medium of human rights, and promoting international cooperation
between them, than it was about providing individuals with redress for human rights violations by national public authorities.

When it was first established, the Convention system had three main institutions. The
European Commission of Human Rights was the first port of call for both state and individual applicants. It ascertained the facts, determined if the admissibility criteria were
satisfied, and explored the possibility of friendly settlement. If no settlement could be
found the Commission expressed a non-binding opinion concerning whether or not the
Convention had been violated. Then, providing the jurisdiction of the European Court
of Human Rights—the second institution which began operating in 1959—had been
accepted by the state or states concerned, the case could be referred by the Commission,

the respondent state, or the state of which the applicant was a national, but not by individual applicants themselves, to the Court for a legally binding decision. The Committee
of Ministers, the third institution, also decided cases over which the European Court did
not have jurisdiction and those that the Commission did not refer to the Court. Both the
Commission and the Court were then staffed by part-time judges.

For most of its first 30 years the ECHR had very little impact on victims of human rights
abuses, and was almost entirely ignored by lawyers, politicians, jurists and other commentators. Only 800 or so individual applications were received by the Strasbourg institutions per year. But from the mid-1980s onwards things began to change dramatically.
First, it became clear that inter-state complaints—about two dozen in the Convention's
entire history[19]—were largely a dead letter, not least because litigation is a hostile act in
most circumstances and, therefore, not an ideal vehicle for cultivating international interdependence. Second, in sharp contrast, the rate of individual applications began to rise
steeply. By the late 1990s it was already clear that this had reached crisis proportions and
by 2012 there were over 65,000, more than the grand total for the first four decades.[20]
On 1 January 2013 over 128,000 applications were awaiting a decision regarding admissibility (compared with 151,600 at the beginning of the previous year), more than half of
which had been lodged against four states. Russia (22.3 per cent) and Ukraine (8.2 per
cent) joined the Convention system in the 1990s, while the other two, Turkey (13.2 per
cent) and Italy (11.1 per cent), were amongst the original signatories.[21] This inundation of
individual applications was due partly to the third significant change: the huge expansion
in the number of states belonging to the Council of Europe, from a mere ten in 1950 to 46
by the end of the 1990s and 47, with a combined population of 800 million, by the end of
the first decade of the twenty-first century. All the former communist states of Central and
Eastern Europe, except Belarus, are now members. A fourth change, and one of the key
factors in the rising application rate, is the fact that the ECHR is now much better known
by lawyers and by the general public throughout Europe.

In response to the rising application rate, the judicial process was reformed by Protocol
No 11 with effect from 1 November 1998. The European Commission of Human Rights
was abolished and the restructured Court became a professional full-time institution with
responsibility for the formal receipt of applications, ascertaining the facts, deciding if the
admissibility criteria were satisfied, seeking friendly resolution, delivering legally binding
judgments, and issuing advisory opinions[22] at the request of the Committee of Ministers.
Protocol No 11 also stripped the Committee of Ministers of its power to settle cases on the
merits, a responsibility deemed incompatible with the now enhanced judicial character of
the complaints processes, and limited its role to supervising the execution of the Court's
judgments. Both the right of individual petition and acceptance of the Court's jurisdiction also became compulsory, although by the 1990s each had already been voluntarily
endorsed by all member states.

---

[19] Committee of Ministers, Protocol No 14 to the Convention for the Protection of Human Rights and
Fundamental Freedoms, Amending the Control System of the Convention, Explanatory Report (12 May
2004) para 11.

[20] European Court of Human Rights, Annual Report 2012, 156, available at: <http://echr.coe.int/
Documents/Annual_report_2012_ENG.pdf>. European Court of Human Rights, Analysis of Statistics 2012,
para B., available at: <http://echr.coe.int/Documents/Stats_analysis_2012_ENG.pdf>.

[21] Annual Report 2012, n 20, 151.

[22] To date, the Committee of Ministers has made three requests for advisory opinions and the Court has
delivered two; see European Court of Human Rights, Annual Report 2011, 11, footnote 1, available at: <http://
echr.coe.int/Documents/Annual_report_2011_ENG.pdf>.

However, by 2000, Protocol No 11 was already officially recognized as inadequate, not least because the consequences of the post-communist enlargement had not been adequately anticipated. In May 2004 another modest reform package, Protocol No 14, was unanimously approved by all states parties. The most significant changes are to the applications and enforcement of judgments processes, considered further in Section 4.3. But by early 2005 it had already become clear that these changes would not make much difference to the rising tide of applications and that something more radical was required. So, in May 2005, a Group of Wise Persons was appointed to make further proposals. Their report, made public in November 2006, contained nothing substantially new, largely recycled ideas already rejected in the course of the Protocol No 14 debate, and assumed that Protocol No 14 would soon come into effect.[23] But in December 2006, to everyone's great surprise and in spite of the fact that the Russian government had already approved it, the Russian parliament refused to ratify Protocol No 14, ostensibly because of objections to admissibility decisions being made by 'single-judge formations'. This caused great consternation in Strasbourg and, notwithstanding intense diplomatic pressure, by May 2009 the Russian parliament had still not been persuaded to change its mind. As a result, the Council of Europe provided an interim set of optional measures intended to apply to the other 46 states. Derived from Protocol No 14, Protocol No 14bis enabled admissibility decisions to be taken by single judge formations and for cases where the Convention had patently been violated to be judged on the merits by three-judge committees. The European Court also sought to manage its mushrooming workload by prioritizing applications according to the seriousness and urgency of the complaint. However, again to everyone's surprise, in January 2010 both chambers of the Russian parliament voted in favour of ratifying Protocol No 14, which came into effect on 1 June 2010.

But this has not, by any means, concluded the reform process. Various proposals for further changes were considered at a series of High Level Conferences on the Future of the European Court of Human Rights held in Interlaken in 2010, Izmir in 2011, and Brighton in 2012. As a result, a fifteenth Protocol was opened for signature on 24 June 2013.[24] When it comes into effect this will require candidates for appointment to the European Court to be under the age of 65 when the three-person lists are requested by PACE, abolish the right of parties to veto relinquishment of litigation to the Grand Chamber, shorten from six to four months the time limit within which applications to the Court must be made from the last decision by the national legal system on the matter, include a reference to subsidiarity, the margin of appreciation, and Strasbourg's supervisory jurisdiction in the Preamble to the Convention, and remove the requirement from Article 35(3)(b) that an application should have been 'duly considered by a domestic tribunal' before it can be rejected as inadmissible on the grounds that the applicant has suffered 'no significant disadvantage'. A further optional protocol, No 16—which permitted national courts to request, in on-going litigation, discretionary, non-binding advisory opinions from the Grand Chamber regarding matters of principle relating to the interpretation and application of Convention rights—was adopted by the Committee of Ministers on 10 July 2013 and opened for signature on 2 October 2013.[25]

---

[23] Report of the Group of Wise Persons to the Committee of Ministers, Cm(2006)203 (15 November 2006).

[24] Available at: <http://conventions.coe.int/Treaty/en/Treaties/html/213.htm>.

[25] Available at: <http://www.conventions.coe.int/Treaty/EN/Treaties/Html/Prot16ECHR.htm>.

4.3 COMPLAINTS PROCEDURES

4.3.1 Inter-state applications

The inter-state applications process is set out in Figure 20.1. Although very infrequently used, and less than a resounding success in correcting alleged violations, it is not yet totally moribund and can have considerable symbolic significance.[26] In 2009 and 2011 respectively, applications made by Georgia against Russia—the former concerning multiple alleged violations of the Convention rights of Georgians living in the Russian Federation and the latter connected with the armed conflict of 2008—were ruled admissible by the European Court of Human Rights.[27]

Under the inter-state process an applicant state lodges a complaint against a respondent state with the Registry of the Court which, as a result of Protocol No 14, can initiate the friendly settlement procedure (see Section 4.4.1) at any stage of the proceedings and not just post-admissibility as under Protocol No 11. Having received an application the Registry informs the Court's President who notifies the respondent state and allocates the complaint to one of the Court's five Sections. A seven-judge Chamber, including the judges elected in respect of applicant and respondent states, is then constituted to consider admissibility, the requirements for which are much less exacting than those for individual petitions. The ECHR must have been binding on the applicant and respondent states, and applicable to the persons concerned within the jurisdiction of the respondent state, at the material time and place. Except where the allegation concerns legislation or an ongoing administrative practice all domestic remedies must have been exhausted. The application must also be lodged with the Court within a period of six months from the date on which the final decision on the relevant subject matter was taken in the respondent state's legal system. As already noted, this will be reduced to four months when Protocol No 15 comes into effect. While a prima facie case is not required in the formal sense, inter-state applications will be rejected as inadmissible if the allegations concerned are wholly unsubstantiated. Protocol No 14 also enables the Court to ask the Committee of Ministers to reduce the number of judges on Chambers to five. The processes of friendly settlement, judgment of the merits, and the roles of the Court's Grand Chamber and the Committee of Ministers are substantially the same as under the individual applications process as amended by Protocol No 14 (see Sections 4.4 and 4.5).

4.3.2 Individual applications

Protocol No 11 became redundant for individual applications when Protocol No 14 came into effect on 1 June 2010. It is, therefore, not necessary to discuss it in detail here. But, in order fully to appreciate what has since changed, a brief review is nevertheless required. Under Protocol No 11 the management of formal applications was the responsibility of a Judge Rapporteur assisted by a case-processing lawyer from the Registry. The Judge Rapporteur examined and prepared the file, including requiring documents and further particulars from the parties, and channelled the complaint for an admissibility decision—together with proposals about its disposal—either to a three-judge committee, if it appeared to be clearly inadmissible, or to a Chamber of seven judges if its inadmissibility was not so clear. Under Article 28 ECHR a committee could, and still can, by unanimous vote, declare an application inadmissible, or strike it off the list, 'where such decision can be taken without further examination',[28] a fate which, pre-Protocol No 14, typically

---

[26] Greer, n 3, 24–8.

[27] *Georgia v Russia (No 1)* (2011) 52 EHRR SE14; *Georgia v Russia (No. 2)* (2012) 54 EHRR SE10.

[28] ECHR, Art 28(1)(a).

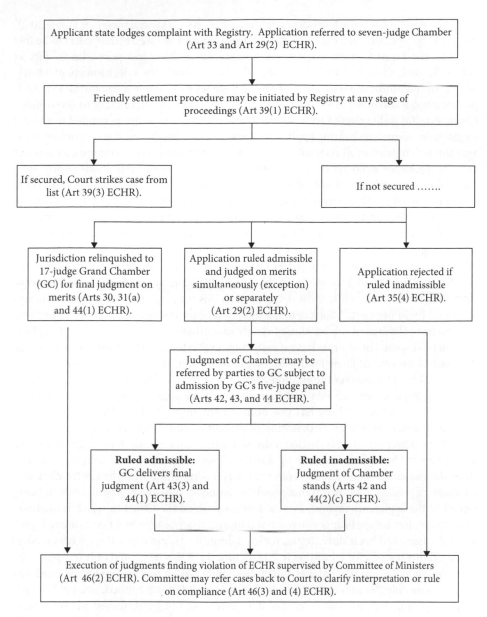

Figure 20.1 The inter-state applications process

befell between 80 and 90 per cent of applications rejected as inadmissible or struck off.[29] Cases which could not be settled unanimously were referred to a seven-judge Chamber for a decision about admissibility and merits, accompanied by a report from the Judge Rapporteur summarizing the facts, indicating the issues raised, and making a proposal as to what should happen next, for example a decision against admissibility or further correspondence with the parties.

[29] Report of the Evaluation Group to the Committee of Ministers on the European Court of Human Rights, EG Court 1 (2001) (27 September 2001) para 28.

Protocol No 14 alters the individual applications process in several ways (see Figure 20.2). First, it is now possible for the friendly settlement procedure (see Section 4.4.1) to be initiated by the Registry at any stage of the proceedings and not just post-admissibility as before. Second, all formal applications are allocated, initially for a decision about admissibility, by 'non-judicial rapporteurs' from the Registry to: a 'single judge formation' comprising a judge and non-judicial rapporteur; to three-judge committees; or to seven-judge Chambers. The judge elected with respect to a particular state is not permitted to sit on a single-judge formation hearing applications against that state. While the rapporteur manages the file containing all relevant documents, the judge can, as already indicated, reject as inadmissible, or strike off the Court's list, the vast majority of applications (where such a decision can be taken without further examination), and direct the remainder to a committee or Chamber. The Court's statistics show a sustained and significant increase in the number of cases rejected at the filtering stage since the single judge procedure came into effect. For example, in 2012, 48,350 of the 65,150 formal applications were allocated to a single judge formation on the grounds that they were likely to be declared inadmissible, while the remainder were identified as Chamber or Committee cases.[30] The total number declared inadmissible or struck of the list (86,201) constituted a 70 per cent increase from the previous year while those disposed of in this manner by single judge formations increased by 74 per cent.[31] Subject to additional Registry resources, the Court expects by 2015 to have eliminated the backlog of clearly inadmissible applications and for applications to be disposed of at a rate increasingly comparable to those received.[32] From 1999 to 2010 only 4 per cent of formal individual applications were declared admissible.[33]

Protocol No 14 preserves the existing admissibility tests and adds a new one. As before, individual applications can be ruled inadmissible if the applicant was not a victim of a Convention violation, redress has not been sought through the national legal system as far as it could have been ('exhaustion of domestic remedies'), more than six months have elapsed between the last national decision on the matter and formal application to Strasbourg (to be reduced to four by Article 4 Protocol No 15), the complaint is substantially the same as one already examined, it is incompatible with the Convention, it is an abuse of process, and/or it is 'manifestly ill-founded' (obviously has no hope of being settled in the applicant's favour). Protocol No 14 enabled the Court to reject as inadmissible complaints by applicants where no significant disadvantage had been suffered, provided the issue had been 'duly considered' by a domestic tribunal and there were no other human rights reasons for admitting it.[34] Until June 2012 this test could only be applied by Chambers and the Grand Chamber and by November 2012 it was known to have rendered inadmissible only 29 cases and to have been considered, but not applied, in a further 19.[35] As already indicated, the 'duly considered' requirement will be abolished when Protocol No 15 comes into effect.[36]

Under Protocol No 14, unanimous committees of three judges are now able simultaneously to settle admissibility and the merits of applications disclosing clear-cut violations according

[30] Analysis of Statistics 2012, n 20, para A.   [31] Analysis of Statistics 2012, n 20, para C.2.
[32] CDDH report, n 7, paras 21 and 22.
[33] European Court of Human Rights, Annual Report 2010, 155, available at: <http://echr.coe.int/Documents/Annual_report_2010_ENG.pdf>. 'Applications declared admissible' as a percentage of 'Applications declared admissible' plus 'Applications declared inadmissible or struck out'.
[34] Art 35(3)(b); Protocol No 15, Art 5 deletes the phrase 'and provided that no case may be rejected on this ground which has not been duly considered by a domestic tribunal'; see Greer, 'The New Admissibility Criterion', in Besson (ed), *The European Court of Human Rights after Protocol 14: Preliminary Assessment and Perspectives* (Schulthess, 2011).
[35] CDDH report, n 7, paras 29, 30.   [36] Art 5.

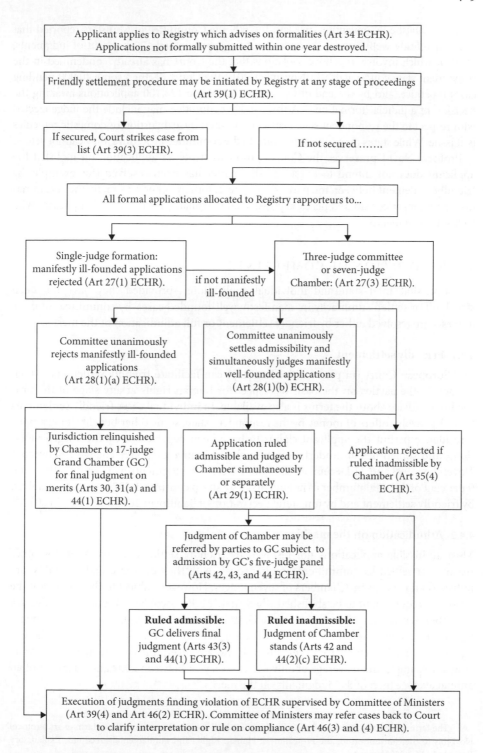

Applicant applies to Registry which advises on formalities (Art 34 ECHR).
Applications not formally submitted within one year destroyed.

Friendly settlement procedure may be initiated by Registry at any stage of proceedings
(Art 39(1) ECHR).

If secured, Court strikes case from list (Art 39(3) ECHR).

If not secured ....

All formal applications allocated to Registry rapporteurs to...

Single-judge formation: manifestly ill-founded applications rejected (Art 27(1) ECHR).

if not manifestly ill-founded

Three-judge committee or seven-judge Chamber: (Art 27(3) ECHR).

Committee unanimously rejects manifestly ill-founded applications (Art 28(1)(a) ECHR).

Committee unanimously settles admissibility and simultaneously judges manifestly well-founded applications (Art 28(1)(b) ECHR).

Jurisdiction relinquished by Chamber to 17-judge Grand Chamber (GC) for final judgment on merits (Arts 30, 31(a) and 44(1) ECHR).

Application ruled admissible and judged by Chamber simultaneously or separately (Art 29(1) ECHR).

Application rejected if ruled inadmissible by Chamber (Art 35(4) ECHR).

Judgment of Chamber may be referred by parties to GC subject to admission by GC's five-judge panel (Arts 42, 43, and 44 ECHR).

Ruled admissible: GC delivers final judgment (Arts 43(3) and 44(1) ECHR).

Ruled inadmissible: Judgment of Chamber stands (Arts 42 and 44(2)(c) ECHR).

Execution of judgments finding violation of ECHR supervised by Committee of Ministers (Art 39(4) and Art 46(2) ECHR). Committee of Ministers may refer cases back to Court to clarify interpretation or rule on compliance (Art 46(3) and (4) ECHR).

Figure 20.2 The individual applications process

to well-established Convention case law. In 2009 the Committee of Ministers reported that such 'manifestly well-founded' cases account for approximately 70 per cent of judgments, most of which involve 'repetitive' violations that the Court has already condemned in the respondent state concerned.[37] In November 2012 the Court deemed some 40,000 pending cases repetitive, and by the end of December there were 128,100 applications awaiting the decision of a judicial formation.[38] A three-judge committee may include the judge elected with respect to the respondent state, particularly when the exhaustion of domestic remedies is at issue. While states may contest recourse to the committee procedure, they cannot veto it.

Protocol No 14 preserves the Court's power to strike an application off its list if the applicant does not intend to pursue it, the matter has been resolved (for example, by friendly settlement between the parties), or where, for any other reason, further examination is no longer considered necessary. Legal aid is available for individual applicants who lack sufficient means.

4.4 RESOLUTION OF COMPLAINTS

All admissible inter-state and individual applications—provided they have not been struck off or settled summarily in 'manifestly well-founded cases' by committees of three judges—are resolved either by friendly settlement or full adjudication of the merits.

4.4.1 Friendly settlement

The European Court (in practice the Registry) can facilitate friendly settlement, which is open to the parties on the basis of respect for human rights at any stage of the proceedings. Advice about the terms is also available. In individual cases friendly settlements typically involve offers of money by the respondent state, some other benefit (for example, a residence permit the applicant claims to have been deprived of by the alleged violation), and sometimes an undertaking to make legislative or policy changes. Between 1 November 1998 and 31 December 2008 there were 898 judgments by friendly settlement, 9 per cent of the total number of judgments.[39] By sharp contrast, 1,532 cases were resolved by friendly settlement and by unilateral declaration of liability in 2011 and 1,909 in 2012.[40]

4.4.2 Adjudication on the merits

Most admissible applications not resolved by friendly settlement, struck off for other reasons, or settled by committees simultaneously with the decision on admissibility, are judged on the merits by Chambers of seven judges. However, subject to the consent of the parties (a requirement to be abolished when Article 3 Protocol No 15 comes into effect), a Chamber may relinquish jurisdiction to a Grand Chamber of 17 judges where the application raises a serious question affecting the interpretation of the ECHR or where there is a prospect of a departure from previous case law. However, this is extremely rare, occurring, for example, in an average of only five cases a year between 2002 and 2005, out of an annual average then of 843 judgments on the merits.[41]

---

[37] The term 'manifestly well-founded', unlike 'manifestly ill-founded', is not an official term of art. Protocol No 14bis to the Convention for the Protection of Human Rights and Fundamental Freedoms, Explanatory Report (27 May 2009) para 16.

[38] CDDH report, n 7, para 25; ECtHR, Annual Report 2012, n 20, 150.

[39] ECtHR, Annual Report 2008, 137, 139, available at: <http://echr.coe.int/Documents/Annual_report_2008_ENG.pdf>.   [40] Analysis of Statistics 2012, n 20, Table 4.

[41] Mowbray, 'An Examination of the Work of the Grand Chamber of the European Court of Human Rights' [2007] PL 507, 509; Annual Report 2012, n 20, 157.

Between 1959 and 1999 the Court delivered fewer than 1,000 judgments, yet by the end of December 2012 the grand total had risen to just under 16,000.[42] Since 2005, when the annual number of judgments first exceeded 1,000, the Court has delivered an annual average of 1,385, dropping to 1,157 in 2011 and 1,093 in 2012.[43] Between 1959 and 2012 judgments on the merits accounted for 90 per cent of all judgments—including those concerning friendly settlement, striking out, just satisfaction, revision, preliminary objections, and lack of jurisdiction—and 93 per cent of judgments on the merits resulted in a finding of at least one violation.[44] Nearly half the Court's judgments between its establishment in 1959 and 2012 concern four states: Turkey (2,870), Italy (2,229), Russia (1,346), and Poland (1,019).[45] The provisions of the Convention most frequently found to have been violated between 1959 and 2011 are the right to fair trial under Article 6 (45.01 per cent of judgments finding a violation), the right to peaceful enjoyment of possessions under Article 1 of Protocol No. 1 (13.35 per cent), and the right to liberty and security under Article 5 (11.46 per cent).[46] In 2011 the Court classified 64 per cent of its own judgments as of 'little legal interest' with the remaining 36 per cent as either making a 'significant contribution' or not merely applying existing case-law.[47]

Judgments on the merits—which rely mostly on written submissions from the parties but in certain cases also upon oral public hearings—are drafted by a Judge Rapporteur, assisted by the judge elected in respect of the respondent state or, in some cases, by a drafting committee, and put to a vote of all judges sitting on the particular panel. Typically they contain summaries of the facts, the history of the dispute including a review of relevant domestic law, the arguments presented by both parties, relevant provisions of the ECHR, the Court's reasoned verdict, a concise statement of the substantive result, plus concurring and dissenting opinions if any.

In urgent cases, where serious consequences such as death or torture could ensue before the matter is resolved, a Chamber may 'indicate to the parties any interim measure which it considers should be adopted'.[48] As a result of the judgment of the Grand Chamber in *Mamatkulov and Askarov v Turkey*,[49] the Court regards interim measures as binding on respondent states with, in most cases, failure to comply constituting a violation of the obligation under Article 34 ECHR not to hinder the right of individual application. Breaches are, however, uncommon. Between 2008 and 2012 the Court received an annual average of 2,822 requests for interim measures; 23.3 per cent were granted, 53 per cent refused, and 23.7 per cent were deemed to fall outside the scope of the provision.[50]

In judging the merits, the primary issue the Court has to consider is whether, on the evidence presented, the respondent state has violated the ECHR. This involves interpreting the alleged misconduct in context and determining what the sparse and abstract statements of the relevant rights mean. A handful of Convention rights are subject to no express exceptions and cannot be suspended under Article 15, while the remainder are

---

[42] Annual Report 2011, n 22, 12: Annual Report 2012, n 20, 157.   [43] Annual Report 2012, n 20, 157.

[44] 'Judgments on the merits' refers to 'Judgments finding at least one violation' plus 'Judgments finding no violation'; European Court of Human Rights, Violation by Article and by State 1959–2012, available at: <http://echr.coe.int/Documents/Stats_violation_1959_2012_ENG.pdf>.

[45] Violation by Article and by State 1959–2012, n 44; Annual Report 2012, n 20, 154–5.

[46] ECtHR, Overview 1959–2011, 5, available at: <http://echr.coe.int/Documents/Overview_2011_ENG.pdf>.

[47] Annual Report 2011, n 22, 87.

[48] Rules of Court, Rule 39. See also Harby, 'The changing nature of interim measures before the European Court of Human Rights' [2010] *EHRLR* 73.   [49] (2005) 41 EHRR 25.

[50] European Court of Human Rights, Rule 39 requests granted and refused in 2008, 2009, and 2010, 2011 and 2012 by responding state, available at: <http://echr.coe.int/Documents/Stats_art_39_2008_2012_ENG.pdf>.

subject to various express limitations and can also be suspended under Article 15. The Court also applies a dozen or so 'principles of interpretation' not found in the text of the Convention itself but identified and developed in the process of litigation over the years.[51] These are rooted in the 'teleological principle', derived from Articles 31 to 33 of the Vienna Convention on the Law of Treaties, which requires the text of international treaties to be interpreted in good faith according to the ordinary meaning of their terms in context—unless any special meaning was intended by the parties—and in the light of the overall object and purpose of the treaty in question. But, unlike most international treaties which are merely reciprocal agreements between states, the ECHR is a 'constitutional instrument of European public order in the field of human rights', which creates a 'network of mutual bilateral undertakings... [and] ... objective obligations'.[52] The principle of effective protection of individual rights holds that, given the primary function of the ECHR, rights should be interpreted broadly and exceptions narrowly. This is linked to the principle of non-abuse of rights and limitations, which prohibits states and others from undermining the protection of rights by abusing either the rights themselves or their limitations. However, the principles of implied rights and implied limitations allow some scope for extensions of rights, and also inherent but not extensive limitations, to be read into the text. The principle of positive obligations allows the Court to interpret the ECHR in a manner that imposes obligations upon states actively to protect Convention rights and not merely the negative obligation to avoid violating them.

Armed with the principle of autonomous interpretation the Court can define some of the Convention's key terms in order to prevent states conveniently re-defining their way around their obligations, for instance, by re-designating crimes as mere 'administrative infractions'. Similarly, the principle of evolutive, or dynamic, interpretation enables outmoded conceptions of how terms in the Convention were originally understood to be abandoned when significant, durable, and—according to the principle of commonality—pan-European changes in the climate of European public opinion have occurred, for example that homosexuality and transsexualism are aspects of private life requiring respect from public authorities.[53] The twin principles of subsidiarity and supervision (expressly incorporated in the preamble to the Convention by Article 1 Protocol No 15), indicate that the role of the Court is subsidiary to that of member states and is limited to determining whether the Convention has been violated rather than acting as final court of appeal or fourth instance.

The principle of proportionality limits interference with Convention rights to that which is least intrusive in pursuit of a legitimate objective, while the closely related 'doctrine' of the margin of appreciation (expressly incorporated into the preamble by Article 1 Protocol No 15), refers to the room for manoeuvre the Strasbourg institutions are prepared to accord national authorities in fulfilling their Convention obligations. Pervasive in the ECHR are the closely related principles of legality, the rule of law, and procedural fairness—which seek to subject the exercise of public power to effective, formal legal constraints in order to avoid arbitrariness—and the principle of democracy, which assumes that human rights flourish best in the context of democratic political institutions and a tolerant social climate.

While the Court generally seeks to remain faithful to its own previous decisions, these are not formally binding precedents, nor is there much doctrinal exposition as in the common law tradition. Most judgments on the merits, therefore, amount to little more than

---

[51] See Greer, n 3, ch 4.
[52] *Ireland v UK* (1980) 2 EHRR 25, para 239; *Austria v Italy* (1961) YB 116, 138.   [53] See Chapter 15.

decisions on the facts where the precise circumstances of the dispute are held to constitute or not to constitute a violation of the ECHR, but which establish little of general application beyond. Moreover, judgments against respondent states typically declare only that the ECHR has been violated because the Court considers itself less well placed than national authorities to be more prescriptive about what precisely should be done to correct it. Even if a judgment finds a violation, an award of compensation is not automatic and, although some general principles have been identified, the relevant case law is not consistent.[54]

However, primarily in order to stem floods of similar complaints, over the past decade or so, the Court has shown greater willingness, in several 'pilot judgments', to indicate the type of remedial action required to correct a violation. For example, in *Broniowski v Poland* the Grand Chamber held that the applicant's right to the peaceful enjoyment of possessions under Article 1 Protocol No 1 had been breached by the expropriation of his property coupled with the payment of inadequate compensation. While this was, in itself, not an unprecedented outcome, the judgment added that, since the violation 'originated in a widespread problem which resulted from a malfunctioning of Polish legislation and administrative practice...which has affected and remains capable of affecting a large number of persons',[55] appropriate measures were required to secure an adequate right of compensation or redress, not simply for the particular applicant, but for all similar claimants.[56] Subsequent applications complaining of violations stemming from the same state of affairs can, therefore, be directed back to the Polish authorities to settle according to the terms of the *Broniowski* judgment without the Court having to reconsider the merits afresh in each case. However, according to a recent study, pilot judgments have only been 'relatively successful' in some contexts and less so in others.[57] They are not, therefore, the panacea for the problem of case overload that some may have hoped.

A Chamber's verdict, whether unanimous or by majority, usually disposes of the matter. However, exceptional cases may be referred by one or more of the parties to a Grand Chamber of 17 judges within three months of the original judgment. Technically, such referrals are not 'appeals' but 're-hearings' and are conditional upon the approval of the Grand Chamber's five-judge 'admissibility' panel, which is obliged to accede to them where the case raises 'a serious question affecting the interpretation or application of the Convention or the Protocols thereto, or a serious issue of general importance'.[58] Judgments of Chambers become final under three circumstances: when the parties declare that they will not request a reference to the Grand Chamber, three months after the date of judgment if a reference to a Grand Chamber has not been made, or where a reference to a Grand Chamber has been made but the five-judge panel has rejected it. Between 2002 and 2005 an annual average of 116 cases were referred to the Grand Chamber. But 91 per cent were rejected as inadmissible and, of the 23 judgments the Grand Chamber delivered, 13 confirmed the original verdict.[59]

4.5 SUPERVISION OF THE EXECUTION OF JUDGMENTS

Supervision of the execution of judgments against respondent states is the responsibility of the Committee of Ministers, which considers whether the obligation under Article 46(1)

---

[54] Harris *et al.*, *Harris, O'Boyle and Warbrick: Law of the European Convention on Human Rights* (OUP, 2009) 856.

[55] (2005) 40 EHRR 495, para 189.   [56] (2005) 40 EHRR 495, para 200.

[57] Leach et al., *Responding to Systematic Human Rights Violations: An Analysis of 'Pilot Judgments' of the European Court of Human Rights and their Impact at National Level* (Intersentia, 2010) 178.

[58] ECHR, Art 43(2).   [59] Mowbray, n 41, 512, 513, and 518.

ECHR, to 'abide by the final judgment of the Court', has been discharged. Since this is a matter for negotiation, the respondent state effectively participates in supervising enforcement against itself. Judgments, including those involving friendly settlement, are referred to the Committee by the Directorate General of Human Rights and Rule of Law, one of three Directorates General of the Council of Europe's Secretariat, and are entered on the agendas of special human rights meetings of the Committee. Not surprisingly, the Court's workload problems are also mirrored in the enforcement process with about 3,000 cases scheduled for each session, only 20–40 of which are actually debated.[60] At its human rights meetings the Committee first invites the respondent state to provide it with information about the remedial measures taken in response to the judgment. Applicants are not represented, but are entitled to communicate with the Committee about the implementation of individual measures including the payment of compensation.

In the past the Committee's view about what constituted sufficient evidence of execution varied from case to case with little apparent rationale.[61] But it is now said to require more convincing evidence that the source of the violation has been effectively tackled.[62] Cases are listed for reconsideration at six-monthly intervals until the Committee is satisfied that the breach has been properly addressed. While awaiting final execution of judgments, interim resolutions can be passed which may simply note that execution has not yet occurred, report progress and encourage completion, or threaten the respondent state with more serious measures if full compliance is further delayed. When it is satisfied that any compensation has been paid, and that any other necessary measures have been introduced, the Committee of Ministers publicly certifies that its responsibilities under Article 46(2) ECHR have been discharged. This can take years, for example over eight-and-a-half in the notoriously protracted case of *Marckx v Belgium*, which involved discrimination between legitimate and illegitimate children in the law of affiliation.[63] States may find it difficult to correct the systemic source of a violation for various reasons including: a lack of clarity in the Court's judgment, political problems, the daunting scale of the reforms required, managing complex legislative procedures, budgetary issues, adverse public opinion, the possible impact of compliance on obligations deriving from other institutions, and bureaucratic inertia.[64]

Under Articles 46(2) and 46(3) ECHR the Court may be involved in the supervision of the execution of its own judgments in two ways, each activated by a two-thirds majority vote of the Committee of Ministers. First, where execution is hindered by problems in determining what the judgment means, the Court may be called upon to provide further clarification. Second, the Committee will be able to refer cases back to the Grand Chamber where doubts have arisen about the respondent state's compliance with the original judgment. Under these arrangements there will be no prospect of re-opening the original verdict or of financial penalties. Up until the end of 2012 neither procedure had been used.[65]

At the end of the supervision of the execution of judgments process, there is very little the Council of Europe can do with a state persistently in violation, short of suspending its

---

[60] Harris *et al.*, n 54, 872.

[61] Tomkins, 'The Committee of Ministers: Its Roles under the European Convention on Human Rights' [1995] *EHRLR* 49, 59–60; Klerk, 'Supervision of the Execution of the Judgments of the European Court of Human Rights—The Committee of Ministers' Role under Article 54 of the European Convention on Human Rights' (1998) 45 *Netherlands ILR* 65, 77–8.

[62] Lambert-Abdelgawad, *The Execution of Judgments of the European Court of Human Rights* (Council of Europe Publishing, 2008) 37–8.   [63] Tomkins, n 61, 61.

[64] Steering Committee for Human Rights (CDDH), Guaranteeing the long-term effectiveness of the control system of the European Convention on Human Rights—Addendum to the final report containing CDDH proposals (long version) (9 April 2003) 34.   [65] CDDH report, n 7, paras 27, 36, and 37.

voting rights on the Committee or expelling it from the Council of Europe altogether—each of which is likely to prove counterproductive in all but the most extreme circumstances.

5 THE EUROPEAN UNION

For European integrationists, the Council of Europe was a missed opportunity and a bitter disappointment. Jean Monnet, the French Planning Commissioner, regarded it as 'entirely valueless' and President de Gaulle found it 'simply ridiculous'.[66] The French Foreign Minister, Robert Schuman, therefore, proposed a European Coal and Steel Community, founded in 1951 by six member states, the primary goal of which was the integration of the French and German coal and steel industries in order to prevent another Franco–German war. Developing this idea, the European Economic Community (EEC) was created in 1957, establishing a common market among member states, and in 1965 the amalgamation of the EEC with the European Coal and Steel Community and the European Atomic Energy Community (also founded in 1957) created the European Communities (EC). Further developments in 1992 transformed the EC into the, by then, 12-member European Union (EU). Retaining the distinctive identity of the EC as the 'First Pillar', the establishment of the EU added a 'Second Pillar' (a Common Foreign and Security Policy), and a 'Third Pillar' (Justice and Home Affairs) embracing such issues as asylum and immigration, drugs, judicial cooperation on civil and criminal justice, and police cooperation on terrorism and international crime. The 'three pillars' were, however, abandoned on 1 December 2009 when the EU acquired a consolidated legal personality under the Treaty of Lisbon. By 2013, new members, mostly from the former communist bloc, also brought the number of EU states to 28, over half that of the Council of Europe.

For much of its 40-year history the EEC/EC showed little overt interest in human rights.[67] This was largely for three reasons. First, although the EEC/EC always regarded the ideals of democracy, human rights, and the rule of law as important and desirable, human rights were not initially seen as a priority for European economic integration. Second, it was, in any case, assumed that they were adequately addressed by the Council of Europe and the ECHR to which all members of the EEC/EC, but not the EEC/EC itself, also belonged. Third, the principal judicial organ of the EEC/EC, the European Court of Justice (ECJ, now the Court of Justice of the European Union (CJEU)), in Luxembourg, generally interpreted EEC/EU law as it applied to member states—although not as it applied to the institutions of the Union itself—in accordance with the ECHR and the jurisprudence of the Strasbourg institutions.

However, for several reasons, towards the end of the twentieth century the profile of human rights increased in the EU, albeit in an ad hoc rather than systematic manner. First, it became clear that the success of European integration hinged upon the supremacy of Community/EU law. A rebellion threatened since the 1970s by national constitutional courts, fearing the risks this posed to national constitutional rights, increasingly compelled the ECJ/CJEU to articulate its own fundamental rights jurisprudence. Second, the EU began to require respect for human rights as a condition of entering into formal trading and other relationships with non-EU states. It, therefore, became increasingly difficult

---

[66] Simpson, *Human Rights and the End of Empire—Britain and the Genesis of the European Convention* (OUP, 2001) 646.

[67] The author would like to express his gratitude to Patrick Ormerod, Christine Reynolds, and Phil Syrpis for drawing attention to some minor errors in a previous draft of this section.

for the EU not to have a developed human rights policy for its own internal affairs. Third, human rights are inextricably interwoven with issues which arose under the Third Pillar, now the Area of Freedom, Security and Justice. Fourth, in the late 1990s, the provision of a formal human rights document and more effective human rights monitoring arrangements were seen as offering a solution to the EU's 'legitimacy crisis' caused by the widening gap between the élite-led deepening and widening vision of European integration, on the one hand, and the needs and aspirations of Europe's citizens, on the other. Fifth, Protocol No 14 to the ECHR enables the EU to become a party to the Convention,[68] while Article 6(2) of the Consolidated Version of the Treaty on European Union requires the EU to accede to the ECHR. In the summer of 2010 the Steering Committee on Human Rights and the European Commission were each given a mandate by, respectively, the Council of Europe's Committee of Ministers and the EU, to negotiate a treaty enabling the EU to become a party to the ECHR, but not a member of the Council of Europe. Although negotiations proved difficult, a Draft Accession Agreement, made public on 5 April 2013, was nevertheless reached.[69] The unanimity required from member states in both the Council of Europe and the EU to bring this project to fruition does not, however, appear to be imminent.[70] But, once the EU becomes a member of the Convention system, individuals will be able to complain to the European Court of Human Rights that it, and/or one or more of its member states acting under EU authority, have violated their ECHR rights.

5.1 HUMAN RIGHTS AND THE COURT OF JUSTICE OF THE EUROPEAN UNION

The EU operates on the basis that 'fundamental rights form an integral part of the general principles of [its] law', and that 'respect for human rights is ... a condition of the lawfulness' of Community/Union acts.[71] In theory, therefore, violations of fundamental rights can be litigated before the CJEU: by EU institutions against each other; by member states against each other; by the Commission against member states; by individuals and subnational organizations with legal personality against EU institutions; and by individuals and subnational organizations with legal personality against member states through preliminary references from national courts in on-going litigation. However, in practice it is rare for any of this to happen. For their part, individuals can complain to the CJEU about a violation of their fundamental rights by EU institutions in one of two ways. First, under Article 263 of the Consolidated Version of the Treaty on the Functioning of the European Union, 'any natural or legal person' can initiate proceedings for review of the legality of acts of EU institutions against 'an act addressed' to, or which is 'of direct and individual concern', to them. But this is a very difficult test to satisfy since the ECJ/CJEU has interpreted it to mean that the applicant has been affected 'by reason of certain attributes which are peculiar to them or by reason of circumstances in which they are differentiated from all other persons'.[72] The second route is more indirect. Under Article 267, a national court

---

[68] Art 59(2), ECHR; Eckes, 'EU Accession to the ECHR: Between Autonomy and Adaptation' (2013) 76 *MLR* 254.

[69] Council of Europe, Fifth negotiation meeting between the CDDH ad hoc negotiation group and the European Commission on the accession of the European Union to the European Convention on Human Rights, Final Report to the CDDH, Appendix 1, 47+1(2013)008rev2 (10 June 2012).

[70] Douglas-Scott, 'The European Union and Human Rights after the Treaty of Lisbon' (2011) 11 *HRLR* 645, 658–69.

[71] *Opinion 2/94 on Accession by the Community to the ECHR* [1996] ECR I-1759, paras 33 and 34.

[72] Case 25/62, *Plaumann & Co v Commission* [1963] ECR 95, 107.

may ask the CJEU for a preliminary ruling on whether EU law, including that relating to fundamental rights, has been violated. But this is not available to litigants 'as a matter of right'.[73] Although neither of these routes requires an 'exhaustion of domestic remedies' as under the ECHR, each is, nevertheless, an expensive and protracted process. It is hardly surprising, therefore, that the CJEU has heard few human rights complaints from individual applicants or that judicial review in Luxembourg has led to the annulment of only a handful of EU measures on human rights grounds.[74] Finally, the jurisdiction of the CJEU over actions of EU institutions and member states is limited. Although activities under the Area of Freedom, Security and Justice are included, the CJEU has no jurisdiction at all in relation to the EU's common foreign and security policy, which potentially raises human rights issues.

5.2 THE CHARTER OF FUNDAMENTAL RIGHTS

The Treaty of Nice 2001 both inaugurated the process of providing the EU with more formal constitutional foundations and provided it with its first formal statement of rights, the Charter of Fundamental Rights ('EU Charter'), which collects together, in a single document, rights which the EU has already recognized in various other disparate sources.[75] However, it was not until the Treaty of Lisbon 2009 that the EU Charter became legally binding on member states, subject to exemptions granted to the UK and Poland by Protocol No 30.

The EU Charter differs from the ECHR in five principal ways. First, it includes rights contained in the ECHR but not in precisely the same terms. For example, Article 6 EU Charter provides the right to liberty and security of the person in a single clause— 'everyone has the right to liberty and security of the person'—while Article 5 ECHR has no less than five clauses, one of which has six further sub-clauses (12 elements in total) for the same right. Article 52(3) EU Charter requires the meaning and scope of rights found in both the Charter and ECHR to be interpreted in the same way as those found in the latter. But, as the Council of Europe's Steering Committee for Human Rights put it, 'experience tends to show that it is difficult to avoid contradictions where two differently worded texts on the same subject-matter are interpreted by two different courts'.[76] However, this has not happened so far in any CJEU case.

Second, the ECHR is largely confined to civil and political rights. The EU Charter, on the other hand, also includes a wide range of social, economic, cultural, and citizenship rights, similar in kind to those found in the European Social Charter discussed in Section 3.3.

Third, the ECHR provides different limitation clauses for each right. Article 52 EU Charter, on the other hand, sets out general limitations on all substantive Charter rights in the following terms. They must be provided for by law, respect the essence of the rights and freedoms in question, and be subject to the principle of proportionality. They must also be necessary and genuinely meet objectives of the general interest recognized by the EU or the need to protect the rights and freedoms of others. Those Charter rights that

---

[73] Case C-50/00 P, *Unión de Pequeños Agricultores v Council* [2002] ECR I-6677, para 42.

[74] Douglas-Scott, n 70, 679–80.

[75] Douglas-Scott, n 70, 650–8; see also Defeis, 'Human Rights, the European Union, and the Treaty Route: From Maastricht to Lisbon' (2012) 35 *Fordham Int'l LJ* 1207.

[76] Steering Committee for Human Rights (CDDH), Study of Technical and Legal Issues of a Possible EC/EU Accession to the European Convention on Human Rights, DG-II(2002)006 [CDDH(2002)010 Addendum 2] (25–8 June 2002) para 80.

derive from EU Treaties must also be exercised under the conditions and within the limits defined by those treaties.

The fourth difference between the ECHR and the EU Charter is that the former generally binds member states in any and all of their activities, while Article 51(1) EU Charter indicates that it is addressed to the institutions of the EU, and, as far as the formulation and implementation of EU law are concerned, also to member states.

Finally, since the EU Charter does not provide any additional right of individual petition, the only recourse to the CJEU open to individual litigants for a breach of a Charter right remains the existing limited ones described in Section 5.1.

However, even before it acquired formal legal status, the EU Charter was already being used as a point of reference by national courts and by EU institutions, including the CJEU. It now operates as the primary source for human rights in the EU, which have become 'one of the most significant areas of EU law'.[77]

5.3 THE FUNDAMENTAL RIGHTS AGENCY AND THE COMMISSIONER FOR JUSTICE, FUNDAMENTAL RIGHTS AND CITIZENSHIP

Developing an idea first approved in 2003, the EU formally proposed, in June 2005, to expand the remit of its European Centre on Racism and Xenophobia to create a Fundamental Rights Agency (FRA), which came into operation on 1 January 2007.[78] Using the Charter as its main point of reference, attempting to avoid overlap with the Council of Europe, and networking with national institutions, the FRA is intended to discharge the following functions: to be an independent centre of expertise on fundamental rights issues through data collection, analysis, and networking; to provide relevant institutions and authorities of the EU and its member states with assistance and expertise when implementing EU law relating to fundamental rights; and to advise Union institutions and member states on how best to prepare and implement fundamental rights-related Union legislation. However, the FRA has no powers to examine individual complaints, to issue regulations, or to carry out 'normative monitoring' for the purposes of Article 7 EU Treaty. In 2010 the European Commission's Justice, Freedom and Security portfolio was divided between the new posts of Commissioner for Justice, Fundamental Rights and Citizenship, and Commissioner for Home Affairs, each with responsibility for policy development in their respective fields.

6 CONCLUSION

As a result of lack of agreement, particularly between the UK and France, over the purpose and shape of pan-European institutions in the aftermath of the Second World War, Europe now has two overlapping transnational legal processes intended to protect human rights. The better-known ECHR and the European Court of Human Rights, often mistakenly believed to be EU institutions, continue to face an as yet unresolved problem stemming from the steadily rising individual application rate. While Protocol No 14 has certainly alleviated this, further reforms in addition to those provided by Protocol Nos 15 and 16

---

[77] Douglas-Scott, n 70, 645.

[78] See Sokhi-Bulley, 'The Fundamental Rights Agency of the European Union: A New Panopticism' (2011) 11 *HRLR* 683.

are, nevertheless, still likely to be required. The results of an official review into ECHR procedure are expected in 2015, and a decision about the need for more profound change is promised by the end of 2019.

As the twenty-first century unfolds, the EU is also likely to expand and develop its human rights mission, bringing the rationales for both systems of international human rights law, how they should relate to each other, and why Europe should have two rather than one, under increasing scrutiny. There can, however, be little doubt that the European nation-state remains the most important arena for the legal protection of human rights. Assuming civil peace, a distribution of resources which is at least not gravely inequitable, and effectively regulated markets, human rights are most likely to be protected by genuinely democratic and rights-sensitive national legislative and executive institutions, independent, professional, and rights-aware national judiciaries, and by the provision of national justiciable constitutional rights. The main human rights-related functions of both the Council of Europe and the EU are, therefore, to attempt to encourage the development of all these elements where they have not yet firmly taken root in Europe, and to contribute to their preservation and protection where they have.

FURTHER READING

ALSTON and DE SCHUTTER (eds), *Monitoring Fundamental Rights in the EU: The Contribution of the Fundamental Rights Agency* (Hart Publishing, 2005).

BATES, *The Evolution of the European Convention on Human Rights: From Its Inception to the Creation of a Permanent Court of Human Rights* (Oxford University Press, 2010).

CHRISTOFFERSEN and MADSEN (eds), *The European Court of Human Rights between Law and Politics* (Oxford University Press, 2011).

DE BECO (ed), *Human Rights Monitoring Mechanisms of the Council of Europe* (Routledge, 2012).

FØLLESDAL et al. (eds), *Constituting Europe: The European Court of Human Rights in a National, European and Global Context* (Cambridge University Press, 2013).

GREER, *The European Convention on Human Rights: Achievements, Problems and Prospects* (Cambridge University Press, 2006).

GREER and WILDHABER, 'Revisiting the Debate about 'Constitutionalising' the European Court of Human Rights' (2012) 12 *HRLR* 655.

GREER and WILLIAMS, 'Human Rights in the Council of Europe and the EU: Towards "Individual", "Constitutional", or "Institutional" Justice?' (2009) 15 *ELJ* 463.

GRABENWARTER (ed), *The European Convention on Human Rights: A Commentary* (Hart, 2013).

HARRIS et al., *Harris, O'Boyle and Warbrick: Law of the European Convention on Human Rights* (Oxford University Press, 2009).

LOCKE, 'EU accession to the ECHR: implications for judicial review in Strasbourg' (2010) 35 *ELR* 777.

MOWBRAY, *Cases, Materials and Commentary on the European Convention on Human Rights* (Oxford University Press, 2012).

TORRES PÉREZ, *Conflicts of Rights in the European Union: A Theory of Supranational Adjudication* (Oxford University Press, 2009).

WILLIAMS, 'Fundamental Rights in the New European Union' in Barnard (ed), *The Fundamentals of EU Law Revisited: Assessing the Impact of the Constitutional Debate* (Oxford University Press, 2007).

USEFUL WEBSITES

Council of Europe: <http://www.coe.int>

European Court of Human Rights: <http://www.echr.coe.int/echr>

European Commissioner for Human Rights: <http://www.coe.int/t/commissioner>

European Union: <http://europa.eu>

Charter of Fundamental Rights: <http://ec.europa.eu/justice_home/unit/charte/index_en.html>

European Union Agency for Fundamental Rights: <http://www.fra.europa.eu/fra>

Court of Justice of the European Union: <http://curia.europa.eu>

Organization for Security and Cooperation in Europe: <http://www.osce.org/>

21

AFRICA

Christof Heyns and Magnus Killander

SUMMARY

The national protection of human rights in Africa is monitored not only by the UN system but also through an extensive framework of regional instruments adopted by the African Union and its predecessor, the Organization of African Unity, as well as sub-regional organizations such as the Economic Community of West African States, the East African Community, and the Southern African Development Community. However, the African Commission on Human and Peoples' Rights, established in 1987, remains the main human rights body of the continent. An African Human Rights Court has been established to complement the work of the Commission.

1 INTRODUCTION

The African continent of today is characterized, inter alia, by the coexistence of traditional and modern strands of society. As is the case in traditional societies across the world, recognition of values such as human dignity, a prohibition of harm to others, and the ideals of benevolent governance may be found in many African societies—the same norms that underlie much of the modern notion of human rights. However, the idea of enforcement of these norms is typically absent or not well developed in traditional societies. To the extent that people may be considered to be the bearers of human rights in such societies, these rights are rights in the weak sense of the word—the corresponding duty they impose is at best a moral or an aspirational one. Abusive leaders (or governments) have to be endured 'like the weather'.

On the other hand, in terms of the modern notion of human rights, the duties imposed by these rights—which could be described as rights in the strong sense of the word—are regarded as enforceable. 'Enforcement' in this context primarily (and ideally) refers to enforcement through law, but behind legal enforcement there is also the claim—either explicit or implicit—that if all other attempts to secure the rights fail, the point may be reached where self-help can be employed to ensure their realization. The concept of human rights does not operate in an anarchistic framework—it recognizes a general obligation to obey the law. But where the line is crossed and human rights violations are at stake, the duty to obey the law is at some point considered to have broken down.[1]

---

[1] Heyns, 'A "Struggle Approach" to Human Rights' in Heyns and Stefiszyn (eds), *Human Rights, Peace and Justice in Africa: A Reader* (Pretoria University Law Press, 2006) 15.

While there is an increasing recognition of human rights in Africa not only in the weak but also in the strong sense of the word, the continent is still facing a myriad of challenges to the full realization of the human rights of its people. This is despite widespread formal commitment to human rights across the continent in the form of bills of rights, establishment of national human rights institutions, declarations by intergovernmental organizations, and the establishment of a regional human rights system.

Human rights violations in Africa, as elsewhere, take many forms. State repression was the hallmark of colonial rule in many parts of Africa. After independence, opposition politicians, journalists, and human rights defenders continue to be persecuted in many countries on the continent. However, human rights violations are not limited to the state. Many human rights violations, which in particular affect women and children, take place in private. These violations may take the form of domestic violence or be a result of harmful traditional practices such as female genital mutilation. While these violations take place in the private sphere, the state still has an important role in addressing the situation by legislation, education, and an institutional framework that supports the victims. Armed conflicts that may or may not involve the state also give rise to serious human rights violations.

In fact, it could be argued that because the human rights ethos recognizes that at some point self-help or even resistance can be employed to validate rights claims, it can foster a climate in which people take the law into their own hands to pursue what they construe as legitimate human rights claims, even if these beliefs are not shared by others, who may in turn defend their own views. The mixture of traditional and modern societies in Africa provides an often unstable environment for the notion of human rights to take root.

Poverty and human rights violations go hand in hand in Africa, as is the case in other parts of the world.[2] However, the situation is particularly pronounced in Africa in view of the high levels of poverty. Most African countries have not made significant progress towards achievement of the Millennium Development Goals (MDGs) and in the realization of other socio-economic rights. While improvement in governance offers the best chance for the realization of socio-economic rights in Africa, a more equitable globalization process would also be beneficial. The global economic crisis also risks further diminishing resources available for the realization of human rights on the continent.

This chapter examines the role played by African regional intergovernmental organizations, in particular the African Union (AU), in the realization of human rights. The focus is on the African Charter on Human and Peoples' Rights (ACHPR or Charter) and the main organs, the Commission and the Court, which have been established to ensure its implementation.

2 HISTORICAL OVERVIEW

The Charter of the Organization of African Unity (OAU Charter), adopted in 1963, made few references to human rights. However, the Charter did set the task for the new organization of enforcing human rights norms by recognizing the goal of bringing an end to colonialism and apartheid in Africa. In the late 1970s, in the wake of the mass murders by the regimes of, for example, Idi Amin in Uganda, the OAU started to pay some attention to the human rights situation in its member states.

[2] See Chapter 28.

In 1978 President Jawara of The Gambia made the following statement before the UN General Assembly:

> With the attainment of self-determination and independence, it would be ironic indeed if the freedom gained from the defeat of colonialism should...be denied our people by our own leaders. After centuries of a deliberate policy of dehumanisation, subjugation, and oppression, the minimum our people expect and must have is the full enjoyment of their political, economic, social, and cultural rights... It should be the duty of all of us to...ensure that...the people enjoy...their civil and political rights.[3]

Over the following years President Jawara, one of the few democratically elected leaders in Africa at the time, played a leading role in the development of the ACHPR, which is also known as the Banjul Charter, after the capital of The Gambia. The OAU Assembly adopted the ACHPR in 1981 and it entered into force in 1986. In 1987 the OAU Assembly elected the 11 members of the African Commission on Human and Peoples' Rights. The Commission recommended that, to guard its independence, the Secretariat of the Commission should not be located at the headquarters of the OAU in Addis Ababa, Ethiopia. A year later, the OAU Assembly decided that the Secretariat of the Commission should be located in Banjul.

With democratic elections in South Africa in April 1994, the OAU had finally succeeded in its main objective of the liberation of Africa from colonialism and apartheid. It was felt that the OAU was in need of transformation and in 2000 the OAU Assembly adopted the Constitutive Act of the AU. The AU was launched in Durban, South Africa, in 2002. The headquarters of the AU remain in Addis Ababa, Ethiopia.

The main principles of the OAU were sovereign equality and 'non-interference in the internal affairs of states'.[4] These principles have been retained in the AU Constitutive Act. However, it is noticeable that a number of new objectives have been added in the Act. These include the objective to 'promote and protect human and peoples' rights in accordance with the ACHPR and other relevant human rights instruments'.[5] In addition to the commitments set out in the Constitutive Act, the AU established a new institutional framework with a mandate that includes the realization of human rights. The new institutions include the African Court on Human and Peoples' Rights, the Pan-African Parliament, the Peace and Security Council, the New Partnership for Africa's Development, and the African Peer Review Mechanism.

There are no entry requirements in terms of human rights practices for states to join the AU, and all the members of the OAU became members of the AU without scrutiny of their human rights records. However, there is at least a theoretical possibility that violations of human rights may lead to suspension from the AU and other sanctions.[6] AU inaction in the face of gross human rights violations in, for example, Darfur, Sudan, and Zimbabwe, however, illustrates that the principle of non-interference still dominates. In fact the AU has only used its power to sanction member states after military coups. For example, the AU Peace and Security Council in February 2009 imposed sanctions, including travel restrictions and freezing of assets, against the leaders of the Mauritanian military regime following the coup in August 2008.[7] In contrast, a sitting head of state runs little risk of being castigated by his peers in respect of how much he (to date, only two African heads of state have been women) has manipulated an election to stay in power. Many current

---

[3] Alhaji Sir Dawda Kairaba Jawara, Statement at the 33rd session of the UN General Assembly, 22 September 1978, quoted in Touray, *The Gambia and the World—A History of the Foreign Policy of Africa's Smallest State 1965–1995* (Institut für Afrika-Kunde, 2000) 161.   [4] OAU Charter, Art 3.

[5] AU Constitutive Act, Art 3.   [6] AU Constitutive Act, Art 23.

[7] See communiqués of the 163rd and 168th meeting of the AU Peace and Security Council annexed to Letter dated 10 February 2009 from the Chargé d'affaires of the Permanent Mission of the Libyan Arab Jamahiriya to the UN addressed to the President of the Security Council, S/2009/85 (11 February 2009).

African presidents first came to power through military coups. Most of them have then tried to legitimize their rule through elections. For example, the democratically elected President Jawara of The Gambia, mentioned above, was deposed in a military coup in 1994 by the 29-year-old Yahya Jammeh who has remained in power ever since, and has turned The Gambia into an increasingly repressive state.

Concern over human rights in Africa by intergovernmental organizations is not limited to the AU. The UN plays a major role through treaty bodies, special procedures, field presences, and so on. Impunity is being addressed, among other matters, through the work of the International Criminal Court and the International Criminal Tribunal for Rwanda (ICTR). In addition, sub-regional African intergovernmental organizations have taken an increased interest in human rights. The AU has recognized eight Regional Economic Communities (RECs) as building blocks towards an African Economic Community.[8] The most active of these in the field of human rights is the Economic Community of West African States (ECOWAS).[9] The ECOWAS Community Court of Justice can hear complaints about human rights violations in member states without the requirement of exhaustion of local remedies. Among its case law can be mentioned cases dealing with arbitrary detention in The Gambia and slavery in Niger.[10] The East African Court of Justice (EACJ) does not have explicit jurisdiction to deal with complaints of human rights violations, but has nevertheless dealt with human rights issues that were considered to constitute violations of their respective founding treaties.[11] The same applied to the Tribunal of the Southern African Development Community (SADC) before it was finally dissolved by the SADC Summit in 2012.[12] Some RECs have also been active in human rights standard-setting. For example, a SADC Protocol on Gender and Development was adopted in 2008.

At the domestic level, all 54 member states of the AU have written constitutions which recognize human rights.[13]

3 THE AFRICAN CHARTER AND OTHER RELEVANT TREATIES

The ACHPR has been ratified by all 54 member states of the AU, except South Sudan.

3.1 NORMS RECOGNIZED IN THE AFRICAN CHARTER

The ACHPR goes further than the primary regional human rights conventions of Europe and the Americas in recognizing not only civil and political rights, but also economic, social, and cultural rights and not only individual rights but also peoples' rights. The Charter also provides for duties.

---

[8] Assembly/AU/Dec.112 (VII) (July 2006).

[9] On the human rights mandate of the RECs, see Viljoen, *International Human Rights Law in Africa* (OUP, 2012) 469.

[10] *Manneh v The Gambia*, ECW/CCJ/JUD/03/08 (5 June 2008); (2008) AHRLR 171; *Koraou v Niger*, ECW/CCJ/JUD/06/08 (27 October 2008); (2008) AHRLR 182.

[11] *Katabazi* and *Others v Secretary General of the East African Community and Another* [2007] EACJ 3; (2007) AHRLR 119 (EAC 2007); *Campbell (Pvt) Ltd and others v Zimbabwe* [2007] SADCT 1 (28 November 2008); (2008) AHRLR 199.

[12] Final communiqué of the 32nd Summit of the SADC Heads of State and Government, Maputo, Mozambique (18 August 2012) para 24.

[13] Heyns and Kaguongo, 'Constitutional Human Rights Law in Africa' (2006) 22 *S African JHR* 673.

A number of shortcomings in respect of the provisions concerning civil and political rights in the ACHPR when compared to other international instruments can be noted. For example, the right to privacy and the right against forced labour are not explicitly mentioned in the Charter. Fair trial rights and the right of political participation are provided for in less detail than in other human rights treaties. However, the African Commission has, in resolutions and in its decisions on cases, interpreted the Charter in line with established international practice. Thus, the ACHPR has been interpreted to encompass some of the rights or aspects of rights not explicitly included. For example, the content of the fair trial rights in the ACHPR has been expounded by the African Commission in its detailed Principles and Guidelines on the Right to a Fair Trial and Legal Assistance in Africa, which were adopted in 2003.

The inclusion in the ACHPR of socio-economic rights alongside civil and political rights emphasizes the indivisibility of human rights and the importance of developmental issues, which are obviously important matters in the African context. At the same time it should be noted that a modest number of socio-economic rights are explicitly included in the Charter. It only recognizes 'a right to work under equitable and satisfactory conditions' (Article 15), a right to health (Article 16), and a right to education (Article 17). Among rights not explicitly included are the rights to food, water, social security, and housing. The socio-economic rights in the ACHPR have generally received scant attention from the African Commission. However in its 2001 decision in *SERAC v Nigeria*, the Commission dealt extensively with the issue.[14] In this case, which dealt with gross human rights violations in the oil-rich Ogoniland region of Nigeria, the African Commission deduced an implicit right to 'housing or shelter' in the ACHPR from the provisions on health, property, and family life in the Charter. Similarly, a right to food was read into the right to dignity. It should also be noted that in 2004 the Commission established a Working Group on Economic, Social and Cultural Rights.

In contrast to the individual rights in the Charter, peoples' rights are more fully developed in the ACHPR than in the UN covenants, which set out only a right to self-determination. According to the Charter, all 'peoples' have a right to be equal (Article 19); to existence and self-determination (Article 20); to freely dispose of their wealth and natural resources (Article 21); to economic, social, and cultural development (Article 22); to peace and security (Article 23); and to a satisfactory environment (Article 24). Clearly, part of the motivation for the recognition of 'peoples' rights' lies in the fact that, historically, entire 'peoples' in Africa have been colonized and otherwise exploited. 'Peoples' can, thus, refer to the whole population of the country. For example, the African Commission has held that a military coup constituted not only a violation of the right to political participation in Article 13, but also violated the right to self-determination in Article 20.[15] Peoples' rights may also be exercised by a part of the population of a state 'bound together by their historical, traditional, racial, ethnic, cultural, linguistic, religious, ideological, geographical, economic identities and affinities, or other bonds.'[16]

In *Katangese Peoples' Congress v Zaire*, the claimant requested that the African Commission recognize the independence of the Katanga province in the then Zaire (now Democratic Republic of the Congo). The Commission held:

In the absence of concrete evidence of violations of human rights to the point that the territorial integrity of Zaire should be called to question and in the absence of evidence that

[14] 155/96, 15th Activity Report of the ACommHPR (2001–2); (2001) AHRLR 60.

[15] 147/95 and 149/96, *Jawara v The Gambia*, 13th Activity Report of the ACommHPR (1999–2000); (2000) AHRLR 107 para 73.

[16] 266/03, *Gunme and Others v Cameroon*, 26th Activity Report of the ACommHPR (2009); (2009) AHRLR 9 para 171.

the people of Katanga are denied the right to participate in government as guaranteed by article 13(1) of the African Charter, the Commission holds the view that Katanga is obliged to exercise a variant of self-determination that is compatible with the sovereignty and territorial integrity of Zaire.[17]

The African Commission upheld this position in a case against Cameroon in which it held that grievances of the Anglophone part of Cameroon against the dominant Francophone part should not be 'resolved through secession but through a comprehensive national dialogue'.[18]

In *SERAC v Nigeria*, discussed already, the African Commission found the Nigerian government guilty of violating Article 21 ACHPR by giving 'the green light to private actors, and the oil companies in particular, to devastatingly affect the well-being of the Ogonis'.[19] In this case, the Commission also found a violation of the right to a satisfactory environment in Article 24 ACHPR. The *Endorois* case, decided in 2009, dealt with the rights of indigenous people in Kenya. Among other violations, the Commission found that Kenya had violated the right to economic, social, and cultural development (Article 22) of the Endorois people.[20]

3.2 DUTIES AND LIMITATIONS

Articles 27, 28, and 29 ACHPR provide for individual duties towards the community. These range from duties towards the family, such as the maintenance of parents 'in case of need', to duties towards the state. The African Commission has not pronounced itself on the content of these duties except for its application of Article 27(2) ('the rights and freedoms of each individual shall be exercised with due regard to the rights of others, collective security, morality, and common interest') as a general limitation clause.

Article 9(2) provides that '[e]very individual shall have the right to express and disseminate his opinions within the law'. The right seems to recognize the right in question only to the extent that it is not infringed upon by national law. Freedom of conscience and religion in Article 8, freedom of association in Article 10, freedom of assembly in Article 11, and freedom of movement in Article 12 are similarly restricted. This type of limitation is often referred to as a claw-back clause.[21] However, the African Commission has held that provisions in the ACHPR that allow rights to be limited 'in accordance with law', should be understood to require such limitations to be provided by domestic legal provisions that comply with the standards set by Article 27(2) and with international human rights law standards.

3.3 PROTECTION OF WOMEN, CHILDREN, AND VULNERABLE GROUPS

Article 18(2) ACHPR places a duty on the state to assist the family as 'the custodian of morals and traditional values recognized by the community'. However, such values

---

[17] 75/92, 8th Activity Report of the ACommHPR (1994–1995); (2000) AHRLR 72 para 6.

[18] *Gunme*, n 16, para 203.   [19] *SERAC*, n 14, para 58.

[20] 276/2003, *Centre for Minority Rights Development (Kenya) and Minority Rights Group International on behalf of Endorois Welfare Council v Kenya*, 27th Activity Report of the ACommHPR (2009); (2009) AHRLR 75.

[21] See Chapter 5.

may not discriminate as this would violate the general prohibition of discrimination in Article 2 and the specific prohibition of discrimination against women in Article 18(3), which also provides for the protection of the rights of women and children 'as stipulated in international declarations and conventions'. Article 18(4) provides for 'special measures of protection' for the aged and disabled.

The OAU Assembly in 1990 adopted the African Charter on the Rights and Welfare of the Child (Children's Charter). The Children's Charter can be seen as a regional response to the UN Convention on the Rights of the Child (CRC), adopted less than a year before the African treaty. The Children's Charter provides some increased protection compared to the CRC, including further protections for child soldiers, as well as protections against child marriages and for internally displaced children. Unlike the CRC, the Children's Charter also provides for duties for children.[22]

A separate Committee on the Rights and Welfare of the Child was established under the Children's Charter. The 11 members of the Committee were elected in July 2001 and the first meeting of the Committee was held in 2002. States have to report to the Committee within two years of the entry into force of the convention for the state party concerned and every three years thereafter. However, despite the fact that the Committee was established in 2001, it only began to consider the reports it had received in 2008.[23] Apart from state reporting, the Children's Charter also provides for a communication procedure. The Committee does not have its own secretariat, and is serviced by the Department for Social Affairs at the AU Commission in Addis Ababa. The Committee has considered a number of state reports and in 2011 handed down its first decision with regard to a communication, dealing with the right to nationality of Nubian children in Kenya.[24]

In 2003, the AU Assembly adopted the Protocol to the African Charter on Human and Peoples' Rights on the Rights of Women (Women's Protocol). Through its 24 substantive provisions, the Women's Protocol provides much more comprehensive protection than the UN Convention on the Elimination of All Forms of Discrimination Against Women (CEDAW). For example, the Women's Protocol includes provisions on domestic violence, trafficking, elimination of harmful practices, reproductive rights, HIV and AIDS, inheritance, and protection of elderly women. However, during the drafting of the Protocol, there were many controversial issues, including the question of polygamy, which is recognized and practised in many African countries. For example, South African President Zuma has four wives, and King Mswati III of Swaziland, one of the world's last absolute monarchs, has 14 known wives. The CEDAW Committee has held that polygamy violates the right to equality in marriage.[25] In contrast, Article 6(c) Women's Protocol provides that 'monogamy is encouraged as the preferred form of marriage and that the rights of women in marriage and family, including in polygamous marital relationships are promoted and protected'. The African Commission and the African Court are responsible for monitoring the implementation of the Women's Protocol.

The OAU Convention Governing the Specific Aspects of Refugee Problems in Africa adopted in 1969 can be seen as the first African human rights treaty. The convention was a response to the 1967 Protocol, which extended the application of the UN Refugee Convention to the whole world. The African Convention includes a broader definition

---

[22] Viljoen, n 9, 393–4.

[23] Mezmur and Sloth-Nielsen, 'An Ice-Breaker: State Party Reports and the 11th session of the African Committee of Experts on the Rights and Welfare of the Child' (2008) 8 *African HRLJ* 596.

[24] 002/09, *IHRDA and Open Society Justice Initiative (OSJI) (on behalf of children of Nubian descent in Kenya) v Kenya* (22 March 2011).

[25] CEDAW Committee, General Recommendation 21, HRI/GEN/1/Rev.9 (Vol II) 337, para 14.

of 'refugee' than the UN Convention, extending the protection to those seeking refuge because of 'external aggression, occupation, foreign domination or events seriously disturbing public order'.[26]

The AU has adopted a number of treaties of relevance to human rights in recent years such as the Convention on Preventing and Combating Corruption, the African Youth Charter, the African Charter on Democracy, Elections and Governance, and the AU Convention for the Protection and Assistance of Internally Displaced Persons in Africa.

4 THE PROTECTIVE MECHANISMS

4.1 THE AFRICAN COMMISSION

4.1.1 Structure and composition

Article 30 ACHPR provides for the establishment of the African Commission on Human and Peoples' Rights. The African Commission was established in 1987 following the entry into force of the Charter in 1986. According to Article 45 ACHPR, the mandate of the Commission includes promoting human rights through research, dissemination of information, and cooperation with other human rights bodies. The Commission also has a mandate to interpret the provisions of the Charter and consider complaints against a state alleging that it has violated the ACHPR. The Commission has also been given the mandate to consider state reports on implementation of the Charter.

The African Commission consists of 11 Commissioners who serve in their individual capacities and are nominated by states parties to the Charter and elected by the AU Assembly. The independence of the Commission has sometimes been questioned as a number of civil servants and ambassadors have served on it. However, in a *note verbale* to the member states in April 2005 the AU Commission provided guidelines that excluded senior civil servants and diplomatic representatives from being elected.[27] These guidelines have been followed with regard to new appointments to the Commission. The Commission meets twice a year in regular sessions for a period of up to two weeks, alternating its meetings between its headquarters in Banjul and other African capitals.

4.1.2 The complaints procedure

Both states and individuals may bring complaints to the African Commission alleging violations of the ACHPR by states parties. The inter-state complaint procedure by which one state brings a complaint about an alleged human rights violation by another state is not often used. Only one such case has been decided by the Commission. In *Democratic Republic of the Congo v Burundi, Rwanda and Uganda*,[28] the Commission held that the three respondent states had violated a number of individual and peoples' rights during the presence of their armed forces on Congolese territory.

Articles 55, 56, 57, and 58 ACHPR deal with 'other communications', that is, communications not submitted by a state. While the Charter is silent on who can bring such communications, the Commission has in its practice accepted complaints from individuals as

---

[26] OAU Convention Governing the Specific Aspects of the Refugee Problem in Africa, Art I(2).
[27] BC/OLC/66/VolXVIII (5 April 2005).   [28] 227/99, 20th Activity Report of the ACommHPR (2006).

well as from NGOs. From the case law of the Commission it is clear that the complainant does not need to be a victim or a family member of a victim.[29]

Article 56 ACHPR lists the admissibility criteria. These include that communications should indicate the author, be compatible with the Charter, not be written in disparaging or insulting language, not be based exclusively on media reports, be submitted within reasonable time, and not deal with a situation which has already been settled. In practice, the most important criterion for admissibility is the exhaustion of local remedies. The Commission has stated that for a case not to be admissible local remedies must be available, effective, sufficient, and not unduly prolonged.[30] In *Purohit and Another v The Gambia*, a case dealing with detention in a mental health institution, the Commission gave a potentially far-reaching decision on the exhaustion of local remedies when it held that:

> [t]he category of people being represented in the present communication are likely to be people picked up from the streets or people from poor backgrounds and as such it cannot be said that the remedies available in terms of the Constitution are realistic remedies for them in the absence of legal aid services.[31]

The criterion of submission within reasonable time has become increasingly important as the Commission has narrowed its definition of what constitutes reasonable time so as to effectively apply the six-month rule inscribed in the European and Inter-American Conventions.

When a complaint is lodged, the state in question is asked to respond in writing to the allegations against it. If it does not respond, and the admissibility criteria are met, the Commission proceeds on the basis of the facts as provided by the complainant. If a state has responded the Commission gives the complainant an opportunity to respond to the arguments by the state. The communication is then scheduled for a hearing at one of the sessions of the Commission. The complainant and respondent state are invited to make presentations at the hearing, which is not public.

If the Commission finds a violation it may make recommendations. These may include that continuing violations should stop (for example, prisoners be released), or specific laws be amended or repealed. However, often the recommendations are rather vague, and the state party is merely urged to 'take all necessary steps to comply with its obligations under the Charter'.

The ACHPR does not contain a provision on interim or provisional measures. However, the Rules of Procedure of the Commission grant the Commission the power to grant provisional measures. The Commission has used provisional measures in a number of cases, for example when an execution has been imminent, often without success. It has held that the breaching of provisional measures constitutes a violation of Article 1 ACHPR.

The Commission has handed down approximately 200 decisions on communications since it was established in 1987, including cases that were declared inadmissible or discontinued due to withdrawal or loss of contact with the complainant. The individual complaints procedure is, thus, not used as frequently as would have been expected on a continent with the type of human rights problems that Africa experiences. This could, to some extent, be attributed to a lack of awareness about the system (see Figure 21.1). Even where there is awareness, however, there is often not much faith that the system will make a difference. One reason for this may be that the Commission's recommendations are often

---

[29] *SERAC*, n 14, para 49.   [30] *Jawara*, n 15, paras 28–40.
[31] 241/01, *Purohit and Another v The Gambia*, 16th Activity Report of the ACommHPR (2002–2003); (2003) AHRLR 96 para 37.

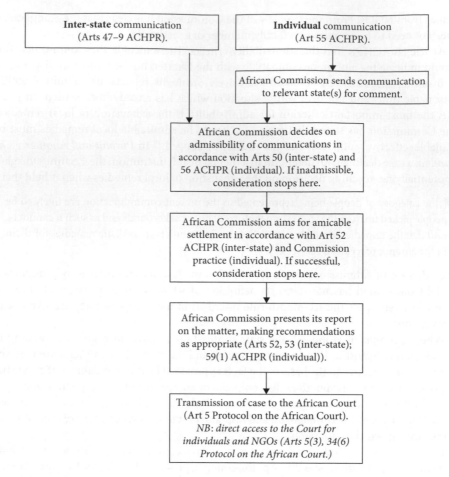

Figure 21.1 The African Charter communications procedure

vague and that the Commission lacks a system of follow-up to its recommendations. It should be noted that while the Commission sometimes recommends compensation to the complainant it does not decide on the amount to award. It is also noticeable that, despite the relatively low number of cases, the Commission often takes more than five years to decide a case.

4.1.3 Consideration of state reports

Each state party is required to submit a report every two years on its efforts to comply with the ACHPR. Reporting has been very tardy, and some states have never submitted a report. Reporting under the Charter allows the state to measure its legislation, policies, and practices against the norms of the ACHPR ('introspection'). This introspection is followed by 'inspection' by the African Commission in which it measures the performance of the state in question against the Charter. The objective is to facilitate a 'constructive dialogue' between the Commission and the states. The dialogue takes place at the public sessions of the African Commission.

NGOs are allowed to submit shadow or alternative reports, but the impact of this avenue is diminished by the lack of access of NGOs to the state reports to which they are supposed to respond. However, recently the Commission has begun to publish the state reports for the upcoming session on its website. Since 2001 the Commission has adopted concluding observations after considering the reports. However, the usefulness of the concluding observations is diminished by the fact that they are not widely disseminated by the Commission.

4.1.4 Special Rapporteurs and working groups

The Commission has appointed a number of Special Rapporteurs to deal with thematic human rights issues. The Special Rapporteurs are always members of the Commission. The Commission has also appointed working groups, some of which include members who are not Commissioners.

In the mid-1990s the Commission adopted the first Special Rapporteur mandates: the Special Rapporteur on extrajudicial, summary, or arbitrary executions; the Special Rapporteur on prisons and conditions of detention; and the Special Rapporteur on the rights of women. The position of Special Rapporteur on extrajudicial, summary, or arbitrary executions has been defunct since 2001, though the mandate of the Working Group on the Death Penalty was expanded in 2012 to include issues that fell under the mandate of this Special Rapporteur. The Commission has more recently appointed Special Rapporteurs on freedom of expression and access to information; refugees and internally displaced persons; and human rights defenders. The Commission has also established a committee to monitor the implementation of the Guidelines and Measures for the Prohibition and Prevention of Torture, Cruel, Inhuman or Degrading Treatment or Punishment in Africa (Robben Island Guidelines); and Working Groups on Indigenous People or Communities; Economic, Social and Cultural Rights; the Death Penalty; and the Rights of Older Persons and Persons with Disabilities in Africa.[32]

The Special Rapporteurs and Working Groups follow developments in the area covered by their mandate and engage with NGOs. They may issue press releases or write letters to governments when they receive reliable information about violations of the ACHPR. The Special Rapporteurs also undertake on-site visits and produce reports with recommendations to governments.

4.1.5 On-site visits

The Commission has conducted a number of on-site visits or missions. These can be divided into promotional and protective missions. Protective missions may be linked to a case under consideration by the Commission or to a situation of massive violations of human rights. Promotional missions help to give the Commission an understanding of the human rights situation in a country through meetings with governments and NGO representatives. They are often aimed at spreading knowledge about the Commission and its work. The missions are generally conducted by one or two members of the Commission, sometimes the Special Rapporteur on a specific issue, together with a legal officer from the Secretariat. Mission reports are adopted by the Commission as a whole at its sessions. Many reports have never been published, in print or on the internet, which diminishes their impact.

4.1.6 Resolutions

The African Commission has adopted resolutions on a number of human rights issues in Africa. In addition to country-specific and other ad hoc resolutions, it has adopted

---

[32] Final communiqué of the 45th ordinary session of the ACommHPR held in Banjul, The Gambia, 13–27 May 2009, para 31.

resolutions on topics such as fair trial; freedom of association; human and peoples' rights education; humanitarian law; contemporary forms of slavery; antipersonnel mines; prisons in Africa; the independence of the judiciary; the electoral process and participatory governance; the International Criminal Court; the death penalty; torture; HIV and AIDS; maternal mortality; and freedom of expression. The Commission, in turn, has relied on these resolutions in its case law. Some of the resolutions, for example the Principles and Guidelines on the Right to a Fair Trial and Legal Assistance in Africa, are quite elaborate and can be seen as regional equivalents of the general comments adopted by the UN treaty bodies.

4.1.7 Relationship with NGOs

NGOs have often been instrumental in bringing cases to the African Commission. Sometimes they submit shadow reports, propose agenda items at the outset of Commission sessions, and provide logistical and other support to the Commission, for example by placing interns at the Commission and providing support to the Special Rapporteurs and missions of the Commission. NGO workshops are arranged prior to Commission sessions, and many NGOs participate actively in the public sessions of the Commission. NGOs also collaborate with the Commission in developing resolutions and new normative instruments. NGOs that wish actively to engage with the Commission need to apply for observer status, which to date has been granted to more than 400 African and international NGOs.[33]

4.1.8 Interaction with AU political bodies

The activity reports of the Commission, which reflect the decisions, resolutions, and other acts of the African Commission, are submitted to the AU summit, which is held twice a year. The activity report must be adopted by the AU Assembly before it can be published. Controversy arose in 2004 when Zimbabwe managed to delay the publication of a case against it due to lack of consultation by the Commission. At around the same time there was debate over the publication of country-specific resolutions.[34] For a few years the AU Assembly and Executive Council reverted to their previous practice of serving as a rubber stamp for the Activity Report of the Commission before there was renewed controversy over the contents of a report leading to a delay in publication of two reports that were finally made public in January 2012. The principle that the very people in charge of the institutions whose human rights practices are at stake—the heads of state—take the final decision on publicity, undermines the legitimacy of the system. This is not to deny that constructive engagement by the AU political organs could be used to put pressure on states to comply with the decisions of the Commission.

4.2 THE AFRICAN COURT ON HUMAN AND PEOPLES' RIGHTS

4.2.1 Background

The only monitoring mechanism included in the ACHPR is the African Commission. In 1994, the OAU Assembly adopted a resolution requesting the Secretary-General of the OAU to convene a Meeting of Experts to consider the establishment of an African Court

---

[33] Final communiqué, n 32, para 23.

[34] Killander, 'Confidentiality v Publicity: Interpreting Article 59 of the African Charter on Human and Peoples' Rights' (2006) 6 *African HRLJ* 572.

on Human and Peoples' Rights. The decision to strengthen the regional human rights system with the establishment of a court should be seen in the context of the increased focus on human rights both in Africa and worldwide in the early 1990s. The Protocol on the African Court on Human and Peoples' Rights was adopted in Addis Ababa, Ethiopia, in 1998 (Protocol on the African Court). The Protocol entered into force in January 2004. Less than half the member states of the AU have ratified the Protocol. The seat of the court is in Arusha, Tanzania. In its first judgment, in December 2009, the Court declared it had no jurisdiction in the case before it as Senegal did not allow direct access to the Court for individuals.

The AU Assembly decided at its summit in July 2004 that the African Human Rights Court should merge with the African Court of Justice. The reason behind the merger was seemingly a need to rationalize the AU structures to save money. The Court of Justice is one of the organs of the AU provided for in the Constitutive Act but it has not been established. It was meant to function as a court adjudicating disputes arising from the increasing integration of the member states of the AU. In July 2008 the AU Assembly adopted the Protocol on the Statute of the African Court of Justice and Human Rights. When this Protocol enters into force, the new court will replace the current African Human Rights Court. Once established, the new court will have one human rights section and one general affairs section. A draft Protocol extending the jurisdiction of the Court to cover international criminal law had as of August 2013 not yet been adopted.

4.2.2 Composition

The African Court on Human and Peoples' Rights 'complements' the protective mandate of the African Commission under the Charter. The court consists of 11 judges nominated by states parties to the Protocol, and elected by the Assembly. Only the president holds a full-time appointment. The Protocol on the African Court provides that the judges are appointed in their individual capacities, and that their independence is guaranteed. Special provision is made in Article 18 Protocol on the African Court that '[t]he position of judge of the Court is incompatible with any activity that might interfere with the independence or impartiality of such a judge'. A judge will not be allowed to sit in a case if that judge is a national of a state which is a party to the case. The first judges were elected by the Assembly in January 2006.

4.2.3 Procedure

In the majority of cases the Commission will take a case to the African Court if it has found a violation and established that the state has not complied with its recommendations. Individuals and those who act on their behalf will be able to take cases directly to the African Court only in respect of those states that have made an additional declaration specifically authorizing them to do so. Only six states, Burkina Faso, Ghana, Malawi, Mali, Rwanda, and Tanzania, have made such a declaration. This opt-in process for direct access to the Court will remain the same under the merged court. Despite having a number of cases in its docket, the Court only handed down its first judgment on the merits in June 2013.

In respect of the Court's findings, the Protocol on the African Court determines that '[i]f the Court finds that there has been a violation of a human or peoples' right, it shall make appropriate orders to remedy the violation, including the payment of fair compensation or reparation.'[35] The Protocol provides that the Council of Ministers (now the

---

[35] Protocol on the African Court, Art 27(1).

AU Executive Council) shall monitor the execution of the judgments of the Court.[36] The Court may adopt provisional measures in cases of 'extreme gravity and urgency' when 'irreparable harm to persons' would otherwise ensue.[37]

In addition to its contentious jurisdiction, the African Court may also deliver advisory opinions at the request of the AU, any of its organs, or any 'African organisation recognised by the [AU]'.[38] It is unclear whether 'African organisations' include NGOs or is simply a reference to the Regional Economic Communities. The merged court will have advisory jurisdiction only at the request of AU organs.[39]

4.3 THE AU MAIN ORGANS AND HUMAN RIGHTS

4.3.1 Overview

The African human rights system is not limited to the African Commission, the African Court, and the Children's Committee. The AU also has the following main organs: the Assembly of Heads of State and Government, the Executive Council, the Permanent Representative Committee, the Pan-African Parliament, the African Court of Justice, the AU Commission (which replaced the OAU Secretariat), Specialised Technical Committees, the Economic, Social and Cultural Council, financial institutions, and the Peace and Security Council. A number of these organs have human rights mandates.

4.3.2 Pan-African Parliament

The Pan-African Parliament (PAP) shall 'ensure the full participation of African peoples in the development and economic integration of the continent'. One of the Parliament's objectives is to '[p]romote the principles of human rights and democracy in Africa'. The PAP has held sessions twice a year since its inception in 2004. Each state party to the Protocol establishing the Parliament sends five national parliamentarians to the PAP, which is based in Midrand, South Africa. Currently the powers of the Parliament are purely consultative and advisory. In the implementation of its human rights mandate, the PAP has sent fact-finding missions to, for example, Darfur, and election observation missions to many AU member states. The PAP electoral observation mission to the Zimbabwe presidential election in 2008 concluded that the elections had not been free and fair. In contrast, the AU Assembly avoided criticizing the election. This episode is symptomatic of the general lack of impact of the PAP.

4.3.3 The Economic, Social and Cultural Council

The Economic, Social and Cultural Council (ECOSOCC) is an advisory organ made up of representatives nominated by civil society organizations of member states. One of ECOSOCC's objectives is to '[p]romote and defend a culture of good governance, democratic principles and institutions, popular participation, human rights and freedoms as well as social justice'. The statutes of ECOSOCC were adopted by the AU Assembly in July 2004. Since then ECOSOCC has been busy establishing its structures rather than establishing itself as a voice of civil society engaging with and putting issues such as human rights on the AU agenda.

---

[36] Protocol on the African Court, Art 29(2).   [37] Protocol on the African Court, Art 27(2).
[38] Protocol on the African Court, Art 4(1).
[39] Statute of the African Court of Justice and Human Rights, Art 53(1).

4.3.4 Peace and Security Council

The attempts to develop mechanisms to deal with conflict in Africa are also of importance in trying to prevent massive human rights violations. The Protocol on the Peace and Security Council (PSC), adopted in 2002, entered into force in 2003. The PSC has a rotating membership of representatives of 15 AU member states. The criteria for membership include 'respect for constitutional governance...as well as the rule of law and human rights'. Article 4 PSC Protocol provides that the Council shall be guided by the AU Constitutive Act, the UN Charter, and the Universal Declaration of Human Rights. The Protocol further provides that one of the Council's objectives is to 'promote and encourage democratic practices, good governance and the rule of law, protect human rights and fundamental freedoms, respect for the sanctity of human life and international humanitarian law, as part of efforts for preventing conflicts'.

Article 19 PSC Protocol provides that the PSC 'shall seek close cooperation with the African Commission'. Nonetheless, from the activity reports of the Commission and the communiqués of the PSC, it appears that the two organs have not often collaborated, despite references to PSC resolutions in the Commission's country-specific resolutions.

4.4 THE AFRICAN PEER REVIEW MECHANISM

The Declaration on Democracy, Political, Economic and Corporate Governance (Governance Declaration) was adopted at the final OAU Assembly in Durban in 2002. The Governance Declaration provided for the establishment of an African Peer Review Mechanism (APRM) 'to promote adherence to and fulfilment of the commitments' in the Declaration.

The APRM grew out of the New Partnership for Africa's Development (NEPAD), adopted by the AU in 2001 as the development framework for the Union. The secretariats of the APRM and NEPAD are based in Midrand, South Africa. The highest decision-making body in the APRM is the APRM Forum consisting of the heads of state and government of the participating states. A panel of eminent persons with seven members oversees the review process and a member of this panel is chosen to lead the review team on its country mission.

Section 10 Governance Declaration provides as follows:

> In the light of Africa's recent history, respect for human rights has to be accorded an importance and urgency all of its own. One of the tests by which the quality of a democracy is judged is the protection it provides for each individual citizen and for the vulnerable and disadvantaged groups. Ethnic minorities, women and children have borne the brunt of the conflicts raging on the continent today. We undertake to do more to advance the cause of human rights in Africa generally and, specifically, to end the moral shame exemplified by the plight of women, children, the disabled and ethnic minorities in conflict situations in Africa.

The APRM process consists of a self-evaluation by the state that has signed up to be reviewed and a review by an international review team. The outcome of the process is a national Programme of Action with time-bound action points to redress identified shortcomings.

The international review process consists of five stages. First, a background study is carried out by the secretariat assisted by consultants. This stage also includes a support mission to the country that will be reviewed. In the second stage, a review team led by one of the eminent persons visits the country for discussions with all stakeholders, after which the team prepares its report (third stage). A number of partner institutions and independent consultants participate in the review mission and assist in the preparation of the report. The fourth stage consists of the submission of the report to the APRM Forum and the discussion among peers. The fifth stage is the publication of the report and further discussion in other AU institutions such as the Pan-African Parliament. After concluding the reviews, participating states submit annual reports to the Forum on the implementation of the Programme of Action.

The APRM is voluntary and according to the APRM Annual Report for 2011, 30 out of 54 AU member states had signed the Memorandum of Understanding, which forms the legal basis for the review. Of these, less than half had reached the fourth stage of the process.

Many observers have emphasized the necessity for civil society to engage the APRM if the mechanism is to make any difference on the ground. The possibilities for such engagement vary greatly between participating states, as do the approaches to the independence of the national process from government interference.

The APRM integrates the political level of the AU in a way that other parts of the African human rights system have not done. As in other parts of the world, African leaders have not shown a great interest in criticizing their peers. Hence, there are reasons to be sceptical about whether 'peer pressure' will be employed in the process and whether the provisions on sanctions as a last resort against a recalcitrant state will ever be used. However, to focus solely on the pressure exercised at this level would be to underestimate the process as a whole.

There has not been much cooperation between the APRM and the African Commission on Human and Peoples' Rights, which is unfortunate. For example, despite the relevance of the APRM for the realization of human rights, no member of the African Commission has participated in a country review mission. The documents guiding the APRM process are cumbersome and repetitive and do not sufficiently address human rights.

5 CONCLUSION

Human rights protection in Africa clearly has a long way to go, and the mechanisms for their protection have been criticized by many commentators. All too often human rights violations are merely endured—like the weather—or it is left to those whose rights are infringed to seek their own redress, resulting in more violations. At the same time, the progress that has been made and the role of the official recognition of the concept of human rights on all levels on the continent—the regional, sub-regional, and the national—have to be recognized as steps in the right direction. By and large, the standards have been set and the foundations for the enforcement mechanisms have been laid.

The challenge remains primarily one of implementation—not only of the human rights standards and systems, but also of those policies aimed at addressing the root causes of human rights violations, such as poverty. However, it remains a challenge to develop a more closely shared understanding of the nature and scope of what human rights claims legitimately entail on the continent, because ultimately people will take the law into their own hands to defend what they regard as their rights.

FURTHER READING

EBOBRAH, 'Litigating Human Rights before Sub-Regional Courts in Africa: Prospects and Challenges' (2009) 17 *African JCIL* 79.

EBOBRAH, 'Towards a Positive Application of Complementarity in the African Human Rights System: Issues of Functions and Relations' (2011) 22 *EJIL* 663.

EVANS and MURRAY (eds), *The African Charter on Human and Peoples' Rights: The System in Practice, 1986–2006* (Cambridge University Press, 2008).

HEYNS (ed), *Human Rights Law in Africa* (Martinus Nijhoff, 2004).

HEYNS and KILLANDER (eds), *Compendium of Key Human Rights Documents of the African Union* (Pretoria University Law Press, 5th edition 2013).

HEYNS and KILLANDER, 'The African Regional Human Rights System' in Gómez Isa and de Feyter (eds), *International Human Rights Law in a Global Context* (University of Deusto, 2009).

KILLANDER, 'The African Peer Review Mechanism and Human Rights: The First Reviews and the Way Forward' (2008) 30 *HRQ* 41.

KILLANDER, 'African Human Rights Law in Theory and Practice' in Joseph and McBeth

(eds), *Research Handbook on International Human Rights Law* (Edward Elgar, 2010).

KILLANDER and ABEBE, 'Human Rights Developments in the African Union during 2010 and 2011' (2012) 12 *AHRLJ* 199.

KUFUOR, *The African Human Rights System: Origin and Evolution* (Palgrave Macmillan, 2010).

OUGUERGOUZ, *The African Charter on Human and Peoples' Rights: A Comprehensive Agenda for Human Rights* (Kluwer Law International, 2003).

SSENYONJO (ed), *The African Regional Human Rights System* (Martinus Nijhoff Publishers, 2012).

VILJOEN, *International Human Rights Law in Africa* (Oxford University Press, 2nd edition 2012).

VILJOEN, 'Human Rights in Africa: Normative, Institutional and Functional Complementarity and Distinctiveness' (2011) 18 *SAJIA* 191.

VILJOEN and LOUW, 'State Compliance with the Recommendations of the African Commission on Human and Peoples' Rights, 1993–2004' (2007) 101 *AJIL* 1.

USEFUL WEBSITES

African Commission on Human and Peoples' Rights: <http://www.achpr.org/>

African Committee on the Rights and Welfare of the Child: <http://acerwc.org/>

African Court on Human and Peoples' Rights: <http://www.african-court.org/en/>

African Human Rights Case Law Analyser: <http://caselaw.ihrda.org/>

African Union: <http://www.africa-union.org>

Centre for Human Rights, University of Pretoria: <http://www.chr.up.ac.za>

22

WITHIN THE STATE

Andrew Byrnes and Catherine Renshaw

SUMMARY

This chapter outlines the role and responsibility of the state for promoting and protecting human rights. The chapter first details the state's obligation to implement internationally guaranteed human rights and describes the different processes by which customary international law norms and international human rights treaties become part of domestic law. The chapter then discusses the principal domestic legal sources of protection of human rights: constitutional and legislative provisions as well as the common law. Finally, the discussion turns to some of the key institutions within the state that have a role in the protection and promotion of human rights: the courts, the executive, the legislature, ombudsmen, and national human rights institutions.

1 INTRODUCTION

The primacy of the state in the protection and fulfilment of internationally guaranteed human rights is the fundamental starting point of international human rights law. In the words of former UN High Commissioner for Human Rights, Louise Arbour: 'States remain the primary actors, the key conduits through which human rights must be realised. The obligation to respect and enforce human rights rests on states.'[1] As explained in Chapters 4 to 6, states are bound by human rights treaties and customary international law to ensure respect for, and the full enjoyment of, human rights of those persons subject to their jurisdiction. States carry out these obligations through a combination of legislative, institutional, judicial, administrative, financial, and other types of measures. Precisely which measures are used will depend on the specific treaty provision or customary international law obligation, and the political structure and practices of the state concerned. The touchstone for implementation of human rights obligations is ultimately a substantive one—not merely whether necessary laws, institutions, and procedures are in place, but whether they ensure that persons within the state's jurisdiction in fact enjoy the rights guaranteed.

This chapter considers the various methods of protection of human rights at the national level, with a particular focus on legal protections and institutions with a specific

---

[1] Statement by Ms Louise Arbour, UN High Commissioner for Human Rights, on the opening of the 61st Session of the Commission on Human Rights (Geneva, 14 March 2005).

rights mandate. Whether those individuals subject to the jurisdiction of the state enjoy human rights in reality depends on a range of factors, including the nature and content of substantive human rights protections applicable within the domestic system, the role of political and legal institutions in the implementation and enforcement of rights, the resources available to ensure the fulfilment of rights, the availability of remedies for violations of rights, the role of the media and other independent commentators, and the perception of the importance of rights among the members of the community and on the national political agenda.

Section 2 deals with *substantive* protections—the nature, status, and scope of human rights protections under national law. These include the incorporation or other use of international human rights norms in domestic law, constitutional guarantees of rights, human rights legislation, protection under the general law, including the concept of the rule of law, and the common law. Section 3 deals with *institutional* protections of human rights. It briefly outlines the types of institutions which commonly play a role in the implementation, monitoring, and protection of human rights, including the courts, the executive, the legislature, as well as mechanisms such as ombudsmen and national human rights institutions.

2 SUBSTANTIVE PROTECTIONS

A fundamental aspect of ensuring the fulfilment of human rights is their formal legal protection under national law. A state party to an international human rights treaty is in general not required directly to implement the provisions of the treaty into domestic law. What is required is that the protection and fulfilment of the rights guaranteed by the treaty are secured through domestic law and practice. While the level of domestic protection should not fall short of the international obligation, it can provide more generous protection.

There are a number of forms that legal protection of human rights may take in domestic legal systems, including:

1. the incorporation of treaty or customary international law protections into domestic law;
2. constitutional guarantees of human rights;
3. legislative protection of human rights, whether in the form of general human rights legislation or subject-specific legislation; and
4. protection of human rights through the common law in common law jurisdictions.

In addition to human rights-specific protection, human rights can also be protected by laws which provide remedies for violations. Examples include defamation laws as protection of the right to privacy; landlord and tenant laws as protection of the right to property and the right to adequate housing; and criminal procedure laws as protection of the rights of the accused and victims of crimes. The positive obligation of the state to fulfil human rights may also be embodied in legislative frameworks, which give effect to rights and, in turn, may provide individual or group remedies for failure to ensure the enjoyment of these rights. Examples include legislation on education giving effect to the right to education; public housing legislation to ensure the right to adequate housing; and food safety and consumer protection laws as protection of the rights to life, health, and an adequate standard of living.

Underpinning all these is the protection afforded by concepts such as the rule of law, the *Rechtsstaatsprinzip*, or the principle of legality—essentially the principle that the exercise of the power of the state must be referable to a positive grant of constitutionally derived power and be subject to review and restraint by independent courts. Procedures such as the writ of habeas corpus in common law jurisdictions and the comparable *amparo* or *tutela* in some civil law jurisdictions are examples of remedies for violations of the principle of legality. The protection afforded by systems of administrative law also complements direct rights protection under domestic law (for example, the presumption that a statute does not authorize the making of regulations that infringe on fundamental rights and the resulting invalidity of infringing regulations).

2.1 INCORPORATION OF INTERNATIONAL HUMAN RIGHTS NORMS INTO DOMESTIC LAW

Human rights treaties—and to a lesser extent customary international law rules—can provide significant protection when they are incorporated into domestic law and are capable of being invoked before judicial, administrative, or other authorities. A person may be able to rely on each of these types of international law norms in a domestic legal system to challenge alleged violations of rights, though treaty-based norms are of greater practical importance. The extent of protection they afford depends in large part on their status in national law. Discussions of the place of international law in domestic legal systems often distinguish between *monist* systems, in which international law norms form part of domestic law without the need for legislative transformation, and *dualist* systems, according to which international and national law are two different systems, and rules of international law must be adopted or transformed by legislative enactment before they form part of the domestic legal order. In relation to customary international law rules, most legal systems have monist elements: these rules are automatically received into domestic law, though the effect of that reception varies considerably. When it comes to treaties, the variety of constitutional arrangements does not reflect a simplistic monist/dualist dichotomy.

2.1.1 Customary international law

In most dualist systems, in particular most common law jurisdictions, customary international law is accepted as 'part of the law of the land' or as 'a relevant source of law'. However, this is generally only to the extent that the applicable rule of customary international law is not inconsistent with binding judicial precedent or a legislative rule.

Under most monist systems, including most civil law systems, customary international law forms part of domestic law, its hierarchical status depending on the particular constitutional arrangements. In many civil law systems, constitutional provisions explicitly provide that customary international law rules form part of national law. In others, such as Argentina, no specific provision exists, but customary international law has been recognized by courts as part of the domestic legal order.[2] Customary international law rules may have a constitutional status, an enhanced statutory status (so that they prevail over all statutes, both prior and subsequent), or the same status as an ordinary statute. For example, Article 25 Basic Law of the Federal Republic of Germany provides: 'The general rules of public international law shall be an integral part of federal law. They shall take

---

[2] Vinuesa, 'Direct Applicability of Human Rights Conventions within the Internal Legal Order: The Situation in Argentina' in Conforti and Francioni (eds), *Enforcing International Human Rights in Domestic Courts* (Martinus Nijhoff, 1997) 149, 159–60.

precedence over the laws and shall directly create rights and duties for the inhabitants of the federal territory.' This provision has the effect that rules of customary international law are part of federal law and prevail over federal statutes and the laws of the *Bundesländer* (the federal states).

2.1.2 Human rights treaties in monist jurisdictions

The extent to which persons can rely on human rights treaties as part of domestic law will depend on the place of those treaties in the national legal system and on whether the treaty or specific provisions of it, even when part of domestic law, are *directly applicable*. In this regard, it is common to contrast monist and dualist states. Yet this classification conceals a range of constitutional arrangements that defy such an easy categorization.

In some states, ratification of, or accession to, a treaty—the formal indication of a state's intention to be bound by that treaty as a matter of international law—triggers the incorporation of the treaty into the domestic legal system. This may simply follow ratification by the executive, as a result of an express or implied constitutional or statutory rule governing reception of treaties. In other cases, prior legislative approval of the ratification may be required before the treaty is received as part of domestic law. For example, under the US Constitution, the President must receive the advice and consent of two-thirds of the Senate before the USA can ratify the treaty at the international level and before it can become the 'supreme law of the land'. In other states, there are constitutional requirements that the legislature approve by ordinary law the international ratification of a treaty before it can become part of domestic law. In a sense, all these models are 'monist' in that, once the required steps are taken, the provisions of the treaty become part of domestic law.

Under other systems, the usual practice is to adopt a law 'ratifying' a specific treaty (rather than relying on a general rule of reception that applies to all treaties), as a result of which the treaty then becomes part of the domestic legal system. 'Ratifying' is used here in the sense of formal legislative approval at the national level and is different from the act of ratification which takes effect on the international plane, indicating the state's consent to be bound by the treaty.

Civil law jurisdictions with systems under which treaties become part of national law by one of the aforementioned routes include Brazil, Egypt, France, Japan, Mexico, Namibia, the Netherlands, the Russian Federation, and Switzerland. For example, Article 93 Netherlands Constitution provides: 'Provisions of treaties and of resolutions by international institutions which may be binding on all persons by virtue of their contents shall become binding after they have been published.' A number of common law states, such as Cyprus and Nepal, have also adopted such an approach.[3]

Another mechanism for reception of treaties as domestic law in a particular area—sometimes known as 'sector monism'—is a legislative provision providing that international treaties prevail over the provisions of existing legislation in that area should an inconsistency arise. For example, Section 15 Finnish Criminal Code provides:

> If an international treaty binding on Finland or another statute or regulation that is internationally binding on Finland in some event restricts the scope of application of the criminal law of Finland, such a restriction applies as agreed. The provisions in this chapter notwithstanding, the restrictions on the scope of application of Finnish law based on generally recognised rules of international law also apply.[4]

---

[3] Constitution of Cyprus, Art 169(3) and Nepal Treaty Act 2047 [1990], Art 9(1).
[4] See also Norwegian Criminal Procedure Act, s 4.

In some states, ratified treaties generally, or a specific treaty, are given constitutional status. For example, in Austria, the European Convention on Human Rights (ECHR) has constitutional status, as do human rights treaties in a number of Latin American states (for example, Argentina[5]). In other states treaties may be given supra-constitutional status. For example, in the Netherlands treaties that conflict with the Constitution may be approved by a two-thirds parliamentary majority and will then prevail over provisions of the Constitution.[6] In still other states the status may be less than constitutional but superior to other laws, whether pre-existing or subsequent. For example, Article 7(1) Constitution of Costa Rica provides: 'Public treaties, international agreements and concordats duly approved by the Legislative Assembly shall have a higher authority than the laws upon their enactment or from the day that they designate.'

In most other states, including the USA, the provisions of the treaty will be given effect as ordinary national laws, prevailing over existing inconsistent laws but subject to being overridden by subsequent national laws. In federal systems in which treaties become part of the law of the land with the status of a federal legislative norm, they will prevail over both prior and subsequent state or provincial legislation and federal subordinate legislation. Germany and the USA are examples: directly applicable treaties prevail over inconsistent laws of the *Bundesländer* or of the constituent states of the USA, respectively.

Even if a treaty forms part of national law, there are additional requirements before it may be relied on directly as a source of rights by an individual. In particular, it must be 'directly applicable' or 'self-executing'.[7] Whether a treaty or a specific provision is directly applicable depends on a number of factors, including the intention of the drafters of the treaty (whether or not they intended that detailed implementing legislation would be required) and the nature of the treaty provision (in particular whether it is sufficiently precise to be applied directly or whether it is vague and general such that it requires further implementing legislation to give it content). It is possible for some provisions of a treaty to be considered directly applicable while others are not. For example, the Swiss Federal Supreme Court has held that Articles 7(1) and 12 Convention on the Rights of the Child (CRC) (rights of the child to registration on birth, a name, a nationality, and to know his or her parents; right of the child to be heard in proceedings) are directly applicable, while other provisions such as Articles 23 and 26 (right of disabled children to enjoy a full and decent life; right of the child to benefit from social security) are not.[8]

Treaties incorporated into domestic law can provide important protection of human rights, either on their own or as a complement to constitutional protections of rights. For example, in most member states of the Council of Europe the ECHR forms part of domestic law directly and can be invoked before the courts and other authorities. The courts of states parties to the ECHR regularly invoke its provisions as a direct source of rights or to inform their interpretation of constitutionally guaranteed rights. The same is true of the courts of many member states of the Organization of American States, for which the American Convention on Human Rights (ACHR) and other treaties are part of the domestic legal order, occasionally with constitutional status. UN and other regional human rights treaties as well as International Labour Organization (ILO) conventions may also provide protection not otherwise available under domestic law.

There are many examples of cases in which treaties have been successfully invoked before national courts. For example, in a case before the French Council of State, a resident

---

    [5] Constitution of Argentina, Art 75(22).   [6] Constitution of the Netherlands, Art 91(3).
    [7] See Kaiser, 'Treaties, Direct Applicability' in *Max Planck Encyclopedia of Public International Law*, available at: <http://www.mpepil.com>.
    [8] *Bundesamt für Sozialversicherungen v K*, 8C_295/2008 (22 November 2008) para 4.2.

of France who had brought her four-year-old child to live with her without seeking official permission challenged an administrative decision to expel the child, on the ground that the expulsion would be contrary to the CRC. The court held that treaties could be directly relied on to challenge administrative action, found that the decision to separate the child from her mother would undermine the child's best interests contrary to Article 3 CRC, and annulled the decision.[9] Another example is the decision of the Supreme Court of Argentina in the *Campodónico de Beviacqua* case, in which a challenge had been brought against a governmental decision to stop providing medication to a child who suffered from a severe immunological condition and who was dependent on the drug. The Court held that the right to health in the International Covenant on Economic, Social and Cultural Rights (ICESCR) and the Constitution of Argentina required the government to continue to provide the drug to the child.[10]

National courts have rarely had difficulty in finding most *civil and political rights* guarantees directly applicable. For example, the Dutch courts have held the right to be tried without undue delay (Article 14(3)(c) International Covenant on Civil and Political Rights (ICCPR)) to be directly applicable,[11] as have the Belgian courts in relation to the right to be informed of the nature of the charges for which one has been arrested (Article 14(3)(a) ICCPR)[12] and the right to free assistance of an interpreter (Article 14(3)(f) ICCPR).[13]

The courts of many states have also directly enforced a wide variety of treaty provisions relating to *economic and social rights*, be it in direct reliance on a treaty such as the ICESCR or an ILO convention as the primary norm, as a parallel source to a national law, or as an interpretive guide to national constitutional or legislative provisions. Other courts have not been so ready to find economic and social rights directly applicable, particularly where reliance is placed on the ICESCR. This reluctance has arisen not only from concern about the nature and justiciability of individual economic and social rights, but in particular from the terms of the ICESCR, under which states parties undertake to realize the rights guaranteed 'progressively'.[14] For example, in a case involving a challenge to an increase in university fees to be paid by students on the ground that it was inconsistent with Article 13(2)(c) ICESCR, the Swiss Federal Supreme Court held that in general the rights guaranteed by the ICESCR are not directly applicable. Rather than creating a justiciable right that could be invoked before the national courts, the treaty addressed not the individual but rather the legislator and did not provide a precise standard that could be applied by a national court.[15]

This approach seems to be based on an understanding of the obligations under the Covenant that does not reflect more recent analysis or international and national jurisprudence. The work of the Committee on Economic, Social and Cultural Rights, in particular, has pointed out the directly applicable aspects of many of the rights in the ICESCR.[16] Other courts (in particular, but not only, in Latin America) have found that the 'progressive

---

[9] Conseil d'État, Section, *Mlle Cinar* (22 September 1997), available at International Labour Organization, *Use of International Law by Domestic Courts: Compendium of Court Decisions* (December 2007) Case No 56: <http://compendium.itcilo.org/en>.

[10] Supreme Court of Argentina, *Campodónico de Beviacqua, Ana Carina c/ Ministerio de Salud y Acción Social Secretaría de Programas de Salud y Banco de Drogas Neoplásicas* (24 October 2000).

[11] Eg Court of Appeal of Arnhem, *Public Prosecutor v X* (1980) 11 *Netherlands YB of IL* 301.

[12] Cour de Cassation, *Pasikrisie belge*, 1984, I, 524 (17 January 1984) cited in Maresceau, 'Belgium' in Jacobs and Roberts (eds), *The Effect of Treaties in Domestic Law* (Sweet & Maxwell, 1987) 1, 18.

[13] Cour de Cassation, *Pasikrisie belge*, 1985, I, 239 (16 October 1984) cited in Maresceau, n 12, 18.

[14] See Chapter 7.

[15] *Verband Studierender an der Universität Zürich et al. v Regierungsrat des Kantons Zürich*, BGE 120 Ia 1, para 5c.

[16] See Chapters 10 and 12.

implementation' obligation under the ICESCR is no bar to finding that provisions of the ICESCR are directly applicable. For example, in *Mariela Viceconte v Estado Nacional (Ministerio de Salud y Ministerio de Economía de la Nación)*, a case involving a claim based on Article 12(2)(c) ICESCR in relation to the government's failure to arrange the production of a vaccine against Argentinean haemorrhagic fever, the Federal Administrative Court of Appeals of Argentina found a violation of the ICESCR and ordered the state to arrange for production of the vaccine.[17]

2.1.3 Human rights treaties in dualist jurisdictions

In systems which are dualist, the executive act of ratifying a treaty does not bring the treaty directly into domestic law. Rather, the treaty must be adopted by some authoritative legislative act (a statute, delegated or secondary legislation, or a decree) in order to be directly invoked before national courts. This reflects the principle that the law of the land should only be changed by acts of the legislature and not by executive acts alone. Most jurisdictions with a common law heritage follow this approach, including many members of the Commonwealth such as Australia, Canada, India, New Zealand, Nigeria, Tanzania, and the UK, as well as jurisdictions such as Ireland and the Hong Kong Special Administrative Region of China. A number of civil law states, such as Denmark, Norway, and Sweden, also have such systems.

In many such jurisdictions the legislative enactment of a human rights treaty as a whole into domestic law is relatively rare. Examples include the UK Human Rights Act 1998, the Irish European Convention on Human Rights Act 2003, the Nigerian African Charter on Human and Peoples' Rights (Ratification and Enforcement) Act 1983, and the Hong Kong Bill of Rights Ordinance 1991. The more common practice is either to fulfil the substantive treaty obligations by way of enactment of laws that are consistent with the treaty (sometimes drawing on its terms) or to enact specific parts of the treaty as directly enforceable national law. Thus, it is not the treaty provision itself that can be directly invoked as part of domestic law but the national legislative provisions that have transformed it into domestic law.

2.1.4 The relevance of unincorporated human rights treaties

Even in jurisdictions in which treaties do not form part of domestic law unless they have been specifically incorporated, or where an incorporated treaty provision is not directly applicable or self-executing, human rights treaty provisions may still have an impact on judicial and executive decision-making and on the legislative process. In many states, courts have adopted approaches that allow unincorporated treaties to be taken into account. In the context of common law dualist systems, the Bangalore Principles on the Domestic Application of International Human Rights Norms (1988) and subsequent reaffirmations of them by many judges have underlined the possibility, and responsibility, of courts to draw on international law standards when there is uncertainty or a gap in domestic law. Principle 7 Bangalore Principles states that:

> it is within the proper nature of the judicial process and well-established judicial functions for national courts to have regard to international obligations which a country undertakes—whether or not they have been incorporated into domestic law—for the purpose of removing ambiguity or uncertainty from national constitutions, legislation or common law.

---

[17] No 31.777/96, judgment of 2 June 1998, available at: <http://www.escr-net.org/caselaw/>.

There are a number of ways in which unincorporated treaties (as well as customary international law standards) have been used in this indirect way. These include: presumptions that, where reasonably possible, legislation or constitutional provisions should be interpreted in a manner consistent with a state's obligations under international human rights law;[18] requirements for decision-makers to take into account a relevant unincorporated treaty in the exercise of administrative discretion;[19] creation of a legitimate expectation that decision-makers will apply the provisions of a treaty;[20] taking an unincorporated treaty into account in the development of the common law where the common law is unclear;[21] or drawing on such a treaty to identify the demands of public policy.

These possibilities are not confined to states with a common law system. Most legal systems adopt the principle of statutory interpretation that the legislature is presumed not to have legislated in a manner inconsistent with the state's international obligations. International norms may also be drawn on in determining the content of national conceptions of public policy or *ordre public*.

2.2 CONSTITUTIONAL GUARANTEES OF HUMAN RIGHTS

2.2.1 Development of constitutional rights

Constitutional guarantees of human rights can be found today in the overwhelming majority of national constitutions, though the scope and efficacy of these guarantees vary widely. Most constitutions set out to describe (and to limit) the power of those who govern and the way in which power is exercised, by protecting individual rights against the potentially intrusive power of the state and preventing the oppression of minorities or those without power through majoritarian political processes. As political documents often drafted in the wake of oppression, revolution, and the arrival of new political orders, national constitutions frequently embody the desire of their drafters to distinguish the new order from the old. The rights of those marginalized under past systems of law, for example indigenous peoples or women, are often explicitly protected in new constitutions. At the same time, new constitutions are sometimes seen as a bulwark against the exercise of power by the incoming governments of states newly independent of their colonial masters. In some cases, constitutions may also provide protection against the violation of rights by non-state actors.

The different emphasis placed on rights in various national constitutions reflects, to a significant extent, the issues which preoccupied the nation at the period in history during which the constitution was drafted. The Spanish Constitution, for example, drafted after 36 years of Franco's dictatorship, grants rights of association but is careful to note that 'secret and paramilitary associations are prohibited' (Article 22). Fiji's 1997 Constitution, drafted in the wake of two racially motivated coups d'état (and abrogated by the military in 2009), declared the right to freedom from discrimination, but was careful to preserve as lawful positive or affirmative measures to assist indigenous Fijians and Rotumans, perceived to have been disadvantaged under the former political order.

---

[18] Eg *Vishaka v State of Rajasthan* [1997] INSC 665, (1997) 6 SCC 241 (Supreme Court of India).

[19] Eg *R v Director of Immigration, ex parte Simon Yin Xiang-jiang & Others* (1994) 4 HKPLR 264 (Hong Kong Court of Appeal).

[20] Eg *Minister for Immigration & Ethnic Affairs v Teoh* [1995] HCA 20, (1995) 183 CLR 273 (High Court of Australia).

[21] Eg *Mabo v Queensland (No 2)* (1992) 175 CLR 1, 42 (High Court of Australia).

2.2.2 Content of constitutional rights

Typically, constitutionally-protected rights address three principal concerns. First, they protect the right to choose political representatives. Second, they restrain the state from unduly interfering with individual liberties and property. Third, they place a duty on the state to assist the individual or group to realize their potential ('pursue happiness') through the opportunity to pursue economic, social, and cultural rights. Rights protected in modern constitutions have been influenced by international human rights instruments, above all the Universal Declaration of Human Rights (UDHR), the ICCPR, and the ICESCR. Many national courts draw on such instruments to interpret constitutional guarantees, sometimes as a matter of interpretive practice, in other cases in accordance with a constitutional stipulation such as that contained in Article 10(2) Constitution of Spain that '[p]rovisions relating to the fundamental rights and liberties recognized by the Constitution shall be construed in conformity with the Universal Declaration of Human Rights and international treaties and agreements thereon ratified by Spain'.

Most constitutions protect political rights (such as universal suffrage and the right to vote by secret ballot) and civil rights (such as freedom from torture, freedom from unreasonable searches and seizures, freedom of expression, and equality before the law). Economic, social, and cultural rights are less commonly found in constitutions and, where present, are often couched only in aspirational terms, as a duty on the part of the state to 'promote' certain rights rather than to 'guarantee' them. For example, the Indian Constitution places economic, social, and cultural rights in a separate section to civil and political rights and describes them as 'Directive Principles of State Policy'.[22] The Constitution provides that these principles 'shall not be enforceable in any court' but are nevertheless 'fundamental in the governance of the country and it shall be the duty of the state to apply these principles in making laws'. Judicial interpretation of constitutional rights has often functioned to expand the substantive content of rights. The US Constitution, for example, does not explicitly mention a right to privacy, but the Supreme Court has derived such a right from other provisions of the Constitution, extending it into areas which include personal autonomy over reproductive decisions. In *Roe v Wade* it famously held that the right protected a woman's decision to terminate her pregnancy in certain circumstances.[23] The Indian courts, constrained from directly enforcing economic, social, and cultural rights, have by interpretation expanded the content of (justiciable) civil and political rights to encompass economic, social, and cultural rights. For example, the obligation on the state to provide free and compulsory education (a 'Directive Principle of State Policy' only), was held by the Supreme Court to be a 'fundamental right' guaranteed by the right to life and hence justiciable.[24] The right to life in Article 21 of the Constitution has been held to include the rights to live with dignity, to livelihood, and to health.[25] In a similar vein, the Supreme Court of Pakistan has held that the right to life in the Constitution of Pakistan includes the right to a healthy environment.[26]

The South African Constitution provides a leading modern example of constitutional guarantees of wide-ranging economic and social rights that are subject to review by the

---

[22] The model was the Constitution of Ireland, and the same approach has been adopted in the constitutions of Bangladesh, Nepal, Pakistan, and Sri Lanka.

[23] 410 US 113 (1973).

[24] *Unni Krishnan JP v State of Andhra Pradesh* [1993] INSC 60, (1993) 1 SCC 645.

[25] *Francis Coralie Mullin v The Administrator, Union of Territory Delhi* [1981] INSC 12, (1981) 2 SCR 516, 529. See Muralidhar, 'India: The Expectations and Challenges of Judicial Enforcement of Social Rights' in Langford (ed), *Social Rights Jurisprudence: Emerging Trends in International and Comparative Law* (CUP, 2008) 102, 103.   [26] *Shehla Zia v WAPDA*, PLD 1994 SC 693.

courts. The rights guaranteed in the Bill of Rights include the right to adequate housing, the right to healthcare services, and rights to sufficient food, water, social security, and education. The obligation of the state is in general 'to take reasonable legislative and other measures, within its available resources, to achieve the progressive realisation' of the rights, but there are also unqualified guarantees against arbitrary eviction and refusal of emergency medical treatment. In a series of important cases, the South African courts have developed a standard for the reasonableness review of legislation and government policy in relation to a number of these constitutional guarantees.[27]

Many modern constitutions set out the permissible limitations that may be imposed on the exercise of protected rights, often drawing on the framework contained in international treaties. Generally, the state must demonstrate that any restriction is adopted in pursuit of a legitimate aim (for example, 'to protect the rights and freedoms of others', to ensure 'national security', or to protect 'public order'), is provided for by law, and is a reasonable and proportionate restriction on the exercise of the right. Even where limitations are not expressly provided for in the text of a constitution, courts frequently imply similar limitations when adjudicating on the meaning and scope of a particular right.

2.3 LEGISLATIVE PROTECTION OF HUMAN RIGHTS

2.3.1 Legislative bills of rights

Fundamental rights protections are not always entrenched constitutionally. They can also be adopted by governments as ordinary pieces of legislation, with the same status as any other Act of Parliament. Important recent examples of such legislation include the New Zealand Bill of Rights Act 1990, the UK Human Rights Act 1998, and Israel's Basic Law: Human Dignity and Liberty 1992.[28] An earlier version of a statutory bill of rights was the Canadian Bill of Rights of 1960, which was largely ineffectual and was ultimately superseded by constitutional protection in the form of the Canadian Charter of Rights and Freedoms 1982. The decisions in these jurisdictions to adopt legislative bills of rights rather than constitutional ones reflect a variety of factors: the difficulty of achieving constitutional change due to complex amendment procedures; concerns about the impact that a constitutional bill of rights may have on the process of representative democracy (in particular perceptions that it involves the transfer to the judiciary of responsibility for decisions that are properly made by elected legislatures); concerns about freezing rights in constitutional form; and what is politically possible in a given context.

These legislative bills of rights commonly focus on the protection of civil and political rights, with limited inclusion of social, economic, and cultural rights (although the UK Human Rights Act includes protection of the right to property and the right to education). They usually provide that legislation is to be interpreted so far as possible to conform to the rights guaranteed. If this is not possible, the courts are not empowered to strike down the legislation, but may make a 'declaration of incompatibility', which invites parliament to reconsider the legislation. Recent examples of such bills of rights—sometimes described as 'parliamentary' or 'dialogue' bills of rights—have the goal of developing a 'culture of human rights' in government and the legislature. They aim to achieve this by requiring

---

[27] See Motala and Ramaphosa, *Constitutional Law: Analysis and Cases* (OUP, 2002) 389–413; and Liebenberg, *Socio-economic Rights: Adjudication Under a Transformative Constitution* (Juta, 2010).

[28] Ireland has also adopted a legislative bill of rights (the European Convention on Human Rights Act 2003), despite having a constitutional guarantee of rights. There are also a number of sub-national legislative bills of rights based on the ICCPR, eg the Human Rights Act 2004 of the Australian Capital Territory and the Victorian Charter of Human Rights and Responsibilities 2006.

executive certification that bills are consistent (or not) with human rights, and in some cases by establishing parliamentary procedures for close scrutiny of bills and other aspects of government policy in light of human rights standards, combined with a procedure for the legislature to revisit its policy decisions following an adverse finding by a court in the form of a declaration of incompatibility. The Joint Committee on Human Rights of the UK Parliament is a leading example of the possibilities for enhanced legislative scrutiny of human rights issues developed as a result of the new wave of 'parliamentary'/'dialogue' bills of rights.[29]

There are two obvious weaknesses to legislative protection of rights. The first is that legislation is capable of being repealed or amended by a later act of the legislature. The second is that parliament is able to pass legislation that is directly inconsistent with the legislative bill of rights and this later, inconsistent, legislation will prevail. However, in practice, courts, as well as legislators, have tended to view legislative bills of rights as having a status different from that of a normal piece of legislation—a quasi-constitutional or enhanced status. For example, the New Zealand courts have treated the New Zealand Bill of Rights Act as 'not entrenched but not an ordinary Statute either'.[30] In formal terms, however, these statutes still are subject to repeal or overriding just as any other ordinary statute.

2.3.2 Legislative protection of human rights through other means

Legislative protection of human rights is not confined to bills of rights or general human rights statutes. In many jurisdictions there exists extensive legislative protection of rights, particularly in fields such as discrimination, privacy, or labour rights. For example, many states have enacted legislation that prohibits discrimination on the grounds of race or ethnic origin, sex, pregnancy, marital status, sexual orientation, disability, and other grounds. Sometimes these laws take the form of a statute that covers one such ground or closely related grounds, as with the Australian federal Racial Discrimination Act 1975 and Sex Discrimination Act 1984, both of which give effect in part to relevant international treaties.[31] Or they take the form of a general anti-discrimination statute that covers multiple grounds of discrimination. Other legislation of this sort may combine prohibitions of discrimination in certain areas with programmatic and institutional measures, as is the case with the Indian Persons with Disabilities (Equal Opportunities, Protection of Rights and Full Participation) Act 1995. In many cases such legislation is accompanied by the establishment of institutions that have an implementation or monitoring role, which may have responsibility for resolving complaints of violations. Examples include the Dutch Equal Treatment Commission, the UK Equality and Human Rights Commission, and the various Scandinavian Equality Ombudsmen.

2.4 COMMON LAW PROTECTION OF HUMAN RIGHTS

For states with a common law heritage, the common law (judicial decisions determining the rights of persons in particular cases brought before the courts) contains principles that can

---

[29] For the Joint Committee's work, see: <http://www.parliament.uk/business/committees/committees-a-z/joint-select/human-rights-committee/>. See also Klug, *Report on the Working Practices of the JCHR*, Appendix 1 to JCHR, *The Committee's Future Working Practices, Twenty-third Report of Session 2005–06* (July 2006); and Hiebert, 'Parliament and the Human Rights Act: Can the JCHR Help Facilitate a Culture of Rights?' (2006) 4 *IJ Con L* 1.

[30] *Herewini v Ministry of Transport* (1992) 9 CRNZ 307, 326 (Fisher J).

[31] In 2012, the Australian government proposed consolidating the various federal anti-discrimination laws into a consolidated statute, without success. See the *Human Rights and Anti-Discrimination Bill 2012 – Exposure Draft Legislation*, November 2012.

provide significant protection against encroachment on human rights by the state. However, common law rules and presumptions must give way to a clear expression of legislative intent to displace or override them. The common law can operate to protect human rights in three key respects. First, it is a repository of rights developed in case law by judges. Second, the law-making function of judges enables them to apply principles of international human rights law when they interpret legislation or apply the common law in cases that come before them. A state's international obligations under treaties such as the ICCPR and the ICESCR are relevant to judicial approaches to statutory interpretation. Third, judges in some jurisdictions have found that the common law can operate to protect civil and political rights that exist in free and democratic societies, such as the right to freedom of communication.

The common law approach to interpreting legislation proceeds on the basis of the 'basic principle that Parliament did not intend to invade fundamental rights, freedoms and immunities'.[32] Thus, there are (rebuttable) presumptions that parliament did not intend to retrospectively change rights, infringe personal liberty, alter criminal law practices based on the principle of a fair trial, exclude the right to claim self-incrimination, authorize the commission of a tort, or interfere with the course of justice.[33] As with all common law rules or presumptions, these protections can be overridden by a legislature that is intent on doing so, and there are many examples of this occurring, in areas as diverse as counter-terrorism legislation and mental health legislation. Even long-established protections in the criminal process are not immune from being cut back, as is evidenced, for example, by recent efforts, some of which have been successful, to introduce limitations to the protection against 'double jeopardy' in criminal cases, the principle that an individual should not be in jeopardy of punishment by the state twice for the same offence.[34]

3 INSTITUTIONAL PROTECTIONS

All the organs of the state have a responsibility for observing and promoting human rights in their respective spheres of responsibility. Institutions that play an important role in the monitoring and enforcement of human rights include the courts, the legislature, and the executive as well as a range of further bodies, which may or may not have a specific human rights mandate, including ombudsmen and national human rights institutions.

3.1 THE COURTS

As is apparent from Section 2, domestic courts may play an important role in protecting human rights through applying human rights guarantees contained in international or national law, interpreting legislation in a human rights-sensitive manner, and developing the common law. Courts with general jurisdiction will have the potential to protect human rights within the area of law they administer (for example, administrative, criminal, or civil law). In some jurisdictions there may be specialized courts or administrative tribunals with a human rights jurisdiction—most frequently seen in the area of anti-discrimination

---

[32] Spigelman, 'The Common Law Bill of Rights' in Spigelman, *Statutory Interpretation and Human Rights* (University of Queensland Press, 2008) 3, 24.

[33] Spigelman, n 32, 26–9.

[34] See McNamara, 'Rolling Back an Established Right: "Reforming" the Rule against Double Jeopardy' in McNamara, *Human Rights Controversies: The Impact of Legal Form* (Taylor & Francis, 2007) 37–98.

law or industrial law.[35] In those states that guarantee human rights at the constitutional level, courts may protect human rights through constitutional review.

Under some legal systems, courts have the power to review the constitutionality of laws enacted by the legislature. The early and well-known example of the US Supreme Court in *Marbury v Madison* (1803), in which that court held it had the power to review the constitutionality of legislation, has influenced arrangements in many states. Constitutional review may take place before *any* court in some systems such as Australia, Canada, India, and the USA. In others, including Germany and Indonesia, the jurisdiction to review constitutionality may be vested in a constitutional court, the exclusive function of which is that of constitutional review. In yet others, such as South Africa, there may be a shared constitutional jurisdiction among the courts of general jurisdiction and a constitutional court, with the latter having the final say.

Some jurisdictions will permit a challenge to the constitutionality of a law to be launched only *after* a law has been enacted (Australia, Canada, Malaysia, and the USA), while others provide for constitutional review only *before* a law is enacted or commences operation (Sri Lanka and, until recently, France).[36] In these latter jurisdictions, the courts often also have the power to review the constitutionality or legality of executive acts, even if they cannot rule on the constitutionality of enacted laws. Some jurisdictions will limit constitutional challenges to cases in which an individual can show a particular interest in the case, while others also allow members of parliament, political parties, or state organs to seek rulings on constitutionality in the abstract (as with the *abstrakte Normenkontrolle* jurisdiction of the German Federal Constitutional Court).[37]

The scope and effectiveness of constitutional protection of rights by courts will depend on the courts' independence and their perception of their role as defenders of rights and place in the constitutional division of powers, as well as the extent of access to court in practice and the respect for court decisions shown by the government and the legislature.

3.2 THE EXECUTIVE

The role of the executive in protecting human rights is also critical. The executive should have procedures in place to ensure that it takes into account both its positive and negative obligations in relation to human rights when deciding on its policy priorities and in assessing the appropriateness of its approach to implementing them. Many states have detailed assessment procedures for ensuring that draft laws are consistent with human rights, both within the bureaucracy and also when proposals are put to cabinet for approval (for example, through requirements in cabinet procedures that the human rights implications of draft legislation be clearly identified).

3.3 THE LEGISLATURE

Legislatures also have an important role to play, both as guarantors of human rights through enactment of legislation and also as monitors of proposals put before them. The means by which legislatures carry out human rights monitoring vary widely.[38] Some legislatures

---

[35] Eg the Norwegian Equality Tribunal and the former New South Wales Equal Opportunity Tribunal.

[36] As the result of the passage of the *Constitutional Law on the Modernization of the Institutions of the Fifth Republic* of 23 July 2008, the Conseil Constitutionnel has a limited role of review of constitutionality of laws, when matters are referred to it by other courts.

[37] Steinberger, *Models of Constitutional Jurisdiction* (Council of Europe Press, 1993).

[38] Inter-Parliamentary Union, PARLINE Database: Parliamentary Human Rights Bodies, available at: <http://www.ipu.org/parline-e/Instance-hr.asp>.

have established a legislative committee with a specific human rights mandate to review legislative proposals (and sometimes other aspects of government policy and conduct) for human rights consistency. The UK Joint Committee on Human Rights is one such example. The Australian Parliamentary Joint Committee on Human Rights, established in 2012,[39] is another: this body has the function of scrutinizing all new legislative proposals and existing legislation in light of the seven principal UN human rights treaties to which Australia is party. Other legislatures have established scrutiny of bills committees that have the responsibility to identify and draw to the attention of the legislature whether legislative proposals 'trespass unduly on personal rights and liberties' or violate a range of other standards.[40] Yet other legislatures may consider human rights issues in other substantive legislative committees, for example ones focusing on legal and constitutional affairs, foreign affairs and trade, or home affairs.

In some states, the role of ensuring that legislation conforms to the constitution may reside exclusively in the legislature instead of the courts. In China, for example, the Standing Committee of the National People's Congress has the power to issue formal, binding opinions on the interpretation of the Constitution. Furthermore, as noted already, in some of the systems with constitutional judicial review, members of parliament are authorized to seek rulings on the constitutionality of proposed legislation before its enactment or entry into force.

3.4 OTHER BODIES

There are many other types of national institutions that can contribute to the protection and enjoyment of human rights. Some of these may have an explicit human rights mandate, while others do not. Examples of institutions that do not necessarily have a specific human rights mandate but that may nonetheless protect human rights in fact include ombudsmen, parliamentary commissioners for administration (who may be entrusted with the task of monitoring public administration and responding to complaints of maladministration), public advocates, inspectors of prisons, data protection mechanisms, and telecommunications and broadcasting regulatory authorities. Institutions with a specific human rights mandate may include human rights commissions, equality bodies, ombudsmen with a specific human rights mandate, and public bodies or offices with responsibility for overseeing government.

3.4.1 Ombudsmen

The institution of the ombudsman has its roots in Scandinavia but has been taken up in many states.[41] While the original ombudsman institution developed in Sweden, its Norwegian and Danish variants have been particularly influential. The traditional model of an ombudsman has been an independent institution that is established by and answerable to parliament, with the power to consider complaints and conduct investigations on its

[39] The Committee is established by the Human Rights (Parliamentary Scrutiny) Act 2011 (Cth). See <http://www.aph.gov.au/Parliamentary_Business/Committees/Senate_Committees?url=humanrights_ctte/index.htm>.
[40] Eg the Australian Senate's Standing Committee on Scrutiny of Bills. See <http://www.aph.gov.au/parliamentary_business/committees/senate_committees?url=scrutiny/index.htm>.
[41] See generally Reif, *The Ombudsman, Good Governance and the International Human Rights System* (Martinus Nijhoff, 2004); Gregory and Giddings (eds), *Righting Wrongs: The Ombudsman in Six Continents* (IOS Press, 2000); Hossain, Besselink, Selassie, and Völker (eds), *Human Rights Commissions and Ombudsman Offices: National Experiences Throughout the World* (Kluwer, 2000).

own initiative, and to make recommendations to government rather than to adopt binding decisions. In terms of mandate, there are two main models of ombudsman (though some ombudsmen are hybrids of the two): the classical ombudsman and the human rights ombudsman.[42] It was estimated in 2003 that there were about 110 states in the world with classical or hybrid ombudsman institutions.[43]

Classical ombudsmen have jurisdiction to oversee government administration and to consider complaints of unfair, unjust, or poor administration. Such bodies are an important means of ensuring that citizens have an affordable and accessible avenue of complaining about administrative conduct. They do not generally have an explicit human rights mandate, but their actions may assist complainants in realizing their rights (for instance, a fair hearing by a government decision-maker or the granting of a social security benefit) and ensuring that constitutional and other legal guarantees of human rights are observed. In some cases, classical ombudsmen make explicit use of international and national human rights norms in their work. The institution of the classical ombudsman is to be found in all regions of the world.[44]

Human rights ombudsmen, on the other hand, have an explicit human rights mandate (and possibly a general maladministration mandate). This may be a specialized mandate focusing on specific human right issues. For example, the Norwegian Gender Equality Ombud had a specific role under the Gender Equality Act, while in Sweden there were until 2009 four Ombuds working in the area of equality and non-discrimination (the Ombudsman against Ethnic Discrimination, the Ombudsman against Discrimination on Grounds of Sexual Orientation, the Equal Opportunities Ombudsman, and the Children's Ombudsman)—these have now been replaced with one Equality Ombudsman with jurisdiction over all these issues. Similarly, a number of states have children's ombudsmen or commissioners. Alternatively, the mandate may be a more general human rights mandate, in which case the ombudsman institution may be very similar to a national human rights institution in its coverage.

Both classical and human rights ombudsmen can provide substantive protection for human rights, by explicitly applying and enforcing domestic and international human rights norms, or by applying standards of good administration without express reference to human rights norms.[45]

3.4.2 National human rights institutions

In the past 20 years, national human rights institutions (NHRIs) have become increasingly significant actors in promoting and protecting human rights within the state. These institutions, established by constitution or legislation, carry out dual functions in relation to the state. Their first role is to work with government in attempting to ensure that legislation complies with the state's international human rights obligations or constitutional guarantees, to educate government officials about human rights, and to advise government about the human rights implications of government action. Their second role is to critique government action that violates human rights and to provide remedies—be it

---

[42] Reif, n 41, 8–9.   [43] Reif, n 41, 11.

[44] Examples include the Swedish Parliamentary Ombudsmen (Riksdagens ombudsmän), the UK's Parliamentary Commissioner for Administration (and similar institutions in many Commonwealth jurisdictions), the Australian Commonwealth Ombudsman, and the institution of the Defensor del Pueblo that is to be found in Spain and many Latin American states. See generally Reif, n 41, 187–92.

[45] Reif, n 41, 103–12, provides an overview of the ways in which both classical ombudsmen and human rights ombudsmen can use domestic and international human rights norms in their work.

through conciliation or adjudication—to individuals whose rights have been violated. The first role requires NHRIs to be able to work closely and effectively with government. The second role requires them to be staunchly independent of government. The experience of NHRIs over the past 20 years suggests that the balance between the two roles is sometimes a difficult one to achieve.[46]

Nonetheless, NHRIs have been and continue to be established in all regions of the world, in very different political circumstances. One of the key factors driving their establishment is recognition that remedies for breaches of international human rights provided at the international level (for example, by the UN treaty-based bodies empowered to receive individual complaints) are inaccessible to most people. For reasons of access and afford-ability, remedies must be provided at the national level.

Recognizing that some states may attempt to establish NHRIs as mere human rights 'window-dressing', in 1993 the UN General Assembly adopted the Paris Principles, a set of standards aimed at ensuring the independence and effectiveness of NHRIs.[47] The Paris Principles provide guidelines as to the composition of NHRIs (requiring that they be representative of the pluralism in society) and the appointment of commission members (requiring that they have a clearly defined term of appointment and transparent procedures for appointment and dismissal). They further require NHRIs to be given competence to promote and protect human rights and as broad a mandate as possible, which is to be clearly anchored in a constitutional or legislative text. In addition, they provide that NHRIs should be empowered to:

- make recommendations and report to government on matters concerning human rights (including in relation to legislative or administrative provisions and any situation of human rights violations they decide to take up);

- promote conformity of national laws and practices with international human rights standards;

- encourage ratification of international human rights treaties and implementation of international standards;

- contribute to reporting procedures under international instruments;

- assist in the formulation and execution of human rights teaching and research and increase public awareness through information and education; and

- cooperate with the UN, regional institutions, and national institutions of other states.

As well as these functions, many NHRIs have 'quasi-judicial' powers, such as the power to compel production of documents and giving of evidence, powers of investigation, and the power to conciliate complaints. Some NHRIs refer complaints to appropriate authorities for investigation or institution of legal proceedings. Where this is the case, NHRIs often possess the power to appear in courts and tribunals as *amicus curiae* in order to bring relevant principles of human rights law to the attention of the court. Many NHRIs also have the power to undertake public inquiries into human rights issues. Public inquiries have proved an effective way for NHRIs, with limited resources and subjected to multiple demands, to make a significant impact in certain areas. The publicity attached to these inquiries and the fact that they are undertaken by an organ

---

[46] See Smith, 'The Unique Position of National Human Rights Institutions: A Mixed Blessing' (2006) 28 *HRQ* 904.

[47] Principles Relating to the Status and Functions of National Institutions for the Promotion and Protection of Human Rights, GA Res 48/134, Annex (1993).

within the state often make it politically difficult for governments to ignore their find-ings and recommendations.

Despite their location within the state and their susceptibility to lack of independence from the government, NHRIs have the potential to be effective actors in strengthening human rights protection. Their ability to pursue issues and hold inquiries of their own accord sets them apart from the courts, which must wait for rights-relevant cases to be brought before them in order that they can make determinations that support the develop-ment of human rights law.

4 CONCLUSION

Securing the enjoyment of human rights within the state is a complex process, involving the interaction between substantive norms of human rights and their status in the domes-tic legal system, the availability and effectiveness of a range of institutions (including those with a specific human rights mandate), the legitimacy of human rights discourse among political leaders and the community, and the level of stability in a given society. All meas-ures for the domestic protection of human rights rely for their efficacy on the allocation by the state of sufficient resources. The provision of legal aid and funding for public interest litigation, a judiciary, a legal profession, and a community educated in human rights are all essential to the realization of human rights.

FURTHER READING

ALSTON (ed), *Promoting Human Rights Through Bills of Right: Comparative Perspectives* (Clarendon Press, 1999).

CARVER, 'A New Answer to an Old Question: National Human Rights Institutions and the Domestication of International Law' (2010) 10 *HRLR* 1.

CONFORTI and FRANCIONI (eds), *Enforcing International Human Rights in Domestic Courts* (Martinus Nijhoff, 1997).

FATIMA, *Using International Law in Domestic Courts* (Hart, 2005).

FENWICK, *Civil Liberties and Human Rights* (Routledge-Cavendish, 2007).

GARGARELLA, DOMINGO, and ROUX (eds), *Courts and Social Transformation in New Democracies: An Institutional Voice for the Poor?* (Ashgate, 2006).

GOODMAN and PEGRAM (eds), *Human Rights, State Compliance, and Social Change:* *Assessing National Human Rights Institutions* (Cambridge University Press, 2012).

HOSSAIN, BESSELINK, SELASSIE, and VÖLKER (eds), *Human Rights Commissions and Ombudsman Offices: National Experiences Throughout the World* (Kluwer, 2000).

JAYAWICKRAMA, *The Judicial Application of Human Rights Law: National, Regional and International Jurisprudence* (Cambridge University Press, 2002).

LANGFORD (ed), *Social Rights Jurisprudence: Emerging Trends in International and Comparative Law* (Cambridge University Press, 2008).

SIMMONS, *Mobilizing for Human Rights: International Law in Domestic Politics* (Cambridge University Press, 2009).

SMITH, 'The Unique Position of National Human Rights Institutions: A Mixed Blessing?' (2006) 28 *HRQ* 904.

USEFUL WEBSITES

Asia Pacific Forum of National Human Rights Institutions: <**http://www.asiapacificforum.net**>

Interights, *Commonwealth and International Human Rights Case Law Databases*: <**http://www.interights.org/database-search/index.htm**>

International Labour Organization, *Use of International Law by Domestic Courts: Compendium of Court Decisions*: <**http://compendium.itcilo.org/en**>

Inter-Parliamentary Union, *PARLINE Database: Parliamentary Human Rights Bodies*: <**http://www.ipu.org/parline-e/Instance-hr.asp**>

National Human Rights Institutions Forum: <**http://www.nhri.net**>

Oxford Reports on International Law in Domestic Courts: <**http://www.oxfordlawreports.com/home**>

Venice Commission of the Council of Europe, *CODICES, the Infobase on Constitutional Case-Law of the Venice Commission:* <**http://www.codices.coe.int/**>

World Legal Information Institute (database of national and international case law): <**http://www.worldlii.org**>

PART V

LINKAGES

23

INTERNATIONAL HUMANITARIAN LAW

Sandesh Sivakumaran

SUMMARY

International humanitarian law is concerned with the regulation of armed conflict. It is closely related to international human rights law. Although the two come from different historical backgrounds, they have common values, primarily those of respect for, and dignity of, the human person. International human rights law does not cease to apply in time of armed conflict. The continued applicability of international human rights law provides added value but also creates difficulties. Given the applicability of both international human rights law and international humanitarian law in time of armed conflict, it is important to discern the relationship between them.

1 INTRODUCTION

The principal body of international law that applies in time of armed conflict is international humanitarian law. International humanitarian law seeks to balance the violence inherent in an armed conflict with the dictates of humanity. It protects the civilian population from the ravages of conflict and establishes limitations on the means and methods of combat. International human rights law does not cease to apply in situations of armed conflict. Rather, it continues to apply alongside international humanitarian law. This continued applicability complements international humanitarian law and offers distinct advantages as far as the protection of the human person is concerned. It also poses some difficulties, not least identifying the exact relationship between the two bodies of law.

Section 2 considers the nature of international humanitarian law and identifies some of its cardinal principles and key rules. Section 3 explores the similarities and differences between international humanitarian law and international human rights law, comparing and contrasting their historical origins and conceptual approaches.

Given that international humanitarian law applies in situations of armed conflict, whether there is a need for international human rights law also to apply is the subject of Section 4. As these two bodies of law coexist, it is crucial to ascertain the relationship between them. Accordingly, this forms the subject of Section 5. Section 6 considers some of the difficulties with the application of international human rights law in time of armed conflict.

2 WHAT IS INTERNATIONAL
HUMANITARIAN LAW?

The principal body of law that applies in time of armed conflict operates under different names: international humanitarian law, the law of war, or the law of armed conflict. It is the body of law which seeks to balance the violence inherent in armed conflict with the dictates of humanity. It belies the idea that 'when the guns go off the law becomes silent'. It is, quite simply, 'the last lifeline, when nothing else stands between mankind and a relapse into savagery'.[1]

International humanitarian law is comprised of treaties—principally, the Hague Regulations of 1899 and 1907, the Geneva Conventions of 1949, and the Protocols Additional to the Geneva Conventions of 1977—and customary international law.[2] Different rules govern international armed conflicts (traditionally fought between two or more states[3]), situations of belligerent occupation (the placing of territory under the authority of a hostile army), and non-international armed conflicts (fought between a state and a non-state armed group or between two or more armed groups, usually within the boundaries of a state). Treaty rules largely govern international armed conflicts and belligerent occupations, with only one provision of the four Geneva Conventions—Article 3, common to all four Conventions—and one principal treaty—Additional Protocol II—regulating the conduct of non-international armed conflicts. Non-international armed conflicts do benefit from detailed regulation at the level of customary international law but this is not to quite the same extent as international armed conflicts. This is because states viewed, and to some degree continue to view, non-international armed conflicts as matters of domestic concern, jealously guarding their sovereignty.

The cardinal principles of international humanitarian law are those of distinction and unnecessary suffering.[4] The principle of distinction requires that combatants (or fighters, in the language of non-international armed conflict) be distinguished from civilians, and civilian objects be distinguished from military objectives. The principle of unnecessary suffering prohibits the use of means (weapons) and methods (tactics) of warfare that are of a nature to cause suffering or injury beyond that which is required for its military purpose. Underlying these principles are the fundamental tenets of humanity, military necessity, and chivalry.

The principal provisions of international humanitarian law seek to afford a measure of protection to civilians and other persons *hors de combat* (literally 'outside of combat'; primarily military personnel no longer fighting due to sickness, injury, or capture) and to place certain restrictions on the means and methods of warfare. Ideas of military necessity are imbued in the provisions and, as such, a state cannot justify violation of the rules by claiming that it was militarily necessary for it to do so. The rules of international

---

[1] Quentin-Baxter, 'Human Rights and Humanitarian Law—Confluence or Conflict?' (1985) 9 *Australian YIL* 94, 103.

[2] For a useful list of treaties, see: <http://www.icrc.org/ihl.nsf/INTRO?OpenView>. For customary international law, see Henckaerts and Doswald-Beck, *Customary International Humanitarian Law* (CUP, 2005).

[3] Pursuant to the Protocol Additional to the Geneva Conventions of 12 August 1949, and relating to the Protection of Victims of International Armed Conflicts (Additional Protocol I), Art 1(4), wars of national liberation, which are fought between states and national liberation movements are also international armed conflicts. However, in practice, the provision has never been used.

[4] *Legality of the Threat or Use of Nuclear Weapons, Advisory Opinion* [1996] ICJ Rep 226, para 78.

humanitarian law are tailored for an exceptional situation—the state of war. Accordingly, there is no possibility of derogating from them on the basis of strategic expedience or necessity.

Let us consider some of the key rules.

Protections afforded to civilians and persons hors de combat: the guiding principle is one of humane treatment. This guarantee encompasses such prohibitions as violence to life and person, outrages upon personal dignity, the taking of hostages, collective punishments, slavery, and forcible displacement.[5] Special protections are in place for particular categories of persons including the wounded and sick, medical and religious personnel, women, and children.[6]

Targeting: the civilian population and civilian objects shall not be made the object of attack.[7] Indiscriminate attacks are similarly prohibited.[8] Equally forbidden are attacks that would violate the principle of proportionality, namely that the incidental loss of civilian life and damage to civilian property should not be excessive in relation to the concrete and direct military advantage anticipated.[9] In the event that an attack takes place, feasible precautions must be taken to avoid injury to the civilian population and damage to civilian objects.[10]

Means and methods of combat: the means of injuring the enemy are not unlimited. Some weapons are specifically prohibited, such as poison, biological and bacteriological weapons, gas, and other chemical weapons.[11] Weapons that are indiscriminate by nature or are of a nature to cause unnecessary suffering are similarly prohibited.[12] Equally, the methods of combat are not unlimited. For example, it is prohibited to order that there shall be no survivors, to kill those who have expressed a desire to surrender, and to make improper use of flags and uniforms.[13]

3 DIFFERENT HISTORIES; SHARED VALUES

International humanitarian law is sometimes described as the human rights law of armed conflict. Such a description has the potential to mislead, for, although the two bodies of law share some of the same purposes, they are historically different and indeed remain distinct.

International human rights law flourished in the immediate aftermath of the Second World War, with the adoption of the Universal Declaration of Human Rights (UDHR).

---

[5] Eg Additional Protocol I, Art 75; Protocol Additional to the Geneva Conventions of 12 August 1949, and relating to the Protection of Victims of Non-International Armed Conflicts (Additional Protocol II), Art 4; Customary International Humanitarian Law (CIHL), Rules 87–105. The CIHL Rules are available at: <http://www.icrc.org/ihl.nsf/FULL/612?OpenDocument>.

[6] Eg Additional Protocol I, Arts 10, 15, 76, 77; Additional Protocol II, Arts 7–9; CIHL, Rules 109–11, 25-30, 134–8.

[7] Additional Protocol I, Arts 51(2), 52(1); Additional Protocol II, Art 13(2) (the civilian population); CIHL, Rules 1 and 7.   [8] Additional Protocol I, Art 51(4); CIHL, Rule 11.

[9] Additional Protocol I, Art 51(5)(b); CIHL, Rule 14.

[10] Additional Protocol I, Art 57; CIHL, Rules 15–24.

[11] Eg Geneva Protocol for the Prohibition of the Use in War of Asphyxiating, Poisonous or Other Gases, and of Bacteriological Methods of Warfare (1925); Convention on the Prohibition of the Development, Production and Stockpiling of Bacteriological (Biological) and Toxin Weapons and Their Destruction (1972); Convention on the Prohibition of the Development, Production, Stockpiling and Use of Chemical Weapons and on Their Destruction (1993); CIHL, Rules 72–6.   [12] Additional Protocol I, Art 35(2); CIHL, Rules 70–1.

[13] Additional Protocol I, Arts 40, 41, 39; CIHL, Rules 46, 58–63.

It has since been followed by the International Covenant on Civil and Political Rights (ICCPR) and the International Covenant on Economic, Social and Cultural Rights as well as numerous treaties, declarations, and the like. International humanitarian law's first flourish took place in the 1860s with the conclusion of the Instructions for the Government of Armies of the United States in the Field (Lieber Code) (1863), the Geneva Convention for the Amelioration of the Condition of the Wounded in Armies in the Field (1864), and the St Petersburg Declaration Renouncing the Use, in Time of War, of Explosive Projectiles Under 400 Grammes Weight (1868).

At a conceptual level, international humanitarian law applies between two or more competing factions (states and/or armed groups). International human rights law, however, regulates the relationship between the state and the individual. International humanitarian law operates on the basis of equality of obligation of the parties; while the fundamental premise of international human rights law is the unequal relationship between the governor and the governed.

More markedly, the two sets of rules differ in their substance. Take the right to life. The right not to be arbitrarily deprived of one's life is fundamental to international human rights law,[14] the supreme right on which all others are built. International humanitarian law accepts the killing of combatants and fighters as inherent in an armed conflict and tolerates the killing of civilians in certain circumstances. For example, a military objective may not be attacked if the attack 'may be expected to cause incidental loss of civilian life, injury to civilians, damage to civilian objects, or a combination thereof, which would be excessive in relation to the concrete and direct military advantage anticipated'.[15] Accordingly, incidental civilian casualties are tolerated provided they are not excessive in comparison with the anticipated military advantage. Thus, the rules of international humanitarian law, humanitarian though they may be, take as their starting point the combatant's privilege, namely the right to kill.

Given these differences, there was little interaction between the two bodies of law in the period immediately after 1945. Some of the great instruments of both areas were adopted at around the same time: the UDHR was adopted in 1948 and the four Geneva Conventions in 1949. Yet few persons participated in the drafting of both sets of instruments and the impact of the one on the other was minimal. Whilst international human rights law largely developed within the United Nations (UN) system, international humanitarian law developed outside, primarily through its guardian, the International Committee of the Red Cross (ICRC). Historically, the ICRC was wary of associating itself with the, politicized, UN; while the UN, having outlawed the threat or use of force in its Charter, was concerned about considering the law that applies during war lest it be thought that such outlawry was doomed from the outset.[16]

It took until 1968 and the International Conference on Human Rights in Tehran for the two bodies of law to come into close contact with one another. During that conference, convened by the UN in the International Year for Human Rights, a resolution was passed that called on all states to ratify the international humanitarian law treaties then in existence and requested the General Assembly to invite the Secretary-General to prepare a study on various aspects of international humanitarian law.[17]

---

[14] See Chapter 9.   [15] Additional Protocol I, Art 51(5)(b); CIHL, Rule 14.

[16] Such was the concern that the International Law Commission—tasked by the UN with codifying and progressively developing international law—felt unable to place the revision of the law of armed conflict on its work agenda despite the urgent need for its revision as evidenced by the Second World War. See *1949 Yearbook of the International Law Commission* 281, para 18 (UN, 1956).

[17] 'Human Rights in Armed Conflicts', Res XXIII of the International Conference on Human Rights, Tehran (12 May 1968), reprinted in Schindler and Toman (eds), *The Laws of Armed Conflicts* (Martinus Nihoff, 2004) 347; GA Res 2444 (XXIII) (19 December 1968).

Since the Tehran Conference, there has been greater interaction between international human rights and humanitarian law. International human rights law has influenced international humanitarian law and vice versa. The fundamental guarantees of the 1977 Additional Protocols, prohibiting murder, torture, and the like are a reflection of international human rights law and are inspired by that body of law.[18] The 1989 Convention on the Rights of the Child (CRC)—a human rights instrument—requires states parties to 'respect and to ensure respect for rules of international humanitarian law applicable to them in armed conflicts which are relevant to the child'.[19] The Optional Protocol thereto on the Involvement of Children in Armed Conflict, unusually for a human rights instrument, refers to armed groups, namely that they 'should not, under any circumstances, recruit or use in hostilities persons under the age of 18 years'.[20]

The mutual influence of the two sets of rules and the closer association between the bodies working with them is, in many respects, unsurprising given that they share similar goals, namely respect for, and dignity of, the human person. The idea of human dignity is at the very heart of international human rights law, human rights being derived from the 'inherent dignity of the human person'.[21] In international humanitarian law, the prohibition on 'outrages upon personal dignity' is based on this idea of human dignity.[22] It is also infused throughout that body of law. The Martens clause, for example, a residual clause contained in most humanitarian law instruments, provides that 'in cases not covered by the law in force, the human person remains under the protection of the principles of humanity and the dictates of the public conscience'.[23]

4 REASONS FOR THE APPLICATION OF HUMAN RIGHTS LAW IN ARMED CONFLICT

Given that a body of international law—international humanitarian law—is designed to regulate armed conflict, it is legitimate to ask whether there is need for another body of international law—international human rights law—also to apply. Aside from the difference in substantive content, which is in itself an important reason, there are at least three other factors that suggest there is indeed a role for international human rights law to play in time of armed conflict.

4.1 NON-APPLICABILITY OF INTERNATIONAL HUMANITARIAN LAW

It has been remarked that, 'the first line of defense against international humanitarian law is to deny that it applies at all'.[24] International humanitarian law presupposes the existence of an armed conflict; a declared war, which is nowadays rare; or occupation of territory, which usually, though not always, results from an armed conflict. An armed conflict, in turn, exists 'whenever there is a resort to armed force between States or protracted armed violence between governmental authorities and organized armed groups or between such

---

[18] Additional Protocol I, Art 75; Additional Protocol II, Art 4.   [19] CRC, Art 38(1).
[20] Optional Protocol to the Convention on the Rights of the Child on the Involvement of Children in Armed Conflict, Art 4(1).   [21] ICCPR, preamble; ICESCR, preamble.
[22] Eg Common Art 3(1)(c).   [23] Eg Additional Protocol II, preamble.
[24] Baxter, 'Some Existing Problems of Humanitarian Law' (1975) 14 *Military Law and the Law of War Review* 297, 298.

groups within a State'.[25] In order to deny the applicability of international humanitarian law, states sometimes contest the very existence of an armed conflict. This has been the approach, for example, of the Russian government in respect of the situation in Chechnya (1999–2009). Events may be characterized as internal tensions or disturbances ('troubles' or 'riots'), or the non-state armed group may be portrayed by the government as criminals or terrorists (as was the case with the armed groups of the National Transitional Council (NTC) of Libya (2011) and the Free Syrian Army (2012–)).

One of the key difficulties in this area is that no single, authoritative body is mandated to determine issues such as the existence of an armed conflict, the characterization of that conflict as international or non-international, or whether territory can be described as occupied. These questions, and others, are left to the individual state and the armed group for their own determinations; yet such determinations will hardly be undertaken in a neutral manner. The views of third states and UN bodies may be influential, though, ultimately, they will not be determinative in the application of international humanitarian law by the parties. The pronouncements of international courts and tribunals may be authoritative but they are likely to be handed down some years after the conflict in question—for example, the International Criminal Tribunals for the former Yugoslavia and for Rwanda.

A further problem with the applicability of international humanitarian law to armed conflicts is that additional pre-requisites have to be satisfied before certain rules become applicable. For example, for the provisions of Additional Protocol II to apply as a matter of treaty law, the armed conflict must take place:

> [I]n the territory of a High Contracting Party between its armed forces and dissident armed forces or other organized armed groups which, under responsible command, exercise such control over a part of its territory as to enable them to carry out sustained and concerted military operations and to implement this Protocol.[26]

The requirement of such territorial control on the part of the armed group as to enable it to implement the Protocol may constitute a threshold that is difficult for some groups to surmount. As such, the treaty rules of Additional Protocol II will not always be applicable, such as in the early stages of the conflict in Syria (2012). The Protocol also requires the armed conflict to be waged between armed forces of the state and dissident armed forces, or armed forces of the state and an armed group. Thus, a non-international armed conflict fought between two or more armed groups without the involvement of the state—such as the armed conflict in Somalia in the 1990s, which, at the time, did not have a central government—would not benefit from the protections afforded by the Protocol.

Given the uncertainty surrounding the existence of an armed conflict and the denial of the applicability of international humanitarian law, there is a very real need for a body of international law to be applicable at all times. International human rights law, thus, has an important role to play. It is true that a state may derogate from certain provisions of international human rights law, but a detailed regime governs the derogation process.[27] The difference in starting point between international human rights law and international humanitarian law reveals the potential importance of the former. The default presumption for international human rights law is that it applies, and for international humanitarian law that it does not. International humanitarian law does not apply until the existence of

---

[25] *Prosecutor v Tadić*, Decision on the Defence Motion for Interlocutory Appeal on Jurisdiction, IT-94-1-AR72, 2 October 1995, para 70.

[26] Additional Protocol II, Art 1(1).   [27] See Chapter 5.

an armed conflict is established. International human rights law does apply until the state derogates from it and continues to apply subject to the limited extent of the derogation.

Even with the applicability of international human rights law, there has been some concern over a potential lacuna in the international legal regulation of internal tensions and disturbances. International humanitarian law would not be applicable to such a situation given that the violence falls short of an armed conflict. Many provisions of international human rights law would not be applicable were the state to consider the tensions a grave public emergency and derogate from certain of its obligations. In light of such a potential lacuna, a group of experts has drafted a 'Declaration of Minimum Humanitarian Standards' outlining the fundamental standards of humanity applicable regardless of the situation,[28] but this has not garnered the full support of states.

4.2 DUTY TO INVESTIGATE

Although a duty to investigate the loss of life does not appear in the text of the principal human rights treaties, it has been read into certain provisions of human rights law. The European Court of Human Rights, for example, has held that the obligation to protect the right to life, coupled with a state's general duty to secure Convention rights pursuant to Article 1 of the European Convention on Human Rights (ECHR) implies that 'there should be some form of effective official investigation when individuals have been killed as a result of the use of force'.[29] Other bodies have taken a similar position.[30] The investigation is required to be prompt, thorough, and effective and should be undertaken by an independent and impartial body.[31] An investigation seeks to avoid the creation of a climate of impunity, which so often provides the setting for further violations. The obligation to investigate does not cease just because the loss of life occurred during a military operation: 'neither the prevalence of violent armed clashes nor the high incidence of fatalities can displace the obligation'.[32]

The general obligation to investigate the loss of life does not, as yet, form part of the corpus of international humanitarian law. In certain specified situations—such as in the case of deaths of prisoners of war,[33] and in response to allegations of war crimes[34]—a duty to investigate exists, but no general duty to investigate the loss of life can be identified. This is because of the different contexts in which the requirement to investigate operates. In peacetime, it is exceptional for an individual to be killed at the hands of the state; whereas in time of conflict, it is unexceptional, indeed it is in the nature of the conflict. Nonetheless, there are cogent reasons as to why international humanitarian law *should* contain a more general duty to investigate and, of late, there is some authority for the existence of such a duty. Notably, the Israeli Supreme Court has said that a 'thorough investigation' is to be performed in the event that a civilian suspected of taking an active part in hostilities is attacked.[35] It would seem, then, that international humanitarian law

---

[28] Report of the Secretary-General prepared pursuant to Commission Resolution 1995/29, E/CN.4/1996/80 (28 November 1995), Annex.   [29] *Isayeva v Russia* (2005) 41 EHRR 38, para 209.

[30] *Myrna Mack Chang v Guatemala*, IACtHR Series C No 101 (25 November 2003) para 157; 74/92, *Commission Nationale des Droits de l'Homme et des Libertés v Chad*, 9th Activity Report of the ACommHPR (1995) para 22.

[31] Eg HRC, General Comment 31, HRI/GEN/I/Rev.9 (Vol I) 243, para 15; *Isayeva*, n29, paras 209–14.

[32] *Kaya v Turkey* (1999) 28 EHRR 1, paras 87 and 91.

[33] Geneva Convention Relative to the Treatment of Prisoners of War of August 12, 1949 (Third Geneva Convention), Art 121.   [34] CIHL, Rule 158.

[35] *The Public Committee Against Torture in Israel v The Government of Israel*, HCJ 769/02 (2006) para 40.

is moving in this direction but that it is not there just yet. Until such time, international human rights law fills the gap, but must do so in a manner that appreciates the different contexts of armed conflict and peace.[36]

4.3 ENFORCEMENT

One of the principal means of enforcing international humanitarian law is the prosecution of individual offenders for breach of that law.[37] Prosecution may take place at the domestic level and, particularly with the advent of the permanent International Criminal Court, at the international level. Prosecution is not a remedy for all the world's ills: the International Criminal Court is of limited jurisdiction while domestic prosecutions are few and far between.

In addition to prosecutions, there are various non-judicial means by which to enforce international humanitarian law. The International Humanitarian Fact-Finding Commission is competent to inquire into any factual allegations of serious violations of the Geneva Conventions or Additional Protocols; however, in practice, it has never been used.[38] The ICRC is the pre-eminent organization working in the field of international humanitarian law and seeks to protect and assist those affected by armed conflict.[39] The ICRC operates on the basis of confidentiality, which allows it to gain access to situations when such access is denied to other organizations, but this also usually prevents it from publicizing violations. Belligerent reprisals—by which a serious violation of international humanitarian law by state A can be met with retaliatory action on the part of state B, subject to certain conditions, which would otherwise have constituted a breach of international humanitarian law—may be carried out so as to induce compliance with the rules on the part of state A. However, such retaliatory action could result in the loss of life or cause injury or suffering to persons not involved in the conflict and so the legality of belligerent reprisals in the form of attacks on civilians has been questioned.[40]

There are many more enforcement mechanisms in the human rights field. Individuals may institute proceedings before a regional human rights court, a regional human rights commission, or a human rights treaty body mandated to hear their complaint. One state may file a complaint against another state before an empowered institution. Human rights treaty bodies scrutinize reports submitted by states parties to the principal human rights treaties on the measures they have taken to give effect to the treaty rights. The Human Rights Council reviews the human rights record of all member states of the UN every four years. Special Rapporteurs or Independent Experts of the Human Rights Council conduct fact-finding missions, prepare reports, and respond to individual complaints.[41] Numerous national and international NGOs monitor human rights violations and 'name and shame'

---

[36] See *The Public Commission to Examine the Maritime Incident of 31 May 2010, The Turkel Commission, Second Report, Israel's Mechanisms for Examining and Investigating Complaints and Claims of Violations of the Laws of Armed Conflict According to International Law* (February 2013) 118–46.   [37] See Chapter 24.

[38] Additional Protocol I, Art 90; Report of the International Fact-Finding Commission 1991–6. See: <http://www.ihffc.org>.

[39] See: <http://www.icrc.org>.

[40] For the view that customary international law prohibits such reprisals, see *Prosecutor v Kupreškić et al.*, Judgment, IT-95-16-T, 14 January 2000, paras 527–36. However, this position seems to have been rejected, implicitly, in *Prosecutor v Martić*, Judgment, IT-95-11-A, 8 October 2008, paras 263–7. Treaty law applicable to international armed conflicts does contain this proscription (Additional Protocol I, Art 51(6)) but a number of states have entered reservations to it.   [41] See Chapter 18.

governments. The applicability of human rights law to situations of armed conflict is useful, then, for its enforcement mechanisms.

If human rights law is being applied with the primary aim of using its enforcement mechanisms, an alternative approach would be to bypass the applicable law and use the enforcement mechanisms to monitor not just human rights law but also humanitarian law. For a time, the Inter-American Commission on Human Rights did just this, applying international humanitarian law directly to several matters before it. In the *Abella* case, for example, the Inter-American Commission characterized violence at the *La Tablada* military base in Argentina as an armed conflict and proceeded to assess the events against the standards of international humanitarian law.[42] However, such an approach raises issues of lack of expertise and overstepping of mandates. For the latter reason, the Inter-American Court of Human Rights held that neither it nor the Commission had the competence to apply directly international humanitarian law.[43] Rather, it could use international humanitarian law in its interpretation of the American Convention on Human Rights.[44] Despite some criticism on the part of certain states, UN entities—the Special Rapporteur on extrajudicial, summary or arbitrary executions and the Working Group on Arbitrary Detention, to name but two—continue to apply and enforce international humanitarian law.[45] The mandate of many of these entities, not being limited to international human rights law, makes that decision sensible.[46]

5 THE RELATIONSHIP BETWEEN THE TWO BODIES OF LAW

That international human rights law applies in armed conflict is, today, beyond question. This is clear from the human rights treaties themselves. The ICCPR, for example, provides that a state party to the ICCPR may derogate from certain of its obligations '[i]n time of public emergency which threatens the life of the nation', a phrase that includes armed conflict.[47] Other, non-derogable, obligations continue to bind the state: armed conflict does not give a free pass to torture, enslave, and the like. A number of human rights treaties— the African Charter on Human and Peoples' Rights for one—do not contain derogation clauses. In respect of these treaties, no derogation is permitted; the whole host of obligations remain applicable.[48] As the International Court of Justice (ICJ) put it:

> [T]he protection offered by human rights conventions does not cease in case of armed conflict, save through the effect of provisions for derogation of the kind to be found in Article 4 of the International Covenant on Civil and Political Rights.[49]

---

[42] Case 11.137, *Abella v Argentina*, IACommHR Report No 55/97 (18 November 1997), paras 156, 176–89.

[43] *Las Palmeras v Colombia*, IACtHR Series C No 67 (4 February 2000) paras 32–4.

[44] *Bámaca-Velásquez v Guatemala*, IACtHR Series C No 70 (25 November 2000) para 209.

[45] Eg Report of the Special Rapporteur on extrajudicial, summary or arbitrary executions, E/CN.4/2005/7 (22 December 2004) paras 41–54; Report of the Working Group on Arbitrary Detention, E/CN.4/2003/8 (16 December 2002) paras 61–4.

[46] For a defence of the competence of UN human rights bodies over international humanitarian law, see Alston, Morgan-Foster, and Abresch, 'The Competence of the UN Human Rights Council and its Special Procedures in relation to Armed Conflicts: Extrajudicial Executions in the "War on Terror" ' (2008) 19 *EJIL* 183.

[47] ICCPR, Art 4; ECHR, Art 15; and ACHR, Art 27 specifically mention 'war'.

[48] *Commission Nationale des Droits de l'Homme et des Libertés*, n 30, para 21.

[49] *Legal Consequences of the Construction of a Wall in the Occupied Palestinian Territory* (Advisory Opinion) [2004] ICJ Rep 136, para 106. This was reiterated by the Court a few years later, in *Armed Activities on the Territory of the Congo* (*Democratic Republic of the Congo v Uganda*) [2005] ICJ Rep 168, para 216.

The applicability of international human rights law to situations of armed conflict is also acknowledged by international humanitarian law treaties. The rules in Additional Protocol I relating to the treatment of persons in the power of a party to the conflict, for example, are described as being additional to 'other applicable rules of international law relating to the protection of fundamental human rights during international armed conflict'.[50] In the context of non-international armed conflict, the preamble to Additional Protocol II recalls that 'international instruments relating to human rights offer a basic protection to the human person'.[51] Accordingly, influential international law and human rights bodies such as the ICJ, the International Law Commission, and the Human Rights Committee have confirmed that international human rights law continues to apply in time of armed conflict.[52]

Far more difficult—and still unsettled—is the precise relationship between international human rights law and international humanitarian law. The most authoritative, though ultimately inconclusive, statement on point is the pronouncement of the ICJ in its *Wall* advisory opinion. In that case, the ICJ was asked by the General Assembly to pronounce on the 'legal consequences arising from the construction of the wall being built by Israel, the occupying Power, in the Occupied Palestinian Territory... considering the rules and principles of international law'.[53] The rules and principles of international law in question included international human rights law and international humanitarian law. Accordingly, the ICJ had to consider the relationship between them. On this, the ICJ opined that:

> As regards the relationship between international humanitarian and human rights law, there are... three possible situations: some rights may be exclusively matters of international humanitarian law; others may be exclusively matters of human rights law; yet others may be matters of both these branches of international law.[54]

It is worth exploring this statement in more detail.[55]

5.1 RIGHTS EXCLUSIVELY MATTERS OF INTERNATIONAL HUMANITARIAN LAW

It is only natural that international humanitarian law, that body of law particularly designed to regulate hostilities, contains rights that are not to be found in international human rights law. Take, for example, occupied territory. International humanitarian law contains a detailed body of rules relating to the law of belligerent occupation. The law of belligerent occupation strikes a delicate balance between the rights of the occupied, the occupying power, and the displaced sovereign. The rules relating to the requisitioning of property are a case in point. As regards 'public buildings, real estate, forests, and agricultural estates belonging to the hostile State, and situated in the occupied country', the occupying power is the usufruct, being able to use and enjoy but not damage or alter them. The occupying power can take into its possession certain property belonging to the sovereign 'which may be used for military operations' but requisitions from the general

---

[50] Additional Protocol I, Art 72.   [51] Additional Protocol II, preamble.
[52] *Legality of the Threat or Use of Nuclear Weapons* (Advisory Opinion) [1996] ICJ Rep 226, para 25; Fragmentation of International Law: Difficulties arising from the Diversification and Expansion of International Law, Report of the Study Group of the International Law Commission, A/CN.4/L.682 (4 April 2006) para 104; General Comment 31, n 31, para 11.   [53] *Wall*, n 49, para 1.
[54] *Wall*, n 49, para 106. This, too, was reiterated in *DRC v Uganda*, n 49, para 216.
[55] See Dinstein, 'Human Rights in Armed Conflict: International Humanitarian Law' in Meron (ed), *Human Rights in International Law* (Clarendon Press, 1985) 345.

population are prohibited 'except for the needs of the army of occupation'.[56] These rules reflect the competing interests of the different actors—the occupied, the occupying power, and the displaced sovereign. This tripartite relationship does not map neatly onto classical international human rights law, which regulates the relationship between the state and the individual. Accordingly, many of the features of the law of occupation are not replicated in international human rights law.

5.2 RIGHTS EXCLUSIVELY MATTERS OF INTERNATIONAL HUMAN RIGHTS LAW

Equally, there are rights grounded in international human rights law that are nowhere to be found in international humanitarian law. The right not to be imprisoned on the ground of inability to fulfil a contractual obligation and the right to recognition as a person before the law are rights featured in the ICCPR from which there may be no derogation.[57] International humanitarian law contains no equivalent provisions. The American Convention on Human Rights lists as non-derogable the rights of the family and the right to a name.[58] Again, there are no equivalent rules in international humanitarian law.

5.3 RIGHTS MATTERS OF BOTH INTERNATIONAL HUMAN RIGHTS LAW AND INTERNATIONAL HUMANITARIAN LAW

In the majority of situations, a particular right will be grounded in both international human rights law and international humanitarian law. In such instances, the principle of *lex specialis* governs, such that the more specific rule will take precedence over the more general.[59] There are two variants of the *lex specialis* principle. The first applies in the event of a conflict between two norms. In this situation, the specific rule *modifies* the general rule to the extent of the inconsistency between them. The general rule does not fall away. It remains in the background and applicable to the extent that it does not conflict with the specific rule. The second variant applies when one norm is of greater specificity than the other norm, or is more tailored to the particular circumstances at hand, but there is no inconsistency between them. Here, the more specific rule is but an *application* of the more general rule. Although it may be useful to distinguish between these variants, a firm distinction between modification and application is difficult to draw and somewhat artificial.

5.3.1 *Lex specialis* as modification

The first variant of the *lex specialis* principle is the modification of the general rule by the specific rule to the extent of any inconsistency between them. Recall our example of the right to life in international human rights law. The ICCPR protects against the arbitrary deprivation of life. This begs the question of when a deprivation of life is considered arbitrary. Does the use of nuclear weapons in armed conflict, for example, constitute an arbitrary deprivation of life? The ICJ has considered this issue:

> In principle, the right not arbitrarily to be deprived of one's life applies also in hostilities. The test of what is an arbitrary deprivation of life, however, then falls to be determined by

---

[56] Regulations respecting the Laws and Customs of War on Land, annexed to Convention (IV) respecting the Laws and Customs of War on Land, The Hague, 1907, Arts 55, 53, and 52 respectively.

[57] ICCPR, Arts 11 and 16.   [58] ACHR, Arts 17 and 18.

[59] See Fragmentation of International Law, n 52, paras 56–122.

the applicable *lex specialis*, namely, the law applicable in armed conflict which is designed to regulate the conduct of hostilities. Thus, whether a particular loss of life, through the use of a certain weapon in warfare, is to be considered an arbitrary deprivation of life contrary to Article 6 of the Covenant [ICCPR], can only be decided by reference to the law applicable in armed conflict and not deduced from the terms of the Covenant itself.[60]

In this instance, the relevant rules of international humanitarian law constituted the *leges specialis* and so trumped, to the extent of the inconsistency, the equivalent rule found in international human rights law. Although this will be the usual case, it is important to note that this passage cannot be read as holding, as is sometimes thought, that the *body* of international humanitarian law always constitutes the *lex specialis*. The Court was considering one particular right—the right to life—and one particular aspect of that right—its compatibility with the use of nuclear weapons.[61] It does not follow that the entire body of international human rights law is the *lex generalis* and the full corpus of international humanitarian law the *lex specialis*. Generalizations cannot be made at the level of the overarching body; it comes down to an analysis of the individual rule. Competing rules have to be identified and the specificity between them ascertained. Should the relevant rule of international human rights law—or, for that matter, any other applicable body of law, such as international environmental law—contain the more specific rule, it would modify the general rule of international humanitarian law to the extent of the inconsistency between them. The conflict set out here is readily resolvable because of the word 'arbitrary'. Sometimes, however, it is more difficult to resolve conflicts of norms.

Consider the example of internment. International humanitarian law allows for internment in certain situations.[62] For its part, the ECHR provides for the right to liberty and security of the person, subject to certain listed exceptions, of which internment is not one.[63] A conflict, thus, exists between these two norms. It may be thought that, as the rules of international humanitarian law were tailored to meet the specificities of the armed conflict situation, with the extra security concerns that exist during such times, the international humanitarian law rules constitute the *leges speciales*.[64] However, the European Court of Human Rights in *Al-Jedda* took a different view, holding that international humanitarian law contains a power to intern rather than an obligation to do so. This needs to be compared with the ECHR, which contains an obligation to respect the liberty of the person. Accordingly, a state can respect both rules by not interning and, therefore, a conflict of norms does not exist. Were this to prohibit internment in situations in which the ECHR is applicable, it would be a cause for concern as being unrealistic. However, the ECHR leaves open the possibility for internment when it refers to internment as 'a matter of last resort'.[65]

5.3.2 *Lex specialis* as application

The second variation of the *lex specialis* principle is the application of the more specific rule as a detailed or tailored version of the general rule. Here, there is no conflict between

---

[60] *Nuclear Weapons*, n 52, para 25.

[61] In the *Wall* advisory opinion, n 49, the Court did refer to taking into consideration international humanitarian law 'as *lex specialis*' (para 106). However, when the Court reproduced the passage in *DRC v Uganda*, n 49, the relevant sentence was omitted (para 216).

[62] Geneva Convention relative to the Protection of Civilian Persons in Time of War of August 12, 1949, Arts 41–3; Third Geneva Convention, Art 21.   [63] ECHR, Art 5(1).

[64] Another approach is that the norm conflict is unresolvable: Milanovic, 'A Norm Conflict Perspective on the Relationship between International Humanitarian Law and Human Rights Law' (2010) 14 *JCSL* 459, 474–6.

[65] *Al-Jedda v the United Kingdom* (2011) 53 EHRR 23, para 107.

the two rules. Rather, one provision is the more detailed version of the other or the more appropriate in the circumstances.

Consider the right to a fair trial in the context of non-international armed conflict. The ICCPR provides for a lengthy list of fair trial guarantees.[66] For its part, Article 3, common to the four Geneva Conventions, requires the provision of 'judicial guarantees which are recognized as indispensable by civilized peoples'. No list of the required guarantees is provided. Additional Protocol II does contain such a list but that list is not self-contained. Rather, it refers to 'all necessary rights and means of defence'.[67] In order to interpret that clause, it is necessary to turn to the relevant rules of international human rights law, which form the *leges speciales* on point. The point here is that there is no conflict between the relevant rules of international human rights law and international humanitarian law. One contains a detailed body of regulation; the other, somewhat vague standards. In order to give content to the general rule, we need to apply its more specific counterpart.

Care needs to be taken when importing ideas from one body of law into another, for they may be appropriate in one context but not in another. Some modification may be required in order to render the idea being transferred suitable to the body of law in which it now finds itself. As the International Criminal Tribunal for the former Yugoslavia has had occasion to observe, 'notions developed in the field of human rights can be transposed in international humanitarian law only if they take into consideration the specificities of the latter body of law'.[68]

For example, the use of torture is prohibited in both international human rights law and international humanitarian law. Torture is subject to a detailed definition in international human rights law; in international humanitarian law it is undefined. The international human rights law definition provides that torture is:

> any act by which severe pain or suffering, whether physical or mental, is intentionally inflicted on a person for such purposes as obtaining from him or a third person information or a confession, punishing him for an act he or a third person has committed or is suspected of having committed, or intimidating or coercing him or a third person, or for any reason based on discrimination of any kind, when such pain or suffering is inflicted by or at the instigation of or with the consent or acquiescence of a public official or other person acting in an official capacity. It does not include pain or suffering arising only from, inherent in or incidental to lawful sanctions.[69]

Given that the term 'torture' is undefined in international humanitarian law, at first sight, this ready-made definition looks useful. Closer inspection, however, reveals a problem. The definition requires 'a public official or other person acting in an official capacity'. Armed groups fighting in non-international armed conflicts are generally not going to be considered public officials or persons acting in an official capacity. Does this mean members of armed groups are not covered by the prohibition on torture? Clearly it could not be so. Thus, this particular aspect of the definition has been considered inapplicable for the purposes of the definition of torture under international humanitarian law.[70]

---

[66] ICCPR, Arts 14–15. See Chapter 13.   [67] Additional Protocol II, Art 6(2)(a).
[68] *Prosecutor v Kunarac et al.*, Judgment, IT-96-23-T, 22 February 2001, para 471.
[69] UN Convention against Torture, Art 1(1).   [70] *Kunarac* Trial Judgment, n 68, para 496.

5.4 AN ALTERNATIVE APPROACH: REGULATION THROUGH APPLICATION OF INTERNATIONAL HUMAN RIGHTS LAW

In recent years, an alternative approach has been suggested, that of a human rights-based law of armed conflict. Although primarily a construct of scholars, the European Court of Human Rights has adopted what may be termed a human rights approach to non-international armed conflict, regulating the conduct of hostilities through the application of not humanitarian law but human rights law.[71] The case of *Isayeva v Russia* is the leading case on point. That case concerned an aerial attack on a village just outside Grozny, Chechnya, as rebels were passing through it in retreat from the besieged Grozny. The applicant's son and other family members were killed by a bomb during the attack. In considering whether there was a violation of the right to life, the European Court held that '[a]ny use of force must be no more than "absolutely necessary" for the achievement of one or more of the purposes set out in' the ECHR and 'strictly proportionate to the achievement of the permitted aims'.[72] The European Court, thus, applied rules of human rights law to events arising out a non-international armed conflict even though the relevant humanitarian law on point differs.

In international humanitarian law, civilians shall not be made the object of attacks; but combatants and fighters may be lawfully targeted as may persons taking a direct part in hostilities for such time as they do so. The ECHR, on the other hand, provides for the right to life but goes on to provide that deprivation of life shall not constitute a violation 'when it results from the use of force which is no more than absolutely necessary' in certain specified situations (in defence of a person, lawful arrest or detention, or to quell a riot).[73] This rule applies to combatants, fighters, and civilians alike, such that only force that is 'absolutely necessary' may be directed even against a fighter. The exact consequences of this rule are yet to be seen but the implication is that lethal force may not be used against a fighter in situations in which it is feasible to arrest him.[74] Accordingly, to kill a fighter when it would have been possible to capture him may be a violation of human rights law. This is an important divergence from the position under international humanitarian law and it reflects the different starting points of the two bodies of law: for human rights law it is the right to life; for humanitarian law, the right to kill in certain circumstances.

It should not be assumed from this that human rights law always affords greater protections than international humanitarian law. In certain instances, the reverse is true. For example, expanding bullets are permitted to be used in peace time, but their use is prohibited during armed conflicts.[75]

6 DIFFICULTIES WITH THE APPLICATION OF INTERNATIONAL HUMAN RIGHTS LAW TO ARMED CONFLICT

The application of human rights law to armed conflict gives rise to at least three distinct difficulties.

---

[71] *Isayeva*, n 29. See Abresch, 'A Human Rights Law of Internal Armed Conflict: The European Court of Human Rights in Chechnya' (2005) 16 *EJIL* 741.

[72] *Isayeva*, n 29, para 173.   [73] ECHR, Art 2.

[74] See *de Guerrero v Colombia*, CCPR/C/15/D/45/1979 (31 March 1982), paras 13.2–13.3.

[75] Hague Declaration concerning Expanding Bullets, 1899; CIHL, Rule 77.

6.1 ASYMMETRICAL OBLIGATIONS BETWEEN THE PARTIES

Human rights are traditionally considered to govern the relationship between the state and the individual. The state is the holder of the obligation and the individual the beneficiary of the right. It should be recalled that, in non-international armed conflicts—and the vast majority of conflicts in the world today are of such a character—the conflict is fought between a state and an armed group or between two or more armed groups. Injecting human rights standards into the equation may be, then, to impose additional obligations for one side (the state) but not the other (the non-state armed group). This inequality of obligation does not bode well for compliance: one party to the conflict is unlikely to abide by obligations that are not binding on the other. Once parties start to violate their obligations, there is the danger that, all too quickly, things will spiral out of control.

An alternative approach would be to impose human rights obligations on both parties to the conflict, that is to say, on armed groups as well as states. This has the advantage of parity of obligation, but it represents a shift in the conceptualization of human rights.[76] There is certainly evidence of some movement in this direction,[77] but it is too early to reach a definitive conclusion.

The imposition of human rights obligations on armed groups presupposes that those groups have the capacity to satisfy their obligations. This cannot be taken for granted, with certain human rights standards going beyond the reach of many armed groups. Human rights obligations may have to be limited to a subset of armed groups, such as those in control of a quantum of territory, for example the Revolutionary Armed Forces of Colombia (FARC) who controlled a sizeable tract of land in Colombia, or the Liberation Tigers of Tamil Eelam (LTTE), which had effective control over the north and east of Sri Lanka. However, even this shift is likely to face opposition from certain states, unhappy with the state-like treatment being accorded to armed groups and any legitimacy this may afford them.

6.2 DIFFERENTIAL OBLIGATIONS WITHIN A COALITION

Large-scale international armed conflicts, such as the early years of the recent armed conflicts in Afghanistan and Iraq, often involve coalitions of states. They may also involve regional military alliances, such as the North Atlantic Treaty Organization (NATO) or the Economic Community of West African States Monitoring Group (ECOMOG). In such conflicts, individuals of several states fight alongside one another. Simplicity dictates that they would be bound by the same legal rules. Yet, states—even close allies—are not party to the same human rights treaties. Those that are may have entered reservations to particular provisions or have different understandings of the same rule. In addition, states outside a particular regional grouping would not be party to the regional human rights treaty to which other members of the coalition or organization are bound. These differing obligations pose difficult questions. For example, can troops from state A, which is party to the ECHR, lawfully transfer an individual in their custody to state B, which is not party to the ECHR, if that individual may face the death penalty in state B? This was at issue in the *Al-Saadoon* case before the ECtHR.[78] In that case, Al-Saadoon and Mufdhi, who

---

[76] See Chapter 26.

[77] See *Elmi v Australia*, CAT/C/22/D/120/1998 (14 May 1999); Institut de Droit International, 'The Application of International Humanitarian Law and Fundamental Human Rights in Armed Conflicts in which Non-State Entities are Parties' (Berlin, 1999); Report of the Special Rapporteur on extrajudicial, summary or arbitrary executions, Mission to Sri Lanka, E/CN.4/2006/53/Add.5 (27 March 2006), paras 25–7. See generally, Clapham, *Human Rights Obligations of Non-State Actors* (OUP, 2006), ch 7.

[78] *Al-Saadoon and Mufdhi v UK* (2010) 51 EHRR 9.

were being held by UK troops in Iraq, were transferred to the Iraqi authorities for trial. The transfer was undertaken pursuant to a treaty concluded between the UK and Iraq. However, the ECtHR held that the transfer violated the UK's obligations under the ECHR and Protocol No 13 due to the real risk that the individuals would be sentenced to death. The case is a good example of the difficulties that arise when different parties to a conflict are bound by different conventional obligations.

6.3 SPHERE OF APPLICABILITY: THE EXTRATERRITORIAL APPLICATION OF HUMAN RIGHTS TREATIES

States frequently fight outside their territorial boundaries. They do so as a matter of course in international armed conflicts; they also do so when they intervene on behalf of one side or another in an otherwise non-international armed conflict. The question that this raises is whether, when a state acts outside its own territory, it continues to be bound by its human rights obligations.

Many human rights treaties do not contain a provision delimiting their territorial application. In respect of these treaties, the presumption is that they have extraterritorial effect.[79] Other treaties contain a clause to the effect that a state party is under an obligation 'to respect and to ensure to all individuals within its territory and subject to its jurisdiction the rights recognized' therein.[80] The 'and' is to be read disjunctively such that the obligation arises in respect of those individuals 'within its territory' and, in addition, those individuals 'subject to its jurisdiction'.[81] The question remains as to the meaning of the term 'jurisdiction'. On this, there is varied authority.[82]

The Human Rights Committee has opined that 'a State party must respect and ensure the rights laid down in the [ICCPR] to anyone within the power or effective control of that State Party, even if not situated within the territory of the State Party'.[83] In the *Al-Skeini* case, the ECtHR held that jurisdiction for the purposes of the ECHR is primarily territorial. The Court went on to hold that certain extra-territorial acts of a state may constitute an exercise of its jurisdiction. This includes where state agents operate outside the state's territorial borders and exercise control over individuals, and where a state exercises effective control over an area outside its territory.[84]

The point here is that when a state engages in an armed conflict that takes place abroad, it is not always going to be bound by its human rights obligations. Thus, before we get to the stage of ascertaining the relationship between international human rights law and international humanitarian law, we first have to answer the question of whether international human rights law is even applicable.

7 CONCLUSION

International human rights law applies in time of armed conflict. This much is clear. Although existing alongside international humanitarian law, there is good reason for its application, not least the mechanisms for its enforcement. The exact relationship between

---

[79] *Application of the International Convention on the Elimination of All Forms of Racial Discrimination* (*Georgia v Russian Federation*), Provisional Measures Order [2008] ICJ Rep, para 109.

[80] This is the language of ICCPR, Art 2.   [81] See *Wall*, n 49, para 111; *DRC v Uganda*, n 49, para 216.

[82] See Chapter 6.   [83] General Comment 31, n 31, para 10.

[84] *Al-Skeini and Others v UK* (2011) 53 EHRR 18, paras 130–40.

international human rights law and international humanitarian law is still to be worked out. It is generally accepted that 'some rights may be exclusively matters of international humanitarian law; others may be exclusively matters of human rights law; yet others may be matters of both these branches of international law' but beyond this there is little agreement. Some difficulties with the application of international human rights law to situations of armed conflict remain. Despite this continued uncertainty, cognizance should be taken of the fundamental shift in the issue. The question is no longer *whether* international human rights law applies in time of armed conflict but *how* it applies. This movement from applicability to application is a significant one and is reflective of a more general trend towards what has been described as the 'humanization of international humanitarian law'.[85]

FURTHER READING

ABRESCH, 'A Human Rights Law of Internal Armed Conflict: The European Court of Human Rights in Chechnya' (2005) 16 *EJIL* 741.

BEN-NAFTALI (ed), *International Humanitarian Law and International Human Rights Law* (Oxford University Press, 2011).

DINSTEIN, 'Human Rights in Armed Conflict: International Humanitarian Law' in Meron (ed), *Human Rights in International Law:* (Clarendon Press, 1985).

DOSWALD-BECK and VITÉ, 'International Humanitarian Law and Human Rights Law' (1993) 293 *IRRC* 94.

DROEGE, The Interplay between International Humanitarian Law and International Human Rights Law in Situations of Armed Conflict' (2007) 40 *Israel LR* 310.

FLECK (ed), *The Handbook of International Humanitarian Law* (Oxford University Press, 2008).

KRIEGER, 'A Conflict of Norms: The Relationship between Humanitarian Law and Human Rights Law in the ICRC Customary Study' (2006) 11 *JCSL* 265.

LUBELL, 'Challenges in Applying Human Rights Law to Armed Conflict' (2005) 87 *IRRC* 737.

MERON, 'The Humanization of Humanitarian Law' (2000) 90 *AJIL* 239.

MILANOVIC, 'A Norm Conflict Perspective on the Relationship between International Humanitarian Law and Human Rights Law' (2010) 14 *JSCL* 459.

PROVOST, *International Human Rights and Humanitarian Law* (Cambridge University Press, 2002).

SIVAKUMARAN, *The Law of Non-International Armed Conflict* (Oxford University Press, 2010) ch 3.

USEFUL WEBSITES

Crimes of War: <http://www.crimesofwar.org>

International Committee of the Red Cross: <http://www.icrc.org>

International Humanitarian Fact-Finding Commission: <http://www.ihffc.org>

---

[85] See Meron, 'The Humanization of Humanitarian Law' (2000) 94 *AJIL* 239.

24

INTERNATIONAL CRIMINAL LAW

Robert Cryer

SUMMARY

There are many links between human rights and international criminal law, and many human rights lawyers and activists are conversant with international criminal law. This chapter seeks to introduce the ideas behind international criminal law, the crimes themselves, and the interplay of those crimes with human rights law. It then looks to the main examples of prosecutions of international crimes and the non-prosecutorial options that have been adopted. It concludes with an analysis of the pros and cons of using international criminal law to protect human rights.

1 INTRODUCTION

International criminal law[1] has a great deal in common with international human rights law. Both are, at least in part, of post-Second World War vintage, as they were part of the response to, and attempted safeguard against, depredations of the type that characterized the Nazi era. Also both, unlike the bulk of international law, attempt to deal more or less directly with individuals. Broadly speaking, if international human rights law deals with the rights that are granted to individuals, international criminal law deals with their duties.[2]

The underlying idea of the parts of international criminal law that are of relevance to human rights is that certain conduct is seen as so unacceptable that it is not simply a matter of domestic jurisdiction, but something of concern to all. However, the level of consensus on this differs amongst the various forms of conduct that are of interest to international criminal law, and as such, two different tracks have developed within international criminal law.

The first is direct international criminalization (international crimes in the narrow sense). These are crimes that are directly created by international law and are covered by the famous pronouncement of the Nuremberg International Military Tribunal (IMT) that:

> Individuals have international duties which transcend the national obligations of obedience imposed by the individual State... [C]rimes against international law are committed

---

[1] The term itself is a controversial one, with various different meanings. Here it will be used primarily to cover those crimes directly criminalized by international law. See Cryer, Friman, Robinson, and Wilmshurst, *An Introduction to International Criminal Law and Procedure* (CUP, 2010) ch 1.

[2] For a classic discussion of this see Lauterpacht, 'The Subjects of the Law of Nations Part I' (1947) 63 *LQR* 439; Lauterpacht, 'The Subjects of the Law of Nations Part II' (1948) 64 *LQR* 97.

by men, not by abstract entities, and only by punishing individuals who commit such crimes can the provisions of international law be enforced.[3]

Such international crimes may be prosecuted by international courts without reference to domestic law and, with the possible exception of the crime of aggression, by any state in the world on the basis of universal jurisdiction, as a matter of international law.[4] Only four crimes can currently claim this status: genocide, crimes against humanity, war crimes, and aggression. It is possible that individual acts of torture or terrorism that do not otherwise fall under the definition of one of these four crimes may be added to this list; some commentators are of the view that they are already directly criminalized by international law,[5] a view that has been adopted about terrorism by one 'internationalised' court.[6] However, there is no agreement yet that they are, and the better view is that they are not.

The second way of involving international law in criminalization occurs when so-called 'transnational crimes' are created. Such crimes involve treaty-based regimes that require states to create crimes within their domestic legal order and often require states either to prosecute those who are found on their territory and who are suspected of such offences, or to extradite them to a state willing to prosecute them (a duty often called, if a little inaccurately, *aut dedere aut judicare*). Here, therefore, the obligation is on states rather than on individuals directly.

There are a large number of treaties of this sort, which require states domestically to criminalize conduct. To the extent to which the conduct described in those treaties overlaps with human rights norms, they can be seen as part of human rights protection. The UN Convention against Torture and the UN Convention against Enforced Disappearance are two examples of such treaties. Not all transnational crimes are relevant to human rights. The law relating, for example, to cutting undersea cables contained in the Convention for the Protection of Submarine Cables does not have any direct human rights implications. These treaties, whether relevant to human rights or not, do not create crimes in and of themselves. The *locus* of the criminal liability for the individual is the domestic, rather than the international, legal order.[7] They will not be covered in depth here.

2 HUMAN RIGHTS LAW AND INTERNATIONAL CRIMES

The overlaps between human rights and international criminal law occur both in their substantive norms and underlying philosophies.[8] There are some questions regarding whether

---

[3] Nuremberg IMT, 'Judgment and Sentence' (1947) 41 *AJIL* 172, 221, 223.

[4] See Cryer, Friman, Robinson, and Wilmshurst, n 1, ch 3.

[5] Cassese *et al.*, *Cassese's International Criminal Law* (OUP, 2013) chs 7–8.

[6] Special Tribunal for Lebanon, Interlocutory Decision on the Applicable Law: Terrorism, Conspiracy, Homicide, Perpetration, Cumulative Charging, STL-11-01-17 *bis*, 16 February 2011. See Saul, 'Legislating from a Radical Hague: The United Nations Special Tribunal for Lebanon Invents an International Crime of Transnational Terrorism' (2011) 24 *LJIL* 677.

[7] Although the International Convention for the Protection of All Persons from Enforced Disappearance, Art 5, accepts that such conduct may amount to an international crime in the relevant context.

[8] Gasser, 'The Changing Relationship Between International Criminal Law, Human Rights Law and Humanitarian Law', in Doria *et al.* (eds), *The Legal Regime of the International Criminal Court: Essays in Honour of Professor Igor Blischenko* (Kluwer, 2009) 1111; Teitel, *Humanity's Law* (OUP, 2011).

human rights and international criminal law are as coherent as many say. Robinson, for example, notes that:

> Many of the prohibitions of ICL [international criminal law] are drawn from, and similar to, prohibitions in human rights and humanitarian law. Faced with familiar-looking provisions, ICL practitioners often assume that the ICL norms are coextensive with their human rights or humanitarian law counterparts, and uncritically transplant concepts and jurisprudence from other domains to flesh out their content. Such assumptions overlook the fact that these bodies of law have different purposes and consequences and thus entail different philosophical commitments.[9]

It is true that human rights law and international criminal law are not identical, but nor are they utterly separate, and international criminal tribunals have relied on human rights jurisprudence quite heavily, particularly in their early phases.[10] Human rights courts have also drawn upon the work of international criminal tribunals,[11] and, to varying extents, taken on a supervisory role in relation to national prosecutions of international crimes.[12] A useful inter-judicial dialogue can serve to improve both areas of law where human rights lawyers and international criminal lawyers are mindful of the context in which the bodies of law apply.

As stated in Section 1, there are four international crimes in the sense used here: genocide, crimes against humanity, war crimes, and aggression. This section will attempt to explain the overlaps between the substantive crimes and human rights law.

2.1 GENOCIDE

Genocide was created as a separate international crime in the 1940s. The term was coined by Raphaël Lemkin in his *Axis Rule in Occupied Europe*.[13] Although the term was mentioned in the indictment at Nuremberg, it was not prosecuted separately there. In 1946, however, the UN General Assembly, in Resolution 96(I) stated that:

> Genocide is a denial of the right of existence of entire human groups,...such denial of the right of existence shocks the conscience of mankind, results in great losses to humanity in the form of cultural and other contributions represented by these human groups, and is contrary to moral law and to the spirit and aims of the United Nations.... The General Assembly, therefore...affirms that genocide is a crime under international law.

Genocide 'is a crime simultaneously directed against individual victims, the group to which they belong, and human diversity'.[14] The drafting of the Convention on the Prevention and Punishment of the Crime of Genocide (Genocide Convention) was completed in 1948. Article I Genocide Convention confirms that 'genocide...is a crime under international law.' As early as 1951, the year the Convention came into force, the International Court of Justice (ICJ) stated that 'the principles underlying the Convention are principles which are recognized by civilized nations as binding on States, even without any conventional obligation'.[15] The ICJ has more recently declared that the prohibition of genocide is 'assuredly'

---

[9] Robinson, 'The Identity Crisis of International Criminal Law' (2008) 21 *LJIL* 925, 946.

[10] See Cryer, 'The Interplay of International Human Rights and International Humanitarian Law: The Approach of the ICTY' (2009) 14 *JCSL* 511; Symposium, 'The Influence of the European Court of Human Rights on International Criminal Law' (2011) 9 *JICJ* 571.   [11] *Jorgić v Germany* (2008) 47 EHRR 6.

[12] Huneeus, 'International Criminal Law by Other Means: The Quasi-Criminal Jurisdiction of the Human Rights Courts' (2013) 107 *AJIL* 1.

[13] (Carnegie Endowment, 1944).   [14] Cryer, Friman, Robinson, and Wilmshurst, n 1, 203.

[15] *Reservations to the Convention on the Prevention and Punishment of the Crime of Genocide* (Advisory Opinion) [1951] ICJ Rep 15, 23.

an example of a norm having reached *jus cogens* status.[16] The term has considerable political weight, and its application to particular circumstances is legally and politically contentious.[17]

2.1.1 Definition

Article II Genocide Convention contains the classic definition of genocide, which is:

[A]ny of the following acts committed with intent to destroy, in whole or in part, a national, ethnical, racial or religious group, as such:

(a) Killing members of the group;

(b) Causing serious bodily or mental harm to members of the group;

(c) Deliberately inflicting on the group conditions of life calculated to bring about its physical destruction in whole or in part;

(d) Imposing measures intended to prevent births within the group;

(e) Forcibly transferring children of the group to another group.

This definition was repeated in the Statutes of the International Criminal Tribunal for the former Yugoslavia (ICTY) and the International Criminal Tribunal for Rwanda (ICTR),[18] and, despite some attempts to 'fix' the definition during the drafting of the Statute of the International Criminal Court (ICC), is essentially repeated in Article 6 of that Statute.[19] Like all crimes, genocide is made up of an external element (the conduct element) and an internal element (the mental element).

2.1.2 External element

There is a common theme between all the underlying acts of genocide except, perhaps, the forcible transfer of children. This is that the acts are related to physical, not cultural, destruction of the group. When the Genocide Convention was being drafted, there were those who suggested that 'cultural genocide' should be included. This was rejected though. There have been some attempts to revive this notion. However, they were not accepted by the ICTY[20] and the ICJ agreed with that Tribunal in the *Bosnian Genocide* case.[21]

The physical acts of genocide have clear overlaps with human rights law. Killing and inflicting serious bodily or mental harm (which can include sexual offences)[22] and deliberately inflicting conditions of life calculated to bring about a group's physical destruction raise fairly clear human rights issues. These types of acts can amount to a violation of civil and political rights. In certain circumstances, they can, particularly inflicting conditions of life calculated to bring about the destruction of a group, also amount to a violation of economic, social, and cultural rights, such as the right to health and the right to food.[23]

---

[16] *Case Concerning Armed Activities on the Territory of the Congo* (New Application: 2002) (*DRC v Rwanda*) [2006] ICJ Rep 6, para 64.

[17] Luban, 'Calling Genocide by Its Rightful Name: Lemkin's Word, Darfur, and the UN Report' (2006–7) 7 *Chicago JIL* 303.   [18] ICTY Statute, Art 4; ICTR Statute, Art 2.

[19] See von Hebel and Robinson, 'Crimes Within the Jurisdiction of the Court' in Lee (ed), *The International Criminal Court: The Making of the Rome Statute, Issues, Negotiations, Results* (Kluwer, 1999) 79, 89.

[20] *Prosecutor v Krstić*, Judgment, IT-98-33-T, 2 August 2001, para 580 and (on appeal) Judgment, IT-98-33-A, 19 April 2004, para 25.

[21] *Case Concerning Application of the Convention on the Prevention and Punishment of the Crime of Genocide* (*Bosnia and Herzegovina v Serbia and Montenegro*) [2007] ICJ Rep 43, para 344.

[22] Eg *Prosecutor v Akayesu*, Judgment, IT-96-4-T, 2 September 1998, para 731.

[23] The Elements of Crimes for the ICC state that such conduct 'may include, but is not necessarily restricted to, deliberate deprivation of resources indispensable for survival, such as food or medical services, or systematic expulsion from homes'.

Imposing measures intended to prevent births within the group would certainly implicate issues of private, home, and family life, as well as likely being inhuman and degrading. The same is true of the transfer of children.

2.1.3 Protected groups

The Genocide Convention expressly limits itself to protecting 'national, ethnical, racial and religious' groups. In General Assembly Resolution 96(I), other groups, such as political and social groups, were included. However, they were not included in the Convention. Some argue that the definition of genocide should be expanded to cover political killings. There are understandable reasons for this.[24] However, crimes against humanity do cover political killings, and it is questionable whether or not political groups are equivalent to the national, ethnic, racial, and religious groups to which they are sometimes equated, as there is a permanence and immutability about those groups that does not apply to political groups.[25]

Determining the existence and membership of groups is not as simple as the Genocide Convention might imply. This has caused interpretative problems, for example whether the terms 'national, ethnical, racial or religious' are to be interpreted separately or together. The ICTR, in its first major case, *Akayesu*, tried to define each of the terms separately. This led to problems. On such an interpretation it was difficult to see the Hutus and Tutsis as different groups, yet they clearly saw themselves as being so.[26] More recently, and more authoritatively, the ICTY, after a detailed review of the relevant materials held that:

> The preparatory work of the Convention shows that setting out such a list was designed more to describe a single phenomenon, roughly corresponding to what was recognised, before the second world war, as 'national minorities', rather than to refer to several distinct prototypes of human groups. To attempt to differentiate each of the named groups on the basis of scientifically objective criteria would thus be inconsistent with the object and purpose of the Convention.[27]

This is the preferable approach given the difficulty of determining groups precisely.[28] The question of perceived difference (as, for example, in the 'Arab'/'African' divide in Darfur) has led to the adoption of a test that relies on the reality of the distinction in the eyes of the relevant population. If such a group is considered to exist in the relevant cultural context, then the perception of the perpetrator that the victim is a member of that group suffices for them to be considered a member for the purposes of genocide.[29]

2.1.4 The context of genocide

Some take the view that genocide, of its essence, requires a plan or policy.[30] The ICTY has taken the view that there could, in theory, be a 'lone *génocidaire*' acting outside any plan;[31]

---

[24] Van Schaack, 'The Crime of Political Genocide: Repairing the Genocide Convention's Blind Spot' (1997) 106 *Yale LJ* 2259; Nersessian, *Genocide and Political Groups* (OUP, 2010).

[25] There was an attempt to read the convention as protecting all 'stable and permanent groups' in the *Akayesu* case, but this was a clear misreading of the Convention and its *travaux préparatoires*. See Cryer, Friman, Robinson, and Wilmshurst, n 1, 169–71.

[26] *Akayesu*, n 24, paras 511–15. It was this that led the Chamber to claim that the Convention protected all 'stable and permanent' groups.   [27] *Krstić* Trial Chamber, n 22, para 556.

[28] Although see Wilson, *Writing History in International Criminal Trials* (CUP, 2011) ch 7.

[29] Eg *Prosecutor v Semanza*, Judgment, ICTR-97-20-T, 15 May 2003, para 317.

[30] Vest, 'A Structure-Based Concept of Genocidal Intent' (2007) 5 *JICJ* 781.

[31] *Prosecutor v Jelesić*, Judgment, IT-95-10-A, 5 July 2001, para 48.

a finding that has been criticized.[32] The drafters of the ICC Statute took a middle path, creating guidance for the ICC to the effect that '[t]he conduct took place in the context of a manifest pattern of similar conduct directed against that group or was conduct that could itself effect such destruction'.[33] There are two aspects to this. Fulfilling either suffices for genocide. The first is that there are other people undertaking similar acts against the relevant group, although not necessarily with genocidal intent.[34] The second was designed to cover an example such as where one person obtained a nuclear weapon and used it against a protected group.[35] The ICC has upheld the applicability of this element of the crime,[36] but the ICTY has held that it does not reflect customary international law.[37]

2.1.5 Internal element

Genocide is distinguished from other crimes by its particular mental element. The perpetrator must act with the intent 'to destroy, in whole or in part, a national, ethnical, racial or religious group, as such'. This is not simply a discriminatory intent, it is an eliminationist one. The Tribunals to date have taken a fairly strong line on this and so many charges relating to 'ethnic cleansing' in the former Yugoslavia have failed, as it was not proved that the policy was to destroy, rather than to discriminate against and remove the groups from particular areas.[38] There are difficulties involved in determining what amounts to a group and how large the 'part' of the group has to be for this aspect of the crime, although the ICTY, ICJ, and ICC all agree that it must be 'substantial'.[39]

2.2 CRIMES AGAINST HUMANITY

The second set of international crimes are crimes against humanity. These were first prosecuted before the Nuremberg IMT, where they were defined, in Article 6(c), as:

> murder, extermination, enslavement, deportation, and other inhumane acts committed against any civilian population, before or during the war; or persecutions on political, racial or religious grounds in execution of or in connection with any crime within the jurisdiction of the Tribunal, whether or not in violation of the domestic law of the country where perpetrated.

The most widely ratified definition of crimes against humanity is that in Article 7 ICC Statute. This reads:

> 1. For the purpose of this Statute, 'crime against humanity' means any of the following acts when committed as part of a widespread or systematic attack directed against any civilian population, with knowledge of the attack:
>
> (a) Murder;
>
> (b) Extermination;
>
> (c) Enslavement;

---

[32] Schabas, 'The Jelesic Case and the *Mens Rea* of the Crime of Genocide' (2001) 14 *LJIL* 125.

[33] Eg Elements of Crimes, Art 6(1)(a), Element 4, ICC/ASP/1/3.

[34] Oosterveld, 'Context of Genocide' in Lee *et al.* (eds), *The International Criminal Court: Elements of Crimes and Rules of Procedure and Evidence* (Transnational, 2001) 44, 47–8.   [35] Oosterveld, n 34, 46.

[36] *Prosecutor v al Bashir*, Decision on the Prosecution's Application for a Warrant of Arrest Against Omar al-Bashir, Pre-Trial Chamber 1, ICC-02/05-01/09, 4 March 2009, paras 126–8.

[37] *Prosecutor v Krstić*, Judgment, IT-98-33-A, 19 April 2004, para 224.

[38] See also *Bosnian Genocide*, n 23, para 190.

[39] *Bosnian Genocide*, n 23, para 198; *al Bashir*, n 38, para 146.

(d) Deportation or forcible transfer of population;

(e) Imprisonment or other severe deprivation of physical liberty in violation of funda-
     mental rules of international law;

(f) Torture;

(g) Rape, sexual slavery, enforced prostitution, forced pregnancy, enforced sterilization,
     or any other form of sexual violence of comparable gravity;

(h) Persecution against any identifiable group or collectivity on political, racial,
     national, ethnic, cultural, religious, gender ... or other grounds that are univer-
     sally recognized as impermissible under international law, in connection with
     any act referred to in this paragraph or any crime within the jurisdiction of
     the Court;

(i) Enforced disappearance of persons;

(j) The crime of apartheid;

(k) Other inhumane acts of a similar character intentionally causing great suffering, or
     serious injury to body or to mental or physical health.[40]

Contrary to the Nuremberg definition, crimes against humanity do not need to be linked
to an armed conflict and are, therefore, committable in peacetime.[41] There are, in essence,
two types of crimes against humanity: 'murder-type' crimes against humanity and 'persecutive' crimes against humanity.[42] Broadly speaking, the latter consist of all crimes against
humanity that are covered by Article 7(1)(h) while the former consist of all the others in
Article 7(1). Both types have clear human rights implications.

2.2.1 Context: widespread or systematic attack

Although acts that come within the purview of crimes against humanity, at least when
undertaken by state actors, are almost always violations of human rights law, they must
have an additional contextual element to amount to crimes against humanity. They must
be committed against the backdrop of, and have a nexus to, a widespread or systematic
attack against the civilian population. The terms have been most authoritatively defined
by the ICTY: '[w]idespread refers to the large-scale nature of the attack and the number
of victims, while the phrase "systematic" refers to the organized nature of the acts of violence and the improbability of their random occurrence'.[43] The ICC appears to agree with
the ICTY on this.[44] It ought to be noted, in addition, that the attack does not have to be a
military attack.[45]

2.2.2 Context: policy

It can be argued that the requirement that crimes against humanity be widespread or systematic also implies a separate requirement: that there was a policy to commit these acts.

---

[40] Although it must be noted that this definition is not necessarily entirely reflective of customary international law on point.

[41] Ratner, Abrams, and Bischoff, *Accountability for Human Rights Atrocities in International Law: Beyond the
Nuremberg Legacy* (OUP, 2009) 52–9.

[42] Schwelb, 'Crimes Against Humanity' (1946) 23 *BYIL* 178, 190 (although Schwelb (rightly) rejects most of
the legal differences between them, as will be seen, only the *mens rea* really differs).

[43] *Prosecutor v Kunarac, Kovač and Vuković*, Judgment, IT-96-23/1-A, 12 June 2002, para 94.

[44] *Al Bashir*, n 38, para 81.   [45] *Kunarac*, n 45, para 86.

That position was rejected as a matter of customary law by the ICTY in the *Kunarac* case.[46] However, the requirement is clearly present in the ICC Statute.[47] The debate in relation to the ICC has concentrated on what type of 'organization' can have such a policy.[48] The relationship between this and the human rights obligations of non-state actors is an issue that has not yet been fully determined.

2.2.3 External element

The physical acts that, when committed in context, amount to crimes against humanity all raise clear human rights issues. Torture and disappearances, for example, are both the subject of separate human rights/transnational criminal law treaties. Similarly, murder and deprivation of liberty in violation of fundamental standards of international law are clear violations of human rights.[49] The most detailed discussion of the interrelationship has occurred, however, with respect to 'persecutive' crimes against humanity. The Appeals Chamber of the ICTY has defined such crimes as:

> [A]n act or omission which:
>
> 1. discriminates in fact and which denies or infringes upon a fundamental right laid down in international customary or treaty law (the *actus reus*); and
>
> 2. was carried out deliberately with the intention to discriminate....[50]

The ICTY has been careful, however, not to indicate a complete overlap between crimes against humanity and human rights law, opining that cases from human rights and refugee law 'cannot provide a basis for individual criminal responsibility. It would be contrary to the principle of legality to convict someone of persecution based on a definition found in international refugee law or human rights law'[51] as they were created for different purposes. However, it used human rights instruments to assist with the task of defining 'persecution'.[52] As another ICTY Trial Chamber has said '[i]n practice, not every denial of a fundamental human right will be serious enough to constitute a crime against humanity'.[53] On the other hand, the ICTY has determined that violations of socio-economic rights, such as the right to employment and medical care, can form the basis of persecutive crimes against humanity.[54]

---

[46] *Kunarac*, n 45, para 98.

[47] ICC Statute, Art 7(2)(a) defines 'attack against any civilian population' as being 'a course of conduct involving the multiple commission of acts referred to in paragraph 1 against any civilian population, pursuant to or in furtherance of a State or organizational policy to commit such attack'.

[48] Werle and Burghardt, 'Do Crimes Against Humanity Require the Participation of a State or "State-Like" Organization?' (2012) 10 *JICJ* 1151; Kress, 'On the Outer Limits of Crimes against Humanity: The Concept of Organization within the Policy Requirement: Some Reflections on the March 2010 ICC Kenya Decision' (2010) 23 *LJIL* 855.

[49] On the overlap in relation to enslavement, see *Prosecutor v Kunarac, Kovač and Vuković*, Judgment, IT-96-23-T, 22 February 2001, paras 518 ff.

[50] *Prosecutor v Blaskić*, Judgment, IT-95-14-A, 29 July 2004, para 131.

[51] *Prosecutor v Kupreškić, Kupreškić, Kupreškić, Papić and Šntić*, Judgment, IT-95-16-T, 14 January 2000, para 589.

[52] *Prosecutor v Kupreškić, Kupreškić, Kupreškić, Papić and Šntić*, para 621. Although see *Prosecutor v Stakić*, Judgment, IT-97-24-T, 31 July 2003, para 721, which is more sceptical of the use of such instruments.

[53] *Prosecutor v Krajišnik*, Judgment, IT-00-39-T, 27 September 2006, para 735. This has been accepted by the ICTY Appeals Chamber. See eg *Prosecutor v Brđanin*, Judgment, IT-99-36-A, 3 April 2007, para 296.

[54] *Prosecutor v. Brđanin*, Judgement, IT-99-36-A, 3 April 2007, paras 292–297.

The fact that words can, in some circumstances, be part of the conduct element of 'persecutive' crimes against humanity has led to some discussion in the ICTR. In the *RTLM* Appeal the majority said that:

[H]ate speech targeting a population on the basis of ethnicity, or any other discriminatory ground, violates the right to respect for the dignity of the members of the targeted group as human beings, and therefore constitutes 'actual discrimination'. ... However, ... other persons need to intervene before such violations can occur; a speech cannot, in itself, directly kill members of a group, imprison or physically injure them. .... [That said] ... it is not necessary that every individual act underlying the crime of persecution should be of a gravity corresponding to other crimes against humanity: ... It is the cumulative effect of all the underlying acts of the crime of persecution which must reach a level of gravity equivalent to that for other crimes against humanity.[55]

Judge Meron, however, argued that the majority did not take sufficient account of freedom of expression.[56]

Turning to the ICC, the drafters of the Elements of Crimes were concerned that crimes against humanity (in particular, but not only, persecutions and 'other inhumane acts') could be used to criminalize all human rights violations. Therefore, they included a statement in those elements designed to limit that possibility:

Since article 7 pertains to international criminal law, its provisions ... must be strictly construed, taking into account that crimes against humanity as defined in article 7 are among the most serious crimes of concern to the international community as a whole, warrant and entail individual criminal responsibility, and require conduct which is impermissible under generally applicable international law, as recognized by the principal legal systems of the world.[57]

This was included specifically at the behest of a small number of states that felt their existing practices might amount to crimes against humanity.

2.2.4 Internal element

The internal element of the crime is, first, that the person had the mental element required for the underlying crime (murder etc). In addition they have to have knowledge of the broader context in which their crimes are committed, that is, that their actions took place in the context of a widespread or systematic attack on the civilian population. In the Appeal in *Tadić* it was said that:

The acts of the accused must comprise part of a pattern of widespread or systematic crimes directed against a civilian population and ... the accused must have *known* that his acts fit into such a pattern. There is nothing in the Statute, however, which mandates the imposition of a *further* condition that the acts in question must not be committed for purely personal reasons, except to the extent that this condition is a consequence or a re-statement of the other two conditions mentioned.[58]

---

[55] *Prosecutor v Nahimana, Barayagwiza and Ngeze*, Judgment, ICTR-99-52-A, 28 November 2007, paras 986–7.

[56] *Prosecutor v Nahimana, Barayagwiza and Ngeze*, Separate and Partially Dissenting Opinion of Judge Meron, paras 5–16.

[57] Elements of Crimes, n 35, Introduction to Elements for Art 7.

[58] *Prosecutor v Tadić*, Judgment, IT-94-1-A, 15 July 1999, para 248.

In contrast to the ICTY Statute, the ICTR Statute explicitly requires a discriminatory intent.[59] Although some thought this to be a part of the ICTY definition, it is now accepted that it is not, not least because the ICC Statute does not reflect such a condition. There is one exception: for 'persecutive' crimes against humanity the perpetrator must have a discriminatory, although not necessarily persecutory, intention.[60]

2.3 WAR CRIMES

War crimes are the oldest of the international crimes. They are serious violations of international humanitarian law, for which there is individual criminal responsibility. The relationship between humanitarian law and human rights law, and the main norms humanitarian law contains, are covered in Chapter 23. Suffice it to say here that war crimes can only be committed in times of armed conflict.

Humanitarian law (and, thus, war crimes law) is often split into 'Geneva' and 'Hague' law, the former dealing with the protection of those not taking part in a conflict and the latter dealing with targeting and weapon use. The two categories are not clear at the boundaries, but this still provides a useful way of dividing the area. The basic norms of 'Geneva' law can be found in Common Article 3 Geneva Conventions. This is a distillation of the four Geneva Conventions of 1949, and is now considered applicable to all armed conflicts.[61] It reads (in part):

[E]ach Party to the conflict shall be bound to apply, as a minimum, the following provisions:

(1) Persons taking no active part in the hostilities, including members of armed forces who have laid down their arms and those placed *hors de combat* by sickness, wounds, detention, or any other cause, shall in all circumstances be treated humanely, without any adverse distinction founded on race, colour, religion or faith, sex, birth or wealth, or any other similar criteria. To this end, the following acts are and shall remain prohibited at any time and in any place whatsoever with respect to the above-mentioned persons:

(a) violence to life and person, in particular murder of all kinds, mutilation, cruel treatment and torture;

(b) taking of hostages;

(c) outrages upon personal dignity, in particular humiliating and degrading treatment;

(d) the passing of sentences and the carrying out of executions without previous judgment pronounced by a regularly constituted court, affording all the judicial guarantees which are recognized as indispensable by civilized peoples.

The human rights implications of much of this are clear. Torture and humiliating and degrading treatment are also prohibited by international human rights law, although the definition may not be quite the same. Murder, at least by state officials, and fair trial rights are also familiar to human rights law, and it is unsurprising that many human rights advocates refer to humanitarian law.

---

[59] ICTR Statute, Art 3. [60] *Blaškić* Appeal, n 53, paras 164–5.
[61] Different law applies in international and non-international armed conflicts, although there is increasing overlap between them.

Many human rights lawyers are less comfortable with 'Hague' law. This law has some principles with which few would quarrel, such as that of unnecessary suffering, and the banning of poison, gas, and biological weapons. However, the law of war crimes (and humanitarian law), despite prohibiting direct attacks on civilians, permits proportionate incidental civilian deaths ('collateral damage') that are the result of an attack on a lawful military target. Many in the human rights community are uncomfortable with this, and the possibility of differing interpretations between human rights lawyers and military officials is something that the ICTY has accepted:

> The answers to these questions [on proportionality] are not simple. It may be necessary to resolve them on a case by case basis, and the answers may differ depending on the background and values of the decision maker. It is unlikely that a human rights lawyer and an experienced combat commander would assign the same relative values to military advantage and to injury to non-combatants.[62]

Of course, not all murders and the like that occur in wartime are war crimes. People still get involved in brawls when there are armed conflicts. Therefore, for such an activity to amount to a war crime there has to be some nexus between the conflict and the violation. As the ICTY has said, 'what distinguishes a war crime from a purely domestic offence is that a war crime is shaped by and dependent upon the environment—the armed conflict—in which it was committed'.[63] It, therefore, stated that there had to be a nexus, which meant that:

> The armed conflict need not have been causal to the commission of the crime, but the existence of an armed conflict must, at a minimum, have played a substantial part in the perpetrator's ability to commit it, his decision to commit it, the manner in which it was committed or the purpose for which it was committed. ... In determining whether or not the act in question is sufficiently related to the armed conflict, the Trial Chamber may take into account, *inter alia*, the following factors: the fact that the perpetrator is a combatant; the fact that the victim is a non-combatant; the fact that the victim is a member of the opposing party; the fact that the act may be said to serve the ultimate goal of a military campaign; and the fact that the crime is committed as part of or in the context of the perpetrator's official duties.[64]

This aspect of war crimes law is also present in the Elements of Crimes for the ICC, although the definition is slightly different.[65]

2.4 AGGRESSION

Aggression is sometimes described as the 'supreme international crime'[66] (although others would reserve this moniker for genocide), and it is probably also the most controversial. It was prosecuted before the Nuremberg and Tokyo IMTs, as well as a number of national tribunals after the Second World War, but at no point in those proceedings was a definition authoritatively set down. It took the General Assembly until 1974 to draft a definition of the concept (not necessarily the crime) of aggression (Resolution 3314). The only international criminal tribunal after the Nuremberg and Tokyo IMTs to have jurisdiction over aggression is the ICC. Article 5(1) ICC Statute provides that aggression is a crime within

---

[62] Final Report to the Prosecutor by the Committee Established to Review the NATO Bombing Campaign Against the Federal Republic of Yugoslavia, available at: <http://www.icty.org/sid/10052#IVA64d>, para 50.

[63] *Kunarac*, n 45, para 58.   [64] *Kunarac*, n 45, paras 58–9.

[65] Elements of Crimes, n 35, Introduction and eg Elements for Art 8(2)(a)(i), 4–5.

[66] Nuremberg Judgment, n 3, 186.

the jurisdiction of the Court, but Article 5(2) requires, for the ICC to exercise that jurisdiction, that the Statute be amended to include a definition of the crime.[67]

This was not thought to be likely at the time, but, confounding expectations, in 2010 the Review Conference of the ICC Statute (in Kampala, Uganda) adopted an amendment to that Statute containing a definition, though the amendment is not yet in force. The definition provides that aggression is 'the planning, preparation, initiation or execution, by a person in a position effectively to exercise control over or to direct the political or military action of a State, of an act of aggression which, by its character, gravity and scale, constitutes a manifest violation of the Charter of the United Nations.'[68] Although achieving a definition at all is a major development in international criminal law, aspects of the definition, as well as the jurisdiction of the ICC over this crime, remain complex and controversial.[69]

Although the Nuremberg IMT asserted that aggression differed from other international crimes 'in that it contained within itself the accumulated evil of the whole',[70] the relationship of aggression to human rights is perhaps the least clear. The criminalization of aggression can be seen as contributing to the right to peace (to the extent that the right exists separately to other human rights),[71] or at least operating in tandem to it. That said, the negotiations in Kampala were not based on the right to peace, nor was there much, if any, talk of it there.

3 PROSECUTIONS: INTERNATIONAL AND NATIONAL

Prosecutions are often, and not necessarily inaccurately, thought to be important from the point of view of human rights protection. For example, in the *Velasquez-Rodriguez* case, the Inter-American Court of Human Rights held that the failure to investigate the disappearance of the applicant's son and punish those responsible was part of the violation of his right to life.[72] In the European system, a failure to undertake a proper investigation can be a violation of the right to life.[73] It is increasingly, albeit controversially, thought that, in the circumstances of international crimes, the rights of the victims include a right to see those who have committed such crimes prosecuted. As will be seen, this is probably a little in advance of the current state of international law, but such views have gained considerable ground in the last decade, especially with respect to high-ranking offenders.[74]

There is a long, although not always illustrious, history of the prosecution of war crimes, both at the national and international level. There were initially plans to try German war

---

[67] See Schabas, *The International Criminal Court* (OUP, 2010) 108–15.

[68] RC/Res.6. (Article 8bis). This Article also contains a number of examples drawn from GA Res 3314.

[69] See the special issue 'After Kampala, Aggression' (2012) 10 *JICJ* 1-288.

[70] Nuremberg Judgment, n 3, 186.

[71] Tehindrazanarivelo and Kolb 'Peace, Right to, International Protection' in Wolfrum (ed), *The Max Planck Encyclopaedia of International Law* (OUP, 2012) Vol VIII, 153, 155.

[72] *Velasquez-Rodriguez v Honduras*, IACtHR Series C No 4 (29 July 1988).

[73] *McCann v UK* (1995) 21 EHRR 67, para 161 (although in this case the investigation was considered sufficient).

[74] *Prosecutor v Kondewa*, Decision on Lack of Jurisdiction/Abuse of Process: Amnesty Provided by the Lomé Accord, SCSL-2004-14-AR72(E) 25 May 2004, separate opinion of Robertson J, para 48.

criminals by the Allies after the First World War.[75] However, these floundered and only a small number of those defendants were tried in Leipzig, Germany, in proceedings considered strongly skewed towards the defence.[76]

Probably the most well-known prosecutions of the twentieth century occurred after the Second World War, when the Nuremberg and Tokyo IMTs were set up to try the major Axis war criminals in both spheres of that conflict. It is possible to trace the beginnings of modern international criminal law to the Nuremberg IMT, which tried Nazi leaders for war crimes, crimes against humanity, and aggression. The latter charge caused the most controversy, on the basis that the offence probably did not exist in international law at the time. However, it is questionable whether international law contained an absolute prohibition of retroactive criminal legislation at the time and later instruments such as the European Convention on Human Rights (ECHR) and the International Covenant on Civil and Political Rights (ICCPR) contain savings clauses that were in part designed to avoid the implication that the Nuremberg Charter violated human rights. For example, Article 15 ICCPR provides both that '[n]o one shall be held guilty of any criminal offence on account of any act or omission which did not constitute a criminal offence under national *or international* law at the time when it was committed' and that 'nothing in this article shall prejudice the trial and punishment of any person for any act or omission which, at the time when it was committed, was criminal according to the general principles of law recognized by the community of nations'.[77]

Overall, the general view of the Nuremberg IMT has been quite positive, in part because the President of the Tribunal, Sir Geoffrey Lawrence, exercised a firm but fair hand over the proceedings.[78] History has not been so kind to the Tokyo IMT, the fair trial standards of which have, in particular, been singled out for criticism.[79] There were also large numbers of domestic trials in countries occupied during the Second World War.

During the Cold War there was little movement on a permanent international criminal court, and national prosecutions for international crimes, such as that of Adolf Eichmann in Jerusalem in 1960,[80] were the exception rather than the rule. A seminal moment in international criminal justice came in 1993, however, when the Security Council created the ICTY. It did so in Resolution 837, using an innovative interpretation of its powers under Chapter VII UN Charter.[81] It acted similarly in 1994 to create the ICTR. Both had their difficulties in the beginning and had slow starts, particularly in the absence of cooperation from a number of states. However, the picture has slowly brightened, and both tribunals, despite some criticism of their approaches to fair trial,[82] have prosecuted a number of high-ranking leaders and catalysed the development of international criminal law more generally. They are now entering their dotage, however, and have begun the process

---

[75] Treaty of Versailles, Arts 227–9.

[76] See eg Bass, *Stay the Hand of Vengeance* (Princeton UP, 2000) ch 3.

[77] Emphasis added. See Gallant, *The Principle of Legality in International and Comparative Law* (CUP, 2008) ch 4b.   [78] Tusa and Tusa, *The Nuremberg Trial* (BBC Books, 1995) 112.

[79] See generally Boister and Cryer, *The Tokyo International Military Tribunal: A Reappraisal* (OUP, 2008).

[80] *A-G of Israel v Eichmann* (1968) 36 ILR 18.

[81] See *Prosecutor v Tadić*, Decision on the Defence Interlocutory Appeal on Jurisdiction, IT-94-1-AR72, 2 October 1995, paras 34–5.

[82] McDermott, 'Rights in Reverse: A Critical Analysis of Fair Trial Rights Under International Criminal Law', in Schabas, McDermott, and Hayes (eds), *The Ashgate Research Companion to International Criminal Law: Critical Perspectives* (Ashgate, 2013) 165.

of having their functions replaced by 'residual mechanisms' to deal with issues such as parole and commutation of sentence.

The largest development in international prosecution of international crimes was the creation of the ICC. The ICC Statute was drafted in Rome in 1998.[83] Despite opposition from some states (most notably, but not limited to, the USA) the Statute entered into force in 2002. It currently has 122 states parties. The ICC, although permanent, does not have jurisdiction over all international crimes. It can prosecute war crimes, crimes against humanity, genocide, and may possibly in the future also be able to conduct proceedings related to aggression,[84] but only in relation to crimes committed by nationals of states parties or on their territories.[85] The only exception to this is if the Security Council refers a situation to the Court. The Security Council has done this twice, in Resolutions 1593 and 1970, which referred the situation in Darfur, Sudan, and Libya, respectively to the ICC.

The jurisdiction of the ICC, unlike that of the ICTY and ICTR, is intended to be 'complementary' to that of states. In other words, the ICC can act only if states are 'unwilling or unable genuinely' to prosecute the offences themselves.[86] The precise meaning of these terms is the subject of some controversy and litigation before the Court.[87] In addition to Darfur and Libya, the Court is currently dealing with situations in the Democratic Republic of Congo, Kenya, the Central African Republic, Mali, Côte d'Ivoire, and Uganda. The fact that these are all African states has caused some to criticize the Court,[88] although others have leapt to the ICC's defence on point.[89] Few would argue, though, that the length of time trials have taken and defendants spend in pre-trial custody are exemplary.[90]

The principle of complementarity is meant to reflect the primary role of national jurisdictions in prosecuting international crimes. It is true that states may assert universal jurisdiction over genocide, war crimes, and crimes against humanity (the position on aggression is less certain).[91] Indeed, in some circumstances (in particular for grave breaches of the Geneva Conventions), they are obliged to do so. In practice, however, the states of nationality of perpetrators tend to be unwilling to prosecute, and territorial states are often also unwilling or unable to prosecute offenders themselves. In spite of something of an upturn in prosecution by third states, they often would prefer to remain inactive. The prosecutions that have occurred tend to be of suspects from conflicts where there is already a practical consensus on the necessity of prosecuting suspects.[92]

---

[83] There is also the significant development of 'internationalized' courts such as the Special Court for Sierra Leone and the Extraordinary Chambers for Prosecuting the Khmer Rouge in Cambodia. See Cryer, Friman, Robinson, and Wilmshurst, n 1, ch 9.

[84] ICC Statute, Art 5(1)(2). The crimes are defined in Arts 6–8. The ICC can only assert jurisdiction over aggression if the Statute is amended to include a definition of that crime.

[85] ICC Statute, Art 12.   [86] ICC Statute, Art 17.

[87] Eg *Prosecutor v Katanga and Ngudjolo*, Judgment on the Appeal of Mr Germain Katanga against the Oral Decision of Trial Chamber II of 12 June 2009 on the Admissibility of the Case, ICC-01/04-01/07-1497, 25 September 2009.

[88] Oola, 'Bashir and the ICC: The Aura or Audition of International Justice in Africa?', Oxford Transitional Justice Research Working Paper, available at: <http://www.csls.ox.ac.uk/documents/OolaFin.pdf>.

[89] Ambos, 'Expanding the focus of the 'African Criminal Court' in Schabas *et al.*, n 87, 499.

[90] McDermott, n 87.   [91] Cryer, Friman, Robinson, and Wilmshurst, n 1, 50–62.

[92] Langer, 'The Diplomacy of Universal Jurisdiction: The Political Branches and the Transnational Prosecution of International Crimes' (2001) 105 *AJIL* 1.

4 NON-PROSECUTORIAL OPTIONS

There are ways of dealing with international crimes other than by prosecution. The legality of some of them has come under fire in the last decade, from human rights groups in particular, but there is probably still room for them to play at least a complementary role for some offenders. In addition, it ought not to be thought that prosecution is a panacea for all of the consequences of international crimes and human rights violations.

4.1 AMNESTIES

Amnesties are probably the most controversial option that does not involve prosecutions. Indeed, they prevent them. There are serious arguments about the lawfulness of amnesties under international law, both where there are treaties that create obligations to prosecute (for example the Geneva Conventions for grave breaches and the Genocide Convention for that crime) and under human rights law. In the former case, it is clear that a duty to prosecute is violated by a domestic law preventing prosecution.[93] With regard to human rights law, there are significant arguments that amnesties, certainly unconditional ones, are contrary to various human rights obligations such as the duty to investigate losses of life attributable to the state and the right of access to courts.[94] However, it is by no means clear that the case can yet be made that amnesties are always unlawful. It is true that the Inter-American Court of Human Rights has taken a strong line against amnesties, observing that:

> This Court considers that all amnesty provisions, provisions on prescription and the establishment of measures designed to eliminate responsibility are inadmissible, because they are intended to prevent the investigation and punishment of those responsible for serious human rights violations such as torture, extrajudicial, summary or arbitrary execution and forced disappearance, all of them prohibited because they violate non-derogable rights recognized by international human rights law.[95]

Some take the view that this case has determined a more generally applicable norm against amnesties in international law,[96] but this may be stretching that court's jurisprudence a little too far. Other tribunals have not been as assertive.[97] The position on point was probably best summed up by the Special Court for Sierra Leone when it said that:

> [T]hat there is a crystallising international norm that a government cannot grant amnesty for serious violations of crimes under international law is amply supported by materials placed before the Court [but the view] that it has crystallised may not be entirely correct . . . it is accepted that such a norm is developing under international law.[98]

---

[93] Although on traditional principles of international law an amnesty in one state would not prevent another state from prosecuting.

[94] Orentlicher, 'Settling Accounts: The Duty to Prosecute Human Rights Violations of a Former Regime' (1991) 100 *Yale LJ* 2537.

[95] *Barrios Altos Case (Chumbipuma Aguierre et al. v Peru)* IACtHR Series C No 75 (2001) para 41.

[96] Laplante, 'Outlawing Amnesty: The Return of Criminal Justice to Transitional Justice Schemes' (2008–2009) 48 *Virginia JIL* 915.

[97] See generally Seibert-Fohr, *Prosecuting Serious Human Rights Violations* (OUP, 2009).

[98] *Prosecutor v Kallon and Kamara*, Decision on Challenge to Jurisdiction: Lomé Amnesty Accord, SCSL-2004-15-AR72(E) and SCSL-2004-16-AR72(E), 13 March 2004, para 82. Although see Akhavan, 'Whither National Courts? The Rome Statute's Missing Half: Towards An Expand and Enforceable Obligation For the National Repression of International Crimes' (2010) 8 *JICJ* 1245.

The merits of amnesties are hotly contested, with some claiming that they foster reconcili-ation and others saying they allow powerful perpetrators, literally, to get away with mur-der, and create a culture of impunity that will only encourage future violations.

4.2 TRUTH AND RECONCILIATION COMMISSIONS

Amnesties can be accompanied by truth and reconciliation commissions and, where they are, there is often more sympathy for the amnesty. This was the case for the South African system, which was set up in the aftermath of apartheid. In South Africa, a failure to fully inform the Truth and Reconciliation Commission of the crimes committed could lead to a refusal of amnesty and indeed did in some cases.[99] The merits and demerits of truth and reconciliation commissions are hotly contested. Some see them as providing the ground-work for later reconciliation; others do not feel that there can be a shared state-authorized truth. Much depends on the composition, mandate, and functioning of such bodies. It is sometimes suggested that lustration (the collective removal of people from their jobs) is an appropriate method of dealing with international crimes, but any collective measure is likely to be questionable on human rights grounds, especially the right to have rights and duties adjudicated at law.[100]

5 CONCLUSION

There is much to be said for using international criminal law to vindicate human rights. For example, as the Nuremberg IMT implied in its famous statement referenced in Section 1,[101] using criminal law actually brings home to high-level leaders that they personally, rather than only the impersonal state, will bear the consequences of their deci-sions. There is also the possibility that civil human rights claims will not provide for a sufficient sense of justice for the victims.[102] Another advantage that has been suggested is the possibility that victims will find testimony cathartic, although this is controversial.[103] Furthermore, it is at least arguable that subjecting facts to forensic scrutiny can later pre-vent denial of those atrocities.[104] However, whether prosecutions can have a significant deterrent effect on the commission of later human rights violations is a matter which is more the subject of, often sceptical, speculation rather than scientific proof.[105]

Perhaps the shadow side of this is that prosecutions for international crimes are, for a variety of reasons, selective, and so not all of those who commit such crimes can be prosecuted. Indeed, as has been noted here, not all human rights violations are also international crimes (although most, but, perhaps, not all, international crimes would probably amount to human rights violations when committed by states). Furthermore, when prosecuting international crimes, it is important to remember that prosecutions for

---

[99] Prosecutions have not been notable by their successes though. See Bubenzer, *Post-TRC Prosecutions in South Africa* (Martinus Nijhoff, 2009).

[100] ICCPR, Art 14; *Casanovas v France*, CCPR/C/51/D/441/1990 (26 July 1994).   [101] Text at n 3.

[102] Although for the argument that this represents only one understanding of justice, see Clarke, *Fictions of Justice: The International Criminal Court and the Challenge of Legal Pluralism in Sub-Saharan Africa* (CUP, 2009).

[103] Stover, *The Witnesses* (Penn State Press, 2007).

[104] Cohen, *States of Denial: Knowing About Atrocities and Suffering* (Polity, 2001).

[105] Harhoff, 'Sense and Sensibility in Sentencing: Taking Stock of International Criminal Punishment', in Engdahl and Wrange (eds), *Law at War: The Law as it Was and the Law as it Should Be: Liber Amicorum Ove Bring* (Martinus Nijhoff, 2008) 121, 127.

international crimes can also, themselves, involve violations of human rights, as the trial of Saddam Hussein showed.[106] That said, international criminal law can, and often does, walk hand in hand with human rights law and practice.

FURTHER READING

BASSIOUNI (ed), *International Criminal Law Vols I–III* (Martinus Nijhoff, 2008).

CASSESE ET AL., *Cassese's International Criminal Law* (Oxford University Press, 2013).

CASSESE ET AL. (eds), *The Oxford Companion to International Criminal Justice* (Oxford University Press, 2009).

CRYER, FRIMAN, ROBINSON, and WILMSHURST, *An Introduction to International Criminal Law and Procedure* (Cambridge University Press, 2010).

HUNEEUS, 'International Criminal Law by Other Means: The Quasi-Criminal Jurisdiction of the Human Rights Courts' (2013) 107 *AJIL* 1.

RATNER, ABRAMS, and BISCHOFF, *Accountability for Human Rights Atrocities in International Law: Beyond the Nuremberg Legacy* (Oxford University Press, 2009).

SCHABAS, *The International Criminal Court* (OUP, 2010).

SCHABAS, *An Introduction to the International Criminal Court* (Cambridge University Press, 2011).

USEFUL WEBSITES

International Criminal Tribunal for the former Yugoslavia: <http://www.icty.org>

International Criminal Tribunal for Rwanda: <http://www.ictr.org>

International Criminal Court: <http://www.icc-cpi.int>

---

[106] Bhuta, 'Fatal Errors: The Trial and Appeal Judgments in the *Dujail* case' (2008) 6 *JICJ* 39.

25

INTERNATIONAL REFUGEE LAW

Alice Edwards

SUMMARY[1]

International refugee law is concerned with the status and standards of treatment of refugees. The two legal regimes of international human rights law and international refugee law emerged from the same historical background of the Second World War, in which millions of persons were displaced as a result of conflict and persecution. The two regimes are, thus, closely related yet also distinct. International human rights law informs and reinforces international refugee law and the rights of refugees. At the same time, the specific rights provided by international refugee law, based on the special character of refugees, remain the primary source of their protection.

1 INTRODUCTION

The primary sources of the rights of refugees are found in the instruments and customary norms making up international refugee law, centring on the 1951 Convention relating to the Status of Refugees (Refugee Convention). International refugee law defines who is and is not a refugee and specifies the range of rights to which they are entitled. In recognition of the special character of refugees, as persons who are outside their country of origin or nationality and are at risk of persecution, the Refugee Convention was drafted to capture the specific rights and needs of refugees and the obligations on host states to provide protection to such persons. International human rights law, in contrast, is a set of rights that are applicable to all persons, regardless of their immigration or other status. As such, international refugee law and international human rights law operate in parallel, with many similar provisions and safeguards. This simultaneous application of the two regimes poses some problems in determining which rights apply to refugees in which circumstances. This can only be resolved at the level of the individual right, rather than at the level of the regime. Such resolutions must be subject to the guiding ethos that the higher standard ought to prevail, in recognition of the inherent dignity of refugees and the aim of the Refugee Convention to ensure refugees the widest possible exercise of their fundamental rights.[2]

Section 2 explains the purpose and scope of international refugee law. Section 3 identifies the five fundamental elements of the Refugee Convention, and also explains other

---

[1] The views expressed in this chapter are the personal views of the author and do not necessarily reflect those of the United Nations or the UNHCR.

[2] Refugee Convention, preamble and Art 5.

important parameters of international refugee law more broadly. Section 4 explores the relationship between the two bodies of law at the macro-level, while Sections 5–8 deal with specific aspects of refugee law—namely, the definition of a refugee, the prohibition of *refoulement*, refugee rights, and the ending of refugee status and solutions—and analyse how international human rights law informs them.

2 WHAT IS INTERNATIONAL REFUGEE LAW?

International refugee law is the body of law that regulates the status and rights of refugees and the securing of long-term solutions to their situation. Its purpose is to ensure that refugees who are outside their countries of origin or nationality receive protection of their basic rights, which they no longer enjoy from their own governments.

International refugee law is made up of treaties and customary international law, centring on the Refugee Convention and the 1967 Protocol relating to the Status of Refugees (1967 Protocol), as well as regional refugee and other protection instruments. In terms of customary international law, from among the range of rights contained in the Refugee Convention, only the prohibition on *refoulement*,[3] or return to countries of origin where the refugee faces a threat to their life or freedom, has crystallized into a customary norm.[4]

While the Refugee Convention and the 1967 Protocol are the principal treaties at the global level, and are widely ratified, a number of regional refugee instruments also exist. These are: the Organization of African Unity's (now African Union) 1969 Convention governing the Specific Aspects of Refugee Problems in Africa (OAU Refugee Convention), the Cartagena Declaration on Refugees,[5] and the European Union's *asylum acquis*, the latter being composed of a series of directives and regulations inter alia on refugee and subsidiary protection,[6] reception, and asylum procedures.

Refugee law is informed by international human rights law, which also forms an integral part of the regime. The Refugee Convention is a human rights treaty in the sense that it codifies the rights that refugees are to enjoy and the correlative obligations on states to respect, protect, and fulfil those rights. It is, though, distinct from the main human rights treaties as it is a specific regime for the protection of a specific class of human being, namely refugees. The protections of international human rights law supplement the refugee regime in multiple ways, as detailed in this chapter.

The mandate and functions of the UN High Commissioner for Refugees (UNHCR) also comprise part of international refugee law. UNHCR is a global humanitarian and non-political organization with the specific mandate granted by the UN General Assembly to provide international protection to refugees and, together with governments, to seek

---

[3] Art 33(1).

[4] See, in particular, Declaration of States Parties to the 1951 Convention and or Its 1967 Protocol relating to the Status of Refugees, HCR/MMSP/2001/09 (16 January 2002) para. 4.

[5] Adopted by the Colloquium on the International Protection of Refugees in Central America, Mexico and Panama, 22 November 1984.

[6] 'Subsidiary protection' covers persons who have reasons for being outside their country of origin owing to a real risk of serious harm arising from '(a) the death penalty or execution; (b) torture or inhuman or degrading treatment or punishment; or (c) serious and individual threat to a civilian's life or person by reason of indiscriminate violence in situations of international or internal armed conflict.' They are entitled to the rights and benefits outlined in the EU Directive 2011/95/EU of the European Parliament and of the Council of 13 December 2011 on standards for the qualification of third-country nationals or stateless persons as beneficiaries of international protection, for a uniform status for refugees or for persons eligible for subsidiary protection, and for the content of the protection granted (recast), 20 December 2011, OJ L 337, 9–26, Arts 2 and 15.

solutions to the situation of refugees. Part of this mandate includes supervising the application of international conventions for the protection of refugees.[7] It does this through a range of measures including producing authoritative legal and policy guidelines and positions, intervening as *amicus curiae* before international and national courts, engaging in diplomatic interventions with governments, and monitoring states' implementation of their treaty obligations. In turn, states parties to the Refugee Convention and/or 1967 Protocol are required to cooperate with UNHCR in the exercise of its functions and to inform it of any laws or regulations enacted relating to refugees.[8]

3 FUNDAMENTAL ELEMENTS OF INTERNATIONAL REFUGEE LAW

International refugee law is premised on the human right 'to seek and enjoy in other countries asylum from persecution' found in Article 14(1) of the Universal Declaration of Human Rights (UDHR). Although it is widely held that there is no obligation on states parties to the Refugee Convention 'to grant' asylum, because the Convention does not contain such an explicit obligation, this is an outdated view. It is clear that the purpose of the Refugee Convention is precisely to provide international protection (or asylum) to persons defined as refugees and in the form outlined in the Convention.

The Refugee Convention can be broken down into five fundamental elements. First, the Refugee Convention *defines* a refugee as anyone who 'is outside their country of origin owing to a well-founded fear of being persecuted for reasons of race, religion, nationality, membership of a particular social group or political opinion.'[9] Although the definition was originally limited to refugees fleeing events in Europe prior to 1 January 1951, the 1967 Protocol 'amended' the Convention to allow states to lift these geographical and temporal caveats, turning the Convention into a truly universal treaty.[10] The regional instruments expand this definition to cover persons in flight from events such as armed conflict, massive or systematic human rights violations, or serious disturbances of public order.[11]

The Refugee Convention definition does not apply to persons for whom there are serious reasons to believe they have committed acts which exclude them from refugee protection, such as war crimes, crimes against humanity, or serious ordinary crimes.[12]

Palestinian refugees are also not in principle covered by the Refugee Convention, being instead protected and assisted by the international community via a special regime under the auspices of the UN Relief and Works Agency for Palestine Refugees in the Near East (UNRWA), which operates in Gaza, the West Bank, Jordan, Lebanon, and Syria.[13] Palestinian refugees may, however, benefit from refugee status under the Refugee Convention automatically when the protection or assistance of UNRWA has ceased. Such protection or assistance may be considered ceased, for example, if the Palestinian refugee is outside UNRWA's areas of operation and is unable to re-avail him- or herself of that protection or assistance for reasons beyond his or her control.[14]

---

[7] Statute of the Office of the United Nations High Commissioner for Refugees, GA Res 428(V), A/RES/428(V) (14 December 1950), para 8(1).   [8] Refugee Convention, Arts 35 and 36.
[9] Art 1(A)(2).   [10] 1967 Protocol, Art 1.
[11] OAU Refugee Convention, Art 1(2); Cartagena Declaration on Refugees, Art 3.
[12] Refugee Convention, Art 1F.   [13] Refugee Convention, Art 1D.
[14] UNHCR, Observations in the case C-364/11 El Kott and Others regarding the interpretation of Article 1D of the 1951 Convention and Article 12(1)(a) of the Qualification Directive, 27 October 2011, available at: <http://www.refworld.org/docid/4eaa95d92.html>.

Second, the *principle of non-discrimination* provides that individuals who are protected by the Convention should enjoy the same rights regardless of immigration or other status except where distinctions can be objectively justified. This is captured in Article 3 of the Convention, which requires that all refugees shall enjoy Convention rights regardless of 'race, religion or country of origin'.

Third, *the principle of non-refoulement* protects refugees from return to threats to life or freedom (discussed in Section 6).

Fourth, there is a *guarantee of non-penalization* of asylum-seekers and refugees who show 'good cause' for illegal entry or stay.[15] Penalties in this sense include both criminal and administrative penalties such as fines or detention. Noting that persons in flight are rarely able to satisfy immigration entry requirements, the Conference of Plenipotentiaries to the Refugee Convention observed that 'good cause' would include fleeing persecution, but there could be other good causes for why a refugee would need to enter a country without official authorization, such as for reasons of family unity.[16]

The fifth fundamental principle is that refugees are to enjoy the *widest possible exercise of their fundamental rights*.[17] Articles 3 to 34 Refugee Convention contain a number of rights entitlements for refugees (discussed in Section 7), while Article 2 notes that refugees are subject to the laws and regulations of the host country and they have a duty to respect them.

In addition to the five fundamental elements of the Refugee Convention, a further key principle of refugee law is that of *finding solutions for refugees* (discussed in Section 8).

Unlike some human rights treaties, the Refugee Convention does not contain a general derogation clause permitting rights to be suspended in a state of emergency.[18] However, the Convention permits—via Article 9—derogation in respect of 'particular persons' who pose a threat to national security 'in times of war or other exceptional circumstances.' This means that particular persons who pose a threat to national security may be subject to security measures, such as restrictions on their freedom of movement and internment or confiscation of property. The suspension of their rights continues until refugee status is granted, or, even after refugee status is granted, where it is considered necessary in the individual's circumstances. Article 8 ensures, however, that such security measures are not applied to refugees solely on the basis of their nationality.[19]

4 RELATIONSHIP BETWEEN THE TWO BODIES OF LAW

Borne out of the evils of the Second World War, in which millions of Jews and others were subjected to persecution forcing them to seek safety across international frontiers, both modern refugee law and human rights law share common roots. However, each body of law responds to different, albeit related, problems: human rights law aims to ensure that such events will never happen again by creating a global regime of fundamental rights,

---

[15] Refugee Convention, Art 31(1).
[16] Refugee Convention, Art 31; Goodwin-Gill, 'Article 31 of the 1951 Convention Relating to the Status of Refugees: Non-Penalization, Detention, and Protection', in Feller, Türk, and Nicholson (eds), *Refugee Protection in International Law* (CUP, 2003) 185.
[17] Refugee Convention, preamble.   [18] On derogations see Chapter 5.
[19] For more on derogation and the 1951 Convention, see Davy, 'Article 8: Exemption from Exceptional Measures', in Zimmerman (ed), *The 1951 Convention relating to the Status of Refugees and its 1967 Protocol: A Commentary* (OUP, 2011) 755; Davy, 'Article 9: Provisional Measures', in Zimmerman 781. On the application of derogation in mass influx situations, see Edwards, 'Temporary Protection, Derogation and the 1951 Refugee Convention' (2012) 13 *Melbourne JIL* 1.

whilst refugee law responds to the displacement of persons caused when such rights are violated. The regimes are, thus, complementary yet distinct.

The Refugee Convention is a human rights instrument of a particular scope—protecting the rights of a specific category of protected person, the refugee. Post-dating the UDHR, but predating the main human rights treaties, the preambular paragraphs of the Refugee Convention recall the UN Charter, the UDHR, and 'the principle that human beings shall enjoy fundamental rights'. Coupled with Article 5, which provides that '[n]othing in this Convention shall be deemed to impair any rights and benefits granted by a Contracting State to refugees apart from this Convention', the Refugee Convention is the floor but not the ceiling for the rights of refugees. Accordingly, it is necessary to consider those developments in human rights law that are applicable to refugees.

Although states were adamant that the International Covenant on Civil and Political Rights (ICCPR) should not contain a right to asylum equivalent to Article 14 UDHR, the right to seek and enjoy asylum from persecution is implicit in the very existence of the Refugee Convention. The European Court of Human Rights appears to have adopted this view in its judgment in the case of *MSS v Belgium and Greece*: 'Belgium and Greece have ratified the *1951 Geneva Convention relating to the Status of Refugees*... which defines the circumstances in which a State *must grant* refugee status to those who request it, as well as the rights and duties of such persons.'[20] Moreover, at the regional level, the right to asylum has been located squarely within human rights instruments,[21] and is also explicit in the OAU Refugee Convention.[22]

The application of human rights instruments to refugees has been consistently recognized by the UN General Assembly, which has called inter alia on states to respect the rights of refugees.[23] Human rights treaty bodies have also dealt with refugee issues.[24] In fact, refugees and asylum-seekers are increasingly resorting to human rights mechanisms in the absence of an individual complaints procedure under the Refugee Convention.[25] Furthermore, the Executive Committee of the High Commissioner for Refugees' Programme has consistently 'reiterate[d]... the obligation to treat asylum-seekers and refugees in accordance with applicable human rights and refugee law standards as set out in relevant international instruments'.[26]

International human rights law thus intersects with refugee law in at least three main ways:

- refugees include those fleeing their countries of origin or nationality on account of serious human rights violations;
- international refugee law is a rights-granting instrument, which is informed by human rights standards; and,
- at the same time, as human beings refugees are also entitled to benefit from the general human rights regime as far as it applies.

---

[20] *MSS v Belgium and Greece* (2011) 53 EHRR 28, 263 (emphasis added).

[21] American Declaration on the Rights and Duties of Man, Art XXVII; American Convention on Human Rights, Art 22(7); African Charter on Human and Peoples' Rights, Art 12(3); European Union Charter of Fundamental Rights, Art 18.

[22] OAU Refugee Convention, Art 2.

[23] Eg, UNHCR, Thematic Compilation of General Assembly and ECOSOC Resolutions (September 2011), available at: <http://www.unhcr.org/3e958fcf4.html>.

[24] Eg Committee on the Rights of the Child, General Comment No 6 on the Treatment of Unaccompanied and Separated Children outside their Country of Origin, 2005, HRI/GEN/1/Rev.9 (Vol II) 441.

[25] Edwards, 'Peter Pan's Fairies and Genie Bottles: The UN Human Rights Treaty Bodies and Supervision of the 1951 Convention', in Simeon (ed), *The UNHCR and the Supervision of International Refugee Law* (CUP, 2013) 159.

[26] Executive Committee Conclusion No 82 (XLVIII) on 'Safeguarding Asylum' (1997) para (d)(vi). See also, Conclusion No 19 (XXXI) on 'Temporary Refuge' (1980) para (e); Conclusion No 22 (XXXII) on 'Protection of Asylum Seekers in Situations of Large-Scale Influx' (1981) para B; Conclusion No 36 (XXXVI) on 'General [Matters]' (1985) para (f).

Goodwin-Gill and McAdam have noted that '[r]efugee [l]aw is an incomplete legal regime of protection, imperfectly covering what ought to be a situation of exception.'[27] International human rights law can, thus, usefully serve to fill gaps in the refugee protection architecture. At the same time, as noted by Hathaway, the rights in the Refugee Convention in a number of ways go beyond those available in international human rights law, at least as far as the human rights regime applies to non-nationals. Hathaway refers, in particular, to the detailed set of socio-economic rights provided to refugees in the Refugee Convention (see Section 7).[28]

The only exception to the generally held view that the Refugee Convention, while being a human rights instrument, is the primary tool of refugee protection is that of Chetail. He claims that human rights law should be the primary source of refugee rights, rather than the inverse, asserting that human rights law has broadly eclipsed the protections in the Refugee Convention.[29] Chetail's article, although thought-provoking, only focuses on the positive aspects of human rights law, in other words, where it strengthens refugee rights in the Refugee Convention. Some of the shortcomings in human rights law are ignored, such as the limitations on economic rights to non-nationals in the International Covenant on Economic, Social and Cultural Rights (ICESCR), which would not be permitted under the Refugee Convention.[30] Likewise, he downplays the range of rights that are tailored to the specific circumstances of refugees in the Refugee Convention, despite the fact that they do not find expression in human rights instruments.[31]

Apart from filling gaps, developments in international human rights law have also had a bearing on the understanding of key terms in the Refugee Convention, in particular the definition of a refugee.

5 HUMAN RIGHTS AND REFUGEE STATUS

As already noted, a Convention refugee is someone who is outside their country of origin owing to a fear of persecution on account of one or more of five grounds. The definition of a refugee in Article 1A(2) Refugee Convention is the subject of volumes of court judgments and legal treatises. The two pivotal aspects of the definition are (i) persecution and (ii) the grounds or reasons for that persecution.

Persecution is generally understood to include, at a minimum, threats to life or freedom.[32] The term covers serious human rights violations, such as torture, arbitrary detention, arbitrary prosecution, and other 'serious harm'.[33] Not every human rights violation is a form of persecution however. The drafters intended international protection to be

---

[27] Goodwin-Gill and McAdam, *The Refugee in International Law* (OUP, 2007) 1.

[28] Hathaway, *The Rights of Refugees under International Law* (CUP, 2005).

[29] Chetail, 'Are refugee rights human rights? An unorthodox questioning of the relations between refugee law and human rights law', in Rubio Martin (ed), *Migrations and Human Rights* (OUP, 2013) (forthcoming).

[30] See Edwards, 'Human Rights, Refugees and the Right to "Enjoy" Asylum' (2005) 17 *IJRL* 297, which looks at two specific rights—the right to work and the right to family life or unity—and acknowledges that human rights law can fill the gaps in the Refugee Convention.

[31] These rights include exemption from usual requirements as to length of stay in enjoyment of rights (Art 6), continuity of lawful residence (Art 10), refugee seamen (Art 11), movable and immovable property (Art 13), recognition of foreign diplomas (Art 19), welfare rights (Arts 20 to 24), special administrative assistance (Article 25), travel documents (Art 28), exemption from fiscal charges (Art 29), transfer of assets (Art 30), non-penalization for illegal entry or stay (Art 31), and naturalization (Art 34).

[32] Refugee Convention, Art 33; UNHCR, *Handbook on Procedures and Criteria for Determining Refugee Status* (UNHCR, 1979, reissued 2011) para 51.   [33] UNHCR, n 32.

made available only to victims of those violations considered to be sufficiently serious to satisfy the threshold of persecution. As a regime predicated on the absence or loss of state protection, such that sanctuary in another country is needed, the regime of refugee law is not appropriate to respond to all human rights violations. Rather, human rights violations that are not sufficiently serious to evidence a fracturing of protection between the individual and his or her state should be dealt with instead under national laws and redress mechanisms.

While human rights law is an important source of defining forms of persecution, rigid reliance on it to understand the terms in the refugee definition should be avoided. This is because not all known forms of persecution have been codified in human rights instruments yet; and the means and methods of persecution are limited only by human depravity and imagination. A further reason against tying the definition too closely to human rights law is that doing so can add an additional legal layer of proof to the granting of status. It is worth noting in this regard that there is no explicit human rights violation of persecution in any of the main international human rights conventions.

As not all human rights violations have yet been codified as such, 'serious harm' has been used as a 'catch-all'. Before the mid-1990s, for example, sexual and gender-based violence (SGBV) against women and girls was not considered an issue for human rights law, and as of today, there is no explicit universal treaty prohibition. Yet clearly SGBV is serious harm, and has been increasingly recognized as a form of persecution.[34] Keeping the definition of persecution open allows the regime to accommodate both new human rights violations of sufficient severity and serious harms that are not yet viewed as human rights violations but which threaten one's life or freedom and are, thus, persecutory. Grave breaches of the laws of war could also amount to persecution, drawing on international humanitarian law.[35]

What about discrimination? Is discrimination persecution? While the grounds of persecution import discrimination as an integral part of the refugee definition, being subjected to discrimination per se is not sufficient for refugee status. The exception is cumulative forms of discrimination that lead to intolerable hardship. Lesser forms of discrimination—while clearly being human rights violations—are not persecution.[36]

The second pivotal aspect of the Convention definition are the 'grounds' on which an individual is at risk of being persecuted, namely 'race, religion, nationality, membership of a particular social group or political opinion'. These are clearly reminiscent of the proscribed grounds of discrimination in international law but are more limited. The ICCPR provisions on non-discrimination (Articles 2 and 26), for example, have an extensive list of proscribed grounds, including discrimination on account of 'other status'.[37] The Refugee Convention definition, in contrast, is limited to the five specific grounds. The most flexible, albeit least understood, ground is that of 'membership of a particular social group'.

---

[34] Eg *Islam (A.P.) v Secretary of State for the Home Department; R v Immigration Appeal Tribunal and Another, Ex Parte Shah (A.P.) (Conjoined appeals)* [1999] 2 WLR 1015; *Minister for Immigration and Multicultural Affairs v Khawar* [2002] HCA 14. Both cases accepted that domestic violence constituted a form of persecution in the context of Pakistan because of the absence of state protection.

[35] Edwards, 'Crossing Legal Borders: The Interface Between Refugee Law, Human Rights Law and Humanitarian Law in the "International Protection" of Refugees', in Arnold and Quenivet (eds), *International Humanitarian Law and International Human Rights: Towards a New Merger in International Law* (Martinus Nijhoff, 2008). On international humanitarian law, see Chapter 23.

[36] UNHCR Handbook, n 32, paras 54–5.

[37] 'Other status' has, for example, been used by the Human Rights Committee to deal with discrimination against refugees, asylum-seekers, or stateless persons; all statuses that are not listed explicitly: HRC, General Comment No 31, HRI/GEN/1/Rev.9 (Vol I) 243, paras 10 and 12.

Added at the last moment during the Conference of Plenipotentiaries that drafted the Convention, there is no drafting history to draw from to inform its meaning. In fact, two distinct, yet similar, tests have emerged in national jurisprudence.

The first, based on the ordinary meaning of the phrase, asks whether someone is perceived in society at large as a member of a social group. This approach is linked to human rights but in a less obvious way than the second approach.[38] The second approach, in identifying that the five Convention grounds are united by each being a 'protected characteristic', draws on human rights concepts such as human dignity to explain who is to be protected.[39] Through the social group ground, the scope of refugee protection has been expanded to slowly become more aligned with other proscribed grounds of discrimination under international human rights law, and cases that have been successful under the 'membership of a particular social group' ground have included those based on age, gender, sexual orientation, and family membership, as well as those involving child soldiers and victims of trafficking. This has allowed, for instance, female victims of domestic violence, or those subjected to female genital mutilation or forced marriage, to be granted refugee protection.[40] Notably economic or social standing has not yet been widely accepted as a ground for refugee status.[41]

6 REFUGEE *NON-REFOULEMENT* AND HUMAN RIGHTS

Concerned with the protection of refugees from persecution at the hands of their own governments, the cardinal provision in the Refugee Convention is Article 33—the 'refugee *non-refoulement*' clause. As already noted, states have accepted that *non-refoulement* of refugees is a norm of customary international law.[42] Article 33 has two parts: Article 33(1) protects a refugee from expulsion or return 'in any manner whatsoever' to where he or she would face threats to his or her life or freedom on account of race, religion,

---

[38] Examples of this approach include: *Applicant A v Minister for Immigration and Ethnic Affairs* (1997) 190 CLR 225 (rejecting that being parents wishing to have more than one child in contravention of China's one child policy constitutes a social group); compared with *Chen Shi Hai v The Minister for Immigration and Multicultural Affairs* [2000] HCA 19 (accepting that 'black children' or children born outside of China's one child policy were a social group because of the distinct treatment and discrimination faced by such children).

[39] The 'protected characteristics' test was elaborated in *Matter of Acosta*, A-24159781, US Board of Immigration Appeals, 1 March 1985, para 11: 'member of a group of persons, all of whom share a common, immutable characteristic, i.e., a characteristic that either is beyond the power of the individual members of the group to change or is so fundamental to their identities or consciences that it ought not be required to be changed'; and *Canada (Attorney General) v Ward* [1993] 2 S.C.R. 689: 'In distilling the contents of the head of "particular social group", account should be taken of the general underlying themes of the defence of human rights and anti-discrimination that form the basis for the international refugee protection initiative. A good working rule for the meaning of "particular social group" provides that this basis of persecution consists of three categories: (1) groups defined by an innate, unchangeable characteristic; (2) groups whose members voluntarily associate for reasons so fundamental to their human dignity that they should not be forced to forsake the association; and (3) groups associated by a former voluntary status, unalterable due to its historical permanence.'

[40] *Islam; Khawar*, n 34; *Secretary of State for the Home Department (Respondent) v K (FC) (Appellant); Fornah (FC) (Appellant) v Secretary of State for the Home Department (Respondent)* [2006] UKHL 46.

[41] See Foster, *International Refugee Law and Socio-Economic Rights: Refuge from Deprivation* (CUP, 2007).

[42] Declaration of States Parties to the 1951 Convention and or Its 1967 Protocol relating to the Status of Refugees, HCR/MMSP/2001/09 (16 January 2002) para 4.

nationality, membership of a particular social group, or political opinion; Article 33(2) permits a number of exceptions to the prohibition.

The obligation in Article 33(1) applies to all refugees, including those who have been recognized as such as well as to asylum-seekers whose status has not yet been determined. It includes not only direct *refoulement* where a refugee is sent home directly, but also indirect or 'chain *refoulement*', that is, where the refugee is returned to an interim country despite the fact that it is reasonably foreseeable that that state is likely to return him or her to their country of origin. Refugee *non-refoulement* also applies to rejection at the frontiers of states. Although this appears to conflict with the general principle in international law that states have the right to control the entry of non-nationals into their territory and their stay therein, allowing states to reject asylum-seekers at the border, or closing their borders in the event of a mass influx of asylum-seekers, would render meaningless the refugee *non-refoulement* obligation. In other words, Article 33 is an exception to the general discretion of states in respect of immigration control.

Given the overlap between the refugee *non-refoulement* norm and the prohibition on return under international human rights law to torture or other forms of inhuman or degrading treatment,[43] human rights law and regional human rights courts have helped strengthen and reaffirm the prohibition of *refoulement* for asylum-seekers and refugees. In the case of *Hirsi v Italy*, for example, the European Court of Human Rights determined that the Italian practice of 'push backs' in the Mediterranean Sea to Libya—that is, the turning back of boats carrying asylum-seekers and migrants (in this case including 11 Somali and 13 Eritrean nationals)—was unlawful and in violation of its obligations under Article 3 ECHR—the prohibition on *refoulement* to torture—because, despite credible information of risks of torture and ill-treatment in Libya, the Italian government continued to carry out its policy. While the Court did not rule on whether the 'push backs' also violated Article 33 of the Refugee Convention, the Court did cite the provision as part of the applicable legal framework, and further took note of the fact that Libya is not a party to the Refugee Convention in assessing Italy's liability.[44]

Likewise, the Inter-American Commission on Human Rights, having being asked to give an opinion on the interception by the US of boats carrying Haitian asylum-seekers, decided that the US practices interfered with the Haitians' right to seek asylum in other countries (that is, countries other than the US in the region) and, in pushing them back to their country of origin, violated a number of rights set out in the American Declaration on Human Rights.[45] Although the petitioners raised Article 33 of the Refugee Convention as part of their submissions, the Commission stated that it lacked jurisdiction to assess the US' compliance with it.[46] Notably, the US Supreme Court had earlier ruled that the Refugee Convention obligation of *non-refoulement* did not extend to the Haitian 'boat people' on the high seas as they were not considered within the jurisdiction of the US.[47] This remains the position in the US regarding interception of asylum-seekers on the high seas.

The jurisdictional question was also raised in the UK House of Lords' *Roma Rights* case. The Law Lords held that the principle of refugee *non-refoulement* did not apply to persons of Roma ethnicity who had been prevented by UK officials in the Czech Republic from boarding a plane to the UK where they wished to seek asylum. The House of Lords relied in

---

[43] See Chapter 6.

[44] *Hirsi Jamaa and Others v Italy*, Application no 27765/09, Judgment of 23 February 2012.

[45] Case 10.675, *The Haitian Centre for Human Rights et al. v United States*, IACommHR Report No 51/96 (13 March 1997).   [46] *The Haitian Centre*, n 45, para. 76.

[47] *Chris Sale, Acting Commissioner, Immigration and Naturalization Service, et al. v. Haitian Centers Council, Inc., et al.*, (1993) 509 US 155.

part on the fact that the individuals had not yet left their country of nationality and so were not 'outside' it in order to be treated as refugees and for the obligations under the Refugee Convention to become activated.[48] The case was not pursued to the European Court, but it would be interesting to see how such a case would be decided today in light of *Hirsi v. Italy*.

In sum, the position at international law on the scope of refugee *non-refoulement* under Article 33(1) of the Refugee Convention, especially as it concerns actions taken on the high seas, is unsettled, in part because of the lack of case law dealing with the Refugee Convention directly. Nonetheless, the most recent case law of the European Court of Human Rights in recognizing obligations of *non-refoulement* to asylum-seekers and refugees, albeit under the ECHR, helps to understand the limits and obligations in the parallel principle in the Refugee Convention. It is interesting to note that the UNHCR intervened as an *amicus curiae* in several of the cases, applying a mixture of Refugee Convention and human rights arguments.[49]

Article 33(2) is an exception to Article 33(1) in that it permits the lawful *refoulement* of refugees in two limited cases: in respect of refugees for 'whom there are reasonable grounds for regarding as a danger to the security of the country' as well as those 'who, having been convicted by a final judgment of a particularly serious crime, constitute[] a danger to the community of that country'. Despite these exceptions, Article 33(2) has been rendered largely irrelevant by developments in international human rights law, where *non-refoulement* to certain violations such as torture, are considered absolute, without exception and with no derogation.[50] At the regional level, it is also the case that Article II OAU Convention does not contain the national security exception and, thus, in Africa, the exceptions to *refoulement* do not apply. So while Article 33(2) has historical significance, states that rely on this exception are likely to be found in violation of their other obligations, and particularly those under international human rights law.

There are, thus, two main distinctions between refugee *non-refoulement* and human rights *non-refoulement*:

– The scope of the protection: in refugee law, *refugees* are protected against return to threats to life or freedom, or other serious human rights violations or serious harm amounting to persecution; in human rights law, *all individuals* are protected against return to a range of rights violations, the scope of which is still undergoing development. At a minimum, human rights law prohibits return to torture or other forms of inhuman or degrading treatment.

– The exceptions to *non-refoulement*: the Refugee Convention permits lawful *refoulement* in specific circumstances, whereas human rights *non-refoulement* to certain risks (such as torture) is absolute. The latter has rendered the exceptions in Article 33(2) Refugee Convention largely irrelevant.

Despite these distinctions, human rights law and courts are increasingly being used to provide protection against return to refugees and asylum-seekers.

---

[48] *R v. Immigration Officer at Prague Airport and Another, Ex parte European Roma Rights Centre and Others,* [2004] UKHL 55, 9 December 2004.

[49] See UN High Commissioner for Refugees, Submission by the Office of the United Nations High Commissioner for Refugees in the case of Hirsi and Others v. Italy, March 2010, available at: <http://www.unhcr.org/refworld/docid/4b97778d2.html>; UN High Commissioner for Refugees, *The European Roma Rights Center and Others (Appellants) v. (1) The Immigration Officer at Prague Airport, (2) The Secretary of State for the Home Department (Respondents), and the Office of the United Nations High Commissioner for Refugees (Intervener). Skeleton Argument on Behalf of the Intervener (UNHCR),* 30 January 2003, available at: <http://www.refworld.org/docid/3e5ba6d45.html>.

[50] Eg, *Chahal v UK* (1997) 23 EHRR 413; *Soering v UK* (1989) 11 EHRR 439.

7 THE PROTECTIONS ACCORDED TO REFUGEES

The Refugee Convention is not only a status-defining instrument. It also contains a range of rights to which refugees are entitled. Articles 3 to 34 list a range of civil rights—such as freedom of religion (Article 3), property rights (Articles 13 and 14), freedom of association (Article 15), and access to courts (Article 16), as well as economic, social, and cultural rights—such as employment rights (Articles 17 to 19) and welfare, social security, and education rights (Articles 20 to 24). The 'structure of entitlement' in the Convention has two specific layers.

First, not all rights are immediately applicable; rather their applicability is dependent upon the length of stay in the territory ('attachment'). There are four general categories of attachment, namely 'simple presence', 'lawful presence', 'lawful residence', and 'habitual residence'.[51] Very few rights included in the Refugee Convention explicitly apply to asylum-seekers, that is, those who have not yet been determined to be refugees. Articles 31 (non-penalization) and 33 (*non-refoulement*) are two such provisions. It is, however, arguable that all those provisions without an indicated level of attachment also apply to asylum-seekers, such as the right to education for children (Article 22), based on the argument that refugee status is declaratory rather than determinative—that is, determining a person to be a refugee does not *make* him or her a refugee, but rather such determination simply *recognizes* that he or she is a refugee (and, in most cases, was a refugee at the time of entry to the territory).[52] This concept is important given the time lag between one's application for refugee status and the final determination of that application.

The second structure of entitlement is that the rights are to be enjoyed on an equivalent basis to three types of legal persons: nationals, 'most favoured nationals' (that is, the standards applicable to the most favoured foreigners, such as permanent residents or particular nationalities benefiting from preferred treatment under regional arrangements, such as EU or ECOWAS nationals), or 'aliens generally' (that is, other non-nationals). In fact, the Refugee Convention is an elaborate mixture of rights, and one needs to analyse carefully each right in question to determine its full and proper scope.

Given that the Refugee Convention is a treaty that is dedicated to setting the standards of treatment of refugees, how is it that recourse to human rights law is permitted as a matter of international law? And why is it needed at all?

In response to the first question, there are two main arguments for importing human rights standards into refugee law. First, Article 5 Refugee Convention, already mentioned, stresses that '[n]othing in this Convention shall be deemed to impair any rights and benefits granted by a Contracting State to refugees apart from this Convention'. The *travaux préparatoires* relating to Article 5 indicate that it was inserted as an attempt to safeguard more generous practices of some states that had been assumed voluntarily.[53] A modern reading of the provision would incorporate new obligations assumed under international law as applicable to refugees, unless specific reservations were made to those treaties.

The second argument is that human rights treaties are applicable to 'everyone' and to 'all human beings' and are in only very few instances 'category-specific' (eg citizens' rights to political participation in Article 25 ICCPR). As such, they apply to refugees as human beings per se. The main exception is in respect of economic rights: Article 2(3) ICESCR allows developing countries—where 80 per cent of the world's refugees are hosted[54]—to

---

[51] Goodwin-Gill and McAdam, n 27, 524–8.   [52] UNHCR Handbook, n 32, para 28.
[53] *The Refugee Convention, 1951: The Travaux Preparatoires Analysed with a Commentary by Dr Paul Weis*, 37, available at: <http://www.unhcr.org/4ca34be29.html>. See also, Skordas, 'Article 5', in Zimmerman, n 19, 669.
[54] UNHCR, *Global Trends 2011*, available at: <http://www.unhcr.org/4fd6f87f9.html>.

make an exception with respect to extending economic rights to non-nationals, subject to some safeguards.[55]

Moving to the question of why recourse to human rights law is needed, the answer is that the Refugee Convention, despite having an extensive list of rights, many of which do not find expression in human rights law, does not deal with all the issues facing refugees. While it could be argued that certain rights were omitted because refugees were not meant to benefit from them, this does not make sense across the board. For example, the prohibition on torture is not contained in the Refugee Convention but it would never be suggested that refugees could be tortured. In fact, human rights law is regularly used to fill gaps in the refugee protection architecture. There is considerable jurisprudence explaining how various human rights provisions apply to refugees.[56]

That said, it needs to be noted that the ways in which the two regimes work in respect of rights is distinct. Refugee law provides for the gradual accumulation of rights over time in the country of asylum, subject to a number of standards—such as that refugees are to enjoy the same educational rights as nationals, but only rights to wage-earning employment on a par with non-nationals generally. Human rights law does not work in this way, and although the ICESCR speaks of 'progressive realization', this is different from the gradual accumulation of rights based on length of stay. Progressive realization relates to the state's obligation to progressively implement rights,[57] whereas in the Refugee Convention the emphasis is on the right of refugees to enjoy more rights the longer they are in the territory of a state of asylum.

8 THE END OF REFUGEE STATUS AND SOLUTIONS FOR REFUGEES

Neither UNHCR's Statute, which calls on UNHCR to find, together with governments, solutions for refugees, nor the Refugee Convention intended for refugee status to be life-long. As an anomaly to normal citizen–state relations, the reattachment to a state—either through repatriation to one's country of origin, local integration/naturalization in the country of asylum, or resettlement to a third country—is considered to bring about the end of refugee status.

The Refugee Convention stipulates both individual and general conditions under which refugee status formally comes to an end. Article 1C(1)–(4) outlines the circumstances in which individual action triggers the cessation of status, such as voluntary re-establishment in one's country of origin. Article 1C(5)–(6), by contrast, ceases the status of a refugee where fundamental and durable changes in the country of origin indicate that protection is no longer needed. This is known as general cessation.[58] The prevailing general human rights conditions in the country of origin form part of the general cessation assessment.

---

[55] See Edwards, Human Rights, n 30, for an exploration of how this works in respect of the right to work.

[56] Edwards, n 30.   [57] On progressive realization see Chapter 7.

[58] UNHCR, Guidelines on International Protection: Cessation of Refugee Status under Article 1C(5) and (6) of the 1951 Convention relating to the Status of Refugees (The 'Ceased Circumstances' Clauses), HCR/GIP/03/03 (10 February 2003). There are exceptions to cessation for those with a continuing need for international protection or owing to compelling reasons of previous persecution cannot be expected to return: see [19]–[21]. See also, *Minister for Immigration and Multicultural and Indigenous Affairs v QAAH of 2004* (2006) 231 CLR 1, 53.

General cessation has been declared 25 times on a group basis between 1973 and 2008,[59] while two more cessation declarations took effect in 2012.[60]

Of the three traditional durable solutions, the Refugee Convention is oriented towards 'assimilation and naturalization' in the country of asylum (Article 34), also called local integration. This is the most common solution for refugees in industrialized countries, where permanent residency and later citizenship are made available to refugees usually within three to five years of being granted status. Commonly, access to citizenship is on more favourable terms than other migrants in recognition of refugees' loss of state protection. However, granting residency or citizenship is not an obligation and realization of this goal has become increasingly elusive in other parts of the world. As such, the international community has developed different strategies to find 'solutions' for refugees.

The repatriation of refugees to their countries of origin on a voluntary basis when conditions permit has been seen by some states to be the preferred option for many large-scale refugee situations. Historic examples of voluntary repatriation include the 300,000 Cambodian refugees repatriated from Thailand in time for national elections in 1993, the more than 5.7 million Afghan refugees who have returned voluntarily to Afghanistan since 2001, and the 155,000 Liberians who returned home from Guinea in 2012.

Resettlement to third countries, whereby refugees are relocated as both a protection and burden-sharing measure, has been a modern response offered by some states. Currently, 27 countries offer approximately 80,000 resettlement places annually, although the largest number of resettlement places are allocated by traditionally known 'immigration countries' such as the US, Australia, and Canada. As a protection response, resettlement works to remove vulnerable refugees from countries where they remain at risk. Resettlement has also been used to unlock protracted refugee situations or to respond to large-scale crises.

The 1980s Comprehensive Plan of Action in which hundreds of thousands of Indo-Chinese refugees were resettled to Australia, Canada, the US, and other countries is an example of a collective effort to find solutions for refugees. It was also a life-saving arrangement which allowed the 'boat people' to be disembarked temporarily into South East Asian countries, with the agreement that they would be resettled elsewhere. A smaller scale example of group resettlement involved the so-called 'Lost Boys of the Sudan', in which 3,600 young Sudanese boys living in refugee camps in Kenya and Ethiopia were resettled to the US in 2001. The ongoing resettlement programme of Bhutanese refugees from Nepal, now numbering 69,000 who have been resettled refugees since 2007, has dual aims: to find permanent solutions for the large majority, while moving from humanitarian assistance to sustainable development in Nepal for the refugee-hosting and impacted areas, and promoting peaceful coexistence between communities.[61]

In recent years some consideration has been paid to another solution, namely giving refugees access to international migration options for work purposes; however, such schemes have yet to be operationalized. The idea is that such access would allow refugees to apply for national migration schemes in other countries. Its aim is to give opportunities

---

[59] Siddiqui, 'Reviewing the Application of the Cessation Clause of the *1951 Refugee Convention relating to the Status of Refugees* in Africa', Working Paper No 76, Refugee Studies Centre, University of Oxford (August 2011), Annex 1, at 52.

[60] These two situations included Angolan and Liberian refugees; a third situation of pre-1999 Rwandan refugees remains subject to the implementation by host governments: 'UNHCR Working to Help Conclude Three African Refugee Situations', UNHCR Media Release (7 February 2012), available at: <http://www.unhcr.org/4f3125cc9.html>.

[61] Further details are available on the country pages of UNHCR's website: <http://www.unhcr.org>.

to refugees to 'migrate out' of their situation and to be able to realize their full potential. This stands in contrast to the situation facing many of the world's refugees, who are denied work rights in their countries of asylum, or may even be housed in camps with limited freedom of movement.[62]

Finding solutions for refugees is not straightforward, and goes well beyond legal provisions. In fact, identifying durable solutions for refugees often requires political solutions to the many intractable and cyclical conflicts causing refugee flight.

8 CONCLUSION

Refugee rights are human rights. The Refugee Convention and regional refugee instruments are human rights instruments in so far as they grant rights to refugees. They are also refugee-specific instruments, which were designed to reflect the particular circumstances of refugees, such circumstances not being as easily reflected in the main human rights instruments. Sharing as background a history of persecution and oppression, human rights law sets the standards against which states' behaviour towards those within their jurisdiction are to be judged, while the Refugee Convention was intended to ensure protection of persons who could no longer obtain the protection of their own states. The two regimes are, therefore, distinct and, at the same time, mutually reinforcing.

FURTHER READING

ANKER, 'Refugee law, Gender, and the Human Rights Paradigm' (2002) 15 *Harvard HRJ* 133.

EDWARDS and FERSTMAN (eds), *Human Security and Non-Citizens: Law, Policy and International Affairs* (Cambridge University Press, 2010).

FELLER, TÜRK, and NICHOLSON (eds), *Refugee Protection in International Law: UNHCR's Global Consultations on International Protection* (Cambridge University Press, 2003).

LAMBERT (ed), *International Refugee Law* (Ashgate, 2010).

MUSALO, 'Claims for Protection Based on Religion or Belief: Analysis and Proposed Conclusions' (2004) 16 *IJRL* 165.

PLENDER and MOLE, 'Beyond the Geneva Convention: Constructing a *de facto* right of asylum from international human rights instruments', in Nicholson and Twomey (eds), *Refugee Rights and Realities* (Cambridge University Press, 1999.

SHACKNOVE, 'Who is a refugee?' (1985) 95 *Ethics* 274.

WEISSBRODT, *The Human Rights of Non-Citizens* (Oxford University Press, 2008), chs 5 and 7.

ZIMMERMAN (ed), *Commentary on the 1951 Convention relating to the Status of Refugees* (Oxford University Press, 2011).

---

[62] See, UNHCR and the International Labour Organization (ILO), Workshop on Labour Mobility for Refugees: Summary Conclusions, 11–12 September 2012, available at: <http://www.unhcr.org/refworld/pdfid/508e4fa72.pdf>.

USEFUL WEBSITES

Forced Migration Online: <http://www.forcedmigration.org/>

Refworld: <http://www.unhcr.org/cgi-bin/texis/vtx/refworld/rwmain>

The Refugee Law Reader: <http://www.refugeelawreader.org/>

Refugee Caselaw: <http://www.refugeecaselaw.org/Home.aspx>

Center for Gender and Refugee Studies: <http://cgrs.uchastings.edu/>

PART VI
CHALLENGES

26

NON-STATE ACTORS

Andrew Clapham

SUMMARY

It is increasingly recognized that human rights law has to address the challenge posed by non-state actors. This chapter starts with a reflection on how the term 'non-state actor' is used and why it is appropriate to look at the impact of non-state actors on the enjoyment of human rights. It then recalls the 'positive obligations' of states to protect those within their jurisdiction from abuses by non-state actors. Finally, it considers the human rights obligations of different non-state actors: international organizations, certain non-state actors under international criminal law, corporations, and armed non-state entities. The chapter argues that we should meet the following challenges: extending and translating certain norms so that they clearly denote the obligations of non-state actors; creating and adapting specific institutions to ensure jurisdiction over the activities of non-state actors; and adjusting our assumptions about who are the duty-bearers in the human rights regime.

1 INTRODUCTION

Even though the term 'non-state actor' can be defined quite simply as any entity that is not a state, it deserves some explanation. In some contexts the term is used to refer to benign civil society groups working for human rights—and it has become commonplace (even a cliché) to refer to the need to 'involve non-state actors in the conversation'. In other contexts, however, the term is understood to refer to some very 'uncivil' groups determined to acquire weapons of mass destruction and target them against a civilian population. The differing use of the term can be confusing not only in terms of understanding what is being alluded to, but also in comprehending the legal obligations involved.

Depending on the context, international law provides that states are either obliged to punish non-state actors or, alternatively, obliged to cooperate with them.[1] Although some commentators have sought to avoid ambiguity and focus the discussion by referring to those non-state actors that violate human rights as non-state perpetrators,[2] to follow this path so early in our discussion would obscure the fact that there are increasing expectations that non-state actors of all kinds should not only refrain from violations, but also work to

---

[1] See AU Convention for the Protection and Assistance of Internally Displaced Persons in Africa (2009), Art 1; SC Res 1540, S/RES/1540 (28 April 2004); Cotonou Agreement between the Members of the African, Caribbean and Pacific Group of States and the European Community and its Member States (2000), Art 6.

[2] Spirer and Spirer, 'Accounting for Human Rights Violations by Non-State Actors' in Andreopoulos, Arat, and Juvilier (eds), *Non-State Actors in the Human Rights Universe* (Kumarian Press, 2006) 43.

protect and promote human rights. Like states, non-state actors are seen as embodying the paradox that their capacity to violate contains within it the potential for protection. Recent scholarship has started to map the landscape so that actors are seen as both the source of human rights violations and the engines for pressuring other actors to advance human rights. In this way, non-state actors can be the 'source and target of pressure at the same time' and such pressure can support or breach human rights.[3]

But even if we admit that the expression 'non-state actor' means different things in different contexts, and that all such actors have the potential either to violate or to promote human rights, there is another problem we need to address. The problem is that the human rights regime has developed along state-centric lines. Human rights treaties were traditionally written by states as sets of obligations for states. The accompanying monitoring mechanisms that provide for state accountability are based on traditional rules of state responsibility. To adjust this system, and to revise the assumptions that have grown up around it, tends to trigger considerable resistance.

Why would lawyers and governments want to exclude non-state actors from the state-centric regime of international law in general, and human rights law in particular? There are a number of reasons. First, with regard to armed opposition groups (also sometimes characterized as 'terrorists'), it is argued that suggesting such groups have human rights obligations under international law lends them a state-like status, which renders them somehow 'legitimate'. This apparent enhanced legitimacy is considered by some governments to be undesirable. Second, in some circumstances, governments may be wary of allowing international organizations to assume state-like features by taking on international obligations, such as those relating to human rights. This has been the case, for example, with regard to the attitude of some governments towards the European Union playing a greater role as the bearer of human rights obligations. Third, corporations and international financial institutions such as the World Bank and the International Monetary Fund are usually not keen to take on a raft of responsibilities that they see as properly the responsibilities of states. In particular, in the imagined extension of all human rights obligations to corporations, there is a perceived danger of undermining or diluting the responsibilities of states. For example, in 2006, John Ruggie, the United Nations (UN) Secretary-General's Special Representative on business and human rights, advised the UN Commission on Human Rights that: 'Corporations are not democratic public interest institutions and…making them, in effect, co-equal duty bearers for the broad spectrum of human rights…may undermine efforts to build indigenous social capacity and to make governments more responsible to their own citizenry.'[4]

We have, then, two perceived problems: a 'legitimacy' problem and a 'dilution' problem. These problems can be quite easily overcome. We can suggest that armed opposition groups and their members are increasingly accused of violations of international humanitarian law and even convicted of war crimes. Highlighting violations of these obligations ought to be seen as de-legitimizing rather than anything else. The problem of legitimizing armed groups evaporates if we decouple human rights from the idea that human rights supposedly emerge from an essential link between governments and their citizens. When we see human rights as rights rather than self-imposed governmental duties, and when we envisage the rights project as founded on better protection for human dignity rather than privileges granted by states, we can start to see how we might imagine human rights obligations for non-state actors. Rather than concentrating on abstract questions of legitimacy

---

[3] Arat, 'Looking beyond the State But Not Ignoring It', in Andreopoulos *et al.*, n 2, 8.

[4] Interim Report of the Special Representative of the Secretary-General on the Issue of Human Rights and Transnational Corporations and Other Business Enterprises, E/CN.4/2006/97 (22 February 2006) para 68.

we can take a more sentimental approach and imagine ourselves in the shoes of a victim. From the victim's perspective, the inhuman and degrading treatment is an assault on dignity whether it is suffered at the hands of a policeman, a rebel commander, or a private security company. With regards to dilution, we can suggest that corporations, international financial institutions, and development agencies have to respect human rights in ways that complement the responsibilities of states, rather than replacing state obligations.

We are already moving in this direction. It is worth considering the report on the 'Alliance of Civilizations', which fixes expectations on non-state actors without seeming to be worried about legitimacy. At the same time, the report cautions about demonizing non-state actors and leaving states out of the picture, thus, addressing worries about dilution:

> A full and consistent adherence to human rights standards forms the foundation for stable societies and peaceful international relations. These rights include the prohibition against physical and mental torture; the right to freedom of religion; and the right to freedom of expression and association.... The integrity of these rights rests on their universal and unconditional nature. These rights should therefore be considered inviolable and all states, international organisations, non-state actors, and individuals, under all circumstances, must abide by them....
>
> Extremism and terrorism are not motivated solely by exclusivist interpretations of religion, nor are non-state actors alone in employing them... a cursory look at the twentieth century indicates that no single group, culture, geographic region, or political orientation has a monopoly on extremism and terrorist acts.[5]

The most promising theoretical basis for human rights obligations for non-state actors is to remind ourselves that the foundational basis of human rights is best explained as rights which belong to the individual in recognition of each person's inherent dignity. The implication is that these natural rights should be respected by everyone and every entity. Moreover, we should recall that the Universal Declaration of Human Rights is written as a proclamation of rights; the obligations of states were not agreed upon at that time. The word 'state' hardly appears in the Declaration. Furthermore, if we leave aside the treaty regimes, with their state-centred monitoring mechanisms, and concentrate on general principles of international law or customary international law, it becomes apparent that even though the jurisdictional clauses of the treaty bodies preclude complaints against non-state actors, the substantive norms themselves may easily be adapted to apply to non-state actors. Before turning to the actual state of human rights law, let us look at four dynamics that challenge the traditional state-focused approach to human rights law.

2 THE CHALLENGE OF NON-STATE ACTORS

2.1 GLOBALIZATION

The globalization of the world economy and means of communication have highlighted the power of large corporations and their limited accountability in law for human rights abuses.[6] There exist today increased possibilities for enterprises to outsource different links in the manufacturing chain, by relying on supplies from subcontractors all over the world. In addition, competition between states to attract foreign direct investment has

---

[5] Alliance of Civilizations: Report of the High Level Group (13 November 2006) paras 2.3 and 3.12.

[6] Eg Amnesty International, *Undermining Freedom of Expression in China: The Role of Yahoo!, Microsoft and Google* (2006); Flint, 'Don't be Evil?' (2006) 27 *Business LRev* 102–4.

sometimes resulted in pressure on labour rights, in particular in the garment sector and in special export-processing zones, with minimal regulation or control over employer practices. Moreover, foreign companies working in the extractive industry have had to resort to special security arrangements in the host state. This practice has led to serious questions about violence at the hands of public and private security guards in this context. The emerging framework for ensuring greater responsibility in these areas is international human rights law.[7]

In a first phase, emphasis was put on the state's duty to protect individuals from such non-state actors. However, this has proven inadequate. Imagine a corporation incorporated in one state with abusive security services operating in another state or a company supplying arms to abusive regimes abroad, risks to health from the chemical or extractive industries operating in developing countries, or the complaints against US private military contractors for killings and allegations of torture in Iraq.[8] In each case to rely on the states concerned to protect people from such abuses is unworkable. Accordingly, a second approach has been suggested, namely that corporate activity should be simply dealt with by national legal tools such as tort or contract law. Transnational activity, with links to multiple jurisdictions, ought to make it easy to find an accountability mechanism; but the opposite is the case.[9] Globalization reminds us that corporate actors have the possibility to operate from multiple jurisdictions, which will not necessarily ensure that they are held accountable for human rights abuses. It also reminds us that governments competing for investment have shown little inclination to develop accountability for corporate abuses.

2.2 PRIVATIZATION

The privatization of sectors such as health, education, prisons, water, communications, security forces, and military training has forced us to think again about the applicability of human rights law to the private sector. Many assume that something which is privatized remains subject to human rights law as the concept of human rights is related to so-called 'public functions'. But this assumption is not borne out in practice. First, the whole point of privatization is to remove certain activity from the state-run sphere, increasing flexibility and usually diminishing accountability. The usual consequence is that the protections that have developed with regard to state activity no longer apply and, although in theory new private remedies should apply, such remedies tend not to include human rights protection in name. The same act, therefore, gets relabelled. What was once a human rights violation becomes a civil wrong, a tort, or a breach of contract. Second, the new entity, which has taken on the former responsibilities of the state, has something that the state did not have. The new non-state entity may have competing human rights, which can be enforced or weighed against anyone claiming their rights against this non-state actor. So, for example, the owners and managers of a private shopping mall dominating a town centre will be able to claim respect for the enjoyment of their private property when protestors claim freedom of expression and assembly in that privatized space.[10]

---

[7] Eg Voluntary Principles on Security and Human Rights (2000).

[8] See International Commission of Jurists, *Report of the Expert Legal Panel on Corporate Complicity in International Crimes*, available at: <http://www.business-humanrights.org/Updates/Archive/ICJPaneloncomplicity>.

[9] See the Corporate Responsibility Coalition, *The Reality of Rights: Barriers to Accessing Remedies When Business Operates Beyond Borders* (London School of Economics and Political Science, 2009).

[10] *Appleby v UK* (2003) 37 EHRR 38.

2.3 FRAGMENTATION OF STATES

The increase in the number of internal armed conflicts involves a third phenomenon: the fragmentation of states as non-state actors take control of territory and populations. Such an exercise of power by armed opposition groups has led to greater expectations of them. The demands go beyond international humanitarian law and individual responsibility under international criminal law. As we shall see, the Special Rapporteurs of the UN Human Rights Council already report on human rights violations by all sides to an armed conflict, and the state/non-state actor boundary again seems less and less relevant. In this context we should also consider the assumption of state-like tasks carried out by the UN in situations of territorial administration such as those of Kosovo and East Timor. This has led to new developments with regard to the applicability of human rights law to the UN and other international organizations in the context of their protection work.

2.4 FEMINIZATION

The developments surrounding the international human rights of women have led to a complete reappraisal of the way in which the public/private divide has been constructed to delimit human rights law. Some treaties now specifically require the state to take action to protect women in the 'private sphere' or to guarantee women's rights in public and private life.[11] International obligations and commitments have been reconfigured through the prism of due diligence, to ensure that they cover daily harm to women and not only a narrow range of concerns of men. The feminization of human rights has shifted the emphasis to issues of violence against women, certain unfair labour practices, sexual exploitation, trafficking, and 'traditional practices' such as honour killings.

3 THE LEGAL FRAMEWORK

All human rights treaties contain positive obligations that oblige states to protect those within their jurisdiction from harms committed by non-state actors.[12] Different treaty bodies and international courts have addressed the extent of these obligations in different contexts. The Human Rights Committee has stated in relation to the International Covenant on Civil and Political Rights (ICCPR) that:

> the positive obligations on States Parties to ensure Covenant rights will only be fully discharged if individuals are protected by the State, not just against violations of Covenant rights by its agents, but also against acts committed by private persons or entities that would impair the enjoyment of Covenant rights in so far as they are amenable to application between private persons or entities. There may be circumstances in which a failure to ensure Covenant rights as required by article 2 [ICCPR] would give rise to violations by States Parties of those rights, as a result of States Parties' permitting or failing to take appropriate measures or to exercise due diligence to prevent, punish, investigate or redress the harm caused by such acts by private persons or entities.[13]

There is a rich vein of case law that allows us to determine the extent to which it is reasonable to expect states not only to punish but also to prevent non-state actors from interfering

---

[11] See Chapter 16.   [12] See Chapter 5.
[13] HRC, General Comment 31, HRI/GEN/1/Rev.9 (Vol 1) 243.

with the enjoyment of human rights under human rights treaties.[14] There are a number
of possibilities through which states may give effect to their positive obligation to protect
individuals from harms committed by non-state actors.

First, some states may give effect to certain international human rights by simply incorporating treaty rights and obligations into their national legal orders. In some situations
this may mean that the human rights obligation applies to certain non-state actors even in
the absence of special legislation.[15]

A second possibility is that the jurisdiction in question allows for human rights claims
against private entities in its constitution (such as South Africa) or has some legislation
that is applied to facilitate human rights claims against non-state actors.

The growing number of cases being litigated under the US Alien Tort Statute (also known
as the Alien Tort Claims Act) is significant in this context. The Alien Tort Statute confers
upon US federal district courts original jurisdiction over 'any civil action by an alien for a
tort only, committed in violation of the law of nations', wherever it may have taken place.[16] It
has proven perfectly possible to bring a suit against a corporation for violating international
law as the principal perpetrator. For example, cases have been brought against contractors
providing interpretation and interrogation services to the USA at Abu Ghraib prison in Iraq
in respect of torture and inhuman or degrading treatment[17] and against Blackwater (a private military contractor) alleging war crimes in connection with the killing of civilians.[18]

US courts have been gradually refining the list of violations of the 'law of nations' that will
be justiciable in this context. Recent rulings have determined that genocide, slave trading, slavery, forced labour, and war crimes are actionable even in the absence of any connection to the
state.[19] In addition, according to the *Kadic v Karadzic* judgment, where rape, torture, and summary execution are committed, these crimes 'are actionable under the Alien Tort Act, without
regard to state action, to the extent they were committed in pursuit of genocide or war crimes'.[20]
In fact, even though US courts, including the Supreme Court, have determined that violations
of the 'law of nations' under this statute must be those that are 'specific, universal and obligatory' and have suggested that the drafters of the Alien Tort Statute probably had in mind a narrow set of violations such as piracy or an assault on an ambassador, the list is not exhaustive, as
international law continues to evolve.[21] Claims concerning adult labour conditions have been
held not to meet the requisite threshold. In 2007, in a case against the Bridgestone Corporation
concerning conditions at their plant in Liberia, a US court determined:

> [T]here is a broad international consensus that at least some extreme practices called 'forced
> labor' violate universal and binding international norms. But the adult plaintiffs in this case
> allege labor practices that lie somewhere on a continuum that ranges from those clear violations
> of international law (slavery or labor forced at the point of soldiers' bayonets) to more ambigu-
> ous situations involving poor working conditions and meager or exploitative wages.[22]

---

[14] Eg *X and Y v The Netherlands* (1985) 8 EHRR 235; *Velásquez Rodriguez v Honduras*, IACtHR Series
C No 4 (29 July 1988); 204/97, *Mouvement Burkinabé des Droits de l'Homme et des Peuples v Burkina Faso*,
ACommHPR; see generally Clapham, *Human Rights Obligations of Non-State Actors* (OUP, 2006) chs 8 and 9.

[15] Eg the situation in the Netherlands: Jägers and van der Heijden, 'Corporate Human Rights Violations: the
Feasibility of Civil Recourse in the Netherlands' (2008) 33 *Brooklyn JIL* 834, 856. For more examples see Oliver
and Fedtke (eds), *Human Rights and the Private Sphere* (Routledge-Cavendish, 2007).

[16] 28 USC § 1350.

[17] *Ibrahim et al. v Titan et al.*; *Saleh et al. v Titan et al.*, Case 1:05-cv-01165-JR (Order of 6 November 2007).

[18] *Abtan et al. v Blackwater Worldwide et al.*, Case 1:07-cv-01831 (RBW), filed 26 November 2007.

[19] *Wiwa v Royal Dutch Shell Petroleum (Shell)*, Case 96 civ 8386 (KMV), Opinion and Order of 28 February
2002, 39. See also *Doe I v Unocal Corporation* (2002) 395 F 3d 932, paras 3 ff.

[20] *Kadic v Karadzic* (1995) 70 F 3d 232, 243–4.

[21] *Sosa v Alvarez-Machain et al.* (2004) 542 US 692, 732 and 734–7.

[22] *Roe et al. v Bridgestone Corporation et al.* (2007) 492 F Supp 2d 988, 1010.

In the 2013 case of *Kiobel v Royal Dutch Petroleum*, the US Supreme Court avoided the question as to whether or not a corporation could be a defendant in a case concerning a violation of the 'law of nations'. Instead, it focused on the presumption against extraterritorial application of legislation and required that claims demonstrate a nexus with the USA. The nexus has to be more than 'mere corporate presence' and the opinion concludes that 'where the claims touch and concern the territory of the United States, they must do so with sufficient force to displace the presumption against extraterritorial application.'[23] At the time of writing a number of similar cases were pending before US courts and the judgments in those cases will shape the extent to which Alien Tort Statute cases can continue to be brought, both with regard to the need for a nexus to the USA, and with regard to the scope of the human rights obligations that are considered sufficiently specific, universal, and obligatory to form the substance of a complaint in this context.[24]

A third possibility is that the incorporating legislation addresses the issue of non-state actors explicitly. This is the case for the Human Rights Act 1998 in the UK. Section 6, entitled 'Acts of public authorities', provides in part:

(1) It is unlawful for a public authority to act in a way which is incompatible with a Convention [ECHR] right....

(3) In this section 'public authority' includes—

    (a) a court or tribunal, and

    (b) any person certain of whose functions are functions of a public nature,

    but does not include either House of Parliament or a person exercising functions in connection with proceedings in Parliament.

(4) In subsection (3) 'Parliament' does not include the House of Lords in its judicial capacity.

(5) In relation to a particular act, a person is not a public authority by virtue only of subsection (3)(b) if the nature of the act is private.

So a non-state actor with functions of a public nature carrying out acts that are not of a private nature has human rights obligations under the Act. Interpreting this conundrum has given rise to a rich stream of case law and has split the then Judicial Committee of the House of Lords in the context of a complaint against a residential care home,[25] and led to new legislation.[26]

Stepping back from the detailed interpretations in these cases, the question of whether to apply human rights to non state actors has forced judges to reflect on the foundational rationale for human rights—to protect individual dignity—and admit that it does not matter from which side of the public/private divide the harm comes. At this point we find that opinions divide, not only on whether certain functions such as education, healthcare, restaurants, rented accommodation, social housing, shopping malls, telephone services, residential care for the elderly, detention, and security are 'obviously' public functions, but also on the question of how much power judges should have to interpret such 'new' obligations for private actors. Our answer depends in part on our approach to human rights: must they be granted

---

[23] *Kiobel v Royal Dutch Petroleum* (2013) 569 US, Slip Opinion 14. See also the concurring opinions for an approach which looks to the nationality of the parties to the dispute and the need to avoid the USA becoming a safe haven for torturers and other 'common enemies of mankind'.

[24] Eg *DaimlerChrysler AG v Bauman*, US Supreme Court Docket No 11-965 (under appeal before US Supreme Court); *Rio Tinto PLC v Sarei*, US Supreme Court Docket No 11-649 (under appeal before US Supreme Court); *John Doe VIII et al. v Exxon Mobil et al.* (pending before DC Circuit).

[25] *YL (by her litigation friend the Official Solicitor) (FC) (Appellant) v Birmingham City Council and others (Respondents)* [2007] UKHL 27.

[26] See Social Care Act 2009, s 145. See also Dickson, *Human Rights and the United Kingdom Supreme Court* (OUP, 2013) 85–8.

through the authoritative process of law-making? Or are they inherent in the individual, generated from a basic obligation on us all to protect human dignity and autonomy?

In a case brought by Naomi Campbell against Mirror Group Newspapers for a breach of her privacy in respect of publication of a photograph of her leaving Narcotics Anonymous, the issue arose as to the weight (if any) to be given to her right to privacy as opposed to the freedom of expression and information claims made by the newspaper. In the past such a claim might have been seen as having nothing to do with human rights due to the absence of a state actor. Today, the expectations are different. Lord Hoffmann reflected this in his speech:

> What human rights law has done is to identify private information as something worth pro-tecting as an aspect of human autonomy and dignity. And this recognition has raised ines-capably the question of why it should be worth protecting against the state but not against a private person. There may of course be justifications for the publication of private information by private persons which would not be available to the state—I have particularly in mind the position of the media, to which I shall return in a moment—but I can see no logical ground for saying that a person should have less protection against a private individual than he would have against the state for the publication of personal information for which there is no justifi-cation. Nor, it appears, have any of the other judges who have considered the matter.[27]

Baroness Hale, in the same case, drew the logical conclusion that as the courts are pub-lic authorities, all their decisions should apply human rights law even in actions brought against non-state actors:

> Neither party to this appeal has challenged the basic principles which have emerged from the Court of Appeal in the wake of the Human Rights Act 1998. The 1998 Act does not create any new cause of action between private persons. But if there is a relevant cause of action applicable, the court as a public authority must act compatibly with both parties' Convention rights.[28]

Lastly, in other situations, legislation has been *interpreted* to cover human rights claims brought against non-state actors. We can find a pervasive percolation of human rights val-ues into judicial reasoning and constitutional interpretation, in ways that indirectly apply human rights obligations to non-state actors.[29]

4 THE OBLIGATIONS OF INTERNATIONAL ORGANIZATIONS

A traditional starting point for the assertion that international organizations have inter-national obligations is the International Court of Justice's statement that international organizations are subject to 'general rules of international law.[30] As Christian Tomuschat points out:

> Substantively, international organizations may be characterized as common agencies oper-ated by States for the fulfilment of certain common tasks. Now, if States acting individually

---

[27] *Campbell v MGN Limited* [2004] UKHL 22, para 50.   [28] *Campbell*, para 132.

[29] See Gardbaum, 'The "Horizontal Effect" of Constitutional Rights' (2003) 102 *Michigan LRev* 387; Barak, 'Constitutional Human Rights and Private Law' in Friedmann and Barak-Erez (eds), *Human Rights in Private Law* (Hart Publishing, 2001) 13; Tushnet, 'The Issue of State Action/Horizontal Effect in Comparative Constitutional Law' (2003) 1 *Intl J Const L* 79.

[30] *Interpretation of the Agreement of 25 March 1951 Between the WHO and Egypt* [1980] ICJ Rep 73, 89–90.

have been subjected to certain rules thought to be indispensable for maintaining orderly relations within the international community, there is no justification for exempting international organizations from the scope *ratione personae* of such rules.[31]

Many would agree with Tomuschat that, even if states can limit the powers of the organization they create, they 'cannot thereby shield their creation from becoming liable towards other subjects of international law on account of [their] activities'.[32] This reasoning has been reflected in the approach of the European Court of Human Rights:

> The Court is of the opinion that where States establish international organisations in order to pursue or strengthen their cooperation in certain fields of activities, and where they attribute to these organisations certain competences and accord them immunities, there may be implications as to the protection of fundamental rights. It would be incompatible with the purpose and object of the Convention [ECHR], however, if the Contracting States were thereby absolved from their responsibility under the Convention in relation to the field of activity covered by such attribution. It should be recalled that the Convention is intended to guarantee not theoretical or illusory rights, but rights that are practical and effective.[33]

But this approach, developed in the context of employment relations, with regard to international entities such as the European Space Agency, has been revisited in complaints regarding peace operations in Kosovo. The issue arose in stark terms in the context of applications brought by Agim and Bekir Behrami against France, and Ruzhdi Saramati against France, Germany, and Norway in the European Court of Human Rights.[34] The complaint of the Behramis concerned the right to life under Article 2 European Convention on Human Rights (ECHR) and related to the failure of the French Kosovo Force (the NATO Force, KFOR) personnel to clear undetonated cluster bomb units. With regard to Saramati the complaint concerned his detention by the UN Interim Administration Mission in Kosovo (UNMIK) on suspicion of attempted murder. The question of whether these acts were attributable to the relevant states or to an international organization arose before the Court.

The European Court of Human Rights engaged in a detailed examination of the respective responsibilities of UNMIK and KFOR and concluded 'that issuing detention orders fell within the security mandate of KFOR and that the supervision of de-mining fell within UNMIK's mandate'.[35] The Court held that it could not attribute any responsibility to the states that provided the relevant units to these peace operations. The implication of the judgment is that the remedy lies at the level of the UN and the Security Council that had authorized both operations. However, whether or not these acts should be attributed to the UN or to NATO, there is no reason the acts should be *solely* attributable to such an organization. As a Special Rapporteur of the International Law Commission, Giorgio Gaja, put it: '[O]ne may argue that attribution of conduct to an international organization does not necessarily exclude attribution of the same conduct to a State, nor does, vice versa, attribution to a State rule out attribution to an international organization.'[36]

---

[31] Tomuschat, 'International Law: Ensuring the Survival of Mankind on the Eve of a New Century: General Course on Public International Law' (1999) 281 *RdC* 9, 34–5.   [32] Tomuschat, n 31, 129–30.

[33] *Waite and Kennedy v Germany* (2000) 30 EHRR 261, para 67.

[34] *Behrami and Behrami v France; Saramati v France, Germany and Norway* (2007) 45 EHRR SE10.

[35] *Behrami and Behrami*, n 34, para 127.

[36] Special Rapporteur, Second Report on Responsibility of International Organizations, A/CN.4/541 (2 April 2004) para 7 (footnotes omitted); see now Nollkaemper, 'Dual Attribution: Liability of the Netherlands for Conduct of Dutchbat in Srebrenica' (2011) 9 *JICJ* 1143.

The idea that international organizations have human rights obligations has been reinforced by the UN human rights treaty bodies. For example, general comments prepared by the Committee on Economic, Social and Cultural Rights on topics such as the right to health, the right to food, the right to water, and the right to work, now include the duty of states to protect individuals from non-state actors that might infringe on the enjoyment of these rights. The Committee also has a chapter at the end of its General Comments entitled 'Obligations of Actors Other than State Parties'. This includes, for example, in the context of the right to work, recommendations for 'individuals, local communities, trade unions, civil society and private sector organisations'.[37] Special attention is given to 'private enterprises—national and multinational'. The respective general comment goes on to address the role of 'the ILO [International Labour Organization] and the other specialized agencies of the United Nations, the World Bank, regional development banks, the International Monetary Fund, the World Trade Organization and other relevant bodies within the United Nations system'.

Now that it is plain that international organizations have human rights obligations, the question arises of how to build accountability mechanisms that would help to influence their behaviour and provide redress for victims. One option is to ensure that human rights treaties allow for international organizations to become contracting parties. This is currently the case for both the Convention on the Rights of Persons with Disabilities and its Optional Protocol. The Convention explains that it allows for 'regional integration organizations' to become parties where those organizations are 'constituted by sovereign States of a given region, to which its member States have transferred competence in respect of matters governed by this Convention'.[38] The European Community has so far only signed the Convention. In the same way, Protocol No 14 ECHR allows for the European Union to become a party to the Convention and its Protocols so that complaints could eventually be brought against the Union before the European Court of Human Rights.[39]

5 INTERNATIONAL CRIMINAL RESPONSIBILITY OF NON-STATE ACTORS

It is more and more likely that international criminal law will become primarily concerned with non-state actors as opposed to state officials. The Statute of the International Criminal Court provides that its jurisdiction can be triggered by a state party that refers a situation in which relevant crimes appear to have been committed.[40] Four states have referred their own situations to the court. In all four situations—Uganda, Central African Republic, the Democratic Republic of the Congo, and Mali—the government concerned is cooperating in order to see non-state actors tried before the Court. Thus, the first trials before the International Criminal Court have been for acts committed by rebel leaders rather than for acts committed by state actors.[41]

Similarly, the only prosecution in the UK for the international crime of torture concerned an Afghan, non-state, warlord who had been fighting the government.[42] Attempts

---

[37] CESCR, General Comment 18, HRI/GEN/1/Rev.9 (Vol I) 243.   [38] Arts 42–4.

[39] For the draft agreement on accession, see Fifth Negotiation Meeting between the CDDH and Ad Hoc Negotiation Group and the European Commission on the Accession of the European Union to the European Convention on Human Rights: Final report to CDDH, 47+1(2013) 008.   [40] Art 14.

[41] See Chapter 24.   [42] *R v Zardad* Central Criminal Court (7 April 2004). See Clapham, n 14, 342–3.

to try government officials for international crimes in foreign courts have been met with multiple jurisdictional and immunity-based hurdles. Belgium and Spain both came under serious political pressure when they attempted to exercise national jurisdiction over foreign governmental officials. Although this migration of international law from state actors to non-state actors has mostly been observed at the level of individual criminal responsibility, there is no convincing conceptual reason why it should not be extended to cover corporate actors and rebel groups as such.[43]

6 CORPORATE SOCIAL RESPONSIBILITY AND THE MOVE TOWARDS ACCOUNTABILITY

Some activists have drawn a distinction between corporate responsibility and corporate accountability. According to the NGO CorpWatch: 'Corporate responsibility refers to any attempt to get corporations to behave responsibly on a voluntary basis, out of either ethical or bottom-line considerations.'[44] Corporate accountability (or compliance), on the other hand, 'refers to requiring corporations to behave according to societal norms or face consequences'.[45] Christian Aid now states that it 'is advocating giving "teeth" to the ethical commitments of companies by moving beyond corporate social responsibility, which does not and cannot go far enough, to corporate social accountability, to ensure that companies have a legal obligation to uphold international standards'.[46]

Some businesses have expressed human rights commitments, from a desire to:

- protect reputation;
- reduce risk of disruption through strikes, protests, and boycotts;
- enhance their attractiveness for future and current employees;
- and because it is the 'right thing to do'.

Major companies now have human rights policies as a matter of course and few now claim openly (as they used to do) that 'human rights are none of our business'. In fact in some sectors the move towards developing principles to guide the companies in fulfilling their responsibilities and developing accountability has led to innovative studies such as the ones undertaken by Paul Hunt, the former UN Special Rapporteur on the right to health. His reports take us beyond a generalized claim that companies have human rights responsibilities into the detail of what sort of measures they are expected to take, for example 'to make medicine as accessible as possible' subject to the 'capacity' of the company at issue.[47]

Three further factors are forcing greater attention to the human rights implications of corporate activity. First, the decision by some governments to link export credit

---

[43] For a debate on this issue, see (2008) 6 *JICJ* 899–979; Nollkaemper and van der Wilt (eds), *System Criminality in International Law* (CUP, 2009).

[44] Karliner and Bruno, 'Responsibility vs. accountability', *International Herald Tribune* (1 July 2002) 14.

[45] Karliner and Bruno, n 44.

[46] Christian Aid, *Behind the Mask: The Real Face of Corporate Social Responsibility* (2004) 56.

[47] Report of the Special Rapporteur on the right of everyone to the enjoyment of the highest attainable standard of physical and mental health, A/HRC/11/12/Add.2 (5 May 2009) para 37; Report of the Special Rapporteur on the right of everyone to the enjoyment of the highest attainable standard of physical and mental health, A/63/263 (11 August 2008) paras 8–18; Human Rights Guidelines for Pharmaceutical Companies in relation to Access to Medicines, A/63/263 (11 August 2008), Annex.

guarantees to human rights impacts.[48] Second, studies and mechanisms being developed by international organizations such as the UN, the ILO, and the Organisation for Economic Co-operation and Development (OECD) are reinforcing the notion that companies have international responsibilities. Worthy of particular mention are the multiple studies produced by the Special Representative of the UN Secretary-General, John Ruggie, and the possibility of complaining to an OECD National Contact Point that a company has failed to respect human rights.[49] Third, human rights compliance is increasingly factored into investment decisions, in particular by funds which advertise an ethical investment dimension. Perhaps the most interesting process in this respect is the Norwegian Council on Ethics for the Government Pension Fund—Global. Under the Council's ethical guidelines, '[u]pon request of the Ministry of Finance, the Council issues recommendations on whether an investment may constitute a violation of Norway's obligations under international law'.[50] While the concern is expressed as a question of Norway's obligations under international law, in effect it is a review of a company's respect for international human rights or humanitarian law, and recommendations for disinvestment may be made even in the absence of a violation of international law.[51]

The concept that has become central to understanding the expectations on companies in this context is that of complicity. Three factors can be said to have combined to reinforce the importance of this concept.

First, since the late 1990s, human rights NGOs have become more interested in reporting on the behaviour of multinational corporations. They found themselves, however, confronted with a legal conundrum. Unlike ethical investors or those in the corporate social responsibility movement, international human rights organizations were starting from a position of cataloguing violations of international human rights law. These violations were usually expressed in terms of violations of the human rights treaties which the relevant state had ratified. The legal methodology did not seem suited to complaining about the behaviour of corporations. Accordingly, Amnesty International formulated 'Human Rights Principles for Companies' (1998), which included a policy recommendation that companies should establish procedures to ensure that all operations are assessed for their potential impact on human rights and safeguards are put in place to ensure that company staff are never complicit in human rights abuses.[52] Similarly, without radically altering the traditional understanding of human rights law, groups such as Human Rights Watch argued that, although corporations did not have obligations as parties to human rights treaties, the states in which they were operating did have such obligations, and the behaviour of the corporations could be seen as contributing to violations by those states. As such, it made sense to talk about the corporations being 'complicit' in such violations.[53]

---

[48] Eg UK Export Credit Guarantees Department, *Mission and Status Review* 1999–2000 (HMSO, 2000) Cm 4790; Recommendation of the Council on Common Approaches for Officially Supported Export Credits and Environmental and Social Due Diligence (the 'OECD Common Approaches') TAD/ECG(2012)5, 28 June 2012.

[49] See Report of the Special Representative of the Secretary-General on the issue of human rights and transnational corporations and other business enterprises, A/HRC/8/5 (7 April 2008); OECD, *OECD Guidelines for Multinational Enterprises 2011 Edition* (OECD, 2011).

[50] Section 4.3.

[51] Recommendation concerning whether the weapons systems Spider and Intelligent Munition System (IMS) might be contrary to international law (20 September 2005).

[52] See also Irene Khan, 'Understanding Corporate Complicity: Extending the Notion beyond Existing Laws' (2006), available at: <http://www.amnesty.org/en/library/asset/POL34/001/2006/en/c866d1a9-d44b-11dd-8 743-d305bea2b2c7/pol340012006en.pdf>.

[53] Eg Human Rights Watch, *Oil Companies Complicit in Nigerian Abuses* (1999); Human Rights Watch, *The Enron Corporation: Corporate Complicity in Human Rights Violations* (1999).

Second, in 1999, the then UN Secretary-General Kofi Annan launched what became the Global Compact with a speech in Davos. He addressed business leaders in the following terms:

> You can uphold human rights and decent labour and environmental standards directly, by your own conduct of your own business. Indeed, you can use these universal values as the cement binding together your global corporations, since they are values people all over the world will recognize as their own. You can make sure that in your own corporate practices you uphold and respect human rights; and that you are not yourselves complicit in human rights abuses.[54]

The Global Compact was developed the following year and operates within the UN as a 'policy platform and a practical framework for companies that are committed to sustainability and responsible business practices'.[55] Its first two principles are: 'Principle 1: Businesses should support and respect the protection of internationally proclaimed human rights; and Principle 2: make sure that they are not complicit in human rights abuses.'[56]

Third, the growing number of cases being litigated under the Alien Tort Statute has focused attention on the scope of corporate complicity in human rights violations.[57] In 2009, one of the longest running cases, the complaint against Shell for complicity in human rights violations in Nigeria, was settled for the sum of US$15.5 million. As we have seen there may now be less scope for such claims under the Alien Tort Statute where there is little or no nexus to the USA, but the notion of corporate complicity is likely to continue to feature in litigation against companies. In sum, businesses are increasingly expected to comply with a broad range of human rights obligations. The UN and the OECD offer a certain degree of analysis and the prospect of monitoring, while there is an emerging sense of accountability due to the Alien Tort Statute and the prospect of litigation in other jurisdictions. These legal developments should, however, be seen for what they are: simply the beginnings of an awareness that companies have human rights responsibilities.[58] It would be naive to believe that human rights law has already met the challenge of preventing and punishing human rights abuses committed by companies. The challenge to translate the obligations, develop the monitoring and accountability mechanisms, and overturn assumptions remains on-going.[59]

7 ARMED OPPOSITION GROUPS

While international humanitarian law is now seen as 'obviously' applicable to the non-state party to an internal armed conflict there is an apparent problem with the application of

---

[54] Press Release, SG/SM/6881 (1 February 1999).

[55] *UN Global Compact: Corporate Citizenship in the World Economy* (UN, 2008) 1.

[56] UN Global Compact Office and OHCHR, *Embedding Human Rights in Business Practice* (2004), available at: <http://www.unglobalcompact.org/docs/news_events/8.1/EHRBPII_Final.pdf>.

[57] Alien Tort Statute, n 16.

[58] For a rejection of the notion that all international human rights obligations apply to corporations, see Vásquez, 'Direct vs Indirect Obligations of Corporations Under International Law' (2005) 43 *Columbia J Trans L* 927.

[59] See generally the work around the 'Guiding Principles on Business and Human Rights: Implementing the United Nations "Protect, Respect and Remedy" Framework', A/HRC/17/31 (21 March 2011); for the background to these principles and an explanation of the process see Ruggie, *Just Business: Multinational Corporations and Human Rights* (WW Norton, 2013).

human rights law to such armed groups.[60] This is for two main reasons. First, because in contrast to international humanitarian law, human rights law is seen as applicable only to states. Human rights treaties only rarely address non-state armed groups.[61] In contrast, international humanitarian law is considered to apply to the non-state party to the conflict. In 2004 the Appeals Chamber of the Special Court for Sierra Leone simply held that 'it is well settled that all parties to an armed conflict, whether states or non-state actors, are bound by international humanitarian law, even though only states may become parties to international treaties'.[62] Second, there is a perception that engaging with rebel groups on human rights issues lends them a certain legitimacy. This is in part related to the first issue: by claiming that a group has violated human rights one is implying that they are a state-like entity because it is presumed that only states have human rights obligations.

Both these obstacles are being eroded. As with corporations, the human rights monitoring mechanisms are starting to include reporting on non-state armed groups in their range of activities. Although several commentators insist that only states have human rights obligations in this context,[63] and that non-state actors are exclusively bound by international humanitarian law, this is being challenged. The challenge comes in the form of increasing demands by the Security Council for armed groups to respect human rights, in the reports of the various truth commissions (such as those in Guatemala and Sierra Leone) which detail the human rights violations committed by non-state actors, and the failure to explain why international humanitarian law has the theoretical potential to bind non-state actors while human rights law does not.[64]

Let us turn to three practical applications of human rights obligations to armed non-state actors: first, the work of the Security Council with regard to children's rights; second, the work of the UN special mechanisms; and third, the work of one NGO, Geneva Call.

7.1 THE UN SECURITY COUNCIL ON CHILDREN AND ARMED CONFLICT

The UN's work on children and armed conflict has led to an innovative approach, which details violations by non-state actors. Reports by the UN Secretary-General to the Security Council on certain situations now list the non-state actors concerned and whether they are involved in any of six grave violations:

(1) Killing or maiming of children;

(2) Recruiting or using child soldiers;

(3) Attacks against schools or hospitals;

(4) Rape or other grave sexual violence against children;

(5) Abduction of children;

(6) Denial of humanitarian access for children.

---

[60] For a discussion of some of the theories that have been proposed to justify the application of human rights law to armed groups, see Sivakumaran, *The Law of Non-International Armed Conflict* (OUP, 2012) 95–100.

[61] One exception being the Optional Protocol to the CRC on the involvement of children in armed conflict. See below for an application in the case of Syria.

[62] *Prosecutor v Sam Hinga Norman*, Decision on Preliminary Motion Based on Lack of Jurisdiction (Child Recruitment), SCSL-2004-14-AR72(E) (31 May 2004) para 22.

[63] Moir, *The Law of Internal Armed Conflict* (CUP, 2002) 194; Zegveld, *Accountability of Armed Opposition Groups in International Law* (CUP, 2002) 53.

[64] See Clapham, 'Human Rights Obligations of Non-State Actors in Conflict Situations' (2006) 88 *IRRC* 491, 495–508.

The UN Secretary-General's initial report explains that these violations are based on international norms, commitments that have been made by the parties to the conflict, national laws, and peace agreements.[65] Subsequent reports on various country situations have detailed the 'grave violations of children's rights' committed by the non-state actors concerned.[66] These reports dedicate as much, if not more, space to the violations committed by the non-state actors as they do to addressing the states concerned. The mechanism vis-à-vis the non-state actors works not only through naming and shaming but by encouraging them to submit an 'action plan' to the Security Council. In this way, the groups can be removed from the list of violators. One non-state armed group that has supplied such an action plan and claimed to no longer be a violator is the Forces Nouvelles (FAFN) in Côte d'Ivoire. It was de-listed by the Security Council in 2008.[67] The Security Council also has in mind that it could adopt:

> country-specific resolutions, targeted and graduated measures, such as, inter alia, a ban on the export and supply of small arms and light weapons and of other military equipment and on military assistance, against parties to situations of armed conflict which are on the Security Council's agenda and are in violation of applicable international law relating to the rights and protection of children in armed conflict.[68]

Although the focus started with the recruitment of child soldiers, the Security Council has requested the Secretary-General to include in his reports 'those parties to armed conflict that engage, in contravention of applicable international law, in patterns of killing and maiming of children and/or rape and other sexual violence against children, in situations of armed conflict'.[69] Even if the reports refer in general terms to the rules of international law that are actually being violated, the prospect of follow-up sanctions by the Security Council is premised on the idea that these groups have violated international law and not simply a set of moral or political imperatives.

This activity is complemented by the Special Representative of the Secretary-General on children and armed conflict whose work not only feeds into the reports to the Security Council but also relies on country visits, engagement with non-state actors, and facilitation of commitments by those armed groups.[70] Let us look, however, at the work of the UN special procedures more generally.

7.2 UN SPECIAL PROCEDURES

The former UN Special Rapporteur on extrajudicial, summary, or arbitrary executions, Philip Alston, grappled with the question of the human rights obligations of armed non-state actors in the context of his report on Sri Lanka. He concluded in the following terms:

> Human rights law affirms that both the Government and the LTTE [Liberation Tigers of Tamil Eelam] must respect the rights of every person in Sri Lanka. Human rights norms operate on three levels—as the rights of individuals, as obligations assumed by States, and as legitimate expectations of the international community. The Government has assumed

---

[65] Report of the Secretary-General on Children and Armed Conflict, S/2005/72 (9 February 2005).
[66] Eg Report of the Secretary-General on Children and Armed Conflict, S/2009/158 (26 March 2009).
[67] See Conclusions on Children and Armed Conflict in Côte d'Ivoire, S/AC.51/2008/5 (1 February 2008).
[68] SC Res 1612 (26 July 2005) para 9.   [69] SC Res 1882 (4 August 2009).
[70] Eg Report of the Special Representative of the Secretary-General for Children and Armed Conflict, A/63/227 (6 August 2008).

the binding legal obligation to respect and ensure the rights recognized in the International Covenant on Civil and Political Rights (ICCPR). As a non-State actor, the LTTE does not have legal obligations under ICCPR, but it remains subject to the demand of the international community, first expressed in the Universal Declaration of Human Rights, that every organ of society respect and promote human rights.[71]

Alston went on to include specific human rights recommendations addressed to the non-state actor.[72] This approach was also applied in the joint report on Lebanon and Israel by a group of four Special Rapporteurs.[73]

More recently, the Commission of Inquiry on Syria applied a limited set of human rights obligations to the armed non-state groups. The Commission stated with regard to the Free Syrian Army (FSA) that:

> [A]t a minimum, human rights obligations constituting peremptory international law (*ius cogens*) bind States, individuals and non-State collective entities, including armed groups. Acts violating *ius cogens* – for instance, torture or enforced disappearances – can never be justified.
>
> FSA leaders abroad also assured the commission that the FSA was committed to conducting its operations in accordance with human rights and international law. They requested guidance in shaping rules of engagement consistent with this undertaking. The FSA leadership indicated to the commission that commanders in the field currently made their own rules of engagement in accordance with the training received in the Syrian Armed Forces.[74]

In a more recent report, the Commission went further in the context of enforced disappearances and stated:

> [a]lthough anti-Government armed groups are per se not a party to the Convention [International Convention for the Protection of All Persons from Enforced Disappearance], their actions may be assessed against customary international legal principles, and they are subject to criminal liability for enforced disappearance amounting to a crime against humanity.[75]

Using the expression 'customary legal principles' suggests a set of human rights principles that do not necessarily have to be proven as customary international rules developed specifically for non-state actors, but rather fundamental standards that ought to apply to all actors in all circumstances.

---

[71] Report of the Special Rapporteur on extrajudicial, summary or arbitrary executions, Philip Alston, Mission to Sri Lanka, E/CN.4/2006/53/Add.5 (27 March 2006) para 25.

[72] Alston, n 71, para 85. See also the letter addressed directly to the LTTE concerning prevention of killings, lack of investigations, and the application of the death penalty: 'Allegation letter sent 21 November 2005', E/CN.4/53/Add.1 (27 March 2006) 320.

[73] Report of the Special Rapporteur on extrajudicial, summary or arbitrary executions; the Special Rapporteur on the right of everyone to the enjoyment of the highest attainable standard of physical and mental health; the Representative of the Secretary-General on human rights of internally displaced persons; and the Special Rapporteur on adequate housing as a component of the right to an adequate standard of living, A/HRC/2/7 (2 October 2006) para 19.

[74] Report of the Independent International Commission of Inquiry on the Syrian Arab Republic, A/HRC/19/69 (22 February 2012) paras 106–7. See also the approach of the Report of the International Commission of Inquiry to investigate all Alleged Violations of International Human Rights Law in the Libyan Arab Jamahiriya, A/HRC/17/44 (1 June 2011).

[75] Report of the Independent International Commission of Inquiry on the Syrian Arab Republic, A/HRC/22/59 (5 February 2013) para 85.

In related developments, the UN High Commissioner for Human Rights and the UN Human Rights Council have had to confront the violence in Mali. In 2013 the Council condemned:

> the excesses and abuses committed in the Republic of Mali, particularly in the north of the country, by, among others, the rebels, terrorist groups and other organized transnational crime networks, which include violence against women and children, summary and extra-judicial executions, hostage-taking, pillaging, destruction of cultural and religious sites and recruitment of child soldiers, as well as all other human rights violations.[76]

The High Commissioner's January 2013 report on Mali goes further than the Commission of Inquiry on Syria, mentioned already, and catalogues a series of human rights violations committed by the armed groups including extrajudicial and summary executions; torture and other cruel, inhuman, or degrading treatment; arbitrary arrests and detentions; recruitment of child soldiers; sexual abuse; attacks on property; violations of freedom of expression and of the right to information; violations of the right to education; violations of the right to health; violations of cultural rights; and violation of the right to freedom of religion.[77]

On the basis of these reports and resolutions, we might conclude that the practice of the UN Human Rights Council is to investigate and condemn violations of human rights by armed groups in more or less the same terms as those used for states. Although findings that human rights treaties have been violated usually refer to states, even here there are new developments with the Commission of Inquiry on Syria concluding in 2013 that '[a]nti-Government armed groups are also responsible for using children under the age of 18 in hostilities in violation of the CRC-OPAC [Optional Protocol to the Convention on the Rights of the Child], which by its terms applies to non-State actors.' The summary also makes the same point: 'Both Government-affiliated militia and anti-Government armed groups were found to have violated the Optional Protocol to the Convention on the Rights of the Child on the involvement of children in armed conflict, to which the Syrian Arab Republic is a party.'[78]

7.3 NGOS AND THE EXAMPLE OF GENEVA CALL

Engagement with such groups is not, however, limited to UN human rights mechanisms. NGOs increasingly report on human rights abuses committed by armed non-state actors. Recent Human Rights Watch reports on Hamas and Fatah have built on the approach developed by the Special Rapporteurs and emphasize the commitment of the Palestinian Authority to human rights and the fact that these groups are seen to be in control of territory.[79] In other situations, human rights law is transposed from the state-based treaty provisions in ways that allude to customary international law. In one case where a non-state actor's justice system was found wanting, the report stated: 'The fairness of any justice system should be tested against international human rights law criteria that include independence, impartiality, and competency of judges, presumption of innocence, right

---

[76] HR Council Res 22/18, A/HRC/RES/22/18 (10 April 2013). See also, on Syria, HR Council Res 22/24, A/HRC/RES/22/24 (12 April 2013), para 4.

[77] Report of the United Nations High Commissioner for Human Rights on the situation of human rights in Mali, A/HRC/22/33 (7 January 2013).

[78] Report of the Commission of Inquiry on Syria, n 75, para 44 and p 2.

[79] Human Rights Watch, *Internal Fight: Palestinian Abuses in Gaza and the West Bank* (2008); Human Rights Watch, *Under Cover of War: Hamas Political Violence in Gaza* (2009).

to legal counsel and adequate time for preparation of defense, and the right to appeal.'[80] Amnesty International's reports similarly address its concerns to the armed non-state actors in terms which go beyond the strict obligations found under the laws of war.[81]

The International Campaign to Ban Landmines, having recognized the limits of the Ottawa Treaty to address the possession and use of landmines by non-state actors, set up its own working group, which led eventually to the establishment of the NGO, Geneva Call.[82] Geneva Call has engaged armed groups in 'Deeds of Commitment' regarding a 'total ban on anti-personnel mines and for cooperation in mine action.'[83] Geneva Call has extended its use of such deeds of commitments to cover 'the protection of children from the effects of armed conflict' and 'the prohibition of sexual violence in situations of armed conflict and towards the elimination of gender discrimination.' Having negotiated the signature of the Deed, Geneva Call receives the armed non-state actors' regular reports, monitors compliance with the Deed, and, in the context of land mines, helps arrange mine action including demining and destruction of stocks. It is worth inquiring at this point what might be the incentives for a non-state actor to bind itself to such a Deed.

First, rebel groups realize the advantages of being seen to abide by international norms in the context of moves towards peace negotiations. Second, it is much easier to criticize governments and their armed forces for committing international crimes if the group has policies in place to avoid and punish such crimes. Third, factions may be able to distinguish themselves from other armed groups and thus 'get ahead' in terms of dialogue with the government or other actors. Lastly, in some circumstances, entering into such commitments will facilitate access to assistance from the international community in the form of mine clearance.

Such explicit recognition of specific obligations by the groups themselves helps to transform the debate about the human rights obligations of non-state actors. If armed groups are prepared to take on such obligations, arguments about their non-applicability under international law lose much of their force. States may fear the legitimacy that such commitments seem to imply, and international lawyers may choose to accord them no value, but from a victim's perspective such commitments may indeed be worth more than the paper they are written on.

8 CONCLUSION

This chapter has covered three challenges posed by non-state actors. First, there is a need to find ways to translate existing norms to create appropriate obligations for non-state actors. This work has started in that it is now clear that individual non-state actors will be prosecuted for certain international crimes. Furthermore, corporations and armed groups are increasingly expected to respect not only international criminal law but human rights obligations as well. The second challenge concerns the development of monitoring and accountability. As we have seen, while the jurisdictional state-centric limits of the traditional human rights courts and bodies remain, the UN and NGOs have developed their

---

[80] Human Rights Watch, '*Being Neutral is Our Biggest Crime': Government, Vigilante, and Naxalite Abuses in India's Chhattisgarh State* (2008) 98. Compare Sivakumaran, 'Courts of Armed Opposition Groups: Fair Trials or Summary Justice?' (2009) 7 *JICJ* 489.

[81] Eg Amnesty International, *Haiti: Abuse of Human Rights: Political Violence as the 200th Anniversary of Independence Approaches* (2003).

[82] See Busé, 'Non-State Actors and their Significance' (2001) 5 *J Mine Action*, available at: <http://maic.jmu.edu/Journal/5.3/features/maggie_buse_nsa/maggie_buse.htm>.

[83] For the Deed of Commitment, see: <http://www.genevacall.org/resources/deed-of-commitment/deed-of-commitment.htm>.

own ways of monitoring non-state actors, and the most recent proposal for a world court of human rights proposes that non-state actors could make declarations bringing themselves within the jurisdiction of this court.[84] Lastly, it is suggested that a further challenge is to question our own assumptions about what it means to talk about human rights and who has human rights obligations. It is hoped that those readers who have reached this point may be starting to meet this last challenge.

FURTHER READING

ALSTON (ed), *Non-State Actors and Human Rights* (Oxford University Press, 2005).

BELLAL and CASEY-MASLEN, *Rules of Engagement: Promoting the Protection of Civilians Through Dialogue with Armed Non-State Actors*, (Geneva Academy of International Humanitarian Law and Human Rights, 2011).

BELLAL, GIACCA, and CASEY-MASLEN, 'International Law and Armed Non-State Actors in Afghanistan' (2011) 93 *IRRC* 47.

BIANCHI (ed), *Non-State Actors and International Law* (Ashgate, 2009).

CLAPHAM, *Human Rights Obligations of Non-State Actors* (Oxford University Press, 2006).

CLAPHAM (ed), *Human Rights and Non-State Actors* (Elgar Publishing, 2013).

CONSTANTINEIDES, 'Human Rights Obligations and Accountability of Armed Opposition Groups: The Practice of the UN Security Council' (2010) 4 *HR and International Legal Discourse* 89.

DE SCHUTTER (ed), *Transnational Corporations and Human Rights* (Hart Publishing, 2006).

HESSBRUEGGE, 'Human Rights Violations Arising from Conduct of Non-State Actors' (2005) 11 *Buffalo HRLR* 21.

JOSEPH, *Corporations and Transnational Human Rights Litigation* (Hart Publishing, 2004).

NOLAN, 'Addressing Economic and Social Rights Violations by Non-state Actors through the Role of the State: A Comparison of Regional Approaches to the "Obligation to Protect"' (2009) 9 *HRLR* 225.

OECD WATCH, *10 Years On: Assessing the contribution of the OECD Guidelines for Multinational Enterprises to responsible business conduct* (2010).

OLIVER and FEDTKE (eds), *Human Rights and the Private Sphere* (Routledge-Cavendish, 2007).

SIVAKUMARAN, 'Lessons from the Law of Armed Conflict from Commitments of Armed Groups: Identification of Legitimate Targets and Prisoners of War' (2011) 93 *IRRC* 463.

USEFUL WEBSITES

Business and Human Rights Resource Centre: <**http://www.business-humanrights.org/Home**>

Geneva Call: <**http://www.genevacall.org/**>

OECD Watch: <**http://oecdwatch.org/**>

Rule of Law in Armed Conflicts Project: <**http://www.adh-geneva.ch/RULAC/**>

Transnational and Non-State Armed Groups Project: <**http://www.armed-groups.org/home.aspx**>

---

[84] See in particular the Commentary to Article 4: '[T]his provision primarily aims at transnational corporations, international non-profit organizations, organized opposition movements and autonomous communities within States or within a group of States. An "Entity" does not necessarily have to be a juridical person recognized under domestic or international law. Finally, it is up to the Court to decide whether it has jurisdiction in relation to a particular "Entity" or not.' *A World Court of Human Rights – Consolidated Statute and Commentary* (Neuer Wissenschaftlicher Verlag, 2010) 33–4.

27

TERRORISM

Martin Scheinin

SUMMARY

Terrorism, and measures to combat terrorism, pose major challenges to the international protection of human rights. Those challenges relate to both the substance of human rights norms and their scope of application. While the focus of attention has been on a number of specific human rights and the rights of those who are suspected of involvement in terrorism, everyone's human rights are, to a lesser or greater extent, affected by counter-terrorism measures. Acts of terrorism, in turn, constitute a serious form of crime and often result in the destruction of human rights.

1 INTRODUCTION

Particularly in the era after the atrocious terrorist attacks in the USA on 11 September 2001 (9/11), a whole wave of counter-terrorism measures have been introduced. While human rights are not always absolute, and public security may form a legitimate ground for introducing certain limitations, it would be a mistake to conclude that security generally trumps human rights. A more nuanced legal analysis is required in order to respond to the challenges of complying with human rights while at the same time effectively combating terrorism. Those challenges appear not only at the level of domestic law, where increased security has often been the justification for measures that restrict human rights. At the international level, the UN Security Council has identified international terrorism as a threat to peace and security, and resorted to its far-reaching powers under Chapter VII of the UN Charter. Shortly after 9/11 it adopted Resolution 1373, imposing a whole set of legally binding counter-terrorism obligations upon states, and established a new subsidiary body, the Counter-Terrorism Committee (CTC).[1] Another subsidiary body, the 1267 Sanctions Committee, administers a regime of listing individuals and entities for targeted sanctions for their association with al-Qaida.[2]

Section 2 addresses the question of whether terrorism constitutes a violation of human rights, or whether the notion of human rights violations can only be applied to action by states. Section 3 deals with challenges to the applicability of human rights law in the fight

---

[1] SC Res 1373 (28 September 2001).

[2] By way of Security Council Resolutions 1988 and 1989 (17 June 2011), the earlier combined al-Qaida and Taliban sanctions regime was split into two separate mechanisms. Resolution 1989 now constitutes the basis for listing individuals or entities associated with al-Qaida and is administered by the 1267 Sanctions Committee.

against terrorism, particularly since 9/11. Section 4 focuses on the notion of terrorism and in particular the risks created to human rights protection by vague or over-inclusive definitions of terrorism. The main section of the chapter, Section 5, deals with some of the major challenges posed by counter-terrorism measures to substantive human rights protections. While all human rights are affected by a global wave of new counter-terrorism laws and measures, some human rights have been at the forefront. Section 6 addresses the issue of listing of terrorists by the UN, which poses a challenge of an institutional nature. Is the Security Council bound by international human rights standards, and how can the sanctions resulting from its listing of terrorists be made subject to judicial or other independent review? The final section, Section 7, suggests that the unprecedented post-9/11 wave of counter-terrorism laws and measures that infringed upon human rights has calmed down and that governments and intergovernmental organizations are increasingly recognizing that full compliance with human rights in the fight against terrorism is not only morally and legally correct but in the long term also the most effective way of combating terrorism.

2 IS TERRORISM A VIOLATION OF HUMAN RIGHTS?

Human rights are usually seen as vertical norms between the state and a private beneficiary (in most cases an individual person). However, changes in the world order, often referred to as globalization, have resulted in an awareness of the existence of other public and private actors that are equally as powerful as states in their capacity directly to affect the enjoyment of human rights.[3] Terrorism is one such challenge emanating from non-state actors. It is generally defined as deadly or otherwise serious violence against 'civilians', that is, members of the general population or a segment of it, for the purpose of spreading fear amongst the population, or to compel the authorities to do, or refrain from doing, something. Acts of terrorism adversely affect several human rights, including the right to life, the right to physical integrity, the right to health, the right to property, in cases of hostage-taking the right to liberty, and so on. Terrorism has, therefore, been rightly described as the destruction, or the antithesis, of human rights.

However, this does not necessarily mean that terrorist acts amount to a *violation* of human rights. Resolutions adopted by intergovernmental organizations in response to the threat of terrorism apply different approaches to the issue of whether the perpetrators of acts of terrorism may be described as violating human rights. Variation in the wording of such resolutions reflects different doctrinal and political positions on the question of whether only states may commit human rights violations, or whether such violations can also be attributed to non-state actors. For example, the 2005 resolution of the then UN Commission on Human Rights that created the mandate of the Special Rapporteur on human rights and counter-terrorism referred in its preamble to acts, methods, and practices of terrorism being 'aimed at the destruction of human rights', while deploring the occurrence of human rights 'violations'—by states—in the context of their fight against terrorism.[4] However, the same Commission on Human Rights had on other occasions adopted resolutions that speak of human rights 'violations' committed by terrorists.[5] The current

---

[3] See Chapter 26.   [4] CHR Res 2005/80 (21 April 2005).
[5] Eg CHR Res 2004/44 (19 April 2004). In the preamble, the Commission expresses serious concern 'at the gross violations of human rights perpetrated by terrorists'.

Special Rapporteur (at the time of writing) on human rights and counter-terrorism takes the view that the word 'violations' should be used with regard to terrorists themselves.[6]

Although the general public may feel perplexed by such inconsistencies and by the insistence of many human rights experts to reserve the notion of human rights violations to states alone, there is, in the view of the present author, good reason for maintaining the distinction between terrorism as *destruction* of human rights and a more straight-forward reference to human rights *violations* by states, at least for the time being. The legally binding normative framework of human rights law is established in human rights treaties. Those treaties are clearly based on human beings as their beneficiaries and states parties as bearers of the corresponding obligations. Even where human rights norms have evolved to the status of customary law, their substance addresses the relationship between a state and an individual and it is not self-evident that such customary norms would, with the same content, be binding upon other actors beyond states. Further, all monitoring mechanisms under human rights treaties are geared towards making *states* accountable for human rights violations. When human rights treaty bodies find a human rights violation, this represents the end result of the application of the treaty in a concrete case or situation and includes an attribution of state responsibility for a breach of its obligations. Under other, non-treaty-based procedures, such as the special procedures of the Human Rights Council, a finding of a human rights violation entails a pronouncement that a state has acted in breach of its obligations under international human rights law.

No similar treaty-based or other monitoring mechanisms generally exist in respect of *non-state* actors. Hence, even assuming that the notion of human rights violations could meaningfully be applied in respect of terrorists, there are no mechanisms through which the actors in question could be made accountable. To a limited extent, the development of international criminal law has come to serve as a substitute for the inability of human rights mechanisms to address the destruction of human rights by non-state actors. For instance, many of the crimes for which an individual can be prosecuted and punished under the Rome Statute of the International Criminal Court have a direct destructive effect on the enjoyment of human rights. In some instances, the Rome Statute may be applicable in respect of specific acts of terrorism.[7] In addition, several international con-ventions and protocols address particular forms of terrorism—such as hostage-taking, or hijacking of an airplane—and require states parties to criminalize the acts in question.[8]

If, in the future, a mechanism such as a World Court of Human Rights,[9] with jurisdic-tion over both states and non-state actors, was established, then it will make more sense to speak about terrorist organizations being responsible for human rights *violations*. Without

---

[6] See Report of the Special Rapporteur on human rights and counter-terrorism (Ben Emmerson), A/HRC/20/14 (4 June 2012) para 12: 'Some still argue that terrorists, rebels and other belligerents cannot com-mit violations of international human rights law unless the degree of organization, territorial control and State recognition involved in a conflict situation has escalated to the level of a full-blown insurgency or internal armed conflict. However, it is a central tenet of international human rights law that it must keep pace with a changing world. Some of the gravest violations of human rights are nowadays committed by, or on behalf of, non-State actors operating in conflict situations of one kind or another, including by domestic and international terrorist networks. If international human rights law is to keep pace with these changes, the victims of acts of terrorism must now be recognized as victims of grave violations of international human rights law.' (footnotes omitted).

[7] Eg Rome Statute of the International Criminal Court, Art 7(1) (listing eg torture and disappearance as crimes against humanity).

[8] For a summary of the 14 major conventions and protocols dealing with terrorism, see: <http://www.un.org/en/terrorism/instruments.shtml>.

[9] Kozma, Nowak, and Scheinin, *A World Court of Human Rights – Consolidated Statute and Commentary* (Neuer Wissenschaftlicher Verlag, 2010).

such a mechanism, there is no forum in which, and no procedure through which, to establish a violation and attribute it to a particular non-state actor.

3 APPLICABILITY OF HUMAN RIGHTS LAW IN THE FIGHT AGAINST TERRORISM

The applicability of human rights law to the fight against terrorism has been challenged in two ways. First, some states have argued that this fight amounts to an armed conflict or that it justifies the proclamation of a state of emergency and, therefore, makes it possible to derogate from certain human rights. Second, some states have argued that international human rights law does not apply to counter-terrorism measures taken outside the state's own territory.

3.1 TIMES OF ARMED CONFLICT OR EMERGENCY

Some governments have sought to justify their unilateral exceptions to international human rights norms by referring to a 'war' against terrorism, which triggers the application of international humanitarian law.[10] Such a position is usually factually incorrect, since acts of terrorism on their own constitute neither an international armed conflict between two or more states, nor a non-international armed conflict between a state and a non-state actor capable of conducting armed hostilities. Instead, terrorism should primarily be seen as a serious form of crime and fought within a law-enforcement paradigm. Therefore, the full applicability of human rights law as the proper legal framework for the rights of terrorist suspects or other persons affected by counter-terrorism measures should be the point of departure.

It is possible, however, that for a limited period of time and in respect of a specific geographic area non-state actors referred to as 'terrorists' may be engaged in an armed conflict. The prime example is Afghanistan in late 2001, when members of al-Qaida were engaged in an armed conflict against the USA, siding with the local Taliban that constituted the de facto government of Afghanistan.[11] But even in such rare circumstances human rights law remains applicable, although it may need to be interpreted in the light of more specific rules contained in international humanitarian law.[12]

Major terrorist attacks, or another situation in which a terrorist organization manages to destabilize public order in a state, may constitute a threat to 'the life of the nation' in the sense of the derogation clauses contained in many human rights treaties. Consequently, a state may officially proclaim a state of emergency and introduce measures that derogate from certain human rights.[13] For instance, declaring a curfew for a city, introducing checkpoints on major roads, restrictions on mass demonstrations, and closer inspection of postal packages may, within the exigencies of the situation, constitute lawful derogations in respect of the normal scope of freedom of movement, the right to peaceful assembly, and the right to privacy as guaranteed by the International Covenant on Civil and Political

---

[10] For international humanitarian law and its relationship with human rights law, see Chapter 23.
[11] See Report of the Special Rapporteur on human rights and counter-terrorism, A/HRC/6/17/Add.3 (22 November 2007) in particular para 9.
[12] Report of the Special Rapporteur, n 11, para 7. See Chapter 23.   [13] See Chapter 5.

Rights (ICCPR). Such measures must be temporary and their aim must be the restoration of normalcy, including the protection of human rights.

As has been elaborated by the Human Rights Committee in its General Comment on states of emergency, the power of a state to derogate from some provisions of the ICCPR does not mean a power to suspend completely the application of these provisions. Rather, any derogation is subject to the requirements of necessity and proportionality. Not only must there be full respect for non-derogable human rights, but also the rights that are subject to derogation must remain protected as far as possible and may include non-derogable dimensions.[14]

3.2 EXTRATERRITORIAL APPLICABILITY OF HUMAN RIGHTS LAW

A separate, but in practice often simultaneously presented, challenge to the applicability of human rights in the counter-terrorism context is the argument that human rights obligations are territorial in scope, limited to a state's own territory where it exercises full jurisdiction. For example, governments may establish detention centres abroad and argue that constitutional guarantees or human rights treaties do not apply there.

While this argument has some support in the text of Article 2(1) ICCPR,[15] consistent practice by the Human Rights Committee demonstrates that a state must comply with the Covenant wherever it factually exercises powers that affect the enjoyment of the rights enshrined in the ICCPR.[16] Thus, even if that provision were to be taken as excluding the obligation to 'legislate' for other countries or their population,[17] this cannot form a justification to engage extraterritorially in outright human rights violations such as arbitrary detention, torture, or other cruel, inhuman, or degrading treatment.[18]

In summary, human rights law continues to apply during situations of armed conflict or a state of emergency, and it applies also to a state's conduct abroad. Closer analysis may be needed as to how the norms of human rights law and international humanitarian law inform the proper interpretation of each other during times of armed conflict, what derogations from certain human rights norms may be permitted as necessary and proportionate within the exigencies of a state of emergency, and what the exact scope of a state's human rights obligations is when its agents are operating outside its own territory. These considerations, however, do not change the basic rule that human rights law continues to apply in any of these circumstances.

4 THE NOTION OF TERRORISM AND ITS MISUSE

'One man's freedom fighter is another man's terrorist', attributed to the British author Gerald Seymour, is an oft-heard and somewhat cynical reference to the degree of

---

[14] HRC, General Comment 29, HRI/GEN/1/Rev.9 (Vol 1) 234 (27 May 2008). See also Chapter 5.

[15] ICCPR, Art 2(1) provides: 'Each State Party to the present Covenant undertakes to respect and to ensure to all individuals within its territory and subject to its jurisdiction the rights recognized in the present Covenant'.

[16] Eg Lopez Burgos v Uruguay, CCPR/C/13/D/52/1979 (29 July 1981); Gueye et al. v France, CCPR/C/35/D/196/1985 (6 April 1989); HRC, Concluding observations: Israel, CCPR/C/79/Add.93 (18 August 1998); HRC, Concluding observations: Israel, CCPR/CO/78/ISR (21 August 2003); HRC, General Comment 31, HRI/GEN/1/Rev.9 (Vol I) 243 (27 May 2008) para 10. See further Chapter 6.

[17] This was the expression used in 1950 by the US representative, Mrs Eleanor Roosevelt, in the drafting of the ICCPR. See Third Periodic Report of the US to the HRC, CCPR/C/USA/3 (28 November 2005) annex I.

[18] Report of the Special Rapporteur on human rights and counter-terrorism, A/HRC/6/17/Add.3 (22 November 2007) para 8.

opportunism employed when using the word 'terrorism'. Although the UN has adopted a whole series of international treaties related to specific forms of terrorism, such as hostage-taking, nuclear terrorism, or terrorist bombings,[19] work towards a comprehensive convention against terrorism is still underway and not very likely to yield results soon. Governments have not been able to agree on the definition of terrorism. Differing views persist, inter alia, with regard to whether states can commit acts of terrorism and whether the quest for self-determination precludes an act from being a form of terrorism.

Particularly in the aftermath of 9/11, governments have increasingly resorted to vague and broad definitions of terrorism. While this may have been triggered partly by a desire to respond to an unspecific threat, all too often governments intended to target individuals or groups that do not deserve to be labelled as terrorist, such as political opposition groups, radical trade unions, vocal but non-violent separatist movements, indigenous peoples, religious minorities, or even human rights defenders. At least for a while, the global consensus about the imperative of combating terrorism was so compelling that authoritarian governments could get away with their repressive practices whenever they renamed their opponents as 'terrorists'.

Of particular concern to the international protection of human rights is that in the aftermath of 9/11, and in the absence of a universal and comprehensive definition of the term, repeated calls by the international community, including the Security Council, for action to combat terrorism, could be understood as leaving it to individual states to define what is meant by the term 'terrorism'. This aggravates the potential for unintended human rights abuses and even the deliberate misuse of the term. There is a clear risk that the international community's use of the term 'terrorism', without defining it, results in the unintentional international legitimization of conduct undertaken by oppressive regimes, through delivering the message that the international community wants strong action against terrorism however defined. Besides situations where some states resort to the deliberate misuse of the term, there is reason for concern about the more frequent adoption in domestic anti-terrorism legislation of terminology that is not properly confined to the countering of terrorism.[20]

Legal definitions of terrorism should refer to the methods used, not the underlying aim. What transforms political or ideological aspirations into terrorism is the decision by one or more morally responsible individuals to employ the morally inexcusable tactics of deadly or otherwise serious violence against 'civilians', that is, innocent bystanders. With the qualification that hostage-taking entails a threat of serious violence and should, therefore, be included in the definition, terrorism and terrorist crimes should always be defined so that such violence forms a mandatory element of the definition.[21]

Amongst Security Council resolutions calling for action against terrorism, Resolution 1566 comes closest to defining terrorism by including the following three cumulative conditions:

(1) acts, including against civilians, committed with the intention of causing death or serious bodily injury, or the taking of hostages; and

---

[19] For a list of these treaties, see: <http://www.un.org/en/terrorism/instruments.shtml>.

[20] Eg Reports of the Special Rapporteur on human rights and counter-terrorism, A/HRC/4/26/Add.2 (16 November 2006) paras 11–18; A/HRC/4/26/Add.3 (14 December 2006) paras 12–17; A/HRC/6/17/Add.2 (7 November 2007) paras 23–4; A/HRC/10/3/Add.2 (16 December 2008) paras 6–14; A/HRC/16/51 (22 December 2010). The last-mentioned report is the final report by the current author as the first Special Rapporteur on human rights and counter-terrorism, identifying ten areas of best practice in the fight against terrorism, including a model national law definition of terrorism (at para 28).

[21] Report of the Special Rapporteur on counter-terrorism and human rights, E/CN.4/2006/98 (28 December 2005).

(2) irrespective of whether motivated by considerations of a political, philosophical, ideological, racial, ethnic, religious, or other similar nature, also committed for the purpose of provoking a state of terror in the general public or in a group of persons or particular persons, intimidating a population, or compelling a government or an international organization to do or to abstain from doing any act; and

(3) such acts constituting offences within the scope of and as defined in the international conventions and protocols relating to terrorism.[22]

As to the third cumulative element, that only acts constituting offences within existing terrorism-related conventions may fall under the terrorism definition, there is a qualification to be made. Where a state is responding to an international call to suppress terrorism, this third cumulative element is essential in determining what type of conduct is to be suppressed. However, states may feel compelled to implement additional counter-terrorism measures according to regional or domestic threats. Where there is evidence that a state must respond to domestic or regional terrorist threats it may, therefore, have genuine reasons to proscribe acts that fall outside the scope of offences under the existing universal terrorism-related conventions.

However, any national definitions of crimes must meet the requirement of legality, enshrined in the non-derogable provision of Article 15 ICCPR. In the absence of an internationally agreed definition of terrorism, this provision has come to serve, together with the prohibition against discrimination, as the basis for a checklist for the conformity of definitions of terrorism or terrorist crimes with human rights. Besides the obvious element of a prohibition against the retroactive application of the criminal law, Article 15 ICCPR also includes the requirements of *nullum crimen sine lege* (all elements of a crime must be defined by the law), *nulla poena sine lege* (all punishments must be defined by the law), accessibility (the law must be publicly available), precision (the line between permitted and prohibited conduct must be clear), and foreseeability (the law must enable an individual to anticipate the consequences of his or her conduct). The safest way to secure compliance with these requirements is to base any definitions of terrorist crimes on an exhaustive list of already defined serious violent crimes. Criminalization of terrorist intent as such, or circular definitions that refer back to the word 'terror', or definitions that generally cover crimes against the state, regularly fail the test under Article 15 ICCPR.

5 SUBSTANTIVE CHALLENGES TO HUMAN RIGHTS LAW IN THE FIGHT AGAINST TERRORISM

Governments have often felt tempted to depart from ordinary laws, normal procedures, or the fundamental rights of the individual when confronted with acts of terrorism or the threat of them. Since 9/11, an unprecedented wave of special legislation or special powers has emerged all over the world, and practically all human rights have been under attack or 'reconsideration'. While most human rights are not absolute but allow for some limitations to protect public security, in many cases governments have gone beyond these permissible limitations, resulting in human rights violations. This section gives an overview of some of the most frequent areas of problematic practices.

---

[22] SC Res 1566 (8 October 2004) para 3. For the view that customary international law contains a norm defining the international crime of terrorism, at least in peacetime, see, Special Tribunal for Lebanon, Interlocutory Decision on the Applicable Law, STL-11-01/1 (16 February 2011), in particular para 85.

As a graphic illustration of the effects of counter-terrorism measures upon human rights, reference can be made to a pyramid. At its top, a relatively small number of individuals—in many cases real or suspected terrorists—are subjected to grave human rights violations, such as torture or extra-judicial execution. At the bottom of the pyramid, all members of society are confronted with new interferences with some of their human rights because of counter-terrorism legislation. Typically, everyone's right to privacy is affected by new rules on interception of communications, databases and data retention, and exchange of personal information across borders.[23] Between the top and the base of the pyramid, certain groups of individuals are affected more than the average citizen by counter-terrorism measures, and many of these interferences easily escalate into violations of human rights law.[24] Immigrants or ethnic or religious minorities are often targeted by counter-terrorism measures affecting a broad range of human rights. Persons fleeing persecution in their own country are confronted with tighter controls of international borders in the name of countering terrorism, effectively preventing them from exercising their human right to leave their own country.[25] Even human rights defenders may find themselves targeted, as associations, public gatherings, and fundraising are subject to tighter control by the authorities.

By using the metaphor of a pyramid it is made clear that the perception that insistence on the importance of human rights in the fight against terrorism would seek to defend the terrorists is wrong. Everyone's human rights are affected to a lesser or greater degree by counter-terrorism measures, and keeping all counter-terrorism legislation under careful public scrutiny is the best way to ensure that measures justified as targeting the 'real terrorists' do not result in the erosion of human rights in general.

5.1 FREEDOM FROM TORTURE AND CRUEL, INHUMAN, OR DEGRADING TREATMENT

The prohibition against torture or any other form of cruel, inhuman, or degrading treatment or punishment is an absolute human right that allows for no exception, even during times of emergency.[26] Accordingly, it is very rare that states would actually legislate to allow for torture. Proposals of legalized forms of torture, such as courts being empowered to issue 'torture warrants' in order to administer lawful torture in a 'ticking-bomb scenario' (which assumes that the police have captured a terrorist who refuses to reveal the location of a time bomb that will soon detonate and kill thousands of innocent people), have remained hypothetical.[27] Furthermore, governments will normally deny that extra-legal torture is used by their law enforcement or intelligence agencies or military forces. Nevertheless, the practice of subjecting terrorist suspects or their presumed associates to torture or related practices became widespread after 9/11 and many long-term patterns of using torture against terrorist suspects were also revealed.[28]

---

[23] See Report of the Special Rapporteur on human rights and counter-terrorism, A/HRC/13/37 (28 December 2009).

[24] For an assessment of the gender impact of counter-terrorism, see Report of the Special Rapporteur on human rights and counter-terrorism, A/64/211 (3 August 2009).

[25] See Report of the Special Rapporteur on human rights and counter-terrorism, A/62/263 (15 August 2007).

[26] UNCAT, Arts 1 and 2(2); ICCPR, Arts 7 and 4(2). See also Chapter 9.

[27] For a critique of a broad interpretation of what constitutes a 'ticking bomb', see Report of the Special Rapporteur on human rights and counter-terrorism, A/HRC/6/17/Add.4 (16 November 2007) paras 20–1.

[28] Eg Amnesty International, Saudi Arabia: Assaulting Human Rights in the Name of Counter-Terrorism (22 July 2009).

There are various ways in which many governments have ended up compromising the absolute prohibition against torture. First, denial of the extraterritorial applicability of the Convention against Torture (UNCAT) and the ICCPR has been used as an argument by the USA to cover the engagement in torture of military forces or intelligence agencies abroad. Second, some states, such as the UK, have relied on information obtained by torture 'for operational purposes' and various forms of cooperation with states that practise torture to circumvent existing rules about torture. Third, by using notions such as 'enhanced interrogation techniques' (USA) or 'moderate physical pressure' (Israel) some governments have tried to shift the barrier between what is prohibited and what is permitted. Fourth, some governments have tried to relax the standard for sending a person to another country under the risk of torture or other ill-treatment, by proposing the replacement of an absolute prohibition in situations of 'real risk' with a 'balancing test', a 'more likely than not' standard, or shifting the responsibility to the receiving state through the use of diplomatic assurances.[29] Finally, there has been a lack of investigation and accountability in cases where allegations of torture of terrorist suspects were made. In Spain, for instance, the authorities have maintained that allegations of ill-treatment are standard operating methods of terrorist organizations and, therefore, prima facie unfounded.

In a report dealing with the role of intelligence agencies and their oversight bodies in countering terrorism, the Special Rapporteur on human rights and counter-terrorism applied the principles of state responsibility and concluded that any form of collusion in torture or other prohibited treatment by intelligence agencies amounts to a human rights violation.[30]

5.2 RIGHT TO LIBERTY AND RIGHT TO A FAIR TRIAL

In the counter-terrorism context, practices breaching the prohibition against torture are often coupled with, and shielded by, secret or arbitrary detention and the denial of a fair trial. The right to liberty of the person and the right to a fair trial are guaranteed, respectively, by Articles 9 and 14 ICCPR.[31] Resort by governments to emergency powers while countering terrorism constitutes a major challenge to these guarantees, as neither of these provisions is on the list of non-derogable rights contained in Article 4(2) ICCPR. Only the requirement of legality in the field of criminal law of Article 15 ICCPR, including the principles of *nullum crimen sine lege* and the prohibition against retroactive criminal laws, is explicitly listed as non-derogable. However, in its General Comments on states of emergency and the right to a fair trial, the Human Rights Committee has clarified that the rights to liberty and a fair trial nevertheless include dimensions from which there can never be derogation.[32] Arbitrary detention and denial of court review over any form of detention are prohibited at all times. The fundamental principles of fair trial, including

---

[29] While many states, including Canada and the USA, demonstrate elements of this trend, the most systematic effort towards 'reconsidering' the rule of *non-refoulement* was made by the UK and several other states in *Saadi v Italy* (2009) 49 EHRR 30. The Grand Chamber of the European Court of Human Rights maintained its position that the rule is absolute. Amnesty International, n 28, paras 137–9.

[30] Report of the Special Rapporteur on human rights and counter-terrorism, A/HRC/10/3 (4 February 2009).

[31] See Chapter 13.

[32] HRC, General Comment 29, n 14, in particular paras 12–16; HRC, General Comment 32, HRI/GEN/1/ Rev.9 (Vol 1) 248 (27 May 2008) in particular para 6. The Human Rights Committee is currently considering a new draft General Comment on the right to liberty and security of the person, CCPR/C/107/R.3 (28 January 2013).

the presumption of innocence and the requirement that only a court can order a criminal punishment, must equally be respected during a state of emergency.

As a consequence, laws and practices that are applied in the name of combating terrorism may be in violation of the rights to liberty and a fair trial. Secret or unacknowledged detention automatically violates the prohibition against arbitrary detention and in some cases also amounts to prohibited disappearance of the person.[33] Even narrowly crafted provisions on *incommunicado* detention, or on delays in effective court review over the lawfulness of detention, easily result in breaches of Article 9 ICCPR. This risk can be demonstrated by a reference to Spain, which despite international criticism continues to apply a regime of *incommunicado* detention, denying terrorist suspects contact with a freely chosen lawyer during the initial period of detention. Instead, detainees are represented by a state-appointed lawyer whom they will usually not meet. The compatibility of such a regime with international human rights law is doubtful and will depend on the merits of the reasons given for denying freely chosen legal representation and the ability of the appointed lawyer to independently and effectively protect the rights of the detainee, including against any form of torture or other prohibited treatment.[34]

The US detention facility at Guantánamo Bay has become a notorious symbol of practices of long-term detention of terrorist suspects without trial. Many other states continue also to detain terrorist suspects or their presumed associates without trial or even any criminal charges. Hence, the first fundamental dimension of the right to a fair trial, access to a court, is denied and as a consequence the persons concerned cannot exercise any of their fair trial rights. Some governments, including the US administration, have referred to the war paradigm as the framework for their counter-terrorism measures, seeking to justify long-term detention without trial as long as the 'war on terror' or 'war against al-Qaida' continues. Under a law-enforcement paradigm that treats terrorism as a serious crime, however, it is evident that the purpose of detaining terrorist suspects must be the investigation of their alleged crimes in preparation of a criminal trial.

Even in countries in which terrorist suspects *are* brought before a court for trial, there may be serious deviations from international human rights standards. Through special legislation, terrorism cases may be dealt with by military or special courts. The trying of civilians by a military court as such is problematic under the right to a fair trial. Moreover, outright violations of Article 14 ICCPR may result from the lack of independence and impartiality of the judges of a military or special court and from undue interference by the executive in deciding that a case will be tried by a military or special court, in the worst cases even after acquittal by an ordinary court. In addition, trials before military or special courts may involve restrictions on the rights of the defence, including in respect of secret evidence, denial of full communication between client and counsel, and breaches of the principle of equality of arms, for instance through restrictions on access by the defence to exculpatory evidence. As to the last-mentioned example, terrorist trials often involve a huge amount of primary material such as transcripts of intercepted telephone calls. If only the prosecution has access to the full records and if it presents to the court only a carefully selected sample, this may result in bias against the defence who may wish to contest the value of the excerpts as evidence by putting them into a broader context. However, this may only be possible if access to exculpatory evidence not presented by the prosecution to the court is provided to the defence, under terms that allow its proper examination.

---

[33] See International Convention for the Protection of All Persons from Enforced Disappearance, Art 2.

[34] See Report of the Special Rapporteur on counter-terrorism and human rights, A/HRC/10/3/Add.2 (16 December 2008).

A general solution to the challenges related to the detention and trial of terrorist suspects can be identified in the 'principle of normalcy'. Terrorism should be treated as a serious form of crime, which is subject to ordinary laws on criminal procedure and dealt with by ordinary courts. This is a recommended course of action for avoiding the temptation to engage in practices that violate international human rights law.[35]

5.3 RIGHT TO NON-DISCRIMINATION

As demonstrated by the pyramid metaphor referred to at the beginning of Section 5, not everyone's human rights are equally affected by counter-terrorism measures. An alarming trend in the post-9/11 era has been the increased use of 'terrorist profiling' as a significant component of states' counter-terrorism efforts.[36] The European Union recommended in 2002 to its member states to develop 'terrorist profiles', defined as 'a set of physical, psychological or behavioural variables, which have been identified as typical of persons involved in terrorist activities and which may have some predictive value in that respect'.[37]

Profiling has been applied, for instance, in the context of data-mining initiatives, that is, searches of personal data sets according to presumed characteristics of suspects. But it also occurs in less explicit forms. For example, law-enforcement agents often rely on sets of physical characteristics when deciding whom to stop and search for counter-terrorism purposes. Even when there are no explicit instructions to target specific groups, stop-and-search powers may disproportionately affect persons of a certain ethnic or religious appearance.

When law-enforcement agents use broad profiles that reflect unexamined generalizations, their practices may constitute disproportionate interferences with human rights. In particular, profiling based on stereotypical assumptions that persons of a certain 'race', national or ethnic origin, or religion are particularly likely to be involved in terrorism may lead to practices that are incompatible with the principle of non-discrimination. Such profiling is also ineffective. An illustrative case is the so-called *Rasterfahndung* programme, initiated by the German authorities in the wake of 9/11 to identify terrorist 'sleepers'. The German police forces collected personal records of several million individuals from public and private databases. The criteria for the search included: being male, age 18–40, current or former student, Muslim denomination, and a link through birth or nationality to one of several specified countries with a predominantly Muslim population. Approximately 32,000 persons were identified as potential terrorist sleepers and more closely examined. In none of these cases did the *Rasterfahndung* lead to bringing criminal charges for terrorism-related offences. The programme was eventually found to be unconstitutional by the German Constitutional Court.[38]

In the UK, police forces have relied on profiles based on a person's ethnic and/or religious appearance when conducting stops, document checks, or searches for counter-terrorism purposes. Accordingly, stops and searches under section 44 of the Terrorism Act 2000, which authorized the police in designated areas to stop and search people without having to show reasonable suspicion, disproportionately affected ethnic minorities. Between

---

[35] For a systematic assessment of the right to a fair trial in the context of countering terrorism, see Report of the Special Rapporteur on counter-terrorism and human rights, A/63/223 (6 August 2008). For the 'principle of normalcy' as one element of best practice in countering terrorism, see Report of the Special Rapporteur on counter-terrorism and human rights, A/HRC/16/51 (22 December 2010) paras 17–21.

[36] Report of the Special Rapporteur on human rights and counter-terrorism, A/HRC/4/26 (29 January 2007).

[37] Council of the EU, Draft Council Recommendation on the development of terrorist profiles, 11858/3/02 REV 3 (18 November 2002).   [38] Bundesverfassungsgericht, 1 BvR 518/02, 4 April 2006.

2001/02 and 2002/03, for example, the number of persons of Asian ethnicity subjected to section 44 searches rose by 302 per cent, with a further rise of 202 per cent between 2006/07 and 2009/10, as compared to a rise of 118 per cent and, respectively, 115 per cent for white people. In 2003/04, Asian people were about 3.6 times more likely and black people about 4.3 times more likely to be stopped and searched under counter-terrorism legislation than white people. Yet the measures resulted in only a handful of arrests.[39]

At worst, terrorist profiling is not only legally and morally wrong and ineffective, it may even be counterproductive. Terrorist organizations can easily evade the profiles employed by the authorities and adjust their tactics accordingly, for instance when recruiting suicide bombers and choosing them for a mission. Profiling may also have negative effects on the targeted minorities. Their stigmatization may result in a feeling of alienation and end up facilitating recruitment to terrorism from within the group.

The Special Rapporteur on human rights and counter-terrorism has, therefore, recommended abandonment of profiling based on group characteristics and its replacement with a combination of universal controls affecting everyone equally, genuinely random searches coupled with proper monitoring to secure that they do not transform into unregulated de facto targeting of specific groups, and profiling based on individual conduct instead of group membership.[40]

5.4 OTHER HUMAN RIGHTS

The examples given in Section 5.3 all relate to well-known and widely discussed human rights impacts of counter-terrorism measures. However, it is important to understand that all human rights are affected, to a greater or lesser extent, and in respect of a smaller or larger group of individuals, by counter-terrorism measures.

An under-explored issue relates to the effect of counter-terrorism measures upon economic, social, and cultural rights.[41] While the equal status, indivisibility, and interdependence of all human rights has been broadly acknowledged,[42] the discourse on human rights and counter-terrorism has tended to focus on civil and political rights. Even among the UN human rights treaty bodies, the Human Rights Committee and the Committee against Torture have been much more systematic than the other treaty bodies in questioning and assessing states' compliance with human rights while countering terrorism. The Committee on Economic, Social and Cultural Rights has very rarely given attention to counter-terrorism measures.

A prime example that demonstrates the need for a systematic assessment is the construction of a wall or barrier into the Occupied Palestinian Territory (OPT) by Israel, the occupying power. Explained as a security measure against the risk of suicide terrorists trying to enter Israel or to attack Israeli settlements inside the OPT, the wall or barrier has resulted not only in the construction of a major physical barrier between Israel and the OPT but also in a whole architecture of associated obstacles, barriers, walls, checkpoints, and so on within the OPT.[43] As a consequence, Palestinian individuals find their everyday life devastated through multiple forms of hardship, many of which are directly related to

---

[39] Report of the Special Rapporteur on human rights and counter-terrorism, A/HRC/4/26 (29 January 2007) para 37; Home Office, *Statistics on Race and the Criminal Justice System 2010* (2011) 43.

[40] Report of the Special Rapporteur, n 39, paras 83–9.

[41] See Report of the Special Rapporteur on human rights and counter-terrorism, A/HRC/6/17 (21 November 2007).   [42] See Chapter 7.

[43] See Report of the Special Rapporteur on human rights and counter-terrorism, A/HRC/6/17/Add.4 (16 November 2007).

their enjoyment of economic, social, and cultural rights. For instance, access to hospitals, schools, water resources, olive groves, and other places of work are all adversely affected and in many cases to a degree that amounts to a violation of, respectively, the rights to health, education, water, an adequate standard of living, and work. In its advisory opinion on the Israeli wall, the International Court of Justice concluded that Israel was in breach of international law, including of the Covenant on Economic, Social and Cultural Rights, through the construction of the wall.[44]

The case of the Israeli wall illustrates that economic, social, and cultural rights must also be taken into account when societies design their security infrastructure, including their measures against terrorism. But economic, social, and cultural rights also have another important role in ensuring responses to terrorism conform to human rights. Violations of human rights in general have been identified in the UN Global Counter-Terrorism Strategy as one of the conditions conducive to the spread of terrorism.[45] Amongst the other identified conducive conditions there are many that have direct links with economic, social, and cultural rights. Hence, long-term work for the promotion of the full enjoyment of economic, social, and cultural rights can be seen as an important element in building societies without terrorism.[46]

6 AN INSTITUTIONAL CHALLENGE: TERRORIST LISTING BY THE SECURITY COUNCIL

While states are responsible for many violations of human rights in the name of countering terrorism, the listing of terrorist individuals or entities is one of the rare occasions where the UN itself engages in action that has a direct effect upon individuals. Therefore, the question of the UN's compliance with human rights arises.[47]

In Resolution 1373, the Security Council identified the terrorist attacks of 9/11, 'like any act of international terrorism', as a threat to international peace and security. Acting under Chapter VII of the UN Charter, it imposed upon all member states a range of legally binding obligations to counter terrorism, including an obligation to report on their measures to a new body, the CTC. This Committee is composed of the diplomatic representatives of the 15 states that at any given time serve as members of the Security Council.

Despite its fundamental role in UN action against terrorism, Resolution 1373 did not result in the blacklisting of terrorists by the UN. The UN is not involved in any general listing of terrorists. Instead, the listing system in place is based on the earlier Security Council Resolution 1267 of 1999 and is today limited to individuals or entities belonging to or associated with al-Qaida. The list of al-Qaida terrorists maintained by a separate Security Council committee, the 1267 Sanctions Committee, includes close to 300 individuals or entities.[48] As Resolution 1267 was also adopted under Chapter VII of the UN Charter,

---

[44] *Legal Consequences of the Construction of a Wall in the Occupied Palestinian Territories* (Advisory Opinion) [2004] ICJ Rep 136, para 116.

[45] GA Res 60/288 (20 September 2006).

[46] For a broader discussion on the role of economic, social, and cultural rights in the context of countering terrorism, see the Report of the Special Rapporteur on human rights and counter-terrorism, A/HRC/6/17 (21 November 2007).

[47] See Report of the Special Rapporteur on human rights and counter-terrorism, A/65/258 (6 August 2010). See, also, Chapter 26.

[48] See List established and maintained by the 1267 Committee with respect to individuals, groups, undertakings and other entities associated with Al-Qaida: <http://www.un.org/sc/committees/1267/pdf/AQList.pdf>.

the implementation of the resolution and the listing decisions by the 1267 Committee is often perceived by states as a Charter obligation that under Article 103 of the Charter trumps competing treaty obligations, including those emanating from human rights treaties. Article 103 proclaims the primacy of Charter obligations over any other agreement to which a state is party. As a consequence, many governments take the view that national authorities enjoy no discretion whatsoever in implementing the sanctions but must without hesitation freeze the assets, and prevent international travel, of any person put on the 1267 terrorist list. Some governments, as well as many scholars and human rights experts, however, argue that as long as there is no effective independent review of listing and delisting decisions at the UN level, member states must secure such review in respect of their own measures implementing the UN-imposed sanctions.[49]

Against this background it is natural that there is persistent concern that the Security Council itself must comply with human rights when listing or delisting persons. Several rounds of improvement have already been made, including Security Council Resolution 1822 of 2008, which introduced a duty to inform the person of the reasons for his or her placement on the list, as well as a mandatory two-year review by the 1267 Committee of all the entries in the list. However, these piecemeal improvements did not remedy the main shortcomings of the 1267 listing procedure.

In October 2008, the Human Rights Committee concluded that Belgium had violated Articles 17 (right to privacy) and 12 (freedom of movement) ICCPR in respect of a Belgian couple, because it had initiated their listing as terrorists by the 1267 Committee, and was subsequently unable to have them delisted even though no case had been proven against them.[50] On 20 July 2009, the 1267 Committee finally removed the couple from its list. This decision by the 1267 Committee is indicative of a broader acknowledgement that there is a need for judicial or other independent review of terrorist listing. Although Belgium was unable to reach a delisting decision earlier, it managed to obtain consensus within the 1267 Committee, after the Human Rights Committee had concluded that because it initiated the listing, Belgium was responsible for a human rights violation. The subsequent decision to delist these individuals can be seen as a recognition of the Committee's possibility to conduct indirect quasi-judicial review over the consequences of the listing by the Security Council, as long as a state that has ratified the Optional Protocol to the ICCPR can be shown to have had a strong enough role in initiating (or implementing) the listing.

Further reforms have been introduced, inter alia, through Security Council Resolutions 1989 of 2011 and 2083 of 2012. Yet listing decisions are still taken by a political body composed of diplomatic representatives of the 15 member states of the Security Council. States do not necessarily disclose any real evidence for a listing proposal even to each other but may be acting on the basis of secret intelligence information, even if a 'statement of case' is nowadays required.[51] An independent delisting Ombudsperson acts upon requests by listed individuals or entities and may recommend delisting.[52] Remarkably, the

---

Pursuant to Security Council Resolution 1988, individuals and entities associated with the Taliban were removed from the 1267 sanctions list and put on a separate Taliban list, which is maintained by a separate Committee of the Security Council but not categorized as a terrorist list. See List of individuals and entities established pursuant to Security Council Resolution 1988 (2011): <http://www.un.org/sc/committees/1988/pdf/1988List.pdf>.

[49] See Report of the Special Rapporteur on human rights and counter-terrorism, A/61/267 (16 August 2006) in particular para 39. See also *Nada v Switzerland* (2013) 56 EHRR 18, in particular para 212 (where the Court 'further finds that there was nothing in the Security Council resolutions to prevent the Swiss authorities from introducing mechanisms to verify the measures taken at national level pursuant to those resolutions.')

[50] *Sayadi and Vinck v Belgium*, CCPR/C/94/D/1472/2006 (29 December 2008).

[51] SC Res 2083 (17 December 2012), para 11. [52] SC Res 2083, n 51, para 19.

delisting recommendation by the Ombudsperson becomes a decision to delist by default, unless either the 1267 Committee by consensus decides to retain the listing or any member state of the Security Council refers the case to the full Security Council where normal voting rules apply, so that delisting will require a qualified majority and can be blocked by any of the five permanent members.[53] Independently of delisting requests sent to the Ombudsperson, the 1267 will review every entry on the list every three years.[54]

Despite the gradual improvements towards transparency and adequate procedure, the terrorist listing procedure of the 1267 Committee fails to meet the requirements of a 'fair and clear procedure', a notion used to describe the level of procedural guarantees that one can expect an intergovernmental organization to deliver, not to speak of full compliance with the right to a fair trial, as would be required if a state were to impose criminal sanctions. Hence, calls for judicial review, either of the listing itself at the UN level or of the implementation of the sanctions at the national (or EU) level, are still vocal.

Important indications of this broad trend of calling for judicial review are the *Kadi* ruling by the European Court of Justice, quashing EU-level implementation of sanctions imposed by the 1267 Committee due to insufficient procedural guarantees,[55] the subsequent *Nada* ruling by the European Court of Human Rights,[56] and a UN General Assembly resolution adopted annually since 2008, urging states 'while ensuring full compliance with their international obligations', to include 'adequate human rights guarantees' in their national procedures for the listing of terrorist individuals and entities.[57] This statement should be seen as an appeal to states to implement UN-imposed sanctions against terrorists not blindly but subject to adequate human rights guarantees. Equally importantly, since 2008 the Security Council itself has repeatedly acknowledged that the UN should comply with human rights when listing individuals.[58]

7 CONCLUSION: IS THE PENDULUM ALREADY SWINGING BACK?

The terrorist acts of 9/11 have led to the worst backlash in the international protection of human rights since the inclusion of the notion of human rights in the UN Charter, in the aftermath of the Second World War. In this sense, terrorism can be seen as the antithesis of human rights. Still, one needs to remember that what constitutes the backlash is the reaction and overreaction by governments that have introduced a whole wave of retrogressive measures in respect of human rights in the aftermath of 9/11. Furthermore,

---

[53] SC Res 2083, n 51, para 21.   [54] SC Res 2083, n 51, para 42.

[55] Joined Cases C-402/05 P and C-415/05 P, *Kadi and Al Barakaat International Foundation v Council of the European Union*, [2008] ECR I-6351. The 1267 Committee decided on 5 October 2012 to delist Mr Kadi, after he had been subject to a travel ban and assets freeze for 11 years. In a new ruling of 18 July 2013, the European Court of Justice affirmed the rationale of its own earlier judgment.   [56] n 49.

[57] GA Res 63/185 (3 March 2009) para 19. For the latest such resolution, see GA Res 66/171 (30 March 2012) para 12.

[58] See SC Res 1822 (30 June 2008) ('Reaffirming the need to combat by all means, in accordance with the Charter of the United Nations and international law, including applicable international human rights, refugee, and humanitarian law, threats to international peace and security caused by terrorist acts, stressing in this regard the important role the United Nations plays in leading and coordinating this effort'). See also GA Res 63/185, n 57, para 27 (reiterating the importance of all states using 'adequate procedures' when implementing the sanctions). For the most recent resolution repeating these statements see SC Res 2083 (17 December 2012) preamble and para 43.

the terrorist attacks were more a triggering cause than a structural one. Many of the human-rights-hostile practices employed by governments in the name of countering terrorism existed prior to 2001 in some parts of the world, albeit that those practices have now become much more widespread.

What has been disheartening in the backlash is the ease with which governments that were known as champions of the international concern for human rights have changed course and become generators of legal arguments and doctrines that seek to deny the applicability or substantive contents of human rights law when they engage in measures against terrorism. Such constructions try to turn the clock back by more than 60 years, to times when human rights were not yet recognized as a matter of concern for the international community. Even worse, some Western governments, such as the Bush administration of the USA and the Blair-Brown government in the UK, appeared at times to try to turn the clock back by 200 years, to times before Immanuel Kant, by reducing a human person to a mere means, instead of treating every individual always as an end. Mass murderers are recognized as an end in the traditional criminal law system, which aims at establishing the facts, the culpability of the person, and the punishment. But suspected terrorists—or even persons only suspected of knowing something of relevance—are reduced to a means when they are tortured to extract information, without any intention to bring them before a court for their possible crimes. Whether a government itself tortures or whether it is complicit in creating an international industry of torture for the production of intelligence information does not matter.

However, there are many signs that the pendulum is swinging back and the damage triggered by the terrorist acts of 9/11 is being assessed and the process of repairs started. For instance, both in the USA and the UK important steps have been taken to depart from earlier human-rights-hostile practices. Within the UN Security Council and other important engines of counter-terrorism measures, it is gradually understood that violating human rights in the name of countering terrorism is not only wrong in legal and moral terms but also counterproductive for any effective strategy against terrorism, as respect for, and promotion of, human rights are acknowledged as important elements in building societies without terrorism.

If it took ten years to turn the clock back by 60 or 200 years, it may take 30 years to repair the damage and to reach a situation where the commitment to respect the human rights of each and every human person in any situation is again universally accepted. But once that is achieved, we will not be in the same situation as before 9/11. We will be wiser than then, and conscious of the fact that much of the seeming universal acceptance of human rights was mere lip service.

FURTHER READING

CAMERON, 'UN Targeted Sanctions, Legal Safeguards and the European Convention on Human Rights' (2003) 72 *NJIL* 159.

DOSWALD-BECK, *Human Rights in Times of Conflict and Terrorism* (Oxford University Press, 2011).

DUFFY, *The 'War on Terror' and the Framework of International Law* (Cambridge University Press, 2005).

FARER, *Confronting Global Terrorism and American Neo-Conservativism: The Framework of a Liberal Grand Strategy* (Oxford University Press, 2008).

INTERNATIONAL COMMISSION OF JURISTS, *Assessing Damage, Urging Action: Report of the Eminent Jurists Panel on Terrorism, Counter-terrorism and Human Rights* (Geneva, 2009).

Jenkins, Henriksen and Jacobsen (eds), *The Long Decade: How 9/11 Has Changed the Law* (Oxford University Press, 2013).

Moeckli, *Human Rights and Non-discrimination in the 'War on Terror'* (Oxford University Press, 2008).

Saul, *Defining Terrorism in International Law* (Oxford University Press, 2006).

United Nations, Reports by the UN Special Rapporteur on the promotion and protection of human rights and fundamental freedoms while countering terrorism, UN documents A/60/370, E/CN.4/2006/98, A/61/267, A/HRC/4/26, A/62/263, A/HRC/6/17, A/63/223, A/HRC/10/3, A/HRC/13/37, A/66/258, A/HRC/16/51, A/66/310, A/HRC/20/14, A/67/396, A/HRC/22/52, and addenda, 2005–13.

USEFUL WEBSITES

Reports by the UN Special Rapporteur on human rights and counter-terrorism: <http://www.ohchr.org/EN/Issues/Terrorism/Pages/Annual.aspx>

UN website on countering terrorism: <http://www.un.org/terrorism>

Website on prevention of terrorism by the UN Office on Drugs and Crime: <http://www.unodc.org/unodc/en/terrorism/index.html>

28

POVERTY

Stephen P Marks

SUMMARY

This chapter addresses the challenge posed by poverty to the protection of human rights. Human rights define the entitlements considered necessary for a life of dignity in society, including the right to an adequate standard of living, that is, the right to be free from poverty. At this high level of abstraction, the elimination of poverty and realization of human rights are similar in that both clarify what needs to be done so that all human beings enjoy minimal standards of a decent existence. The context for this inquiry is the consensus regarding the imperative of poverty reduction and human rights realization, and the contested interpretations of the impact of globalization and financial crises on poverty and human rights. This context will be set out first, followed by a discussion of how international legal discourses on human rights and poverty issues diverge and, finally, how they converge.

1 INTRODUCTION

Human rights have emerged in national and international legal systems as a means of enhancing the lives of people in a position to claim their rights. But what do these rights mean for the one-fifth of humanity who live in misery and lack the basic necessities in terms of income, health, education, food, and employment? Without a minimal level of social and economic status, the extremely poor might be expected to see human rights as a luxury beyond their reach. For them the elimination of poverty is likely to be perceived as the highest priority in the human rights struggle.

There are deep political and even ideological issues involved in the relationship between the elimination of poverty and the struggle for human rights. It has been argued that 'the present global institutional order is foreseeably associated with such massive incidence of avoidable severe poverty, its (uncompensated) imposition manifests an on-going human rights violation—arguably the largest such violation ever committed in human history'.[1] Others have argued that the development of a middle class who exercise economic freedoms under competitive capitalism without state interference should come first and then political freedom and democracy will follow. A survey of attitudes of lower and middle class people in 13 countries confirms the hypothesis that '[e]conomic well-being is linked

---

[1] Pogge, 'Severe Poverty as a Human Rights Violation' in Pogge (ed), *Freedom from Poverty as a Human Right: Who Owes What to the Very Poor?* (OUP, 2007) 52.

with support for democracy'[2] and '[m]iddle-class respondents often assign a higher priority to free speech than do those in the lower income group'.[3] Although it may appear tautological, the survey found that 'lower-income respondents were more likely than their wealthier fellow citizens to prioritize avoiding hunger and poverty'.[4] Are the poor indifferent to human rights beyond the economic and social rights that enhance their economic well-being? Is the way out of poverty to provide economic freedoms under competitive capitalism to favour the classes that benefit most from economic growth on the assumption that it is on those classes that the affirmation of human rights must rely and that a rising tide (middle- and upper-class income) lifts all boats (including the poor)? Or is it the responsibility of the state to redistribute wealth so as to eliminate poverty and guarantee all human rights—including economic and social rights—to all, including the poor?

This chapter addresses the relationship between human rights and models of development in response to these questions. If, as the classical liberal model might suggest, human rights are a luxury that comes to people who have risen out of poverty, then it is likely to be limited to what Karl Marx called 'bourgeois freedoms', those that protect the interests of the middle class and the rich against those of the poor. The first challenge regarding the relationship between poverty and human rights is, therefore, to explore whether, and to what extent, human rights is a regime that is hostile to the interests of the poor. Such would be the case if a narrow interpretation of human rights consisting exclusively of negative freedoms (civil and political rights) were used, rather than the nearly universally accepted understanding of human rights as integrating civil, cultural, economic, political, and social rights.[5] In other words, if human rights were limited to those rights that protect the interests and wealth of people with resources, then the poor would rightfully be suspicious of them.

While the narrow understanding may still have proponents today (as will be seen), the more widely accepted understanding of human rights is not only that they embrace economic, social, and cultural dimensions but that they also empower the poor in their struggle against the obstacles to their liberation from misery. As the former Secretary-General of Amnesty International put it, '[h]uman rights are claims that the weak advance to hold the powerful accountable, and that is why poverty is first and foremost about rights'.[6] From this perspective—and this is the real challenge raised by this chapter—poverty is a human rights issue in terms of ends and means. The *end* of human rights is to ensure for all—rich and poor—equal rights, including those called 'economic, social and cultural rights', among which is, in the words of Article 25 of the Universal Declaration of Human Rights (UDHR), the right of everyone 'to a standard of living adequate for the health and well-being of himself and of his family, including food, clothing, housing and medical care and necessary social services, and the right to security in the event of unemployment, sickness, disability, widowhood, old age or other lack of livelihood in circumstances beyond his control'. The *means* of human rights—awareness by rights-holders through learning and accountability of duty-bearers through laws, policies, and enforcement mechanisms—provide anti-poverty campaigns tools for mobilization and action. Unless and until these

---

[2] Pew Global Attitudes Project, *The Global Middle Class: Views on Democracy, Religion, Values, and Life Satisfaction in Emerging Nations* (Pew Research Center, 2009) 2. The countries in the study were Argentina, Brazil, Bulgaria, Chile, Egypt, India, Malaysia, Mexico, Poland, Russia, South Africa, Ukraine, and Venezuela.

[3] *The Global Middle Class*, n 2, 14.   [4] *The Global Middle Class*, n 2, 15.

[5] Vienna Declaration and Programme of Action, A/CONF.157/23 (25 June 1993) para 5; World Summit outcome document, GA Res 60/1 (24 October 2005) para 9.

[6] Khan, *The Unheard Truth: Poverty and Human Rights* (WW Norton, 2009) 21.

ends and means guide popular awareness and the functioning of institutions, poverty will pose a serious challenge to the protection, and perhaps the very concept, of human rights.

2 HUMAN RIGHTS AND POVERTY IN THE GLOBAL ECONOMY

At the outset, it is necessary to define the meaning of 'poverty' and explore its relationship to human rights, development, and social justice. Equally important as background to the topic of this chapter is the context of globalization.

2.1 POVERTY AND ITS SIGNIFICANCE FOR HUMAN RIGHTS

Development practitioners and scholars distinguish between extreme (or absolute) poverty and relative poverty. Extreme poverty is measured as the number of people living on an income below the current threshold set by the World Bank at US$1.25 per day (in 2005 prices). This threshold is the average of the national poverty lines in the poorest 10–20 countries. According to 2013 estimates, this number declined from 1.91 billion people in 1981 (52.2 per cent of the world population) to 1.22 billion people in 2010 (20.6 per cent).[7] The World Bank considers that '[t]he developing world has already attained the first Millennium Development Goal (MDG) target of halving the 1990 poverty rate by 2015',[8] which is the case if one compares the 1990 extreme poverty rate of 43.1 per cent to that in 2010 of 20.6 per cent. Notwithstanding this achievement, even if the current rate of progress is to be maintained, about 1 billion people will still live in extreme poverty in 2015, according to United Nations (UN) estimates.[9] It is also worth noting that 'the output and living standards of the developing world as a whole have been growing at faster rates than for the rich world since the turn of the century, reversing a prior pattern of little or no progress toward economic convergence'.[10] As the authors of a World Bank publication on absolute poverty measures note, 'the developing world outside China has seen little or no sustained progress in reducing the number of poor, with rising poverty counts in some regions, notably Sub-Saharan Africa'.[11] Nevertheless, the World Bank Group President Jim Yong Kim announced in April 2013 that '[w]e are at an auspicious moment in history when the successes of past decades and an increasingly favourable economic outlook combine to give developing countries a chance—for the first time ever—to end extreme poverty within a generation'.[12] Thus, according to Kim, this goal can be reached by 2030 if sustained high growth is maintained in South Asia and Sub-Saharan Africa, inequality is curbed primarily through job creation, and

[7] World Bank, *World Development Indicators 2013*, available at: <http://databank.worldbank.org/data/download/WDI-2013-ebook.pdf>.

[8] World Bank, 'Poverty', available at: <http://www.worldbank.org/en/topic/poverty>.

[9] UN, *Millennium Development Goals Report 2012* (2012) 7.

[10] Ravallion, 'How Long Will It Take to Lift One Billion People Out of Poverty?', World Bank Policy Research Working Paper 6325 (January 2013) 6.

[11] Chen and Ravallion, *Absolute Poverty Measures for the Developing World, 1981–2004*,World Bank Report WPS4211 (World Bank Development Research Group, 2007) 1.

[12] World Bank, 'World Bank Group President Calls for a World Free of Poverty', Press Release (2 April 2013) available at: <http://www.worldbank.org/en/news/press-release/2013/04/02/world-bank-group-president-calls-world-free-poverty>.

potential new food, fuel, or financial crises and climatic disasters are averted or mitigated. The idea of ending poverty by 2030 is gaining support.[13]

When one uses a US$2.00 threshold of poverty, there was a small decline from 2.59 billion in 1981 to 2.40 billion in 2010, although as a percentage of the global population the share decreases from 69.2 per cent in 1981 to 47 per cent in 2005. Regional differences are considerable. For example, in Sub-Saharan Africa the number of people living below US$2.00 per day went from 294 million in 1981 to 557 million in 2005, although that represents a change from 74 to 73 per cent of the population. In contrast, in the East Asia and Pacific region, including China, those living below US$2.00 decreased from 1.28 billion (95.4 per cent) in 1981 to 0.73 billion (38.7 per cent) in 2005.[14] However, the global financial crisis, which began in 2008, stalled this progress, especially for poorer countries.

Poverty can be measured according to absolute poverty lines or relative poverty lines. Absolute poverty lines set a floor such as the current thresholds used by the World Bank of US$1.25 and US$2.00) as the minimum amount required to secure the necessities for life, or a level of per capita caloric intake. Relative poverty lines measure, for example, the bottom 10 per cent of the income distribution or a certain fraction of median income, such as the fortieth percentile. The Human Poverty Index ranks countries according to an index of several factors, which differ between developing and developed countries. While calculating the number of people living on extremely low income is a convenient way of identifying poverty, it is widely acknowledged that the definition of poverty is broader than income data. As the Nobel prize-winning economist Amartya Sen put it, '[the] identification of poverty with low income is well established, but there is, by now, quite a substantial literature on its inadequacies'.[15] He notes four types of contingencies that determine variations in the impact of (low) income and that cause us to appreciate that poverty is more than just low income: individual physical characteristics, environmental conditions, social conditions, and behavioural expectations within the community.[16] These characteristics vary by individual, family, and society such that a given level of income may result in one person living in poverty in terms of their capability to lead a life they value, compared to another with the same income but whose functionings (the term used by Sen for what you actually do) provide a higher level of happiness or well-being. In sum, 'real poverty (in terms of capability deprivation) can easily be much more intense than we can deduce from income data'.[17]

UN human rights bodies, in particular the Committee on Economic, Social and Cultural Rights, share the critique of a statistically determined definition of poverty. In its statement on poverty, the Committee endorsed a 'multi-dimensional understanding of poverty, which reflects the indivisible and interdependent nature of all human rights' and defined poverty 'as a human condition characterized by sustained or chronic deprivation of the resources, capabilities, choices, security and power necessary for the enjoyment of an adequate standard of living'.[18]

Whether measured in relative or absolute terms or in terms of capabilities, the problem of global poverty is staggering in its magnitude and affects both developing and developed countries. It has attracted the attention of the human rights community for decades, if not centuries. For Jean-Jacques Rousseau 'it is plainly contrary to the law of nature...that the

---

[13] Eg 'Towards the end of poverty', *The Economist* (1 June 2013) 11, 22–24.

[14] Chen and Ravallion, *The Developing World is Poorer than We Thought, but no Less Successful in the Fight Against Poverty* (World Bank Development Research Group, 2008) 41–33.

[15] Sen, *The Idea of Justice* (Allen Lane, 2009) 254.   [16] Sen, n 15, 255–6.   [17] Sen, n 15, 256.

[18] CESCR, Statement on Poverty and the ICESCR, E/C.12/2001/10 (10 May 2001) para 8.

privileged few should gorge themselves with superfluities, while the starving multitude are in want of the bare necessities of life'.[19]

In preparation for the adoption in 1948 of the UDHR, the UN Educational, Scientific and Cultural Organization (UNESCO) convened a Committee on the Philosophical Principles of the Rights of Man to reflect on an eventual declaration of human rights, which stated, 'one group of rights is essentially connected with the provision of means of subsistence, through [one's] own efforts or, where they are insufficient, through the resources of society'.[20] In 1968, on the occasion of the twentieth anniversary of the UDHR, the International Conference on Human Rights proclaimed that '[t]he widening gap between the economically developed and developing countries impedes the realization of human rights in the international community'.[21] Thus, the basic idea that poverty and underdevelopment are human rights concerns has been part of the rhetoric of human rights since the founding of the contemporary human rights movement and even before. The UN High Commissioner for Human Rights declared in 1998 that extreme poverty was the worst violation of human rights.[22]

2.2 DEVELOPMENT, SOCIAL JUSTICE, AND HUMAN RIGHTS

Poverty and human rights are related in the context of development, whether defined as an increase in aggregate production of goods and services (economic growth) or in more social terms of improvement of the well-being and quality of life for a community (human development). Definitions of development vary across the spectrum from increase in material wealth at one end to greater freedom to be and do what one values at the other. This latter concept overlaps with that of capabilities in Sen's book *Development as Freedom*. Development strategies have evolved from earlier formulations focusing on modernization, industrialization, and growth, to the current view that even growth-based strategies must prioritize poverty reduction.

Another definitional issue that should be clarified at the outset is the overlap and distinction between human rights and 'social justice'. While social justice is part of the vocabulary of both development and human rights, the focus of much of the social justice movement is to challenge unjust structures (structural violence); support communities of poor, vulnerable, and marginalized people, using methodologies of community development and empowerment; and challenge the processes of international economic integration ('globalization') by which the rich get richer and the poor get poorer. A human rights approach to addressing poverty may well find merit in such approaches but would focus more on an accountability framework for pursuing social justice and refer to explicit human rights norms rather than a broad appeal to notions of redistributive or egalitarian justice.

Human rights are claims on those in authority with respect to protection of the dignity and well-being of the human person. Human rights approaches, especially when applied

---

[19] Rousseau, *The Social Contract and Discourses* (DGH Cole tr, 1782, Campbell, 1973) 117.

[20] UNESCO, *Human Rights: Comments and Interpretations. A Symposium Convened by UNESCO*, UNESCO/PHS/3, (rev) Appendix II (25 July 1948) 11. The published version of the work of the Committee appears in Maritain, *Universal Declaration of Human Rights: Comments and Interpretations* (UNESCO, 1949).

[21] Proclamation of Teheran, Final Act of the International Conference on Human Rights, Teheran, A/CONF.32/41, 3 (13 May 1968) para 12.

[22] 'I am often asked what is the most serious form of human rights violations in the world today, and my reply is consistent: extreme poverty.' UNDP, *Poverty Reduction and Human Rights: A Practice Note* (UNDP, 2003) iv.

by courts of law, tend to focus on claims of individuals anchored in binding law rather than redressing broader injustices and concern for the welfare of the poor. The latter are regarded as policy matters to be determined by other branches of government. In one sense, human rights is narrower than the general commitment to social justice in that it is based on specific norms agreed upon as enforceable human rights. It is at the same time more general insofar as it protects rights for all, not just the poor. Therefore, social justice, which has various definitions, is used here in its focus on reducing inequalities and eliminating poverty, whereas human rights is concerned with poverty among other problems that affect people's capacity to lead meaningful lives. The two tend to overlap when addressing the consequences of globalization.

2.3 THE CONTEXT OF POVERTY AND HUMAN RIGHTS: GLOBALIZATION

The term 'globalization' is often used to refer to the increased interconnectedness of people across borders and, in economic terms, to those features of the global economy that favour liberalization of trade in goods and services, the operations of giant transnational corporations, deregulation and privatization, virtually unrestricted capital flows, and the macroeconomic policies of international financial institutions. Globalization also suggests the dominant 'neo-liberal' model of development, that is, one that relies on the self-correcting and wealth-generating power of markets. From this perspective, it has been argued that most of the credit for the success in recent decades in reducing poverty 'must go to capitalism and free trade, for they enable economies to grow—and it was growth, principally that has eased destitution.'[23]

The phenomenon of 'globalization' in the economic sense has proved to be highly controversial. Ferocious opposition has come from pro-poor, anti-globalization movements outraged by the motivating force of greed behind the behaviour of the economically and militarily powerful and by the devastating impact of the process in terms of widening economic and social disparities, destruction of non-renewable resources, ecological devastation, and homogenization of culture. The violence of their opposition was felt in Seattle, Geneva, Washington, Hong Kong, Mexico City, and other locations of World Trade Organization (WTO) ministerial meetings and annual sessions of the G-20 and the Bretton Woods Institutions (the International Monetary Fund (IMF) and the World Bank), which are seen as icons of the harm brought about by globalization. The economic analyses supporting anti-globalization build on older neo-Marxist analysis of the global class struggle, dependency theory seeing the 'centre' as exploiting the 'periphery', and similar frameworks for pinpointing the injustice inflicted on the poor by the rich.

Many mainstream economists argue that globalization 'works' and is eventually an antidote to poverty. Some argue that 'the cure for poverty is economic growth'[24] or writing off debt and vastly increasing aid from donor to poor-country governments. What is interesting from the perspective of human rights and poverty is that human rights tends to be part of the strategies contesting globalization and absent from the discourse of its supporters. This preference is symptomatic of a deeper divergence of poverty reduction and human rights agendas.

---

[23] 'Towards the end of poverty', *The Economist* (1 June 2013) 11.
[24] Coyle, *The Soulful Science: What Economists Really Do and Why it Matters* (Princeton UP, 2007) 72.

3 DIVERGENCE OF POVERTY REDUCTION AND HUMAN RIGHTS AGENDAS

To a certain extent, the divergence in perspective between the human rights and poverty reduction discourses can be explained by the dominance of law, political science, and philosophy among those who theorize about and develop policies on human rights and the dominance of economics among those who theorize about and develop poverty reduction strategies. Some of these divergent ways of thinking are explored in Section 3.1, which examines how economists think about poverty and human rights. Section 3.2 analyses the thinking of governors of central banks and ministers of finance.

3.1 RESISTANCE TO HUMAN RIGHTS DISCOURSE IN ECONOMIC THINKING

Economists and economic decision-makers only rarely invoke human rights concepts, although many are open to related notions. Some economists tend to consider their professional role as value-neutral, offering the tools of analysis to be applied to policies set by others. Other economists address moral dimensions of economic issues, but avoid human rights language. Jeffrey Sachs proposed to end extreme poverty by 2025 through a nine-step programme that he places in the historical trajectory of the ending of slavery, colonialism, segregation, and apartheid. Although all of these were human rights movements, he does not call them that.[25] He does not explicitly make the link between the human rights causes of the past and the current cause of poverty elimination. Economists often apply notions of minimum standards, transparency, participation, and the like in the context of development policy, without relating them to a human rights framework. Thus, in the economics literature on international trade, there has been much discussion about appropriate mechanisms to promote labour standards, including addressing child labour in developing countries.[26] Likewise, the literature on public services has highlighted how a lack of transparency, insufficient accountability, and corrupt government officials will increase social wastage and distort economic and service delivery outcomes.[27] Other research has focused on matters of 'process', correlating economic performance with democracy and the rule of law.[28]

These analyses are illustrative of the divergence between human rights and economic thinking insofar as the authors grapple with many of the same concerns as are used in human rights (fairness, accountability, transparency, labour standards, child labour, democracy, rule of law) without reference to the respective standards contained in international human rights instruments. Nobel prize-winning economist Joseph Stiglitz, in his influential book *Making Globalization Work*, contrasted how at the national level 'we argue for and against different policies on the basis of whether they are just, whether they hurt the poor, whether their burden falls disproportionately on those less well off', whereas in the international arena, 'not only do we fail to do the analysis, we almost never argue for a

---

[25] Sachs, *The End of Poverty: Economic Possibilities for Our Time* (Penguin Press, 2005) 360–8.

[26] Eg Edmonds and Pavcnik, *International Trade and Child Labor: Cross-country evidence* (National Bureau of Economic Research, 2004).

[27] Eg Shleifer and Vishny, 'Corruption' (1993) 108 *Quarterly J of Economics* 599.

[28] Eg Rigobon and Rodrik, *Rule of Law, Democracy, Openness and Income: Estimating the Interrelationships* (Kennedy School of Government, Harvard University, 2004).

policy on the basis of fairness'.[29] He does allude in his conclusion to the UDHR but only as something the founding fathers of the USA would be pleased with, rather than as the inaugural document to a rather extensive set of international instruments relevant to reducing what he calls the 'gap between economic and political globalization'.[30]

Furthermore, there are many points of tension between mainstream economic thinking and human rights-centred approaches when it comes to defining development goals or implementing anti-poverty policy. One such point of tension is that growth-oriented economic analysis tends to disregard the impact of income on the realization of such human rights as the rights to health, education, and cultural and political freedoms. Economic analysis and policy interventions are fundamentally about making *choices* among alternatives in a world of limited resources. In contrast, the language of human rights (and associated *obligations* towards bearers of rights) appears less forgiving about choices and options. Rights language tends to be used by economists when it enhances, rather than limits choices. As Sen has said:

> In economics the concept of rights is often invoked...however...[n]o intrinsic importance is attached to the existence or fulfilment of rights, and they have been judged by their ability to achieve good consequences, among which the fulfilment of rights have not figured.[31]

Indeed, human rights principles are quite different from rankings of social arrangements based on utilitarian and Rawlsian principles that are favoured by economists. Part of the appeal to economists of John Rawls, one of the leading rights theorists of the twentieth century, is probably the use of the fiction of a 'rational' person making choices, which is typical of economists. In his influential *A Theory of Justice*, Rawls imagines such a person choosing behind a 'veil of ignorance' the fairest social arrangement in assigning rights and duties and distribution of advantages in society. He hypothesizes that such a free and rational person would choose, first, a principle of equal enjoyment of basic liberties (civil and political rights in international human rights language, language which Rawls does not use) and, second, equality of opportunity to occupy offices and positions under a social arrangement that provides the greatest benefit to the least advantaged members of society. This hypothetical and ahistorical reasoning is not unlike models that are developed in economics and it is not surprising that the economics literature draws on Rawls and uses rights language without reference to the human rights that, in historical fact, have been agreed upon. There is certainly value in economic analysis using a model of a society of only two individuals deemed to act rationally in order to isolate choices, before extrapolating to social arrangements, without considering the messier arrangements that actually exist. This démarche of Rawls and other rights theorists is appealing to economists but often pays no heed to the actual human rights that have been defined through historical social processes.

When, almost 30 years after his *A Theory of Justice*, Rawls does allude to 'human rights', he does so in a somewhat idiosyncratic way. In *The Law of Peoples*, he explains that human rights 'set a necessary, though not sufficient, standard for the decency of domestic political and social institutions', but only Articles 3 to 18 UDHR (those relating to civil and political rights) contain 'human rights proper'; while economic, social, and cultural rights, which 'presuppose specific kinds of institutions', presumably are not 'human rights proper'.[32] Elsewhere, he enumerates human rights as the rights to life (including 'the means of

---

[29] Stiglitz, *Making Globalization Work* (WW Norton, 2006) 278.
[30] Stiglitz, n 29, 292.   [31] Sen, *On Ethics and Economics* (Blackwell, 1988) 49.
[32] Rawls, *The Law of Peoples* (Harvard UP, 1999) 80, n 23.

subsistence'), liberty, and 'formal equality as expressed by the rules of natural justice'.[33] This interpretation is quite remote from the human rights that are guaranteed by international law and reinforces the perceived tension between human rights (understood as civil and political rights) and a concern for poverty (focusing more on redistribution). Mainstream human rights thinking and international human rights instruments adopted by the UN and regional organizations have no hesitation in regarding health, education, work, social security, and housing as 'human rights proper' and, therefore, of direct value to promoting poverty elimination, which the Rawlsian framework does not.

Another point of tension between human rights and economic thinking is that, even when the importance of goals other than that of economic growth is recognized in economic analysis, there is a temptation to consider civil and political rights as optional goods that can await a sufficient level of economic growth. The holistic human rights approach would not accept such a trade-off. Economic literature has come down on both sides of this issue. There are scholarly articles, both theoretical and empirical, that suggest that priority attention to political rights, for instance, can make a positive contribution to economic growth.[34] Others suggest that economic growth is more likely to pave the way for institutional, including political, development—and that prioritizing political freedom may not be the best strategy for developing countries to pursue economic growth.[35] There seems to be little doubt that political freedoms are positively related to economic growth and that rising living standards foster democratic freedoms, while declining living standards subvert them. However, as Benjamin Friedman has said:

> That there is usually more freedom in countries with higher per capita incomes does not by itself reveal whether having a high income leads a society to value and therefore provide these freedoms, or whether having widespread rights and liberties enables a country to achieve a higher level of income—in other words, whether a high material standard of living fosters freedom, or freedom facilitates economic success.[36]

The more interesting question is how adherence to human rights principles can instrumentally contribute to the effectiveness of economic policy interventions, including those aimed at growth and efficiency.

Thus, there is no simple answer to the question of how economists think about poverty and human rights. Some attempt to be value-neutral; some favour eliminating poverty through redistribution; some apply the concept of development as freedom; but most favour raising the condition of the poor through market-based growth. The latter group tends to dominate in high-level decision-making among central bankers and treasury departments.

3.2 THE PERSPECTIVE OF CENTRAL BANKS AND MINISTRIES OF FINANCE

The divergence between human rights and poverty reduction agendas is perhaps best represented by the Group of Twenty (G20).[37] Founded in 1999, it claims to represent around

---

[33] Rawls, n 32, 65.

[34] Eg Kaufmann, 'Human Rights, Governance, and Development: An Empirical Perspective' (2006) 8 *Development Outreach* 15, 15–20 and references cited therein.

[35] Eg Glaeser *et al.*, *Do Institutions Cause Growth?* (National Bureau of Economic Research, 2004).

[36] Friedman, *The Moral Consequences of Economic Growth* (Alfred A Knopf, 2005) 314.

[37] The members of the G20 are the finance ministers and central bank governors of 19 countries: Argentina, Australia, Brazil, Canada, China, France, Germany, India, Indonesia, Italy, Japan, Mexico, Russia, Saudi Arabia, South Africa, South Korea, Turkey, UK, and USA. The European Union is also a member and senior officials of the International Monetary Fund (IMF) and the World Bank participate in G20 meetings.

two-thirds of the world's population and 90 per cent of world gross domestic product. It describes itself as 'the premier forum for international cooperation on the most important issues of the global economic and financial agenda',[38] which do not include human rights. The G20 finance ministers and central bank governors meet once a year. Typical of their approach is the Statement on Global Development Issues adopted at their meeting in China in 2005. Neither 'human rights' nor 'human development' are mentioned in that document and 'good governance' is only mentioned in relation to sound economic policies and accountability. The statement does say, 'we are committed to strengthening the dialogue on varying development philosophies, strategies, and policies, from which all countries can benefit'.[39] Human rights did not fare any better at the meeting in Australia in 2006, which adopted a set of country-specific actions to implement the G20 Accord for Sustained Growth of 2004, none of which mentions directly or indirectly human rights, equity, human development, or good governance. Similarly, the final communiqué of the meeting of ministers and governors held in South Africa in 2007 makes no mention of 'human rights' or even 'right', and the word 'human' is never attached to development (it is used once in 'human capital'). Development is mentioned 11 times, usually next to growth, which is mentioned 18 times. The essence of the communiqué is expressed in the 'collective determination to achieve balanced and sustainable growth'.

Following the 2008 financial crisis, the G20 began meeting at the summit level of heads of state and government. The focus on growth continued, including under the Russian presidency in 2013, which organized the agenda around 'three overarching priorities, aimed at starting the new cycle of economic growth: [g]rowth through quality jobs and investment; [g]rowth through trust and transparency; [g]rowth through effective regulation.'[40] In contrast, a group of independent researchers called Civil 20 prepared, for the 2013 St Petersburg summit, 'an independent analysis and proposals for a dialogue between a wide range of stakeholders and the G20 governors on the G20 concerted policies and actions to improve economic equality within their countries and beyond.'[41] In its report, Civil 20 included among the 'Common Principles and Policies for All' the following:

> Affirm the need to strengthen the public policy foundations. These consist of good governance and basic human rights, specifically, universal access to the rule of law, anti-corruption, anti-tax evasion, and equal access to essential food, water, health care and rights of movement for citizens within the country. This requires expanding the G20 agenda to substantially take up the issues of water, health and mobility.[42]

Much of the concern of Civil 20 echoes the G20 acknowledgement of 'the human dimension to the crisis', as it was called in the Global Plan for Recovery and Reform, adopted by the Second G20 Leaders' Summit in London in 2009. Once again, there was no reference to human development or human rights, only the rather feeble

---

[38] See: <http://www.g20.org/docs/about/about_G20.html>.

[39] G20 Statement on Global Development Issues (Xianghe, Hebei, China, 2005) para 3, available at: <http://www.g20.utoronto.ca/2005/2005development.html>.

[40] Priorities of Russia's G20 presidency in 2013, available at: <http://www.g20.org/docs/g20_russia/priorities.html>.

[41] G20 Research Group at the University of Toronto and the International Organizations and International Cooperation Institute of the National Research University Higher School of Economics, *Sustained and Balanced Growth Requires Equitable Policies, Draft Report*, available at: <https://www.hse.ru/data/2013/05/14/1299928420/Equality%20Report%20final.pdf>.

[42] G20 Research Group, n 41, 28.

commitment 'to support those affected by the crisis by creating employment opportunities and through income support measures.'[43] This was echoed in the Pittsburgh
Summit the same year with its reference to 'collective responsibility to mitigate the
social impact of the crisis' and the pledge to cooperate 'to improve access to food, fuel,
and finance for the poor'.[44] The underlying philosophy of the summit is expressed in
the statement: 'the only sure foundation for sustainable globalisation and rising prosperity for all is an open world economy based on market principles, effective regulation, and strong global institutions'.[45] Critiquing the London communiqué of the G20,
two human rights scholars noted:

> The crisis, its human impact, and the proposed solutions are also issues of international
> human rights law—and in particular of state obligations to take collective action to create a
> global economic system amenable to the fulfilment of basic rights to subsistence, security,
> and freedom.[46]

A similar focus on growth and markets as the solution to poverty characterizes the pronouncements of the G8 and the World Economic Forum in Davos, Switzerland. These
settings and the G20 illustrate an ambiguity regarding human rights and poverty. The
confrontation is not between the morally indignant voices of the poor against a band
of greedy capitalists meeting in some boardroom in Washington or London. Many in
the anti-globalization movement do indeed claim to speak for the poor, but so do the
representatives of the G20 governments, which include India and China, as well as
Argentina, Mexico, South Africa, and the European Union. These are not the forces of
evil against the forces of good. They are the principal actors in the global economy and
they send contradictory messages about the proposition that human rights have anything to do with poverty. It is little wonder, therefore, that human rights do not figure
prominently among the approaches to poverty in vogue in policy pronouncements on
the international financing of development. The critique by the human rights community of the G20 approach is found, among others in the work of 'Righting Finance',
which noted in 2011 that 'human rights considerations have no place in their discussions or statements' but that 'their actions have significant impacts on the realization
and enjoyment of human rights, and the members of the G20 are Nation-states that
cannot disregard their human rights obligations in any forum, including multilateral
economic institutions.'[47]

However, the situation is changing progressively as human rights specialists learn
more about the economic analyses of poverty and development economists learn about
the compatibility of their goals with those of human rights and the instrumental value
of human rights for poverty reduction. These trends have opened the space—still fairly
restricted—for the convergence of human rights and poverty reduction agendas.

[43] The Global Plan for Recovery and Reform, para 26, available at: <http://www.g20.utoronto.
ca/2009/2009communique0402.html>.

[44] G20 Leaders Statement: The Pittsburgh Summit (Pittsburgh, 2009), paras 34 and 38, available at: <http://
www.g20.utoronto.ca/2009/2009communique0925.html>.

[45] G20 Leaders Statement, n 44.

[46] Fukuda-Parr and Salomon, 'A Human Rights Analysis of the G20 Communique: Recent Awareness of the
"Human Cost" Is Not Quite Enough,' Carnegie Council online, available at: <http://www.carnegiecouncil.org/
publications/ethics_online/0033.html>.

[47] Rightingfinance, 'The Group of 20, Financial Regulation and Human Rights' available at: <http://www.
rightingfinance.org/?p=97>.

4 CONVERGENCE OF POVERTY REDUCTION AND HUMAN RIGHTS AGENDAS

Section 3 illustrated several ways in which human rights concerns diverge from those of development and poverty reduction. This section addresses the convergence—or at least the trends that demonstrate mutually reinforcing relations—between human rights and anti-poverty agendas, beginning in Section 4.1 with some economic thinking that is congruent with human rights and continuing in Section 4.2 with policies to combat poverty using human rights tools.

4.1 TRENDS IN ECONOMIC THINKING CONGRUENT WITH HUMAN RIGHTS

Apart from the economic studies referred to already, which deal with fairness, transparency, and participation, there is another strand of development economics that acknowledges human rights as providing goals for development: the development ethics movement. The International Development Ethics Association (IDEA), for example, defines its members as 'a cross-cultural group of philosophers, social scientists, and practitioners who apply ethical reflection to global development goals and strategies and to North/South relations'. They advocate a normative approach to development-based theories 'that appeal to social justice, human rights, basic needs, and theological understandings of the human condition'.[48] In 1989, IDEA adopted the Mérida Declaration, which enumerates among their guiding ethical principles 'the absolute respect for the dignity of the human person, regardless of gender, ethnic group, social class, religion, age or nationality'.[49] Leading development economists, such as David A Crocker, Paul Streeten, and especially Denis Goulet, spearheaded this movement. Human rights and poverty are central to their concerns, although human rights as such is rarely an operative concept in their work.

The principal exception to the divergence between human rights and economic thinking, however, is the 'human development and capabilities' approach, theorized primarily by Amartya Sen and Martha Nussbaum. This approach has been embraced by the UN Development Programme (UNDP) in its *Human Development Report* and is promoted by an association of academics and practitioners called the Human Development and Capability Association (HDCA). The openness to human rights of this perspective is due to the centrality of the concept of development as freedom and expanding choices. In the words of the *Human Development Report*:

> Human development shares a common vision with human rights. The goal is human freedom. And in pursuing capabilities and realizing rights, this freedom is vital. People must be free to exercise their choices and to participate in decision-making that affects their lives. Human development and human rights are mutually reinforcing, helping to secure the well-being and dignity of all people, building self-respect and the respect of others.[50]

The farther one moves from trade, finance, and treasury departments of governments, including in their multilateral settings of the WTO and the G20, and the closer one gets to bilateral and multilateral fora for addressing poverty, the more relevant human rights

---

[48] See: <http://developmentethics.org/about-2/what-is-development-ethics/>.
[49] See: <http://developmentethics.org/announcements/declarations-2/>.
[50] UNDP, *Human Development Report 2001*, 9.

considerations become. This continuum runs from the G20 to the World Bank Group and regional development banks to broad-based deliberative bodies (such as the global conferences and summits, and the UN Economic and Social Council), to development aid agencies and programmes (such as the UK Department for International Development (DFID) and UNDP), to UN human rights bodies (such as the Human Rights Council and the Third Committee of the General Assembly), to human rights treaty regimes. To illustrate the gap, compare the various G20 communiqués discussed in Section 3.2, representing one end of this continuum, with the statement of the Committee on Economic, Social and Cultural Rights on poverty, cited in Section 2.1, representing the other end. In the Committee's statement regretted 'that the human rights dimensions of poverty eradication policies rarely receive the attention they deserve. This neglect is especially regrettable because a human rights approach to poverty can reinforce anti-poverty strategies and make them more effective.'[51]

The World Conference on Human Rights, in its 1993 Vienna Declaration, stated that '[t]he existence of widespread extreme poverty inhibits the full and effective enjoyment of human rights; its immediate alleviation and eventual elimination must remain a high priority for the international community'.[52] It further affirmed:

> [E]xtreme poverty and social exclusion constitute a violation of human dignity and . . . urgent steps are necessary to achieve better knowledge of extreme poverty and its causes, including those related to the problem of development, in order to promote the human rights of the poorest, and to put an end to extreme poverty and social exclusion and to promote the enjoyment of the fruits of social progress. It is essential for States to foster participation by the poorest people in the decision-making process by the community in which they live, the promotion of human rights and efforts to combat extreme poverty.[53]

4.2 HUMAN RIGHTS APPROACHES IN POVERTY REDUCTION POLICIES

Human rights have become part of the international development agenda, including poverty reduction, through the introduction of human rights approaches into UN development cooperation, poverty reduction strategies, the Millennium Development Goals, and bilateral development programmes. Each of these is examined in this section, before turning to the most systematic approach to integrating poverty and human rights, namely by considering development itself as a human right.

4.2.1 UN development cooperation

In 2003, representatives from across the UN defined a Common Understanding on a Human Rights-based Approach to Development Cooperation.[54] This document became a standard reference for translating normative human rights commitments of member states into development cooperation policies and projects of UN agencies, funds, and programmes. In his report *Strengthening of the United Nations: An Agenda for Further Change*, the UN Secretary-General called human rights 'a bedrock requirement for the realization of the Charter's vision of a just and peaceful world'. He listed, among 36 actions

---

[51] CESCR, n 18, para 2.
[52] Vienna Declaration and Programme of Action, A/CONF.157/23 (25 June 1993) para 14.
[53] Vienna Declaration, n 52, para 25.
[54] UN Development Group, 'The Human Rights Based Approach to Development Cooperation: Towards a Common Understanding Among UN Agencies' (7 May 2003), available at: <http://www.unescobkk.org/fileadmin/user_upload/appeal/human_rights/UN_Common_understanding_RBA.pdf>.

to realize this vision, 'Action 2' on joint UN efforts at the country level, which was based on the Action 2 Plan of Action, adopted by 21 heads of UN departments and agencies.[55] This Plan, which ended in 2009, integrated human rights into humanitarian, development, and peacekeeping work throughout the UN system. The Action 2 Interagency Task Force, consisting of the Office of the High Commissioner for Human Rights (OHCHR), UNDP, the UN Population Fund (UNFPA), the UN Children's Fund (UNICEF), and the UN Development Fund for Women (UNIFEM), worked towards clarifying, and training staff in, this approach, including through launching the Action 2 Global Programme. In 2007, the UN Common Learning Package on Human Rights-Based Approach (HRBA) was issued, building on the experience of all agencies.[56] In the four years of its operation, Action 2 supported over 60 UN country teams and their national partners in capacity-building to integrate human rights into their work.[57] In late 2009, the UN Development Group Human Rights Mainstreaming Mechanism (UNDG-HRM) replaced Action 2 with the overarching objective 'to further institutionalize human rights mainstreaming efforts in the UN development system and to strengthen system-wide coherence'.[58] The programme includes a UN Practitioners Portal on Human Rights Based Approaches to Programming (HRBAP)[59] and a Multi-Partner Human Rights Mainstreaming Trust Fund.[60]

4.2.2 Poverty reduction strategies

Since the Asian financial crisis in the 1990s, there has been a rethinking in the World Bank and the IMF of their earlier policies of structural adjustment, sometimes taking into account the human rights impact of such policies, but mostly to avoid social impacts that reduce the productivity of workers and the stability of regimes. Health and education are frequently cited as suffering the most from structural adjustment programmes. More recently, the focus of these institutions has been on the Poverty Reduction Strategy process to reduce the debt of Highly Indebted Poor Countries (HIPC) that have submitted Poverty Reduction Strategy Papers (PRSPs). Launched in September 1999, the PRSP approach 'results in a comprehensive country-based strategy for poverty reduction' and reflects 'a recognition by the IMF and the World Bank of the importance of ownership as well as the need for a greater focus on poverty reduction'.[61]

In a concept note, the High Commissioner for Human Rights drew the World Bank's attention to the following:

> In linking a Poverty Reduction Strategy to a universal normative framework and State obligations emanating from the human rights instruments, the goals of the Poverty Reduction Strategy could be sustained with enhanced accountability of the relevant stake-holders. The universal nature of human rights, their mobilization potential and their emphasis on legal obligations to respect, protect and promote human rights, while encouraging national ownership and people's empowerment makes the human rights framework a useful tool to strengthen the accountability and equity dimensions of the Poverty Reduction Strategies.[62]

---

[55] Strengthening of the United Nations: An Agenda for Further Change, A/57/387 (9 September 2002).
[56] Available at: <http://www.undg.org/index.cfm?P=531>.
[57] Report of the UN High Commissioner for Human Rights, A/64/36 (6 August 2009), para 93.
[58] UN Development Group, UNDG Human Rights Mainstreaming Mechanism Summary of the Operational Plan 2011-2013 (18 October 2011) 2.
[59] <http://hrbaportal.org>.   [60] <http://mptf.undp.org/factsheet/fund/HRM00>.
[61] IMF Factsheet, available at: <http://www.imf.org/external/np/exr/facts/prsp.htm>.
[62] OHCHR, Comments on the Concept Note. Joint World Bank and IMF Report on Poverty Reduction Strategy Papers—Progress in Implementation 2005 PRS Review, available at: <http://siteresources.worldbank.org/INTPRS1/Resources/PRSP-Review/un_ohchr.pdf>.

The issue had already been raised by the Commission on Human Rights, which in 1990 requested its Sub-Commission to consider the relationship between human rights and poverty.[63] The Sub-Commission appointed a Special Rapporteur on human rights and extreme poverty, whose report was published in 1996, followed in 1998 by the appointment of an Independent Expert on human rights and extreme poverty. In a related development, and in direct response to a request from the Chair of the Committee on Economic, Social and Cultural Rights, the High Commissioner commissioned in 2001 guidelines for the integration of human rights into poverty reduction strategies, a 60-page document setting out basic principles of a human rights approach to: (1) the process of formulating a poverty reduction strategy; (2) determining the content of a poverty reduction strategy; and (3) guiding the monitoring and accountability aspects of poverty reduction strategies.[64]

More recently, standards on human rights and poverty reduction have been adopted by the UN Human Rights Council. The Special Rapporteur (then Independent Expert) on extreme poverty and human rights prepared 'Guiding Principles on extreme poverty and human rights', which were adopted by the Council on 27 September 2012.[65] They are designed for policy-makers and other actors to align public policies with international law and the objective of poverty reduction.

4.2.3 Millennium Development Goals

Following the commitments made by heads of state at the Millennium Summit in 2000, all governments and international institutions have set specific targets for poverty reduction in the Millennium Development Goals (MDGs). While these goals are important to development planning, they have tended to ignore commitments made by states to human rights and the rule of law. The MDGs define the priorities for the international community and guide much of the technical cooperation and assistance provided by bilateral and multilateral donors. They are a set of eight goals with 18 numerical targets and over 40 quantifiable indicators, most of which are to be met by 2015. These MDGs are:

1. eradicate extreme poverty and hunger;
2. achieve universal primary education;
3. promote gender equality and empower women;
4. reduce child mortality;
5. improve maternal health;
6. combat HIV/AIDS, malaria, and other diseases;
7. ensure environmental sustainability; and
8. develop a global partnership for development.

The High Commissioner for Human Rights has focused attention on the relationship between the MDGs and human rights by disseminating charts on the intersection of human rights treaty obligations and the MDGs and has published *Claiming the MDGs: A Human Rights Approach*, which is an exhaustive analysis of how human rights can contribute to the MDGs.[66] Similarly, the UNDP has published a primer called *Human Rights and the*

---

[63] CHR, Human Rights and Extreme Poverty, E/CN.4/Res/1990/15 (23 February 1990) 5.

[64] Hunt, Nowak, and Osmani, *Draft Guidelines: A Human Rights Approach to Poverty Reduction Strategies* (OHCHR, 2002). See also Hunt, Nowak, and Osmani, *Human Rights and Poverty Reduction Strategies: Human Rights and Poverty Reduction: A Conceptual Framework* (OHCHR, 2003).

[65] HR Council Res 21/11.   [66] OHCHR, *Claiming the MDGs: A Human Rights Approach* (2008).

Millennium Development Goals: Making the Link,[67] and various national development agencies have published their own human rights approaches to MDGs.[68]

Recent reflections on human rights and the MDGs—and, therefore, on human rights and poverty—have focused on integrating human rights more meaningfully into the post-2015 development agenda.[69] At the conclusion of the June 2012 UN Conference on Sustainable Development (Rio+20), the heads of state and government affirmed 'the importance of…respect for all human rights, including the right to development and the right to an adequate standard of living'[70] along with eight other references to human rights. The UN Secretary General's High-Level Panel of Eminent Persons on the Post-2015 Development Agenda was set up to make recommendations 'regarding the vision and shape of a Post-2015 development agenda that will help respond to the global challenges of the 21st century, building on the MDGs and with a view to ending poverty', to be considered by the General Assembly at the end of 2013.[71] The UN System Task Team, created in September 2011 to support UN system-wide preparations for the post-2015 UN development agenda recommended a 'vision for the future that rests on the core values of human rights, equality and sustainability'.[72] According to its report, these three principles 'would constitute the common, underlying elements necessary to address and resolve, through transformative change, the global trends and challenges that people will face in the post-2015 era. They provide the foundation of an agenda for achieving a better life for all human beings, and would serve to inspire and assist each society in determining how best to pursue this vision'.[73]

The final report of the High-Level Panel, however, seems to take a step back from the Task Team. Rather than basing the report on the three core values, the panel, 'convinced of the need for a new paradigm', decided that the post-2015 development agenda should be 'driven by five big, transformative shifts', including, as part of the first shift 'Leave no one behind', ensuring 'that no person—regardless of ethnicity, gender, geography, disability, race or other status—is denied universal human rights and basic economic opportunities'.[74] The second shift has to do with sustainable development in the context of climate change and environmental degradation; the third with jobs and growth; the fourth with peace and accountable institutions; and the fifth with a new global partnership based on solidarity, cooperation, and mutual accountability. The fourth shift reflects the panel's ambiguity regarding human rights: the statement 'Freedom from fear, conflict and violence is the most fundamental human right' later becomes 'Freedom from conflict and

---

[67] UNDP, *Human Rights and the Millennium Development Goals: Making the Link* (Oslo Governance Centre, 2007).

[68] Eg the Swedish International Development Agency (available at: <http://www.sida.se/English?About-us/Organization/Policy/>); the UK's DFID (available at: <https://www.gov.uk/government/organisations/department-for-international-development/about>); the US MCC (<http://www.mcc.gov/pages/about>); Canada's CIDA (available at: <http://www.acdi-cida.gc.ca/acdi-cida/acdi-cida.nsf/en/JUD-13173118-GPM>); and Denmark's DANIDA (available at: <http://um.dk/en/danida-en/goals/mdg/>).

[69] Darrow, 'Millennium Development Goals: Milestones or Millstones - Human Rights Priorities for the Post-2015 Development Agenda' (2012) 15 *Yale Human Rights and Development LJ* 55.

[70] GA Res 66/288 (27 July 2012) para 8.

[71] Terms of Reference for the High-Level Panel of Eminent Persons on the Post-2015 Development Agenda, available at: <http://www.un.org/sg/management/pdf/ToRpost2015.pdf>.

[72] UN, *Realizing the future we want for all: Report to the Secretary-General* (June 2012) i.

[73] UN, n 72, 23.

[74] High-Level Panel Of Eminent Persons on the Post-2015 Development Agenda, *A New Global Partnership: Eradicate Poverty and Transform Economies Through Sustainable Development: The Report of the High-Level Panel of Eminent Persons on the Post-2015 Development Agenda*, (UN, 2013) Executive Summary and 7.

violence is the most fundamental human entitlement.[75] That theme also refers to 'the rule of law, property rights, freedom of speech and the media, open political choice, access to justice, and accountable government and public institutions'. The fifth shift also mentions—in passing—that the principles established at the Rio+20 Summit included 'universality, equity, sustainability, solidarity, human rights, the right to development and responsibilities shared in accordance with capabilities.'[76] In addition to a reference to '[t]he universal human rights and fundamental freedoms of migrants',[77] there is also the following statement: 'We envision a world where the principles of equity, sustainability, solidarity, respect for human rights and shared responsibilities in accordance with respective capabilities, has been brought to life by our common action.'[78] The language becomes more directly relevant to a human rights-based approach to poverty reduction in Annex II on 'Evidence of Impact and Explanation of Illustrative Goals', which includes the following under Goal 10 (Ensure Good Governance and Effective Institutions):

> The Universal Declaration of Human Rights, signed over 60 years ago, set out the fundamental freedoms and human rights that form the foundations of human development. It reiterated a simple and powerful truth – that every person is born free and equal in dignity and rights. This truth is at the very heart of a people-centered agenda, and reminds us how high we can reach, if we reaffirm the value of every person on this planet. It is through people that we can transform our societies and our economies and form a global partnership.[79]

While the panel does not propose new goals and indicators, it does list among the 'examples of some of the issues raised' in relation to the theme of 'Governance and Human Rights' the following:

- Existing human rights norms, operational standards and commitments are a non-negotiable normative base of the new framework; development policies, programs and practice at all levels reflect obligations under international human rights law

- Strengthen access to justice and judicial accountability for human rights; national human rights monitoring bodies and quasi-judicial regulatory bodies are supported with the mandate, capacities and resources required to monitor violations of human rights and to act on complaints

- Systematic integration of national reporting on development goals in reports to the Universal Periodic Review of the Human Rights Council and to international human rights treaty monitoring bodies is promoted

- International cooperation and technical and financial assistance is consistent with human rights obligations and due diligence to prevent human rights abuses.[80]

While referenced in an annex listing issues raised during consultations but not retained, these reasonable and explicitly human rights dimensions of the post-2015 development agenda will be lost unless the momentum is regained. Indeed, the relationship between human rights and poverty in the MDG process began with the 2000 Millennium Declaration establishing the link, but the MDGs which followed de-linked them. Sakiko Fukuda-Parr saw the Declaration as a 'statement of a "human rights-based" vision of development as both an end and a process', which 'conceptualizes poverty as a dehumanizing human condition,

---

[75] *A New Global Partnership*, n 74, Executive Summary and 9.   [76] *A New Global Partnership*, n 74, 9.
[77] *A New Global Partnership*, n 74, 18.   [78] *A New Global Partnership*, n 74, 27.
[79] *A New Global Partnership*, n 74, 50.   [80] *A New Global Partnership*, n 74, 61.

in the human rights and capabilities perspectives rather than in the utilitarian perspective of material deprivation'.[81] While the Declaration 'reflects a human rights perspective on poverty as a problem that imposes obligations on states and the international community to put in place adequate social arrangements to eliminate it', the MDGs 'do not reflect the meaning of poverty as an affront to human dignity in the human rights and capabilities perspective'.[82] In order to 'recapture the narrative of development as a process of national development and expansion of human dignity as envisioned in the Millennium Declaration' she argues, a 'new set of quantitative goals is needed to reset the narrative of development as sustainable, equitable and human rights–based development'.[83] A similar position was taken by UN official and scholar Mac Darrow, who proposed that the 'international human rights framework can serve a vital purpose in helping to ensure that the negotiations towards 2015 focus on legitimate *ends* of human development, corresponding to internationally agreed upon human rights norms, rather than context-specific and contested *means*'.[84] The UN High Commissioner for Human Rights, Navi Pillay, pushed the human rights focus very hard.[85] So did many NGOs, such as Human Rights Watch, which proposed 'six elements, which are distinct but mutually reinforcing, [and] should be comprehensively incorporated into a sustainable and human rights-respecting Post-2015 Development Agenda',[86] and the Centre for Economic and Social Rights, which published with the OHCHR a study on human rights accountability post-2015.[87] A joint statement, endorsed by 19 leading human rights organizations in 2013, called for human rights to be placed at the core of the new development agenda.[88] Nevertheless, some governments feared that '[p]ushing too hard on human rights in the next set of development goals could jeopardise agreement on the post-2015 agenda'.[89]

4.2.4 Bilateral development cooperation

The trend of national development agencies to adopt human rights approaches has been studied by the Organisation for Economic Co-operation and Development (OECD), which has determined that 'human rights offer a coherent normative framework which can guide development assistance'.[90] The advantages identified by the OECD relate to adaptability to different political and cultural environments, the potential for operationalizing human rights principles, relevance to good governance and meaningful participation, poverty reduction, and aid effectiveness.[91] The growing trend among scholars, development NGOs, and international institutions to use the human rights-based approach to

---

[81] Fukuda-Parr, 'Recapturing the Narrative of International Development', UN Research Institute for Social Development Research Paper No. 2012–5 (July 2012) 6.   [82] Fukuda-Parr, n 81.

[83] Fukuda-Parr, n 81, 11.   [84] Darrow, n 69, 105.

[85] Eg Opening Remarks by Ms Navi Pillay, Global Thematic Consultation: 'Governance and the post-2015 development agenda', 28 February – 01 March 2013, in Johannesburg, South Africa, available at: <http://www.worldwewant2015.org/fr/node/316193>.

[86] Eg Human Rights Watch, 'Letter to the High-level Panel of Eminent Persons on the Post-2015 Development Agenda' (24 March 2013) available at: <http://www.hrw.org/news/2013/03/24/letter-high-level-panel-eminent-persons-post-2015-development-agenda>.

[87] Centre for Economic and Social Rights and OHCHR, *Who Will Be Accountable? Human Rights and the Post-2015 Development Agenda* (UN, 2013).

[88] 'New development goals must have human rights at their core' (6 May 2013), available at: <http://www.rightingfinance.org/?p=402>.

[89] Tran, 'Human rights could be faultline in post-2015 development agenda', *The Guardian* (21 November 2012), available at: <http://www.guardian.co.uk/global-development/2012/nov/21/human-rights-faultline-development-agenda?CMP=twt_fd>.

[90] World Bank and OECD, *Integrating Human Rights into Development: Donor Approaches, Experiences, and Challenges* (World Bank, 2013) 69.

[91] World Bank, n 90, 58–68.

development and poverty reduction both integrates concepts that already had currency in development theory, such as accountability and transparency, in the context of good governance, and adds a dimension with which development practitioners were less familiar, especially the explicit reference to government obligations deriving from international human rights law.

Efforts to integrate human rights have been less successful in relation to the Paris Declaration on Aid Effectiveness, adopted in 2005 by ministers or senior officials of some 85 developed and developing countries and heads of 20 bilateral and multilateral development agencies. The Declaration seeks to reform the delivery of aid and outlines the five overarching principles of ownership, alignment, harmonization, managing for development results, and mutual accountability, with agreed upon indicators, targets, timetables, and processes to monitor implementation. Each of these principles has been examined critically from the human rights perspective in a paper commissioned from the Overseas Development Institute by the OECD, which argues for using human rights to broaden the scope and content of the Paris Declaration commitments and indicators on mutual accountability.[92] Many see the Paris Declaration as donor-driven, with insufficient local ownership or mutual accountability with respect to implementation and the assessment of its effectiveness. More important from the perspective of this chapter is the very minimal attention given to human rights in the context of using aid to address poverty. Although human rights are not mentioned in the Paris Declaration, they are referred to twice in the Accra Agenda for Action, adopted by the Third High-Level Forum on Aid Effectiveness, held in Accra, Ghana, in 2008. Thus, the Agenda states that 'gender equality, respect for human rights, and environmental sustainability are cornerstones for achieving enduring impact on the lives and potential of poor women, men, and children. It is vital that all our policies address these issues in a more systematic and coherent way'.[93] The Fourth High Level Forum on Aid Effectiveness, held in 2011 in Busan, Republic of Korea, adopted the Busan Partnership for Effective Development Cooperation, which refers to 'our agreed international commitments on human rights, decent work, gender equality, environmental sustainability and disability'[94] and to rights-based approaches of civil society organizations, which 'play a vital role in enabling people to claim their rights',[95] but does not add to the human rights content of the Accra Agenda for Action.

4.2.5 The right to development

One of the greatest challenges for an economic approach to poverty is to accept the proposition that development itself—essentially an economic process—can be regarded as a human right—an essentially legal and governance concept. The challenge from the beginning has been to translate the hopeful but ambiguous language of the UN Declaration on the Right to Development (1986)[96] into concepts that are meaningful to economists and useful to the rethinking of the development process and poverty reduction strategies. Most developing states use the right to development to voice their concerns about the negative impact of certain aspects of international trade, unequal access to technology, and the crushing debt burden; they promote the idea of an international convention to

---

[92] Foresti, Booth, and O'Neil, *Aid Effectiveness and Human Rights: Strengthening the Implementation of the Paris Declaration* (Overseas Development Institute, 2006).

[93] The Accra High Level Forum (HLF3) and the Accra Agenda for Action, para 3, available at: <http://www.oecd.org/dac/effectiveness/theaccrahighlevelforumhlf3andtheaccraagendaforaction.htm>.

[94] Fourth High Level Forum on Aid Effectiveness, para 11, available at: <http://www.oecd.org/dac/effectiveness/fourthhighlevelforumonaideffectiveness.htm>.

[95] Fourth High Level Forum, n 94, para 22.   [96] GA Res 41/128 (4 December 1986).

establish binding obligations to facilitate development. In contrast, most donor states see the right to development as a way of improving the governance and rule-of-law performance of recipient states.

The real test is whether the right to development can help define a middle ground between these two contrasting positions, on which consensus can be sustained and practical outcomes achieved. The High-Level Task Force on the implementation of the right to development (which functioned under Human Rights Council resolutions from 2004 to 2010) attempted to bridge this gap between political posturing and practical policy in its report to the Working Group on the Right to Development in 2010. It defined the right to development as 'the right of peoples and individuals to the constant improvement of their well-being and to a national and global enabling environment conducive to just, equitable, participatory and human-centred development respectful of all human rights.'[97] The Task Force proposed three components or attributes, which not only clarify the meaning of the right, but specify how it can be instrumental in responding to poverty. The three attributes correspond to the concepts of policy, process, and outcome. What policy must be advanced to realize the right to development? The answer in attribute 1 is a 'comprehensive and human-centred development policy'. How should this right be advanced? The answer, given in attribute 2, is through 'participatory human rights processes'. What should be the outcome of action to realize this right? The answer, in attribute 3, is 'social justice in development'. The principal distinguishing feature is that the first attribute relates to commitment (to a particular concept of development), the second to rules and principles (human rights, participation, accountability, and transparency), and the third to distributional outcomes (fair distribution of the benefits and burdens of development). The Task Force also provided criteria, sub-criteria, and indicators to further specify what is expected of national and international development policy and practice conducive to the right to development.

Responsibility for the right to development is complicated by the fact that states have not translated their commitment to this right into decision-making in their international partnerships aimed at poverty reduction and, without an explicit mandate, it is unlikely that national and international policies and programmes will incorporate the right to development. Most poverty reduction strategies are based on political and legal commitments, such as PRSPs, with clear incentives to comply with standards and procedures, often resulting in targeted funding or debt forgiveness. The right to development has no such incentives and is only compelling for those who find the principles on which it is based to be compelling.

The right to development is guaranteed in two regional human rights treaties, namely in Article 22 of the African Charter on Human and Peoples' Rights and Article 37 of the Arab Charter on Human Rights. However, none of the institutions that monitor implementation of these treaties had taken any significant steps to hold states parties accountable according to these provisions until the African Commission on Human and Peoples' Rights issued its landmark decision concerning the violation of the right to development as a result of an eviction of an indigenous group from a wildlife reserve in Kenya.[98]

The politics of the right to development is largely a matter of balancing the national and international dimensions of this right, since each dimension reflects the preference of different groups of states. In theory and in the wording of the Declaration, both are

---

[97] A/HRC/15/WG.2/TF/2.Add.2 (2 February 2010) Annex.
[98] 276/03, *Centre for Minority Rights Development (Kenya) and Minority Rights Group International on behalf of Endorois Welfare Council v Kenya*, 27th Activity Report of the ACommHPR (2009).

complementary rather than conflicting. The right to development requires that governments that reject international scrutiny of their national policies must accept human
rights as part of their national development and those governments that support human
rights in development but reject efforts to challenge their power in international economic
relations must be willing to address the unjust structures of the global economy through
genuine development agendas, including negotiated and agreed modifications in terms of
trade, investment, and aid, allowing developing countries to overcome the disadvantages
of history and draw the full benefit of their natural and human resources. Thus, the greatest challenge in bringing the right to development into the realm of practice is for all states
to embrace the indivisibility and interdependence of 'all the aspects of the right to development' as set forth in Article 9 of the Declaration and to agree to development agendas
consistent with the affirmation in Article 4 that, 'as a complement to the efforts of developing countries, effective international co-operation is essential in providing these countries with appropriate means and facilities to foster their comprehensive development'. The
right to development has so far proved to be too broad in scope and too demanding in
terms of structural change to be a significant factor in the practice of poverty reduction. It
remains, nevertheless, the most systematic human rights framework for addressing issues
of poverty at the normative level.

5 CONCLUSION

There are two reasons why those who favour the growth model of development resist what
they see as the well-intentioned but misguided intrusion of human rights into pro-poor
development work. The first is the conviction that economic progress suffers as a result of
advancing human rights before a sufficient level of prosperity has been reached. However,
the examples of countries that developed rapidly under conditions of human rights deprivation and that liberalized later (for example, Brazil, Chile, South Korea, and Taiwan) are
far too complex to be probative, and counter-examples can be found, such as Costa Rica,
Ghana, India, Senegal, and Thailand, that did not impose systematic human right deprivation as the price of economic development. The second is that those who have primary
responsibility over the economy—ministers of finance and planning, corporate executives,
shareholders, and academic economists—often assume that human rights are merely matters of legal disputes or strident claims of the political opposition to the government they
represent or with which they cooperate.

   However, in response to the challenges posed at the beginning of this chapter, there
are compelling reasons why human rights are both definitional of and instrumental to
anti-poverty objectives. The definitional component is the common purpose of both
human rights and development, which specialists in both fields usually articulate in terms
of human welfare. The instrumental component is the relationship between human rights
and forms of empowerment that make anti-poverty measures sustainable and equitable.

   A powerful justification for human rights in the anti-poverty agenda relates to the
proposition that human rights define the same objective as pro-poor development, for
which human development is a convenient proxy. From the capability perspective, both
human development and human rights increase freedom. From the utilitarian perspective, both enhance human well-being. However, the similarity is diminished if development is defined merely in terms of growth in production and consumption of goods and
services, which is the case in particular of the G20 process discussed in Section 3. Growth
is desirable but not as an end in itself; it is a means towards various possible ends. If the
end is the enrichment of the few at the expense of the many and of the planet, then it will

not help the poor. If it is a means toward sustainable and equitable development, then it must be governed so as to reach that end. Another way of understanding the relationship between the means and ends of development is to recall that, '[e]conomic growth is often promoted as a means to alleviate poverty; yet even when growth does materialize, its benefits are unevenly distributed and rarely accrue to the poor.'[99]

Thus, the first step in clarifying in practical terms the meaning of poverty in the context of human rights is to note that pro-poor human development, like human rights, is a process that enables choices by all people to lead a life they value and, thus, enhances their well-being. Human rights are also about creating an environment in which people can develop their full potential and lead creative lives by, in the words of the UDHR, assuring 'the dignity and worth of the human person' and promoting 'social progress and better standards of life in larger freedom.'[100] The ultimate objective of both human development and human rights is, therefore, well-being as understood in both fields. The greatest obstacle to those choices is poverty, which is both capability deprivation and a measure of the denial of human rights.

Although the word is overused, empowerment has a special significance in this context. Human rights can be seen as a strategy for empowerment if 'empowerment' is understood as social and economic transformation by and for the poor. Such a strategy brings the human rights and anti-poverty agendas together. This transformative strategy sometimes goes by the name of human rights education and learning. The UDHR was proclaimed 'to the end that every individual and every organ of society, keeping this Declaration constantly in mind, shall strive by teaching and education to promote respect for these rights.'[101] When education and learning are transformative, poor people take charge of their own lives and become subjects rather than objects of history; they build on human rights obligations of states to challenge unjust power relations and claim their rights. Where contrary interests are entrenched, this struggle is difficult but it targets the root causes of poverty, which is where the struggle belongs.

These empowerment outcomes of human rights education and mobilization are surprisingly consistent with the empowerment strategy of the World Bank, insofar as it seeks 'the expansion of assets and capabilities of poor people to participate in, negotiate with, influence, control, and hold accountable institutions that affect their lives.'[102] As noted by its former Vice President, Gobind Nankani, 'much of the poverty work of the World Bank and other donors is informed by the same notions of equality and non-discrimination that are central to human rights and empowerment approaches to development.'[103] The economic empowerment of people to be subjects rather than objects of their own history, to know, claim, and realize the full range of their human rights is both morally desirable and the principal means to realize what Article 28 UDHR refers to as the right to 'a social and international order in which the rights and freedoms set forth in this Declaration can be fully realized'. The combats against poverty and for human rights come together in the vision of such a social and international order.

---

[99] Millen, Irwin, and Yong Kim, 'Conclusion: Pessimism of the Intellect, Optimism of the Will', in Yong Kim, Millen, Irwin, and Gershman, *Dying for Growth: Global Inequality and the Health of the Poor* (Common Courage Press, 2000) 383.

[100] UDHR, preambular para 5.   [101] Preambular para 8.

[102] Narayan (ed), *Empowerment and Poverty Reduction: A Sourcebook* (World Bank, 2002).

[103] Alsop (ed), *Power, Rights, and Poverty: Concepts and Connections* (World Bank and DFID, 2004) 8.

FURTHER READING

ALSTON and ROBINSON (eds), *Human Rights and Development: Toward Mutual Reinforcement* (Oxford University Press, 2005).

ANDREASSEN and MARKS (eds), *Development as a Human Right: Legal, Political and Economic Dimensions* (Intersentia, 2010).

COLLIER, *The Bottom Billion: Why the Poorest Countries Are Failing and What Can Be Done About It* (Oxford University Press, 2007).

DARROW, 'The Millennium Development Goals: Milestones or Millstones? Human Rights Priorities for the Post-2015 Development', (2012) 15 *Yale HR and Development LJ* 55.

FERRAZ, 'Poverty and Human Rights' (2008) 28 *OJLS* 585.

GAURI and GLOPPEN, 'Human Rights-Based Approaches to Development: Concepts, Evidence, and Policy' (2012) 44 *Polity* 485.

GREADY and VANDENHOLE (eds), *Human Rights and Development in the New Millennium: Towards a Theory of Change* (Routledge, forthcoming 2014).

HUNT, NOWAK, and OSMANI, *Human Rights and Poverty Reduction Strategies: Human Rights and Poverty Reduction: A Conceptual Framework* (OHCHR, 2003).

KHAN, *The Unheard Truth: Poverty and Human Rights*, (WW Norton, 2009).

LANGFORD, SUMNER, and YAMIN, *Millennium Development Goals and Human Rights: Past, Present and Future* (Cambridge University Press, 2013).

OSMANI, 'Poverty and Human Rights: Building on the Capability Approach' (2005) 6 *J of Human Development* 205.

OHCHR, *Claiming the MDGs: A Human Rights Approach* (UN, 2008).

OHCHR, *Realizing the Right to Development: Essays in Commemoration of 25 Years of the United Nations Declaration on the Right to Development* (UN, 2013).

POGGE, *World Poverty and Human Rights* (Polity Press, 2008).

SALOMON, *Global Responsibility for Human Rights: World Poverty and the Development of International Law* (Oxford University Press, 2007).

SEN, *Development as Freedom* (Alfred A Knopf, 2000).

SEN, 'Human Rights and Capabilities' (2005) 6 *J of Human Development* 151.

UVIN, *Human Rights and Development* (Kumarian Press, 2004).

USEFUL WEBSITES

Special Rapporteur on extreme poverty and human rights: <http://www.ohchr.org/EN/Issues/Poverty/Pages/SRExtremePovertyIndex.aspx>

International Network for Economic, Social and Cultural Rights: <http://www.escr-net.org/>

World Bank: <http://www.worldbank.org/>

Oxfam International: <http://www.oxfam.org>

MDG Gap: <http://www.un.org/esa/policy/mdggap/index.html>

UN Development Programme, Millennium Development Goals: <http://www.undp.org/content/undp/en/home/mdgoverview/>

Centre for Economic and Social Rights: <http://www.cesr.org>

29

ENVIRONMENTAL DEGRADATION

Malgosia Fitzmaurice

SUMMARY

This chapter investigates the challenges environmental degradation poses for human rights protection. Two human rights approaches to combating environmental degradation are discussed. First, the idea of substantive environmental human rights is examined. Such rights are explicitly provided for in the African Charter on Human and Peoples' Rights as well as in the San Salvador Protocol to the American Convention on Human Rights. Other efforts to imply substantive environmental human rights are critically analysed. There are, however, concerns with the development and use of substantive environmental human rights. Therefore, there have been efforts to develop procedural environmental human rights. Such efforts include the Aarhus Convention, environmental impact assessments, as well as the creative approaches of the European Court of Human Rights to imply that such a right exists within the framework of existing rights. Procedural environmental human rights provide the best way forward for meeting the challenges of environmental degradation.

1 INTRODUCTION

This chapter addresses the challenges environmental degradation poses for human rights protection, examining whether substantive and procedural environmental rights can overcome them. The main issue is whether human rights constitute an efficient and practical tool that can be used to combat environmental degradation.

The link between the enjoyment of human rights and the environment in which we live was addressed for the first time in 1972 at the UN Conference on the Human Environment. The Declaration of the Conference (Stockholm Declaration) recognizes that 'man's environment [is] essential to his well-being and to the enjoyment of basic human rights', such as the right to life. It is clear that:

> The harm caused to individuals and communities by degraded environments—from unsafe drinking water to disappearing wild life—is increasingly seen by many people as a question of 'rights' being violated...Protection of the environment can no longer be seen as simply a policy choice.[1]

---

[1] Kravchenko and Bonine, *Human Rights and the Environment: Cases, Law, and Policy* (Carolina Academic Press, 2008) 3.

Degradation of the environment, by which we mean the deterioration in environmental quality from ambient concentrations of pollutants and other activities and processes, such as improper land use and natural disasters,[2] can cause violations of human rights. For example, the Office of the UN High Commissioner for Human Rights (OHCHR) has investigated the varied effects of climate change on the enjoyment of human rights. In a 2009 report to the Human Rights Council, the impact of climate change on several human rights, including the rights to life, adequate food, water, adequate housing, health, and self-determination, was examined.[3] The report notes that the effects of climate change, including heatwaves, floods, and other natural phenomena, will pose direct and indirect threats to the right to life and the closely related rights to adequate food, water, health, and housing. Climate change will have disastrous effects on the right to food as its production will decrease, particularly at lower latitudes. It is estimated that 600 million people will face malnutrition. It will cause a shortage of water supplies, adversely impacting on the availability of drinking water and resulting in an increase in water-related diseases. Therefore, it may be said that climate change also constitutes a grave challenge to the right to health. The report also details the impact climate change will have on the right to adequate housing. For example, rising sea levels and the erosion of livelihoods will result in increased migration to cities and a corresponding increase in the number of hazardous dwellings. Finally, climate change will adversely affect the right to self-determination, especially for indigenous peoples, whose traditional livelihood depends on access to land and natural resources. Women and children, who constitute the most vulnerable groups during natural disasters and whose health and livelihoods are the most endangered, will be disproportionately affected.

Despite recognizing the link between climate change and human rights violations, the OHCHR was rather sceptical regarding the viability of litigation for violations of human rights caused by climate change. It identified several issues that render such litigation very difficult, including the multiplicity of causes for environmental degradation and the multitude of states contributing to climate change, which make establishing responsibility in international law very problematic.[4] This is not only a theoretical concern. It has proven difficult in practice to establish such responsibility. A petition to the Inter-American Commission from Inuit Tribes in the Arctic Regions of the US and Canada claimed that global warming caused by the activities of the US had caused a number of human rights violations. However, the Commission came to the conclusion that is was impossible to process the complaint because, on the basis of the information submitted, it was unable to determine whether the alleged facts constitute a violation of the rights protected by the American Declaration of the Rights and Duties of Man.[5]

The threat to the enjoyment of human rights posed by environmental degradation has also been considered by the Committee on Economic, Social and Cultural Rights. In its General Comment 14, the Committee observed that the steps that should be taken to realize the right to health, and in particular 'the improvement of all aspects of environmental and industrial hygiene', include 'preventive measures in respect of occupational accidents and diseases; the requirement to ensure an adequate supply of safe and potable water and basic sanitation; the prevention and reduction of the population's exposure to harmful

---

[2] OECD Glossary of Statistical Terms, available at: <http://stats.oecd.org/glossary/detail.asp?ID=821>.
[3] Report of the OHCHR on the relationship between climate change and human rights, A/HRC/10/61 (15 January 2009).
[4] Report of the OHCHR, n 3, para 91.
[5] See Center for International Environmental Law, Inuit Petition Recasts Climate Change Debate, available at: <http://www.ciel.org/Climate_Change/Inuit.html>.

substances such as radiation and harmful chemicals or other detrimental environmental conditions that directly or indirectly impact upon human health.'[6] Comparable comments have been made in relation to the right to water.[7]

Similarly, the effect of dumping of toxic waste on the enjoyment of human rights has been widely acknowledged. In 1995, the Commission on Human Rights established a Special Rapporteur to investigate this link. In 1996, the Rapporteur reported that environmental degradation following the dumping of toxic waste would impact on the enjoyment of the rights to self-determination, life, health, food, safe and healthy working conditions, housing, information, participation, and freedom of association, as well as cultural rights.[8] These adverse effects have been repeatedly emphasized in Commission on Human Rights and Human Rights Council resolutions.[9]

There is clearly a negative link between environmental degradation and the enjoyment of human rights. The question then arises, can human rights be used as an effective tool to deal with environmental degradation? How should, and indeed does, human rights address this challenge? One answer is through the use of substantive environmental rights, that is, the right to a clean and healthy environment. A different approach is to use procedural environmental rights that guarantee access to information, participation in decision-making, and access to justice in environmental matters. Each of these approaches and their merits will be discussed in the rest of this chapter.

2 SUBSTANTIVE ENVIRONMENTAL RIGHTS

There are very few human rights treaties that grant a direct right to a clean and healthy environment. Only the African Charter on Human and Peoples' Rights (ACHPR) and the San Salvador Protocol to the American Convention on Human Rights in the Area of Economic, Social and Cultural Rights (San Salvador Protocol) do so. Despite this, there has been some progress at the UN level in drafting 'soft law' documents that suggest that there might be a substantive human right to a clean and healthy environment. Furthermore, the European Court of Human Rights has found that such a right can be derived within the prism of existing human rights.

2.1 AFRICAN CHARTER

The first treaty to accord a direct right to a clean and healthy environment was the ACHPR. Article 24 provides peoples with a right to 'a general satisfactory environment favourable to their development'. This provision was one of the bases of a claim in the *Ogoniland* case before the African Commission on Human and Peoples' Rights.[10] The complainants alleged that the Nigerian government had directly participated in unsustainable oil development

---

[6] CESCR, General Comment 14, HRI/GEN/1/Rev.9 (Vol 1) 78, para 25.

[7] CESCR, General Comment 15, HRI/GEN/1/Rev.9 (Vol 1) 97. See also Fitzmaurice, 'The Human Right to Water' (2007) 18 *Fordham Envm LR* 537.

[8] Preliminary report of the Special Rapporteur on the adverse effects of the illicit movement of toxic and dangerous products and wastes on the enjoyment of human rights, E/CN.4/1996/17 (22 February 1996) para 132.

[9] Eg HR Council Res 9/1 (5 September 2008); HR Council Res 12/18 (2 October 2009).

[10] 155/96, *Social and Economic Rights Action Center and the Center for Economic and Social Rights v Nigeria*, 15th Activity Report of the ACommHPR (2001–2002) ('*Ogoniland*'). See Shelton, 'Decision Regarding Communication 155/96 (Social and Economic Rights Action Centre/Centre for Economic and Social Rights v Nigeria). Case No ACHPR/COMM/A044/1' (2002) 96 *AJIL* 937; Coomans, 'The Ogoni Case before the African Commission on Human and Peoples' Rights' (2003) 52 *ICLQ* 749.

practices in Ogoniland. It was also claimed that the state-owned oil company had caused environmental degradation, including widespread contamination of soil, water, and air, the destruction of homes, the burning of crops, and the killing of farm animals. These actions, in turn, had led to health problems amongst the Ogoni people. As such, violations of the rights to health, a healthy environment, housing, and food were alleged.

The African Commission held that a satisfactory environment is one that is clean and safe and promotes health. Similarly, the right to health imposes obligations on states to 'take the necessary measures to protect the health of their people'.[11] In the view of the Commission, states must *respect* these rights by refraining from directly threatening the health and the environment of their citizens, as well as *protect* them by adopting measures to prevent pollution and ecological degradation. In addition, states parties must *fulfil* the right to a satisfactory environment by adopting reasonable measures to prevent pollution and ecological degradation, to promote conservation, and to pursue the concept of sustainable development and use of natural resources.

Concluding that although Nigeria had the right to make use of its natural resources, including oil, the Commission held that Nigeria had breached its human rights obligations in relation to those living in the Ogoni region and that 'the pollution and environmental degradation to a level humanly unacceptable has made living in [Ogoniland] a nightmare'.[12] The Commission not only saw environmental degradation as leading to the violation of other rights, but as a human rights violation in itself because of its impact on the quality of life. It further stated that 'an environment degraded by pollution and defaced by destruction of all beauty and variety is as contrary to satisfactory living conditions and development as the breakdown of the fundamental ecologic equilibria is harmful to physical and moral health'.[13]

Although the decision in the *Ogoniland* case is truly remarkable, particularly as it confirms the justiciable nature of Article 24, the African Commission's restricted regulatory powers and the poor record of compliance with its recommendations limit the practical usefulness of its attempts to remedy environmental degradation in the African region.

2.2 SAN SALVADOR PROTOCOL TO THE AMERICAN CONVENTION ON HUMAN RIGHTS

Article 11 San Salvador Protocol provides for a right to a healthy environment:

1. Everyone shall have a right to live in a healthy environment and to have access to basic public services.

2. The States Parties shall promote the protection, preservation, and improvement of the environment.

However, the Inter-American human rights institutions have limited powers in respect of this right. They can only receive annual reports from states on their observance of this right as there is no provision for individual applications to the Inter-American Commission or Court regarding alleged violations of the San Salvador Protocol.

Despite this, the Commission and the Court have linked environmental degradation and human rights on numerous occasions when deciding cases regarding indigenous rights.[14] In such cases, the Commission has stressed that the importance of economic

---

[11] ACHPR, Art 16.   [12] *Ogoniland*, n 10, para 67.   [13] *Ogoniland*, n 10, para 51.

[14] Case 7615, *Yanomami v Brazil*, IACommHR Res 12/85 (5 March 1985); *Mayagna (Sumo) Awas Tigni Community v Nicaragua*, IACtHR Series C No 79 (31 August 2001); Case 12/053, *Maya Indigenous Community of the Toledo District v Belize*, IACommHR Report No 40/40 (12 October 2004).

development should not override environmental considerations. However, it is questionable whether these decisions will have an impact beyond the particular context of indigenous peoples' rights to their traditional lands.[15]

The *La Oroya* case is the first case in which the Inter-American Commission has considered the responsibility of a state for the breach of human rights of a non-indigenous community caused by the contamination of the environment.[16] In 2006, a coalition of NGOs filed a petition on behalf of a group of inhabitants of La Oroya to the Commission. The petition alleged that Peru had violated the following Articles of the ACHR: 4 (life), 5 (personal integrity), 11 (honour and dignity), 13 (freedom of thought and expression), 8 (fair trial), and 25 (judicial protection), in connection with the duties of the state in Articles 1(1) and 1(2). The petition also alleged violations of Articles 10 (health) and 11 (healthy environment) of the San Salvador Protocol. Specifically, the petitioners alleged that the metallurgical complex, owned by the American company Doe Run, had caused severe environmental contamination of La Oroya, including exposure to lead, arsenic, cadmium, as well as sulphur dioxide pollution. The actions of the Peruvian state, and its failure to act in light of its knowledge about the grave situation in the area since 1999, had led to violations of the rights of the inhabitants of La Oroya. In 2007, the Inter-American Commission granted precautionary measures obliging the Peruvian state to provide medical diagnoses and treatment to 65 inhabitants of La Oroya because they suffered from a series of health problems from the environmental contamination caused by the metallurgical complex. In 2009 the Commission decided that the complaint was admissible. However, the Commission held that it could only examine the complaints under the ACHR and that the allegations of violations of the San Salvador Protocol were outside its competence; instead the Commission was mandated to take into account the San Salvador Protocol 'in interpreting the scope and intent of the American Convention.'[17] A decision on the merits is still awaited.

2.3 PROGRESS AT THE UN

Several 'soft law' instruments have been adopted by the UN, which suggest the possibility of a substantive environmental human right. The first suggestions of such a right can be traced to Principle 1 Stockholm Declaration, which provides that:

> Man is both creature and moulder of his environment, which gives him physical sustenance and affords him the opportunity for intellectual, moral, social and spiritual growth. In the long and tortuous evolution of the human race on this planet a stage has been reached when, through the rapid acceleration of science and technology, man has acquired the power to transform his environment in countless ways and on an unprecedented scale. Both aspects of man's environment, the natural and the man-made, are essential to his well-being and to the enjoyment of basic human rights the right to life itself [sic].

Many saw this as an incipient environmental human right. However, although '[t]his grand statement might have provided the basis for subsequent elaboration of a human right to environmental quality, ... its real-world impact has been noticeably modest'.[18]

---

[15] Boyle, 'Human Rights or Environmental Rights? A Reassessment' (2007) 18 *Fordham Envm LR* 471, 476.

[16] Case 1473.06, *Community of La Oroya v Peru*, IACommHR Report No 76/09 (5 August 2009). See Spieler, 'The La Oroya Case: the Relationship Between Environmental Degradation and Human Rights Violations' (2010) 18 *HR Brief* 19.

[17] *Community of La Oroya*, n 16, para 54.   [18] Boyle, n 15, 473.

In 1992, world leaders met again at the UN Conference on the Environment and World Development. There were great expectations that this conference would produce a document that included an explicit human right to a clean environment. However, these hopes were dashed as no compromise could be found as to its content. Instead, the Rio Declaration 1992 maintained the position taken in Stockholm, that: 'Human beings are at the centre of concerns for sustainable development. They are entitled to a healthy and productive life in harmony with nature.'

In 1989, in preparation for the Rio Conference, a Special Rapporteur on environment and development was appointed by the Sub-Commission on Prevention of Discrimination and Protection of Minorities. The Special Rapporteur, Fatma Zohra Ksentini, addressed the link between human rights and environmental degradation in her 1994 final report. She stated that the environment, development, democracy, and human rights are the fundamental building blocks of modern society. Endorsing the view that environmental rights are protected by existing human rights, she reported that there was universal acceptance of the right to a satisfactory environment at national, regional, and international levels. The Special Rapporteur recommended the adoption of the Draft Declaration of Principles on Human Rights and the Environment, which had been drafted by academics and NGOs.[19] Presuming that environmental human rights exist, the Draft Declaration builds on the Stockholm and Rio Declarations and provides that:

1. Human rights, an ecologically sound environment, sustainable development and peace are interdependent and indivisible.

2. All persons have the right to a secure, healthy and ecologically sound environment. This right and other human rights, including civil, cultural, economic, political and social rights, are universal, interdependent and indivisible.

Containing a wide range of both substantive and procedural environmental rights, the Draft Declaration includes rights to freedom from pollution, environmental degradation, and activities that adversely affect the environment, threaten life, health, livelihood, well-being, or sustainable development within, across, or outside national boundaries. There are also rights to the protection and preservation of the air, water, soil, sea ice, flora, and fauna, and the essential processes and areas necessary to maintain high biological diversity and ecosystems. The Declaration also proclaims the right to safe and healthy food and water, a healthy working environment, as well as adequate housing. The Declaration was not adopted by the Commission on Human Rights and, to date, has not been considered by the Human Rights Council.

More recently the Human Rights Council has reaffirmed the relationship between human rights on the environment.[20] It has also now appointed an Independent Expert on the issue of human rights obligations relating to the enjoyment of a safe, clean, healthy, and sustainable environment who is to study the human rights obligations relating to a safe, clean, healthy, and sustainable environment and identify best practice relating to the use of human rights in environmental policy-making.[21]

---

[19] Report by the Special Rapporteur on environment and development, E/CN.4/Sub.2/1994/9 (6 July 1994).
[20] HR Council Res 16/11 (24 March 2011); HR Council Res 7/23 (28 March 2008); HR Council Res 10/4 (25 March 2009); and HR Council Res 18/22 (30 September 2011) on climate change and human rights.
[21] HR Council Res 19/10 (19 April 2012).

2.4 INDIRECT SUBSTANTIVE ENVIRONMENTAL RIGHTS

As the Special Rapporteur on environment and development reported, rights to a clean and healthy environment may be drawn from other human rights: civil and political, as well as economic, social, and cultural rights. Some favour civil and political rights as more useful in realizing a healthy and clean environment as '[i]nternational courts and tribunals are likely to be more easily persuaded that civil and political rights are capable of creating practical and enforceable obligations in relation to environmental and related matters'.[22] Recourse to existing political and civil rights gives individuals, groups, and NGOs access to existing information as well as tried and tested remedies and political processes. Others argue for the mobilization of second generation rights, that is economic, social, and cultural rights, over first generation rights in the protection of the environment as many of these rights have a direct bearing upon environmental conditions. However, the translation of economic, social, and cultural rights 'into specific environmental standards will never be an easy task'.[23] Although he prefers this approach, Anderson has stated that '[d]espite their advantages, the existing system for implementing and monitoring second generation rights construe these rights rather narrowly, and continue to approach environmental questions only indirectly'.[24]

The European Court of Human Rights has been very active in determining a right to a clean and healthy environment within existing civil and political human rights, and this approach will be examined in Section 2.4.1.

2.4.1 European Convention on Human Rights

The European Convention on Human Rights (ECHR) does not contain a direct substantive environmental human right and the first few cases regarding environmental degradation were regarded as inadmissible. For example, *X and Y v Federal Republic of Germany* was the first 'environmental' case to come before the Council of Europe institutions, and was deemed inadmissible by the European Commission on Human Rights on the basis that the ECHR did not include a right to the preservation of nature.[25]

However, more recently, the jurisprudence of the European Court of Human Rights has undergone a fundamental change regarding environmental issues. The Court has given effect to environmental rights indirectly through its interpretation of the protections accorded to other rights set out within the ECHR, including Articles 2 (right to life), 3 (freedom from torture), 8 (right to respect for private and family life), and 10 (freedom of expression), as well as Article 1 Protocol 1 (right to property). Dealing with environmental degradation in this manner is particularly challenging as there is competition between those rights explicitly protected by the ECHR and the protection of the environment which is not.

Most cases have been brought under Article 8 ECHR, the right to respect for private and family life, home, and correspondence. This right is qualified and may be restricted if this is 'necessary in a democratic society', understood as requiring that 'the interference corresponds to a pressing social need and...is proportionate to the legitimate aim pursued. The reasons given to justify the interference must be "relevant" and "sufficient".[26] The first 'environmental' case brought before the European Court concerned noise pollution

---

[22] Sands, *Principles of International Environmental Law* (Manchester University Press, 2001) 297.

[23] Sands, n 22.

[24] Anderson, 'Human Rights Approaches to Environmental Protection: An Overview' in Boyle and Anderson, *Human Rights Approaches to Environmental Protection* (OUP, 1996) 6.

[25] 15 DR 161 (1976).   [26] *Olsson v Sweden* (1988) 11 EHRR 259. See Chapter 5.

from aircraft arriving and leaving London airports. In *Powell and Raynor v UK*, the Court balanced the competing interests of the individuals who were disturbed by flights to and from Heathrow airport and those of the community at large, including the economic importance of the airport as a source of employment and the development of trade and communications. The European Court concluded that although the quality of life of the applicants had been disturbed, this was necessary for the well-being of the community.[27]

Lopez Ostra v Spain is considered to be a ground-breaking case.[28] In 1988, a tannery company erected a waste treatment plant on municipal grounds (with state subsidies), without a licence for activities, which may be classified as causing a nuisance, 12 metres from the applicant's apartment. The applicant alleged the impairment of both her health and that of her family due to fumes generated by the tannery. She had to be re-housed. The European Court held that environmental pollution, even without causing serious damage to health, could affect the well-being of individuals and impede enjoyment of their private and family life. Spain had not struck a proper balance between the well-being of the applicants and the general economic benefits brought by the waste treatment plant. Although the plant was privately owned, there was a positive obligation to regulate private actions carried out on state territory in order to protect private and family life and the home. This was the first time that the European Court had found a violation of the ECHR on the basis of environmental pollution.

The case of *Hatton v UK* also concerned state responsibility for pollution caused by private industry. This case was a disappointment from the point of view of environmental protection and human rights. The European Court adopted a very restrictive approach to the link between environmental degradation and human rights, exhibiting a more deferential attitude towards states than in the *Lopez Ostra* case. The case concerned night flights to and from Heathrow Airport which, it was argued by the applicants, disturbed their sleep. The UK government had introduced the use of noise quotas in order to minimize the disturbance caused by night flights. The case was first heard by a Chamber of the Court in 2001.[29] Referring to the 'fair balance' that must be struck between the competing interests of the individual and the community as a whole, the Chamber admitted that the state enjoyed a certain margin of appreciation in determining the steps to be taken to ensure compliance with the ECHR. The Chamber found that despite the margin of appreciation left to the UK government, the implementation of the noise quota scheme failed to strike a fair balance between the country's economic well-being and the applicants' effective enjoyment of their right to respect for their homes and family lives; therefore, violating Article 8 ECHR. The UK government requested the referral of the case to the Grand Chamber. The Grand Chamber stated in no uncertain terms that 'there is no explicit right under the Convention to a clean and quiet environment' and that only 'where the individual is directly and seriously affected by noise or other pollution' may an issue arise under Article 8.[30] Finding that there was no violation of Article 8, the Grand Chamber reiterated the fundamentally subsidiary role of the Court: national authorities have direct democratic legitimacy and are better placed than an international tribunal to assess local needs and conditions. In matters of general policy, which may involve different opinions contained within democratic society, the actions of domestic policy-makers to ensure compliance with the ECHR should be given a wide margin of appreciation.

A minority of judges appended a powerful joint dissenting opinion.[31] The dissenting judges argued that the 'evolutive' interpretation of the ECHR leads to the construction of

---

[27] (1990) 12 EHRR 355.   [28] (1994) 20 EHRR 27.
[29] (2002) 34 EHRR 1.   [30] (2003) 37 EHRR 28, para 96.
[31] Joint Dissenting Opinion of Judges Costa, Ress, Türmen, Zupančič, and Steiner, *Hatton v UK*, n 30.

an environmental human right on the basis of Article 8. They asserted that the European Court has confirmed on several occasions, including in *Lopez Ostra*, that Article 8 embraces the right to a healthy environment: 'the Convention and the Court have increasingly taken the view that Article 8 embraces the right to a healthy environment, and therefore to protection against nuisance caused by harmful chemicals, offensive smells, agents which precipitate respiratory ailments, noise and so on'.[32] They felt that, unfortunately, the Grand Chamber's judgment in *Hatton* appeared to deviate from these developments, appearing to take a step backwards, and that the UK government had not sufficiently substantiated the economic importance of Heathrow Airport for the country.

The European Court adopted a very restrictive and deferential view towards the state's position regarding environmental human rights and the possibility of redressing environmental degradation through this means in *Hatton*. The Court took into consideration the fact that the UK government had acted in conformity with national laws concerning night flights. By contrast, in *Lopez Ostra* the authorities had failed to comply with domestic law as there was no licence for the tannery.

This line of reasoning was also present in *Fadeyeva v Russia* in which the Court noted the breach of national laws by the defendant state. The European Court clarified in *Fadeyeva v Russia* that not every instance of environmental degradation will constitute a breach of Article 8 ECHR.[33] The case concerned air pollution from a Soviet steel plant which had been privatized. In order for pollution to raise an issue under Article 8, the Court reiterated the principles it had set out in its earlier cases. First, the deleterious effects of the pollution must directly affect the applicant's home, family, or private life; and, second, the adverse effects must have reached a certain minimum level if they are to fall within the scope of Article 8. The minimum level to be reached is not general but relative and depends on all the circumstances, including the intensity and duration of the nuisance, its physical or mental effects, and the general environmental context (for example, there would be no claim under Article 8 if the harm complained of was negligible in comparison to the environmental hazards inherent to life in every modern city). The Court held that the emissions from the industrial plant had affected the applicant's health, making her more vulnerable to various diseases, as well as affecting the enjoyment of her home. Taken together, the effects of the pollution were of a level to bring it within the scope of Article 8. A violation of Article 8 was found as the state had made no efforts to provide the applicant with an effective solution to the dangers of the steel plant's emissions.[34]

The European Court has also examined the obligations of states under Article 2, which protects the right to life, where environmental pollution has had, or may have, lethal effects. So, for example, in *Öneryıldız v Turkey*,[35] and *Budayeva and Others v Russia*,[36] the Court found a causal link between gross negligence attributable to the state and the loss of human lives which resulted from environmental degradation. In both cases the relevant states had failed to fulfil their positive obligations to protect the right to life. The Court held that where 'dangerous activities' are embarked upon which may have potentially lethal consequences, including those that cause environmental degradation, there must be enhanced national regulation. National authorities must govern the licensing, setting up, operation, security, and supervision of such activities and make it compulsory for all concerned to take practical measures to ensure the effective protection of citizens whose lives might be endangered by the inherent risks. These preventive measures include the public's right to information. Appropriate

---

[32] Joint Dissenting Opinion, n 31, para 2.   [33] (2007) 45 EHRR 10.

[34] Similar issues were raised in *Ledyaeva v Russia* App nos 53157/99, 53247/99, 53695/00 and 56850/00, Judgment of 26 October 2006; and *Dubetska and Others v Ukraine* App no 30499/03, Judgment of 9 September 2010.

[35] (2005) 41 EHRR 20.

[36] App nos 15339/02, 21166/02, 20058/02, and 15343/02 , Judgment of 16 October 2003.

procedures, considering the technical aspects of the activity, for the purpose of identifying shortcomings in the processes concerned and any errors committed by those responsible at different levels must be established. The Court also stated that in the context of dangerous activities, the scope of positive obligations under Article 2 largely overlaps with those under Article 8. As in many other cases concerned with environmental issues, the choice of measures to be taken falls within states' margin of appreciation. The Court stressed in the *Budayeva* case that, where environmental disasters have occurred, the scope of the positive obligation imputable to the state depends on the origin of the disaster and whether its risks were susceptible to mitigation. Furthermore, the Court observed that if the infringement of the right to life or physical integrity is not caused intentionally, the positive obligation to set up an effective judicial inquiry does not necessarily entail criminal proceedings and may be satisfied if impartial civil, administrative, or even disciplinary remedies are at the disposal of victims.

An interesting case element resulted from the catastrophe of the ship *Prestige*.[37] In November 2002, while sailing off the Spanish coast the *Prestige* released into the Atlantic Ocean the 70,000 tons of fuel oil it was carrying. The applicant, Mr Mangouras, the captain of the ship, was the subject of a criminal investigation and was remanded in custody for 83 days with bail fixed at 3,000,000 Euros (which was paid the by ship owner's insurers). Mr Mangouras complained of a violation of Article 5(3) ECHR, specifically claiming that the amount of bail required was excessively high and had been fixed without regard for his personal situation. The European Court found no violation and said that new realities had to be taken into consideration, namely the growing and legitimate concern both in Europe and internationally in relation to environmental offences and the tendency to use criminal law as a means of enforcing the environmental obligations imposed by European and international law. The Court concluded that, given the exceptional nature of the case and the huge environmental damage caused by the marine pollution, the bail amount required was in line with the level of liability incurred, so as to ensure that those responsible had no incentive to evade justice.

The above discussion demonstrates a willingness of the European Court to remedy environmental degradation through human rights, despite the lack of a specific environmental right in the ECHR. However, the numerous requirements which 'an environmental claim' must fulfil to fall under the scope of Article 8 ECHR are challenging. It would be overstating the case to consider that there is a substantive environmental right under the ECHR. Rather, as the Court said in *Kyrtatos v Greece*, no provision of the European Convention is designed to protect the environment itself, unless the rights of individuals are directly affected.[38]

2.4.2 Other international treaties

There are other treaties that grant indirect substantive environmental rights. One such treaty is the International Labour Organization (ILO) Convention No 169 concerning Indigenous and Tribal Peoples in Independent Countries. Of particular importance are Article 14, regarding ownership and possession of land, and Article 15, regarding the right to participate in the use, management, and conservation of natural resources. These provisions were the main reason for the lack of widespread ratification of the Convention. These indirect environmental human rights should be viewed from the perspective of the culture and religion of indigenous peoples for whom the link with land and the environment and natural resources is frequently part and parcel of their identity as human beings. They are

---

[37] *Mangouras v Spain* (2012) 54 EHRR 25.　　[38] (2005) 40 EHRR 16.

also linked to the question of self-determination. Therefore, environmental rights are at the heart of protections for indigenous populations.

2.5 SUBSTANTIVE ENVIRONMENTAL RIGHTS AT THE NATIONAL LEVEL

Although at present more than 100 national constitutions contain a right to a healthy, decent, or good environment, the role these provisions play in remedying environmental degradation is not altogether clear. Formulations regarding such a right vary considerably. They may refer to the duty of authorities to provide a healthy and balanced environment or go further and impose a duty on citizens to cooperate in the protection of the environment for present and future generations. For example, Article 24 of the Constitution of the Republic of South Africa provides that:

Everyone has the right to an environment that is not harmful to their health or well-being; and to have the environment protected, for the benefit of present and future generations, through reasonable legislative and other measures that prevent pollution and ecological degradation; promote conservation; and secure ecologically sustainable development and use of natural resources while promoting justifiable economic and social development.

Constitutional rights may be a very useful tool in challenging regulations and executive action which negatively impact the environment, but only if such rights are justiciable. For example, a case was brought before the Supreme Court of the Philippines regarding commercial logging agreements, which had a deleterious effect on the rainforest. In *Oposa v Factoran*, 44 children argued that their right, and the rights of generations yet unborn, under the constitution to a balanced and healthful ecology was being violated.[39] The Supreme Court held that:

Each generation has a responsibility to the next to preserve that rhythm and harmony for the full enjoyment of a balanced and healthful ecology... the minors' assertion of their right to a sound environment constitutes, at the same time, the performance of their obligation to ensure the protection of that right for the generations to come.[40]

The Supreme Court was of the view that the children had standing before national courts on the issue and thus confirmed the justiciable nature of the environmental right.

A progressive approach to environmental rights based on a broad interpretation of the right to life has been taken by the courts of India. In 1991, in the case of *Subhash Kumar v State of Bihar*, the Supreme Court of India observed that the 'right to life guaranteed by article 21 [of the Constitution] includes the right of enjoyment of pollution-free water and air for full enjoyment of life'.[41] In this case, the Supreme Court also recognized the right to a wholesome environment as part of the fundamental right to life. It held that municipalities and a large number of other governmental agencies must take adequate steps to prevent pollution. This approach has since been followed by courts in Bangladesh,[42] Pakistan,[43] and Colombia.[44] In addition, the Constitution (Forty Second Amendment)

---

[39] GR No 101083 (30 July 1993).

[40] *Oposa v Factoran*, n 39. However, Judge Feliciano in his Separate Opinion forcefully argued that such a right is too general and vague to constitute a ground for a legal action.

[41] AIR 1991 SC 420, para 7.

[42] Eg *Dr M Farooque v Secretary, Ministry of Communication, Government of the People's Republic of Bangladesh and 12 Others*, WP No 300 of 1995.

[43] Eg *The Employees of the Pakistan Law Commission v Ministry of Works*, 1994 SCMR 1548.

[44] Eg *Victor Ramon Castrillon Vega v Federacio Nacional de Algodoneros y Corporacion Autonoma Regional del Cesar* (1997) Case No 4577.

Act 1976 has explicitly incorporated environmental protection and improvement as a part of state policy so that Article 48A Indian Constitution, a directive principle of state policy, provides that '[t]he State shall endeavour to protect and improve the environment and to safeguard the forests and wild life of the country'.

2.6 IS THERE A NEED FOR A SUBSTANTIVE ENVIRONMENTAL RIGHT?

Do we need a substantive environmental human right? This is a highly controversial issue that has attracted much debate.[45] One of the main critics of this approach, Handl, has argued that it is far from clear that environmental human rights and environmental protection share common objectives.[46] Handl raises several concerns regarding the use of a substantive environmental human right as a solution to the problem of environmental degradation.

First, he argues that, to date, the normative content of such a putative environmental human right has not been defined. Any definition is likely to be qualitatively different from, for instance, the right to health.[47] A clean environment would be difficult to conceptualize as an inalienable right, as environmental protection measures are subject to the reordering of national socio-economic priorities to meet public policy objectives, such as ensuring continued 'development' or 'saving jobs'.[48] Environmental rights will also differ according to the area where they arise, that is, whether they relate to the North or the South.[49]

Second, he argues that any attempt to establish criteria for the evaluation of state compliance with obligations stemming from generic environmental human rights would encounter political and technical difficulties. Where would the division of labour between human rights and environmental institutions lie? What would be the appropriate locus of decision-making: the international or national level? However, others maintain that adhering to a strict division of labour between environmental and human rights institutions, which deal with similar or at least comparable issues, is to duplicate efforts and leads to the depletion of available resources.[50]

Third, Handl expresses concern regarding the democratic legitimacy of a human rights-based approach to environmental issues. A generic environmental human right would serve as a powerful tool for socio-economic engineering by human rights decision-making bodies. Implementation of the right could lead to internationalized decision-making in sensitive areas that traditionally belong to the state. However, it may be noted that many other human rights share this characteristic. Therefore, it does not appear that this feature sets apart environmental human rights from other human rights.

Handl looks to the regional human rights systems for evidence that the relationship between environmental degradation and human rights either remains not fully accepted as an operational normative concept (ECHR), or is formulated in ambiguous language,

---

[45] Eg Boyle and Anderson (eds), n 24; Boyle, n 15; Handl, 'Human Rights and Protection of the Environment: A Mildly "Revisionist" View' in Cançado Trindade (ed), *Human Rights, Sustainable Development and the Environment* (Instituto Interamericano de Derechos, 1992) 117; and Handl, 'Human Rights and Protection of the Environment' in Eide, Krause, and Rosas (eds), *Economic, Social and Cultural Rights* (Kluwer Law International, 2001) 303.

[46] Handl in Eide, Krause, and Rosas, n 45, 309.   [47] Handl, n 45, 315.

[48] Handl in Cançado Trindade, n 45, 117–42.   [49] Handl in Cançado Trindade, n 45, 126.

[50] Taillant, 'Environmental Advocacy and the Inter-American Human Rights System' in Picolatti and Taillant (eds), *Linking Human Rights and the Environment* (University of Arizona Press, 2003) 118.

due to inherent conflicts with economic development (ACHPR).[51] He also notes that there is little evidence that states will be willing to use Article 11 San Salvador Protocol as a vehicle to push the environmental agenda.[52]

Others have also been critical of adopting a generic environmental human right. They argue that such a right is only human-oriented and does not consider the intrinsic right of the environment itself for protection.[53] Boyle has noted that the implications of the argument for anthropocentricity are essentially structural. They imply a need for the integration of human claims to a decent environment within a wider spectrum of decision-making processes that is based on balancing of the interests of human beings, the environment, and authorities through international cooperation and supervisory institutions. Boyle submits that such decision-making processes should take into consideration the competing interests of future generations and other states and the collective interest in common spaces and wildlife preservation. The right to environment and the right of the environment are two concepts that are impossible to reconcile. Therefore, the question remains:

> should we continue to think about human rights and the environment within the existing framework of human rights law in which the protection of humans is the central focus— essentially a greening of the rights to life, private life, and property—or has the time come to talk directly about environmental rights—in other words a right to have the environment itself protected? Should we transcend the anthropocentric in favour of the eco-centric?[54]

Some would argue that the 'eco-centric' approach is the only proper way to consider environmental rights.[55]

A further unresolved issue is the classification of such a putative environmental human right. Such a right is 'understood to represent aspects of a first generation, a second generation right, or to represent a mix thereof' and this indeterminacy is based upon the ambiguity of the content of the right.[56] Whilst some have argued that to classify the right to a clean environment in the group of social, economic, and cultural rights would give it a normative quality,[57] in general the right has been categorized as a so-called 'third generation' human right.[58] Third generation rights are said to include the rights to development, peace, and co-ownership of the common heritage of mankind and are primarily viewed as being collective in nature with regard to both their object and subject. Human rights experts consider them immensely vague[59] and it has been argued that they are so vast they encompass anything and anybody.[60] Therefore, some have argued that a generic environmental human right 'would scarcely be a "human" right in an orthodox sense'.[61]

As indicated by the serious criticism and doubts presented here, it is clear that substantive environmental human rights are not a straightforward means to remedy environmental

---

[51] Handl in Eide, Krause, and Rosas, n 45.   [52] Handl in Eide, Krause, and Rosas, n 45.
[53] Boyle, 'The Role of Human Rights in the Protection of the Environment' in Boyle and Anderson, n 24, 43 and 51–3; Handl in Cançado Trinidade, n 45, 138. See also, Redgwell, 'Life, Universe and Everything: A Critique of Anthropocentric Rights' in Boyle and Anderson, n 24, 71.   [54] Boyle, n 15, 473.
[55] Rodriguez-Rivera, 'Is the Human Right to Environment Recognised under International Law? It Depends on the Source' (2001) 12 *Colo J Intl Envm L & Policy* 1, 11–12.
[56] Handl in Eide, Kraus, and Rosas, n 45, 313.
[57] Merrills, 'Environmental Protection and Human Rights: Conceptual Aspects' in Boyle and Anderson, n 24, 25.
[58] Alston, 'A Third Generation of Solidarity Rights: Progressive Development or Obfuscation of International Human Rights' (1982) 29 *Netherlands ILR* 307, 309; Vasak, 'For the Third Generation of Human Rights: The Right of Solidarity', Inaugural Lecture to the 10th Study Session of the International Institute of Human Rights, Strasbourg (2–27 July 1979).
[59] Boyle, n 53, 46.   [60] Alston, n 58, 317.   [61] Boyle, n 53, 48.

degradation. In Section 3 we will examine another approach to dealing with the problem of environmental degradation: procedural environmental rights.

3 PROCEDURAL ENVIRONMENTAL RIGHTS

The definition of procedural environmental rights is included in Principle 10 Rio Declaration 1992:

> Environmental issues are best handled with participation of all concerned citizens, at the relevant level. At the national level, each individual shall have appropriate access to information concerning the environment that is held by public authorities, including information on hazardous materials and activities in their communities, and the opportunity to participate in decision-making processes. States shall facilitate and encourage public awareness and participation by making information widely available. Effective access to judicial and administrative proceedings, including redress and remedy, shall be provided.

Procedural rights are based on three pillars: a right to information, a right to participate, and a right to access to justice. They can be 'understood as a refinement of established political or civil human rights or as novel human rights'.[62] They are an expression of democracy, where democracy concerns 'the role of people in governance'.[63] Although it may be premature to claim that such rights are binding on states as part of customary international law, it appears that there has been a gradual expansion of the participation of civil society in environmental matters.[64] Procedural environmental rights are of fundamental importance in the protection of the environment as they bestow on individuals and civil society rights that can be used, through various ways, to influence, shape, and evaluate state activities which may have an adverse impact on the environment. Through the participation of civil society, a degree of transparency in environmental matters can be achieved.

Procedural environmental rights have been realized in a number of ways. There is the Convention on Access to Information, Public Participation in Decision-making and Access to Justice in Environmental Matters (Aarhus Convention), which develops the three pillars of a procedural environmental right: the right to information, the right to participation in environmental decision-making, and the right to access to justice (discussed in Section 3.1). There is also the 1993 North American Agreement on Environmental Cooperation, which is a side agreement to the North American Free Trade Agreement between Canada, Mexico, and the US. This agreement obliges states parties to grant public access to certain information concerning environmental matters. The 2003 African Convention on the Conservation of Nature includes provisions on participatory and procedural rights in environmental matters and provides for dissemination of environmental information and access to such information.[65] In addition, environmental impact assessment (EIA)

---

[62] Handl in Eide, Krause, and Rosas, n 45, 318.

[63] Franck, *Fairness in International Law and Institutions* (OUP, 1995) 83.

[64] International Law Association, 'Final Report on the Status of the Universal Declaration of Human Rights in National and International Law' (1994) 546, 548. See Fitzmaurice, 'Some Reflections on Public Participation in Environmental Matters' (2002) 2 *NSA & IL* 1.

[65] In depth on this subject see, Jonas Ebbesson, Draft Paper on: Partcipatory and Procedural Rights in Environmental Matters: State of Play, High Level Expert Meeting of the New Future of Human Rights and the Environment: Moving the Global Agenda Forward, Co-organised by UNEP and OHCHR (2009), available at: <http://www.unep.org/environmentalgovernance/Portals/8/documents/Paper%20participatory%20 procedural%20rights.pdf>.

procedures have been developed and the European Court of Human Rights and African Commission on Human and Peoples' Rights have found violations of an indirect procedural environmental right.

3.1 THE AARHUS CONVENTION

The Aarhus Convention was drafted within the UN Economic Commission for Europe (UNECE).[66] Any UN member state can accede to the Convention; at the time of writing there are 46 states parties. The Convention links the substantive right to a clean environment with a procedural one, guaranteeing all three limbs of the right: the right to information, the right to participate in environmental decision-making, and the right to access to justice. The preamble of the Convention states that everyone has the 'the right to live in an environment adequate to his or her health and well-being', and the Convention recognizes that this can only be realized with the broad participation of civil society acting in the public interest.[67]

3.1.1 Right to information

The Aarhus Convention provides a very broad definition of environmental information. The general public is entitled, without proving a special interest, to access to information regarding the state of the environment, public health, and other factors impacting on the environment. This right is to be realized by both public authorities and private entities that exercise public responsibility in the field of conservation. Article 4 grants the right to request and obtain information and Article 5 imposes an obligation on states to collect and disseminate it. However, Article 5(3) Aarhus Convention limits the right to information by according states a much-criticized discretion to refuse to disseminate information if it is not available in electronic form. The right to information has been implemented extensively by states parties to the Aarhus Convention.

In 2003 a Protocol to the Aarhus Convention on Pollutant Release and Transfer Registers was adopted. The Protocol obliges states parties to establish and maintain a publicly accessible electronic national pollutant release and transfer register and sets out the minimum requirements for these registers. States parties must ensure that there are no impediments to access, such as reasons for access being required. The UNECE has required information to be disseminated in a number of other environmental situations. For example, the 1992 Convention on the Protection and Use of Transboundary Watercourses and International Lakes contains provisions regarding access to information, whilst the 1999 Protocol to this Convention on Water and Health confirmed the need for access to information and public participation in decision-making concerning water and health, and obliged states to ensure that certain information is made available to the public within a reasonable time, with refusal to disclose only being accepted on certain grounds. Similarly, the 1991 Convention on Transboundary Effects of Industrial Activities (Industrial Accident Convention) requires states to ensure that adequate information is given to the public in areas capable of being affected by an industrial accident arising out of a hazardous activity.

---

[66] The UNECE was set up as one of the five regional commissions of the UN in 1947 by the Economic and Social Council. For more information on the UNECE, see: <http://www.unece.org>.

[67] For a good outline of the Aarhus Convention, see Redgwell, 'Access to Environmental Justice' in Francioni (ed), *Access to Justice as a Human Right* (OUP, 2007) 153.

3.1.2 Right to participate in environmental decision-making

Article 6 Aarhus Convention provides a very far-reaching participatory right in environmental decision-making, with a focus on certain industries, such as the energy sector, production of metals, mineral extraction, chemical processing, and waste management. Public participation during the preparation of plans and programmes relating to the environment is provided for in Article 7, while Article 8 provides that states 'shall strive to promote effective participation at an appropriate stage, and while options are still open, during the preparation by public authorities of executive regulations and other generally applicable rules that may have a significant effect on the environment'. However, it has been noted that this second pillar of public participation has not been implemented as extensively as the right to information.

The adoption of the 2003 Kiev Protocol on Strategic Environmental Assessment was an attempt to further develop Articles 7 and 8 Aarhus Convention. However, the Protocol does not address public participation generally,[68] but only information and public participation within the context of an EIA. EIAs traditionally involve the procedural rights of information and public participation in relation to certain activities which would impact on the environment. They have their roots in the USA where they were first used in 1968. Historically, they were seen as part and parcel of environmental law and not treated as part of a procedural human right. Even in 1991, the Espoo Convention on Environmental Impact Assessment in a Transboundary Context, another UNECE initiative, treated the EIA as a tool of environmental law and requires states parties to disseminate EIA documentation to the public for comment and to take these comments into account when making final decisions. However, since then the rights realized by EIAs have begun to be viewed as part of a procedural human right, not purely an environmental procedure.

3.1.3 Access to justice

Article 9 Aarhus Convention grants the right of access to national courts to challenge decisions relating to the provision of information and public participation. Such a right is based on the assumptions of wide participation of civil society in environmental affairs and a balancing of interests between the government and society. This right has found its expression, and is already well established, in civil and political rights.[69] Access to justice, as defined by the Aarhus Convention, is a means of correcting erroneous administrative decisions on environmental issues by a court or another independent and impartial body established by law.[70] The right to access to justice may be triggered (1) by any person if her or his request for environmental information has been ignored, refused, or not dealt with in accordance with the Convention (Article 9(1)), or (2) by any member of the public who has a sufficient interest or maintains impairment of a right (Article 9(2)).

Article 9(2) provides that what constitutes 'a person with a sufficient interest' and the 'impairment of a right' is to be determined in accordance with the requirements of national law, bearing in mind the objective of giving broad access to justice. Standing should be granted to NGOs and they are to be considered in national law as persons with 'a sufficient interest'. Thus, public interest litigation in access to environmental justice is of particular

---

[68] Kravchenko and Bonine, n 1, 285.
[69] Franck, n 63, 98, states that the conception of democratic entitlement may be dated from the General Assembly's adoption of the UDHR. See also Ebbesson, 'The Notion of Public Participation in International Environmental Law' (1997) 8 *YIEnvmL* 62.
[70] Aarhus Convention, Art 9(3).

importance. Certain jurisdictions allow *actio popularis* to be used in civil claims, such as those concerning consumer and environmental protection, whilst in some jurisdictions the existence of the right to life in national constitutions is interpreted as granting standing in *actio popularis* proceedings.[71] However, it is worth noting that in some states there has been a movement backwards to the traditional practice of standing based on interest.[72] Thus, this pillar of the Aarhus Convention is still not fully implemented. Considering how national laws stand at present, such a state of affairs, at least in some states, will continue for a considerable period of time.

3.1.4 The Aarhus Compliance Committee

A Compliance Committee, a quasi-judicial body, further strengthens the procedural right of access to environmental justice within the context of the Aarhus Convention. It consists of independent experts who decide on alleged breaches by states parties of provisions of the Convention. There is a requirement that national remedies have been exhausted before the Committee can examine complaints. The unique feature of this compliance mechanism, which sets it apart from similar mechanisms set up under environmental agreements, is that environmental NGOs can bring complaints of alleged violations of the Aarhus Convention to the attention of the Committee.[73] However, the decisions of the Compliance Committee are not binding, and so the effectiveness of this procedure is rather weak. Nevertheless, the public nature of these proceedings can put considerable pressure on a state that is not in compliance.

An example encompassing all relevant characteristics of this system is a case concerning Turkmenistan, which was initiated by a Moldovan NGO on behalf of the population of Turkmenistan. The communication alleged that Turkmenistan's new Law on Public Association was in breach of the Aarhus Convention provisions relating to recognition and support of environmental NGOs, and non-discrimination as to citizenship, nationality, and domicile of the members of the public.[74] The communication observed several restrictions that the law of Turkmenistan imposed on freedom of public association and noted the possibility for a public association to be liquidated by a court decision with no right of appeal. It was further alleged that the legislation provided the basis for the Ministry of Justice to abolish the majority of environmental NGOs in Turkmenistan, leaving only the NGO led by the Turkmen Deputy Prime Minister. The Compliance Committee made a preliminary decision on admissibility and the communication was forwarded to Turkmenistan for a reply. No response was received.

The Compliance Committee adopted a decision that Turkmenistan was in breach of certain provisions of the Aarhus Convention. It also found that Turkmenistan had failed to comply with the general requirements of establishing a clear, transparent, and consistent legal framework to implement the Aarhus Convention. It adopted a set of recommendations, which were submitted to the Meeting of the Parties of the Aarhus Convention.

---

[71] *Drustva Ecology Slovenje*, Case No U-I-30/95. See Bruch and King, 'Constitutional Procedural Rights: Enhancing Civil Society's Role in Good Governance' in Bruch (ed), *The New 'Public': Globalisation of Public Participation* (Environmental Law Institute, 2002) 36.

[72] Eg Verschuuren, 'The Role of the Judiciary in the Environmental Governance in the Netherlands' in Kotze and Paterson (eds), *The Role of the Judiciary in Environmental Governance: Comparative Perspectives* (Kluwer Law International, 2009); Tolsma, de Graaf, and Jans, 'The Rise and Fall of Access to Justice in the Netherlands' (2009) 21 *JEnvmL* 315.

[73] Fitzmaurice, 'Environmental Justice through International Compliant Procedures? Comparing the Aarhus Convention and the North American Agreement on Environmental Matters' in Ebbeson and Okowa (eds), *Environmental Law and Justice in Context* (CUP, 2009) 211.

[74] Aarhus Convention, Arts 3(4) and 3(9).

These included amending the Act on Public Associations with a view to bringing all its provisions into compliance with the Convention, immediately taking appropriate interim measures to ensure compliance with the Convention, carrying out these measures with the involvement of civil society, and submitting a report to the Compliance Committee on the measures taken to implement the recommendations. The proceedings, which were open and involved all parties concerned, related, inter alia, to the development of the awareness of the public as to the use of the rights granted by the Convention, which include inquiries about the progress made. Turkmenistan was also granted the possibility to address the Compliance Committee for assistance. This case clearly indicates the constitutive elements of justice: very strong—if not crucial—participation of NGOs, transparency for all parties involved, and openness and fairness.

3.2 INDIRECT PROCEDURAL ENVIRONMENTAL RIGHTS

The practice of the European Court of Human Rights in relation to procedural environmental rights is based on an interpretation of Articles 8 and 10 ECHR. Recent developments of the jurisprudence of the Court indicate that the content of these rights is similar in scope to the rights granted by the Aarhus Convention. The right to receive information has been interpreted by the Court in several cases: *Guerra and others v Italy*,[75] *Taskin v Turkey*,[76] *Tatar v Romania*,[77] *Öneryıldız v Turkey*, and *Budayeva v Russia*. In each of these cases the European Court stressed the essential duty of a state to provide environmental information, broadly understood, concerning environmental hazards, as well as environmental procedures, which are necessary to initiate and conduct projects such as EIAs. In *Guerra* the Court was of the view that providing relevant information to the applicants, all of whom lived in the vicinity of the factory, could have a bearing on their private and family life and physical integrity protected under Article 8 ECHR. Furthermore, the Court reiterated that Article 10 ECHR 'basically prohibits a government from restricting a person from receiving information that others wish or may be willing to impart to him.'[78] However, that freedom was interpreted restrictively and cannot be construed as imposing on a state, in circumstances such as those in *Guerra*, a positive obligation to collect and disseminate information of its own motion.

In *Taskin*, the European Court took the view that 'whilst Article 8 contains no explicit procedural requirements, the decision-making process leading to measures of interference must be fair and such as to afford due respect to the interests of the individual as safeguarded by Article 8.'[79] As such the participation of those affected by environmental issues in the decision-making process will be essential for compliance with Article 8 ECHR, as well as Article 6 Aarhus Convention.[80] In *Tatar*, the Court explicitly referred to the rights of information and participation guaranteed by the Aarhus Convention. The Court stated that these were breached by prohibiting interested persons from obtaining information and participating in environmental decision-making. However, this right of participation in decision-making is only available to persons whose Convention rights have been affected and not to everyone. The European Court also alluded to EIAs as a necessary requirement to evaluate the effect of a proposed activity on the environment and the rights of the individual.

There is no express procedural environmental right under the African Charter. However, in the *Ogoniland* case, the African Commission on Human and Peoples'

---

[75] (1998) 26 EHRR 357.   [76] (2006) 42 EHRR 50.
[77] App no 67021/01, Judgment of 27 January 2009.
[78] n 75, para 41.   [79] n 76, para 118.   [80] Boyle, n 15, 496.

Rights drew such a right from Article 24 ACHPR, which grants a substantive environmental right. The Commission gave the substantive right a meaningful content by supporting the rights of the public to information and participation in environmental matters.[81] In particular, it decided that states should follow certain environmental procedures such as EIAs, involve the public in a manner that encompasses the three limbs of the procedural environmental right, and monitor potentially harmful activities. According to Shelton, such a comprehensive approach should become a blueprint 'for merging environmental protection, economic development, and guarantees of human rights'.[82]

4 CONCLUSION

This chapter has analysed the challenges posed by environmental degradation to the realization of human rights. Substantive and procedural environmental human rights were explored as possible solutions to the problem of environmental degradation. It is clear that the human rights approach to environmental degradation faces many challenges. The normative content of a substantive environmental human right is not well defined and its global acceptance is doubtful. Environmental rights can be derived from other existing human rights. Such an approach, however, as developed by the European Court of Human Rights, has been limited to cases of direct harm to individual interests and states are given a wide margin of appreciation.

The way forward, it appears, lies in reliance on procedural environmental human rights, which are not nearly as controversial as the substantive right and widely accepted and implemented. A cross-fertilization of ideas between various human rights systems might mean that the approach to environmental information and participation, as professed by the European Court of Human Rights in *Taskin*, may acquire global acceptance.[83] Similarly, the very broadly conceived participatory rights in the Aarhus Convention may gain worldwide acceptance,[84] especially as they impose on states parties a duty to spread the ideas therein at international fora. Application of procedural rights is steadily growing, even in institutions traditionally criticized for their inadequate respect for the environment and human rights, such as multilateral development banks. The use of a participatory right, however, is not devoid of challenges, as procedural rights alone are not sufficient to counterbalance a presumption in favour of development and economic interests.[85]

Generally, it appears that within the domestic context, environmental procedural rights have the potential for successful implementation in practice, as they can be enforced by NGOs and individuals, and may be used to influence the shaping of domestic policy. Public law litigation may help to overcome the intrinsic anthropocentricity of environmental rights, 'to the extent that rights can be exercised on behalf of the environment or of its non-human components, and not solely for human benefit'.[86]

---

[81] Shelton, n 8, 939.   [82] Shelton, n 8, 942.   [83] Boyle, n 15, 504–5.

[84] The Aarhus Convention does not exclude participation of non-UNECE states as parties. The amendment to the Espoo Convention also provides for such a possibility.

[85] Hayward, *Constitutional Environmental Rights* (OUP, 2005) 180.

[86] Birnie, Boyle, and Redgwell, *International Law and the Environment* (OUP, 2009) 298.

FURTHER READING

ANTON and SHELTON, *Environmental Protection and Human Rights* (Cambridge University Press, 2011).

BOYLE, 'Human Rights or Environmental Rights? A Reassessment' (2007) 18 *Fordham Envm LR* 471.

BOYLE, 'Human Rights and the Environment: Where Next?' (2012) 23 *EJIL* 613.

BOYLE and ANDERSON (eds), *Human Rights Approaches to Environmental Protection* (Oxford University Press, 1996).

FITZMAURICE, 'Some Reflections on Public Participation in Environmental Matters as a Human Right in International Law' (2002) 2 *NSA & IL* 1.

FITZMAURICE and MARSHALL, 'The Human Right to a Clean Environment—Phantom or Reality? The European Court of Human Rights and English Courts Perspective on balancing Rights in Environmental Cases' (2007) 76 *Nordic JIL* 103.

FRANCIONI, 'International Human Rights in an Environmental Horizon' (2010) 21 *EJIL* 41.

HANDL, 'Human Rights and Protection of the Environment' in Eide, Krause, and Rosas (eds), *Economic, Social and Cultural Rights* (Kluwer Law International, 2001) 303.

KNOX, 'Climate Change and Human Rights Law' (2009) 50 *Virginia JIL* 163.

MOGERA, 'An Update on the Aarhus Convention and its Continued Global Relevance' (2005) 14 *Rev EC & I Envm L* 138.

OHCHR, Report on the relationship between climate change and human rights, A/HRC/10/61 (15 January 2001).

PALLEMAERTS, 'A Human Rights Perspective on Current Environmental Issues and their Management: Evolving International Legal and Political Discourse of Human Environment, the Individual and the State' (2008) 2 *HR & IL Discourse* 149.

PEDERSEN, 'European Environmental Human Rights and Environmental Rights: A Long Time Coming?' (2008) 21 *Georgetown I Envm LR* 1.

PALMER and ROBB (eds), *International Environmental Law Reports, Vol 3: Human Rights and Environment* (Cambridge University Press, 2001).

SAN JOSÉ, *Environmental Protection and the European Convention on Human Rights* (Council of Europe, 2005).

SHELTON, 'Human Rights, Environmental Rights and the Right to the Environment' (1991) 28 *Stanford JIL* 103.

SHELTON, *Human Rights and the Environment* (Edward Elgar Publishing, 2011).

SHELTON, 'Human Rights and the Environment: What Specific Environmental Rights Have Been Recognized?' (2006) 35 *Denver JIL & P* 129.

STEC, '"Aarhus Environmental Rights" in Eastern Europe' (2005) 5 *YB E Envm L* 1.

TURNER, *A Substantive Environmental Right: An Examination of the Legal Obligations of Decision-Makers Towards the Environment* (Kluwer Law International, 2009).

USEFUL WEBSITES

OHCHR, Human Rights and Climate Change: <http://www.ohchr.org/EN/Issues/HRAndClimateChange/Pages/HRClimateChangeIndex.aspx>

OHCHR, Human Rights and the Environment: <http://www2.ohchr.org/english/issues/environment/environ/index.htm>

OHCHR, Independent Expert on Human Rights and the Environment: <http://www.ohchr.org/EN/Issues/Environment/IEEnvironment/Pages/IEenvironmentIndex.aspx>

UNECE, Aarhus Convention: <http://www.unece.org/env/pp/welcome.html>

INDEX

Introductory Note

References such as '178–9' indicate (not necessarily continuous) discussion of a topic across a range of pages. Wherever possible in the case of topics with many references, these have either been divided into sub-topics or only the most significant discussions of the topic are listed. Because the entire work is about 'human rights', the use of this term (and certain others which occur constantly throughout the book) as an entry point has been restricted. Information will be found under the corresponding detailed topics.

Aarhus Compliance
    Committee 606
Aarhus Convention on Access
    to Information, Public
    Participation in
    Decision-making and Access
    to Justice in Environmental
    Matters 590, 603–8
    Protocol on Pollutant Release
    and Transfer Registers 604
aboriginal peoples 345
abortion 121, 325
absolute rights 110, 345
access to justice 274, 603–5, 608
accountability 113, 130, 138,
    534, 541, 580–3, 585–6
    corporate 541
    mutual 582, 585
ACHPR, see African Charter on
    Human and Peoples' Rights
    (ACHPR)
ACHR, see American
    Convention on Human
    Rights (ACHR)
actio popularis 117, 382, 401,
    606
adequate food 103, 152, 196,
    199–202, 207, 209, 591
adequate housing 149, 152,
    203–4, 209–10, 305, 459, 591
adequate standard of
    living 195–215
    children 207
    climate change 591
    definition 195–6
    duties of individual 197
    equality 199
    food, see right to food
    freedom from want 196
    health, see right to health
    housing, see right to housing
    human dignity 196
    indigenous peoples 208–9
    international action 213–15
    national strategies 202, 207

normative content 199–206
obligations 199
poverty 567; see also poverty
progressive
    implementation 212–13
relationship with other
    human rights 210–12
social security, see right to
    social security
state obligations 198
water, see right to water
women 207; see also women's
    rights
administration of justice
    due process 259
    fair trial, see fair trial
    freedom from arbitrary
        detention, see freedom
        from arbitrary detention
    freedom from enforced
        disappearance, see
        enforced disappearance
    right to liberty 259, 269
    security of the person 259;
        see also security of the
        person
advisory jurisdiction 398, 411,
    454
affirmative action 170–1
Africa 3, 117, 339, 441–57, 511,
    568–70, 575–7
    African Union, see African
        Union (AU)
    human rights
        protection 441–3, 456
    Millennium Development
        Goals (MDGs) 581;
    see also Millennium
        Development Goals
        (MDGs)
    poverty 442; see also poverty
    sub-regional
        organizations 441, 444
African Charter on Human
    and Peoples' Rights

(ACHPR) 161–3, 174–6,
    187–90, 278–80, 282–3,
    336–7, 442–52
    adoption 443
    civil and political rights 444
    duties 446
    economic, social and cultural
        rights 444–5
    environment, right to 446,
        590, 601, 603
    equality 161, 164, 166
    fair trial 444
    interpretation 445
    jurisdiction 132
    prohibition on forced
        labour 444
    prohibition on torture and
        ill-treatment 174, 176
    scope of rights 184, 200, 205,
        240, 251, 336, 444–5
    self-determination 336
    territorial scope 132
    Women's Protocol 447
African Charter on the
    Rights and Welfare of the
    Child
    Committee on Rights and
        Welfare of the Child 447
    protections 447
African Commission on
    Human and Peoples'
    Rights 125, 166, 189–90, 200,
    203, 445–56, 592–3
    complaints procedure 448–9
    function 441, 443
    interaction with African
        Union bodies 452
    non-governmental
        organizations (NGOs) 451
    on-site visits 450–1
    resolutions 451
    state reports 449–50
    structure 448
    working groups 450
African Court of Justice 453–4

African Court on Human and Peoples' Rights 443, 452–4
African Peer Review Mechanism (APRM) 443, 455–6
African Union (AU) 441–3, 514
  African Charter on Human and Peoples' Rights (ACHPR), *see* **African Charter on Human and Peoples' Rights (ACHPR)**
  African Charter on the Rights and Welfare of the Child, *see* **African Charter on the Rights and Welfare of the Child**
  African Commission on Human and Peoples' Rights, *see* **African Commission on Human and People's Rights**
  Assembly 447–8, 452–4
  Economic, Social and Cultural Council (ECOSOCC) 454
  history 441–3, 453
  Pan-African Parliament (PAP) 443, 454, 456
  refugees 447
aggression 29, 147, 497–8, 506–9
  crime of 82, 497
aid effectiveness 584–5
AIDS 153, 210, 349, 447, 452
alien subjugation, domination and exploitation 338, 340–1
Alien Tort Claims Act 536, 543
American Convention on Human Rights (ACHR) 113–15, 132–3, 161–3, 188–91, 265–7, 276–83, 398–413
  adoption 400
  denunciation 114
  equality 161
  fair trial 278–80, 282
  freedom of assembly 234
  individual petitions 401–2
  integrity of the person 175
  jurisdiction 131–2
  member states 400
  national implementation 400–1, 462
  prohibition on torture and ill-treatment 174, 176
  Protocol to Abolish the Death Penalty 400
  San Salvador Protocol, 295, 435, 624, 593, 601

scope of rights 184, 241, 400
territorial scope 132
American Declaration on the Rights and Duties of Man
  equality 161
  scope of rights 399
Americas 62, 251, 261, 266, 398–413, 444
amnesties 510–11
Amnesty International 83, 175, 253, 408, 533, 542, 557–8
anti-poverty agendas 578, 587–8
anti-Semitism 230
apartheid 3, 78, 81, 442–3, 502, 511, 573
APRM, *see* **African Peer Review Mechanism (APRM)**
Arab Charter on Human Rights 161, 219, 225, 231, 241, 251, 260
Arab Spring 227, 236
arbitrariness 235, 263, 278, 432
arbitrary deprivation 85, 184, 186, 188, 489–90
  assisted suicide 186
  beginning of life 186
  components 186–91
  death penalty 184, 187–91, 193; *see also* **death penalty**
  end of life 186
  environmental concerns 591, 596, 598, 600
  euthanasia 186
  extrajudicial killings 186–7, 191, 193
  law enforcement measures 186–7, 191–3
  legal status 184, 186
  limitations 111
  obligations 191
  relationship with other human rights 192
  sources 184
  Special Rapporteur on Extrajudicial Killings 184
  UN Basic Principles on the Use of Force and Firearms 186–7
arbitrary detention, *see* **freedom from arbitrary detention**
arbitrary executions 93, 149, 184, 188, 451, 487, 545–6
Argentina 121, 132–3, 268, 404, 460, 462–3, 487
Aristotle 158
armed conflicts 85–7, 392, 479–90, 492–5, 505–6, 544–5, 553–4

belligerent occupation 480
belligerent reprisals 486
dictates of humanity 479–80
difficulties with application of human rights law to 492–5
human rights 479–80, 487–93
internal/non-international armed conflicts 480, 484, 488, 534, 543
international armed conflicts 479, 493
methods of combat 479–80
reasons for application of human rights law 483–7
armed forces 80, 234, 409, 448, 484, 505, 548
armed groups 480, 482–4, 491, 493, 544–8
  organized 483–4; *see also* **armed opposition groups**
armed non-state actors 544–8
armed opposition groups 532, 535, 543–8
  engagement 548
  human rights obligations 532, 543–4
  international human rights law 491, 493, 543
  international humanitarian law 479, 483, 544
  legitimacy 532, 544
  monitoring 544, 546
arrest 130, 186–7, 261, 263–5, 268–9, 492, 501
art 226, 288, 290, 295, 430
artificial entities 122–3
artistic freedom 292, 295–6
artistic productions 210, 287, 297, 299–300
ASEAN Human Rights Declaration 161, 219, 225, 234
assets 197, 202, 326, 393, 443, 518, 563
asylum 263, 313, 435, 515, 517, 521, 524
asylum-seekers 263, 516–17, 519, 521–3
atrocities 67, 69, 180, 511
AU, *see* **African Union**
Australia 30, 120, 122–3, 263–4, 470–1, 525, 575–6
Austria 92, 124, 168–9, 229, 309–12, 325, 327
authors 18, 29, 36–7, 46, 51, 296–301, 313–14
autonomy 6, 35, 37, 44–5, 342, 348–9, 351–2

available resources 92, 144, 204, 239, 293, 297, 467

Badinter Committee 343–4, 346, 349, 351
bail 267, 599
balance 50, 121, 218, 230, 300, 365, 479–80
  fair 168, 224, 597
Bangalore Principles on the Domestic Application of International Human Rights Norms 464
Belarus 122, 125, 190, 233, 236, 367, 424
Belgium 21, 100–1, 130, 166–7, 240, 517, 563
Bentham, Jeremy 21, 55–8, 60, 70
Bill of Rights Act 1990 (New Zealand) 467
bills of rights 17, 20–3, 30, 442, 467–8
birth 21, 121, 161–5, 199, 209, 253, 499–500
blasphemy 230–1
bonded labour 11, 197, 247, 253
Bosnia-Herzegovina 78, 81, 116, 342, 344, 351, 501
boycotts 232, 344, 541
Bulgaria 26, 87, 92, 112, 222, 264–6, 325
burka 223
Burke, Edmund 20–1
Burkina Faso 269, 346–7, 453, 536

Cambodia 367, 390
Cameroon 182, 264, 341, 390, 445–6
Canada 121–3, 189–90, 221–2, 334, 342, 345, 470
  Charter of Rights and Freedoms 467
capacity building 6, 362, 366, 375, 389
capital punishment, see death penalty
Cartagena Declaration on Refugees 514–15
categories of human rights 143–55
  civil and political rights 144–5
  composite rights 155
  economic, social and cultural rights 144–5, 148, 155
  freedom rights 145
  new human rights 154
  one-dimensional rights 147, 155

rights of collectivities 145–7, 155
  rights of individuals 98, 100, 120–2, 145–6, 155
  welfare rights 145
CEDAW, see Convention on the Elimination of All Forms of Discrimination Against Women (CEDAW)
censorship 218, 227, 291, 295
Central African Republic 509, 540
central banks 573
  view on poverty and human rights 575–7
CERD, see Committee on the Elimination of Racial Discrimination (CERD)
Charter of Fundamental Rights of the European Union 161, 219, 251, 260, 291, 437, 437–8
  citizenship rights 438
  compliance 438
  equality 161
  scope of rights 251
Chechnya 484, 492
chemical weapons 481
children 152–3, 196–7, 207–8, 308–10, 377–8, 380–1, 462–3
  adequate standard of living 207; see also adequate standard of living
  adoption 309
  child labour 240, 250–2, 254–7, 573
  child marriages 327, 447
  child mortality 206, 208, 581
  child pornography 78, 304, 377
  child prostitution 304
  child soldiers 447, 520, 544–5, 547
  Convention on the Rights of the Child (CRC), see Convention on the Rights of the Child (CRC)
  custody 277, 309
  fair trial 283
  healthcare 206–7
  killing or maiming 544–5
  unborn children 121
Chile 30, 93, 104, 225, 298, 305, 408
China 30, 187, 253, 327, 520, 569–70, 575–7
citizenship 438, 525, 606
civil and political rights; see also International Covenant on Civil and Political Rights (ICCPR)

African Charter on Human and Peoples' Rights (ACHPR) 444
American Convention on Human Rights (ACHR) 401
categorization 143–4, 148, 155
constitutional protections 466
European Convention on Human Rights (ECHR) 422–3
civil society 4–6, 60–1, 360, 364, 379, 386, 389
  organizations 202, 364, 372, 454, 585
civilian populations 151, 176, 180, 185, 479, 481, 501–4
civilians
  armed conflicts 480, 482, 486
  military trials, involving 275–6, 559
  protection 373, 393, 480, 492
  war crimes 506, 536
CJEU, see Court of Justice of the European Union (CJEU)
clean environment 335, 595–6, 601–2, 604
clean water 208–9, 337
climate change 5, 582, 591, 595
Cold War 62, 417–18, 421, 508
collectivities, rights of 143, 145–7
Colombia 102, 180, 187, 192, 404, 410–11, 492–3
colonial boundaries 346–7
colonial powers 339–40, 342, 347
colonial territories 338–41, 345–6, 354
colonialism 62, 68, 338, 340, 442–3, 573
combatants 9, 480, 482, 492, 506
Commission on Human Rights (UN) 89–90, 93, 132, 204, 214, 325, 360–1
Committee against Torture 175–179, 310, 330, 380–3, 561
Committee on Economic, Social and Cultural Rights 591–2
Committee on the Elimination of Discrimination against Women 323, 326, 328, 380–1
Committee on the Elimination of Racial Discrimination (CERD) 92, 153, 167, 170, 329, 377–9, 382

Committee on the Rights of
Persons with Disabilities 380
common law 23, 111, 263,
458–9, 464–5, 468–9
communism 61, 418
compensation 10, 266, 282, 384,
408, 423, 433–4
competence 27, 80–1, 88, 251,
380–1, 402–3, 487
complaints procedures 90, 214,
241, 370–2, 380–1, 384, 387
collective 418
individual 385, 449, 517
compulsory education 240,
244–5, 466
primary 145, 239, 243–4
compulsory labour 253–5
Conference on Security and
Cooperation in Europe
(CSCE) 246, 417
confessions 178, 181, 192, 279,
491
conscience 3, 114, 150, 196,
217–21, 223–5, 401
conscientious objection 220, 224
consent 17–19, 77, 79–80,
99–100, 108–9, 309, 381
consequentialist theories 42,
58
consistency 83, 87–8, 158–60, 387
constitutional guarantees of
human rights 105, 459, 462,
465–7, 470
constitutional rights 345, 418,
435, 439, 465–6, 538, 600
constitutionality 470–1
constitutions 19–20, 22–3, 214,
462, 464–7, 471–2, 600
consular assistance 189, 411
contempt of court 186, 263
contextualization 48–9
contractual obligations 114,
150, 262, 489
Convention concerning the
Protection of the World
Cultural and Natural
Heritage 291–2
Convention for the Protection
of Cultural Property in the
Event of Armed Conflict 291
Convention for the
Safeguarding of Intangible
Cultural Heritage 292
Convention on the
Elimination of All Forms
of Discrimination Against
Women (CEDAW) 80–1,
92, 105, 124, 170–2, 317–18,
322–8; see also women's
rights

adoption 316–17, 322
adoption Committee 80, 92,
170, 308, 318, 323–8, 447
discrimination 322–3
equal pay 323
reservations 105, 317
substantive protections 78,
160, 171, 205, 239,
321, 380
Convention on the Prevention,
Punishment and Eradication
of Violence Against Women
(CPPEVAW) 93, 326–7, 400
Convention on the Prevention
and Punishment of the
Crime of Genocide 99; see
also genocide
Convention on the Protection
and Promotion of the
Diversity of Cultural
Expressions 292
Convention on the Protection
of the Underwater Cultural
Heritage 292
Convention on the Rights of
Persons with Disabilities
(CRPD) 77–8, 160,
163, 250, 260,
270–1, 377
Convention on the Rights of
the Child (CRC) 160–3, 196,
207–8, 240, 447, 462–3, 483
equality 160
fair trial 271, 283
right to education 240
right to work 250
sexual orientation 307
conversion 221–2
core obligations 7, 151, 155,
248, 256, 293, 300
core rights 59, 143, 150–2,
155, 174
corporal punishment 182, 187,
192, 240
corporate accountability 541
corporate complicity 534, 543
corporate social
responsibility 541–3
corporations
analogy to state 532
corporate responsibility
541–2
globalization 571
human rights entitlement 122
human rights
obligations 544
transnational 135, 367, 369,
542, 549, 572
Costa Rica 158, 403–4, 406,
411–12, 462, 587

Côte d'Ivoire 365–7, 509, 545
Council of Europe 92–3, 130–1,
210, 228, 291–2, 416–22, 434–9
creation 417–18
European Convention for the
Prevention of Torture and
Inhuman or Degrading
Treatment or Punishment
(ECPT) 418, 420–1
European Convention on
Human Rights (ECHR), see
European Convention on
Human Rights (ECHR)
European Framework
Convention for the
Protection of National
Minorities 417, 421
European Social Charter, see
European Social Charter
functions 417
institutions 418–19
Counter-Terrorism Committee
(CTC) 393, 550, 562
counter-terrorism
measures 550–1, 553,
556–7, 559–61, 565; see also
terrorism
applicability of human rights
law 553–4
Counter-Terrorism Committee
(CTC) 550, 562
derogation 554; see also
derogation
detention 558–60
economic, social, and cultural
rights 561–2
emergency 554
extra 554
fair trial 558
non-discrimination 560–1
profiling 560–1
terrorist listing 562–5
torture 176, 557–8
Court of Justice of the
European Union
(CJEU) 435–8, 564
CPPEVAW, see Convention on
the Prevention, Punishment
and Eradication of Violence
Against Women (CPPEVAW)
CRC, see Convention on the
Rights of the Child (CRC)
Crimea 342
crimes against humanity 28–9,
151, 176, 180, 497–8, 500–5,
508–9
definition 147, 151, 175–6,
179–80, 185, 499, 504
prosecution 28–9, 151, 497,
501

criminal law 111, 150, 461, 511, 556, 558, 599
criminal offences 111, 230, 259, 266, 268, 282–3, 508
criminal trials 271–2, 276, 278, 284, 559
criminalization 269–70, 306–7, 309, 496–7, 504, 507, 552
critiques 34–5, 41, 53–71, 374
  conceptual 54–5
  cultural relativism 62–4
  feminist 54–5, 65–7, 70, 320
  Marxist 55, 60–2, 70
  particularist 54, 62–5
  post-colonial 68–70
  practical 54–5
  realist 55, 69–70
  utilitarian 54, 58–9, 70
CRPD, see Convention on the Rights of Persons with Disabilities (CRPD)
cruel and unusual punishments 20, 175
cruel treatment 176, 505
CSCE, see Conference on Security and Cooperation in Europe (CSCE)
CTC, see Counter-Terrorism Committee (CTC)
Cuba 25, 30, 132, 236, 268, 367, 398
cultural development 146, 336, 342–3, 352, 445–6
cultural diversity 289–90, 293, 352
cultural expressions 289, 292, 294
cultural goods 291–2
cultural heritage 291–4, 300–1
cultural identity 203, 248, 288, 291, 293–5, 300, 353
cultural life 210, 286–97, 300–1, 313
  definition 288–90
  right to take part in, see right to take part in cultural life
cultural practices 206–7, 273, 287–8, 291, 293, 295, 324–5
cultural relativism 53, 62–4, 70
cultural rights 135–6, 143–52, 203–7, 209–14, 245–9, 286–301, 561–2
  right to take part in cultural life 290–6
cultural survival 353
cultural traditions 294–5, 317, 324
culture 11, 62–4, 68, 208, 286–96, 301, 348–51
  definition 290

high 288–9
popular 289
custody 125–6, 176, 180–1, 186, 260, 268, 493
children 277, 309
customary international law 24–5, 81–7, 91–2, 107, 120, 161, 480–2
  as source of law 81–3
Cyprus 89, 113, 129, 168, 180, 306, 461
  Northern 107, 109, 113, 129
Czech Republic 120, 165–6, 169–70, 243, 521
Czechoslovakia 26, 31

Dalits 153, 155, 209
Darfur 365–6, 393, 443, 454, 499–500, 509
de Gouges, Olympe 65, 69
death penalty 80, 115–16, 174–5, 183–5, 187–93, 281–2, 451–2; see also right to life
  abolition 80, 187–8
  European Convention on Human Rights (ECHR) 423
  fair trial 189–90, 192
  minimum possible suffering 190–1
  personal limitations 191, 193
  procedural limitations 189–90, 193
  substantive limitations 188–9, 193
decent work 249, 254, 256, 585
Declaration of the Rights of Man and Citizen (France) 18–23, 53, 55–7, 60, 65
Declaration of the Rights of Woman 65–6
defamation 229
  of religions 231, 375
democracy 29, 51–2, 112, 228–9, 454–5, 567–8, 573
  liberal 55, 417–18
  representative 399–400, 467
democratic legitimacy 218, 597, 601
Democratic Republic of the Congo (DRC) 84, 90, 126, 132, 134, 365–7, 487–8
democratic society 96, 111–12, 218–19, 222–3, 234–6, 278, 596–7
denial of justice, flagrant 128, 272
dependence condition 38, 47, 49
deportation 121, 128, 262, 382, 422

deprivation of liberty 181, 192, 261–3, 268, 281, 330, 503; see also freedom from arbitrary detention
  conditions of detention 265, 267
  detention 260–3
  permissible 262–4
derogation 57, 84, 98, 113–14, 487, 516, 554
  armed conflict 484, 487
  derogable rights 113
  non-derogable rights, 136, 144, 182, 222, 231, 313–4, 530, 532, 554, 556, 558
  terrorism 553
descent 163, 209–10
detainees 8, 89, 137, 178, 181, 264–8, 559; see also deprivation of liberty and freedom from arbitrary detention
  criminal charges 264
  Guantánamo Bay 133, 137, 401, 559
  pre-trial detention 267
  procedural protections 264–5
  prohibition on torture and ill-treatment, see torture
  prompt judicial proceedings 267
  substantive protections 264–5, 267, 559
  UN Standard Minimum Rules for the Treatment of Prisoners 181
detention, see deprivation of liberty; freedom from arbitrary detention
detention facilities 265–6, 411
developing countries 121, 201, 204, 206, 208, 298–9, 587
development, see right to development; poverty reduction
differential treatment 158, 163–4, 166, 168–9, 220, 274, 309
dignity, see human dignity
diplomatic protection 448, 562–3
direct applicability 460–3
direct discrimination 157, 160, 164, 164–6, 169, 322
directive principles 214–15, 466
disabilities 163, 211, 250–1, 288, 373–5, 377, 380–2
disadvantaged groups 159–60, 171, 203, 293, 327, 455

disappearance, *see* enforced
disappearance
discrimination 157–70,
198–203, 307–10, 316–17,
322–3, 325–8, 377–82; *see also*
equality
differential treatment, *see*
differential treatment
direct 157, 159–60, 164,
164–6, 169, 322
elimination of 145, 152, 255,
373
indirect 157–60, 164, 164–6,
169, 172, 209
intended 164, 166
intersectional 163, 324, 327,
329
justifications 164, 166
prohibited grounds 162, 164,
519–20
racial 78, 116, 122, 124,
160–1, 170, 329
reverse 171, 323
unintended 164, 166
discriminatory intention 166
displaced persons 327, 367,
369, 451, 546
diversity
cultural 289–90, 293, 352
religious 222
domestic courts 22, 104, 233,
403, 413, 460, 469–70; *see also*
domestic protection
domestic law 16–17, 21, 23, 49,
106–7, 252, 458–64
domestic protection 16–23,
32, 458–74; *see also*
constitutional protections
executive action 470
institutional protections 473
judicial protection 469–70
national human rights
institutions (NHRIs), *see*
**national human rights
institutions (NHRIs)**
ombudsmen, *see* **ombudsmen**
substantive protections 458–69
domestic violence 92–3, 102,
124, 183, 325–6, 329–30,
519–20
domination 336, 338, 340–1, 448
drinking water 203, 208, 367,
590–1
dualism 464
due diligence 92–3, 102, 124,
138, 183, 191, 325–6
Dunant, Henry 24
duty-bearers 37, 40, 52, 119–20,
531, 568
Dworkin, Ronald 42, 46, 50–1

ECHR, *see* European
Convention on Human
Rights (ECHR)
economic, social and cultural
rights; *see also* International
Covenant on Economic,
Social and Cultural Rights
(ICESCR)
African Charter on Human
and Peoples' Rights
(ACHPR) 444–5
categorization 144–5
Charter of Fundamental
Rights of the European
Union 437
domestic protection 463,
465–7
equality 172
justiciability 148–9
Limburg Principles 149
monitoring 149
San Salvador Protocol 400
Economic and Social Council
(ECOSOC) 149, 185, 360,
362, 365, 376, 579
economic globalization 213,
249, 301
economic survival 208, 327
ECOSOC, *see* Economic and
Social Council (ECOSOC)
Ecuador 181, 187, 268, 292–3,
353, 388, 404
education 3–4, 78, 148–9, 170,
238–49, 256–7, 293–5; *see also*
right to education
aims 242
compulsory 240, 244–5, 466
human rights 6, 103, 242,
362, 372, 389, 588
primary 145, 239, 243–8
educational institutions 160,
240–1, 243, 246–7
private 245–6, 249
public 240, 243, 247
effective control 119–20, 125,
129–33, 136–8, 266, 401, 493–4
Egypt 128, 279, 461, 538, 568
EIAs, *see* environmental impact
assessments (EIAs)
elections 120, 344, 361, 374,
395, 443–4, 454
emergency 110, 113–14, 266,
268–9, 271, 553–4, 557–9
detention powers 268–9
public 113, 150, 177, 423,
485, 487
employees 252, 254, 256–7, 376,
541, 600
employers 211, 231–2, 244, 250,
252, 254, 256–7

employment 121, 134, 159–60,
170, 250–2, 254–6, 323–4
rights 121, 523
empowerment 67, 248, 328,
571, 587–8
enforced disappearance 93,
125, 151–2, 154, 269–70,
380–1, 546
International Convention
for the Protection of All
Persons from Enforced
Disappearance 77, 497
scope 154, 399
enforcement 7, 24–5, 32, 40,
117, 147–8, 441
human rights 48, 116, 469
and international
humanitarian law 486–7
law, *see* **law enforcement**
mechanisms 11, 456, 486–7,
568
enjoyment of rights 19–20,
161–3, 197–9, 293–4, 296–7,
319–20, 590–2
effective 143, 388, 579, 597
equal 171, 307, 322, 574
full 103, 352, 443, 458, 562,
600
Enlightenment 17–18, 68, 157
enslavement 501, 503
environmental degradation 54,
582, 590–609
Aarhus Convention 603
access to justice 605, 608
African Charter on Human
and Peoples' Rights
(ACHPR) 446, 590, 592–3,
601, 608
air pollution 598
climate change 591
dumping toxic waste 592
environmental impact
assessments (EIAs) 590,
605
European Convention
on Human Rights
(ECHR) 596
noise pollution 597
procedural environmental
rights 605, 608
Rio Declaration on the
Environment and World
Development 595, 603
Stockholm Declaration
on the Human
Environment 590–1, 593,
595
substantive environmental
rights 599–602
sustainable development 593

environmental impact
assessments (EIAs) 590, 603,
605, 607–8
environmental rights 594–6,
599–603, 608
procedural 121, 590, 592,
595, 603, 607
equal moral status 44–7, 51
equal political status 45–6
equality 44–6, 157–61, 163–4,
169–72, 198–9, 273–6,
318–22; see also discrimination
of arms 273–4, 280, 381, 559
autonomous norms 162–3
before the law 159, 163, 274–5
formal 158–60, 164, 171, 575
in international law 160–4
meaning 157–9
of opportunity 159
political 45–6, 49
of results 159
scope 161–3
sources 161
subordinate norms 162
substantive 158–60, 171, 318,
320–4, 331
women 317, 319–20, 322–4,
327–9, 331
equity 85, 576, 580, 583
erga omnes obligations 101, 340
Eritrea 341, 348, 367, 372
Ethiopia 117, 341, 443, 453, 525
ethnic cleansing 151, 501
ethnic minorities 218, 248,
455, 560
ethnic origin/ethnicity 163,
168, 202, 230, 239, 247, 560–1
EU, see European Union (EU)
Europe
Council of Europe, see
Council of Europe
European Union, see
European Union (EU)
Organization for Security and
Cooperation in Europe
(OSCE), see Organization
for Security and
Cooperation in Europe
(OSCE)
European Commission of
Human Rights 100, 121, 168,
177, 277, 423–4
European Committee of Social
Rights (ECSR) 420
European Convention
for the Prevention of
Torture and Inhuman
or Degrading Treatment
or Punishment, 1987
(ECPT) 418, 420–1

European Convention on Human
Rights (ECHR)
125–32, 161–4, 184–92,
276–83, 417–20, 422–38, 596–9
complaints procedure 426–34
Council of Europe 422–5,
433–4
death penalty 423
denunciation clauses 114
deprivation of liberty 261, 263
derogations 113, 423, 431
equality 423
fair trial 271–2, 278–80, 282,
422; see also fair trial
freedom from arbitrary
detention 422; see also
freedom from arbitrary
detention
freedom of assembly 234,
423; see also freedom of
assembly
freedom of opinion and
expression 422, 596; see
also freedom of opinion
and expression
freedom of thought,
conscience and
religion 422; see also
freedom of thought,
conscience and religion
incorporation into domestic
law 462
inhuman and degrading
treatment 176–8, 182, 422;
see also torture
jurisdiction 129–31, 136
margin of appreciation 65,
105, 597; see also margin of
appreciation
reservations 107
scope of rights 422–3
territorial scope 129–32
European Court of Human
Rights (ECtHR) 164–7,
177–83, 222–7, 229–33,
261–4, 382–4, 423–8
European Court of Justice
(ECJ), see Court of Justice of
the European Union (CJEU)
European Framework
Convention for the
Protection of National
Minorities 421
European Social Charter
Revised 251, 254–5, 257, 288
right to education 240
right to work 251, 254
European Union (EU) 120,
225, 343–4, 416–17, 435–9,
514, 540

Charter of Fundamental
Rights, see Charter of
Fundamental Rights of the
European Union
Court of Justice of the
European Union
(CJEU) 435–8, 564
Fundamental Rights Agency
(FRA) 438
history 435–6
evictions 133, 203–4, 209, 586
exclusion 45, 50, 153, 155, 182,
210, 223
executions
arbitrary 93, 149, 184, 188,
451, 487, 545–6
extra-judicial 399, 547, 557
expeditious disposal of
proceedings 276–7
expertise 6, 149, 370, 372–3,
376, 389, 438
experts 6, 16, 88, 93, 313–14,
360–1, 367–8
human rights 76, 236, 287,
305, 552, 563, 602
independent 4–5, 149, 214,
367, 376, 486, 606
exploitation 170, 249, 292,
299–300, 338, 340–1
of natural resources 292–3
expulsion 128, 224, 463, 499,
520
extent of responsibility 125
extra-judicial executions 399,
547, 557
extradition 84, 101, 128, 177,
183, 262, 395
extrajudicial killings 186–7,
191, 193
extraterritoriality 119, 132
extraterritorial
application 129, 132, 537
extraterritorial
jurisdiction 119–20
extraterritorial
obligations 127, 134, 136,
150
extreme poverty 149, 212, 215,
569, 571, 579, 581

fair balance 168, 224, 597
fair hearing 276–7, 284, 472; see
also fair trial
fair trial 111, 128, 189–90,
192–3, 259, 270–84, 558–60;
see also administration of
justice
children 283
civil rights and
obligations 271–2

fair trial (*contd*):
  competent tribunal 275
  counter-terrorism
    measures 558–60; *see also*
    terrorism
  criminal proceedings 271–2,
    278–84
  equality before the
    courts 273–6, 280
  fair and public hearing 275,
    276–8
  generally applicable
    guarantees 272–8
  impartiality 275–6
  independent tribunal 275
  international criminal
    tribunals 271
  military courts 275–6
  no punishment without
    law 283, 556, 558–9
  scope and type of
    obligations 271–2
  sources of right 270–1
  substantive protection 271–2
  suit at law 271–2
family members 181, 190, 256,
  269, 309, 373, 449
family planning 207, 324–6
Federal Republic of Yugoslavia
  (FRY) 126, 130, 506
feminism 65–7, 71, 324
feminist critiques 54–5, 65–7,
  70, 320
feminization 329, 535
finance ministries, view
  on poverty and human
  rights 575–7
financial resources 238, 277,
  388, 390, 413
Finland 26–7, 235, 350, 461
First World War, *see* World
  War I
flagrant denial of justice 128, 272
food, *see* right to food
Food and Agriculture
  Organization of the UN
  (FAO) 201
forced evictions, *see* evictions
forced labour 25, 250, 253–5,
  445, 536
forced marriage 520
foreign nationals 116, 268,
  411, 420
formal equality 158–60, 164,
  171, 575
formal sources of law 75–6, 80,
  89, 91–2, 94
foundationalism 36
FRA, *see* Fundamental Rights
  Agency (FRA)

fragmentation of states 535
Framework Convention on the
  Value of Cultural Heritage
  for Society 292
France 17–19, 21, 61, 81, 84,
  224, 539
Free Syrian Army (FSA) 484, 546
freedom from arbitrary
  detention 184, 225, 259–70,
  310–11, 369, 487, 558–9
  arbitrariness 263
  deprivation of liberty, *see*
    deprivation of liberty
  detainees, *see* detainees
  guarantees to those deprived
    of their liberty 264–8
  permissible deprivations of
    liberty 262–4
  procedural remedies 264
  scope and types of
    obligations 261–2
  sources of right 260–1
freedom from torture, *see*
  prohibition of torture and
  ill-treatment
freedom from want 29, 195, 215
freedom of assembly 234–6
freedom of association 231–4
freedom of belief, *see* freedom
  of religion or belief
freedom of conscience 219–20,
  422
freedom of expression, *see*
  freedom of opinion and
  expression
freedom of information 228–9
freedom of movement 137, 148,
  235, 261, 423, 446, 516
  legality 263
  permissible deprivation 264
  right to liberty 260–1, 268
freedom of opinion and
  expression 20, 29, 143,
  195–6, 225–31, 583
  freedom of information 227,
    229; *see also* freedom of
    information
  limitations 228–30
  media freedom 226–7
freedom of religion or
  belief 42, 104, 129, 195, 218,
  219–25, 249
freedom of speech, *see* freedom
  of opinion and expression
freedom of thought 114, 150,
  217–21, 223–5, 236, 333, 422
French Declaration of
  the Rights of Man, *see*
  Declaration of the Rights of
  Man and Citizen (France)

French Revolution 20–1, 60,
  418
friendly settlement 383, 403,
  405, 422–3, 426, 430–1, 434
  procedures 403, 426–9
full enjoyment 103, 352, 443,
  458, 562, 600
fundamental freedoms 4–6, 77,
  217, 316, 322–3, 359–60, 583
fundamental rights 11, 29, 32,
  225, 290–1, 436–8, 516–17
Fundamental Rights Agency
  (FRA) 438

Gambia 166, 443–5, 449, 451
gender 171, 317, 318–31, 373;
  see also sex discrimination
  stereotypes 318, 324, 330, 332
gender identity 93, 153, 163,
  303–15, 318, 332, 375; *see also*
  sexual orientation
General Assembly, *see* United
  Nations (UN), General
  Assembly
general comments/
  recommendations 80–1,
  89, 328
general obligations 110, 162,
  246, 441, 485
general principles of law 75, 85,
  292–3, 508
Geneva Call 544, 548
Geneva Conventions 24, 31, 176,
  291, 348, 480–2, 490–1
genocide 31, 84–5, 147, 151,
  334–5, 497–501, 536
  definition 508
  International Convention
    on the Prevention and
    Punishment of the Crime
    of Genocide 30, 78,
    99–100, 108–9, 115–16,
    497–500, 510
Georgia 116, 426, 494
Germany 26–9, 116, 229,
  278–9, 283, 306, 539
girls 66, 206, 224, 243–4, 317,
  331, 519; *see also* women
globalization 213, 249, 253,
  292, 389, 533–4, 571–2
  economic 213, 249, 301
good governance 454–5, 471,
  576, 584–5, 606
governance 10, 60, 63, 214, 342,
  348, 398
  good 454–5, 471, 576, 584–5,
    606
Greece 26, 84, 114, 178, 218,
  222–3, 517
Grenada 132

group rights 198, 333–54
relevance 335
v rights of individuals 334–5
Guantánamo Bay 133, 137,
401, 559
Guatemala 168, 180, 182, 409,
485, 487

habeas corpus 16, 20, 266, 269,
460
Habeas Corpus Act 17
happiness 19, 58, 466, 570
harmonization 368, 384, 386–7,
396, 585
hate speech 170, 230–1
HDCA, see Human
Development and Capability
Association (HDCA)
headscarves 223
health 148, 195–6, 198–9,
205–9, 212–15, 298–301,
591–5; see also right to health
mental 149, 205, 260, 264,
311, 449, 541
public 111–12, 205, 228, 235,
248, 345, 604
services 134, 205, 207, 209, 349
healthcare 4, 59, 145, 159, 170,
196, 207–10; see also health,
services
healthy environment 145, 337,
466, 592–4, 596, 598
heritage, cultural 291–4, 300–1
hierarchy of human rights 84,
150–1, 155
High Commissioner for Human
Rights 5, 93, 359, 386, 388,
392–3, 580–1
high culture, see culture, high
hijab 218, 223–4
history 15–32
Hobbes, Thomas 17
holocaust denial 230
homelessness 204, 305
homosexuality 112, 235, 303–6,
309–11, 432
Honduras 93, 102, 124, 183,
266, 269, 399–400
hostilities 80, 230, 293, 295,
485, 488–90, 492
housing, adequate, see adequate
housing; see also right to
housing
HRC, see Human Rights
Council (HRC)
human development 296, 571,
576, 578, 583–4, 587–8
Human Development and
Capability Association
(HDCA) 578

human dignity 10–11, 34–7,
46–7, 150–1, 174–5, 196, 483
human nature 34, 44
human rights, see Introductory
note and detailed entries
human rights abuses 329–32,
398, 401–4, 413–14, 533–4,
542–3, 547–8
Human Rights Act 1998
(UK) 22–3, 83, 130–1, 463,
467–8, 537–8
human rights bodies 70, 99, 106,
167, 192–3, 269–70, 487–8
international 105, 107, 117,
151, 164, 168, 275–6
national 82–5, 87–8, 214,
266, 362–4, 372, 374–5,
378–80, 436, 438, 458–9,
462–4, 472–4
Human Rights Committee 162,
334, 381, 383
Human Rights Council
(HRC) 4–5, 89–91, 181–2,
314, 359–64, 366–75, 388–94
Advisory Committee 372–3
complaint procedure 370–2
composition 361
creation 361
responses to urgent
situations 365–6
special procedures 367–70
Universal Periodic Review
(UPR), see Universal
Periodic Review (UPR)
human rights discourse 70, 145,
153, 322, 360, 474, 573
human rights education 6, 103,
242, 362, 372, 389, 588
human rights movement 7,
252, 303, 571, 573
human rights obligations, see
obligations
human rights theory 35–6, 38,
40, 43, 50, 52, 70
human rights treaty bodies 80,
92, 101, 133, 376, 386–7, 395
human rights violations 87–8,
127–9, 319–22, 441–5,
510–12, 518–19, 550–2
gross 153, 443, 445
serious 32, 442, 510, 517–18,
522
systematic 399, 433, 515
Human Rights Watch 7, 89,
401, 542, 547, 584
humanitarian law, see
international
humanitarian law
Hungary 26, 92, 124, 169, 228,
235–6, 265

hunger 4, 199–202, 206, 212,
581

ICC, see International Criminal
Court (ICC)
ICCPR, see International
Covenant on Civil and
Political Rights (ICCPR)
ICERD, see International
Convention on the
Elimination of All Forms
of Racial Discrimination
(ICERD)
ICESCR, see International
Covenant on Economic,
Social and Cultural Rights
(ICESCR)
ICJ, see International Court of
Justice (ICJ)
ICRC, see International
Committee of the Red Cross
(ICRC)
ICTR, see International
Criminal Tribunal for
Rwanda (ICTR)
ICTY, see International
Criminal Tribunal for the
former Yugoslavia (ICTY)
identity
cultural 203, 248, 288, 291,
293–5, 300, 353
gender 93, 153, 163, 303–15,
318, 332, 375
ill-treatment 174–8, 180–4,
190–3, 260, 269, 279, 558
ILO, see International Labour
Organization (ILO)
IMF, see International
Monetary Fund (IMF)
immediate obligation 144, 200,
213, 238, 245–6, 255
immunity, state 85, 274
implementation of human
rights obligations 101–5
incommunicado detention 181,
189, 266, 559
incorporation into domestic
law 460–4
independent experts 4–5, 149,
214, 367, 376, 486, 606
Indian Constitution 466, 601
indigenous peoples 146, 152–3,
207–9, 288, 292–5, 300–1,
350–4; see also aboriginal
peoples
adequate standard of
living 208–9
definition 351
displacement 209
environmental rights 598

indigenous peoples (*contd*):
rights of 153, 333, 350–4
self-determination 146, 341, 354
UN Declaration on the Rights of Indigenous Peoples 146, 260
indirect discrimination 157–8, 160, 164–6, 169, 172, 209
indivisibility of human rights 143–4, 147–50, 155, 238, 249, 257
integrity
of the person 174–93, 594
physical 212, 333–4, 410, 551, 599, 607
territorial 233, 346, 445–6
intellectual property 297–9
Inter-American Commission on Human Rights
complaints procedure 398–9, 402–13
country studies 398, 403
function 399
rapporteurs 403
structure 402
thematic studies 403
Inter-American Convention on the Prevention, Punishment and Eradication of Violence Against Women (CPPEVAW) 400
Inter-American Court of Human Rights
advisory jurisdiction 398, 404–12
contentious cases 382, 384, 403, 406–7, 413
interim measures 382, 409
jurisdiction 404, 413
reparations 407
structure 404
Inter-American human rights system 398–9, 402, 411–14, 601
inter-state complaints 80, 381, 403, 424
interdependence of human rights 143, 147–50, 155, 238, 249, 257
interim measures 382, 410, 431, 449
internal self-determination 342–3, 345, 351
International Bill of Rights 15, 23, 30–1, 55, 78, 144, 174
International Committee of the Red Cross (ICRC) 24, 482, 486

International Convention on the Elimination of All Forms of Racial Discrimination (ICERD) 78, 124, 162–3, 170–2, 375, 377, 381
denunciation clause 114
equality 160
fair trial 271, 273
freedom of opinion and expression 225
right to health 205
women's rights 329
International Convention on the Protection of the Rights of All Migrant Workers and Members of Their Families (ICRMW)
complaint mechanism 380
equality 160
fair trial 270
freedom from arbitrary detention 260
International Court of Justice (ICJ) 83–7, 99–100, 116–17, 339–41, 346–7, 395, 487–9
Statute 75–7, 81, 85–6, 88–90
International Covenant on Civil and Political Rights (ICCPR)
corporal punishment 182
equality 160
fair trial, right to 271–2, 274, 278–80, 282; *see also* **fair trial**
freedom from arbitrary detention 260
freedom of assembly 234
freedom of association 230
freedom of opinion and expression 225
freedom of thought, conscience and religion 219–20
Human Rights Committee; *see also* **Human Rights Committee**
jurisdiction 134
limitation clause 111
minority rights 145, 349
non-derogable rights 114, 151
origins 31
prohibition of torture and ill-treatment 182
reservations 105–7, 110
right to life 185
right to work 250
self-determination 335–6, 338–9, 345; *see also* **self-determination**
sexual orientation 288

special measures of protection 171
territorial scope 133–4
withdrawal 114–15
women 320–1, 328–9
International Covenant on Economic, Social and Cultural Rights (ICESCR) 149–51, 199–205, 239–50, 254–6, 287–91, 294–9, 463–4
adequate standard of living 196
Committee on Economic, Social and Cultural Rights 149, 151
equality 160
freedom of association 231
jurisdiction 134–7
Limburg Principles 150
Optional Protocol 78, 80, 149, 215, 380
origins 31
progressive realization 144–5
right to education 239–40
right to food 199
right to health 205
right to work 249
self-determination 335–6, 338–9, 345; *see also* **self-determination**
sexual orientation 307
territorial scope 134–6
women 320–1, 329
International Criminal Court (ICC) 126, 175–6, 499, 501–4, 506–9, 540, 552
Statute 176, 179–80, 279, 501, 503, 505–7, 509
international criminal law 87, 151, 176–7, 271, 453, 496–512, 531
aggression 497
amnesties, *see* **amnesties**
crimes against humanity, *see* **crimes against humanity**
genocide, *see* **genocide**
human rights law and international crimes 497–507
International Criminal Tribunal for Rwanda (ICTR) 176, 444, 499–500, 504, 508–9
International Criminal Tribunal for the former Yugoslavia (ICTY) 84, 87, 175–7, 491, 498–503, 506, 508–9

international dimension of human rights
after Second World War 28–31
before Second World War 23–8
international human rights bodies 105, 107, 117, 151, 164, 168, 275–6
international human rights treaties 77, 87–8, 96, 98, 105–6, 114, 458–9
international humanitarian law 8–9, 24, 176–7, 479–95, 505–6, 542–5, 553–4; see also armed conflicts
definition 480–1
difficulties with application of human rights law to armed conflicts 492–5
and duty to investigate 485–6
and enforcement 486–7
non-applicability 483–5
reasons for application of human rights law in armed conflicts 483–7
relationship with human rights law 487–91
and shared values 481–3
International Labour Organization (ILO) 231–2, 249–52, 254–5, 257, 319, 462–3, 540
International Military Tribunal at Nuremberg, see Nuremberg Tribunal
International Monetary Fund (IMF) 394, 531–2, 539–40, 572, 575, 580
international organizations 5–6, 25, 76, 125–7, 398, 531–2, 538–40
accountability 540
obligations 538–40
international peace 27, 346, 392, 418, 562, 564
international refugee law 503, 513–26
definition 514–15
end of refugee status and solutions for refugees 524–6
fundamental elements 515–16
non-refoulement and human rights 520–2
protections accorded to refugees 523–4
refugee status and human rights 518–20

relationship with human rights law 516–18
International Relations realism 57
Internet 218, 226–8, 230, 289, 451
internment 490, 516
interrelatedness of human rights 143, 147–50, 155, 238, 249, 257
invalid reservations 108–10
inventors 286, 288, 297, 300–1
investment plans 292, 353–4
Iraq 125, 130, 132–3, 342, 371, 393, 493–4
Ireland 113, 121, 126, 178–9, 214, 273–4, 466–7
Islam 222, 230, 519–20
Islamophobia 230
Israel 86, 133–4, 137, 365–6, 485, 554, 561–2
Italy 28, 84, 100, 122, 177, 431–2, 521–2

Jamaica 189–90, 265, 281, 384
Jawara, Alhaji Sir Dawda Kairaba 443–4
Jefferson, Thomas 18–19
Jordan 128, 191, 515
judicial decisions 11, 75–6, 86–90, 383, 468
judiciary 123, 270–1, 275–6, 452, 467, 474, 606
jurisdiction
advisory 398, 411, 454
dependent territories 129
detainees 136–7
effective control 119, 129–30, 132, 136–8
over persons 136–7
right to prescribe/enforce laws 119
state authority 119
territorial scope 119, 129–30, 133, 136, 138
jus cogens 106, 151, 161, 177, 185, 193, 339–40
as source of law 84–5
justiciability of human rights 148–50, 196, 214, 238, 462–4, 466, 600
justifications 34–52, 164, 167, 169–70, 228–9, 235, 538–9
moral and legal rights 39–41
objective and reasonable 167, 274, 412
plurality 41–3
reasons for justifying human rights 36–9

and strength of human rights 49–52
test 52, 167–8, 171–2
and universality of human rights 47–9

Kant, Immanuel 18, 565
Katanga 445–6, 509
Kenya 68, 130, 446–7, 509, 525, 586
kettling 261
knowledge 248, 268, 275, 286, 289, 294–5, 299
traditional 292, 294, 299–300
Kosovo 90, 125, 341–2, 539

labour 197, 202, 240, 244, 249, 251, 601
bonded, see bonded labour
conditions 249–52
slave 84
Lauterpacht, Hersch 15, 29, 31–2, 496
law enforcement 8, 111, 186, 209, 310, 557
officers/officials 91, 174, 176, 185–6, 267, 310
lawful residence 518
lawful sanctions 179, 182, 491
lawyers 3, 10, 98–9, 181, 280, 424, 506
League of Nations 25–7, 82, 246, 418
legal aid 273, 281, 381, 430, 474
legal assistance 271, 273, 278, 281, 407, 445, 452
legal representation 189, 281, 316, 332, 407, 559
legality 38, 83–4, 86, 150, 219, 263, 460
leges speciales, see lex specialis
legislative protection of human rights 333, 459, 467–8
legislatures 23, 86, 123, 169, 458–9, 464–5, 467–71
legitimacy 38, 42, 47–8, 77, 87–8, 347, 532–3
democratic 218, 597, 601
psychological 43
lesbians 153, 303–5, 312, 326; see also homosexuality
lex specialis 489–92
liberal democracy 55, 417–18
liberalism 17, 19, 55, 66, 157, 159
Liberia 21, 117, 367, 536
liberty 10–11, 18–20, 57, 60–1, 259–66, 268–70, 558–9
deprivation of, see deprivation of liberty

Libya 105, 347, 390, 393, 484, 509, 521
life, see right to life
Limburg Principles 149
limitation clauses 112, 437
general 111, 446
limitations 96, 111–12
permitted 111, 218, 235, 467, 556
substantive 188–9, 193
linguistic minorities 27, 91, 146, 209, 246, 348–9
livelihood 103, 195, 198, 200, 208, 211, 591
living standards, see adequate standard of living
Locke, John 17–18, 21, 39
Luxembourg 273, 418, 435, 437

Magna Carta 16, 23, 31–2, 259, 284
mainstreaming 76, 171, 316, 318, 328–31, 391, 580
Mali 253, 342, 346, 366–7, 390, 392, 547
margin of appreciation 65, 96, 104–5, 597–9
marginalized groups 206, 296, 330, 349
marital status 163–4, 254, 322–3, 325–6, 468
marriage 65, 309, 311–12, 320, 326, 447
children 327, 447
same-sex 311–12
Marx, Karl 21, 60–2, 68–9, 568
Marxist critique 55, 60–2, 70
material interests 210, 286–8, 297, 299–301
Mauritania 253, 276
MDGs, see Millennium Development Goals (MDGs)
media 7–8, 76, 145, 226–9, 275, 368–9, 417
medical care 8, 195–6, 256, 266, 411, 503, 568
medicines 209, 292, 299–300, 541
mental health 149, 205, 260, 264, 311, 449, 541
Mérida Declaration 578
Mexico 92–3, 116, 268, 380, 384, 411, 461
middle class 567–8
migrant workers 152, 160, 249–51, 260, 268, 377–8, 404
migrants 149, 256, 294, 301, 327, 367, 521
military coups 115, 443–5
military courts 275–6, 559

Mill, John Stuart 59
Millennium Development Goals (MDGs) 135, 244, 389, 442, 569, 579, 581–4
minorities 26–7, 146, 218–19, 288, 293–5, 335, 348–51; see also indigenous peoples
definition 348–9
ethnic 218, 248, 455, 560
linguistic 27, 91, 146, 209, 246, 348–9
national 26–7, 162–3, 240, 246, 349–50, 417–18, 420–3
religious 26, 243, 555, 557
rights of, see minority rights
sexual 104, 169, 303, 310–11, 314
minority groups 146, 305, 350–1
minority rights 27, 91, 146, 219, 246, 335, 349–51
protection 25–8
self-determination 367, 387; see also self-determination
UN Declaration on the Rights of Persons belonging to National, Ethnic, Religious and Linguistic Minorities 91, 145, 246, 348–50
minority treaties 26–7
Moldova 129–30, 137, 222
monism 460–4
Montesquieu, Baron de 18
moral duties 40, 48
moral interests 40, 50, 210, 286–8, 297, 299–301
moral justifications 35–6, 38–9, 41, 43, 47, 50
moral pluralism 48–9
moral relativism 47–8
moral rights 35, 38–41, 45
moral status, equal 44–7, 51
morality 36, 38, 40–3, 46–8, 59, 63, 111
morals 111–12, 223, 228, 235, 245, 255, 307
murder 4, 84, 102, 185–6, 190–1, 501, 503–6
Muslims 221–2, 224, 230–1; see also Islam
mutual accountability 582, 585

Namibia 168–9, 339, 461
national courts 83–5, 214, 266, 380, 436, 438, 462–4
interaction between 87–8
national human rights institutions (NHRIs) 82, 362–4, 372, 374–5, 378–80, 458–9, 472–4; see also ombudsmen

national minorities 26–7, 162–3, 240, 246, 349–50, 417–18, 420–3
national protection, see domestic protection
national security 111–12, 218, 223, 228–9, 233, 235, 516
nationality 62, 65, 67, 100, 163–4, 343, 513–17
NATO, see North Atlantic Treaty Organization (NATO)
natural disasters 114, 291, 591
natural law 38, 77, 412
natural resources 5, 198, 200, 207–8, 353, 593, 599–600
natural rights 16–18, 20–1, 56–8, 70, 533
nineteenth century challenges 21
naturalistic fallacy 34, 44
naturalization 158, 167, 411–12, 518, 525
nature of human rights 38, 46, 49, 81, 96, 101, 143
indivisibility 143–4, 150, 155, 238, 249, 257
Nazi regime 25, 28–9, 175, 229–30, 496
ne bis in idem 283
negative freedoms 232, 568
negative obligations 59, 102, 158, 182, 191, 238, 256–7
neo-liberalism 55, 71
Nepal 380, 461, 466, 525
Netherlands 125–7, 162, 164, 168–9, 282, 461–2, 536
new human rights 143, 152–5
New Zealand 264, 309, 464, 468
NGOs, see non-governmental organizations (NGOs)
NHRIs, see national human rights institutions (NHRIs)
Nicaragua 83, 208, 403–4, 593
Niger 253, 347, 444
Nigeria 125, 190, 200, 203, 235, 445–6, 592–3
non-binding instruments 91–2, 260
non-citizens 120–1, 153
non-derogable rights 107, 113–14, 150, 185, 269, 510, 558
non-discrimination 10, 93, 121, 157–73, 198–9, 250, 321–2; see also discrimination; equality
in international law 160–4

non-governmental
organizations (NGOs)
362–4, 369, 371–4, 378–9,
419–20, 449–52, 547–8; *see
also* Geneva Call and Human
Rights Watch
non-nationals 120–1, 136, 518,
521, 523–4
non-refoulement 129, 183,
520–3; *see also* refoulement
non-religious justifications of
human rights 41–2
non-state actors 11, 54, 83, 90,
94, 531–49, 551–3
accountability 535–8, 543
armed 544–8
armed opposition groups, *see*
armed opposition groups
challenges posed by 533–5
corporate social
responsibility, *see*
**corporate social
responsibility**
definition 531–2
globalization, *see*
globalization
human rights obligations 90,
503, 548
international criminal
responsibility 540–1
international organizations,
see **international
organizations**
legal framework 535–8
privatization, *see*
privatization
terrorism 551–2; *see also*
terrorism
US Alien Tort Statute 537
violations 551–2
normalcy 113, 554, 560
North American Agreement
on Environmental
Cooperation 603
North Atlantic Treaty
Organization (NATO) 130,
493, 539
Northern Cyprus 107, 109,
113, 129
Northern Ireland 178,
191, 343
Norway 16, 21, 121, 125, 280,
539, 542
nuclear weapons 83–4, 86, 480,
488–90, 501
nulla poena sine lege 283, 556
nullem crimen sine lege 114,
283, 556, 558
Nuremberg Tribunal 29, 496–7,
501, 507–8, 511

OAS, *see* Organization of
American States (OAS)
objective and reasonable
justification 167, 274, 412
obligations 96–111, 113–18,
197–200, 244–7, 255–7,
291–3, 493–4
contractual 114, 150, 262,
489
core 7, 151, 155, 248, 256,
293, 300
derogations 113–14
extraterritorial 127, 134,
136, 150
implementation 101–5
international
organizations 538–40
limitations 110–13
nature 96–118
negative 59, 102, 158, 182,
191, 238, 256–7
positive 59, 137, 182–3,
191–2, 238, 535–6, 597–9
remedies for violations 115–17
special character of human
rights obligations 98–101
state 150, 170, 197–8, 202,
204–5, 214, 251
observers 362, 364, 372, 374,
420, 456
occupation 130, 253–5, 348,
351, 448, 483, 489
Office of the UN High
Commissioner for Human
Rights (OHCHR) 4–5, 136,
365–6, 369–71, 388–92,
580–1, 591; *see also* High
Commissioner for Human
Rights
advisory services 388
field presences 390
mandate 380
resources 388
right to development 388
technical cooperation 388
training activities 388
voluntary funds 390
Ogoniland 125, 445,
592–3, 607
OHCHR, *see* Office of the UN
High Commissioner for
Human Rights (OHCHR)
ombudsmen 419, 458–9, 469,
471–2; *see also* national
human rights institutions
(NHRIs)
omissions 90, 119, 123, 125,
132, 182–3, 508
opinio juris 81–3, 85–6, 89,
93, 339

oppression 4, 17–18, 26, 57,
333–4, 337, 465
Organisation for Economic
Co-operation and Development
(OECD) 542–3, 585
Organization for Security and
Cooperation in Europe
(OSCE) 210, 342, 416–17
establishment 416
High Commissioner on
National Minorities 417
mandate 416
minority rights 349; *see also*
minorities
Office for Democratic
Institutions and Human
Rights (ODHIR) 416
Office of the Special
Representative and
Coordinator for Combating
Trafficking in Human
Beings 416–17
OSCE Representative on the
Freedom of the Media 417
Organization of African Unity
(OAU) 441–4, 452, 514–15,
517; *see also* **African
Union (AU)**
Organization of American
States (OAS) 91, 115, 226,
266, 398–402, 404–6, 410–13
American Convention
on Human Rights, *see*
**American Convention on
Human Rights (ACHR)**
American Declaration on the
Rights and Duties of Man,
see **American Declaration
on the Rights and Duties
of Man**
challenges 412–13
Charter 399–400, 402
Charter of the Organization of
American States 399–401
creation 399
General Assembly 398, 400,
402, 410, 412
Inter-American Commission
on Human Rights, *see*
**Inter-American
Commission on Human
Rights**
Inter-American Court of
Human Rights, *see* **Inter-
American Court of
Human Rights**
Legal Assistance Fund 412
membership 398–9
San Salvador Protocol, *see*
San Salvador Protocol

Organization of Islamic
 Cooperation 314
organized armed groups 483–4
OSCE, see Organization for
 Security and Cooperation in
 Europe (OSCE)
overcrowding 182, 411

Paine, Thomas 20
Pakistan 11, 314, 341, 466, 519,
 600
Pan-African Parliament
 (PAP) 443, 454, 456
PAP, see Pan-African
 Parliament
Paraguay 122, 208–9, 270, 408,
 410
parents 145, 197, 207–8, 220,
 223, 239–41, 244–5
Paris Declaration on Aid
 Effectiveness 585
Paris Principles Relating to the
 Status of National Human
 Rights Institutions 473
parochialism 47–8
particularism 53, 64–5, 70
particularist critique 62–5
passports 133, 137, 267
patents 298–9
peace 26–7, 145–7, 291–2,
 390–1, 393–5, 399–400, 507
 agreements 78, 343, 545
 international 27, 346, 392,
 418, 562, 564
Peace and Security Council
 (PSC) 443, 454–5
peaceful assembly 111, 234–6,
 367, 553
peaceful enjoyment of
 possessions 423, 431, 433
peacekeeping 125, 389–90,
 392, 580
peacekeeping forces 125
peer review 361, 363,
 443, 455
peremptory norms 84, 151,
 174, 177, 271
periodic reports 107, 117, 297,
 307–10, 324, 330, 376
Permanent Court of
 International Justice 27,
 86, 246
persecution 28, 311, 313,
 501–4, 513, 515–20, 522
personal capacity 78, 367–8
personal dignity, see human
 dignity
personal integrity, see integrity
 of the person
personhood 43–4, 46

Peru 79, 180–1, 263, 276,
 292–3, 408, 594
Philippines 92, 229, 342, 382,
 600
philosophy 19, 21, 36, 46, 58,
 60, 320
physical integrity 212, 333–4,
 410, 551, 599, 607
Pinochet, Augusto 88,
 177, 183
Pittsburgh Summit 577
pluralism 40, 43, 112, 168, 222,
 473
 moral 48–9
 political 234
poison 481, 506
Poland 26–7, 31, 181, 235, 431,
 433, 437
police 59, 102–3, 181–2, 187,
 209–10, 234–5, 409
political emancipation 60–1
political equality 45–6, 49
political freedom 567, 574–5
political participation 120, 248,
 333, 445, 523
political parties 122, 217, 231,
 233–4, 470
political pluralism 234
political status 146, 336, 341–2,
 352
politicization 360, 396
pollution 206, 593, 595, 597–8,
 600
polygamy 447
popular culture 289
Portugal 129, 309, 340, 347
positive action 135, 158, 170–2,
 323
positive discrimination, see
 reverse discrimination
positive law 21, 334
 transformation of human
 rights into 18–20
positive obligations 59, 137,
 182–3, 191–2, 238, 535–6,
 597–9
post-colonial critiques 67–70
poverty 3, 5, 36, 213, 389,
 442, 567–89; see also
 poverty reduction; right to
 development
 definition/measurement 570
 extreme 149, 212, 215, 569,
 571, 579, 581
 as human rights
 violation 567–8
 significance for human
 rights 569–71
poverty reduction 248, 567,
 571–3, 575, 577–81, 583–8

bilateral development
 cooperation 581, 585
 central banks 575, 577
 convergence of poverty
 reduction and human
 rights agendas 578–88
 divergence of poverty
 reduction and human
 rights agendas 573–7
 economic theory 574–5,
 578–9
 globalization 571–2
 Millennium Development
 Goals (MDGs) 581
 ministries of finance 577
 strategies 573, 579–81,
 585–6
 UN development
 cooperation 579
power 17–20, 61–3, 133, 443–4,
 465, 470–1, 473
 exercise of 77, 227, 465, 535
pre-trial detention 267, 279
preferential treatment 160,
 171–2
pregnancy 206–7, 243, 254, 317,
 323, 466, 468
presumption of innocence 20,
 267, 279, 547, 559
primary education 239, 243–8
prisoners 91, 176–8, 181,
 187, 260, 266, 401; see also
 detainees
 of war 24, 84, 485
privacy 110, 125, 229, 303,
 305–7, 320–1, 538
private actors 102, 123–5,
 261–2, 323, 330, 446, 537; see
 also non-state actors
private educational
 institutions 245–6, 249
private interests 60, 300–1
private life 229, 306, 432, 535,
 598, 602
private property 60, 272, 534
private sphere 55, 102, 112, 124,
 138, 317, 535–6
privatization 292, 534, 572
procedural rights 274, 603,
 605, 608
 environmental 121, 590, 592,
 595, 603, 607
progressive realization 92, 134,
 144–5, 202, 238–40,
 463, 524
prohibited grounds of
 distinction 163–4
prohibition of torture and
 ill-treatment; see also
 torture

Committee against Torture, *see* **Committee against Torture**
components 177–82
European Committee for the Prevention of Torture and Inhuman or Degrading Treatment or Punishment 176
legal status 176
obligations 182–3
relationship with other human rights 183
sources 176
Special Rapporteur 176–7
Sub-Committee on the Prevention of Torture 176
UN Convention against Torture and Other Cruel, Inhuman or Degrading Treatment 1984 (UNCAT) 77, 176, 178–9, 192
UN Declaration against Torture or Other Cruel, Inhuman or Degrading Treatment or Punishment (UNDAT) 178
UN Standard Minimum Rules for the Treatment of Prisoners 181–2
property 18–19, 125–6, 161–5, 210, 317, 466–7, 488; *see also* **intellectual property**
private 60, 272, 534
proportionality 112, 167–8, 186–8, 193, 224, 506, 554
prostitution 170, 197
Protocol on Pollutant Release and Transfer Registers 604
provisional measures of protection 116, 382, 385, 402, 404, 410–12, 449
PSC, *see* **Peace and Security Council (PSC)**
psychological legitimacy 43
public educational institutions 240, 243, 247
public emergency 113, 150, 177, 423, 485, 487
public functions 408–9, 534, 537
public health 111–12, 205, 228, 235, 248, 345, 604
public hearings 270, 273, 276, 407, 409, 431
public order 56, 59, 111–12, 167, 176, 184, 235
European 101, 107, 432
public sphere 55, 102, 322–3

publicity 7, 278, 401, 404, 452, 473
punishment 29, 150–2, 174–9, 181–3, 281–3, 420–2, 498–9
capital, *see* **death penalty**
cruel and unusual 20, 175

al-Qaida 126, 550, 553, 559, 562
quadrilogue 419
quasi-judicial bodies 313, 583, 606
Québec 122, 342–3, 345

racial discrimination 78, 116, 122, 124, 160–1, 170, 329
rape 87, 180, 191, 274, 304, 331, 502, 536, 544–5
ratification 77, 105, 109–10, 129, 161, 168, 461–4
Rawls, John 50, 574–5
realism 26, 48, 53, 56–7, 71
realist critique 55–7, 70
realization of human rights 259, 391, 442–3, 456, 474, 567, 571
reciprocity 96, 98–100, 109–11, 403
reconciliation 154, 366, 511
redress 10–11, 20, 121, 124, 266, 313–14, 455–6
reforms 8, 361, 379, 384, 387, 391, 576–7
refoulement 128–9, 135, 514, 521–2; *see also* **non-refoulement**
chain 521
refugee status 78, 203, 513–17, 523–4
end of, and solutions for refugees 524–6
and human rights 518–20
refugees 28, 78, 203, 327, 394, 448, 513–26; *see also* **international refugee law**
rights 513–14, 517–18, 526
regional human rights
courts 79, 85, 93, 395, 486, 521
instruments 79, 81, 161, 176, 195, 211, 326
systems 88, 384, 414, 442, 453, 601
regional treaties 77, 93, 130, 175, 271, 333, 349
relativism 48, 62–4
cultural 53, 62–4, 70
moral 47–8
religion 26–7, 42, 145–6, 161–5, 168–9, 217–24, 348–51
defamation of 231, 375

freedom of, *see* **freedom of religion or belief**
religious dress 218, 223–4
religious groups 221–2, 230, 243, 295, 499–501
religious minorities 26, 243, 555, 557
religious symbols 218–19, 224
remuneration 207, 251, 254, 275, 317
equal 145, 254, 256
rendition 69, 262
reparations 10, 91, 93, 151, 154, 353, 408–9, 414
repatriation 524–5
representative democracy 399–400, 467
representatives 5, 360, 367, 374, 395, 402, 454–5
diplomatic 448, 562–3
reprisals 116, 374, 394, 410, 486
reproductive rights 207, 325, 447
reputation 88, 228–9, 300, 319, 360
reservations 79, 81, 83, 96, 98–100, 105–10, 317
consequences 108–10
invalid 108–10
permissibility 106–8
responsibility for assessment 108
resettlement 524–5
residence 148, 401
habitual 523
lawful 518
responsibility to protect 151
retroactive criminal legislation 508
right of self-determination, *see* **self-determination**
right to an adequate standard of living, *see* **adequate standard of living**
right to development 135, 146–8, 335, 388, 585; *see also* **poverty reduction**
right to education 239–49
accessibility 243
aims of education 242
language of own choice 245
moral/religious education 241
primary education 246
private education 241
realization 247, 257
relationship with other human rights 248–9
sources 239–41
state education 241

right to education (*contd*):
   types of obligations 246–8
   UNESCO Convention
      against Discrimination in
      Education 239
right to food 103, 148–9,
   195–203, 209, 212–15,
   296–301, 591–3; *see also*
   adequate food
   components 200–1
   developing countries 201
   realization 201–2
   sources 199
   water 199–200; *see also* **right
      to water**
   World Food Summit 201
right to health
   components 205–6
   maternal health 206
   realization 206
right to housing 148, 170,
   195–9, 202–4, 206–7, 212–15,
   591–3; *see also* **adequate
   housing**
   climate change 591
   components 203–4
   sources 202
right to information 604; *see
   also* **freedom of information**
right to life 121, 150–1, 174–5,
   184–93, 466, 492, 598–600
   arbitrary deprivation 85, 184,
      186, 188, 489–90
   assisted suicide 186
   beginning of life 186
   components 186–91
   death penalty 184, 187–91,
      193; *see also* **death
      penalty**
   end of life 186
   environmental
      concerns 591, 596, 598,
      600
   euthanasia 186
   extrajudicial killings
      186–7, 191, 193
   law enforcement
      measures 186–7, 191–3
   legal status 184, 186
   limitations 111
   obligations 191
   relationship with other
      human rights 192
   sources 184
   Special Rapporteur
      on Extrajudicial
      Killings 184
   UN Basic Principles on
      the Use of Force and
      Firearms 186–7

components 186–90
legal status 185
relationship with other
   human rights 192
scope 185–6
sources 184
types of obligation 191–2
right to science 288, 296–7
right to self-determination, *see*
   self-determination
right to social security 162,
   196, 210–12, 251, 256, 445,
   462
right to take part in cultural
   life 290–6
   groups requiring special
      attention 294–5
   limitations 295–6
right to truth 154
right to water 199, 201; *see also*
   right to food
right to work 238, 249–57
   allocation of resources 257
   child labour 254–5
   claim to employment 252
   conditions of work 254
   decent work 254, 256
   equality 254–6
   forced labour 253–5
   freedom of association 255
   International Labour
      Organization (ILO),
      see **International Labour
      Organization (ILO)**
   migrant workers 249–50
   realization 255, 257
   relationship with other
      human rights 256–7
   right to seek work 253
   slavery 253
   sources 249–52
   unemployment 249
rights of minorities 27, 91, 219,
   246, 288, 335, 349
Roma 153, 165, 170, 209, 243
Roosevelt, Franklin D. 29, 31,
   143, 195
Rousseau, Jean-Jacques 18
Russia 89, 129–30, 168–9, 191,
   310, 426, 598
Russian Federation 116,
   188, 191, 274, 279,
   310, 426

same-sex marriage 311–12
same-sex partnerships 306,
   308–10, 326
science 62, 67, 286–8, 293–4,
   296–7, 301, 572–3
   right to, *see* **right to science**

scientific progress 210, 286–7,
   296–7, 300–1
scope of application 119–38
   territorial 129–37
Second World War, *see* **World
   War II**
Security Council, *see* **United
   Nations (UN), Security
   Council**
security forces 174, 186–7, 191,
   236, 394, 534
security of the person 270
self-determination 146–8,
   335–9, 341–3, 348–9, 351–3,
   445–6, 591–2
   African Charter on Human
      and Peoples' Rights
      (ACHPR) 445
   application of right 338–41
   colonial context 338–9
   concept 146–7, 151, 335–6
   consultation 343–4
   Declaration on Principles of
      International Law 342, 345
   definitions 336–8
   exercise of right 341–4
   external self-
      determination 342
   independence 354
   indigenous peoples 340,
      591–2; *see also* **indigenous
      peoples**
   internal 342–3, 345, 351
   limitations 344–8, 354
   minority rights 334, 354; *see
      also* **minorities**
   non-colonial context 340
   procedures 343–4
   recognition 337–8
   and rights of others 345
   secession 342, 344
   territorial integrity 345–7
self-executing human rights
   norms 460–4
self-government 266, 339, 341,
   352
self-identification 337–8, 349,
   351
Senegal 84, 93, 101, 177, 183,
   395, 453
September 11 attacks 8, 262,
   550, 555, 558, 565
Serbia 81, 116, 130–1, 229, 341,
   351, 499
serious harm 514, 518–19, 522
sex 65–6, 161–5, 168–9, 304,
   307–8, 312, 322–5; *see also*
   gender
   discrimination 66, 69, 168,
      320–2, 326–7, 329–30, 585

sex workers 319, 326
sexual activity 306–7, 309–10
sexual minorities 104, 169, 303, 310–11, 314
sexual orientation 67, 93, 153, 163–4, 230, 303–15, 330
  criminal prosecutions 305
  death penalty 304
  discrimination 164, 303, 307–9
  perceived 303, 305, 313
  privacy 303, 305
  prohibition of torture and ill-treatment 309
  same-sex relationships 304–7, 312
  transgender persons 304
  treaty-monitoring bodies 305
  vulnerability 303–4, 306–9
  Yogyakarta Principles 303–4, 313
sexual violence 67, 329, 331, 392, 502, 544–5, 548
shadow reports 379, 452
shaming 8–9, 545
Sharia 105, 233
Sierra Leone 190, 509–10, 544
Singapore 64
slave labour 84
slave trade 24–5, 536
slavery 22, 24–5, 68, 84, 253, 367, 536
slaves 22, 24–5, 253
social assistance 197, 211, 251
Social Charter, see European Social Charter
social contract 17–18, 77
social development 196, 198, 207, 336, 600
social groups 290, 500, 515, 519–21
social justice 4, 10–11, 55, 214, 249, 252, 571–2
social origin 114, 161–5, 199, 308, 423
social relativism 48
social rights 145, 212–13, 254, 463, 466, 568, 592
social security 148, 162, 196–9, 210–12, 251, 256, 313; see also right to social security
social services, necessary 195–6, 568
soft law 75, 91, 175, 184, 193, 380, 592–4
  sources 92, 176, 185
soldiers 24, 272, 536
  child 447, 520, 544–5, 547
solidarity 55, 240, 348, 582–3, 602
  international 367, 373
solitary confinement 182, 268

Somalia 341, 367, 484
sources of law 75–94
  customary international law 81–3
  formal 75–6, 80, 89, 91–2, 94
  general principles of law 85
  judicial decisions 86–8
  jus cogens 84–5; see also jus cogens
  resolutions of international institutions 90–1
  treaties 77–81
  work of treaty bodies 89–90
  writings of jurists 88–9
South Africa 3, 81, 117, 239, 443, 454–5, 575–7
  Constitution 466
South Korea 575, 587
sovereignty 15, 17, 28, 30–1, 97, 343–4, 347
Soviet Union 22, 28, 30–1, 60–1, 190, 340, 349; see also Russia
Spain 16, 21, 100, 124, 466, 558–9, 597
  Constitution 465–6
Special Court for Sierra Leone 510, 544
special measures 171, 447
special procedures 89, 149, 310–11, 313, 373–5, 392–3, 395–6
  Human Rights Council (HRC) 367–70
  system 360, 367–9, 375
special protection 251, 283, 321, 348, 410, 481
special sessions 361–2, 365–6, 374, 406
specific practices 181–2
  terrorist suspects 557–8
  war crimes 175–6; see also war crimes
specificity 79, 319, 331, 378, 386–7, 489–91
spouses 326, 412, 423
Sri Lanka 123, 263, 269–70, 365–6, 394, 493, 545–6
stability 25, 346, 400, 417, 474, 580
  regional 27
stakeholders 363–5, 368–9, 374, 378–80, 385–6, 455, 576
standard of living, see adequate standard of living
state actions within organization 127
  jurisdiction 119–20, 137
  private actors 123, 138

state actors 502, 538, 540–1; see also non-state actors
state agents 125, 132, 269, 410, 494
state compliance 361, 405, 408–10, 419–20, 601
state immunity 85, 274
state obligations 150, 170, 197, 202, 204–5, 214, 251
  adequate standard of living 198
  duty to fulfil 102–3, 123, 247, 255, 459
  duty to protect 101–3, 123, 247, 255
  duty to respect 101–3, 123, 247, 255
state responsibility
  acts of agents 123
  acts of other states 128–9
  attribution 119, 123
stereotypes 305, 321, 330
  gender 318, 324, 330, 332
structural change 387, 587
subjugation 338, 340–1, 443
subordinate norms 161–2, 320
subsidiarity 425, 432
subsidiary bodies 90, 361, 374, 394, 550
subsistence 43, 151, 336, 571, 575, 577
substantive equality 158–60, 171, 318, 320–4, 331
Sudan 365, 367, 393, 443, 509, 525
suicide 185–6, 192, 208
  terrorists 561
Suriname 263, 292, 353
survival 4, 57–8, 143, 152, 208, 499
  cultural 353
suspected terrorists 187, 263, 393, 557, 565
sustainability 581–3, 585
sustainable
  development 145, 525, 582, 593, 595, 600–1
Swaziland 275, 447
Sweden 21, 128, 164, 212, 277–8, 350, 471–2
Switzerland 107, 126–7, 277, 281, 291, 334, 461–3
symbols 221, 223, 230
  religious 218–19, 224
Syria 314, 365–7, 375, 392–3, 484, 515, 546–7

Taliban 126, 243, 553, 563
Tanzania 453, 464, 525

technologies 207, 290, 296–7, 325, 387, 585, 594
temporary gatherings 217, 235
tenure 203–4, 275, 369, 372
territorial boundaries 338, 346, 348–9, 494
territorial control 131, 134, 136, 484, 535, 547, 552
territorial integrity 233, 346, 445–6
territorial scope of application 129–37
terrorism 9, 126, 229–30, 268, 497, 532–3, 550–65; see also counter-terrorism measures
applicability of human rights law in fight against 553–4
counter-terrorism measures 550–1, 553, 556–7, 559–61, 565
definition 551, 554–6
as a human rights violation 550–3
international criminal law 552
misuse of notion 554–6
September 11 263, 550, 558, 565; see also September 11 attacks
substantive challenges to human rights law in fight against 556–62
suspected terrorists 187, 263, 393, 557, 565
terrorist listing 551, 562–4
terrorists, see terrorism
suicide 561
Thompson, EP 61
ticking bomb scenario 59, 176, 557
Tokyo Tribunal
terrorism 497; see also terrorism
torture 496; see also prohibition against torture and ill-treatment
transnational crimes 497
truth and reconciliation commissions, see truth and reconciliation commissions
war crimes, see war crimes
tolerance 54, 63, 222, 242, 417
torture 58–9, 174–84, 192, 279–80, 376–82, 420–2, 557–9; see also prohibition of torture and ill-treatment
armed opposition groups 491–2
corporal punishment 182, 192

crimes against humanity 176, 180; see also crimes against humanity
definition 177–80, 182, 192, 383, 491
evidence obtained by 279
integrity of the person 174–5
international crime 86–7, 540
interrogation techniques 177–8, 536, 558
toxic waste 367, 592
trade-offs 42, 49–51, 58
Trade Related Aspects of Intellectual Property Rights (TRIPS) 298
trade union rights 231–2, 241, 249–50, 252
trade unions 145, 148, 217, 231–2, 250, 256–7, 420
traditional knowledge 292, 294, 299–300
traditions 8, 22–3, 47, 55, 290, 294–5, 352–4
cultural 294–5, 317, 324
Transdniestria 130, 137
transnational corporations 135, 367, 369, 542, 549, 572
transnational crimes 497, 503
transparency 113, 227–8, 399, 408, 564, 573, 585–6
transsexuals 303, 306, 310, 432
treaties
derogations, see derogations
importance 79
law of treaties 77–81, 105–10, 113–15
reservations, see reservations
revitalization of system 79–81
as sources of law 77–81
unincorporated 464–5
treaty-based bodies, see United Nations (UN), treaty-based bodies
treaty bodies 80–2, 89–90, 308, 363–4, 376–9, 381–7, 395–6
members 378–9, 381, 386–7
tribal peoples 288, 351, 353, 599
Trinidad and Tobago 115, 177, 188–90, 266, 400, 413
tripartite typology 101–3
TRIPS, see Trade Related Aspects of Intellectual Property Rights (TRIPS)
truth and reconciliation commissions 511
Tunisia 236
turbans 165, 224
Turkey 107, 109–10, 113, 129–30, 180–1, 225–6, 233

Turkmenistan 606–7
tyranny 17–18

UDHR, see Universal Declaration of Human Rights (UDHR)
Uganda 132–4, 177, 442, 448, 487–8, 490, 494
UN, see United Nations (UN)
unborn 121, 600
UNDAT, see United Nations (UN), Declaration against Torture
unemployment 62, 195, 198, 211, 249, 252, 256
UNESCO (UN Educational, Scientific and Cultural Organisation) 78, 239, 243, 247, 289–90, 296, 571
Convention against Discrimination in Education 239
UNHCR, see United Nations (UN), High Commissioner for Refugees
unincorporated human rights treaties 464–5
United Kingdom (UK) 121, 177, 490
United Nations (UN) 29–31, 77–80, 338–40, 359–96, 482, 542–5, 561–2
Charter 29–31, 77, 318–19, 335–6, 339–40, 359–60, 393–4
Commission on Human Rights; see also Human Rights Council
establishment 30, 360
special procedures system 592
Sub-Commission on the Protection and Promotion of Human Rights 360
Convention against Torture and Other Cruel, Inhuman or Degrading Treatment (UNCAT) 78, 271, 330, 380–1, 497
Declaration against Torture (UNDAT) 178–9
Declaration on the Rights of Indigenous Peoples 2007 146, 260
Declaration on the Rights of Persons Belonging to National, Ethnic, Religious and Linguistic Minorities 1992 91, 146, 246

Development Programme (UNDP) 571, 578–82
Economic and Social Council (ECOSOC) 149, 185, 360, 362, 365, 370, 376
General Assembly 30–1, 75–6, 78, 83, 361–2, 373–5, 384–92
High Commissioner for Human Rights 5, 93, 359, 386, 388, 392–3, 580–1; *see also* Office of the UN High Commissioner for Human Rights (OHCHR)
High Commissioner for Refugees (UNHCR) 514–15, 517–18, 522–4
Human Rights Committee, *see* Human Rights Committee
Human Rights Council, *see* Human Rights Council
interim administration in Kosovo (UNMIK) 90, 125, 539
mainstreaming human rights 76, 171
Secretary-General 4, 6, 77, 115, 144, 394–5, 542–5
Security Council 125–7, 390–4, 508–9, 539, 544–5, 555, 562–4
resolutions 90, 125–7, 339, 390, 393, 550, 562–3
Working Group on Children and Armed Conflict 544–5
Standard Minimum Rules for the Treatment of Prisoners 181–2, 260, 271
system 6, 78, 360, 362, 370, 379, 390–1
treaty-based bodies 375–87
Common Core Document 387
complaints procedure 380–4; 387
coordination, harmonization, reform, and strengthening 384–7
General Comments 379–80
inquiries 380–1
reforms 387
state reports/ reporting 376–9, 387
working methods 387, 395
United States 19–20, 22–5, 132–3, 341–2, 399–401, 461–2, 536–7
Bill of Rights 21–3

Constitution 20, 23, 461, 466
Declaration of Independence 18, 20–1, 23, 157
Universal Declaration of Human Rights (UDHR) 30–2, 55–7, 145–6, 195–6, 218–21, 287–9, 319–20
adequate standard of living 195
adoption 30–1, 55, 359
equality 3, 160
fair trial 270
freedom from arbitrary detention 260
freedom of assembly 234
freedom of association 230
freedom of opinion and expression 225
freedom of thought, conscience and religion 220
general limitation clause 111
influence 32, 55
prohibition on torture and ill-treatment 175
right to education 239–40
right to food 199
right to health 205
right to life 187
status 30–1
women 320
Universal Declaration on Cultural Diversity 289–90
universal human rights 5, 55, 63, 107, 215, 250, 316
universal jurisdiction 183, 497, 509
Universal Periodic Review (UPR) 5, 82, 307, 361–6, 373–4, 389, 395
universalism 63–5, 70
universality 47, 63, 106, 313, 320, 362, 413
unlawful detention 126, 130, 266
UNMIK, *see* United Nations (UN), interim administration in Kosovo
UPR, *see* Universal Periodic Review (UPR)
Uruguay 133, 137, 171, 180, 554
USSR, *see* Soviet Union
uti possidetis juris 346
utilitarian critique 54, 56, 58–9, 70
utilitarian theories 574
utilitarianism 55–6, 58–60, 70, 584, 587
utility 42, 50, 58–9, 314
Uzbekistan 190, 223

VCLT, *see* Vienna Convention on the Law of Treaties (VCLT)
VDPA, *see* Vienna Declaration and Programme of Action (VDPA)
Venezuela 115, 187, 275, 401, 411, 413, 568
Venice Statement on the Right to Enjoy the Benefits of Scientific Progress and its Applications 296–7
victims' rights 153–4
Vienna Convention on the Law of Treaties (VCLT) 79, 84, 97, 105–6, 108–10, 115–16, 432
Vienna Declaration and Programme of Action (VDPA) 147, 157, 210, 359, 568, 579
Vienna World Conference on Human Rights, *see* World Conference on Human Rights
violence 80–1, 92–3, 230–1, 295, 304, 324–7, 479–81
domestic 92–3, 102, 124, 183, 325–6, 329–30, 519–20
sexual 67, 329, 331, 392, 502, 544–5, 548
violence against women 327, 535
Virginia Declaration of Rights 19, 23
vocational guidance 255–6, 327
vocational training 240, 251, 256
Voltaire 18
voluntary commitments 363–4
vulnerability 186, 209, 264, 303–4, 326–7
vulnerable groups 169, 204, 207, 209, 246, 273, 404

war crimes 29, 120, 176, 179–80, 497–8, 505–9, 536
War on Terror 70, 177, 487, 559; *see also* counter-terrorism measures
water 134–5, 148–9, 198–9, 201–2, 215, 576, 591–3; *see also* right to water
drinking 203, 208, 367, 590–1
wealth 82, 89, 125, 168, 213, 215, 445
welfare 19, 42, 50, 58, 147, 208, 447
Western Sahara 339, 344, 347

withdrawal 81, 98, 114–15, 137, 364, 449
witnesses 126, 191, 267, 274, 281, 407, 410
wives 273, 319, 321, 447; *see also* spouses
women, *see* women's rights
women's rights 11, 22, 155, 295, 316–31, 375, 535
  adequate standard of living 206–7
  anti-trafficking measures 319, 535
  cultural traditions 317, 324
  discrimination 322–4, 326, 329, 331
  domestic violence 329
  equality 317, 319–20, 322–4, 327–9, 331
  fair trial 273
  gender mainstreaming 316, 318, 331
  honour killings 11, 535
  International Convention on the Elimination of All Forms of Discrimination Against Women (CEDAW), *see* International Convention on the Elimination of All Forms of Discrimination Against Women (CEDAW)
  limitations 324–5
  marginalization 316, 318, 328–9
  maternal health 207–8, 317
  privacy rights 321
  prohibition of torture and ill-treatment 330
  protective responses 329–31
  realization 316, 318
  right to life 325, 329
  security of the person 326
  sexual exploitation 535
  violence against women 325, 327, 535
work-related rights, *see* right to work
workplace 224, 251, 257, 312
World Bank 197, 394, 532, 540, 569, 579–80, 588
World Conference on Human Rights (1993) 92, 146–7, 157, 328, 359, 388, 579

World Food Summit 201
World Summit (2005) 148, 151, 390, 392, 568
World Trade Organization (WTO) 127, 298, 394, 539–40, 572, 578
  Trade Related Aspects of Intellectual Property Rights (TRIPS) 298
World War I 25–6, 28, 246, 249, 335, 418, 508
World War II 15–16, 23, 25–6, 28–9, 418, 481–2, 508
writings of publicists 89
WTO, *see* World Trade Organization (WTO)

Yogyakarta Principles 303, 313–14
Yugoslavia 26, 31, 116, 176–7, 340, 346, 349

Zaire 189, 264, 445–6
Zambia 188, 277
Zimbabwe 374, 443–4, 452, 454